Y0-BWS-109

NAICS/SIC Code
United States Manual 1997

2nd Edition

NAICS/SIC Code
United States Manual 1997

2nd Edition

Being the North American Industry Classification System of 1997 as used jointly by the United States, Canada and Mexico, replacing the Standard Industry Classification (SIC) Code Manual of 1987 effective 1/1/97

Tables 1, 2 and 4 by
U.S. Office of Management and Budget

Table 3 by
Mike Frerichs, Editor

An exact reprint of GPO's Tables 1, 2 and 4 and Claitor's Table 3 by
CLAITOR'S PUBLISHING DIVISION
P.O. Box 261333, Baton Rouge, LA 70826-1333
800-274-1403 (In LA 504-344-0476)
e mail: claitors@claitors.com
World Wide Web: http://www.claitors.com

ISBN Number 1-57980-100-5 IRCB 1997-3 vol. 11
ISBN Number 1-57980-101-3 NAICS 1997 paperbound
ISBN Number 1-57980-040-3 NAICS 1997 hardbound

Published and for sale by
CLAITOR'S PUBLISHING DIVISION
3165 S. Acadian at I-10, P.O. Box 261333
Baton Rouge, LA 70826-1333
Tel: 800-274-1403 (In LA 504-344-0476)
Fax: 504-344-0480
Internet address:
e mail: claitors@claitors.com
World Wide Web: http://www.claitors.com

Table of Contents

About This Manual

This manual is basically in four tables:

TABLE 1. 1997 NAICS Matched to 1987 SIC.

If you know the NAICS code number, this is your quickest route to identify the code. You will find related industries nearby with their classification numbers.

TABLE 2. 1987 SIC Matched to 1997 NAICS.

If you have the old 1987 SIC code number, this table will give you the new NAICS code number.

TABLE 3. 1997/1987 NAICS/SIC Alphabetical and Key Word/Phrase Index Including Both 1997 NAICS and 1987 SIC

If you know the category, key word, or phrase of the industry or something close to it, this alphabetical arrangement will give you the new NAICS code (as well as the old SIC code). Then, if desired, go to Table 1 for more information and associated industries.

TABLE 4. Alphabetical Arrangement of Old SIC Codes.

This information might be helpful in identifying the codes used on pre-1997 documents. However, you may find Table 3 to be more useful for this purpose.

Armed with the above descriptions, you should have no difficulty in using this manual. We would appreciate your suggestions and comments.

— Editor

OFFICE OF MANAGEMENT AND BUDGET

1997 North American Industry Classification System — 1987 Standard Industrial Classification Replacement

AGENCY: Office of Management and Budget, Executive Office of the President.

ACTION: Notice of final decision.

SUMMARY: This notice presents the Office of Management and Budget's final decisions for the adoption of the North American Industry Classification System (NAICS) for the United States, a new economic classification system that replaces the 1987 Standard Industrial Classification (SIC) for statistical purposes. NAICS is a system for classifying establishments by type of economic activity. Its purposes are: (1) to facilitate the collection, tabulation, presentation, and analysis of data relating to establishments, and (2) to promote uniformity and comparability in the presentation of statistical data describing the economy. NAICS will be used by Federal statistical agencies that collect or publish data by industry. It is also expected to be widely used by State agencies, trade associations, private businesses, and other organizations.

The Instituto Nacional de Estadística, Geografía e Informatíca (INEGI) of Mexico, Statistics Canada, and the United States Office of Management and Budget (OMB), through its Economic Classification Policy Committee (ECPC), have collaborated on NAICS to make the industrial statistics produced in the three countries comparable. NAICS is the first industry classification system developed in accordance with a single principle of aggregation, the principle that producing units that use similar production processes should be grouped together in the classification. The fresh view of establishment data that this restructuring will provide should engender insights into the increasingly interrelated evolution of our economies. NAICS also reflects in a much more explicit way the enormous changes in technology and in the growth and diversification of services that have marked recent decades. Industry statistics compiled using NAICS will also be comparable with statistics compiled according to the latest revision of the United Nations' International Standard Industrial Classification (ISIC, Revision 3) for some sixty high level groupings.

NAICS will provide a consistent framework for the collection, tabulation, presentation, and analysis of industrial statistics used by government policy analysts, by academics and researchers, by the business community, and by the public. Because of differing national economic and institutional structures as well as limited resources and time for constructing NAICS, however, the NAICS structure has not been made entirely comparable at the individual industry level across all three countries. For some sectors and subsectors, the statistical agencies of the three countries have agreed to harmonize NAICS based on sectoral boundaries rather than on a detailed industry structure. Those sectors or subsectors are: utilities; construction; wholesale trade; retail trade; finance and insurance; real estate; waste management and remediation services; other services that include personal and laundry services, and religious, grantmaking, civic, and professional and similar organizations; and public administration. To ensure comparability between

Canada and the United States, the two countries have agreed on an industry structure and hierarchy for each sector listed above except for construction, wholesale trade, and public administration. In some cases within these sectors, the United States will provide for additional industries at the national level to reflect important industries in the United States that will not be shown separately in Canada. To distinguish the three countries' versions of NAICS, they are called NAICS Canada, NAICS Mexico (SCIAN Mexico, in Spanish), and NAICS United States.

In developing NAICS United States, OMB has published a total of seven previous Federal Register notices advising the public of the work of the ECPC and seeking comment on that work. The March 31, 1993, Federal Register notice (pp. 16990-17004) announced OMB's intention to revise the SIC for 1997, the establishment of the Economic Classification Policy Committee, and the process for revising the SIC. The July 26, 1994, Federal Register notice (pp. 38092-38096) set forth the concepts for the new system and the decision to develop NAICS in cooperation with Statistics Canada and INEGI. That notice also included a request for the public to submit recommendations for the industries to be included in the new system. The deadline for submitting proposals for new or revised industries was November 7, 1994.

After considering all proposals from the public, consulting with a large number of U.S. data users and industry groups, and undertaking extensive discussions with INEGI and Statistics Canada, a new industrial structure for NAICS that would apply to all three North American countries was developed. A series of five Federal Register notices sought comment on the structure of the system. These notices are described in more detail in the Supplementary Information section below.

As intimated by the description below of the NAICS development process, the actual classification presented at the end of this notice in Tables 1 and 2 reveals only the tip of the work carried out by dedicated individuals from INEGI, Statistics Canada, and U.S. statistical agencies. It is through their efforts, painstaking analysis, and spirit of accommodation that NAICS has emerged as a harmonized international classification of economic activities. This has been an immense undertaking that has required the time, energy, creativity, and cooperation of numerous people and organizations throughout the three countries. The work that has been accomplished is a testament to the individual and collective willingness of many persons and organizations both inside and outside government to contribute to the development of NAICS.

EFFECTIVE DATE: Federal statistical data published for reference years beginning on or after January 1, 1997, will be published using the new NAICS United States codes. NAICS is scheduled to go into effect in 1997 in Canada and the United States, and in 1998 in Mexico. Publication of the 1997 NAICS United States Manual is planned for December 1997. Use of NAICS for nonstatistical purposes (e.g., administrative, regulatory, or taxation) will be determined by the agency or agencies that have chosen to use the SIC for nonstatistical purposes. Readers interested in the effective dates for the use of NAICS for nonstatistical purposes should contact the relevant agency to determine its plans, if any, for a transition from use of the SIC to NAICS.

ADDRESSES: Please send correspondence about the final decisions to: Katherine K.

Wallman, Chief Statistician, Office of Management and Budget, New Executive Office Building, 725 17th Street, NW, Room 10201, Washington, D.C. 20503, telephone number: (202) 395-3093, FAX number: (202) 395-7245.

ELECTRONIC AVAILABILITY AND CORRESPONDENCE: This document is available on the Internet from the Census Bureau Internet site via WWW browser, ftp, and E-mail.

To obtain this document via WWW browser, connect to "http://www.census.govj then select "Subjects A to Z," then select "N," then select "NAICS (North American Industry Classification System)." This WWW page contains previous NAICS United States Federal Register notices and related documents as well.

To obtain this document via ftp, log into ftp.census.gov as anonymous, and retrieve the files "naicsfr8.pdf," "naicsfr8tbl1.pdf," and "naicsfr8tbl2.pdf" from the "/pub/epcd/naics" directory. (That directory also contains previous NAICS United States Federal Register notices and related documents.)

To obtain this document via Internet E-mail, send a message to majordomo@census.gov with the body text as follows: "get gatekeeper naics.txt". Instructions for obtaining this and other NAICS United States documents will be delivered as a message attachment.

Correspondence may be sent via Internet E-mail to OMB at naics@a1.eop.gov (do not include any capital letters in the address).

FOR FURTHER INFORMATION CONTACT: Paul Bugg, 10201 New Executive Office Bldg., Washington, D.C. 20503, E-mail address: bugg_p@a1.eop.gov, telephone number: (202) 395-3093, FAX number: (202) 395-7245. Inquiries about the content of industries or requests for electronic copies of the tables should be made to Carole Ambler, Coordinator, Economic Classification Policy Committee, Bureau of the Census,

Room 2633-3, Washington, D.C. 20233, E-mail address: cambler@ccmail.census.gov, telephone number: (301) 457-2668, FAX number: (301) 457-1343.

SUPPLEMENTARY INFORMATION:

NAICS Development Process

The Standard Industrial Classification (SIC) was originally developed in the 1930's to classify establishments by the type of activity in which they are primarily engaged and to promote the comparability of establishment data describing various facets of the U.S. economy. The SIC covers the entire field of economic activities by defining industries in accordance with the composition and structure of the economy. Over the years, it was revised periodically to reflect the economy's changing industry composition and organization. OMB last updated the SIC in 1987.

In recent years, rapid changes in both the U.S. and world economies brought the SIC under increasing criticism. The 1991 International Conference on the Classification of Economic Activities provided a forum for exploring the issues and for considering new approaches to classifying economic activity.

In July 1992, the Office of Management and Budget established the Economic Classification Policy Committee chaired by the Bureau of Economic Analysis, U.S. Department of Commerce, with representatives from the Bureau of the Census, U.S. Department of Commerce, and the Bureau of Labor Statistics, U.S. Department of Labor. OMB charged the ECPC with conducting a "fresh slate" examination of economic classifications for statistical purposes and determining the desirability of developing a new industry classification system for the United States based on a single economic concept. A March 31, 1993, Federal Register notice (pp. 16990-17004) announced OMB's intention to revise the SIC for 1997, the establishment of the Economic Classification Policy Committee, and the process for revising the SIC. The ECPC published six issue papers relating to industrial classification for comment. Those papers are as follows:

Issues Paper No. 1 - Conceptual Issues
Issues Paper No. 2 - Aggregation Structures and Hierarchies
Issues Paper No. 3 - Collectibility of Data
Issues Paper No. 4 - Criteria for Determining Industries
Issues Paper No. 5 - The Impact of Classification Revisions on Time Series
Issues Paper No. 6 - Services Classifications

In addition to these issue papers, two research reports were published providing further information on industry classifications. The first report was part of a comparative review of Canadian and U.S. SIC concepts. The ECPC and Statistics Canada reviewed the existing structure of detailed "4-digit" industries in the 1987 U.S. SIC and the 1980 Canadian SIC for conformance to economic concepts. The results of the U.S. review are contained in ECPC Report No. 1., "Economic Concepts Incorporated in the Standard Industrial Classification Industries of the United States," and the Canadian results are contained in "The Conceptual Basis of the Standard Industrial Classification," Standards Division, Statistics Canada. The second ECPC report evaluated U.S. industries using the new "index of heterogeneity" to assess whether establishments in existing 1987 4-digit industries met the conditions for the production-oriented classification concept, as presented in ECPC Issues Paper No. 1. The ECPC Report No. 2 is titled "The Heterogeneity Index: A Quantitative Tool to Support Industrial Classification.j

A July 26, 1994, Federal Register notice (pp. 38092-38096) announced that the ECPC was developing NAICS in cooperation with INEGI and Statistics Canada and proposed that NAICS replace the 1980 Canadian SIC, the Mexican Classification of Activities and Products (1994) (CMAP), the industry classification system of Mexico, and the 1987 SIC in the United States. The notice requested comments on that proposal and on the structure of the new system. That notice also included the concepts of the new system and the principles upon which the three countries proposed to develop NAICS, as follows:

(1) NAICS will be erected on a production-oriented, or supply-based, conceptual framework. This means that producing units that use identical or similar production processes will be grouped together in NAICS.

(2) The system will give special attention to developing production-oriented classifications for (a) new and emerging industries, (b) service industries in general, and (c) industries engaged in the production of advanced technologies.

(3) Time series continuity will be maintained to the extent possible. However, changes in the economy and proposals from data users must be considered. In addition, adjustments will be required for sectors where Canada, Mexico, and the United States presently have incompatible industry classification definitions in order to produce a common industry system for all three North American countries.

(4) The system will strive for compatibility with the 2-digit level of the International Standard Industrial Classification of All Economic Activities (ISIC, Rev. 3) of the United Nations.

In response to the July 26, 1994, Federal Register notice, the ECPC received 125 public responses to the call for proposals for new and revised industries, plus 8 responses from 6 State government agencies, and 9 responses from 6 Federal Government agencies. These formal responses contained several hundred proposals. Additional proposals and suggestions for change arose from the extensive ECPC public outreach program, which consisted of meetings and other communications with industry, data user, and data respondent groups. Other proposals for modifications such as changing industry definitions and clarifying boundaries, came from U.S. statistical agency personnel who worked on NAICS, reflecting accumulated public comments and criticism, over a number of years, of the U.S. SIC system. The ECPC also received a number of proposals to eliminate U.S. industries, or to combine them with other industries.

Comments to the ECPC from these sources ranged over many aspects of the 1987 SIC system. For example, approximately 20 percent of the formal letters received concerned ambiguities in the titles and definitions of the 1987 SIC industries, and incomplete or out-of-date product lists. More than 40 respondents requested better-defined product detail within existing industries, without necessarily requesting changes to industry boundaries. These product-oriented requests and suggestions are being handled through the redesign of forms where product information is collected in the 1997 Economic Censuses.

Another group of responses to the notice were proposals for a "separate, market-oriented product grouping system" (July 26, 1994, Federal Register, p. 38095). These proposals were submitted as industry proposals but, after analysis by the ECPC, were found more appropriately to be market-oriented product groupings, and have been held over for action during production of the product coding system discussed below.

Proposals were also received for changing or modifying the boundaries of existing industries, without necessarily creating a new industry. In addition, changes to 1987 SIC industry definitions were frequently required to bring about compatibility with the Canadian and Mexican classifications (as were corresponding changes in those countries' classification systems). Those changes are listed and described in five Federal Register notices that portray portions of the proposed NAICS United States system. These notices are described more fully below. Some changes that were required for international compatibility interacted with proposed changes from the U.S. public, and in some cases the two kinds of changes resulted in a broader rethinking of the entire portion of the structure.

The ECPC established seven subcommittees composed of senior economists, statisticians, and classification specialists representing 14 of the Federal agencies that use the SIC. Subcommittees were established for Agriculture; Mining and Manufacturing; Construction; Distribution Networks (retail trade; wholesale trade; and transportation, communications, and utilities); Finance, Insurance, and Real Estate; Business and Personal Services; and Health, Social Assistance, and Public Administration. They were responsible for developing the proposed structure of NAICS in cooperation with representatives from INEGI and Statistics Canada. The ECPC also established the U.S. Coordinating Committee that was responsible for coordinating the work of the U.S. subcommittees and the work with INEGI and Statistics Canada.

The structure of NAICS was developed in a series of meetings among the three countries. Public proposals for individual industries from all three countries were considered for acceptance if the proposed industry was based on the production-oriented concept of NAICS.

As groups of subsectors of NAICS were completed and agreed upon by the three countries, the ECPC published the proposed industries for those subsectors for public comment in the Federal Register. Five successive Federal Register notices were published asking for comment. A first notice published in the Federal Register, July 26, 1995 (pp. 38436-38452), requested comment on proposed industry structures for petroleum and coal product manufacturing, chemical manufacturing, and rubber and plastics manufacturing; for broadcasting and telecommunications; and for food services and drinking places and accommodations. A second Federal Register notice published on February 6, 1996 (pp. 4524-4578), requested comment on proposed industry structures for crop production, animal production, forestry and logging; textile mills, textile product mills, apparel manufacturing, and leather and allied product manufacturing; food manufacturing and beverage and tobacco product manufacturing; fabricated metal product manufacturing; machinery manufacturing; electrical equipment, appliance and component manufacturing; and transportation equipment manufacturing. A third Federal Register notice published on May 28, 1996 (pp. 26558-26668), requested comment on proposed industry structures for health and social assistance; educational services; computers and electronics product manufacturing; furniture manufacturing; printing and related support activities; professional, technical and scientific services; performing arts, spectator sports and related industries; museums, historical sites and similar institutions; recreation, amusement and gambling; information; wood product manufacturing, except furniture; rental and leasing; repair and maintenance; management and support; transportation; mining; paper manufacturing; nonmetallic minerals manufacturing; primary metal manufacturing; miscellaneous manufacturing; and postal service and couriers. A fourth Federal Register notice published on July 5, 1996 (pp. 35384-35515), requested comment on proposed industry structures for finance and insurance; wholesale trade; retail trade; construction; utilities; waste management and remediation services; real estate; lessors of other nonfinancial assets; personal and laundry services; and religious, grant making, civic, and other membership organizations. That notice also requested comments on the proposed hierarchy and coding system for NAICS. Finally, a fifth Federal Register notice published on November 5, 1996 (pp. 57006-57183), announced the ECPC's final recommendations to OMB for the complete structure of

NAICS United States, including the hierarchy and coding system, and asked for public comments. Final comments were due on December 20, 1996. Changes incorporated into the new system based on comments in response to the November 5, 1996, notice are presented in the section below containing OMB's Final Decisions.

In response to those notices, the ECPC received approximately 400 additional comments. A significant number of these comments supported the development of NAICS, expressed the view that NAICS is a significant improvement over the SIC system, or supported the inclusion in NAICS of specific industries. Other comments requested clarification of a concept or industry title. Of the few who commented on the proposed coding system, over one-half supported the 6-digit system that has been adopted. Over one-half of the comments received requested changes to the proposed system. Some of these proposed changes were requests for new or revised industries even though the deadline for receiving such requests was November 7, 1994. However, the ECPC did consider these new requests. There were also requests for title changes. Each comment was carefully considered, as were comments received by INEGI and Statistics Canada. After consultation with INEGI and Statistics Canada, changes based on the comments were incorporated into the ECPC's final recommendations to OMB for NAICS United States as presented in the November 5, 1996, Federal Register notice (pp. 57006-57183).

NAICS Structure

NAICS is organized in a hierarchical structure, much like the existing U.S. SIC. The 1987 SIC employs a 4-digit coding system, in which the first two digits designate a "major group" that in NAICS is known as a "subsector," the third digit designates the industry group, and the fourth digit designates the industry. For example, in the 1987 U.S. SIC, the two digits 26 designate the major group for the manufacture of "Paper and Allied Products," within which the digits 262 designate an industry group titled "Paper Mills," which contains one 4-digit industry, SIC 2621, also titled "Paper Mills."

NAICS employs a 6-digit coding system in which the first two digits designate the sector (the NAICS term "sector" is replacing the term "division" used in the 1987 SIC), the third digit designates the subsector, the fourth digit designates the industry group, the fifth digit represents the NAICS industry (the most detailed level at which comparable data will be available for Canada, Mexico, and the United States), and the sixth digit designates individual country-level national industries. Using the paper mill example above, in NAICS United States industry 322121 the two initial digits 32 designate a manufacturing sector and the three digits 322 designate the paper manufacturing subsector. Within 322 is the industry group 3221, Pulp, Paper, and Paperboard Mills, within which is NAICS industry 32212, Paper Mills. There are two U.S. national industries under Paper Mills: 322121, Paper (except Newsprint) Mills, and 322122, Newsprint Mills.

The NAICS coding system was expanded to six digits from the four digits used in the SIC for two reasons. First, it is desirable that the first character or characters in a coding system designate the sector. A modern economy is too complex to be described adequately with the nine or ten sectors permitted by using only a single digit in a coding system. For example, NAICS has 20 sectors. Accordingly, the first two digits are used to designate the sector in NAICS.

Second, the NAICS agreements among the ECPC, INEGI, and Statistics Canada permit each country to designate detailed industries, below the level of a five-digit NAICS industry, to meet national needs. The United States will have such national industry detail in many places in the new classification. The sixth digit in the NAICS United States codes designates the U.S. detailed national industries.

Thus NAICS will have a six-digit coding system in which the first two digits designate the NAICS sector, and the third, fourth, fifth, and sixth digits designate, respectively, the NAICS subsector, industry group, and industry, and U.S. national industry (if any). Although the 1997 NAICS United States industries will now have six digits compared with four digits for 1987 U.S. SIC industries, there will not be a uniform corresponding increase in classification detail that the 1997 NAICS United States provides compared with the 1987 U.S. SIC. As explained above, the two additional digits primarily allow for more sectors and for individual country-level detailed national industries.

NAICS United States Highlights

The 1987 U.S. SIC (excluding Nonclassifiable Establishments) includes 10 divisions subdivided into 1004 4-digit industries, of which 125 are nonmanufacturing goods producing industries (agriculture, mining, construction, and electric, natural gas, and water utility industries); 459 are manufacturing industries; and 420 are service producing industries. In contrast, the 1997 NAICS United States (excluding Unclassified Establishments) has 20 sectors subdivided into 1174 5-digit and/or 6-digit industries, of which 132 are nonmanufacturing goods producing industries (agriculture, mining, construction, and electric, natural gas, and water utility industries); 473 are manufacturing industries; and 569 are service producing industries. Most of the 170 industry increase between the 1987 U.S. SIC and the 1997 NAICS United States is in the service producing industries with a net increase of 149 industries, although there are net increases of seven industries in the Agriculture, Forestry, Hunting, and Fishing sector; one in Utilities; two in Construction; and 14 in Manufacturing. There is a net decrease of three industries in Mining.

Most of the changes in the Agriculture, Forestry, Hunting, and Fishing sector and the Mining sector are the result of changes necessary to achieve comparability with Canada and Mexico. The Utilities sector was reorganized to reflect the changing regulatory and technological structure of the industries within that sector.

The Manufacturing sector was reorganized to promote international comparability and to recognize technological changes occurring in that sector. For example, a new subsector, Computer and Electronic Product Manufacturing, was created to bring together industries producing electronic products and their components. The manufacture of computers, communications equipment, audio and video equipment, and semiconductors is grouped into the same subsector because of the inherent technological similarities of their production processes, and the likelihood that these technologies will continue to converge in the future. An important change is that the reproduction of packaged software is placed in this sector, rather than in the services sector, because the reproduction of packaged software is a manufacturing process, and the product moves through the wholesale and retail distribution systems like any other manufactured product. NAICS acknowledges the importance of these electronic industries, their rapid growth over the past several years, and the likelihood that these industries will, in the future, become even more important in the economies of the three North American countries.

NAICS creates a new sector, Information, that groups industries that primarily create and disseminate products with intellectual property content. In addition, the NAICS Information sector brings together those activities that transform information into a commodity that is produced and distributed, and activities that provide the means for distributing those products, other than through traditional wholesale-retail distribution channels. A few of the newly revised industries in this sector include: database and directory publishers; software publishers; music publishers; paging services; cellular and other wireless telecommunications services; telecommunications resellers; and satellite telecommunications. Also included in the Information sector are newspaper, periodical, and book publishers (but not printing, which is still included in manufacturing); motion picture and sound recording industries; and libraries and archives. There are 34 industries in the Information sector, 20 of which are new.

NAICS divides the 1987 SIC Services division into eight new sectors. One of the new sectors is the Professional, Scientific and Technical Services sector, which comprises establishments engaged in activities where human capital is the major input. The industries within this sector are defined by the expertise and training of the service provider. The sector includes such industries as offices of lawyers; engineering services; environmental consulting services; advertising agencies; and translation and interpretation services. Forty-eight industries comprise this sector, 29 of which are recognized for the first time.

The new sector, Health Care and Social Assistance, recognizes the merging of the boundaries of health care and social assistance. The industries in this new sector are arranged in an order that reflects the range and extent of health care and social assistance provided. Some new industries are family planning centers, out-patient mental health and substance abuse centers, HMO medical centers, diagnostic imaging centers, continuing care retirement communities, and homes for the elderly. This sector has 39 industries, 27 of which are new.

A new sector for Arts, Entertainment, and Recreation greatly expands the number of industries provided for these services. There are 25 industries in this sector, 19 of which are new.

Another new sector is Accommodation and Foodservices that combines eating and drinking places (formerly in Retail Trade) with accommodations (formerly in the Services division). There are 15 industries in this sector, 10 of which are new. Some new industries recognized in this sector are casino hotels, bed and breakfast inns, full-service restaurants, and limited-service restaurants.

Other new sectors that were created from industries in the 1987 SIC Services division are Real Estate and Rental and Leasing that has 24 industries, 15 of which are new; Administrative and Support, Waste Management and Remediation Services that has

43 industries, 29 of which are new; Educational Services that has 17 industries, 12 of which are new; and Other Services (except Public Administration) that has 52 industries, 19 of which are new.

Product Classification System

The July 26, 1994, Federal Register notice (p. 38095) specifies that market-oriented, or demand-based groupings of economic data are required for many purposes; some of these purposes may not be well served by a production-oriented industry classification system. The ECPC committed to a program that will provide improved data for purposes that require market-orient groupings.

The first part of that commitment was to expand the lists of commodities and services that would be available from the 1997 Economic Census. A Product Code Task Force was formed and charged with improving the basic lists of products and commodities and with constructing new detailed codes that will be compatible across U.S. statistical agencies and that will also mesh to the extent possible with international detailed commodity or product systems. In the manufacturing area, the investment goods product detail (1987 SIC major groups 35-38) has been revised to better compare to the international Harmonized System product detail. In addition, the Census Bureau and Bureau of Labor Statistics have developed a plan to provide more comparable product data from their statistical programs. In the nongoods producing industries, additional product detail has been added for certain industries, including professional, scientific, and technical services; software publishing; and communications.

The second part of the ECPC commitment was to develop a product classification system for use by all U.S. government statistical agencies in 2002. Preliminary plans are now being developed to begin the process of creating a product classification system. It is planned to develop this system in cooperation with INEGI and Statistics Canada.

OMB's Final Decisions

After taking into consideration comments submitted in response to the November 5, 1996, Federal Register notice, as well as benefits and costs, and after consultation with the ECPC, INEGI, and Statistics Canada, OMB has made the final determination of the scope and substance of NAICS United States. In general, OMB accepted the ECPC's final recommendations published in the November 5, 1996, Federal Register notice. However, in response to public comment and additional information gained in consultation with the ECPC, INEGI, and Statistics Canada, OMB made some changes to the ECPC's recommendations for NAICS United States.

OMB received 37 public responses and 6 responses from State government agencies to the November 5, 1996, Federal Register notice. Comments to OMB from these sources can be grouped into a few categories. Almost half the letters requested further changes to the NAICS United States structure, including title changes. OMB carefully considered these requests and any changes accepted are noted below. Seven of the letters specifically supported NAICS United States and thanked the ECPC for its work. Three of the letters objected to the reclassification of auxiliaries, which also is addressed below. The remainder of the letters requested clarification of industry content, discussed detailed implementation issues, or spoke of regulatory concerns. The ECPC is currently preparing a response for each of these letters.

In response to comments and consultation, OMB has made the following determinations:

Mining - NAICS United States 213112, Support Activities for Oil and Gas Field Exploration, and 213113, Other Oil and Gas Field Support Activities, have been combined and numbered and titled, 213112, Support Activities for Oil and Gas Field Operations. Since geophysical mapping and surveying has been moved to NAICS 54136, Geophysical Survey and Mapping Services, the remaining activities in the original NAICS United States 213112, Support Activities for Oil and Gas Field Exploration, are too small to support a separate industry. Because of the above change, the following industries have been renumbered: Support Activities for Coal Mining, is now 213113; Support Activities for Metal Mining is now 213114; and Support Activities for Non-Metallic Minerals (except Fuels) is now 213115.

Manufacturing - NAICS subsector 337 Furniture and Related Product Manufacturing has been revised. The new structure changes from an emphasis on furniture manufacture by type of material, i.e., wood, metal, and other materials, to one by type of furniture, i.e., household, office and other. A separate NAICS industry also was created for kitchen cabinet and countertop manufacturing. This change better represents the way the furniture industry is structured and is consistent with the production principle on which NAICS is based. The creation of many detailed furniture manufacturing NAICS industries for the three countries was not possible, however, because the internal structure of furniture manufacturing differs from country to country. For example, the production of institutional furniture (furniture for schools, libraries, etc.) combined with the production of household furniture takes place in a significant number of establishments in one country and does not in another; similarly, the combined production of custom architectural woodwork and millwork and of office furniture takes place in a significant number of establishments in one country and does not in another.

NAICS United States 321912, Hardwood Dimension Mills, and 321913, Softwood Cut Stock, Resawing Lumber, and Planing, are combined into NAICS United States 321912, Cut Stock, Resawing Lumber, and Planing. The processes used to produce the products of these industries are the same or similar, the major difference being the use of hardwood versus softwood. Therefore, the industries are combined. NAICS United States 339117, Eyeglass and Contact Lens Manufacturing, is combined with NAICS United States 339115, Ophthalmic Goods Manufacturing. There is no production distinction between these two industries and thus they are combined.

NAICS United States 331421 has been renamed Copper Rolling, Drawing, and Extruding and NAICS United States 331422 has been renamed Copper Wire (except Mechanical) Drawing. This clarifies the fact that brass mills producing mechanical wire are included in 331421 and wire mills producing wire are classified in 331422. Other title changes in manufacturing are: 311225 is retitled Fats and Oils Refining and Blending; 325188 is retitled All Other Basic Inorganic Chemical Manufacturing; 325199 is retitled All Other Basic Organic Chemical Manufacturing; 325221 is retitled Cellulosic Organic Fiber Manufacturing; 32552 is retitled Adhesive Manufacturing; 32731 is retitled Cement Manufacturing; 336322 is retitled Other Motor Vehicle Electrical and Electronic Equipment Manufacturing; and 339911 is retitled Jewelry (except Costume) Manufacturing.

Retail - NAICS United States 453999, All Other Miscellaneous Store Retailers (except Tobacco Stores) is renumbered to 453998. There is no change in the title.

Transportation and Warehousing - NAICS 48121, Nonscheduled Chartered Air Transportation, and NAICS 48122, Nonscheduled Specialty Air Transportation, have been combined and numbered and titled, 48121, Nonscheduled Air Transportation. Since some of the typical activities performed by establishments providing a combination of specialty air transportation or flying services overlap with establishments providing nonscheduled chartered air transportation of passengers and/or cargo, the three countries agreed to combine these establishments into one NAICS industry. The U.S. national industries within NAICS 48121, Nonscheduled Air Transportation, are as follows: NAICS United States 481211, Nonscheduled Chartered Passenger Air Transportation; NAICS United States 481212, Nonscheduled Chartered Freight Air Transportation; and NAICS United States 481219, Other Nonscheduled Air Transportation.

The following NAICS industry groups and industries are retitled: 4852 is retitled Interurban and Rural Bus Transportation; 48521 is retitled Interurban and Rural Bus Transportation; 4854 is retitled School and Employee Bus Transportation; 48541 is retitled School and Employee Bus Transportation; NAICS United States 488112 is retitled and renumbered 488119, Other Airport Operations; 49311 is retitled General Warehousing and Storage Facilities; 49312 is retitled Refrigerated Warehousing and Storage Facilities; 49313 is retitled Farm Product Warehousing and Storage Facilities; and 49319 is retitled Other Warehousing and Storage Facilities.

Finance and Insurance - NAICS 52593 has been retitled Real Estate Investment Trusts.

Professional, Scientific, and Technical Services - NAICS United States 541199 has been retitled All Other Legal Services; NAICS 54143 has been retitled Graphic Design Services; and 54182 has been retitled Public Relations Agencies.

Management of Companies and Enterprises - NAICS United States 551113 has been renumbered 551114, Corporate, Subsidiary and Regional Managing Offices.

Administrative and Support Services - NAICS United States 561431 has been renumbered and retitled 561439, Other Business Service Centers (including Copy Shops) and NAICS United States 561432 has been renumbered 561431, Private Mail Centers.

Accommodation and Foodservices - NAICS 72233 has been retitled Mobile Foodservices.

Other Services (except Public Administration) - NAICS United States 811121 has been retitled Automotive Body, Paint, and Interior Repair and Maintenance and NAICS industry group 8122 has been retitled Death Care Services.

Auxiliaries - Three private sector commentors and one State agency objected to classifying auxiliary establishments (those establishments that primarily produce support services not intended for use outside the enterprise) based on their primary activity rather than maintaining the historic SIC treatment of classifying auxiliary establishments based on the industry classification of the establishments they primarily serve. Two State government agencies supported the change. Those who objected acknowledge that there are problems associated with the 1987 SIC classification of auxiliaries, but are concerned about the loss of employment in manufacturing industries if auxiliary establishments such as accounting offices, administrative and corporate offices, and warehouses are classified according to their primary activity.

NAICS, however, is based on the economic principle that establishments should be grouped together based on their production processes, i.e., units that use identical or similar production processes in producing a good or service should be grouped together. For example, classifying a data processing services establishment of an automobile producer that performs services for its automobile assembly plants in the automobile industry violates that principle. The data processing center's production process is much more like that of establishments in NAICS 51421, Data Processing Services, than those establishments in NAICS United States 336111, Automobile Manufacturing.

In addition, more and more of these auxiliary establishments are selling their services to establishments outside their enterprise. For example, the 1992 Economic Censuses reported that auxiliary establishments had more than $142 billion in outside sales, more than doubling the $64 billion reported in 1987. These sales are not reflected in the industries in which they occur, but rather in the industries that the auxiliary establishment primarily serves, thereby understating the receipts of many service industries. Therefore, NAICS will classify auxiliary establishments based on their primary activity.

To address the concern about the apparent loss of manufacturing employment, the Census Bureau will code auxiliary establishments for the 1997 Economic Censuses both by primary activity and by the industry of the establishments they primarily serve, thereby providing a link between the 1992 and 1997 data.

NAICS United States Implementation

The NAICS United States replacement of the SIC is effective January 1, 1997. The first data to be available on a NAICS United States basis will be from the 1997 Economic Censuses to be published in early 1999. For most programs, data will be introduced over several years. Data series may not always be revised for years before the respective program's implementation of NAICS United States.

INEGI, OMB, and Statistics Canada have put in place a process for ensuring that the implementation of NAICS is comparable across all three countries. Regularly scheduled meetings among the three countries will ensure that there is a smooth transition to NAICS in all three countries. In addition, the three countries plan to continually review and update NAICS to ensure that new activities are promptly recognized and to extend NAICS to the 5-digit industry level in those sectors where agreement is now at only the sector, subsector, or industry group level.

Time Series Continuity

The standard approach to preserving time series continuity after classification revisions is to create linkages where the series break. This is accomplished by producing the data series using both the old and new classifications for a given period of transition.

With the dual classifications of data, the full impact of the revision can be assessed. Data producers then may measure the reallocation of the data at aggregate industry levels and develop a concordance between the new and old series for that given point in time. The concordance creates a crosswalk between the old and new classification systems. This link between the 1987 U.S. SIC and the 1997 NAICS United States will be developed by the statistical agencies in the U.S.

NAICS Nonstatistical Use

NAICS was designed, as was the SIC before it, solely for statistical purposes. Although it is expected that NAICS, like the SIC, will also be used for various nonstatistical purposes (e.g., administrative, regulatory, or taxation), the requirements of government agencies that use it for nonstatistical purposes have played no role in its development.

Consequently, as has been the case with the SIC (Statistical Policy Directive No. 8, Standard Industrial Classification of Establishments), NAICS shall not be used in any administrative, regulatory, or tax program unless the head of the agency administering that program has first determined that the use of such industry definitions is appropriate to the implementation of the program's objectives. If the terms, "North American Industry Classification System," "NAICS," or "NAICS United States" are to be used in the operative text of any law or regulation to define industry (or trade or commerce), language similar to the following should be used to assure sufficient flexibility: "An industry or grouping of industries shall mean a North American Industry Classification System industry or grouping of industries as defined by the Office of Management and Budget subject to such modifications with respect to individual industries or groupings of industries as the Secretary (Administrator) may determine to be appropriate for the purpose of this Act (regulation).j

1997 NAICS United States Industry Structure and Relationship to 1987 SIC

Table 1 below presents the final decisions for the entire structure of the 1997 NAICS United States classification system including both 5-digit NAICS and 6-digit NAICS United States national detail industries. It shows the hierarchy and the coding system in 1997 NAICS United States sequence; it also relates the 1997 NAICS United States to the 1987 U.S. SIC.

Table 2 is in 1987 U.S. SIC sequence and relates the 1987 U.S. SIC industries to the 1997 NAICS United States including the 6-digit U.S. national detail industries. All OMB final changes to the structure of the 1997 NAICS United States based on public comment and consultation with the ECPC, INEGI, and Statistics Canada are included in Tables 1 and 2.

Table 1. 1997 NAICS Matched to 1987 SIC

1997 NAICS United States Structure, Including Relationship to 1987 U.S. SIC

Table 1 - 1997 NAICS United States Matched to 1987 U.S. SIC

1997 NAICS Code	1997 NAICS United States and U.S. Description	Status Code	1987 SIC Code	1987 U.S. SIC Description
11	Agriculture, Forestry, Fishing and Hunting			
111	Crop Production			
1111	Oilseed and Grain Farming			
11111	Soybean Farming	E	0116	Soybeans
11112	Oilseed (except Soybean) Farming	N	*0119	Cash Grains, NEC (oilseed, except soybean farming)
11113	Dry Pea and Bean Farming	N	*0119	Cash Grains, NEC (dry pea and bean farms)
11114	Wheat Farming	E	0111	Wheat
11115	Corn Farming	R	0115	Corn
			*0119	Cash Grains, NEC (popcorn farming)
11116	Rice Farming	E	0112	Rice
11119	Other Grain Farming			
111191	Oilseed and Grain Combination Farming	N	*0119	Cash Grains, NEC (oilseed and grain combination farms)
111199	All Other Grain Farming	R	*0119	Cash Grains, NEC (except popcorn, soybean, and dry pea and bean, and oilseed and grain combination farms)
1112	Vegetable and Melon Farming			
11121	Vegetable and Melon Farming			
111211	Potato Farming	E	0134	Irish Potatoes
111219	Other Vegetable (except Potato) and Melon Farming	R	0161	Vegetables and Melons
			*0139	Field Crops Except Cash Grains (sweet potatoes and yams)
1113	Fruit and Tree Nut Farming			
11131	Orange Groves	N	*0174	Citrus Fruits (orange groves and farms)
11132	Citrus (except Orange) Groves	R	*0174	Citrus Fruits (except, orange groves and farms)
11133	Noncitrus Fruit and Tree Nut Farming			
111331	Apple Orchards	N	*0175	Deciduous Tree Fruits (apple orchards and farms)
111332	Grape Vineyards	E	0172	Grapes
111333	Strawberry Farming	N	*0171	Berry Crops (strawberry farms)
111334	Berry (except Strawberry) Farming	R	*0171	Berry Crops (except strawberry farms)
111335	Tree Nut Farming	E	0173	Tree Nuts
111336	Fruit and Tree Nut Combination Farming	N	*0179	Fruits and Tree Nuts, NEC (combination farms)
111339	Other Noncitrus Fruit Farming	R	*0175	Deciduous Tree Fruits (except apple orchards and farms)

The definitions of status codes are as follows: E--existing industry; L--nonexistent (null set) industry in U.S.; N--new industry; R--revised industry; and * means "part of" The abbreviation NEC is used for Not Elsewhere Classified.

1997 NAICS Code	1997 NAICS United States and U.S. Description	Status Code	1987 SIC Code	1987 U.S. SIC Description
			*0179	Fruit and Tree Nuts, NEC (except combination farms)
1114	Greenhouse, Nursery and Floriculture Production			
11141	Food Crops Grown Under Cover			
111411	Mushroom Production	N	*0182	Food Crops Grown Under Cover (mushrooms, growing of)
111419	Other Food Crops Grown Under Cover	R	*0182	Food Crops Grown Under Cover (except mushroom, growing of)
11142	Nursery and Floriculture Production			
111421	Nursery and Tree Production	N	*0181	Ornamental Floriculture and Nursery Products (nursery farming)
			*0811	Timber Tracts (short rotation woody crops)
111422	Floriculture Production	N	*0181	Ornamental Floriculture and Nursery Products (floriculture farming)
1119	Other Crop Farming			
11191	Tobacco Farming	E	0132	Tobacco
11192	Cotton Farming	E	0131	Cotton
11193	Sugarcane Farming	N	*0133	Sugarcane and Sugar Beets (sugarcane farms)
11194	Hay Farming	N	*0139	Field Crops, Except Cash Grains, NEC (hay farms)
11199	All Other Crop Farming			
111991	Sugar Beet Farming	N	*0133	Sugarcane and Sugar Beets (sugar beet farms)
111992	Peanut Farming	N	*0139	Field Crops, Except Cash Grains, NEC (peanut farms)
111998	All Other Miscellaneous Crop Farming	R	*0139	Field Crops, Except Cash Grains, NEC (except peanut, sweet potato, yam and hay farms)
			0191	General Farms, Primarily Crop
			*0831	Forest Products (maple sap, gathering of)
			*0919	Miscellaneous Marine Products (plant aquaculture)
			*2099	Food Preparations, NEC (reducing maple sap to maple syrup)
112	Animal Production			
1121	Cattle Ranching and Farming			
11211	Beef Cattle Ranching and Farming, including Feedlots			
112111	Beef Cattle Ranching and Farming	R	0212	Beef Cattle, Except Feedlots (cattle farms)
			*0241	Dairy Farms (dairy heifer replacement farms)
112112	Cattle Feedlots	E	0211	Beef Cattle Feedlots (cattle farms)
11212	Dairy Cattle and Milk Production	R	*0241	Dairy Farms
11213	Dual Purpose Cattle Ranching and Farming	L		
1122	Hog and Pig Farming			
11221	Hog and Pig Farming	E	0213	Hogs
1123	Poultry and Egg Production			
11231	Chicken Egg Production	E	0252	Chicken Eggs
11232	Broilers and Other Meat Type Chicken Production	E	0251	Broiler, Fryers, and Roaster Chickens
11233	Turkey Production	E	0253	Turkey and Turkey Eggs
11234	Poultry Hatcheries	E	0254	Poultry Hatcheries
11239	Other Poultry Production	E	0259	Poultry and Eggs, NEC
1124	Sheep and Goat Farming			

11241	Sheep Farming	N	*0214	Sheep and Goats (sheep farms)
11242	Goat Farming	N	*0214	Sheep and Goats (goat farms)
1125	Animal Aquaculture			
11251	Animal Aquaculture			
112511	Finfish Farming and Fish Hatcheries	N	*0273	Animal Aquaculture (finfish farms)
			*0921	Fish Hatcheries and Preserves (finfish hatcheries)
112512	Shellfish Farming	N	*0273	Animal Aquaculture (shellfish farms)
			*0921	Fish Hatcheries and Preserves (shellfish hatcheries)
112519	Other Animal Aquaculture	R	*0273	Animal Aquaculture (except finfish and shellfish)
1129	Other Animal Production			
11291	Apiculture	N	*0279	Animal Specialties, NEC (apiculture)
11292	Horse and Other Equine Production	E	0272	Horse and Other Equine
11293	Fur-Bearing Animal and Rabbit Production	E	0271	Fur-Bearing Animals and Rabbits
11299	All Other Animal Production	R	0219	General Livestock, Except Dairy and Poultry
			*0279	Animal Specialties, NEC (except apiculture)
			0291	General Farms, Primarily Livestock and Animal Specialties
113	Forestry and Logging			
1131	Timber Tract Operations			
11311	Timber Tract Operations	R	*0811	Timber Tracts (long term timber farms)
1132	Forest Nurseries and Gathering of Forest Products			
11321	Forest Nurseries and Gathering of Forest Products	E	*0831	Forest Nurseries and Gathering of Forest Products (forest products, except gathering of maple sap)
1133	Logging			
11331	Logging	E	2411	Logging
114	Fishing, Hunting and Trapping			
1141	Fishing			
11411	Fishing			
114111	Finfish Fishing	E	0912	Finfish
114112	Shellfish Fishing	E	0913	Shellfish
114119	Other Marine Fishing	R	*0919	Miscellaneous Marine Products (except plant aquaculture)
1142	Hunting and Trapping			
11421	Hunting and Trapping	E	0971	Hunting and Trapping, and Game Propagation
115	Support Activities for Agriculture and Forestry			
1151	Support Activities for Crop Production			
11511	Support Activities for Crop Production			
115111	Cotton Ginning	E	0724	Cotton Ginning
115112	Soil Preparation, Planting, and Cultivating	R	0711	Soil Preparation Services
			*0721	Crop Planting, Cultivating, and Protecting (other)

1997 NAICS Code	1997 NAICS United States and U.S. Description	Status Code	1987 SIC Code	1987 U.S. SIC Description
115113	Crop Harvesting, Primarily by Machine	E	0722	Crop Harvesting, Primarily by Machine
115114	Postharvest Crop Activities (except Cotton Ginning)	E	0723	Crop Preparation Services For Market, Except Cotton Ginning
115115	Farm Labor Contractors and Crew Leaders	E	0761	Farm Labor Contractors and Crew Leaders
115116	Farm Management Services	E	0762	Farm Management Services
1152	Support Activities for Animal Production			
11521	Support Activities for Animal Production	N	*0751	Livestock Services, Except Veterinary (except custom slaughtering)
			*0752	Animal Specialty Services, Except Veterinary (horses and equines services and animal production breeding)
			*7699	Repair Services, NEC (farriers)
1153	Support Activities for Forestry			
11531	Support Activities for Forestry	R	0851	Forestry Services
21	Mining			
211	Oil and Gas Extraction			
2111	Oil and Gas Extraction			
21111	Oil and Gas Extraction			
211111	Crude Petroleum and Natural Gas Extraction	E	1311	Crude Petroleum and Natural Gas
211112	Natural Gas Liquid Extraction	E	1321	Natural Gas Liquids
212	Mining (except Oil and Gas)			
2121	Coal Mining			
21211	Coal Mining			
212111	Bituminous Coal and Lignite Surface Mining	E	1221	Bituminous Coal and Lignite Surface Mining
212112	Bituminous Coal Underground Mining	E	1222	Bituminous Coal Underground Mining
212113	Anthracite Mining	E	1231	Anthracite Mining
2122	Metal Ore Mining			
21221	Iron Ore Mining	E	1011	Iron Ores
21222	Gold Ore and Silver Ore Mining			
212221	Gold Ore Mining	E	1041	Gold Ores
212222	Silver Ore Mining	E	1044	Silver Ores
21223	Copper, Nickel, Lead and Zinc Mining			
212231	Lead Ore and Zinc Ore Mining	E	1031	Lead and Zinc Ores
212234	Copper Ore and Nickel Ore Mining	R	1021	Copper Ores
			*1061	Ferroalloy Ores, Except Vanadium (nickel)
21229	Other Metal Ore Mining			
212291	Uranium-Radium-Vanadium Ore Mining	E	1094	Uranium-Radium-Vanadium Ores
212299	All Other Metal Ore Mining	R	*1061	Ferroalloy Ores, Except Vanadium (other ferroalloys except nickel)
			1099	Miscellaneous Metal Ores, NEC
2123	Non-Metallic Mineral Mining and Quarrying			

21231	Stone Mining and Quarrying			
212311	Dimension Stone Mining and Quarrying	E	1411	Dimension Stone
212312	Crushed and Broken Limestone Mining and Quarrying	E	1422	Crushed and Broken Limestone
212313	Crushed and Broken Granite Mining and Quarrying	E	1423	Crushed and Broken Granite
212319	Other Crushed and Broken Stone Mining and Quarrying	R	1429	Crushed and Broken Stone, NEC
			*1499	Miscellaneous Nonmetallic Minerals, Except Fuels (bituminous limestone and bituminous sandstone)
21232	Sand, Gravel, Clay, and Ceramic and Refractory Minerals Mining and Quarrying			
212321	Construction Sand and Gravel Mining	E	1442	Construction Sand and Gravel
212322	Industrial Sand Mining	E	1446	Industrial Sand
212324	Kaolin and Ball Clay Mining	E	1455	Kaolin and Ball Clay
212325	Clay and Ceramic and Refractory Minerals Mining	E	1459	Clay, Ceramic, and Refractory Minerals, NEC
21239	Other Non-Metallic Mineral Mining and Quarrying			
212391	Potash, Soda, and Borate Mineral Mining	E	1474	Potash, Soda, and Borate Minerals
212392	Phosphate Rock Mining	E	1475	Phosphate Rock
212393	Other Chemical and Fertilizer Mineral Mining	E	1479	Chemical and Fertilizer Mineral Mining, NEC
212399	All Other Non-Metallic Mineral Mining	R	*1499	Miscellaneous Nonmetallic Minerals, Except Fuels (except bituminous limestone and bituminous sandstone)
213	Support Activities for Mining			
2131	Support Activities for Mining			
21311	Support Activities for Mining			
213111	Drilling Oil and Gas Wells	E	1381	Drilling Oil and Gas Wells
213112	Support Activities for Oil and Gas Operations	R	*1382	Oil and Gas Field Exploration Services (except geophysical mapping and surveying and aerial geophysical exploration)
			1389	Oil and Gas Field Services, NEC
213113	Support Activities for Coal Mining	E	1241	Coal Mining Services
213114	Support Activities for Metal Mining	R	*1081	Metal Mining Services (except geophysical surveying)
213115	Support Activities for Non-Metallic Minerals (except Fuels)	E	*1481	Nonmetallic Minerals Services, Except Fuels (except geophysical surveying)
22	Utilities			
221	Utilities			
2211	Electric Power Generation, Transmission and Distribution			
22111	Electric Power Generation			
221111	Hydroelectric Power Generation	N	*4911	Electric Services (hydroelectric power generation)
			*4931	Electric and Other Services Combined (hydroelectric power generation)
			*4939	Combination Utilities, NEC (hydroelectric power generation)

1997 NAICS Code	1997 NAICS United States and U.S. Description	Status Code	1987 SIC Code	1987 U.S. SIC Description
221112	Fossil Fuel Electric Power Generation	N	*4911	Electric Services (fossil fuel power generation)
			*4931	Electric and Other Services Combined (fossil fuel power generation)
			*4939	Combination Utilities, NEC (fossil fuel power generation)
221113	Nuclear Electric Power Generation	N	*4911	Electric Services (nuclear electric power generation)
			*4931	Electric and Other Services Combined (nuclear power generation)
			*4939	Combination Utilities, NEC (nuclear power generation)
221119	Other Electric Power Generation	N	*4911	Electric Services (other electric power generation)
			*4931	Electric and Other Services Combined (other electric power generation)
			*4939	Combination Utilities, NEC (other electric power generation)
22112	Electric Power Transmission, Control and Distribution			
221121	Electric Bulk Power Transmission and Control	N	*4911	Electric Services (electric power transmission and control)
			*4931	Electric and Other Services Combined (electric power transmission and control)
			*4939	Combination Utilities, NEC (electric power transmission and control)
221122	Electric Power Distribution	N	*4911	Electric Services (electric power distribution)
			*4931	Electric and Other Services Combined (electric power distribution)
			*4939	Combination Utilities, NEC (electric power distribution)
2212	Natural Gas Distribution			
22121	Natural Gas Distribution	R	*4923	Natural Gas Transmission and Distribution (distribution)
			4924	Natural Gas Distribution
			4925	Mixed, Manufactured, or Liquefied Petroleum Gas Production and/or Distribution (natural gas distribution)
			*4931	Electronic and Other Services Combined (natural gas distribution)
			4932	Gas and Other Services Combined (natural gas distribution)
			*4939	Combination Utilities, NEC (natural gas distribution)
2213	Water, Sewage and Other Systems			
22131	Water Supply and Irrigation Systems	R	4941	Water Supply
			4971	Irrigation Systems
22132	Sewage Treatment Facilities	E	4952	Sewerage Systems
22133	Steam and Air-Conditioning Supply	E	4961	Steam and Air-Conditioning Supply
23	Construction			
233	Building, Developing and General Contracting			
2331	Land Subdivision and Land Development			
23311	Land Subdivision and Land Development	E	6552	Land Subdividers and Developers, Except Cemeteries
2332	Residential Building Construction			
23321	Single Family Housing Construction	R	1521	General contractors-Single-Family Houses
			*1531	Operative Builders (single-family housing construction)

23322	Multifamily Housing Construction	R	*1522	General Contractors-Residential Building, Other Than Single-Family (except hotel and motel construction)
			*1531	Operative Builders (multi-family housing construction)
2333	Nonresidential Building Construction			
23331	Manufacturing and Industrial Building Construction	R	*1531	Operative Builders (manufacturing and light industrial building construction)
			*1541	General Contractors-Industrial Buildings and Warehouses (except warehouse construction)
23332	Commercial and Institutional Building Construction	R	*1522	General Contractors-Residential Building Other than Single-Family (hotel and motel construction)
			*1531	Operative Builders (commercial and institutional building construction)
			*1541	General Contractors-Industrial Buildings and Warehouses (warehouse construction)
			1542	General Contractor-Nonresidential Buildings, Other than Industrial Buildings and Warehouses
234	Heavy Construction			
2341	Highway, Street, Bridge and Tunnel Construction			
23411	Highway and Street Construction	E	1611	Highway and Street Construction, Except Elevated Highways
23412	Bridge and Tunnel Construction	E	1622	Bridge, Tunnel, and Elevated Highway Construction
2349	Other Heavy Construction			
23491	Water, Sewer, and Pipeline Construction	N	*1623	Water, Sewer, Pipeline, and Communications and Power Line Construction (water and sewer mains and pipelines construction)
23492	Power and Communication Transmission Line Construction	N	*1623	Water, Sewer, Pipelines, and Communications and Power Line Construction (communications and power line construction)
23493	Industrial Nonbuilding Structure Construction	N	*1629	Heavy Construction, NEC (industrial nonbuilding structures construction)
23499	All Other Heavy Construction	R	*1629	Heavy Construction, NEC (except industrial nonbuilding structures construction)
			*7353	Construction Equipment Rental and Leasing (with operator)
235	Special Trade Contractors			
2351	Plumbing, Heating and Air-Conditioning Contractors			
23511	Plumbing, Heating and Air-Conditioning Contractors	E	1711	Plumbing, Heating and Air-Conditioning
2352	Painting and Wall Covering Contractors			
23521	Painting and Wall Covering Contractors	R	1721	Painting and Paper Hanging
			*1799	Special Trade Contractors, NEC (paint and wallpaper, stripping and wallpaper removal contractors)
2353	Electrical Contractors			
23531	Electrical Contractors	R	*1731	Electrical Work (except burglar and fire alarm installation)
2354	Masonry, Drywall, Insulation, and Tile Contractors			
23541	Masonry and Stone Contractors	E	1741	Masonry, Stone Setting and Other Stone Work

1997 NAICS Code	1997 NAICS United States and U.S. Description	Status Code	1987 SIC Code	1987 U.S. SIC Description
23542	Drywall, Plastering, Acoustical and Insulation Contractors	R	1742	Plastering, Drywall, Acoustical, and Insulation Work
			*1743	Terrazzo, Tile, Marble and Mosaic work (fresco work)
			*1771	Concrete Work (stucco construction)
23543	Tile, Marble, Terrazzo and Mosaic Contractors	R	*1743	Terrazzo, Tile, Marble, and Mosaic Work (except fresco work)
2355	Carpentry and Floor Contractors			
23551	Carpentry Contractors	E	1751	Carpentry Work
23552	Floor Laying and Other Floor Contractors	E	1752	Floor Laying and Other Floor Work, NEC
2356	Roofing, Siding and Sheet Metal Contractors			
23561	Roofing, Siding and Sheet Metal Contractors	E	1761	Roofing, Siding, and Sheet Metal Work
2357	Concrete Contractors			
23571	Concrete Contractors	R	*1771	Concrete Work (except stucco construction)
2358	Water Well Drilling Contractors			
23581	Water Well Drilling Contractors	E	1781	Water Well Drilling
2359	Other Special Trade Contractors			
23591	Structural Steel Erection Contractors	E	1791	Structural Steel Erection
23592	Glass and Glazing Contractors	R	1793	Glass and Glazing Work
			*1799	Specialty Trade Contractors, NEC (tinting glass work)
23593	Excavation Contractors	E	1794	Excavation Work
23594	Wrecking and Demolition Contractors	E	1795	Wrecking and Demolition Work
23595	Building Equipment and Other Machinery Installation Contractors	E	1796	Installation of Erection of Building Equipment, NEC
23599	All Other Special Trade Contractors	R	*1799	Special Trade Contractors, NEC (except paint and wallpaper stripping, wall paper removal contractors, and tinting glass work)
31-33	Manufacturing			
311	Food Manufacturing			
3111	Animal Food Manufacturing			
31111	Animal Food Manufacturing			
311111	Dog and Cat Food Manufacturing	E	2047	Dog and Cat Food
311119	Other Animal Food Manufacturing	R	*2048	Prepared Feeds and Feed Ingredients for Animals and Fowls, Except Dogs and Cats (except slaughtering animals for pet food)
3112	Grain and Oilseed Milling			
31121	Flour Milling and Malt Manufacturing			
311211	Flour Milling	R	*2034	Dehydrated Fruits, Vegetables and Soup Mixes (vegetable flour)
			2041	Flour and Other Grain Mill Products
311212	Rice Milling	E	2044	Rice Milling
311213	Malt Manufacturing	E	2083	Malt
31122	Starch and Vegetable Fats and Oils Manufacturing			
311221	Wet Corn Milling	E	2046	Wet Corn Milling
311222	Soybean Processing	R	*2075	Soybean Oil Mills (soybean processing)

		R	*2079	Shortening, Table Oils, Margarine, and Other Edible Fats and Oils, NEC (processing soybean oil from soybeans crushed in the same establishment)
311223	Other Oilseed Processing	N	*2074	Cottonseed Oil Mills (cottonseed processing)
		R	*2079	Shortening, Table Oils, Margarine and Other Edible Fats and Oils, NEC (processing vegetable oils, except soybeans, from oilseeds crushed in the same establishment)
			*2076	Vegetable Oil Mills, Except Corn, Cottonseed, and Soybean (oilseed processing)
311225	Fats and Oils Refining and Blending	R	*2077	Animal and Marine Fats and Oil, NEC (vegetable oil foods)
			*2074	Cottonseed Oil Mills (processing purchased cottonseed oil)
			*2075	Soybean Oil Mills (processing purchased soybean oil)
			*2076	Vegetable Oil Mills, Except Corn, Cottonseed, and Soybean (processing purchased vegetable oils)
			*2079	Shortening, Table Oils, Margarine, and Other Edible Fats and Oils, NEC (processing fats and oils from purchased fats and oils)
31123	Breakfast Cereal Manufacturing	R	*2043	Cereal Breakfast Foods (breakfast cereal)
3113	Sugar and Confectionery Product Manufacturing			
31131	Sugar Manufacturing			
311311	Sugarcane Mills	E	2061	Cane Sugar, Except Refining
311312	Cane Sugar Refining	E	2062	Cane Sugar Refining
311313	Beet Sugar Manufacturing	E	2063	Beet Sugar
31132	Chocolate and Confectionery Manufacturing from Cacao Beans	E	2066	Chocolate and Cocoa Products
31133	Confectionery Manufacturing from Purchased Chocolate	N	*2064	Candy and Other Confectionery Products (chocolate confectionery)
31134	Non-Chocolate Confectionery Manufacturing	N	*2064	Candy and Other Confectionery Products (non-chocolate confectionery)
			2067	Chewing Gum
			*2099	Food Preparations, NEC (marshmallow creme)
3114	Fruit and Vegetable Preserving and Specialty Food Manufacturing			
31141	Frozen Food Manufacturing			
311411	Frozen Fruit, Juice and Vegetable Manufacturing	E	2037	Frozen Fruits, Fruit Juices, and Vegetables
311412	Frozen Specialty Food Manufacturing	E	2038	Frozen Specialties, NEC
31142	Fruit and Vegetable Canning, Pickling and Drying			
311421	Fruit and Vegetable Canning	R	2033	Canned Fruits, Vegetables, Preserves, Jams, and Jellies
			*2035	Pickled Fruits and Vegetables, Vegetable Sauces, and Seasonings and Salad Dressings (pickled fruits and vegetables)
311422	Specialty Canning	R	*2032	Canned Specialties (except canned puddings)

1997 NAICS Code	1997 NAICS United States and U.S. Description	Status Code	1987 SIC Code	1987 U.S. SIC Description
311423	Dried and Dehydrated Food Manufacturing	R	*2034	Dried and Dehydrated Fruits, Vegetables and Soup Mixes (except vegetable flour)
			*2099	Food Preparation, NEC (bouillon)
3115	Dairy Product Manufacturing			
31151	Dairy Product (except Frozen) Manufacturing			
311511	Fluid Milk Manufacturing	E	2026	Fluid Milk
311512	Creamery Butter Manufacturing	E	2021	Creamery Butter
311513	Cheese Manufacturing	E	2022	Natural, Processed, and Imitation Cheese
311514	Dry, Condensed, and Evaporated Dairy Product Manufacturing	E	2023	Dry, Condensed and Evaporated Dairy Products
31152	Ice Cream and Frozen Dessert Manufacturing	E	2024	Ice Cream and Frozen Desserts
3116	Meat Product Manufacturing			
31161	Animal Slaughtering and Processing			
311611	Animal (except Poultry) Slaughtering	R	*0751	Livestock Services, Except Veterinary (custom slaughtering)
			2011	Meat Packing Plants
			*2048	Prepared Feeds and Feed Ingredients for Animals and Fowls, Except Dogs and Cats (animal slaughtering for pet food)
311612	Meat Processed from Carcasses	R	2013	Sausages and Other Prepared Meats
			*5147	Meat and Meat Products (boxed beef)
311613	Rendering and Meat By-product Processing	N	*2077	Animal and Marine Fats and Oils (animal fats and oils)
311615	Poultry Processing	R	*2015	Poultry Slaughtering and Processing (poultry processing)
3117	Seafood Product Preparation and Packaging			
31171	Seafood Product Preparation and Packaging			
311711	Seafood Canning	R	*2077	Animal and Marine Fats and Oils (canned marine fats and oils)
			2091	Canned and Cured Fish and Seafood
311712	Fresh and Frozen Seafood Processing	R	*2077	Animal and Marine Fats and Oils (fresh and frozen marine fats and oils)
			2092	Prepared Fresh or Frozen Fish and Seafood
3113	Bakeries and Tortilla Manufacturing			
31181	Bread and Bakery Product Manufacturing			
311811	Retail Bakeries	N	*5461	Retail Bakeries (bread, cake and related products baked and sold on premise)
311812	Commercial Bakeries	R	2051	Bread and Other Bakery Products, Except Cookies and Crackers
			*2052	Cookies and Crackers (unleavened bread)
311813	Frozen Bakery Product Manufacturing	E	2053	Frozen Bakery Products, Except Bread
31182	Cookie, Cracker, and Pasta Manufacturing			
311821	Cookie and Cracker Manufacturing	R	*2052	Cookies and Crackers (except unleavened bread and pretzels)
311822	Flour Mixes and Dough Manufacturing from Purchased Flour	E	2045	Prepared Flour Mixes and Doughs
311823	Pasta Manufacturing	E	2098	Macaroni, Spaghetti, Vermicelli and Noodles
31183	Tortilla Manufacturing	N	*2099	Food Preparations, NEC (tortillas)

3119	Other Food Manufacturing			
31191	Snack Food Manufacturing			
311911	Roasted Nuts and Peanut Butter Manufacturing	R	2068	Salted and Roasted Nuts and Seeds
			*2099	Food Preparations, NEC (peanut butter)
311919	Other Snack Food Manufacturing	R	*2052	Cookies and Crackers (pretzels)
			2096	Potato Chips, Corn Chips, and Similar Snacks
31192	Coffee and Tea Manufacturing	N	*2043	Cereal Breakfast Foods (coffee substitute)
			*2095	Roasted Coffee (roasted coffee)
			*2099	Food Preparations, NEC (tea)
31193	Flavoring Syrup and Concentrate Manufacturing	R	*2087	Flavoring Extracts and Flavoring Syrups (flavoring syrup and concentrate)
31194	Seasoning and Dressing Manufacturing			
311941	Mayonnaise, Dressing and Other Prepared Sauce Manufacturing	N	*2035	Pickled Fruits and Vegetables, Vegetable Seasonings, and Sauces and Salad Dressings (sauces and salad dressing)
			*2099	Food Preparations, NEC (vinegar)
311942	Spice and Extract Manufacturing	N	*2087	Flavoring Extracts and Flavoring Syrups (flavoring extracts)
			*2095	Roasted Coffee (coffee extracts)
			*2099	Food Preparations, NEC (spices, dip mix, salad dressing mix, and seasoning mix)
			*2899	Chemical Preparations, NEC (table salt)
31199	All Other Food Manufacturing			
311991	Perishable Prepared Food Manufacturing	N	*2099	Food Preparations, NEC (perishable prepared food)
311999	All Other Miscellaneous Food Manufacturing	R	*2015	Poultry Slaughtering and Processing (egg processing)
			*2032	Canned Specialties (canned puddings)
			*2087	Flavoring Extracts and Flavoring Syrups (powered drink mix)
			*2099	Food Preparations, NEC (except bouillon, marshmallow creme, spices, extracts, peanut butter, perishable prepared foods, tortillas, tea, spices, dip mix, salad dressing mix, seasoning mix, and vinegar)
312	Beverage and Tobacco Product Manufacturing			
3121	Beverage Manufacturing			
31211	Soft Drink and Ice Manufacturing			
312111	Soft Drink Manufacturing	R	*2086	Bottled and Canned Soft Drinks and Carbonated Water (except bottled water)
312112	Bottled Water Manufacturing	N	*2086	Bottled and Canned Soft Drinks and Carbonated Water (bottled water)
312113	Ice Manufacturing	E	2097	Manufactured Ice
31212	Breweries	E	2082	Malt Beverages
31213	Wineries	E	2084	Wines, Brandy, and Brandy Spirits
31214	Distilleries	E	2085	Distilled and Blended Liquors

1997 NAICS Code	1997 NAICS United States and U.S. Description	Status Code	1987 SIC Code	1987 U.S. SIC Description
3122	Tobacco Manufacturing			
31221	Tobacco Stemming and Redrying	R	*2141	Tobacco Stemming and Redrying (redrying and stemming)
31222	Tobacco Product Manufacturing			
312221	Cigarette Manufacturing	E	2111	Cigarettes
312229	Other Tobacco Product Manufacturing	N	2121	Cigars
			2131	Chewing and Smoking Tobacco and Snuff
			*2141	Tobacco Stemming and Redrying (reconstituted tobacco)
313	Textile Mills			
3131	Fiber, Yarn, and Thread Mills			
31311	Fiber, Yarn, and Thread Mills			
313111	Yarn Spinning Mills	R	2281	Yarn Spinning Mills
			*2299	Textile Goods, NEC (yarn of flax, hemp, jute, and ramie)
313112	Yarn Texturing, Throwing and Twisting Mills	R	*2282	Yarn Texturing, Throwing, Winding Mills (except spooling purchased yarns)
313113	Thread Mills	R	*2284	Thread Mills (except finishing)
			*2299	Textile Goods, NEC (thread of hemp, linen, and ramie)
3132	Fabric Mills			
31321	Broadwoven Fabric Mills	N	2211	Broadwoven Fabric Mills, Cotton
			2221	Broadwoven Fabric Mills, Manmade Fiber and Silk
			*2231	Broadwoven Fabric Mills, Wool (Including Dyeing and Finishing)(except wool finishing)
			*2299	Textile Goods, NEC (broadwoven fabrics of jute, linen, hemp, and ramie)
31322	Narrow Fabric Mills and Schiffli Machine Embroidery			
313221	Narrow Fabric Mills	R	2241	Narrow Fabric and Other Smallware Mills: Cotton, Wool, Silk and Manmade Fiber
			*2299	Textile Goods, NEC (narrow woven fabric of jute, linen, hemp, and ramie)
313222	Schiffli Machine Embroidery	E	2397	Schiffli Machine Embroideries
31323	Nonwoven Fabric Mills	R	2297	Nonwoven Fabrics
			*2299	Textile Goods, NEC (nonwoven felt)
31324	Knit Fabric Mills			
313241	Weft Knit Fabric Mills	R	*2257	Weft Knit Fabric Mills (except finishing)
			*2259	Knitting Mills NEC (finished articles of weft knit fabric)
313249	Other Knit Fabric and Lace Mills	R	*2258	Lace and Warp Knit Fabric Mills (except finishing)
			*2259	Knitting Mills NEC (finished articles of warp knit fabric)
3133	Textile and Fabric Finishing and Fabric Coating Mills			
31331	Textile and Fabric Finishing Mills			

313311	Broadwoven Fabric Finishing Mills	N	*2231	Broadwoven Fabric Mills, Wool (wool broadwoven fabric finishing)
			2261	Finishers of Broadwoven Fabrics of Cotton
			2262	Finishers of Broadwoven Fabrics of Manmade Fiber and Silk
			*2269	Finishers of Textiles, NEC (broadwoven fabric finishing)
			*5131	Piece Goods and Notions (broadwoven converters)
313312	Textile and Fabric Finishing (except Broadwoven Fabric) Mills	N	*2231	Broadwoven Fabric Mills, Wool (wool finishing except broadwoven fabric)
			*2257	Weft Knit Fabric Mills (finishing)
			*2258	Lace and Warp Knit Fabric Mills (finishing)
			*2269	Finishers of Textiles, NEC (except broadwoven fabric finishing)
			*2282	Yarn Texturizing, Throwing, Twisting, and Winding Mills (spooling purchased yarn)
			*2284	Thread Mills (thread finishing)
			*2299	Textile Goods, NEC (finishing hard fiber thread and yarn)
			*5131	Piece Goods and Notions (converters, except broadwoven)
31332	Fabric Coating Mills	R	2295	Coated Fabrics, Not Rubberized
			*3069	Fabricated Rubber Products, NEC (rubberized fabric)
314	Textile Product Mills			
3141	Textile Furnishings Mills			
31411	Carpet and Rug Mills	E	2273	Carpets and Rugs
31412	Curtain and Linen Mills			
314121	Curtain and Drapery Mills	R	2391	Curtains and Draperies
			*5714	Drapery, Curtain, and Upholstery Stores (custom drapes)
314129	Other Household Textile Product Mills	R	*2392	Housefurnishings, Except Curtains and Draperies (except mops and bags)
3149	Other Textile Product Mills			
31491	Textile Bag and Canvas Mills			
314911	Textile Bag Mills	R	*2392	Housefurnishings, Except Curtains and Draperies (blanket, laundry, and wardrobe bags)
			2393	Textile Bags
314912	Canvas and Related Product Mills	E	2394	Canvas and Related Products
31499	All Other Textile Product Mills			
314991	Rope, Cordage and Twine Mills	E	2298	Cordage and Twine
314992	Tire Cord and Tire Fabric Mills	E	2296	Tire Cord and Fabrics

1997 NAICS Code	1997 NAICS United States and U.S. Description	Status Code	1987 SIC Code	1987 U.S. SIC Description
314999	All Other Miscellaneous Textile Product Mills	R	*2299	Textile Goods, NEC (other textile products)
			*2395	Pleating, Decorative and Novelty Stitching, and Tucking for the Trade (except apparel contractors)
			*2396	Automotive Trimmings, Apparel Findings, and Related Products (textile products except automotive and apparel trim and printing on apparel)
			*2399	Fabricated Textile Products, NEC (except apparel, automotive seat belts, and seat and tire covers)
315	Apparel Manufacturing			
3151	Apparel Knitting Mills			
31511	Hosiery and Sock Mills			
315111	Sheer Hosiery Mills	R	2251	Women's Full-Length and Knee-Length Hosiery, Except socks
			*2252	Hosiery, NEC (girls' hosiery)
315119	Other Hosiery and Sock Mills	R	*2252	Hosiery, NEC (socks)
31519	Other Apparel Knitting Mills			
315191	Outerwear Knitting Mills	R	2253	Knit Outerwear Mills
			*2259	Knitting Mills, NEC (gloves and mittens)
315192	Underwear and Nightwear Knitting Mills	R	2254	Knit Underwear and Nightwear Mills
			*2259	Knitting Mills, NEC (girdles)
3152	Cut and Sew Apparel Manufacturing			
31521	Cut and Sew Apparel Contractors			
315211	Men's and Boys' Cut and Sew Apparel Contractors	N	*2311	Men's and Boys' Suits, Coats, and Overcoats (contractors)
			*2321	Men's and Boys' Shirts, Except Work Shirts (contractors)
			*2322	Men's and Boys' Underwear and Nightwear (contractors)
			*2325	Men's and Boys' Trousers and Slacks (contractors)
			*2326	Men's and Boys' Work Clothing (contractors)
			*2329	Men's and Boys' Clothing, NEC (contractors)
			*2341	Women's, Misses', Children's, and Infants' Underwear and Nightwear (boys' contractors)
			*2361	Girls', Children's, and Infants' Dresses, Blouses and Shirts (boys' contractors)
			*2369	Girls', Children's, and Infants' Outerwear, NEC (boys' contractors)

			*2384	Robes and Dressing Gowns (men's and boys' contractors)
			*2385	Waterproof Outerwear (men's and boys' contractors)
			*2389	Apparel and Accessories, NEC (contractors)
			*2395	Pleating, Decorative and Novelty Stitching, and Tucking for the Trade (men's and boy's apparel contractors)
315212	Women's and Girls' Cut and Sew Apparel Contractors	N	*2331	Women's, Misses', and Juniors' Blouses and Shirts (contractors)
			*2335	Women's, Misses' and Juniors' Dresses (contractors)
			*2337	Women's, Misses', and Juniors' Suits, Skirts, and Coats (contractors)
			*2339	Women's, Misses', and Juniors' Outerwear, NEC (contractors)
			*2341	Women's, Misses', Children's, and Infants' Underwear and Nightwear (contractors)
			*2342	Brassieres, Girdles, and Allied Garments (contractors)
			*2361	Girls', Children's, and Infants' Dresses, Blouses, and Shirts (girls' contractors)
			*2369	Girls', Children's, and Infants' Outerwear, NEC (girls' and infants' contractors)
			*2384	Robes and Dressing Gowns (women's, girls', and infants'
			*2385	Waterproof Outerwear (women's, girls', and infants' contractors)
			*2389	Apparel and Accessories, NEC (contractors)
			*2395	Pleating, Decorative and Novelty Stitching, and Tucking for the Trade (women's and girls' apparel contractors)
31522	Men's and Boys' Cut and Sew Apparel Manufacturing			
315221	Men's and Boys' Cut and Sew Underwear and Nightwear Manufacturing	R	*2322	Men's and Boys' Underwear and Nightwear (except contractors)
			*2341	Women's, Misses', Children's, and Infants' Underwear and Nightwear (boys' except contractors)
			*2369	Girls', Children's, and Infants' Outerwear, NEC (boys' robes except contractors)
			*2384	Robes and Dressing Gowns (men's except contractors)
315222	Men's and Boys' Cut and Sew Suit, Coat and Overcoat Manufacturing	R	*2311	Men's and Boys' Suits, Coats, and Overcoats (except contractors)

1997 NAICS Code	1997 NAICS United States and U.S. Description	Status Code	1987 SIC Code	1987 U.S. SIC Description
			*2369	Girls', Children's, and Infants' Outerwear, NEC (boys' suits and coats except contractors)
			*2385	Waterproof Outerwear (men's and boys' raincoats except contractors)
315223	Men's and Boys' Cut and Sew Shirt (except Work Shirt) Manufacturing	R	*2321	Men's and Boys' Shirts, Except Work Shirts (except contractors)
			*2361	Girls', Children's, and Infants' Dresses, Blouses, and Shirts (boys' shirts except contractors)
315224	Men's and Boys' Cut and Sew Trouser, Slack and Jean Manufacturing	R	*2325	Men's and Boys' Trousers and Slacks (except contractors)
			*2369	Girls', Children's, and Infants' Outerwear, NEC (boys' trousers, slacks, and jeans except contractors)
315225	Men's and Boys' Cut and Sew Work Clothing Manufacturing	R	*2326	Men's and Boys' Work Clothing (except contractors)
315228	Men's and Boys' Cut and Sew Other Outerwear Manufacturing	R	*2329	Men's and Boys' Clothing, NEC (men's and boys' other outerwear except contractors)
			*2369	Girls', Children's, and Infants' Outerwear, NEC (boys' other outerwear except contractors)
			*2385	Waterproof Outerwear (except contractors)
31523	Women's and Girls' Cut and Sew Apparel Manufacturing			
315231	Women's and Girls' Cut and Sew Lingerie, Loungewear and Nightwear Manufacturing	R	*2341	Women's, Misses', Children's, and Infants' Underwear and Nightwear (women and girls' except contractors)
			*2342	Brassieres, Girdles, and Allied Garments (except contractors)
			*2369	Girls', Children's, and Infants' Outerwear, NEC (girls' robes except contractors)
			*2384	Robes and Dressing Gowns (women's except contractors)
			*2389	Apparel and Accessories, NEC (garters and garter belts)
315232	Women's and Girls' Cut and Sew Blouse and Shirt Manufacturing	R	*2331	Women's, Misses', and Juniors' Blouses and Shirts (except contractors)
			*2361	Girls', Children's, and Infants' Dresses, Blouses and Shirts (girls' blouses and shirts except contractors)
315233	Women's and Girls' Cut and Sew Dress Manufacturing	R	*2335	Women's, Misses', and Juniors' Dresses (except contractors)
			*2361	Girls', Children's, and Infants' Dresses, Blouses and Shirts (girls' dresses except contractors)
315234	Women's and Girls' Cut and Sew Suit, Coat, Tailored Jacket and Skirt Manufacturing	R	*2337	Women's, Misses', and Juniors' Suits, Skirts, and Coats (except contractors)
			*2369	Girls', Children's, and Infants' Outerwear, NEC (girls' suits, coats, jackets, and skirts except contractors)
			*2385	Waterproof Outerwear (women's and girls' raincoats except contractors)

NAICS	Title	Status	SIC	Description
315238	Women's and Girls' Cut and Sew Other Outerwear Manufacturing	R	*2339	Women's, Misses', and Juniors' Outerwear, NEC (except contractors)
			*2369	Girls', Children's, and Infants' Outerwear, NEC (girls' except contractors)
			*2385	Waterproof Outerwear (other women's and girls' outerwear except contractors)
31529	Other Cut and Sew Apparel Manufacturing			
315291	Infants' Cut and Sew Apparel Manufacturing	R	*2341	Women's, Misses', Children's, and Infants' Underwear and Nightwear (infants' except contractors)
			*2361	Girls', Children's, and Infants' Dresses, Blouses, and Shirts (infants' except contractors)
			*2369	Girls', Children's, and Infants' Outerwear, NEC (infants' except contractors)
			*2385	Waterproof Outerwear (infants' outerwear except contractors)
315292	Fur and Leather Apparel Manufacturing	R	2371	Fur Goods
			2386	Leather and Sheep-lined Clothing
315299	All Other Cut and Sew Apparel Manufacturing	R	*2329	Men's and Boys' Outerwear, NEC (athletic uniforms except contractors)
			*2339	Women's, Misses', and Juniors' Outerwear, NEC (athletic uniforms except contractors)
			*2389	Apparel and Accessories, NEC (academic and clerical outerwear, except contractors)
3159	Apparel Accessories and Other Apparel Manufacturing			
31599	Apparel Accessories and Other Apparel Manufacturing			
315991	Hat, Cap and Millinery Manufacturing	E	2353	Hats, Caps, and Millinery
315992	Glove and Mitten Manufacturing	R	2381	Dress and Work Gloves, Except Knit and All-Leather
			3151	Leather Gloves and Mittens
315993	Men's and Boys' Neckwear Manufacturing	E	2323	Men's and Boys' Neckwear
315999	Other Apparel Accessories and Other Apparel Manufacturing	N	*2339	Women's, Misses', and Juniors' Outerwear, NEC (scarves)
			*2385	Waterproof Outerwear (aprons, bibs, and other miscellaneous waterproof items)
			2387	Apparel Belts
			*2389	Apparel and Accessories, NEC (handkerchiefs, arm bands, etc.)
			*2396	Automotive Trimmings, Apparel Findings, and Related Products (apparel findings and trimming)
			*2399	Fabricated Textile Products, NEC (apparel and apparel accessories)
316	Leather and Allied Product Manufacturing			
3161	Leather and Hide Tanning and Finishing			

1997 NAICS Code	1997 NAICS United States and U.S. Description	Status Code	1987 SIC Code	1987 U.S. SIC Description
31611	Leather and Hide Tanning and Finishing	R	3111	Leather Tanning and Finishing
			*3999	Manufacturing Industries, NEC (fur dressing and finishing)
3162	Footwear Manufacturing			
31621	Footwear Manufacturing			
316211	Rubber and Plastics Footwear Manufacturing	E	3021	Rubber and Plastics Footwear
316212	House Slipper Manufacturing	E	3142	House Slippers
316213	Men's Footwear (except Athletic) Manufacturing	E	3143	Men's Footwear, Except Athletic
316214	Women's Footwear (except Athletic) Manufacturing	E	3144	Women's Footwear, Except Athletic
316219	Other Footwear Manufacturing	E	3149	Footwear Except Rubber, NEC
3169	Other Leather and Allied Product Manufacturing			
31699	Other Leather and Allied Product Manufacturing			
316991	Luggage Manufacturing	E	3161	Luggage
316992	Women's Handbag and Purse Manufacturing	E	3171	Women's Handbags and Purses
316993	Personal Leather Good (except Women's Handbag and Purse) Manufacturing	E	3172	Personal Leather Goods, Except Women's Handbags and Purses
316999	All Other Leather Good Manufacturing	R	*3131	Boot and Shoe Cut Stock and Findings (except wood heels and metal buckles)
			3199	Leather Goods, NEC
321	Wood Product Manufacturing			
3211	Sawmills and Wood Preservation			
32111	Sawmills and Wood Preservation			
321113	Sawmills	R	*2421	Sawmills and Planing Mills, General
			*2429	Special Product Sawmills, NEC
321114	Wood Preservation	E	2491	Wood Preserving
3212	Veneer, Plywood and Engineered Wood Product Manufacturing			
32121	Veneer, Plywood, and Engineered Wood Product Manufacturing			
321211	Hardwood Veneer and Plywood Manufacturing	E	2435	Hardwood Veneer and Plywood
321212	Softwood Veneer and Plywood Manufacturing	E	2436	Softwood Veneer and Plywood
321213	Engineered Wood Member (except Truss) Manufacturing	R	*2439	Structural Wood Members, NEC (except trusses)
321214	Truss Manufacturing	N	*2439	Structural Wood Members, NEC (trusses)
321219	Reconstituted Wood Product Manufacturing	E	2493	Reconstituted Wood Products
3219	Other Wood Product Manufacturing			
32191	Millwork			
321911	Wood Window and Door Manufacturing	N	*2431	Millwork (wood windows and doors)

321912	Cut Stock, Resawing Lumber, and Planing	N	*2421	Sawmills and Planing Mills, General (lumber manufacturing from purchased lumber, softwood cut stock, wood lath, fence pickets, and planing mill products)
			*2426	Hardwood Dimension and Flooring Mills (except flooring)
			*2429	Special Product Sawmills, NEC (stave manufacturing from purchased lumber)
			*2439	Structural Wood Members, NEC (lumber member manufacturing from purchased lumber)
321918	Other Millwork (including Flooring)	R	*2426	Hardwood Dimension and Flooring Mills (hardwood flooring)
			*2421	Sawmills and Planing Mills, General (softwood flooring)
			*2431	Millwork (except wood doors and windows)
32192	Wood Container and Pallet Manufacturing	N	2441	Nailed and Lock Corner Wood Boxes and Shook
			2448	Wood Pallets and Skids
			2449	Wood Containers, NEC
			*2499	Wood Products, NEC (wood tubs and vats, jewelry and cigar boxes)
32199	All Other Wood Product Manufacturing			
321991	Manufactured Home (Mobile Home) Manufacturing	E	2451	Mobile Homes
321992	Prefabricated Wood Building Manufacturing	E	2452	Prefabricated Wood Buildings and Components
321999	All Other Miscellaneous Wood Product Manufacturing	R	*2426	Hardwood Dimension and Flooring Mills (wood stock and turnings)
			*2499	Wood Products, NEC (other wood products)
			*3131	Boot and Shoe Cut Stock and Findings (wood heels)
			*3999	Manufacturing Industries, NEC (burnt wood articles and other wood products)
			*2421	Sawmills and Planing Mills, General (kiln drying)
			*2429	Special Product Sawmills, NEC (excelsior and cooperage headings)
322	Paper Manufacturing			
3221	Pulp, Paper, and Paperboard Mills			
32211	Pulp Mills	R	*2611	Pulp Mills (pulp producing mills only)
32212	Paper Mills			
322121	Paper (except Newsprint) Mills	R	*2611	Pulp Mills (pulp mills producing paper)
			*2621	Paper Mills (except newsprint mills)
322122	Newsprint Mills	N	*2621	Paper Mills (newsprint mills)
3221[illegible]	Paperboard Mills	R	*2611	Pulp Mills (pulp mills producing paperboard)
			2631	Paperboard Mills
3222	Converted Paper Product Manufacturing			
32221	Paperboard Container Manufacturing			
322211	Corrugated and Solid Fiber Box Manufacturing	E	2653	Corrugated and Solid Fiber Boxes
322212	Folding Paperboard Box Manufacturing	E	2657	Folding Paperboard Boxes, Including Sanitary

1997 NAICS Code	1997 NAICS United States and U.S. Description	Status Code	1987 SIC Code	1987 U.S. SIC Description
322213	Setup Paperboard Box Manufacturing	E	2652	Setup Paperboard Boxes
322214	Fiber Can, Tube, Drum, and Similar Products Manufacturing	E	2655	Fiber Cans, Tubes, Drums, and Similar Products
322215	Non-Folding Sanitary Food Container Manufacturing	R	2656	Sanitary Food Containers, Except Folding
			*2679	Converted Paper and Paperboard Products, NEC (egg cartons and other containers from purchased paper)
32222	Paper Bag and Coated and Treated Paper Manufacturing			
322221	Coated and Laminated Packaging Paper and Plastics Film Manufacturing	R	*2671	Packaging Paper and Plastics Film, Coated and Laminated (single-web paper, paper multiweb laminated rolls and sheets for packaging uses)
322222	Coated and Laminated Paper Manufacturing	R	2672	Coated and Laminated Paper, NEC
			*2679	Converted Paper and Paperboard Products, NEC (wallpaper and gift wrap paper)
322223	Plastics, Foil, and Coated Paper Bag Manufacturing	R	*2673	Plastics, Foil, and Coated Paper Bags (coated or multiweb laminated bags)
322224	Uncoated Paper and Multiwall Bag Manufacturing	E	2674	Uncoated Paper and Multiwall Bags
322225	Laminated Aluminum Foil Manufacturing for Flexible Packaging Uses	N	*3497	Metal Foil and Leaf (laminated aluminum foil rolls and sheets for flexible packaging uses)
32223	Stationery Product Manufacturing			
322231	Die-Cut Paper and Paperboard Office Supplies Manufacturing	N	*2675	Die-Cut Paper and Paperboard and Cardboard (file folders, tabulating cards, and other paper and paperboard office supplies)
			*2679	Converted Paper and Paperboard Products, NEC (paper supplies for business machines and other paper office supplies)
322232	Envelope Manufacturing	E	2677	Envelopes
322233	Stationery, Tablet, and Related Product Manufacturing	E	2678	Stationery, Tablets, and Related Products
32229	Other Converted Paper Product Manufacturing			
322291	Sanitary Paper Product Manufacturing	E	2676	Sanitary Paper Products
322292	Surface-Coated Paperboard Manufacturing	N	*2675	Die-Cut Paper and Paperboard and Cardboard (pasted, lined, laminated, or surface-coated paperboard)
322298	All Other Converted Paper Product Manufacturing	R	*2675	Die-Cut Paper and Paperboard and Cardboard (die-cut paper and paperboard products, except office supplies)
			*2679	Converted Paper and Paperboard Products, NEC (other converted paper and paperboard products such as paper filters, crepe paper, and laminated and tiled wallboard)
323	Printing and Related Support Activities			
3231	Printing and Related Support Activities			
32311	Printing			

323110	Commercial Lithographic Printing	R	*2752	Commercial Printing, Lithographic (except quick printing)
			*2771	Greeting Cards (lithographic printing of greeting cards)
			*2782	Blankbooks, Loose-leaf Binders and Devices (lithographic printing of checkbooks)
			*3999	Manufacturing Industries, NEC (lithographic printing of eyeglass frames for the trade)
323111	Commercial Gravure Printing	R	2754	Commercial Printing, Gravure
			*2771	Greeting Cards (gravure printing of greeting cards)
			*2782	Blankbooks, Loose-leaf Binders and Devices (gravure printing of checkbooks)
			*3999	Manufacturing Industries, NEC (gravure printing of eyeglass frames for the trade)
323112	Commercial Flexographic Printing	N	*2759	Commercial Printing, NEC (flexographic printing)
			*2771	Greeting Cards (flexographic printing of greeting cards)
			*2782	Blankbooks, Loose-leaf Binders and Devices (flexographic printing of checkbooks)
			*3999	Manufacturing Industries, NEC (flexographic printing of eyeglass frames for the trade)
323113	Commercial Screen Printing	N	*2396	Automotive Trimmings, Apparel Findings, and Related Products (printing and embossing on fabric articles)
			*2759	Commercial Printing, NEC (screen printing)
			*2771	Greeting Cards (screen printing of greeting cards)
			*2782	Blankbooks, Loose-leaf Binders and Devices (screen printing of checkbooks)
			*3999	Manufacturing Industries, NEC (screen printing of eyeglass frames for the trade)
323114	Quick Printing	N	*2752	Commercial Printing, Lithographic (quick printing)
			*2759	Commercial Printing, NEC (quick printing)
323115	Digital Printing	N	*2759	Commercial Printing, NEC (digital printing, except quick printing)
323116	Manifold Business Form Printing	E	2761	Manifold Business Forms
323117	Book Printing	E	2732	Book Printing
323118	Blankbook, Loose-leaf Binder and Device Manufacturing	R	*2782	Blankbooks, Loose-leaf Binders and Devices (except checkbooks)
323119	Other Commercial Printing	R	*2759	Commercial Printing, NEC (other commercial printing except quick printing)
			*2771	Greeting Cards (other printing of greeting cards)
			*2782	Blankbooks, Loose-leaf Binders and Devices (other printing of checkbooks)
			*3999	Manufacturing Industries, NEC (other printing of eyeglass frames for the trade)

1997 NAICS Code	1997 NAICS United States and U.S. Description	Status Code	1987 SIC Code	1987 U.S. SIC Description
32312	Support Activities for Printing			
323121	Tradebinding and Related Work	E	2789	Bookbinding and Related Work
323122	Prepress Services	R	2791	Typesetting
			2796	Platemaking and Related Services
324	Petroleum and Coal Products Manufacturing			
3241	Petroleum and Coal Products Manufacturing			
32411	Petroleum Refineries	E	2911	Petroleum Refining
32412	Asphalt Paving, Roofing and Saturated Materials Manufacturing			
324121	Asphalt Paving Mixture and Block Manufacturing	E	2951	Asphalt Paving Mixtures and Blocks
324122	Asphalt Shingle and Coating Materials Manufacturing	E	2952	Asphalt Felts and Coatings
32419	Other Petroleum and Coal Products Manufacturing			
324191	Petroleum Lubricating Oil and Grease Manufacturing	E	2992	Lubricating Oils and Greases
324199	All Other Petroleum and Coal Products Manufacturing	R	2999	Products of Petroleum and Coal, NEC
			*3312	Blast Furnaces and Steel Mills (coke ovens)
325	Chemical Manufacturing			
3251	Basic Chemical Manufacturing			
32511	Petrochemical Manufacturing	N	*2865	Cyclic Organic Crudes and Intermediates, and Organic Dyes and Pigments (aromatics)
			*2869	Industrial Organic Chemicals, NEC (aliphatics)
32512	Industrial Gas Manufacturing	R	2813	Industrial Gases
			*2869	Industrial Organic Chemicals, NEC (fluorocarbon gases)
32513	Dye and Pigment Manufacturing			
325131	Inorganic Dye and Pigment Manufacturing	N	*2816	Inorganic Pigments (except bone and lamp black)
			*2819	Industrial Inorganic Chemicals, NEC (inorganic dyes)
325132	Organic Dye and Pigment Manufacturing	N	*2865	Cyclic Organic Crudes and Intermediates, and Organic Dyes and Pigments (organic dyes and pigments)
32518	Other Basic Inorganic Chemical Manufacturing			
325181	Alkalies and Chlorine Manufacturing	E	2812	Alkalies and Chlorine
325182	Carbon Black Manufacturing	R	*2816	Inorganic pigments (bone and lamp black)
			2895	Carbon Black
325188	All Other Basic Inorganic Chemical Manufacturing	R	*2819	Industrial Inorganic Chemicals, NEC (except activated carbon and charcoal, alumina, and inorganic industrial dyes)
			*2869	Industrial Organic Chemicals, NEC (carbon bisulfide)
32519	Other Basic Organic Chemical Manufacturing			
325191	Gum and Wood Chemical Manufacturing	E	2861	Gum and Wood Chemicals
325192	Cyclic Crude and Intermediate Manufacturing	R	*2865	Cyclic Organic Crudes and Intermediates and Organic Dyes and Pigments (except aromatics and organic dyes and pigments)

325193	Ethyl Alcohol Manufacturing	N	*2869	Industrial Organic Chemicals (ethyl alcohol)
325199	All Other Basic Organic Chemical Manufacturing	R	*2869	Industrial Organic Chemicals, NEC (except aliphatics, carbon bisulfide, ethyl alcohol, and fluorocarbon gases)
			*2899	Chemical and Chemical Preparations, NEC (fatty acids)
3252	Resin, Synthetic Rubber, and Artificial and Synthetic Fibers and Filaments Manufacturing			
32521	Resin and Synthetic Rubber Manufacturing			
325211	Plastics Material and Resin Manufacturing	E	2821	Plastics Materials, Synthetic and Resins, and Nonvulcanizable Elastomers
325212	Synthetic Rubber Manufacturing	E	2822	Synthetic Rubber
32522	Artificial and Synthetic Fibers and Filaments Manufacturing			
325221	Cellulosic Organic Fiber Manufacturing	E	2823	Cellulosic Manmade Fibers
325222	Noncellulosic Organic Fiber Manufacturing	E	2824	Manmade Organic Fibers, Except Cellulosic
3253	Pesticide, Fertilizer and Other Agricultural Chemical Manufacturing			
32531	Fertilizer Manufacturing			
325311	Nitrogenous Fertilizer Manufacturing	E	2873	Nitrogenous Fertilizers
325312	Phosphatic Fertilizer Manufacturing	E	2874	Phosphatic Fertilizers
325314	Fertilizer (Mixing Only) Manufacturing	E	2875	Fertilizers, Mixing Only
32532	Pesticide and Other Agricultural Chemical Manufacturing	E	2879	Pesticides and Agricultural Chemicals, NEC
3254	Pharmaceutical and Medicine Manufacturing			
32541	Pharmaceutical and Medicine Manufacturing			
325411	Medicinal and Botanical Manufacturing	E	2833	Medicinal Chemicals and Botanical Products
325412	Pharmaceutical Preparation Manufacturing	R	2834	Pharmaceutical Preparations
			*2835	In-Vitro and In-Vivo Diagnostic Substances (except in-vitro diagnostic)
325413	In-Vitro Diagnostic Substance Manufacturing	N	*2835	In-Vitro and In-Vivo Diagnostic Substances (in-vitro diagnostic substances)
325414	Biological Product (except Diagnostic) Manufacturing	E	2836	Biological Products, Except Diagnostic Substance
3255	Paint, Coating, Adhesive, and Sealant Manufacturing			
32551	Paint and Coating Manufacturing	R	2851	Paints, Varnishes, Lacquers, Enamels and Allied Products
			*2899	Chemicals and Chemical Preparations, NEC (frit)
32552	Adhesive Manufacturing	E	2891	Adhesives and Sealants
3256	Soap, Cleaning Compound and Toilet Preparation Manufacturing			
32561	Soap and Cleaning Compound Manufacturing			
325611	Soap and Other Detergent Manufacturing	R	2841	Soaps and Other Detergents, Except Specialty Cleaners
			*2844	Toilet Preparations (toothpaste)

1997 NAICS Code	1997 NAICS United States and U.S. Description	Status Code	1987 SIC Code	1987 U.S. SIC Description
325612	Polish and Other Sanitation Good Manufacturing	E	2842	Specialty Cleaning, Polishing, and Sanitary Preparations
325613	Surface Active Agent Manufacturing	E	2843	Surface Active Agents, Finishing Agents, Sulfonated Oils, and Assistants
32562	Toilet Preparation Manufacturing	R	*2844	Perfumes, Cosmetics, and Other Toilet Preparations (except toothpaste)
3259	Other Chemical Product Manufacturing			
32591	Printing Ink Manufacturing	E	2893	Printing Ink
32592	Explosives Manufacturing	E	2892	Explosives
32599	All Other Chemical Product Manufacturing			
325991	Custom Compounding of Purchased Resin	E	3087	Custom Compounding of Purchased Plastics Resin
325992	Photographic Film, Paper, Plate and Chemical Manufacturing	N	*3861	Photographic Equipment and Supplies (photographic films, paper, plates and chemicals)
325998	All Other Miscellaneous Chemical Product Manufacturing	R	*2819	Industrial Inorganic Chemicals, NEC (activated carbon and charcoal)
			*2899	Chemicals and Chemical Preparations NEC (except frit and table salt)
			*3952	Lead Pencils and Art Goods (drawing inks and india ink)
			*3999	Manufacturing Industries, NEC (matches)
326	Plastics and Rubber Products Manufacturing			
3261	Plastics Product Manufacturing			
32611	Unsupported Plastics Film, Sheet and Bag Manufacturing			
326111	Unsupported Plastics Bag Manufacturing	N	*2673	Plastics, Foil, and Coated Paper Bags (plastics bags)
326112	Unsupported Plastics Packaging Film and Sheet Manufacturing	N	*2671	Packaging Paper and Plastics Film, Coated, and Laminated (plastics packaging film and sheet)
326113	Unsupported Plastics Film and Sheet (except Packaging) Manufacturing	E	3081	Unsupported Plastics Film and Sheets
32612	Plastics Pipe, Pipe Fitting, and Unsupported Profile Shape Manufacturing			
326121	Unsupported Plastics Profile Shape Manufacturing	R	3082	Unsupported Plastics Profile Shapes
			*3089	Plastics Product, NEC (plastics sausage casings)
326122	Plastics Pipe and Pipe Fitting Manufacturing	R	3084	Plastics Pipe
			*3089	Plastics Products, NEC (pipe fittings)
32613	Laminated Plastics Plate, Sheet and Shape Manufacturing	E	3083	Laminated Plastics Plate, Sheet and Profile Shapes
32614	Polystyrene Foam Product Manufacturing	N	*3086	Plastics Foam Products (polystyrene foam products)
32615	Urethane and Other Foam Product (except Polystyrene) Manufacturing	N	*3086	Plastics Foam Products (urethane foam products)
32616	Plastics Bottle Manufacturing	E	3085	Plastics Bottles
32619	Other Plastics Product Manufacturing			
326191	Plastics Plumbing Fixture Manufacturing	E	3088	Plastics Plumbing Fixtures

326192	Resilient Floor Covering Manufacturing	R	*3069	Fabricated Rubber Products, NEC (rubber resilient floor coverings)
			3996	Linoleum, Asphalted-Felt-Base, and Other Hard Surface Floor Coverings, NEC
326199	All Other Plastics Product Manufacturing	R	*3089	Plastics Products, NEC (except plastics pipe fittings and plastics sausage casings)
			*3999	Manufacturing Industries, NEC (plastics products such as combs, hair curlers, etc.)
3262	Rubber Product Manufacturing			
32621	Tire Manufacturing			
326211	Tire Manufacturing (except Retreading)	E	3011	Tires and Inner Tubes
326212	Tire Retreading	N	*7534	Tire Retreading and Repair Shops (rebuilding)
32622	Rubber and Plastics Hoses and Belting Manufacturing	E	3052	Rubber and Plastics Hose and Belting
32629	Other Rubber Product Manufacturing			
326291	Rubber Product Manufacturing for Mechanical Use	E	3061	Molded, Extruded, and Lathe-Cut Mechanical Rubber Goods
326299	All Other Rubber Product Manufacturing	R	*3069	Fabricated Rubber Products, NEC (except rubberized fabric and rubber resilient floor covering)
327	Nonmetallic Mineral Product Manufacturing			
3271	Clay Product and Refractory Manufacturing			
32711	Pottery, Ceramics, and Plumbing Fixture Manufacturing			
327111	Vitreous China Plumbing Fixture and China and Earthenware Fittings and Bathroom Accessories Manufacturing	E	3261	Vitreous China Plumbing Fixtures and China and Earthenware Fittings and Bathroom Accessories
327112	Vitreous China, Fine Earthenware and Other Pottery Product Manufacturing	N	3262	Vitreous China Table and Kitchen Articles
			3263	Fine Earthenware (Whiteware) Table and Kitchen Articles
			3269	Pottery Products, NEC
327113	Porcelain Electrical Supply Manufacturing	E	3264	Porcelain Electrical Supplies
32712	Clay Building Material and Refractories Manufacturing			
327121	Brick and Structural Clay Tile Manufacturing	E	3251	Brick and Structural Clay Tile
327122	Ceramic Wall and Floor Tile Manufacturing	E	3253	Ceramic Wall and Floor Tile
327123	Other Structural Clay Product Manufacturing	E	3259	Structural Clay Products, NEC
327124	Clay Refractory Manufacturing	E	3255	Clay Refractories
327125	Nonclay Refractory Manufacturing	E	3297	Nonclay Refractories
3272	Glass and Glass Product Manufacturing			
32721	Glass and Glass Product Manufacturing			
327211	Flat Glass Manufacturing	E	3211	Flat Glass
327212	Other Pressed and Blown Glass and Glassware Manufacturing	E	3229	Pressed and Blown Glass and Glassware, NEC
327213	Glass Container Manufacturing	E	3221	Glass Containers

1997 NAICS Code	1997 NAICS United States and U.S. Description	Status Code	1987 SIC Code	1987 U.S. SIC Description
327215	Glass Product Manufacturing Made of Purchased Glass	E	3231	Glass Products Made of Purchased Glass
3273	Cement and Concrete Product Manufacturing			
32731	Cement Manufacturing	E	3241	Cement, Hydraulic
32732	Ready-Mix Concrete Manufacturing	E	3273	Ready-Mixed Concrete
32733	Concrete Pipe, Brick and Block Manufacturing			
327331	Concrete Block and Brick Manufacturing	E	3271	Concrete Block and Brick
327332	Concrete Pipe Manufacturing	N	*3272	Concrete Products, Except Block and Brick (concrete pipe)
32739	Other Concrete Product Manufacturing	N	*3272	Concrete Products, Except Block and Brick (concrete products, except dry mix concrete and pipe)
3274	Lime, Gypsum and Gypsum Product Manufacturing			
32741	Lime Manufacturing	E	3274	Lime
32742	Gypsum and Gypsum Product Manufacturing	R	3275	Gypsum Products
			*3299	Nonmetallic Mineral Products, NEC (moldings, ornamental and architectural plaster work)
3279	Other Nonmetallic Mineral Product Manufacturing			
32791	Abrasive Product Manufacturing	R	*3291	Abrasive Products (except steel wool with or without soap)
32799	All Other Nonmetallic Mineral Product Manufacturing			
327991	Cut Stone and Stone Product Manufacturing	E	3281	Cut Stone and Stone Products
327992	Ground or Treated Mineral and Earth Manufacturing	E	3295	Minerals and Earths, Ground or Otherwise Treated
327993	Mineral Wool Manufacturing	E	3296	Mineral Wool
327999	All Other Miscellaneous Nonmetallic Mineral Product Manufacturing	R	*3272	Concrete Products, Except Block and Brick (dry mixture concrete)
			*3292	Asbestos Products (except brake pads and linings)
			*3299	Nonmetallic Mineral Products, NEC (except moldings, ornamental and architectural plaster work)
331	Primary Metal Manufacturing			
3311	Iron and Steel Mills and Ferroalloy Manufacturing			
33111	Iron and Steel Mills and Ferroalloy Manufacturing			
331111	Iron and Steel Mills	N	*3312	Steel Works, Blast Furnaces (Including Coke Ovens), and Rolling Mills (except coke ovens not integrated with steel mills)
			*3399	Primary Metal Products, NEC (ferrous powder, paste, flakes, etc.)
331112	Electrometallurgical Ferroalloy Product Manufacturing	R	*3313	Electrometallurgical Products, Except Steel (ferroalloys)
3312	Steel Product Manufacturing from Purchased Steel			
33121	Iron and Steel Pipes and Tubes Manufacturing from Purchased Steel	E	3317	Steel Pipe and Tubes
33122	Rolling and Drawing of Purchased Steel			
331221	Cold-Rolled Steel Shape Manufacturing	E	3316	Cold-Rolled Steel Sheet, Strip and Bars
331222	Steel Wire Drawing	R	*3315	Steel Wiredrawing and Steel Nails and Spikes (steel wire drawing)

3313	Alumina and Aluminum Production and Processing			
33131	Alumina and Aluminum Production and Processing			
331311	Alumina Refining	N	*2819	Industrial Inorganic Chemicals, NEC (alumina)
331312	Primary Aluminum Production	E	3334	Primary Production of Aluminum
331314	Secondary Smelting and Alloying of Aluminum	N	*3341	Secondary Smelting and Refining of Nonferrous Metals (aluminum)
			*3399	Primary Metal Products, NEC (aluminum powder, paste, flakes, etc.)
331315	Aluminum Sheet, Plate and Foil Manufacturing	E	3353	Aluminum Sheet, Plate, and Foil
331316	Aluminum Extruded Product Manufacturing	E	3354	Aluminum Extruded Products
331319	Other Aluminum Rolling and Drawing	R	3355	Aluminum Rolling and Drawing, NEC
			*3357	Drawing and Insulating of Nonferrous Wire (aluminum wire drawing)
3314	Nonferrous Metal (except Aluminum) Production and Processing			
33141	Nonferrous Metal (except Aluminum) Smelting and Refining			
331411	Primary Smelting and Refining of Copper	E	3331	Primary Smelting and Refining of Copper
331419	Primary Smelting and Refining of Nonferrous Metal (except Copper and Aluminum)	E	3339	Primary Smelting and Refining of Nonferrous Metals, Except Copper and Aluminum
33142	Copper Rolling, Drawing, Extruding, and Alloying			
331421	Copper Rolling, Drawing and Extruding	E	3351	Rolling, Drawing, and Extruding of Copper
331422	Copper Wire (except Mechanical) Drawing	N	*3357	Drawing and Insulating of Nonferrous Wire (copper wire drawing)
331423	Secondary Smelting, Refining, and Alloying of Copper	R	*3341	Secondary Smelting and Refining of Nonferrous Metals (copper)
			*3399	Primary Metal Products, NEC (copper powders, flakes, paste, etc.)
33149	Nonferrous Metals (except Copper and Aluminum) Rolling, Drawing, Extruding and Alloying			
331491	Nonferrous Metal (except Copper and Aluminum) Rolling, Drawing and Extruding	R	3356	Rolling, Drawing and Extruding of Nonferrous Metals, Except Copper and Aluminum
			*3357	Drawing and Insulating of Nonferrous Wire (wire drawing except copper or aluminum)
331492	Secondary Smelting, Refining, and Alloying of Nonferrous Metal (except Copper and Aluminum)	N	*3313	Electrometallurgical Products, Except Steel (except copper and aluminum)
			*3341	Secondary Smelting and Reining of Nonferrous Metals (except copper and aluminum)
			*3399	Primary Metal Products, NEC (except copper and aluminum)
3315	Foundries			
33151	Ferrous Metal Foundries			
331511	Iron Foundries	R	3321	Gray and Ductile Iron Foundries

1997 NAICS Code	1997 NAICS United States and U.S. Description	Status Code	1987 SIC Code	1987 U.S. SIC Description
			3322	Malleable Iron Foundries
331512	Steel Investment Foundries	E	3324	Steel Investment Foundries
331513	Steel Foundries, (except Investment)	E	3325	Steel Foundries, NEC
33152	Nonferrous Metal Foundries			
331521	Aluminum Die-Castings	E	3363	Aluminum Die-Castings
331522	Nonferrous (except Aluminum) Die-Castings	E	3364	Nonferrous Die-Castings, Except Aluminum
331524	Aluminum Foundries	E	3365	Aluminum Foundries
331525	Copper Foundries	E	3366	Copper Foundries
331528	Other Nonferrous Foundries	E	3369	Nonferrous Foundries, Except Aluminum and Copper
332	Fabricated Metal Product Manufacturing			
3321	Forging and Stamping			
33211	Forging and Stamping			
332111	Iron and Steel Forging	E	3462	Iron and Steel Forgings
332112	Nonferrous Forging	E	3463	Nonferrous Forgings
332114	Custom Roll Forming	N	*3449	Miscellaneous Structural Metal Work (custom roll forming)
332115	Crown and Closure Manufacturing	E	3466	Crowns and Closures
332116	Metal Stamping	N	*3469	Metal Stampings, NEC (except kitchen utensils, pots and pans for cooking and coins)
332117	Powder Metallurgy Part Manufacturing	N	*3499	Fabricated Metal Products, NEC (powder metallurgy)
3322	Cutlery and Hand Tool Manufacturing			
33221	Cutlery and Hand Tool Manufacturing			
332211	Cutlery and Flatware (except Precious) Manufacturing	N	3421	Cutlery
			*3914	Silverware, Plated Ware, and Stainless Steel Ware (cutlery and flatware except precious)
332212	Hand and Edge Tool Manufacturing	R	3423	Hand and Edge Tools, Except Machine Tools and Handsaws
			*3523	Farm Machinery and Equipment (hand hair clippers for animals)
			*3524	Lawn and Garden Tractors and Home Lawn and Garden Equipment (nonpowered lawnmowers)
			*3545	Cutting Tools, Machine Tools Accessories, and Machinist Precision Measuring Devices (precision measuring devices)
			*3799	Transportation Equipment, NEC (wheelbarrows)
			*3999	Manufacturing Industries, NEC (tape measures)
332213	Saw Blade and Handsaw Manufacturing	E	3425	Saw Blades and Handsaws
332214	Kitchen Utensil, Pot and Pan Manufacturing	N	*3469	Metal Stampings, NEC (kitchen utensils, pots, and pans for cooking)
3323	Architectural and Structural Metals Manufacturing			
33231	Plate Work and Fabricated Structural Product Manufacturing			

332311	Prefabricated Metal Building and Component Manufacturing	E	3448	Prefabricated Metal Buildings and Components
332312	Fabricated Structural Metal Manufacturing	R	3441	Fabricated Structural Metal
			*3449	Miscellaneous Structural Metal Work (fabricated bar joists and concrete reinforcing bars)
332313	Plate Work Manufacturing	N	*3443	Fabricated Plate Work (Boiler Shops) (fabricated plate work and metal weldments)
33232	Ornamental and Architectural Metal Products Manufacturing			
332321	Metal Window and Door Manufacturing	R	3442	Metal Doors, Sash, Frames, Molding and Trim
			*3449	Miscellaneous Structural Metal Work (curtain wall)
332322	Sheet Metal Work Manufacturing	R	*3444	Sheet Metal Work (ducts, flumes, flooring, siding, dampers, etc.)
332323	Ornamental and Architectural Metal Work Manufacturing	R	3446	Architectural and Ornamental Metal Work
			*3449	Miscellaneous Structural Metal Work (metal plaster bases)
			*3523	Farm Machinery and Equipment (corrals, stalls, and holding gates)
3324	Boiler, Tank, and Shipping Container Manufacturing			
33241	Power Boiler and Heat Exchanger Manufacturing	N	*3443	Fabricated Plate Work (Boiler Shops) (power boilers and heat exchangers)
33242	Metal Tank (Heavy Gauge) Manufacturing	N	*3443	Fabricated Plate Work (Boiler Shops) (heavy gauge tanks)
33243	Metal Can, Box, and Other Metal Container (Light Gauge) Manufacturing			
332431	Metal Can Manufacturing	E	3411	Metal Cans
332439	Other Metal Container Manufacturing	R	3412	Metal Shipping Barrels, Drums, Kegs, and Pails
			*3429	Hardware, NEC (vacuum and insulated bottles, jugs, and chests)
			*3444	Sheet Metal Work (metal bins and vats)
			*3499	Fabricated Metal Products, NEC (metal boxes)
			*3537	Industrial Trucks, Tractors, Trailers, and Stackers (metal air cargo containers)
3325	Hardware Manufacturing			
33251	Hardware Manufacturing	R	*3429	Hardware, NEC (hardware, except hose nozzles, and vacuum and insulated bottles, jugs and chests)
			*3499	Fabricated Metal Products, NEC (safe and vault locks)
3326	Spring and Wire Product Manufacturing			
33261	Spring and Wire Product Manufacturing			
332611	Steel Spring (except Wire) Manufacturing	E	3493	Steel Springs, Except Wire
332612	Wire Spring Manufacturing	R	*3495	Wire Springs (except watch and clock springs)
332618	Other Fabricated Wire Product Manufacturing	R	*3315	Steel Wiredrawing and Steel Nails and Spikes (nails, spikes, paper clips and wire not made in wiredrawing plants)
			*3399	Primary Metal Products, NEC (nonferrous nails, brads, staples, etc.)

1997 NAICS Code	1997 NAICS United States and U.S. Description	Status Code	1987 SIC Code	1987 U.S. SIC Description
			3496	**Miscellaneous Fabricated Wire Products**
3327	Machine Shops, Turned Product, and Screw, Nut and Bolt Manufacturing			
33271	Machine Shops	N	*3599	Industrial and Commercial Machinery and Equipment, NEC (machine shops)
33272	Turned Product and Screw, Nut and Bolt Manufacturing			
332721	Precision Turned Product Manufacturing	E	3451	Screw Machine Products
332722	Bolt, Nut, Screw, Rivet and Washer Manufacturing	E	3452	Bolts, Nuts, Screws, Rivets, and Washers
3328	Coating, Engraving, Heat Treating and Allied Activities			
33281	Coating, Engraving, Heat Treating, and Allied Activities			
332811	Metal Heat Treating	E	3398	Metal Heat Treating
332812	Metal Coating, Engraving (except Jewelry and Silverware), and Allied Services to Manufacturers	R	*3479	Coating, Engraving, and Allied Services, NEC (except jewelry, silverware, and flatware engraving and etching)
332813	Electroplating, Plating, Polishing, Anodizing and Coloring	R	*3399	Primary Metal Products, NEC (laminating steel)
			3471	Electroplating, Plating, Polishing, Anodizing, and Coloring
3329	Other Fabricated Metal Product Manufacturing			
33291	Metal Valve Manufacturing			
332911	Industrial Valve Manufacturing	E	3491	Industrial Valves
332912	Fluid Power Valve and Hose Fitting Manufacturing	R	3492	Fluid Power Valves and Hose Fittings
			*3728	Aircraft Parts and Auxiliary Equipment, NEC (fluid power aircraft subassemblies)
332913	Plumbing Fixture Fitting and Trim Manufacturing	R	*3432	Plumbing Fixture Fittings and Trim (except shower rods)
332919	Other Metal Valve and Pipe Fitting Manufacturing	R	*3429	Hardware, NEC (hose nozzles)
			*3494	Valves and Pipe Fittings, NEC (except metal pipe hangers and supports)
			*3499	Fabricated Metal Products, NEC (metal aerosol valves)
33299	All Other Fabricated Metal Product Manufacturing			
332991	Ball and Roller Bearing Manufacturing	E	3562	Ball and Roller Bearings
332992	Small Arms Ammunition Manufacturing	E	3482	Small Arms Ammunition
332993	Ammunition (except Small Arms) Manufacturing	E	3483	Ammunition, Except for Small Arms
332994	Small Arms Manufacturing	E	3484	Small Arms
332995	Other Ordnance and Accessories Manufacturing	E	3489	Ordnance and Accessories, NEC
332996	Fabricated Pipe and Pipe Fitting Manufacturing	E	3498	Fabricated Pipe and Pipe Fittings
332997	Industrial Pattern Manufacturing	E	3543	Industrial Patterns
332998	Enameled Iron and Metal Sanitary Ware Manufacturing	E	3431	Enameled Iron and Metal Sanitary Ware
332999	All Other Miscellaneous Fabricated Metal Product Manufacturing	R	*3291	Abrasive Products (steel wool with or without soap)
			*3432	Plumbing Fixture Fittings and Trim (metal shower rods)
			*3494	Valves and Pipe Fittings, NEC (metal pipe hangers and supports)

			*3497	Metal Foil and Leaf (foil and foil containers)
			*3499	Fabricated Metal Products, NEC (other metal products)
			*3537	Industrial Trucks, Tractors, Trailers, and Stackers (metal pallets)
			*3599	Industrial and Commercial Machinery and Equipment, NEC (flexible metal hose)
			*3999	Manufacturing Industries, NEC (other miscellaneous metal products, such as combs, hair curlers, etc.)
333	Machinery Manufacturing			
3331	Agriculture, Construction, and Mining Machinery Manufacturing			
33311	Agricultural Implement Manufacturing			
333111	Farm Machinery and Equipment Manufacturing	R	*3523	Farm Machinery and Equipment (except corrals, stalls, holding gates, hand clippers for animals, and farm conveyors/elevators)
333112	Lawn and Garden Tractor and Home Lawn and Garden Equipment Manufacturing	R	*3524	Lawn and Garden Tractors and Home Lawn and Garden Equipment (except nonpowered lawnmowers)
33312	Construction Machinery Manufacturing	R	*3531	Construction Machinery and Equipment (except railway track maintenance equipment; winches, aerial work platforms; and automotive wreckers hoists)
33313	Mining and Oil and Gas Field Machinery Manufacturing			
333131	Mining Machinery and Equipment Manufacturing	E	3532	Mining Machinery and Equipment, Except Oil and Gas Field Machinery and Equipment
333132	Oil and Gas Field Machinery and Equipment Manufacturing	E	3533	Oil and Gas Field Machinery and Equipment
3332	Industrial Machinery Manufacturing			
33321	Sawmill and Woodworking Machinery Manufacturing	E	3553	Woodworking Machinery
33322	Rubber and Plastics Industry Machinery Manufacturing	N	*3559	Special Industry Machinery, NEC (rubber and plastics manufacturing machinery)
33329	Other Industrial Machinery Manufacturing			
333291	Paper Industry Machinery Manufacturing	E	3554	Paper Industries Machinery
333292	Textile Machinery Manufacturing	E	3552	Textile Machinery
333293	Printing Machinery and Equipment Manufacturing	E	3555	Printing Trades Machinery and Equipment
333294	Food Product Machinery Manufacturing	E	3556	Food Products Machinery
333295	Semiconductor Machinery Manufacturing	N	*3559	Special Industry Machinery, NEC (semiconductor machinery manufacturing)
333298	All Other Industrial Machinery Manufacturing	R	*3559	Special Industry Machinery, NEC (except rubber and plastics manufacturing machinery, semiconductor manufacturing machinery, and automotive maintenance equipment)
			*3639	Household Appliances, NEC (household sewing machines)
3333	Commercial and Service Industry Machinery Manufacturing			
33331	Commercial and Service Industry Machinery Manufacturing			

1997 NAICS Code	1997 NAICS United States and U.S. Description	Status Code	1987 SIC Code	1987 U.S. SIC Description
333311	Automatic Vending Machine Manufacturing	E	3581	Automatic Vending Machines
333312	Commercial Laundry, Drycleaning and Pressing Machine Manufacturing	E	3582	Commercial Laundry, Drycleaning and Pressing Machines
333313	Office Machinery Manufacturing	N	*3578	Calculating and Accounting Machinery, Except Electronic Computers (except point of sales terminals and funds transfer devices)
			*3579	Office Machines, NEC (except timeclocks, time stamps, pencil sharpeners, stapling machines, etc.)
333314	Optical Instrument and Lens Manufacturing	E	3827	Optical Instruments and Lenses
333315	Photographic and Photocopying Equipment Manufacturing	N	*3861	Photographic Equipment and Supplies (except photographic film, paper, plates and chemicals)
333319	Other Commercial and Service Industry Machinery Manufacturing	R	*3559	Special Industry Machinery, NEC (automotive maintenance equipment)
			3589	Service Industry Machinery, NEC
			*3599	Industrial and Commercial Machinery and Equipment, NEC (carnival amusement park equipment)
			*3699	Electrical Machinery, Equipment and Supplies, NEC (electronic teaching machines and flight simulators)
3334	Ventilation, Heating, Air-Conditioning and Commercial Refrigeration Equipment Manufacturing			
33341	Ventilation, Heating, Air-Conditioning and Commercial Refrigeration Equipment Manufacturing			
333411	Air Purification Equipment Manufacturing	N	*3564	Industrial and Commercial Fans and Blowers and Air Purification Equipment (air purification equipment)
333412	Industrial and Commercial Fan and Blower Manufacturing	R	*3564	Industrial and Commercial Fans and Blowers and Air Purification Equipment (fans and blowers)
333414	Heating Equipment (except Electric and Warm Air Furnaces) Manufacturing	R	3433	Heating Equipment, Except Electric and Warm Air Furnaces
			*3634	Electric Housewares and Fans (wall and baseboard heating units for permanent installation)
333415	Air-Conditioning and Warm Air Heating Equipment and Commercial and Industrial Refrigeration Equipment Manufacturing	R	*3443	Fabricated Plate Work (Boiler Shops) (metal cooling towers)
			*3585	Air-Conditioning and Warm Air Heating Equipment and Commercial and Industrial Refrigeration Equipment (except motor vehicle air-conditioning)
3335	Metalworking Machinery Manufacturing			
33351	Metalworking Machinery Manufacturing			
333511	Industrial Mold Manufacturing	R	*3544	Special Dies and Tools, Die Sets, Jigs and Fixtures, and Industrial Molds (industrial molds)
333512	Machine Tool (Metal Cutting Types) Manufacturing	E	3541	Machine Tools, Metal Cutting Type

333513	Machine Tool (Metal Forming Types) Manufacturing	E	3542	Machine Tools, Metal Forming Type
333514	Special Die and Tool, Die Set, Jig and Fixture Manufacturing	R	*3544	Special Dies and Tools, Die Sets, Jigs and Fixtures, and Industrial Molds (except molds)
333515	Cutting Tool and Machine Tool Accessory Manufacturing	R	*3545	Cutting Tools, Machine Tool Accessories, and Machinists' Precision Measuring Devices (except precision measuring devices)
333516	Rolling Mill Machinery and Equipment Manufacturing	E	3547	Rolling Mill Machinery and Equipment
333518	Other Metalworking Machinery Manufacturing	E	3549	Metalworking Machinery, NEC
3336	Engine, Turbine, and Power Transmission Equipment Manufacturing			
33361	Engine, Turbine and Power Transmission Equipment Manufacturing			
333611	Turbine and Turbine Generator Set Unit Manufacturing	E	3511	Steam, Gas, and Hydraulic Turbines, and Turbine Generator Set Units
333612	Speed Changer, Industrial High-Speed Drive and Gear Manufacturing	E	3566	Speed Changers, Industrial High-Speed Drives, and Gears
333613	Mechanical Power Transmission Equipment Manufacturing	E	3568	Mechanical Power Transmission Equipment, NEC
333618	Other Engine Equipment Manufacturing	R	*3519	Internal Combustion Engines, NEC (except stationary engine radiators)
			*3699	Electrical Machinery, Equipment and Supplies, NEC (outboard electric motors)
3339	Other General Purpose Machinery Manufacturing			
33391	Pump and Compressor Manufacturing			
333911	Pump and Pumping Equipment Manufacturing	R	3561	Pumps and Pumping Equipment
			*3743	Railroad Equipment (locomotive fuel lubricating or cooling medium pumps)
333912	Air and Gas Compressor Manufacturing	E	3563	Air and Gas Compressors
333913	Measuring and Dispensing Pump Manufacturing	E	3586	Measuring and Dispensing Pumps
33392	Material Handling Equipment Manufacturing			
333921	Elevator and Moving Stairway Manufacturing	E	3534	Elevators and Moving Stairways
333922	Conveyor and Conveying Equipment Manufacturing	R	*3523	Farm Machinery and Equipment (farm conveyors and elevators)
			3535	Conveyors and Conveying Equipment
333923	Overhead Traveling Crane, Hoist and Monorail System Manufacturing	R	3536	Overhead Traveling Cranes, Hoists, and Monorail Systems
			*3531	Construction Machinery and Equipment (winches, aerial work platforms, and automobile wrecker hoists)
333924	Industrial Truck, Tractor, Trailer and Stacker Machinery Manufacturing	R	*3537	Industrial Trucks, Tractors, Trailers, and Stackers (except metal pallets and metal air cargo containers)
33399	All Other General Purpose Machinery Manufacturing			
333991	Power-Driven Hand Tool Manufacturing	E	3546	Power-Driven Handtools

1997 NAICS Code	1997 NAICS United States and U.S. Description	Status Code	1987 SIC Code	1987 U.S. SIC Description
333992	Welding and Soldering Equipment Manufacturing	R	*3548	Electric and Gas Welding and Soldering Equipment (except transformers for arc-welding)
333993	Packaging Machinery Manufacturing	E	3565	Packaging Machinery
333994	Industrial Process Furnace and Oven Manufacturing	E	3567	Industrial Process Furnaces and Ovens
333995	Fluid Power Cylinder and Actuator Manufacturing	E	3593	Fluid Power Cylinders and Actuators
333996	Fluid Power Pump and Motor Manufacturing	E	3594	Fluid Power Pumps and Motors
333997	Scale and Balance (except Laboratory) Manufacturing	E	3596	Scales and Balances, Except Laboratory
333999	All Other General Purpose Machinery Manufacturing	R	*3599	Industrial and Commercial Machinery and Equipment, NEC (other industrial and commercial machinery and equipment)
			3569	General Industrial Machinery and Equipment, NEC
334	Computer and Electronic Product Manufacturing			
3341	Computer and Peripheral Equipment Manufacturing			
33411	Computer and Peripheral Equipment Manufacturing			
334111	Electronic Computer Manufacturing	E	3571	Electronic Computers
334112	Computer Storage Device Manufacturing	E	3572	Computer Storage Devices
334113	Computer Terminal Manufacturing	E	3575	Computer Terminals
334119	Other Computer Peripheral Equipment Manufacturing	R	3577	Computer Peripheral Equipment, NEC
			*3578	Calculating and Accounting Machines, Except Electronic Computers (point of sale terminals and fund transfer devices)
			*3699	Electrical Machinery, Equipment and Supplies, NEC (bar code scanners)
3342	Communications Equipment Manufacturing			
33421	Telephone Apparatus Manufacturing	R	*3661	Telephone and Telegraph Apparatus (except telephone transformers and consumer external modems)
33422	Radio and Television Broadcasting and Wireless Communications Equipment Manufacturing	R	3663	Radio and Television Broadcasting and Communication Equipment
			*3679	Electronic Components, NEC (communication equipment)
33429	Other Communications Equipment Manufacturing	E	3669	Communications Equipment, NEC
3343	Audio and Video Equipment Manufacturing			
33431	Audio and Video Equipment Manufacturing	E	3651	Household Audio and Video Equipment
3344	Semiconductor and Other Electronic Component Manufacturing			
33441	Semiconductor and Other Electronic Component Manufacturing			
334411	Electron Tube Manufacturing	E	3671	Electron Tubes
334412	Printed Circuit Board Manufacturing	E	3672	Printed Circuit Boards
334413	Semiconductor and Related Device Manufacturing	E	3674	Semiconductors and Related Devices
334414	Electronic Capacitor Manufacturing	E	3675	Electronic Capacitors
334415	Electronic Resistor Manufacturing	E	3676	Electronic Resistors

334416	Electronic Coil, Transformer, and Other Inductor Manufacturing	R	*3661	Telephone and Telegraph Apparatus (telephone transformers)
			3677	Electronic Coils, Transformers, and Other Inductors
			*3825	Instruments for Measuring and Testing of Electricity and Electrical Signals (portable instrument transformers)
334417	Electronic Connector Manufacturing	E	3678	Electronic Connectors
334418	Printed Circuit/Electronics Assembly Manufacturing	N	*3679	Electronic Components, NEC (printed circuit/electronic assembly manufacturing)
			*3661	Telephone and Telegraph Apparatus (consumer external modems)
334419	Other Electronic Component Manufacturing	R	*3679	Electronic Components, NEC (other electronic components)
3345	Navigational, Measuring, Medical, and Control Instruments Manufacturing			
33451	Navigational, Measuring, Medical, and Control Instruments Manufacturing			
334510	Electromedical and Electrotherapeutic Apparatus Manufacturing	R	*3842	Orthopedic, Prosthetic and Surgical Appliances and Supplies (electronic hearing aids)
			*3845	Electromedical and Electrotherapeutic Apparatus (other electromedical and electrotherapeutic apparatus)
334511	Search, Detection, Navigation, Guidance, Aeronautical, and Nautical System and Instrument Manufacturing	E	3812	Search, Detection, Navigation, Guidance, Aeronautical, and Nautical Systems and Instruments
334512	Automatic Environmental Control Manufacturing for Residential, Commercial and Appliance Use	E	3822	Automatic Controls for Regulating Residential and Commercial Environments and Appliances
334513	Instruments and Related Products Manufacturing for Measuring, Displaying, and Controlling Industrial Process Variables	E	3823	Industrial Instruments for Measurement, Display, and Control of Process Variables; and Related Products
334514	Totalizing Fluid Meter and Counting Device Manufacturing	E	3824	Totalizing Fluid Meters and Counting Devices
334515	Instrument Manufacturing for Measuring and Testing Electricity and Electrical Signals	R	*3825	Instruments for Measuring and Testing of Electricity and Electrical Signals (except portable instrument transformers)
334516	Analytical Laboratory Instrument Manufacturing	E	3826	Laboratory Analytical Instruments
334517	Irradiation Apparatus Manufacturing	R	3844	X-Ray Apparatus and Tubes and Related Irradiation Apparatus
			*3845	Electromedical and Electrotherapeutic Apparatus (CT and CAT Scanners)
334518	Watch, Clock, and Part Manufacturing	R	*3495	Wire Springs (clock and watch springs)
			*3579	Office Machines, NEC (time clocks and other time recording devices)
			3873	Watches, Clocks, Clockwork Operated Devices, and Parts
334519	Other Measuring and Controlling Device Manufacturing	R	*3829	Measuring and Controlling Devices, NEC (except medical thermometers)

1997 NAICS Code	1997 NAICS United States and U.S. Description	Status Code	1987 SIC Code	1987 U.S. SIC Description
3346	Manufacturing and Reproducing Magnetic and Optical Media			
33461	Manufacturing and Reproducing Magnetic and Optical Media			
334611	Software Reproducing	N	*7372	Prepackaged Software (reproduction of software)
334612	Prerecorded Compact Disc (except Software), Tape, and Record Reproducing	N	*3652	Phonograph Records and Prerecorded Audio Tapes and Disks (reproduction of all other media except video)
			*7819	Services Allied to Motion Picture Production (reproduction of video)
334613	Magnetic and Optical Recording Media Manufacturing	E	3695	Magnetic and Optical Recording Media
335	Electrical Equipment, Appliance and Component Manufacturing			
3351	Electric Lighting Equipment Manufacturing			
33511	Electric Lamp Bulb and Part Manufacturing	E	3641	Electric Lamp Bulbs and Tubes
33512	Lighting Fixture Manufacturing			
335121	Residential Electric Lighting Fixture Manufacturing	E	3645	Residential Electric Lighting Fixtures
			*3999	Manufacturing Industries, NEC (lamp shades of paper or textile)
335122	Commercial, Industrial and Institutional Electric Lighting Fixture Manufacturing	E	3646	Commercial, Industrial, and Institutional Electric Lighting Fixtures
335129	Other Lighting Equipment Manufacturing	R	3648	Lighting Equipment, NEC
			*3699	Electrical Machinery, Equipment, and Supplies, NEC (Christmas tree lighting sets and electric insect lamps)
3352	Household Appliance Manufacturing			
33521	Small Electrical Appliance Manufacturing			
335211	Electric Housewares and Household Fan Manufacturing	R	*3634	Electric Housewares and Fans (except wall and baseboard heating units for permanent installation)
335212	Household Vacuum Cleaner Manufacturing	R	3635	Household Vacuum Cleaners
			*3639	Household Appliances, NEC (floor waxing and floor polishing machines)
33522	Major Appliance Manufacturing			
335221	Household Cooking Appliance Manufacturing	E	3631	Household Cooking Equipment
335222	Household Refrigerator and Home Freezer Manufacturing	E	3632	Household Refrigerators and Home and Farm Freezers
335224	Household Laundry Equipment Manufacturing	E	3633	Household Laundry Equipment
335228	Other Major Household Appliance Manufacturing	R	*3639	Household Appliances, NEC (except floor waxing and floor polishing machines, and household sewing machines)
3353	Electrical Equipment Manufacturing			
33531	Electrical Equipment Manufacturing			
335311	Power, Distribution and Specialty Transformer Manufacturing	R	*3548	Electric and Gas Welding and Soldering Equipment (transformers for arc-welders)

NAICS	Title	Status	SIC	SIC Title
335312	Motor and Generator Manufacturing	R	3612	Power, Distribution, and Speciality Transformers
			3621	Motors and Generators
			*7694	Armature Rewinding Shops (remanufacturing)
335313	Switchgear and Switchboard Apparatus Manufacturing	E	3613	Switchgear and Switchboard Apparatus
335314	Relay and Industrial Control Manufacturing	E	3625	Relays and Industrial Controls
3359	Other Electrical Equipment and Component Manufacturing			
33591	Battery Manufacturing			
335911	Storage Battery Manufacturing	E	3691	Storage Batteries
335912	Dry and Wet Primary Battery Manufacturing	E	3692	Primary Batteries, Dry and Wet
33592	Communication and Energy Wire and Cable Manufacturing			
335921	Fiber Optic Cable Manufacturing	N	*3357	Drawing and Insulating of Nonferrous Wire (fiber optic cable-insulating only)
335929	Other Communication and Energy Wire Manufacturing	N	*3357	Drawing and Insulating of Nonferrous Wire (communication and energy wire, except fiber optic-insulating only)
33593	Wiring Device Manufacturing			
335931	Current-Carrying Wiring Device Manufacturing	E	3643	Current-Carrying Wiring Devices
335932	Noncurrent-Carrying Wiring Device Manufacturing	E	3644	Noncurrent-Carrying Wiring Devices
33599	All Other Electrical Equipment and Component Manufacturing			
335991	Carbon and Graphite Product Manufacturing	E	3624	Carbon and Graphite Products
335999	All Other Miscellaneous Electrical Equipment and Component Manufacturing	R	3629	Electrical Industrial Apparatus, NEC
			*3699	Electrical Machinery, Equipment, and Supplies, NEC (other electrical industrial apparatus)
336	Transportation Equipment Manufacturing			
3361	Motor Vehicle Manufacturing			
33611	Automobile and Light Duty Motor Vehicle Manufacturing			
336111	Automobile Manufacturing	N	*3711	Motor Vehicles and Passenger Car Bodies (automobiles)
336112	Light Truck and Utility Vehicle Manufacturing	N	*3711	Motor Vehicles and Passenger Car Bodies (light trucks and utility vehicles)
33612	Heavy Duty Truck Manufacturing	N	*3711	Motor Vehicles and Passenger Car Bodies (heavy duty trucks)
3362	Motor Vehicle Body and Trailer Manufacturing			
33621	Motor Vehicle Body and Trailer Manufacturing			
336211	Motor Vehicle Body Manufacturing	R	*3711	Motor Vehicles and Passenger Car Bodies (kit car and other passenger car bodies)
			3713	Truck and Bus Bodies
			*3714	Motor Vehicle Parts and Accessories (dumptruck lifting mechanisms and fifth wheels)

1997 NAICS Code	1997 NAICS United States and U.S. Description	Status Code	1987 SIC Code	1987 U.S. SIC Description
336212	Truck Trailer Manufacturing	E	3715	Truck Trailers
336213	Motor Home Manufacturing	E	3716	Motor Homes
336214	Travel Trailer and Camper Manufacturing	R	3792	Travel Trailers and Campers
			*3799	Transportation Equipment, NEC (automobile, boat, utility and light truck trailers)
3363	Motor Vehicle Parts Manufacturing			
33631	Motor Vehicle Gasoline Engine and Engine Parts Manufacturing			
336311	Carburetor, Piston, Piston Ring and Valve Manufacturing	E	3592	Carburetors, Pistons, Piston Rings, and Valves
336312	Gasoline Engine and Engine Parts Manufacturing	N	*3714	Motor Vehicle Parts and Accessories (gasoline engines and engine parts including rebuilt)
33632	Motor Vehicle Electrical and Electronic Equipment Manufacturing			
336321	Vehicular Lighting Equipment Manufacturing	E	3647	Vehicular Lighting Equipment
336322	Other Motor Vehicle Electrical and Electronic Equipment Manufacturing	R	*3679	Electronic Components, NEC (electronic control modules for motor vehicles)
			3694	Electrical Equipment for Internal Combustion Engines
			*3714	Motor Vehicle Parts and Accessories (wiring harness sets, other than ignition; block heaters and battery heaters; instrument board assemblies; permanent defrosters; windshield washer-wiper mechanisms; cruise control mechanisms; and other electrical equipment for internal combustion engines)
33633	Motor Vehicle Steering and Suspension Components (except Spring) Manufacturing	N	*3714	Motor Vehicle Parts and Accessories (steering and suspension parts)
33634	Motor Vehicle Brake System Manufacturing	N	*3292	Asbestos Products (asbestos brake linings and pads)
			*3714	Motor Vehicle Parts and Accessories (brake and brake systems, including assemblies)
33635	Motor Vehicle Transmission and Power Train Parts Manufacturing	N	*3714	Motor Vehicle Parts and Accessories (transmissions and power train parts, including rebuilding)
33636	Motor Vehicle Fabric Accessories and Seat Manufacturing	N	*2396	Automotive Trimmings, Apparel Findings, and Related Products (textile motor vehicle trimming)
			*2399	Fabricated Textile Products, NEC (seat belts, and seat and tire covers)
			*2531	Public Building and Related Furniture (seats for motor vehicles)
33637	Motor Vehicle Metal Stamping	E	3465	Automotive Stampings
33639	Other Motor Vehicle Parts Manufacturing			
336391	Motor Vehicle Air-Conditioning Manufacturing	N	*3585	Air-Conditioning and Warm Air Heating Equipment and Commercial and Industrial Refrigeration Equipment (motor vehicle air-conditioning)
336399	All Other Motor Vehicle Parts Manufacturing	R	*3519	Internal Combustion Engines, NEC (stationary engine radiators)

			*3599	Industrial and Commercial Machinery and Equipment, NEC (gasoline, oil and intake filters for internal combustion engines, except for motor vehicles)
			*3714	Motor Vehicle Parts and Accessories (except truck and bus bodies, trailers, engine and engine parts, motor vehicle electrical and electronic equipment, motor vehicle steering and suspension components, motor vehicle brake systems, and motor vehicle transmission and power train parts)
3364	Aerospace Product and Parts Manufacturing			
33641	Aerospace Product and Parts Manufacturing			
336411	Aircraft Manufacturing	E	3721	Aircraft
336412	Aircraft Engine and Engine Parts Manufacturing	E	3724	Aircraft Engines and Engine Parts
336413	Other Aircraft Part and Auxiliary Equipment Manufacturing	R	*3728	Aircraft Parts and Auxiliary Equipment, NEC (except fluid power aircraft subassemblies)
336414	Guided Missile and Space Vehicle Manufacturing	E	3761	Guided Missiles and Space Vehicles
336415	Guided Missile and Space Vehicle Propulsion Unit and Propulsion Unit Parts Manufacturing	E	3764	Guided Missile and Space Vehicle Propulsion Units and Propulsion Unit Parts
336419	Other Guided Missile and Space Vehicle Parts and Auxiliary Equipment Manufacturing	E	3769	Guided Missile and Space Vehicle Parts and Auxiliary Equipment
3365	Railroad Rolling Stock Manufacturing			
33651	Railroad Rolling Stock Manufacturing	R	*3531	Construction Machinery and Equipment (railway track maintenance equipment)
			*3743	Railroad Equipment (except locomotive fuel lubricating or cooling medium pumps)
3366	Ship and Boat Building			
33661	Ship and Boat Building			
336611	Ship Building and Repairing	E	3731	Ship Building and Repairing
336612	Boat Building	R	*3732	Boat Building and Repairing (boat building)
3369	Other Transportation Equipment Manufacturing			
33699	Other Transportation Equipment Manufacturing			
336991	Motorcycle, Bicycle and Parts Manufacturing	R	*3944	Games, Toys, and Children's Vehicles, Except Dolls and Bicycles (metal tricycles)
			3751	Motorcycles, Bicycles and Parts
336992	Military Armored Vehicle, Tank and Tank Component Manufacturing	R	*3711	Motor Vehicles and Passenger Car Bodies (military armored vehicles)
			3795	Tanks and Tank Components
336999	All Other Transportation Equipment Manufacturing	R	*3799	Transportation Equipment, NEC (except automobile, boat, utility light truck trailers, and wheelbarrows)
337	Furniture and Related Product Manufacturing			

1997 NAICS Code	1997 NAICS United States and U.S. Description	Status Code	1987 SIC Code	1987 U.S. SIC Description
3371	Household and Institutional Furniture and Kitchen Cabinet Manufacturing			
33711	Wood Kitchen Cabinet and Counter Top Manufacturing	R	2434	Wood Kitchen Cabinets
			*2541	Wood Office and Store Fixtures, Partitions, Shelving, and Lockers (counter tops)
			*5712	Furniture Stores (custom wood cabinets)
33712	Household and Institutional Furniture Manufacturing			
337121	Upholstered Household Furniture Manufacturing	R	2512	Wood Household Furniture, Upholstered
			*2515	Mattress, Foundations, and Convertible Beds (convertible sofas)
			*5712	Furniture (custom made upholstered household furniture except cabinets)
337122	Nonupholstered Wood Household Furniture Manufacturing	E	2511	Wood Household Furniture, Except Upholstered
			*5712	Furniture Stores (custom made wood household furniture except cabinets)
337124	Metal Household Furniture Manufacturing	E	2514	Metal Household Furniture
337125	Household Furniture (except Wood and Metal) Manufacturing	E	2519	Household Furniture, NEC
337127	Institutional Furniture Manufacturing	R	*2531	Public Building and Related Furniture (furniture made for public buildings)
			*2599	Furniture and Fixtures, NEC (except hospital beds)
			*3952	Lead Pencils, Crayons, and Artist's Materials (drafting tables and boards)
			*3999	Manufacturing Industries, NEC (beauty and barber chairs)
337129	Wood Television, Radio, and Sewing Machine Cabinet Manufacturing	E	2517	Wood Television, Radio, Phonograph, and Sewing Machine Cabinets
3372	Office Furniture (including Fixtures) Manufacturing			
33721	Office Furniture (including Fixtures) Manufacturing			
337211	Wood Office Furniture Manufacturing	E	2521	Wood Office Furniture
337212	Custom Architectural Woodwork and Millwork Manufacturing	N	*2541	Wood Office and Store Fixtures, Partitions, Shelving, and Lockers (architectural woodwork, millwork, and fixtures)
337214	Nonwood Office Furniture Manufacturing	E	2522	Office Furniture, Except Wood
337215	Showcase, Partition, Shelving, and Locker Manufacturing	N	2542	Office and Store Fixtures, Partitions, Shelving and Lockers, Except Wood
			*2541	Wood Office and Store Fixtures, Partitions, Shelving, and Lockers (except counter tops, custom architectural woodwork, millwork and fixtures)
			*2426	Hardwood Dimension and Flooring Mills (wood furniture frames)
			*3499	Fabricated Metal Products, NEC (metal furniture frames)
3379	Other Furniture Related Product Manufacturing			

33791	Mattress Manufacturing	R	*2515	Mattresses, Foundations and Convertible Beds (mattresses and foundations)
33792	Blind and Shade Manufacturing	E	2591	Drapery Hardware and Window Blinds and Shades
339	Miscellaneous Manufacturing			
3391	Medical Equipment and Supplies Manufacturing			
33911	Medical Equipment and Supplies Manufacturing			
339111	Laboratory Apparatus and Furniture Manufacturing		*3829	Measuring and Controlling Devices, NEC (medical thermometers)
339112	Surgical and Medical Instrument Manufacturing	R	3841	Surgical and Medical Instruments and Apparatus
			*3829	Measuring and Controlling Devices, NEC (medical thermometers)
339113	Surgical Appliance and Supplies Manufacturing	R	*2599	Furniture and Fixtures, NEC (hospital beds)
			*3842	Orthopedic, Prosthetic, and Surgical Appliances and Supplies (except electronic hearing aids)
339114	Dental Equipment and Supplies Manufacturing	E	3843	Dental Equipment and Supplies
339115	Ophthalmic Goods Manufacturing	R	3851	Opthalmic Goods
			*5995	Optical Goods Stores (optical laboratories grinding of lenses to prescription)
339116	Dental Laboratories	E	8072	Dental Laboratories
3399	Other Miscellaneous Manufacturing			
33991	Jewelry and Silverware Manufacturing			
339911	Jewelry (except Costume) Manufacturing	R	*3469	Metal Stamping, NEC (stamping coins)
			*3479	Coating, Engraving, and Allied Services, NEC (jewelry engraving and etching, including precious metal)
			3911	Jewelry, Precious Metal
339912	Silverware and Plated Ware Manufacturing	R	*3479	Coating, Engraving, and Allied Services, NEC (silver and plated ware engraving and etching)
			*3914	Silverware, Plated Ware, and Stainless Steel Ware (except nonprecious metal cutlery and flatware)
339913	Jewelers' Material and Lapidary Work Manufacturing	E	3915	Jewelers' Findings and Materials, and Lapidary Work
339914	Costume Jewelry and Novelty Manufacturing	R	*3479	Coating, Engraving, and Allied Services, NEC (costume jewelry engraving and etching)
			*3499	Fabricated Metal Products, NEC (trophies of nonprecious metals)
			3961	Costume Jewelry and Costume Novelties, Except Precious Metal
33992	Sporting and Athletic Goods Manufacturing	E	3949	Sporting and Athletic Goods, NEC
33993	Doll, Toy, and Game Manufacturing			
339931	Doll and Stuffed Toy Manufacturing	E	3942	Dolls and Stuffed Toys
339932	Game, Toy, and Children's Vehicle Manufacturing	R	*3944	Games, Toys, and Children's Vehicles, Except Dolls and Bicycles (except metal tricycles)
33994	Office Supplies (except Paper) Manufacturing			
339941	Pen and Mechanical Pencil Manufacturing	E	3951	Pens, Mechanical Pencils, and Parts
339942	Lead Pencil and Art Good Manufacturing	R	*2531	Public Buildings and Related Furniture (blackboards)

1997 NAICS Code	1997 NAICS United States and U.S. Description	Status Code	1987 SIC Code	1987 U.S. SIC Description
			*3579	Office Machines, NEC (pencil sharpeners, staplers and other office equipment)
			*3952	Lead Pencils, Crayons, and Artists' Materials (except drawing and india ink, and drafting tables and boards)
339943	Marking Device Manufacturing	E	3953	Marking Devices
339944	Carbon Paper and Inked Ribbon Manufacturing	E	3955	Carbon Paper and Inked Ribbons
33995	Sign Manufacturing	E	3993	Signs and Advertising Specialties
33999	All Other Miscellaneous Manufacturing			
339991	Gasket, Packing, and Sealing Device Manufacturing	E	3053	Gaskets, Packing, and Sealing Devices
339992	Musical Instrument Manufacturing	E	3931	Musical Instruments
339993	Fastener, Button, Needle and Pin Manufacturing	R	3965	Fasteners, Buttons, Needles, and Pins
			*3131	Boat and Shoe Cut Stock and Findings (metal buckles)
339994	Broom, Brush and Mop Manufacturing	R	3991	Brooms and Brushes
			*2392	Housefurnishings, Except Curtains and Draperies (mops, floor and dust)
339995	Burial Casket Manufacturing	E	3995	Burial Caskets
339999	All Other Miscellaneous Manufacturing	R	*2499	Wood Products, NEC (mirror and picture frames)
			*3999	Manufacturing Industries, NEC (other miscellaneous products not specially provided for previously)
42	Wholesale Trade			
421	Wholesale Trade, Durable Goods			
4211	Motor Vehicle and Motor Vehicle Part and Supplies Wholesalers			
42111	Automobile and Other Motor Vehicle Wholesalers	E	5012	Automobiles and Other Motor Vehicles
42112	Motor Vehicle Supplies and New Part Wholesalers	R	*5013	Motor Vehicle Supplies and New Parts (except parts sold via retail methods)
42113	Tire and Tube Wholesalers	R	*5014	Tires and Tubes (except tires sold via retail method)
42114	Motor Vehicle Part (Used) Wholesalers	E	5015	Motor Vehicle Parts, Used
4212	Furniture and Home Furnishing Wholesalers			
42121	Furniture Wholesalers	R	*5021	Furniture (except furniture sold via retail method)
42122	Home Furnishing Wholesalers	R	*5023	Homefurnishings (except homefurnishings sold via retail method)
4213	Lumber and Other Construction Materials Wholesalers			
42131	Lumber, Plywood, Millwork and Wood Panel Wholesalers	R	*5031	Lumber, Plywood, Millwork, and Wood Panels (except construction materials sold via retail method)
			*5211	Lumber and Other Building Materials Dealers - Retail (construction materials sold by establishments "known as retail in the trade" selling via wholesale method)
42132	Brick, Stone and Related Construction Material Wholesalers	R	*5032	Brick, Stone, and Related Construction Materials (except construction materials sold via retail method)
42133	Roofing, Siding and Insulation Material Wholesalers	E	5033	Roofing, Siding, and Insulation Materials
42139	Other Construction Material Wholesalers	R	*5039	Construction Materials, NEC (sold via wholesale method)

4214	Professional and Commercial Equipment and Supplies Wholesalers			
42141	Photographic Equipment and Supplies Wholesalers	E	5043	Photographic Equipment and Supplies
42142	Office Equipment Wholesalers	E	5044	Office Equipment
42143	Computer and Computer Peripheral Equipment and Software Wholesalers	R	*5045	Computers and Computer Peripherals Equipment and Software (except computers, equipment, and software sold via retail method)
42144	Other Commercial Equipment Wholesalers	E	5046	Commercial Equipment, NEC
42145	Medical, Dental and Hospital Equipment and Supplies Wholesalers	R	*5047	Medical, Dental and Hospital Equipment and Supplies (except medical, dental, and hospital equipment and supplies sold via retail method)
42146	Ophthalmic Goods Wholesalers	E	5048	Ophthalmic Goods
42149	Other Professional Equipment and Supplies Wholesalers	R	*5049	Professional Equipment and Supplies, NEC (except religious and school supplies sold via retail method)
4215	Metal and Mineral (except Petroleum) Wholesalers			
42151	Metal Service Centers and Offices	E	5051	Metals Service Centers and Offices
42152	Coal and Other Mineral and Ore Wholesalers	E	5052	Coal and Other Mineral and Ores
4216	Electrical Goods Wholesalers			
42161	Electrical Apparatus and Equipment, Wiring Supplies and Construction Material Wholesalers	R	*5063	Electrical Apparatus and Equipment, Wiring Supplies and Construction Materials (except electrical supplies sold via retail method)
42162	Electrical Appliance, Television and Radio Set Wholesalers	E	5064	Electrical Appliances, Television and Radio Sets
42169	Other Electronic Parts and Equipment Wholesalers	E	5065	Electronic Parts and Equipment, NEC
4217	Hardware, and Plumbing and Heating Equipment and Supplies Wholesalers			
42171	Hardware Wholesalers	E	5072	Hardware
42172	Plumbing and Heating Equipment and Supplies (Hydronics) Wholesalers	R	*5074	Plumbing and Heating Equipment and Supplies (Hydronics) (except plumbing equipment sold via retail method)
42173	Warm Air Heating and Air-Conditioning Equipment and Supplies Wholesalers	E	5075	Warm Air Heating and Air-Conditioning Equipment and Supplies
42174	Refrigeration Equipment and Supplies Wholesalers	E	5078	Refrigeration Equipment and Supplies
4218	Machinery, Equipment and Supplies Wholesalers			
42181	Construction and Mining (except Petroleum) Machinery and Equipment Wholesalers	E	5082	Construction and Mining (Except Petroleum) Machinery and Equipment
42182	Farm and Garden Machinery and Equipment Wholesalers	R	*5083	Farm and Garden Machinery and Equipment (except lawn and garden equipment sold via retail method)
42183	Industrial Machinery and Equipment Wholesalers	R	5084	Industrial Machinery and Equipment
			*5085	Industrial Supplies (fluid power accessories)
42184	Industrial Supplies Wholesalers	R	*5085	Industrial Supplies (except fluid power accessories)

1997 NAICS Code	1997 NAICS United States and U.S. Description	Status Code	1987 SIC Code	1987 U.S. SIC Description
42185	Service Establishment Equipment and Supplies Wholesalers	R	*5087	Service Establishment Equipment and Supplies (except sales of the service establishment equipment and supplies sold via retail method.
42186	Transportation Equipment and Supplies (except Motor Vehicle) Wholesalers	E	5088	Transportation Equipment and Supplies, Except Motor Vehicles
4219	Miscellaneous Durable Goods Wholesalers			
42191	Sporting and Recreational Goods and Supplies Wholesalers	E	5091	Sporting and Recreational Goods and Supplies
42192	Toy and Hobby Goods and Supplies Wholesalers	E	5092	Toys and Hobby Goods and Supplies
42193	Recyclable Material Wholesalers	E	5093	Scrap and Waste Materials
42194	Jewelry, Watch, Precious Stone and Precious Metal Wholesalers	E	5094	Jewelry, Watches, Precious Stones, and Precious Metals
42199	Other Miscellaneous Durable Goods Wholesalers	R	5099	Durable Goods, NEC
			*7822	Motion Picture and Video Tape Distribution (prerecorded video tapes - distribution)
422	Wholesale Trade, Nondurable Goods			
4221	Paper and Paper Product Wholesalers			
42211	Printing and Writing Paper Wholesalers	E	5111	Printing and Writing Paper
42212	Stationary and Office Supplies Wholesalers	R	*5112	Stationery and Office Supplies (except stationary and office supplies sold via retail method)
42213	Industrial and Personal Service Paper Wholesalers	E	5113	Industrial and Personal Service Paper
4222	Drug, Drug Proprietaries and Druggists' Sundries Wholesalers			
42221	Drug, Drug Proprietaries and Druggists' Sundries Wholesalers	E	5122	Drugs, Drug Proprietaries, and Druggists' Sundries
4223	Apparel, Piece Goods, and Notions Wholesalers			
42231	Piece Goods, Notions and Other Dry Goods Wholesalers	R	*5131	Piece Goods, Notions, and Other Dry Goods (except piece goods converters)
42232	Men's and Boys' Clothing and Furnishings Wholesalers	E	5136	Men's and Boys' Clothing and Furnishings
42233	Women's, Children's, and Infants' and Accessories Wholesalers	E	5137	Women's, Children's, and Infants' Clothing and Accessories
42234	Footwear Wholesalers	E	5139	Footwear
4224	Grocery and Related Product Wholesalers			
42241	General Line Grocery Wholesalers	E	5141	Groceries, General Line
42242	Packaged Frozen Food Wholesalers	E	5142	Packaged Frozen Foods
42243	Dairy Product (except Dried or Canned) Wholesalers	E	5143	Dairy Products, Except Dried or Canned
42244	Poultry and Poultry Product Wholesalers	E	5144	Poultry and Poultry Products
42245	Confectionery Wholesalers	E	5145	Confectionery
42246	Fish and Seafood Wholesalers	E	5146	Fish and Seafoods
42247	Meat and Meat Product Wholesalers	R	*5147	Meats and Meat Products (except boxed beef)
42248	Fresh Fruit and Vegetable Wholesalers	E	5148	Fresh Fruits and Vegetables

42249	Other Grocery and Related Products Wholesalers	E	5149	Groceries and Related Products, NEC
4225	Farm Product Raw Material Wholesalers			
42251	Grain and Field Bean Wholesalers	E	5153	Grain and Field Beans
42252	Livestock Wholesalers	E	5154	Livestock
42259	Other Farm Product Raw Material Wholesalers	E	5159	Farm-Product Raw Materials, NEC
4226	Chemical and Allied Products Wholesalers			
42261	Plastics Materials and Basic Forms and Shapes Wholesalers	E	5162	Plastics Materials and Basic Forms and Shapes
42269	Other Chemical and Allied Products Wholesalers	E	5169	Chemicals and Allied Products, NEC
4227	Petroleum and Petroleum Products Wholesalers			
42271	Petroleum Bulk Stations and Terminals	R	*5171	Petroleum Bulk Stations and Terminals (except petroleum sold via retail method)
42272	Petroleum and Petroleum Products (except Bulk Stations and Terminals) Wholesalers	E	5172	Petroleum and Petroleum Products Wholesalers, Except Bulk Stations and Terminals
4228	Beer, Wine, and Distilled Alcoholic Beverage Wholesalers			
42281	Beer and Ale Wholesalers	E	5181	Beer and Ale
42282	Wine and Distilled Alcoholic Beverage Wholesalers	E	5182	Wine and Distilled Alcoholic Beverages
4229	Miscellaneous Nondurable Goods Wholesalers			
42291	Farm Supplies Wholesalers	R	*5191	Farm Supplies (except lawn and garden supplies sold via retail method)
42292	Book, Periodical and Newspaper Wholesalers	E	5192	Books, Periodicals, and Newspapers
42293	Flower, Nursery Stock and Florists' Supplies Wholesalers	E	*5193	Flowers, Nursery Stock, and Florists' Supplies (except nursery stock sold via retail method)
42294	Tobacco and Tobacco Product Wholesalers	E	5194	Tobacco and Tobacco Products
42295	Paint, Varnish and Supplies Wholesalers	R	*5198	Paints, Varnishes, and Supplies (except paints, etc. sold via retail method)
			*5231	Paint, Glass and Wallpaper Stores (sold via wholesale method)
42299	Other Miscellaneous Nondurable Goods Wholesalers	R	*5199	Nondurable Goods, NEC (except specialty advertising)
44-45	Retail Trade			
441	Motor Vehicle and Parts Dealers			
4411	Automobile Dealers			
44111	New Car Dealers	E	5511	Motor Vehicle Dealers (New and Used)
44112	Used Car Dealers	E	5521	Motor Vehicle Dealers (Used Only)
4412	Other Motor Vehicle Dealers			
44121	Recreational Vehicle Dealers	E	5561	Recreational Vehicle Dealers
44122	Motorcycle, Boat and Other Motor Vehicle Dealers			
441221	Motorcycle Dealers	E	5571	Motorcycle Dealers
441222	Boat Dealers	E	5551	Boat Dealers
441229	All Other Motor Vehicle Dealers	E	5599	Automotive Dealers, NEC
4413	Automotive Parts, Accessories and Tire Stores			

1997 NAICS Code	1997 NAICS United States and U.S. Description	Status Code	1987 SIC Code	1987 U.S. SIC Description
44131	Automotive Parts and Accessories Stores	N	*5013	Motor Vehicle Supplies and New Parts (Wholesale) (auto parts sold via retail method)
			*5731	Radio, Television, and Consumer Electronics Stores (automobile radios)
			*5531	Auto and Home Supply Stores (except tires and tubes)
44132	Tire Dealers	N	*5014	Tires and Tubes (Wholesale) (tires and tubes sold via retail method)
			*5531	Auto and Home Supply Stores (tires and tubes)
442	Furniture and Home Furnishings Stores			
4421	Furniture Stores			
44211	Furniture Stores	R	*5021	Furniture (Wholesale) (sold via the retail method)
			*5712	Furniture Stores (except custom furniture and cabinets)
4422	Home Furnishings Stores			
44221	Floor Covering Stores	R	*5023	Homefurnishings (Wholesale) (floor covering sold via retail method)
			5713	Floor Coverings Stores
44229	Other Home Furnishings Stores			
442291	Window Treatment Stores	N	*5714	Drapery, Curtain, and Upholstery Stores (drapery and curtain stores)
			*5719	Miscellaneous Homefurnishings Stores (blinds and shades)
442299	All Other Home Furnishings Stores	R	*5719	Miscellaneous Homefurnishings Stores (except pottery and crafts made and sold on site and frame shops, and window furnishings)
443	Electronics and Appliance Stores			
4431	Electronics and Appliance Stores			
44311	Appliance, Television and Other Electronics Stores			
443111	Household Appliance Stores	R	5722	Household Appliance Stores
			*5999	Miscellaneous Retail Stores, NEC (personal appliance stores)
			*7623	Refrigeration and Air-Conditioning Service and Repair Shops (sales location providing supporting refrigerator repair services as major source of receipts)
			*7629	Electrical and Electronic Repair Shops, NEC (Services) (Sales location providing supporting appliance repair services as major source of receipts)
443112	Radio, Television and Other Electronics Stores	R	*5731	Radio, Television, and Consumer Electronics Stores (except auto radios)
			*5999	Miscellaneous Retail Stores, NEC (typewriters and telephones)
			*7622	Radio and Television Repair Shops (sales locations providing supporting repair services as major source of receipts)
44312	Computer and Software Stores	R	*5045	Computers and Computer Peripheral Equipment and Software (sold via retail method)

			*7378	Computer Maintenance and Repair (sales locations providing supporting repair services as major source of receipts)`
			5734	Computer and Computer Software Stores
44313	Camera and Photographic Supplies Stores	E	5946	Camera and Photographic Supply Stores
444	Building Material and Garden Equipment and Supplies Dealers			
4441	Building Material and Supplies Dealers			
44411	Home Centers	N	*5211	Lumber and Other Building Materials Dealers (home center stores)
44412	Paint and Wallpaper Stores	R	*5198	Paints, Varnishes, and Supplies (sold via retail method)
			*5231	Paint, Glass, and Wallpaper Stores (paint and wallpaper)
44413	Hardware Stores	E	5251	Hardware Stores
44419	Other Building Material Dealers	R	*5031	Lumber, Plywood, Millwork, and Wood Panels (Wholesale) (sold via retail method)
			*5032	Brick, Stone, and Related Construction Materials (Wholesale) (sold via retail method)
			*5039	Construction Materials, NEC (Wholesale) (glass sold via retail method)
			*5063	Electrical Apparatus and Equipment, Wiring Supplies, and Construction Materials (Wholesale) (sold via retail method)
			*5074	Plumbing and Heating Equipment and Supplies (Hydronics) (sold via retail method)
			*5211	Lumber and Other Building Materials Dealers (except home centers)
			*5231	Paint, Glass, and Wallpaper Stores (glass)
4442	Lawn and Garden Equipment and Supplies Stores			
44421	Outdoor Power Equipment Stores	N	*5083	Farm and Garden Machinery and Equipment (Wholesale) (sold via retail method)
			*5261	Retail Nurseries, Lawn and Garden Supply Stores (outdoor power equipment)
44422	Nursery and Garden Centers	R	*5191	Farm Supplies (sold via retail method)
			*5193	Flowers, Nursery Stock, and Florists' Supplies (sold via retail method)
			*5261	Retail Nurseries, Lawn and Garden Supply Stores (except outdoor power equipment and cut Christmas trees)
445	Food and Beverage Stores			
4451	Grocery Stores			
44511	Supermarkets and Other Grocery (except Convenience) Stores	N	*5411	Grocery Stores (except convenience stores and grocery stores with substantial general merchandise)
44512	Convenience Stores	N	*5411	Grocery Stores (convenience stores without gas)
4452	Specialty Food Stores			
44521	Meat Markets	R	*5421	Meat and Fish (Seafood) Markets, Including Freezer Provisioners (meat except freezer provisioners)

1997 NAICS Code	1997 NAICS United States and U.S. Description	Status Code	1987 SIC Code	1987 U.S. SIC Description
			*5499	Miscellaneous Food Stores (poultry and poultry products)
44522	Fish and Seafood Markets	N	*5421	Meat and Fish (Seafood) Markets, Including Freezer Provisioners (seafood)
44523	Fruit and Vegetable Markets	E	5431	Fruit and Vegetable Markets
44529	Other Specialty Food Stores			
445291	Baked Goods Stores	R	*5461	Retail Bakeries (selling only)
445292	Confectionery and Nut Stores	E	5441	Candy, Nut and Confectionery Stores
445299	All Other Specialty Food Stores	R	*5499	Miscellaneous Food Stores (except food supplements, poultry stores, and stores with food for immediate consumption)
			5451	Dairy Products Stores
4453	Beer, Wine and Liquor Stores			
44531	Beer, Wine and Liquor Stores	E	5921	Liquor Stores
446	Health and Personal Care Stores			
4461	Health and Personal Care Stores			
44611	Pharmacies and Drug Stores	E	5912	Drug Stores and Proprietary Stores
44612	Cosmetics, Beauty Supplies and Perfume Stores	N	*5087	Service Establishment Equipment and Supplies (beauty and barber supplies sold via retail method)
			*5999	Miscellaneous Retail Stores, NEC (cosmetics and perfumes)
44613	Optical Goods Stores	R	*5995	Optical Goods Stores (except labs grinding prescription lenses)
44619	Other Health and Personal Care Stores			
446191	Food (Health) Supplement Stores	N	*5499	Miscellaneous Food Stores (food supplements)
446199	All Other Health and Personal Care Stores	N	*5047	Medical, Dental, and Hospital Equipment and Supplies (sold via retail method)
			*5999	Miscellaneous Retail Stores, NEC (hearing aids and artificial limbs)
447	Gasoline Stations			
4471	Gasoline Stations			
44711	Gasoline Stations with Convenience Stores	N	*5541	Gasoline Service Station (gasoline station with convenience store)
			*5411	Grocery Stores (convenience store with gas)
44719	Other Gasoline Stations	N	*5541	Gasoline Service Station (gasoline station without convenience store)
448	Clothing and Clothing Accessories Stores			
4481	Clothing Stores			
44811	Men's Clothing Stores	R	*5611	Men's and Boys' Clothing and Accessory Stores (clothing stores)
44812	Women's Clothing Stores	E	5621	Women's Clothing Stores
44813	Children's and Infants' Clothing Stores	E	5641	Children's and Infants' Wear Stores
44814	Family Clothing Stores	E	5651	Family Clothing Stores
44815	Clothing Accessories Stores	N	*5611	Men's and Boys' Clothing and Accessory Stores (accessories)
			*5632	Women's Accessory and Specialty Stores (accessories)
			*5699	Miscellaneous Apparel and Accessory Stores (accessories)

44819	Other Clothing Stores	R	*5699	Miscellaneous Apparel and Accessory Stores (miscellaneous apparel)
			*5632	Women's Accessory and Specialty Stores (specialty stores)
4482	Shoe Stores			
44821	Shoe Stores	E	5661	Shoe Stores
4483	Jewelry, Luggage, and Leather Goods Stores			
44831	Jewelry Stores	R	*5999	Miscellaneous Retailer, NEC (rough gems)
			5944	Jewelry Stores
44832	Luggage and Leather Goods Stores	E	5948	Luggage and Leather Goods Stores
451	Sporting Goods, Hobby, Book and Music Stores			
4511	Sporting Goods, Hobby and Musical Instrument Stores			
45111	Sporting Goods Stores	R	*7699	Repair Shops and Related Services, NEC (bicycle sales locations providing supporting repair services as major source of receipts)
			5941	Sporting Goods Stores and Bicycle Shops
45112	Hobby, Toy and Game Stores	E	5945	Hobby, Toy, and Game Stores
45113	Sewing, Needlework and Piece Goods Stores	R	*5714	Drapery, Curtain, and Upholstery Stores (upholstery materials)
			5949	Sewing, Needlework, and Piece Goods Stores
45114	Musical Instrument and Supplies Stores	E	5736	Musical Instruments Stores
4512	Book, Periodical and Music Stores			
45121	Book Stores and News Dealers			
451211	Book Stores	E	5942	Book Stores
451212	News Dealers and Newsstands	E	5994	News Dealers and Newsstands
45122	Prerecorded Tape, Compact Disc and Record Stores	E	5735	Record and Prerecorded Tape Stores
452	General Merchandise Stores			
4521	Department Stores			
45211	Department Stores	E	5311	Department Stores
4529	Other General Merchandise Stores			
45291	Warehouse Clubs and Superstores	N	*5399	Miscellaneous General Merchandise Stores (warehouse clubs and supermarket/general merchandise combination)
			*5411	Grocery Stores (grocery stores and supermarkets selling substantial amounts of nonfood items)
45299	All Other General Merchandise Stores	R	*5399	Miscellaneous General Merchandise Stores (except warehouse club and supermarket/general merchandise combination)
			5331	Variety Stores
453	Miscellaneous Store Retailers			
4531	Florists			
45311	Florists	E	5992	Florists
4532	Office Supplies, Stationery and Gift Stores			
45321	Office Supplies and Stationery Stores	R	*5049	Professional Equipment and Supplies, NEC (school and church supplies sold via retail method)
			*5112	Stationery and Office Supplies (sold via retail method)

1997 NAICS Code	1997 NAICS United States and U.S. Description	Status Code	1987 SIC Code	1987 U.S. SIC Description
			5943	Stationery Stores
45322	Gift, Novelty and Souvenir Stores	E	5947	Gift, Novelty, and Souvenir Shops
4533	Used Merchandise Stores			
45331	Used Merchandise Stores	R	*5932	Used Merchandise Stores (except pawn shops)
4539	Other Miscellaneous Store Retailers			
45391	Pet and Pet Supplies Stores	N	*5999	Miscellaneous Retail Stores, NEC (pet and pet supplies)
45392	Art Dealers	N	*5999	Miscellaneous Retail Stores, NEC (art dealer)
45393	Manufactured (Mobile) Home Dealers	E	5271	Mobile Home Dealers
45399	All Other Miscellaneous Store Retailers			
453991	Tobacco Stores	E	5993	Tobacco Stores and Stands
453998	All Other Miscellaneous Store Retailers (except Tobacco Stores)	R	*5999	Miscellaneous Retail Stores, NEC (except art, pet and pet supplies, hearing aids, artificial limbs, cosmetics, telephones, typewriters, personal appliances and rough gems)
			*5261	Retail Nurseries, Lawn and Garden Supply Stores (cut Christmas trees)
454	Nonstore Retailers			
4541	Electronic Shopping and Mail-Order Houses			
45411	Electronic Shopping and Mail-Order Houses	E	5961	Catalog and Mail-Order Houses
4542	Vending Machine Operators			
45421	Vending Machine Operators	E	5962	Automatic Merchandise Machine Operators
4543	Direct Selling Establishments			
45431	Fuel Dealers			
454311	Heating Oil Dealers	R	*5171	Petroleum Bulk Stations and Terminals (heating oil sold to final consumer)
			5983	Fuel Oil Dealers
454312	Liquefied Petroleum Gas (Bottled Gas) Dealers	R	*5171	Petroleum Bulk Stations and Terminals (LP gas sold to final consumer)
			5984	Liquefied Petroleum Gas (Bottled Gas) Dealers
454319	Other Fuel Dealers	E	5989	Fuel Dealers, NEC
45439	Other Direct Selling Establishments	R	*5421	Meat and Fish (Seafood) Markets, Including Freezer Provisioners (freezer provisioners)
			*5963	Direct Selling Establishments (except mobile food services)
48-49	Transportation and Warehousing			
481	Air Transportation			
4811	Scheduled Air Transportation			
48111	Scheduled Air Transportation			
481111	Scheduled Passenger Air Transportation	N	*4512	Air Transportation, Scheduled (passenger)
481112	Scheduled Freight Air Transportation	N	*4512	Air Transportation, Scheduled (freight)
4812	Nonscheduled Air Transportation			
48121	Nonscheduled Air Transportation			
481211	Nonscheduled Chartered Passenger Air Transportation	N	*4522	Air Transportation, Nonscheduled (passenger)

481212	Nonscheduled Chartered Freight Air Transportation	N	*4522	Air Transportation, Nonscheduled (freight)
481219	Other Nonscheduled Air Transportation	N		Establishments that use general purpose aircraft to provide a variety of specialized flying services, such as the following:
			*0721	Crop Planting, Cultivating, and Protecting (crop dusting)
			*7319	Advertising, NEC (aerial advertising)
			*7335	Commercial Photography (aerial photography)
482	Rail Transportation			
4821	Rail Transportation			
48211	Rail Transportation			
482111	Line-Haul Railroads	E	4011	Railroads, Line-Haul Operating
482112	Short Line Railroads	N	*4013	Railroad Switching and Terminal Establishments (belt line and logging railroads)
483	Water Transportation			
4831	Deep Sea, Coastal and Great Lakes Water Transportation			
48311	Deep Sea, Coastal and Great Lakes Water Transportation			
483111	Deep Sea Freight Transportation	E	4412	Deep Sea Foreign Transportation of Freight
483112	Deep Sea Passenger Transportation	R	*4481	Deep Sea Transportation of Passengers, Except by Ferry (deep sea activities)
483113	Coastal and Great Lakes Freight Transportation	R	4424	Deep Sea Domestic Transportation of Freight
			4432	Freight Transportation on the Great Lakes - St. Lawrence Seaway
			*4492	Towing and Tugboat Services (coastal barge operations)
483114	Coastal and Great Lakes Passenger Transportation	R	*4481	Deep Sea Transportation of Passengers, Except by Ferry (coastal activities)
			*4482	Ferries (coastal and Great Lakes)
4832	Inland Water Transportation			
48321	Inland Water Transportation			
483211	Inland Water Freight Transportation	R	4449	Water Transportation of Freight, NEC
			*4492	Towing and Tugboat Services (inland barge operations)
483212	Inland Water Passenger Transportation	R	*4482	Ferries (inland)
			*4489	Water Transportation of Passengers, NEC (water taxi)
484	Truck Transportation			
4841	General Freight Trucking			
48411	General Freight Trucking, Local	N	*4212	Local Trucking without Storage (general freight)
			*4214	Local Trucking with Storage (general freight)
48412	General Freight Trucking, Long-Distance			
484121	General Freight Trucking, Long-Distance, Truckload	N	*4213	Trucking, Except Local (general freight, truckload)
484122	General Freight Trucking, Long-Distance, Less Than Truckload	N	*4213	Trucking, Except Local (general freight, less than truckload)
4842	Specialized Freight Trucking			
48421	Used Household and Office Goods Moving	N	*4212	Local Trucking Without Storage (household goods moving)
			*4213	Trucking, Except Local (household goods moving)

1997 NAICS Code	1997 NAICS United States and U.S. Description	Status Code	1987 SIC Code	1987 U.S. SIC Description
			*4214	Local Trucking With Storage (household goods moving)
48422	Specialized Freight (except Used Goods) Trucking, Local	N	*4212	Local Trucking without Storage (specialized freight)
			*4214	Local Trucking with Storage (specialized freight)
48423	Specialized Freight (except Used Goods) Trucking, Long-Distance	N	*4213	Trucking, Except Local (specialized freight)
485	Transit and Ground Passenger Transportation			
4851	Urban Transit Systems			
48511	Urban Transit Systems			
485111	Mixed Mode Transit Systems	N	*4111	Local and Suburban Transit (mixed mode)
485112	Commuter Rail Systems	N	*4111	Local and Suburban Transit (commuter rail)
485113	Bus and Motor Vehicle Transit Systems	N	*4111	Local and Suburban Transit (bus and motor vehicle)
485119	Other Urban Transit Systems	N	*4111	Local and Suburban Transit (other than mixed mode, commuter rail, and bus and motor vehicle)
4852	Interurban and Rural Bus Transportation			
48521	Interurban and Rural Bus Transportation	E	4131	Intercity and Rural Bus Transportation
4853	Taxi and Limousine Service			
48531	Taxi Service	E	4121	Taxicabs
48532	Limousine Service	N	*4119	Local Passenger Transportation, NEC (limousine rental with driver and automobile rental with driver)
4854	School and Employee Bus Transportation			
48541	School and Employee Bus Transportation	R	4151	School Buses
			*4119	Local Passenger Transportation, NEC (employee transportation)
4855	Charter Bus Industry			
48551	Charter Bus Industry	R	4141	Local Charter Bus Service
			4142	Bus Charter Services, Except Local
4859	Other Transit and Ground Passenger Transportation			
48599	Other Transit and Ground Passenger Transportation			
485991	Special Needs Transportation	N	*4119	Local Passenger Transportation, NEC (special needs transportation)
485999	All Other Transit and Ground Passenger Transportation	R	*4111	Local and Suburban Transit (airport transportation service)
			*4119	Local Passenger Transportation, NEC (hearse rental with driver and carpool and vanpool operation)
486	Pipeline Transportation			
4861	Pipeline Transportation of Crude Oil			
48611	Pipeline Transportation of Crude Oil	E	4612	Crude Petroleum Pipelines
4862	Pipeline Transportation of Natural Gas			
48621	Pipeline Transportation of Natural Gas	R	4922	Natural Gas Transmission
			*4923	Natural Gas Transmission and Distribution (transmission)
4869	Other Pipeline Transportation			
48691	Pipeline Transportation of Refined	E	4613	Refined Petroleum Pipelines

	Petroleum Products			
48699	All Other Pipeline Transportation	E	4619	Pipelines, NEC
487	Scenic and Sightseeing Transportation			
4871	Scenic and Sightseeing Transportation, Land			
48711	Scenic and Sightseeing Transportation, Land	N	*4119	Local Passenger Transportation, NEC (sightseeing buses and cable and cog railways, except scenic)
			*4789	Transportation Services, NEC (horse-drawn cabs and carriages)
			*7999	Amusement and Recreation Services, NEC (scenic transport operations, land)
4872	Scenic and Sightseeing Transportation, Water			
48721	Scenic and Sightseeing Transportation, Water	N	*4489	Water Transportation of Passengers, NEC (airboats, excursion boats, and sightseeing boats)
			*7999	Amusement and Recreation Services, NEC (charter fishing)
4879	Scenic and Sightseeing Transportation, Other			
48799	Scenic and Sightseeing Transportation, Other	N	*4522	Air Transportation, Non-Scheduled (sightseeing planes)
			*7999	Amusement and Recreation Services, NEC (aerial tramways, scenic and amusement)
488	Support Activities for Transportation			
4881	Support Activities for Air Transportation			
48811	Airport Operations			
488111	Air Traffic Control	N	*4581	Airports, Flying Fields, and Airport Terminal Services (private air traffic control)
			*9621	Regulation and Administration of Transportation Programs (government air traffic control)
488119	Other Airport Operations	N	*4581	Airports, Flying Fields, and Airport Terminal Services (airfreight handling at airports, hangar operations, airport terminal services, aircraft storage, airports, and flying fields)
			*4959	Sanitary Services, NEC (vacuuming of runways)
48819	Other Support Activities for Air Transportation	N	*4581	Airports, Flying Fields, and Airport Terminal Services (aircraft servicing and repairing)
4882	Support Activities for Rail Transportation			
48821	Support Activities for Rail Transportation	R	*4013	Railroad Switching and Terminal Establishments (all but short line railroads)
			*4741	Rental of Railroad Cars (grain leveling in railroad cars, grain trimming for railroad equipment, precooling of fruits and vegetables in connection with transportation, and railroad car cleaning, icing, ventilating, and heating)
			*4789	Transportation Services, NEC (car loading and unloading; cleaning of railroad ballasts; dining, parlor, sleeping, and other car operations; and railroad maintenance)
4883	Support Activities for Water Transportation			

1997 NAICS Code	1997 NAICS United States and U.S. Description	Status Code	1987 SIC Code	1987 U.S. SIC Description
48831	Port and Harbor Operations	N	*4491	Marine Cargo Handling (dock and pier operations)
			*4499	Water Transportation Services, NEC (lighthouse operations)
48832	Marine Cargo Handling	R	*4491	Marine Cargo Handling (all but dock and pier operations)
48833	Navigational Services to Shipping	N	*4492	Towing and Tugboat Services (all but barge operations)
			*4499	Water Transportation Services, NEC (piloting vessels in and out of harbors and marine salvage)
48839	Other Support Activities for Water Transportation	R	*4499	Water Transportation Services, NEC (all but lighthouse operations, piloting vessels in and out of harbors, boat and ship rental, and marine salvage)
			*4785	Fixed Facilities and Inspection and Weighing Services for Motor Vehicle Transportation (marine cargo checkers)
			*7699	Repair Shops and Related Services, NEC (ship scaling)
4884	Support Activities for Road Transportation			
48841	Motor Vehicle Towing	N	*7549	Automotive Services, Except Repair and Carwashes (towing)
48849	Other Support Activities for Road Transportation	R	4173	Terminal and Service Facilities for Motor Vehicle Passenger Transportation
			4231	Terminal and Joint Terminal Maintenance Facilities for Motor Freight Transportation
			*4785	Fixed Facilities and Inspection and Weighing Services for Motor Vehicle Transportation (all but marine cargo checkers)
4885	Freight Transportation Arrangement			
48851	Freight Transportation Arrangement	R	*4731	Arrangement of Transportation of Freight and Cargo (except freight rate auditors and tariff consultants)
4889	Other Support Activities for Transportation			
48899	Other Support Activities for Transportation			
488991	Packing and Crating	E	4783	Packing and Crating
488999	All Other Support Activities for Transportation	R	*4729	Arrangement of Passenger Transportation, NEC (arrangement of carpools and vanpools)
			*4789	Transportation Services, NEC (pipeline terminals and stockyards for transportation)
491	Postal Service			
4911	Postal Service			
49111	Postal Service	E	4311	United States Postal Service
492	Couriers and Messengers			
4921	Couriers			
49211	Couriers	R	*4215	Courier Services, Except by Air (hub and spoke intercity delivery)
			4513	Air Courier Services
4922	Local Messengers and Local Delivery			
49221	Local Messengers and Local Delivery	N	*4215	Courier Services, Except by Air (local delivery)
493	Warehousing and Storage Facilities			

4931	Warehousing and Storage Facilities			
49311	General Warehousing and Storage Facilities	R	*4225	General Warehousing and Storage (all but self-storage miniwarehouse warehousing)
			*4226	Special Warehousing and Storage, NEC (warehousing in foreign trade zones)
49312	Refrigerated Warehousing and Storage Facilities	R	4222	Refrigerated Warehousing and Storage
			*4226	Special Warehousing and Storage, NEC (fur storage)
49313	Farm Product Warehousing and Storage Facilities	E	4221	Farm Product Warehousing and Storage
49319	Other Warehousing and Storage Facilities	R	*4226	Special Warehousing and Storage, NEC (all but fur storage and warehousing in foreign trade zones)
51	Information			
511	Publishing Industries			
5111	Newspaper, Periodical, Book and Database Publishers			
51111	Newspaper Publishers	E	2711	Newspapers: Publishing or Publishing and Printing
51112	Periodical Publishers	E	2721	Periodicals: Publishing or Publishing and Printing
51113	Book Publishers	R	*2731	Books: Publishing or Publishing and Printing (except music books)
51114	Database and Directory Publishers	N	*2741	Miscellaneous Publishing (database publishers)
51119	Other Publishers			
511191	Greeting Card Publishers	R	*2771	Greeting Cards (publishing greeting cards)
511199	All Other Publishers	R	*2741	Miscellaneous Publishing (except database and sheet music publishing)
5112	Software Publishers			
51121	Software Publishers	R	*7372	Prepackaged Software (software publishing)
512	Motion Picture and Sound Recording Industries			
5121	Motion Picture and Video Industries			
51211	Motion Picture and Video Production	E	7812	Motion Picture and Video Tape Production
51212	Motion Picture and Video Distribution	R	*7822	Motion Picture and Video Tape Distribution (except video tape and cassette wholesalers)
			*7829	Services Allied to Motion Picture Distribution (film libraries)
51213	Motion Picture and Video Exhibition			
512131	Motion Picture Theaters, Except Drive-Ins.	E	7832	Motion Picture Theaters, Except Drive-In
512132	Drive-In Motion Picture Theaters	E	7833	Drive-In Motion Picture Theaters
51219	Post Production and Other Motion Picture and Video Industries			
512191	Teleproduction and Other Post-Production Services	N	*7819	Services Allied to Motion Picture Production (teleproduction and post-production services)

1997 NAICS Code	1997 NAICS United States and U.S. Description	Status Code	1987 SIC Code	1987 U.S. SIC Description
512199	Other Motion Picture and Video Industries	N	*7819	Services Allied to Motion Picture Production (except casting bureaus, wardrobe and equipment rental, talent payment services, teleproduction and other post-production services, reproduction of videos, and film distributors and other related motion picture production services)
			*7829	Services Allied to Motion Picture Distribution (except film libraries)
5122	Sound Recording Industries			
51221	Record Production	N	*8999	Services, NEC (record production)
51222	Integrated Record Production/Distribution	N	*3652	Phonograph Records and Prerecorded Audio Tapes and Disks (integrated record companies, except duplication only)
51223	Music Publishers	N	*2731	Books: Publishing or Publishing and Printing (music books)
			*2741	Miscellaneous Publishing (sheet music publishing)
			*8999	Services, NEC (music publishing)
51224	Sound Recording Studios	N	*7389	Business Services, NEC (recording studios)
51229	Other Sound Recording Industries	N	*7389	Business Services, NEC (audio taping services)
			*7922	Theatrical Producers (Except Motion Picture) and Miscellaneous Theatrical Services (producers of radio programs)
513	Broadcasting and Telecommunications			
5131	Radio and Television Broadcasting			
51311	Radio Broadcasting			
513111	Radio Networks	N	*4832	Radio Broadcasting Stations (networks)
513112	Radio Stations	N	*4832	Radio Broadcasting Stations (except networks)
51312	Television Broadcasting	N	4833	Television Broadcasting Stations
5132	Cable Networks and Program Distribution			
51321	Cable Networks	N	*4841	Cable and Other Pay Television Services (cable networks)
51322	Cable and Other Program Distribution	N	*4841	Cable and Other Pay Television Services (except cable networks)
5133	Telecommunications			
51331	Wired Telecommunications Carriers	N	*4813	Telephone Communications, Except Radiotelephone (except resellers)
			4822	Telegraph and Other Message Communications
51332	Wireless Telecommunications Carriers (except Satellite)			
513321	Paging	N	*4812	Radiotelephone Communications (paging carriers)
513322	Cellular and Other Wireless Telecommunications	N	*4812	Radiotelephone Communications (cellular carriers)
			*4899	Communications Services, NEC (radio dispatch)
51333	Telecommunications Resellers	N	*4812	Radio Communications (paging and cellular resellers)
			*4813	Telephone Communications, Except Radiotelephone (resellers)
51334	Satellite Telecommunications	N	*4899	Communications Services, NEC (satellite communications)
51339	Other Telecommunications	N	*4899	Communications Services, NEC (except radio dispatch, satellite communications)
514	Information Services and Data Processing Services			

NAICS	Title	Status	SIC	SIC Title
5141	Information Services			
51411	News Syndicates	E	7383	News Syndicates
51412	Libraries and Archives	E	8231	Libraries
51419	Other Information Services			
514191	On-Line Information Services	E	7375	Information Retrieval Services
514199	All Other Information Services	N	*8999	Services, NEC (miscellaneous information providers)
5142	Data Processing Services			
51421	Data Processing Services	E	7374	Computer Processing and Data Preparation and Processing Services
52	Finance and Insurance			
521	Monetary Authorities - Central Bank			
5211	Monetary Authorities - Central Bank			
52111	Monetary Authorities - Central Bank	E	6011	Federal Reserve Banks
522	Credit Intermediation and Related Activities			
5221	Depository Credit Intermediation			
52211	Commercial Banking	R	*6021	National Commercial Banks (banking)
			*6022	State Commercial Banks (banking)
			6029	Commercial Banks, NEC
			*6081	Branches and Agencies of Foreign Banks (banking)
52212	Savings Institutions	R	6035	Savings Institutions, Federally Chartered
			6036	Savings Institutions, Not Federally Chartered
52213	Credit Unions	R	6061	Credit Unions, Federally Chartered
			6062	Credit Unions, Not Federally Chartered
52219	Other Depository Credit Intermediation	N	*6022	State Commercial Banks (private and industrial banking)
5222	Non-Depository Credit Intermediation			
52221	Credit Card Issuing	N	*6021	National Commercial Banks (credit card issuing)
			*6022	State Commercial Banks (credit card issuing)
			*6141	Personal Credit Institutions (credit card issuing)
52222	Sales Financing	N	*6141	Personal Credit Institutions (installment sales finance)
			*6153	Short-Term Business Credit Institutions, Except Agricultural (business sales finance).
			*6159	Miscellaneous Business Credit Institutions (finance leasing)
52229	Other Non-Depository Credit Intermediation			
522291	Consumer Lending	R	*6141	Personal Credit Institutions (except installment sales finance and credit card issuing)
522292	Real Estate Credit	R	*6162	Mortgage Bankers and Loan Correspondents (mortgage bankers and originators)
522293	International Trade Financing	N	*6081	Branches and Agencies of Foreign Banks (international trade financing)
			6082	Foreign Trade and International Banking Institutions
			*6111	Federal and Federally-Sponsored Credit Agencies (trade banks)

1997 NAICS Code	1997 NAICS United States and U.S. Description	Status Code	1987 SIC Code	1987 U.S. SIC Description
522294	Secondary Market Financing	N	*6159	Miscellaneous Business Credit Institutions (trade banks)
			*6111	Federal and Federally Sponsored Credit Agencies (except trade banks)
522298	All Other Non-Depository Credit Intermediation	N	*5932	Used Merchandise Stores (pawnshops)
			*6081	Branches and Agencies of Foreign Banks (agencies)
			*6111	Federal and Federally-Sponsored Credit Agencies (except trade banks and secondary market financing)
			*6153	Short-Term Business Credit Institutions, Except Agricultural (except credit card service and business sales finance)
			*6159	Miscellaneous Business Credit Institutions (except trade banks and finance leasing)
5223	Activities Related to Credit Intermediation			
52231	Mortgage and Other Loan Brokers	E	6163	Loan Brokers
52232	Financial Transactions Processing, Reserve, and Clearing House Activities	N	6019	Central Reserve Depository Institutions, NEC
			*6099	Functions Related to Depository Banking, NEC (electronic funds transfer networks and clearing house associations)
			*6153	Short-Term Business Credit Institutions, Except Agricultural (credit card service)
			*7389	Business Services, NEC (credit card service)
52239	Other Activities Related to Credit Intermediation	N	*6099	Functions Related to Depository Banking, NEC (except money orders, electronic funds transfer networks and clearing houses, foreign currency exchanges, escrow and fiduciary agencies and deposit brokers)
			*6162	Mortgage Bankers and Loan Correspondents (mortgage servicing)
523	Securities, Commodity Contracts and Other Intermediation and Related Activities			
5231	Securities and Commodity Contracts Intermediation and Brokerage			
52311	Investment Banking and Securities Dealing	N	*6211	Security Brokers, Dealers, and Flotation Companies (securities dealers and underwriters)
52312	Securities Brokerage	N	*6211	Security Brokers, Dealers, and Flotation Companies (security brokers)
52313	Commodity Contracts Dealing	N	*6099	Functions Related to depository Banking, NEC (foreign currency exchange)
			*6799	Investors, NEC (commodity contract trading companies)
			*6221	Commodity Contracts Brokers and Dealers (commodity dealers)
52314	Commodity Brokerage	N	*6221	Commodity Contracts Brokers and Dealers (commodity brokers)
5232	Securities and Commodity Exchanges			
52321	Securities and Commodity Exchanges	E	6231	Security and Commodity Exchanges
5239	Other Financial Investment Activities			

52391	Miscellaneous Intermediation	N	*6211	Securities Brokers, Dealers and Flotation Companies (except securities and commodity dealers)
			*6799	Investors, NEC (venture capital companies)
52392	Portfolio Management	N	*6282	Investment Advice (portfolio managers)
			*6371	Pension, Health, and Welfare Funds (managers)
			*6733	Trust, Except Educational, Religious, and Charitable (managers)
			*6799	Investors, NEC (pool operators)
52393	Investment Advice	R	*6282	Investment Advice (except portfolio managers)
52399	All Other Financial Investment Activities			
523991	Trust, Fiduciary and Custody Activities	N	*6021	National Commercial Banks (trust services)
			*6022	State Commercial Banks (trust services)
			6091	Nondeposit Trust Facilities
			*6099	Functions Related to Depository Banking, NEC (escrow and fiduciary agencies)
			*6289	Services Allied With the Exchange of Securities or Commodities, NEC (securities custodians)
			*6733	Trusts, Except Educational, Religious, and Charitable (administrators of private estates)
523999	Miscellaneous Financial Investment Activities	R	*6099	Functions Related to Depository Banking, NEC (deposit brokers)
			*6211	Security Brokers, Dealers, and Flotation Companies (other except security and commodity)
			*6289	Services Allied With the Exchange of Securities or Commodities, NEC (except security custodians)
			*6799	Investors, NEC (except pool operators and venture capital companies)
			*6792	Oil Royalty Traders (investors on own account)
524	Insurance Carriers and Related Activities			
5241	Insurance Carriers			
52411	Direct Life, Health and Medical Insurance Carriers			
524113	Direct Life Insurance Carriers	R	*6311	Life Insurance (life insurers-direct)
524114	Direct Health and Medical Insurance Carriers	R	*6324	Hospital and Medical Service Plans (health and medical insurers-direct)
			*6321	Accident and Health Insurance (health and medical insurers-direct)
52412	Direct Insurance (except Life, Health, and Medical) Carriers			
524126	Direct Property and Casualty Insurance Carriers	R	*6331	Fire, Marine, and Casualty Insurance (fire, marine, and casualty insurers-direct)
			*6351	Surety Insurance (financial responsibility insurers-direct)
524127	Direct Title Insurance Carriers	R	*6361	Title Insurance (title insurers-direct)
524128	Other Direct Insurance (except Life, Health and Medical) Carriers	E	6399	Insurance Carriers, NEC

1997 NAICS Code	1997 NAICS United States and U.S. Description	Status Code	1987 SIC Code	1987 U.S. SIC Description
52413	Reinsurance Carriers	N	*6311	Life Insurance (reinsurers)
			*6321	Accident and Health Insurance (reinsurers)
			*6324	Hospital and Medical Service Plans (reinsurers)
			*6331	Fire, Marine, and Casualty Insurance (reinsurers)
			*6351	Surety Insurance (reinsurers)
			*6361	Title Insurance (reinsurers)
5242	Agencies, Brokerages and Other Insurance Related Activities			
52421	Insurance Agencies and Brokerages	R	*6411	Insurance Agents, Brokers and Service (insurance agents and brokers)
52429	Other Insurance Related Activities			
524291	Claims Adjusters	N	*6411	Insurance Agents, Brokers and Service (insurance claims adjusters)
524292	Third Party Administration for Insurance and Pension Funds	N	*6371	Pension, Health, and Welfare Funds (administrators)
524298	All Other Insurance Related Activities	N	*6411	Insurance Agents, Brokers and Service (processors)
			*6411	Insurance Agents, Brokers and Service (except processors, agents and brokers, and claims adjusters)
525	Funds, Trusts and Other Financial Vehicles (U.S. Only)			
5251	Insurance and Employee Benefit Funds			
52511	Pension Funds	N	*6371	Pension, Health, and Welfare Funds (pension funds)
52512	Health and Welfare Funds	N	*6371	Pension, Health, and Welfare Funds (health and welfare funds)
52519	Other Insurance Funds	N	*6321	Accident and Health Insurance (self insurers)
			*6324	Hospital and Medical Service Plans (self insurers)
			*6331	Fire, Marine, and Casualty Insurance (self insurers)
			*6733	Trusts, Except Educational, Religious, and Charitable (vacation funds for employees)
5259	Other Investment Pools and Funds			
52591	Open-End Investment Funds	E	6722	Management Investment Offices, Open-End
52592	Trusts, Estates, and Agency Accounts	N	*6733	Trusts, Except Educational, Religious, and Charitable (personal trusts, estates, and agency accounts)
52593	Real Estate Investment Trusts	E	6798	Real Estate Investment Trusts
52599	Other Financial Vehicles	E	6726	Unit Investment Trusts, Face-Amount Certificate Offices, and Closed-End Management Investment Offices
53	Real Estate and Rental and Leasing			
531	Real Estate			
5311	Lessors of Real Estate			
53111	Lessors of Residential Buildings and Dwellings	R	6513	Operators of Apartment Buildings
			6514	Operators of Dwellings Other Than Apartment Buildings
53112	Lessors of Nonresidential Buildings (except Miniwarehouses)	N	*6512	Operators of Nonresidential Buildings (other except stadium and arena owners)
53113	Lessors of Miniwarehouses and Self Storage Units	E	*4225	General Warehousing and Storage (miniwarehouses and self-storage units)

53119	Lessors of Other Real Estate Property	R	6515	Operators of Residential Mobile Home Sites
			6517	Lessors of Railroad Property
			6519	Lessors of Real Property, NEC
5312	Offices of Real Estate Agents and Brokers			
53121	Offices of Real Estate Agents and Brokers	N	*6531	Real Estate Agents Managers (agents and brokers)
5313	Activities Related to Real Estate			
53131	Real Estate Property Managers			
531311	Residential Property Managers	N	*6531	Real Estate Agents and Managers (managers-residential, real estate)
531312	Nonresidential Property Managers	N	*6531	Real Estate Agents and Managers (managers-nonresidential, real estate)
53132	Offices of Real Estate Appraisers	N	*6531	Real Estate Agents and Managers (appraisers)
53139	Other Activities Related to Real Estate	N	*6531	Real Estate Agents and Managers (except real estate managers, condominium management, cemetery management, agents and brokers, and appraisers)
532	Rental and Leasing Services			
5321	Automotive Equipment Rental and Leasing			
53211	Passenger Car Rental and Leasing			
532111	Passenger Car Rental	E	7514	Passenger Car Rental
532112	Passenger Car Leasing	E	7515	Passenger Car Leasing
53212	Truck, Utility Trailer, and RV (Recreational Vehicle) Rental and Leasing	N	7513	Truck Rental and Leasing Without Drivers
			7519	Utility Trailers and Recreational Vehicle Rental
5322	Consumer Goods Rental			
53221	Consumer Electronics and Appliances Rental	N	*7359	Equipment Rental and Leasing, NEC (appliances, TV, VCR, and electronic equipment rental)
53222	Formal Wear and Costume Rental	N	*7299	Miscellaneous Personal Services, NEC (formal wear and costume rental)
			*7819	Services Allied to Motion Picture Production (wardrobe rental for motion picture film production)
53223	Video Tape and Disc Rental	E	7841	Video Tape Rental
53229	Other Consumer Goods Rental			
532291	Home Health Equipment Rental	N	*7352	Medical Equipment Rental and Leasing (home health furniture and equipment rental and leasing)
532292	Recreational Goods Rental	N	*7999	Amusement and Recreation Services, NEC (canoe, pleasure boats, bicycles, motorcycles, moped, go carts, etc. rental)
532299	All Other Consumer Goods Rental	R	*7359	Equipment Rental and Leasing, NEC (except transportation equipment, industrial equipment, and consumer electronics, appliances and home and garden equipment)
5323	General Rental Centers			
53231	General Rental Centers	N	*7359	Equipment Rental and Leasing, NEC (general rental centers)

1997 NAICS Code	1997 NAICS United States and U.S. Description	Status Code	1987 SIC Code	1987 U.S. SIC Description
5324	Commercial and Industrial Machinery and Equipment Rental and Leasing			
53241	Construction, Transportation, Mining and Forestry Machinery and Equipment Rental and Leasing			
532411	Commercial Air, Rail, and Water Transportation Equipment Rental and Leasing	N	*4499	Water Transportation Services, NEC (boat and ship rental, commercial)
			*4741	Rental of Railroad Cars (rental of railroad cars)
			*7359	Equipment Rental and Leasing, NEC (airplane rental and leasing)
532412	Construction, Mining and Forestry Machinery and Equipment Rental and Leasing	R	*7353	Heavy Construction Equipment Rental and Leasing (without operators)
			*7359	Equipment Rental and Leasing, NEC (oil field and well drilling equipment)
53242	Office Machinery and Equipment Rental and Leasing	N	*7359	Equipment Rental and Leasing (office machine rental and leasing)
			7377	Computer Rental and Leasing
53249	Other Commercial and Industrial Machinery and Equipment Rental and Leasing	N	*7352	Medical Equipment Rental and Leasing (medical machinery and equipment)
			*7359	Equipment Rental and Leasing, NEC (industrial truck and equipment rental and leasing)
			*7819	Services Allied to Motion Picture Production (motion picture equipment rental)
			*7922	Theatrical Producers (Except Motion Picture) and Miscellaneous Theatrical Services (theatrical equipment rental)
533	Owners and Lessors of Other Non-Financial Assets			
5331	Owners and Lessors of Other Non-Financial Assets			
53311	Owners and Lessors of Other Non-Financial Assets	R	*6792	Oil Royalty Traders (except investors on own account)
			6794	Patent Owners and Lessors
54	Professional, Scientific and Technical Services			
541	Professional, Scientific and Technical Services			
5411	Legal Services			
54111	Offices of Lawyers	E	8111	Legal Services
54112	Offices of Notaries	L		Null Set for U.S.
54119	Other Legal Services			
541191	Title Abstract and Settlement Offices	E	6541	Title Abstract Offices
541199	All Other Legal Services	N	*7389	Business Services, NEC (process services, patent agents, notaries public, paralegal services)
5412	Accounting, Tax Preparation, Bookkeeping and Payroll Services			
54121	Accounting, Tax Preparation, Bookkeeping and Payroll Services			
541211	Offices of Certified Public Accountants	N	*8721	Accounting, Auditing, and Bookkeeping Services (auditing accountants)

541213	Tax Preparation Services	E	7291	Tax Return Preparation Services
541214	Payroll Services	N	*7819	Services Allied to Motion Picture Production (talent payment services)
			*8721	Accounting, Auditing, and Bookkeeping Services (payroll services)
541219	Other Accounting Services	N	*8721	Accounting, Auditing, and Bookkeeping Services (other accounting services)
5413	Architectural, Engineering and Related Services			
54131	Architectural Services	E	8712	Architectural Services
54132	Landscape Architectural Services	R	*0781	Landscape Counseling and Planning (except horticultural consulting)
54133	Engineering Services	E	8711	Engineering Services
54134	Drafting Services	N	*7389	Business Services, NEC (drafting service)
54135	Building Inspection Services	N	*7389	Business Services, NEC (home and building inspection services)
54136	Geophysical Surveying and Mapping Services	N	*8713	Surveying Services (geophysical surveying)
			*1081	Metal Mining Services (geophysical surveying)
			*1382	Oil and Gas Field Exploration Services (geophysical surveying and mapping)
			*1481	Nonmetallic Minerals Services, Except Fuels (geophysical surveying)
54137	Surveying and Mapping (except Geophysical) Services	N	*7389	Business Services, NEC (map making services)
			*8713	Surveying Services (except geophysical surveying)
54138	Testing Laboratories	R	*8734	Testing Laboratories (except veterinary testing laboratories)
5414	Specialized Design Services			
54141	Interior Design Services	N	*7389	Business Services, NEC (interior design)
54142	Industrial Design Services	N	*7389	Business Services, NEC (industrial design)
54143	Graphic Design Services	R	7336	Commercial Art and Graphic Design
			*8099	Health and Allied Services, NEC (medical artists)
54149	Other Specialized Design Services	N	*7389	Business Services, NEC (fashion, furniture, and other design services)
5415	Computer Systems Design and Related Services			
54151	Computer Systems Design and Related Services			
541511	Custom Computer Programming Services	E	7371	Computer Programming Services
541512	Computer Systems Design Services	N	7373	Computer Integrated Systems Design
			*7379	Computer Related Services, NEC (computer systems consultants)
541513	Computer Facilities Management Services	E	7376	Computer Facilities Management Services
541519	Other Computer Related Services	R	*7379	Computer Related Services, NEC (except computer systems consultants)
5416	Management, Scientific and Technical Consulting Services			
54161	Management Consulting Services			

1997 NAICS Code	1997 NAICS United States and U.S. Description	Status Code	1987 SIC Code	1987 U.S. SIC Description
541611	Administrative Management and General Management Consulting Services	N	*8742	Management Consulting Services (administrative management and general management consulting)
541612	Human Resources and Executive Search Consulting Services	N	*8742	Management Consulting Services (human resources and personnel management consulting)
			*7361	Employment Agencies (executive placement services)
			*8999	Services, NEC (actuarial consulting)
541613	Marketing Consulting Services	N	*8742	Management Consulting Services (marketing consulting)
541614	Process, Physical, Distribution and Logistics Consulting Services	N	*8742	Management Consulting Services (manufacturing management, physical distribution, and site location consulting)
541618	Other Management Consulting Services	N	*4731	Arrangement of Transportation of Freight and Cargo (freight rate-auditors and tariff consulting)
			*8748	Business Consulting Services, NEC (safety consulting)
54162	Environmental Consulting Services	N	*8999	Services, NEC (environmental consultants)
54169	Other Scientific and Technical Consulting Services	N	*0781	Landscape Counseling and Planning (horticulture consulting)
			*8748	Business Consulting Services, NEC (agriculture, economic, radio, and traffic consultants)
			*8999	Services, NEC (nuclear consultants, geologists, and physicists)
5417	Scientific Research and Development Services			
54171	Research and Development in the Physical Sciences and Engineering Sciences	N	*8731	Commercial Physical and Biological Research (physical and engineering sciences)
			*8733	Noncommercial Research Organizations (physical and engineering services)
54172	Research and Development in the Life Sciences	N	*8731	Commercial Physical and Biological Research (life sciences)
			*8733	Noncommercial Research Organizations (life sciences)
54173	Research and Development in the Social Sciences and Humanities	N	*8732	Commercial Economic, Sociological, and Educational Research (social sciences and humanities)
			*8733	Noncommercial Research Organizations (social sciences and humanities)
5418	Advertising and Related Services			
54181	Advertising Agencies	E	7311	Advertising Agencies
54182	Public Relations Agencies	E	8743	Public Relations Services
54183	Media Buying Agencies	N	*7319	Advertising, NEC (media buying services)
54184	Media Representatives	E	7313	Radio, Television, and Publishers' Advertising Representatives
54185	Display Advertising	N	7312	Outdoor Advertising Services
			*7319	Advertising, NEC (display advertising, except outdoor)
54186	Direct Mail Advertising	E	7331	Direct Mail Advertising Services
54187	Advertising Material Distribution Services	N	*7319	Advertising, NEC (advertising materials distributor)
54189	Other Services Related to Advertising	N	*7319	Advertising, NEC (except media buying, display advertising, except outdoor; and advertising material distributors)
			*5199	Nondurable Goods, NEC (advertising specialities goods distributors)

			*7389	Business Services, NEC (sign painting and other advertising related business services)
5419	Other Professional, Scientific and Technical Services			
54191	Marketing Research and Public Opinion Polling	N	*8732	Commercial Economic, Sociological, and Educational Research (market research and opinion research)
54192	Photographic Services			
541921	Photography Studios, Portrait	E	7221	Photographic Studios, Portrait
541922	Commercial Photography	R	*7335	Commercial Photography (except when combined with a variety of aircraft based services)
			*8099	Health and Allied Services, NEC (medical photography)
54193	Translation and Interpretation Services	N	*7389	Business Services, NEC (translation and interpretation services)
54194	Veterinary Services	R	0741	Veterinary Services for Livestock
			0742	Veterinary Services for Animal Specialties
			*8734	Testing Laboratories (veterinary testing laboratories)
54199	All Other Professional, Scientific and Technical Services	N	*7389	Business Services (appraisers, except insurance and real estate, and miscellaneous professional, scientific, and technical services)
55	Management of Companies and Enterprises			
551	Management of Companies and Enterprises			
5511	Management of Companies and Enterprises			
55111	Management of Companies and Enterprises			
551111	Offices of Bank Holding Companies	E	6712	Offices of Bank Holding Companies
551112	Offices of Other Holding Companies	E	6719	Offices of Holding Companies, NEC
551114	Corporate, Subsidiary and Regional Managing Offices	N		These establishments were included as auxiliaries in the 1987 Standard Industrial Classification
56	Administrative and Support, Waste Management and Remediation Services			
561	Administrative and Support Services			
5611	Office Administrative Services			
56111	Office Administrative Services	R	*8741	Management Services (except construction management)
5612	Facilities Support Services			
56121	Facilities Support Services	E	8744	Facilities Support Management Services
5613	Employment Services			
56131	Employment Placement Agencies	R	*7361	Employment Agencies (except executive placing services)
			*7819	Services Allied to Motion Pictures Production(casting bureaus)
			*7922	Theatrical Producers and Miscellaneous Theatrical Services (casting agencies)
56132	Temporary Help Services	N	*7363	Help Supply Services (except employee leasing service)
56133	Employee Leasing Services	N	*7363	Help Supply Services (except temporary help service)

1997 NAICS Code	1997 NAICS United States and U.S. Description	Status Code	1987 SIC Code	1987 U.S. SIC Description
5614	Business Support Services			
56141	Document Preparation Services	N	*7338	Secretarial and Court Reporting (except court reporting)
56142	Telephone Call Centers			
561421	Telephone Answering Services	N	*7389	Business Services, NEC (telephone answering)
561422	Telemarketing Bureaus	N	*7389	Business Services, NEC (telemarketing bureaus and telephone soliciting)
56143	Business Service Centers			
561431	Private Mail Centers	N	*7389	Business Services, NEC (private mail centers and mail box rental)
561439	Other Business Service Centers (including Copy Shops)	R	7334	Photocopying and Duplicating Services
			*7389	Business Services, NEC (business service centers, except private mail centers and mail box rental)
56144	Collection Agencies	R	*7322	Adjustment and Collection Services (except adjustment bureaus)
56145	Credit Bureaus	E	7323	Credit Reporting Services
56149	Other Business Support Services			
561491	Repossession Services	N	*7322	Adjustment and Collection (adjustment bureaus)
			*7389	Business Services, NEC (recovery and repossession services)
561492	Court Reporting and Stenotype Services	N	*7338	Secretarial and Court Reporting (except secretarial)
561499	All Other Business Support Services	N	*7389	Business Services, NEC (business support services except telephone answering, telemarketing bureaus, private mail centers and repossession services)
5615	Travel Arrangement and Reservation Services			
56151	Travel Agencies	E	4724	Travel Agencies
56152	Tour Operators	E	4725	Tour Operators
56159	Other Travel Arrangement and Reservation Services			
561591	Convention and Visitors Bureaus	N	*7389	Business Services, NEC (convention and visitors bureaus, tourist information bureaus)
561599	All Other Travel Arrangement and Reservation Services	N	*4729	Arrangement of Passenger Transportation, NEC (except arrangement of vanpools and carpools)
			*7389	Business Services, NEC (reservation systems: hotel & restaurants)
			*7999	Amusement and Recreation Services, NEC (ticket agencies)
			*8699	Membership Organizations, NEC (motor clubs)
5616	Investigation and Security Services			
56161	Investigation, Guard and Armored Car Services			
561611	Investigation Services	N	*7381	Detective, Guard, and Armored Car Services (detective services)
561612	Security Guards and Patrol Services	N	*7381	Detective, Guard, and Armored Car Services (guard services)
561613	Armored Car Services	N	*7381	Detective, Guard, and Armored Car Services (armored car services)
56162	Security Systems Services			
561621	Security Systems Services (except Locksmiths)	R	7382	Security Systems Services

			*1731	Electrical Work (burglar and fire alarm installation)
561622	Locksmiths	N	*7699	Repair Shops and Related Services, NEC (locksmith shops)
5617	Services to Buildings and Dwellings			
56171	Exterminating and Pest Control Services	R	*4959	Sanitary Services, NEC (mosquito eradication)
			*7342	Disinfecting and Pest Control Services (exterminating and pest control)
56172	Janitorial Services	R	*7342	Disinfecting and Pest Control Services (except exterminating)
			7349	Building Cleaning and Maintenance Services, NEC
			*4581	Airports, Flying Fields, and Airport Terminal Services (airplane cleaning and janitorial services)
56173	Landscaping Services	R	0782	Lawn and Garden Services
			0783	Ornamental Shrub and Tree Services
56174	Carpet and Upholstery Cleaning Services	E	7217	Carpet and Upholstery Cleaning
56179	Other Services to Buildings and Dwellings	N	*7389	Business Services, NEC (swimming pool cleaning and maintenance)
			*7699	Repair Shops and Related Services, NEC (furnace, duct, chimney, gutter, and drain cleaning services)
5619	Other Support Services			
56191	Packaging and Labeling Services	N	*7389	Business Services, NEC (packaging and labeling services)
56192	Convention and Trade Show Organizers	N	*7389	Business Services, NEC (convention and trade show services)
56199	All Other Support Services	N	*7389	Business Services, NEC (other support services except packaging and labeling, convention and trade shows services, convention and visiter bureaus, tourist information bureaus)
562	Waste Management and Remediation Services			
5621	Waste Collection			
56211	Waste Collection			
562111	Solid Waste Collection	N	*4212	Local Trucking Without Storage (solid waste collection without disposal)
			*4953	Refuse Systems (solid waste collection)
562112	Hazardous Waste Collection	N	*4212	Local Trucking Without Storage (hazardous waste collection without disposal)
			*4953	Refuse Systems (hazardous waste collection)
562119	Other Waste Collection	N	*4212	Local Trucking Without Storage (other waste collection without disposal)
			*4953	Refuse Systems (other waste collection when combined with disposal)
5622	Waste Treatment and Disposal			
56221	Waste Treatment and Disposal			
562211	Hazardous Waste Treatment and Disposal	N	*4953	Refuse Systems (hazardous waste treatment and disposal)
562212	Solid Waste Landfill	N	*4953	Refuse Systems (solid waste landfills)
562213	Solid Waste Combustors and Incinerators	N	*4953	Refuse Systems (solid waste combustors and incinerators)

1997 NAICS Code	1997 NAICS United States and U.S. Description	Status Code	1987 SIC Code	1987 U.S. SIC Description
562219	Other Nonhazardous Waste Treatment and Disposal	N	*4953	Refuse Systems (other nonhazardous waste treatment and disposal)
5629	Remediation and Other Waste Management Services			
56291	Remediation Services	N	*1799	Special Trade Contractors, NEC (asbestos abatement and lead paint removal contractors)
			*4959	Sanitary Services, NEC (remediation services)
56292	Materials Recovery Facilities	N	*4953	Refuse Systems (materials recovery facilities)
56299	All Other Waste Management Services			
562991	Septic Tank and Related Services	N	*7359	Equipment Rental and Leasing, NEC (portable toilet rental)
			*7699	Repair Shops and Related Services, NEC (cesspool cleaning, sewer cleaning and rodding)
562998	All Other Miscellaneous Waste Management Services	R	*4959	Sanitary Services, NEC (all but remediation services, malaria control, mosquito eradication, snowplowing, street sweeping, and airport runway vacuuming)
61	Educational Services			
611	Educational Services			
6111	Elementary and Secondary Schools			
61111	Elementary and Secondary Schools	E	8211	Elementary and Secondary Schools
6112	Junior Colleges			
61121	Junior Colleges	E	8222	Junior Colleges and Technical Institutes
6113	Colleges, Universities and Professional Schools			
61131	Colleges, Universities and Professional Schools	E	8221	Colleges, Universities, and Professional Schools
6114	Business Schools and Computer and Management Training			
61141	Business and Secretarial Schools	E	8244	Business and Secretarial Schools
61142	Computer Training	R	*8243	Data Processing Schools (except computer repair training)
61143	Professional and Management Development Training	N	*8299	Schools and Educational Services, NEC (professional and management development training)
6115	Technical and Trade Schools			
61151	Technical and Trade Schools			
611511	Cosmetology and Barber Schools	N	*7231	Beauty Shops (beauty and cosmetology schools)
			*7241	Barber Shops (barber colleges)
611512	Flight Training	N	*8249	Vocational Schools, NEC (aviation schools, excluding flying instruction)
			*8299	Schools and Educational Services, NEC (flying instruction)
611513	Apprenticeship Training	N	*8249	Vocational Schools, NEC (vocational apprenticeship training)
611519	Other Technical and Trade Schools	N	*8249	Vocational Schools, NEC (except aviation and flight training and apprenticeship training)
			*8243	Data Processing Schools (computer repair training)
6116	Other Schools and Instruction			
61161	Fine Arts Schools	N	*8299	Schools and Educational Services, NEC (art, drama, and music schools)

			*7911	Dance Studios, Schools, and Halls (dance instructors, and professional and other dance schools)
61162	Sports and Recreation Instruction	N	*7999	Amusement and Recreation Services, NEC (baseball, basketball, bowling, gymnastic, judo, karate, parachute, scuba and skin diving, skating, ski, swimming, tennis, and other sports instruction; and sports instructional schools and camps)
61163	Language Schools	N	*8299	Schools and Educational Services, NEC (language schools)
61169	All Other Schools and Instruction			
611691	Exam Preparation and Tutoring	N	*8299	Schools and Educational Services, NEC (exam preparation and tutoring)
611692	Automobile Driving Schools	N	*8299	Schools and Educational Services, NEC (automobile driving instruction)
611699	All Other Miscellaneous Schools and Instruction	N	*8299	Schools and Educational Services, NEC (except professional and management training, aviation and flight training, fine arts schools, language schools, exam preparation and tutoring, automobile driving schools, and educational support services)
6117	Educational Support Services			
61171	Educational Support Services	N	*8299	Schools and Educational Services NEC (except instruction)
			*8748	Business Consulting Services, NEC (educational test development and evaluation services, educational testing services, and educational consultants)
62	Health Care and Social Assistance			
621	Ambulatory Health Care Services			
6211	Offices of Physicians			
62111	Offices of Physicians			
621111	Offices of Physicians (except Mental Health Specialists)	N	*8011	Offices and Clinics of Doctors of Medicine (except mental health specialists)
			*8031	Offices and Clinics of Doctors of Osteopathy (except mental health specialists)
621112	Offices of Physicians, Mental Health Specialists	N	*8011	Offices and Clinics of Doctors of Medicine (mental health specialists)
			*8031	Offices and Clinics of Doctors of Osteopathy (mental health specialists)
6212	Offices of Dentists			
62121	Offices of Dentists	E	8021	Offices and Clinics of Dentists
6213	Offices of Other Health Practitioners			
62131	Offices of Chiropractors	E	8041	Offices and Clinics of Chiropractors
62132	Offices of Optometrists	E	8042	Offices and Clinics of Optometrists
62133	Offices of Mental Health Practitioners (except Physicians)	N	*8049	Offices and Clinics of Health Practitioners, NEC (mental health practitioners except physicians)

1997 NAICS Code	1997 NAICS United States and U.S. Description	Status Code	1987 SIC Code	1987 U.S. SIC Description
62134	Offices of Physical, Occupational and Speech Therapists and Audiologists	N	*8049	Offices and Clinics of Health Practitioners, NEC (physical, occupational, speech therapists, and audiologists)
62139	Offices of All Other Health Practitioners			
621391	Offices of Podiatrists	E	8043	Offices and Clinics of Podiatrists
621399	Offices of All Other Miscellaneous Health Practitioners	N	*8049	Offices and Clinics of Health Practitioners, NEC (except mental health practitioners, physical, occupational, speech therapists, and audiologists)
6214	Outpatient Care Centers			
62141	Family Planning Centers	N	*8093	Speciality Outpatient Facilities, NEC (family planning centers)
			*8099	Health and Allied Services, NEC (childbirth preparation)
62142	Outpatient Mental Health and Substance Abuse Centers	N	*8093	Specialty Outpatient Facilities, NEC (mental health facilities)
62149	Other Outpatient Care Centers			
621491	HMO Medical Centers	N	*8011	Offices and Clinics of Doctors of Medicine (HMO Medical Centers)
621492	Kidney Dialysis Centers	E	8092	Kidney Dialysis Centers
621493	Freestanding Ambulatory Surgical and Emergency Centers	N	*8011	Offices and Clinics of Doctors of Medicine (surgical and emergency centers)
621498	All Other Outpatient Care Centers	N	*8093	Specialty Outpatient Facilities, NEC (except family planning and mental health centers)
6215	Medical and Diagnostic Laboratories			
62151	Medical and Diagnostic Laboratories			
621511	Medical Laboratories	R	*8071	Medical Laboratories (except diagnostic imaging centers)
621512	Diagnostic Imaging Centers	N	*8071	Medical Laboratories (diagnostic imaging centers)
6216	Home Health Care Services			
62161	Home Health Care Services	E	8082	Home Health Care Services (home health agencies)
6219	Other Ambulatory Health Care Services			
62191	Ambulance Services	N	*4119	Local Passenger Transportation, NEC (land ambulance)
			*4522	Air Transportation, Nonscheduled (air ambulance)
62199	All Other Ambulatory Health Care Services			
621991	Blood and Organ Banks	N	*8099	Health and Allied Services, NEC (blood and organ banks)
621999	All Other Miscellaneous Ambulatory Health Care Services	N	*8099	Health and Allied Services, NEC (except blood and organ banks, medical artists, medical photography, and childbirth preparation classes)
622	Hospitals			
6221	General Medical and Surgical Hospitals			
62211	General Medical and Surgical Hospitals	R	8062	General Medical and Surgical Hospitals
			*8069	Specialty Hospitals, Except Psychiatric (childrens' hospitals)
6222	Psychiatric and Substance Abuse Hospitals			
62221	Psychiatric and Substance Abuse Hospitals	R	8063	Psychiatric Hospitals
			*8069	Specialty Hospitals, Except Psychiatric (substance abuse hospitals)

6223	Specialty (except Psychiatric and Substance Abuse) Hospitals			
62231	Specialty (except Psychiatric and Substance Abuse) Hospitals	R	*8069	Specialty Hospitals, Except Psychiatric (except childrens' and substance abuse hospitals)
623	Nursing and Residential Care Facilities			
6231	Nursing Care Facilities			
62311	Nursing Care Facilities	N	*8051	Skilled Nursing Care Facilities (except continuing care retirement communities)
			*8052	Intermediate Care Facilities (except continuing care retirement communities and mental retardation facilities)
			*8059	Nursing and Personal Care Facilities, NEC (except continuing care retirement communities)
6232	Residential Mental Retardation, Mental Health and Substance Abuse Facilities			
62321	Residential Mental Retardation Facilities	N	*8052	Intermediate Care Facilities (mental retardation facilities)
62322	Residential Mental Health and Substance Abuse Facilities	N	*8361	Residential Care (mental health and substance abuse facilities)
6233	Community Care Facilities for the Elderly			
62331	Community Care Facilities for the Elderly			
623311	Continuing Care Retirement Communities	N	*8051	Skilled Nursing Care Facilities (continuing care retirement communities)
			*8052	Intermediate Care Facilities (continuing care retirement communities)
			*8059	Nursing and Personal Care Facilities, NEC (continuing care retirement communities)
623312	Homes for the Elderly	N	*8361	Residential Care (homes for the elderly)
6239	Other Residential Care Facilities			
62399	Other Residential Care Facilities	N	*8361	Residential Care (except mental health and substance abuse facilities, homes for the elderly)
624	Social Assistance			
6241	Individual and Family Services			
62411	Child and Youth Services	N	*8322	Individual and Family Social Services (child and youth services)
			*8641	Civic, Social, and Fraternal Organizations (youth development organizations)
62412	Services for the Elderly and Persons with Disabilities	N	*8322	Individual and Family Social Services (services for the elderly and disabled)
62419	Other Individual and Family Services	N	*8322	Individual and Family Social Services (except services for children, youth, elderly, disabled; food, housing, emergency and relief)
6242	Community Food and Housing, and Emergency and Other Relief Services			
62421	Community Food Services	N	*8322	Individual and Family Social Services (food services)

1997 NAICS Code	1997 NAICS United States and U.S. Description	Status Code	1987 SIC Code	1987 U.S. SIC Description
62422	Community Housing Services			
624221	Temporary Shelters	N	*8322	Individual and Family Social Services (temporary shelter)
624229	Other Community Housing Services	N	*8322	Individual and Family Social Services (housing services except temporary shelter)
62423	Emergency and Other Relief Services	N	*8322	Individual and Family Social Services (emergency and relief services)
6243	Vocational Rehabilitation Services			
62431	Vocational Rehabilitation Services	E	8331	Job Training and Vocational Rehabilitation Services
6244	Child Day Care Services			
62441	Child Day Care Services	R	8351	Child Day Care Services
			*7299	Miscellaneous Personal Services, NEC (babysitting)
71	Arts, Entertainment and Recreation			
711	Performing Arts, Spectator Sports and Related Industries			
7111	Performing Arts Companies			
71111	Theater Companies and Dinner Theaters	N	*5812	Eating Places (dinner theaters)
			*7922	Theatrical Producers (Except Motion Pictures) and Miscellaneous Theatrical Services (theater companies, opera companies)
71112	Dance Companies	N	*7922	Theatrical Producers (Except Motion Pictures) and Miscellaneous Theatrical Services (ballet and dance companies)
71113	Musical Groups and Artists	N	*7929	Bands, Orchestras, Actors, and Entertainment Groups (musical groups and artists and orchestras)
71119	Other Performing Arts Companies	N	*7929	Bands, Orchestras, Actors, and Entertainment Groups, (except musical groups, artists, actors, and actresses)
			*7999	Amusement and Recreation Services, NEC (circus companies)
7112	Spectator Sports			
71121	Spectator Sports			
711211	Sports Teams and Clubs	N	*7941	Professional Sports Clubs and Promoters (professional sports clubs)
711212	Race Tracks	N	*7948	Racing, Including Track Operations (track operations)
711219	Other Spectator Sports	N	*7941	Professional Sports Clubs and Promoters (except sports clubs, stadium operators, sports promoters and agents)
			*7948	Racing, Including Track Operations (except track operators)
			*7999	Amusement and Recreation Services, NEC (professional athletes)
7113	Promoters of Performing Arts, Sports and Similar Events			
71131	Promoters of Performing Arts, Sports and Similar Events with Facilities	N	*6512	Operators of Nonresidential Buildings (stadium and arena owners)
			*7922	Theatrical Procedures (Except Motion Pictures) and Miscellaneous Theatrical Services (theater operators)
			*7941	Professional Sports Clubs and Promoters (stadium operators)

71132	Promoters of Performing Arts, Sports and Similar Events without Facilities	N	*7922	Theatrical Producers (Except Motion Pictures) and Miscellaneous Theatrical Services (theatrical promoters)
			*7941	Professional Sports Clubs and Promoters (sports promoters)
7114	Agents and Managers for Artists, Athletes, Entertainers and Other Public Figures			
71141	Agents and Managers for Artists, Athletes, Entertainers and Other Public Figures	N	*7389	Business Services, NEC (agents and brokers for authors and artists)
			*7922	Theatrical Producers (Except Motion Pictures) and Miscellaneous Theatrical Services (theatrical agents)
			*7941	Professional Sports Clubs and Promoters (sports agents)
7115	Independent Artists, Writers, and Performers			
71151	Independent Artists, Writers, and Performers	N	*7819	Services Allied to Motion Picture Production (film directors and related motion picture production services, independent)
			*7929	Bands, Orchestras, Actors, and Other Entertainers and Entertainment Services (actors and actresses)
			*8999	Services, NEC (authors, artists, and related technical services independent)
712	Museums, Historical Sites and Similar Institutions			
7121	Museums, Historical Sites and Similar Institutions			
71211	Museums	R	*8412	Museums and Art Galleries (except historic and heritage sites)
71212	Historical Sites	N	*8412	Museums and Art Galleries (historic and heritage sites)
71213	Zoos and Botanical Gardens	R	*8422	Arboreta and Botanical and Zoological Gardens (except nature parks and reserves)
71219	Nature Parks and Other Similar Institutions	N	*7999	Amusement and Recreation Services, NEC (caverns and miscellaneous commercial parks)
			*8422	Arboreta and Botanical and Zoological Gardens (nature parks and reserves)
713	Amusement, Gambling and Recreation Industries			
7131	Amusement Parks and Arcades			
71311	Amusement and Theme Parks	E	7996	Amusement Parks
71312	Amusement Arcades	R	*7993	Coin-Operated Amusement Devices (amusement arcades)
7132	Gambling Industries			
71321	Casinos (except Casino Hotels)	N	*7999	Amusement and Recreation Services, NEC (casinos, except hotel casinos)
71329	Other Gambling Industries	N	*7993	Coin-Operated Amusement Devices (slot machine operators)
			*7999	Amusement and Recreation Services, NEC (lottery, bingo, bookie, and other gambling operations)
7139	Other Amusement and Recreation Industries			
71391	Golf Courses and Country Clubs	N	7992	Public Golf Courses
			*7997	Membership Sports and Recreation Clubs (golf clubs)
71392	Skiing Facilities	N	*7999	Amusement and Recreation Services, NEC (skiing facilities)

1997 NAICS Code	1997 NAICS United States and U.S. Description	Status Code	1987 SIC Code	1987 U.S. SIC Description
71393	Marinas	E	4493	Marinas
71394	Fitness and Recreational Sports Centers	N	7991	Physical Fitness Facilities
			*7997	Membership Sports and Recreation Clubs (recreation clubs with facilities)
			*7999	Amusement and Recreation Services, NEC (nonmembership recreation facilities)
71395	Bowling Centers	E	7933	Bowling Centers
71399	All Other Amusement and Recreation Industries	N	*7911	Dance Studios, Schools, and Halls (except instruction)
			*7993	Amusement and Recreation Services, NEC (except amusement arcades and slot machine operators)
			*7997	Membership Sports and Recreation Clubs (recreation clubs without facilities)
			*7999	Amusement and Recreation Services, NEC (except circuses, professionals, athletes, caverns and other commercial parks, skiing facilities, casinos and other gambling operations, amusement and recreation facilities, sports instruction, sports equipment rental, ticket agencies, and amusement or scenic transport operations)
72	Accommodation and Foodservices			
721	Accommodation			
7211	Traveler Accommodation			
72111	Hotels (except Casino Hotels) and Motels	R	*7011	Hotels and Motels (hotels and motels, except casino hotels)
			*7041	Organization Hotels and Lodging Houses, on Membership Basis (hotels)
72112	Casino Hotels	N	*7011	Hotels and Motels (casino hotels)
72119	Other Traveler Accommodation			
721191	Bed and Breakfast Inns	N	*7011	Hotels and Motels (bed and breakfast inns)
721199	All Other Traveler Accommodation	N	*7011	Hotels and Motels (except hotels, motels and bed and breakfast inns)
7212	RV (Recreational Vehicle) Parks and Recreational Camps			
72121	RV (Recreational Vehicle) Parks and Recreational Camps			
721211	RV (Recreational Vehicle) Parks and Campgrounds	E	7033	Recreational Vehicle Parks and Campgrounds
721214	Recreational and Vacation Camps	E	7032	Sporting and Recreational Camps
7213	Rooming and Boarding Houses			
72131	Rooming and Boarding Houses	R	7021	Rooming and Boarding Houses
			*7041	Organization Hotels and Lodging Houses, on Membership Basis (except hotels)
722	Foodservices and Drinking Places			
7221	Full-Service Restaurants			
72211	Full-Service Restaurants	N	*5812	Eating Places (full-service restaurants)
7222	Limited-Service Eating Places			

NAICS	Title	Status	SIC	SIC Title
72221	Limited-Service Eating Places			
722211	Limited-Service Restaurants	N	*5812	Eating Places (limited-service restaurants)
			*5499	Miscellaneous Food Stores (coffee shops making and serving food and beverages for immediate consumption)
722212	Cafeterias	N	*5812	Eating Places (cafeterias)
722213	Snack and Nonalcoholic Beverage Bars	N	*5812	Eating Places (snack and nonalcoholic beverage bars)
			*5461	Retail Bakeries (snacks)
7223	Special Foodservices			
72231	Foodservice Contractors	N	*5812	Eating Places (food service contractors)
72232	Caterers	N	*5812	Eating Places (caterers)
72233	Mobile Foodservices	N	*5963	Direct Selling Establishments (mobile food wagons)
7224	Drinking Places (Alcoholic Beverages)			
72241	Drinking Places (Alcoholic Beverages)	E	5813	Drinking Places (alcoholic beverages)
81	Other Services (except Public Administration)			
811	Repair and Maintenance			
8111	Automotive Repair and Maintenance			
81111	Automotive Mechanical and Electrical Repair and Maintenance			
811111	General Automotive Repair	E	7538	General Automotive Repair Shops
811112	Automotive Exhaust System Repair	E	7533	Automotive Exhaust System Repair Shops
811113	Automotive Transmission Repair	E	7537	Automotive Transmission Repair Shops
811118	Other Automotive Mechanical and Electrical Repair and Maintenance	E	7539	Automotive Repair Shops, NEC
81112	Automotive Body, Paint, Interior and Glass Repair			
811121	Automotive Body, Paint and Interior Repair and Maintenance	E	7532	Top, Body, and Upholstery Repair Shops and Paint Shops
811122	Automotive Glass Replacement Shops	E	7536	Automotive Glass Replacement Shops
81119	Other Automotive Repair and Maintenance			
811191	Automotive Oil Change and Lubrication Shops	N	*7549	Automotive Services, Except Repair and Carwashes (lubricating service, automotive)
811192	Car Washes	E	7542	Carwashes
811198	All Other Automotive Repair and Maintenance	R	*7534	Tire Retreading and Repair Shops (repair)
			*7549	Automotive Services, Except Repair and Carwashes (except lubricating and towing)
8112	Electronic and Precision Equipment Repair and Maintenance			
81121	Electronic and Precision Equipment Repair and Maintenance			
811211	Consumer Electronics Repair and Maintenance	N	*7622	Radio and Television Repair Shops (stereo, TV, VCR, and radio)

1997 NAICS Code	1997 NAICS United States and U.S. Description	Status Code	1987 SIC Code	1987 U.S. SIC Description
			*7629	Electrical and Electronic Repair Shops, NEC (consumer equipment except computer, TV, stereo, VCR, and radio)
811212	Computer and Office Machine Repair and Maintenance	N	*7378	Computer Maintenance and Repair (except sales location, providing supporting repair services as major source of revenue)
			*7629	Electrical and Electronic Repair Shops, NEC (business and office machine repair, electrical)
			*7699	Repair Shops and Related Services, NEC (typewriter repair)
811213	Communication Equipment Repair and Maintenance	N	*7622	Radio and Television Repair Shops (telecommunication equipment repair)
			*7629	Electrical and Electronic Repair Shops, NEC (telephone set repair)
811219	Other Electronic and Precision Equipment Repair and Maintenance	N	*7629	Electrical and Electronic Repair Shops, NEC (electrical measuring instrument repair and calibration, medical equipment repair, electrical)
			*7699	Repair Shops and Related Services, NEC (dental instrument repair, laboratory instrument repair, medical equipment and other electronic and precision equipment repair, except typewriters)
8113	Commercial and Industrial Machinery and Equipment (except Automotive and Electronic) Repair and Maintenance			
81131	Commercial and Industrial Machinery and Equipment (except Automotive and Electronic) Repair and Maintenance	R	*7699	Repair Shops and Related Services, NEC (other non-automotive transportation equipment and industrial machines and equipment)
			*7623	Refrigerator and Air-Conditioning Service and Repair Shops (commercial refrigerator equipment repair)
			*7694	Armature Rewinding Shops (repair)
8114	Personal and Household Goods Repair and Maintenance			
81141	Home and Garden Equipment and Appliance Repair and Maintenance			
811411	Home and Garden Equipment Repair and Maintenance	N	*7699	Repair Shops and Related Services, NEC (lawnmower repair shops, sharpening and repairing knives, saws and tools)
811412	Appliance Repair and Maintenance	N	*7623	Refrigeration and Air-Conditioning Service and Repair Shops (except commercial)
			*7629	Electrical and Electronic Repair Shops, NEC (appliance repair, electrical; washing machine repair; electric razor repair)
			*7699	Repairs Shops and Related Services, NEC (gas appliance repair service, sewing machine repair, stove repair shops, and other non-electrical appliance)
81142	Reupholstery and Furniture Repair	E	7641	Reupholstery and Furniture Repair
81143	Footwear and Leather Goods Repair	R	7251	Shoe Repair and Shoeshine Parlors
			*7699	Repair Shops and Related Services (leather goods repair shops, luggage repair shops, pocketbook repair shops)
81149	Other Personal and Household Goods Repair and Maintenance	N	*3732	Boat Building and Repairing (pleasure boat repair)

NAICS	Title	Status	SIC	SIC Title
			*7219	Laundry and Garment Services, NEC (alteration and repair)
			7631	Watch, Clock, and Jewelry Repair
			7692	Welding Repair
			*7699	Repair Shops and Related Services, NEC (except industrial, electronic, home and garden, appliance, and leather goods)
812	Personal and Laundry Services			
8121	Personal Care Services			
81211	Hair, Nail, and Skin Care Services			
812111	Barber Shops	R	*7241	Barber Shops (except barber colleges)
812112	Beauty Salons	R	*7231	Beauty Shops (except beauty and cosmetology schools and manicure and pedicure salons)
812113	Nail Salons	N	*7231	Beauty Shops (manicure and pedicure salons)
81219	Other Personal Care Services			
812191	Diet and Weight Reducing Centers	N	*7299	Miscellaneous Personal Services, NEC (diet and weight reducing services)
812199	Other Personal Care Services	N	*7299	Miscellaneous Personal Services, NEC, (personal care services)
8122	Death Care Services			
81221	Funeral Homes	R	*7261	Funeral Services and Crematories (funeral homes and services)
81222	Cemeteries and Crematories	R	*6531	Real Estate Agents and Managers (cemetery management)
			6553	Cemetery Subdividers and Developers
			*7261	Funeral Services and Crematories (except funeral homes)
8123	Laundry Services			
81231	Coin-Operated Laundries and Drycleaners	E	7215	Coin-Operated Laundry and Drycleaning
81232	Drycleaning and Laundry Services (except Coin-Operated)			
812321	Laundries, Family and Commercial	E	7211	Power Laundries, Family and Commercial
812322	Drycleaning Plants	E	7216	Drycleaning Plants, Except Rug Cleaning
81233	Linen and Uniform Supply			
812331	Linen Supply	R	7213	Linen Supply
			*7219	Laundry and Garment Services, NEC, (diaper service)
812332	Industrial Launderers	E	7218	Industrial Launderers
81239	Other Laundry Services			
812391	Garment Pressing, and Agents for Laundries	E	7212	Garment Pressing and Agents for Laundries
812399	All Other Laundry Services	R	*7219	Laundry and Garment Services, NEC (except diaper service and clothing alteration and repair)
8129	Other Personal Services			
81291	Pet Care (except Veterinary) Services	R	*0752	Animal Speciality Services, Except Veterinary (pet care services, except veterinary)
81292	Photo Finishing			
812921	Photo Finishing Laboratories (except One-Hour)	N	*7384	Photofinishing Laboratories (except one-hour)
812922	One-Hour Photo Finishing	N	*7384	Photofinishing Laboratories (one-hour)

1997 NAICS Code	1997 NAICS United States and U.S. Description	Status Code	1987 SIC Code	1987 U.S. SIC Description
81293	Parking Lots and Garages	E	7521	Automobile Parking
81299	All Other Personal Services	R	*7299	Miscellaneous Personal Services, NEC (except diet and weight reducing services, personal care services, and formal wear and costume rental service)
			*7389	Miscellaneous Business Services (bail handling)
813	Religious, Grantmaking, Civic, and Professional and Similar Organizations			
8131	Religious Organizations			
81311	Religious Organizations	E	8661	Religious Organizations
8132	Grantmaking and Giving Services			
81321	Grantmaking and Giving Services			
813211	Grantmaking Foundations	E	6732	Educational, Religious, and Charitable Trust
813212	Voluntary Health Organizations	N	*8399	Social Services, NEC (voluntary health organizations)
813219	Other Grantmaking and Giving Services	N	*8399	Social Services, NEC (grantmaking and giving)
8133	Social Advocacy Organizations			
81331	Social Advocacy Organizations			
813311	Human Rights Organizations	N	*8399	Social Services, NEC (human rights organizations and)
813312	Environment, Conservation and Wildlife Organizations	N	*8399	Social Services, NEC (environment, conservation, and wildlife advocacy)
			*8699	Membership Organizations, NEC (humane societies)
813319	Other Social Advocacy Organizations	N	*8399	Social Services, NEC (except human rights, environment, conservation and wildlife organizations, grantmaking and giving, and voluntary health organizations)
8134	Civic and Social Organizations			
81341	Civic and Social Organizations	N	*8641	Civic, Social, and Fraternal Organizations (except condominium and homeowner associations, and youth development organizations)
			*8699	Membership Organizations, NEC (farm granges)
8139	Business, Professional, Labor, Political, and Other Organizations			
81391	Business Associations	R	8611	Business Associations
			*8699	Membership Organizations, NEC (farm business organizations)
81392	Professional Organizations	E	8621	Professional Membership Organizations
81393	Labor Unions and Similar Labor Organizations	E	8631	Labor Unions and Similar Labor Organizations
81394	Political Organizations	E	8651	Political Organizations
81399	Other Similar Organizations	R	*6531	Real Estate Agents and Managers (condominium associations)
			*8641	Civic, Social, and Fraternal Organizations (condominium and homeowner associations)
			*8699	Membership Organizations, NEC (except farm business organizations, farm granges, and environmental, conservation, and wildlife organizations)

814	Private Households			
8141	Private Households			
81411	Private Households	E	8811	Private Households
92	Public Administration			Public Administration
921	Executive, Legislative, Public Finance and General Government			
9211	Executive, Legislative, Public Finance and General Government			
92111	Executive Offices	E	9111	Executive Offices
92112	Legislative Bodies	E	9121	Legislative Bodies
92113	Public Finance	E	9311	Public Finance, Taxation, and Monetary Policy
92114	Executive and Legislative Offices, Combined	E	9131	Executive and Legislative Office, Combined
92115	American Indian and Alaska Native Tribal Governments	N	*8641	Civic, Social, and Fraternal Organizations (pt) (Indian Tribal Councils)
92119	All Other General Government	E	9199	General Government, NEC
922	Justice, Public Order, and Safety			
9221	Justice, Public Order, and Safety			
92211	Courts	E	9211	Courts
92212	Police Protection	E	9221	Police Protection
92213	Legal Counsel and Prosecution	E	9222	Legal Counsel and Prosecution
92214	Correctional Institutions	E	9223	Correctional Institutions
92215	Parole Offices and Probation Offices	N	*8322	Individual and Family Social Services (parole and probation offices)
92216	Fire Protection	E	9224	Fire Protection
92219	All Other Justice, Public Order, and Safety	E	9229	Public Order and Safety, NEC
923	Administration of Human Resource Programs			
9231	Administration of Human Resource Programs			
92311	Administration of Education Programs	E	9411	Administration of Educational Programs
92312	Administration of Public Health Programs	E	9431	Administration of Public Health Programs
92313	Administration of Social, Human Resource and Income Maintenance Programs	E	9441	Administration of Social, Human Resource and Income Maintenance Programs
92314	Administration of Veteran's Affairs	E	9451	Administration of Veteran's Affairs, Except Health Insurance
924	Administration of Environmental Quality Programs			
9241	Administration of Environmental Quality Programs			
92411	Air and Water Resource and Solid Waste Management	E	9511	Air and Water Resource and Solid Waste Management
92412	Land, Mineral, Wildlife, and Forest Conservation	E	9512	Land, Mineral, Wildlife, and Forest Conservation

1997 NAICS Code	1997 NAICS United States and U.S. Description	Status Code	1987 SIC Code	1987 U.S. SIC Description
925	Administration of Housing Programs, Urban Planning, and Community Development			
9251	Administration of Housing Programs, Urban Planning, and Community Development			
92511	Administration of Housing Programs	E	9531	Administration of Housing Programs
92512	Administration of Urban Planning and Community and Rural Development	E	9532	Administration of Urban Planning and Community and Rural Development
926	Administration of Economic Programs			
9261	Administration of Economic Programs			
92611	Administration of General Economic Programs	E	9611	Administration of General Economic Programs
92612	Regulation and Administration of Transportation Programs	R	9621	Regulations and Administration of Transportation Programs (except air traffic control)
92613	Regulation and Administration of Communications, Electric, Gas, and Other Utilities	E	9631	Regulation and Administration of Communications, Electric, Gas, and Other Utilities
92614	Regulation of Agricultural Marketing and Commodities	E	9641	Regulation of Agricultural Marketing and Commodities
92615	Regulation, Licensing, and Inspection of Miscellaneous Commercial Sectors	E	9651	Regulation, Licensing, and Inspection of Miscellaneous Commercial Sectors
927	Space Research and Technology			
9271	Space Research and Technology			
92711	Space Research and Technology	E	9661	Space Research and Technology
928	National Security and International Affairs			
9281	National Security and International Affairs			
92811	National Security	E	9711	National Security
92812	International Affairs	E	9721	International Affairs
99	Unclassified Establishments			
999	Unclassified Establishments			
9999	Unclassified Establishments			
99999	Unclassified Establishments	E	9999	Nonclassifiable Establishments

The definitions of status codes are as follows: E--existing industry; L--nonexistent (null set) industry in U.S.; N--new industry; R--revised industry; and * means "part of". The abbreviation NEC is used for Not Elsewhere Classified.

Table 2. 1987 SIC Matched to 1997 NAICS

Table 2 - 1987 U.S. SIC Matched to 1997 NAICS United States

1987 SIC Code	1987 SIC Description	1997 NAICS Code	1997 NAICS United States Description
0111	Wheat	11114	Wheat Farming
0112	Rice	11116	Rice Farming
0115	Corn	11115	Corn Farming (pt)
0116	Soybeans	11111	Soybean Farming
0119	Cash Grains, NEC		
	Dry Pea and Bean Farms	11113	Dry Pea and Bean Farming
	Oilseed, Except Soybean, Farms	11112	Oilseed (except Soybean) Farming
	Popcorn Farms	11115	Corn Farming (pt)
	Combination Oilseed and Grain Farms	111191	Oilseed and Grain Combination Farming
	Other Farms	111199	All Other Grain Farming
0131	Cotton	11192	Cotton farming
0132	Tobacco	11191	Tobacco Farming
0133	Sugarcane and Sugar Beets		
	Sugar Beets	111991	Sugar Beet Farming
	Sugarcane	11193	Sugarcane Farming
0134	Irish Potatoes	111211	Potato Farming
0139	Field Crops, Except Cash Grains, NEC		
	Hay Farms	11194	Hay Farming
	Peanut Farming	111992	Peanut Farming

The abbreviation "pt" means "part of"; @ means time series break has been created that is greater than 3% of the 1992 value of shipments for the 1987 industry. The abbreviation NEC is used for Not Elsewhere Classified.

1987 SIC Code	1987 SIC Description	1997 NAICS Code	1997 NAICS United States Description
	Sweet Potatoes and Yams	111219	Other Vegetable (except Potato) and Melon Farming (pt)
	Other Field Crop Farms	111998	All Other Miscellaneous Crop Farming (pt)
0161	Vegetables and Melons	111219	Other Vegetable (except Potato) and Melon Farming (pt)
0171	Berry Crops		
	Strawberry Farms	111333	Strawberry Farming
	Other Berry Farms	111334	Berry (except Strawberry) Farming
0172	Grapes	111332	Grape Vineyards
0173	Tree Nuts	111335	Tree Nut Farming
0174@	Citrus Fruits		
	Orange Groves and Farms	11131	Orange Groves
	Other Citrus Groves and Farms	11132	Citrus (except Orange) Groves
0175	Deciduous Tree Fruits		
	Apple Orchard and Farms	111331	Apple Orchards
	Other Farms	111339	Other Noncitrus Fruit Farming (pt)
0179@	Fruits and Tree Nuts, NEC		
	Combination Fruit and Tree Nut Farms	111336	Fruit and Tree Nut Combination Farming
	Other Farms	111339	Other Noncitrus Fruit Farming (pt)
0181@	Ornamental Floriculture and Nursery Products		
	Floriculture Farming	111422	Floriculture Production
	Nursery Farming	111421	Nursery and Tree Production (pt)
0182	Food Crops Grown Under Cover		
	Mushroom, Growing Of	111411	Mushroom Production

	Other Food Crops Grown Under Cover	111419	Other Food Crops Grown Under Cover
0191@	General Farms, Primarily Crop	111998	All Other Miscellaneous Crop Farming (pt)
0211	Beef Cattle Feedlots	112112	Cattle Feedlots
0212	Beef Cattle, Except Feedlots	112111	Beef Cattle Ranching and Farming (pt)
0213	Hogs	11221	Hog and Pig Farming
0214	Sheep and Goats		
	Sheep Farms	11241	Sheep Farming
	Goat Farms	11242	Goat Farming
0219@	General Livestock, Except Dairy and Poultry	11299	All Other Animal Production (pt)
0241	Dairy Farms		
	Dairy Heifer Replacement Farms	112111	Beef Cattle Ranching and Farming (pt)
	Dairy Farms	11212	Dairy Cattle and Milk Production
0251	Broiler, Fryers, and Roaster Chickens	11232	Broilers and Other Meat-Type Chicken Production
0252	Chicken Eggs	11231	Chicken Egg Production
0253	Turkey and Turkey Eggs	11233	Turkey Production
0254	Poultry Hatcheries	11234	Poultry Hatcheries
0259	Poultry and Eggs, NEC	11239	Other Poultry Production
0271	Fur-Bearing Animals and Rabbits	11293	Fur-Bearing Animal and Rabbit Production
0272	Horses and Other Equines	11292	Horse and Other Equine Production
0273	Animal Aquaculture		
	Finfish Farming	112511	Finfish Farming and Fish Hatcheries (pt)
	Shellfish Farming	112512	Shellfish Farming (pt)

1987 SIC Code	1987 SIC Description	1997 NAICS Code	1997 NAICS United States Description
	Other Animal Aquaculture	112519	Other Animal Aquaculture
0279@	Animal Specialities, NEC		
	Apiculture	11291	Apiculture
	Other	11299	All Other Animal Production (pt)
0291@	General Farms, Primarily Livestock and Animal Specialties	11299	All Other Animal Production (pt)
0711	Soil Preparation Services	115112	Soil Preparation, Planting and Cultivating (pt)
0721	Crop Planting, Cultivating and Protecting		
	Crop Dusting (using general purpose aircraft)	481219	Other Nonscheduled Air Transportation (pt)
	Other (including crop dusting using special purpose aircraft)	115112	Soil Preparation, Planting and Cultivating (pt)
0722	Crop Harvesting, Primarily by Machine	115113	Crop Harvesting, Primarily By Machine
0723	Crop Preparation Services For Market, except Cotton Ginning	115114	Postharvest Crop Activities (except Cotton Ginning)
0724	Cotton Ginning	115111	Cotton Ginning
0741	Veterinary Service For Livestock	54194	Veterinary Services(pt)
0742	Veterinary Services for Animal Specialties	54194	Veterinary Services (pt.)
0751@	Livestock Services, Except Veterinary		
	Custom Slaughtering	311611	Animal (except Poultry) Slaughtering (pt)
	Other Livestock Service, Except Veterinary	11521	Support Activities for Animal Production (pt)
0752@	Animal Specialty Services, Except Veterinary		
	Horses and Equines Services and Animal Production Breeding	11521	Support Activities for Animal Production (pt)
	Pet Care Services	81291	Pet Care (except Veterinary) Services

0761	Farm Labor Contractors and Crew Leaders	115115	Farm Labor Contractors and Crew Leaders
0762	Farm Management Services	115116	Farm Management Services
0781	Landscape Counseling and Planning		
	Horticulture Consulting	54169	Other Scientific and Technical Consulting Services (pt)
	Landscape Architectural Services	54132	Landscape Architectural Services
0782	Lawn and Garden Services	56173	Landscaping Services (pt)
0783	Ornamental Shrub and Tree Services	56173	Landscaping Services (pt)
0811@	Timber Tracts		
	Short Rotation Woody Crops	111421	Nursery and Tree Production (pt)
	Long Term Timber Farming	11311	Timber Tract Operations
0831@	Forest Nurseries and Gathering of Forest Products		
	Maple Sap	111998	All Other Miscellaneous Crop Farming (pt)
	Other Forest Products	11321	Forest Nurseries and Gathering of Forest Products
0851	Forestry Services	11531	Support Activities for Forestry
0912	Finfish	114111	Finfish Fishing
0913	Shellfish	114112	Shellfish Fishing
0919	Miscellaneous Marine Products		
	Except Plant Aquaculture	114119	Other Marine Fisning
	Plant Aquaculture	111998	All Other Miscellaneous Crop Farming (pt)
0921@	Fish Hatcheries and Preserves		
	Finfish Hatcheries	112511	Finfish Farming and Fish Hatcheries (pt)
	Shellfish Hatcheries	112512	Shellfish Farming (pt)

1987 SIC Code	1987 SIC Description	1997 NAICS Code	1997 NAICS United States Description
0971	Hunting, Trapping, and Game Propagation	11421	Hunting and Trapping
1011	Iron Ores	21221	Iron Ore Mining
1021	Copper Ores	212234	Copper Ore and Nickel Ore Mining (pt.)
1031	Lead and Zinc Ores	212231	Lead Ore and Zinc Ore Mining
1041	Gold Ores	212221	Gold Ore Mining
1044	Silver Ores	212222	Silver Ore Mining
1061	Ferroalloy Ores, Except Vanadium		
	Nickel Ore Mining	212234	Copper Ore and Nickel Ore Mining (pt.)
	Other Ferroalloys (except nickel)	212299	Other Metal Ore Mining (pt)
1081	Metal Mining Services		
	Metal Mining (except geophysical surveying)	213114	Support Activities for Metal Mining
	Geophysical Surveying	54136	Geophysical Surveying and Mapping Services (pt)
1094	Uranium-Radium-Vanadium Ores	212291	Uranium-Radium-Vanadium Ore Mining
1099	Miscellaneous Metal Ores, NEC	212299	Other Metal Ore Mining (pt)
1221	Bituminous Coal and Lignite Surface Mining	212111	Bituminous Coal and Lignite Surface Mining
1222	Bituminous Coal Underground Mining	212112	Bituminous Coal Underground Mining
1231	Anthracite Mining	212113	Anthracite Mining
1241	Coal Mining Services	213113	Support Activities for Coal Mining
1311	Crude Petroleum and Natural Gas	211111	Crude Petroleum and Natural Gas Extraction
1321	Natural Gas Liquids	211112	Natural Gas Liquid Extraction
1381	Drilling Oil and Gas Wells	213111	Drilling Oil and Gas Wells
1382	Oil and Gas Field Exploration Services		

	Geophysical Mapping and Surveying	54136	Geophysical Surveying and Mapping Services (pt)
	Other Oil and Gas Field Exploration Services	213112	Support Activities for Oil and Gas Field Operations (pt)
1389	Oil and Gas Field Services, NEC	213112	Support Activities for Oil and Gas Field Operations (pt)
1411	Dimension Stone	212311	Dimension Stone Mining and Quarry
1422	Crushed and Broken Limestone	212312	Crushed and Broken Limestone Mining and Quarrying
1423	Crushed and Broken Granite	212313	Crushed and Broken Granite Mining and Quarrying
1429	Crushed and Broken Stone, NEC	212319	Other Crushed and Broken Stone Mining and Quarrying (pt)
1442	Construction Sand and Gravel	212321	Construction Sand and Gravel Mining
1446	Industrial Sand	212322	Industrial Sand Mining
1455	Kaolin and Ball Clay	212324	Kaolin and Ball Clay Mining
1459	Clay, Ceramic, and Refractory Minerals, NEC	212325	Clay and Ceramic and Refractory Minerals Mining
1474	Potash, Soda, and Borate Minerals	212391	Potash, Soda, and Borate Mineral Mining
1475	Phosphate Rock	212392	Phosphate Rock Mining
1479	Chemical and Fertilizer Mineral Mining, NEC	212393	Other Chemical and Fertilizer Mineral Mining
1481	Nonmetallic Minerals Services Except Fuels		
	Nonmetallic Minerals Services, except fuels (except geophysical surveying)	213115	Support Activities for Non-metallic Minerals, (except Fuels)
	Geophysical Surveying Services	54136	Geophysical Surveying and Mapping Services (pt)
1499	Miscellaneous Nonmetallic Minerals, Except Fuels		
	Bituminous Limestone and Bituminous Sandstone	212319	Other Crushed and Broken Stone Mining or Quarrying (pt)
	Except Bituminous Limestone and Bituminous Sandstone	212399	All Other Non-Metallic Mineral Mining
1521@	General Contractors-Single-Family Houses	23321	Single Family Housing Construction (pt)

1987 SIC Code	1987 SIC Description	1997 NAICS Code	1997 NAICS United States Description
1522@	General Contractors-Residential Buildings, Other Than Single-Family		
	Hotel and Motel Construction	23332	Commercial and Institutional Building Construction (pt)
	Except Hotel and Motel Construction	23322	Multifamily Housing Construction (pt)
1531@	Operative Builders		
	Single-Family Housing	23321	Single Family Housing Construction (pt)
	Multi-Family Housing	23322	Multifamily Housing Construction (pt)
	Manufacturing and Light Industrial Buildings	23331	Manufacturing and Industrial Building Construction (pt)
	Commercial and Institutional Buildings	23332	Commercial and Institutional Building Construction (pt)
1541@	General Contractors-Industrial Buildings and Warehouses		
	Warehouse Construction	23332	Commercial and Institutional Building Construction (pt)
	Except Warehouse Construction	23331	Manufacturing and Industrial Building Construction (pt)
1542@	General Contractors-Nonresidential Buildings, Other than Industrial Buildings and Warehouses	23332	Commercial and Institutional Building Construction (pt)
1611	Highway and Street Construction, Except Elevated Highways	23411	Highway and Street Construction
1622	Bridge, Tunnel, and Elevated Highway Construction	23412	Bridge and Tunnel Construction
1623	Water, Sewer, Pipeline, and Communications and Power Line Construction		
	Water, Sewer and Pipelines	23491	Water, Sewer and Pipeline Construction
	Power and Communication Transmission Lines	23492	Power and Communication Transmission Line Construction
1629	Heavy Construction, NEC		
	Industrial Nonbuilding Structures Construction	23493	Industrial Nonbuilding Structure Construction
	Except Industrial Nonbuilding Structures Construction	23499	All Other Heavy Construction (pt)

1711	Plumbing, Heating, and Air-Conditioning	23511	Plumbing, Heating and Air-Conditioning Contractors
1721@	Painting and Paper Hanging	23521	Painting and Wall Covering Contractors (pt)
1731@	Electrical Work		
	Burglar and Fire Alarm Installation	561621	Security Systems Services (except Locksmiths) (pt)
	Except Burglar and Fire Alarm Installation	23531	Electrical Contractors
1741	Masonry, Stone Setting and Other Stone Work	23541	Masonry and Stone Contractors
1742	Plastering, Drywall, Acoustical and Insulation Work	23542	Drywall, Plastering, Acoustical and Insulation Contractors (pt)
1743	Terrazzo, Tile, Marble, and Mosaic Work		
	Fresco Work	23542	Drywall, Plastering, Acoustical and Insulation Contractors (pt)
	Except Fresco Work	23543	Tile, Marble, Terrazzo and Mosaic Contractors
1751	Carpentry Work	23551	Carpentry Contractors
1752	Floor Laying and Other Floor Work, NEC	23552	Floor Laying and Other Floor Contractors
1761	Roofing, Siding, and Sheet Metal Work	23561	Roofing, Siding, and Sheet Metal Contractors
1771@	Concrete Work		
	Stucco Construction	23542	Drywall, Plastering, Acoustical and Insulation Contractors (pt)
	Except Stucco Construction	23571	Concrete Contractors
1781	Water Well Drilling	23581	Water Well Drilling Contractors
1791	Structural Steel Erection	23591	Structural Steel Erection Contractors
1793	Glass and Glazing Work	23592	Glass and Glazing Contractors (pt)
1794	Excavation Work	23593	Excavation Contractors
1795	Wrecking and Demolition Work	23594	Wrecking and Demolition Contractors
1796	Installation or Erection of Building Equipment, NEC	23595	Building Equipment and Other Machinery Installation Contractors

1987 SIC Code	1987 SIC Description	1997 NAICS Code	1997 NAICS United States Description
1799@	Special Trade Contractors, NEC		
	Paint and Wallpaper Stripping and Wallpaper Removal Contractors	23521	Painting and Wall Covering Contractors (pt)
	Tinted Glass Work	23592	Glass and Glazing Contractors (pt)
	Asbestos Abatement and Lead Paint Removal Contractors	56291	Remediation Services (pt)
	All Other Special Trade Contractors	23599	All Other Special Trade Contractors
2011	Meat Packing Plants	311611	Animal (except Poultry) Slaughtering (pt)
2013	Sausages and Other Prepared Meats	311612	Meat Processed from Carcasses (pt)
2015@	Poultry Slaughtering and Processing		
	Poultry Processing	311615	Poultry Processing
	Egg Processing	311999	All Other Miscellaneous Food Manufacturing (pt)
2021	Creamery Butter	311512	Creamery Butter Manufacturing
2022	Natural, Processed, and Imitation Cheese	311513	Cheese Manufacturing
2023	Dry, Condensed, and Evaporated Dairy Products	311514	Dry, Condensed, and Evaporated Dairy Product Manufacturing
2024	Ice Cream and Frozen Desserts	31152	Ice Cream and Frozen Dessert Manufacturing
2026	Fluid Milk	311511	Fluid Milk Manufacturing
2032	Canned Specialties		
	Canned Specialties	311422	Specialty Canning
	Canned Pudding	311999	All Other Miscellaneous Food Manufacturing (pt)
2033@	Canned Fruits, Vegetables, Preserves, Jams, and Jellies	311421	Fruit and Vegetable Canning (pt)
2034	Dried and Dehydrated Fruits, Vegetables, and Soup Mixes		
	Dried and Dehydrated Fruit, Vegetable, and Soup Mixes	311423	Dried and Dehydrated Food Manufacturing (pt)

	Vegetable Flours	311211	Flour Milling (pt)
2035	Pickled Fruits and Vegetables, Vegetables Sauces and Seasonings, and Salad Dressings		
	Pickled Fruits and Vegetables	311421	Fruit and Vegetable Canning (pt)
	Sauces and Salad Dressings	311941	Mayonnaise, Dressing, and Other Prepared Sauce Manufacturing (pt)
2037	Frozen Fruits, Fruit Juices, and Vegetables	311411	Frozen Fruit, Juice, and Vegetable Processing
2038	Frozen Specialties, NEC	311412	Frozen Specialty Food Manufacturing
2041	Flour and Other Grain Mill Products	311211	Flour Milling (pt)
2043	Cereal Breakfast Foods		
	Coffee Substitute	31192	Coffee and Tea Manufacturing (pt)
	Breakfast Cereal	31123	Breakfast Cereal Manufacturing
2044	Rice Milling	311212	Rice Milling
2045	Prepared Flour Mixes and Doughs	311822	Flour Mixes and Dough Manufacturing from Purchased Flour
2046	Wet Corn Milling	311221	Wet Corn Milling
2047	Dog and Cat Food	311111	Dog and Cat Food Manufacturing
2048	Prepared Feed and Feed Ingredients for Animals and Fowls, Except Dogs and Cats		
	Animal Slaughtering for Pet Food	311611	Animal (except Poultry) Slaughtering (pt)
	Except Slaughtering Animals for Pet Food	311119	Other Animal Food Manufacturing
2051	Bread and Other Bakery Products, Except Cookies and Crackers	311812	Commercial Bakeries (pt)
2052@	Cookies and Crackers		
	Cookie and Cracker	311821	Cookie and Cracker Manufacturing
	Pretzels	311919	Other Snack Food Manufacturing (pt)

1987 SIC Code	1987 SIC Description	1997 NAICS Code	1997 NAICS United States Description
	Unleavened Bread	311812	Commercial Bakeries (pt)
2053	Frozen Bakery Products, Except Bread	311813	Frozen Bakery Product Manufacturing
2061	Cane Sugar, Except Refining	311311	Sugarcane Mills
2062	Cane Sugar Refining	311312	Cane Sugar Refining
2063	Beet Sugar	311313	Beet Sugar Manufacturing
2064@	Candy and Other Confectionery Products		
	Chocolate Confectionery	31133	Confectionery Manufacturing from Purchased Chocolate
	Non-Chocolate Confectionery Manufacturing	31134	Non-Chocolate Confectionery Manufacturing (pt)
2066	Chocolate and Cocoa Products	31132	Chocolate and Confectionery Manufacturing from Cacao Beans
2067@	Chewing Gum	31134	Non-Chocolate Confectionery Manufacturing (pt)
2068@	Salted and Roasted Nuts and Seeds	311911	Roasted Nuts and Peanut Butter Manufacturing (pt)
2074@	Cottonseed Oil Mills		
	Cottonseed Processing	311223	Other Oilseed Processing (pt)
	Processing Purchased Cottonseed Oil	311225	Fats and Oils Refining and Blending (pt)
2075	Soybean Oil Mills		
	Soybean Processing	311222	Soybean Processing (pt)
	Processing Purchased Soybean Oil	311225	Fats and Oils Refining and Blending (pt)
2076@	Vegetable Oil Mills, Except Corn, Cottonseed, and Soybeans		
	Vegetable Oilseed Processing, except Corn, Cottonseed, and Soybeans	311223	Other Oilseed Processing (pt)
	Processing Purchased Vegetable Oils, except Corn, Cottonseed, and Soybeans	311225	Fats and Oils Refining and Blending (pt)
2077@	Animal and Marine Fats and Oils		

	Animal Fats and Oils	311613	Rendering and Meat By-product Processing
	Canned Marine Fats and Oils	311711	Seafood Canning (pt)
	Fresh and Frozen Marine Fats and Oils	311712	Fresh and Frozen Seafood Processing (pt)
	Vegetable Oil Foots	311225	Fats and Oils Refining and Blending (pt)
2079	Shortening, Table Oils, Margarine, and Other Edible Fats and Oils, NEC		
	Processing Fats and Oils from Purchased Fats and Oils	311225	Fats and Oils Refining and Blending (pt)
	Processing Soybean Oil from Soybeans Crushed in the Same Establishment	311222	Soybean Processing (pt)
	Processing Vegetable Oils, except Soybeans, from Oilseeds Crushed in the Same Establishment	311223	Other Oilseed Processing (pt)
2082	Malt Beverages	31212	Breweries
2083	Malt	311213	Malt Manufacturing
2084	Wines, Brandy, and Brandy Spirits	31213	Wineries
2085	Distilled and Blended Liquors	31214	Distilleries
2086	Bottled and Canned Soft Drinks and Carbonated Waters		
	Soft Drinks	312111	Soft Drink Manufacturing
	Bottled Water	312112	Bottled Water Manufacturing
2087@	Flavoring Extracts and Flavoring Syrups NEC		
	Flavoring Syrup and Concentrate	31193	Flavoring Syrup and Concentrate Manufacturing
	Flavoring Extracts	311942	Spice and Extract Manufacturing (pt)
	Powered Drink Mix	311999	All Other Miscellaneous Food Manufacturing (pt)
2091@	Canned and Cured Fish and Seafood	311711	Seafood Canning (pt)

1987 SIC Code	1987 SIC Description	1997 NAICS Code	1997 NAICS United States Description
2092@	Prepared Fresh or Frozen Fish and Seafoods	311712	Fresh and Frozen Seafood Processing (pt)
2095@	Roasted Coffee		
	Roasted Coffee	31192	Coffee and Tea Manufacturing (pt)
	Coffee Extracts	311942	Spice and Extract Manufacturing (pt)
2096@	Potato Chips, Corn Chips, and Similar Snacks	311919	Other Snack Food Manufacturing (pt)
2097	Manufactured Ice	312113	Ice Manufacturing
2098	Macaroni, Spaghetti, Vermicelli, and Noodles	311823	Pasta Manufacturing
2099	Food Preparations, NEC		
	Bouillon	311423	Dried and Dehydrated Food Manufacturing (pt)
	Reducing Maple Sap to Maple Syrup	111998	All Other Miscellaneous Crop Farming (pt)
	Marshmallow Creme	31134	Non-Chocolate Confectionery Manufacturing (pt)
	Peanut Butter	311911	Roasted Nuts and Peanut Butter Manufacturing (pt)
	Perishable Prepared Food	311991	Perishable Prepared Food Manufacturing
	Tortillas	31183	Tortilla Manufacturing
	Tea	31192	Coffee and Tea Manufacturing (pt)
	Vinegar, Dip Mix, Salad Dressing Mix and Seasoning Mix	311941	Mayonnaise, Dressing, and Other Prepared Sauce Manufacturing (pt)
	Spices and Extracts	311942	Spice and Extract Manufacturing (pt)
	Other	311999	All Other Miscellaneous Food Manufacturing (pt)
2111	Cigarettes	312221	Cigarette Manufacturing
2121	Cigars	312229	Other Tobacco Product Manufacturing (pt)
2131@	Chewing and Smoking Tobacco and Snuff	312229	Other Tobacco Product Manufacturing (pt)
2141@	Tobacco Stemming and Redrying		

	Reconstituted Tobacco	312229	Other Tobacco Product Manufacturing (pt)
	Redrying and Stemming	31221	Tobacco Stemming and Redrying
2211@	Broadwoven Fabric Mills, Cotton	31321	Broadwoven Fabric Mills (pt)
2221@	Broadwoven Fabric Mills, Manmade Fiber and Silk	31321	Broadwoven Fabric Mills (pt)
2231@	Broadwoven Fabric Mills, Wool (Including Dyeing and Finishing)		
	Except Wool Finishing	31321	Broadwoven Fabric Mills (pt)
	Wool Broadwoven Fabric Finishing	313311	Broadwoven Fabric Finishing Mills (pt)
	Wool Finishing, Except Broadwoven Fabric	313312	Textile and Fabric Finishing (except Broadwoven Fabric) Mills (pt)
2241	Narrow Fabric and Other Smallware Mills: Cotton, Wool, Silk, and Manmade Fiber	313221	Narrow Fabric Mills (pt)
2251@	Women's Full-Length and Knee-Length Hosiery, Except Socks	315111	Sheer Hosiery Mills (pt)
2252 @	Hosiery, NEC		
	Girls' Hosiery	315111	Sheer Hosiery Mills (pt)
	Socks	315119	Other Hosiery and Sock Mills
2253@	Knit Outerwear Mills	315191	Outerwear Knitting Mills (pt)
2254	Knit Underwear and Nightwear Mills	315192	Underwear and Nightwear Knitting Mills (pt)
2257@	Weft Knit Fabric Mills		
	Except Finishing	313241	Weft Knit Fabric Mills (pt)
	Finishing	313312	Textile and Fabric Finishing (except Broadwoven Fabric) Mills (pt)
2258@	Lace and Warp Knit Fabric Mills		
	Except Finishing	313249	Other Knit Fabric and Lace Mills (pt)
	Finishing	313312	Textile and Fabric Finishing (except Broadwoven Fabric) Mills (pt)

1987 SIC Code	1987 SIC Description	1997 NAICS Code	1997 NAICS United States Description
2259@	Knitting Mills, NEC		
	Knit Gloves and Mittens	315191	Outerwear Knitting Mills (pt)
	Girdles	315192	Underwear and Nightwear Knitting Mills (pt)
	Finished Articles of Weft Knit Fabric	313241	Weft Knit Fabric Mills (pt)
	Finished Articles of Warp Knit Fabric	313249	Other Knit Fabric and Lace Mills (pt)
2261@	Finishers of Broadwoven Fabrics of Cotton	313311	Broadwoven Fabric Finishing Mills (pt)
2262@	Finishers of Broadwoven Fabrics of Manmade Fiber and Silk	313311	Broadwoven Fabric Finishing Mills (pt)
2269@	Finishers of Textiles, NEC		
	Broadwoven Finishing	313311	Broadwoven Fabric Finishing Mills (pt)
	Except Broadwoven Finishing	313312	Textile and Fabric Finishing (except Broadwoven Fabric) Mills (pt)
2273	Carpets and Rugs	31411	Carpet and Rug Mills
2281@	Yarn Spinning Mills	313111	Yarn Spinning Mills (pt)
2282@	Yarn Texturizing, Throwing, Twisting, and Winding Mills		
	Except Spooling Purchased Yarn	313112	Yarn Texturing, Throwing and Twisting Mills
	Spooling Purchased Yarn	313312	Textile and Fabric Finishing (except Broadwoven Fabric) Mills (pt)
2284@	Thread Mills		
	Except Finishing	313113	Thread Mills (pt)
	Finishing	313312	Textile and Fabric Finishing (except Broadwoven Fabric) Mills (pt)
2295@	Coated Fabrics, Not Rubberized	31332	Fabric Coating Mills (pt)
2296	Tire Cord and Fabrics	314992	Tire Cord and Tire Fabric Mills
2297@	Nonwoven Fabrics	31323	Nonwoven Fabric Mills (pt)
2298	Cordage and Twine	314991	Rope, Cordage and Twine Mills

2299@	Textile Goods, NEC		
	Broadwoven Fabric of Jute, Linen, Hemp, and Ramie	31321	Broadwoven Fabric Mills (pt)
	Nonwoven Felt	31323	Nonwoven Fabric Mills (pt)
	Finishing Thread and Yarn of Flax, Hemp, Jute, Linen, and Ramie	313312	Textile and Fabric Finishing (except Broadwoven Fabrics) Mills (pt)
	Narrow Woven Fabric of Jute, Linen, Hemp, and Ramie	313221	Narrow Fabric Mills (pt)
	Thread of Hemp, Linen, and Ramie	313113	Thread Mills (pt)
	Yarn of Flax, Hemp, Jute, and Ramie	313111	Yarn Spinning Mills (pt)
	Other Textile Goods	314999	All Other Miscellaneous Textile Product Mills (pt)
2311@	Men's and Boys' Suits, Coats and Overcoats		
	Contractors	315211	Men's and Boys' Cut and Sew Apparel Contractors (pt)
	Except Contractors	315222	Men's and Boys' Cut and Sew Suit, Coat, and Overcoat Manufacturing (pt)
2321@	Men's and Boys' Shirts, Except Work Shirts		
	Contractors	315211	Men's and Boys' Cut and Sew Apparel Contractors (pt)
	Except Contractors	315223	Men's and Boys' Cut and Sew Shirt, (except Work Shirt) Manufacturing (pt)
2322@	Men's and Boys' Underwear and Nightwear		
	Contractors	315211	Men's and Boys' Cut and Sew Apparel Contractors (pt)
	Except Contractors	315221	Men's and Boys' Cut and Sew Underwear and Nightwear Manufacturing (pt)
2323	Men's and Boys' Neckwear	315993	Men's and Boys' Neckwear Manufacturing
2325@	Men's and Boys' Trousers and Slacks		
	Contractors	315211	Men's and Boys' Cut and Sew Apparel Contractors (pt)

1987 SIC Code	1987 SIC Description	1997 NAICS Code	1997 NAICS United States Description
	Except Contractors	315224	Men's and Boys' Cut And Sew Trouser, Slack, And Jean Manufacturing (pt)
2326@	Men's and Boys' Work Clothing		
	Contractors	315211	Men's and Boys' Cut and Sew Apparel Contractors (pt)
	Except Contractors	315225	Men's and Boys' Cut and Sew Work Clothing Manufacturing
2329@	Men's and Boys' Clothing, NEC		
	Contractors	315211	Men's and Boys' Cut and Sew Apparel Contractors (pt)
	Except Contractors	315228	Men's and Boys' Cut and Sew Other Outerwear Manufacturing (pt)
	Athletic Uniforms	315299	All Other Cut and Sew Apparel Manufacturing (pt)
2331@	Women's, Misses', and Juniors' Blouses and Shirts		
	Contractors	315212	Women's and Girls' Cut and Sew Apparel Contractors (pt)
	Except Contractors	315232	Women's and Girls' Cut and Sew Blouse and Shirt Manufacturing (pt)
2335@	Women's, Misses' and Junior's Dresses		
	Contractors	315212	Women's and Girls' Cut and Sew Apparel Contractors (pt)
	Except Contractors	315233	Women's and Girls' Cut and Sew Dress Manufacturing (pt)
2337@	Women's, Misses' and Juniors' Suits, Skirts and Coats		
	Contractors	315212	Women's and Girls' Cut and Sew Apparel Contractors (pt)
	Except Contractors	315234	Women's and Girls' Cut and Sew Suit, Coat, Tailored Jacket, and Skirt Manufacturing (pt)
2339@	Women's, Misses' and Juniors' Outerwear, NEC		
	Scarves	315999	Other Apparel Accessories and Other Apparel Manufacturing (pt)
	Contractors	315212	Women's and Girls' Cut and Sew Apparel Contractors (pt)
	Athletic Uniforms	315299	All Other Cut and Sew Apparel Manufacturing (pt)

	All Other, Except Contractors	315238	Women's and Girls' Cut and Sew Other Outerwear Manufacturing (pt)
2341@	Women's, Misses, Children's, and Infants' Underwear and Nightwear		
	Women and Girls' Contractors	315212	Women's and Girls' Cut and Sew Apparel Contractors (pt)
	Boys' Contractors	315211	Men's and Boys' Cut and Sew Apparel Contractors (pt)
	Women's and Girls', Except Contractors	315231	Women's and Girls' Cut and Sew Lingerie, Loungewear, and Nightwear Manufacturing (pt)
	Boys' Except Contractors	315221	Men's and Boys' Cut and Sew Underwear and Nightwear Manufacturing (pt)
	Infants', Except Contractors	315291	Infants' Cut and Sew Apparel Manufacturing (pt)
2342@	Brassieres, Girdles, and Allied Garments		
	Contractors	315212	Women's and Girls' Cut and Sew Apparel Contractors (pt)
	Except contractors	315231	Women's and Girls' Cut and Sew Lingerie, Loungewear, and Nightwear Manufacturing (pt)
2353	Hats, Caps, and Millinery	315991	Hat, Cap, and Millinery Manufacturing
2361@	Girls', Children's and Infants' Dresses, Blouses and Shirts		
	Infants' Dresses, Blouses, and Shirts	315291	Infants' Cut and Sew Apparel Manufacturing (pt)
	Boys' Shirts	315223	Men's and Boys' Cut and Sew Shirt, (except Work Shirt) Manufacturing (pt)
	Boys' Shirt Contractors	315211	Men's and Boys' Cut and Sew Apparel Contractors (pt)
	Girls' Blouses and Shirts	315232	Women's and Girls' Cut and Sew Blouse and Shirt Manufacturing (pt)
	Girls' Dresses	315233	Women's and Girls' Cut and Sew Dress Manufacturing (pt)
	Girls' Contractors	315212	Women's and Girls' Cut and Sew Apparel Contractors (pt)
2369@	Girls', Children's and Infants' Outerwear, NEC		
	Infants' Outerwear, NEC	315291	Infants' Cut and Sew Apparel Manufacturing (pt)

1987 SIC Code	1987 SIC Description	1997 NAICS Code	1997 NAICS United States Description
	Boys' Suits and Coats	315222	Men's and Boys' Cut and Sew Suit, Coat, and Overcoat Manufacturing (pt)
	Boys' Trousers and Slacks	315224	Men's and Boys' Cut and Sew Trouser, Slack, and Jean Manufacturing (pt)
	Boys' Outerwear, NEC	315228	Men's and Boys' Cut and Sew Other Outerwear Manufacturing (pt)
	Boys' Robes	315221	Men's and Boys' Cut and Sew Underwear and Nightwear Manufacturing (pt)
	Boys' Contractors	315211	Men's and Boys' Cut and Sew Apparel Contractors (pt)
	Girls' Suits, Coats, Skirts, Etc.	315234	Women's and Girls' Cut and Sew Suit, Coat, Tailored Jacket, and Skirt Manufacturing (pt)
	Girls' Outerwear, NEC	315238	Women's and Girls' Cut and Sew Other Outerwear Manufacturing (pt)
	Girls' Robes	315231	Women's and Girls' Cut and Sew Lingerie, Loungewear, and Nightwear Manufacturing (pt)
	Girls' Contractors	315212	Women's and Girls' Cut and Sew Apparel Contractors (pt)
2371	Fur Goods	315292	Fur and Leather Apparel Manufacturing (pt)
2381@	Dress and Work Gloves, Except Knit and All-Leather	315992	Glove and Mitten Manufacturing (pt
2384@	Robes and Dressing Gowns		
	Women's Except Contractors	315231	Women's and Girls' Cut and Sew Lingerie, Loungewear, and Nightwear Manufacturing (pt)
	Men's Except Contractors	315221	Men's and Boys' Cut and Sew Underwear and Nightwear Manufacturing (pt)
	Men's and Boys' Contractors	315211	Men's and Boys' Cut and Sew Apparel Contractors (pt)
	Women's and Girls' Contractors	315212	Women's and Girls' Cut and Sew Apparel Contractors (pt)
2385@	Waterproof Outerwear		
	Raincoats (Men's and Boys')	315222	Men's and Boys' Cut and Sew Suit, Coat, and Overcoat Manufacturing (pt)

	Raincoats (Women's and Girls')	315234	Women's and Girls' Cut and Sew Suit, Coat, Tailored Jacket, and Skirt Manufacturing (pt)
	Other Men's and Boys' Outerwear	315228	Men's and Boys' Cut and Sew Other Outerwear Manufacturing (pt)
	Other Women's and Girls' Outerwear	315238	Women's and Girls' Cut and Sew Other Outerwear Manufacturing (pt)
	Infants' Waterproof Outerwear Except Contractors	315291	Infants' Cut and Sew Apparel Manufacturing (pt)
	Aprons, Bibs, and Other Miscellaneous Waterproof Items	315999	Other Apparel Accessories and Other Apparel Manufacturing (pt)
	Contractors (Men's and Boys')	315211	Men's and Boys' Cut and Sew Apparel Contractors (pt)
	Contractors (Women's and Girls')	315212	Women's and Girls' Cut and Sew Apparel Contractors (pt)
2386@	Leather and Sheep-Lined Clothing	315292	Fur and Leather Apparel Manufacturing (pt)
2387@	Apparel Belts	315999	Other Apparel Accessories and Other Apparel Manufacturing (pt)
2389@	Apparel and Accessories, NEC		
	Handkerchiefs, Arm bands, etc.	315999	Other Apparel Accessories and Other Apparel Manufacturing (pt)
	Academic and Clerical Outerwear	315299	All Other Cut and Sew Apparel Manufacturing (pt)
	Garters and Garter Belts	315231	Women's and Girls' Cut and Sew Lingerie, Loungewear, and Nightwear Manufacturing (pt)
	Women' Contractors	315212	Women's and Girls' Cut and Sew Apparel Contractors (pt)
	Men's Contractors	315211	Mens' and Boys' Cut and Sew Apparel Contractors (pt)
2391	Curtains and Draperies	314121	Curtain and Drapery Mills (pt)
2392@	Housefurnishings, Except Curtains and Draperies		
	Blanket, Laundry, and Wardrobe Bags	314911	Textile Bag Mills (pt)
	Mops, Floor and Dust	339994	Broom, Brush and Mop Manufacturing (pt)
	Other Housefurnishings	314129	Other Household Textile Product Mills
2393@	Textile Bags	314911	Textile Bag Mills (pt)

1987 SIC Code	1987 SIC Description	1997 NAICS Code	1997 NAICS United States Description
2394	Canvas and Related Products	314912	Canvas and Related Product Mills
2395@	Pleating, Decorative and Novelty Stitching, and Tucking for the Trade		
	Pleating and Stitching, Except Apparel Contractors	314999	All Other Miscellaneous Textile Product Mills (pt)
	Men's and Boys' Apparel Contractors	315211	Mens' and Boys' Cut and Sew Apparel Contractors (pt)
	Women's and Girls' Apparel Contractors	315212	Women's and Girls' Cut and Sew Apparel Contractors (pt)
2396@	Automotive Trimmings, Apparel Findings, and Related Products		
	Textile Automotive Trimmings	33636	Motor Vehicle Fabric Accessories and Seat Manufacturing (pt)
	Apparel Findings and Trimmings	315999	Other Apparel Accessories, and Other Apparel Manufacturing (pt)
	Printing and Embossing on Fabric Articles	323113	Commercial Screen Printing (pt)
	Other Apparel Products	314999	All Other Miscellaneous Textile Product Mills (pt)
2397	Schiffli Machine Embroideries	313222	Schiffli Machine Embroidery
2399	Fabricated Textile Products, NEC		
	Seat Belts and Seat and Tire Covers	33636	Motor Vehicle Fabric Accessories and Seat Manufacturing (pt)
	Apparel and Apparel Accessories	315999	Other Apparel Accessories and Other Apparel Manufacturing (pt)
	Other Fabricated Textile Products	314999	All Other Miscellaneous Textile Product Mills (pt)
2411	Logging	11331	Logging
2421@	Sawmills and Planing Mills, General		
	Lumber Manufacturing from Purchased Lumber, Softwood Cut Stock, Wood Lathe and Planing Mill Products	321912	Cut Stock, Resawing Lumber, and Planing (pt)
	Sawmills	321113	Sawmills (pt)
	Softwood Flooring	321918	Other Millwork (including Flooring) (pt)

	Kiln Drying	321999	All Other Miscellaneous Wood Product Manufacturing (pt)
2426 @	Hardwood Dimension and Flooring Mills		
	Hardwood Flooring	321918	Other Millwork (including Flooring) (pt)
	Wood Stock and Turnings	321999	All Other Miscellaneous Wood Product Manufacturing (pt)
	Wood Furniture Frames	337215	Showcase, Partition, Shelving, and Locker Manufacturing (pt)
	Other Hardwood Dimension Except Flooring	321912	Cut Stock, Resawing Lumber, and Planing (pt)
2429@	Special Product Sawmills, NEC		
	Sawmills	321113	Sawmills (pt)
	Stave Manufacturing from Purchased Lumber	321912	Cut Stock, Resawing Lumber, and Planing (pt)
	Excelsior and Cooperage Headings	321999	All Other Miscellaneous Wood Product Manufacturing (pt)
2431	Millwork		
	Wood Windows and Doors	321911	Wood Window and Door Manufacturing
	Except Wood Window and Doors	321918	Other Millwork (including Flooring) (pt)
2434	Wood Kitchen Cabinets	33711	Wood Kitchen Cabinet and Counter Top Manufacturing (pt)
2435	Hardwood Veneer and Plywood	321211	Hardwood Veneer and Plywood Manufacturing
2436	Softwood Veneer and Plywood	321212	Softwood Veneer and Plywood Manufacturing
2439@	Structural Wood Members, NEC		
	Lumber Member Manufacturing from Purchased Lumber	321912	Cut Stock, Resawing Lumber, and Planing (pt)
	Trusses	321214	Truss Manufacturing
	Except Trusses and Lumber Member Manufacturing from Purchased Lumber	321213	Engineered Wood Member (except Truss) Manufacturing
2441	Nailed and Lock Corner Wood Boxes and Shook	32192	Wood Container and Pallet Manufacturing (pt)

1987 SIC Code	1987 SIC Description	1997 NAICS Code	1997 NAICS United States Description
2448	Wood Pallets and Skids	32192	Wood Container and Pallet Manufacturing (pt)
2449	Wood Containers, NEC	32192	Wood Container and Pallet Manufacturing (pt)
2451	Mobile Homes	321991	Manufactured Home (Mobile Home) Manufacturing
2452	Prefabricated Wood Buildings and Components	321992	Prefabricated Wood Building Manufacturing
2491	Wood Preserving	321114	Wood Preservation
2493	Reconstituted Wood Products	321219	Reconstituted Wood Product Manufacturing
2499	Wood Products, NEC		
	Mirror and Picture Frames	339999	All Other Miscellaneous Manufacturing (pt)
	Wood Tubs and Vats, Jewelry and Cigar Boxes	32192	Wood Container and Pallet Manufacturing (pt)
	Other Wood Products	321999	All Other Miscellaneous Wood Product Manufacturing (pt)
2511	Wood Household Furniture, Except Upholstered	337122	Wood Household Furniture (except Upholstered) Manufacturing (pt)
2512	Wood Household Furniture, Upholstered	337121	Upholstered Household Furniture Manufacturing (pt)
2514	Metal Household Furniture	337124	Metal Household Furniture Manufacturing
2515	Mattresses, Foundations, and Convertible Beds		
	Mattresses and Foundations	33791	Mattress Manufacturing
	Convertible Sofas	337121	Upholstered Household Furniture Manufacturing (pt)
2517	Wood Television, Radio, Phonograph and Sewing Machine Cabinets	337129	Wood Television, Radio, and Sewing Machine Cabinet Manufacturing
2519	Household Furniture, NEC	337125	Household Furniture (except Wood and Metal) Manufacturing
2521	Wood Office Furniture	337211	Wood Office Furniture Manufacturing
2522	Office Furniture, Except Wood	337214	Nonwood Office Furniture Manufacturing
2531@	Public Building and Related Furniture		
	Seats for Motor Vehicles	33636	Motor Vehicle Fabric Accessories and Seat Manufacturing (pt)

	Furniture Made for Public Buildings	337127	Institutional Furniture Manufacturing (pt)
	Blackboards	339942	Lead Pencil and Art Good Manufacturing (pt)
2541	Wood Office and Store Fixtures, Partitions, Shelving, and Lockers		
	Counter Tops	33711	Wood Kitchen Cabinet and Counter Top Manufacturing (pt)
	Custom Architectural Woodwork, Millwork and Fixtures	337212	Custom Architectural Woodwork, and Millwork Manufacturing
	Except Counter Tops, Custom Architectural Woodwork, Millwork, and Fixtures	337215	Showcase, Partition, Shelving, and Locker Manufacturing (pt)
2542	Office and Store Fixtures, Partitions Shelving, and Lockers, Except Wood	337215	Showcase, Partition, Shelving, and Locker Manufacturing (pt)
2591	Drapery Hardware and Window Blinds and Shades	33792	Blind and Shade Manufacturing
2599@	Furniture and Fixtures, NEC		
	Hospital Beds	339113	Surgical Appliance and Supplies Manufacturing (pt)
	Except Hospital Beds	337127	Institutional Furniture Manufacturing (pt)
2611	Pulp Mills		
	Pulp Producing Mills Only	32211	Pulp Mills
	Pulp Mills Producing Paper	322121	Paper (except Newsprint) Mills (pt)
	Pulp Mills Producing Paperboard	32213	Paperboard Mills (pt)
2621@	Paper Mills		
	Except Newsprint Mills	322121	Paper (except Newsprint) Mills (pt)
	Newsprint Mills	322122	Newsprint Mills
2631	Paperboard Mills	32213	Paperboard Mills (pt)
2652	Setup Paperboard Boxes	322213	Setup Paperboard Box Manufacturing

1987 SIC Code	1987 SIC Description	1997 NAICS Code	1997 NAICS United States Description
2653	Corrugated and Solid Fiber Boxes	322211	Corrugated and Solid Fiber Box Manufacturing
2655	Fiber Cans, Tubes, Drums, and Similar Products	322214	Fiber Can, Tube, Drum, and Similar Products Manufacturing
2656	Sanitary Food Containers, Except Folding	322215	Non-Folding Sanitary Food Container Manufacturing (pt)
2657	Folding Paperboard Boxes, Including Sanitary	322212	Folding Paperboard Box Manufacturing
2671	Packaging Paper and Plastics Film, Coated and Laminated		
	Single-Web Paper, Paper Multiweb Laminated Rolls and Sheets for Packaging Uses	322221	Coated and Laminated Packaging Paper and Plastics Film Manufacturing
	Plastics Packaging Film and Sheet	326112	Unsupported Plastics Packaging Film and Sheet Manufacturing
2672	Coated and Laminated Paper, NEC	322222	Coated and Laminated Paper Manufacturing (pt)
2673	Plastics, Foil, and Coated Paper Bags		
	Coated or Multiweb Laminated Bags	322223	Plastics, Foil, and Coated Paper Bag Manufacturing
	Plastics Bags	326111	Unsupported Plastics Bag Manufacturing
2674	Uncoated Paper and Multiwall Bags	322224	Uncoated Paper and Multiwall Bag Manufacturing
2675@	Die-Cut Paper and Paperboard and Cardboard		
	File Folders, Tabulating Cards, and Other Paper and Paperboard Office Supplies	322231	Die-Cut Paper and Paperboard Office Supplies Manufacturing (pt)
	Pasted, Lined, Laminated, or Surface-Coated Paperboard	322292	Surface-Coated Paperboard Manufacturing
	Die-Cut Paper and Paperboard Products, Except Office Supplies	322298	All Other Converted Paper Product Manufacturing (pt)
2676	Sanitary Paper Products	322291	Sanitary Paper Product Manufacturing
2677	Envelopes	322232	Envelope Manufacturing
2678	Stationery, Tablets, and Related Products	322233	Stationery, Tablet, and Related Product Manufacturing
2679@	Converted Paper and Paperboard Products, NEC		

	Egg Cartons and Other Containers from Purchased Paper	322215	Non-Folding Sanitary Food Container Manufacturing (pt)
	Wallpaper and Gift Wrap Paper	322222	Coated and Laminated Paper Manufacturing (pt)
	Paper Supplies for Business Machines and Other Paper Office Supplies	322231	Die-Cut Paper and Paperboard Office Supplies Manufacturing (pt)
	Other Converted Paper and Paperboard Products such as Paper Filters, Crepe Paper, and Laminated and Tiled Wallboard	322298	All Other Converted Paper Product Manufacturing (pt)
2711	Newspapers: Publishing, or Publishing and Printing	51111	Newspaper Publishers
2721	Periodicals: Publishing, or Publishing and Printing	51112	Periodical Publishers
2731	Books: Publishing, or Publishing and Printing		
	Music Book Publishing	51223	Music Publishers (pt)
	All Other Book Publishers	51113	Book Publishers
2732	Book Printing	323117	Book Printing
2741	Miscellaneous Publishing		
	Database Publishing	51114	Database and Directory Publishers
	Sheet Music Publishers	51223	Music Publishers (pt)
	Miscellaneous Publishing, Except Database	511199	All Other Publishers
2752@	Commercial Printing, Lithographic		
	Quick Printing	323114	Quick Printing (pt)
	Except Quick Printing	323110	Commercial Lithographic Printing (pt)
2754	Commercial Printing, Gravure	323111	Commercial Gravure Printing (pt)
2759@	Commercial Printing, NEC		
	Screen Printing	323113	Commercial Screen Printing (pt)

1987 SIC Code	1987 SIC Description	1997 NAICS Code	1997 NAICS United States Description
	Flexographic Printing	323112	Commercial Flexographic Printing (pt)
	Quick Printing	323114	Quick Printing (pt)
	Digital Printing,, except Quick Printing	323115	Digital Printing
	Other Commercial Printing	323119	Other Commercial Printing (pt)
2761	Manifold Business Forms	323116	Manifold Business Form Printing
2771@	Greeting Cards		
	Lithographic Printing of Greeting Cards	323110	Commercial Lithographic Printing (pt)
	Gravure Printing of Greeting Cards	323111	Commercial Gravure Printing (pt)
	Flexographic Printing of Greeting Cards	323112	Commercial Flexographic Printing (pt)
	Screen Printing of Greeting Cards	323113	Commercial Screen Printing (pt)
	Other Printing of Greeting Cards	323119	Other Commercial Printing (pt)
	Publishing Greeting Cards	511191	Greeting Card Publishers
2782@	Blankbooks, Loose-leaf Binders and Devices		
	Lithographic Printing of Checkbooks	323110	Commercial Lithographic Printing (pt)
	Gravure Printing of Checkbooks	323111	Commercial Gravure Printing (pt)
	Flexographic Printing of Checkbooks	323112	Commercial Flexographic Printing (pt)
	Screen Printing of Checkbooks	323113	Commercial Screen Printing (pt)
	Other Printing of Checkbooks	323119	Other Commercial Printing (pt)
	Blankbooks, Loose-leaf Binders and Devices	323118	Blankbook, Loose-leaf Binder and Device Manufacturing
2789	Bookbinding and Related Work	323121	Tradebinding and Related Work
2791@	Typesetting	323122	Prepress Services (pt)
2796@	Platemaking and Related Services	323122	Prepress Services (pt)

2812	Alkalies and Chlorine	325181	Alkalies and Chlorine Manufacturing
2813	Industrial Gases	32512	Industrial Gas Manufacturing (pt)
2816	Inorganic Pigments		
	Inorganic Pigments, Except Bone and Lamp Black	325131	Inorganic Dye and Pigment Manufacturing (pt)
	Bone and Lamp Black	325182	Carbon Black Manufacturing (pt)
2819@	Industrial Inorganic Chemicals, NEC		
	Activated Carbon and Charcoal	325998	All Other Miscellaneous Chemical Product Manufacturing (pt)
	Alumina	331311	Alumina Refining
	Inorganic Dyes	325131	Inorganic Dye and Pigment Manufacturing (pt)
	Other	325188	All Other Basic Inorganic Chemical Manufacturing (pt)
2821	Plastics Material Synthetic Resins, and Nonvulcanizable Elastomers	325211	Plastics Material and Resin Manufacturing
2822	Synthetic Rubber	325212	Synthetic Rubber Manufacturing
2823	Cellulosic Manmade Fibers	325221	Cellulosic Organic Fiber Manufacturing
2824	Manmade Organic Fibers, Except Cellulosic	325222	Noncellulosic Organic Fiber Manufacturing
2833	Medicinal Chemicals and Botanical Products	325411	Medicinal and Botanical Manufacturing
2834	Pharmaceutical Preparations	325412	Pharmaceutical Preparation Manufacturing (pt)
2835@	In Vitro and In Vivo Diagnostic Substances		
	Diagnostic Substances, Except In-Vitro Diagnostic	325412	Pharmaceutical Preparation Manufacturing (pt)
	In-Vitro Diagnostic Substances	325413	In-Vitro Diagnostic Substance Manufacturing
2836	Biological Products, Except Diagnostic Substances	325414	Biological Product (except Diagnostic) Manufacturing
2841	Soaps and Other Detergents, Except Speciality Cleaners	325611	Soap and Other Detergent Manufacturing (pt)
2842	Speciality Cleaning, Polishing, and Sanitary Preparations	325612	Polish and Other Sanitation Good Manufacturing

1987 SIC Code	1987 SIC Description	1997 NAICS Code	1997 NAICS United States Description
2843	Surface Active Agents, Finishing Agents, Sulfonated Oils, and Assistants	325613	Surface Active Agent Manufacturing
2844	Perfumes, Cosmetics, and Other Toilet Preparations		
	Toilet Preparations, Except Toothpaste	32562	Toilet Preparation Manufacturing
	Toothpaste	325611	Soap and Other Detergent Manufacturing (pt)
2851	Paints, Varnishes, Lacquers, Enamels, and Allied Products	32551	Paint and Coating Manufacturing (pt)
2861	Gum and Wood Chemicals	325191	Gum and Wood Chemical Manufacturing
2865@	Cyclic Organic Crudes and Intermediates, and Organic Dyes and Pigments		
	Aromatics	32511	Petrochemical Manufacturing (pt)
	Organic Dyes and Pigments	325132	Organic Dye and Pigment Manufacturing
	Other	325192	Cyclic Crude and Intermediate Manufacturing
2869@	Industrial Organic Chemicals, NEC		
	Aliphatics	32511	Petrochemical Manufacturing (pt)
	Carbon Bisulfide	325188	All Other Inorganic Chemical Manufacturing (pt)
	Ethyl Alcohol	325193	Ethyl Alcohol Manufacturing
	Fluorocarbon Gases	32512	Industrial Gas Manufacturing (pt)
	Other	325199	All Other Basic Organic Chemical Manufacturing (pt)
2873	Nitrogenous Fertilizers	325311	Nitrogenous Fertilizer Manufacturing
2874	Phosphatic Fertilizers	325312	Phosphatic Fertilizer Manufacturing
2875	Fertilizers, Mixing Only	325314	Fertilizer (Mixing Only) Manufacturing
2879	Pesticides and Agricultural Chemicals, NEC	32532	Pesticide and Other Agricultural Chemical Manufacturing
2891	Adhesives and Sealants	32552	Adhesive Manufacturing

2892	Explosives	32592	Explosives Manufacturing
2893	Printing Ink	32591	Printing Ink Manufacturing
2895	Carbon Black	325182	Carbon Black Manufacturing (pt)
2899	Chemicals and Chemical Preparations, NEC		
	Frit	32551	Paint and Coating Manufacturing (pt)
	Table Salt	311942	Spice and Extract Manufacturing (pt)
	Fatty Acids	325199	All Other Basic Organic Chemical Manufacturing (pt)
	Other	325998	All Other Miscellaneous Chemical Product Manufacturing (pt)
2911	Petroleum Refining	32411	Petroleum Refineries
2951	Asphalt Paving Mixtures and Blocks	324121	Asphalt Paving Mixture and Block Manufacturing
2952	Asphalt Felts and Coatings	324122	Asphalt Shingle and Coating Materials Manufacturing
2992	Lubricating Oils and Greases	324191	Petroleum Lubricating Oil and Grease Manufacturing
2999	Products of Petroleum and Coal, NEC	324199	All Other Petroleum and Coal Products Manufacturing (pt)
3011	Tires and Inner Tubes	326211	Tire Manufacturing (except Retreading)
3021	Rubber and Plastics Footwear	316211	Rubber and Plastics Footwear Manufacturing
3052	Rubber and Plastics Hose and Belting	32622	Rubber and Plastics Hoses and Belting Manufacturing
3053	Gaskets, Packing, and Sealing Devices	339991	Gasket, Packing, and Sealing Device Manufacturing
3061	Molded, Extruded, and Lathe-Cut Mechanical Rubber Products	326291	Rubber Product Manufacturing for Mechanical Use
3069	Fabricated Rubber Products, NEC		
	Rubberized Fabric	31332	Fabric Coating Mills (pt)
	Rubber Resilient Floor Covering	326192	Resilient Floor Covering Manufacturing (pt)
	Other	326299	All Other Rubber Product Manufacturing

1987 SIC Code	1987 SIC Description	1997 NAICS Code	1997 NAICS United States Description
3081	Unsupported Plastics Film and Sheet	326113	Unsupported Plastics Film and Sheet (except Packaging) Manufacturing
3082	Unsupported Plastics Profile Shapes	326121	Unsupported Plastics Profile Shape Manufacturing (pt)
3083	Laminated Plastics Plate, Sheet, and Profile Shapes	32613	Laminated Plastics Plate, Sheet, and Shape Manufacturing
3084@	Plastic Pipe	326122	Plastic Pipe and Pipe Fitting Manufacturing (pt)
3085	Plastics Bottles	32616	Plastics Bottle Manufacturing
3086	Plastics Foam Products		
	Urethane Foam Products	32615	Urethane and Other Foam Product (except Polystyrene) Manufacturing
	Polystyrene Foam Products	32614	Polystyrene Foam Product Manufacturing
3087	Custom Compounding of Purchased Plastics Resins	325991	Custom Compounding of Purchased Resin
3088	Plastics Plumbing Fixtures	326191	Plastics Plumbing Fixtures Manufacturing
3089	Plastics Products, NEC		
	Pipe Fittings	326122	Plastics Pipe and Pipe Fitting Manufacturing (pt)
	Plastics Sausage Casings	326121	Unsupported Plastics Profile Shape Manufacturing (pt)
	Other	326199	All Other Plastics Product Manufacturing (pt)
3111	Leather Tanning and Finishing	31611	Leather and Hide Tanning and Finishing (pt)
3131@	Boot and Shoe Cut Stock and Findings		
	Wood Heels	321999	All Other Miscellaneous Wood Product Manufacturing (pt)
	Metal Buckles	339993	Fastener, Button, Needle, and Pin Manufacturing (pt)
	Except Wood Heels and Metal Buckles	316999	All Other Leather Good Manufacturing (pt)
3142	House Slippers	316212	House Slipper Manufacturing
3143	Men's Footwear, Except Athletic	316213	Men's Footwear (except Athletic) Manufacturing
3144	Women's Footwear, Except Athletic	316214	Women's Footwear (except Athletic) Manufacturing

3149	Footwear, Except Rubber, NEC	316219	Other Footwear Manufacturing
3151	Leather Gloves and Mittens	315992	Glove and Mitten Manufacturing (pt)
3161	Luggage	316991	Luggage Manufacturing
3171	Women's Handbags and Purses	316992	Women's Handbag and Purse Manufacturing
3172	Personal Leather Goods, Except Women's Handbags and Purses	316993	Personal Leather Good (except Women's Handbag and Purse) Manufacturing
3199@	Leather Goods, NEC	316999	All Other Leather Good Manufacturing (pt)
3211	Flat Glass	327211	Flat Glass Manufacturing
3221	Glass Containers	327213	Glass Container Manufacturing
3229	Pressed and Blown Glass and Glassware, NEC	327212	Other Pressed and Blown Glass and Glassware Manufacturing
3231	Glass Products, Made of Purchased Glass	327215	Glass Product Manufacturing Made of Purchased Glass
3241	Cement, Hydraulic	32731	Cement Manufacturing
3251	Brick and Structural Clay Tile	327121	Brick and Structural Clay Tile Manufacturing
3253	Ceramic Wall and Floor Tile	327122	Ceramic Wall and Floor Tile Manufacturing
3255	Clay Refractories	327124	Clay Refractory Manufacturing
3259	Structural Clay Products, NEC	327123	Other Structural Clay Product Manufacturing
3261	Vitreous China Plumbing Fixtures and China and Earthenware Fittings and Bathroom Accessories	327111	Vitreous China Plumbing Fixture and China and Earthenware Fittings and Bathroom Accessories Manufacturing
3262	Vitreous China Table and Kitchen Articles	327112	Vitreous China, Fine Earthenware and Other Pottery Product Manufacturing (pt)
3263	Fine Earthenware (Whiteware) Table and Kitchen Articles	327112	Vitreous China, Fine Earthenware and Other Pottery Product Manufacturing (pt)
3264	Porcelain Electrical Supplies	327113	Porcelain Electrical Supply Manufacturing
3269	Pottery Products, NEC	327112	Vitreous China, Fine Earthenware, and Other Pottery Product Manufacturing (pt)

1987 SIC Code	1987 SIC Description	1997 NAICS Code	1997 NAICS United States Description
3271	Concrete Block and Brick	327331	Concrete Block and Brick Manufacturing
3272@	Concrete Products, Except Block and Brick		
	Dry Mixture Concrete	327999	All Other Miscellaneous Nonmetallic Mineral Product Manufacturing (pt)
	Concrete Pipes	327332	Concrete Pipe Manufacturing
	Other Concrete Products	32739	Other Concrete Product Manufacturing
3273	Ready-Mixed Concrete	32732	Ready-Mix Concrete Manufacturing
3274	Lime	32741	Lime Manufacturing
3275	Gypsum Products	32742	Gypsum and Gypsum Product Manufacturing (pt)
3281	Cut Stone and Stone Products	327991	Cut Stone and Stone Product Manufacturing
3291	Abrasive Products		
	Steel Wool With or Without Soap	332999	All Other Miscellaneous Fabricated Metal Product Manufacturing (pt)
	Abrasive Products (Except Steel Wool With or Without Soap)	32791	Abrasive Product Manufacturing
3292	Asbestos Products		
	Asbestos Brake Linings and Pads	33634	Motor Vehicle Brake System Manufacturing (pt)
	Other Asbestos Products	327999	All Other Miscellaneous Nonmetallic Mineral Product Manufacturing (pt)
3295	Minerals and Earths, Ground or Otherwise Treated	327992	Ground or Treated Mineral and Earth Manufacturing
3296	Mineral Wool	327993	Mineral Wool Manufacturing
3297	Nonclay Refractories	327125	Nonclay Refractory Manufacturing
3299@	Nonmetallic Mineral Products, NEC		
	Moldings, Ornamental and Architectural Plaster Work	32742	Gypsum and Gypsum Product Manufacturing (pt)

	Other Nonmetallic Mineral Products	327999	All Other Miscellaneous Nonmetallic Mineral Product Manufacturing (pt)
3312@	Steel Works, Blast Furnaces (Including Coke Ovens), and Rolling Mills		
	Coke Ovens, Not Integrated With Steel Mills	324199	All Other Petroleum and Coal Products Manufacturing (pt)
	Except Coke Ovens Not Integrated with Steel Mills	331111	Iron and Steel Mills (pt)
3313@	Electrometallurgical Products, Except Steel		
	Ferroalloys	331112	Electrometallurgical Ferroalloy Product Manufacturing
	Nonferrous Alloys	331492	Secondary Smelting, Refining, and Alloying of Nonferrous Metals (except Copper and Aluminum) (pt)
3315@	Steel Wiredrawing and Steel Nails and Spikes		
	Steel Wire Drawing	331222	Steel Wire Drawing
	Nails, Spikes, Paper Clips, and Wire, Not Made in Wire Drawing Plants	332618	Other Fabricated Wire Product Manufacturing (pt)
3316	Cold-Rolled Steel Sheet, Strip, and Bars	331221	Cold-Rolled Steel Shape Manufacturing
3317	Steel Pipe and Tubes	33121	Iron and Steel Pipes and Tubes Manufacturing from Purchased Steel
3321	Gray and Ductile Iron Foundries	331511	Iron Foundries (pt)
3322	Malleable Iron Foundries	331511	Iron Foundries (pt)
3324	Steel Investment Foundries	331512	Steel Investment Foundries
3325	Steel Foundries, NEC	331513	Steel Foundries (except Investment)
3331	Primary Smelting and Refining of Copper	331411	Primary Smelting and Refining of Copper
3334	Primary Production of Aluminum	331312	Primary Aluminum Production
3339	Primary Smelting and Refining of Nonferrous Metals, Except Copper and Aluminum	331419	Primary Smelting and Refining of Nonferrous Metals (except Copper and Aluminum)
3341@	Secondary Smelting and Refining of Nonferrous Metals		

1987 SIC Code	1987 SIC Description	1997 NAICS Code	1997 NAICS United States Description
	Aluminum	331314	Secondary Smelting and Alloying of Aluminum (pt)
	Copper	331423	Secondary Smelting, Refining, and Alloying of Copper (pt)
	Except Aluminum and Copper	331492	Secondary Smelting, Refining, and Alloying of Nonferrous Metals (except Copper and Aluminum) (pt)
3351	Rolling, Drawing, and Extruding of Copper	331421	Copper Rolling, Drawing, and Extruding
3353	Aluminum Sheet, Plate, and Foil	331315	Aluminum Sheet, Plate, and Foil Manufacturing
3354	Aluminum Extruded Products	331316	Aluminum Extruded Product Manufacturing
3355	Aluminum Rolling and Drawing, NEC	331319	Other Aluminum Rolling and Drawing, (pt)
3356	Rolling, Drawing, and Extruding of Nonferrous Metals, Except Copper and Aluminum	331491	Nonferrous Metal (except Copper and Aluminum) Rolling. Drawing, and Extruding (pt)
3357@	Drawing and Insulating of Nonferrous Wire		
	Aluminum Wire Drawing	331319	Other Aluminum Rolling and Drawing (pt)
	Copper Wire Drawing	331422	Copper Wire (except Mechanical) Drawing
	Wire Drawing Except Copper or Aluminum	331491	Nonferrous Metal (except Copper and Aluminum) Rolling, Drawing, and Extruding (pt)
	Fiber Optic Cable - Insulating Only	335921	Fiber Optic Cable Manufacturing
	All Other	335929	Other Communication and Energy Wire Manufacturing
3363	Aluminum Die-Castings	331521	Aluminum Die-Castings
3364	Nonferrous Die-Castings, Except Aluminum	331522	Nonferrous (except Aluminum) Die-Castings
3365	Aluminum Foundries	331524	Aluminum Foundries
3366	Copper Foundries	331525	Copper Foundries
3369	Nonferrous Foundries, Except Aluminum and Copper	331528	Other Nonferrous Foundries
3398	Metal Heat Treating	332811	Metal Heat Treating
3399@	Primary Metal Products, NEC		

	Ferrous Powder, Paste, Flakes, etc.	331111	Iron and Steel Mills (pt)
	Aluminum Powder, Paste, Flakes, etc.	331314	Secondary Smelting and Alloying of Aluminum (pt)
	Copper Powder, Flakes, Paste, etc.	331423	Secondary Smelting, Refining and Alloying of Copper (pt)
	Other Nonferrous Powder, Paste, Flakes, etc.	331492	Secondary Smelting, Refining, and Alloying of Nonferrous Metals (except Copper and Aluminum) (pt)
	Nonferrous Nails, Brads, Staples, etc.	332618	Other Fabricated Wire Product Manufacturing (pt)
	Laminated Steel	332813	Electroplating, Plating, Polishing, Anodizing, and Coloring (pt)
3411	Metal Cans	332431	Metal Can Manufacturing
3412	Metal Shipping Barrels, Drums, Kegs and Pails	332439	Other Metal Container Manufacturing (pt)
3421	Cutlery	332211	Cutlery and Flatware (except Precious) Manufacturing (pt)
3423	Hand and Edge Tools, Except Machine Tools and Handsaws	332212	Hand and Edge Tool Manufacturing (pt)
3425	Saw Blades and Handsaws	332213	Saw Blade and Handsaw Manufacturing
3429@	Hardware, NEC		
	Vacuum and Insulated Bottles, Jugs, and Chests	332439	Other Metal Container Manufacturing (pt)
	Hose Nozzles	332919	Other Metal Valve and Pipe Fitting Manufacturing (pt)
	Hardware, Except Hose Nozzles, and Vacuum and Insulated Bottles, Jugs, and Chests	33251	Hardware Manufacturing (pt)
3431	Enameled Iron and Metal Sanitary Ware	332998	Enameled Iron and Metal Sanitary Ware Manufacturing
3432	Plumbing Fixture Fittings and Trim		
	Plumbing Fixtures Fittings and Trim, Except Metal Shower Rods	332913	Plumbing Fixture Fitting and Trim Manufacturing
	Metal Shower Rods	332999	All Other Miscellaneous Fabricated Metal Product Manufacturing (pt)
3433	Heating Equipment, Except Electric and Warm Air Furnaces	333414	Heating Equipment Manufacturing, (except Electric and Warm Air Furnaces) (pt)

1987 SIC Code	1987 SIC Description	1997 NAICS Code	1997 NAICS United States Description
3441	Fabricated Structural Metal	332312	Fabricated Structural Metal Manufacturing (pt)
3442	Metal Doors, Sash, Frames, Molding, and Trim Manufacturing	332321	Metal Window and Door Manufacturing (pt)
3443@	Fabricated Plate Work (Boiler Shops)		
	Fabricated Plate Work and Metal Weldments	332313	Plate Work Manufacturing
	Power Boilers and Heat Exchanges	33241	Power Boiler and Heat Exchanger Manufacturing
	Heavy Gauge Tanks	33242	Metal Tank (Heavy Gauge) Manufacturing
	Metal Cooling Towers	333415	Air-Conditioning and Warm Air Heating Equipment and Commercial and Industrial Refrigeration Equipment Manufacturing (pt)
3444	Sheet Metal Work		
	Ducts, Flumes, Flooring. Siding, Dampers, etc.	332322	Sheet Metal Work Manufacturing
	Metal Bins and Vats	332439	Other Metal Container Manufacturing (pt)
3446	Architectural and Ornamental Metal Work	332323	Ornamental and Architectural Metal Work Manufacturing (pt)
3448	Prefabricated Metal Buildings and Components	332311	Prefabricated Metal Building and Component Manufacturing
3449@	Miscellaneous Structural Metal Work		
	Custom Roll Forming	332114	Custom Roll Forming
	Fabricated Bar Joists and Concrete Reinforcing Bars	332312	Fabricated Structural Metal Manufacturing (pt)
	Curtain Wall	332321	Metal Window and Door Manufacturing (pt)
	Metal Plaster Bases	332323	Ornamental and Architectural Metal Work Manufacturing (pt)
3451	Screw Machine Products	332721	Precision Turned Product Manufacturing
3452	Bolts, Nuts, Screws, Rivets, and Washers	332722	Bolt, Nut, Screw, Rivet, and Washer Manufacturing
3462	Iron and Steel Forgings	332111	Iron and Steel Forging
3463	Nonferrous Forgings	332112	Nonferrous Forging

3465	Automotive Stamping	33637	Motor Vehicle Metal Stamping
3466	Crowns and Closures	332115	Crown and Closure Manufacturing
3469	Metal Stamping, NEC		
	Stamping Coins	339911	Jewelry (except Costume) Manufacturing, (pt)
	Metal Stamping, NEC (Except Kitchen Utensils, Pots and Pans for Cooking and Coins)	332116	Metal Stamping
	Kitchen Utensils and Pots and Pans for Cooking	332214	Kitchen Utensil, Pot and Pan Manufacturing
3471	Electroplating, Plating, Polishing, Anodizing, and Coloring	332813	Electroplating, Plating, Polishing, Anodizing, and Coloring (pt)
3479	Coating, Engraving, and Allied Services, NEC		
	Jewelry Engraving and Etching, Costume Jewelry	339914	Costume Jewelry and Novelty Manufacturing (pt)
	Jewelry Engraving and Etching, Precious Metal	339911	Jewelry (except Costume) Manufacturing (pt)
	Silverware and Flatware Engraving and Etching	339912	Silverware and Plated Ware Manufacturing (pt)
	Other Coating, Engraving and Allied Services	332812	Metal Coating, Engraving (except Jewelry and Silverware), and Allied Services to Manufacturers
3482	Small Arms Ammunition	332992	Small Arms Ammunition Manufacturing
3483	Ammunition, Except for Small Arms	332993	Ammunition (except Small Arms) Manufacturing
3484	Small Arms	332994	Small Arms Manufacturing
3489	Ordnance and Accessories, NEC	332995	Other Ordnance and Accessories Manufacturing
3491	Industrial Valves	332911	Industrial Valve Manufacturing
3492	Fluid Power Valves and Hose Fittings	332912	Fluid Power Valve and Hose Fitting Manufacturing (pt)
3493	Steel Springs, Except Wire	332611	Steel Spring (except Wire) Manufacturing
3494	Valves and Pipe Fittings, NEC		
	Except Metal Pipe Hangers and Supports	332919	Other Metal Valve and Pipe Fitting Manufacturing (pt)

1987 SIC Code	1987 SIC Description	1997 NAICS Code	1997 NAICS United States Description
	Metal Pipe Hangers and Supports	332999	All Other Miscellaneous Fabricated Metal Product Manufacturing (pt)
3495	Wire Springs		
	Wire Springs (Except Watch and Clock Springs)	332612	Wire Spring Manufacturing
	Watch and Clock Springs	334518	Watch, Clock, and Part Manufacturing (pt)
3496	Miscellaneous Fabricated Wire Products	332618	Other Fabricated Wire Product Manufacturing (pt)
3497	Metal Foil and Leaf		
	Laminated Aluminum Foil Rolls/Sheets for Flexible Packaging Uses	322225	Laminated Aluminum Foil Manufacturing for Flexible Packaging Uses
	Foil and Foil Containers	332999	All Other Miscellaneous Fabricated Metal Product Manufacturing (pt)
3498	Fabricated Pipe and Pipe Fittings	332996	Fabricated Pipe and Pipe Fitting Manufacturing
3499	Fabricated Metal Products, NEC		
	Metal Furniture Frames	337215	Showcase, Partition, Shelving, and Locker Manufacturing (pt)
	Powder Metallurgy	332117	Powder Metallurgy Part Manufacturing
	Metal Boxes	332439	Other Metal Container Manufacturing (pt)
	Safe and Vault Locks	33251	Hardware Manufacturing (pt)
	Metal Aerosol Valves	332919	Other Metal Valve and Pipe Fitting Manufacturing (pt)
	Trophies of Nonprecious Metals	339914	Costume Jewelry and Novelty Manufacturing (pt)
	Other Metal Products	332999	All Other Miscellaneous Fabricated Metal Product Manufacturing (pt)
3511	Steam, Gas, and Hydraulic Turbines, and Turbine Generator Set Units	333611	Turbine and Turbine Generator Set Unit Manufacturing
3519	Internal Combustion Engines, NEC		
	Stationary Engine Radiators	336399	All Other Motor Vehicle Parts Manufacturing (pt)
	Except Stationary Engine Radiators	333618	Other Engine Equipment Manufacturing (pt)

3523@	Farm Machinery and Equipment		
	Farm Machinery and Equipment (Except Corrals, Stalls, Holding Gates, Hand Hair Clippers for Animals, Farm Conveyors, and Elevators)	333111	Farm Machinery and Equipment Manufacturing
	Corrals, Stalls, Holding Gates	332323	Ornamental and Architectural Metal Work Manufacturing (pt)
	Hand Hair Clippers for Animals	332212	Hand and Edge Tool Manufacturing(pt)
	Farm Conveyors and Farm Elevators, Stackers, and Bale Throwers	333922	Conveyor and Conveying Equipment Manufacturing (pt)
3524	Lawn and Garden Tractors and Home Lawn and Garden Equipment		
	Lawn and Garden Tractors and Home Lawn and Garden Equipment (Except Nonpowered Lawnmowers)	333112	Lawn and Garden Tractor and Home Lawn and Garden Equipment Manufacturing
	Nonpowered Lawnmowers	332212	Hand and Edge Tool Manufacturing (pt)
3531@	Construction Machinery and Equipment		
	Railway Track Maintenance Equipment	33651	Railroad Rolling Stock Manufacturing (pt)
	Winches, Aerial Work Platforms, and Automotive Wrecker Hoists	333923	Overhead Traveling Crane, Hoist, and Monorail System Manufacturing (pt)
	Other Construction Machinery and Equipment	33312	Construction Machinery Manufacturing
3532	Mining Machinery and Equipment, Except Oil and Gas Field Machinery and Equipment	333131	Mining Machinery and Equipment Manufacturing
3533	Oil and Gas Field Machinery and Equipment	333132	Oil and Gas Field Machinery and Equipment Manufacturing
3534	Elevators and Moving Stairways	333921	Elevator and Moving Stairway Manufacturing
3535	Conveyors and Conveying Equipment	333922	Conveyor and Conveying Equipment Manufacturing (pt)
3536	Overhead Traveling Cranes, Hoists and Monorail Systems	333923	Overhead Traveling Crane, Hoist and Monorail System Manufacturing (pt)

1987 SIC Code	1987 SIC Description	1997 NAICS Code	1997 NAICS United States Description
3537	Industrial Trucks, Tractors, Trailers, and Stackers		
	Industrial Trucks, Tractors, Trailers, and Stackers (Except Metal Pallets and Air Cargo Containers)	333924	Industrial Truck, Tractor, Trailer, and Stacker Machinery Manufacturing
	Metal Pallets	332999	All Other Miscellaneous Fabricated Metal Product Manufacturing (pt)
	Metal Air Cargo Containers	332439	Other Metal Container Manufacturing (pt)
3541	Machine Tools, Metal Cutting Type	333512	Machine Tool (Metal Cutting Types) Manufacturing
3542	Machine Tools, Metal Forming Type	333513	Machine Tool (Metal Forming Types) Manufacturing
3543	Industrial Patterns	332997	Industrial Pattern Manufacturing
3544	Special Dies and Tools, Die Sets, Jigs and Fixtures, and Industrial Molds		
	Except Industrial Molds	333514	Special Die and Tool, Die Set, Jig, and Fixture Manufacturing
	Industrial Molds	333511	Industrial Mold Manufacturing
3545@	Cutting Tools, Machine Tool Accessories, and Machinists' Precision Measuring Devices		
	Cutting Tools, Machine Tool Accessories, and Machinists' Precision Measuring Devices (Except Precision Measuring Devices)	333515	Cutting Tool and Machine Tool Accessory Manufacturing
	Precision Measuring Devices	332212	Hand and Edge Tool Manufacturing (pt)
3546	Power-Driven Handtools	333991	Power-Driven Hand Tool Manufacturing
3547	Rolling Mill Machinery and Equipment	333516	Rolling Mill Machinery and Equipment Manufacturing
3548@	Electric and Gas Welding and Soldering Equipment		
	Except Transformers for Arc-Welding	333992	Welding and Soldering Equipment Manufacturing
	Transformers for Arc-Welding	335311	Power, Distribution, and Specialty Transformer Manufacturing (pt)
3549	Metalworking Machinery, NEC	333518	Other Metalworking Machinery Manufacturing
3552	Textile Machinery	333292	Textile Machinery Manufacturing

3553	Woodworking Machinery	33321	Sawmill and Woodworking Machinery Manufacturing
3554	Paper Industries Machinery	333291	Paper Industry Machinery Manufacturing
3555	Printing Trades Machinery and Equipment	333293	Printing Machinery and Equipment Manufacturing
3556	Food Products Machinery	333294	Food Product Machinery Manufacturing
3559@	Special Industry Machinery, NEC		
	Rubber and Plastics Manufacturing Machinery	33322	Rubber and Plastics Industry Machinery Manufacturing
	Automotive Maintenance Equipment	333319	Other Commercial and Service Industry Machinery Manufacturing (pt)
	Semiconductor Machinery Manufacturing	333295	Semiconductor Manufacturing Machinery
	Except Rubber and Plastics Manufacturing Machinery, Semiconductor Manufacturing Machinery and Automotive Maintenance Equipment	333298	All Other Industrial Machinery Manufacturing (pt)
3561	Pumps and Pumping Equipment	333911	Pump and Pumping Equipment Manufacturing (pt)
3562	Ball and Roller Bearings	332991	Ball and Roller Bearing Manufacturing
3563	Air and Gas Compressors	333912	Air and Gas Compressor Manufacturing
3564	Industrial and Commercial Fans and Blowers and Air Purification Equipment		
	Air Purification Equipment	333411	Air Purification Equipment Manufacturing
	Fans and Blowers	333412	Industrial and Commercial Fan and Blower Manufacturing
3565	Packaging Machinery	333993	Packaging Machinery Manufacturing
3566	Speed Changers, Industrial High-Speed Drives, and Gears	333612	Speed Changer, Industrial High-Speed Drive, and Gear Manufacturing
3567	Industrial Process Furnaces and Ovens	333994	Industrial Process Furnace and Oven Manufacturing
3568	Mechanical Power Transmission Equipment, NEC	333613	Mechanical Power Transmission Equipment Manufacturing
3569	General Industrial Machinery and Equipment, NEC	333999	All Other General Purpose Machinery Manufacturing (pt)
3571	Electronic Computers	334111	Electronic Computer Manufacturing

1987 SIC Code	1987 SIC Description	1997 NAICS Code	1997 NAICS United States Description
3572	Computer Storage Devices	334112	Computer Storage Device Manufacturing
3575	Computer Terminals	334113	Computer Terminal Manufacturing
3577	Computer Peripheral Equipment, NEC	334119	Other Computer Peripheral Equipment Manufacturing (pt)
3578@	Calculating and Accounting Machines, Except Electronic Computers		
	Point of Sales Terminals and Fund Transfer Devices	334119	Other Computer Peripheral Equipment Manufacturing (pt)
	Calculating and Accounting Machines, Except Point of Sales Terminals and Fund Transfer Devices	333313	Office Machinery Manufacturing (pt)
3579@	Office Machines, NEC		
	Pencil Sharpeners, Staplers, and Other Office Equipment	339942	Lead Pencil and Art Good Manufacturing (pt)
	Time Clocks and Other Time Recording Devices	334518	Watch, Clock, and Part Manufacturing (pt)
	Other Office Machines	333313	Office Machinery Manufacturing (pt)
3581	Automatic Vending Machines	333311	Automatic Vending Machine Manufacturing
3582	Commercial Laundry, Drycleaning, and Pressing Machines	333312	Commercial Laundry, Drycleaning, and Pressing Machine Manufacturing
3585	Air-Conditioning and Warm Air Heating Equipment and Commercial and Industrial Refrigeration Equipment		
	Motor Vehicle Air Conditioning	336391	Motor Vehicle Air Conditioning Manufacturing
	Except Motor Vehicle Air Conditioning	333415	Air Conditioning and Warm Air Heating Equipment and Commercial and Industrial Refrigeration Equipment Manufacturing (pt)
3586	Measuring and Dispensing Pumps	333913	Measuring and Dispensing Pump Manufacturing
3589	Service Industry Machinery, NEC	333319	Other Commercial and Service Industry Machinery Manufacturing (pt)
3592	Carburetors, Pistons, Piston Rings and Valves	336311	Carburetor, Piston, Piston Ring and Valve Manufacturing
3593	Fluid Power Cylinders and Actuators	333995	Fluid Power Cylinder and Actuator Manufacturing

3594	Fluid Power Pumps and Motors	333996	Fluid Power Pump and Motor Manufacturing
3596	Scales and Balances, Except Laboratory	333997	Scale and Balance (except Laboratory) Manufacturing
3599@	Industrial and Commercial Machinery and Equipment, NEC		
	Gasoline, Oil and Intake Filters for Internal Combustion Engines, Except Motor Vehicle	336399	All Other Motor Vehicle Part Manufacturing (pt)
	Flexible Metal Hose	332999	All Other Miscellaneous Fabricated Metal Product Manufacturing (pt)
	Carnival Amusement Park Equipment	333319	Other Commercial and Service Industry Machinery Manufacturing (pt)
	Machine Shops	33271	Machine Shops
	Other Industrial and Commercial Machinery and Equipment	333999	All Other General Purpose Machinery Manufacturing (pt)
3612	Power, Distribution, and Specialty Transformers	335311	Power, Distribution, and Specialty Transformer Manufacturing (pt)
3613	Switchgear and Switchboard Apparatus	335313	Switchgear and Switchboard Apparatus Manufacturing
3621	Motors and Generators	335312	Motor and Generator Manufacturing (pt)
3624	Carbon and Graphite Products	335991	Carbon and Graphite Product Manufacturing
3625	Relays and Industrial Controls	335314	Relay and Industrial Control Manufacturing
3629	Electrical Industrial Apparatus, NEC	335999	All Other Miscellaneous Electrical Equipment and Component Manufacturing (pt)
3631	Household Cooking Equipment	335221	Household Cooking Appliance Manufacturing
3632	Household Refrigerators and Home and Farm Freezers	335222	Household Refrigerator and Home Freezer Manufacturing
3633	Household Laundry Equipment	335224	Household Laundry Equipment Manufacturing
3634	Electric Housewares and Fans		
	Except Wall and Baseboard Heating Units for Permanent Installation	335211	Electric Housewares and Household Fan Manufacturing

1987 SIC Code	1987 SIC Description	1997 NAICS Code	1997 NAICS United States Description
	Wall and Baseboard Heating Units For Permanent Installation	333414	Heating Equipment (except Electric and Warm Air Furnaces) Manufacturing (pt)
3635	Household Vacuum Cleaners	335212	Household Vacuum Cleaner Manufacturing (pt)
3639	Household Appliances, NEC		
	Floor Waxing and Floor Polishing Machines	335212	Household Vacuum Cleaner Manufacturing (pt)
	Household Sewing Machines	333298	All Other Industrial Machinery Manufacturing (pt)
	Other Household Appliances	335228	Other Major Household Appliance Manufacturing
3641	Electric Lamp Bulbs and Tubes	33511	Electric Lamp Bulb and Part Manufacturing
3643	Current-Carrying Wiring Devices	335931	Current-Carrying Wiring Device Manufacturing
3644	Noncurrent-Carrying Wiring Devices	335932	Noncurrent-Carrying Wiring Device Manufacturing
3645	Residential Electric Lighting Fixtures	335121	Residential Electric Lighting Fixture Manufacturing (pt)
3646	Commercial, Industrial, and Institutional Electric Lighting Fixtures	335122	Commercial, Industrial, and Institutional Electric Lighting Fixture Manufacturing
3647	Vehicular Lighting Equipment	336321	Vehicular Lighting Equipment Manufacturing
3648@	Lighting Equipment, NEC	335129	Other Lighting Equipment Manufacturing (pt)
3651	Household Audio and Video Equipment	33431	Audio and Video Equipment Manufacturing
3652	Phonograph Records and Prerecorded Audio Tapes and Disks		
	Reproduction of Recording Media	334612	Prerecorded Compact Disc (Except Software), Tape and Record Reproducing (pt)
	Integrated Record Companies, Except Duplication Only	51222	Integrated Record Production/Distribution
3661	Telephone and Telegraph Apparatus		
	Telephone and Telegraph Apparatus, Except Telephone Transformers, and Consumer External Modems	33421	Telephone Apparatus Manufacturing

	Telephone Transformers	334416	Electronic Coil, Transformer, and Other Inductor Manufacturing (pt)
	Consumer External Modems	334418	Printed Circuit/Electronics Assembly Manufacturing (pt)
3663	Radio and Television Broadcasting and Communication Equipment	33422	Radio and Television Broadcasting and Wireless Communications Equipment Manufacturing (pt)
3669	Communications Equipment, NEC	33429	Other Communication Equipment Manufacturing
3671	Electron Tubes	334411	Electron Tube Manufacturing
3672	Printed Circuit Boards	334412	Printed Circuit Board Manufacturing
3674	Semiconductors and Related Devices	334413	Semiconductor and Related Device Manufacturing
3675	Electronic Capacitors	334414	Electronic Capacitor Manufacturing
3676	Electronic Resistors	334415	Electronic Resistor Manufacturing
3677	Electronic Coils, Transformers, and Other Inductors	334416	Electronic Coil, Transformer, and Other Inductor Manufacturing (pt)
3678	Electronic Connectors	334417	Electronic Connector Manufacturing
3679	Electronic Components, NEC		
	Communication Equipment	33422	Radio and Television Broadcasting and Wireless Communications Equipment Manufacturing (pt)
	Printed Circuit/Electronics Assembly	334418	Printed Circuit/Electronics Assembly Manufacturing (pt)
	Electronic Control Modules for Motor Vehicles	336322	Other Motor Vehicle Electrical and Electronic Equipment Manufacturing (pt)
	Other Electronic Components	334419	Other Electronic Component Manufacturing
3691	Storage Batteries	335911	Storage Battery Manufacturing
3692	Primary Batteries, Dry and Wet	335912	Dry and Wet Primary Battery Manufacturing
3694	Electrical Equipment for Internal Combustion Engines	336322	Other Motor Vehicle Electrical and Electronic Equipment Manufacturing (pt)
3695	Magnetic and Optical Recording Media	334613	Magnetic and Optical Recording Media Manufacturing

1987 SIC Code	1987 SIC Description	1997 NAICS Code	1997 NAICS United States Description
3699	Electrical Machinery, Equipment, and Supplies, NEC		
	Electronic Teaching Machines and Flight Simulators	333319	Other Commercial and Service Industry Machinery Manufacturing (pt)
	Outboard Electric Motors	333618	Other Engine Equipment Manufacturing (pt)
	Bar Code Scanners	334119	Other Computer Peripheral Equipment Manufacturing (pt)
	Lasers		Classify According to Function
	Christmas Tree Lighting Sets and Electric Insect Lamps	335129	Other Lighting Equipment Manufacturing (pt)
	Other Electrical Machinery, Equipment, and Supplies	335999	All Other Miscellaneous Electrical Equipment and Component Manufacturing (pt)
3711@	Motor Vehicles and Passenger Car Bodies		
	Automobiles	336111	Automobile Manufacturing
	Light Truck and Utility Vehicles	336112	Light Truck and Utility Vehicle Manufacturing
	Heavy Duty Trucks	33612	Heavy Duty Truck Manufacturing
	Kit Car and Other Passenger Car Bodies	336211	Motor Vehicle Body Manufacturing (pt)
	Military Armored Vehicles	336992	Military Armored Vehicle, Tank, and Tank Component Manufacturing (pt)
3713	Truck and Bus Bodies	336211	Motor Vehicle Body Manufacturing (pt)
3714@	Motor Vehicle Parts and Accessories		
	Dump-Truck Lifting Mechanisms and Fifth Wheels	336211	Motor Vehicle Body Manufacturing (pt)
	Gasoline Engines Including Rebuilt and Engine Parts Including Rebuilt for Motor Vehicles	336312	Gasoline Engine and Engine Parts Manufacturing

	Wiring Harness Sets, Other than Ignition; Block Heaters and Battery Heaters; Instrument Board Assemblies; Permanent Defroster; Windshield Washer-Wiper Mechanisms; Cruise Control Mechanisms; and Other Electrical Equipment for Internal Combustion Engines	336322	Other Motor Vehicle Electrical and Electronic Equipment Manufacturing (pt)
	Steering and Suspension Parts	33633	Motor Vehicle Steering and Suspension Components (except Spring) Manufacturing
	Brake and Brake Systems, Including Assemblies	33634	Motor Vehicle Brake System Manufacturing (pt)
	Transmissions and Power Train Parts, Including Rebuilding	33635	Motor Vehicle Transmission and Power Train Parts Manufacturing
	Other Motor Vehicle Parts	336399	All Other Motor Vehicle Parts Manufacturing (pt)
3715	Truck Trailers	336212	Truck Trailer Manufacturing
3716	Motor Homes	336213	Motor Home Manufacturing
3721	Aircraft	336411	Aircraft Manufacturing
3724	Aircraft Engines and Engine Parts	336412	Aircraft Engine and Engine Parts Manufacturing
3728	Aircraft Parts and Auxiliary Equipment, NEC		
	Fluid Power Aircraft Subassemblies	332912	Fluid Power Valve and Hose Fitting Manufacturing (pt)
	Except Fluid Power Aircraft Subassemblies	336413	Other Aircraft Part and Auxiliary Equipment Manufacturing
3731	Ship Building and Repairing	336611	Ship Building and Repairing
3732	Boat Building and Repairing		
	Boat Repair	81149	Other Personal and Household Goods Repair and Maintenance (pt)
	Boat Building	336612	Boat Building
3743	Railroad Equipment		
	Locomotive Fuel Lubricating or Cooling Medium Pumps	333911	Pump and Pumping Equipment Manufacturing (pt)

1987 SIC Code	1987 SIC Description	1997 NAICS Code	1997 NAICS United States Description
	Other Railroad Equipment	33651	Railroad Rolling Stock Manufacturing (pt)
3751	Motorcycles, Bicycles, and Parts	336991	Motorcycle, Bicycle, and Parts Manufacturing (pt)
3761	Guided Missiles and Space Vehicles	336414	Guided Missile and Space Vehicle Manufacturing
3764	Guided Missile and Space Vehicle Propulsion Units and Propulsion Unit Parts	336415	Guided Missile and Space Vehicle Propulsion Unit and Propulsion Unit Parts Manufacturing
3769	Guided Missile Space Vehicle Parts and Auxiliary Equipment, NEC	336419	Other Guided Missile and Space Vehicle Parts and Auxiliary Equipment Manufacturing
3792	Travel Trailers and Campers	336214	Travel Trailer and Camper Manufacturing (pt)
3795	Tanks and Tank Components	336992	Military Armored Vehicle, Tank, and Tank Component Manufacturing (pt)
3799@	Transportation Equipment, NEC		
	Automobile, Boat, Utility and Light Truck Trailers	336214	Travel Trailer and Camper Manufacturing (pt)
	Wheelbarrows	332212	Hand and Edge Tool Manufacturing (pt)
	Other Transportation Equipment	336999	All Other Transportation Equipment Manufacturing
3812	Search, Detection, Navigation, Guidance, Aeronautical, and Nautical Systems and Instruments	334511	Search, Detection, Navigation, Guidance, Aeronautical, and Nautical System and Instrument Manufacturing
3821	Laboratory Apparatus and Furniture	339111	Laboratory Apparatus and Furniture Manufacturing
3822	Automatic Controls for Regulating Residential and Commercial Environments and Appliances	334512	Automatic Environmental Control Manufacturing for Regulating Residential, Commercial, and Appliance Use
3823	Industrial Instruments for Measurement, Display, and Control of Process Variables; and Related Products	334513	Instruments and Related Product Manufacturing for Measuring Displaying, and Controlling Industrial Process Variables
3824	Totalizing Fluid Meters and Counting Devices	334514	Totalizing Fluid Meter and Counting Device Manufacturing
3825	Instruments for Measuring and Testing of Electricity and Electrical Signals		
	Portable Instrument Transformers	334416	Electronic Coil, Transformer, and Other Inductor Manufacturing (pt)

	Except Portable Instrument Transformers	334515	Instrument Manufacturing for Measuring and Testing Electricity and Electrical Signals
3826	Laboratory Analytical Instruments	334516	Analytical Laboratory Instrument Manufacturing
3827	Optical Instruments and Lenses	333314	Optical Instrument and Lens Manufacturing
3829	Measuring and Controlling Devices, NEC		
	Medical Thermometers	339112	Surgical and Medical Instrument Manufacturing (pt)
	Except Medical Thermometers	334519	Other Measuring and Controlling Device Manufacturing
3841	Surgical and Medical Instruments and Apparatus	339112	Surgical and Medical Instrument Manufacturing (pt)
3842@	Orthopedic, Prosthetic, and Surgical Appliances and Supplies		
	Orthopedic, Prosthetic, and Surgical Appliances and Supplies, except Electronic Hearing Aids	339113	Surgical Appliance and Supplies Manufacturing (pt)
	Electronic Hearing Aids	334510	Electromedical and Electrotherapeutic Apparatus Manufacturing (pt)
3843	Dental Equipment and Supplies	339114	Dental Equipment and Supplies Manufacturing
3844	X-Ray Apparatus and Tubes and Related Irradiation Apparatus	334517	Irradiation Apparatus Manufacturing (pt)
3845	Electromedical and Electrotherapeutic Apparatus		
	CT and CAT Scanners	334517	Irradiation Apparatus Manufacturing (pt)
	Other Electromedical and Electrotherapeutic Apparatus	334510	Electromedical and Electrotherapeutic Apparatus Manufacturing (pt)
3851	Ophthalmic Goods	339115	Ophthalmic Goods Manufacturing (pt)
3861	Photographic Equipment and Supplies		
	Photographic Equipment and Supplies (Except Photographic Film, Paper, Plate and Chemicals)	333315	Photographic and Photocopying Equipment Manufacturing
	Photographic Film, Paper, Plates and Chemicals	325992	Photographic Film, Paper, Plate and Chemical Manufacturing

1987 SIC Code	1987 SIC Description	1997 NAICS Code	1997 NAICS United States Description
3873	Watches, Clocks, Clockwork Operated Devices and Parts	334518	Watch, Clock, and Part Manufacturing (pt)
3911	Jewelry, Precious Metal	339911	Jewelry (except Costume) Manufacturing (pt)
3914	Silverware, Plated Ware, and Stainless Steel Ware		
	Cutlery and Flatware Except Precious	332211	Cutlery and Flatware (except Precious) Manufacturing (pt)
	Silverware, Plated Ware, and Stainless Steel Ware (Except Nonprecious Metal Cutlery and Flatware)	339912	Silverware and Plated Ware Manufacturing (pt)
3915	Jewelers' Findings and Materials, and Lapidary Work	339913	Jewelers' Material and Lapidary Work Manufacturing
3931	Musical Instruments	339992	Musical Instrument Manufacturing
3942	Dolls and Stuffed Toys	339931	Doll and Stuffed Toy Manufacturing
3944	Games, Toys, and Children's Vehicles, Except Dolls and Bicycles		
	Metal Tricycles	336991	Motorcycle, Bicycle and Parts Manufacturing (pt)
	Other Games, Toys and Children's Vehicles	339932	Game, Toy, and Children's Vehicle Manufacturing
3949	Sporting and Athletic Goods, NEC	33992	Sporting and Athletic Good Manufacturing
3951	Pens, Mechanical Pencils and Parts	339941	Pen and Mechanical Pencil Manufacturing
3952@	Lead Pencils, Crayons, and Artist's Materials		
	Drafting Tables and Boards	337127	Institutional Furniture Manufacturing (pt)
	Drawing and India Ink	325998	All Other Miscellaneous Chemical Manufacturing (pt)
	Other	339942	Lead Pencil and Art Good Manufacturing (pt)
3953	Marking Devices	339943	Marking Device Manufacturing
3955	Carbon Paper and Inked Ribbons	339944	Carbon Paper and Inked Ribbon Manufacturing
3961	Costume Jewelry and Costume Novelties, Except Precious Metals	339914	Costume Jewelry and Novelty Manufacturing (pt)
3965	Fasteners, Buttons, Needles, and Pins	339993	Fastener, Button, Needle and Pin Manufacturing (pt)

3991	Brooms and Brushes	339994	Broom, Brush and Mop Manufacturing (pt)
3993	Signs and Advertising Specialties	33995	Sign Manufacturing
3995	Burial Caskets	339995	Burial Casket Manufacturing
3996	Linoleum, Asphalted-Felt-Base, and Other Hard Surface Floor Coverings, NEC	326192	Resilient Floor Covering Manufacturing (pt)
3999	Manufacturing Industries, NEC		
	Beauty and Barber Chairs	337127	Institutional Furniture Manufacturing (pt)
	Burnt Wood Articles	321999	All Other Miscellaneous Wood Product Manufacturing (pt)
	Fur Dressing and Bleaching	31611	Leather and Hide Tanning and Finishing (pt)
	Lamp Shades of Paper or Textile	335121	Residential Electric Lighting Fixture Manufacturing (pt)
	Matches	325998	All Other Miscellaneous Chemical Product Manufacturing (pt)
	Metal Products, Such As Combs, Hair Curlers, Etc.	332999	All Other Miscellaneous Fabricated Metal Product Manufacturing (pt)
	Plastics Products, Such As Combs, Hair Curlers, Etc.	326199	All Other Plastics Product Manufacturing (pt)
	Flexographic Printing Eyeglass Frames for the Trade	323112	Commercial Flexographic Printing (pt)
	Gravure Printing Eyeglass Frames for the Trade	323111	Commercial Gravure Printing (pt)
	Lithographic Printing Eyeglass Frames for the Trade	323110	Commercial Lithographic Printing (pt)
	Screen Printing of Eyeglass Frames for the Trade	323113	Commercial Screen Printing (pt)
	Other Printing of Eyeglass Frames for the Trade	323119	Other Commercial Printing (pt)
	Tape Measures	332212	Hand and Edge Tool Manufacturing (pt)
	Other	339999	All Other Miscellaneous Manufacturing (pt)
4011	Railroads, Line-haul Operating	482111	Line-Haul Railroads
4013@	Railroad Switching and Terminal Establishments		
	Beltline and Logging Railroads	482112	Short Line Railroads

1987 SIC Code	1987 SIC Description	1997 NAICS Code	1997 NAICS United States Description
	Other	48821	Support Activities for Rail Transportation (pt)
4111@	Local and Suburban Transit		
	Mixed Mode Transit Systems	485111	Mixed Mode Transit Systems
	Commuter Rail Systems	485112	Commuter Rail Systems
	Bus and Motor Vehicle Transit Systems	485113	Bus and Motor Vehicle Transit Systems
	Other Urban Transit Systems	485119	Other Urban Transit Systems
	Airport Limousine Transportation	485999	All Other Transit and Ground Passenger Transportation (pt)
4119@	Local Passenger Transportation, NEC		
	Ambulances	62191	Ambulance Service (pt)
	Employee Transportation	48541	School and Employee Bus Transportation (pt)
	Sightseeing Buses and Cable and Cog Railways, Except Scenic	48711	Scenic and Sightseeing Transportation , Land (pt)
	Special Needs Transportation	485991	Special Needs Transportation
	Hearse Rental with Driver and Carpool and Vanpool Operations	485999	All Other Transit and Ground Passenger Transportation (pt)
	Automobile Rental with Driver and Limousine Rental with Driver	48532	Limousine Service
4121	Taxicabs	48531	Taxi Service
4131	Intercity and Rural Bus Transportation	48521	Interurban and Rural Bus Transportation
4141@	Local Bus Charter Service	48551	Charter Bus Industry (pt)
4142	Bus Charter Service, Except Local	48551	Charter Bus Industry (pt)
4151	School Buses	48541	School and Employee Bus Transportation (pt)
4173@	Terminal and Service Facilities for Motor Vehicle Passenger Transportation	48849	Other Support Activities for Road Transportation (pt)

4212@	Local Trucking Without Storage		
	Solid Waste Collection Without Disposal	562111	Solid Waste Collection (pt)
	Hazardous Waste Collection Without Disposal	562112	Hazardous Waste Collection (pt)
	Other Waste Collection Without Disposal	562119	Other Waste Collection (pt)
	Local General Freight Trucking Without Storage	48411	General Freight Trucking, Local (pt)
	Household Goods Moving Without Storage	48421	Used Household and Office Goods Moving (pt)
	Local Specialized Freight Trucking Without Storage	48422	Specialized Freight (except Used Goods) Trucking, Local (pt)
4213@	Trucking, Except Local		
	Long-distance Truckload General Freight Trucking	484121	General Freight Trucking, Long-Distance, Truckload
	Long-distance Less Than Truckload General Freight Trucking	484122	General Freight Trucking, Long-Distance, Less Than Truckload
	Long-distance Household Goods Moving	48421	Used Household and Office Goods Moving (pt)
	Long-distance Specialized Freight Trucking	48423	Specialized Freight (except Used Goods) Trucking, Long-Distance
4214@	Local Trucking with Storage		
	Local General Freight Trucking with Storage	48411	General Freight Trucking, Local (pt)
	Local Household Goods Moving	48421	Used Household and Office Goods Moving (pt)
	Local Specialized Freight Trucking with Storage	48422	Specialized Freight (except Used Goods) Trucking, Local (pt)
4215@	Couriers Services Except by Air		
	Hub and Spoke Intercity Delivery	49211	Couriers (pt)
	Local Delivery	49221	Local Messengers and Local Delivery
4221	Farm Product Warehousing and Storage	49313	Farm Product Warehousing and Storage Facilities
4222	Refrigerated Warehousing and Storage	49312	Refrigerated Warehousing and Storage Facilities (pt)
4225	General Warehousing and Storage		

1987 SIC Code	1987 SIC Description	1997 NAICS Code	1997 NAICS United States Description
	General Warehousing and Storage	49311	General Warehousing and Storage Facilities (pt)
	Miniwarehouses and Self-Storage Units	53113	Lessors of Miniwarehouses and Self Storage Units
4226	Special Warehousing and Storage, NEC		
	Fur Storage	49312	Refrigerated Warehousing and Storage Facilities (pt)
	General Warehousing in Foreign Trade Zones	49311	General Warehousing and Storage Facilities (pt)
	Other	49319	Other Warehousing and Storage Facilities
4231@	Terminal and Joint Terminal Maintenance Facilities for Motor Freight Transportation	48849	Other Support Activities for Road Transportation (pt)
4311	United States Postal Service	49111	Postal Service
4412	Deep Sea Foreign Transportation of Freight	483111	Deep Sea Freight Transportation
4424@	Deep Sea Domestic Transportation of Freight	483113	Coastal and Great Lakes Freight Transportation (pt)
4432@	Freight Transportation on the Great Lakes - St. Lawrence Seaway	483113	Coastal and Great Lakes Freight Transportation (pt)
4449	Water Transportation of Freight, NEC	483211	Inland Water Freight Transportation (pt)
4481	Deep Sea Transportation of Passengers, Except by Ferry		
	Deep Sea Passenger Transportation	483112	Deep Sea Passenger Transportation
	Coastal and Great Lakes Passenger Transportation	483114	Coastal and Great Lakes Passenger Transportation (pt)
4482@	Ferries		
	Coastal and Great Lakes Ferries	483114	Coastal and Great Lakes Passenger Transportation (pt)
	Inland Water Ferries	483212	Inland Water Passenger Transportation (pt)
4489	Water Transportation of Passengers, NEC		
	Water Taxis	483212	Inland Water Passenger Transportation (pt)
	Airboats, Excursion Boats, and Sightseeing Boats	48721	Scenic and Sightseeing Transportation, Water (pt)

4491	Marine Cargo Handling		
	Dock and Pier Operations	48831	Port and Harbor Operations (pt)
	Except Dock and Pier Operations	48832	Marine Cargo Handling
4492@	Towing and Tugboat Services		
	Coastal and Great Lakes Barge Operations	483113	Coastal and Great Lakes Freight Transportation (pt)
	Inland Water Barge Operations	483211	Inland Water Freight Transportation (pt)
	Except Barge Operations	48833	Navigational Services to Shipping (pt)
4493	Marinas	71393	Marinas
4499@	Water Transportation Services, NEC		
	Boat and Ship Rental	532411	Commercial Air, Rail, and Water Transportation Equipment Rental and Leasing (pt)
	Lighthouse Operations	48831	Port and Harbor Operations (pt)
	Marine Salvage and Piloting Vessels In and Out of Harbors	48833	Navigational Services to Shipping (pt)
	Other	48839	Other Support Activities for Water Transportation (pt)
4512	Air Transportation, Scheduled		
	Scheduled Passenger Air Transportation	481111	Scheduled Passenger Air Transportation
	Scheduled Freight Air Transportation	481112	Scheduled Freight Air Transportation
4513@	Air Courier Services	49211	Couriers (pt)
4522@	Air Transportation, Nonscheduled		
	Air Ambulance	62191	Ambulance Services (pt)
	Nonscheduled Charter Freight Air Transportation	481212	Nonscheduled Chartered Freight Air Transportation
	Nonscheduled Charter Passenger Air Transportation	481211	Nonscheduled Chartered Passenger Air Transportation

1987 SIC Code	1987 SIC Description	1997 NAICS Code	1997 NAICS United States Description
	Sightseeing Aircraft	48799	Scenic and Sightseeing Transportation , Other (pt)
4581	Airports, Flying Fields, and Airport Terminal Services		
	Air Traffic Control	488111	Air Traffic Control (pt)
	Airfreight Handling at Airports, Hangar Operations, Airport Terminal Services, Aircraft Storage, Airports, and Flying Fields	488119	Other Airport Operations (pt)
	Aircraft Cleaning and Janitorial Services	56172	Janitorial Services (pt)
	Aircraft Servicing and Repairing	48819	Other Support Activities for Air Transportation
4612	Crude Petroleum Pipelines	48611	Pipeline Transportation of Crude Oil
4613	Refined Petroleum Pipelines	48691	Pipeline Transportation of Refined Petroleum Products
4619	Pipelines, NEC	48699	All Other Pipeline Transportation
4724	Travel Agencies	56151	Travel Agencies
4725	Tour Operators	56152	Tour Operators
4729@	Arrangement of Passenger Transportation, NEC		
	Arrangement of Carpools and Vanpools	488999	All Other Support Activities for Transportation (pt)
	Except Arrangement of Carpools and Vanpools	561599	All Other Travel Arrangement and Reservation Services (pt)
·731	Arrangement of Transportation of Freight and Cargo		
	Freight Rate Auditors and Tariff Consultants	541618	Other Management Consulting Services (pt)
	Except Freight Rate Auditors and Tariff Consultants	48851	Freight Transportation Arrangement
4741@	Rental of Railroad Cars		
	Rental of Railroad Cars	532411	Commercial Air, Rail, and Water Transportation Equipment Rental and Leasing (pt)

	Grain Leveling in Railroad Cars, Grain Trimming for Railroad Equipment, Precooling of Fruits and Vegetables in Connection with Transportation, and Railroad Car Cleaning, Icing, Ventilating and Heating	48821	Support Activities for Rail Transportation (pt)
4783	Packing and Crating	488991	Packing and Crating
4785	Fixed Facilities and Inspection and Weighing Services for Motor Vehicle Transportation		
	Marine Cargo Checkers	48839	Other Support Activities for Water Transportation (pt)
	Except Marine Cargo Checkers	48849	Other Support Activities for Road Transportation (pt)
4789	Transportation Services, NEC		
	Pipeline Terminals and Stockyards for Transportation	488999	All Other Support Activities for Transportation (pt)
	Horse-drawn Cabs and Carriages	48711	Scenic and Sightseeing Transportation, Land (pt)
	Other	48821	Support Activities for Rail Transportation (pt)
4812@	Radiotelephone Communications		
	Paging Carriers	513321	Paging
	Cellular Carriers	513322	Cellular and Other Wireless Telecommunications (pt)
	Paging and Cellular Resellers	51333	Telecommunications Resellers (pt)
4813@	Telephone Communications, Except Radiotelephone		
	Except Resellers	51331	Wired Telecommunications Carriers (pt)
	Resellers	51333	Telecommunications Resellers (pt)
4822@	Telegraph and Other Message Communications	51331	Wired Telecommunications Carriers (pt)
4832	Radio Broadcasting Stations		
	Networks	513111	Radio Networks
	Stations	513112	Radio Stations

1987 SIC Code	1987 SIC Description	1997 NAICS Code	1997 NAICS United States Description
4833	Television Broadcasting Stations	51312	Television Broadcasting
4841	Cable and Other Pay Television Services		
	Cable Networks	51321	Cable Networks
	Except Cable Networks	51322	Cable and Other Program Distribution
4899	Communications Services, NEC		
	Radio Dispatch	513322	Cellular and Other Wireless Telecommunications (pt)
	Satellite Communications	51334	Satellite Telecommunications
	Except Radio Dispatch and Satellite Communications	51339	Other Telecommunications
4911	Electric Services		
	Hydroelectric Power Generation	221111	Hydroelectric Power Generation (pt)
	Electric Power Generation by Fossil Fuels	221112	Fossil Fuel Electric Power Generation (pt)
	Electric Power Generation by Nuclear Fuels	221113	Nuclear Electric Power Generation (pt)
	Other Electric Power Generation	221119	Other Electric Power Generation (pt)
	Electric Power Transmission and Control	221121	Electric Bulk Power Transmission and Control (pt)
	Electric Power Distribution	221122	Electric Power Distribution (pt)
4922	Natural Gas Transmission	48621	Pipeline Transportation of Natural Gas (pt)
4923@	Natural Gas Transmission and Distribution		
	Distribution	22121	Natural Gas Distribution (pt)
	Transmission	48621	Pipeline Transportation of Natural Gas (pt)
4924@	Natural Gas Distribution	22121	Natural Gas Distribution (pt)
4925@	Mixed, Manufactured, or Liquefied Petroleum Gas Production and/or Distribution	22121	Natural Gas Distribution (pt)
4931@	Electric and Other Services Combined		

	Hydroelectric Power Generation When Combined with Other Services	221111	Hydroelectric Power Generation (pt)
	Electric Power Generation by Fossil Fuels When Combined with Other Services	221112	Fossil Fuel Electric Power Generation (pt)
	Electric Power Generation by Nuclear Fuels When Combined with Other Services	221113	Nuclear Electric Power Generation (pt)
	Other Electric Power Generation When Combined with Other Services	221119	Other Electric Power Generation (pt)
	Electric Power Transmission When Combined with Other Services	221121	Electric Bulk Power Transmission and Control (pt)
	Electric Power Distribution When Combined with Other Services	221122	Electric Power Distribution (pt)
	Natural Gas When Combined with Electric Services	22121	Natural Gas Distribution (pt)
4932@	Gas and Other Services Combined	22121	Natural Gas Distribution (pt)
4939@	Combination Utilities, NEC		
	Hydroelectric Power Generation When Combined with Other Services	221111	Hydroelectric Power Generation (pt)
	Electric Power Generation by Fossil Fuels When Combined with Other Services	221112	Fossil Fuel Electric Power Generation (pt)
	Electric Power Generation by Nuclear Fuels When Combined with Other Services	221113	Nuclear Electric Power Generation (pt)
	Other Power Generation When Combined with Other Services	221119	Other Electric Power Generation (pt)
	Electric Power Transmission When Combined with Other Services	221121	Electric Bulk Power Transmission and Control (pt)
	Electric Power Distribution When Combined with Other Services	221122	Electric Power Distribution (pt)

1987 SIC Code	1987 SIC Description	1997 NAICS Code	1997 NAICS United States Description
	Natural Gas Distribution when Combined with Other Services	22121	Natural Gas Distribution (pt)
4941	Water Supply	22131	Water Supply and Irrigation Systems (pt)
4952	Sewerage Systems	22132	Sewage Treatment Facilities
4953	Refuse Systems		
	Solid Waste Collection When Combined with Disposal	562111	Solid Waste Collection (pt)
	Hazardous Waste Collection When Combined with Disposal	562112	Hazardous Waste Collection (pt)
	Materials Recovery Facilities	56292	Materials Recovery Facilities
	Other Waste Collection When Combined with Disposal	562119	Other Waste Collection (pt)
	Hazardous Waste Treatment and Disposal	562211	Hazardous Waste Treatment and Disposal
	Solid Waste Landfills	562212	Solid Waste Landfills
	Solid Waste Combustors and Incinerators	562213	Solid Waste Combustors and Incinerators
	Other Nonhazardous Waste Treatment and Disposal	562219	Other Nonhazardous Waste Treatment and Disposal
4959	Sanitary Services, NEC		
	Vacuuming of Airport Runways	488119	Other Airport Operations (pt)
	Remediation Services	56291	Remediation Services (pt)
	Malaria Control and Mosquito Eradication	56171	Exterminating and Pest Control Services (pt)
	Other	562998	All Other Miscellaneous Waste Management Services
4961	Steam and Air-Conditioning Supply	22133	Steam and Air-Conditioning Supply
4971@	Irrigation Systems	22131	Water Supply and Irrigation Systems (pt)
5012	Automobiles and Other Motor Vehicles	42111	Automobile and Other Motor Vehicle Wholesalers
5013	Motor Vehicle Supplies and New Parts		

	Sold Via Retail Method	44131	Automotive Parts and Accessories Stores (pt) - Retail
	Sold Via Wholesale Method	42112	Motor Vehicle Supplies and New Part Wholesalers
5014	Tires and Tubes		
	Sold Via Retail Method	44132	Tire Dealers (pt.) - Retail
	Sold Via Wholesale Method	42113	Tire and Tube Wholesalers
5015	Motor Vehicle Parts, Used	42114	Motor Vehicle Part (Used) Wholesalers
5021	Furniture		
	Sold Via Retail Method	44211	Furniture Stores (pt)
	Sold Via Wholesale Method	42121	Furniture Wholesalers
5023	Home Furnishings		
	Sold Via Retail Method	44221	Floor Covering Stores (pt)
	Sold Via Wholesale Method	42122	Home Furnishing Wholesalers
5031	Lumber, Plywood, Millwork, and Wood Panels		
	Sold Via Retail Method	44419	Other Building Material Dealers (pt)
	Sold Via Wholesale Method	42131	Lumber, Plywood, Millwork, and Wood Panel Wholesalers (pt)
5032	Brick, Stone and Related Construction Materials		
	Sold Via Retail Method	44419	Other Building Material Dealers (pt)
	Sold Via Wholesale Method	42132	Brick, Stone and Related Construction Material Wholesalers
5033	Roofing, Siding, and Insulation Materials	42133	Roofing, Siding, and Insulation Material Wholesalers
5039	Construction Materials, NEC		
	Sold Via Retail Method	44419	Other Building Material Dealers (pt)
	Sold Via Wholesale Method	42139	Other Construction Material Wholesalers

1987 SIC Code	1987 SIC Description	1997 NAICS Code	1997 NAICS United States Description
5043	Photographic Equipment and Supplies	42141	Photographic Equipment and Supplies Wholesalers
5044	Office Equipment	42142	Office Equipment Wholesalers
5045	Computers and Computer Peripheral Equipment and Software		
	Sold Via Wholesale Method	42143	Computer and Computer Peripheral Equipment and Software Wholesalers
	Sold Via Retail Method	44312	Computer and Software Stores (pt) - Retail
5046	Commercial Equipment, NEC	42144	Other Commercial Equipment Wholesalers
5047	Medical, Dental, and Hospital Equipment and Supplies		
	Sold Via Wholesale Method	42145	Medical, Dental and Hospital Equipment and Supplies Wholesalers
	Sold Via Retail Method	446199	All Other Health and Personal Care Stores (pt) - Retail
5048	Ophthalmic Goods	42146	Ophthalmic Goods Wholesalers
5049	Professional Equipment and Supplies, NEC		
	Sold Via Wholesale Method	42149	Other Professional Equipment and Supplies Wholesalers
	Religious and School Supplies Sold Via Retail Method	45321	Office Supplies and Stationery Stores (pt) - Retail
5051	Metals Service Centers and Offices	42151	Metals Service Centers and Offices
5052	Coal and Other Minerals and Ores	42152	Coal and Other Mineral and Ore Wholesalers
5063	Electrical Apparatus and Equipment Wiring Supplies, and Construction Materials		
	Sold Via Retail Method	44419	Other Building Material Dealers (pt)
	Sold Via Wholesale Method	42161	Electrical Apparatus and Equipment, Wiring Supplies and Construction Material Wholesalers
5064	Electrical Appliances, Television and Radio Sets	42162	Electrical Appliance, Television and Radio Set Wholesalers
5065	Electronic Parts and Equipment, Not Elsewhere Classified	42169	Other Electronic Parts and Equipment Wholesalers

5072	Hardware	42171	Hardware Wholesalers
5074	Plumbing and Heating Equipment and Supplies (Hydronics)		
	Sold Via Retail Method	44419	Other Building Material Dealers (pt)
	Sold Via Wholesale Method	42172	Plumbing and Heating Equipment and Supplies (Hydronics) Wholesalers
5075	Warm Air Heating and Air-Conditioning Equipment and Supplies	42173	Warm Air Heating and Air-Conditioning Equipment and Supplies Wholesalers
5078	Refrigeration Equipment and Supplies	42174	Refrigeration Equipment and Supplies Wholesalers
5082	Construction and Mining (Except Petroleum) Machinery and Equipment	42181	Construction and Mining (except Petroleum) Machinery and Equipment Wholesalers
5083	Farm and Garden Machinery and Equipment		
	Sold Via Wholesale Method	42182	Farm and Garden Machinery and Equipment Wholesalers
	Garden and Lawn Equipment Sold Via Retail Method	44421	Outdoor Power Equipment Stores (pt) - Retail
5084	Industrial Machinery and Equipment	42183	Industrial Machinery and Equipment Wholesalers (pt)
5085	Industrial Supplies		
	Fluid Power Accessories	42183	Industrial Machinery and Equipment Wholesalers (pt)
	Except Fluid Power Accessories	42184	Industrial Supplies Wholesalers
5087	Service Establishment Equipment and Supplies		
	Sold Via Wholesale Method	42185	Service Establishment Equipment and Supplies Wholesalers
	Sold Via Retail Method	44612	Cosmetics, Beauty Supplies, and Perfume Stores (pt)
5088	Transportation Equipment and Supplies, Except Motor Vehicles	42186	Transportation Equipment and Supplies (except Motor Vehicles) Wholesalers
5091	Sporting and Recreational Goods and Supplies	42191	Sporting and Recreational Goods and Supplies Wholesalers
5092	Toys and Hobby Goods and Supplies	42192	Toy and Hobby Goods and Supplies Wholesalers

1987 SIC Code	1987 SIC Description	1997 NAICS Code	1997 NAICS United States Description
5093	Scrap and Waste Materials	42193	Recyclable Material Wholesalers
5094	Jewelry, Watches, Precious Stones, and Precious Metals	42194	Jewelry, Watch , Precious Stone, and Precious Metal Wholesalers
5099	Durable Goods, NEC	42199	Other Miscellaneous Durable Goods Wholesalers (pt)
5111	Printing and Writing Paper	42211	Printing and Writing Paper Wholesalers
5112	Stationery and Office Supplies		
	Sold Via Retail Method	45321	Office Supplies and Stationery Stores (pt)
	Sold Via Wholesale Method	42212	Stationery and Office Supplies Wholesalers
5113	Industrial and Personal Service Paper	42213	Industrial and Personal Service Paper Wholesalers
5122	Drugs, Drug Proprietaries, and Druggists' Sundries	42221	Drugs, Drug Proprietaries, and Druggists' Sundries Wholesalers
5131	Piece Goods, Notions, and Other Dry Goods		
	Piece Good Converters, Broadwoven Fabrics	313311	Broadwoven Fabric Finishing Mills (pt)
	Piece Good Converters, Except Broadwoven Fabrics	313312	Textile and Fabric Finishing (except Broadwoven Fabric) Mills (pt)
	Except Converters	42231	Piece Goods, Notions, and Other Dry Goods Wholesalers
5136	Men's and Boys' Clothing and Furnishings	42232	Men's and Boys' Clothing and Furnishings Wholesalers
5137	Women's Children's and Infants' Clothing and Accessories	42233	Women's, Children's, and Infants' Clothing and Accessories Wholesalers
5139	Footwear	42234	Footwear Wholesalers
5141	Groceries, General Line	42241	General Line Grocery Wholesalers
5142	Packaged Frozen Foods	42242	Packaged Frozen Food Wholesalers
5143	Dairy Products, Except Dried or Canned	42243	Dairy Products (except Dried or Canned) Wholesalers
5144	Poultry and Poultry Products	42244	Poultry and Poultry Product Wholesalers
5145	Confectionery	42245	Confectionery Wholesalers
5146	Fish and Seafoods	42246	Fish and Seafood Wholesalers

5147	Meats and Meat Products		
	Boxed Beef	311612	Meat Processed from Carcasses (pt)
	Except Boxed Beef	42247	Meat and Meat Product Wholesalers
5148	Fresh Fruits and Vegetables	42248	Fresh Fruit and Vegetable Wholesalers
5149	Groceries and Related Products, NEC	42249	Other Grocery and Related Product Wholesalers
5153	Grain and Field Beans	42251	Grain and Field Bean Wholesalers
5154	Livestock	42252	Livestock Wholesalers
5159	Farm-Product Raw Materials, NEC	42259	Other Farm Product Raw Material Wholesalers
5162	Plastics Materials and Basic Forms and Shapes	42261	Plastics Materials and Basic Forms and Shapes Wholesalers
5169	Chemicals and Allied Products, NEC	42269	Other Chemical and Allied Products Wholesalers
5171	Petroleum Bulk Stations and Terminals		
	Heating Oil Sold Via Retail Method	454311	Heating Oil Dealers (pt)
	LP Gas Sold Via Retail Method	454312	Liquefied Petroleum Gas (Bottled Gas) Dealers (pt)
	Sold Via Wholesale Method	42271	Petroleum Bulk Stations and Terminals
5172	Petroleum and Petroleum Products Wholesalers, Except Bulk Stations and Terminals	42272	Petroleum and Petroleum Products (except Bulk Stations and Terminals) Wholesalers
5181	Beer and Ale	42281	Beer and Ale Wholesalers
5182	Wine and Distilled Alcoholic Beverages	42282	Wine and Distilled Alcoholic Beverage Wholesalers
5191	Farm Supplies		
	Lawn and Garden Supplies Sold Via Retail Method	44422	Nursery and Garden Centers (pt) - Retail
	Except Lawn and Garden Supplies Sold Via Retail Method	42291	Farm Supplies Wholesalers
5192	Books, Periodicals, and Newspapers	42292	Book, Periodical and Newspaper Wholesalers

1987 SIC Code	1987 SIC Description	1997 NAICS Code	1997 NAICS United States Description
5193	Flowers, Nursery Stock, and Florists' Supplies		
	Sold Via Wholesale Method	42293	Flower, Nursery Stock and Florists' Supplies Wholesalers
	Sold Via Retail Method	44422	Nursery and Garden Centers (pt) - Retail
5194	Tobacco and Tobacco Products	42294	Tobacco and Tobacco Product Wholesalers
5198	Paint, Varnishes, and Supplies		
	Sold Via Wholesale Method	42295	Paint, Varnish and Supplies Wholesalers (pt)
	Sold Via Retail Method	44412	Paint and Wallpaper Stores (pt) - (Retail)
5199	Nondurable Goods, NEC		
	Advertising Specialties Goods Distributors	54189	Other Services Related to Advertising (pt)
	Except Specialty Advertising	42299	Other Miscellaneous Nondurable Goods Wholesalers
5211	Lumber and Other Building Materials Dealers		
	Home Centers	44411	Home Centers
	Sold Via Wholesale Method	42131	Lumber, Plywood, Millwork and Wood Panel Wholesalers (pt)
	Sold Via Retail Method, Except Home Centers and Glass	44419	Other Building Material Dealers (pt)
5231	Paint, Glass, and Wallpaper Stores		
	Paint and Wallpaper Sold Via Wholesale Method	42295	Paint, Varnish and Supplies Wholesalers (pt)
	Glass Stores	44419	Other Building Material Dealers (pt)
	Paint and Wallpaper Sold Via Retail Method	44412	Paint and Wallpaper Stores (pt)
5251	Hardware Stores	44413	Hardware Stores
5261	Retail Nurseries, Lawn and Garden Supply Stores		
	Except Cut Christmas Trees and Outdoor Power Equipment	44422	Nursery and Garden Centers (pt)

	Cut Christmas Trees	453998	All Other Miscellaneous Store Retailers (except Tobacco Stores) (pt)
	Outdoor Power Equipment Stores	44421	Outdoor Power Equipment Stores (pt)
5271	Mobile Home Dealers	45393	Manufactured (Mobile) Home Dealers
5311	Department Stores	45211	Department Stores
5331	Variety Stores	45299	All Other General Merchandise Stores (pt)
5399	Miscellaneous General Merchandise Stores		
	Warehouse Clubs and General Merchandise Combination Stores	45291	Warehouse Clubs and Superstores (pt)
	All Other General Merchandise Stores	45299	All Other General Merchandise Stores (pt)
5411	Grocery Stores		
	Convenience Stores with Gas	44711	Gasoline Stations with Convenience Stores (pt)
	Supermarkets and Grocery Stores with Little General Merchandise	44511	Supermarkets and Other Grocery (except Convenience) Stores
	Supermarkets and Grocery Stores with Substantial General Merchandise	45291	Warehouse Clubs and Superstores (pt)
	Convenience Stores without Gas	44512	Convenience Stores
5421	Meat and Fish (Seafood) Markets, Including Freezer Provisioners		
	Freezer Provisioners	45439	Other Direct Selling Establishments (pt)
	Meat Markets	44521	Meat Markets (pt)
	Fish and Seafood Markets	44522	Fish and Seafood Markets
5431	Fruit and Vegetable Markets	44523	Fruit and Vegetable Markets
5441	Candy, Nut, and Confectionery Stores	445292	Confectionary and Nut Stores
5451	Dairy Products Stores	445299	All Other Specialty Food Stores (pt)

1987 SIC Code	1987 SIC Description	1997 NAICS Code	1997 NAICS United States Description
5461	Retail Bakeries		
	Donut Shops, Pretzel Shops, Cookie Shops, Bagel Shops, and Other Such Shops that Make and Sell for Immediate Consumption	722213	Snack and Nonalcoholic Beverage Bars (pt)
	Bakeries That Make and Sell at the Same Location	311811	Retail Bakeries
	Sales Only of All Other Baked Goods	445291	Baked Goods Stores
5499	Miscellaneous Food Stores		
	Poultry and Poultry Products	44521	Meat Markets (pt)
	Coffee Shops Making and Serving Food and Beverages for Immediate Consumption	722211	Limited-Service Restaurants (pt)
	Food Supplement Stores	446191	Food (Health) Supplement Stores
	All Other Miscellaneous Food Stores	445299	All Other Specialty Food Stores (pt)
5511	Motor Vehicle Dealers (New and Used)	44111	New Car Dealers
5521	Motor Vehicle Dealers (Used Only)	44112	Used Car Dealers
5531	Auto and Home Supply Stores		
	Tire Dealers	44132	Tire Dealers (pt)
	All Other Auto and Home Supply Stores	44131	Automotive Parts and Accessories Stores (pt)
5541	Gasoline Service Stations		
	Convenience Store with Gas	44711	Gasoline Stations with Convenience Store (pt)
	Except with Convenience Stores	44719	Other Gasoline Stations
5551	Boat Dealers	441222	Boat Dealers
5561	Recreational Vehicle Dealers	44121	Recreational Vehicle Dealers
5571	Motorcycle Dealers	441221	Motorcycle Dealers
5599	Automotive Dealers, NEC	441229	All Other Motor Vehicle Dealers

5611	Men's and Boys' Clothing and Accessory Stores		
	Men's Clothing Stores	44811	Men's Clothing Stores
	Men's Accessory Stores	44815	Clothing Accessories Stores (pt)
5621	Women's Clothing Stores	44812	Women's Clothing Stores
5632	Women's Accessory and Specialty Stores		
	Specialty Stores	44819	Other Clothing Stores (pt)
	Accessory Stores	44815	Clothing Accessories Stores (pt)
5641	Children's and Infants' Wear Stores	44813	Children's and Infants' Clothing Stores
5651	Family Clothing Stores	44814	Family Clothing Stores
5661	Shoe Stores	44821	Shoe Stores
5699	Miscellaneous Apparel and Accessory Stores		
	Custom Tailors and Seamstresses	315	Included in Apparel Manufacturing Subsector Based on Type of Garment Produced
	Miscellaneous Apparel	44819	Other Clothing Stores (pt)
	Miscellaneous Accessories	44815	Clothing Accessories Stores (pt)
5712	Furniture Stores		
	Custom Made Furniture, Except Cabinets and Upholstered	337122	Nonupholstered Wood Household Furniture Manufacturing (pt)
	Custom Wood Cabinets	33711	Wood Kitchen Cabinet and Counter Top Manufacturing (pt)
	Upholstered Custom Made Furniture	337121	Upholstered Household Furniture Manufacturing (pt)
	Except Custom Cabinet and Furniture Builders	44211	Furniture Stores (pt.)
5713	Floor Covering Stores	44221	Floor Covering Stores (pt)
5714	Drapery, Curtain, and Upholstery Stores		

1987 SIC Code	1987 SIC Description	1997 NAICS Code	1997 NAICS United States Description
	Drapery and Curtain Stores	442291	Window Treatment Stores (pt)
	Upholstery Stores	45113	Sewing, Needlework and Piece Goods Stores (pt)
	Custom Drapes	314121	Curtain and Drapery Mills (pt)
5719	Miscellaneous Homefurnishings Stores		
	Blinds and Shades	442291	Window Treatment Stores (pt)
	Pottery and Crafts Made and Sold on Site		Included in Manufacturing sector based on article produced
	Except Blinds, Shades, and Pottery and Crafts Made and Sold on Site	442299	All Other Home Furnishings Stores
5722	Household Appliance Stores	443111	Household Appliance Stores (pt)
5731	Radio, Television, and Consumer Electronics Stores		
	Except Auto Radio Stores	443112	Radio, Television, and Other Electronics Stores (pt)
	Auto Radio Stores	44131	Automotive Parts and Accessories Stores (pt)
5734	Computer and Computer Software Stores	44312	Computer and Software Stores (pt)
5735	Record and Prerecorded Tape Stores	45122	Prerecorded Tape, Compact Disc and Record Stores
5736	Musical Instrument Stores	45114	Musical Instrument and Supplies Stores
5812@	Eating and Drinking Places		
	Full Service Restaurants	72211	Full-Service Restaurants
	Limited Service Restaurants	722211	Limited-Service Restaurants (pt)
	Cafeterias	722212	Cafeterias
	Snack Nonalcoholic Beverage Bars	722213	Snack and Nonalcoholic Beverage Bars (pt)
	Food Service Contractors	72231	Foodservice Contractors
	Caterers	72232	Caterers
	Dinner Theaters	71111	Theater Companies and Dinner Theaters (pt)

5813	Drinking Places (Alcoholic Beverages)	72241	Drinking Places (Alcoholic Beverages)
5912	Drug Stores and Proprietary Stores	44611	Pharmacies and Drug Stores
5921	Liquor Stores	44531	Beer, Wine and Liquor Stores
5932	Used Merchandise Stores		
	Pawn Shops	522298	All Other Non-Depository Credit Intermediation (pt)
	Except pawn shops	45331	Used Merchandise Stores
5941	Sporting Goods Stores and Bicycle Shops	45111	Sporting Goods Stores (pt)
5942	Book Stores	451211	Book Stores
5943	Stationery Stores	45321	Office Supplies and Stationery Stores (pt)
5944	Jewelry Stores	44831	Jewelry Stores (pt)
5945	Hobby, Toy, and Game Shops	45112	Hobby, Toy and Game Stores
5946	Camera and Photographic Supply Stores	44313	Camera and Photographic Supplies Stores
5947	Gift, Novelty, and Souvenir Shops	45322	Gift, Novelty and Souvenir Stores
5948	Luggage and Leather Goods Stores	44832	Luggage and Leather Goods Stores
5949	Sewing, Needlework, and Piece Goods Stores	45113	Sewing, Needlework and Piece Goods Stores (pt)
5961	Catalog and Mail-Order Houses	45411	Electronic Shopping and Mail-Order Houses
5962	Automatic Merchandising Machine Operator	45421	Vending Machine Operators
5963	Direct Selling Establishments		
	Mobile Food Wagons	72233	Mobile Foodservices
	All Other Direct Selling Establishments	45439	Other Direct Selling Establishments (pt)
5983	Fuel Oil Dealers	454311	Heating Oil Dealers (pt)
5984	Liquefied Petroleum Gas (Bottled Gas) Dealers	454312	Liquefied Petroleum Gas (Bottled Gas) Dealers (pt)

1987 SIC Code	1987 SIC Description	1997 NAICS Code	1997 NAICS United States Description
5989	Fuel Dealers, NEC	454319	Other Fuel Dealers
5992	Florists	45311	Florists
5993	Tobacco Stores and Stands	453991	Tobacco Stores
5994	News Dealers and Newsstands	451212	News Dealers and Newsstands
5995	Optical Goods Stores		
	Optical Stores Grinding Prescription Lenses, except 1-Hour Labs	339115	Ophthalmic Goods Manufacturing (pt)
	Except Optical Laboratories Grinding Prescription Lenses	44613	Optical Goods Stores
5999	Miscellaneous Retail Stores, NEC		
	Cosmetic Stores	44612	Cosmetics, Beauty Supplies and Perfume Stores (pt)
	Hearing Aid and Artificial Limb Stores	446199	All Other Health and Personal Care Stores (pt)
	Pets and Pet Supply Stores	45391	Pet and Pet Supplies Stores
	Art Dealers	45392	Art Dealers
	Personal Appliance Stores	443111	Household Appliance Stores (pt)
	Telephone and Typewriter Stores	443112	Radio, Television and Other Electronics Stores (pt.)
	Rough Gem Stores	44831	Jewelry Stores (pt)
	Other Miscellaneous Retail Stores	453998	All Other Miscellaneous Store Retailers (except Tobacco Stores) (pt)
6011	Federal Reserve Banks	52111	Monetary Authorities-Central Banks
6019@	Central Reserve Depository Institutions, NEC	52232	Financial Transactions Processing, Reserve, and Clearing House Activities (pt)
6021@	National Commercial Banks		
	Commercial Banks	52211	Commercial Banking (pt)
	Credit Card Issuing	52221	Credit Card Issuing (pt)

	Trust Services	523991	Trust, Fiduciary and Custody Activities (pt)
6022@	State Commercial Banks		
	Commercial Banks	52211	Commercial Banking (pt)
	Credit Card Issuing	52221	Credit Card Issuing (pt)
	Private and Industrial Banking	52219	Other Depository Intermediation
	Trust Services	523991	Trust, Fiduciary and Custody Activities (pt)
6029@	Commercial Banks, NEC	52211	Commercial Banking (pt)
6035@	Savings Institutions, Federally Chartered	52212	Savings Institutions (pt)
6036@	Savings institutions, Not Federally Chartered	52212	Savings Institutions (pt)
6061@	Credit Unions, Federally Chartered	52213	Credit Unions (pt)
6062@	Credit Unions, Not Federally Chartered	52213	Credit Unions (pt)
6081@	Branches and Agencies of Foreign Banks		
	International Trade Financing	522293	International Trade Financing (pt)
	Branches of Foreign Banks	52211	Commercial Banking (pt)
	Agencies of Foreign Banks	522298	All Other Non-Depository Credit Intermediation (pt)
6082@	Foreign Trade and International Banking Institutions	522293	International Trade Financing (pt)
6091@	Nondeposit Trust Facilities	523991	Trust, Fiduciary, and Custody Activities (pt)
6099@	Functions Related to Deposit Banking, NEC		
	Clearinghouses and Electronic Funds Transfer	52232	Financial Transactions Processing, Reserve, and Clearing House Activities (pt)
	Foreign Currency Exchange	52313	Commodity Contracts Dealing (pt)
	Escrow and Fiduciary Agencies	523991	Trust, Fiduciary, and Custody Activities (pt)
	Deposit Brokers	523999	Miscellaneous Financial Investment Activities (pt)

1987 SIC Code	1987 SIC Description	1997 NAICS Code	1997 NAICS United States Description
	Other	52239	Other Activities Related to Credit Intermediation (pt)
6111@	Federal and Federally Sponsored Credit Agencies		
	Trade Banks	522293	International Trade Financing (pt)
	Secondary Market Financing	522294	Secondary Market Financing
	Other	522298	All Other Non-Depository Credit Intermediation (pt)
6141@	Personal Credit Institutions		
	Credit Card Issuing	52221	Credit Card Issuing (pt)
	Installment Sales Financing	52222	Sales Financing (pt)
	Other	522291	Consumer Lending
6153@	Short-Term Business Credit Institutions, Except Agricultural		
	Business Sales Finance	52222	Sales Financing (pt)
	Credit Card Service	52232	Financial Transactions Processing, Reserve, and Clearing House Activities (pt)
	Other	522298	All Other Non-Depository Credit Intermediation (pt)
6159@	Miscellaneous Business Credit Institutions		
	Finance Leasing, Without Operating Leasing	52222	Sales Financing (pt)
	Finance Leasing and Operating Leasing Combined	532	Included in Rental and Leasing Services subsector by Type of Equipment and Method of Operation
	Trade Banks	522293	International Trade Financing (pt)
	All Other	522298	All Other Non-Depository Credit Intermediation (pt)
6162@	Mortgage Bankers and Loan Correspondents		
	Mortgage Bankers and Originators	522292	Real Estate Credit
	Mortgage Servicing	52239	Other Activities Related to Credit Intermediation (pt)

6163	Loan Brokers	52231	Mortgage and Other Loan Brokers
6211@	Security Brokers, Dealers, and Flotation Companies		
	Security Dealers and Underwriters	52311	Investment Banking and Securities Dealing
	Security Brokers	52312	Securities Brokerage
	Dealers, Except Securities and Commodities	52391	Miscellaneous Intermediation (pt.)
	Other	523999	Miscellaneous Financial Investment Activities (pt.)
6221@	Commodity Contracts Brokers and Dealers		
	Commodity Dealers	52313	Commodity Contracts Dealing (pt)
	Commodity Brokers	52314	Commodity Brokerage
6231	Security and Commodity Exchanges	52321	Securities and Commodity Exchanges
6282@	Investment Advice		
	Portfolio Managers	52392	Portfolio Management (pt)
	Other	52393	Investment Advice
6289@	Services Allied With the Exchange of Securities or Commodities, NEC		
	Securities Custodians	523991	Trust, Fiduciary, and Custody Activities (pt)
	Other	523999	Miscellaneous Financial Investment Activities (pt)
6311@	Life Insurance		
	Life Insurers-Direct	524113	Direct Life Insurance Carriers
	Reinsurance Carriers, Life	52413	Reinsurance Carriers (pt)
6321@	Accident and Health Insurance		
	Accident and Health Insurers-Direct	524114	Direct Health and Medical Insurance Carriers (pt)
	Self Insurers	52519	Other Insurance Funds (pt)

1987 SIC Code	1987 SIC Description	1997 NAICS Code	1997 NAICS United States Description
	Reinsurance Carriers, Accident and Health	52413	Reinsurance Carriers (pt)
6324@	Hospital and Medical Service Plans		
	Accident and Health Insurers-Direct	524114	Direct Health and Medical Insurance Carriers (pt)
	Self Insurers	52519	Other Insurance Funds (pt)
	Reinsurance Carriers, Health and Medical	52413	Reinsurance Carriers (pt)
6331@	Fire, Marine, and Casualty Insurance		
	Fire, Marine, and Casualty Insurers-Direct	524126	Direct Property and Casualty Insurance Carriers (pt)
	Self Insurers	52519	Other Insurance Funds (pt)
	Reinsurance Carriers, Fire, Marine, and Casualty	52413	Reinsurance Carriers (pt)
6351@	Surety Insurance		
	Financial Responsibility Insurers-Direct	524126	Direct Property and Casualty Insurance Carriers (pt)
	Reinsurance Carriers, Financial Responsibility	52413	Reinsurance Carriers (pt)
6361@	Title Insurance		
	Title Insurers-Direct	524127	Direct Title Insurance Carriers
	Reinsurance Carriers, Title	52413	Reinsurance Carriers (pt)
6371@	Pension, Health, and Welfare Funds		
	Managers	52392	Portfolio Management (pt)
	Administrators	524292	Third Party Administration for Insurance and Pension Funds (pt)
	Pension Funds	52511	Pension Funds
	Health and Welfare Funds	52512	Health and Welfare Funds
6399	Insurance Carriers, NEC	524128	Other Direct Insurance (except Life, Health, and Medical) Carriers
6411@	Insurance Agents, Brokers, and Service		

	Insurance Agents and Brokers	52421	Insurance Agencies and Brokerages
	Claim Adjusters	524291	Claims Adjusters
	Claim Processors	524292	Third Party Administrators for Insurance and Pension Funds (pt)
	Other	524298	All Other Insurance Related Activities
6512	Operators of Nonresidential Buildings		
	Stadium and Arena Owners	71131	Promoters of Performing Arts, Sports and Similar Events with Facilities (pt)
	Except Stadium and Arena Owners	53112	Lessors of Nonresidential Buildings (except Miniwarehouses)
6513@	Operators of Apartment Buildings	53111	Lessors of Residential Buildings and Dwellings (pt)
6514@	Operators of Dwellings Other Than Apartment Buildings	53111	Lessors of Residential Buildings and Dwellings (pt)
6515@	Operators of Residential Mobile Home Sites	53119	Lessors of Other Real Estate Property(pt)
6517@	Lessors of Railroad Property	53119	Lessors of Other Real Estate Property (pt)
6519@	Lessors of Real Property, NEC	53119	Lessors of Other Real Estate Property (pt)
6531@	Real Estate Agents and Managers		
	Real Estate Agents and Brokers	53121	Offices of Real Estate Agents and Brokers
	Condominium Associations	81399	Other Similar Organizations (pt)
	Residential Property Managers	531311	Residential Property Managers
	Nonresidential Property Managers	531312	Nonresidential Property Managers
	Real Estate Appraisers	53132	Offices of Real Estate Appraisers
	Cemetery Management	81222	Cemeteries and Crematories (pt)
	Other	53139	Other Activities Related to Real Estate
6541	Title Abstract Offices	541191	Title Abstract and Settlement Offices
6552	Land Subdividers and Developers, Except Cemeteries	23311	Land Subdivision and Land Development

1987 SIC Code	1987 SIC Description	1997 NAICS Code	1997 NAICS United States Description
6553@	Cemetery Subdividers and Developers	81222	Cemeteries and Crematories (pt.)
6712	Offices of Bank Holding Companies	551111	Offices of Bank Holding Companies
6719	Offices of Holding Companies, NEC	551112	Offices of Other Holding Companies
6722	Management Investment Offices, Open-End	52591	Open-End Investment Funds
6726	Unit Investment Trusts, Face-Amount Certificate Offices, and Closed-End Management Investment Offices	52599	Other Financial Vehicles
6732	Education, Religious, and Charitable Trusts	813211	Grantmaking Foundations
6733@	Trusts, Except Educational, Religious, and Charitable		
	Managers	52392	Portfolio Management (pt)
	Administrators of Private Estates	523991	Trust, Fiduciary, and Custody Services (pt)
	Vacation Funds for Employees	52519	Other Insurance Funds (pt)
	Personal Trusts, Estates, and Agency Accounts	52592	Trusts, Estates, and Agency Accounts
6792@	Oil Royalty Traders		
	Investors on Own Account	523999	Miscellaneous Financial Investment Activities (pt.)
	Oil Royalty Trading Companies	53311	Owners and Lessors of Other Non-Financial Assets (pt)
6794	Patent Owners and Lessors	53311	Owners and Lessors of Other Non-Financial Assets (pt)
6798	Real Estate Investment Trusts	52593	Real Estate Investment Trusts
6799@	Investors, NEC		
	Venture Capital Companies	52391	Miscellaneous Intermediation (pt)
	Pool Operators	52392	Portfolio Management (pt)
	Commodity Contract Trading Companies	52313	Commodity Contracts Dealing (pt)
	Other	523999	Miscellaneous Financial Investment Activities (pt)
7011	Hotels and Motels		

	Hotels and Motels, except Casino Hotels	72111	Hotels (except Casino Hotels) and Motels (pt)
	Casino Hotels	72112	Casino Hotels
	Bed and Breakfast Inns	721191	Bed and Breakfast Inns
	Other	721199	All Other Traveler Accommodation
7021	Rooming and Boarding Houses	72131	Rooming and Boarding Houses (pt)
7032	Sporting and Recreational Camps	721214	Recreational and Vacation Camps
7033	Recreational Vehicle Parks and Campsites	721211	RV (Recreational Vehicle Parks) and Campgrounds
7041@	Organization Hotels and Lodging Houses, on Membership Basis		
	Organization Hotels	72111	Hotels (except Casino Hotels) and Motels (pt)
	Other	72131	Rooming and Boarding Houses (pt)
7211	Power Laundries, Family and Commercial	812321	Laundries, Family and Commercial
7212	Garment Pressing, and Agents for Laundries	812391	Garment Pressing and Agents for Laundries
7213@	Linen Supply	812331	Linen Supply (pt.)
7215	Coin-Operated Laundry and Drycleaning	81231	Coin-Operated Laundries and Drycleaners
7216	Drycleaning Plants, Except Rug Cleaning	812322	Drycleaning Plants
7217	Carpet and Upholstery Cleaning	56174	Carpet and Upholstery Cleaning Services
7218	Industrial Launderers	812332	Industrial Launderers
7219@	Laundry and Garment Services, NEC		
	Diaper Service	812331	Linen Supply (pt)
	Clothing Alteration and Repair	81149	Other Personal and Household Goods Repair and Maintenance (pt)
	Except Diaper Service and Clothing Alteration and Repair	812399	All Other Laundry Services

1987 SIC Code	1987 SIC Description	1997 NAICS Code	1997 NAICS United States Description
7221	Photographic Studios, Portrait	541921	Photographic Studios, Portrait
7231@	Beauty Shops		
	Beauty Shops and Salons	812112	Beauty Salons
	Manicure and Pedicure Salons	812113	Nail Salons
	Beauty and Cosmetology Schools	611511	Cosmetology and Barber Schools (pt)
7241	Barber Shops		
	Barber Shops	812111	Barber Shops
	Barber Colleges	611511	Cosmetology and Barber Schools (pt)
7251	Shoe Repair Shops and Shoeshine Parlors	81143	Footwear and Leather Goods Repair (pt)
7261	Funeral Services and Crematories		
	Funeral Homes	81221	Funeral Homes
	Except Funeral Homes	81222	Cemeteries and Crematories (pt)
7291	Tax Return Preparation Services	541213	Tax Preparation Services
7299@	Miscellaneous Personal Services, NEC		
	Babysitting Services	62441	Child Day Care Services (pt)
	Diet and Weight Reducing Services	812191	Diet and Weight Reducing Centers
	Formal Wear and Costume Rental	53222	Formal Wear and Costume Rental (pt)
	Personal Care Services	812199	Other Personal Care Services
	All Other Miscellaneous Personal Services, NEC	81299	All Other Personal Services (pt)
7311	Advertising Agencies	54181	Advertising Agencies
7312	Outdoor Advertising Services	54185	Display Advertising (pt)
7313	Radio, Television, and Publishers' Advertising Representatives	54184	Media Representatives

7319	Advertising, NEC		
	Aerial Advertising	481219	Other Nonscheduled Air Transportation (pt)
	Media Buying Services	54183	Media Buying Agencies
	Display Advertising, Except Outdoor	54185	Display Advertising (pt)
	Advertising Materials Distributor Services	54187	Advertising Material Distribution Services
	Other	54189	Other Services Related to Advertising (pt.)
7322	Adjustment and Collection Services		
	Collection Services	56144	Collection Agencies
	Adjustment Bureaus	561491	Repossession Services (pt)
7323	Credit Reporting Services	56145	Credit Bureaus
7331	Direct Mail Advertising Services	54186	Direct Mail Advertising
7334	Photocopying and Duplicating Services	561439	Business Service Centers (including Copy Shops)
7335	Commercial Photography		
	Aerial Photography	481219	Other Nonscheduled Air Transportation (pt)
	Except When Combined With a Variety of Aircraft-based Services	541922	Commercial Photography (pt)
7336	Commercial Art and Graphic Design	54143	Graphic Design Services (pt)
7338	Secretarial and Court Reporting Services		
	Secretarial Services	56141	Document Preparation Services
	Court Reporting Services	561492	Court Reporting and Stenotype Services
7342	Disinfecting and Pest Control Services		
	Disinfecting Services	56172	Janitorial Services (pt)
	Exterminating and Pest Control Services	56171	Exterminating and Pest Control Services (pt)

1987 SIC Code	1987 SIC Description	1997 NAICS Code	1997 NAICS United States Description
7349	Building Cleaning and Maintenance Services, NEC	56172	Janitorial Services (pt)
7352@	Medical Equipment Rental and Leasing		
	Home Health Furniture and Equipment Rental and Leasing	532291	Home Health Equipment Rental
	Medical Machinery Rental and Leasing	53249	Other Commercial and Industrial Machinery and Equipment Rental and Leasing (pt)
7353@	Heavy Construction Equipment Rental and Leasing		
	With Operator	23499	All Other Heavy Construction (pt)
	Without Operator	532412	Construction, Mining and Forestry Machinery and Equipment Rental and Leasing (pt)
7359@	Equipment Rental and Leasing, NEC		
	Consumer Electronics and Appliances Rental	53221	Consumer Electronics and Appliances Rental
	General Rental Centers	53231	General Rental Centers
	Residential Furniture, Party Supplies, and All Other Miscellaneous Consumer Goods Rental and Leasing	532299	All Other Consumer Goods Rental
	Oilfield and Well Drilling Machinery and Equipment Rental and Leasing	532412	Construction, Mining and Forestry Machinery and Equipment Rental and Leasing (pt)
	Airplane Rental and Leasing	532411	Commercial Air, Rail, and Water Transportation Equipment Rental and Leasing (pt)
	Portable Toilet Rental	562991	Septic Tank and Related Services (pt)
	Office Machinery and Equipment Rental and Leasing	53242	Office Machinery and Equipment Rental and Leasing (pt)
	Industrial Trucks Rental and Leasing	53249	Other Commercial and Industrial Machinery and Equipment Rental and Leasing (pt)
7361@	Employment Agencies		
	Executive Placing Services	541612	Human Resources and Executive Search Consulting Services (pt)
	Except Executive Placing Services	56131	Employment Placement Agencies (pt)

7363	Help Supply Services		
	Temporary Help Supply	56132	Temporary Help Services
	Employee Leasing Services	56133	Employee Leasing Services
7371	Computer Programming Services	541511	Custom Computer Programming Services
7372	Prepackaged Software		
	Software Publishing	51121	Software Publishers
	Reproduction of Software	334611	Software Reproducing
7373	Computer Integrated Systems Design	541512	Computer Systems Design Services (pt)
7374	Computer Processing and Data Preparation and Processing Services	51421	Data Processing Services
7375	Information Retrieval Services	514191	On-Line Information Services
7376	Computer Facilities Management Services	541513	Computer Facilities Management Services
7377	Computer Rental and Leasing	53242	Office Machinery and Equipment Rental and Leasing (pt)
7378	Computer Maintenance and Repair		
	Sales Locations Providing Supporting Repair Services as Major Source of Revenue	44312	Computer and Software Stores (pt)
	All Other Repair and Maintenance	811212	Computer and Office Machine Repair and Maintenance (pt)
7379	Computer Related Services, NEC		
	Computer Systems Consultants	541512	Computer Systems Design Services (pt.)
	Except Computer Systems Consultants	541519	Other Computer Related Services
7381	Detective, Guard, and Armored Car Services		
	Detective Services	561611	Investigation Services
	Guard Services	561612	Security Guards and Patrol Services

1987 SIC Code	1987 SIC Description	1997 NAICS Code	1997 NAICS United States Description
	Armored Car Services	561613	Armored Car Services
7382	Security Systems Services	561621	Security Systems Services (except Locksmiths) (pt)
7383	News Syndicates	51411	New Syndicates
7384	Photofinishing Laboratories		
	Photofinishing Laboratories (Except One-Hour)	812921	Photo Finishing Laboratories (except One-Hour)
	One-Hour Photofinishing	812922	One-Hour Photo Finishing
7389	Business Services, NEC		
	Sound Recording Studios	51224	Sound Recording Studios
	Audio Taping Services	51229	Other Sound Recording Industries (pt.)
	Process Services, Patent Agents, Notaries Public and Paralegal Services	541199	All Other Legal Services
	Bail Handling	81299	All Other Personal Services (pt)
	Mapmaking Services	54137	Surveying and Mapping (except Geophysical) Services (pt)
	Interior Design	54141	Interior Design Services
	Industrial Design	54142	Industrial Design Services
	Drafting Service	54134	Drafting Services
	Fashion, Furniture and Other Design Services	54149	Other Specialized Design Services
	Sign Painting and Other Advertising Related Business Services	54189	Other Services Related to Advertising (pt)
	Translation and Interpretation Services	54193	Translation and Interpretation Services
	Home and Building Inspection Services	54135	Building Inspection Services
	Appraisers, Except Insurance and Real Estate, and Miscellaneous Professional, Scientific, and Technical Services	54199	All Other Professional, Scientific and Technical Services

	Agents and Brokers for Authors and Artists	71141	Agents and Managers for Artists, Athletes, Entertainers and Other Public Figures (pt)
	Telephone Answering Services	561421	Telephone Answering Services
	Telemarketing Bureaus and Telephone Soliciting Services	561422	Telemarketing Bureaus
	Private Mail Centers and Mail Box Rental	561431	Private Mail Centers
	Business Service Centers, except Private Mail Centers and Mail Box Rental	561439	Other Business Service Centers (including Copy Shops)
	Recovery and Repossess	561491	Repossession Services (pt)
	Packaging and Labeling Services	56191	Packaging and Labeling Services
	Swimming Pool Cleaning and Maintenance	56179	Other Services to Buildings and Dwellings (pt)
	Hotel and Restaurant Reservation Services	561599	All Other Travel Arrangement and Reservation Services (pt)
	Convention and Trade Show Services	56192	Convention and Trade Show Organizers
	Convention and Visitors Bureaus and Tourist Information Service	561591	Convention and Visitors Bureaus
	Credit Card Services	52232	Financial Transactions, Processing, Reserve and Clearing House Activities (pt)
	Business Support Services, Except Telephone Answering, Telemarketing Bureaus, Private Mail Centers, and Repossession Services	561499	All Other Business Support Services
	All Other Support Services	56199	All Other Support Services
7513	Truck Rental and Leasing, Without Drivers	53212	Truck, Utility Trailer and RV (Recreational Vehicle) Rental and Leasing (pt)
7514	Passenger Car Rental	532111	Passenger Cars Rental
7515	Passenger Car Leasing	532112	Passenger Cars Leasing

1987 SIC Code	1987 SIC Description	1997 NAICS Code	1997 NAICS United States Description
7519	Utility Trailer and Recreational Vehicle Rental	53212	Truck, Utility Trailer and RV (Recreational Vehicles) Rental and Leasing (pt)
7521	Automobile Parking	81293	Parking Lots and Garages
7532	Top, Body, and Upholstery Repair Shops and Paint Shops	811121	Automotive Body, Paint, and Interior Repair and Maintenance
7533	Automotive Exhaust System Repair Shops	811112	Automotive Exhaust System Repair
7534@	Tire Retreading and Repair Shops		
	Retreading	326212	Tire Retreading
	Repair	811198	All Other Automotive Repair and Maintenance (pt)
7536	Automotive Glass Replacement Shops	811122	Automotive Glass Replacement Shops
7537	Automotive Transmission Repair Shops	811113	Automotive Transmission Repair
7538	General Automotive Repair Shops	811111	General Automotive Repair
7539	Automotive Repair Shops, NEC	811118	Other Automotive Mechanical and Electrical Repair and Maintenance
7542	Carwashes	811192	Car Washes
7549@	Automotive Services, Except Repair and Carwashes		
	Lubricating Services, Automotive	811191	Automotive Oil Change and Lubrication Shops
	Towing	48841	Motor Vehicle Towing
	Except Lubricating Services and Towing	811198	All Other Automotive Repair and Maintenance (pt)
7622	Radio and Television Repair Shops		
	Stereo, TV, VCR, and Radio Repair	811211	Consumer Electronics Repair and Maintenance (pt)
	Telecommunication Equipment Repair	811213	Communication Equipment Repair and Maintenance (pt)
	Radio and TV Sales Locations Providing Supporting Repair Services As Major Source of Revenue	443112	Radio, Television and Other Electronics Stores (pt)
7623	Refrigeration and Air-Conditioning Services and Repair Shops		

	Refrigerator and A/C Sales Locations Providing Supporting Repair Service as Major Source of Revenue	443111	Household Appliance Stores (pt)
	Commercial Refrigerator Equipment Repair	81131	Commercial and Industrial Machinery and Equipment (except Automotive and Electronic) Repair and Maintenance (pt)
	Except Commercial	811412	Appliance Repair and Maintenance (pt)
7629	Electrical and Electronic Repair Shops, NEC		
	Appliance Sales Locations Providing Supporting Repair Services As Major Source of Revenue	443111	Household Appliance Stores (pt)
	Business and Office Machine Repair, Electrical	811212	Computer and Office Machine Repair and Maintenance (pt)
	Telephone Set Repair	811213	Communication Equipment Repair and Maintenance (pt)
	Electrical Measuring Instrument Repair and Calibration, Medical Equipment Repair, Electrical	811219	Other Electronic and Precision Equipment Repair and Maintenance (pt)
	Appliance Repair, Electrical; Washing Machine Repair; Electric Razor Repair	811412	Appliance Repair and Maintenance (pt)
	Consumer Electronic Equipment Repair Except Computer, Radio, Television, Stereo, and VCR	811211	Consumer Electronics Repair and Maintenance (pt)
7631@	Watch, Clock, and Jewelry Repair	81149	Other Personal and Household Goods Repair and Maintenance (pt)
7641	Reupholster and Furniture Repair	81142	Reupholstery and Furniture Repair
7692@	Welding Repair	81149	Other Personal and Household Goods Repair and Maintenance (pt)
7694@	Armature Rewinding Shops		
	Repair	81131	Commercial and Industrial Machinery and Equipment (except Automotive and Electronic) Repair and Maintenance (pt)
	Remanufacturing	335312	Motor and Generator Manufacturing (pt)
7699	Repair Shops and Related Services, NEC		
	Locksmith Shops	561622	Locksmiths
	Cesspool Cleaning, Sewer Cleaning and Rodding	562991	Septic Tank and Related Services (pt)

1987 SIC Code	1987 SIC Description	1997 NAICS Code	1997 NAICS United States Description
	Furnace Ducts, Chimney and Gutter Cleaning Services	56179	Other Services to Buildings and Dwellings (pt)
	Ship Scaling	48839	Other Supporting Activities for Water Transportation (pt)
	Bicycle Sales Locations Providing Supporting Repair Services As Major Source of Revenue	45111	Sporting Goods Stores (pt)
	Other Non-Automotive Transportation Equipment and Industrial Machinery and Equipment	81131	Commercial and Industrial Machinery and Equipment (except Automotive and Electronic) Repair and Maintenance (pt)
	Farriers	11521	Support Activities for Animal Production (pt)
	Typewriter Repair	811212	Computer and Office Machine Repair and Maintenance (pt)
	Dental Instrument Repair, Laboratory Instrument Repair, Medical Equipment and Other Electronic and Precision Equipment Repair, Except Typewriters	811219	Other Electronic and Precision Equipment Repair and Maintenance (pt)
	Lawnmower Repair Shops, Sharpening and Repairing Knives, Saws and Tools	811411	Home and Garden Equipment Repair and Maintenance
	Gas Appliance Repair Service, Sewing Machine Repair, Stove Repair Shops, and Other Non-Electrical Appliances	811412	Appliance Repair and Maintenance (pt)
	Leather Goods Repair Shops, Luggage Repair Shops, Pocketbook Repair Shops	81143	Footwear and Leather Goods Repair (pt)
	Except Industrial, Electronic, Home and Garden, Appliance, Locksmith, and Leather Goods	81149	Other Personal and Household Goods Repair and Maintenance (pt)
7812	Motion Picture and Video Tape Production	51211	Motion Picture and Video Production
7819	Services Allied to Motion Picture Production		
	Teleproduction and Post-Production Services	512191	Teleproduction and Other Post-Production Services
	Casting Bureaus	56131	Employment Placement Agencies (pt)
	Wardrobe Rental (Motion Pictures)	53222	Formal Wear and Costumes Rental (pt)
	Rental of Motion Picture Equipment	53249	Other Commercial and Industrial Machinery and Equipment Rental and Leasing (pt)

	Talent Payment Services	541214	Payroll Services (pt)
	Film Directors and Related Motion Picture Production Services, Independent	71151	Independent Artists, Writers, and Performers (pt)
	Reproduction of Video	334612	Prerecorded Compact Disc (Except Software), Tape, and Record Manufacturing (pt)
	All Other Services	512199	Other Motion Picture and Video Industries (pt)
7822	Motion Picture and Video Tape Distribution		
	Prerecorded Video Tapes (Wholesaling of)	42199	Other Miscellaneous Durable Goods Wholesalers (pt)
	All Other	51212	Motion Picture and Video Distribution (pt)
7829	Services Allied to Motion Picture Distribution		
	Except Film Libraries	512199	Other Motion Picture and Video Industries (pt)
	Film Libraries	51212	Motion Picture and Video Distribution (pt)
7832	Motion Picture Theaters, Except Drive-Ins.	512131	Motion Picture Theaters, Except Drive-In
7833	Drive-In Motion Picture Theaters	512132	Drive-In Motion Picture Theaters
7841	Video Tape Rental	53223	Video Tapes and Disc Rental
7911@	Dance Studios, Schools, and Halls		
	Dance Studios and Halls	71399	All Other Amusement and Recreation Industries (pt)
	Dance Schools	61161	Fine Arts Schools (pt)
7922@	Theatrical Producers (Except Motion Picture) and Miscellaneous Theatrical Services		
	Casting Agencies	56131	Employment Placement Agencies (pt)
	Theater and Opera Companies	71111	Theater Companies and Dinner Theaters (pt)
	Theatrical Agents	71141	Agents and Managers for Artists, Athletes, Entertainers and Other Public Figures (pt)

1987 SIC Code	1987 SIC Description	1997 NAICS Code	1997 NAICS United States Description
	Ballet and Dance Companies	71112	Dance Companies
	Theater Operators	71131	Promoters of Performing Arts, Sports, and Similar Events with Facilities (pt)
	Theatrical Promoters	71132	Promoters of Performing Arts, Sports, and Similar Events without Facilities (pt)
	Producers of Radio Programs	51229	Other Sound Recording Industries (pt)
	Theatrical Equipment Rental	53249	Other Commercial and Industrial Machinery and Equipment Rental and Leasing (pt)
7929@	Bands, Orchestras, Actors, and Other Entertainers and Entertainment Groups		
	Musical Groups and Artists, Orchestras	71113	Musical Groups and Artists
	Actors and Actresses	71151	Independent Artists, Writers, and Performers (pt)
	Except Musical Groups and Artists, Actors and Actresses	71119	Other Performing Arts Companies (pt)
7933	Bowling Centers	71395	Bowling Centers
7941@	Professional Sports Clubs and Promoters		
	Professional Sports Clubs	711211	Sports Teams and Clubs
	Sports Agents	71141	Agents and Managers for Artists, Athletes, Entertainers , and Other Public Figures (pt)
	Sports Promoters	71132	Promoters of Arts, Sports and Similar Events without Facilities (pt)
	Stadium Operators	71131	Promoters of Arts, Sports, and Similar Events with Facilities (pt)
	Except Sports Clubs, Stadium Operators, Sports Promoters, and Agents	711219	Other Spectator Sports (pt)
7948@	Racing, Including Track Operations		
	Racetrack Operators	711212	Race Tracks
	Racing, except Track Operators	711219	Other Spectator Sports (pt)

7991@	Physical Fitness Facilities	71394	Fitness and Recreational Sports Centers (pt)
7992@	Public Golf Courses	71391	Golf Courses and Country Clubs (pt)
7993@	Coin Operated Amusement Devices		
	Amusement Arcades	71312	Amusement Arcades
	Gambling (Slot Machine) Operators	71329	Other Gambling Industries (pt)
	Except Amusement Arcades and Slot Machine Operators	71399	All Other Amusement and Recreation Industries (pt)
7996	Amusement Parks	71311	Amusement and Theme Parks
7997@	Membership Sports and Recreation Clubs		
	Golf Clubs	71391	Golf Courses and Country Clubs (pt)
	Recreation Clubs with Facilities	71394	Fitness and Recreational Sports Centers (pt)
	Recreation Clubs Without Facilities	71399	All Other Amusement and Recreation Industries (pt)
7999	Amusement and Recreation Services, NEC		
	Ticket Agencies	561599	All Other Travel Arrangement and Reservation Services (pt)
	Aerial Tramways, Scenic and Amusement	48799	Scenic and Sightseeing Transportation, Other (pt)
	Circus Companies	71119	Other Performing Arts Companies (pt)
	Professional Athletes	711219	Other Spectator Sports (pt)
	Skiing Facilities	71392	Skiing Facilities
	Nonmembership Recreation Facilities	71394	Fitness and Recreational Sports Centers (pt)
	Casinos, except Casino Hotels	71321	Casinos (except Casino Hotels)
	Lottery, Bingo, Bookie and Other Gaming Operations	71329	Other Gambling Industries (pt)
	Caverns and Miscellaneous Commercial Parks	71219	Nature Parks and Other Similar Institutions (pt)
	Sports Instruction	61162	Sports and Recreation Instruction

1987 SIC Code	1987 SIC Description	1997 NAICS Code	1997 NAICS United States Description
	Sports Equipment Rental	532292	Recreational Goods Rental
	Scenic Transport Operations, Land	48711	Scenic and Sightseeing Transportation, Land (pt)
	Charter Fishing	48721	Scenic and Sightseeing Transportation, Water (pt)
	Amusement and Recreation Services, NEC (except circuses, professional athletes, caverns, and other commercial parks, skiing facilities, casinos and other gambling operations, amusement and recreation facilities, sports instruction, sports equipment rental, and amusement or scenic transport operations)	71399	All Other Amusement and Recreation Industries (pt)
8011@	Offices and Clinics of Doctors of Medicine		
	Surgical and Emergency Centers	621493	Freestanding Ambulatory Surgical and Emergency Centers
	HMO Medical Centers	621491	HMO Medical Centers
	Offices of Physicians, Mental Health Specialists	621112	Offices of Physicians, Mental Health Specialists (pt)
	Offices of Physicians Except Mental Health	621111	Offices of Physicians, (except Mental Health Specialists) (pt)
8021	Offices and Clinics of Dentists	62121	Offices of Dentists
8031@	Offices and Clinics of Doctors of Osteopathy		
	Offices of Doctors of Osteopathy, Except Mental Health	621111	Offices of Physicians (except Mental Health Specialists) (pt)
	Offices of Doctors of Osteopathy, Mental Health Specialists	621112	Offices of Physicians, Mental Health Specialists (pt)
8041	Offices and Clinics of Chiropractors	62131	Offices of Chiropractors
8042	Offices and Clinics of Optometrists	62132	Offices of Optometrists
8043	Offices and Clinics of Podiatrists	621391	Offices of Podiatrists
8049	Offices and Clinics of Health Practitioners, NEC		
	Mental Health Practitioners, Except Physicians	62133	Offices of Mental Health Practitioners (except Physicians)

	Offices of Physical, Occupational, and Speech Therapists and Audiologists	62134	Offices of Physical, Occupational, and Speech Therapists and Audiologists
	Other Offices of Heath Practitioners	621399	Offices of All Other Miscellaneous Health Practitioners
8051@	Skilled Nursing Care Facilities		
	Continuing Care Retirement Communities	623311	Continuing Care Retirement Communities (pt)
	All Other Skilled Nursing Care Facilities	62311	Nursing Care Facilities (pt)
8052@	Intermediate Care Facilities		
	Continuing Care Retirement Communities	623311	Continuing Care Retirement Communities (pt)
	Mental Retardation Facilities	62321	Residential Mental Retardation Facilities
	Other Intermediate Care Facilities	62311	Nursing Care Facilities (pt)
8059@	Nursing and Personal Care Facilities, NEC		
	Continuing Care Retirement Communities	623311	Continuing Care Retirement Communities (pt)
	Other Nursing and Personal Care Facilities	62311	Nursing Care Facilities (pt)
8062@	General Medical and Surgical Hospitals	62211	General Medical and Surgical Hospitals (pt)
8063@	Psychiatric Hospitals	62221	Psychiatric and Substance Abuse Hospitals (pt)
8069@	Specialty Hospitals, Except Psychiatric		
	Children's Hospitals	62211	General Medical and Surgical Hospitals (pt)
	Psychiatric and Substance Abuse Hospitals	62221	Psychiatric and Substance Abuse Hospitals (pt)
	Other Specialty Hospitals	62231	Specialty (except Psychiatric and Substance Abuse) Hospitals
8071	Medical Laboratories		
	Diagnostic Imaging Centers	621512	Diagnostic Imaging Centers
	Medical Laboratories, Except Diagnostic Imaging Centers	621511	Medical Laboratories

1987 SIC Code	1987 SIC Description	1997 NAICS Code	1997 NAICS United States Description
8072	Dental Laboratories	339116	Dental Laboratories
8082	Home Health Care Services	62161	Home Health Care Services
8092	Kidney Dialysis Centers	621492	Kidney Dialysis Centers
8093	Specialty Outpatient Facilities, NEC		
	Family Planning Centers	62141	Family Planning Centers (pt)
	Outpatient Mental Health Facilities	62142	Outpatient Mental Health and Substance Abuse Centers
	Other Specialty Outpatient Facilities	621498	All Other Outpatient Care Facilities
8099@	Health and Allied Services, NEC		
	Blood and Organ Banks	621991	Blood and Organ Banks
	Medical artists	54143	Graphic Design Services (pt)
	Medical Photography	541922	Commercial Photography (pt)
	Childbirth Preparation Classes	62141	Family Planning Centers (pt)
	Other Health and Allied Services	621999	All Other Miscellaneous Ambulatory Health Care Services
8111	Legal Services	54111	Offices of Lawyers
8211	Elementary and Secondary Schools	61111	Elementary and Secondary Schools
8221	Colleges, Universities, and Professional Schools	61131	Colleges, Universities and Professional Schools
8222	Junior Colleges and Technical Institutes	61121	Junior Colleges
8231	Libraries	51412	Libraries and Archives
8243	Data Processing Schools		
	Computer Repair Training	611519	Other Technical and Trade Schools (pt)
	Except Computer Repair Training	61142	Computer Training
8244	Business and Secretarial Schools	61141	Business and Secretarial Schools

8249@	Vocational Schools, NEC		
	Vocational Apprenticeship Training	611513	Apprenticeship Training
	Aviation Schools	611512	Flight Training (pt)
	Other Technical and Trade Schools	611519	Other Technical and Trade Schools (pt)
8299@	Schools and Educational Services, NEC		
	Flying Instruction	611512	Flight Training (pt)
	Automobile Driving Instruction	611692	Automobile Driving Schools
	Curriculum Development, Educational	61171	Educational Support Services (pt)
	Exam Preparation and Tutoring	611691	Exam Preparation and Tutoring
	Art Drama and Music Schools	61161	Fine Arts Schools (pt)
	Language Schools	61163	Language Schools
	Professional and Management Development Training	61143	Professional and Mangement Development Training Schools
	All Other Schools and Educational Services, NEC	611699	All Other Miscellaneous Schools and Instruction
8322	Individual and Family Social Services		
	Child and Youth Services	62411	Child and Youth Services (pt)
	Community Food Services	62421	Community Food Services
	Community Housing Services, Except Temporary Shelters	624229	Other Community Housing Services
	Emergency and Other Relief Services	62423	Emergency and Other Relief Services
	Services for the Elderly and Persons with Disabilities	62412	Services for the Elderly and Persons with Disabilities
	Temporary Shelter	624221	Temporary Shelters
	Parole Offices and Probation Offices	92215	Parole Offices and Probation Offices
	Other Individual and Family Services	62419	Other Individual and Family Services

1987 SIC Code	1987 SIC Description	1997 NAICS Code	1997 NAICS United States Description
8331	Job Training and Vocational Rehabilitation Services	62431	Vocational Rehabilitation Services
8351	Child Day Care Services	62441	Child Day Care Services (pt)
8361	Residential Care		
	Homes for the Elderly	623312	Homes for the Elderly
	Mental Health and Substance Abuse Facilities	62322	Residential Mental Health and Substance Abuse Facilities
	Other Residential Care	62399	Other Residential Care Facilities
8399	Social Services, NEC		
	Voluntary Health Organizations	813212	Voluntary Health Organizations
	Grantmaking and Giving	813219	Other Grantmaking and Giving Services
	Human Rights Organizations	813311	Human Rights Organizations
	Environment, Conservation, and Wildlife Organizations	813312	Environment, Conservation and Wildlife Organizations (pt)
	All Other Social Advocacy Organizations	813319	Other Social Advocacy Organizations
8412	Museums and Art Galleries		
	Museums	71211	Museums
	Historical and Heritage Sites	71212	Historical Sites
8422	Arboreta and Botanical or Zoological Gardens		
	Botanical and Zoological Gardens	71213	Zoos and Botanical Gardens
	Nature Parks and Reserves	71219	Nature Parks and Other Similar Institutions (pt)
8611	Business Associations	81391	Business Associations (pt)
8621	Professional Membership Organizations	81392	Professional Organizations
8631	Labor Unions and Similar Labor Organizations	81393	Labor Unions and Similar Labor Organizations
8641	Civic, Social, and Fraternal Associations		

	Civic and Social Associations	81341	Civic and Social Organizations (pt)
	Homeowner and Condominium Associations	81399	Other Similar Organizations(pt)
	American Indian and Alaskan Native Tribal Governments	92115	American Indian and Alaska Native Tribal Governments
	Youth Development Organizations	62411	Child and Youth Services (pt)
8651	Political Organizations	81394	Political Organizations
8661	Religious Organizations	81311	Religious Organizations
8699@	Membership Organizations, NEC		
	Farm Granges	81341	Civic and Social Organizations (pt)
	Farm Business Organizations	81391	Business Associations (pt)
	Humane Societies	813312	Environment, Conservation, and Wildlife Organizations (pt)
	Motor Clubs	561599	All Other Travel Arrangement and Reservation Services (pt)
	Except Farm Granges, Farm Business Organizations and Environmental Conservation and Wildlife Organizations	81399	Other Similar Organizations (pt)
8711	Engineering Services	54133	Engineering Services
8712	Architectural Services	54131	Architectural Services
8713	Surveying Services		
	Geophysical Surveying Services	54136	Geophysical Surveying and Mapping Services (pt)
	Except Geophysical Surveying	54137	Surveying and Mapping (except Geophysical) Services (pt)
8721@	Accounting, Auditing, and Bookkeeping Services		
	Auditing Accountants	541211	Offices of Certified Public Accountants
	Payroll Services	541214	Payroll Services (pt)
	Other Accounting Services	541219	Other Accounting Services

1987 SIC Code	1987 SIC Description	1997 NAICS Code	1997 NAICS United States Description
8731@	Commercial Physical and Biological Research		
	Physical and Engineering Sciences	54171	Research and Development in the Physical Sciences and Engineering Sciences (pt)
	Life Sciences	54172	Research and Development in the Life Sciences (pt)
8732@	Commercial Economic, Sociological, and Educational Research		
	Social Sciences and Humanities	54173	Research and Development in the Social Sciences and Humanities (pt)
	Market Research and Opinion Research	54191	Marketing Research and Public Opinion Polling
8733@	Noncommercial Research Organizations		
	Physical and Engineering Services	54171	Research and Development in the Physical Sciences and Engineering Sciences (pt)
	Life Sciences	54172	Research and Development in the Life Sciences (pt)
	Social Sciences and Humanities	54173	Research and Development in the Social Sciences and Humanities (pt)
8734	Testing Laboratories		
	Veterinary Testing Labs	54194	Veterinary Services (pt)
	Except Veterinary Testing Labs	54138	Testing Laboratories
8741@	Management Services		
	Except Construction Management Services	56111	Office Administrative Services
	Construction Management Services	23	Included in Construction Sector By Type of Construction
8742@	Management Consulting Services		
	Administrative and General Management Consulting	541611	Administrative Management and General Management Consulting Services
	Human Resources and Personnel Management Consulting	541612	Human Resources and Executive Search Services (pt)
	Marketing Consulting	541613	Marketing Consulting Services

	Manufacturing Management, Physical Distribution, and Site Location Consulting	541614	Process, Physical, Distribution and Logistics Consulting Services
8743	Public Relations Services	54182	Public Relations Agencies
8744	Facilities Support Management Services	56121	Facilities Support Services
8748@	Business Consulting Services, NEC		
	Educational Test Development and Evaluation Services, Educational Testing, and Educational Consulting	61171	Educational Support Services (pt)
	Safety Consulting	541618	Other Management Consulting Services (pt)
	Agriculture Consulting, Economic Consultants, Radio Consultants, Traffic Consultants	54169	Other Scientific and Technical Consulting Services (pt)
8811	Private Households	81411	Private Households
8999@	Services, NEC		
	Authors, Artists, and Related Technical Services, Independent	71151	Independent Artists, Writers, and Performers (pt)
	Record Production	51221	Record Production
	Nuclear Consultants, Consulting Geologists, and Consulting Physicists	54169	Other Scientific and Technical Consulting Services (pt)
	Music Publishing	51223	Music Publishers (pt)
	Actuarial Consulting	541612	Human Resources and Executive Search Consulting Services (pt)
	All Other Information Providers	514199	All Other Information Services
	Environmental Consultants	54162	Environmental Consulting Services
9111	Executive Offices	92111	Executive Offices
9121	Legislative Bodies	92112	Legislative Bodies
9131	Executive and Legislative Offices, Combined	92114	Executive and Legislative Offices, Combined

1987 SIC Code	1987 SIC Description	1997 NAICS Code	1997 NAICS United States Description
9199	General Government, NEC	92119	All Other General Government
9211	Courts	92211	Courts
9221	Police Protection	92212	Police Protection
9222	Legal Counsel and Prosecution	92213	Legal Counsel and Prosecution
9223	Correctional Institutions	92214	Correctional Institutions
9224	Fire Protection	92216	Fire Protection
9229	Public Order and Safety, NEC	92219	All Other Justice, Public Order, and Safety
9311	Public Finance, Taxation, and Monetary Policy	92113	Public Finance
9411	Administration of Educational Programs	92311	Administration of Education Programs
9431	Administration of Public Health Programs	92312	Administration of Public Health Programs
9441	Administration of Social, Human Resource and Income Maintenance Programs	92313	Administration of Social, Human Resource and Income Maintenance Programs
9451	Administration of Veteran's Affairs, Except Health Insurance	92314	Administration of Veteran's Affairs
9511	Air and Water Resource and Solid Waste Management	92411	Air and Water Resource and Solid Waste Management
9512	Land, Mineral, Wildlife, and Forest Conservation	92412	Land, Mineral, Wildlife, and Forest Conservation
9531	Administration of Housing Programs	92511	Administration of Housing Programs
9532	Administration of Urban Planning and Community and Rural Development	92512	Administration of Urban Planning and Community and Rural Development
9611	Administration of General Economic Programs	92611	Administration of General Economic Programs
9621	Regulations and Administration of Transportation Programs		
	Air Traffic Control	488111	Air Traffic Control (pt)
	Except Air Traffic Control	92612	Regulation and Administration of Transportation Programs

9631	Regulation and Administration of Communications, Electric, Gas, and Other Utilities	92613	Regulation and Administration of Communications, Electric, Gas, and Other Utilities
9641	Regulation of Agricultural Marketing and Commodity	92614	Regulation of Agricultural Marketing and Commodity
9651	Regulation, Licensing, and Inspection of Miscellaneous Commercial Sectors	92615	Regulation, Licensing, and Inspection of Miscellaneous Commercial Sectors
9661	Space Research and Technology	92711	Space Research and Technology
9711	National Security	92811	National Security
9721	International Affairs	92812	International Affairs
9999	Nonclassifiable Establishments	99999	Unclassified Establishments

The abbreviation "pt" means "part of"; @ means time series break has been created that is greater than 3% of the 1992 value of shipments for the 1987 industry. The abbreviation NEC is used for Not Elsewhere Classified.

Sally Katzen,
Administrator, Office of Information and Regulatory Affairs.
[FR Doc. 97–8101 Filed 4–8–97; 8:45 am]
BILLING CODE 3110–01–C

Table 3. 1997/1987 NAICS Alphabetical and Key Word/Phrase Index

Editor's Note:

This following index has been prepared as an aid to the reader in locating appropriate NAICS codes by key word and phrase. This index was generated by cross-indexing the NAICS codes to the key word and phrase index appearing in the *1987 Standard Industrial Classification Manual*. Since the original key word index was based on SIC codes, some redundancies and loosely construed classifications may appear in sub-categories to alphabetical listings. NAICS titles have also been rephrased in order to yield a more logical alphabetical listing. Please verify your look-ups against Table 1 to insure that they match the appropriate NAICS syntax and standard.

NAICS titles have been merged into the key word index. They appear in bold type. Abbreviations have also been used to identify industry sectors in which the listings appear. A table of abbreviations used appears in the adjoining column.

Glossary of Abbreviations:

NAICS	INDUSTRY SECTOR TITLE	ABBREV.
48-49	Transportation and Warehousing	*trans*
31-33	Manufacturing	*mfg*
44-45	Retail Trade	*retail*
11	Agriculture, Forestry, Fishing, and Hunting	*ag*
21	Mining	*mining*
22	Utilities	*util*
23	Construction	*const*
42	Wholesale Trade	*whlse*
51	Information	*info*
52	Finance and Insurance	*fin*
53	Real Estate and Rental and Leasing	*real*
54	Professional, Scientific and Technical Services	*prof*
55	Management of Companies and Enterprises	*manag*
56	Administrative and Support, Waste Management and Remediation Services	*admin*
61	Educational Services	*educ*
62	Health Care and Social Assistance	*hlth*
71	Arts, Entertainment and Recreation	*arts*
72	Accommodation and Foodservices	*accom*
81	Other Services (except Public Administration)	*serv*
92	Public Administration	*pub*
99	Unclassified Establishments	*uncl*

Table 3. 1997/1987 NAICS Alphabetical and Key Word/Phrase Index

ALPHABETICAL INDEX	NAICS	SIC
Abdominal supporters, braces, and trusses: Surgical Appliance and Supplies—*mfg*	339113	3842
Abrasion testing machines: Measuring and Controlling Device, Other—*mfg*	334519	3829
Surgical and Medical Instrument—*mfg*	339112	3829
Abrasive buffs, bricks, cloth, paper, sticks, stones, wheels, etc.: Abrasive Product—*mfg*	32791	3291
Fabricated Metal Product, All Other Miscellaneous—*mfg*	332999	3291
Abrasive coated products: Abrasive Product—*mfg*	32791	3291
Fabricated Metal Product, All Other Miscellaneous—*mfg*	332999	3291
Abrasive grains, natural and artificial: Abrasive Product—*mfg*	32791	3291
Fabricated Metal Product, All Other Miscellaneous—*mfg*	332999	3291
Abrasive points, wheels, and disks–dental: Dental Equipment and Supplies—*mfg*	339114	3843
Abrasive Product Manufacturing	**32791**	**3291**
Abrasive sand mining: Industrial Sand—*mining*	212322	1446
Abrasives: Industrial Supplies—*whlse*	42184	5085
Abrasives, aluminous: Abrasive Product—*mfg*	32791	3291
Fabricated Metal Product, All Other Miscellaneous—*mfg*	332999	3291
Absorbent cotton, sterilized: Surgical Appliance and Supplies—*mfg*	339113	3842
Absorbent paper: Newsprint Mills—*mfg*	322122	2621
Paper (except Newsprint) Mills—*mfg*	322121	2621
Absorbers, gas: Air-Conditioning and Warm Air Heating Equipment and Commercial and Industrial Refrigeration Equipment—*mfg*	333415	3443
Metal Tank (Heavy Gauge)—*mfg*	33242	3443
Plate Work— *mfg*	332313	3443
Power Boiler and Heat Exchanger—*mfg*	33241	3443
Absorption analyzers, industrial process type–e.g., infrared, X-ray: Instruments and Related Products for Measuring, Displaying, and Controlling Industrial Process Variables—*mfg*	334513	3823
Abstract companies, title: Title Abstract and Settlement Offices—*prof*	541191	6541
Abutment construction–general contractors: Bridge and Tunnel—*const*	23412	1622
Academic caps and gowns: Cut and Sew Apparel, All Other—*mfg*	315299	2389
Academies, elementary and secondary schools: Elementary and Secondary Schools—*educ*	61111	8211
Academies, service (college): Colleges, Universities and Professional Schools—*educ*	61131	8221
Accelerating waveguide structures: Electrical Equipment and Component, All Other Miscellaneous—*mfg*	335999	3699
Engine Equipment, Other—*mfg*	333618	3699
Acceleration indicators and systems components, aerospace types: Search, Detection, Navigation, Guidance, Aeronautical, and Nautical System and Instrument—*mfg*	334511	3812
Accelerators, rubber processing–cyclic and acyclic: Basic Organic Chemical, All Other—*mfg*	325199	2869
Accelerometers, except aerospace type: Measuring and Controlling Device, Other—*mfg*	334519	3829
Surgical and Medical Instrument—*mfg*	339112	3829
Accident and health insurance: Direct Health and Medical Insurance Carriers—*fin*	524114	6321
Insurance Funds, Other—*fin*	52519	6321
Reinsurance Carriers—*fin*	52413	6321
Accommodation	**721**	
Accommodation and Foodservices	**72**	
Accordions and parts: Musical Instrument—*mfg*	339992	3931
Account books: Blankbook, Loose-leaf Binder and Device—*mfg*	323118	2782
Flexographic Printing, Commercial—*mfg*	323112	2782
Gravure Printing, Commercial—*mfg*	323111	2782
Lithographic Printing, Commercial—*mfg*	323110	2782
Printing, Other Commercial—*mfg*	323119	2782
Screen Printing, Commercial—*mfg*	323113	2782
Accounting machines: Office Equipment—*whlse*	42142	5044
Accounting machines, operator paced: Computer Peripheral Equipment, Other—*mfg*	334119	3578
Office Machinery—*mfg*	333313	3578
Accounting service: Accounting Services, Other—*prof*	541219	8721
Certified Public Accountants, Offices Of—*prof*	541211	8721
Payroll Services—*prof*	541214	8721
Accounting Services, Other	**541219**	**8721**
Accounting, Tax Preparation, Bookkeeping and Payroll Services	**5412**	
Accounting, Tax Preparation, Bookkeeping and Payroll Services	**54121**	
Accumulators (industrial pressure vessels): Air-Conditioning and Warm Air Heating Equipment and Commercial and Industrial Refrigeration Equipment—*mfg*	333415	3443
Metal Tank (Heavy Gauge)—*mfg*	33242	3443
Plate Work—*mfg*	332313	3443
Power Boiler and Heat Exchanger—*mfg*	33241	3443
Acetal resins: Plastics Material and Resin—*mfg*	325211	2821
Acetaldehyde: Basic Organic Chemical, All Other—*mfg*	325199	2869
Acetate broadwoven fabrics: Broadwoven Fabric Mills—*mfg*	31321	2221
Acetate fibers: Cellulosic Organic Fiber—*mfg*	325221	2823

ALPHABETICAL INDEX	NAICS	SIC
Acetate filament yarn–throwing, twisting, winding, or spooling: Textile and Fabric Finishing (except Broadwoven Fabric) Mills—*mfg*	313312	2282
Yarn Texturing, Throwing and Twisting Mills—*mfg*	313112	2282
Acetate of lime, natural: Gum and Wood Chemical—*mfg*	325191	2861
Acetate yarn, made from purchased staple–spun: Yarn Spinning Mills—*mfg*	313111	2281
Acetate, cellulose (plastics): Plastics Material and Resin—*mfg*	325211	2821
Acetates, except natural acetate of lime: Basic Organic Chemical, All Other—*mfg*	325199	2869
Acetic acid, synthetic: Basic Organic Chemical, All Other—*mfg*	325199	2869
Acetic anhydride: Basic Organic Chemical, All Other—*mfg*	325199	2869
Acetin: Basic Organic Chemical, All Other—*mfg*	325199	2869
Acetone, natural: Gum and Wood Chemical—*mfg*	325191	2861
Acetone, synthetic: Basic Organic Chemical, All Other—*mfg*	325199	2869
Acetylene: Industrial Gas—*mfg*	32512	2813
Acetylene cylinders: Air-Conditioning and Warm Air Heating Equipment and Commercial and Industrial Refrigeration Equipment—*mfg*	333415	3443
Metal Tank (Heavy Gauge)—*mfg*	33242	3443
Plate Work—*mfg*	332313	3443
Power Boiler and Heat Exchanger—*mfg*	33241	3443
Acid bottles, rubber: Fabric Coating Mills—*mfg*	31332	3069
Rubber Product, All Other—*mfg*	326299	3069
Acid dyes, synthetic: Organic Dye and Pigment—*mfg*	325132	2865
Petrochemical—*mfg*	32511	2865
Acid esters and amines: Basic Organic Chemical, All Other—*mfg*	325199	2869
Acid oil, produced in petroleum refineries: Petroleum Refineries—*mfg*	32411	2911
Acid resist for etching: Basic Organic Chemical, All Other—*mfg*	325199	2899
Chemical Product, All Other Miscellaneous—*mfg*	325998	2899
Acid waste, collection and disposal of: Hazardous Waste Collection—*admin*	562112	4953
Hazardous Waste Treatment and Disposal—*admin*	562211	4953
Materials Recovery Facilities—*admin*	56292	4953
Nonhazardous Waste Treatment and Disposal, Other—*admin*	562219	4953
Waste Collection, Other—*admin*	562119	4953
Acid, battery: Basic Organic Chemical, All Other—*mfg*	325199	2899
Chemical Product, All Other Miscellaneous—*mfg*	325998	2899
Acid, pyroligneous: Gum and Wood Chemical—*mfg*	325191	2861
Acidizing wells on a contract basis: Oil and Gas Operations Support Activities—*mining*	213112	1389
Acidophilus milk: Fluid Milk—*mfg*	311511	2026
Acids: Chemical and Allied Products, Other—*whlse*	42269	5169
Acids, coal tar–derived from coal tar distillation: Cyclic Crude and Intermediate—*mfg*	325192	2865
Petrochemical—*mfg*	32511	2865

ALPHABETICAL INDEX	NAICS	SIC
Acids, fatty–oleic, margaric, and stearic: Basic Organic Chemical, All Other—*mfg*	325199	2899
Chemical Product, All Other Miscellaneous—*mfg*	325998	2899
Acids, inorganic–except nitric or phosphoric: Basic Inorganic Chemical, All Other—*mfg*	325188	2819
Chemical Product, All Other Miscellaneous—*mfg*	325998	2819
Acids, naphthenic–produced in petroleum refineries: Petroleum Refineries—*mfg*	32411	2911
Acids, naphtholsulfonic: Cyclic Crude and Intermediate—*mfg*	325192	2865
Petrochemical—*mfg*	32511	2865
Acids, organic: Basic Organic Chemical, All Other—*mfg*	325199	2869
Acoustical board and tile, mineral wool: Mineral Wool—*mfg*	327993	3296
Acoustical plaster, gypsum: Gypsum and Gypsum Product—*mfg*	32742	3275
Acoustical suspension systems, metal: Ornamental and Architectural Metal Work—*mfg*	332323	3446
Acoustical tile cleaning service: Janitorial Services—*admin*	56172	7349
Acoustical work–contractors: Drywall, Plastering, Acoustical and Insulation Contractors—*const*	23542	1742
Acrolein: Basic Organic Chemical, All Other—*mfg*	325199	2869
Acrylate type rubbers: Synthetic Rubber—*mfg*	325212	2822
Acrylate–butadiene rubbers: Synthetic Rubber—*mfg*	325212	2822
Acrylic and modacrylic filament yarn–throwing, winding, or spooling: Textile and Fabric Finishing (except Broadwoven Fabric) Mills—*mfg*	313312	2282
Yarn Texturing, Throwing and Twisting Mills—*mfg*	313112	2282
Acrylic broadwoven fabrics: Broadwoven Fabric Mills—*mfg*	31321	2221
Acrylic fibers: Noncellulosic Organic Fiber—*mfg*	325222	2824
Acrylic resins: Plastics Material and Resin—*mfg*	325211	2821
Acrylic rubbers: Synthetic Rubber—*mfg*	325212	2822
Acrylic yarn, made from purchased staple–spun: Yarn Spinning Mills—*mfg*	313111	2281
Acrylonitrile: Basic Organic Chemical, All Other—*mfg*	325199	2869
Acrylonitrile fibers: Noncellulosic Organic Fiber—*mfg*	325222	2824
Acrylonitrile-butadiene–styrene resins: Plastics Material and Resin—*mfg*	325211	2821
Actinometers, meteorological: Measuring and Controlling Device, Other—*mfg*	334519	3829
Activated carbon and charcoal: Basic Inorganic Chemical, All Other—*mfg*	325188	2819
Chemical Product, All Other Miscellaneous—*mfg*	325998	2819
Activity centers, elderly or handicapped: Child and Youth Services—*hlth*	62411	8322
Community Food Services—*hlth*	62421	8322
Community Housing Services, Other—*hlth*	624229	8322
Emergency and Other Relief Services—*hlth*	62423	8322
Individual and Family Services, Other—*hlth*	62419	8322
Services for the Elderly and Persons with Disabilities—*hlth*	62412	8322

Description	NAICS	SIC
Temporary Shelters—*hlth*	624221	8322
Actors: Independent Artists, Writers, and Performers—*arts*	71151	7929
Musical Groups and Artists—*arts*	71113	7929
Performing Arts Companies, Other—*arts*	71119	7929
Actresses: Independent Artists, Writers, and Performers—*arts*	71151	7929
Musical Groups and Artists—*arts*	71113	7929
Performing Arts Companies, Other—*arts*	71119	7929
Actuators, fluid power–hydraulic and pneumatic: Fluid Power Cylinder and Actuator—*mfg*	333995	3593
Acupuncturists, except M.D.–offices of: Health Practitioners, Offices Of Miscellaneous—*hlth*	621399	8049
Physical, Occupational and Speech Therapists and Audiologists, Offices Of—*hlth*	62134	8049
Adapter assemblies, hydromatic propeller: Aircraft Part and Auxiliary Equipment, Other—*mfg*	336413	3728
Fluid Power Valve and Hose Fitting—*mfg*	332912	3728
Adapters for multiweapon rack loading on aircraft: Fabricated Metal Product, All Other Miscellaneous—*mfg*	332999	3537
Industrial Truck, Tractor, Trailer and Stacker Machinery—*mfg*	333924	3537
Metal Container, Other—*mfg*	332439	3537
Adapters, bombcluster: Ammunition (except Small Arms)—*mfg*	332993	3483
Adding machine rolls, paper: Coated and Laminated Paper—*mfg*	322222	2679
Converted Paper Product, All Other—*mfg*	322298	2679
Adding machines: Computer Peripheral Equipment, Other—*mfg*	334119	3578
Office Equipment—*whlse*	42142	5044
Office Machinery—*mfg*	333313	3578
Additive alloys, except copper: Electrometallurgical Ferroalloy Product—*mfg*	331112	3313
Secondary Smelting, Refining, and Alloying of Nonferrous Metal (except Copper and Aluminum)—*mfg*	331492	3313
Address labeling machines: Office Machinery—*mfg*	333313	3579
Address list compilers: Direct Mail Advertising—*prof*	54186	7331
Addressing machines: Office Equipment—*whlse*	42142	5044
Addressing machines, plates and plate embossers: Office Machinery—*mfg*	333313	3579
Addressing service: Direct Mail Advertising—*prof*	54186	7331
Adhesive Manufacturing	**32552**	**2891**
Adhesive tape and plasters, medicated or nonmedicated: Surgical Appliance and Supplies—*mfg*	339113	3842
Adhesives: Adhesive—*mfg*	32552	2891
Adhesives, plastics: Adhesive—*mfg*	32552	2891
Adipic acid: Basic Organic Chemical, All Other—*mfg*	325199	2869
Adipic acid esters: Basic Organic Chemical, All Other—*mfg*	325199	2869
Adiponitrile: Basic Organic Chemical, All Other—*mfg*	325199	2869
Adiprene: Synthetic Rubber—*mfg*	325212	2822
Adjustment bureaus, except insurance adjustment agencies: Collection Agencies—*admin*	56144	7322
Repossession Services—*admin*	561491	7322
Adjustment services, insurance: Claims Adjusters—*fin*	524291	6411
Insurance Agencies and Brokerages—*fin*	52421	6411
Insurance Related Activities, All Other—*fin*	524298	6411
Third Party Administration for Insurance and Pension Funds—*fin*	524292	6411
Administration building construction general contractors: Building, Commercial and Institutional—*const*	23332	1542
Administrative and Support Services	**561**	
Administrative Management and General Management Consulting Services	**541611**	**8742**
Administrative management consultants: Administrative Management and General Management Consulting Services—*prof*	541611	8742
Human Resources and Executive Search Consulting Services—*prof*	541612	8742
Marketing Consulting Services—*prof*	541613	8742
Process, Physical, Distribution and Logistics Consulting Services—*prof*	541614	8742
Administrators of private estates (nonoperating): Insurance Funds, Other—*fin*	52519	6733
Portfolio Management—*fin*	52392	6733
Trust, Fiduciary and Custody Activities—*fin*	523991	6733
Trusts, Estates, and Agency Accounts—*fin*	52592	6733
Adobe brick: Structural Clay Product, Other—*mfg*	327123	3259
Adoption services: Child and Youth Services—*hlth*	62411	8322
Individual and Family Services, Other—*hlth*	62419	8322
Adrenal derivatives–bulk, uncompounded: Medicinal and Botanical—*mfg*	325411	2833
Adrenal pharmaceutical preparations: Pharmaceutical Preparation—*mfg*	325412	2834
Adult day care centers: Community Housing Services, Other—*hlth*	624229	8322
Emergency and Other Relief Services—*hlth*	62423	8322
Individual and Family Services, Other—*hlth*	62419	8322
Services for the Elderly and Persons with Disabilities—*hlth*	62412	8322
Temporary Shelters—*hlth*	624221	8322
Advertisement typesetting: Prepress Services—*mfg*	323122	2791
Advertising Agencies	**54181**	**7311**
Advertising and newspaper mats: Printing Machinery and Equipment—*mfg*	333293	3555
Advertising and Related Services	**5418**	
Advertising consultants (agencies): Advertising Agencies—*prof*	54181	7311
Advertising displays, except printed: Sign—*mfg*	33995	3993
Advertising Material Distribution Services	**54187**	**7319**
Advertising posters, lithographed: Lithographic Printing, Commercial—*mfg*	323110	2752
Quick Printing—*mfg*	323114	2752
Advertising service, outdoor: Display Advertising—*prof*	54185	7312
Advertising specialties: Advertising, Other Services Related to—*prof*	54189	5199
Sign—*mfg*	33995	3993
Advertising, Other Services Related to	**54189**	**5199**

ALPHABETICAL INDEX	NAICS	SIC
Advertising, aerial: Advertising Material Distribution Services—*prof*	54187	7319
Advertising, Other Services Related to—*prof*	54189	7319
Display Advertising—*prof*	54185	7319
Media Buying Agencies—*prof*	54183	7319
Nonscheduled Air, Other—*trans*	481219	7319
Advertising, billboard: Display Advertising—*prof*	54185	7312
Advertising, direct mail: Direct Mail Advertising—*prof*	54186	7331
Advisory commissions, executive: Executive Offices—*pub*	92111	9111
Advisory commissions, legislative: Legislative Bodies—*pub*	92112	9121
Advocacy groups: Environment, Conservation and Wildlife Organizations—*serv*	813312	8399
Grantmaking and Giving Services, Other—*serv*	813219	8399
Human Rights Organizations—*serv*	813311	8399
Social Advocacy Organizations, Other—*serv*	813319	8399
Voluntary Health Organizations—*serv*	813212	8399
Adzes: Hand and Edge Tool—*mfg*	332212	3423
Aerating machines, for beverages: Packaging Machinery—*mfg*	333993	3565
Aerial advertising: Advertising Material Distribution Services—*prof*	54187	7319
Advertising, Other Services Related to—*prof*	54189	7319
Display Advertising—*prof*	54185	7319
Media Buying Agencies—*prof*	54183	7319
Nonscheduled Air, Other—*trans*	481219	7319
Aerial cameras: Photographic and Photocopying Equipment—*mfg*	333315	3861
Photographic Film, Paper, Plate and Chemical—*mfg*	325992	3861
Aerial dusting and spraying: Nonscheduled Air, Other—*trans*	481219	721
Soil Preparation, Planting, and Cultivating—*ag*	115112	721
Aerial geophysical exploration, oil and gas field–on a contract basis: Geophysical Surveying and Mapping Services—*prof*	54136	1382
Oil and Gas Operations Support Activities—*mining*	213112	1382
Aerial photographic service, except map making: Nonscheduled Air, Other—*trans*	481219	7335
Photography, Commercial—*prof*	541922	7335
Aerial tramways, except amusement and scenic: Transit and Ground Passenger, All Other—*trans*	485999	4119
Transportation, Special Needs—*trans*	485991	4119
Aerial work platforms, hydraulic or electric truck or carrier mounted: Construction Machinery—*mfg*	33312	3531
Overhead Traveling Crane, Hoist and Monorail System—*mfg*	333923	3531
Railroad Rolling Stock—*mfg*	33651	3531
Aerobic dance and exercise classes: Fitness and Recreational Sports Centers—*arts*	71394	7991
Aeronautical equipment and supplies: Transportation Equipment and Supplies (except Motor Vehicle)—*whlse*	42186	5088
Aerosol valves, metal: Other Metal Valve and Pipe Fitting, Other—*mfg*	332919	3499
Aerospace Product and Parts Manufacturing	**33641**	

ALPHABETICAL INDEX	NAICS	SIC
Aftercooler shells: Air-Conditioning and Warm Air Heating Equipment and Commercial and Industrial Refrigeration Equipment—*mfg*	333415	3443
Metal Tank (Heavy Gauge)—*mfg*	33242	3443
Plate Work—*mfg*	332313	3443
Power Boiler and Heat Exchanger—*mfg*	33241	3443
Aftercoolers, steam jet: Air-Conditioning and Warm Air Heating Equipment and Commercial and Industrial Refrigeration Equipment—*mfg*	333415	3443
Metal Tank (Heavy Gauge)—*mfg*	33242	3443
Plate Work—*mfg*	332313	3443
Power Boiler and Heat Exchanger—*mfg*	33241	3443
Agar culture media, except in vitro and in vivo: Biological Product (except Diagnostic)—*mfg*	325414	2836
Agar–agar (ground): Medicinal and Botanical—*mfg*	325411	2833
Agate mining: Crushed and Broken Stone and Quarrying, Other—*mining*	212319	1499
Non-Metallic Mineral, All Other—*mining*	212399	1499
Agencies of foreign banks: Banking, Commercial—*fin*	52211	6081
International Trade Financing—*fin*	522293	6081
Non-Depository Credit Intermediation, All Other—*fin*	522298	6081
Agents and brokers for authors and nonperforming artists: Agents and Managers for Artists, Athletes, Entertainers and Other Public Figures—*arts*	71141	7389
Agents and Managers for Artists, Athletes, Entertainers and Other Public Figures	**71141**	**7922**
Agents and Managers for Artists, Athletes, Entertainers and Other Public Figures	**7114**	
Agents for mutual funds: Financial Investment Activities, Miscellaneous—*fin*	523999	6211
Intermediation, Miscellaneous—*fin*	52391	6211
Investment Banking and Securities Dealing—*fin*	52311	6211
Securities Brokerage—*fin*	52312	6211
Agents or managers for entertainers: Agents and Managers for Artists, Athletes, Entertainers and Other Public Figures—*arts*	71141	7922
Employment Placement Agencies—*admin*	56131	7922
Promoters of Performing Arts, Sports and Similar Events without Facilities—*arts*	71132	7922
Agents, farm or business loan: Mortgage and Other Loan Brokers—*fin*	52231	6163
Agents, real estate: Real Estate Agents and Brokers, Offices Of—*real*	53121	6531
Agents, retail–for laundries and drycleaners: Garment Pressing, and Agents for Laundries—*serv*	812391	7212
Agents, shipping: Freight Arrangement—*trans*	48851	4731
Agents, talent–theatrical: Agents and Managers for Artists, Athletes, Entertainers and Other Public Figures—*arts*	71141	7922

Entry	NAICS	SIC
Employment Placement Agencies—*admin*	56131	7922
Promoters of Performing Arts, Sports and Similar Events without Facilities—*arts*	71132	7922
Aggregate: Brick, Stone and Related Material—*whlse*	42132	5032
Building Material Dealers, Other—*retail*	44419	5032
Aggregate spreaders: Construction Machinery—*mfg*	33312	3531
Overhead Traveling Crane, Hoist and Monorail System—*mfg*	333923	3531
Railroad Rolling Stock—*mfg*	33651	3531
Aggressins, except in vitro and in vivo: Biological Product (except Diagnostic)—*mfg*	325414	2836
Agreement Corporations: International Trade Financing—*fin*	522293	6082
Agricultural (crop and livestock) insurance: Direct Property and Casualty Insurance Carriers—*fin*	524126	6331
Insurance Funds, Other—*fin*	52519	6331
Reinsurance Carriers—*fin*	52413	6331
Agricultural chemicals: Farm Supplies—*whlse*	42291	5191
Nursery and Garden Centers—*retail*	44422	5191
Agricultural consulting: Educational Support Services—*educ*	61171	8748
Management Consulting Services, Other—*prof*	541618	8748
Scientific and Technical Consulting Services, Other—*prof*	54169	8748
Agricultural disinfectants: Pesticide and Other Agricultural Chemical—*mfg*	32532	2879
Agricultural edge tools, hand: Hand and Edge Tool—*mfg*	332212	3423
Agricultural equipment repair: Machinery and Equipment (except Automotive and Electronic) Repair and Maintenance, Commercial and Industrial—*serv*	81131	7699
Agricultural gypsum: Gypsum and Gypsum Product—*mfg*	32742	3275
Agricultural hand sprayers: Farm Machinery and Equipment—*mfg*	333111	3523
Hand and Edge Tool—*mfg*	332212	3523
Agricultural handtools–hoes, rakes, spades, hay forks, etc.: Hand and Edge Tool—*mfg*	332212	3423
Agricultural Implement Manufacturing	**33311**	
Agricultural implements and machinery: Farm Machinery and Equipment—*mfg*	333111	3523
Agricultural lime: Lime—*mfg*	32741	3274
Agricultural limestone: Farm Supplies—*whlse*	42291	5191
Nursery and Garden Centers—*retail*	44422	5191
Agricultural limestone, ground: Crushed and Broken Limestone and Quarrying—*mining*	212312	1422
Agricultural loan companies: International Trade Financing—*fin*	522293	6159
Non-Depository Credit Intermediation, All Other—*fin*	522298	6159
Sales Financing—*fin*	52222	6159
Agricultural machinery: Farm and Garden Machinery and Equipment—*whlse*	42182	5083
Outdoor Power Equipment Stores—*retail*	44421	5083
Agricultural Marketing and Commodities, Regulation of	**92614**	**9641**
Agricultural pesticides: Pesticide and Other Agricultural Chemical—*mfg*	32532	2879
Agricultural properties, lessors of: Lessors of Other Real Estate Property—*real*	53119	6519
Agricultural research, commercial: Research and Development in the Life Sciences—*prof*	54172	8731
Research and Development in the Physical Sciences and Engineering Sciences—*prof*	54171	8731
Agriculture and Forestry Support Activities	**115**	
Agriculture extension services: Agricultural Marketing and Commodities, Regulation of—*pub*	92614	9641
Agriculture fair boards: Agricultural Marketing and Commodities, Regulation of—*pub*	92614	9641
Agriculture, Construction, and Mining Machinery Manufacturing	**3331**	
Agriculture, Forestry, Fishing, and Hunting	**11**	
Aid to families with dependent children (AFDC): Child and Youth Services—*hlth*	62411	8322
Community Food Services—*hlth*	62421	8322
Community Housing Services, Other—*hlth*	624229	8322
Emergency and Other Relief Services—*hlth*	62423	8322
Individual and Family Services, Other—*hlth*	62419	8322
Services for the Elderly and Persons with Disabilities—*hlth*	62412	8322
Temporary Shelters—*hlth*	624221	8322
Aigin products: Basic Organic Chemical, All Other—*mfg*	325199	2869
Ailerons, aircraft: Aircraft Part and Auxiliary Equipment, Other—*mfg*	336413	3728
Fluid Power Valve and Hose Fitting—*mfg*	332912	3728
Aiming circles (fire control equipment): Optical Instrument and Lens—*mfg*	333314	3827
Aininoazotoluene: Cyclic Crude and Intermediate—*mfg*	325192	2865
Petrochemical—*mfg*	32511	2865
Air and Gas Compressor Manufacturing	**333912**	**3563**
Air and Water Resource and Solid Waste Management	**92411**	**9511**
Air brake and air line hose, rubber or rubberized fabric: Rubber and Plastics Hoses and Belting—*mfg*	32622	3052
Air brakes, motor vehicle: Motor Vehicle Brake System—*mfg*	33634	3714
Motor Vehicle Parts, All Other—*mfg*	336399	3714
Air brakes, railway: Pump and Pumping Equipment—*mfg*	333911	3743
Railroad Rolling Stock—*mfg*	33651	3743
Air cargo carriers, nonscheduled: Ambulance Services—*hlth*	62191	4522
Nonscheduled Chartered Freight Air—*trans*	481212	4522
Nonscheduled Chartered Passenger Air—*trans*	481211	4522
Scenic and Sightseeing, Other—*trans*	48799	4522
Air cargo carriers, scheduled: Scheduled Freight Air—*trans*	481112	4512
Scheduled Passenger Air—*trans*	481111	4512
Air circuit breakers: Switchgear and Switchboard Apparatus—*mfg*	335313	3613
Air cleaning systems: Air Purification Equipment—*mfg*	333411	3564
Industrial and Commercial Fan and Blower—*mfg*	333412	3564
Air cowls, scoops, or airports (ship ventilators), sheet metal: Metal Container, Other—*mfg*	332439	3444

ALPHABETICAL INDEX	NAICS	SIC
Sheet Metal Work—*mfg*	332322	3444
Air cushions, canvas: Canvas and Related Product Mills—*mfg*	314912	2394
Air ducts, sheet metal: Building Material Dealers, Other—*retail*	44419	5039
Construction Material, Other—*whlse*	42139	5039
Air flow controllers, air-conditioning and refrigeration–except valves: Automatic Environmental Control for Residential, Commercial and Appliance Use—*mfg*	334512	3822
Air Force: National Security—*pub*	92811	9711
Air intake filters, internal combustion engine–except motor vehicle: Fabricated Metal Product, All Other Miscellaneous—*mfg*	332999	3599
General Purpose Machinery , All Other—*mfg*	333999	3599
Machine Shops—*mfg*	33271	3599
Machinery, Other Commercial and Service Industry—*mfg*	333319	3599
Air mattresses, plastics: Plastics Pipe and Pipe Fitting—*mfg*	326122	3089
Plastics Product, All Other—*mfg*	326199	3089
Unsupported Plastics Profile Shape—*mfg*	326121	3089
Air passenger carriers, nonscheduled: Ambulance Services—*hlth*	62191	4522
Nonscheduled Chartered Freight Air—*trans*	481212	4522
Nonscheduled Chartered Passenger Air—*trans*	481211	4522
Scenic and Sightseeing, Other—*trans*	48799	4522
Air passenger carriers, scheduled: Scheduled Freight Air—*trans*	481112	4512
Scheduled Passenger Air—*trans*	481111	4512
Air pollution control agencies: Air and Water Resource and Solid Waste Management—*pub*	92411	9511
Air pollution control equipment and supplies: Warm Air Heating and Air-Conditioning Equipment and Supplies—*whlse*	42173	5075
Air preheaters, nonrotating–plate type: Air-Conditioning and Warm Air Heating Equipment and Commercial and Industrial Refrigeration Equipment—*mfg*	333415	3443
Metal Tank (Heavy Gauge)—*mfg*	33242	3443
Plate Work—*mfg*	332313	3443
Power Boiler and Heat Exchanger—*mfg*	33241	3443
Air purification and dust collection equipment: Air Purification Equipment—*mfg*	333411	3564
Industrial and Commercial Fan and Blower—*mfg*	333412	3564
Air Purification Equipment Manufacturing	**333411**	**3564**
Air purifiers, portable: Electric Housewares and Household Fan—*mfg*	335211	3634
Heating Equipment (except Electric and Warm Air Furnaces)—*mfg*	333414	3634
Air receiver tanks, metal plate: Air-Conditioning and Warm Air Heating Equipment and Commercial and Industrial Refrigeration Equipment—*mfg*	333415	3443
Metal Tank (Heavy Gauge)—*mfg*	33242	3443
Plate Work—*mfg*	332313	3443
Power Boiler and Heat Exchanger—*mfg*	33241	3443
Air scoops, aircraft: Aircraft Engine and Engine Parts—*mfg*	336412	3724

ALPHABETICAL INDEX	NAICS	SIC
Air separators (machinery): General Purpose Machinery , All Other—*mfg*	333999	3569
Air supported rubber structures: Fabric Coating Mills—*mfg*	31332	3069
Rubber Product, All Other—*mfg*	326299	3069
Air system balancing and testing–contractors: Plumbing, Heating and Air-Conditioning Contractors—*const*	23511	1711
Air taxi services: Ambulance Services—*hlth*	62191	4522
Nonscheduled Chartered Freight Air—*trans*	481212	4522
Nonscheduled Chartered Passenger Air—*trans*	481211	4522
Scenic and Sightseeing, Other—*trans*	48799	4522
Air Traffic Control	**488111**	**9621**
Air traffic control operations: Air Traffic Control—*trans*	488111	9621
Air traffic control radar systems and equipment: Search, Detection, Navigation, Guidance, Aeronautical, and Nautical System and Instrument—*mfg*	334511	3812
Air traffic control, except government: Air Traffic Control—*trans*	488111	4581
Air Transportation	**481**	
Air Transportation Support Activities	**4881**	
Air Transportation, Other Support Activities for	**48819**	**4581**
Air, Rail, and Water Transportation Equipment Rental and Leasing, Commercial	**532411**	**4741**
Air-conditioner repair, automotive: Automotive Mechanical and Electrical Repair and Maintenance, Other—*serv*	811118	7539
Air-conditioner repair, self-contained units–except automotive: Appliance Repair and Maintenance—*serv*	811412	7623
Household Appliance Stores—*retail*	443111	7623
Machinery and Equipment (except Automotive and Electronic) Repair and Maintenance, Commercial and Industrial—*serv*	81131	7623
Air-conditioners, motor vehicle: Air-Conditioning and Warm Air Heating Equipment and Commercial and Industrial Refrigeration Equipment—*mfg*	333415	3585
Motor Vehicle Air-Conditioning—*mfg*	336391	3585
Air-conditioning and heating combination units: Air-Conditioning and Warm Air Heating Equipment and Commercial and Industrial Refrigeration Equipment—*mfg*	333415	3585
Motor Vehicle Air-Conditioning—*mfg*	336391	3585
Air-Conditioning and Warm Air Heating Equipment and Commercial and Industrial Refrigeration Equipment Manufacturing	**333415**	**3585**
Air-conditioning compressors: Air-Conditioning and Warm Air Heating Equipment and Commercial and Industrial Refrigeration Equipment—*mfg*	333415	3585
Motor Vehicle Air-Conditioning—*mfg*	336391	3585
Air-conditioning condensers and condensing units: Air-Conditioning and Warm Air Heating Equipment and Commercial and Industrial Refrigeration Equipment—*mfg*	333415	3585
Motor Vehicle Air-Conditioning—*mfg*	336391	3585

Description	NAICS	SIC
Air-conditioning equipment, automobile–sale and installation: Automotive Parts and Accessories Stores—*retail*	44131	5531
Air-conditioning equipment, except room units: Warm Air Heating and Air-Conditioning Equipment and Supplies—*whlse*	42173	5075
Air-conditioning room units, self-contained: Electrical Appliance, Television and Radio Set—*whlse*	42162	5064
Household Appliance Stores—*retail*	443111	5722
Air-conditioning supply services: Steam and Air-Conditioning Supply—*util*	22133	4961
Air-conditioning units, complete–domestic and industrial: Air-Conditioning and Warm Air Heating Equipment and Commercial and Industrial Refrigeration Equipment—*mfg*	333415	3585
Motor Vehicle Air-Conditioning—*mfg*	336391	3585
Air-conditioning, with or without sheet metal work–contractors: Plumbing, Heating and Air-Conditioning Contractors—*const*	23511	1711
Airboats (swamp buggy rides): Inland Water Passenger—*trans*	483212	4489
Scenic and Sightseeing, Water—*trans*	48721	4489
Airborne integrated data systems/flight recorders: Search, Detection, Navigation, Guidance, Aeronautical, and Nautical System and Instrument—*mfg*	334511	3812
Airborne radio communications equipment: Radio and Television Broadcasting and Wireless Communications Equipment—*mfg*	33422	3663
Aircraft: Aircraft—*mfg*	336411	3721
Aircraft and automotive wire and cable, nonferrous: Aluminum Rolling and Drawing, Other—*mfg*	331319	3357
Communication and Energy Wire, Other—*mfg*	335929	3357
Copper Wire (except Mechanical) Drawing—*mfg*	331422	3357
Fiber Optic Cable—*mfg*	335921	3357
Nonferrous Metal (except Copper and Aluminum) Rolling, Drawing and Extruding—*mfg*	331491	3357
Aircraft and parts: Transportation Equipment and Supplies (except Motor Vehicle)—*whlse*	42186	5088
Aircraft armament, except guns: Aircraft Part and Auxiliary Equipment, Other—*mfg*	336413	3728
Fluid Power Valve and Hose Fitting—*mfg*	332912	3728
Aircraft arresting device system: Aircraft Part and Auxiliary Equipment, Other—*mfg*	336413	3728
Fluid Power Valve and Hose Fitting—*mfg*	332912	3728
Aircraft artillery: Ordnance and Accessories, Other—*mfg*	332995	3489
Aircraft assemblies, subassemblies, and parts, except engines: Aircraft Part and Auxiliary Equipment, Other—*mfg*	336413	3728
Fluid Power Valve and Hose Fitting—*mfg*	332912	3728
Aircraft body assemblies and parts: Aircraft Part and Auxiliary Equipment, Other—*mfg*	336413	3728
Fluid Power Valve and Hose Fitting—*mfg*	332912	3728
Aircraft cleaning and janitorial service: Airport Operations, Other—*trans*	488119	4581
Janitorial Services—*admin*	56172	4581
Aircraft electrical equipment repair, except radio: Communication Equipment Repair and Maintenance—*serv*	811213	7629
Electronic and Precision Equipment Repair and Maintenance, Other—*serv*	811219	7629
Aircraft Engine and Engine Parts Manufacturing	**336412**	**3724**
Aircraft engine cradles: Fabricated Metal Product, All Other Miscellaneous—*mfg*	332999	3537
Industrial Truck, Tractor, Trailer and Stacker Machinery—*mfg*	333924	3537
Metal Container, Other—*mfg*	332439	3537
Aircraft engines and engine parts: Transportation Equipment and Supplies (except Motor Vehicle)—*whlse*	42186	5088
Aircraft engines and engine parts, internal combustion and jet propulsion: Aircraft Engine and Engine Parts—*mfg*	336412	3724
Aircraft equipment and supplies: Transportation Equipment and Supplies (except Motor Vehicle)—*whlse*	42186	5088
Aircraft flight instruments: Search, Detection, Navigation, Guidance, Aeronautical, and Nautical System and Instrument—*mfg*	334511	3812
Aircraft floor coverings, except rubber or plastics: Carpet and Rug Mills—*mfg*	31411	2273
Aircraft fo!gings, ferrous–not made in rolling mills: Iron and Steel Forging—*mfg*	332111	3462
Aircraft forgings, nonferrous–not made in hot-rolling nlls: Nonferrous Forging—*mfg*	332112	3463
Aircraft fueling services: Petroleum and Petroleum Products (except Bulk Stations and Terminals)—*whlse*	42272	5172
Aircraft hardware: Hardware—*mfg*	33251	3429
Aircraft inspection: Air Traffic Control—*trans*	488111	9621
Transportation Programs, Regulation and Administration of—*pub*	92612	9621
Aircraft lighting flxtures: Vehicular Lighting Equipment—*mfg*	336321	3647
Aircraft loading hoists: Fabricated Metal Product, All Other Miscellaneous—*mfg*	332999	3537
Industrial Truck, Tractor, Trailer and Stacker Machinery—*mfg*	333924	3537
Metal Container, Other—*mfg*	332439	3537
Aircraft Manufacturing	**336411**	**3721**
Aircraft Part and Auxiliary Equipment Manufacturing, Other	**336413**	**3728**
Aircraft power transmission equipment: Aircraft Part and Auxiliary Equipment, Other—*mfg*	336413	3728
Fluid Power Valve and Hose Fitting—*mfg*	332912	3728
Aircraft propeller parts: Aircraft Part and Auxiliary Equipment, Other—*mfg*	336413	3728
Fluid Power Valve and Hose Fitting—*mfg*	332912	3728
Aircraft propellers, variable and fixed pitch: Aircraft Part and Auxiliary Equipment, Other—*mfg*	336413	3728
Fluid Power Valve and Hose Fitting—*mfg*	332912	3728
Aircraft radio equlpment repair: Communication Equipment Repair and Maintenance—*serv*	811213	7622
Consumer Electronics Repair and Maintenance—*serv*	811211	7622
Radio, Television and Other Electronics Stores—*retail*	443112	7622
Aircraft seats: Motor Vehicle Fabric Accessories and Seat—*mfg*	33636	2531

ALPHABETICAL INDEX	NAICS	SIC
Aircraft servicing and repairing, except on a factory basis: Air, Other Support Activities for—*trans*	48819	4581
Airport Operations, Other—*trans*	488119	4581
Aircraft storage at airports: Airport Operations, Other—*trans*	488119	4581
Aircraft upholstery repair: Air, Other Support Activities for—*trans*	48819	4581
Aircurtains (blower): Air Purification Equipment—*mfg*	333411	3564
Industrial and Commercial Fan and Blower—*mfg*	333412	3564
Airfoils, aircraft engine: Aircraft Engine and Engine Parts—*mfg*	336412	3724
Airframe assemblies, except for guided missiles: Aircraft Part and Auxiliary Equipment, Other—*mfg*	336413	3728
Fluid Power Valve and Hose Fitting—*mfg*	332912	3728
Airframe assemblies, for guided missiles: Guided Missile and Space Vehicle Parts and Auxiliary Equipment, Other—*mfg*	336419	3769
Airframe equipment instruments: Search, Detection, Navigation, Guidance, Aeronautical, and Nautical System and Instrument—*mfg*	334511	3812
Airfreight handling at airports: Air, Other Support Activities for—*trans*	48819	4581
Airline ticket offices, not operated by transportation companies: Transportation, All Other Support Activities—*trans*	488999	4729
Travel Arrangement and Reservation Services, All Other—*admin*	561599	4729
Airlocks: Air-Conditioning and Warm Air Heating Equipment and Commercial and Industrial Refrigeration Equipment—*mfg*	333415	3443
Metal Tank (Heavy Gauge)—*mfg*	33242	3443
Plate Work—*mfg*	332313	3443
Power Boiler and Heat Exchanger—*mfg*	33241	3443
Airplane brake expanders: Aircraft Part and Auxiliary Equipment, Other—*mfg*	336413	3728
Fluid Power Valve and Hose Fitting—*mfg*	332912	3728
Airplane cloth, cotton: Broadwoven Fabric Mills—*mfg*	31321	2211
Airplane models, except toy and hobby models: Fabricated Metal Product, All Other Miscellaneous—*mfg*	332999	3999
Plastics Product, All Other—*mfg*	326199	3999
Wood Product, All Other Miscellaneous—*mfg*	321999	3999
Airplane models, toy and hobby: Game, Toy, and Children's Vehicle—*mfg*	339932	3944
Airplane rental and leasing: Air, Rail, and Water Equipment Rental and Leasing, Commercial—*real*	532411	7359
Airplanes, fixed or rotary wing: Aircraft—*mfg*	336411	3721
Airplanes, janitorial services on: Airport Operations, Other—*trans*	488119	4581
Janitorial Services—*admin*	56172	4581
Airplanes, toy: Game, Toy, and Children's Vehicle—*mfg*	339932	3944
Airport hangar rental: Airport Operations, Other—*trans*	488119	4581
Airport leasing, if not operating airport: Lessors of Other Real Estate Property—*real*	53119	6519
Airport leasing, if operating airport: Airport Operations, Other—*trans*	488119	4581

ALPHABETICAL INDEX	NAICS	SIC
Airport lighting transformers: Power, Distribution and Specialty Transformer—*mfg*	335311	3612
Airport limousine scheduled service: Bus and Motor Vehicle Transit Systems—*trans*	485113	4111
Transit and Ground Passenger, All Other—*trans*	485999	4111
Airport Operations	**48811**	
Airport Operations, Other	**488119**	**4959**
Airport runway construction–general contractors: Highway and Street—*const*	23411	1611
Airport terminal services: Airport Operations, Other—*trans*	488119	4581
Janitorial Services—*admin*	56172	4581
Airport transportation service, local–road or rail: Bus and Motor Vehicle Transit Systems—*trans*	485113	4111
Commuter Rail Systems—*trans*	485112	4111
Mixed Mode Transit Systems—*trans*	485111	4111
Transit and Ground Passenger, All Other—*trans*	485999	4111
Urban Transit Systems, Other—*trans*	485119	4111
Airports: Airport Operations, Other—*trans*	488119	4581
Airships: Aircraft—*mfg*	336411	3721
Airspeed instrumentation (aeronautical instruments): Search, Detection, Navigation, Guidance, Aeronautical, and Nautical System and Instrument—*mfg*	334511	3812
Alabaster mining: Crushed and Broken Stone and Quarrying, Other—*mining*	212319	1499
Non-Metallic Mineral, All Other—*mining*	212399	1499
Alarm signal systems: Building Material Dealers, Other—*retail*	44419	5063
Electrical Apparatus and Equipment, Wiring Supplies and Material—*whlse*	42161	5063
Albums: Blankbook, Loose-leaf Binder and Device—*mfg*	323118	2782
Flexographic Printing, Commercial—*mfg*	323112	2782
Gravure Printing, Commercial—*mfg*	323111	2782
Lithographic Printing, Commercial—*mfg*	323110	2782
Printing, Other Commercial—*mfg*	323119	2782
Screen Printing, Commercial—*mfg*	323113	2782
Albums (photo) and scrapbooks: Office Supplies and Stationery Stores—*retail*	45321	5112
Stationary and Office Supplies—*whlse*	42212	5112
Alcohol for medicinal and beverage purposes, ethyl or grain: Distilleries—*mfg*	31214	2085
Alcohol resins, polyvinyl: Plastics Material and Resin—*mfg*	325211	2821
Alcohol treatment, outpatient clinics: Family Planning Centers—*hlth*	62141	8093
Outpatient Care Centers, All Other—*hlth*	621498	8093
Outpatient Mental Health and Substance Abuse Centers—*hlth*	62142	8093
Alcohol, aromatic: Basic Organic Chemical, All Other—*mfg*	325199	2869
Ethyl Alcohol—*mfg*	325193	2869
Alcohol, fatty–powdered: Basic Organic Chemical, All Other—*mfg*	325199	2869
Ethyl Alcohol—*mfg*	325193	2869

Description	NAICS	SIC
Alcohol, industrial: Chemical and Allied Products, Other—*whlse*	42269	5169
Alcohol, methyl–natural: Gum and Wood Chemical—*mfg*	325191	2861
Alcohol, methyl–synthetic (methanol): Basic Organic Chemical, All Other—*mfg*	325199	2869
Ethyl Alcohol—*mfg*	325193	2869
Alcohol, wood–natural (methanol): Gum and Wood Chemical—*mfg*	325191	2861
Alcoholic beverage control boards: Regulation, Licensing, and Inspection of Miscellaneous Commercial Sectors—*pub*	92615	9651
Alcoholism counseling, nonresidential–except medical treatment: Child and Youth Services—*hlth*	62411	8322
Community Housing Services, Other—*hlth*	624229	8322
Emergency and Other Relief Services—*hlth*	62423	8322
Individual and Family Services, Other—*hlth*	62419	8322
Parole Offices and Probation Offices—*pub*	92215	8322
Temporary Shelters—*hlth*	624221	8322
Alcoholism rehabilitation centers, residential–with health care incidental: Residential Care Facilities, Other—*hlth*	62399	8361
Residential Mental Health and Substance Abuse Facilities—*hlth*	62322	8361
Alcoholism rehabilitation hospitals: General Medical and Surgical Hospitals—*hlth*	62211	8069
Hospitals (except Psychiatric and Substance Abuse), Specialty—*hlth*	62231	8069
Psychiatric and Substance Abuse Hospitals—*hlth*	62221	8069
Alcohols, industrial–denatured (nonbeverage): Basic Organic Chemical, All Other—*mfg*	325199	2869
Ethyl Alcohol—*mfg*	325193	2869
Alcohols, polyhydric: Basic Organic Chemical, All Other—*mfg*	325199	2869
Ethyl Alcohol—*mfg*	325193	2869
Ale: Beer and Ale—*whlse*	42281	5181
Breweries—*mfg*	31212	2082
Alfalfa: Farm Supplies—*whlse*	42291	5191
Nursery and Garden Centers—*retail*	44422	5191
Alfalfa farms: Crop Farming, All Other Miscellaneous—*ag*	111998	139
Hay Farming—*ag*	11194	139
Alfalfa, cubed: Animal Food, Other—*mfg*	311119	2048
Alfalfa, prepared as feed for animals: Animal Food, Other—*mfg*	311119	2048
Alidades, surveying: Measuring and Controlling Device, Other—*mfg*	334519	3829
Surgical and Medical Instrument—*mfg*	339112	3829
Alighting assemblies (landing gear), aircraft: Aircraft Part and Auxiliary Equipment, Other—*mfg*	336413	3728
Fluid Power Valve and Hose Fitting—*mfg*	332912	3728
Alkali metals: Basic Inorganic Chemical, All Other—*mfg*	325188	2819
Chemical Product, All Other Miscellaneous—*mfg*	325998	2819
Alkalies: Chemical and Allied Products, Other—*whlse*	42269	5169
Alkalies and Chlorine Manufacturing	**325181**	**2812**
Alkalies, not produced at mines: Alkalies and Chlorine—*mfg*	325181	2812
Alkaline cell storage batteries: Storage Battery—*mfg*	335911	3691
Alkaloids and salts: Medicinal and Botanical—*mfg*	325411	2833
Alkyd resins: Plastics Material and Resin—*mfg*	325211	2821
Alkylated diphenylamines, mixed: Cyclic Crude and Intermediate—*mfg*	325192	2865
Petrochemical—*mfg*	32511	2865
Alkylated phenol, mixed: Cyclic Crude and Intermediate—*mfg*	325192	2865
Petrochemical—*mfg*	32511	2865
Alkylates, produced in petroleum refineries: Petroleum Refineries—*mfg*	32411	2911
All terrain vehicles (ATV): Transportation Equipment, All Other—*mfg*	336999	3799
All-terrain vehicles: Motorcycle Dealers—*retail*	441221	5571
Allergenic extracts, except in vitro and in vivo: Biological Product (except Diagnostic)—*mfg*	325414	2836
Allergens: Biological Product (except Diagnostic)—*mfg*	325414	2836
Alley construction–general contractors: Highway and Street—*const*	23411	1611
Alligator farms: Animal Production, All Other—*ag*	11299	279
Apiculture—*ag*	11291	279
Alloy steel castings, except investment: Steel Foundries, (except Investment)—*mfg*	331513	3325
Allyl resins: Plastics Material and Resin—*mfg*	325211	2821
Almond groves and farms: Tree Nut Farming—*ag*	111335	173
Almond hulling and shelling: Postharvest Crop Activities (except Cotton Ginning)—*ag*	115114	723
Almond pastes: Roasted Nuts and Peanut Butter—*mfg*	311911	2099
Alpacas, cotton: Broadwoven Fabric Mills—*mfg*	31321	2211
Alpacas, mohair–woven: Broadwoven Fabric Finishing Mills—*mfg*	313311	2231
Broadwoven Fabric Mills—*mfg*	31321	2231
Textile and Fabric Finishing (except Broadwoven Fabric) Mills—*mfg*	313312	2231
Altars, cut stone: Cut Stone and Stone Product—*mfg*	327991	3281
Altars, except stone and concrete: Institutional Furniture—*mfg*	337127	2531
Alterations and garment repair: Personal and Household Goods Repair and Maintenance, Other—*serv*	81149	7219
Alternator and generator testers: Electronic Coil, Transformer, and Other Inductor—*mfg*	334416	3825
Instrument for Measuring and Testing Electricity and Electrical Signals—*mfg*	334515	3825
Alternators, motor vehicle: Motor Vehicle Electrical and Electronic Equipment, Other—*mfg*	336322	3694
Altimeters, aeronautical: Search, Detection, Navigation, Guidance, Aeronautical, and Nautical System and Instrument—*mfg*	334511	3812
Altitude testing chambers: General Purpose Machinery , All Other—*mfg*	333999	3569
Alum mining: Potash, Soda, and Borate Mineral—*mining*	212391	1474
Alumina: Alumina Refining—*mfg*	331311	2819
Alumina and Aluminum Production and Processing	**33131**	
Alumina and Aluminum Production and Processing	**3313**	
Alumina fused refractories: Nonclay Refractory—*mfg*	327125	3297
Alumina porcelain insulators: Porcelain Electrical Supply—*mfg*	327113	3264
Alumina Refining	**331311**	**2819**

ALPHABETICAL INDEX	NAICS	SIC
Aluminous abrasives: Abrasive Product—*mfg*	32791	3291
Fabricated Metal Product, All Other Miscellaneous—*mfg*	332999	3291
Aluminum and aluminum-base alloy castings, except die-castings: Aluminum Foundries—*mfg*	331524	3365
Aluminum atomized powder: Electroplating, Plating, Polishing, Anodizing and Coloring—*mfg*	332813	3399
Fabricated Wire Product, Other—*mfg*	332618	3399
Secondary Smelting and Alloying of Aluminum—*mfg*	331314	3399
Aluminum bars, rods, ingots, sheets, pipes, plates, etc.: Metal Service Centers and Offices—*whlse*	42151	5051
Aluminum chloride: Alumina Refining—*mfg*	331311	2819
Aluminum coating of metal products for trade not done in rolling mills: Costume Jewelry and Novelty—*mfg*	339914	3479
Jewelry (except Costume)—*mfg*	339911	3479
Metal Coating, Engraving (except Jewelry and Silverware), and Allied Services to Manufacturers—*mfg*	332812	3479
Silverware and Plated Ware—*mfg*	339912	3479
Aluminum compounds: Alumina Refining—*mfg*	331311	2819
Aluminum die-casting, including alloys: Aluminum Die-Castings—*mfg*	331521	3363
Aluminum Die-Castings	**331521**	**3363**
Aluminum Extruded Product Manufacturing	**331316**	**3354**
Aluminum extrusion ingot, secondary: Secondary Smelting and Alloying of Aluminum—*mfg*	331314	3341
Aluminum forgings, not made in hot-rollmg mills: Nonferrous Forging—*mfg*	332112	3463
Aluminum Foundries	**331524**	**3365**
Aluminum hydroxide (alumina trihydrate): Alumina Refining—*mfg*	331311	2819
Aluminum ingots and primary production shapes, from bauxite or alumina: Primary Aluminum Production—*mfg*	331312	3334
Aluminum ore mining: Metal Ore, All Other—*mining*	212299	1099
Aluminum oxide: Alumina Refining—*mfg*	331311	2819
Aluminum oxide (fused) abrasives: Abrasive Product—*mfg*	32791	3291
Fabricated Metal Product, All Other Miscellaneous—*mfg*	332999	3291
Aluminum plant construction–general contractors: Building, Commercial and Institutional—*const*	23332	1541
Manufacturing and Industrial Building—*const*	23331	1541
Aluminum Rolling and Drawing, Other	**331319**	**3357**
Aluminum Sheet, Plate and Foil Manufacturing	**331315**	**3353**
Aluminum smelting and refining, secondary: Secondary Smelting and Alloying of Aluminum—*mfg*	331314	3341
Aluminum sulfate: Alumina Refining—*mfg*	331311	2819
Aluminumware: Home Furnishing—*whlse*	42122	5023
Aluminumware stores: Home Furnishings Stores, All Other—*retail*	442299	5719
Window Treatment Stores—*retail*	442291	5719
Alums: Alumina Refining—*mfg*	331311	2819
Basic Inorganic Chemical, All Other—*mfg*	325188	2819

ALPHABETICAL INDEX	NAICS	SIC
Chemical Product, All Other Miscellaneous—*mfg*	325998	2819
Alunite mining: Chemical and Fertilizer Mineral, Other—*mining*	212393	1479
Amalgamators (metallurgical and mining machinery): Mining Machinery and Equipment—*mfg*	333131	3532
Amalgams, dental: Dental Equipment and Supplies—*mfg*	339114	3843
Amateur radio communications equipment: Electronic Parts and Equipment, Other—*whlse*	42169	5065
Amblygonite mining: Chemical and Fertilizer Mineral, Other—*mining*	212393	1479
Ambulance bodies: Motor Vehicle Body—*mfg*	336211	3713
Ambulance service, road: Ambulance Services—*hlth*	62191	4119
Ambulance Services	**62191**	**4522**
Ambulance services, air: Ambulance Services—*hlth*	62191	4522
Nonscheduled Chartered Freight Air—*trans*	481212	4522
Nonscheduled Chartered Passenger Air—*trans*	481211	4522
Ambulances: Automobile and Other Motor Vehicle—*whlse*	42111	5012
Ambulances (motor vehicles): Automobile—*mfg*	336111	3711
Heavy Duty Truck—*mfg*	33612	3711
Light Truck and Utility Vehicle—*mfg*	336112	3711
Military Armored Vehicle, Tank and Tank Component—*mfg*	336992	3711
Motor Vehicle Body—*mfg*	336211	3711
Ambulatory Health Care Services	**621**	
Ambulatory Health Care Services, All Other	**62199**	
Ambulatory Health Care Services, All Other Miscellaneous	**621999**	**8099**
Ambulatory Health Care Services, Other	**6219**	
Ambulatory surgical centers: Freestanding Ambulatory Surgical and Emergency Centers—*hlth*	621493	8011
HMO Medical Centers—*hlth*	621491	8011
Physicians (except Mental Health Specialists), Offices Of—*hlth*	621111	8011
Physicians, Mental Health Specialists, Offices Of—*hlth*	621112	8011
American Indian and Alaska Native Tribal Governments	**92115**	**8641**
Amethyst mining: Crushed and Broken Stone and Quarrying, Other—*mining*	212319	1499
Non-Metallic Mineral, All Other—*mining*	212399	1499
Amines of polyhydric alcohols, and of fatty and other acids: Basic Organic Chemical, All Other—*mfg*	325199	2869
Amino acid analyzers, laboratory type: Analytical Laboratory Instrument—*mfg*	334516	3826
Aminoanthraquinone: Cyclic Crude and Intermediate—*mfg*	325192	2865
Petrochemical—*mfg*	32511	2865
Aminoazobenzene: Cyclic Crude and Intermediate—*mfg*	325192	2865
Petrochemical—*mfg*	32511	2865
Aminophenol: Cyclic Crude and Intermediate—*mfg*	325192	2865
Petrochemical—*mfg*	32511	2865
Ammeters: Electronic Coil, Transformer, and Other Inductor—*mfg*	334416	3825
Instrument for Measuring and Testing Electricity and Electrical Signals—*mfg*	334515	3825

Description	NAICS	SIC
Ammonia alum: Basic Inorganic Chemical, All Other—*mfg*	325188	2819
Chemical Product, All Other Miscellaneous—*mfg*	325998	2819
Ammonia applicators and attachments (agricultural machinery): Farm Machinery and Equipment—*mfg*	333111	3523
Ammonia liquor: Nitrogenous Fertilizer—*mfg*	325311	2873
Ammonia, anhydrous: Nitrogenous Fertilizer—*mfg*	325311	2873
Ammonia, except for fertilizer: Chemical and Allied Products, Other—*whlse*	42269	5169
Ammonia, household: Polish and Other Sanitation Good—*mfg*	325612	2842
Ammonium chloride, hydroxide, and molybdate: Basic Inorganic Chemical, All Other—*mfg*	325188	2819
Chemical Product, All Other Miscellaneous—*mfg*	325998	2819
Ammonium compounds, except for fertilizer: Basic Inorganic Chemical, All Other—*mfg*	325188	2819
Chemical Product, All Other Miscellaneous—*mfg*	325998	2819
Ammonium nitrate and sulfate: Nitrogenous Fertilizer—*mfg*	325311	2873
Ammonium perchlorate: Basic Inorganic Chemical, All Other—*mfg*	325188	2819
Chemical Product, All Other Miscellaneous—*mfg*	325998	2819
Ammonium phosphates: Phosphatic Fertilizer—*mfg*	325312	2874
Ammonium thiosulfate: Basic Inorganic Chemical, All Other—*mfg*	325188	2819
Chemical Product, All Other Miscellaneous—*mfg*	325998	2819
Ammunition: Sporting Goods Stores—*retail*	45111	5941
Ammunition (except Small Arms) Manufacturing	**332993**	**3483**
Ammunition and component parts, more than 30 mm. (or more than 1.18 inch): Ammunition (except Small Arms)—*mfg*	332993	3483
Ammunition and component parts, small arms–30 mm. (or 1.18 inch) or less: Small Arms Ammunition—*mfg*	332992	3482
Ammunition and explosives loading machinery: Industrial Machinery, All Other—*mfg*	333298	3559
Machinery, Other Commercial and Service Industry—*mfg*	333319	3559
Ammunition belts, sporting type–of all materials: Sporting and Athletic Goods—*mfg*	33992	3949
Ammunition boxes, metal: Metal Container, Other—*mfg*	332439	3499
Ammunition boxes, wood: Wood Container and Pallet—*mfg*	32192	2441
Ammunition cans or tubes, paperboard laminated with metal foil: Fiber Can, Tube, Drum, and Similar Products—*mfg*	322214	2655
Ammunition carts, machine gun: Small Arms—*mfg*	332994	3484
Ammunition loading and assembling plants: Ammunition (except Small Arms)—*mfg*	332993	3483
Ammunition, except sporting: Durable Goods, Other Miscellaneous—*whlse*	42199	5099
Ammunition, sporting: Sporting and Recreational Goods and Supplies—*whlse*	42191	5091
Ampere-hour meters: Electronic Coil, Transformer, and Other Inductor—*mfg*	334416	3825
Instrument for Measuring and Testing Electricity and Electrical Signals—*mfg*	334515	3825
Amphibian motor vehicles, except tanks: Automobile—*mfg*	336111	3711
Heavy Duty Truck—*mfg*	33612	3711
Light Truck and Utility Vehicle—*mfg*	336112	3711
Military Armored Vehicle, Tank and Tank Component—*mfg*	336992	3711
Motor Vehicle Body—*mfg*	336211	3711
Amphibian tanks, military: Military Armored Vehicle, Tank and Tank Component—*mfg*	336992	3795
Amplifiers–radio, public address, or musical instrument: Audio and Video Equipment—*mfg*	33431	3651
Amplifiers–RF power and IF: Radio and Television Broadcasting and Wireless Communications Equipment—*mfg*	33422	3663
Amplifiers; magnetic, pulse, and maser: Electrical Equipment and Component, All Other Miscellaneous—*mfg*	335999	3699
Ampoules, glass: Glass Container—*mfg*	327213	3221
Amusement and Recreation Industries, All Other	**71399**	**7997**
Amusement and Recreation Industries, Other	**7139**	
Amusement and Theme Parks	**71311**	**7996**
Amusement Arcades	**71312**	**7993**
Amusement centers and parks (not fairs, circuses, or carnivals): Amusement and Theme Parks—*arts*	71311	7996
Amusement concessions: Amusement and Recreation Industries, All Other—*arts*	71399	7999
Amusement device parlors, coin-operated: Amusement and Recreation Industries, All Other—*arts*	71399	7993
Amusement Arcades—*arts*	71312	7993
Gambling Industries, Other—*arts*	71329	7993
Amusement machines, coin-operated–except coin-operated phonographs: Fabricated Metal Product, All Other Miscellaneous—*mfg*	332999	3999
Amusement machines, coin-operated–operation of: Amusement and Recreation Industries, All Other—*arts*	71399	7993
Amusement Arcades—*arts*	71312	7993
Gambling Industries, Other—*arts*	71329	7993
Amusement parks: Amusement and Theme Parks—*arts*	71311	7996
Amusement Parks and Arcades	**7131**	
Amusement rides: Amusement and Recreation Industries, All Other—*arts*	71399	7999
Amusement rides for carnivals: Fabricated Metal Product, All Other Miscellaneous—*mfg*	332999	3599
General Purpose Machinery , All Other—*mfg*	333999	3599
Machine Shops—*mfg*	33271	3599
Machinery, Other Commercial and Service Industry—*mfg*	333319	3599
Amusement, Gambling and Recreation Industries	**713**	
Amyl acetate and alcohol: Basic Organic Chemical, All Other—*mfg*	325199	2869
Amytal (explosives): Explosives—*mfg*	32592	2892
Analgesic: Pharmaceutical Preparation—*mfg*	325412	2834
Analog-to-digital converters, electronic instrumentation type: Electronic Coil, Transformer, and Other Inductor—*mfg*	334416	3825
Instrument for Measuring and Testing Electricity and Electrical Signals—*mfg*	334515	3825

ALPHABETICAL INDEX	NAICS	SIC
Analytical instruments–photometers, Spectrographs, and chromatographic instruments: Office Supplies and Stationery Stores—*retail*	45321	5049
Professional Equipment and Supplies, Other—*whlse*	42149	5049
Analytical Laboratory Instrument Manufacturing	**334516**	**3826**
Analyzers for testing electrical characteristics: Electronic Coil, Transformer, and Other Inductor—*mfg*	334416	3825
Instrument for Measuring and Testing Electricity and Electrical Signals—*mfg*	334515	3825
Analyzers, industrial process tvpe: Instruments and Related Products for Measuring, Displaying, and Controlling Industrial Process Variables—*mfg*	334513	3823
Anamometers: Measuring and Controlling Device, Other—*mfg*	334519	3829
Surgical and Medical Instrument—*mfg*	339112	3829
Anchors, forged–not made in rolling mills: Iron and Steel Forging—*mfg*	332111	3462
Andalusite mining: Clay and Ceramic and Refractory Minerals—*mining*	212325	1459
Andirons: Hardware—*mfg*	33251	3429
Anesthesia apparatus: Surgical and Medical Instrument—*mfg*	339112	3841
Anesthesiologists, offices of: Freestanding Ambulatory Surgical and Emergency Centers—*hlth*	621493	8011
HMO Medical Centers—*hlth*	621491	8011
Physicians (except Mental Health Specialists), Offices Of—*hlth*	621111	8011
Physicians, Mental Health Specialists, Offices Of—*hlth*	621112	8011
Anesthetics, in bulk form: Medicinal and Botanical—*mfg*	325411	2833
Anesthetics, packaged: Pharmaceutical Preparation—*mfg*	325412	2834
Angiourographic diagnostic agents: In-Vitro Diagnostic Substance—*mfg*	325413	2835
Pharmaceutical Preparation—*mfg*	325412	2835
Angle irons, hardware: Hardware—*mfg*	33251	3429
Angle rings: Cutting Tool and Machine Tool Accessory—*mfg*	333515	3545
Hand and Edge Tool—*mfg*	332212	3545
Angle-of-attack instrumentation: Search, Detection, Navigation, Guidance, Aeronautical, and Nautical System and Instrument—*mfg*	334511	3812
Angle-of-yaw instrumentation: Search, Detection, Navigation, Guidance, Aeronautical, and Nautical System and Instrument—*mfg*	334511	3812
Anhydrous ammonia: Nitrogenous Fertilizer—*mfg*	325311	2873
Anhydrous butterfat: Creamery Butter—*mfg*	311512	2021
Anidex fibers: Noncellulosic Organic Fiber—*mfg*	325222	2824
Aniline: Cyclic Crude and Intermediate—*mfg*	325192	2865
Petrochemical—*mfg*	32511	2865
Aniline oil: Cyclic Crude and Intermediate—*mfg*	325192	2865
Petrochemical—*mfg*	32511	2865
Animal (except Poultry) Slaughtering	**311611**	**2011**
Animal and fish traps, made from purchased wire: Fabricated Wire Product, Other—*mfg*	332618	3496
Animal Aquaculture	**1125**	
Animal Aquaculture	**11251**	
Animal Aquaculture, Other	**112519**	**273**
Animal black: Carbon Black—*mfg*	325182	2816
Inorganic Dye and Pigment—*mfg*	325131	2816
Animal cemetery operation: Cemeteries and Crematories—*serv*	81222	6553
Animal clippers, hand and electric: Farm Machinery and Equipment—*mfg*	333111	3523
Hand and Edge Tool—*mfg*	332212	3523
Animal exhibits: Nature Parks and Other Similar Institutions—*arts*	71219	8422
Zoos and Botanical Gardens—*arts*	71213	8422
Animal feeds, except pet: Farm Supplies—*whlse*	42291	5191
Nursery and Garden Centers—*retail*	44422	5191
Animal feeds, prepared–except dog and cat: Animal Food, Other—*mfg*	311119	2048
Animal fiber yarn–twisting, winding, or spooling: Textile and Fabric Finishing (except Broadwoven Fabric) Mills—*mfg*	313312	2282
Yarn Texturing, Throwing and Twisting Mills—*mfg*	313112	2282
Animal Food Manufacturing	**3111**	
Animal Food Manufacturing	**31111**	
Animal Food Manufacturing, Other	**311119**	**2048**
Animal hair: Farm Product Raw Material, Other—*whlse*	42259	5159
Animal hospitals for livestock: Veterinary Services—*prof*	54194	741
Animal hospitals for pets and other animal specialties: Veterinary Services—*prof*	54194	742
Animal humane societies: Environment, Conservation and Wildlife Organizations—*serv*	813312	8699
Animal oils, except medicinal grade: Fats and Oils Refining and Blending—*mfg*	311225	2077
Fresh and Frozen Seafood Processing—*mfg*	311712	2077
Rendering and Meat By-product Processing—*mfg*	311613	2077
Seafood Canning—*mfg*	311711	2077
Animal oils, medicinal grade–refined and concentrated: Medicinal and Botanical—*mfg*	325411	2833
Animal Production	**112**	
Animal Production Support Activities	**1152**	
Animal Production Support Activities	**11521**	**752**
Animal Production, All Other	**11299**	**279**
Animal Production, Other	**1129**	
Animal remedies: Pharmaceutical Preparation—*mfg*	325412	2834
Animal shelters: Animal Production Support Activities—*ag*	11521	752
Pet Care (except Veterinary) Services—*serv*	81291	752
Animal shows in circuses, fairs, and carnivals: Amusement and Recreation Industries, All Other—*arts*	71399	7999
Animal Slaughtering and Processing	**31161**	

Entry	NAICS	SIC
Animal specialty and livestock farms, general: Animal Production, All Other—*ag*	11299	291
Animal trapping, commercial: Hunting and Trapping—*ag*	11421	971
Animal traps, iron and steel–except wire: Hardware—*mfg*	33251	3429
Anise oil: Spice and Extract—*mfg*	311942	2899
Ankle supports, orthopedic: Surgical Appliance and Supplies—*mfg*	339113	3842
Anklets, hosiery: Hosiery and Sock Mills, Other—*mfg*	315119	2252
Sheer Hosiery Mills—*mfg*	315111	2252
Annato extract: Gum and Wood Chemical—*mfg*	325191	2861
Annealing boxes, pots, and covers: Air-Conditioning and Warm Air Heating Equipment and Commercial and Industrial Refrigeration Equipment—*mfg*	333415	3443
Metal Tank (Heavy Gauge)—*mfg*	33242	3443
Plate Work—*mfg*	332313	3443
Power Boiler and Heat Exchanger—*mfg*	33241	3443
Annealing of metal for the trade: Metal Heat Treating—*mfg*	332811	3398
Announcements, engraved: Digital Printing—*mfg*	323115	2759
Flexographic Printing, Commercial—*mfg*	323112	2759
Printing, Other Commercial—*mfg*	323119	2759
Quick Printing—*mfg*	323114	2759
Announcers, radio and television service: Independent Artists, Writers, and Performers—*arts*	71151	8999
Annunciators, relay and solid-state types–industrial display: Instruments and Related Products for Measuring, Displaying, and Controlling Industrial Process Variables—*mfg*	334513	3823
Anode metal: Metal Service Centers and Offices—*whlse*	42151	5051
Anodizing equipment (except rolling mill lines): Industrial Machinery, All Other—*mfg*	333298	3559
Machinery, Other Commercial and Service Industry—*mfg*	333319	3559
Anodizing of metals and formed products, for the trade: Electroplating, Plating, Polishing, Anodizing and Coloring—*mfg*	332813	3471
Answering machines, telephone: Electrical Appliance, Television and Radio Set—*whlse*	42162	5064
Ant poisons: Pesticide and Other Agricultural Chemical—*mfg*	32532	2879
Antacids: Pharmaceutical Preparation—*mfg*	325412	2834
Antenna installation, except household type–contractors: Trade Contractors, All Other Special—*const*	23599	1799
Antenna stores, household: Automotive Parts and Accessories Stores—*retail*	44131	5731
Radio, Television and Other Electronics Stores—*retail*	443112	5731
Antennas, household–installation and service: Communication Equipment Repair and Maintenance—*serv*	811213	7622
Consumer Electronics Repair and Maintenance—*serv*	811211	7622
Radio, Television and Other Electronics Stores—*retail*	443112	7622
Antennas, receiving–automobile, home, and portable: Electronic Component, Other—*mfg*	334419	3679
Motor Vehicle Electrical and Electronic Equipment, Other—*mfg*	336322	3679
Printed Circuit/Electronics Assembly—*mfg*	334418	3679
Radio and Television Broadcasting and Wireless Communications Equipment—*mfg*	33422	3679
Antennas, satellite–home type: Electronic Component, Other—*mfg*	334419	3679
Printed Circuit/Electronics Assembly—*mfg*	334418	3679
Radio and Television Broadcasting and Wireless Communications Equipment—*mfg*	33422	3679
Antennas, transmitting and communications: Radio and Television Broadcasting and Wireless Communications Equipment—*mfg*	33422	3663
Anthelmintics: Pharmaceutical Preparation—*mfg*	325412	2834
Anthracene: Cyclic Crude and Intermediate—*mfg*	325192	2865
Petrochemical—*mfg*	32511	2865
Anthracite mine tunneling–on a contrast basis: Coal Support Activities—*mining*	213113	1241
Anthracite Mining	**212113**	**1231**
Anthracite mining services on a contract basis: Coal Support Activities—*mining*	213113	1241
Anthraquinone dyes: Organic Dye and Pigment—*mfg*	325132	2865
Petrochemical—*mfg*	32511	2865
Anti-hog-cholera serums: Biological Product (except Diagnostic)—*mfg*	325414	2836
Antiaircraft artillery: Ordnance and Accessories, Other—*mfg*	332995	3489
Antibiotics, packaged: Pharmaceutical Preparation—*mfg*	325412	2834
Antibiotics–bulk uncompounded: Medicinal and Botanical—*mfg*	325411	2833
Antifreeze compounds, except industrial alcohol: Basic Organic Chemical, All Other—*mfg*	325199	2899
Chemical Product, All Other Miscellaneous—*mfg*	325998	2899
Antifriction bearing metals, lead-base–primary: Primary Smelting and Refining of Nonferrous Metal (except Copper and Aluminum)—*mfg*	331419	3339
Antigens: Biological Product (except Diagnostic)—*mfg*	325414	2836
Antihistamine preparations: Pharmaceutical Preparation—*mfg*	325412	2834
Antimonial lead refining, secondary: Secondary Smelting and Alloying of Aluminum—*mfg*	331314	3341
Secondary Smelting, Refining, and Alloying of Copper—*mfg*	331423	3341
Secondary Smelting, Refining, and Alloying of Nonferrous Metal (except Copper and Aluminum)—*mfg*	331492	3341
Antimony ore mining: Metal Ore, All Other—*mining*	212299	1099
Antimony refining, primary: Primary Smelting and Refining of Nonferrous Metal (except Copper and Aluminum)—*mfg*	331419	3339
Antioxidants, rubber processing–cyclic and acyclic: Basic Organic Chemical, All Other—*mfg*	325199	2869
Antipoverty boards: Grantmaking and Giving Services, Other—*serv*	813219	8399
Human Rights Organizations—*serv*	813311	8399
Social Advocacy Organizations, Other—*serv*	813319	8399
Voluntary Health Organizations—*serv*	813212	8399
Antipyretics: Pharmaceutical Preparation—*mfg*	325412	2834
Antique and classic automobile restoration: Automotive Body, Paint and Interior Repair and Maintenance—*serv*	811121	7532

ALPHABETICAL INDEX	NAICS	SIC
Antique autos: Used Car Dealers—*retail*	44112	5521
Antique furniture: Non-Depository Credit Intermediation, All Other—*fin*	522298	5932
Used Merchandise Stores—*retail*	45331	5932
Antique furniture repair and restoration: Reupholstery and Furniture Repair—*serv*	81142	7641
Antique home furnishings: Non-Depository Credit Intermediation, All Other—*fin*	522298	5932
Used Merchandise Stores—*retail*	45331	5932
Antique stores: Non-Depository Credit Intermediation, All Other—*fin*	522298	5932
Used Merchandise Stores—*retail*	45331	5932
Antiscaling compounds, boiler: Basic Organic Chemical, All Other—*mfg*	325199	2899
Chemical Product, All Other Miscellaneous—*mfg*	325998	2899
Antiseptics: Drug, Drug Proprietaries and Druggists' Sundries—*whlse*	42221	5122
Antiseptics, medicinal: Pharmaceutical Preparation—*mfg*	325412	2834
Antiserums: Biological Product (except Diagnostic)—*mfg*	325414	2836
Antisubmarine and torpedo nets, made from purchased wire: Fabricated Wire Product, Other—*mfg*	332618	3496
Antisubmarine projectors (ordnance): Ordnance and Accessories, Other—*mfg*	332995	3489
Antitank rocket launchers: Ordnance and Accessories, Other—*mfg*	332995	3489
Antitoxins: Biological Product (except Diagnostic)—*mfg*	325414	2836
Antivenin: Biological Product (except Diagnostic)—*mfg*	325414	2836
Anvils, forged–not made in rolling mills: Iron and Steel Forging—*mfg*	332111	3462
Apartment building construction–general contractors: Building, Commercial and Institutional—*const*	23332	1522
Multifamily Housing—*const*	23322	1522
Apartment buildings (five or more housing units), operators of: Lessors of Residential Buildings and Dwellings—*real*	53111	6513
Apartment hotels, operators of: Lessors of Residential Buildings and Dwellings—*real*	53111	6513
Apatite mining: Phosphate Rock—*mining*	212392	1475
Apiaries: Animal Production, All Other—*ag*	11299	279
Apiculture—*ag*	11291	279
Apiculture	**11291**	**279**
Aplite mining: Clay and Ceramic and Refractory Minerals—*mining*	212325	1459
Apothecaries: Pharmacies and Drug Stores—*retail*	44611	5912
Apparatus wire and cord–made in wire drawing plants: Aluminum Rolling and Drawing, Other—*mfg*	331319	3357
Communication and Energy Wire, Other—*mfg*	335929	3357
Copper Wire (except Mechanical) Drawing—*mfg*	331422	3357
Fiber Optic Cable—*mfg*	335921	3357
Nonferrous Metal (except Copper and Aluminum) Rolling, Drawing and Extruding—*mfg*	331491	3357
Apparel Accessories and Apparel Manufacturing, Other	**315999**	**2385**
Apparel Accessories and Other Apparel Manufacturing	**31599**	
Apparel Accessories and Other Apparel Manufacturing	**3159**	
Apparel accessory stores, men's and boys': Clothing Accessories Stores—*retail*	44815	5611
Men's Clothing Stores—*retail*	44811	5611
Apparel accessory stores, women's: Clothing Accessories Stores—*retail*	44815	5632
Clothing Stores, Other—*retail*	44819	5632
Apparel belts, men's and boys': Men's and Boys' Clothing and Furnishings—*whlse*	42232	5136
Apparel belts–women's and children's: Women's, Children's, and Infants' and Accessories—*whlse*	42233	5137
Apparel Contractors, Cut and Sew	**31521**	
Apparel Contractors, Men's and Boys' Cut and Sew	**315211**	**2321**
Apparel Contractors, Women's and Girls' Cut and Sew	**315212**	**2335**
Apparel filling–cotton mill waste, kapok, and related materials: Broadwoven Fabric Mills—*mfg*	31321	2299
Narrow Fabric Mills—*mfg*	313221	2299
Nonwoven Fabric Mills—*mfg*	31323	2299
Textile and Fabric Finishing (except Broadwoven Fabric) Mills—*mfg*	313312	2299
Textile Product Mills, All Other Miscellaneous—*mfg*	314999	2299
Thread Mills—*mfg*	313113	2299
Yarn Spinning Mills—*mfg*	313111	2299
Apparel findings and trimmings: Apparel Accessories and Apparel, Other—*mfg*	315999	2396
Textile Product Mills, All Other Miscellaneous—*mfg*	314999	2396
Apparel Knitting Mills	**3151**	
Apparel Knitting Mills, Other	**31519**	
Apparel Manufacturing	**315**	
Apparel Manufacturing, Cut and Sew	**3152**	
Apparel Manufacturing, Cut and Sew, All Other	**315299**	**2339**
Apparel Manufacturing, Cut and Sew, Other	**31529**	
Apparel Manufacturing, Infant's Cut and Sew	**315291**	**2361**
Apparel Manufacturing, Men's and Boys' Cut and Sew	**31522**	
Apparel Manufacturing, Women's and Girls' Cut and Sew	**31523**	
Apparel webbing: Narrow Fabric Mills—*mfg*	313221	2241
Apparel, fur: Fur and Leather Apparel—*mfg*	315292	2371
Apparel, Piece Goods, and Notions Wholesalers	**4223**	
Apple Orchards	**111331**	**175**
Apple orchards and farms: Apple Orchards—*ag*	111331	175
Noncitrus Fruit Farming, Other—*ag*	111339	175
Applejack: Distilleries—*mfg*	31214	2085

Appliance cords for e.g., electric irons, grills, waffle irons: Electrical Equipment and Component, All Other Miscellaneous—*mfg*	335999	3699
Appliance mechanical rubber goods–molded, extruded, and lathe-cut: Rubber Product for Mechanical Use—*mfg*	326291	3061
Appliance parts, porcelain enameled: Kitchen Utensil, Pot and Pan—*mfg*	332214	3469
Appliance regulators, except switches: Automatic Environmental Control for Residential, Commercial and Appliance Use—*mfg*	334512	3822
Appliance rental and leasing: Consumer Electronics and Appliances Rental—*real*	53221	7359
Appliance Repair and Maintenance	**811412**	**7629**
Appliance repair, electrical: Appliance Repair and Maintenance—*serv*	811412	7629
Household Appliance Stores—*retail*	443111	7629
Appliance timers: Watch, Clock, and Part—*mfg*	334518	3873
Appliance, Television and Other Electronics Stores	**44311**	
Applications software programming, custom: Custom Computer Programming Services, Custom—*prof*	541511	7371
Applications software, computer–prepackaged: Publishers—*info*	51121	7372
Software Reproducing—*mfg*	334611	7372
Applicators, cotton tipped: Surgical Appliance and Supplies—*mfg*	339113	3842
Applicators, wood: Manufacturing, All Other Miscellaneous—*mfg*	339999	2499
Wood Container and Pallet—*mfg*	32192	2499
Wood Product, All Other Miscellaneous—*mfg*	321999	2499
Appliqueing, for the trade: Men's and Boys' Cut and Sew Apparel Contractors—*mfg*	315211	2395
Textile Product Mills, All Other Miscellaneous—*mfg*	314999	2395
Women's and Girls' Cut and Sew Apparel Contractors—*mfg*	315212	2395
Appraisal of damaged cars-by independent adjusters: Claims Adjusters—*fin*	524291	6411
Insurance Agencies and Brokerages—*fin*	52421	6411
Insurance Related Activities, All Other—*fin*	524298	6411
Third Party Administration for Insurance and Pension Funds—*fin*	524292	6411
Appraisers, real estate: Real Estate Agents and Brokers, Offices Of—*real*	53121	6531
Real Estate Appraisers, Offices Of—*real*	53132	6531
Apprenticeship Training	**611513**	**8249**
Apricot orchards and farms: Apple Orchards—*ag*	111331	175
Noncitrus Fruit Farming, Other—*ag*	111339	175
Apron supply service: Linen Supply—*serv*	812331	7213
Aprons, breast (harness): Apparel Accessories and Apparel, Other—*mfg*	315999	2399
Aprons, except rubberized and plastics: Apparel Accessories and Apparel, Other—*mfg*	315999	2339
Cut and Sew Apparel, All Other—*mfg*	315299	2339
Women's and Girls' Cut and Sew Apparel Contractors—*mfg*	315212	2339
Women's and Girls' Cut and Sew Other Outerwear—*mfg*	315238	2339
Aprons, leather–e.g., blacksmiths', welders': Leather Good, All Other—*mfg*	316999	3199
Aprons, textile machinery–leather: Leather Good, All Other—*mfg*	316999	3199
Aprons, vulcanized rubber and rubberized fabric: Fabric Coating Mills—*mfg*	31332	3069
Rubber Product, All Other—*mfg*	326299	3069
Aprons, waterproof–except vulcanized rubber: Apparel Accessories and Apparel, Other—*mfg*	315999	2385
Infants' Cut and Sew Apparel—*mfg*	315291	2385
Men's and Boys' Cut and Sew Apparel Contractors—*mfg*	315211	2385
Men's and Boys' Cut and Sew Other Outerwear—*mfg*	315228	2385
Men's and Boys' Cut and Sew Suit, Coat and Overcoat—*mfg*	315222	2385
Women's and Girls' Cut and Sew Apparel Contractors—*mfg*	315212	2385
Women's and Girls' Cut and Sew Other Outerwear—*mfg*	315238	2385
Women's and Girls' Cut and Sew Suit, Coat, Tailored Jacket and Skirt—*mfg*	315234	2385
Aprons, work, except rubberized and plastics: Men's and Boys' Cut and Sew Apparel Contractors—*mfg*	315211	2326
Men's and Boys' Cut and Sew Work Clothing—*mfg*	315225	2326
Aqua ammonia, household: Polish and Other Sanitation Good—*mfg*	325612	2842
Aqua ammonia, made in ammonia plants: Nitrogenous Fertilizer—*mfg*	325311	2873
Aquarium accessories, metal: Fabricated Metal Product, All Other Miscellaneous—*mfg*	332999	3499
Aquarium accessories, plastics: Plastics Pipe and Pipe Fitting—*mfg*	326122	3089
Plastics Product, All Other—*mfg*	326199	3089
Unsupported Plastics Profile Shape—*mfg*	326121	3089
Aquariums: Nature Parks and Other Similar Institutions—*arts*	71219	8422
Zoos and Botanical Gardens—*arts*	71213	8422
Aquariums and reflectors, made from purchased glass: Glass Product Made of Purchased Glass—*mfg*	327215	3231
Aqueduct construction–general contractors: Power and Communication Transmission Line—*const*	23492	1623
Water, Sewer, and Pipeline—*const*	23491	1623
Arbitration and conciliation services: Legal Services, All Other—*prof*	541199	7389
Arbor presses: Machine Tool (Metal Forming Types)—*mfg*	333513	3542
Arboreta: Nature Parks and Other Similar Institutions—*arts*	71219	8422
Zoos and Botanical Gardens—*arts*	71213	8422
Arborist services: Landscaping Services—*admin*	56173	783
Arbors (machine tool accessories): Cutting Tool and Machine Tool Accessory—*mfg*	333515	3545
Hand and Edge Tool—*mfg*	332212	3545
Arc lamp units, electrotherapeutic–except infrared and ultraviolet: Electromedical and Electrotherapeutic Apparatus—*mfg*	334510	3845
Irradiation Apparatus—*mfg*	334517	3845
Arc lamps, except electrotherapeutic: Lighting Equipment, Other—*mfg*	335129	3648
Arc lighting fixtures: Lighting Equipment, Other—*mfg*	335129	3648

ALPHABETICAL INDEX	NAICS	SIC
Arc-welder transformers (separate): Power, Distribution and Specialty Transformer—*mfg*	335311	3548
Welding and Soldering Equipment—*mfg*	333992	3548
Arc-welders, transformer-rectifier: Power, Distribution and Specialty Transformer—*mfg*	335311	3548
Welding and Soldering Equipment—*mfg*	333992	3548
Arc-welding generators: Power, Distribution and Specialty Transformer—*mfg*	335311	3548
Welding and Soldering Equipment—*mfg*	333992	3548
Arc-welding generators, a.c. and d.c.: Power, Distribution and Specialty Transformer—*mfg*	335311	3548
Welding and Soldering Equipment—*mfg*	333992	3548
Arcades, amusement: Amusement and Recreation Industries, All Other—*arts*	71399	7993
Amusement Arcades—*arts*	71312	7993
Gambling Industries, Other—*arts*	71329	7993
Arch supports, orthopedic: Surgical Appliance and Supplies—*mfg*	339113	3842
Archeological expeditions: Research and Development in the Life Sciences—*prof*	54172	8733
Research and Development in the Physical Sciences and Engineering Sciences—*prof*	54171	8733
Research and Development in the Social Sciences and Humanities—*prof*	54173	8733
Archery equipment: Sporting and Athletic Goods—*mfg*	33992	3949
Sporting and Recreational Goods and Supplies—*whlse*	42191	5091
Archery ranges, operation of: Fitness and Recreational Sports Centers—*arts*	71394	7999
Arches, laminated lumber: Cut Stock, Resawing Lumber, and Planing—*mfg*	321912	2439
Engineered Wood Member (except Truss)—*mfg*	321213	2439
Truss—*mfg*	321214	2439
Architects' equipment and supplies: Office Supplies and Stationery Stores—*retail*	45321	5049
Professional Equipment and Supplies, Other—*whlse*	42149	5049
Architectural Services	**54131**	**8712**
Architectural and Structural Metals Manufacturing	**3323**	
Architectural block, concrete–e.g., fluted, screen, split, slump, ground face: Concrete Block and Brick—*mfg*	327331	3271
Architectural engineering services: Architectural Services—*prof*	54131	8712
Architectural metal work: Building Material Dealers, Other—*retail*	44419	5039
Construction Material, Other—*whlse*	42139	5039
Architectural metal work, ferrous and nonferrous: Ornamental and Architectural Metal Work—*mfg*	332323	3446
Architectural sculptures, plaster of paris–factory production only: Gypsum and Gypsum Product—*mfg*	32742	3299
Nonmetallic Mineral Product, All Other Miscellaneous—*mfg*	327999	3299

ALPHABETICAL INDEX	NAICS	SIC
Architectural sculptures–gypsum, clay or papier mache: Gypsum and Gypsum Product—*mfg*	32742	3299
Nonmetallic Mineral Product, All Other Miscellaneous—*mfg*	327999	3299
Architectural services: Architectural Services—*prof*	54131	8712
Architectural sheet metal work–contractors: Roofing, Siding and Sheet Metal Contractors—*const*	23561	1761
Architectural terra cotta: Structural Clay Product, Other—*mfg*	327123	3259
Architectural Woodwork and Millwork Manufacturing, Custom	**337212**	**2541**
Architectural, Engineering and Related Services	**5413**	
Arctics, rubber or rubber soled fabric: Rubber and Plastics Footwear—*mfg*	316211	3021
Area and sports luminaries: Lighting Equipment, Other—*mfg*	335129	3648
Areaways, basement window–concrete: Concrete Pipe—*mfg*	327332	3272
Concrete Product, Other—*mfg*	32739	3272
Nonmetallic Mineral Product, All Other Miscellaneous—*mfg*	327999	3272
Arenas, boxing and wrestling (sports promotion)–professional: Agents and Managers for Artists, Athletes, Entertainers and Other Public Figures—*arts*	71141	7941
Promoters of Performing Arts, Sports and Similar Events with Facilities—*arts*	71131	7941
Promoters of Performing Arts, Sports and Similar Events without Facilities—*arts*	71132	7941
Spectator Sports, Other—*arts*	711219	7941
Sports Teams and Clubs—*arts*	711211	7941
Argillite, dimension: Dimension Stone and Quarrying—*mining*	212311	1411
Argon: Industrial Gas—*mfg*	32512	2813
Arm bands, elastic: Apparel Accessories and Apparel, Other—*mfg*	315999	2389
Armature relays: Relay and Industrial Control—*mfg*	335314	3625
Armature rewinding: Machinery and Equipment (except Automotive and Electronic) Repair and Maintenance, Commercial and Industrial—*serv*	81131	7694
Motor and Generator—*mfg*	335312	7694
Armatures, industrial: Motor and Generator—*mfg*	335312	3621
Armatures, motor vehicle: Motor Vehicle Electrical and Electronic Equipment, Other—*mfg*	336322	3694
Arming and fusing devices for missiles: Ammunition (except Small Arms)—*mfg*	332993	3483
Armor plate, forged iron and steel–not made in rolling mills: Iron and Steel Forging—*mfg*	332111	3462
Armor plate, made in steel works or rolling mills: Iron and Steel Mills—*mfg*	331111	3312
Petroleum and Coal Productsa, All Other—*mfg*	324199	3312
Armored cable or conductor, nonferrous: Aluminum Rolling and Drawing, Other—*mfg*	331319	3357
Communication and Energy Wire, Other—*mfg*	335929	3357
Copper Wire (except Mechanical) Drawing—*mfg*	331422	3357

Description	NAICS	SIC
Nonferrous Metal (except Copper and Aluminum) Rolling, Drawing and Extruding—*mfg*	331491	3357
Armored Car Services	**561613**	**7381**
Army: National Security—*pub*	92811	9711
Aromatic chemicals: Chemical and Allied Products, Other—*whlse*	42269	5169
Aromatic chemicals, made in petroleum refineries: Petroleum Refineries—*mfg*	32411	2911
Arrangement of carpools and vanpools: Transportation, All Other Support Activities—*trans*	488999	4729
Travel Arrangement and Reservation Services, All Other—*admin*	561599	4729
Arrestors and coils, lightning: Current-Carrying Wiring Device—*mfg*	335931	3643
Arrows, archery: Sporting and Athletic Goods—*mfg*	33992	3949
Arsenates–calcium, copper, and lead-formulated: Pesticide and Other Agricultural Chemical—*mfg*	32532	2879
Arsenic mineral mining: Chemical and Fertilizer Mineral, Other—*mining*	212393	1479
Arsenites, formulated: Pesticide and Other Agricultural Chemical—*mfg*	32532	2879
Art and illustration, commercial: Nonscheduled Air, Other—*trans*	481219	7335
Photography, Commercial—*prof*	541922	7335
Art and ornamental ware, pottery: Vitreous China, Fine Earthenware and Other Pottery Product—*mfg*	327112	3269
Art councils: Civic and Social Organizations—*serv*	81341	8699
Art Dealers	**45392**	**5999**
Art galleries, not primarily selling: Museums—*arts*	71211	8412
Art glass, made from purchased glass: Glass Product Made of Purchased Glass—*mfg*	327215	3231
Art glassware, made in glass-making plants: Pressed and Blown Glass and Glassware, Other—*mfg*	327212	3229
Art goods: Nondurable Goods, Other Miscellaneous—*whlse*	42299	5199
Art goods–plaster of paris, papier-mache, and scagliola: Gypsum and Gypsum Product—*mfg*	32742	3299
Nonmetallic Mineral Product, All Other Miscellaneous—*mfg*	327999	3299
Art marble, concrete: Concrete Product, Other—*mfg*	32739	3272
Nonmetallic Mineral Product, All Other Miscellaneous—*mfg*	327999	3272
Art needlework: Men's and Boys' Cut and Sew Apparel Contractors—*mfg*	315211	2395
Textile Product Mills, All Other Miscellaneous—*mfg*	314999	2395
Women's and Girls' Cut and Sew Apparel Contractors—*mfg*	315212	2395
Art restoration: Scientific and Technical Consulting Services, Other—*prof*	54169	8999
Art schools, commercial: Apprenticeship Training—*educ*	611513	8249
Technical and Trade Schools, Other—*educ*	611519	8249
Art schools, except commercial: Fine Arts Schools—*educ*	61161	8299
Art squares, textile fiber: Carpet and Rug Mills—*mfg*	31411	2273
Art squares–twisted paper, grass, reed, coir, sisal, jute, and rag: Carpet and Rug Mills—*mfg*	31411	2273
Artichokes in olive oil, canned: Fruit and Vegetable Canning—*mfg*	311421	2033
Artificial and Synthetic Fibers and Filaments Manufacturing	**32522**	

Description	NAICS	SIC
Artificial flowers: Flower, Nursery Stock and Florists' Supplies—*whlse*	42293	5193
Nursery and Garden Centers—*retail*	44422	5193
Artificial horizon instrumentation: Search, Detection, Navigation, Guidance, Aeronautical, and Nautical System and Instrument—*mfg*	334511	3812
Artificial insemination services–animal specialties: Animal Production Support Activities—*ag*	11521	752
Pet Care (except Veterinary) Services—*serv*	81291	752
Artificial insemination services–livestock: Animal Production Support Activities—*ag*	11521	751
Artificial limb stores: Health and Personal Care Stores, All Other—*retail*	446199	5999
Artificial nucleation (cloud seeding): Environmental Consulting Services—*prof*	54162	8999
Artificial turf installation–contractors: Trade Contractors, All Other Special—*const*	23599	1799
Artillery ammunition and component parts, more than 30 mm. (or more than 1.18inch): Ammunition (except Small Arms)—*mfg*	332993	3483
Artillery ammunition and component parts, more than 80 mm. (or more than 1.18 inch): Ammunition (except Small Arms)—*mfg*	332993	3483
Artillery parts for artillery more than 30 mm. (or more than 1.18 inch): Ordnance and Accessories, Other—*mfg*	332995	3489
Artillery parts for artillery more than 80 mm. (or more than 1.18 inch): Ordnance and Accessories, Other—*mfg*	332995	3489
Artillery, more than 30 mm. (or more than 1.18 inch)–aircraft, antiaircraft, field, naval, and tank: Ordnance and Accessories, Other—*mfg*	332995	3489
Artists' brushes, hand: Broom, Brush and Mop—*mfg*	339994	3991
Artists' materials: Nondurable Goods, Other Miscellaneous—*whlse*	42299	5199
Artists' materials, except drafting instruments: Chemical Product, All Other Miscellaneous—*mfg*	325998	3952
Lead Pencil and Art Good—*mfg*	339942	3952
Artists' studios, except commercial and medical: Independent Artists, Writers, and Performers—*arts*	71151	8999
Artists, commercial: Graphic Design Services—*prof*	54143	7336
Artists, except commercial and medical: Independent Artists, Writers, and Performers—*arts*	71151	8999
Artists, medical: Graphic Design Services—*prof*	54143	8099
Arts, Entertainment and Recreation	**71**	
Asbestos cement products–e.g., siding, pressure pipe, conduits, ducts: Motor Vehicle Brake System—*mfg*	33634	3292
Nonmetallic Mineral Product, All Other Miscellaneous—*mfg*	327999	3292
Asbestos mining: Crushed and Broken Stone and Quarrying, Other—*mining*	212319	1499
Non-Metallic Mineral, All Other—*mining*	212399	1499
Asbestos paper and asbestos filled paper: Newsprint Mills—*mfg*	322122	2621

ALPHABETICAL INDEX	NAICS	SIC
Paper (except Newsprint) Mills—*mfg*	322121	2621
Asbestos products–except packing and gaskets: Motor Vehicle Brake System—*mfg*	33634	3292
Nonmetallic Mineral Product, All Other Miscellaneous—*mfg*	327999	3292
Ascots: Men's and Boys' Neckwear—*mfg*	315993	2323
Ashcans, stamped and pressed metal: Kitchen Utensil, Pot and Pan—*mfg*	332214	3469
Ashes, collection and disposal of: Solid Waste Collection—*admin*	562111	4953
Solid Waste Combustors and Incinerators—*admin*	562213	4953
Solid Waste Landfill—*admin*	562212	4953
Waste Collection, Other—*admin*	562119	4953
Ashlar, cast stone: Concrete Pipe—*mfg*	327332	3272
Concrete Product, Other—*mfg*	32739	3272
Nonmetallic Mineral Product, All Other Miscellaneous—*mfg*	327999	3272
Ashtrays, glass: Pressed and Blown Glass and Glassware, Other—*mfg*	327212	3229
Ashtrays, pottery: Vitreous China, Fine Earthenware and Other Pottery Product—*mfg*	327112	3269
Asides (explosives): Explosives—*mfg*	32592	2892
Asparagus farms: Vegetable (except Potato) and Melon Farming, Other—*ag*	111219	161
Aspartome: Basic Organic Chemical, All Other—*mfg*	325199	2869
Asphalt (native) mining: Crushed and Broken Stone and Quarrying, Other—*mining*	212319	1499
Non-Metallic Mineral, All Other—*mining*	212399	1499
Asphalt and asphaltic materials–liquid and solid-produced in petroleum refineries: Petroleum Refineries—*mfg*	32411	2911
Asphalt and asphaltic mixtures for paving, not made in refineries: Asphalt Paving Mixture and Block—*mfg*	324121	2951
Asphalt felts and coatings: Roofing, Siding and Insulation Material—*whlse*	42133	5033
Asphalt floor tile: Nonmetallic Mineral Product, All Other Miscellaneous—*mfg*	327999	3292
Asphalt mixtures: Brick, Stone and Related Material—*whlse*	42132	5032
Building Material Dealers, Other—*retail*	44419	5032
Asphalt paints: Paint and Coating—*mfg*	32551	2851
Asphalt paper–laminated: Newsprint Mills—*mfg*	322122	2621
Paper (except Newsprint) Mills—*mfg*	322121	2621
Asphalt paving blocks, not made in petroleum refineries: Asphalt Paving Mixture and Block—*mfg*	324121	2951
Asphalt Paving Mixture and Block Manufacturing	**324121**	**2951**
Asphalt Paving, Roofing and Saturated Materials Manufacturing	**32412**	
Asphalt paving–roads, public sidewalks, and streets–contractors: Highway and Street—*const*	23411	1611
Asphalt plants, including travel–mix type: Construction Machinery—*mfg*	33312	3531
Overhead Traveling Crane, Hoist and Monorail System—*mfg*	333923	3531

ALPHABETICAL INDEX	NAICS	SIC
Railroad Rolling Stock—*mfg*	33651	3531
Asphalt rock mining: Crushed and Broken Stone and Quarrying, Other—*mining*	212319	1499
Non-Metallic Mineral, All Other—*mining*	212399	1499
Asphalt roof cement: Asphalt Shingle and Coating Materials—*mfg*	324122	2952
Asphalt roofing: Roofing, Siding and Insulation Material—*whlse*	42133	5033
Asphalt saturated board: Asphalt Shingle and Coating Materials—*mfg*	324122	2952
Asphalt sheathing: Newsprint Mills—*mfg*	322122	2621
Paper (except Newsprint) Mills—*mfg*	322121	2621
Asphalt Shingle and Coating Materials Manufacturing	**324122**	**2952**
Asphalt tile installation–contractors: Floor Laying and Other Floor Contractors—*const*	23552	1752
Asphalted felt-base floor coverings: Resilient Floor Covering—*mfg*	326192	3996
Asphaltic concrete, not made in petroleum refineries: Asphalt Paving Mixture and Block—*mfg*	324121	2951
Asphalting of private driveways and private parking areas–contractors: Concrete Contractors—*const*	23571	1771
Drywall, Plastering, Acoustical and Insulation Contractors—*const*	23542	1771
Assaying services: Testing Laboratories—*prof*	54138	8734
Assembling complete automobiles, trucks, commercial cars, and buses: Automobile—*mfg*	336111	3711
Heavy Duty Truck—*mfg*	33612	3711
Light Truck and Utility Vehicle—*mfg*	336112	3711
Military Armored Vehicle, Tank and Tank Component—*mfg*	336992	3711
Motor Vehicle Body—*mfg*	336211	3711
Assembly hall furniture: Institutional Furniture—*mfg*	337127	2531
Assembly machines, e.g., rotary transfer, in-line transfer, special purpose–includ ing robotic: Other Metalworking Machinery, Other—*mfg*	333518	3549
Other Metalworking Machinery, Other—*mfg*	333518	3549
Assessment associations, accident and health insurance: Direct Health and Medical Insurance Carriers—*fin*	524114	6321
Insurance Funds, Other—*fin*	52519	6321
Reinsurance Carriers—*fin*	52413	6321
Assessment associations, surety and fidelity insurance: Direct Property and Casualty Insurance Carriers—*fin*	524126	6351
Reinsurance Carriers—*fin*	52413	6351
Assessment associations–fire, marine, and casualty insurance: Direct Property and Casualty Insurance Carriers—*fin*	524126	6331
Insurance Funds, Other—*fin*	52519	6331
Reinsurance Carriers—*fin*	52413	6331
Assessment life insurance organizations: Direct Life Insurance Carriers—*fin*	524113	6311
Reinsurance Carriers—*fin*	52413	6311
Assistants, textile and leather processing: Surface Active Agent—*mfg*	325613	2843

Description	NAICS	SIC
Associated factory mutuals, fire and marine insurance: Direct Property and Casualty Insurance Carriers—*fin*	524126	6331
Insurance Funds, Other—*fin*	52519	6331
Reinsurance Carriers—*fin*	52413	6331
Astringents, medicinal: Pharmaceutical Preparation—*mfg*	325412	2834
Athletic and sporting goods–except clothing, footwear, small arms, and ammunition: Sporting and Athletic Goods—*mfg*	33992	3949
Athletic and sporting goods: except clothing, footwear, small arms, and ammunition: Sporting and Athletic Goods—*mfg*	33992	3949
Athletic clothing: Cut and Sew Apparel, All Other—*mfg*	315299	2329
Athletic field construction–general contractors: Heavy, All Other—*const*	23499	1629
Industrial Nonbuilding Structure—*const*	23493	1629
Athletic field operation (sports promotion): Agents and Managers for Artists, Athletes, Entertainers and Other Public Figures—*arts*	71141	7941
Promoters of Performing Arts, Sports and Similar Events with Facilities—*arts*	71131	7941
Promoters of Performing Arts, Sports and Similar Events without Facilities—*arts*	71132	7941
Spectator Sports, Other—*arts*	711219	7941
Sports Teams and Clubs—*arts*	711211	7941
Athletic footwear: Footwear—*whlse*	42234	5139
Athletic goods: Sporting Goods Stores—*retail*	45111	5941
Athletic goods, except apparel and footwear: Sporting and Recreational Goods and Supplies—*whlse*	42191	5091
Athletic shoe stores: Shoe Stores—*retail*	44821	5661
Athletic shoes, except rubber: Footwear, Other—*mfg*	316219	3149
Athletic socks: Hosiery and Sock Mills, Other—*mfg*	315119	2252
Athletic uniforms: Cut and Sew Apparel, All Other—*mfg*	315299	2339
Atlases, lithographed: Lithographic Printing, Commercial—*mfg*	323110	2752
Atlases–publishing and printing, or publishing only: Publishers, All Other—*info*	511199	2741
Atom smashers (particle accelerators): Electrical Equipment and Component, All Other Miscellaneous—*mfg*	335999	3699
Machinery, Other Commercial and Service Industry—*mfg*	333319	3699
Atomic waste casks: Metal Tank (Heavy Gauge)—*mfg*	33242	3443
Plate Work—*mfg*	332313	3443
Power Boiler and Heat Exchanger—*mfg*	33241	3443
Atomizers, medical: Surgical Appliance and Supplies—*mfg*	339113	3842
Atomizers, other than medical: Fabricated Metal Product, All Other Miscellaneous—*mfg*	332999	3999
Atropine and derivatives: Medicinal and Botanical—*mfg*	325411	2833
Attachments for portable drills: Power-Driven Hand Tool—*mfg*	333991	3546
Attenuatom: Electronic Component, Other—*mfg*	334419	3679
Motor Vehicle Electrical and Electronic Equipment, Other—*mfg*	336322	3679
Printed Circuit/Electronics Assembly—*mfg*	334418	3679
Radio and Television Broadcasting and Wireless Communications Equipment—*mfg*	33422	3679
Attic fans: Air Purification Equipment—*mfg*	333411	3564
Industrial and Commercial Fan and Blower—*mfg*	333412	3564
Attorneys: Lawyers, Offices Of—*prof*	54111	8111
Attorneys general's offices: Legal Counsel and Prosecution—*pub*	92213	9222
Auction rooms general merchandise: Stores (except Tobacco Stores), All Other Miscellaneous—*retail*	453998	5999
Auctioning livestock: Livestock—*whlse*	42252	5154
Audio and Video Equipment Manufacturing	**3343**	
Audio and Video Equipment Manufacturing	**33431**	**3651**
Audio cabinets, wood: Wood Television, Radio, and Sewing Machine Cabinet—*mfg*	337129	2517
Audio range tapes, blank: Magnetic and Optical Recording Media—*mfg*	334613	3695
Audio recorders and players–automotive and household: Audio and Video Equipment—*mfg*	33431	3651
Audiofrequency oscillators: Electronic Coil, Transformer, and Other Inductor—*mfg*	334416	3825
Instrument for Measuring and Testing Electricity and Electrical Signals—*mfg*	334515	3825
Audiological equipment, electromedical: Electromedical and Electrotherapeutic Apparatus—*mfg*	334510	3845
Irradiation Apparatus—*mfg*	334517	3845
Audiologists, offices of: Health Practitioners, Offices Of Miscellaneous—*hlth*	621399	8049
Mental Health Practitioners (except Physicians), Offices Of—*hlth*	62133	8049
Physical, Occupational and Speech Therapists and Audiologists, Offices Of—*hlth*	62134	8049
Audiometers, except medical: Electronic Coil, Transformer, and Other Inductor—*mfg*	334416	3825
Instrument for Measuring and Testing Electricity and Electrical Signals—*mfg*	334515	3825
Audiovisual motion picture program production: Motion Picture and Video Production—*info*	51211	7812
Auditing service, accounts: Accounting Services, Other—*prof*	541219	8721
Certified Public Accountants, Offices Of—*prof*	541211	8721
Payroll Services—*prof*	541214	8721
Auditorium construction–general contractors: Building, Commercial and Institutional—*const*	23332	1542
Auditors, freight rate: Freight Arrangement—*trans*	48851	4731
Management Consulting Services, Other—*prof*	541618	4731
Auger mining equipment: Mining Machinery and Equipment—*mfg*	333131	3532
Auger mining services–bituminous coal, anthracite, and lignite on a contract basis: Coal Support Activities—*mining*	213113	1241
Augers (edge tools): Hand and Edge Tool—*mfg*	332212	3423
Authors: Independent Artists, Writers, and Performers—*arts*	71151	8999
Authors' agents and brokers: Agents and Managers for Artists, Athletes, Entertainers and Other Public Figures—*arts*	71141	7389
Auto courts: Bed and Breakfast Inns—*accom*	721191	7011
Casino Hotels—*accom*	72112	7011

ALPHABETICAL INDEX	NAICS	SIC
Hotels (except Casino Hotels) and Motels—*accom*	72111	7011
Traveler Accommodation, All Other—*accom*	721199	7011
Auto emissions testing, without repairs: Automotive Oil Change and Lubrication Shops—*serv*	811191	7549
Automotive Repair and Maintenance, All Other—*serv*	811198	7549
Motor Vehicle Towing—*trans*	48841	7549
Auto wind lace: Narrow Fabric Mills—*mfg*	313221	2241
Autoclaves, dental: Dental Equipment and Supplies—*mfg*	339114	3843
Autoclaves, hospital and surgical: Surgical Appliance and Supplies—*mfg*	339113	3842
Autoclaves, industrial: Air-Conditioning and Warm Air Heating Equipment and Commercial and Industrial Refrigeration Equipment—*mfg*	333415	3443
Metal Tank (Heavy Gauge)—*mfg*	33242	3443
Plate Work—*mfg*	332313	3443
Power Boiler and Heat Exchanger—*mfg*	33241	3443
Autogiros: Aircraft—*mfg*	336411	3721
Autograph and philatelist supply stores: Stores (except Tobacco Stores), All Other Miscellaneous—*retail*	453998	5999
Autographic register forms, printed: Manifold Business Form Printing—*mfg*	323116	2761
Automated blood and body fluid analyzers, except laboratory: Electromedical and Electrotherapeutic Apparatus—*mfg*	334510	3845
Irradiation Apparatus—*mfg*	334517	3845
Automated clearinghouses: Commodity Contracts Dealing—*fin*	52313	6099
Credit Intermediation, Other Activities Related to—*fin*	52239	6099
Financial Investment Activities, Miscellaneous—*fin*	523999	6099
Financial Transactions Processing, Reserve, and Clearing House Activities—*fin*	52232	6099
Trust, Fiduciary and Custody Activities—*fin*	523991	6099
Automatic chemical analyzers, laboratory type: Analytical Laboratory Instrument—*mfg*	334516	3826
Automatic chucking machines: Machine Tool (Metal Cutting Types)—*mfg*	333512	3541
Automatic Environmental Control Manufacturing for Residential, Commercial and Appliance Use	**334512**	**3822**
Automatic laundry: Coin-Operated Laundries and Drycleaners—*serv*	81231	7215
Automatic pilots: Search, Detection, Navigation, Guidance, Aeronautical, and Nautical System and Instrument—*mfg*	334511	3812
Automatic screw machines: Machine Tool (Metal Cutting Types)—*mfg*	333512	3541
Automatic teller machines (ATM): Computer Peripheral Equipment, Other—*mfg*	334119	3578
Office Machinery—*mfg*	333313	3578
Automatic transmission repair, automotive: Automotive Transmission Repair—*serv*	811113	7537
Automatic Vending Machine Manufacturing	**333311**	**3581**

ALPHABETICAL INDEX	NAICS	SIC
Automats (eating places): Cafeterias—*accom*	722212	5812
Caterers—*accom*	72232	5812
Foodservice Contractors—*accom*	72231	5812
Full-Service Restaurants—*accom*	72211	5812
Limited-Service Restaurants—*accom*	722211	5812
Snack and Nonalcoholic Beverage Bars—*accom*	722213	5812
Theater Companies and Dinner Theaters—*arts*	71111	5812
Automobile accessory dealers: Automotive Parts and Accessories Stores—*retail*	44131	5531
Tire Dealers—*retail*	44132	5531
Automobile agencies (dealers): New Car Dealers—*retail*	44111	5511
Automobile air-conditioning equipment, sale and installation: Automotive Parts and Accessories Stores—*retail*	44131	5531
Tire Dealers—*retail*	44132	5531
Automobile and Light Duty Motor Vehicle Manufacturing	**33611**	
Automobile and Other Motor Vehicle Wholesalers	**42111**	**5012**
Automobile auction: Automobile and Other Motor Vehicle—*whlse*	42111	5012
Automobile battery dealers: Automotive Parts and Accessories Stores—*retail*	44131	5531
Automobile bodies, passenger car: Automobile—*mfg*	336111	3711
Heavy Duty Truck—*mfg*	33612	3711
Light Truck and Utility Vehicle—*mfg*	336112	3711
Military Armored Vehicle, Tank and Tank Component—*mfg*	336992	3711
Motor Vehicle Body—*mfg*	336211	3711
Automobile dead storage: General Warehousing and Storage Facilities—*trans*	49311	4226
Refrigerated Warehousing and Storage Facilities—*trans*	49312	4226
Warehousing and Storage Facilities, Other—*trans*	49319	4226
Automobile Dealers	**4411**	
Automobile driving instruction: Automobile Driving Schools—*educ*	611692	8299
Automobile Driving Schools	**611692**	**8299**
Automobile engine testing equipment, electrical: Automotive Parts and Accessories Stores—*retail*	44131	5013
Motor Vehicle Supplies and New Part—*whlse*	42112	5013
Automobile engines, used-wholesale or retail: Motor Vehicle Part (Used)—*whlse*	42114	5015
Automobile finance leasing: International Trade Financing—*fin*	522293	6159
Non-Depository Credit Intermediation, All Other—*fin*	522298	6159
Sales Financing—*fin*	52222	6159
Automobile floor coverings, except rubber or plastics: Carpet and Rug Mills—*mfg*	31411	2273
Automobile glass: Automotive Parts and Accessories Stores—*retail*	44131	5013
Motor Vehicle Supplies and New Part—*whlse*	42112	5013
Automobile hardware: Hardware—*mfg*	33251	3429
Automobile hose, plastics or rubber: Rubber and Plastics Hoses and Belting—*mfg*	32622	3052
Automobile house trailer chassis: Travel Trailer and Camper—*mfg*	336214	3792

Description	NAICS	SIC
Automobile insurance: Direct Property and Casualty Insurance Carriers—*fin*	524126	6331
Insurance Funds, Other—*fin*	52519	6331
Reinsurance Carriers—*fin*	52413	6331
Automobile leasing, except finance leasing–without drivers: Passenger Car Leasing—*real*	532112	7515
Automobile license tags, stamped metal: Metal Stamping—*mfg*	332116	3469
Automobile lifts (elevators): Elevator and Moving Stairway—*mfg*	333921	3534
Automobile loans (may include automobile insurance): Consumer Lending—*fin*	522291	6141
Credit Card Issuing—*fin*	52221	6141
Sales Financing—*fin*	52222	6141
Automobile Manufacturing	**336111**	**3711**
Automobile owners' associations and clubs: Travel Arrangement and Reservation Services, All Other—*admin*	561599	8699
Automobile parts dealers: Automotive Parts and Accessories Stores—*retail*	44131	5531
Tire Dealers—*retail*	44132	5531
Automobile parts, used-wholesale or retail: Motor Vehicle Part (Used)—*whlse*	42114	5015
Automobile polishes: Polish and Other Sanitation Good—*mfg*	325612	2842
Automobile proving and testing grounds: Testing Laboratories—*prof*	54138	8734
Veterinary Services—*prof*	54194	8734
Automobile recovery service: Repossession Services—*admin*	561491	7389
Automobile rental with drivers: Ambulance Services—*hlth*	62191	4119
Limousine Service—*trans*	48532	4119
Scenic and Sightseeing, Land—*trans*	48711	4119
School and Employee Bus—*trans*	48541	4119
Transit and Ground Passenger, All Other—*trans*	485999	4119
Transportation, Special Needs—*trans*	485991	4119
Automobile rental, without drivers: Passenger Car Rental—*real*	532111	7514
Automobile seat covers: Motor Vehicle Fabric Accessories and Seat—*mfg*	33636	2399
Automobile seat frames, metal: Fabricated Metal Product, All Other Miscellaneous—*mfg*	332999	3499
Automobile seats: Motor Vehicle Fabric Accessories and Seat—*mfg*	33636	2531
Automobile service station equipment: Automotive Parts and Accessories Stores—*retail*	44131	5013
Motor Vehicle Supplies and New Part—*whlse*	42112	5013
Automobile service stations: Gasoline Stations with Convenience Stores—*retail*	44711	5541
Gasoline Stations, Other—*retail*	44719	5541
Automobile skid chains, made from purchased wire: Fabricated Wire Product, Other—*mfg*	332618	3496
Automobile springs: Steel Spring (except Wire)—*mfg*	332611	3493
Automobile tire dealers: Automotive Parts and Accessories Stores—*retail*	44131	5531
Tire Dealers—*retail*	44132	5531
Automobile tires and tubes: Tire and Tube—*whlse*	42113	5014
Tire Dealers—*retail*	44132	5014
Automobile trailer chassis, except travel trailer: Travel Trailer and Camper—*mfg*	336214	3799
Automobile trailers, except house and travel: Travel Trailer and Camper—*mfg*	336214	3799
Automobile trimmings, fabric: Motor Vehicle Fabric Accessories and Seat—*mfg*	33636	2396
Textile Product Mills, All Other Miscellaneous—*mfg*	314999	2396
Automobile wrecker hoists: Construction Machinery—*mfg*	33312	3531
Overhead Traveling Crane, Hoist and Monorail System—*mfg*	333923	3531
Railroad Rolling Stock—*mfg*	33651	3531
Automobile wrecker-truck body: Motor Vehicle Body—*mfg*	336211	3713
Automobiles: Automobile—*mfg*	336111	3711
Automobile and Other Motor Vehicle—*whlse*	42111	5012
Heavy Duty Truck—*mfg*	33612	3711
Light Truck and Utility Vehicle—*mfg*	336112	3711
Military Armored Vehicle, Tank and Tank Component—*mfg*	336992	3711
Motor Vehicle Body—*mfg*	336211	3711
Automobiles and trucks, toy: Game, Toy, and Children's Vehicle—*mfg*	339932	3944
Automobiles, children's pedal driven: Game, Toy, and Children's Vehicle—*mfg*	339932	3944
Automobiles, new and used: New Car Dealers—*retail*	44111	5511
Automobiles, used cars only: Used Car Dealers—*retail*	44112	5521
Automotive accessories: Automotive Parts and Accessories Stores—*retail*	44131	5013
Motor Vehicle Supplies and New Part—*whlse*	42112	5013
Automotive air-conditioners: Warm Air Heating and Air-Conditioning Equipment and Supplies—*whlse*	42173	5075
Automotive ammeters and voltmeters: Electronic Coil, Transformer, and Other Inductor—*mfg*	334416	3825
Instrument for Measuring and Testing Electricity and Electrical Signals—*mfg*	334515	3825
Automotive and aircraft wire and cable, nonferrous: Aluminum Rolling and Drawing, Other—*mfg*	331319	3357
Communication and Energy Wire, Other—*mfg*	335929	3357
Copper Wire (except Mechanical) Drawing—*mfg*	331422	3357
Fiber Optic Cable—*mfg*	335921	3357
Nonferrous Metal (except Copper and Aluminum) Rolling, Drawing and Extruding—*mfg*	331491	3357
Automotive body shops: Automotive Body, Paint and Interior Repair and Maintenance—*serv*	811121	7532
Automotive Body, Paint and Interior Repair and Maintenance	**811121**	**7532**
Automotive Body, Paint, Interior and Glass Repair	**81112**	
Automotive electrical service battery and ignition repair): Automotive Mechanical and Electrical Repair and Maintenance, Other—*serv*	811118	7539
Automotive engines, new: Automotive Parts and Accessories Stores—*retail*	44131	5013

ALPHABETICAL INDEX	NAICS	SIC
Motor Vehicle Supplies and New Part—*whlse*	42112	5013
Automotive Equipment Rental and Leasing	**5321**	
Automotive Exhaust System Repair	**811112**	**7533**
Automotive fabrics, cotton: Broadwoven Fabric Mills—*mfg*	31321	2211
Automotive fabrics, manmade fiber: Broadwoven Fabric Mills—*mfg*	31321	2221
Automotive forgings, ferrous–not made in rolling mills: Iron and Steel Forging—*mfg*	332111	3462
Automotive forgings, nonferrous–not made in hot-rolling mills: Nonferrous Forging—*mfg*	332112	3463
Automotive glass replacement and repair service: Automotive Glass Replacement Shops—*serv*	811122	7536
Automotive Glass Replacement Shops	**811122**	**7536**
Automotive inspection and diagnostic service: Automotive Oil Change and Lubrication Shops—*serv*	811191	7549
Automotive Repair and Maintenance, All Other—*serv*	811198	7549
Motor Vehicle Towing—*trans*	48841	7549
Automotive interior shops: Automotive Body, Paint and Interior Repair and Maintenance—*serv*	811121	7532
Automotive lighting fixtures: Vehicular Lighting Equipment—*mfg*	336321	3647
Automotive Mechanical and Electrical Repair and Maintenance	**81111**	
Automotive Mechanical and Electrical Repair and Maintenance, Other	**811118**	**7539**
Automotive mechanical rubber goods–molded, extruded, and lathe-cut: Rubber Product for Mechanical Use—*mfg*	326291	3061
Automotive mufflers, sale and installation: Automotive Exhaust System Repair—*serv*	811112	7533
Automotive Oil Change and Lubrication Shops	**811191**	**7549**
Automotive paint shops: Automotive Body, Paint and Interior Repair and Maintenance—*serv*	811121	7532
Automotive Parts and Accessories Stores	**44131**	**5531**
Automotive Parts, Accessories and Tire Stores	**4413**	
Automotive parts, new: Automotive Parts and Accessories Stores—*retail*	44131	5013
Motor Vehicle Supplies and New Part—*whlse*	42112	5013
Automotive radio repair shops: Communication Equipment Repair and Maintenance—*serv*	811213	7622
Consumer Electronics Repair and Maintenance—*serv*	811211	7622
Radio, Television and Other Electronics Stores—*retail*	443112	7622
Automotive Repair and Maintenance	**8111**	
Automotive Repair and Maintenance, All Other	**811198**	**7549**
Automotive Repair and Maintenance, Other	**81119**	
Automotive repair shops, general: General Automotive Repair—*serv*	811111	7538
Automotive springs, rebuilding and repair: Automotive Mechanical and Electrical Repair and Maintenance, Other—*serv*	811118	7539
Automotive stampings: Automotive Parts and Accessories Stores—*retail*	44131	5013
Motor Vehicle Supplies and New Part—*whlse*	42112	5013

ALPHABETICAL INDEX	NAICS	SIC
Automotive stampings–e.g., fenders, tops, hub caps, body parts, trim: Motor Vehicle Metal Stamping—*mfg*	33637	3465
Automotive starter and generator repair: Automotive Mechanical and Electrical Repair and Maintenance, Other—*serv*	811118	7539
Automotive supplies: Automotive Parts and Accessories Stores—*retail*	44131	5013
Motor Vehicle Supplies and New Part—*whlse*	42112	5013
Automotive tops (canvas or plastic), installation, repair, or sales and installation: Automotive Body, Paint and Interior Repair and Maintenance—*serv*	811121	7532
Automotive towing service: Automotive Oil Change and Lubrication Shops—*serv*	811191	7549
Automotive Repair and Maintenance, All Other—*serv*	811198	7549
Motor Vehicle Towing—*trans*	48841	7549
Automotive Transmission Repair	**811113**	**7537**
Automotive trim shops: Automotive Body, Paint and Interior Repair and Maintenance—*serv*	811121	7532
Automotive upholstery and trim shops: Automotive Body, Paint and Interior Repair and Maintenance—*serv*	811121	7532
Automotive washing and polishing: Car Washes—*serv*	811192	7542
Automotive wiring harness sets, except ignition: Motor Vehicle Electrical and Electronic Equipment, Other—*mfg*	336322	3714
Motor Vehicle Parts, All Other—*mfg*	336399	3714
Automotive wrecking for scrap: Recyclable Material—*whlse*	42193	5093
Autophones (organs with perforated music rolls: Musical Instrument—*mfg*	339992	3931
Autos, midget–power driven: Transportation Equipment, All Other—*mfg*	336999	3799
Autotransformers for switchboards, except telephone switchboards: Power, Distribution and Specialty Transformer—*mfg*	335311	3612
Autotransformers for telephone switchboards: Electronic Coil, Transformer, and Other Inductor—*mfg*	334416	3661
Printed Circuit/Electronics Assembly—*mfg*	334418	3661
Telephone Apparatus—*mfg*	33421	3661
Autotransformers, electric (power transformers): Power, Distribution and Specialty Transformer—*mfg*	335311	3612
Auxiliary computer storage units: Computer Storage Device—*mfg*	334112	3572
Aviaries (e.g., parakeet, canary, love birds): Animal Production, All Other—*ag*	11299	279
Apiculture—*ag*	11291	279
Aviation clubs, membership: Amusement and Recreation Industries, All Other—*arts*	71399	7997
Aviation schools, excluding flying instruction: Flight Training—*educ*	611512	8249
Technical and Trade Schools, Other—*educ*	611519	8249
Avocado orchards and farms: Fruit and Tree Nut Combination Farming—*ag*	111336	179
Noncitrus Fruit Farming, Other—*ag*	111339	179

Index entry	NAICS	SIC
Awls: Hand and Edge Tool—*mfg*	332212	3423
Awning installation–contractors: Trade Contractors, All Other Special—*const*	23599	1799
Awning repair shops: Buildings and Dwellings, Other Services to—*admin*	56179	7699
Awning shops: Stores (except Tobacco Stores), All Other Miscellaneous—*retail*	453998	5999
Awning stripes, cotton: Broadwoven Fabric Mills—*mfg*	31321	2211
Awnings: Building Material Dealers, Other—*retail*	44419	5039
Construction Material, Other—*whlse*	42139	5039
Awnings, fabric: Canvas and Related Product Mills—*mfg*	314912	2394
Awnings, fiberglass and plastics combination: Plastics Pipe and Pipe Fitting—*mfg*	326122	3089
Plastics Product, All Other—*mfg*	326199	3089
Unsupported Plastics Profile Shape—*mfg*	326121	3089
Awnings, sheet metal: Metal Container, Other—*mfg*	332439	3444
Sheet Metal Work—*mfg*	332322	3444
Awnings, wood: Millwork (including Flooring), Other—*mfg*	321918	2431
Wood Window and Door—*mfg*	321911	2431
Axes: Hand and Edge Tool—*mfg*	332212	3423
Axle housings and shafts, motor vehicle: Motor Vehicle Parts, All Other—*mfg*	336399	3714
Motor Vehicle Steering and Suspension Components (except Spring)—*mfg*	33633	3714
Motor Vehicle Transmission and Power Train Parts—*mfg*	33635	3714
Axle straightening, automotive: Automotive Mechanical and Electrical Repair and Maintenance, Other—*serv*	811118	7539
Axles, motor vehicle: Motor Vehicle Parts, All Other—*mfg*	336399	3714
Motor Vehicle Steering and Suspension Components (except Spring)—*mfg*	33633	3714
Motor Vehicle Transmission and Power Train Parts—*mfg*	33635	3714
Axles, railroad–forged-not made in rolling mills: Iron and Steel Forging—*mfg*	332111	3462
Axles, rolled or forged–made in steel works or rolling mills: Iron and Steel Mills—*mfg*	331111	3312
Petroleum and Coal Productsa, All Other—*mfg*	324199	3312
Axminster carpets: Carpet and Rug Mills—*mfg*	31411	2273
Azine dyes: Organic Dye and Pigment—*mfg*	325132	2865
Petrochemical—*mfg*	32511	2865
Azo dyes: Organic Dye and Pigment—*mfg*	325132	2865
Petrochemical—*mfg*	32511	2865
Azobenzene: Cyclic Crude and Intermediate—*mfg*	325192	2865
Petrochemical—*mfg*	32511	2865
Azoic dyes: Organic Dye and Pigment—*mfg*	325132	2865
Petrochemical—*mfg*	32511	2865
Babbitt metal smelting and refining, Secondary: Secondary Smelting and Alloying of Aluminum—*mfg*	331314	3341
Secondary Smelting, Refining, and Alloying of Copper—*mfg*	331423	3341
Secondary Smelting, Refining, and Alloying of Nonferrous Metal (except Copper and Aluminum)—*mfg*	331492	3341
Babbitt metal, primary: Primary Smelting and Refining of Nonferrous Metal (except Copper and Aluminum)—*mfg*	331419	3339
Baby carriages: Stores (except Tobacco Stores), All Other Miscellaneous—*retail*	453998	5999
Baby foods (including meats), canned: Canning, Specialty—*mfg*	311422	2032
Food, All Other Miscellaneous—*mfg*	311999	2032
Baby formula–fresh, processed, and bottled: Dry, Condensed, and Evaporated Dairy Product—*mfg*	311514	2023
Baby goods: Women's, Children's, and Infants' and Accessories—*whlse*	42233	5137
Baby pants, vulcanized rubber and rubberized fabric: Fabric Coating Mills—*mfg*	31332	3069
Rubber Product, All Other—*mfg*	326299	3069
Baby powder: Soap and Other Detergent—*mfg*	325611	2844
Toilet Preparation—*mfg*	32562	2844
Baby scales: Scale and Balance (except Laboratory)—*mfg*	333997	3596
Babysitting (private households employing babysitters in the home): Private Households—*serv*	81411	8811
Babysitting bureaus: Child Day Care Services—*hlth*	62441	7299
Personal Services, All Other—*serv*	81299	7299
Backfillers, self-propelled: Construction Machinery—*mfg*	33312	3531
Overhead Traveling Crane, Hoist and Monorail System—*mfg*	333923	3531
Railroad Rolling Stock—*mfg*	33651	3531
Backflow preventors: Fabricated Metal Product, All Other Miscellaneous—*mfg*	332999	3432
Plumbing Fixture Fitting and Trim—*mfg*	332913	3432
Backhoes: Construction Machinery—*mfg*	33312	3531
Overhead Traveling Crane, Hoist and Monorail System—*mfg*	333923	3531
Railroad Rolling Stock—*mfg*	33651	3531
Backpacking, hiking, and mountaineering equipment: Sporting Goods Stores—*retail*	45111	5941
Backs for metal household furniture: Metal Household Furniture—*mfg*	337124	2514
Bacon, slab and sliced: Animal (except Poultry) Slaughtering—*mfg*	311611	2011
Meat Processed from Carcasses—*mfg*	311612	2013
Bacterial vaccines: Biological Product (except Diagnostic)—*mfg*	325414	2836
Bacterins, except in vitro and in vivo: Biological Product (except Diagnostic)—*mfg*	325414	2836
Bacteriological laboratories (not manufacturing): Diagnostic Imaging Centers—*hlth*	621512	8071
Medical Laboratories—*hlth*	621511	8071
Bacteriological media, except in vitro and in vivo: Biological Product (except Diagnostic)—*mfg*	325414	2836
Badges for policemen and firemen–metal: Fabricated Metal Product, All Other Miscellaneous—*mfg*	332999	3999
Badges, made from fabric: Apparel Accessories and Apparel, Other—*mfg*	315999	2399

ALPHABETICAL INDEX	NAICS	SIC
Badminton equipment: Sporting and Athletic Goods—*mfg*	33992	3949
Baffles: Air-Conditioning and Warm Air Heating Equipment and Commercial and Industrial Refrigeration Equipment—*mfg*	333415	3443
Metal Tank (Heavy Gauge)—*mfg*	33242	3443
Plate Work—*mfg*	332313	3443
Power Boiler and Heat Exchanger—*mfg*	33241	3443
Bag and envelope making machinery (paper machinery): Paper Industry Machinery—*mfg*	333291	3554
Bag leather: Leather and Hide Tanning and Finishing—*mfg*	31611	3111
Bag loading plants, ammunition: Ammunition (except Small Arms)—*mfg*	332993	3483
Bag opening, filling and closing machines: Packaging Machinery—*mfg*	333993	3565
Bag paper: Newsprint Mills—*mfg*	322122	2621
Paper (except Newsprint) Mills—*mfg*	322121	2621
Bag reclaiming: Recyclable Material—*whlse*	42193	5093
Bag sewing and closing machines (industrial sewing machines): Industrial Machinery, All Other—*mfg*	333298	3559
Machinery, Other Commercial and Service Industry—*mfg*	333319	3559
Bagatelle tables: Sporting and Athletic Goods—*mfg*	33992	3949
Bagel stores: Baked Goods Stores—*retail*	445291	5461
Retail Bakeries—*mfg*	311811	5461
Snack and Nonalcoholic Beverage Bars—*accom*	722213	5461
Bagels: Bakeries, Commercial—*mfg*	311812	2051
Baggage transfer: Freight (except Used Goods) Trucking, Local Specialized—*trans*	48422	4212
Used Household and Office Goods Moving—*trans*	48421	4212
Bagging of tea: Grocery and Related Products, Other—*whlse*	42249	5149
Bagging, jute–made in jute weaving mills: Broadwoven Fabric Mills—*mfg*	31321	2299
Narrow Fabric Mills—*mfg*	313221	2299
Nonwoven Fabric Mills—*mfg*	31323	2299
Textile and Fabric Finishing (except Broadwoven Fabric) Mills—*mfg*	313312	2299
Textile Product Mills, All Other Miscellaneous—*mfg*	314999	2299
Thread Mills—*mfg*	313113	2299
Yarn Spinning Mills—*mfg*	313111	2299
Bags (luggage), regardless of material: Luggage—*mfg*	316991	3161
Bags and bagging: Knit Fabric and Lace Mills, Other—*mfg*	313249	2259
Weft Knit Fabric Mills—*mfg*	313241	2259
Bags and containers, textile–except sleeping bags-insulated or not: Textile Bag Mills—*mfg*	314911	2393
Bags, blanket–plastics: Household Textile Product Mills, Other—*mfg*	314129	2392
Textile Bag Mills—*mfg*	314911	2392
Bags, feed–for horses: Leather Good, All Other—*mfg*	316999	3199
Bags, garment storage–except paper or plastics film: Household Textile Product Mills, Other—*mfg*	314129	2392

ALPHABETICAL INDEX	NAICS	SIC
Textile Bag Mills—*mfg*	314911	2392
Bags, golf: Sporting and Athletic Goods—*mfg*	33992	3949
Bags, laundry: Household Textile Product Mills, Other—*mfg*	314129	2392
Textile Bag Mills—*mfg*	314911	2392
Bags, paper and disposable plastics: Industrial and Personal Service Paper—*whlse*	42213	5113
Bags, paper–uncoated: Uncoated Paper and Multiwall Bag—*mfg*	322224	2674
Bags, plastics–printed only, except lithographed or gravure (bags not made in printing plants): Digital Printing—*mfg*	323115	2759
Flexographic Printing, Commercial—*mfg*	323112	2759
Printing, Other Commercial—*mfg*	323119	2759
Quick Printing—*mfg*	323114	2759
Bags, rosin: Sporting and Athletic Goods—*mfg*	33992	3949
Bags, rubber or rubberized fabric: Fabric Coating Mills—*mfg*	31332	3069
Rubber Product, All Other—*mfg*	326299	3069
Bags, sleeping: Textile Product Mills, All Other Miscellaneous—*mfg*	314999	2399
Bags, striking (punching): Sporting and Athletic Goods—*mfg*	33992	3949
Bags, textile: Nondurable Goods, Other Miscellaneous—*whlse*	42299	5199
Bags, textile–including canvas–except laundry, garment, and sleeping: Textile Bag Mills—*mfg*	314911	2393
Bails, ladle: Air-Conditioning and Warm Air Heating Equipment and Commercial and Industrial Refrigeration Equipment—*mfg*	333415	3443
Metal Tank (Heavy Gauge)—*mfg*	33242	3443
Plate Work—*mfg*	332313	3443
Power Boiler and Heat Exchanger—*mfg*	33241	3443
Bait and tackle shops: Sporting Goods Stores—*retail*	45111	5941
Bait, artificial: Sporting and Recreational Goods and Supplies—*whlse*	42191	5091
Bait, fishing–artificial: Sporting and Athletic Goods—*mfg*	33992	3949
Baked beans without meat–canned: Canning, Specialty—*mfg*	311422	2032
Food, All Other Miscellaneous—*mfg*	311999	2032
Baked Goods Stores	**445291**	**5461**
Bakeries: Baked Goods Stores—*retail*	445291	5461
Retail Bakeries—*mfg*	311811	5461
Snack and Nonalcoholic Beverage Bars—*accom*	722213	5461
Bakeries and Tortilla Manufacturing	**3118**	
Bakeries with baking on the premises: Baked Goods Stores—*retail*	445291	5461
Retail Bakeries—*mfg*	311811	5461
Snack and Nonalcoholic Beverage Bars—*accom*	722213	5461
Bakeries without baking on the premises: Baked Goods Stores—*retail*	445291	5461
Retail Bakeries—*mfg*	311811	5461
Snack and Nonalcoholic Beverage Bars—*accom*	722213	5461
Bakeries, Commercial	**311812**	**2052**
Bakers' cheese: Fluid Milk—*mfg*	311511	2026
Bakers' colors, except synthetic: Flavoring Syrup and Concentrate—*mfg*	31193	2087

Description	NAICS	SIC
Food, All Other Miscellaneous—*mfg*	311999	2087
Spice and Extract—*mfg*	311942	2087
Bakers' equipment, wood: Manufacturing, All Other Miscellaneous—*mfg*	339999	2499
Wood Container and Pallet—*mfg*	32192	2499
Wood Product, All Other Miscellaneous—*mfg*	321999	2499
Bakers' oven construction-general contractors: Heavy, All Other—*const*	23499	1629
Industrial Nonbuilding Structure—*const*	23493	1629
Bakers' service apparel, washable: Men's and Boys' Cut and Sew Apparel Contractors—*mfg*	315211	2326
Men's and Boys' Cut and Sew Work Clothing—*mfg*	315225	2326
Bakery goods, purchased–house-to-house: Direct Selling Establishments, Other—*retail*	45439	5963
Mobile Foodservices—*accom*	72233	5963
Bakery machinery: Food Product Machinery—*mfg*	333294	3556
Bakery products: Grocery and Related Products, Other—*whlse*	42249	5149
Bakery products produced primarily for sale on the premises: Baked Goods Stores—*retail*	445291	5461
Retail Bakeries—*mfg*	311811	5461
Snack and Nonalcoholic Beverage Bars—*accom*	722213	5461
Bakery products, dry–e.g., biscuits, crackers, pretzels: Bakeries, Commercial—*mfg*	311812	2052
Cookie and Cracker—*mfg*	311821	2052
Snack Food, Other—*mfg*	311919	2052
Bakery products, fresh–bread, cakes, doughnuts, and pastries: Bakeries, Commercial—*mfg*	311812	2051
Bakery products, frozen: Packaged Frozen Food—*whlse*	42242	5142
Bakery products, frozen–except bread and bread-type rolls: Frozen Bakery Product—*mfg*	311813	2053
Bakery products, partially cooked–except frozen: Bakeries, Commercial—*mfg*	311812	2051
Baking and frying fats (shortening): Fats and Oils Refining and Blending—*mfg*	311225	2079
Oilseed Processing, Other—*mfg*	311223	2079
Soybean Processing—*mfg*	311222	2079
Baking chocolate: Chocolate and Confectionery from Cacao Beans—*mfg*	31132	2066
Baking japans: Paint and Coating—*mfg*	32551	2851
Baking powder: Food, All Other Miscellaneous—*mfg*	311999	2099
Balances, except laboratory: Equipment, Other Commercial—*whlse*	42144	5046
Scale and Balance (except Laboratory)—*mfg*	333997	3596
Balancing equipment, automotive wheel: Industrial Machinery, All Other—*mfg*	333298	3559
Machinery, Other Commercial and Service Industry—*mfg*	333319	3559
Balconies, metal: Ornamental and Architectural Metal Work—*mfg*	332323	3446
Bale dyeing of cotton broadwoven products: Broadwoven Fabric Finishing Mills—*mfg*	313311	2261
Bale dyeing of manmade fiber and silk broadwoven fabrics: Broadwoven Fabric Finishing Mills—*mfg*	313311	2262
Bale throwers: Conveyor and Conveying Equipment—*mfg*	333922	3523
Farm Machinery and Equipment—*mfg*	333111	3523
Bale ties, made from purchased wire: Fabricated Wire Product, Other—*mfg*	332618	3496
Bale ties, wire: Metal Service Centers and Offices—*whlse*	42151	5051
Balers, farm–e.g., hay, straw, cotton: Farm Machinery and Equipment—*mfg*	333111	3523
Baling hooks: Hand and Edge Tool—*mfg*	332212	3423
Baling machines for scrap metal, paper, and similar materials: General Purpose Machinery , All Other—*mfg*	333999	3569
Ball and Roller Bearing Manufacturing	**332991**	**3562**
Ball bearings and parts: Ball and Roller Bearing—*mfg*	332991	3562
Ball clay mining: Kaolin and Ball Clay—*mining*	212324	1455
Ball joints, except motor vehicle and air craft: Mechanical Power Transmission Equipment—*mfg*	333613	3568
Ball joints, motor vehicle: Motor Vehicle Parts, All Other—*mfg*	336399	3714
Motor Vehicle Steering and Suspension Components (except Spring)—*mfg*	33633	3714
Motor Vehicle Transmission and Power Train Parts—*mfg*	33635	3714
Ballast distributors (railway track equipment): Construction Machinery—*mfg*	33312	3531
Overhead Traveling Crane, Hoist and Monorail System—*mfg*	333923	3531
Railroad Rolling Stock—*mfg*	33651	3531
Ballast forks: Hand and Edge Tool—*mfg*	332212	3423
Ballasts for lighting fixtures: Power, Distribution and Specialty Transformer—*mfg*	335311	3612
Ballet production: Dance Companies—*arts*	71112	7922
Ballet slippers: Footwear, Other—*mfg*	316219	3149
Balling wells on a contract basis: Oil and Gas Operations Support Activities—*mining*	213112	1389
Ballistic missiles, complete: Guided Missile and Space Vehicle—*mfg*	336414	3761
Balloon cloth, cotton: Broadwoven Fabric Mills—*mfg*	31321	2211
Balloon shops: Gift, Novelty and Souvenir Stores—*retail*	45322	5947
Balloons (aircraft): Aircraft—*mfg*	336411	3721
Balloons, advertising and toy–rubber: Fabric Coating Mills—*mfg*	31332	3069
Rubber Product, All Other—*mfg*	326299	3069
Balloons, metal foil laminated with rubber: Fabric Coating Mills—*mfg*	31332	3069
Rubber Product, All Other—*mfg*	326299	3069
Balloons, plastics: Plastics Pipe and Pipe Fitting—*mfg*	326122	3089
Plastics Product, All Other—*mfg*	326199	3089
Unsupported Plastics Profile Shape—*mfg*	326121	3089
Ballpoint pens: Pen and Mechanical Pencil—*mfg*	339941	3951
Ballroom operation: Amusement and Recreation Industries, All Other—*arts*	71399	7911
Fine Arts Schools—*educ*	61161	7911
Balls, rubber–except athletic equipment: Fabric Coating Mills—*mfg*	31332	3069

ALPHABETICAL INDEX	NAICS	SIC
Rubber Product, All Other—*mfg*	326299	3069
Balls, steel: Iron and Steel Mills—*mfg*	331111	3399
Secondary Smelting, Refining, and Alloying of Nonferrous Metal (except Copper and Aluminum)—*mfg*	331492	3399
Balls–baseball, basketball, football, golf, tennis, pool, and bowling: Sporting and Athletic Goods—*mfg*	33992	3949
Balsam needles, gathering of: Crop Farming, All Other Miscellaneous—*ag*	111998	831
Forest Nurseries and Gathering of Forest Products—*ag*	11321	831
Baluns: Electronic Coil, Transformer, and Other Inductor—*mfg*	334416	3677
Banana farms: Fruit and Tree Nut Combination Farming—*ag*	111336	179
Noncitrus Fruit Farming, Other—*ag*	111339	179
Banana ripening for the trade: Fresh Fruit and Vegetable—*whlse*	42248	5148
Band uniforms: Cut and Sew Apparel, All Other—*mfg*	315299	2389
Bandage cloths, cotton: Broadwoven Fabric Mills—*mfg*	31321	2211
Bandage, cheese: Textile Product Mills, All Other Miscellaneous—*mfg*	314999	2399
Bandages: Drug, Drug Proprietaries and Druggists' Sundries—*whlse*	42221	5122
Bandages and dressings, surgical and orthopedic: Surgical Appliance and Supplies—*mfg*	339113	3842
Bandages–plastics, muslin, and plaster of paris: Surgical Appliance and Supplies—*mfg*	339113	3842
Bandeaux: Women's and Girls' Cut and Sew Apparel Contractors—*mfg*	315212	2342
Women's and Girls' Cut and Sew Lingerie, Loungewear and Nightwear—*mfg*	315231	2342
Banding, spindle: Narrow Fabric Mills—*mfg*	313221	2241
Bandoleers: Apparel Accessories and Apparel, Other—*mfg*	315999	2399
Bands, dance: Independent Artists, Writers, and Performers—*arts*	71151	7929
Musical Groups and Artists—*arts*	71113	7929
Performing Arts Companies, Other—*arts*	71119	7929
Bands, plastics: Plastics Pipe and Pipe Fitting—*mfg*	326122	3089
Plastics Product, All Other—*mfg*	326199	3089
Unsupported Plastics Profile Shape—*mfg*	326121	3089
Bands, shell–copper and copper alloy–made in copper rolling mills: Copper Rolling, Drawing and Extruding—*mfg*	331421	3351
Bandsaws, woodworking: Sawmill and Woodworking Machinery—*mfg*	33321	3553
Banjos and parts: Musical Instrument—*mfg*	339992	3931
Bank and turn indicators and components (aeronautical instruments): Search, Detection, Navigation, Guidance, Aeronautical, and Nautical System and Instrument—*mfg*	334511	3812
Bank automatic teller machines: Office Equipment—*whlse*	42142	5044
Bank building construction–general contractors: Building, Commercial and Institutional—*const*	23332	1542
Bank buildings, operation of: Lessors of Nonresidential Buildings (except Miniwarehouses)—*real*	53112	6512
Promoters of Performing Arts, Sports and Similar Events with Facilities—*arts*	71131	6512
Bank chests, metal: Metal Container, Other—*mfg*	332439	3499
Bank deposit insurance: Direct Insurance (except Life, Health and Medical) Carriers, Other—*fin*	524128	6399
Bank fixtures, ornamental metal: Ornamental and Architectural Metal Work—*mfg*	332323	3446
Bank holding companies: Bank Holding Companies, Offices Of—*manag*	551111	6712
Bank Holding Companies, Offices Of	**551111**	**6712**
Bankers, investment: Financial Investment Activities, Miscellaneous—*fin*	523999	6211
Intermediation, Miscellaneous—*fin*	52391	6211
Investment Banking and Securities Dealing—*fin*	52311	6211
Securities Brokerage—*fin*	52312	6211
Banking regulatory agencies: Regulation, Licensing, and Inspection of Miscellaneous Commercial Sectors—*pub*	92615	9651
Banking schools (training in banking): Apprenticeship Training—*educ*	611513	8249
Technical and Trade Schools, Other—*educ*	611519	8249
Banking, Commercial	**52211**	**6022**
Banknotes, engraved: Digital Printing—*mfg*	323115	2759
Flexographic Printing, Commercial—*mfg*	323112	2759
Printing, Other Commercial—*mfg*	323119	2759
Quick Printing—*mfg*	323114	2759
Banks for cooperatives: International Trade Financing—*fin*	522293	6111
Non-Depository Credit Intermediation, All Other—*fin*	522298	6111
Secondary Market Financing—*fin*	522294	6111
Banks, commercial–national: Banking, Commercial—*fin*	52211	6021
Credit Card Issuing—*fin*	52221	6021
Trust, Fiduciary and Custody Activities—*fin*	523991	6021
Banks, commercial–not chartered: Banking, Commercial—*fin*	52211	6029
Banks, commercial–state: Banking, Commercial—*fin*	52211	6022
Credit Card Issuing—*fin*	52221	6022
Depository Credit Intermediation, Other—*fin*	52219	6022
Trust, Fiduciary and Custody Activities—*fin*	523991	6022
Banks, Federal Reserve: Monetary Authorities - Central Bank—*fin*	52111	6011
Banks, savings–Federal: Savings Institutions—*fin*	52212	6035
Banks, savings–not federally chartered: Savings Institutions—*fin*	52212	6036
Banks, toy: Game, Toy, and Children's Vehicle—*mfg*	339932	3944
Banner shops: Stores (except Tobacco Stores), All Other Miscellaneous—*retail*	453998	5999
Banners, made from fabric: Textile Product Mills, All Other Miscellaneous—*mfg*	314999	2399
Bannisters, railings, guards, etc.–made from metal pipe: Ornamental and Architectural Metal Work—*mfg*	332323	3446
Baptismal fonts, cut stone: Cut Stone and Stone Product—*mfg*	327991	3281

Entry	NAICS	SIC
Bar associations: Professional Organizations—*serv*	81392	8621
Bar fixtures, except wood: Showcase, Partition, Shelving, and Locker—*mfg*	337215	2542
Bar fixtures, wood: Architectural Woodwork and Millwork, Custom—*mfg*	337212	2541
Showcase, Partition, Shelving, and Locker—*mfg*	337215	2541
Wood Kitchen Cabinet and Counter Top—*mfg*	33711	2541
Bar furniture: Furniture—*whlse*	42121	5021
Furniture Stores—*retail*	44211	5021
Institutional Furniture—*mfg*	337127	2599
Bar mills: Rolling Mill Machinery and Equipment—*mfg*	333516	3547
Barbecue sauce: Fruit and Vegetable Canning—*mfg*	311421	2033
Barbecues, grills, and braziers for outdoor cooking: Household Cooking Appliance—*mfg*	335221	3631
Barbed and twisted wire–made in wire drawing plants: Fabricated Wire Product, Other—*mfg*	332618	3315
Steel Wire Drawing—*mfg*	331222	3315
Barbed wire, made from purchased wire: Fabricated Wire Product, Other—*mfg*	332618	3496
Barber and beauty shops, combined: Beauty Salons—*serv*	812112	7231
Cosmetology and Barber Schools—*educ*	611511	7231
Nail Salons—*serv*	812113	7231
Barber colleges: Barber Shops—*serv*	812111	7241
Cosmetology and Barber Schools—*educ*	611511	7241
Barber shop equipment: Fabricated Metal Product, All Other Miscellaneous—*mfg*	332999	3999
Barber shop equipment and supplies: Cosmetics, Beauty Supplies and Perfume Stores—*retail*	44612	5087
Service Establishment Equipment and Supplies—*whlse*	42185	5087
Barber Shops	**812111**	**7241**
Barber shops: Cosmetology and Barber Schools—*educ*	611511	7241
Barbers' scissors: Cutlery and Flatware (except Precious)—*mfg*	332211	3421
Barbers' service apparel, washable: Men's and Boys' Cut and Sew Apparel Contractors—*mfg*	315211	2326
Men's and Boys' Cut and Sew Work Clothing—*mfg*	315225	2326
Barbituric acid and derivatives–bulk, uncompounded: Medicinal and Botanical—*mfg*	325411	2833
Barbituric acid pharmaceutical preparations: Pharmaceutical Preparation—*mfg*	325412	2834
Barge sections, prefabricated metal: Fabricated Structural Metal—*mfg*	332312	3441
Barges, building and repairing: Ship Building and Repairing—*mfg*	336611	3731
Barite mining: Chemical and Fertilizer Mineral, Other—*mining*	212393	1479
Barite, ground or otherwise treated: Ground or Treated Mineral and Earth—*mfg*	327992	3295
Barium compounds: Basic Inorganic Chemical, All Other—*mfg*	325188	2819
Chemical Product, All Other Miscellaneous—*mfg*	325998	2819
Barium diagnostic agents: In-Vitro Diagnostic Substance—*mfg*	325413	2835
Pharmaceutical Preparation—*mfg*	325412	2835
Barium ore mining: Chemical and Fertilizer Mineral, Other—*mining*	212393	1479
Barium sulfate, precipitated (blanc fixe): Carbon Black—*mfg*	325182	2816
Barium, ground or otherwise treated: Ground or Treated Mineral and Earth—*mfg*	327992	3295
Bark cloth, cotton: Broadwoven Fabric Mills—*mfg*	31321	2211
Barks, gathering of: Crop Farming, All Other Miscellaneous—*ag*	111998	831
Forest Nurseries and Gathering of Forest Products—*ag*	11321	831
Barley: Grain and Field Bean—*whlse*	42251	5153
Barley farms: Grain Farming, All Other—*ag*	111199	119
Barmen laces: Knit Fabric and Lace Mills, Other—*mfg*	313249	2258
Textile and Fabric Finishing (except Broadwoven Fabric) Mills—*mfg*	313312	2258
Barn cleaners: Farm Machinery and Equipment—*mfg*	333111	3523
Barn stanchions and standards: Farm Machinery and Equipment—*mfg*	333111	3523
Barographs: Measuring and Controlling Device, Other—*mfg*	334519	3829
Surgical and Medical Instrument—*mfg*	339112	3829
Barometers, mercury and aneroid types: Measuring and Controlling Device, Other—*mfg*	334519	3829
Surgical and Medical Instrument—*mfg*	339112	3829
Barometric condensers: Air-Conditioning and Warm Air Heating Equipment and Commercial and Industrial Refrigeration Equipment—*mfg*	333415	3443
Metal Tank (Heavy Gauge)—*mfg*	33242	3443
Plate Work—*mfg*	332313	3443
Power Boiler and Heat Exchanger—*mfg*	33241	3443
Barrel heading and staves, sawed or split: Cut Stock, Resawing Lumber, and Planing—*mfg*	321912	2429
Sawmills—*mfg*	321113	2429
Wood Product, All Other Miscellaneous—*mfg*	321999	2429
Barrels, gun–30 mm. (or 1.18 inch) or less: Small Arms—*mfg*	332994	3484
Barrels, gun–more than 30 mm. (or more than 1.18 inch): Ordnance and Accessories, Other—*mfg*	332995	3489
Barrels, new and reconditioned: Industrial Machinery and Equipment—*whlse*	42183	5085
Industrial Supplies—*whlse*	42184	5085
Barrels, shipping–steel and other metal: Metal Container, Other—*mfg*	332439	3412
Barrels, wood–coopered: Wood Container and Pallet—*mfg*	32192	2449
Barricades, metal: Fabricated Metal Product, All Other Miscellaneous—*mfg*	332999	3499
Bars (alcoholic beverage drinking places): Drinking Places (Alcoholic Beverages)—*accom*	72241	5813
Bars and restaurants owned and operated for members of organizations only: Organizations, Other Similar—*serv*	81399	8641
Bars, aluminum–extruded: Aluminum Extruded Product—*mfg*	331316	3354
Bars, aluminum–rolled: Aluminum Rolling and Drawing, Other—*mfg*	331319	3355

ALPHABETICAL INDEX	NAICS	SIC
Bars, candy–including chocolate covered bars: Confectionery form Purchased Chocolate—*mfg*	31113	2084
Bars, candy–solid chocolate: Chocolate and Confectionery from Cacao Beans—*mfg*	31132	2066
Bars, concrete reinforcing: Metal Service Centers and Offices—*whlse*	42151	5051
Bars, concrete reinforcing–fabricated steel: Fabricated Structural Metal—*mfg*	332312	3449
Metal Window and Door—*mfg*	332321	3449
Ornamental and Architectural Metal Work—*mfg*	332323	3449
Roll Forming, Custom—*mfg*	332114	3449
Bars, copper and copper alloy: Copper Rolling, Drawing and Extruding—*mfg*	331421	3351
Bars, iron–made in steel works or rolling mills: Iron and Steel Mills—*mfg*	331111	3312
Petroleum and Coal Productsa, All Other—*mfg*	324199	3312
Bars, metal: Metal Service Centers and Offices—*whlse*	42151	5051
Bars, prying (handtools): Hand and Edge Tool—*mfg*	332212	3423
Bars, refinery–primary copper: Primary Smelting and Refining of Copper—*mfg*	331411	3331
Bars, steel–cold-rolled-not made in hot-rolling mills: Cold-Rolled Steel Shape—*mfg*	331221	3316
Bars, steel–made in steel works or hot-rolling mills: Iron and Steel Mills—*mfg*	331111	3312
Petroleum and Coal Productsa, All Other—*mfg*	324199	3312
Bars–lead, magnesium, nickel, tin, titanium, zinc, and their alloys: Nonferrous Metal (except Copper and Aluminum) Rolling, Drawing and Extruding—*mfg*	331491	3356
Bartering services for individuals: Personal Services, All Other—*serv*	81299	7299
Barware, glass: Pressed and Blown Glass and Glassware, Other—*mfg*	327212	3229
Barytes pigments: Carbon Black—*mfg*	325182	2816
Inorganic Dye and Pigment—*mfg*	325131	2816
Basalt, crushed and broken: Crushed and Broken Stone and Quarrying, Other—*mining*	212319	1429
Basalt, dimension: Dimension Stone and Quarrying—*mining*	212311	1411
Base maintenance (providing personnel on continuing basis): Facilities Support Services—*admin*	56121	8744
Baseball caps, except plastics: Hat, Cap and Millinery—*mfg*	315991	2353
Baseball clubs, except professional and semiprofessional: Fitness and Recreational Sports Centers—*arts*	71394	7997
Baseball clubs, professional or semiprofessional: Agents and Managers for Artists, Athletes, Entertainers and Other Public Figures—*arts*	71141	7941
Promoters of Performing Arts, Sports and Similar Events with Facilities—*arts*	71131	7941
Promoters of Performing Arts, Sports and Similar Events without Facilities—*arts*	71132	7941
Spectator Sports, Other—*arts*	711219	7941

ALPHABETICAL INDEX	NAICS	SIC
Sports Teams and Clubs—*arts*	711211	7941
Baseball equipment and supplies, except uniforms and footwear: Sporting and Athletic Goods—*mfg*	33992	3949
Baseball instruction schools: Sports and Recreation Instruction—*educ*	61162	7999
Baseball uniforms: Cut and Sew Apparel, All Other—*mfg*	315299	2329
Baseboards, floor–wood: Millwork (including Flooring), Other—*mfg*	321918	2431
Wood Window and Door—*mfg*	321911	2431
Baseboards, metal: Metal Window and Door—*mfg*	332321	3442
Bases, baseball: Sporting and Athletic Goods—*mfg*	33992	3949
Bases, perfume–blending and compounding: Soap and Other Detergent—*mfg*	325611	2844
Toilet Preparation—*mfg*	32562	2844
Basic Chemical Manufacturing	**3251**	
Basic Inorganic Chemical Manufacturing, All Other	**325188**	**2819**
Basic Inorganic Chemical Manufacturing, Other	**32518**	**2819**
Basic Organic Chemical Manufacturing, All Other	**325199**	**2899**
Basic Organic Chemical Manufacturing, Other	**32519**	**2869**
Basket weave fabrics, cotton: Broadwoven Fabric Mills—*mfg*	31321	2211
Basketball clubs, professional or semi professional: Agents and Managers for Artists, Athletes, Entertainers and Other Public Figures—*arts*	71141	7941
Promoters of Performing Arts, Sports and Similar Events with Facilities—*arts*	71131	7941
Promoters of Performing Arts, Sports and Similar Events without Facilities—*arts*	71132	7941
Spectator Sports, Other—*arts*	711219	7941
Sports Teams and Clubs—*arts*	711211	7941
Basketball instruction schools: Sports and Recreation Instruction—*educ*	61162	7999
Basketball uniforms: Cut and Sew Apparel, All Other—*mfg*	315299	2329
Basketballs and basketball equipment and supplies, except uniforms and foot wear: Sporting and Athletic Goods—*mfg*	33992	3949
Baskets, except fruit, vegetable, fish, and bait–(e.g., rattan, reed, straw): Manufacturing, All Other Miscellaneous—*mfg*	339999	2499
Wood Container and Pallet—*mfg*	32192	2499
Wood Product, All Other Miscellaneous—*mfg*	321999	2499
Baskets, fish and bait: Sporting and Athletic Goods—*mfg*	33992	3949
Baskets, fruit and vegetable–e.g., till, berry, climax, round stave: Wood Container and Pallet—*mfg*	32192	2449
Baskets, made from purchased wire: Fabricated Wire Product, Other—*mfg*	332618	3496
Baskets, steel–made in wiredrawing plants: Fabricated Wire Product, Other—*mfg*	332618	3315
Steel Wire Drawing—*mfg*	331222	3315
Baskets, toy: Game, Toy, and Children's Vehicle—*mfg*	339932	3944

Entry	NAICS	SIC
Baskets–reed, rattan, willow, and wood: Nondurable Goods, Other Miscellaneous—*whlse*	42299	5199
Bassinets, reed and rattan: Household Furniture (except Wood and Metal)—*mfg*	337125	2519
Bassoons: Musical Instrument—*mfg*	339992	3931
Bastnasite ore mining: Metal Ore, All Other—*mining*	212299	1099
Batching plants, bituminous: Construction Machinery—*mfg*	33312	3531
Overhead Traveling Crane, Hoist and Monorail System—*mfg*	333923	3531
Railroad Rolling Stock—*mfg*	33651	3531
Batching plants, for aggregate concrete and bulk cement: Construction Machinery—*mfg*	33312	3531
Overhead Traveling Crane, Hoist and Monorail System—*mfg*	333923	3531
Railroad Rolling Stock—*mfg*	33651	3531
Bath houses, independently operated: Fitness and Recreational Sports Centers—*arts*	71394	7999
Bath mitts (washcloths): Household Textile Product Mills, Other—*mfg*	314129	2392
Bath salts: Soap and Other Detergent—*mfg*	325611	2844
Toilet Preparation—*mfg*	32562	2844
Bath sprays, rubber: Fabric Coating Mills—*mfg*	31332	3069
Rubber Product, All Other—*mfg*	326299	3069
Bathing beaches, membership: Fitness and Recreational Sports Centers—*arts*	71394	7997
Bathing beaches, public: Fitness and Recreational Sports Centers—*arts*	71394	7999
Bathing caps and suits, rubber: Fabric Coating Mills—*mfg*	31332	3069
Rubber Product, All Other—*mfg*	326299	3069
Bathing suit stores: Clothing Accessories Stores—*retail*	44815	5699
Clothing Stores, Other—*retail*	44819	5699
Bathing suits: Apparel Accessories and Apparel, Other—*mfg*	315999	2339
Cut and Sew Apparel, All Other—*mfg*	315299	2329
Outerwear Knitting Mills—*mfg*	315191	2253
Women's and Girls' Cut and Sew Apparel Contractors—*mfg*	315212	2339
Women's and Girls' Cut and Sew Other Outerwear—*mfg*	315238	2339
Bathmats and sets, textile: Carpet and Rug Mills—*mfg*	31411	2273
Bathmats, cotton–made in weaving mills: Broadwoven Fabric Mills—*mfg*	31321	2211
Bathmats, rubber: Fabric Coating Mills—*mfg*	31332	3069
Rubber Product, All Other—*mfg*	326299	3069
Bathmats, textile fiber: Carpet and Rug Mills—*mfg*	31411	2273
Bathrobes: Men's and Boys' Cut and Sew Apparel Contractors—*mfg*	315211	2384
Men's and Boys' Cut and Sew Underwear and Nightwear—*mfg*	315221	2384
Outerwear Knitting Mills—*mfg*	315191	2253
Women's and Girls' Cut and Sew Apparel Contractors—*mfg*	315212	2384
Women's and Girls' Cut and Sew Lingerie, Loungewear and Nightwear—*mfg*	315231	2384
Bathroom accessories, vitreous china and earthenware: Vitreous China Plumbing Fixture and China and Earthenware Fittings and Bathroom Accessories—*mfg*	327111	3261
Bathroom fixtures, plastics: Plastics Plumbing Fixture—*mfg*	326191	3088
Bathroom fixtures–enameled iron, cast iron, and pressed metal: Enameled Iron and Metal Sanitary Ware—*mfg*	332998	3431
Bathroom scales: Scale and Balance (except Laboratory)—*mfg*	333997	3596
Baths, turkish: Personal Care Services, Other—*serv*	812199	7299
Baths, whirlpool: Health and Personal Care Stores, All Other—*retail*	446199	5047
Medical, Dental and Hospital Equipment and Supplies—*whlse*	42145	5047
Bathtub refinishing–contractors: Trade Contractors, All Other Special—*const*	23599	1799
Bathtubs, concrete: Concrete Pipe—*mfg*	327332	3272
Concrete Product, Other—*mfg*	32739	3272
Nonmetallic Mineral Product, All Other Miscellaneous—*mfg*	327999	3272
Bathtubs, plastics: Plastics Plumbing Fixture—*mfg*	326191	3088
Bathtubs–enameled iron, cast iron, and prod metal: Enameled Iron and Metal Sanitary Ware—*mfg*	332998	3431
Bathware, plastics–except plumbing fixtures: Plastics Pipe and Pipe Fitting—*mfg*	326122	3089
Plastics Product, All Other—*mfg*	326199	3089
Unsupported Plastics Profile Shape—*mfg*	326121	3089
Batik work (handprinting on textiles): Design Services, Other Specialized—*prof*	54149	7389
Batiste, cotton: Broadwoven Fabric Mills—*mfg*	31321	2211
Baton instruction: Schools and Instruction, All Other Miscellaneous—*educ*	611699	8299
Bats, game–e.g., baseball, softball, cricket: Sporting and Athletic Goods—*mfg*	33992	3949
Batteries, automotive: Automotive Parts and Accessories Stores—*retail*	44131	5013
Motor Vehicle Supplies and New Part—*whlse*	42112	5013
Batteries, except automotive: Building Material Dealers, Other—*retail*	44419	5063
Electrical Apparatus and Equipment, Wiring Supplies and Material—*whlse*	42161	5063
Batteries, primary–dry or wet: Dry and Wet Primary Battery—*mfg*	335912	3692
Batteries, rechargeable: Storage Battery—*mfg*	335911	3691
Batteries, storage: Storage Battery—*mfg*	335911	3691
Battery acid: Basic Organic Chemical, All Other—*mfg*	325199	2899
Chemical Product, All Other Miscellaneous—*mfg*	325998	2899
Battery boxes, jars, and parts–hard rubber: Fabric Coating Mills—*mfg*	31332	3069
Rubber Product, All Other—*mfg*	326299	3069
Battery cable wiring sets for internal combustion engines: Motor Vehicle Electrical and Electronic Equipment, Other—*mfg*	336322	3694
Battery cases, plastics: Plastics Pipe and Pipe Fitting—*mfg*	326122	3089
Plastics Product, All Other—*mfg*	326199	3089
Unsupported Plastics Profile Shape—*mfg*	326121	3089
Battery chargers, rectifying or nonrotating: Electrical Equipment and Component, All Other Miscellaneous—*mfg*	335999	3629

ALPHABETICAL INDEX	NAICS	SIC
Battery charging generators for internal combustion engines: Motor Vehicle Electrical and Electronic Equipment, Other—*mfg*	336322	3694
Battery dealers, automobile: Automotive Parts and Accessories Stores—*retail*	44131	5531
Tire Dealers—*retail*	44132	5531
Battery jars, glass: Pressed and Blown Glass and Glassware, Other—*mfg*	327212	3229
Battery Manufacturing	**33591**	
Battery metal: Nonferrous Metal (except Copper and Aluminum) Rolling, Drawing and Extruding—*mfg*	331491	3356
Battery sealing compounds: Adhesive—*mfg*	32552	2891
Battery separators, wood: Manufacturing, All Other Miscellaneous—*mfg*	339999	2499
Wood Container and Pallet—*mfg*	32192	2499
Wood Product, All Other Miscellaneous—*mfg*	321999	2499
Battery service, automotive: Automotive Mechanical and Electrical Repair and Maintenance, Other—*serv*	811118	7539
Battery testers, electrical: Electronic Coil, Transformer, and Other Inductor—*mfg*	334416	3825
Instrument for Measuring and Testing Electricity and Electrical Signals—*mfg*	334515	3825
Battery wells and boxes, concrete: Concrete Pipe—*mfg*	327332	3272
Concrete Product, Other—*mfg*	32739	3272
Nonmetallic Mineral Product, All Other Miscellaneous—*mfg*	327999	3272
Batts and batting–cotton mill waste, kapok, and related materials: Broadwoven Fabric Mills—*mfg*	31321	2299
Narrow Fabric Mills—*mfg*	313221	2299
Nonwoven Fabric Mills—*mfg*	31323	2299
Textile and Fabric Finishing (except Broadwoven Fabric) Mills—*mfg*	313312	2299
Textile Product Mills, All Other Miscellaneous—*mfg*	314999	2299
Thread Mills—*mfg*	313113	2299
Yarn Spinning Mills—*mfg*	313111	2299
Batts, insulating–paper: Coated and Laminated Paper—*mfg*	322222	2679
Converted Paper Product, All Other—*mfg*	322298	2679
Die-Cut Paper and Paperboard Office Supplies—*mfg*	322231	2679
Non-Folding Sanitary Food Container—*mfg*	322215	2679
Bauxite brick: Nonclay Refractory—*mfg*	327125	3297
Bauxite mining: Metal Ore, All Other—*mining*	212299	1099
Bauxite, refined: Basic Inorganic Chemical, All Other—*mfg*	325188	2819
Chemical Product, All Other Miscellaneous—*mfg*	325998	2819
Bay oil: Spice and Extract—*mfg*	311942	2899
Bay rum: Soap and Other Detergent—*mfg*	325611	2844
Toilet Preparation—*mfg*	32562	2844
Beach chairs and accessories, rental: Recreational Goods Rental—*real*	532292	7999

ALPHABETICAL INDEX	NAICS	SIC
Beach clubs, membership: Fitness and Recreational Sports Centers—*arts*	71394	7997
Beach maintenance cleaning: Airport Operations, Other—*trans*	488119	4959
Exterminating and Pest Control Services—*admin*	56171	4959
Remediation Services—*admin*	56291	4959
Waste Management Services, All Other Miscellaneous—*admin*	562998	4959
Beach sandals, rubber: Rubber and Plastics Footwear—*mfg*	316211	3021
Beach umbrellas: Plastics Product, All Other—*mfg*	326199	3999
Beaches, bathing–public: Fitness and Recreational Sports Centers—*arts*	71394	7999
Beaching gear, aircraft: Aircraft Part and Auxiliary Equipment, Other—*mfg*	336413	3728
Fluid Power Valve and Hose Fitting—*mfg*	332912	3728
Beachwear: Apparel Accessories and Apparel, Other—*mfg*	315999	2339
Cut and Sew Apparel, All Other—*mfg*	315299	2339
Outerwear Knitting Mills—*mfg*	315191	2253
Women's and Girls' Cut and Sew Apparel Contractors—*mfg*	315212	2339
Women's and Girls' Cut and Sew Other Outerwear—*mfg*	315238	2339
Beachwear, men's and boys': Men's and Boys' Clothing and Furnishings—*whlse*	42232	5136
Beaded novelties: Fabricated Metal Product, All Other Miscellaneous—*mfg*	332999	3999
Plastics Product, All Other—*mfg*	326199	3999
Wood Product, All Other Miscellaneous—*mfg*	321999	3999
Beaders, metal (machines): Machine Tool (Metal Forming Types)—*mfg*	333513	3542
Beads, glass reflector–for highway signs and other reflectors: Glass Product Made of Purchased Glass—*mfg*	327215	3231
Beads, unassembled: Fabricated Metal Product, All Other Miscellaneous—*mfg*	332999	3999
Plastics Product, All Other—*mfg*	326199	3999
Wood Product, All Other Miscellaneous—*mfg*	321999	3999
Beaming machines, textile: Textile Machinery—*mfg*	333292	3552
Beaming yarns for the trade: Textile and Fabric Finishing (except Broadwoven Fabric) Mills—*mfg*	313312	2282
Yarn Texturing, Throwing and Twisting Mills—*mfg*	313112	2282
Bean cleaning: Postharvest Crop Activities (except Cotton Ginning)—*ag*	115114	723
Bean elevators, except sales: Farm Product Warehousing and Storage Facilities—*trans*	49313	4221
Bean farms, except dry beans: Vegetable (except Potato) and Melon Farming, Other—*ag*	111219	161
Bean sprouts grown under cover: Food Crops Grown Under Cover, Other—*ag*	111419	182
Mushroom Production—*ag*	111411	182
Bean sprouts, canned: Canning, Specialty—*mfg*	311422	2032
Food, All Other Miscellaneous—*mfg*	311999	2032

Description	NAICS	SIC
Beaneries: Cafeterias—*accom*	722212	5812
Caterers—*accom*	72232	5812
Foodservice Contractors—*accom*	72231	5812
Full-Service Restaurants—*accom*	72211	5812
Limited-Service Restaurants—*accom*	722211	5812
Snack and Nonalcoholic Beverage Bars—*accom*	722213	5812
Theater Companies and Dinner Theaters—*arts*	71111	5812
Beans, baked–with or without meat-canned: Canning, Specialty—*mfg*	311422	2032
Food, All Other Miscellaneous—*mfg*	311999	2032
Beans, dry–bulk: Grain and Field Bean—*whlse*	42251	5153
Beans, inedible: Grain and Field Bean—*whlse*	42251	5153
Beans, unshelled: Grain and Field Bean—*whlse*	42251	5153
Bearing and hearing race forgings, nonferrous–not made in hot-rolling mills: Nonferrous Forging—*mfg*	332112	3463
Bearing piles, iron and steel: Metal Service Centers and Offices—*whlse*	42151	5051
Bearing pullers, handtools: Hand and Edge Tool—*mfg*	332212	3423
Bearings: Industrial Machinery and Equipment—*whlse*	42183	5085
Industrial Supplies—*whlse*	42184	5085
Bearings, ball and roller: Ball and Roller Bearing—*mfg*	332991	3562
Bearings, motor vehicle–except ball and roller: Motor Vehicle Parts, All Other—*mfg*	336399	3714
Motor Vehicle Steering and Suspension Components (except Spring)—*mfg*	33633	3714
Motor Vehicle Transmission and Power Train Parts—*mfg*	33635	3714
Bearings, plain: Mechanical Power Transmission Equipment—*mfg*	333613	3568
Bearings, plastics: Plastics Pipe and Pipe Fitting—*mfg*	326122	3089
Plastics Product, All Other—*mfg*	326199	3089
Unsupported Plastics Profile Shape—*mfg*	326121	3089
Bearings, wood: Manufacturing, All Other Miscellaneous—*mfg*	339999	2499
Wood Container and Pallet—*mfg*	32192	2499
Wood Product, All Other Miscellaneous—*mfg*	321999	2499
Beauticians: Beauty Salons—*serv*	812112	7231
Cosmetology and Barber Schools—*educ*	611511	7231
Nail Salons—*serv*	812113	7231
Beauty and barber shops, combined: Beauty Salons—*serv*	812112	7231
Cosmetology and Barber Schools—*educ*	611511	7231
Nail Salons—*serv*	812113	7231
Beauty culture schools: Beauty Salons—*serv*	812112	7231
Cosmetology and Barber Schools—*educ*	611511	7231
Nail Salons—*serv*	812113	7231
Beauty parlor equipment and supplies: Cosmetics, Beauty Supplies and Perfume Stores—*retail*	44612	5087
Service Establishment Equipment and Supplies—*whlse*	42185	5087
Beauty Salons	**812112**	**7231**
Beauty shops or salons: Beauty Salons—*serv*	812112	7231
Cosmetology and Barber Schools—*educ*	611511	7231
Nail Salons—*serv*	812113	7231

Description	NAICS	SIC
Bed and Breakfast Inns	**721191**	**7011**
Bed and breakfast inns: Casino Hotels—*accom*	72112	7011
Hotels (except Casino Hotels) and Motels—*accom*	72111	7011
Traveler Accommodation, All Other—*accom*	721199	7011
Bed sets, lace: Knit Fabric and Lace Mills, Other—*mfg*	313249	2258
Textile and Fabric Finishing (except Broadwoven Fabric) Mills—*mfg*	313312	2258
Bed tickings, cotton: Broadwoven Fabric Mills—*mfg*	31321	2211
Bedcoverings, electric: Electric Housewares and Household Fan—*mfg*	335211	3634
Heating Equipment (except Electric and Warm Air Furnaces)—*mfg*	333414	3634
Bedding (sheets, blankets, spreads, and pillows): Home Furnishings Stores, All Other—*retail*	442299	5719
Window Treatment Stores—*retail*	442291	5719
Bedding plants, growing of: Floriculture Production—*ag*	111422	181
Nursery and Tree Production—*ag*	111421	181
Bedjackets: Infants' Cut and Sew Apparel—*mfg*	315291	2341
Women's and Girls' Cut and Sew Apparel Contractors—*mfg*	315212	2341
Women's and Girls' Cut and Sew Lingerie, Loungewear and Nightwear—*mfg*	315231	2341
Beds and springs: Furniture Stores—*retail*	44211	5712
Nonupholstered Wood Household Furniture—*mfg*	337122	5712
Upholstered Household Furniture—*mfg*	337121	5712
Wood Kitchen Cabinet and Counter Top—*mfg*	33711	5712
Beds, hospital: Health and Personal Care Stores, All Other—*retail*	446199	5047
Institutional Furniture—*mfg*	337127	2599
Medical, Dental and Hospital Equipment and Supplies—*whlse*	42145	5047
Surgical Appliance and Supplies—*mfg*	339113	2599
Beds, including folding and cabinet beds–household-metal: Metal Household Furniture—*mfg*	337124	2514
Beds, including folding and cabinet beds–household-wood: Nonupholstered Wood Household Furniture—*mfg*	337122	2511
Beds, sleep system ensembles–flotation and adjustable: Mattress—*mfg*	33791	2515
Upholstered Household Furniture—*mfg*	337121	2515
Beds, sofa and chair–on frames of any material: Mattress—*mfg*	33791	2515
Upholstered Household Furniture—*mfg*	337121	2515
Bedsheeting, cotton: Broadwoven Fabric Mills—*mfg*	31321	2211
Bedside stands, wood: Nonupholstered Wood Household Furniture—*mfg*	337122	2511
Bedspreads: Home Furnishing—*whlse*	42122	5023
Knit Fabric and Lace Mills, Other—*mfg*	313249	2259
Weft Knit Fabric Mills—*mfg*	313241	2259
Bedspreads and bed sets: Household Textile Product Mills, Other—*mfg*	314129	2392
Bedspreads, cotton–made in weaving mills: Broadwoven Fabric Mills—*mfg*	31321	2211

ALPHABETICAL INDEX	NAICS	SIC
Bedspreads, lace–made on lace machines: Knit Fabric and Lace Mills, Other—*mfg*	313249	2258
Textile and Fabric Finishing (except Broadwoven Fabric) Mills—*mfg*	313312	2258
Bedspreads, silk and manmade fiber: Broadwoven Fabric Mills—*mfg*	31321	2221
Bedspring frames, metal: Metal Household Furniture—*mfg*	337124	2514
Bedspring frames, wood: Nonupholstered Wood Household Furniture—*mfg*	337122	2511
Bedsprings: Furniture—*whlse*	42121	5021
Furniture Stores—*retail*	44211	5021
Bedsprings, assembled: Mattress—*mfg*	33791	2515
Upholstered Household Furniture—*mfg*	337121	2515
Bee farms: Animal Production, All Other—*ag*	11299	279
Apiculture—*ag*	11291	279
Beef: Animal (except Poultry) Slaughtering—*mfg*	311611	2011
Meat Processed from Carcasses—*mfg*	311612	2013
Beef cattle farms, except feedlots: Beef Cattle Ranching and Farming—*ag*	112111	212
Beef cattle feedlots: Cattle Feedlots—*ag*	112112	211
Beef Cattle Ranching and Farming	**112111**	**241**
Beef Cattle Ranching and Farming, including Feedlots	**11211**	
Beef stew: Meat Processed from Carcasses—*mfg*	311612	2013
Beehive coke oven products: Iron and Steel Mills—*mfg*	331111	3312
Petroleum and Coal Productsa, All Other—*mfg*	324199	3312
Beekeeping supplies: Farm Supplies—*whlse*	42291	5191
Nursery and Garden Centers—*retail*	44422	5191
Beekeeping supplies, wood: Manufacturing, All Other Miscellaneous—*mfg*	339999	2499
Wood Container and Pallet—*mfg*	32192	2499
Wood Product, All Other Miscellaneous—*mfg*	321999	2499
Beeper (radio pager) communications services: Cellular and Other Wireless Telecommunications—*info*	513322	4812
Paging—*info*	513321	4812
Telecommunications Resellers—*info*	51333	4812
Beer (alcoholic beverage): Breweries—*mfg*	31212	2082
Beer and Ale Wholesalers	**42281**	**5181**
Beer and other fermented malt liquors: Beer and Ale—*whlse*	42281	5181
Beer cans, metal: Metal Can—*mfg*	332431	3411
Beer dispensing equipment: Air-Conditioning and Warm Air Heating Equipment and Commercial and Industrial Refrigeration Equipment—*mfg*	333415	3585
Motor Vehicle Air-Conditioning—*mfg*	336391	3585
Beer gardens (drinking places): Drinking Places (Alcoholic Beverages)—*accom*	72241	5813
Beer parlors (tap rooms): Drinking Places (Alcoholic Beverages)—*accom*	72241	5813

ALPHABETICAL INDEX	NAICS	SIC
Beer pump coil cleaning and repair service: Machinery and Equipment (except Automotive and Electronic) Repair and Maintenance, Commercial and Industrial—*serv*	81131	7699
Beer taverns: Drinking Places (Alcoholic Beverages)—*accom*	72241	5813
Beer, birch and root–bottled or canned: Bottled Water—*mfg*	312112	2086
Soft Drink—*mfg*	312111	2086
Beer, packaged: Beer, Wine and Liquor Stores—*retail*	44531	5921
Beer, Wine and Liquor Stores	**4453**	
Beer, Wine and Liquor Stores	**44531**	**5921**
Beer, Wine, and Distilled Alcoholic Beverage Wholesalers	**4228**	
Beer, wine, and liquors–sale for on-premise consumption: Drinking Places (Alcoholic Beverages)—*accom*	72241	5813
Beeswax, processing of: Polish and Other Sanitation Good—*mfg*	325612	2842
Beet farms, except sugar beet: Vegetable (except Potato) and Melon Farming, Other—*ag*	111219	161
Beet farms, sugar: Sugar Beet Farming—*ag*	111991	133
Sugarcane Farming—*ag*	11193	133
Beet pulp, dried: Beet Sugar—*mfg*	311313	2063
Beet Sugar Manufacturing	**311313**	**2063**
Beet sugar, made from sugar beets: Beet Sugar—*mfg*	311313	2063
Belladonna pharmaceutical preparations: Pharmaceutical Preparation—*mfg*	325412	2834
Bellows, hand: Hardware—*mfg*	33251	3429
Bellows, industrial–metal: Fabricated Metal Product, All Other Miscellaneous—*mfg*	332999	3599
General Purpose Machinery , All Other—*mfg*	333999	3599
Machine Shops—*mfg*	33271	3599
Machinery, Other Commercial and Service Industry—*mfg*	333319	3599
Bells (musical instruments): Musical Instrument—*mfg*	339992	3931
Bells, electric: Electrical Equipment and Component, All Other Miscellaneous—*mfg*	335999	3699
Bells, toy: Game, Toy, and Children's Vehicle—*mfg*	339932	3944
Belt and buckle assembly kits: Broadwoven Fabric Finishing Mills—*mfg*	313311	5131
Piece Goods, Notions and Other Dry Goods—*whlse*	42231	5131
Textile and Fabric Finishing (except Broadwoven Fabric) Mills—*mfg*	313312	5131
Belt conveyor systems for general industrial use: Conveyor and Conveying Equipment—*mfg*	333922	3535
Belt dressing: Polish and Other Sanitation Good—*mfg*	325612	2842
Belt laces, leather: Leather Good, All Other—*mfg*	316999	3199
Belt line railroads: Rail Support Activities—*trans*	48821	4013
Short Line Railroads—*trans*	482112	4013
Belting (industrial) reinforcement, cord and fabric: Tire Cord and Tire Fabric Mills—*mfg*	314992	2296
Belting butts, curried or rough: Leather and Hide Tanning and Finishing—*mfg*	31611	3111

Description	NAICS	SIC
Belting leather: Leather and Hide Tanning and Finishing—*mfg*	31611	3111
Belting, chain: Mechanical Power Transmission Equipment—*mfg*	333613	3568
Belting, fabric: Apparel Accessories and Apparel, Other—*mfg*	315999	2399
Belting, hose and packing–industrial: Industrial Machinery and Equipment—*whlse*	42183	5085
Industrial Supplies—*whlse*	42184	5085
Belting, rubber–e.g., conveyor, elevator, transmission: Rubber and Plastics Hoses and Belting—*mfg*	32622	3052
Beltings, woven or braided: Narrow Fabric Mills—*mfg*	313221	2241
Belts and belting for machinery, leather: Leather Good, All Other—*mfg*	316999	3199
Belts, ammunition (sporting goods–of all materials): Sporting and Athletic Goods—*mfg*	33992	3949
Belts, apparel–custom: Clothing Accessories Stores—*retail*	44815	5699
Clothing Stores, Other—*retail*	44819	5699
Belts, apparel–made of any material: Apparel Accessories and Apparel, Other—*mfg*	315999	2387
Belts, cartridge–sporting type: Sporting and Athletic Goods—*mfg*	33992	3949
Belts, conveyor–made from purchased wire: Fabricated Wire Product, Other—*mfg*	332618	3496
Belts, drying–made from purchased wire: Fabricated Wire Product, Other—*mfg*	332618	3496
Belts, machine gun, metallic–30 mm. (or 1.18 inch) or less: Small Arms—*mfg*	332994	3484
Belts, money–made of any material: Apparel Accessories and Apparel, Other—*mfg*	315999	2399
Belts, safety–leather: Leather Good, All Other—*mfg*	316999	3199
Belts–sanitary, surgical, and corrective: Surgical Appliance and Supplies—*mfg*	339113	3842
Benches for public buildings: Institutional Furniture—*mfg*	337127	2531
Benches, cut stone: Cut Stone and Stone Product—*mfg*	327991	3281
Benches, office–except wood: Nonwood Office Furniture—*mfg*	337214	2522
Benches, office–wood: Wood Office Furniture—*mfg*	337211	2521
Benches, work–industrial: Institutional Furniture—*mfg*	337127	2599
Bending and forming machines: Machine Tool (Metal Forming Types)—*mfg*	333513	3542
Bends, pipe–fabricated from purchased metal pipe: Fabricated Pipe and Pipe Fitting—*mfg*	332996	3498
Benevolent insurance associations: Direct Life Insurance Carriers—*fin*	524113	6311
Reinsurance Carriers—*fin*	52413	6311
Bentonite mining: Clay and Ceramic and Refractory Minerals—*mining*	212325	1459
Benzaldehyde: Cyclic Crude and Intermediate—*mfg*	325192	2865
Petrochemical—*mfg*	32511	2865
Benzene hexachioride (BHC): Cyclic Crude and Intermediate—*mfg*	325192	2865
Petrochemical—*mfg*	32511	2865
Benzene, made in chemical plants: Cyclic Crude and Intermediate—*mfg*	325192	2865

Description	NAICS	SIC
Petrochemical—*mfg*	32511	2865
Benzene, produced in petroleum refineries: Petroleum Refineries—*mfg*	32411	2911
Benzoic acid: Cyclic Crude and Intermediate—*mfg*	325192	2865
Petrochemical—*mfg*	32511	2865
Bermuda sprigging services: Landscaping Services—*admin*	56173	782
Berries, machine harvesting of: Crop Harvesting, Primarily by Machine—*ag*	115113	722
Berry (except Strawberry) Farming	**111334**	**171**
Berry and grain separators, farm: Farm Machinery and Equipment—*mfg*	333111	3523
Berry crates, wood–wire-bound: Wood Container and Pallet—*mfg*	32192	2449
Berry cups, veneer and splint: Wood Container and Pallet—*mfg*	32192	2449
Berry farms: Berry (except Strawberry) Farming—*ag*	111334	171
Strawberry Farming—*ag*	111333	171
Beryl mining: Metal Ore, All Other—*mining*	212299	1099
Beryllia porcelain insulators: Porcelain Electrical Supply—*mfg*	327113	3264
Beryllium castings, except die-castings: Nonferrous Foundries, Other—*mfg*	331528	3369
Beryllium die-castings: Nonferrous (except Aluminum) Die-Castings—*mfg*	331522	3364
Beryllium metal: Primary Smelting and Refining of Nonferrous Metal (except Copper and Aluminum)—*mfg*	331419	3339
Beryllium ore mining: Metal Ore, All Other—*mining*	212299	1099
Beryllium oxide: Basic Inorganic Chemical, All Other—*mfg*	325188	2819
Chemical Product, All Other Miscellaneous—*mfg*	325998	2819
Beta-ray irradiation equipment: Irradiation Apparatus—*mfg*	334517	3844
Betatrons: Electrical Equipment and Component, All Other Miscellaneous—*mfg*	335999	3699
Machinery, Other Commercial and Service Industry—*mfg*	333319	3699
Better business bureaus: Business Associations—*serv*	81391	8611
Betting information services: Gambling Industries, Other—*arts*	71329	7999
Beveling of cards: Tradebinding and Related Work—*mfg*	323121	2789
Beverage alcohol, ethyl and grain: Distilleries—*mfg*	31214	2085
Beverage and Tobacco Product Manufacturing	**312**	
Beverage bases: Flavoring Syrup and Concentrate—*mfg*	31193	2087
Food, All Other Miscellaneous—*mfg*	311999	2087
Spice and Extract—*mfg*	311942	2087
Beverage concentrates: Grocery and Related Products, Other—*whlse*	42249	5149
Beverage coolers: Refrigeration Equipment and Supplies—*whlse*	42174	5078
Beverage Manufacturing	**3121**	
Beverage syrups: Flavoring Syrup and Concentrate—*mfg*	31193	2087
Food, All Other Miscellaneous—*mfg*	311999	2087
Spice and Extract—*mfg*	311942	2087
Bias bindings: Apparel Accessories and Apparel, Other—*mfg*	315999	2396
Textile Product Mills, All Other Miscellaneous—*mfg*	314999	2396
Bible schools, not operated by churches: Schools and Instruction, All Other Miscellaneous—*educ*	611699	8299

ALPHABETICAL INDEX	NAICS	SIC
Bibles, house-to-house selling: Direct Selling Establishments, Other—*retail*	45439	5963
Mobile Foodservices—*accom*	72233	5963
Bibs, vulcanized rubber and rubberized fabric: Fabric Coating Mills—*mfg*	31332	3069
Rubber Product, All Other—*mfg*	326299	3069
Bibs, waterproof: Apparel Accessories and Apparel, Other—*mfg*	315999	2385
Infants' Cut and Sew Apparel—*mfg*	315291	2385
Men's and Boys' Cut and Sew Apparel Contractors—*mfg*	315211	2385
Men's and Boys' Cut and Sew Other Outerwear—*mfg*	315228	2385
Men's and Boys' Cut and Sew Suit, Coat and Overcoat—*mfg*	315222	2385
Women's and Girls' Cut and Sew Apparel Contractors—*mfg*	315212	2385
Women's and Girls' Cut and Sew Other Outerwear—*mfg*	315238	2385
Women's and Girls' Cut and Sew Suit, Coat, Tailored Jacket and Skirt—*mfg*	315234	2385
Bichromates and chromates: Basic Inorganic Chemical, All Other—*mfg*	325188	2819
Chemical Product, All Other Miscellaneous—*mfg*	325998	2819
Bicycle and bicycle parts dealers, except motorized: Sporting Goods Stores—*retail*	45111	5941
Bicycle lamps: Vehicular Lighting Equipment—*mfg*	336321	3647
Bicycle repair shops: Personal and Household Goods Repair and Maintenance, Other—*serv*	81149	7699
Sporting Goods Stores—*retail*	45111	7699
Bicycle tires and tubes: Sporting and Recreational Goods and Supplies—*whlse*	42191	5091
Bicycles: Sporting and Recreational Goods and Supplies—*whlse*	42191	5091
Bicycles and parts: Motorcycle, Bicycle and Parts—*mfg*	336991	3751
Bicycles, motorized: Motorcycle Dealers—*retail*	441221	5571
Bidets, vitreous china: Vitreous China Plumbing Fixture and China and Earthenware Fittings and Bathroom Accessories—*mfg*	327111	3261
Bill posting, advertising: Display Advertising—*prof*	54185	7312
Billboard advertising: Display Advertising—*prof*	54185	7312
Billet mills: Rolling Mill Machinery and Equipment—*mfg*	333516	3547
Billets, steel: Iron and Steel Mills—*mfg*	331111	3312
Petroleum and Coal Productsa, All Other—*mfg*	324199	3312
Billfold inserts, plastics: Plastics Pipe and Pipe Fitting—*mfg*	326122	3089
Plastics Product, All Other—*mfg*	326199	3089
Unsupported Plastics Profile Shape—*mfg*	326121	3089
Billfolds, regardless of material: Personal Leather Good (except Women's Handbag and Purse)—*mfg*	316993	3172
Billheads, lithographed: Lithographic Printing, Commercial—*mfg*	323110	2752
Quick Printing—*mfg*	323114	2752
Billiard and pool balls, cues, cue tips, and tables: Sporting and Athletic Goods—*mfg*	33992	3949
Billiard chalk: Sporting and Athletic Goods—*mfg*	33992	3949
Billiard cloths: Broadwoven Fabric Finishing Mills—*mfg*	313311	2231

ALPHABETICAL INDEX	NAICS	SIC
Broadwoven Fabric Mills—*mfg*	31321	2231
Textile and Fabric Finishing (except Broadwoven Fabric) Mills—*mfg*	313312	2231
Billiard parlors: Fitness and Recreational Sports Centers—*arts*	71394	7999
Billiards equipment and supplies: Sporting and Recreational Goods and Supplies—*whlse*	42191	5091
Billing machines: Computer Peripheral Equipment, Other—*mfg*	334119	3578
Office Machinery—*mfg*	333313	3578
Binder and baler twine: Rope, Cordage and Twine Mills—*mfg*	314991	2298
Binders (chemical foundry supplies): Basic Organic Chemical, All Other—*mfg*	325199	2899
Chemical Product, All Other Miscellaneous—*mfg*	325998	2899
Binders' board: Paperboard Mills—*mfg*	32213	2631
Binders, looseleaf: Blankbook, Loose-leaf Binder and Device—*mfg*	323118	2782
Flexographic Printing, Commercial—*mfg*	323112	2782
Gravure Printing, Commercial—*mfg*	323111	2782
Lithographic Printing, Commercial—*mfg*	323110	2782
Printing, Other Commercial—*mfg*	323119	2782
Screen Printing, Commercial—*mfg*	323113	2782
Binding machines, plastics and adhesive–for store or office use: Lead Pencil and Art Good—*mfg*	339942	3579
Office Machinery—*mfg*	333313	3579
Watch, Clock, and Part—*mfg*	334518	3579
Binding only–books, pamphlets, magazines, etc: Tradebinding and Related Work—*mfg*	323121	2789
Binding, textile: Broadwoven Fabric Finishing Mills—*mfg*	313311	5131
Piece Goods, Notions and Other Dry Goods—*whlse*	42231	5131
Textile and Fabric Finishing (except Broadwoven Fabric) Mills—*mfg*	313312	5131
Bindings, bias: Apparel Accessories and Apparel, Other—*mfg*	315999	2396
Textile Product Mills, All Other Miscellaneous—*mfg*	314999	2396
Bindings, cap and hat: Apparel Accessories and Apparel, Other—*mfg*	315999	2396
Textile Product Mills, All Other Miscellaneous—*mfg*	314999	2396
Bindings, textile: Narrow Fabric Mills—*mfg*	313221	2241
Bingo boards (games): Game, Toy, and Children's Vehicle—*mfg*	339932	3944
Bingo parlors: Gambling Industries, Other—*arts*	71329	7999
Binocular cases: Luggage—*mfg*	316991	3161
Binoculars: Optical Instrument and Lens—*mfg*	333314	3827
Stores (except Tobacco Stores), All Other Miscellaneous—*retail*	453998	5999
Binoculars and other optical goods repair: Electronic and Precision Equipment Repair and Maintenance, Other—*serv*	811219	7699
Bins, prefabricated metal plate: Air-Conditioning and Warm Air Heating Equipment and Commercial and Industrial Refrigeration Equipment—*mfg*	333415	3443
Metal Tank (Heavy Gauge)—*mfg*	33242	3443
Plate Work—*mfg*	332313	3443
Power Boiler and Heat Exchanger—*mfg*	33241	3443

Bins, prefabricated–sheet metal: Metal Container, Other—*mfg*	332439	3444
Sheet Metal Work—*mfg*	332322	3444
Biofeedback centers: Family Planning Centers—*hlth*	62141	8093
Outpatient Care Centers, All Other—*hlth*	621498	8093
Outpatient Mental Health and Substance Abuse Centers—*hlth*	62142	8093
Biological and allied products–antitoxins, bacterins, vaccines, viruses, except in vitro and in vivo: Biological Product (except Diagnostic)—*mfg*	325414	2836
Biological laboratories (not manufacturing): Diagnostic Imaging Centers—*hlth*	621512	8071
Medical Laboratories—*hlth*	621511	8071
Biological Product (except Diagnostic) Manufacturing	**325414**	**2836**
Biological research, commercial: Research and Development in the Life Sciences—*prof*	54172	8731
Research and Development in the Physical Sciences and Engineering Sciences—*prof*	54171	8731
Biological research, noncommercial: Research and Development in the Life Sciences—*prof*	54172	8733
Research and Development in the Physical Sciences and Engineering Sciences—*prof*	54171	8733
Research and Development in the Social Sciences and Humanities—*prof*	54173	8733
Biological stains: Petrochemical—*mfg*	32511	2865
Biologicals and allied products: Drug, Drug Proprietaries and Druggists' Sundries—*whlse*	42221	5122
Biopsy instruments and equipment: Surgical and Medical Instrument—*mfg*	339112	3841
Birch beer, bottled or canned: Bottled Water—*mfg*	312112	2086
Soft Drink—*mfg*	312111	2086
Bird cages, made from purchased wire: Fabricated Wire Product, Other—*mfg*	332618	3496
Bird food, prepared: Animal Food, Other—*mfg*	311119	2048
Bird proofing: Exterminating and Pest Control Services—*admin*	56171	7342
Janitorial Services—*admin*	56172	7342
Bird's-eye diaper cloth, cotton: Broadwoven Fabric Mills—*mfg*	31321	2211
Birth certificate agencies: Personal Services, All Other—*serv*	81299	7299
Birth control clinics (family planning): Family Planning Centers—*hlth*	62141	8093
Outpatient Care Centers, All Other—*hlth*	621498	8093
Outpatient Mental Health and Substance Abuse Centers—*hlth*	62142	8093
Birthday cards, except hand painted: Flexographic Printing, Commercial—*mfg*	323112	2771
Gravure Printing, Commercial—*mfg*	323111	2771
Greeting Card Publishers—*info*	511191	2771
Lithographic Printing, Commercial—*mfg*	323110	2771
Printing, Other Commercial—*mfg*	323119	2771
Screen Printing, Commercial—*mfg*	323113	2771
Biscuit cutters (machines): Food Product Machinery—*mfg*	333294	3556
Biscuit dough, canned: Flour Milling—*mfg*	311211	2041
Biscuit mixes and doughs: Flour Mixes and Dough from Purchased Flour—*mfg*	311822	2045
Biscuits, baked–baking powder and raised: Bakeries, Commercial—*mfg*	311812	2051
Biscuits, baked–dry, except baking powder and raised: Bakeries, Commercial—*mfg*	311812	2052
Cookie and Cracker—*mfg*	311821	2052
Snack Food, Other—*mfg*	311919	2052
Bismuth refining, primary: Primary Smelting and Refining of Nonferrous Metal (except Copper and Aluminum)—*mfg*	331419	3339
Bits (edge too's for woodworking): Hand and Edge Tool—*mfg*	332212	3423
Bits for use on lathes, planers, shapers, etc.: Cutting Tool and Machine Tool Accessory—*mfg*	333515	3545
Hand and Edge Tool—*mfg*	332212	3545
Bits, rock–except oil and gas field tools: Mining Machinery and Equipment—*mfg*	333131	3532
Bits, rock–oil and gas field tools: Oil and Gas Field Machinery and Equipment—*mfg*	333132	3533
Bitters (flavoring concentrates): Flavoring Syrup and Concentrate—*mfg*	31193	2087
Food, All Other Miscellaneous—*mfg*	311999	2087
Spice and Extract—*mfg*	311942	2087
Bitumens (native) mining: Crushed and Broken Stone and Quarrying, Other—*mining*	212319	1499
Bituminous batching plants: Construction Machinery—*mfg*	33312	3531
Overhead Traveling Crane, Hoist and Monorail System—*mfg*	333923	3531
Railroad Rolling Stock—*mfg*	33651	3531
Bituminous Coal and Lignite Surface Mining	**212111**	**1221**
Bituminous coal cleaning plants: Bituminous Coal and Lignite Surface—*mining*	212111	1221
Bituminous coal crushing: Bituminous Coal and Lignite Surface—*mining*	212111	1221
Bituminous coal mining services on a con-tract basis: Coal Support Activities—*mining*	213113	1241
Bituminous coal screening plants: Bituminous Coal and Lignite Surface—*mining*	212111	1221
Bituminous coal stripping service–on a contract basis: Coal Support Activities—*mining*	213113	1241
Bituminous coal stripping–except on a contract, fee, or other basis: Bituminous Coal Underground—*mining*	212112	1222
Bituminous Coal Underground Mining	**212112**	**1222**
Bituminous coal washeries: Bituminous Coal and Lignite Surface—*mining*	212111	1221
Bituminous limestone quarrying: Crushed and Broken Stone and Quarrying, Other—*mining*	212319	1499
Bituminous or lignite auger mining service–on a contract basis: Coal Support Activities—*mining*	213113	1241
Bituminous paints: Paint and Coating—*mfg*	32551	2851

ALPHABETICAL INDEX	NAICS	SIC
Bituminous processing equipment: Construction and (except Petroleum) Machinery and Equipment—*whlse*	42181	5082
Bituminous sandstone quarrying: Crushed and Broken Stone and Quarrying, Other—*mining*	212319	1499
Black pigments, except carbon black: Carbon Black—*mfg*	325182	2816
Inorganic Dye and Pigment—*mfg*	325131	2816
Black plate, iron and steel: Metal Service Centers and Offices—*whlse*	42151	5051
Blackberry farms: Berry (except Strawberry) Farming—*ag*	111334	171
Strawberry Farming—*ag*	111333	171
Blackboards, slate: Cut Stone and Stone Product—*mfg*	327991	3281
Blackboards, wood: Institutional Furniture—*mfg*	337127	2531
Lead Pencil and Art Good—*mfg*	339942	2531
Blackings: Polish and Other Sanitation Good—*mfg*	325612	2842
Blackplate: Iron and Steel Mills—*mfg*	331111	3312
Petroleum and Coal Productsa, All Other—*mfg*	324199	3312
Blacksmith shops: Animal Production Support Activities—*ag*	11521	7699
Blacksmiths' aprons, leather: Leather Good, All Other—*mfg*	316999	3199
Blackstrap molasses: Sugarcane Mills—*mfg*	311311	2061
Blacktop work–private driveways and private parking areas–contractors: Concrete Contractors—*const*	23571	1771
Drywall, Plastering, Acoustical and Insulation Contractors—*const*	23542	1771
Blades for graders, scrapers, dozers, and snowplows: Construction Machinery—*mfg*	33312	3531
Overhead Traveling Crane, Hoist and Monorail System—*mfg*	333923	3531
Railroad Rolling Stock—*mfg*	33651	3531
Blades, aircraft propeller–metal or wood: Aircraft Part and Auxiliary Equipment, Other—*mfg*	336413	3728
Fluid Power Valve and Hose Fitting—*mfg*	332912	3728
Blades, knife and razor: Cutlery and Flatware (except Precious)—*mfg*	332211	3421
Blades, saw–for hand or power saws: Saw Blade and Handsaw—*mfg*	332213	3425
Blanc fixe (barium sulfate, precipitated): Carbon Black—*mfg*	325182	2816
Blank cartridges, 30 mm. (or 1.18 inch) or less: Small Arms Ammunition—*mfg*	332992	3482
Blankbook making: Blankbook, Loose-leaf Binder and Device—*mfg*	323118	2782
Flexographic Printing, Commercial—*mfg*	323112	2782
Gravure Printing, Commercial—*mfg*	323111	2782
Lithographic Printing, Commercial—*mfg*	323110	2782
Printing, Other Commercial—*mfg*	323119	2782
Screen Printing, Commercial—*mfg*	323113	2782
Blankbook, Loose-leaf Binder and Device Manufacturing	**323118**	**2782**
Blankbooks: Office Supplies and Stationery Stores—*retail*	45321	5112
Stationary and Office Supplies—*whlse*	42212	5112
Blanket bags, plastic: Household Textile Product Mills, Other—*mfg*	314129	2392
Blanketings, manmade fiber: Broadwoven Fabric Mills—*mfg*	31321	2221
Blankets: Home Furnishing—*whlse*	42122	5023
Household Textile Product Mills, Other—*mfg*	314129	2392
Blankets and blanketings, cotton: Broadwoven Fabric Mills—*mfg*	31321	2211

ALPHABETICAL INDEX	NAICS	SIC
Blankets and blanketings, wool and similar animal fibers: Broadwoven Fabric Finishing Mills—*mfg*	313311	2231
Broadwoven Fabric Mills—*mfg*	31321	2231
Textile and Fabric Finishing (except Broadwoven Fabric) Mills—*mfg*	313312	2231
Blankets, asbestos: Motor Vehicle Brake System—*mfg*	33634	3292
Nonmetallic Mineral Product, All Other Miscellaneous—*mfg*	327999	3292
Blankets, electric: Electric Housewares and Household Fan—*mfg*	335211	3634
Heating Equipment (except Electric and Warm Air Furnaces)—*mfg*	333414	3634
Blankets, horse: Textile Product Mills, All Other Miscellaneous—*mfg*	314999	2399
Blankets, insulating for aircraft–asbestos: Motor Vehicle Brake System—*mfg*	33634	3292
Nonmetallic Mineral Product, All Other Miscellaneous—*mfg*	327999	3292
Blankets, insulating–paper: Coated and Laminated Paper—*mfg*	322222	2679
Converted Paper Product, All Other—*mfg*	322298	2679
Die-Cut Paper and Paperboard Office Supplies—*mfg*	322231	2679
Non-Folding Sanitary Food Container—*mfg*	322215	2679
Blankets, printers'–rubber: Fabric Coating Mills—*mfg*	31332	3069
Rubber Product, All Other—*mfg*	326299	3069
Blanks for electric light bulbs, glass: Pressed and Blown Glass and Glassware, Other—*mfg*	327212	3229
Blanks, button: Fastener, Button, Needle and Pin—*mfg*	339993	3965
Blanks, cutting tool: Cutting Tool and Machine Tool Accessory—*mfg*	333515	3545
Hand and Edge Tool—*mfg*	332212	3545
Blanks, tips and inserts: Industrial Machinery and Equipment—*whlse*	42183	5084
Blanks, tips and inserts–cutting tools: Cutting Tool and Machine Tool Accessory—*mfg*	333515	3545
Hand and Edge Tool—*mfg*	332212	3545
Blanks, wood–for bowling pins, handles, and textile machinery accessories: Cut Stock, Resawing Lumber, and Planing—*mfg*	321912	2426
Millwork (including Flooring), Other—*mfg*	321918	2426
Showcase, Partition, Shelving, and Locker—*mfg*	337215	2426
Wood Product, All Other Miscellaneous—*mfg*	321999	2426
Blast cleaning equipment, dustless–except metalworking: General Purpose Machinery , All Other—*mfg*	333999	3569
Blast furnace products: Iron and Steel Mills—*mfg*	331111	3312
Petroleum and Coal Productsa, All Other—*mfg*	324199	3312
Blast furnace slag: Ground or Treated Mineral and Earth—*mfg*	327992	3295
Blast sand mining: Industrial Sand—*mining*	212322	1446
Blasting mats, rope: Rope, Cordage and Twine Mills—*mfg*	314991	2298
Blasting powder and blasting caps: Explosives—*mfg*	32592	2892
Blasting, except building demolition–contractors: Heavy, All Other—*const*	23499	1629
Industrial Nonbuilding Structure—*const*	23493	1629

Description	NAICS	SIC
Bleach (calcium hypochlorite), industrial: Basic Inorganic Chemical, All Other—*mfg*	325188	2819
Chemical Product, All Other Miscellaneous—*mfg*	325998	2819
Bleach (sodium hypochlorite), industrial: Basic Inorganic Chemical, All Other—*mfg*	325188	2819
Chemical Product, All Other Miscellaneous—*mfg*	325998	2819
Bleacher seating, portable: Institutional Furniture—*mfg*	337127	2531
Bleaches, hair: Soap and Other Detergent—*mfg*	325611	2844
Toilet Preparation—*mfg*	32562	2844
Bleaches, household–liquid or dry: Polish and Other Sanitation Good—*mfg*	325612	2842
Bleaches, industrial: Basic Inorganic Chemical, All Other—*mfg*	325188	2819
Chemical Product, All Other Miscellaneous—*mfg*	325998	2819
Bleaching cotton broadwoven fabrics: Broadwoven Fabric Finishing Mills—*mfg*	313311	2261
Bleaching machinery, textile: Textile Machinery—*mfg*	333292	3552
Bleaching manmade fiber and silk broad-woven fabrics: Broadwoven Fabric Finishing Mills—*mfg*	313311	2262
Bleaching powder, industrial: Basic Inorganic Chemical, All Other—*mfg*	325188	2819
Chemical Product, All Other Miscellaneous—*mfg*	325998	2819
Bleaching raw stock, yarn, and narrow fabrics–except knit and wool: Broadwoven Fabric Finishing Mills—*mfg*	313311	2269
Textile and Fabric Finishing (except Broadwoven Fabric) Mills—*mfg*	313312	2269
Bleaching yarn and fabrics, wool and similar animal fibers–except knit: Broadwoven Fabric Finishing Mills—*mfg*	313311	2231
Broadwoven Fabric Mills—*mfg*	31321	2231
Textile and Fabric Finishing (except Broadwoven Fabric) Mills—*mfg*	313312	2231
Bleaching, kier–continuous machine: Broadwoven Fabric Finishing Mills—*mfg*	313311	2261
Bleed control cabinets (engine testers): Electronic Coil, Transformer, and Other Inductor—*mfg*	334416	3825
Instrument for Measuring and Testing Electricity and Electrical Signals—*mfg*	334515	3825
Blende (zinc) mining: Lead Ore and Zinc Ore—*mining*	212231	1031
Blended flour: Flour Mixes and Dough from Purchased Flour—*mfg*	311822	2045
Blenders, electric: Electric Housewares and Household Fan—*mfg*	335211	3634
Heating Equipment (except Electric and Warm Air Furnaces)—*mfg*	333414	3634
Blending and compounding perfume bases: Soap and Other Detergent—*mfg*	325611	2844
Toilet Preparation—*mfg*	32562	2844
Blending tea: Coffee and Tea—*mfg*	31192	2099
Blimps: Aircraft—*mfg*	336411	3721
Blind and Shade Manufacturing	**33792**	**2591**
Blinds (shutters), wood: Millwork (including Flooring), Other—*mfg*	321918	2431
Wood Window and Door—*mfg*	321911	2431
Blinds, venetian: Blind and Shade—*mfg*	33792	2591
Blinds, vertical: Blind and Shade—*mfg*	33792	2591
Blister copper: Primary Smelting and Refining of Copper—*mfg*	331411	3331
Blister packaging, plastics: Plastics Pipe and Pipe Fitting—*mfg*	326122	3089
Plastics Product, All Other—*mfg*	326199	3089
Unsupported Plastics Profile Shape—*mfg*	326121	3089
Block ice: Ice—*mfg*	312113	2097
Blocks, building: Brick, Stone and Related Material—*whlse*	42132	5032
Building Material Dealers, Other—*retail*	44419	5032
Blocks, concrete and cinder: Concrete Block and Brick—*mfg*	327331	3271
Blocks, copper: Primary Smelting and Refining of Copper—*mfg*	331411	3331
Blocks, engravers'–wood: Printing Machinery and Equipment—*mfg*	333293	3555
Blocks, fire clay: Clay Refractory—*mfg*	327124	3255
Blocks, glass: Pressed and Blown Glass and Glassware, Other—*mfg*	327212	3229
Blocks, hat: Wood Product, All Other Miscellaneous—*mfg*	321999	3999
Blocks, lead–primary: Primary Smelting and Refining of Nonferrous Metal (except Copper and Aluminum)—*mfg*	331419	3339
Blocks, paving–cut stone: Cut Stone and Stone Product—*mfg*	327991	3281
Blocks, sand lime: Gypsum and Gypsum Product—*mfg*	32742	3299
Nonmetallic Mineral Product, All Other Miscellaneous—*mfg*	327999	3299
Blocks, segment–clay: Structural Clay Product, Other—*mfg*	327123	3259
Blocks, swage: Fabricated Metal Product, All Other Miscellaneous—*mfg*	332999	3599
General Purpose Machinery , All Other—*mfg*	333999	3599
Machine Shops—*mfg*	33271	3599
Machinery, Other Commercial and Service Industry—*mfg*	333319	3599
Blocks, tackle–metal: Hardware—*mfg*	33251	3429
Blocks, tackle–wood: Manufacturing, All Other Miscellaneous—*mfg*	339999	2499
Wood Container and Pallet—*mfg*	32192	2499
Wood Product, All Other Miscellaneous—*mfg*	321999	2499
Blocks, tailors' pressing–wood: Manufacturing, All Other Miscellaneous—*mfg*	339999	2499
Wood Container and Pallet—*mfg*	32192	2499
Wood Product, All Other Miscellaneous—*mfg*	321999	2499
Blocks, toy: Game, Toy, and Children's Vehicle—*mfg*	339932	3944
Blocks, wood–for bowling pins, handles, and textile machinery accessories: Cut Stock, Resawing Lumber, and Planing—*mfg*	321912	2426
Millwork (including Flooring), Other—*mfg*	321918	2426
Showcase, Partition, Shelving, and Locker—*mfg*	337215	2426
Wood Product, All Other Miscellaneous—*mfg*	321999	2426
Blocks, zinc, primary: Primary Smelting and Refining of Nonferrous Metal (except Copper and Aluminum)—*mfg*	331419	3339
Blood analysis laboratories: Diagnostic Imaging Centers—*hlth*	621512	8071
Medical Laboratories—*hlth*	621511	8071
Blood and Organ Banks	**621991**	**8099**
Blood banks: Blood and Organ Banks—*hlth*	621991	8099
Blood derivative diagnostic reagents: In-Vitro Diagnostic Substance—*mfg*	325413	2835
Pharmaceutical Preparation—*mfg*	325412	2835

Description	NAICS	SIC
Boards of supervisors: Legislative Bodies—*pub*	92112	9121
Boards of trade, other than security and commodity exchanges: Business Associations—*serv*	81391	8611
Boards, bulletin–wood and cork: Manufacturing, All Other Miscellaneous—*mfg*	339999	2499
Wood Container and Pallet—*mfg*	32192	2499
Wood Product, All Other Miscellaneous—*mfg*	321999	2499
Boards, drawing–artists': Chemical Product, All Other Miscellaneous—*mfg*	325998	3952
Institutional Furniture—*mfg*	337127	3952
Lead Pencil and Art Good—*mfg*	339942	3952
Boards–clip, ironing, meat, and pastry-wood: Manufacturing, All Other Miscellaneous—*mfg*	339999	2499
Wood Container and Pallet—*mfg*	32192	2499
Wood Product, All Other Miscellaneous—*mfg*	321999	2499
Boards–plotting, spotting, and gun fire adjustment: Optical Instrument and Lens—*mfg*	333314	3827
Boat and ship lighting fixtures: Vehicular Lighting Equipment—*mfg*	336321	3647
Boat Building	**336612**	**3732**
Boat cleaning: Air, Rail, and Water Equipment Rental and Leasing, Commercial—*real*	532411	4499
Navigational Services to Shipping—*trans*	48833	4499
Port and Harbor Operations—*trans*	48831	4499
Water, Other Support Activities for—*trans*	48839	4499
Boat cradles: Fabricated Metal Product, All Other Miscellaneous—*mfg*	332999	3537
Industrial Truck, Tractor, Trailer and Stacker Machinery—*mfg*	333924	3537
Metal Container, Other—*mfg*	332439	3537
Boat cushions: Household Textile Product Mills, Other—*mfg*	314129	2392
Boat Dealers	**441222**	**5551**
Boat hiring, except pleasure: Air, Rail, and Water Equipment Rental and Leasing, Commercial—*real*	532411	4499
Navigational Services to Shipping—*trans*	48833	4499
Port and Harbor Operations—*trans*	48831	4499
Water, Other Support Activities for—*trans*	48839	4499
Boat kits, not a model: Boat Building—*mfg*	336612	3732
Personal and Household Goods Repair and Maintenance, Other—*serv*	81149	3732
Boat lifts: Overhead Traveling Crane, Hoist and Monorail System—*mfg*	333923	3536
Boat livery, except pleasure: Air, Rail, and Water Equipment Rental and Leasing, Commercial—*real*	532411	4499
Navigational Services to Shipping—*trans*	48833	4499
Port and Harbor Operations—*trans*	48831	4499
Water, Other Support Activities for—*trans*	48839	4499
Boat rental, commercial: Air, Rail, and Water Equipment Rental and Leasing, Commercial—*real*	532411	4499
Navigational Services to Shipping—*trans*	48833	4499
Port and Harbor Operations—*trans*	48831	4499
Water, Other Support Activities for—*trans*	48839	4499
Boat sections, prefabricated metal: Fabricated Structural Metal—*mfg*	332312	3441
Boat trailers: Transportation Equipment, All Other—*mfg*	336999	3799
Boat yards, storage and incidental repair: Marinas—*arts*	71393	4493
Boating clubs, membership: Fitness and Recreational Sports Centers—*arts*	71394	7997
Boats, except pleasure: Transportation Equipment and Supplies (except Motor Vehicle)—*whlse*	42186	5088
Boats, fiberglass–building and repairing: Boat Building—*mfg*	336612	3732
Personal and Household Goods Repair and Maintenance, Other—*serv*	81149	3732
Boats, nonrigid–plastics: Plastics Pipe and Pipe Fitting—*mfg*	326122	3089
Plastics Product, All Other—*mfg*	326199	3089
Unsupported Plastics Profile Shape—*mfg*	326121	3089
Boats, pleasure–canoes, motorboats, and sailboats: Sporting and Recreational Goods and Supplies—*whlse*	42191	5091
Boats, rigid–plastics: Boat Building—*mfg*	336612	3732
Personal and Household Goods Repair and Maintenance, Other—*serv*	81149	3732
Boats–motorboats, sailboats, rowboats, and canoes-building and repairing: Boat Building—*mfg*	336612	3732
Personal and Household Goods Repair and Maintenance, Other—*serv*	81149	3732
Bobbin blocks and blanks, wood: Cut Stock, Resawing Lumber, and Planing—*mfg*	321912	2426
Millwork (including Flooring), Other—*mfg*	321918	2426
Showcase, Partition, Shelving, and Locker—*mfg*	337215	2426
Wood Product, All Other Miscellaneous—*mfg*	321999	2426
Bobbinet (lace goods): Knit Fabric and Lace Mills, Other—*mfg*	313249	2258
Textile and Fabric Finishing (except Broadwoven Fabric) Mills—*mfg*	313312	2258
Bobbins for textile machinery: Textile Machinery—*mfg*	333292	3552
Bobbins, fiber: Fiber Can, Tube, Drum, and Similar Products—*mfg*	322214	2655
Bobsleds: Sporting and Athletic Goods—*mfg*	33992	3949
Bobtailers, laundry and drycleaning: Garment Pressing, and Agents for Laundries—*serv*	812391	7212
Bodies, aircraft–not complete aircraft: Aircraft Part and Auxiliary Equipment, Other—*mfg*	336413	3728
Fluid Power Valve and Hose Fitting—*mfg*	332912	3728
Bodies, automotive: Automobile and Other Motor Vehicle—*whlse*	42111	5012
Bodies, dump: Motor Vehicle Body—*mfg*	336211	3713
Bodies, passenger automobile: Automobile—*mfg*	336111	3711
Heavy Duty Truck—*mfg*	33612	3711
Light Truck and Utility Vehicle—*mfg*	336112	3711
Military Armored Vehicle, Tank and Tank Component—*mfg*	336992	3711
Motor Vehicle Body—*mfg*	336211	3711
Bodies, truck (motor vehicle): Motor Vehicle Body—*mfg*	336211	3713
Body parts, automotive–stamped: Motor Vehicle Metal Stamping—*mfg*	33637	3465

ALPHABETICAL INDEX	NAICS	SIC
Body powder: Soap and Other Detergent— *mfg*	325611	2844
Toilet Preparation—*mfg*	32562	2844
Body repair, automotive: Automotive Body, Paint and Interior Repair and Maintenance—*serv*	811121	7532
Body shops, automotive: Automotive Body, Paint and Interior Repair and Maintenance—*serv*	811121	7532
Body stockings: Outerwear Knitting Mills—*mfg*	315191	2253
Bofors guns: Ordnance and Accessories, Other—*mfg*	332995	3489
Boiler and pipe, insulation of–contractors: Trade Contractors, All Other Special—*const*	23599	1799
Boiler casings–metal plate: Air-Conditioning and Warm Air Heating Equipment and Commercial and Industrial Refrigeration Equipment—*mfg*	333415	3443
Metal Tank (Heavy Gauge)—*mfg*	33242	3443
Plate Work—*mfg*	332313	3443
Power Boiler and Heat Exchanger—*mfg*	33241	3443
Boiler compounds, antiscaling: Basic Organic Chemical, All Other—*mfg*	325199	2899
Chemical Product, All Other Miscellaneous—*mfg*	325998	2899
Boiler controls–industrial, power, and marine type: Instruments and Related Products for Measuring, Displaying, and Controlling Industrial Process Variables—*mfg*	334513	3823
Boiler couplings and drains, metal: Fabricated Metal Product, All Other Miscellaneous—*mfg*	332999	3494
Other Metal Valve and Pipe Fitting, Other—*mfg*	332919	3494
Boiler covering (heat insulating material),except felt: Motor Vehicle Brake System—*mfg*	33634	3292
Nonmetallic Mineral Product, All Other Miscellaneous—*mfg*	327999	3292
Boiler covering, felt: Broadwoven Fabric Mills—*mfg*	31321	2299
Narrow Fabric Mills—*mfg*	313221	2299
Nonwoven Fabric Mills—*mfg*	31323	2299
Textile and Fabric Finishing (except Broadwoven Fabric) Mills—*mfg*	313312	2299
Textile Product Mills, All Other Miscellaneous—*mfg*	314999	2299
Thread Mills—*mfg*	313113	2299
Yarn Spinning Mills—*mfg*	313111	2299
Boiler erection and installation–contractors: Plumbing, Heating and Air-Conditioning Contractors—*const*	23511	1711
Boiler gauge cocks: Industrial Valve—*mfg*	332911	3491
Boiler insurance: Direct Property and Casualty Insurance Carriers—*fin*	524126	6331
Insurance Funds, Other—*fin*	52519	6331
Reinsurance Carriers—*fin*	52413	6331
Boiler repair shops, except manufacturing: Machinery and Equipment (except Automotive and Electronic) Repair and Maintenance, Commercial and Industrial—*serv*	81131	7699

ALPHABETICAL INDEX	NAICS	SIC
Boiler shop products–industrial boilers, smokestacks, and steel tanks: Air-Conditioning and Warm Air Heating Equipment and Commercial and Industrial Refrigeration Equipment—*mfg*	333415	3443
Metal Tank (Heavy Gauge)—*mfg*	33242	3443
Plate Work—*mfg*	332313	3443
Power Boiler and Heat Exchanger—*mfg*	33241	3443
Boiler tube cleaners: Fabricated Metal Product, All Other Miscellaneous—*mfg*	332999	3599
General Purpose Machinery , All Other—*mfg*	333999	3599
Machine Shops—*mfg*	33271	3599
Machinery, Other Commercial and Service Industry—*mfg*	333319	3599
Boiler tubes, wrought: Iron and Steel Pipes and Tubes from Purchased Steel—*mfg*	33121	3317
Boiler, Tank, and Shipping Container Manufacturing	**3324**	
Boilers, low-pressure heating–steam or hot water: Heating Equipment (except Electric and Warm Air Furnaces)—*mfg*	333414	3433
Boilers, power–industrial: Building Material Dealers, Other—*retail*	44419	5074
Plumbing and Heating Equipment and Supplies (Hydronics)—*whlse*	42172	5074
Boilers, steam and hot water heating: Building Material Dealers, Other—*retail*	44419	5074
Plumbing and Heating Equipment and Supplies (Hydronics)—*whlse*	42172	5074
Boilers–industrial, power, and marine: Air-Conditioning and Warm Air Heating Equipment and Commercial and Industrial Refrigeration Equipment—*mfg*	333415	3443
Metal Tank (Heavy Gauge)—*mfg*	33242	3443
Plate Work—*mfg*	332313	3443
Power Boiler and Heat Exchanger—*mfg*	33241	3443
Bok choy farms: Vegetable (except Potato) and Melon Farming, Other—*ag*	111219	161
Bologna: Meat Processed from Carcasses—*mfg*	311612	2013
Bolt caps, vitreous china and earthenware: Vitreous China Plumbing Fixture and China and Earthenware Fittings and Bathroom Accessories—*mfg*	327111	3261
Bolt, Nut, Screw, Rivet and Washer Manufacturing	**332722**	**3452**
Bolts, metal: Bolt, Nut, Screw, Rivet and Washer—*mfg*	332722	3452
Bolts, nuts, rivets, and screws: Hardware—*whlse*	42171	5072
Bolts, plastics: Plastics Pipe and Pipe Fitting—*mfg*	326122	3089
Plastics Product, All Other—*mfg*	326199	3089
Unsupported Plastics Profile Shape—*mfg*	326121	3089
Bolts, wood–e.g., handle, heading, shingle, stave: Logging—*ag*	11331	2411
Bomb lifts: Fabricated Metal Product, All Other Miscellaneous—*mfg*	332999	3537
Industrial Truck, Tractor, Trailer and Stacker Machinery—*mfg*	333924	3537
Metal Container, Other—*mfg*	332439	3537
Bomb loading and assembling plants: Ammunition (except Small Arms)—*mfg*	332993	3483

Bomb racks, aircraft: Aircraft Part and Auxiliary Equipment, Other—*mfg*	336413	3728
Fluid Power Valve and Hose Fitting—*mfg*	332912	3728
Bomb trucks: Fabricated Metal Product, All Other Miscellaneous—*mfg*	332999	3537
Industrial Truck, Tractor, Trailer and Stacker Machinery—*mfg*	333924	3537
Metal Container, Other—*mfg*	332439	3537
Bombazine, cotton: Broadwoven Fabric Mills—*mfg*	31321	2211
Bombcluster adapters: Ammunition (except Small Arms)—*mfg*	332993	3483
Bombs and parts: Ammunition (except Small Arms)—*mfg*	332993	3483
Bombs, flashlight: Basic Organic Chemical, All Other—*mfg*	325199	2899
Chemical Product, All Other Miscellaneous—*mfg*	325998	2899
Bond and mortgage companies: Credit Intermediation, Other Activities Related to—*fin*	52239	6162
Real Estate Credit—*fin*	522292	6162
Bond dealers and brokers: Financial Investment Activities, Miscellaneous—*fin*	523999	6211
Intermediation, Miscellaneous—*fin*	52391	6211
Investment Banking and Securities Dealing—*fin*	52311	6211
Securities Brokerage—*fin*	52312	6211
Bond paper: Newsprint Mills—*mfg*	322122	2621
Paper (except Newsprint) Mills—*mfg*	322121	2621
Bonded wine cellars, engaged in blending wines: Wineries—*mfg*	31213	2084
Bonded-fiber fabrics, except felt: Nonwoven Fabric Mills—*mfg*	31323	2297
Bonderizing of metal and metal products, for the trade: Costume Jewelry and Novelty—*mfg*	339914	3479
Jewelry (except Costume)—*mfg*	339911	3479
Metal Coating, Engraving (except Jewelry and Silverware), and Allied Services to Manufacturers—*mfg*	332812	3479
Silverware and Plated Ware—*mfg*	339912	3479
Bondholders protective committees: Financial Investment Activities, Miscellaneous—*fin*	523999	6289
Trust, Fiduciary and Custody Activities—*fin*	523991	6289
Bonding for guaranteeing job completion: Direct Property and Casualty Insurance Carriers—*fin*	524126	6351
Reinsurance Carriers—*fin*	52413	6351
Bonding of employees: Direct Property and Casualty Insurance Carriers—*fin*	524126	6351
Reinsurance Carriers—*fin*	52413	6351
Bonding, fidelity or surety: Direct Property and Casualty Insurance Carriers—*fin*	524126	6351
Reinsurance Carriers—*fin*	52413	6351
Bondspersons: Personal Services, All Other—*serv*	81299	7389
Bone black: Carbon Black—*mfg*	325182	2816
Inorganic Dye and Pigment—*mfg*	325131	2816
Bone china: Vitreous China, Fine Earthenware and Other Pottery Product—*mfg*	327112	3262
Bone drills: Surgical and Medical Instrument—*mfg*	339112	3841
Bone plates and screws: Surgical and Medical Instrument—*mfg*	339112	3841
Bone rongeurs: Surgical and Medical Instrument—*mfg*	339112	3841
Book cloth: Broadwoven Fabric Mills—*mfg*	31321	2211
Book club publishing and printing, or publishing only: Book Publishers—*info*	51113	2731
Music Publishers—*info*	51223	2731
Book clubs, not publishing: Electronic Shopping and Mail-Order Houses—*retail*	45411	5961
Book ends, metal: Fabricated Metal Product, All Other Miscellaneous—*mfg*	332999	3499
Book gilding, bronzing, edging, deckling, embossing, and gold stamping: Tradebinding and Related Work—*mfg*	323121	2789
Book matches: Chemical Product, All Other Miscellaneous—*mfg*	325998	3999
Book paper: Newsprint Mills—*mfg*	322122	2621
Paper (except Newsprint) Mills—*mfg*	322121	2621
Book paper, coated: Coated and Laminated Paper—*mfg*	322222	2672
Book Printing	**323117**	**2732**
Book Publishers	**51113**	**2731**
Book Stores	**451211**	**5942**
Book Stores and News Dealers	**45121**	
Book stores selling new books and magazines: Book Stores—*retail*	451211	5942
Book stores, secondhand: Non-Depository Credit Intermediation, All Other—*fin*	522298	5932
Used Merchandise Stores—*retail*	45331	5932
Book tile, clay: Brick and Structural Clay Tile—*mfg*	327121	3251
Book, Periodical and Music Stores	**4512**	
Book, Periodical and Newspaper Wholesalers	**42292**	**5192**
Bookbinders' leather: Leather and Hide Tanning and Finishing—*mfg*	31611	3111
Bookbinders' machines: Printing Machinery and Equipment—*mfg*	333293	3555
Bookbinding–edition, job, library, and trade: Tradebinding and Related Work—*mfg*	323121	2789
Bookcases, household–metal: Metal Household Furniture—*mfg*	337124	2514
Bookcases, household–wood: Nonupholstered Wood Household Furniture—*mfg*	337122	2511
Bookcases, office–except wood: Nonwood Office Furniture—*mfg*	337214	2522
Bookcases, office–wood: Wood Office Furniture—*mfg*	337211	2521
Booking agencies, motion picture: Motion Picture and Video Distribution—*info*	51212	7829
Motion Picture and Video Industries, Other—*info*	512199	7829
Bookkeeping and billing service: Accounting Services, Other—*prof*	541219	8721
Certified Public Accountants, Offices Of—*prof*	541211	8721
Payroll Services—*prof*	541214	8721
Bookkeeping machines: Computer Peripheral Equipment, Other—*mfg*	334119	3578
Office Machinery—*mfg*	333313	3578
Bookmakers, race: Gambling Industries, Other—*arts*	71329	7999
Books: Book, Periodical and Newspaper—*whlse*	42292	5192
Books, mail-order: Electronic Shopping and Mail-Order Houses—*retail*	45411	5961

ALPHABETICAL INDEX	NAICS	SIC
Books, memorandum–except printed: Stationery, Tablet, and Related Product—*mfg*	322233	2678
Books, music–printing or printing and binding, not publishing: Book Printing—*mfg*	323117	2732
Books, music–publishing and printing, or publishing only: Book Publishers—*info*	51113	2731
Music Publishers—*info*	51223	2731
Books–printing or printing and binding, not publishing: Book Printing—*mfg*	323117	2732
Books–publishing and printing, or publishing only: Book Publishers—*info*	51113	2731
Music Publishers—*info*	51223	2731
Boomerangs: Sporting and Athletic Goods—*mfg*	33992	3949
Booster clubs: Civic and Social Organizations—*serv*	81341	8641
Boosters and bursters: Ammunition (except Small Arms)—*mfg*	332993	3483
Boosters, feeder voltage (electric transformers): Power, Distribution and Specialty Transformer—*mfg*	335311	3612
Boot and shoe cut stock and findings: Cosmetics, Beauty Supplies and Perfume Stores—*retail*	44612	5087
Fastener, Button, Needle and Pin—*mfg*	339993	3131
Leather Good, All Other—*mfg*	316999	3131
Service Establishment Equipment and Supplies—*whlse*	42185	5087
Wood Product, All Other Miscellaneous—*mfg*	321999	3131
Boot and shoe lasts, regardless of material: Manufacturing, All Other Miscellaneous—*mfg*	339999	2499
Wood Container and Pallet—*mfg*	32192	2499
Wood Product, All Other Miscellaneous—*mfg*	321999	2499
Boot making and repairing machinery: Industrial Machinery, All Other—*mfg*	333298	3559
Machinery, Other Commercial and Service Industry—*mfg*	333319	3559
Bootblack parlors: Footwear and Leather Goods Repair—*serv*	81143	7251
Booths, spray–prefabricated sheet metal: Metal Container, Other—*mfg*	332439	3444
Sheet Metal Work—*mfg*	332322	3444
Booths, telephone–except wood: Showcase, Partition, Shelving, and Locker—*mfg*	337215	2542
Booths, telephone–wood: Architectural Woodwork and Millwork, Custom—*mfg*	337212	2541
Showcase, Partition, Shelving, and Locker—*mfg*	337215	2541
Wood Kitchen Cabinet and Counter Top—*mfg*	33711	2541
Boots, dress and casual–men's: Men's Footwear (except Athletic)—*mfg*	316213	3143
Boots, horse: Leather Good, All Other—*mfg*	316999	3199
Boots, plastics: Rubber and Plastics Footwear—*mfg*	316211	3021
Boots, rubber or rubber soled fabric: Rubber and Plastics Footwear—*mfg*	316211	3021

ALPHABETICAL INDEX	NAICS	SIC
Boots–women's canvas and leather-except athletic: Women's Footwear (except Athletic)—*mfg*	316214	3144
Borate compounds mining: Potash, Soda, and Borate Mineral—*mining*	212391	1474
Borax (sodium tetraborate): Basic Inorganic Chemical, All Other—*mfg*	325188	2819
Chemical Product, All Other Miscellaneous—*mfg*	325998	2819
Borax mining: Potash, Soda, and Borate Mineral—*mining*	212391	1474
Borax, crude–ground and pulverized: Potash, Soda, and Borate Mineral—*mining*	212391	1474
Bordeaux mixture: Pesticide and Other Agricultural Chemical—*mfg*	32532	2879
Borescopes: Optical Instrument and Lens—*mfg*	333314	3827
Boric acid: Basic Inorganic Chemical, All Other—*mfg*	325188	2819
Chemical Product, All Other Miscellaneous—*mfg*	325998	2819
Boring for building construction–contractors: Trade Contractors, All Other Special—*const*	23599	1799
Boring machine attachments (machine tool accessories): Cutting Tool and Machine Tool Accessory—*mfg*	333515	3545
Hand and Edge Tool—*mfg*	332212	3545
Boring machine tools, metalworking: Machine Tool (Metal Cutting Types)—*mfg*	333512	3541
Boring mills: Machine Tool (Metal Cutting Types)—*mfg*	333512	3541
Boring test holes for metal mining–on acontract basis: Geophysical Surveying and Mapping Services—*prof*	54136	1081
Metal Support Activities—*mining*	213114	1081
Boring test holes for nonmetallic minerals,except fuels–on a contract basis: Geophysical Surveying and Mapping Services—*prof*	54136	1481
Non-Metallic Minerals (except Fuels) Support Activities—*mining*	213115	1481
Boring, drilling, and milling machine combinations: Machine Tool (Metal Cutting Types)—*mfg*	333512	3541
Boron carbide abrasives: Abrasive Product—*mfg*	32791	3291
Fabricated Metal Product, All Other Miscellaneous—*mfg*	332999	3291
Boron compounds, not produced atmines: Basic Inorganic Chemical, All Other—*mfg*	325188	2819
Chemical Product, All Other Miscellaneous—*mfg*	325998	2819
Boron mineral mining: Potash, Soda, and Borate Mineral—*mining*	212391	1474
Borosilicate: Basic Inorganic Chemical, All Other—*mfg*	325188	2819
Chemical Product, All Other Miscellaneous—*mfg*	325998	2819
Bort: Industrial Machinery and Equipment—*whlse*	42183	5085
Industrial Supplies—*whlse*	42184	5085
Bort, crushing: Abrasive Product—*mfg*	32791	3291
Fabricated Metal Product, All Other Miscellaneous—*mfg*	332999	3291
Botanical extracts–powdered, pilular,solid, and fluid, except diagnostics: Pharmaceutical Preparation—*mfg*	325412	2834
Botanical gardens: Nature Parks and Other Similar Institutions—*arts*	71219	8422
Zoos and Botanical Gardens—*arts*	71213	8422

Description	NAICS	SIC
Botanical products, medicinal–ground,graded, and milled: Medicinal and Botanical—*mfg*	325411	2833
Bottle cap board: Paperboard Mills—*mfg*	32213	2631
Bottle caps and tops, die-cut from purchased paper or paperboard: Converted Paper Product, All Other—*mfg*	322298	2675
Die-Cut Paper and Paperboard Office Supplies—*mfg*	322231	2675
Surface-Coated Paperboard—*mfg*	322292	2675
Bottle caps and tops, stamped metal: Crown and Closure—*mfg*	332115	3466
Bottle caps, molded plastics: Plastics Pipe and Pipe Fitting—*mfg*	326122	3089
Plastics Product, All Other—*mfg*	326199	3089
Unsupported Plastics Profile Shape—*mfg*	326121	3089
Bottle clubs (drinking places): Drinking Places (Alcoholic Beverages)—*accom*	72241	5813
Bottle corks: Manufacturing, All Other Miscellaneous—*mfg*	339999	2499
Wood Container and Pallet—*mfg*	32192	2499
Wood Product, All Other Miscellaneous—*mfg*	321999	2499
Bottle covers–willow, rattan, and reed: Manufacturing, All Other Miscellaneous—*mfg*	339999	2499
Wood Container and Pallet—*mfg*	32192	2499
Wood Product, All Other Miscellaneous—*mfg*	321999	2499
Bottle openers, made from purchasedwire: Fabricated Wire Product, Other—*mfg*	332618	3496
Bottle openers, stamped metal: Kitchen Utensil, Pot and Pan—*mfg*	332214	3469
Bottle warmers, household–electric: Electric Housewares and Household Fan—*mfg*	335211	3634
Heating Equipment (except Electric and Warm Air Furnaces)—*mfg*	333414	3634
Bottle warmers, plastics: Plastics Pipe and Pipe Fitting—*mfg*	326122	3089
Plastics Product, All Other—*mfg*	326199	3089
Unsupported Plastics Profile Shape—*mfg*	326121	3089
Bottled gas: Liquefied Petroleum Gas (Bottled Gas) Dealers—*retail*	454312	5984
Bottled Water Manufacturing	**312112**	**2086**
Bottlers' supplies–caps, bottles, etc.: Industrial Machinery and Equipment—*whlse*	42183	5085
Industrial Supplies—*whlse*	42184	5085
Bottles for packing, bottling, and canning:glass: Glass Container—*mfg*	327213	3221
Bottles, glass or plastics: Industrial Machinery and Equipment—*whlse*	42183	5085
Industrial Supplies—*whlse*	42184	5085
Bottles, paper fiber: Fiber Can, Tube, Drum, and Similar Products—*mfg*	322214	2655
Bottles, plastics: Plastics Bottle—*mfg*	32616	3085
Bottles, rubber: Fabric Coating Mills—*mfg*	31332	3069
Rubber Product, All Other—*mfg*	326299	3069
Bottles, vacuum: Metal Container, Other—*mfg*	332439	3429
Bottles, waste: Recyclable Material—*whlse*	42193	5093
Bottling machinery–washing, sterilizing,filling, capping, and labeling: Packaging Machinery—*mfg*	333993	3565
Bottling mineral or spring water-whole-sale: Grocery and Related Products, Other—*whlse*	42249	5149
Bottling wines and liquors: Wine and Distilled Alcoholic Beverage—*whlse*	42282	5182
Boudoir lamps: Residential Electric Lighting Fixture—*mfg*	335121	3645
Bouillon cubes: Dried and Dehydrated Food—*mfg*	311423	2099
Boulder, crushed and broken: Crushed and Broken Stone and Quarrying, Other—*mining*	212319	1429
Boulets (fuel bricks), made with petroleumbinder: Petroleum and Coal Productsa, All Other—*mfg*	324199	2999
Bow ties: Men's and Boys' Neckwear—*mfg*	315993	2323
Bowl covers, plastics: Plastics Pipe and Pipe Fitting—*mfg*	326122	3089
Plastics Product, All Other—*mfg*	326199	3089
Unsupported Plastics Profile Shape—*mfg*	326121	3089
Bowling alley installation and service–contractors: Trade Contractors, All Other Special—*const*	23599	1799
Bowling alleys and accessories: Sporting and Athletic Goods—*mfg*	33992	3949
Bowling center furniture: Institutional Furniture—*mfg*	337127	2599
Bowling Centers	**71395**	**7933**
Bowling equipment: Sporting and Recreational Goods and Supplies—*whlse*	42191	5091
Bowling equipment and supplies: Sporting Goods Stores—*retail*	45111	5941
Bowling instruction: Sports and Recreation Instruction—*educ*	61162	7999
Bowling leagues or teams, except professional and semiprofessional: Fitness and Recreational Sports Centers—*arts*	71394	7997
Bowling pin blanks: Cut Stock, Resawing Lumber, and Planing—*mfg*	321912	2426
Millwork (including Flooring), Other—*mfg*	321918	2426
Showcase, Partition, Shelving, and Locker—*mfg*	337215	2426
Wood Product, All Other Miscellaneous—*mfg*	321999	2426
Bowling pin machines, automatic: Sporting and Athletic Goods—*mfg*	33992	3949
Bowling pins: Sporting and Athletic Goods—*mfg*	33992	3949
Bowls, glass: Pressed and Blown Glass and Glassware, Other—*mfg*	327212	3229
Bowls, wood–turned and shaped: Manufacturing, All Other Miscellaneous—*mfg*	339999	2499
Wood Container and Pallet—*mfg*	32192	2499
Wood Product, All Other Miscellaneous—*mfg*	321999	2499
Bows, archery: Sporting and Athletic Goods—*mfg*	33992	3949
Bows, shoe: Fastener, Button, Needle and Pin—*mfg*	339993	3131
Leather Good, All Other—*mfg*	316999	3131
Wood Product, All Other Miscellaneous—*mfg*	321999	3131
Box cleats, wood: Wood Container and Pallet—*mfg*	32192	2441
Box lumber: Cut Stock, Resawing Lumber, and Planing—*mfg*	321912	2421
Millwork (including Flooring), Other—*mfg*	321918	2421
Sawmills—*mfg*	321113	2421
Wood Product, All Other Miscellaneous—*mfg*	321999	2421
Box lunch stands: Cafeterias—*accom*	722212	5812
Caterers—*accom*	72232	5812
Foodservice Contractors—*accom*	72231	5812
Full-Service Restaurants—*accom*	72211	5812

ALPHABETICAL INDEX	NAICS	SIC
Limited-Service Restaurants—*accom*	722211	5812
Snack and Nonalcoholic Beverage Bars—*accom*	722213	5812
Theater Companies and Dinner Theaters—*arts*	71111	5812
Box lunches for sale off premises: Perishable Prepared Food—*mfg*	311991	2099
Box making machines for paper boxes: Paper Industry Machinery—*mfg*	333291	3554
Box making machines for wooden boxes: Sawmill and Woodworking Machinery—*mfg*	33321	3553
Box shooks: Industrial Machinery and Equipment—*whlse*	42183	5085
Industrial Supplies—*whlse*	42184	5085
Wood Container and Pallet—*mfg*	32192	2441
Box springs, assembled: Mattress—*mfg*	33791	2515
Upholstered Household Furniture—*mfg*	337121	2515
Box tees, leather (shoe cut stock): Fastener, Button, Needle and Pin—*mfg*	339993	3131
Leather Good, All Other—*mfg*	316999	3131
Wood Product, All Other Miscellaneous—*mfg*	321999	3131
Boxboard: Paperboard Mills—*mfg*	32213	2631
Boxed beef: Animal (except Poultry) Slaughtering—*mfg*	311611	2011
Boxes and fittings, electrical: Building Material Dealers, Other—*retail*	44419	5063
Electrical Apparatus and Equipment, Wiring Supplies and Material—*whlse*	42161	5063
Boxes for packing and shipping, metal: Metal Container, Other—*mfg*	332439	3499
Boxes, ammunition–metal: Metal Container, Other—*mfg*	332439	3499
Boxes, annealing: Air-Conditioning and Warm Air Heating Equipment and Commercial and Industrial Refrigeration Equipment—*mfg*	333415	3443
Metal Tank (Heavy Gauge)—*mfg*	33242	3443
Plate Work—*mfg*	332313	3443
Power Boiler and Heat Exchanger—*mfg*	33241	3443
Boxes, cash and stamp–stamped metal: Metal Stamping—*mfg*	332116	3469
Boxes, cigar–wood and part wood: Wood Container and Pallet—*mfg*	32192	2441
Boxes, condenser–metal plate: Air-Conditioning and Warm Air Heating Equipment and Commercial and Industrial Refrigeration Equipment—*mfg*	333415	3443
Metal Tank (Heavy Gauge)—*mfg*	33242	3443
Plate Work—*mfg*	332313	3443
Power Boiler and Heat Exchanger—*mfg*	33241	3443
Boxes, corrugated and solid fiber: Corrugated and Solid Fiber Box—*mfg*	322211	2653
Boxes, crates, etc., other than paper: Industrial Machinery and Equipment—*whlse*	42183	5085
Industrial Supplies—*whlse*	42184	5085
Boxes, electric wiring–junction, outlet, switch, and fuse: Noncurrent-Carrying Wiring Device—*mfg*	335932	3644
Boxes, folding paperboard: Folding Paperboard Box—*mfg*	322212	2657

ALPHABETICAL INDEX	NAICS	SIC
Boxes, hard rubber: Fabric Coating Mills—*mfg*	31332	3069
Rubber Product, All Other—*mfg*	326299	3069
Boxes, hat–except paper or paperboard: Luggage—*mfg*	316991	3161
Boxes, leather: Leather Good, All Other—*mfg*	316999	3199
Boxes, newsboard–metal edged: Setup Paperboard Box—*mfg*	322213	2652
Boxes, paperboard and disposable plastics: Industrial and Personal Service Paper—*whlse*	42213	5113
Boxes, plastics: Plastics Pipe and Pipe Fitting—*mfg*	326122	3089
Plastics Product, All Other—*mfg*	326199	3089
Unsupported Plastics Profile Shape—*mfg*	326121	3089
Boxes, setup paperboard: Setup Paperboard Box—*mfg*	322213	2652
Boxes, sketching and paint: Chemical Product, All Other Miscellaneous—*mfg*	325998	3952
Institutional Furniture—*mfg*	337127	3952
Lead Pencil and Art Good—*mfg*	339942	3952
Boxes, vulcanized fiber: Fiber Can, Tube, Drum, and Similar Products—*mfg*	322214	2655
Boxes, waste: Recyclable Material—*whlse*	42193	5093
Boxes, wood–plain or fabric covered, nailed or lock corner: Wood Container and Pallet—*mfg*	32192	2441
Boxes, wood–wire-bound: Wood Container and Pallet—*mfg*	32192	2449
Boxing equipment: Sporting and Athletic Goods—*mfg*	33992	3949
Boys' camps: Recreational and Vacation Camps—*accom*	721214	7032
Boys' hosiery: Hosiery and Sock Mills, Other—*mfg*	315119	2252
Sheer Hosiery Mills—*mfg*	315111	2252
Boys' towns: Homes for the Elderly—*hlth*	623312	8361
Residential Care Facilities, Other—*hlth*	62399	8361
Residential Mental Health and Substance Abuse Facilities—*hlth*	62322	8361
Bra-slips: Infants' Cut and Sew Apparel—*mfg*	315291	2341
Women's and Girls' Cut and Sew Apparel Contractors—*mfg*	315212	2341
Women's and Girls' Cut and Sew Lingerie, Loungewear and Nightwear—*mfg*	315231	2341
Braces, elastic: Surgical Appliance and Supplies—*mfg*	339113	3842
Braces, orthopedic: Surgical Appliance and Supplies—*mfg*	339113	3842
Bracing of orchard trees and vines: Nonscheduled Air, Other—*trans*	481219	721
Soil Preparation, Planting, and Cultivating—*ag*	115112	721
Brackets, architectural–plaster-factory production only: Gypsum and Gypsum Product—*mfg*	32742	3299
Nonmetallic Mineral Product, All Other Miscellaneous—*mfg*	327999	3299
Brackets, iron and steel: Hardware—*mfg*	33251	3429
Brackets, wood: Millwork (including Flooring), Other—*mfg*	321918	2431
Wood Window and Door—*mfg*	321911	2431
Brads: Hardware—*whlse*	42171	5072
Brads, nonferrous metal (including wire): Fabricated Wire Product, Other—*mfg*	332618	3399
Iron and Steel Mills—*mfg*	331111	3399
Secondary Smelting and Alloying of Aluminum—*mfg*	331314	3399

Description	NAICS	SIC
Secondary Smelting, Refining, and Alloying of Copper—*mfg*	331423	3399
Secondary Smelting, Refining, and Alloying of Nonferrous Metal (except Copper and Aluminum)—*mfg*	331492	3399
Brads, steel–wire or cut: Fabricated Wire Product, Other—*mfg*	332618	3315
Steel Wire Drawing—*mfg*	331222	3315
Braided goods, except wool–bleaching, dyeing, printing, and other finishing: Broadwoven Fabric Finishing Mills—*mfg*	313311	2269
Textile and Fabric Finishing (except Broadwoven Fabric) Mills—*mfg*	313312	2269
Braiding machines, textile: Textile Machinery—*mfg*	333292	3552
Braids, textile: Narrow Fabric Mills—*mfg*	313221	2241
Braids, tubular nylon and plastics: Narrow Fabric Mills—*mfg*	313221	2241
Brake burnishing and washing machines: General Purpose Machinery , All Other—*mfg*	333999	3569
Brake drums: Motor Vehicle Brake System—*mfg*	33634	3714
Motor Vehicle Parts, All Other—*mfg*	336399	3714
Brake fluid, hydraulic: Petroleum Lubricating Oil and Grease—*mfg*	324191	2992
Brake lining, asbestos: Motor Vehicle Brake System—*mfg*	33634	3292
Nonmetallic Mineral Product, All Other Miscellaneous—*mfg*	327999	3292
Brake lining, rubber: Fabric Coating Mills—*mfg*	31332	3069
Rubber Product, All Other—*mfg*	326299	3069
Brake linings, sale and installation: Automotive Mechanical and Electrical Repair and Maintenance, Other—*serv*	811118	7539
Brake pads, asbestos: Motor Vehicle Brake System—*mfg*	33634	3292
Nonmetallic Mineral Product, All Other Miscellaneous—*mfg*	327999	3292
Brake repairing, automotive: Automotive Mechanical and Electrical Repair and Maintenance, Other—*serv*	811118	7539
Brake shoes, railroad–cast iron: Iron Foundries—*mfg*	331511	3321
Brakes and brake parts, motor vehicle: Motor Vehicle Brake System—*mfg*	33634	3714
Motor Vehicle Parts, All Other—*mfg*	336399	3714
Brakes, aircraft: Aircraft Part and Auxiliary Equipment, Other—*mfg*	336413	3728
Fluid Power Valve and Hose Fitting—*mfg*	332912	3728
Brakes, bicycle–friction clutch and other: Motorcycle, Bicycle and Parts—*mfg*	336991	3751
Brakes, electromagnetic: Relay and Industrial Control—*mfg*	335314	3625
Brakes, metal forming: Machine Tool (Metal Forming Types)—*mfg*	333513	3542
Brakes, railway–air and vacuum: Pump and Pumping Equipment—*mfg*	333911	3743
Railroad Rolling Stock—*mfg*	33651	3743
Bran and middlings, except rice: Flour Milling—*mfg*	311211	2041
Bran, rice: Rice Milling—*mfg*	311212	2044
Branches of foreign banks: Banking, Commercial—*fin*	52211	6081
International Trade Financing—*fin*	522293	6081
Non-Depository Credit Intermediation, All Other—*fin*	522298	6081
Branding irons, for marking purposes: Marking Device—*mfg*	339943	3953
Brandy: Wineries—*mfg*	31213	2084
Brandy and brandy spirits: Wine and Distilled Alcoholic Beverage—*whlse*	42282	5182
Brandy spirits: Wineries—*mfg*	31213	2084
Brass die castings: Nonferrous (except Aluminum) Die-Castings—*mfg*	331522	3364
Brass foundries: Copper Foundries—*mfg*	331525	3366
Brass goods, plumbers': Building Material Dealers, Other—*retail*	44419	5074
Fabricated Metal Product, All Other Miscellaneous—*mfg*	332999	3432
Plumbing and Heating Equipment and Supplies (Hydronics)—*whlse*	42172	5074
Plumbing Fixture Fitting and Trim—*mfg*	332913	3432
Brass rolling and drawing: Copper Rolling, Drawing and Extruding—*mfg*	331421	3351
Brass smelting and refining, secondary: Secondary Smelting and Alloying of Aluminum—*mfg*	331314	3341
Secondary Smelting, Refining, and Alloying of Copper—*mfg*	331423	3341
Brassieres: Women's and Girls' Cut and Sew Apparel Contractors—*mfg*	315212	2342
Women's and Girls' Cut and Sew Lingerie, Loungewear and Nightwear—*mfg*	315231	2342
Brasswork, ornamental–structural: Ornamental and Architectural Metal Work—*mfg*	332323	3446
Braziers, barbecue: Household Cooking Appliance—*mfg*	335221	3631
Brazilwood extract: Gum and Wood Chemical—*mfg*	325191	2861
Brazing (hardening) metal for the trade: Metal Heat Treating—*mfg*	332811	3398
Brazing (welding): Personal and Household Goods Repair and Maintenance, Other—*serv*	81149	7692
Brazing fluxes: Basic Organic Chemical, All Other—*mfg*	325199	2899
Chemical Product, All Other Miscellaneous—*mfg*	325998	2899
Bread and Bakery Product Manufacturing	**31181**	
Bread and bread-type roll mixes: Flour Mixes and Dough from Purchased Flour—*mfg*	311822	2045
Bread and bread4ype roll mixes: Flour Milling—*mfg*	311211	2041
Bread crumbs, not made in bakeries: Dried and Dehydrated Food—*mfg*	311423	2099
Bread slicing machines: Food Product Machinery—*mfg*	333294	3556
Bread wrappers, lithographed: Lithographic Printing, Commercial—*mfg*	323110	2752
Quick Printing—*mfg*	323114	2752
Bread wrappers, printed–except lithographed or gravure: Digital Printing—*mfg*	323115	2759
Flexographic Printing, Commercial—*mfg*	323112	2759
Printing, Other Commercial—*mfg*	323119	2759
Quick Printing—*mfg*	323114	2759
Bread wrappers, waxed or laminated: Coated and Laminated Packaging Paper and Plastics Film—*mfg*	322221	2671
Unsupported Plastics Packaging Film and Sheet—*mfg*	326112	2671
Bread wrappers–gravure printing: Gravure Printing, Commercial—*mfg*	323111	2754
Bread wrapping machines: Packaging Machinery—*mfg*	333993	3565
Bread, brown–Boston and other-canned: Bakeries, Commercial—*mfg*	311812	2051

ALPHABETICAL INDEX	NAICS	SIC
Bread, frozen–packaged: Packaged Frozen Food—*whlse*	42242	5142
Bread, including frozen: Bakeries, Commercial—*mfg*	311812	2051
Breaker point sets, internal combustion engine: Motor Vehicle Electrical and Electronic Equipment, Other—*mfg*	336322	3694
Breakers, anthracite: Anthracite—*mining*	212113	1231
Breakers, coal: Mining Machinery and Equipment—*mfg*	333131	3532
Breakers, paving: Construction Machinery—*mfg*	33312	3531
Overhead Traveling Crane, Hoist and Monorail System—*mfg*	333923	3531
Railroad Rolling Stock—*mfg*	33651	3531
Breakers, vacuum–plumbing: Fabricated Metal Product, All Other Miscellaneous—*mfg*	332999	3432
Plumbing Fixture Fitting and Trim—*mfg*	332913	3432
Breakfast bars: Confectionery from Purchased Chocolate—*mfg*	31133	2064
Non-Chocolate Confectionery—*mfg*	31134	2064
Breakfast Cereal Manufacturing	**31123**	**2043**
Breakfast cereals: Grocery and Related Products, Other—*whlse*	42249	5149
Breakfast foods, cereal: Breakfast Cereal—*mfg*	31123	2043
Coffee and Tea—*mfg*	31192	2043
Breakfast sets (furniture), metal: Metal Household Furniture—*mfg*	337124	2514
Breakfast sets (furniture), wood: Nonupholstered Wood Household Furniture—*mfg*	337122	2511
Breakwater construction–general contractors: Heavy, All Other—*const*	23499	1629
Industrial Nonbuilding Structure—*const*	23493	1629
Breast aprons (harness): Apparel Accessories and Apparel, Other—*mfg*	315999	2399
Breechings, metal plate: Air-Conditioning and Warm Air Heating Equipment and Commercial and Industrial Refrigeration Equipment—*mfg*	333415	3443
Metal Tank (Heavy Gauge)—*mfg*	33242	3443
Plate Work—*mfg*	332313	3443
Power Boiler and Heat Exchanger—*mfg*	33241	3443
Breeding of animals, other than cattle, hogs, sheep, goats, and poultry: Animal Production Support Activities—*ag*	11521	752
Pet Care (except Veterinary) Services—*serv*	81291	752
Breeding of livestock: Animal Production Support Activities—*ag*	11521	751
Brentwood (steam bent) products, except furniture: Manufacturing, All Other Miscellaneous—*mfg*	339999	2499
Wood Container and Pallet—*mfg*	32192	2499
Wood Product, All Other Miscellaneous—*mfg*	321999	2499
Breweries	**31212**	**2082**
Brewers' and malteers' machinery: Food Product Machinery—*mfg*	333294	3556
Brewers' grain: Breweries—*mfg*	31212	2082
Brewers' pitch, product of softwood distillation: Gum and Wood Chemical—*mfg*	325191	2861
Bric-a-brac: Fabricated Metal Product, All Other Miscellaneous—*mfg*	332999	3999

ALPHABETICAL INDEX	NAICS	SIC
Plastics Product, All Other—*mfg*	326199	3999
Wood Product, All Other Miscellaneous—*mfg*	321999	3999
Brick and Structural Clay Tile Manufacturing	**327121**	**3251**
Brick and tile dealers: Building Material Dealers, Other—*retail*	44419	5211
Home Centers—*retail*	44411	5211
Brick making machines: Industrial Machinery, All Other—*mfg*	333298	3559
Machinery, Other Commercial and Service Industry—*mfg*	333319	3559
Brick siding, asphalt: Asphalt Shingle and Coating Materials—*mfg*	324122	2952
Brick, abrasive: Abrasive Product—*mfg*	32791	3291
Fabricated Metal Product, All Other Miscellaneous—*mfg*	332999	3291
Brick, adobe: Structural Clay Product, Other—*mfg*	327123	3259
Brick, bauxite: Nonclay Refractory—*mfg*	327125	3297
Brick, carbon: Nonclay Refractory—*mfg*	327125	3297
Brick, clay refractory–fire clay and highalumina: Clay Refractory—*mfg*	327124	3255
Brick, concrete: Concrete Block and Brick—*mfg*	327331	3271
Brick, except refractory: Brick, Stone and Related Material—*whlse*	42132	5032
Building Material Dealers, Other—*retail*	44419	5032
Brick, glass: Pressed and Blown Glass and Glassware, Other—*mfg*	327212	3229
Brick, ladle–clay: Clay Refractory—*mfg*	327124	3255
Brick, refractory–chrome, magnesite,silica, and other nonclay: Nonclay Refractory—*mfg*	327125	3297
Brick, sand lime: Gypsum and Gypsum Product—*mfg*	32742	3299
Nonmetallic Mineral Product, All Other Miscellaneous—*mfg*	327999	3299
Brick, silicon carbide: Nonclay Refractory—*mfg*	327125	3297
Brick, Stone and Related Construction Material Wholesalers	**42132**	**5032**
Brick–common, face, glazed, vitrified, and hollow clay: Brick and Structural Clay Tile—*mfg*	327121	3251
Bricklaying–contractors: Masonry and Stone Contractors—*const*	23541	1741
Bridal dresses or gowns: Women's and Girls' Cut and Sew Apparel Contractors—*mfg*	315212	2335
Women's and Girls' Cut and Sew Dress—*mfg*	315233	2335
Bridal shops, except custom: Women's Clothing Stores—*retail*	44812	5621
Bridal veils: Apparel Accessories and Apparel, Other—*mfg*	315999	2396
Bridge and gate machinery, hydraulic: General Purpose Machinery , All Other—*mfg*	333999	3569
Bridge and Tunnel Construction	**23412**	**1622**
Bridge clubs, membership: Amusement and Recreation Industries, All Other—*arts*	71399	7997
Fitness and Recreational Sports Centers—*arts*	71394	7997
Bridge construction–general contractors: Bridge and Tunnel—*const*	23412	1622
Bridge instruction: Sports and Recreation Instruction—*educ*	61162	7999
Bridge painting–contractors: Painting and Wall Covering Contractors—*const*	23521	1721
Bridge sections, highway–prefabricatedmetal: Fabricated Structural Metal—*mfg*	332312	3441

Bridge sets (cloths and napkins): Household Textile Product Mills, Other—*mfg*	314129	2392
Bridge sets (furniture), metal: Metal Household Furniture—*mfg*	337124	2514
Bridge sets (furniture), wood: Nonupholstered Wood Household Furniture—*mfg*	337122	2511
Bridges and trestles, wood–treated: Wood Preservation—*mfg*	321114	2491
Bridges, billiard and pool: Sporting and Athletic Goods—*mfg*	33992	3949
Bridges, electrical–e.g., Kelvin, Wheat-stone, vacuum tube, and megohm: Electronic Coil, Transformer, and Other Inductor—*mfg*	334416	3825
Instrument for Measuring and Testing Electricity and Electrical Signals—*mfg*	334515	3825
Bridges, highway–operation of: Road, Other Support Activities for—*trans*	48849	4785
Water, Other Support Activities for—*trans*	48839	4785
Bridges, piano: Musical Instrument—*mfg*	339992	3931
Bridle leather: Leather and Hide Tanning and Finishing—*mfg*	31611	3111
Bridle path construction–general contractors: Heavy, All Other—*const*	23499	1629
Industrial Nonbuilding Structure—*const*	23493	1629
Briefcases, regardless of material: Luggage—*mfg*	316991	3161
Briefs: Infants' Cut and Sew Apparel—*mfg*	315291	2341
Women's and Girls' Cut and Sew Apparel Contractors—*mfg*	315212	2341
Women's and Girls' Cut and Sew Lingerie, Loungewear and Nightwear—*mfg*	315231	2341
Briefs, underwear: Men's and Boys' Cut and Sew Apparel Contractors—*mfg*	315211	2322
Men's and Boys' Cut and Sew Underwear and Nightwear—*mfg*	315221	2322
Underwear and Nightwear Knitting Mills—*mfg*	315192	2254
Brimstone mining: Chemical and Fertilizer Mineral, Other—*mining*	212393	1479
Brine: Basic Inorganic Chemical, All Other—*mfg*	325188	2819
Chemical Product, All Other Miscellaneous—*mfg*	325998	2819
Brining of fruits and vegetables: Fruit and Vegetable Canning—*mfg*	311421	2035
Mayonnaise, Dressing and Other Prepared Sauce—*mfg*	311941	2035
Briquettes (fuel bricks)–made with petroleum binder: Petroleum and Coal Productsa, All Other—*mfg*	324199	2999
Briquettes, sawdust or bagasse–nonpetroleum binder: Manufacturing, All Other Miscellaneous—*mfg*	339999	2499
Wood Container and Pallet—*mfg*	32192	2499
Wood Product, All Other Miscellaneous—*mfg*	321999	2499
Bristles: Farm Product Raw Material, Other—*whlse*	42259	5159
Bristles, dressing of: Fabricated Metal Product, All Other Miscellaneous—*mfg*	332999	3999
Bristols, bogus: Paperboard Mills—*mfg*	32213	2631
Bristols, except bogus: Newsprint Mills—*mfg*	322122	2621
Paper (except Newsprint) Mills—*mfg*	322121	2621
Britannia metal, rolling and drawing: Nonferrous Metal (except Copper and Aluminum) Rolling, Drawing and Extruding—*mfg*	331491	3356
Broaches: Industrial Machinery and Equipment—*whlse*	42183	5084
Broaches (machine tool accessories): Cutting Tool and Machine Tool Accessory—*mfg*	333515	3545
Hand and Edge Tool—*mfg*	332212	3545
Broaches, dental: Dental Equipment and Supplies—*mfg*	339114	3843
Broaching machines: Machine Tool (Metal Cutting Types)—*mfg*	333512	3541
Broadcast equipment (including studio),radio and television: Radio and Television Broadcasting and Wireless Communications Equipment—*mfg*	33422	3663
Broadcasting and Telecommunications	**513**	
Broadcasting stations, radio: Radio Networks—*info*	513111	4832
Radio Stations—*info*	513112	4832
Broadcasting stations, television: Television Broadcasting—*info*	51312	4833
Broadcloth, cotton: Broadwoven Fabric Mills—*mfg*	31321	2211
Broadwoven Fabric Finishing Mills	**313311**	**2261**
Broadwoven Fabric Mills	**31321**	**2221**
Broadwoven fabrics: Broadwoven Fabric Finishing Mills—*mfg*	313311	5131
Piece Goods, Notions and Other Dry Goods—*whlse*	42231	5131
Textile and Fabric Finishing (except Broadwoven Fabric) Mills—*mfg*	313312	5131
Broadwoven fabrics, cotton: Broadwoven Fabric Mills—*mfg*	31321	2211
Broadwoven fabrics, silk and manmade fiber: Broadwoven Fabric Mills—*mfg*	31321	2221
Broadwoven fabrics–linen, jute, hemp, and ramie: Broadwoven Fabric Mills—*mfg*	31321	2299
Narrow Fabric Mills—*mfg*	313221	2299
Nonwoven Fabric Mills—*mfg*	31323	2299
Textile and Fabric Finishing (except Broadwoven Fabric) Mills—*mfg*	313312	2299
Textile Product Mills, All Other Miscellaneous—*mfg*	314999	2299
Thread Mills—*mfg*	313113	2299
Yarn Spinning Mills—*mfg*	313111	2299
Brocade, cotton: Broadwoven Fabric Mills—*mfg*	31321	2211
Brocatelle, cotton: Broadwoven Fabric Mills—*mfg*	31321	2211
Broccoli farms: Vegetable (except Potato) and Melon Farming, Other—*ag*	111219	161
Broiler chickens, raising of: Broilers and Other Meat Type Chicken Production—*ag*	11232	251
Broilers and Other Meat Type Chicken Production	**11232**	**251**
Broilers, electric: Electric Housewares and Household Fan—*mfg*	335211	3634
Heating Equipment (except Electric and Warm Air Furnaces)—*mfg*	333414	3634
Brokers of manufactured homes, on site: Real Estate Agents and Brokers, Offices Of—*real*	53121	6531
Brokers, commodity contract: Commodity Brokerage—*fin*	52314	6221
Commodity Contracts Dealing—*fin*	52313	6221
Brokers, custom house: Freight Arrangement—*trans*	48851	4731
Management Consulting Services, Other—*prof*	541618	4731

ALPHABETICAL INDEX	NAICS	SIC
Brokers, farm or business loan: Mortgage and Other Loan Brokers—*fin*	52231	6163
Brokers, insurance: Claims Adjusters—*fin*	524291	6411
Insurance Agencies and Brokerages—*fin*	52421	6411
Insurance Related Activities, All Other—*fin*	524298	6411
Third Party Administration for Insurance and Pension Funds—*fin*	524292	6411
Brokers, real estate: Real Estate Agents and Brokers, Offices Of—*real*	53121	6531
Brokers, security: Financial Investment Activities, Miscellaneous—*fin*	523999	6211
Intermediation, Miscellaneous—*fin*	52391	6211
Investment Banking and Securities Dealing—*fin*	52311	6211
Securities Brokerage—*fin*	52312	6211
Brokers, shipping: Freight Arrangement—*trans*	48851	4731
Management Consulting Services, Other—*prof*	541618	4731
Brokers, transportation: Freight Arrangement—*trans*	48851	4731
Management Consulting Services, Other—*prof*	541618	4731
Bromine, elemental: Basic Inorganic Chemical, All Other—*mfg*	325188	2819
Chemical Product, All Other Miscellaneous—*mfg*	325998	2819
Bromochloromethane: Basic Organic Chemical, All Other—*mfg*	325199	2869
Bronchoscopes, electromedical: Electromedical and Electrotherapeutic Apparatus—*mfg*	334510	3845
Irradiation Apparatus—*mfg*	334517	3845
Bronchoscopes, except electromedical: Surgical and Medical Instrument—*mfg*	339112	3841
Bronze die castings: Nonferrous (except Aluminum) Die-Castings—*mfg*	331522	3364
Bronze foundries: Copper Foundries—*mfg*	331525	3366
Bronze ink: Printing Ink—*mfg*	32591	2893
Bronze rolling and drawing: Copper Rolling, Drawing and Extruding—*mfg*	331421	3351
Bronze smelting and refining, secondary: Secondary Smelting and Alloying of Aluminum—*mfg*	331314	3341
Secondary Smelting, Refining, and Alloying of Copper—*mfg*	331423	3341
Bronze, artists'–mixtures, powders, paints, etc.: Chemical Product, All Other Miscellaneous—*mfg*	325998	3952
Institutional Furniture—*mfg*	337127	3952
Lead Pencil and Art Good—*mfg*	339942	3952
Bronzing and dusting machines for the printing trade: Printing Machinery and Equipment—*mfg*	333293	3555
Bronzing books, cards, or paper: Tradebinding and Related Work—*mfg*	323121	2789
Brooders: Farm Machinery and Equipment—*mfg*	333111	3523
Broom making machinery: Industrial Machinery, All Other—*mfg*	333298	3559
Machinery, Other Commercial and Service Industry—*mfg*	333319	3559
Broom, Brush and Mop Manufacturing	**339994**	**2392**

ALPHABETICAL INDEX	NAICS	SIC
Broom, mop, and paint handles-whole-sale: Nondurable Goods, Other Miscellaneous—*whlse*	42299	5199
Broomcorn: Farm Product Raw Material, Other—*whlse*	42259	5159
Broomcorn farms: Crop Farming, All Other Miscellaneous—*ag*	111998	139
Hay Farming—*ag*	11194	139
Peanut Farming—*ag*	111992	139
Vegetable (except Potato) and Melon Farming, Other—*ag*	111219	139
Brooms: Home Furnishings Stores, All Other—*retail*	442299	5719
Window Treatment Stores—*retail*	442291	5719
Brooms, hand and machine–bamboo, wire, fiber, splint, or other material: Broom, Brush and Mop—*mfg*	339994	3991
Brooms, powered (motor vehicles): Automobile—*mfg*	336111	3711
Heavy Duty Truck—*mfg*	33612	3711
Light Truck and Utility Vehicle—*mfg*	336112	3711
Military Armored Vehicle, Tank and Tank Component—*mfg*	336992	3711
Motor Vehicle Body—*mfg*	336211	3711
Broth, except seafood–canned: Canning, Specialty—*mfg*	311422	2032
Food, All Other Miscellaneous—*mfg*	311999	2032
Brown bread, Boston and other–canned: Bakeries, Commercial—*mfg*	311812	2051
Brown coal mining: Bituminous Coal and Lignite Surface—*mining*	212111	1221
Brown ore mining: Iron Ore—*mining*	21221	1011
Brownprint paper and cloth, sensitized: Photographic and Photocopying Equipment—*mfg*	333315	3861
Photographic Film, Paper, Plate and Chemical—*mfg*	325992	3861
Brownprint reproduction machines and equipment: Photographic and Photocopying Equipment—*mfg*	333315	3861
Photographic Film, Paper, Plate and Chemical—*mfg*	325992	3861
Brownprinting equipment: Office Equipment—*whlse*	42142	5044
Brucine and derivatives: Medicinal and Botanical—*mfg*	325411	2833
Brucite mining: Clay and Ceramic and Refractory Minerals—*mining*	212325	1459
Brush blocks, carbon or molded graphite: Carbon and Graphite Product—*mfg*	335991	3624
Brush blocks, wood–turned and shaped: Cut Stock, Resawing Lumber, and Planing—*mfg*	321912	2426
Millwork (including Flooring), Other—*mfg*	321918	2426
Showcase, Partition, Shelving, and Locker—*mfg*	337215	2426
Wood Product, All Other Miscellaneous—*mfg*	321999	2426
Brush clearing or cutting–contractors: Heavy, All Other—*const*	23499	1629
Industrial Nonbuilding Structure—*const*	23493	1629
Brush handles, plastics: Plastics Pipe and Pipe Fitting—*mfg*	326122	3089
Plastics Product, All Other—*mfg*	326199	3089
Unsupported Plastics Profile Shape—*mfg*	326121	3089
Brushes: Home Furnishings Stores, All Other—*retail*	442299	5719
Window Treatment Stores—*retail*	442291	5719
Brushes and brush stock contacts–carbon and graphite-electric: Carbon and Graphite Product—*mfg*	335991	3624

Entry	NAICS	SIC
Brushes for vacuum cleaners, carpet sweepers, and other rotary machines: Broom, Brush and Mop—*mfg*	339994	3991
Brushes, air–artists': Chemical Product, All Other Miscellaneous—*mfg*	325998	3952
Institutional Furniture—*mfg*	337127	3952
Lead Pencil and Art Good—*mfg*	339942	3952
Brushes, house-to-house or party plan selling: Direct Selling Establishments, Other—*retail*	45439	5963
Mobile Foodservices—*accom*	72233	5963
Brushes, household and industrial: Broom, Brush and Mop—*mfg*	339994	3991
Brushes, rubber: Fabric Coating Mills—*mfg*	31332	3069
Rubber Product, All Other—*mfg*	326299	3069
Brushing machines (metalworking machinery): Machine Tool (Metal Cutting Types)—*mfg*	333512	3541
Bubble formed packaging, plastics: Plastics Pipe and Pipe Fitting—*mfg*	326122	3089
Plastics Product, All Other—*mfg*	326199	3089
Unsupported Plastics Profile Shape—*mfg*	326121	3089
Bubble towers: Air-Conditioning and Warm Air Heating Equipment and Commercial and Industrial Refrigeration Equipment—*mfg*	333415	3443
Metal Tank (Heavy Gauge)—*mfg*	33242	3443
Plate Work—*mfg*	332313	3443
Power Boiler and Heat Exchanger—*mfg*	33241	3443
Bubblers, drinking fountain: Fabricated Metal Product, All Other Miscellaneous—*mfg*	332999	3432
Plumbing Fixture Fitting and Trim—*mfg*	332913	3432
Bucket and scarifier teeth: Construction Machinery—*mfg*	33312	3531
Overhead Traveling Crane, Hoist and Monorail System—*mfg*	333923	3531
Railroad Rolling Stock—*mfg*	33651	3531
Bucket type conveyor systems for general industrial use: Conveyor and Conveying Equipment—*mfg*	333922	3535
Buckets, elevator or conveyor for general industrial use: Conveyor and Conveying Equipment—*mfg*	333922	3535
Buckets, excavating–e.g., clamshell, con-crete, dragline, drag scraper, shovel: Construction Machinery—*mfg*	33312	3531
Overhead Traveling Crane, Hoist and Monorail System—*mfg*	333923	3531
Railroad Rolling Stock—*mfg*	33651	3531
Buckets, fish and bait: Sporting and Athletic Goods—*mfg*	33992	3949
Buckets, plastics: Plastics Pipe and Pipe Fitting—*mfg*	326122	3089
Plastics Product, All Other—*mfg*	326199	3089
Unsupported Plastics Profile Shape—*mfg*	326121	3089
Buckets, wood–coopered: Wood Container and Pallet—*mfg*	32192	2449
Buckle blanks and molds: Fastener, Button, Needle and Pin—*mfg*	339993	3965
Buckles and buckle parts, except shoe buckles: Fastener, Button, Needle and Pin—*mfg*	339993	3965
Buckles, shoe: Fastener, Button, Needle and Pin—*mfg*	339993	3131
Leather Good, All Other—*mfg*	316999	3131
Wood Product, All Other Miscellaneous—*mfg*	321999	3131
Buckram: Broadwoven Fabric Mills—*mfg*	31321	2211
Buckram–varnished, waxed, and impregnated: Fabric Coating Mills—*mfg*	31332	2295
Buckwheat farms: Grain Farming, All Other—*ag*	111199	119
Buckwheat flour: Flour Milling—*mfg*	311211	2041
Budget agencies: Public Finance—*pub*	92113	9311
Buffets (eating places): Cafeterias—*accom*	722212	5812
Caterers—*accom*	72232	5812
Foodservice Contractors—*accom*	72231	5812
Full-Service Restaurants—*accom*	72211	5812
Limited-Service Restaurants—*accom*	722211	5812
Snack and Nonalcoholic Beverage Bars—*accom*	722213	5812
Theater Companies and Dinner Theaters—*arts*	71111	5812
Buffets (furniture): Nonupholstered Wood Household Furniture—*mfg*	337122	2511
Buffing and polishing machines (machine tools): Machine Tool (Metal Cutting Types)—*mfg*	333512	3541
Buffing and polishing wheels, abrasive and nonabrasive: Abrasive Product—*mfg*	32791	3291
Fabricated Metal Product, All Other Miscellaneous—*mfg*	332999	3291
Buffing machines, hand–electric: Power-Driven Hand Tool—*mfg*	333991	3546
Buffing, for the trade: Electroplating, Plating, Polishing, Anodizing and Coloring—*mfg*	332813	3471
Buffings, russet: Leather and Hide Tanning and Finishing—*mfg*	31611	3111
Bugles and parts (musical instruments): Musical Instrument—*mfg*	339992	3931
Builders' hardware: Hardware—*whlse*	42171	5072
Hardware Stores—*retail*	44413	5251
Builders' hardware, including locks and lock sets: Hardware—*mfg*	33251	3429
Builders, operative–on own account: Building, Commercial and Institutional—*const*	23332	1531
Manufacturing and Industrial Building—*const*	23331	1531
Multifamily Housing—*const*	23322	1531
Single Family Housing—*const*	23321	1531
Builders, speculative: Building, Commercial and Institutional—*const*	23332	1531
Manufacturing and Industrial Building—*const*	23331	1531
Multifamily Housing—*const*	23322	1531
Single Family Housing—*const*	23321	1531
Building alterations, industrial and warehouse–general contractors: Building, Commercial and Institutional—*const*	23332	1541
Manufacturing and Industrial Building—*const*	23331	1541
Building alterations, nonresidential–except industrial and warehouses–general contractors: Building, Commercial and Institutional—*const*	23332	1542
Building alterations, residential–except single family–general contractors: Building, Commercial and Institutional—*const*	23332	1522
Multifamily Housing—*const*	23322	1522
Building alterations, single-family–general contractors: Single Family Housing—*const*	23321	1521
Building board, gypsum: Gypsum and Gypsum Product—*mfg*	32742	3275

ALPHABETICAL INDEX	NAICS	SIC
Building cleaning service, interior: Janitorial Services—*admin*	56172	7349
Building components manufacturing plant construction–general contractors: Building, Commercial and Institutional—*const*	23332	1541
Manufacturing and Industrial Building—*const*	23331	1541
Building Construction, Commercial and Institutional	**23332**	**1531**
Building construction, industrial and warehouse–general contractors: Building, Commercial and Institutional—*const*	23332	1541
Manufacturing and Industrial Building—*const*	23331	1541
Building construction, nonresidential–except industrial and warehouses–general contractors: Building, Commercial and Institutional—*const*	23332	1542
Building construction, residential–except single family–general contractors: Building, Commercial and Institutional—*const*	23332	1522
Multifamily Housing—*const*	23322	1522
Building construction, single family–general contractors: Single Family Housing—*const*	23321	1521
Building Equipment and Other Machinery Installation Contractors	**23595**	**1796**
Building front installation, metal-con-tractors: Structural Steel Erection Contractors—*const*	23591	1791
Building glass, flat: Flat Glass—*mfg*	327211	3211
Building Inspection Services	**54135**	**7389**
Building lime: Lime—*mfg*	32741	3274
Building maintenance, except repairs: Janitorial Services—*admin*	56172	7349
Building Material and Garden Equipment and Supplies Dealers	**444**	
Building Material and Supplies Dealers	**4441**	
Building Material Dealers, Other	**44419**	**5032**
Building materials dealers: Building Material Dealers, Other—*retail*	44419	5211
Home Centers—*retail*	44411	5211
Building materials, asbestos–except asbestos paper: Motor Vehicle Brake System—*mfg*	33634	3292
Nonmetallic Mineral Product, All Other Miscellaneous—*mfg*	327999	3292
Building materials, concrete–except block and brick: Concrete Pipe—*mfg*	327332	3272
Concrete Product, Other—*mfg*	32739	3272
Nonmetallic Mineral Product, All Other Miscellaneous—*mfg*	327999	3272
Building materials, fiberglass: Building Material Dealers, Other—*retail*	44419	5039
Construction Material, Other—*whlse*	42139	5039
Building materials, used: Non-Depository Credit Intermediation, All Other—*fin*	522298	5932
Used Merchandise Stores—*retail*	45331	5932
Building oil and gas well foundations on a contract basis: Oil and Gas Operations Support Activities—*mining*	213112	1389
Building paper, laminated: Coated and Laminated Paper—*mfg*	322222	2679
Converted Paper Product, All Other—*mfg*	322298	2679
Die-Cut Paper and Paperboard Office Supplies—*mfg*	322231	2679

ALPHABETICAL INDEX	NAICS	SIC
Non-Folding Sanitary Food Container—*mfg*	322215	2679
Building paper–sheathing, insulation, saturating, and dry felts: Newsprint Mills—*mfg*	322122	2621
Paper (except Newsprint) Mills—*mfg*	322121	2621
Building repairs, industrial–general contractors: Building, Commercial and Institutional—*const*	23332	1541
Manufacturing and Industrial Building—*const*	23331	1541
Building repairs, nonresidential–general contractors: Building, Commercial and Institutional—*const*	23332	1542
Building repairs, residential–except single-family–general contractors: Building, Commercial and Institutional—*const*	23332	1522
Multifamily Housing—*const*	23322	1522
Building repairs, single family–general contractors: Single Family Housing—*const*	23321	1521
Building services monitoring controls, automatic: Automatic Environmental Control for Residential, Commercial and Appliance Use—*mfg*	334512	3822
Building standards agencies: Housing Programs, Administration of—*pub*	92511	9531
Building stone: Brick, Stone and Related Material—*whlse*	42132	5032
Building Material Dealers, Other—*retail*	44419	5032
Building stone, artificial–concrete: Concrete Pipe—*mfg*	327332	3272
Concrete Product, Other—*mfg*	32739	3272
Nonmetallic Mineral Product, All Other Miscellaneous—*mfg*	327999	3272
Building stone, natural–cut-including combination with quarrying: Cut Stone and Stone Product—*mfg*	327991	3281
Building tile, clay: Brick and Structural Clay Tile—*mfg*	327121	3251
Building, Developing and General Contracting	**233**	
Buildings and Dwellings, Other Services to	**56179**	**7699**
Buildings, apartment (five or more housing units)–operators of: Lessors of Residential Buildings and Dwellings—*real*	53111	6513
Buildings, dwelling (four or fewer housing units)–operators of: Lessors of Residential Buildings and Dwellings—*real*	53111	6514
Buildings, mobile–commercial use: Manufactured Home (Mobile Home)—*mfg*	321991	2451
Buildings, nonresidential–operators of: Lessors of Nonresidential Buildings (except Miniwarehouses)—*real*	53112	6512
Promoters of Performing Arts, Sports and Similar Events with Facilities—*arts*	71131	6512
Buildings, prefabricated: Building Material Dealers, Other—*retail*	44419	5211
Home Centers—*retail*	44411	5211
Buildings, prefabricated and portable–wood: Prefabricated Wood Building—*mfg*	321992	2452
Buildings, prefabricated–metal: Prefabricated Metal Building and Component—*mfg*	332311	3448
Built-up mica: Gypsum and Gypsum Product—*mfg*	32742	3299
Nonmetallic Mineral Product, All Other Miscellaneous—*mfg*	327999	3299

Bulbs for electric lights, without filaments or sockets: Pressed and Blown Glass and Glassware, Other—*mfg*	327212	3229
Bulbs for medicine droppers, syringes, atomizers, and sprays–rubber: Fabric Coating Mills—*mfg*	31332	3069
Rubber Product, All Other—*mfg*	326299	3069
Bulbs, electric light–complete: Electric Lamp Bulb and Part—*mfg*	33511	3641
Bulbs, flower and field: Farm Supplies—*whlse*	42291	5191
Nursery and Garden Centers—*retail*	44422	5191
Bulbs, growing of: Floriculture Production—*ag*	111422	181
Nursery and Tree Production—*ag*	111421	181
Bulbs, seed and nursery stock: Nursery and Garden Centers—*retail*	44422	5261
Outdoor Power Equipment Stores—*retail*	44421	5261
Stores (except Tobacco Stores), All Other Miscellaneous—*retail*	453998	5261
Bulldozer rental and leasing: Construction, and Forestry Machinery and Equipment Rental and Leasing—*real*	532412	7353
Heavy, All Other—*const*	23499	7353
Bulldozers, construction: Construction Machinery—*mfg*	33312	3531
Overhead Traveling Crane, Hoist and Monorail System—*mfg*	333923	3531
Railroad Rolling Stock—*mfg*	33651	3531
Bulldozers, metalworking: Machine Tool (Metal Forming Types)—*mfg*	333513	3542
Bullet jackets and cores, 30 mm. (or 1.18 inch) or less: Small Arms Ammunition—*mfg*	332992	3482
Bulletin boards, wood and cork: Manufacturing, All Other Miscellaneous—*mfg*	339999	2499
Wood Container and Pallet—*mfg*	32192	2499
Wood Product, All Other Miscellaneous—*mfg*	321999	2499
Bulletproof vests: Surgical Appliance and Supplies—*mfg*	339113	3842
Bullion, gold–produced at mine, mill, or dredge site: Gold Ore—*mining*	212221	1041
Bullion, precious metals: Jewelry, Watch, Precious Stone and Precious Metal—*whlse*	42194	5094
Bullion, silver–produced at mine or mill site: Silver Ore—*mining*	212222	1044
Bump shops (automotive repair): Automotive Body, Paint and Interior Repair and Maintenance—*serv*	811121	7532
Bumpers and bumperettes, motor vehicle: Motor Vehicle Body—*mfg*	336211	3714
Motor Vehicle Parts, All Other—*mfg*	336399	3714
Bumping posts, railroad–forged-not made in rolling mills: Iron and Steel Forging—*mfg*	332111	3462
Bungs, wood: Manufacturing, All Other Miscellaneous—*mfg*	339999	2499
Wood Container and Pallet—*mfg*	32192	2499
Wood Product, All Other Miscellaneous—*mfg*	321999	2499
Buns, bread-type (e.g., hamburger, hotdog), including frozen: Bakeries, Commercial—*mfg*	311812	2051
Buns, sweet, except frozen: Bakeries, Commercial—*mfg*	311812	2051
Bunting: Broadwoven Fabric Mills—*mfg*	31321	2211
Buoyancy instruments, industrial process type: Instruments and Related Products for Measuring, Displaying, and Controlling Industrial Process Variables—*mfg*	334513	3823
Buoys and floats, plastics: Plastics Pipe and Pipe Fitting—*mfg*	326122	3089
Plastics Product, All Other—*mfg*	326199	3089
Unsupported Plastics Profile Shape—*mfg*	326121	3089
Buoys, cork: Manufacturing, All Other Miscellaneous—*mfg*	339999	2499
Wood Container and Pallet—*mfg*	32192	2499
Wood Product, All Other Miscellaneous—*mfg*	321999	2499
Buoys, metal: Air-Conditioning and Warm Air Heating Equipment and Commercial and Industrial Refrigeration Equipment—*mfg*	333415	3443
Metal Tank (Heavy Gauge)—*mfg*	33242	3443
Plate Work—*mfg*	332313	3443
Power Boiler and Heat Exchanger—*mfg*	33241	3443
Bureaus of criminal investigations: Police Protection—*pub*	92212	9221
Bureaus of standards: Regulation, Licensing, and Inspection of Miscellaneous Commercial Sectors—*pub*	92615	9651
Burglar alarm apparatus, electric: Communications Equipment, Other—*mfg*	33429	3669
Burglar alarm installation–contractors: Electrical Contractors—*const*	23531	1731
Security Systems Services (except Locksmiths)—*admin*	561621	1731
Burglar alarm monitoring and maintenance: Security Systems Services (except Locksmiths)—*admin*	561621	7382
Burglary and theft insurance: Direct Property and Casualty Insurance Carriers—*fin*	524126	6331
Insurance Funds, Other—*fin*	52519	6331
Reinsurance Carriers—*fin*	52413	6331
Burial cases, metal and wood: Burial Casket—*mfg*	339995	3995
Burial Casket Manufacturing	**339995**	**3995**
Burial garments: Cut and Sew Apparel, All Other—*mfg*	315299	2389
Burial insurance societies: Direct Life Insurance Carriers—*fin*	524113	6311
Reinsurance Carriers—*fin*	52413	6311
Burial vaults, concrete and precast terrazo: Concrete Pipe—*mfg*	327332	3272
Concrete Product, Other—*mfg*	32739	3272
Nonmetallic Mineral Product, All Other Miscellaneous—*mfg*	327999	3272
Burial vaults, fiberglass: Burial Casket—*mfg*	339995	3995
Burial vaults, stone: Cut Stone and Stone Product—*mfg*	327991	3281
Burlap: Nondurable Goods, Other Miscellaneous—*whlse*	42299	5199
Burlap, jute: Broadwoven Fabric Mills—*mfg*	31321	2299
Narrow Fabric Mills—*mfg*	313221	2299
Nonwoven Fabric Mills—*mfg*	31323	2299
Textile and Fabric Finishing (except Broadwoven Fabric) Mills—*mfg*	313312	2299
Textile Product Mills, All Other Miscellaneous—*mfg*	314999	2299
Thread Mills—*mfg*	313113	2299
Yarn Spinning Mills—*mfg*	313111	2299
Burlesque companies: Theater Companies and Dinner Theaters—*arts*	71111	7922
Burley mining: Clay and Ceramic and Refractory Minerals—*mining*	212325	1459
Burling and mending wool cloth for the trade: Broadwoven Fabric Finishing Mills—*mfg*	313311	2231
Broadwoven Fabric Mills—*mfg*	31321	2231

ALPHABETICAL INDEX	NAICS	SIC
Textile and Fabric Finishing (except Broadwoven Fabric) Mills—*mfg*	313312	2231
Burls, wood: Logging—*ag*	11331	2411
Burners, fuel oil and distillate oil: Building Material Dealers, Other—*retail*	44419	5074
Plumbing and Heating Equipment and Supplies (Hydronics)—*whlse*	42172	5074
Burners, gas–domestic: Heating Equipment (except Electric and Warm Air Furnaces)—*mfg*	333414	3433
Burners, oil–domestic and industrial: Heating Equipment (except Electric and Warm Air Furnaces)—*mfg*	333414	3433
Burning metal for the trade: Metal Heat Treating—*mfg*	332811	3398
Burnishers and cushions, gilders': Chemical Product, All Other Miscellaneous—*mfg*	325998	3952
Institutional Furniture—*mfg*	337127	3952
Lead Pencil and Art Good—*mfg*	339942	3952
Burnishing and washing machines, brake: General Purpose Machinery , All Other—*mfg*	333999	3569
Burnishing ink: Polish and Other Sanitation Good—*mfg*	325612	2842
Burnishing machines (machine tools): Machine Tool (Metal Cutting Types)—*mfg*	333512	3541
Burnt leather goods for the trade: Leather Good, All Other—*mfg*	316999	3199
Burnt sugar (food color): Flavoring Syrup and Concentrate—*mfg*	31193	2087
Food, All Other Miscellaneous—*mfg*	311999	2087
Spice and Extract—*mfg*	311942	2087
Burnt wood articles: Wood Product, All Other Miscellaneous—*mfg*	321999	3999
Burro farms: Horse and Other Equine Production—*ag*	11292	272
Burrstone quarrying: Crushed and Broken Stone and Quarrying, Other—*mining*	212319	1499
Non-Metallic Mineral, All Other—*mining*	212399	1499
Burs, dental: Dental Equipment and Supplies—*mfg*	339114	3843
Bus and Motor Vehicle Transit Systems	**485113**	**4111**
Bus bar structures: Switchgear and Switchboard Apparatus—*mfg*	335313	3613
Bus bars (electrical conductors): Current-Carrying Wiring Device—*mfg*	335931	3643
Bus bars and trolley ducts: Building Material Dealers, Other—*retail*	44419	5063
Electrical Apparatus and Equipment, Wiring Supplies and Material—*whlse*	42161	5063
Bus bodies, motor vehicle: Motor Vehicle Body—*mfg*	336211	3713
Bus card advertising: Advertising Material Distribution Services—*prof*	54187	7319
Advertising, Other Services Related to—*prof*	54189	7319
Display Advertising—*prof*	54185	7319
Media Buying Agencies—*prof*	54183	7319
Nonscheduled Air, Other—*trans*	481219	7319
Bus charter service, except local: Charter Bus Industry—*trans*	48551	4142
Bus charter service, local: Charter Bus Industry—*trans*	48551	4141

ALPHABETICAL INDEX	NAICS	SIC
Bus line operation, local: Bus and Motor Vehicle Transit Systems—*trans*	485113	4111
Commuter Rail Systems—*trans*	485112	4111
Mixed Mode Transit Systems—*trans*	485111	4111
Transit and Ground Passenger, All Other—*trans*	485999	4111
Urban Transit Systems, Other—*trans*	485119	4111
Bus lines, intercity: Interurban and Rural Bus—*trans*	48521	4131
Bus terminal operation: Road, Other Support Activities for—*trans*	48849	4173
Bus ticket offices, not operated by transportation companies: Transportation, All Other Support Activities—*trans*	488999	4729
Travel Arrangement and Reservation Services, All Other—*admin*	561599	4729
Bus trailers, tractor type: Truck Trailer—*mfg*	336212	3715
Bus washing: Car Washes—*serv*	811192	7542
Bus, truck and trailer forgings, ferrous–not made in rolling mills: Iron and Steel Forging—*mfg*	332111	3462
Buses: Automobile and Other Motor Vehicle—*whlse*	42111	5012
Buses, motor–except trackless trolley: Automobile—*mfg*	336111	3711
Heavy Duty Truck—*mfg*	33612	3711
Light Truck and Utility Vehicle—*mfg*	336112	3711
Military Armored Vehicle, Tank and Tank Component—*mfg*	336992	3711
Motor Vehicle Body—*mfg*	336211	3711
Buses, school–operation of: School and Employee Bus—*trans*	48541	4151
Buses, sightseeing–operation of: Scenic and Sightseeing, Land—*trans*	48711	4119
Transit and Ground Passenger, All Other—*trans*	485999	4119
Buses, trackless trolley: Pump and Pumping Equipment—*mfg*	333911	3743
Railroad Rolling Stock—*mfg*	33651	3743
Bush hooks: Hand and Edge Tool—*mfg*	332212	3423
Bushings and boarings, except die-castings–brass, bronze, and copper: Copper Foundries—*mfg*	331525	3366
Bushings, cast steel–except investment: Steel Foundries, (except Investment)—*mfg*	331513	3325
Bushings, rubber: Fabric Coating Mills—*mfg*	31332	3069
Rubber Product, All Other—*mfg*	326299	3069
Bushings, wood: Manufacturing, All Other Miscellaneous—*mfg*	339999	2499
Wood Container and Pallet—*mfg*	32192	2499
Wood Product, All Other Miscellaneous—*mfg*	321999	2499
Business and Secretarial Schools	**61141**	**8244**
Business Associations	**81391**	**8699**
Business associations, other than civic and social: Business Associations—*serv*	81391	8611
Business brokers (buying and selling business enterprises): Business Support Services, All Other—*admin*	561499	7389
Business colleges and schools, not of college grade: Business and Secretarial Schools—*educ*	61141	8244
Business credit institutions, short-term: Financial Transactions Processing, Reserve, and Clearing House Activities—*fin*	52232	6153

Non-Depository Credit Intermediation, All Other—*fin*	522298	6153
Sales Financing—*fin*	52222	6153
Business economists, commercial: Marketing Research and Public Opinion Polling—*prof*	54191	8732
Research and Development in the Social Sciences and Humanities—*prof*	54173	8732
Business forms: Office Supplies and Stationery Stores—*retail*	45321	5112
Stationary and Office Supplies—*whlse*	42212	5112
Business forms, except manifold, lithographed or gravure printed: Digital Printing—*mfg*	323115	2759
Flexographic Printing, Commercial—*mfg*	323112	2759
Printing, Other Commercial—*mfg*	323119	2759
Quick Printing—*mfg*	323114	2759
Business forms, except manifold–gravure printing: Gravure Printing, Commercial—*mfg*	323111	2754
Business forms, except manifold–lithographed: Lithographic Printing, Commercial—*mfg*	323110	2752
Quick Printing—*mfg*	323114	2752
Business forms, manifold: Manifold Business Form Printing—*mfg*	323116	2761
Business machine repair, electrical: Computer and Office Machine Repair and Maintenance—*serv*	811212	7629
Consumer Electronics Repair and Maintenance—*serv*	811211	7629
Business management services: Office Administrative Services—*admin*	56111	8741
Business research, commercial: Marketing Research and Public Opinion Polling—*prof*	54191	8732
Research and Development in the Social Sciences and Humanities—*prof*	54173	8732
Business Schools and Computer and Management Training	**6114**	
Business Service Centers	**56143**	
Business Service Centers (including Copy Shops), Other	**561439**	**7389**
Business service newsletters–publishing and printing, or publishing only: Database and Directory Publishers—*info*	51114	2741
Music Publishers—*info*	51223	2741
Publishers, All Other—*info*	511199	2741
Business Support Services	**5614**	
Business Support Services, All Other	**561499**	**7389**
Business Support Services, Other	**56149**	
Business, Professional, Labor, Political, and Other Organizations	**8139**	
Businesspersons clubs, civic and social: Civic and Social Organizations—*serv*	81341	8641
Butadiene copolymers, containing lessthan 50 percent butadiene: Plastics Material and Resin—*mfg*	325211	2821
Butadiene rubbers: Synthetic Rubber—*mfg*	325212	2822
Butadiene, made in chemical plants: Basic Organic Chemical, All Other—*mfg*	325199	2869
Butadiene, produced in petroleum refineries: Petroleum Refineries—*mfg*	32411	2911
Butadiene-acrylonitrile copolymers (more than 50 percent butadiene): Synthetic Rubber—*mfg*	325212	2822
Butadiene-styrene copolymers (more than 50 percent butadiene): Synthetic Rubber—*mfg*	325212	2822
Butane (natural) production: Natural Gas Liquid Extraction—*mining*	211112	1321
Butane gas, bottled: Liquefied Petroleum Gas (Bottled Gas) Dealers—*retail*	454312	5984
Butane gas, except bulk stations and terminals: Petroleum and Petroleum Products (except Bulk Stations and Terminals)—*whlse*	42272	5172
Butchers' knives: Cutlery and Flatware (except Precious)—*mfg*	332211	3421
Butchers' store fixtures, except wood: Showcase, Partition, Shelving, and Locker—*mfg*	337215	2542
Butchers' store fixtures, wood: Architectural Woodwork and Millwork, Custom—*mfg*	337212	2541
Showcase, Partition, Shelving, and Locker—*mfg*	337215	2541
Wood Kitchen Cabinet and Counter Top—*mfg*	33711	2541
Butter: Dairy Product (except Dried or Canned)—*whlse*	42243	5143
Butter and other dairy product stores: Food Stores, All Other Specialty—*retail*	445299	5451
Butter cloths: Broadwoven Fabric Mills—*mfg*	31321	2211
Butter crates, wood–wirebound: Wood Container and Pallet—*mfg*	32192	2449
Butter making and butter working machinery: Food Product Machinery—*mfg*	333294	3556
Butter oil: Creamery Butter—*mfg*	311512	2021
Butter powder: Creamery Butter—*mfg*	311512	2021
Butter, creamery and whey: Creamery Butter—*mfg*	311512	2021
Butter, renovated and processed: Perishable Prepared Food—*mfg*	311991	2099
Butterfat, anhydrous: Creamery Butter—*mfg*	311512	2021
Buttermilk emulsion for animal food: Animal Food, Other—*mfg*	311119	2048
Buttermilk, cultured: Fluid Milk—*mfg*	311511	2026
Buttermilk–concentrated, condensed,dried, evaporated, and powdered: Dry, Condensed, and Evaporated Dairy Product—*mfg*	311514	2023
Butters, fruit: Fruit and Vegetable Canning—*mfg*	311421	2033
Button backs and parts: Fastener, Button, Needle and Pin—*mfg*	339993	3965
Button blanks and molds: Fastener, Button, Needle and Pin—*mfg*	339993	3965
Button coloring for the trade: Fastener, Button, Needle and Pin—*mfg*	339993	3965
Buttonhole and eyelet machines and attachments, household: Major Household Appliance, Other—*mfg*	335228	3639
Buttonhole and eyelet machines and attachments, industrial: Industrial Machinery, All Other—*mfg*	333298	3559
Machinery, Other Commercial and Service Industry—*mfg*	333319	3559
Buttonhole making, except fur–for the trade: Men's and Boys' Cut and Sew Apparel Contractors—*mfg*	315211	2395
Textile Product Mills, All Other Miscellaneous—*mfg*	314999	2395
Women's and Girls' Cut and Sew Apparel Contractors—*mfg*	315212	2395
Buttonhole making, fur: Fur and Leather Apparel—*mfg*	315292	2371
Buttons: Broadwoven Fabric Finishing Mills—*mfg*	313311	5131

ALPHABETICAL INDEX	NAICS	SIC
Piece Goods, Notions and Other Dry Goods—*whlse*	42231	5131
Textile and Fabric Finishing (except Broadwoven Fabric) Mills—*mfg*	313312	5131
Buttons, except precious metal and precious or semiprecious stones: Fastener, Button, Needle and Pin—*mfg*	339993	3965
Buttons–Red Cross, union, and identification: Fabricated Metal Product, All Other Miscellaneous—*mfg*	332999	3999
Butyl acetate, alcohol, and propionate: Basic Organic Chemical, All Other—*mfg*	325199	2869
Ethyl Alcohol—*mfg*	325193	2869
Butyl ester solution of 2, 4-D: Basic Organic Chemical, All Other—*mfg*	325199	2869
Butyl rubber: Synthetic Rubber—*mfg*	325212	2822
Butylene, made in chemical plants: Basic Organic Chemical, All Other—*mfg*	325199	2869
Butylene, produced in petroleum refineries: Petroleum Refineries—*mfg*	32411	2911
Buyers of raw farm products, except grain,field beans, and livestock: Farm Product Raw Material, Other—*whlse*	42259	5159
Buyers' clubs: Personal Services, All Other—*serv*	81299	7299
Buying agents, real estate: Real Estate Agents and Brokers, Offices Of—*real*	53121	6531
C-clamps: Hand and Edge Tool—*mfg*	332212	3423
CAB (computer-aided engineering) systems services: Computer Systems Design Services—*prof*	541512	7373
Cabarets: Drinking Places (Alcoholic Beverages)—*accom*	72241	5813
Cabbage farms: Vegetable (except Potato) and Melon Farming, Other—*ag*	111219	161
Cabin environment indicators, transmitters, and sensors: Search, Detection, Navigation, Guidance, Aeronautical, and Nautical System and Instrument—*mfg*	334511	3812
Cabinet hardware, including locks and lock sets: Hardware—*mfg*	33251	3429
Cabinet makers' machinery: Sawmill and Woodworking Machinery—*mfg*	33321	3553
Cabinet work on a custom basis to individual order: Furniture Stores—*retail*	44211	5712
Nonupholstered Wood Household Furniture—*mfg*	337122	5712
Upholstered Household Furniture—*mfg*	337121	5712
Wood Kitchen Cabinet and Counter Top—*mfg*	33711	5712
Cabinet work performed at the construction site: Carpentry Contractors—*const*	23551	1751
Cabinets, dental: Dental Equipment and Supplies—*mfg*	339114	3843
Cabinets, factory: Institutional Furniture—*mfg*	337127	2599
Cabinets, household refrigerator: Household Refrigerator and Home Freezer—*mfg*	335222	3632
Cabinets, kitchen–metal: Metal Household Furniture—*mfg*	337124	2514
Cabinets, kitchen–not built in: Furniture Stores—*retail*	44211	5712
Nonupholstered Wood Household Furniture—*mfg*	337122	5712
Upholstered Household Furniture—*mfg*	337121	5712
Wood Kitchen Cabinet and Counter Top—*mfg*	33711	5712
Cabinets, kitchen–to be installed: Building Material Dealers, Other—*retail*	44419	5211
Home Centers—*retail*	44411	5211
Cabinets, kitchen–wood-factory made to be installed: Wood Kitchen Cabinet and Counter Top—*mfg*	33711	2434
Cabinets, medicine–metal: Metal Household Furniture—*mfg*	337124	2514
Cabinets, office–except wood: Nonwood Office Furniture—*mfg*	337214	2522
Cabinets, office–wood: Wood Office Furniture—*mfg*	337211	2521
Cabinets, radio and television–metal: Metal Household Furniture—*mfg*	337124	2514
Cabinets, radio and television–plastics: Household Furniture (except Wood and Metal)—*mfg*	337125	2519
Cabinets, show and display–refrigerated: Air-Conditioning and Warm Air Heating Equipment and Commercial and Industrial Refrigeration Equipment—*mfg*	333415	3585
Motor Vehicle Air-Conditioning—*mfg*	336391	3585
Cabinets, show, display, and storage–except refrigerated-wood: Architectural Woodwork and Millwork, Custom—*mfg*	337212	2541
Showcase, Partition, Shelving, and Locker—*mfg*	337215	2541
Wood Kitchen Cabinet and Counter Top—*mfg*	33711	2541
Cabinets, show, display, and storage–not refrigerated-except wood: Showcase, Partition, Shelving, and Locker—*mfg*	337215	2542
Cabinets, wood–radio, television, phonograph, and sewing machines: Wood Television, Radio, and Sewing Machine Cabinet—*mfg*	337129	2517
Cabinets, wood–to be installed: Wood Kitchen Cabinet and Counter Top—*mfg*	33711	2434
Cabins and cottages: Bed and Breakfast Inns—*accom*	721191	7011
Casino Hotels—*accom*	72112	7011
Hotels (except Casino Hotels) and Motels—*accom*	72111	7011
Traveler Accommodation, All Other—*accom*	721199	7011
Cabins, tourist: Bed and Breakfast Inns—*accom*	721191	7011
Casino Hotels—*accom*	72112	7011
Hotels (except Casino Hotels) and Motels—*accom*	72111	7011
Traveler Accommodation, All Other—*accom*	721199	7011
Cable and Other Program Distribution	**51322**	**4841**
Cable cars, aerial–except amusement and scenic: Transit and Ground Passenger, All Other—*trans*	485999	4119
Transportation, Special Needs—*trans*	485991	4119
Cable cars, except aerial, amusement and scenic: Bus and Motor Vehicle Transit Systems—*trans*	485113	4111
Commuter Rail Systems—*trans*	485112	4111
Mixed Mode Transit Systems—*trans*	485111	4111
Transit and Ground Passenger, All Other—*trans*	485999	4111
Urban Transit Systems, Other—*trans*	485119	4111

Entry	NAICS	SIC
Cable conduit: Building Material Dealers, Other—*retail*	44419	5063
Electrical Apparatus and Equipment, Wiring Supplies and Material—*whlse*	42161	5063
Cable laying construction–contractors: Power and Communication Transmission Line—*const*	23492	1623
Water, Sewer, and Pipeline—*const*	23491	1623
Cable lifts, amusement or scenic–operated separately from lodges: Skiing Facilities—*arts*	71392	7999
Cable Networks	**51321**	**4841**
Cable Networks and Program Distribution	**5132**	
Cable service, telephone: Telecommunications Resellers—*info*	51333	4813
Wired Telecommunications Carriers—*info*	51331	4813
Cable splicing service, nonelectrical–contractors: Trade Contractors, All Other Special—*const*	23599	1799
Cable splicing, electrical–contractors: Electrical Contractors—*const*	23531	1731
Security Systems Services (except Locksmiths)—*admin*	561621	1731
Cable television equipment: Radio and Television Broadcasting and Wireless Communications Equipment—*mfg*	33422	3663
Cable television hookup–contractors: Electrical Contractors—*const*	23531	1731
Security Systems Services (except Locksmiths)—*admin*	561621	1731
Cable television line construction–contractors: Power and Communication Transmission Line—*const*	23492	1623
Water, Sewer, and Pipeline—*const*	23491	1623
Cable television services: Cable and Other Program Distribution—*info*	51322	4841
Cable Networks—*info*	51321	4841
Cable testing machines: Measuring and Controlling Device, Other—*mfg*	334519	3829
Surgical and Medical Instrument—*mfg*	339112	3829
Cable trays, metal plate: Air-Conditioning and Warm Air Heating Equipment and Commercial and Industrial Refrigeration Equipment—*mfg*	333415	3443
Metal Tank (Heavy Gauge)—*mfg*	33242	3443
Plate Work—*mfg*	332313	3443
Power Boiler and Heat Exchanger—*mfg*	33241	3443
Cable, aluminum–made in rolling mills: Aluminum Rolling and Drawing, Other—*mfg*	331319	3355
Cable, fiber: Rope, Cordage and Twine Mills—*mfg*	314991	2298
Cable, nonferrous–bare, insulated, or armored: Aluminum Rolling and Drawing, Other—*mfg*	331319	3357
Communication and Energy Wire, Other—*mfg*	335929	3357
Copper Wire (except Mechanical) Drawing—*mfg*	331422	3357
Fiber Optic Cable—*mfg*	335921	3357
Nonferrous Metal (except Copper and Aluminum) Rolling, Drawing and Extruding—*mfg*	331491	3357
Cable, steel–insulated or armored: Fabricated Wire Product, Other—*mfg*	332618	3315
Steel Wire Drawing—*mfg*	331222	3315
Cable, uninsulated wire–made from purchased wire: Fabricated Wire Product, Other—*mfg*	332618	3496
Cable, wire–not insulated: Metal Service Centers and Offices—*whlse*	42151	5051
Cablegram services: Wired Telecommunications Carriers—*info*	51331	4822
Cabs for industrial trucks and tractors: Fabricated Metal Product, All Other Miscellaneous—*mfg*	332999	3537
Industrial Truck, Tractor, Trailer and Stacker Machinery—*mfg*	333924	3537
Metal Container, Other—*mfg*	332439	3537
Cabs, agricultural machinery: Farm Machinery and Equipment—*mfg*	333111	3523
Cabs, construction machinery: Construction Machinery—*mfg*	33312	3531
Overhead Traveling Crane, Hoist and Monorail System—*mfg*	333923	3531
Railroad Rolling Stock—*mfg*	33651	3531
Cabs, horse-drawn–for hire: Rail Support Activities—*trans*	48821	4789
Scenic and Sightseeing, Land—*trans*	48711	4789
Transportation, All Other Support Activities—*trans*	488999	4789
Cacao bean products–chocolate, cocoa butter, and cocoa: Chocolate and Confectionery from Cacao Beans—*mfg*	31132	2066
Cacao beans–shelling, roasting, and grinding for making chocolate liquor: Chocolate and Confectionery from Cacao Beans—*mfg*	31132	2066
CAD/CAM systems services: Computer Systems Design Services—*prof*	541512	7373
Caddy cars: Transportation Equipment, All Other—*mfg*	336999	3799
Caddy carts: Sporting and Athletic Goods—*mfg*	33992	3949
Cadmium refining, primary: Primary Smelting and Refining of Nonferrous Metal (except Copper and Aluminum)—*mfg*	331419	3339
Cafes: Cafeterias—*accom*	722212	5812
Caterers—*accom*	72232	5812
Foodservice Contractors—*accom*	72231	5812
Full-Service Restaurants—*accom*	72211	5812
Limited-Service Restaurants—*accom*	722211	5812
Snack and Nonalcoholic Beverage Bars—*accom*	722213	5812
Theater Companies and Dinner Theaters—*arts*	71111	5812
Cafeteria food warming equipment: Machinery, Other Commercial and Service Industry—*mfg*	333319	3589
Cafeteria furniture: Furniture—*whlse*	42121	5021
Furniture Stores—*retail*	44211	5021
Institutional Furniture—*mfg*	337127	2599
Cafeterias	**722212**	**5812**
Caterers—*accom*	72232	5812
Foodservice Contractors—*accom*	72231	5812
Full-Service Restaurants—*accom*	72211	5812
Limited-Service Restaurants—*accom*	722211	5812
Snack and Nonalcoholic Beverage Bars—*accom*	722213	5812
Theater Companies and Dinner Theaters—*arts*	71111	5812
Caffeine and derivatives: Medicinal and Botanical—*mfg*	325411	2833
Caftans: Men's and Boys' Cut and Sew Apparel Contractors—*mfg*	315211	2384
Men's and Boys' Cut and Sew Underwear and Nightwear—*mfg*	315221	2384
Women's and Girls' Cut and Sew Apparel Contractors—*mfg*	315212	2384

ALPHABETICAL INDEX	NAICS	SIC
Women's and Girls' Cut and Sew Lingerie, Loungewear and Nightwear—*mfg*	315231	2384
Cages, mine shaft: Mining Machinery and Equipment—*mfg*	333131	3532
Cages, wire–made from purchased wire: Fabricated Wire Product, Other—*mfg*	332618	3496
Caisson drilling–contractors: Heavy, All Other—*const*	23499	1629
Industrial Nonbuilding Structure—*const*	23493	1629
Caisson limbers: Ordnance and Accessories, Other—*mfg*	332995	3489
Caissons, metal plate: Air-Conditioning and Warm Air Heating Equipment and Commercial and Industrial Refrigeration Equipment—*mfg*	333415	3443
Metal Tank (Heavy Gauge)—*mfg*	33242	3443
Plate Work—*mfg*	332313	3443
Power Boiler and Heat Exchanger—*mfg*	33241	3443
Cake decorating supplies: Stores (except Tobacco Stores), All Other Miscellaneous—*retail*	453998	5999
Cake flour: Flour Milling—*mfg*	311211	2041
Flour Mixes and Dough from Purchased Flour—*mfg*	311822	2045
Cake mixes: Flour Mixes and Dough from Purchased Flour—*mfg*	311822	2045
Cake ornaments, confectionery: Confectionery from Purchased Chocolate—*mfg*	31133	2064
Non-Chocolate Confectionery—*mfg*	31134	2064
Cake, corn oil: Wet Corn Milling—*mfg*	311221	2046
Cakes, bakery, except frozen: Bakeries, Commercial—*mfg*	311812	2051
Cakes, frozen–packaged: Packaged Frozen Food—*whlse*	42242	5142
Cakes, frozen–pound, layer, and cheese: Frozen Bakery Product—*mfg*	311813	2053
Calamine mining: Lead Ore and Zinc Ore—*mining*	212231	1031
Calaverite mining: Gold Ore—*mining*	212221	1041
Calcareous tufa, crushed and broken: Crushed and Broken Limestone and Quarrying—*mining*	212312	1422
Calcareous tufa, dimension: Dimension Stone and Quarrying—*mining*	212311	1411
Calcimines: Paint and Wallpaper Stores—*retail*	44412	5198
Paint, Varnish and Supplies—*whlse*	42295	5198
Calcimines, dry and paste: Paint and Coating—*mfg*	32551	2851
Calcined petroleum coke: Petroleum and Coal Productsa, All Other—*mfg*	324199	2999
Calcining kilns (industrial furnaces): Industrial Process Furnace and Oven—*mfg*	333994	3567
Calcite mining: Crushed and Broken Stone and Quarrying, Other—*mining*	212319	1499
Non-Metallic Mineral, All Other—*mining*	212399	1499
Calcium acetate, product of hardwood distillation: Gum and Wood Chemical—*mfg*	325191	2861
Calcium arsenate and arsenite, formulated: Pesticide and Other Agricultural Chemical—*mfg*	32532	2879

ALPHABETICAL INDEX	NAICS	SIC
Calcium carbide, chloride, and hypochlorite: Basic Inorganic Chemical, All Other—*mfg*	325188	2819
Chemical Product, All Other Miscellaneous—*mfg*	325998	2819
Calcium compounds, inorganic: Basic Inorganic Chemical, All Other—*mfg*	325188	2819
Chemical Product, All Other Miscellaneous—*mfg*	325998	2819
Calcium meta-phosphates: Phosphatic Fertilizer—*mfg*	325312	2874
Calcium metal: Basic Inorganic Chemical, All Other—*mfg*	325188	2819
Chemical Product, All Other Miscellaneous—*mfg*	325998	2819
Calcium oxalate: Basic Organic Chemical, All Other—*mfg*	325199	2869
Calcium salts of sulfonated oils, fats, or greases: Surface Active Agent—*mfg*	325613	2843
Calculating machines: Office Equipment—*whlse*	42142	5044
Calculating machines, operator paced: Computer Peripheral Equipment, Other—*mfg*	334119	3578
Office Machinery—*mfg*	333313	3578
Calculating service, computer: Data Processing Services—*info*	51421	7374
Calendars, gravure printing–not publishing: Gravure Printing, Commercial—*mfg*	323111	2754
Calendars, lithographed–not published: Lithographic Printing, Commercial—*mfg*	323110	2752
Quick Printing—*mfg*	323114	2752
Calendars, printed; except lithographed or gravure: Digital Printing—*mfg*	323115	2759
Flexographic Printing, Commercial—*mfg*	323112	2759
Printing, Other Commercial—*mfg*	323119	2759
Quick Printing—*mfg*	323114	2759
Calendars–publishing and printing, or publishing only: Database and Directory Publishers—*info*	51114	2741
Music Publishers—*info*	51223	2741
Publishers, All Other—*info*	511199	2741
Calendering of cotton broadwoven fabrics: Broadwoven Fabric Finishing Mills—*mfg*	313311	2261
Calendering of manmade fiber and silk broadwoven fabrics: Broadwoven Fabric Finishing Mills—*mfg*	313311	2262
Calendering of wool, mohair, and similar animal fiber fabrics–except knit: Broadwoven Fabric Finishing Mills—*mfg*	313311	2231
Broadwoven Fabric Mills—*mfg*	31321	2231
Textile and Fabric Finishing (except Broadwoven Fabric) Mills—*mfg*	313312	2231
Calf savers (farm equipment): Farm Machinery and Equipment—*mfg*	333111	3523
Hand and Edge Tool—*mfg*	332212	3523
Calf's-foot jelly: Meat Processed from Carcasses—*mfg*	311612	2013
Calibration and certification (testing): Testing Laboratories—*prof*	54138	8734
Veterinary Services—*prof*	54194	8734
Calipers and dividers: Cutting Tool and Machine Tool Accessory—*mfg*	333515	3545

Hand and Edge Tool—*mfg*	332212	3545
Caiks, horseshce–forged-not made in rolling mills: Iron and Steel Forging—*mfg*	332111	3462
Calliopes (steam organs): Musical Instrument—*mfg*	339992	3931
Cambric, cotton: Broadwoven Fabric Mills—*mfg*	31321	2211
Cambric–varnished, waxed, and impregnated: Fabric Coating Mills—*mfg*	31332	2295
Camelback for tire retreading: Tire (except Retreading)—*mfg*	326211	3011
Camera and Photographic Supplies Stores	**44313**	**5946**
Camera carrying bags, regardless of material: Luggage—*mfg*	316991	3161
Camera repair shops: Electronic and Precision Equipment Repair and Maintenance, Other—*serv*	811219	7699
Sporting Goods Stores—*retail*	45111	7699
Camera shops, photographic: Camera and Photographic Supplies Stores—*retail*	44313	5946
Camera stores, video: Automotive Parts and Accessories Stores—*retail*	44131	5731
Radio, Television and Other Electronics Stores—*retail*	443112	5731
Cameras, equipment, and supplies: Photographic Equipment and Supplies—*whlse*	42141	5043
Cameras, microfilm: Photographic and Photocopying Equipment—*mfg*	333315	3861
Photographic Film, Paper, Plate and Chemical—*mfg*	325992	3861
Cameras, still and motion picture: Photographic and Photocopying Equipment—*mfg*	333315	3861
Photographic Film, Paper, Plate and Chemical—*mfg*	325992	3861
Cameras, television: Radio and Television Broadcasting and Wireless Communications Equipment—*mfg*	33422	3663
Camisoles: Infants' Cut and Sew Apparel—*mfg*	315291	2341
Women's and Girls' Cut and Sew Apparel Contractors—*mfg*	315212	2341
Women's and Girls' Cut and Sew Lingerie, Loungewear and Nightwear—*mfg*	315231	2341
Camouflage nets: Broadwoven Fabric Mills—*mfg*	31321	2211
Camouflage nets, not made in weaving mills: Rope, Cordage and Twine Mills—*mfg*	314991	2298
Camp furniture, metal: Metal Household Furniture—*mfg*	337124	2514
Camp furniture, reed and rattan: Household Furniture (except Wood and Metal)—*mfg*	337125	2519
Camp furniture, wood: Nonupholstered Wood Household Furniture—*mfg*	337122	2511
Campers (pickup coaches) for mounting on trucks: Automobile and Other Motor Vehicle—*whlse*	42111	5012
Recreational Vehicle Dealers—*retail*	44121	5561
Campers (recreational vehicles), rental: Truck, Utility Trailer, and RV (Recreational Vehicle) Rental and Leasing—*real*	53212	7519
Campers, for mounting on trucks: Travel Trailer and Camper—*mfg*	336214	3792
Campgrounds: RV (Recreational Vehicle) Parks and Campgrounds—*accom*	721211	7033
Camphor, synthetic: Basic Organic Chemical, All Other—*mfg*	325199	2869
Camping equipment: Sporting and Recreational Goods and Supplies—*whlse*	42191	5091
Sporting Goods Stores—*retail*	45111	5941
Camping tents and equipment: Sporting and Recreational Goods and Supplies—*whlse*	42191	5091
Camping trailers and chassis: Travel Trailer and Camper—*mfg*	336214	3792
Camps, sporting and recreational: Recreational and Vacation Camps—*accom*	721214	7032
Campsites for transients: RV (Recreational Vehicle) Parks and Campgrounds—*accom*	721211	7033
Cams (machine tool accessories): Cutting Tool and Machine Tool Accessory—*mfg*	333515	3545
Hand and Edge Tool—*mfg*	332212	3545
Camshafts, motor vehicle gasoline engine: Gasoline Engine and Engine Parts—*mfg*	336312	3714
Motor Vehicle Parts, All Other—*mfg*	336399	3714
Can keys, made from purchased wire: Fabricated Wire Product, Other—*mfg*	332618	3496
Can lids and ends, metal: Metal Can—*mfg*	332431	3411
Can making machines: Machine Tool (Metal Forming Types)—*mfg*	333513	3542
Can openers, electric: Electric Housewares and Household Fan—*mfg*	335211	3634
Heating Equipment (except Electric and Warm Air Furnaces)—*mfg*	333414	3634
Can openers, except electric: Hand and Edge Tool—*mfg*	332212	3423
Canal barge operations: Inland Water Freight—*trans*	483211	4449
Canal construction–general contractors: Heavy, All Other—*const*	23499	1629
Industrial Nonbuilding Structure—*const*	23493	1629
Canal freight transportation: Inland Water Freight—*trans*	483211	4449
Canal operation: Air, Rail, and Water Equipment Rental and Leasing, Commercial—*real*	532411	4499
Navigational Services to Shipping—*trans*	48833	4499
Port and Harbor Operations—*trans*	48831	4499
Water, Other Support Activities for—*trans*	48839	4499
Canceling machinery, post office: Lead Pencil and Art Good—*mfg*	339942	3579
Office Machinery—*mfg*	333313	3579
Watch, Clock, and Part—*mfg*	334518	3579
Cancer detection program administration: Public Health Programs, Administration of—*pub*	92312	9431
Cancer hospitals: General Medical and Surgical Hospitals—*hlth*	62211	8069
Hospitals (except Psychiatric and Substance Abuse), Specialty—*hlth*	62231	8069
Psychiatric and Substance Abuse Hospitals—*hlth*	62221	8069
Candelabra tubes, fiber: Fiber Can, Tube, Drum, and Similar Products—*mfg*	322214	2655
Candied fruits and fruit peel: Confectionery from Purchased Chocolate—*mfg*	31133	2064
Non-Chocolate Confectionery—*mfg*	31134	2064
Candle pin centers: Bowling Centers—*arts*	71395	7933

ALPHABETICAL INDEX	NAICS	SIC
Candle shops: Stores (except Tobacco Stores), All Other Miscellaneous—*retail*	453998	5999
Candles: Nondurable Goods, Other Miscellaneous—*whlse*	42299	5199
Candlesticks, glass: Pressed and Blown Glass and Glassware, Other—*mfg*	327212	3229
Candy: Confectionery—*whlse*	42245	5145
Candy bars, except solid chocolate: Confectionery from Purchased Chocolate—*mfg*	31133	2064
Non-Chocolate Confectionery—*mfg*	31134	2064
Candy stores: Confectionery and Nut Stores—*retail*	445292	5441
Candy, except solid chocolate: Confectionery from Purchased Chocolate—*mfg*	31133	2064
Non-Chocolate Confectionery—*mfg*	31134	2064
Candy, solid chocolate: Chocolate and Confectionery from Cacao Beans—*mfg*	31132	2066
Cane farms, sugar: Sugar Beet Farming—*ag*	111991	133
Sugarcane Farming—*ag*	11193	133
Cane knives: Hand and Edge Tool—*mfg*	332212	3423
Cane sugar refineries: Cane Sugar Refining—*mfg*	311312	2062
Cane Sugar Refining	**311312**	**2062**
Cane sugar, made from sugarcane: Sugarcane Mills—*mfg*	311311	2061
Cane syrup, made from sugarcane: Sugarcane Mills—*mfg*	311311	2061
Cane syrup, made in sugar refineries from purchased sugar: Cane Sugar Refining—*mfg*	311312	2062
Cane, chair–woven of reed or rattan: Manufacturing, All Other Miscellaneous—*mfg*	339999	2499
Wood Container and Pallet—*mfg*	32192	2499
Wood Product, All Other Miscellaneous—*mfg*	321999	2499
Canes and cane trimmings, except precious metal: Wood Product, All Other Miscellaneous—*mfg*	321999	3999
Canes, orthopedic: Surgical Appliance and Supplies—*mfg*	339113	3842
Canisters, ammunition: Ammunition (except Small Arms)—*mfg*	332993	3483
Canned fish, crustacea, and mollusks: Seafood Canning—*mfg*	311711	2091
Canned fruits and vegetables: Fruit and Vegetable Canning—*mfg*	311421	2033
Canned goods–fruits, vegetables, fish, sea-foods, meats, and milk: Grocery and Related Products, Other—*whlse*	42249	5149
Canned meats, except baby foods and animal feeds: Meat Processed from Carcasses—*mfg*	311612	2013
Canned specialties: Grocery and Related Products, Other—*whlse*	42249	5149
Canning, Specialty	**311422**	**2032**
Cannons, more than 30 mm. (or more than 1.18 inch): Ordnance and Accessories, Other—*mfg*	332995	3489
Cannulae: Surgical and Medical Instrument—*mfg*	339112	3841
Canoe rental: Recreational Goods Rental—*real*	532292	7999
Canoes, building and repairing: Boat Building—*mfg*	336612	3732
Personal and Household Goods Repair and Maintenance, Other—*serv*	81149	3732
Canopies, fabric: Canvas and Related Product Mills—*mfg*	314912	2394
Canopies, sheet metal: Metal Container, Other—*mfg*	332439	3444
Sheet Metal Work—*mfg*	332322	3444
Cans for fruits and vegetables: Industrial Machinery and Equipment—*whlse*	42183	5085
Industrial Supplies—*whlse*	42184	5085
Cans, aluminum: Metal Can—*mfg*	332431	3411
Cans, ash and garbage–stamped and pressed metal: Kitchen Utensil, Pot and Pan—*mfg*	332214	3469
Cans, composite–foil-fiber and other combinations: Fiber Can, Tube, Drum, and Similar Products—*mfg*	322214	2655
Cans, fiber (metal-en or all-fiber): Fiber Can, Tube, Drum, and Similar Products—*mfg*	322214	2655
Cans, metal: Metal Can—*mfg*	332431	3411
Cans, retinning of; not done in rolling mills: Costume Jewelry and Novelty—*mfg*	339914	3479
Jewelry (except Costume)—*mfg*	339911	3479
Metal Coating, Engraving (except Jewelry and Silverware), and Allied Services to Manufacturers—*mfg*	332812	3479
Silverware and Plated Ware—*mfg*	339912	3479
Cant hooks (handtools): Hand and Edge Tool—*mfg*	332212	3423
Cantaloup farms: Vegetable (except Potato) and Melon Farming, Other—*ag*	111219	161
Canton crepes: Broadwoven Fabric Mills—*mfg*	31321	2221
Canton flannels, cotton: Broadwoven Fabric Mills—*mfg*	31321	2211
Cants, resawed (lumber): Cut Stock, Resawing Lumber, and Planing—*mfg*	321912	2421
Millwork (including Flooring), Other—*mfg*	321918	2421
Sawmills—*mfg*	321113	2421
Wood Product, All Other Miscellaneous—*mfg*	321999	2421
Canvas: Broadwoven Fabric Mills—*mfg*	31321	2211
Canvas and Related Product Mills	**314912**	**2394**
Canvas board, artists': Chemical Product, All Other Miscellaneous—*mfg*	325998	3952
Institutional Furniture—*mfg*	337127	3952
Lead Pencil and Art Good—*mfg*	339942	3952
Canvas products: Nondurable Goods, Other Miscellaneous—*whlse*	42299	5199
Canvas products, except bags and knapsacks: Canvas and Related Product Mills—*mfg*	314912	2394
Canvas shoes, rubber soled: Rubber and Plastics Footwear—*mfg*	316211	3021
Canvas, artists'–prepared on frames: Chemical Product, All Other Miscellaneous—*mfg*	325998	3952
Institutional Furniture—*mfg*	337127	3952
Lead Pencil and Art Good—*mfg*	339942	3952
Canvassers (door-to-door), headquarters for retail sale of merchandise: Direct Selling Establishments, Other—*retail*	45439	5963
Mobile Foodservices—*accom*	72233	5963

Description	NAICS	SIC
Cap fronts and visors: Apparel Accessories and Apparel, Other—*mfg*	315999	2396
Textile Product Mills, All Other Miscellaneous—*mfg*	314999	2396
Capacitor and condenser cans and cases–stamped metal: Metal Stamping—*mfg*	332116	3469
Capacitor paper: Newsprint Mills—*mfg*	322122	2621
Paper (except Newsprint) Mills—*mfg*	322121	2621
Capacitors, a.c.–for motors and fluorescent lamp ballasts: Electrical Equipment and Component, All Other Miscellaneous—*mfg*	335999	3629
Capacitors, electronic: Electronic Parts and Equipment, Other—*whlse*	42169	5065
Capacitors, electronic–fixed and variable: Electronic Capacitor—*mfg*	334414	3675
Capacitors, except electronic: Building Material Dealers, Other—*retail*	44419	5063
Electrical Apparatus and Equipment, Wiring Supplies and Material—*whlse*	42161	5063
Capacitors, except electronic–fixed and variable: Electrical Equipment and Component, All Other Miscellaneous—*mfg*	335999	3629
Capes, except fur and vulcanized rubber: Women's and Girls' Cut and Sew Apparel Contractors—*mfg*	315212	2337
Women's and Girls' Cut and Sew Suit, Coat, Tailored Jacket and Skirt—*mfg*	315234	2337
Capes, fur: Fur and Leather Apparel—*mfg*	315292	2371
Capes, vulcanized rubber and rubberized fabric: Fabric Coating Mills—*mfg*	31332	3069
Rubber Product, All Other—*mfg*	326299	3069
Caprolactam: Basic Organic Chemical, All Other—*mfg*	325199	2869
Caps: Outerwear Knitting Mills—*mfg*	315191	2253
Caps and gowns, academic: Cut and Sew Apparel, All Other—*mfg*	315299	2389
Caps and gowns–women's and children's: Women's, Children's, and Infants' and Accessories—*whlse*	42233	5137
Caps and plugs, attachment–electric: Current-Carrying Wiring Device—*mfg*	335931	3643
Caps and tops, bottle–die cut from purchased paper or paperboard: Converted Paper Product, All Other—*mfg*	322298	2675
Die-Cut Paper and Paperboard Office Supplies—*mfg*	322231	2675
Surface-Coated Paperboard—*mfg*	322292	2675
Caps and tops, bottle–stamped metal: Crown and Closure—*mfg*	332115	3466
Caps, blasting and detonating: Explosives—*mfg*	32592	2892
Caps, bolt–vitreous china and earthenware: Vitreous China Plumbing Fixture and China and Earthenware Fittings and Bathroom Accessories—*mfg*	327111	3261
Caps, bomb: Ammunition (except Small Arms)—*mfg*	332993	3483
Caps, cloth: Hat, Cap and Millinery—*mfg*	315991	2353
Caps, for toy pistols: Basic Organic Chemical, All Other—*mfg*	325199	2899
Chemical Product, All Other Miscellaneous—*mfg*	325998	2899
Caps, fur: Fur and Leather Apparel—*mfg*	315292	2371
Caps, heel and toe–leather or metal: Fastener, Button, Needle and Pin—*mfg*	339993	3131
Leather Good, All Other—*mfg*	316999	3131
Wood Product, All Other Miscellaneous—*mfg*	321999	3131
Caps, leather: Fur and Leather Apparel—*mfg*	315292	2386
Caps, men's and boys': Men's and Boys' Clothing and Furnishings—*whlse*	42232	5136
Caps, plastics: Plastics Pipe and Pipe Fitting—*mfg*	326122	3089
Plastics Product, All Other—*mfg*	326199	3089
Unsupported Plastics Profile Shape—*mfg*	326121	3089
Caps, rubber: Fabric Coating Mills—*mfg*	31332	3069
Rubber Product, All Other—*mfg*	326299	3069
Caps–textiles, straw, fur-felt, and wool felt: Hat, Cap and Millinery—*mfg*	315991	2353
Caps–women 5 and children's: Women's, Children's, and Infants' and Accessories—*whlse*	42233	5137
Capstans, ship: Construction Machinery—*mfg*	33312	3531
Overhead Traveling Crane, Hoist and Monorail System—*mfg*	333923	3531
Railroad Rolling Stock—*mfg*	33651	3531
Capsules, gelatin–empty: Basic Organic Chemical, All Other—*mfg*	325199	2899
Chemical Product, All Other Miscellaneous—*mfg*	325998	2899
Car bodies, including fiberglass: Automobile—*mfg*	336111	3711
Heavy Duty Truck—*mfg*	33612	3711
Light Truck and Utility Vehicle—*mfg*	336112	3711
Military Armored Vehicle, Tank and Tank Component—*mfg*	336992	3711
Motor Vehicle Body—*mfg*	336211	3711
Car dumpers, mining: Mining Machinery and Equipment—*mfg*	333131	3532
Car lighters (ferries): Coastal and Great Lakes Passenger—*trans*	483114	4482
Inland Water Passenger—*trans*	483212	4482
Car loading: Rail Support Activities—*trans*	48821	4789
Scenic and Sightseeing, Land—*trans*	48711	4789
Transportation, All Other Support Activities—*trans*	488999	4789
Car seals, metal: Hardware—*mfg*	33251	3429
Car title and tag service: Personal Services, All Other—*serv*	81299	7299
Car Washes	**811192**	**7542**
Car wheels, railroad–chilled cast iron: Iron Foundries—*mfg*	331511	3321
Car wheels, rolled: Iron and Steel Mills—*mfg*	331111	3312
Petroleum and Coal Productsa, All Other—*mfg*	324199	3312
Carafes, plastics: Plastics Pipe and Pipe Fitting—*mfg*	326122	3089
Plastics Product, All Other—*mfg*	326199	3089
Unsupported Plastics Profile Shape—*mfg*	326121	3089
Carbide: Basic Inorganic Chemical, All Other—*mfg*	325188	2819
Chemical Product, All Other Miscellaneous—*mfg*	325998	2819
Carbines, 30 mm. (or 1.18 inch) or less: Small Arms—*mfg*	332994	3484
Carbohydrate plastics: Plastics Material and Resin—*mfg*	325211	2821
Carbohydrates, nitrated (explosives): Explosives—*mfg*	32592	2892
Carbon and Graphite Product Manufacturing	**335991**	**3624**
Carbon arc lamp units, electrotherapeutic–except infrared and ultraviolet: Electromedical and Electrotherapeutic Apparatus—*mfg*	334510	3845
Irradiation Apparatus—*mfg*	334517	3845

ALPHABETICAL INDEX	NAICS	SIC
Carbon bisulfide (disulfide): Basic Organic Chemical, All Other—*mfg*	325199	2869
Carbon black: Carbon Black—*mfg*	325182	2895
Chemical and Allied Products, Other—*whlse*	42269	5169
Carbon Black Manufacturing	**325182**	**2895**
Carbon brick: Nonclay Refractory—*mfg*	327125	3297
Carbon dioxide: Industrial Gas—*mfg*	32512	2813
Carbon paper: Carbon Paper and Inked Ribbon—*mfg*	339944	3955
Office Supplies and Stationery Stores—*retail*	45321	5112
Stationary and Office Supplies—*whlse*	42212	5112
Carbon Paper and Inked Ribbon Manufacturing	**339944**	**3955**
Carbon removing solvent: Basic Organic Chemical, All Other—*mfg*	325199	2899
Chemical Product, All Other Miscellaneous—*mfg*	325998	2899
Carbon specialties for electrical use: Carbon and Graphite Product—*mfg*	335991	3624
Carbon tetrachloride: Basic Organic Chemical, All Other—*mfg*	325199	2869
Carbon, activated: Basic Inorganic Chemical, All Other—*mfg*	325188	2819
Chemical Product, All Other Miscellaneous—*mfg*	325998	2819
Carbonated beverages, nonalcoholic–bottled or canned: Bottled Water—*mfg*	312112	2086
Soft Drink—*mfg*	312111	2086
Carbonates, potassium and sodium–not produced at mines: Alkalies and Chlorine—*mfg*	325181	2812
Carbonized rags: Broadwoven Fabric Mills—*mfg*	31321	2299
Narrow Fabric Mills—*mfg*	313221	2299
Nonwoven Fabric Mills—*mfg*	31323	2299
Textile and Fabric Finishing (except Broadwoven Fabric) Mills—*mfg*	313312	2299
Textile Product Mills, All Other Miscellaneous—*mfg*	314999	2299
Thread Mills—*mfg*	313113	2299
Yarn Spinning Mills—*mfg*	313111	2299
Carbonizing equipment (wool processing machinery): Textile Machinery—*mfg*	333292	3552
Carbonizing of wool, mohair, and similar fibers: Broadwoven Fabric Mills—*mfg*	31321	2299
Narrow Fabric Mills—*mfg*	313221	2299
Nonwoven Fabric Mills—*mfg*	31323	2299
Textile and Fabric Finishing (except Broadwoven Fabric) Mills—*mfg*	313312	2299
Textile Product Mills, All Other Miscellaneous—*mfg*	314999	2299
Thread Mills—*mfg*	313113	2299
Yarn Spinning Mills—*mfg*	313111	2299
Carbons, electric: Carbon and Graphite Product—*mfg*	335991	3624
Carbons, lighting: Carbon and Graphite Product—*mfg*	335991	3624
Carboys, glass: Glass Container—*mfg*	327213	3221
Carburetor repair: Automotive Mechanical and Electrical Repair and Maintenance, Other—*serv*	811118	7539

ALPHABETICAL INDEX	NAICS	SIC
Carburetor, Piston, Piston Ring and Valve Manufacturing	**336311**	**3592**
Carburetors, all types: Carburetor, Piston, Piston Ring and Valve—*mfg*	336311	3592
Card advertising: Advertising Material Distribution Services—*prof*	54187	7319
Advertising, Other Services Related to—*prof*	54189	7319
Display Advertising—*prof*	54185	7319
Media Buying Agencies—*prof*	54183	7319
Nonscheduled Air, Other—*trans*	481219	7319
Card cases, except precious metal: Personal Leather Good (except Women's Handbag and Purse)—*mfg*	316993	3172
Card clothing for textile machines: Textile Machinery—*mfg*	333292	3552
Card cutting: Converted Paper Product, All Other—*mfg*	322298	2675
Die-Cut Paper and Paperboard Office Supplies—*mfg*	322231	2675
Surface-Coated Paperboard—*mfg*	322292	2675
Card punching and sorting machines: Computer Peripheral Equipment, Other—*mfg*	334119	3577
Card rooms: Gambling Industries, Other—*arts*	71329	7999
Card-type conversion equipment, computer peripheral equipment: Computer Peripheral Equipment, Other—*mfg*	334119	3577
Cardboard: Paperboard Mills—*mfg*	32213	2631
Cardboard and products: Industrial and Personal Service Paper—*whlse*	42213	5113
Cardboard foundations and cutouts: Converted Paper Product, All Other—*mfg*	322298	2675
Die-Cut Paper and Paperboard Office Supplies—*mfg*	322231	2675
Surface-Coated Paperboard—*mfg*	322292	2675
Cardboard panels and cutouts: Converted Paper Product, All Other—*mfg*	322298	2675
Die-Cut Paper and Paperboard Office Supplies—*mfg*	322231	2675
Surface-Coated Paperboard—*mfg*	322292	2675
Cardboard–pasted, laminated, lined, and surface coated: Converted Paper Product, All Other—*mfg*	322298	2675
Die-Cut Paper and Paperboard Office Supplies—*mfg*	322231	2675
Surface-Coated Paperboard—*mfg*	322292	2675
Carded fiber, asbestos: Motor Vehicle Brake System—*mfg*	33634	3292
Nonmetallic Mineral Product, All Other Miscellaneous—*mfg*	327999	3292
Carded yarn, cotton: Yarn Spinning Mills—*mfg*	313111	2281
Carding machines, textile: Textile Machinery—*mfg*	333292	3552
Cardiodynameter: Electromedical and Electrotherapeutic Apparatus—*mfg*	334510	3845
Irradiation Apparatus—*mfg*	334517	3845
Cardiographs: Electromedical and Electrotherapeutic Apparatus—*mfg*	334510	3845
Irradiation Apparatus—*mfg*	334517	3845
Cardiophone, electric: Electromedical and Electrotherapeutic Apparatus—*mfg*	334510	3845
Irradiation Apparatus—*mfg*	334517	3845

Description	NAICS	SIC
Cardioscope: Electromedical and Electrotherapeutic Apparatus—*mfg*	334510	3845
Irradiation Apparatus—*mfg*	334517	3845
Cardiotachometer: Electromedical and Electrotherapeutic Apparatus—*mfg*	334510	3845
Irradiation Apparatus—*mfg*	334517	3845
Cards, cut and designed–unprinted: Converted Paper Product, All Other—*mfg*	322298	2675
Die-Cut Paper and Paperboard Office Supplies—*mfg*	322231	2675
Surface-Coated Paperboard—*mfg*	322292	2675
Cards, except greeting cards–engraving of: Digital Printing—*mfg*	323115	2759
Flexographic Printing, Commercial—*mfg*	323112	2759
Printing, Other Commercial—*mfg*	323119	2759
Quick Printing—*mfg*	323114	2759
Cards, except greeting–gravure printing: Gravure Printing, Commercial—*mfg*	323111	2754
Cards, greeting, except hand painted: Flexographic Printing, Commercial—*mfg*	323112	2771
Gravure Printing, Commercial—*mfg*	323111	2771
Greeting Card Publishers—*info*	511191	2771
Lithographic Printing, Commercial—*mfg*	323110	2771
Printing, Other Commercial—*mfg*	323119	2771
Screen Printing, Commercial—*mfg*	323113	2771
Cards, index–die-cut: Converted Paper Product, All Other—*mfg*	322298	2675
Die-Cut Paper and Paperboard Office Supplies—*mfg*	322231	2675
Surface-Coated Paperboard—*mfg*	322292	2675
Cards, jacquard: Converted Paper Product, All Other—*mfg*	322298	2675
Die-Cut Paper and Paperboard Office Supplies—*mfg*	322231	2675
Surface-Coated Paperboard—*mfg*	322292	2675
Cards, jewelers: Converted Paper Product, All Other—*mfg*	322298	2675
Die-Cut Paper and Paperboard Office Supplies—*mfg*	322231	2675
Surface-Coated Paperboard—*mfg*	322292	2675
Cards, lithographed: Lithographic Printing, Commercial—*mfg*	323110	2752
Quick Printing—*mfg*	323114	2752
Cards, plain paper–die-cut or rotary cut from purchased materials: Converted Paper Product, All Other—*mfg*	322298	2675
Die-Cut Paper and Paperboard Office Supplies—*mfg*	322231	2675
Surface-Coated Paperboard—*mfg*	322292	2675
Cards, playing–except lithographed or gravure: Digital Printing—*mfg*	323115	2759
Flexographic Printing, Commercial—*mfg*	323112	2759
Printing, Other Commercial—*mfg*	323119	2759
Quick Printing—*mfg*	323114	2759
Cards, playing–gravure Printing: Gravure Printing, Commercial—*mfg*	323111	2754
Cards, printed–except greeting, lithographed or gravure: Digital Printing—*mfg*	323115	2759
Flexographic Printing, Commercial—*mfg*	323112	2759
Printing, Other Commercial—*mfg*	323119	2759
Quick Printing—*mfg*	323114	2759
Cards, tabulating and time recording–die-cut from purchased paperboard: Converted Paper Product, All Other—*mfg*	322298	2675
Die-Cut Paper and Paperboard Office Supplies—*mfg*	322231	2675
Surface-Coated Paperboard—*mfg*	322292	2675
Cards–beveling, bronzing, deckling, edging, and gilding: Tradebinding and Related Work—*mfg*	323121	2789
Cargo checkers and surveyors, marine: Road, Other Support Activities for—*trans*	48849	4785
Water, Other Support Activities for—*trans*	48839	4785
Cargo nets (cordage): Rope, Cordage and Twine Mills—*mfg*	314991	2298
Cargo salvaging, from distressed vessels: Air, Rail, and Water Equipment Rental and Leasing, Commercial—*real*	532411	4499
Navigational Services to Shipping—*trans*	48833	4499
Port and Harbor Operations—*trans*	48831	4499
Water, Other Support Activities for—*trans*	48839	4499
Cargo vessels, building and repairing: Ship Building and Repairing—*mfg*	336611	3731
Carillon bells: Musical Instrument—*mfg*	339992	3931
Carnival amusement rides: Fabricated Metal Product, All Other Miscellaneous—*mfg*	332999	3599
General Purpose Machinery , All Other—*mfg*	333999	3599
Machine Shops—*mfg*	33271	3599
Machinery, Other Commercial and Service Industry—*mfg*	333319	3599
Carnival and amusement park equipment: Cosmetics, Beauty Supplies and Perfume Stores—*retail*	44612	5087
Service Establishment Equipment and Supplies—*whlse*	42185	5087
Carnotite mining: Uranium-Radium-Vanadium Ore—*mining*	212291	1094
Carousels (merry-go-rounds): Fabricated Metal Product, All Other Miscellaneous—*mfg*	332999	3599
General Purpose Machinery , All Other—*mfg*	333999	3599
Machine Shops—*mfg*	33271	3599
Machinery, Other Commercial and Service Industry—*mfg*	333319	3599
Carpenters' handtools, except saws: Hand and Edge Tool—*mfg*	332212	3423
Carpentry and Floor Contractors	**2355**	
Carpentry Contractors	**23551**	**1751**
Carpentry work–contractors: Carpentry Contractors—*const*	23551	1751
Carpet and furniture cleaning on location: Carpet and Upholstery Cleaning Services—*admin*	56174	7217
Carpet and Rug Mills	**31411**	**2273**
Carpet and Upholstery Cleaning Services	**56174**	**7217**
Carpet cleaning and repairing plants: Carpet and Upholstery Cleaning Services—*admin*	56174	7217
Carpet cleaning on customers' premises: Carpet and Upholstery Cleaning Services—*admin*	56174	7217
Carpet laying or removal service–contractors: Floor Laying and Other Floor Contractors—*const*	23552	1752
Carpet linings, felt–except woven: Broadwoven Fabric Mills—*mfg*	31321	2299
Narrow Fabric Mills—*mfg*	313221	2299
Nonwoven Fabric Mills—*mfg*	31323	2299

ALPHABETICAL INDEX	NAICS	SIC
Textile and Fabric Finishing (except Broadwoven Fabric) Mills—*mfg*	313312	2299
Textile Product Mills, All Other Miscellaneous—*mfg*	314999	2299
Thread Mills—*mfg*	313113	2299
Yarn Spinning Mills—*mfg*	313111	2299
Carpet linings, textile–except felt: Household Textile Product Mills, Other—*mfg*	314129	2392
Carpet stores: Floor Covering Stores—*retail*	44221	5713
Carpet sweepers, except household electric vacuum sweepers: Machinery, Other Commercial and Service Industry—*mfg*	333319	3589
Carpet yarn, cotton: Yarn Spinning Mills—*mfg*	313111	2281
Carpet yarn–wool, mohair, or similar animal fibers: Yarn Spinning Mills—*mfg*	313111	2281
Carpets: Floor Covering Stores—*retail*	44221	5023
Carpets, asphalted felt-base (linoleum): Resilient Floor Covering—*mfg*	326192	3996
Carpets, cork: Manufacturing, All Other Miscellaneous—*mfg*	339999	2499
Wood Container and Pallet—*mfg*	32192	2499
Wood Product, All Other Miscellaneous—*mfg*	321999	2499
Carpets, textile fiber: Carpet and Rug Mills—*mfg*	31411	2273
Carpets–twisted paper, grass, reed, coir, sisal, jute, and rag: Carpet and Rug Mills—*mfg*	31411	2273
Carports, prefabricated–metal: Prefabricated Metal Building and Component—*mfg*	332311	3448
Carriages, baby: Game, Toy, and Children's Vehicle—*mfg*	339932	3944
Carriages, doll: Game, Toy, and Children's Vehicle—*mfg*	339932	3944
Carriages, gun–for artillery more than 30 mm. (or more than 1.18 inch): Ordnance and Accessories, Other—*mfg*	332995	3489
Carriages, horse-drawn–for hire: Rail Support Activities—*trans*	48821	4789
Scenic and Sightseeing, Land—*trans*	48711	4789
Transportation, All Other Support Activities—*trans*	488999	4789
Carrier cases and tables, mail–except wood: Showcase, Partition, Shelving, and Locker—*mfg*	337215	2542
Carrier equipment, radio communications: Radio and Television Broadcasting and Wireless Communications Equipment—*mfg*	33422	3663
Carrier equipment, telephone and telegraph: Electronic Coil, Transformer, and Other Inductor—*mfg*	334416	3661
Printed Circuit/Electronics Assembly—*mfg*	334418	3661
Telephone Apparatus—*mfg*	33421	3661
Carrier trays, wood: Wood Container and Pallet—*mfg*	32192	2441
Carriers, crane: Construction Machinery—*mfg*	33312	3531
Overhead Traveling Crane, Hoist and Monorail System—*mfg*	333923	3531
Railroad Rolling Stock—*mfg*	33651	3531
Carry-out restaurants: Cafeterias—*accom*	722212	5812
Caterers—*accom*	72232	5812
Foodservice Contractors—*accom*	72231	5812

ALPHABETICAL INDEX	NAICS	SIC
Full-Service Restaurants—*accom*	72211	5812
Limited-Service Restaurants—*accom*	722211	5812
Snack and Nonalcoholic Beverage Bars—*accom*	722213	5812
Theater Companies and Dinner Theaters—*arts*	71111	5812
Cars and car equipment, freight or passenger: Pump and Pumping Equipment—*mfg*	333911	3743
Railroad Rolling Stock—*mfg*	33651	3743
Cars for hot metal: Air-Conditioning and Warm Air Heating Equipment and Commercial and Industrial Refrigeration Equipment—*mfg*	333415	3443
Metal Tank (Heavy Gauge)—*mfg*	33242	3443
Plate Work—*mfg*	332313	3443
Power Boiler and Heat Exchanger—*mfg*	33241	3443
Cars, armored: Automobile—*mfg*	336111	3711
Heavy Duty Truck—*mfg*	33612	3711
Light Truck and Utility Vehicle—*mfg*	336112	3711
Military Armored Vehicle, Tank and Tank Component—*mfg*	336992	3711
Motor Vehicle Body—*mfg*	336211	3711
Cars, electric–for highway use: Automobile—*mfg*	336111	3711
Heavy Duty Truck—*mfg*	33612	3711
Light Truck and Utility Vehicle—*mfg*	336112	3711
Military Armored Vehicle, Tank and Tank Component—*mfg*	336992	3711
Motor Vehicle Body—*mfg*	336211	3711
Cars, electric–off-highway: Transportation Equipment, All Other—*mfg*	336999	3799
Cars, industrial–except automotive cars and trucks and mining cars: Fabricated Metal Product, All Other Miscellaneous—*mfg*	332999	3537
Industrial Truck, Tractor, Trailer and Stacker Machinery—*mfg*	333924	3537
Metal Container, Other—*mfg*	332439	3537
Cars, mining: Mining Machinery and Equipment—*mfg*	333131	3532
Cars, new and used: New Car Dealers—*retail*	44111	5511
Cars, play (children's vehicles): Game, Toy, and Children's Vehicle—*mfg*	339932	3944
Cars, used only: Used Car Dealers—*retail*	44112	5521
Carting, by truck or horse-drawn wagon: Freight (except Used Goods) Trucking, Local Specialized—*trans*	48422	4212
General Freight Trucking, Local—*trans*	48411	4212
Solid Waste Collection—*admin*	562111	4212
Carton packing machines: Packaging Machinery—*mfg*	333993	3565
Cartons, folding, except milk cartons–paperboard: Folding Paperboard Box—*mfg*	322212	2657
Cartoon motion picture production: Motion Picture and Video Production—*info*	51211	7812
Cartridge belts, sporting type: Sporting and Athletic Goods—*mfg*	33992	3949
Cartridge cases for ammunition, 30 mm.(or 1.18 inch) or less: Small Arms Ammunition—*mfg*	332992	3482

Cartridge cups, discs, and sheets–copper and copper alloy: Copper Rolling, Drawing and Extruding—*mfg*	331421	3351
Cartridge-activated hand power tools: Power-Driven Hand Tool—*mfg*	333991	3546
Cartridges, 30 mm. (or 1.18 inch) or less: Small Arms Ammunition—*mfg*	332992	3482
Cartridges, refill–for ballpoint pens: Pen and Mechanical Pencil—*mfg*	339941	3951
Carts for lawn and garden use: Hand and Edge Tool—*mfg*	332212	3524
Lawn and Garden Tractor and Home Lawn and Garden Equipment—*mfg*	333112	3524
Carts, caddy: Sporting and Athletic Goods—*mfg*	33992	3949
Carts, doll: Game, Toy, and Children's Vehicle—*mfg*	339932	3944
Carts, golf–hand: Sporting and Athletic Goods—*mfg*	33992	3949
Carts, grocery–made from purchased wire: Fabricated Wire Product, Other—*mfg*	332618	3496
Carts, machine gun and machine gun ammunition: Small Arms—*mfg*	332994	3484
Carts, restaurant: Institutional Furniture—*mfg*	337127	2599
Carved and turned wood (except furni-ture): Manufacturing, All Other Miscellaneous—*mfg*	339999	2499
Wood Container and Pallet—*mfg*	32192	2499
Wood Product, All Other Miscellaneous—*mfg*	321999	2499
Carving machine, woodworking: Sawmill and Woodworking Machinery—*mfg*	33321	3553
Carving sets, with metal handles andblades: Cutlery and Flatware (except Precious)—*mfg*	332211	3914
Silverware and Plated Ware—*mfg*	339912	3914
Carving sets–except all metal: Cutlery and Flatware (except Precious)—*mfg*	332211	3421
Carvings, furniture–wood: Cut Stock, Resawing Lumber, and Planing—*mfg*	321912	2426
Millwork (including Flooring), Other—*mfg*	321918	2426
Showcase, Partition, Shelving, and Locker—*mfg*	337215	2426
Wood Product, All Other Miscellaneous—*mfg*	321999	2426
Carwash equipment and supplies: Cosmetics, Beauty Supplies and Perfume Stores—*retail*	44612	5087
Service Establishment Equipment and Supplies—*whlse*	42185	5087
Carwashes: Car Washes—*serv*	811192	7542
Carwashing machinery, including coin-perated: Machinery, Other Commercial and Service Industry—*mfg*	333319	3589
Case leather: Leather and Hide Tanning and Finishing—*mfg*	31611	3111
Casein fibers: Noncellulosic Organic Fiber—*mfg*	325222	2824
Casein plastics: Plastics Material and Resin—*mfg*	325211	2821
Casein products, molded for the trade: Plastics Pipe and Pipe Fitting—*mfg*	326122	3089
Plastics Product, All Other—*mfg*	326199	3089
Unsupported Plastics Profile Shape—*mfg*	326121	3089
Casein, dry and wet: Dry, Condensed, and Evaporated Dairy Product—*mfg*	311514	2023
Casement cloth, cotton: Broadwoven Fabric Mills—*mfg*	31321	2211
Casements, aluminum: Metal Window and Door—*mfg*	332321	3442
Cases for watches: Watch, Clock, and Part—*mfg*	334518	3873
Cases, filing–except wood: Nonwood Office Furniture—*mfg*	337214	2522
Cases, filing–wood: Wood Office Furniture—*mfg*	337211	2521
Cases, gun and rod (sporting equipment): Sporting and Athletic Goods—*mfg*	33992	3949
Cases, jewelry–regardless of material: Personal Leather Good (except Women's Handbag and Purse)—*mfg*	316993	3172
Cases, luggage: Luggage—*mfg*	316991	3161
Cases, mailing–paper fiber (metal-end or all-fiber): Fiber Can, Tube, Drum, and Similar Products—*mfg*	322214	2655
Cases, musical instrument: Luggage—*mfg*	316991	3161
Cases, packing–wood-nailed or lockcorner: Wood Container and Pallet—*mfg*	32192	2441
Cases, plastics: Plastics Pipe and Pipe Fitting—*mfg*	326122	3089
Plastics Product, All Other—*mfg*	326199	3089
Unsupported Plastics Profile Shape—*mfg*	326121	3089
Cases, shipping–wood-nailed or lockcorner: Wood Container and Pallet—*mfg*	32192	2441
Cases, shipping–wood-wirebound: Wood Container and Pallet—*mfg*	32192	2449
Cases, show and display–refrigerated: Air-Conditioning and Warm Air Heating Equipment and Commercial and Industrial Refrigeration Equipment—*mfg*	333415	3585
Motor Vehicle Air-Conditioning—*mfg*	336391	3585
Cases–cigar, cigarette, and vanity-precious metal: Jewelry (except Costume)—*mfg*	339911	3911
Cases–radio, phonograph, and sewing machine-wood: Wood Television, Radio, and Sewing Machine Cabinet—*mfg*	337129	2517
Cash and stamp boxes, stamped metal: Metal Stamping—*mfg*	332116	3469
Cash grain farms–except wheat, rice, corn,and soybeans: Grain Farming, All Other—*ag*	111199	119
Cash registers: Office Equipment—*whlse*	42142	5044
Cash registers, including adding machines with cash drawers: Computer Peripheral Equipment, Other—*mfg*	334119	3578
Office Machinery—*mfg*	333313	3578
Casing fluids for curing fruits, spices, and tobacco: Basic Organic Chemical, All Other—*mfg*	325199	2869
Casing, boiler–metal plate: Air-Conditioning and Warm Air Heating Equipment and Commercial and Industrial Refrigeration Equipment—*mfg*	333415	3443
Metal Tank (Heavy Gauge)—*mfg*	33242	3443
Plate Work—*mfg*	332313	3443
Power Boiler and Heat Exchanger—*mfg*	33241	3443
Casing-head butane and propane production: Natural Gas Liquid Extraction—*mining*	211112	1321
Casings for missiles and missile components shipping and storage: Guided Missile and Space Vehicle Parts and Auxiliary Equipment, Other—*mfg*	336419	3769

ALPHABETICAL INDEX	NAICS	SIC
Casings, scroll: Air-Conditioning and Warm Air Heating Equipment and Commercial and Industrial Refrigeration Equipment—*mfg*	333415	3443
Metal Tank (Heavy Gauge)—*mfg*	33242	3443
Plate Work—*mfg*	332313	3443
Power Boiler and Heat Exchanger—*mfg*	33241	3443
Casings, sheet metal: Metal Container, Other—*mfg*	332439	3444
Sheet Metal Work—*mfg*	332322	3444
Casino Hotels	**72112**	**7011**
Casino hotels: Bed and Breakfast Inns—*accom*	721191	7011
Hotels (except Casino Hotels) and Motels—*accom*	72111	7011
Traveler Accommodation, All Other—*accom*	721199	7011
Casinos (except Casino Hotels)	**71321**	**7999**
Casket hardware: Metal Container, Other—*mfg*	332439	3429
Caskets, burial: Cosmetics, Beauty Supplies and Perfume Stores—*retail*	44612	5087
Service Establishment Equipment and Supplies—*whlse*	42185	5087
Caskets, metal and wood: Burial Casket—*mfg*	339995	3995
Casks, wood–cooperod: Wood Container and Pallet—*mfg*	32192	2449
Casseroles, electric: Electric Housewares and Household Fan—*mfg*	335211	3634
Heating Equipment (except Electric and Warm Air Furnaces)—*mfg*	333414	3634
Cassettes, prerecorded–audio: Durable Goods, Other Miscellaneous—*whlse*	42199	5099
Cassettes, recording: Electronic Parts and Equipment, Other—*whlse*	42169	5065
Cast iron pipe: Iron Foundries—*mfg*	331511	3321
Metal Service Centers and Offices—*whlse*	42151	5051
Cast steel railroad car wheels: Steel Foundries, (except Investment)—*mfg*	331513	3325
Cast stone, concrete: Concrete Pipe—*mfg*	327332	3272
Concrete Product, Other—*mfg*	32739	3272
Nonmetallic Mineral Product, All Other Miscellaneous—*mfg*	327999	3272
Castable refractories, clay: Clay Refractory—*mfg*	327124	3255
Castable refractories, nonclay: Nonclay Refractory—*mfg*	327125	3297
Casters, furniture: Hardware—*mfg*	33251	3429
Casters, industrial: Hardware—*mfg*	33251	3429
Casting agencies, theatrical–except motion picture: Employment Placement Agencies—*admin*	56131	7922
Casting bureaus, motion picture: Employment Placement Agencies—*admin*	56131	7819
Independent Artists, Writers, and Performers—*arts*	71151	7819
Motion Picture and Video Industries, Other—*info*	512199	7819
Casting bureaus, theatrical–except motion picture: Employment Placement Agencies—*admin*	56131	7922
Casting of plastics for the trade, except foam plastics: Plastics Pipe and Pipe Fitting—*mfg*	326122	3089
Plastics Product, All Other—*mfg*	326199	3089

ALPHABETICAL INDEX	NAICS	SIC
Unsupported Plastics Profile Shape—*mfg*	326121	3089
Castings gray iron and semisteel: Iron Foundries—*mfg*	331511	3321
Castings, aluminum–except die-castings: Aluminum Foundries—*mfg*	331524	3365
Castings, compacted graphite iron: Iron Foundries—*mfg*	331511	3321
Castings, except die-castings and castings of aluminum and copper: Nonferrous Foundries, Other—*mfg*	331528	3369
Castings, except die-castings–brass, bronze, copper, and copper-base alloy: Copper Foundries—*mfg*	331525	3366
Castings, malleable iron: Iron Foundries—*mfg*	331511	3322
Castings, precision, except die-castings–industrial and aircraft use-cobalt-chromium: Nonferrous Foundries, Other—*mfg*	331528	3369
Castings, rough–iron and steel: Metal Service Centers and Offices—*whlse*	42151	5051
Castings, rubber: Fabric Coating Mills—*mfg*	31332	3069
Rubber Product, All Other—*mfg*	326299	3069
Castings, steel–except investment: Steel Foundries, (except Investment)—*mfg*	331513	3325
Castor oil and pomace: Fats and Oils Refining and Blending—*mfg*	311225	2076
Oilseed Processing, Other—*mfg*	311223	2076
Casual shoes, men's–except athletic and rubber footwear: Men's Footwear (except Athletic)—*mfg*	316213	3143
Casualty insurance and reinsurance: Real Estate, Other Activities Related to—*real*	53139	6531
Cat farms: Animal Production, All Other—*ag*	11299	279
Apiculture—*ag*	11291	279
Cat food: Dog and Cat Food—*mfg*	311111	2047
Catalog (order taking) offices of mailorder houses: Electronic Shopping and Mail-Order Houses—*retail*	45411	5961
Catalog paper: Newsprint Mills—*mfg*	322122	2621
Paper (except Newsprint) Mills—*mfg*	322121	2621
Catalog showrooms, general merchandise–except catalog mail-order: General Merchandise Stores, All Other—*retail*	45299	5399
Warehouse Clubs and Superstores—*retail*	45291	5399
Catalogs, printed–except lithographed or gravure (not publishing): Digital Printing—*mfg*	323115	2759
Flexographic Printing, Commercial—*mfg*	323112	2759
Printing, Other Commercial—*mfg*	323119	2759
Quick Printing—*mfg*	323114	2759
Catalogs–gravure printing (not publishing): Gravure Printing, Commercial—*mfg*	323111	2754
Catalogs–publishing and printing, or publishing only: Database and Directory Publishers—*info*	51114	2741
Music Publishers—*info*	51223	2741
Publishers, All Other—*info*	511199	2741
Catalysts, chemical: Basic Inorganic Chemical, All Other—*mfg*	325188	2819
Chemical Product, All Other Miscellaneous—*mfg*	325998	2819

Entry	NAICS	SIC
Catalytic converters, automotive–installation, repair, or sales and installation: Automotive Exhaust System Repair—*serv*	811112	7533
Catapult guns: Ordnance and Accessories, Other—*mfg*	332995	3489
Catapults: Fabricated Metal Product, All Other Miscellaneous—*mfg*	332999	3599
General Purpose Machinery , All Other—*mfg*	333999	3599
Machine Shops—*mfg*	33271	3599
Machinery, Other Commercial and Service Industry—*mfg*	333319	3599
Catch basin cleaning: Septic Tank and Related Services—*admin*	562991	7699
Catch basin covers, concrete: Concrete Pipe—*mfg*	327332	3272
Concrete Product, Other—*mfg*	32739	3272
Nonmetallic Mineral Product, All Other Miscellaneous—*mfg*	327999	3272
Categorical health program administration-govemment: Public Health Programs, Administration of—*pub*	92312	9431
Caterers	**72232**	**5812**
Cafeterias—*accom*	722212	5812
Foodservice Contractors—*accom*	72231	5812
Full-Service Restaurants—*accom*	72211	5812
Limited-Service Restaurants—*accom*	722211	5812
Snack and Nonalcoholic Beverage Bars—*accom*	722213	5812
Theater Companies and Dinner Theaters—*arts*	71111	5812
Catfish farms: Animal Aquaculture, Other—*ag*	112519	273
Finfish Farming and Fish Hatcheries—*ag*	112511	273
Shellfish Farming—*ag*	112512	273
Cathedral glass: Flat Glass—*mfg*	327211	3211
Catheters: Surgical and Medical Instrument—*mfg*	339112	3841
Cathode ray picture tubes: Electronic Parts and Equipment, Other—*whlse*	42169	5065
Cathode ray tube (CRT) teleprinter, multistation: Computer Terminal—*mfg*	334113	3575
Cathode ray tubes: Electron Tube—*mfg*	334411	3671
Catlinite mining: Crushed and Broken Stone and Quarrying, Other—*mining*	212319	1499
Non-Metallic Mineral, All Other—*mining*	212399	1499
Cats: Nondurable Goods, Other Miscellaneous—*whlse*	42299	5199
Catsup: Fruit and Vegetable Canning—*mfg*	311421	2033
Cattle: Livestock—*whlse*	42252	5154
Cattle dips: Pesticide and Other Agricultural Chemical—*mfg*	32532	2879
Cattle feeding farms: Cattle Feedlots—*ag*	112112	211
Cattle feeding, handling, and watering equipment: Conveyor and Conveying Equipment—*mfg*	333922	3523
Farm Machinery and Equipment—*mfg*	333111	3523
Cattle Feedlots	**112112**	**211**
Cattle feodlot operations: Cattle Feedlots—*ag*	112112	211
Cattle oilers (farm equipment): Farm Machinery and Equipment—*mfg*	333111	3523
Cattle raising farms: Beef Cattle Ranching and Farming—*ag*	112111	212
Cattle ranches: Beef Cattle Ranching and Farming—*ag*	112111	212
Cattle Ranching and Farming	**1121**	
Cattle slaughtering plants: Animal (except Poultry) Slaughtering—*mfg*	311611	2011
Cattle spraying: Animal Production Support Activities—*ag*	11521	751
Cauliflower farms: Vegetable (except Potato) and Melon Farming, Other—*ag*	111219	161
Caulking (construction)–contractors: Glass and Glazing Contractors—*const*	23592	1799
Trade Contractors, All Other Special—*const*	23599	1799
Caulking corn pounds: Adhesive—*mfg*	32552	2891
Caulking guns: Hand and Edge Tool—*mfg*	332212	3423
Caulking hammers: Power-Driven Hand Tool—*mfg*	333991	3546
Caulking tools, hand: Hand and Edge Tool—*mfg*	332212	3423
Causeway construction on structural supports–general contractors: Bridge and Tunnel—*const*	23412	1622
Caustic potash: Alkalies and Chlorine—*mfg*	325181	2812
Caustic soda: Alkalies and Chlorine—*mfg*	325181	2812
Chemical and Allied Products, Other—*whlse*	42269	5169
Caviar, canned: Seafood Canning—*mfg*	311711	2091
Cedar chests: Nonupholstered Wood Household Furniture—*mfg*	337122	2511
Ceiling lumber, dressod: Cut Stock, Resawing Lumber, and Planing—*mfg*	321912	2421
Millwork (including Flooring), Other—*mfg*	321918	2421
Sawmills—*mfg*	321113	2421
Wood Product, All Other Miscellaneous—*mfg*	321999	2421
Ceiling squares, concrete: Concrete Pipe—*mfg*	327332	3272
Concrete Product, Other—*mfg*	32739	3272
Nonmetallic Mineral Product, All Other Miscellaneous—*mfg*	327999	3272
Ceiling tile, unsupported plastics: Plastics Pipe and Pipe Fitting—*mfg*	326122	3089
Plastics Product, All Other—*mfg*	326199	3089
Unsupported Plastics Profile Shape—*mfg*	326121	3089
Ceilings, acoustical installation–contractors: Drywall, Plastering, Acoustical and Insulation Contractors—*const*	23542	1742
Ceilings, metal–erection and repair–contractors: Roofing, Siding and Sheet Metal Contractors—*const*	23561	1761
Ceilometers: Measuring and Controlling Device, Other—*mfg*	334519	3829
Surgical and Medical Instrument—*mfg*	339112	3829
Celery farms: Vegetable (except Potato) and Melon Farming, Other—*ag*	111219	161
Celestite mining: Chemical and Fertilizer Mineral, Other—*mining*	212393	1479
Cellophane adhesive tape: Coated and Laminated Paper—*mfg*	322222	2672
Cellos and parts: Musical Instrument—*mfg*	339992	3931
Cellular and Other Wireless Telecommunications	**513322**	**4899**
Cellular radio telephones: Radio and Television Broadcasting and Wireless Communications Equipment—*mfg*	33422	3663
Cellular telephone services: Cellular and Other Wireless Telecommunications—*info*	513322	4812
Paging—*info*	513321	4812
Telecommunications Resellers—*info*	51333	4812

ALPHABETICAL INDEX	NAICS	SIC
Celluloid products, molded for the trade: Plastics Pipe and Pipe Fitting—*mfg*	326122	3089
Plastics Product, All Other—*mfg*	326199	3089
Unsupported Plastics Profile Shape—*mfg*	326121	3089
Cellulose acetate (plastics): Plastics Material and Resin—*mfg*	325211	2821
Cellulose acetate monofflament, yarn, staple, or tow: Cellulosic Organic Fiber—*mfg*	325221	2823
Cellulose acetate, unplasticined: Basic Organic Chemical, All Other—*mfg*	325199	2869
Cellulose fibers, manmade: Cellulosic Organic Fiber—*mfg*	325221	2823
Cellulose fibers, regenerated: Cellulosic Organic Fiber—*mfg*	325221	2823
Cellulose nitrate resins: Plastics Material and Resin—*mfg*	325211	2821
Cellulose propionate (plastics): Plastics Material and Resin—*mfg*	325211	2821
Cellulose, regenerated–except fibers: Plastics Pipe and Pipe Fitting—*mfg*	326122	3089
Plastics Product, All Other—*mfg*	326199	3089
Unsupported Plastics Profile Shape—*mfg*	326121	3089
Cellulosic Organic Fiber Manufacturing	**325221**	**2823**
Cellulosic plastics film and sheet, unsupported: Unsupported Plastics Film and Sheet (except Packaging)—*mfg*	326113	3081
Cement: Brick, Stone and Related Material—*whlse*	42132	5032
Building Material Dealers, Other—*retail*	44419	5032
Cement (cellulose nitrate base): Adhesive—*mfg*	32552	2891
Cement and Concrete Product Manufacturing	**3273**	
Cement bags: Uncoated Paper and Multiwall Bag—*mfg*	322224	2674
Cement kilns, rotary: Industrial Machinery, All Other—*mfg*	333298	3559
Machinery, Other Commercial and Service Industry—*mfg*	333319	3559
Cement making machinery: Industrial Machinery and Equipment—*whlse*	42183	5084
Industrial Machinery, All Other—*mfg*	333298	3559
Machinery, Other Commercial and Service Industry—*mfg*	333319	3559
Cement Manufacturing	**32731**	**3241**
Cement rock, crushed and broken: Crushed and Broken Limestone and Quarrying—*mining*	212312	1422
Cement silos (batch plant): Construction Machinery—*mfg*	33312	3531
Overhead Traveling Crane, Hoist and Monorail System—*mfg*	333923	3531
Railroad Rolling Stock—*mfg*	33651	3531
Cement, clay refractory: Clay Refractory—*mfg*	327124	3255
Cement, dental: Dental Equipment and Supplies—*mfg*	339114	3843
Cement, hydraulic–portland, natural, masonry, and pozzolana: Cement—*mfg*	32731	3241
Cement, Keene's: Gypsum and Gypsum Product—*mfg*	32742	3275
Cement, linoleum: Adhesive—*mfg*	32552	2891
Cement, magnesia: Nonclay Refractory—*mfg*	327125	3297
Cement, mending: Adhesive—*mfg*	32552	2891
Cement, roofmg–asphalt, fibrous plastics: Asphalt Shingle and Coating Materials—*mfg*	324122	2952

ALPHABETICAL INDEX	NAICS	SIC
Cement, rubber: Adhesive—*mfg*	32552	2891
Cement–high temperature, refractory(nonclay): Nonclay Refractory—*mfg*	327125	3297
Cementing oil and gas well casings on a contract basis: Oil and Gas Operations Support Activities—*mining*	213112	1389
Cemeteries and Crematories	**81222**	**6553**
Cemeteries-real estate operation: Cemeteries and Crematories—*serv*	81222	6553
Cemetery associations: Cemeteries and Crematories—*serv*	81222	6553
Cemetery management service: Cemeteries and Crematories—*serv*	81222	6531
Cemetery upkeep, independent: Landscaping Services—*admin*	56173	782
Centering machines: Machine Tool (Metal Cutting Types)—*mfg*	333512	3541
Centerpieces, glass: Pressed and Blown Glass and Glassware, Other—*mfg*	327212	3229
Centers for documentation: Libraries and Archives—*info*	51412	8231
Centers for senior citizens: Child and Youth Services—*hlth*	62411	8322
Community Food Services—*hlth*	62421	8322
Community Housing Services, Other—*hlth*	624229	8322
Emergency and Other Relief Services—*hlth*	62423	8322
Individual and Family Services, Other—*hlth*	62419	8322
Parole Offices and Probation Offices—*pub*	92215	8322
Services for the Elderly and Persons with Disabilities—*hlth*	62412	8322
Temporary Shelters—*hlth*	624221	8322
Central liquidity facility: Financial Transactions Processing, Reserve, and Clearing House Activities—*fin*	52232	6019
Central station construction-general con tractors: Heavy, All Other—*const*	23499	1629
Industrial Nonbuilding Structure—*const*	23493	1629
Central-mixed concrete: Ready-Mix Concrete—*mfg*	32732	3273
Centrifugal purifiers: General Purpose Machinery , All Other—*mfg*	333999	3569
Centrifuges, industrial: General Purpose Machinery , All Other—*mfg*	333999	3569
Ceramic articles for craft shops: Vitreous China, Fine Earthenware and Other Pottery Product—*mfg*	327112	3269
Ceramic construction materials, except refractory: Brick, Stone and Related Material—*whlse*	42132	5032
Building Material Dealers, Other—*retail*	44419	5032
Ceramic fiber: Gypsum and Gypsum Product—*mfg*	32742	3299
Nonmetallic Mineral Product, All Other Miscellaneous—*mfg*	327999	3299
Ceramic glazed brick, clay: Brick and Structural Clay Tile—*mfg*	327121	3251
Ceramic kilns and furnaces: Industrial Process Furnace and Oven—*mfg*	333994	3567
Ceramic tile, floor and wall: Ceramic Wall and Floor Tile—*mfg*	327122	3253
Ceramic wall and floor tile: Brick, Stone and Related Material—*whlse*	42132	5032
Building Material Dealers, Other—*retail*	44419	5032
Ceramic Wall and Floor Tile Manufacturing	**327122**	**3253**
Ceramics schools: Schools and Instruction, All Other Miscellaneous—*educ*	611699	8299

Description	NAICS	SIC
Ceramics supplies: Hobby, Toy and Game Stores—*retail*	45112	5945
Cercal preparations and breakfast foods: Breakfast Cereal—*mfg*	31123	2043
Coffee and Tea—*mfg*	31192	2043
Cereals, cracked grain: Flour Milling—*mfg*	311211	2041
Cerium ore mining: Metal Ore, All Other—*mining*	212299	1099
Cerium salts: Basic Inorganic Chemical, All Other—*mfg*	325188	2819
Chemical Product, All Other Miscellaneous—*mfg*	325998	2819
Cerrusite mining: Lead Ore and Zinc Ore—*mining*	212231	1031
Certificates, security–engraved: Digital Printing—*mfg*	323115	2759
Flexographic Printing, Commercial—*mfg*	323112	2759
Printing, Other Commercial—*mfg*	323119	2759
Quick Printing—*mfg*	323114	2759
Certified public accountants (CPAs): Accounting Services, Other—*prof*	541219	8721
Certified Public Accountants, Offices Of—*prof*	541211	8721
Payroll Services—*prof*	541214	8721
Certified Public Accountants, Offices Of	**541211**	**8721**
Cervical collars: Surgical Appliance and Supplies—*mfg*	339113	3842
Cesium metal: Basic Inorganic Chemical, All Other—*mfg*	325188	2819
Chemical Product, All Other Miscellaneous—*mfg*	325998	2819
Cesspool cleaning: Septic Tank and Related Services—*admin*	562991	7699
Cesspool construction–contractors: Plumbing, Heating and Air-Conditioning Contractors—*const*	23511	1711
Chaffing dispensers, aircraft: Aircraft Part and Auxiliary Equipment, Other—*mfg*	336413	3728
Fluid Power Valve and Hose Fitting—*mfg*	332912	3728
Chafing dishes, electric: Electric Housewares and Household Fan—*mfg*	335211	3634
Heating Equipment (except Electric and Warm Air Furnaces)—*mfg*	333414	3634
Chain fittings: Hardware—*mfg*	33251	3429
Chain ladders, metal: Ornamental and Architectural Metal Work—*mfg*	332323	3446
Chain link fencing, steel–made in wire-drawing plants: Fabricated Wire Product, Other—*mfg*	332618	3315
Steel Wire Drawing—*mfg*	331222	3315
Chain saws, portable: Power-Driven Hand Tool—*mfg*	333991	3546
Chain type saw blades: Saw Blade and Handsaw—*mfg*	332213	3425
Chain, power transmission: Industrial Machinery and Equipment—*whlse*	42183	5085
Industrial Supplies—*whlse*	42184	5085
Mechanical Power Transmission Equipment—*mfg*	333613	3568
Chain, welded–made from purchased wire: Fabricated Wire Product, Other—*mfg*	332618	3496
Chain, wire–made from purchased wire: Fabricated Wire Product, Other—*mfg*	332618	3496
Chains, forged steel–not made in rolling mills: Iron and Steel Forging—*mfg*	332111	3462
Chains, surveyors': Measuring and Controlling Device, Other—*mfg*	334519	3829
Surgical and Medical Instrument—*mfg*	339112	3829
Chainsaws: Hardware Stores—*retail*	44413	5251
Industrial Machinery and Equipment—*whlse*	42183	5084
Chair and couch springs, assembled: Mattress—*mfg*	33791	2515
Upholstered Household Furniture—*mfg*	337121	2515
Chair beds, on frames of any material: Mattress—*mfg*	33791	2515
Upholstered Household Furniture—*mfg*	337121	2515
Chair covers, cloth: Household Textile Product Mills, Other—*mfg*	314129	2392
Chair frames for upholstered furniture,wood: Cut Stock, Resawing Lumber, and Planing—*mfg*	321912	2426
Millwork (including Flooring), Other—*mfg*	321918	2426
Showcase, Partition, Shelving, and Locker—*mfg*	337215	2426
Wood Product, All Other Miscellaneous—*mfg*	321999	2426
Chair frames, metal: Fabricated Metal Product, All Other Miscellaneous—*mfg*	332999	3499
Chair glides: Hardware—*mfg*	33251	3429
Chair pads, except felt: Household Textile Product Mills, Other—*mfg*	314129	2392
Chair seats, hardwood: Cut Stock, Resawing Lumber, and Planing—*mfg*	321912	2426
Millwork (including Flooring), Other—*mfg*	321918	2426
Showcase, Partition, Shelving, and Locker—*mfg*	337215	2426
Wood Product, All Other Miscellaneous—*mfg*	321999	2426
Chair stock, hardwood–turned, shaped, orcarved: Cut Stock, Resawing Lumber, and Planing—*mfg*	321912	2426
Millwork (including Flooring), Other—*mfg*	321918	2426
Showcase, Partition, Shelving, and Locker—*mfg*	337215	2426
Wood Product, All Other Miscellaneous—*mfg*	321999	2426
Chairs, bentwood: Nonupholstered Wood Household Furniture—*mfg*	337122	2511
Chairs, cane: Household Furniture (except Wood and Metal)—*mfg*	337125	2519
Chairs, dentists': Dental Equipment and Supplies—*mfg*	339114	3843
Chairs, household–except upholstered-wood: Nonupholstered Wood Household Furniture—*mfg*	337122	2511
Chairs, household–metal: Metal Household Furniture—*mfg*	337124	2514
Chairs, hydraulic–beauty and barbershop: Cosmetics, Beauty Supplies and Perfume Stores—*retail*	44612	5087
Service Establishment Equipment and Supplies—*whlse*	42185	5087
Chairs, office–except wood: Nonwood Office Furniture—*mfg*	337214	2522
Chairs, office–wood: Wood Office Furniture—*mfg*	337211	2521
Chairs, portable folding: Institutional Furniture—*mfg*	337127	2531
Chairs, tablet arm: Institutional Furniture—*mfg*	337127	2531
Chairs, upholstered on wood frames,except convertible beds: Upholstered Household Furniture—*mfg*	337121	2512
Chairs, wheel: Surgical Appliance and Supplies—*mfg*	339113	3842
Chairs–household, office, and public building: Furniture—*whlse*	42121	5021
Furniture Stores—*retail*	44211	5021
Chalcocite mining: Copper Ore and Nickel Ore—*mining*	212234	1021
Chalcopyrite mining: Copper Ore and Nickel Ore—*mining*	212234	1021

ALPHABETICAL INDEX	NAICS	SIC
Chalk mining, crushed and broken: Crushed and Broken Limestone and Quarrying—*mining*	212312	1422
Chalk, billiard: Sporting and Athletic Goods—*mfg*	33992	3949
Chalk, ground or otherwise treated: Crushed and Broken Limestone and Quarrying—*mining*	212312	1422
Chalk–e.g., carpenters', blackboard, marking, artists', tailors': Chemical Product, All Other Miscellaneous—*mfg*	325998	3952
Institutional Furniture—*mfg*	337127	3952
Lead Pencil and Art Good—*mfg*	339942	3952
Chalkboards, slate: Cut Stone and Stone Product—*mfg*	327991	3281
Chalkboards, wood: Institutional Furniture—*mfg*	337127	2531
Lead Pencil and Art Good—*mfg*	339942	2531
Chambers of Commerce: Business Associations—*serv*	81391	8611
Chambrays: Broadwoven Fabric Mills—*mfg*	31321	2211
Chamfering machines: Machine Tool (Metal Cutting Types)—*mfg*	333512	3541
Chamois leather: Leather and Hide Tanning and Finishing—*mfg*	31611	3111
Nondurable Goods, Other Miscellaneous—*whlse*	42299	5199
Chandeliers, commercial: Electric Lighting Fixture, Commercial, Industrial and Institutional—*mfg*	335122	3646
Chandeliers, residential: Residential Electric Lighting Fixture—*mfg*	335121	3645
Change making machines: Computer Peripheral Equipment, Other—*mfg*	334119	3578
Office Machinery—*mfg*	333313	3578
Channel black: Carbon Black—*mfg*	325182	2895
Channel construction–general contractors: Heavy, All Other—*const*	23499	1629
Industrial Nonbuilding Structure—*const*	23493	1629
Channel cutoff construction–general contractors: Heavy, All Other—*const*	23499	1629
Industrial Nonbuilding Structure—*const*	23493	1629
Channels, furring: Ornamental and Architectural Metal Work—*mfg*	332323	3446
Charcoal: Nondurable Goods, Other Miscellaneous—*whlse*	42299	5199
Charcoal, activated: Basic Inorganic Chemical, All Other—*mfg*	325188	2819
Chemical Product, All Other Miscellaneous—*mfg*	325998	2819
Charcoal, except activated: Gum and Wood Chemical—*mfg*	325191	2861
Charge account service (shopping plates)-collection by individual firms: Business Support Services, All Other—*admin*	561499	7389
Chargers, battery–rectifying or nonrotating: Electrical Equipment and Component, All Other Miscellaneous—*mfg*	335999	3629
Charitable trusts, management of: Grantmaking Foundations—*serv*	813211	6732
Charlotte Russe (bakery product), except frozen: Bakeries, Commercial—*mfg*	311812	2051
Charm schools: Schools and Instruction, All Other Miscellaneous—*educ*	611699	8299
Chart and graph design: Graphic Design Services—*prof*	54143	7336
Chart and graph paper, ruled: Blankbook, Loose-leaf Binder and Device—*mfg*	323118	2782
Flexographic Printing, Commercial—*mfg*	323112	2782
Gravure Printing, Commercial—*mfg*	323111	2782
Lithographic Printing, Commercial—*mfg*	323110	2782
Printing, Other Commercial—*mfg*	323119	2782
Screen Printing, Commercial—*mfg*	323113	2782
Charter Bus Industry	**48551**	**4142**
Charter Bus Industry	**4855**	
Chartering of commercial boats: Air, Rail, and Water Equipment Rental and Leasing, Commercial—*real*	532411	4499
Navigational Services to Shipping—*trans*	48833	4499
Port and Harbor Operations—*trans*	48831	4499
Water, Other Support Activities for—*trans*	48839	4499
Chasers (machine tool accessories): Cutting Tool and Machine Tool Accessory—*mfg*	333515	3545
Hand and Edge Tool—*mfg*	332212	3545
Chases and galleys, printers': Printing Machinery and Equipment—*mfg*	333293	3555
Chasing on metals for the trade, for purposes other than printing: Costume Jewelry and Novelty—*mfg*	339914	3479
Jewelry (except Costume)—*mfg*	339911	3479
Metal Coating, Engraving (except Jewelry and Silverware), and Allied Services to Manufacturers—*mfg*	332812	3479
Silverware and Plated Ware—*mfg*	339912	3479
Chassis for travel and camping trailers: Travel Trailer and Camper—*mfg*	336214	3792
Chassis, automobile trailer–except mobile home and travel trailer: Transportation Equipment, All Other—*mfg*	336999	3799
Travel Trailer and Camper—*mfg*	336214	3799
Chassis, motor vehicle: Automobile—*mfg*	336111	3711
Heavy Duty Truck—*mfg*	33612	3711
Light Truck and Utility Vehicle—*mfg*	336112	3711
Military Armored Vehicle, Tank and Tank Component—*mfg*	336992	3711
Motor Vehicle Body—*mfg*	336211	3711
Chassis, radio and television–stamped metal: Metal Stamping—*mfg*	332116	3469
Chauffeur registries: Employment Placement Agencies—*admin*	56131	7361
Human Resources and Executive Search Consulting Services—*prof*	541612	7361
Chauffeurs' hats and caps, cloth: Hat, Cap and Millinery—*mfg*	315991	2353
Check cashing agencies: Commodity Contracts Dealing—*fin*	52313	6099
Credit Intermediation, Other Activities Related to—*fin*	52239	6099
Financial Investment Activities, Miscellaneous—*fin*	523999	6099
Financial Transactions Processing, Reserve, and Clearing House Activities—*fin*	52232	6099
Trust, Fiduciary and Custody Activities—*fin*	523991	6099
Check clearinghouse associations: Commodity Contracts Dealing—*fin*	52313	6099
Credit Intermediation, Other Activities Related to—*fin*	52239	6099
Financial Investment Activities, Miscellaneous—*fin*	523999	6099

Description	NAICS	SIC
Financial Transactions Processing, Reserve, and Clearing House Activities—*fin*	52232	6099
Trust, Fiduciary and Custody Activities—*fin*	523991	6099
Check validation service: Business Support Services, All Other—*admin*	561499	7389
Financial Transactions Processing, Reserve, and Clearing House Activities—*fin*	52232	7389
Check writing, endorsing, signing, numbering, and protecting machines: Lead Pencil and Art Good—*mfg*	339942	3579
Office Machinery—*mfg*	333313	3579
Watch, Clock, and Part—*mfg*	334518	3579
Checkbook covers, regardless of material: Personal Leather Good (except Women's Handbag and Purse)—*mfg*	316993	3172
Checkbooks: Blankbook, Loose-leaf Binder and Device—*mfg*	323118	2782
Flexographic Printing, Commercial—*mfg*	323112	2782
Gravure Printing, Commercial—*mfg*	323111	2782
Lithographic Printing, Commercial—*mfg*	323110	2782
Printing, Other Commercial—*mfg*	323119	2782
Screen Printing, Commercial—*mfg*	323113	2782
Checkers and checkerboards: Game, Toy, and Children's Vehicle—*mfg*	339932	3944
Checkroom concessions or services: Personal Services, All Other—*serv*	81299	7299
Cheese: Dairy Product (except Dried or Canned)—*whlse*	42243	5143
Cheese analogs: Cheese—*mfg*	311513	2022
Cheese bandages: Textile Product Mills, All Other Miscellaneous—*mfg*	314999	2399
Cheese curls and puffs: Snack Food, Other—*mfg*	311919	2096
Cheese making machinery: Food Product Machinery—*mfg*	333294	3556
Cheese Manufacturing	**311513**	**2022**
Cheese products, imitation or substitutes: Cheese—*mfg*	311513	2022
Cheese spreads, pastes, and chees~like preparations: Cheese—*mfg*	311513	2022
Cheese stores: Food Stores, All Other Specialty—*retail*	445299	5451
Cheese warehouses: Refrigerated Warehousing and Storage Facilities—*trans*	49312	4222
Cheese, cottage: Fluid Milk—*mfg*	311511	2026
Cheese, except cottage cheese: Cheese—*mfg*	311513	2022
Cheese, imitation or substitutes: Cheese—*mfg*	311513	2022
Cheese, mail-order: Electronic Shopping and Mail-Order Houses—*retail*	45411	5961
Cheese, natural–except cottage cheese: Cheese—*mfg*	311513	2022
Cheese, processed: Cheese—*mfg*	311513	2022
Cheesecloth: Broadwoven Fabric Finishing Mills—*mfg*	313311	5131
Broadwoven Fabric Mills—*mfg*	31321	2211
Piece Goods, Notions and Other Dry Goods—*whlse*	42231	5131
Textile and Fabric Finishing (except Broadwoven Fabric) Mills—*mfg*	313312	5131
Chemical and Allied Products Wholesalers	**4226**	
Chemical and Allied Products Wholesalers, Other	**42269**	**5169**
Chemical and Fertilizer Mineral Mining, Other	**212393**	**1479**
Chemical bulk stations and terminals: Chemical and Allied Products, Other—*whlse*	42269	5169
Chemical catalysts: Basic Inorganic Chemical, All Other—*mfg*	325188	2819
Chemical Product, All Other Miscellaneous—*mfg*	325998	2819
Chemical complex or facilities construction–general contractors: Heavy, All Other—*const*	23499	1629
Industrial Nonbuilding Structure—*const*	23493	1629
Chemical cotton (processed cotton linters): Basic Organic Chemical, All Other—*mfg*	325199	2899
Chemical Product, All Other Miscellaneous—*mfg*	325998	2899
Chemical explosives metal forming machines: Machine Tool (Metal Forming Types)—*mfg*	333513	3542
Chemical indicators: Cyclic Crude and Intermediate—*mfg*	325192	2865
Petrochemical—*mfg*	32511	2865
Chemical kilns: Industrial Machinery, All Other—*mfg*	333298	3559
Machinery, Other Commercial and Service Industry—*mfg*	333319	3559
Chemical laboratories, commercial research–except testing: Research and Development in the Life Sciences—*prof*	54172	8731
Research and Development in the Physical Sciences and Engineering Sciences—*prof*	54171	8731
Chemical machinery and equipment: Industrial Machinery, All Other—*mfg*	333298	3559
Machinery, Other Commercial and Service Industry—*mfg*	333319	3559
Chemical Manufacturing	**325**	
Chemical milling job shops: Fabricated Metal Product, All Other Miscellaneous—*mfg*	332999	3599
General Purpose Machinery , All Other—*mfg*	333999	3599
Machine Shops—*mfg*	33271	3599
Machinery, Other Commercial and Service Industry—*mfg*	333319	3599
Chemical milling machines: Machine Tool (Metal Cutting Types)—*mfg*	333512	3541
Chemical porcelain: Vitreous China, Fine Earthenware and Other Pottery Product—*mfg*	327112	3269
Chemical Product Manufacturing, All Other	**32599**	
Chemical Product Manufacturing, All Other Miscellaneous	**325998**	**2899**
Chemical Product Manufacturing, Other	**3259**	
Chemical recovery coke oven products: Iron and Steel Mills—*mfg*	331111	3312
Petroleum and Coal Productsa, All Other—*mfg*	324199	3312
Chemical stoneware (pottery products): Vitreous China, Fine Earthenware and Other Pottery Product—*mfg*	327112	3269
Chemical supplies for foundries: Basic Organic Chemical, All Other—*mfg*	325199	2899
Chemical Product, All Other Miscellaneous—*mfg*	325998	2899
Chemical treatment of soil for crops: Soil Preparation, Planting, and Cultivating—*ag*	115112	711
Chemical warfare gases: Basic Organic Chemical, All Other—*mfg*	325199	2869
Chemical warfare projectiles and components: Ammunition (except Small Arms)—*mfg*	332993	3483

ALPHABETICAL INDEX	NAICS	SIC
Chemically treating wells on a contract basis: Oil and Gas Operations Support Activities—*mining*	213112	1389
Chemicals, agricultural: Farm Supplies—*whlse*	42291	5191
Nursery and Garden Centers—*retail*	44422	5191
Chemicals, industrial and heavy: Chemical and Allied Products, Other—*whlse*	42269	5169
Chemicals, laboratory–inorganic: Basic Inorganic Chemical, All Other—*mfg*	325188	2819
Chemical Product, All Other Miscellaneous—*mfg*	325998	2819
Chemicals, medicinal–organic and inorganic-bulk, uncompounded: Medicinal and Botanical—*mfg*	325411	2833
Chemicals, photographic–preparod: Photographic and Photocopying Equipment—*mfg*	333315	3861
Photographic Film, Paper, Plate and Chemical—*mfg*	325992	3861
Chemises: Infants' Cut and Sew Apparel—*mfg*	315291	2341
Women's and Girls' Cut and Sew Apparel Contractors—*mfg*	315212	2341
Women's and Girls' Cut and Sew Lingerie, Loungewear and Nightwear—*mfg*	315231	2341
Chemists, biological–(not manufacturing) laboratories of: Diagnostic Imaging Centers—*hlth*	621512	8071
Medical Laboratories—*hlth*	621511	8071
Chemists, consulting–not connected with business service laboratories: Scientific and Technical Consulting Services, Other—*prof*	54169	8999
Chenille rugs: Carpet and Rug Mills—*mfg*	31411	2273
Chenilles, tufted textile: Broadwoven Fabric Mills—*mfg*	31321	2211
Cherries, brinod: Fruit and Vegetable Canning—*mfg*	311421	2035
Mayonnaise, Dressing and Other Prepared Sauce—*mfg*	311941	2035
Cherries, maraschino: Fruit and Vegetable Canning—*mfg*	311421	2033
Cherry gum, gathering of: Crop Farming, All Other Miscellaneous—*ag*	111998	831
Forest Nurseries and Gathering of Forest Products—*ag*	11321	831
Cherry orchards and farms: Apple Orchards—*ag*	111331	175
Noncitrus Fruit Farming, Other—*ag*	111339	175
Chessmen and chessboards: Game, Toy, and Children's Vehicle—*mfg*	339932	3944
Chestnut extract: Gum and Wood Chemical—*mfg*	325191	2861
Chestnut gum, gathering of: Crop Farming, All Other Miscellaneous—*ag*	111998	831
Forest Nurseries and Gathering of Forest Products—*ag*	11321	831
Chests for tools, wood: Wood Container and Pallet—*mfg*	32192	2441
Chests, cedar: Nonupholstered Wood Household Furniture—*mfg*	337122	2511
Chests, fire or burglary resistive–metal: Metal Container, Other—*mfg*	332439	3499
Chests, money–steel: Fabricated Metal Product, All Other Miscellaneous—*mfg*	332999	3999
Chests, musical: Fabricated Metal Product, All Other Miscellaneous—*mfg*	332999	3999

ALPHABETICAL INDEX	NAICS	SIC
Chests, safe deposit–metal: Metal Container, Other—*mfg*	332439	3499
Chests, silverware–wood (floor standing): Nonupholstered Wood Household Furniture—*mfg*	337122	2511
Cheviots, cotton: Broadwoven Fabric Mills—*mfg*	31321	2211
Chewing candy, except chewing gum: Confectionery from Purchased Chocolate—*mfg*	31133	2064
Non-Chocolate Confectionery—*mfg*	31134	2064
Chewing gum: Confectionery—*whlse*	42245	5145
Non-Chocolate Confectionery—*mfg*	31134	2067
Chewing gum base: Non-Chocolate Confectionery—*mfg*	31134	2067
Chewing gum machinery: Food Product Machinery—*mfg*	333294	3556
Chewing tobacco: Tobacco and Tobacco Product—*whlse*	42294	5194
Tobacco Product, Other—*mfg*	312229	2131
Chicken brooders: Farm Machinery and Equipment—*mfg*	333111	3523
Chicken broth and soup, canned: Canning, Specialty—*mfg*	311422	2032
Food, All Other Miscellaneous—*mfg*	311999	2032
Chicken coops (crates), wood–wirebound for shipping poultry: Wood Container and Pallet—*mfg*	32192	2449
Chicken coops, prefabricated–wood: Prefabricated Wood Building—*mfg*	321992	2452
Chicken egg farms: Chicken Egg Production—*ag*	11231	252
Chicken Egg Production	**11231**	**252**
Chicken farms or ranches, raising for slaughter: Broilers and Other Meat Type Chicken Production—*ag*	11232	251
Chicken feeders: Farm Machinery and Equipment—*mfg*	333111	3523
Chicken feeds, prepared: Animal Food, Other—*mfg*	311119	2048
Chicken hatcheries: Poultry Hatcheries—*ag*	11234	254
Chickens, processed–fresh, frozen, canned, or cooked: Food, All Other Miscellaneous—*mfg*	311999	2015
Poultry Processing—*mfg*	311615	2015
Chickens–slaughtering and dressing: Food, All Other Miscellaneous—*mfg*	311999	2015
Poultry Processing—*mfg*	311615	2015
Chicks: Farm Product Raw Material, Other—*whlse*	42259	5159
Chicory root, dried: Dried and Dehydrated Food—*mfg*	311423	2099
Chiffoniers and chifforobes: Nonupholstered Wood Household Furniture—*mfg*	337122	2511
Child and Youth Services	**62411**	**8641**
Child care centers: Child Day Care Services—*hlth*	62441	8351
Child Day Care Services	**6244**	
Child Day Care Services	**62441**	**7299**
Child guidance agencies: Child and Youth Services—*hlth*	62411	8322
Community Food Services—*hlth*	62421	8322
Community Housing Services, Other—*hlth*	624229	8322
Emergency and Other Relief Services—*hlth*	62423	8322
Individual and Family Services, Other—*hlth*	62419	8322
Parole Offices and Probation Offices—*pub*	92215	8322

Entry	NAICS	SIC
Services for the Elderly and Persons with Disabilities—*hlth*	62412	8322
Temporary Shelters—*hlth*	624221	8322
Childbirth preparation classes: Family Planning Centers—*hlth*	62141	8099
Children's and Infants' Clothing Stores	**44813**	**5641**
Children's boarding homes: Homes for the Elderly—*hlth*	623312	8361
Residential Care Facilities, Other—*hlth*	62399	8361
Residential Mental Health and Substance Abuse Facilities—*hlth*	62322	8361
Children's dancing schools: Amusement and Recreation Industries, All Other—*arts*	71399	7911
Fine Arts Schools—*educ*	61161	7911
Children's homes: Homes for the Elderly—*hlth*	623312	8361
Residential Care Facilities, Other—*hlth*	62399	8361
Residential Mental Health and Substance Abuse Facilities—*hlth*	62322	8361
Children's hosiery: Hosiery and Sock Mills, Other—*mfg*	315119	2252
Sheer Hosiery Mills—*mfg*	315111	2252
Children's hospitals: General Medical and Surgical Hospitals—*hlth*	62211	8069
Hospitals (except Psychiatric and Substance Abuse), Specialty—*hlth*	62231	8069
Psychiatric and Substance Abuse Hospitals—*hlth*	62221	8069
Children's villages: Homes for the Elderly—*hlth*	623312	8361
Residential Care Facilities, Other—*hlth*	62399	8361
Residential Mental Health and Substance Abuse Facilities—*hlth*	62322	8361
Children's wear stores: Children's and Infants' Clothing Stores—*retail*	44813	5641
Chili con came, canned: Canning, Specialty—*mfg*	311422	2032
Food, All Other Miscellaneous—*mfg*	311999	2032
Chili sauce, tomato: Fruit and Vegetable Canning—*mfg*	311421	2033
Chimes and parts (musical instruments): Musical Instrument—*mfg*	339992	3931
Chimes, electric: Electrical Equipment and Component, All Other Miscellaneous—*mfg*	335999	3699
Chimney blocks, radial clay: Brick and Structural Clay Tile—*mfg*	327121	3251
Chimney caps, concrete: Concrete Pipe—*mfg*	327332	3272
Concrete Product, Other—*mfg*	32739	3272
Nonmetallic Mineral Product, All Other Miscellaneous—*mfg*	327999	3272
Chimney cleaning service: Janitorial Services—*admin*	56172	7349
Chimney construction and maintenance–contractors: Masonry and Stone Contractors—*const*	23541	1741
Chimney pipe and tops, clay: Structural Clay Product, Other—*mfg*	327123	3259
Chimneys, lamp–glass-pressed or blown: Pressed and Blown Glass and Glassware, Other—*mfg*	327212	3229
China: Home Furnishing—*whlse*	42122	5023
China clay mining: Kaolin and Ball Clay—*mining*	212324	1455
China closets: Nonupholstered Wood Household Furniture—*mfg*	337122	2511
China cooking ware: Vitreous China, Fine Earthenware and Other Pottery Product—*mfg*	327112	3262
China firing and decorating, for the trade: Vitreous China, Fine Earthenware and Other Pottery Product—*mfg*	327112	3269
China stores: Home Furnishings Stores, All Other—*retail*	442299	5719
Window Treatment Stores—*retail*	442291	5719

Entry	NAICS	SIC
China tableware, commercial, and house-hold–vitreous: Vitreous China, Fine Earthenware and Other Pottery Product—*mfg*	327112	3262
Chinchilla farms: Fur-Bearing Animal and Rabbit Production—*ag*	11293	271
Chinese foods, canned: Canning, Specialty—*mfg*	311422	2032
Food, All Other Miscellaneous—*mfg*	311999	2032
Chinese noodles: Food, All Other Miscellaneous—*mfg*	311999	2099
Chintz, cotton: Broadwoven Fabric Mills—*mfg*	31321	2211
Chiorobenzene: Cyclic Crude and Intermediate—*mfg*	325192	2865
Petrochemical—*mfg*	32511	2865
Chip spreaders, selfpropelled: Construction Machinery—*mfg*	33312	3531
Overhead Traveling Crane, Hoist and Monorail System—*mfg*	333923	3531
Railroad Rolling Stock—*mfg*	33651	3531
Chipboard (paperboard): Paperboard Mills—*mfg*	32213	2631
Chipboard, pasted: Converted Paper Product, All Other—*mfg*	322298	2675
Die-Cut Paper and Paperboard Office Supplies—*mfg*	322231	2675
Surface-Coated Paperboard—*mfg*	322292	2675
Chipper mills: Cut Stock, Resawing Lumber, and Planing—*mfg*	321912	2421
Millwork (including Flooring), Other—*mfg*	321918	2421
Sawmills—*mfg*	321113	2421
Wood Product, All Other Miscellaneous—*mfg*	321999	2421
Chippers, commercial–brush, limb, and log: Construction Machinery—*mfg*	33312	3531
Overhead Traveling Crane, Hoist and Monorail System—*mfg*	333923	3531
Railroad Rolling Stock—*mfg*	33651	3531
Chipping hammers, electric: Power-Driven Hand Tool—*mfg*	333991	3546
Chiropractors, offices and clinics of: Chiropractors, Offices Of—*hlth*	62131	8041
Chiropractors, Offices Of	**62131**	**8041**
Chisels: Hand and Edge Tool—*mfg*	332212	3423
Chloral: Basic Organic Chemical, All Other—*mfg*	325199	2869
Chlorinated rubbers, natural: Fabric Coating Mills—*mfg*	31332	3069
Rubber Product, All Other—*mfg*	326299	3069
Chlorinated rubbers, synthetic: Synthetic Rubber—*mfg*	325212	2822
Chlorinated solvents: Basic Organic Chemical, All Other—*mfg*	325199	2869
Chlorination tablets and kits (water purification): Pharmaceutical Preparation—*mfg*	325412	2834
Chlorine: Chemical and Allied Products, Other—*whlse*	42269	5169
Chlorine bleaching compounds, household–liquid or dry: Polish and Other Sanitation Good—*mfg*	325612	2842
Chlorine, compressed or liquefied: Alkalies and Chlorine—*mfg*	325181	2812
Chloroacetic acid and metallic salts: Basic Organic Chemical, All Other—*mfg*	325199	2869
Chloroform: Basic Organic Chemical, All Other—*mfg*	325199	2869
Chloronaphthalene: Cyclic Crude and Intermediate—*mfg*	325192	2865
Petrochemical—*mfg*	32511	2865
Chlorophenol: Cyclic Crude and Intermediate—*mfg*	325192	2865
Petrochemical—*mfg*	32511	2865
Chloropicrin: Basic Organic Chemical, All Other—*mfg*	325199	2869
Chloroprene type rubbers: Synthetic Rubber—*mfg*	325212	2822
Chlorosulfonated polyethylenes: Synthetic Rubber—*mfg*	325212	2822

ALPHABETICAL INDEX	NAICS	SIC
Chlorosulfonic acid: Basic Inorganic Chemical, All Other—*mfg*	325188	2819
Chemical Product, All Other Miscellaneous—*mfg*	325998	2819
Chlorotoluene: Cyclic Crude and Intermediate—*mfg*	325192	2865
Petrochemical—*mfg*	32511	2865
Chocolate: Grocery and Related Products, Other—*whlse*	42249	5149
Chocolate and Confectionery Manufacturing from Cacao Beans	**31132**	**2066**
Chocolate bars, from purchased cocoa or chocolate: Confectionery from Purchased Chocolate—*mfg*	31133	2064
Non-Chocolate Confectionery—*mfg*	31134	2064
Chocolate bars, solid–from cacao beans: Chocolate and Confectionery from Cacao Beans—*mfg*	31132	2066
Chocolate candy, except solid chocolate: Confectionery from Purchased Chocolate—*mfg*	31133	2064
Non-Chocolate Confectionery—*mfg*	31134	2064
Chocolate coatings and syrups: Chocolate and Confectionery from Cacao Beans—*mfg*	31132	2066
Chocolate liquor: Chocolate and Confectionery from Cacao Beans—*mfg*	31132	2066
Chocolate milk: Fluid Milk—*mfg*	311511	2026
Chocolate processing machinery: Food Product Machinery—*mfg*	333294	3556
Chocolate syrup: Chocolate and Confectionery from Cacao Beans—*mfg*	31132	2066
Chocolate, instant: Chocolate and Confectionery from Cacao Beans—*mfg*	31132	2066
Chocolate, sweetened or unsweetened: Chocolate and Confectionery from Cacao Beans—*mfg*	31132	2066
Chop suey, canned: Canning, Specialty—*mfg*	311422	2032
Food, All Other Miscellaneous—*mfg*	311999	2032
Choppers, food–commercial types: Food Product Machinery—*mfg*	333294	3556
Chopping and silo filling: Crop Harvesting, Primarily by Machine—*ag*	115113	722
Chow mein, canned: Canning, Specialty—*mfg*	311422	2032
Food, All Other Miscellaneous—*mfg*	311999	2032
Chowder, clam–canned: Seafood Canning—*mfg*	311711	2091
Chowders, fish and seafood–canned: Seafood Canning—*mfg*	311711	2091
Chowders, fish and seafood–frozen: Fresh and Frozen Seafood Processing—*mfg*	311712	2092
Christian Science lecturers: Scientific and Technical Consulting Services, Other—*prof*	54169	8999
Christian Science practitioners, offices of: Health Practitioners, Offices Of Miscellaneous—*hlth*	621399	8049
Mental Health Practitioners (except Physicians), Offices Of—*hlth*	62133	8049
Physical, Occupational and Speech Therapists and Audiologists, Offices Of—*hlth*	62134	8049
Christmas cards, except hand painted: Flexographic Printing, Commercial—*mfg*	323112	2771
Gravure Printing, Commercial—*mfg*	323111	2771

ALPHABETICAL INDEX	NAICS	SIC
Greeting Card Publishers—*info*	511191	2771
Lithographic Printing, Commercial—*mfg*	323110	2771
Printing, Other Commercial—*mfg*	323119	2771
Screen Printing, Commercial—*mfg*	323113	2771
Christmas tree growing: Nursery and Tree Production—*ag*	111421	811
Timber Tract Operations—*ag*	11311	811
Christmas tree lighting sets, electric: Lighting Equipment, Other—*mfg*	335129	3699
Christmas tree ornaments, except electrical and glass: Fabricated Metal Product, All Other Miscellaneous—*mfg*	332999	3999
Plastics Product, All Other—*mfg*	326199	3999
Christmas tree ornaments, from glass: Pressed and Blown Glass and Glassware, Other—*mfg*	327212	3229
Christmas tree ornaments, made from purchased glass: Glass Product Made of Purchased Glass—*mfg*	327215	3231
Christmas trees (natural): Nursery and Garden Centers—*retail*	44422	5261
Outdoor Power Equipment Stores—*retail*	44421	5261
Stores (except Tobacco Stores), All Other Miscellaneous—*retail*	453998	5261
Christmas trees, artificial: Fabricated Metal Product, All Other Miscellaneous—*mfg*	332999	3999
Christmas trees, including artificial: Nondurable Goods, Other Miscellaneous—*whlse*	42299	5199
Chromates and bichromates: Basic Inorganic Chemical, All Other—*mfg*	325188	2819
Chemical Product, All Other Miscellaneous—*mfg*	325998	2819
Chromatographic instruments, laboratory and electric: Analytical Laboratory Instrument—*mfg*	334516	3826
Chromatographs, industrial process type: Instruments and Related Products for Measuring, Displaying, and Controlling Industrial Process Variables—*mfg*	334513	3823
Chrome pigments: chrome green, chrome yellow, chrome orange, and zinc yellow: Carbon Black—*mfg*	325182	2816
Inorganic Dye and Pigment—*mfg*	325131	2816
Chromic acid: Basic Inorganic Chemical, All Other—*mfg*	325188	2819
Chemical Product, All Other Miscellaneous—*mfg*	325998	2819
Chromite mining: Copper Ore and Nickel Ore—*mining*	212234	1061
Metal Ore, All Other—*mining*	212299	1061
Chromium compounds, inorganic: Basic Inorganic Chemical, All Other—*mfg*	325188	2819
Chemical Product, All Other Miscellaneous—*mfg*	325998	2819
Chromium ore mining: Copper Ore and Nickel Ore—*mining*	212234	1061
Metal Ore, All Other—*mining*	212299	1061
Chromium plating of metals and formed products for the trade: Electroplating, Plating, Polishing, Anodizing and Coloring—*mfg*	332813	3471
Chromium refining, primary: Primary Smelting and Refining of Nonferrous Metal (except Copper and Aluminum)—*mfg*	331419	3339

Description	NAICS	SIC
Chromium salts: Basic Inorganic Chemical, All Other—*mfg*	325188	2819
Chemical Product, All Other Miscellaneous—*mfg*	325998	2819
Chronic disease hospitals: General Medical and Surgical Hospitals—*hlth*	62211	8069
Hospitals (except Psychiatric and Substance Abuse), Specialty—*hlth*	62231	8069
Psychiatric and Substance Abuse Hospitals—*hlth*	62221	8069
Chronographs, spring wound: Watch, Clock, and Part—*mfg*	334518	3873
Chronometers, electronic: Measuring and Controlling Device, Other—*mfg*	334519	3829
Surgical and Medical Instrument—*mfg*	339112	3829
Chronometers, spring wound: Watch, Clock, and Part—*mfg*	334518	3873
Chronoscopes-mfg: Analytical Laboratory Instrument—*mfg*	334516	3826
Chucking machines, automatic-mfg: Machine Tool (Metal Cutting Types)—*mfg*	333512	3541
Chucks: drill, lathe, and magnetic (machine tool accessories): Cutting Tool and Machine Tool Accessory—*mfg*	333515	3545
Hand and Edge Tool—*mfg*	332212	3545
Church furniture, concrete: Concrete Pipe—*mfg*	327332	3272
Concrete Product, Other—*mfg*	32739	3272
Nonmetallic Mineral Product, All Other Miscellaneous—*mfg*	327999	3272
Church furniture, cut stone: Cut Stone and Stone Product—*mfg*	327991	3281
Church furniture, except stone or concrete: Institutional Furniture—*mfg*	337127	2531
Church pews: Furniture—*whlse*	42121	5021
Furniture Stores—*retail*	44211	5021
Church, synagogue, and related building construction general contractors: Building, Commercial and Institutional—*const*	23332	1542
Churches: Religious Organizations—*serv*	81311	8661
Chutes, metal plate: Air-Conditioning and Warm Air Heating Equipment and Commercial and Industrial Refrigeration Equipment—*mfg*	333415	3443
Metal Tank (Heavy Gauge)—*mfg*	33242	3443
Plate Work—*mfg*	332313	3443
Power Boiler and Heat Exchanger—*mfg*	33241	3443
Cider presses: Food Product Machinery—*mfg*	333294	3556
Cider, nonalcoholic: Food, All Other Miscellaneous—*mfg*	311999	2099
Cigar and cigarette holders: Fabricated Metal Product, All Other Miscellaneous—*mfg*	332999	3999
Plastics Product, All Other—*mfg*	326199	3999
Cigar boxes, wood and part wood: Wood Container and Pallet—*mfg*	32192	2441
Cigar cases, except precious metal: Personal Leather Good (except Women's Handbag and Purse)—*mfg*	316993	3172
Cigar cases, precious metal: Jewelry (except Costume)—*mfg*	339911	3911
Cigar lighters, electric: Electric Housewares and Household Fan—*mfg*	335211	3634
Heating Equipment (except Electric and Warm Air Furnaces)—*mfg*	333414	3634
Cigar lighters, except precious metal and: Fabricated Metal Product, All Other Miscellaneous—*mfg*	332999	3999
Cigar lighters, precious metal or based metal clad with precious metal and electric: Jewelry (except Costume)—*mfg*	339911	3911
Cigar stores and stands: Tobacco Stores—*retail*	453991	5993
Cigarette and cigar making machines: Industrial Machinery, All Other—*mfg*	333298	3559
Machinery, Other Commercial and Service Industry—*mfg*	333319	3559
Cigarette cases, except precious metal: Personal Leather Good (except Women's Handbag and Purse)—*mfg*	316993	3172
Cigarette cases, precious metal: Jewelry (except Costume)—*mfg*	339911	3911
Cigarette holder mouthpieces, molded: Fabric Coating Mills—*mfg*	31332	3069
Rubber Product, All Other—*mfg*	326299	3069
Cigarette lighters, electric: Electric Housewares and Household Fan—*mfg*	335211	3634
Heating Equipment (except Electric and Warm Air Furnaces)—*mfg*	333414	3634
Cigarette lighters, except precious metal: Fabricated Metal Product, All Other Miscellaneous—*mfg*	332999	3999
Cigarette lighters, precious metal: Jewelry (except Costume)—*mfg*	339911	3911
Cigarette Manufacturing	**312221**	**2111**
Cigarette paper: Newsprint Mills—*mfg*	322122	2621
Paper (except Newsprint) Mills—*mfg*	322121	2621
Cigarette paper, book: Coated and Laminated Paper—*mfg*	322222	2679
Converted Paper Product, All Other—*mfg*	322298	2679
Die-Cut Paper and Paperboard Office Supplies—*mfg*	322231	2679
Non-Folding Sanitary Food Container—*mfg*	322215	2679
Cigarette tow, cellulosic fiber: Cellulosic Organic Fiber—*mfg*	325221	2823
Cigarettes: Cigarette—*mfg*	312221	2111
Tobacco and Tobacco Product—*whlse*	42294	5194
Cigarettes, sale by vending machine: Vending Machine Operators—*retail*	45421	5962
Cigarillos: Tobacco Product, Other—*mfg*	312229	2121
Cigars: Tobacco and Tobacco Product—*whlse*	42294	5194
Tobacco Product, Other—*mfg*	312229	2121
Cinchona and derivatives: Medicinal and Botanical—*mfg*	325411	2833
Cinder block, concrete: Concrete Block and Brick—*mfg*	327331	3271
Cinders: Brick, Stone and Related Material—*whlse*	42132	5032
Building Material Dealers, Other—*retail*	44419	5032
Cinetheodolites: Optical Instrument and Lens—*mfg*	333314	3827
Cinnabar mining: Metal Ore, All Other—*mining*	212299	1099
Circuit boards, television and radio: printed: Printed Circuit Board—*mfg*	334412	3672
Circuit breakers: Building Material Dealers, Other—*retail*	44419	5063
Electrical Apparatus and Equipment, Wiring Supplies and Material—*whlse*	42161	5063
Circuit breakers, air: Switchgear and Switchboard Apparatus—*mfg*	335313	3613
Circuit breakers, power: Switchgear and Switchboard Apparatus—*mfg*	335313	3613

ALPHABETICAL INDEX	NAICS	SIC
Circuit management services for motion picture theaters: Office Administrative Services—*admin*	56111	8741
Circular distributing service: Advertising Material Distribution Services—*prof*	54187	7319
Advertising, Other Services Related to—*prof*	54189	7319
Display Advertising—*prof*	54185	7319
Media Buying Agencies—*prof*	54183	7319
Nonscheduled Air, Other—*trans*	481219	7319
Circular knit fabrics: Broadwoven Fabric Finishing Mills—*mfg*	313311	5131
Piece Goods, Notions and Other Dry Goods—*whlse*	42231	5131
Textile and Fabric Finishing (except Broadwoven Fabric) Mills—*mfg*	313312	5131
Textile and Fabric Finishing (except Broadwoven Fabric) Mills—*mfg*	313312	2257
Weft Knit Fabric Mills—*mfg*	313241	2257
Circulars, lithographed: Lithographic Printing, Commercial—*mfg*	323110	2752
Quick Printing—*mfg*	323114	2752
Circulars, printed: except lithographed or gravure: Digital Printing—*mfg*	323115	2759
Flexographic Printing, Commercial—*mfg*	323112	2759
Printing, Other Commercial—*mfg*	323119	2759
Quick Printing—*mfg*	323114	2759
Circulars: gravure printing: Gravure Printing, Commercial—*mfg*	323111	2754
Circulating libraries: Libraries and Archives—*info*	51412	8231
Circus companies: Amusement and Recreation Industries, All Other—*arts*	71399	7999
Citizens' band (CB) antennas, installation of: Communication Equipment Repair and Maintenance—*serv*	811213	7622
Consumer Electronics Repair and Maintenance—*serv*	811211	7622
Radio, Television and Other Electronics Stores—*retail*	443112	7622
Citizens' band (CB) radios: Radio and Television Broadcasting and Wireless Communications Equipment—*mfg*	33422	3663
Citizens' band radios: Electronic Parts and Equipment, Other—*whlse*	42169	5065
Citizens' unions: Civic and Social Organizations—*serv*	81341	8641
Citral: Basic Organic Chemical, All Other—*mfg*	325199	2869
Citratos: Basic Organic Chemical, All Other—*mfg*	325199	2869
Citric acid: Basic Organic Chemical, All Other—*mfg*	325199	2869
Citronella oil: Spice and Extract—*mfg*	311942	2899
Citronellal: Basic Organic Chemical, All Other—*mfg*	325199	2869
Citrus (except Orange) Groves	**11132**	**174**
Citrus grove cultivation services: Nonscheduled Air, Other—*trans*	481219	721
Soil Preparation, Planting, and Cultivating—*ag*	115112	721
Citrus grove management and maintenance, with or without crop services: Farm Management Services—*ag*	115116	762
Citrus groves and farms: Citrus (except Orange) Groves—*ag*	11132	174
Orange Groves—*ag*	11131	174

ALPHABETICAL INDEX	NAICS	SIC
Citrus processing machinery: Industrial Machinery and Equipment—*whlse*	42183	5084
Citrus seed meal: Animal Food, Other—*mfg*	311119	2048
City and suburban bus line operation: Bus and Motor Vehicle Transit Systems—*trans*	485113	4111
Commuter Rail Systems—*trans*	485112	4111
Mixed Mode Transit Systems—*trans*	485111	4111
Transit and Ground Passenger, All Other—*trans*	485999	4111
Urban Transit Systems, Other—*trans*	485119	4111
City and town councils: Legislative Bodies—*pub*	92112	9121
City and town managers' offices: Executive Offices—*pub*	92111	9111
City planners, except professional engineering: Educational Support Services—*educ*	61171	8748
Management Consulting Services, Other—*prof*	541618	8748
Scientific and Technical Consulting Services, Other—*prof*	54169	8748
Civic and Social Organizations	**8134**	
Civic and Social Organizations	**81341**	**8699**
Civic associations: Civic and Social Organizations—*serv*	81341	8641
Civic center construction–general contractors: Building, Commercial and Institutional—*const*	23332	1542
Civil rights commissions: General Government, All Other—*pub*	92119	9199
Civil service commissions: General Government, All Other—*pub*	92119	9199
Civil service schools: Schools and Instruction, All Other Miscellaneous—*educ*	611699	8299
Civilian courts: Courts—*pub*	92211	9211
Claim adjusters insurance–not employed by insurance companies: Claims Adjusters—*fin*	524291	6411
Insurance Agencies and Brokerages—*fin*	52421	6411
Insurance Related Activities, All Other—*fin*	524298	6411
Third Party Administration for Insurance and Pension Funds—*fin*	524292	6411
Claims Adjusters	**524291**	**6411**
Clam bouillon, broth, chowder, juice–bottled or canned: Seafood Canning—*mfg*	311711	2091
Clamps, hand: Hand and Edge Tool—*mfg*	332212	3423
Clamps, hose: Other Metal Valve and Pipe Fitting, Other—*mfg*	332919	3429
Clamps, machine tool: Cutting Tool and Machine Tool Accessory—*mfg*	333515	3545
Hand and Edge Tool—*mfg*	332212	3545
Clamps, metal: Other Metal Valve and Pipe Fitting, Other—*mfg*	332919	3429
Clamps, surgical: Surgical and Medical Instrument—*mfg*	339112	3841
Clams, digging of: Shellfish Fishing—*ag*	114112	913
Clarifying machinery, mineral: Mining Machinery and Equipment—*mfg*	333131	3532
Clarinets and parts: Musical Instrument—*mfg*	339992	3931
Clasps, shoe: Fastener, Button, Needle and Pin—*mfg*	339993	3131
Leather Good, All Other—*mfg*	316999	3131
Wood Product, All Other Miscellaneous—*mfg*	321999	3131

Description	NAICS	SIC
Classical music groups or artists: Independent Artists, Writers, and Performers—*arts*	71151	7929
Musical Groups and Artists—*arts*	71113	7929
Performing Arts Companies, Other—*arts*	71119	7929
Classifiers, metallurgical and mining: Mining Machinery and Equipment—*mfg*	333131	3532
Clay and Ceramic and Refractory Minerals Mining	**212325**	**1459**
Clay Building Material and Refractories Manufacturing	**32712**	
Clay coated board: Paperboard Mills—*mfg*	32213	2631
Clay construction materials, except refractory: Brick, Stone and Related Material—*whlse*	42132	5032
Building Material Dealers, Other—*retail*	44419	5032
Clay for petroleum refining, chemically processed: Ground or Treated Mineral and Earth—*mfg*	327992	3295
Clay Product and Refractory Manufacturing	**3271**	
Clay refractories: Clay Refractory—*mfg*	327124	3255
Clay Refractory Manufacturing	**327124**	**3255**
Clay, ground or otherwise treated: Ground or Treated Mineral and Earth—*mfg*	327992	3295
Clay, modeling: Chemical Product, All Other Miscellaneous—*mfg*	325998	3952
Institutional Furniture—*mfg*	337127	3952
Lead Pencil and Art Good—*mfg*	339942	3952
Clays (common) quarrying-not in conjunction with manufacturing: Clay and Ceramic and Refractory Minerals—*mining*	212325	1459
Clayworking and tempering machines: Industrial Machinery, All Other—*mfg*	333298	3559
Machinery, Other Commercial and Service Industry—*mfg*	333319	3559
Clean room apparel supply service: Industrial Launderers—*serv*	812332	7218
Clean room construction–general contractors: Building, Commercial and Institutional—*const*	23332	1541
Manufacturing and Industrial Building—*const*	23331	1541
Cleaners, air–motor vehicle: Gasoline Engine and Engine Parts—*mfg*	336312	3714
Motor Vehicle Parts, All Other—*mfg*	336399	3714
Cleaners, boiler tube: Fabricated Metal Product, All Other Miscellaneous—*mfg*	332999	3599
General Purpose Machinery , All Other—*mfg*	333999	3599
Machine Shops—*mfg*	33271	3599
Machinery, Other Commercial and Service Industry—*mfg*	333319	3599
Cleaners, denture: Soap and Other Detergent—*mfg*	325611	2844
Toilet Preparation—*mfg*	32562	2844
Cleaners, electric vacuum–industrial: Machinery, Other Commercial and Service Industry—*mfg*	333319	3589
Cleaners, electric–vacuum-household: Household Vacuum Cleaner—*mfg*	335212	3635
Cleaners, not operating own drycleaning plants: Garment Pressing, and Agents for Laundries—*serv*	812391	7212
Cleaners, paintbrush: Paint and Coating—*mfg*	32551	2851
Cleaning and descaling metal products, for the trade: Electroplating, Plating, Polishing, Anodizing and Coloring—*mfg*	332813	3471
Cleaning and dyeing plants, except rug cleaning: Drycleaning Plants—*serv*	812322	7216
Cleaning and laundry pickup stations, not owned by laundries or cleaners: Garment Pressing, and Agents for Laundries—*serv*	812391	7212
Cleaning and polishing (detailing) new autos for dealers on a contract or fee basis: Car Washes—*serv*	811192	7542
Cleaning and polishing of rice: Rice Milling—*mfg*	311212	2044
Cleaning and polishing preparations: Polish and Other Sanitation Good—*mfg*	325612	2842
Cleaning and repairing plants, rug and carpet: Carpet and Upholstery Cleaning Services—*admin*	56174	7217
Cleaning bricks: Buildings and Dwellings, Other Services to—*admin*	56179	7699
Cleaning building exteriors–contractors: Trade Contractors, All Other Special—*const*	23599	1799
Cleaning equipment, ultrasonic–except medical and dental: Electrical Equipment and Component, All Other Miscellaneous—*mfg*	335999	3699
Machinery, Other Commercial and Service Industry—*mfg*	333319	3699
Cleaning lease tanks, oil and gas field–on a contract basis: Oil and Gas Operations Support Activities—*mining*	213112	1389
Cleaning lines, electrolytic (rolling mill equipment): Rolling Mill Machinery and Equipment—*mfg*	333516	3547
Cleaning machinery, mineral: Mining Machinery and Equipment—*mfg*	333131	3532
Cleaning machines for fruits, grains, and vegetables–farm: Conveyor and Conveying Equipment—*mfg*	333922	3523
Farm Machinery and Equipment—*mfg*	333111	3523
Cleaning new buildings after construction–contractors: Trade Contractors, All Other Special—*const*	23599	1799
Cleaning of dry foods and spices: Grocery and Related Products, Other—*whlse*	42249	5149
Cleaning of railroad cars: Air, Rail, and Water Equipment Rental and Leasing, Commercial—*real*	532411	4741
Rail Support Activities—*trans*	48821	4741
Cleaning plants, bituminous coal: Bituminous Coal and Lignite Surface—*mining*	212111	1221
Cleaning poultry coops: Animal Production Support Activities—*ag*	11521	751
Cleaning railroad ballasts: Rail Support Activities—*trans*	48821	4789
Scenic and Sightseeing, Land—*trans*	48711	4789
Transportation, All Other Support Activities—*trans*	488999	4789
Cleaning wells on a contract basis: Oil and Gas Operations Support Activities—*mining*	213112	1389
Cleansing tissue stock: Newsprint Mills—*mfg*	322122	2621
Paper (except Newsprint) Mills—*mfg*	322121	2621
Cleansing tissues: Sanitary Paper Product—*mfg*	322291	2676
Clearance lamps and reflectors, motor vehicle: Vehicular Lighting Equipment—*mfg*	336321	3647
Clearing of land–general contractors: Heavy, All Other—*const*	23499	1629
Industrial Nonbuilding Structure—*const*	23493	1629

ALPHABETICAL INDEX	NAICS	SIC
Clearinghouse associations–bank or check: Commodity Contracts Dealing—*fin*	52313	6099
Credit Intermediation, Other Activities Related to—*fin*	52239	6099
Financial Investment Activities, Miscellaneous—*fin*	523999	6099
Financial Transactions Processing, Reserve, and Clearing House Activities—*fin*	52232	6099
Trust, Fiduciary and Custody Activities—*fin*	523991	6099
Clearinghouses, commodity exchange: Financial Investment Activities, Miscellaneous—*fin*	523999	6289
Trust, Fiduciary and Custody Activities—*fin*	523991	6289
Clearinghouses, security exchange: Financial Investment Activities, Miscellaneous—*fin*	523999	6289
Trust, Fiduciary and Custody Activities—*fin*	523991	6289
Cleats, porcelain: Porcelain Electrical Supply—*mfg*	327113	3264
Cleavers: Cutlery and Flatware (except Precious)—*mfg*	332211	3421
Clergy's vestments: Cut and Sew Apparel, All Other—*mfg*	315299	2389
Climax baskets: Wood Container and Pallet—*mfg*	32192	2449
Clinical chemistry reagents (including toxicology): In-Vitro Diagnostic Substance—*mfg*	325413	2835
Pharmaceutical Preparation—*mfg*	325412	2835
Clinical chemistry standards and controls (including toxicology): In-Vitro Diagnostic Substance—*mfg*	325413	2835
Pharmaceutical Preparation—*mfg*	325412	2835
Clinical thermometers, including digital: Measuring and Controlling Device, Other—*mfg*	334519	3829
Surgical and Medical Instrument—*mfg*	339112	3829
Clinics of chiropractors: Chiropractors, Offices Of—*hlth*	62131	8041
Clinics of dentists: Dentists, Offices Of—*hlth*	62121	8021
Clinics of optometrists: Optometrists, Offices Of—*hlth*	62132	8042
Clinics of osteopathic physicians: Physicians (except Mental Health Specialists), Offices Of—*hlth*	621111	8031
Physicians, Mental Health Specialists, Offices Of—*hlth*	621112	8031
Clinics of physicians (M.D.): Freestanding Ambulatory Surgical and Emergency Centers—*hlth*	621493	8011
HMO Medical Centers—*hlth*	621491	8011
Physicians (except Mental Health Specialists), Offices Of—*hlth*	621111	8011
Physicians, Mental Health Specialists, Offices Of—*hlth*	621112	8011
Clinics of podiatrists: Podiatrists, Offices Of—*hlth*	621391	8043
Clinics, alcohol and drug treatment–outpatient: Family Planning Centers—*hlth*	62141	8093
Outpatient Care Centers, All Other—*hlth*	621498	8093
Outpatient Mental Health and Substance Abuse Centers—*hlth*	62142	8093
Clinics, mental health–outpatient: Family Planning Centers—*hlth*	62141	8093
Outpatient Care Centers, All Other—*hlth*	621498	8093
Outpatient Mental Health and Substance Abuse Centers—*hlth*	62142	8093
Clip cups, glass: Pressed and Blown Glass and Glassware, Other—*mfg*	327212	3229

ALPHABETICAL INDEX	NAICS	SIC
Clipboards, wood: Manufacturing, All Other Miscellaneous—*mfg*	339999	2499
Wood Container and Pallet—*mfg*	32192	2499
Wood Product, All Other Miscellaneous—*mfg*	321999	2499
Clippers, fingernail and tcenail: Cutlery and Flatware (except Precious)—*mfg*	332211	3421
Clippers, hair–for animal use-hand and electric: Farm Machinery and Equipment—*mfg*	333111	3523
Hand and Edge Tool—*mfg*	332212	3523
Clips and fasteners, made from purchased wire-rnfg: Fabricated Wire Product, Other—*mfg*	332618	3496
Clips, gun–30 mm. (or 1.18 inch) or less: Small Arms—*mfg*	332994	3484
Cloaks, vulcanized rubber and rubborized fabric: Fabric Coating Mills—*mfg*	31332	3069
Rubber Product, All Other—*mfg*	326299	3069
Clock materials and parts, except crystals and jewels: Watch, Clock, and Part—*mfg*	334518	3873
Clock radio and telephone combinations: Audio and Video Equipment—*mfg*	33431	3651
Clock radios: Audio and Video Equipment—*mfg*	33431	3651
Clock repair shops: Personal and Household Goods Repair and Maintenance, Other—*serv*	81149	7631
Clock springs, precision–made from purchased wire: Watch, Clock, and Part—*mfg*	334518	3495
Wire Spring—*mfg*	332612	3495
Clocks: Jewelry, Watch, Precious Stone and Precious Metal—*whlse*	42194	5094
Clocks, assembling of: Watch, Clock, and Part—*mfg*	334518	3873
Clocks, except timeclocks: Watch, Clock, and Part—*mfg*	334518	3873
Clocks, including custom made: Jewelry Stores—*retail*	44831	5944
Closed circuit television equipment: Radio and Television Broadcasting and Wireless Communications Equipment—*mfg*	33422	3663
Closed circuit television services: Cable and Other Program Distribution—*info*	51322	4841
Cable Networks—*info*	51321	4841
Closet bowls, vitreous china: Vitreous China Plumbing Fixture and China and Earthenware Fittings and Bathroom Accessories—*mfg*	327111	3261
Closures, paper and disposable plastics: Industrial and Personal Service Paper—*whlse*	42213	5113
Closures, plastics: Plastics Pipe and Pipe Fitting—*mfg*	326122	3089
Plastics Product, All Other—*mfg*	326199	3089
Unsupported Plastics Profile Shape—*mfg*	326121	3089
Closures, stamped metal: Crown and Closure—*mfg*	332115	3466
Cloth mending, except wool–for the trade: Broadwoven Fabric Finishing Mills—*mfg*	313311	2269
Textile and Fabric Finishing (except Broadwoven Fabric) Mills—*mfg*	313312	2269

Description	NAICS	SIC
Cloth spreading machines: Textile Machinery—*mfg*	333292	3552
Cloth stripping machines: Textile Machinery—*mfg*	333292	3552
Cloth winding reels, wood: Manufacturing, All Other Miscellaneous—*mfg*	339999	2499
Wood Container and Pallet—*mfg*	32192	2499
Wood Product, All Other Miscellaneous—*mfg*	321999	2499
Cloth, abrasive: Abrasive Product—*mfg*	32791	3291
Fabricated Metal Product, All Other Miscellaneous—*mfg*	332999	3291
Cloth, asbestos: Motor Vehicle Brake System—*mfg*	33634	3292
Nonmetallic Mineral Product, All Other Miscellaneous—*mfg*	327999	3292
Cloth, circular knit: Textile and Fabric Finishing (except Broadwoven Fabric) Mills—*mfg*	313312	2257
Weft Knit Fabric Mills—*mfg*	313241	2257
Cloth, photographic–sensitized: Photographic and Photocopying Equipment—*mfg*	333315	3861
Photographic Film, Paper, Plate and Chemical—*mfg*	325992	3861
Cloth, tracing (drafting material): Chemical Product, All Other Miscellaneous—*mfg*	325998	3952
Institutional Furniture—*mfg*	337127	3952
Lead Pencil and Art Good—*mfg*	339942	3952
Cloth, varnished glass: Fabric Coating Mills—*mfg*	31332	2295
Cloth, warp knit-rnitse: Knit Fabric and Lace Mills, Other—*mfg*	313249	2258
Textile and Fabric Finishing (except Broadwoven Fabric) Mills—*mfg*	313312	2258
Cloth, wool–mending for the trade: Broadwoven Fabric Finishing Mills—*mfg*	313311	2231
Broadwoven Fabric Mills—*mfg*	31321	2231
Textile and Fabric Finishing (except Broadwoven Fabric) Mills—*mfg*	313312	2231
Cloth, woven wire–made from purchased wire: Fabricated Wire Product, Other—*mfg*	332618	3496
Cloth–garnet, emery, aluminum oxide, and silicon carbide coated: Abrasive Product—*mfg*	32791	3291
Fabricated Metal Product, All Other Miscellaneous—*mfg*	332999	3291
Cloth-lined paper: Coated and Laminated Paper—*mfg*	322222	2672
Clothes dryer controls, including dryness controls: Automatic Environmental Control for Residential, Commercial and Appliance Use—*mfg*	334512	3822
Clothes dryers (clothes horses), wood: Manufacturing, All Other Miscellaneous—*mfg*	339999	2499
Wood Container and Pallet—*mfg*	32192	2499
Wood Product, All Other Miscellaneous—*mfg*	321999	2499
Clothes dryers, household–electric andgas: Electrical Appliance, Television and Radio Set—*whlse*	42162	5064
Clothes drying frames, wood: Manufacturing, All Other Miscellaneous—*mfg*	339999	2499
Wood Container and Pallet—*mfg*	32192	2499
Wood Product, All Other Miscellaneous—*mfg*	321999	2499
Clothes hangers: Nondurable Goods, Other Miscellaneous—*whlse*	42299	5199
Clothes hangers, plastics: Plastics Pipe and Pipe Fitting—*mfg*	326122	3089
Plastics Product, All Other—*mfg*	326199	3089
Unsupported Plastics Profile Shape—*mfg*	326121	3089
Clothes horses, wood: Manufacturing, All Other Miscellaneous—*mfg*	339999	2499
Wood Container and Pallet—*mfg*	32192	2499
Wood Product, All Other Miscellaneous—*mfg*	321999	2499
Clothes poles, wood: Manufacturing, All Other Miscellaneous—*mfg*	339999	2499
Wood Container and Pallet—*mfg*	32192	2499
Wood Product, All Other Miscellaneous—*mfg*	321999	2499
Clothespins, plastics: Plastics Pipe and Pipe Fitting—*mfg*	326122	3089
Plastics Product, All Other—*mfg*	326199	3089
Unsupported Plastics Profile Shape—*mfg*	326121	3089
Clothespins, wood: Manufacturing, All Other Miscellaneous—*mfg*	339999	2499
Wood Container and Pallet—*mfg*	32192	2499
Wood Product, All Other Miscellaneous—*mfg*	321999	2499
Clothing Accessories Stores	**44815**	**5632**
Clothing accessories–women's, children's, and infants': Women's, Children's, and Infants' and Accessories—*whlse*	42233	5137
Clothing alteration and repair shops: Personal and Household Goods Repair and Maintenance, Other—*serv*	81149	7219
Clothing and Clothing Accessories Stores	**448**	
Clothing rental, except industrial launderers and linen supply: Formal Wear and Costume Rental—*real*	53222	7299
Clothing Stores	**4481**	
Clothing stores, family: Family Clothing Stores—*retail*	44814	5651
Clothing stores, men's and boys': Clothing Accessories Stores—*retail*	44815	5611
Men's Clothing Stores—*retail*	44811	5611
Clothing Stores, Other	**44819**	**5632**
Clothing stores, secondhand: Non-Depository Credit Intermediation, All Other—*fin*	522298	5932
Used Merchandise Stores—*retail*	45331	5932
Clothing, doll: Doll and Stuffed Toy—*mfg*	339931	3942
Clothing, electrically heated: Electrical Equipment and Component, All Other Miscellaneous—*mfg*	335999	3699
Clothing, fire resistant and protective: Surgical Appliance and Supplies—*mfg*	339113	3842
Clothing, fur: Fur and Leather Apparel—*mfg*	315292	2371
Clothing, leather or sheep-lined: Fur and Leather Apparel—*mfg*	315292	2386
Clothing, men's and boys': Men's and Boys' Clothing and Furnishings—*whlse*	42232	5136
Clothing, ready-to-wear–women 's: Women's Clothing Stores—*retail*	44812	5621
Clothing, vulcanized rubber and rubberized fabric: Fabric Coating Mills—*mfg*	31332	3069
Rubber Product, All Other—*mfg*	326299	3069
Clothing, waterproof: Apparel Accessories and Apparel, Other—*mfg*	315999	2385
Infants' Cut and Sew Apparel—*mfg*	315291	2385
Men's and Boys' Cut and Sew Apparel Contractors—*mfg*	315211	2385
Men's and Boys' Cut and Sew Other Outerwear—*mfg*	315228	2385
Men's and Boys' Cut and Sew Suit, Coat and Overcoat—*mfg*	315222	2385

ALPHABETICAL INDEX	NAICS	SIC
Women's and Girls' Cut and Sew Apparel Contractors—*mfg*	315212	2385
Women's and Girls' Cut and Sew Other Outerwear—*mfg*	315238	2385
Women's and Girls' Cut and Sew Suit, Coat, Tailored Jacket and Skirt—*mfg*	315234	2385
Clothing–women's, children's, and infants': Women's, Children's, and Infants' and Accessories—*whlse*	42233	5137
Cloths, drop–fabric: Canvas and Related Product Mills—*mfg*	314912	2394
Cloths, dusting and polishing–chemically treated: Polish and Other Sanitation Good—*mfg*	325612	2842
Cloths, lunch: Household Textile Product Mills, Other—*mfg*	314129	2392
Cloths, saddle: Textile Product Mills, All Other Miscellaneous—*mfg*	314999	2399
Cloud seeding: Environmental Consulting Services—*prof*	54162	8999
Clover farms: Crop Farming, All Other Miscellaneous—*ag*	111998	139
Hay Farming—*ag*	11194	139
Peanut Farming—*ag*	111992	139
Vegetable (except Potato) and Melon Farming, Other—*ag*	111219	139
Clubroom furniture, metal: Metal Household Furniture—*mfg*	337124	2514
Clubroom furniture, wood: Nonupholstered Wood Household Furniture—*mfg*	337122	2511
Clubs, health: Fitness and Recreational Sports Centers—*arts*	71394	7991
Clubs, membership–sports and recreation, except physical fitness: Fitness and Recreational Sports Centers—*arts*	71394	7997
Clubs, police–wood: Manufacturing, All Other Miscellaneous—*mfg*	339999	2499
Wood Container and Pallet—*mfg*	32192	2499
Wood Product, All Other Miscellaneous—*mfg*	321999	2499
Clubs–golf, Indian, etc. (sporting goods): Sporting and Athletic Goods—*mfg*	33992	3949
Clutch facings, ashestos: Motor Vehicle Brake System—*mfg*	33634	3292
Nonmetallic Mineral Product, All Other Miscellaneous—*mfg*	327999	3292
Clutches, except motor vehicle: Mechanical Power Transmission Equipment—*mfg*	333613	3568
Coagulation diagnostic reagents: In-Vitro Diagnostic Substance—*mfg*	325413	2835
Pharmaceutical Preparation—*mfg*	325412	2835
Coagulation products: Biological Product (except Diagnostic)—*mfg*	325414	2836
Coal: Coal and Other Mineral and Ore—*whlse*	42152	5052
Coal and Other Mineral and Ore Wholesalers	**42152**	**5052**
Coal breakers, cutters, and pulverizers: Mining Machinery and Equipment—*mfg*	333131	3532
Coal chutes, prefabricated sheet metal: Metal Container, Other—*mfg*	332439	3444
Sheet Metal Work—*mfg*	332322	3444
Coal dealers: Fuel Dealers, Other—*retail*	454319	5989
Coal gas, derived from chemical recovery coke ovens: Iron and Steel Mills—*mfg*	331111	3312
Petroleum and Coal Productsa, All Other—*mfg*	324199	3312
Coal gasification at the mine site: Crude Petroleum and Natural Gas Extraction—*mining*	211111	1311
Coal liquefaction at the mine site: Crude Petroleum and Natural Gas Extraction—*mining*	211111	1311
Coal Mining	**2121**	
Coal Mining	**21211**	
Coal Mining Support Activities	**213113**	**1241**
Coal mining, anthracite: Anthracite—*mining*	212113	1231
Coal mining, bituminous–surface: Bituminous Coal and Lignite Surface—*mining*	212111	1221
Coal mining, bituminous-underground: Bituminous Coal Underground—*mining*	212112	1222
Coal mining-brown: Bituminous Coal and Lignite Surface—*mining*	212111	1221
Coal pipeline operation: Pipeline, All Other—*trans*	48699	4619
Coal preparation plants, bituminous or lignite: Bituminous Coal and Lignite Surface—*mining*	212111	1221
Coal pyrolysis at the mine site: Crude Petroleum and Natural Gas Extraction—*mining*	211111	1311
Coal tar crudes, derived from chemical recovery coke ovens: Iron and Steel Mills—*mfg*	331111	3312
Petroleum and Coal Productsa, All Other—*mfg*	324199	3312
Coal tar crudes, derived from coal tar distillation: Cyclic Crude and Intermediate—*mfg*	325192	2865
Petrochemical—*mfg*	32511	2865
Coal tar distillates: Cyclic Crude and Intermediate—*mfg*	325192	2865
Petrochemical—*mfg*	32511	2865
Coal tar intermediates: Cyclic Crude and Intermediate—*mfg*	325192	2865
Petrochemical—*mfg*	32511	2865
Coal tar paving materials, not made in petroleum refineries: Asphalt Paving Mixture and Block—*mfg*	324121	2951
Coal tar products, primary and intermediate: Chemical and Allied Products, Other—*whlse*	42269	5169
Coal tar resins: Plastics Material and Resin—*mfg*	325211	2821
Coastal and Great Lakes Freight Transportation	**483113**	**4432**
Coastal and Great Lakes Passenger Transportation	**483114**	**4482**
Coaster brakes, bicycle: Motorcycle, Bicycle and Parts—*mfg*	336991	3751
Coastwise transportation of freight: Coastal and Great Lakes Freight—*trans*	483113	4424
Coat hangers, made from purchased wire: Fabricated Wire Product, Other—*mfg*	332618	3496
Coat linings, fronts, and pads: Apparel Accessories and Apparel, Other—*mfg*	315999	2396
Textile Product Mills, All Other Miscellaneous—*mfg*	314999	2396
Coat linings, fur: Fur and Leather Apparel—*mfg*	315292	2371
Coat supply service: Linen Supply—*serv*	812331	7213
Coat trimmings fabric: Apparel Accessories and Apparel, Other—*mfg*	315999	2396
Textile Product Mills, All Other Miscellaneous—*mfg*	314999	2396

Coated and Laminated Packaging Paper and Plastics Film Manufacturing	**322221**	**2671**
Coated and Laminated Paper Manufacturing	**322222**	**2679**
Coated fabrics: Broadwoven Fabric Finishing Mills—*mfg*	313311	5131
Piece Goods, Notions and Other Dry Goods—*whlse*	42231	5131
Textile and Fabric Finishing (except Broadwoven Fabric) Mills—*mfg*	313312	5131
Coated paper for packaging: Coated and Laminated Packaging Paper and Plastics Film—*mfg*	322221	2671
Unsupported Plastics Packaging Film and Sheet—*mfg*	326112	2671
Coating (hot dipping) of metals and formed products, for the trade: Costume Jewelry and Novelty—*mfg*	339914	3479
Jewelry (except Costume)—*mfg*	339911	3479
Metal Coating, Engraving (except Jewelry and Silverware), and Allied Services to Manufacturers—*mfg*	332812	3479
Silverware and Plated Ware—*mfg*	339912	3479
Coating and finishing machinery, paper: Paper Industry Machinery—*mfg*	333291	3554
Coating and impregnating of fabrics, except rubberzing: Fabric Coating Mills—*mfg*	31332	2295
Coating and wrapping steel pipe: Costume Jewelry and Novelty—*mfg*	339914	3479
Jewelry (except Costume)—*mfg*	339911	3479
Metal Coating, Engraving (except Jewelry and Silverware), and Allied Services to Manufacturers—*mfg*	332812	3479
Silverware and Plated Ware—*mfg*	339912	3479
Coating compounds, tar: Asphalt Shingle and Coating Materials—*mfg*	324122	2952
Coating of concrete structures with plastics–contractors: Glass and Glazing Contractors—*const*	23592	1799
Coating of metals with plastics and resins,for the trade: Costume Jewelry and Novelty—*mfg*	339914	3479
Jewelry (except Costume)—*mfg*	339911	3479
Metal Coating, Engraving (except Jewelry and Silverware), and Allied Services to Manufacturers—*mfg*	332812	3479
Silverware and Plated Ware—*mfg*	339912	3479
Coating of metals with silicon, for thetrade: Costume Jewelry and Novelty—*mfg*	339914	3479
Jewelry (except Costume)—*mfg*	339911	3479
Metal Coating, Engraving (except Jewelry and Silverware), and Allied Services to Manufacturers—*mfg*	332812	3479
Silverware and Plated Ware—*mfg*	339912	3479
Coating, air curing: Paint and Coating—*mfg*	32551	2851
Coating, Engraving, Heat Treating and Allied Activities	**3328**	
Coating, Engraving, Heat Treating, and Allied Activities	**33281**	
Coating, rust preventive: Costume Jewelry and Novelty—*mfg*	339914	3479
Jewelry (except Costume)—*mfg*	339911	3479
Metal Coating, Engraving (except Jewelry and Silverware), and Allied Services to Manufacturers—*mfg*	332812	3479
Silverware and Plated Ware—*mfg*	339912	3479
Coatings, chocolate: Chocolate and Confectionery from Cacao Beans—*mfg*	31132	2066
Coats, except fur and raincoats: Women's and Girls' Cut and Sew Apparel Contractors—*mfg*	315212	2337
Women's and Girls' Cut and Sew Suit, Coat, Tailored Jacket and Skirt—*mfg*	315234	2337
Coats, except tailored or work: Cut and Sew Apparel, All Other—*mfg*	315299	2329
Men's and Boys' Cut and Sew Apparel Contractors—*mfg*	315211	2329
Men's and Boys' Cut and Sew Other Outerwear—*mfg*	315228	2329
Coats, fur: Fur and Leather Apparel—*mfg*	315292	2371
Coats, leather or sheep-lined: Fur and Leather Apparel—*mfg*	315292	2386
Coats, men's and boys': Men's and Boys' Clothing and Furnishings—*whlse*	42232	5136
Coats, oiled fabric and blanket-lined: Cut and Sew Apparel, All Other—*mfg*	315299	2329
Men's and Boys' Cut and Sew Apparel Contractors—*mfg*	315211	2329
Men's and Boys' Cut and Sew Other Outerwear—*mfg*	315228	2329
Coats, service apparel (e.g., medical and lab): Apparel Accessories and Apparel, Other—*mfg*	315999	2339
Cut and Sew Apparel, All Other—*mfg*	315299	2339
Women's and Girls' Cut and Sew Apparel Contractors—*mfg*	315212	2339
Women's and Girls' Cut and Sew Other Outerwear—*mfg*	315238	2339
Coats, tailored: Men's and Boys' Cut and Sew Apparel Contractors—*mfg*	315211	2311
Men's and Boys' Cut and Sew Suit, Coat and Overcoat—*mfg*	315222	2311
Coats–women's, children's, and infants': Women's, Children's, and Infants' and Accessories—*whlse*	42233	5137
Coaxial cable: Building Material Dealers, Other—*retail*	44419	5063
Electrical Apparatus and Equipment, Wiring Supplies and Material—*whlse*	42161	5063
Coaxial cable, nonferrous: Aluminum Rolling and Drawing, Other—*mfg*	331319	3357
Communication and Energy Wire, Other—*mfg*	335929	3357
Copper Wire (except Mechanical) Drawing—*mfg*	331422	3357
Fiber Optic Cable—*mfg*	335921	3357
Nonferrous Metal (except Copper and Aluminum) Rolling, Drawing and Extruding—*mfg*	331491	3357
Cobalt 60 (radioactive): Basic Inorganic Chemical, All Other—*mfg*	325188	2819
Chemical Product, All Other Miscellaneous—*mfg*	325998	2819
Cobalt chloride: Basic Inorganic Chemical, All Other—*mfg*	325188	2819
Chemical Product, All Other Miscellaneous—*mfg*	325998	2819
Cobalt ore mining: Copper Ore and Nickel Ore—*mining*	212234	1061
Metal Ore, All Other—*mining*	212299	1061
Cobalt refining, primary: Primary Smelting and Refining of Nonferrous Metal (except Copper and Aluminum)—*mfg*	331419	3339
Cobalt sulfate: Basic Inorganic Chemical, All Other—*mfg*	325188	2819
Chemical Product, All Other Miscellaneous—*mfg*	325998	2819

ALPHABETICAL INDEX	NAICS	SIC
Cocaine and derivatives: Medicinal and Botanical—*mfg*	325411	2833
Cocks, drain (including basin): Fabricated Metal Product, All Other Miscellaneous—*mfg*	332999	3432
Plumbing Fixture Fitting and Trim—*mfg*	332913	3432
Cocktail lounges: Drinking Places (Alcoholic Beverages)—*accom*	72241	5813
Cocktail mixes, nonalcoholic-mig: Flavoring Syrup and Concentrate—*mfg*	31193	2087
Food, All Other Miscellaneous—*mfg*	311999	2087
Spice and Extract—*mfg*	311942	2087
Cocktails, alcoholic: Distilleries—*mfg*	31214	2085
Cocktails, alcoholic–premixed: Wine and Distilled Alcoholic Beverage—*whlse*	42282	5182
Cocoa butter: Chocolate and Confectionery from Cacao Beans—*mfg*	31132	2066
Cocoa mix, instant: Chocolate and Confectionery from Cacao Beans—*mfg*	31132	2066
Cocoa, powdered–mixed with other substances: Chocolate and Confectionery from Cacao Beans—*mfg*	31132	2066
Coconut oil: Fats and Oils Refining and Blending—*mfg*	311225	2076
Oilseed Processing, Other—*mfg*	311223	2076
Coconut, desiccated and shredded: Dried and Dehydrated Food—*mfg*	311423	2099
Cod oil, sulfonated: Surface Active Agent—*mfg*	325613	2843
Cod, catching of: Finfish Fishing—*ag*	114111	912
Coddington magnifying instruments: Optical Instrument and Lens—*mfg*	333314	3827
Codeine and derivatives: Medicinal and Botanical—*mfg*	325411	2833
Codfish–smoked, salted, dried, and pickled: Seafood Canning—*mfg*	311711	2091
Coffee and Tea Manufacturing	**31192**	**2095**
Coffee concentrates (instant coffee): Coffee and Tea—*mfg*	31192	2095
Spice and Extract—*mfg*	311942	2095
Coffee extracts: Coffee and Tea—*mfg*	31192	2095
Spice and Extract—*mfg*	311942	2095
Coffee farms: Fruit and Tree Nut Combination Farming—*ag*	111336	179
Noncitrus Fruit Farming, Other—*ag*	111339	179
Coffee flavorings and syrups: Flavoring Syrup and Concentrate—*mfg*	31193	2087
Food, All Other Miscellaneous—*mfg*	311999	2087
Spice and Extract—*mfg*	311942	2087
Coffee makers, house'hold–electric: Electric Housewares and Household Fan—*mfg*	335211	3634
Heating Equipment (except Electric and Warm Air Furnaces)—*mfg*	333414	3634
Coffee roasting and grinding machines: Food Product Machinery—*mfg*	333294	3556
Coffee roasting, except by wholesale grocers: Coffee and Tea—*mfg*	31192	2095
Spice and Extract—*mfg*	311942	2095
Coffee shops: Cafeterias—*accom*	722212	5812
Caterers—*accom*	72232	5812
Foodservice Contractors—*accom*	72231	5812

ALPHABETICAL INDEX	NAICS	SIC
Full-Service Restaurants—*accom*	72211	5812
Limited-Service Restaurants—*accom*	722211	5812
Snack and Nonalcoholic Beverage Bars—*accom*	722213	5812
Theater Companies and Dinner Theaters—*arts*	71111	5812
Coffee stores: Food (Health) Supplement Stores—*retail*	446191	5499
Food Stores, All Other Specialty—*retail*	445299	5499
Limited-Service Restaurants—*accom*	722211	5499
Meat Markets—*retail*	44521	5499
Coffee substitutes made from grain: Breakfast Cereal—*mfg*	31123	2043
Coffee and Tea—*mfg*	31192	2043
Coffee tables, wood: Nonupholstered Wood Household Furniture—*mfg*	337122	2511
Coffee urns, commercial: Equipment, Other Commercial—*whlse*	42144	5046
Coffee urns, restaurant type: Machinery, Other Commercial and Service Industry—*mfg*	333319	3589
Coffee, ground–mixed with grain or chicory: Coffee and Tea—*mfg*	31192	2095
Spice and Extract—*mfg*	311942	2095
Coffee, instant and freezedried: Coffee and Tea—*mfg*	31192	2095
Spice and Extract—*mfg*	311942	2095
Coffee–green, roasted, instant, freeze-dried, or extract: Grocery and Related Products, Other—*whlse*	42249	5149
Coffee-cart food service: Direct Selling Establishments, Other—*retail*	45439	5963
Mobile Foodservices—*accom*	72233	5963
Cofferdam construction–general contractors: Heavy, All Other—*const*	23499	1629
Industrial Nonbuilding Structure—*const*	23493	1629
Cog railways, except amusement and scenic: Transit and Ground Passenger, All Other—*trans*	485999	4119
Transportation, Special Needs—*trans*	485991	4119
Coil winding machines for springs: Other Metalworking Machinery, Other—*mfg*	333518	3549
Coil winding service: Machinery and Equipment (except Automotive and Electronic) Repair and Maintenance, Commercial and Industrial—*serv*	81131	7694
Motor and Generator—*mfg*	335312	7694
Coil windings, electronic: Electronic Coil, Transformer, and Other Inductor—*mfg*	334416	3677
Coiled flat springs: Steel Spring (except Wire)—*mfg*	332611	3493
Coilers (metalworking machines): Other Metalworking Machinery, Other—*mfg*	333518	3549
Coils for motors and generators: Motor and Generator—*mfg*	335312	3621
Coils, chokes and other inductors, electronic: Electronic Coil, Transformer, and Other Inductor—*mfg*	334416	3677
Coils, electronic: Electronic Parts and Equipment, Other—*whlse*	42169	5065
Coils, ignition–internal combustion engines: Motor Vehicle Electrical and Electronic Equipment, Other—*mfg*	336322	3694

Coils, pipe–fabricated from purchased metal pipe: Fabricated Pipe and Pipe Fitting—*mfg*	332996	3498
Coils, rod–aluminum-extruded: Aluminum Extruded Product—*mfg*	331316	3354
Coils, sheet–aluminum: Aluminum Sheet, Plate and Foil—*mfg*	331315	3353
Coils, wire–aluminum-made in rolling mills: Aluminum Rolling and Drawing, Other—*mfg*	331319	3355
Coin counters: Computer Peripheral Equipment, Other—*mfg*	334119	3578
Office Machinery—*mfg*	333313	3578
Coin purses, regardless of material: Personal Leather Good (except Women's Handbag and Purse)—*mfg*	316993	3172
Coin shops-retail, except mail-order: Stores (except Tobacco Stores), All Other Miscellaneous—*retail*	453998	5999
Coin wrapping machines: Lead Pencil and Art Good—*mfg*	339942	3579
Office Machinery—*mfg*	333313	3579
Watch, Clock, and Part—*mfg*	334518	3579
Coin-operated amusement machine, except phonographs: Fabricated Metal Product, All Other Miscellaneous—*mfg*	332999	3999
Coin-operated drycleaning: Coin-Operated Laundries and Drycleaners—*serv*	81231	7215
Coin-operated game machines: Durable Goods, Other Miscellaneous—*whlse*	42199	5099
Coin-operated laundries: Coin-Operated Laundries and Drycleaners—*serv*	81231	7215
Coin-Operated Laundries and Drycleaners	**81231**	**7215**
Coin-operated laundry and drycleaning routes: Coin-Operated Laundries and Drycleaners—*serv*	81231	7215
Coin-operated machines selling merchandise: Vending Machine Operators—*retail*	45421	5962
Coin-operated merchandise vending machines: Automatic Vending Machine—*mfg*	333311	3581
Coin-operated phonographs: Audio and Video Equipment—*mfg*	33431	3651
Coin-operated service machine operation–scales, shoeshine, lockers, and blood pressure: Personal Services, All Other—*serv*	81299	7299
Coins: Jewelry, Watch, Precious Stone and Precious Metal—*whlse*	42194	5094
Coins, mail-order: Electronic Shopping and Mail-Order Houses—*retail*	45411	5961
Coir yarns and roving: Broadwoven Fabric Mills—*mfg*	31321	2299
Narrow Fabric Mills—*mfg*	313221	2299
Nonwoven Fabric Mills—*mfg*	31323	2299
Textile and Fabric Finishing (except Broadwoven Fabric) Mills—*mfg*	313312	2299
Textile Product Mills, All Other Miscellaneous—*mfg*	314999	2299
Thread Mills—*mfg*	313113	2299
Yarn Spinning Mills—*mfg*	313111	2299
Coke: Coal and Other Mineral and Ore—*whlse*	42152	5052
Coke oven construction–general contractors: Heavy, All Other—*const*	23499	1629
Industrial Nonbuilding Structure—*const*	23493	1629
Coke oven gas, production and distribution: Natural Gas Distribution—*util*	22121	4925
Coke ovens, byproduct–operated for manufacture or distribution of gas: Natural Gas Distribution—*util*	22121	4925
Coke, petroleum–not produced in petroleum refineries: Petroleum and Coal Productsa, All Other—*mfg*	324199	2999
Coke, petroleum–produced in petroleum refineries: Petroleum Refineries—*mfg*	32411	2911
Coke, produced in beehive ovens: Iron and Steel Mills—*mfg*	331111	3312
Petroleum and Coal Productsa, All Other—*mfg*	324199	3312
Coke, produced in chemical recovery coke ovens: Iron and Steel Mills—*mfg*	331111	3312
Petroleum and Coal Productsa, All Other—*mfg*	324199	3312
Cold drink dispensing equipment, except coin-operated: Air-Conditioning and Warm Air Heating Equipment and Commercial and Industrial Refrigeration Equipment—*mfg*	333415	3585
Motor Vehicle Air-Conditioning—*mfg*	336391	3585
Cold forming type mills (rolling mill machinery): Rolling Mill Machinery and Equipment—*mfg*	333516	3547
Cold kits for labeling with technetium: In-Vitro Diagnostic Substance—*mfg*	325413	2835
Pharmaceutical Preparation—*mfg*	325412	2835
Cold remedies: Pharmaceutical Preparation—*mfg*	325412	2834
Cold storage locker rental: Refrigerated Warehousing and Storage Facilities—*trans*	49312	4222
Cold storage machinery: Refrigeration Equipment and Supplies—*whlse*	42174	5078
Cold storage plant construction–general contractors: Building, Commercial and Institutional—*const*	23332	1541
Manufacturing and Industrial Building—*const*	23331	1541
Cold storage warehousing: Refrigerated Warehousing and Storage Facilities—*trans*	49312	4222
Cold-finished steel bars–not made in hot-rolling mills: Cold-Rolled Steel Shape—*mfg*	331221	3316
Cold-Rolled Steel Shape Manufacturing	**331221**	**3316**
Cold-rolled steel strip, sheet, and bars–not made in hot-rolling mills: Cold-Rolled Steel Shape—*mfg*	331221	3316
Colemanite mining: Potash, Soda, and Borate Mineral—*mining*	212391	1474
Collapsible tubes for viscous products, metal: Fabricated Metal Product, All Other Miscellaneous—*mfg*	332999	3499
Collar and cuff sets: Apparel Accessories and Apparel, Other—*mfg*	315999	2339
Cut and Sew Apparel, All Other—*mfg*	315299	2339
Outerwear Knitting Mills—*mfg*	315191	2253
Women's and Girls' Cut and Sew Apparel Contractors—*mfg*	315212	2339
Women's and Girls' Cut and Sew Other Outerwear—*mfg*	315238	2339
Collar buttons, except precious metal and precious or semiprecious stones: Fastener, Button, Needle and Pin—*mfg*	339993	3965
Collar buttons, precious metal and precious or semiprecious stones: Jewelry (except Costume)—*mfg*	339911	3911

ALPHABETICAL INDEX	NAICS	SIC
Collar leather: Leather and Hide Tanning and Finishing—*mfg*	31611	3111
Collar linings, for men's coats: Apparel Accessories and Apparel, Other—*mfg*	315999	2396
Textile Product Mills, All Other Miscellaneous—*mfg*	314999	2396
Collars (machine tool accessories: Cutting Tool and Machine Tool Accessory—*mfg*	333515	3545
Hand and Edge Tool—*mfg*	332212	3545
Collars and collar pads (harness): Leather Good, All Other—*mfg*	316999	3199
Collars, dog: Leather Good, All Other—*mfg*	316999	3199
Collars, men's: Men's and Boys' Cut and Sew Apparel Contractors—*mfg*	315211	2321
Men's and Boys' Cut and Sew Shirt (except Work Shirt)—*mfg*	315223	2321
Collars, shaft (power transmission equipment): Mechanical Power Transmission Equipment—*mfg*	333613	3568
Collating machines for printing and bookbinding trade use: Printing Machinery and Equipment—*mfg*	333293	3555
Collating machines for store or office use: Lead Pencil and Art Good—*mfg*	339942	3579
Office Machinery—*mfg*	333313	3579
Watch, Clock, and Part—*mfg*	334518	3579
Collecting and distributing agencies operated by cleaning plants: Drycleaning Plants—*serv*	812322	7216
Collecting and distributing agencies, laundry–operated by power laundries: Laundries, Family and Commercial—*serv*	812321	7211
Collecting and distributing agents, laundry and drycleaning: Garment Pressing, and Agents for Laundries—*serv*	812391	7212
Collection Agencies	**56144**	**7322**
Collection agencies, accounts: Collection Agencies—*admin*	56144	7322
Repossession Services—*admin*	561491	7322
Collective bargaining units: Labor Unions and Similar Labor Organizations—*serv*	81393	8631
Collector rings for motors and generators: Motor and Generator—*mfg*	335312	3621
College clearinghouses: Personal Services, All Other—*serv*	81299	7299
Colleges, except junior: Colleges, Universities and Professional Schools—*educ*	61131	8221
Colleges, Universities and Professional Schools	**6113**	
Colleges, Universities and Professional Schools	**61131**	**8221**
Collets (machine tool accessories): Cutting Tool and Machine Tool Accessory—*mfg*	333515	3545
Hand and Edge Tool—*mfg*	332212	3545
Collision shops, automotive: Automotive Body, Paint and Interior Repair and Maintenance—*serv*	811121	7532
Colognes: Soap and Other Detergent—*mfg*	325611	2844
Toilet Preparation—*mfg*	32562	2844
Colonscopes, electromedical: Electromedical and Electrotherapeutic Apparatus—*mfg*	334510	3845

ALPHABETICAL INDEX	NAICS	SIC
Irradiation Apparatus—*mfg*	334517	3845
Color cards, paint–offset printing: Lithographic Printing, Commercial—*mfg*	323110	2752
Quick Printing—*mfg*	323114	2752
Color lakes and toners: Petrochemical—*mfg*	32511	2865
Color lithography: Lithographic Printing, Commercial—*mfg*	323110	2752
Quick Printing—*mfg*	323114	2752
Color pigments, inorganic: Carbon Black—*mfg*	325182	2816
Inorganic Dye and Pigment—*mfg*	325131	2816
Color pigments, organic–except animal black and bone black: Organic Dye and Pigment—*mfg*	325132	2865
Petrochemical—*mfg*	32511	2865
Color printing–except lithographed or gravure: Digital Printing—*mfg*	323115	2759
Flexographic Printing, Commercial—*mfg*	323112	2759
Printing, Other Commercial—*mfg*	323119	2759
Quick Printing—*mfg*	323114	2759
Color printing–gravure: Gravure Printing, Commercial—*mfg*	323111	2754
Color separations for printing: Prepress Services—*mfg*	323122	2796
Colorimeters, laboratory type: Analytical Laboratory Instrument—*mfg*	334516	3826
Coloring and finishing of aluminum and formed products, for the trade: Electroplating, Plating, Polishing, Anodizing and Coloring—*mfg*	332813	3471
Coloring of leather: Leather and Hide Tanning and Finishing—*mfg*	31611	3111
Colorings, food–except synthetic: Flavoring Syrup and Concentrate—*mfg*	31193	2087
Food, All Other Miscellaneous—*mfg*	311999	2087
Spice and Extract—*mfg*	311942	2087
Colors and pigments: Paint and Wallpaper Stores—*retail*	44412	5198
Paint, Varnish and Supplies—*whlse*	42295	5198
Colors for bakers' and confectioners' use, except synthetic: Flavoring Syrup and Concentrate—*mfg*	31193	2087
Food, All Other Miscellaneous—*mfg*	311999	2087
Spice and Extract—*mfg*	311942	2087
Colors in oil, except artists': Paint and Coating—*mfg*	32551	2851
Colors, artists'–water and oxide ceramic glass: Chemical Product, All Other Miscellaneous—*mfg*	325998	3952
Institutional Furniture—*mfg*	337127	3952
Lead Pencil and Art Good—*mfg*	339942	3952
Colors, dry–lakes, toners, or full strength organic colors: Organic Dye and Pigment—*mfg*	325132	2865
Petrochemical—*mfg*	32511	2865
Colors, extended (color lakes): Organic Dye and Pigment—*mfg*	325132	2865
Petrochemical—*mfg*	32511	2865
Colors, food–synthetic: Organic Dye and Pigment—*mfg*	325132	2865
Petrochemical—*mfg*	32511	2865
Colostomy appliances: Surgical Appliance and Supplies—*mfg*	339113	3842

Entry	NAICS	SIC
Columbite mining: Copper Ore and Nickel Ore—*mining*	212234	1061
Metal Ore, All Other—*mining*	212299	1061
Columbium refining, primary: Primary Smelting and Refining of Nonferrous Metal (except Copper and Aluminum)—*mfg*	331419	3339
Columns, concrete: Concrete Pipe—*mfg*	327332	3272
Concrete Product, Other—*mfg*	32739	3272
Nonmetallic Mineral Product, All Other Miscellaneous—*mfg*	327999	3272
Columns, fractionating–metal plate: Air-Conditioning and Warm Air Heating Equipment and Commercial and Industrial Refrigeration Equipment—*mfg*	333415	3443
Metal Tank (Heavy Gauge)—*mfg*	33242	3443
Plate Work—*mfg*	332313	3443
Power Boiler and Heat Exchanger—*mfg*	33241	3443
Columns, papier-mache or plaster of paris: Gypsum and Gypsum Product—*mfg*	32742	3299
Nonmetallic Mineral Product, All Other Miscellaneous—*mfg*	327999	3299
Comb cases, except precious metal: Personal Leather Good (except Women's Handbag and Purse)—*mfg*	316993	3172
Comb mounting, except precious metal: Fabricated Metal Product, All Other Miscellaneous—*mfg*	332999	3999
Plastics Product, All Other—*mfg*	326199	3999
Combat ships, building and repairing: Ship Building and Repairing—*mfg*	336611	3731
Combat vehicles, except trucks: Transportation Equipment and Supplies (except Motor Vehicle)—*whlse*	42186	5088
Combed yarn, cotton: Yarn Spinning Mills—*mfg*	313111	2281
Combination limit and fan controls: Automatic Environmental Control for Residential, Commercial and Appliance Use—*mfg*	334512	3822
Combination oil and hydronic controls: Automatic Environmental Control for Residential, Commercial and Appliance Use—*mfg*	334512	3822
Combines harvester-threshers: Farm Machinery and Equipment—*mfg*	333111	3523
Combing and converting top: Broadwoven Fabric Mills—*mfg*	31321	2299
Narrow Fabric Mills—*mfg*	313221	2299
Nonwoven Fabric Mills—*mfg*	31323	2299
Textile and Fabric Finishing (except Broadwoven Fabric) Mills—*mfg*	313312	2299
Textile Product Mills, All Other Miscellaneous—*mfg*	314999	2299
Thread Mills—*mfg*	313113	2299
Yarn Spinning Mills—*mfg*	313111	2299
Combing machines, textile: Textile Machinery—*mfg*	333292	3552
Combining, agricultural: Crop Harvesting, Primarily by Machine—*ag*	115113	722
Combs, except hard rubber: Fabricated Metal Product, All Other Miscellaneous—*mfg*	332999	3999
Plastics Product, All Other—*mfg*	326199	3999
Wood Product, All Other Miscellaneous—*mfg*	321999	3999
Combs, hard rubber: Fabric Coating Mills—*mfg*	31332	3069
Rubber Product, All Other—*mfg*	326299	3069
Combs, plastics: Plastics Pipe and Pipe Fitting—*mfg*	326122	3089
Plastics Product, All Other—*mfg*	326199	3089
Unsupported Plastics Profile Shape—*mfg*	326121	3089
Combustion control instruments, except commercial and household furnacetype: Instruments and Related Products for Measuring, Displaying, and Controlling Industrial Process Variables—*mfg*	334513	3823
Comets and parts: Musical Instrument—*mfg*	339992	3931
Comfort station operation: Personal Services, All Other—*serv*	81299	7299
Comforters or comfortables: Household Textile Product Mills, Other—*mfg*	314129	2392
Comforters, manmade fiber: Broadwoven Fabric Mills—*mfg*	31321	2221
Comic books–publishing and printing, or publishing only: Periodical Publishers—*info*	51112	2721
Commercial and household tableware and kitchenware–vitreous china: Vitreous China, Fine Earthenware and Other Pottery Product—*mfg*	327112	3262
Commercial and industrial buildings, operators of: Lessors of Nonresidential Buildings (except Miniwarehouses)—*real*	53112	6512
Promoters of Performing Arts, Sports and Similar Events with Facilities—*arts*	71131	6512
Commercial art and illustration: Graphic Design Services—*prof*	54143	7336
Commercial art schcols: Apprenticeship Training—*educ*	611513	8249
Technical and Trade Schools, Other—*educ*	611519	8249
Commercial banks, National: Banking, Commercial—*fin*	52211	6021
Credit Card Issuing—*fin*	52221	6021
Trust, Fiduciary and Custody Activities—*fin*	523991	6021
Commercial banks, not chartered: Banking, Commercial—*fin*	52211	6029
Commercial banks, State: Banking, Commercial—*fin*	52211	6022
Credit Card Issuing—*fin*	52221	6022
Depository Credit Intermediation, Other—*fin*	52219	6022
Trust, Fiduciary and Custody Activities—*fin*	523991	6022
Commercial building construction–general contractors: Building, Commercial and Institutional—*const*	23332	1542
Commercial earthenware, semivitreous: Vitreous China, Fine Earthenware and Other Pottery Product—*mfg*	327112	3263
Commercial lighting fixtures: Electric Lighting Fixture, Commercial, Industrial and Institutional—*mfg*	335122	3646
Commercial paper and accounts receivable, purchasers of: Financial Transactions Processing, Reserve, and Clearing House Activities—*fin*	52232	6153
Non-Depository Credit Intermediation, All Other—*fin*	522298	6153
Sales Financing—*fin*	52222	6153
Commercial photography: Nonscheduled Air, Other—*trans*	481219	7335
Photography, Commercial—*prof*	541922	7335
Commercial printing and newspaper publishing combined: Newspaper Publishers—*info*	51111	2711
Commercial printing, gravure: Gravure Printing, Commercial—*mfg*	323111	2754

ALPHABETICAL INDEX	NAICS	SIC
Commercial printing, lithographic: Lithographic Printing, Commercial—*mfg*	323110	2752
Quick Printing—*mfg*	323114	2752
Commercial printing, offset: Lithographic Printing, Commercial—*mfg*	323110	2752
Quick Printing—*mfg*	323114	2752
Commercial printing–except lithographed or gravure: Digital Printing—*mfg*	323115	2759
Flexographic Printing, Commercial—*mfg*	323112	2759
Printing, Other Commercial—*mfg*	323119	2759
Quick Printing—*mfg*	323114	2759
Commercial stationers (not printers): Office Supplies and Stationery Stores—*retail*	45321	5112
Stationary and Office Supplies—*whlse*	42212	5112
Commercial tableware and kitchenware,fine earthenware: Vitreous China, Fine Earthenware and Other Pottery Product—*mfg*	327112	3263
Commercial utensils, stamped and pressed metal–except cast aluminum: Metal Stamping—*mfg*	332116	3469
Commercial warehouse construction–general contractors: Building, Commercial and Institutional—*const*	23332	1541
Manufacturing and Industrial Building—*const*	23331	1541
Commercials, television–tape or ifim production: Motion Picture and Video Production—*info*	51211	7812
Commissary restaurants: Cafeterias—*accom*	722212	5812
Caterers—*accom*	72232	5812
Foodservice Contractors—*accom*	72231	5812
Full-Service Restaurants—*accom*	72211	5812
Limited-Service Restaurants—*accom*	722211	5812
Snack and Nonalcoholic Beverage Bars—*accom*	722213	5812
Theater Companies and Dinner Theaters—*arts*	71111	5812
Commodity Brokerage	**52314**	**6221**
Commodity brokers (contracts): Commodity Brokerage—*fin*	52314	6221
Commodity Contracts Dealing—*fin*	52313	6221
Commodity contract exchanges: Securities and Commodity Exchanges—*fin*	52321	6231
Commodity contract pool operators: Commodity Contracts Dealing—*fin*	52313	6799
Financial Investment Activities, Miscellaneous—*fin*	523999	6799
Intermediation, Miscellaneous—*fin*	52391	6799
Portfolio Management—*fin*	52392	6799
Commodity contract trading companies: Commodity Contracts Dealing—*fin*	52313	6799
Financial Investment Activities, Miscellaneous—*fin*	523999	6799
Intermediation, Miscellaneous—*fin*	52391	6799
Portfolio Management—*fin*	52392	6799
Commodity Contracts Dealing	**52313**	**6221**
Commodity Credit Corporation: International Trade Financing—*fin*	522293	6111

ALPHABETICAL INDEX	NAICS	SIC
Non-Depository Credit Intermediation, All Other—*fin*	522298	6111
Secondary Market Financing—*fin*	522294	6111
Commodity dealers (contracts): Commodity Brokerage—*fin*	52314	6221
Commodity Contracts Dealing—*fin*	52313	6221
Common sand mining: Construction Sand and Gravel—*mining*	212321	1442
Communicable disease program adminstration-govemment: Public Health Programs, Administration of—*pub*	92312	9431
Communication and Energy Wire and Cable Manufacturing	**33592**	
Communication and Energy Wire Manufacturing, Other	**335929**	**3357**
Communication Equipment Repair and Maintenance	**811213**	**7629**
Communications commissions: Communications, Electric, Gas, and Other Utilities, Regulation and Administration of—*pub*	92613	9631
Communications equipment and parts,telephone and telegraph: Electronic Coil, Transformer, and Other Inductor—*mfg*	334416	3661
Printed Circuit/Electronics Assembly—*mfg*	334418	3661
Telephone Apparatus—*mfg*	33421	3661
Communications equipment installation–contractors: Electrical Contractors—*const*	23531	1731
Security Systems Services (except Locksmiths)—*admin*	561621	1731
Communications Equipment Manufacturing	**3342**	
Communications Equipment Manufacturing, Other	**33429**	**3669**
Communications equipment, except household: Electronic Parts and Equipment, Other—*whlse*	42169	5065
Communications equipment, mobile andmicrowave: Radio and Television Broadcasting and Wireless Communications Equipment—*mfg*	33422	3663
Communications headgear, telephone: Electronic Coil, Transformer, and Other Inductor—*mfg*	334416	3661
Printed Circuit/Electronics Assembly—*mfg*	334418	3661
Telephone Apparatus—*mfg*	33421	3661
Communications wire and cable, nonferrous: Aluminum Rolling and Drawing, Other—*mfg*	331319	3357
Communication and Energy Wire, Other—*mfg*	335929	3357
Copper Wire (except Mechanical) Drawing—*mfg*	331422	3357
Fiber Optic Cable—*mfg*	335921	3357
Nonferrous Metal (except Copper and Aluminum) Rolling, Drawing and Extruding—*mfg*	331491	3357
Communications, Electric, Gas, and Other Utilities, Regulation and Administration of	**92613**	**9631**
Communion tables, wood: Institutional Furniture—*mfg*	337127	2531
Communion wafers: Bakeries, Commercial—*mfg*	311812	2052
Cookie and Cracker—*mfg*	311821	2052
Snack Food, Other—*mfg*	311919	2052
Community action agencies: Grantmaking and Giving Services, Other—*serv*	813219	8399
Social Advocacy Organizations, Other—*serv*	813319	8399
Voluntary Health Organizations—*serv*	813212	8399

Description	NAICS	SIC
Community Care Facilities for the Elderly	**6233**	
Community Care Facilities for the Elderly	**62331**	
Community centers: Child and Youth Services—*hlth*	62411	8322
Community Food Services—*hlth*	62421	8322
Community Housing Services, Other—*hlth*	624229	8322
Emergency and Other Relief Services—*hlth*	62423	8322
Individual and Family Services, Other—*hlth*	62419	8322
Parole Offices and Probation Offices—*pub*	92215	8322
Services for the Elderly and Persons with Disabilities—*hlth*	62412	8322
Temporary Shelters—*hlth*	624221	8322
Community chests: Grantmaking and Giving Services, Other—*serv*	813219	8399
Social Advocacy Organizations, Other—*serv*	813319	8399
Voluntary Health Organizations—*serv*	813212	8399
Community colleges (junior): Junior Colleges—*educ*	61121	8222
Community development agencies: Urban Planning and Community and Rural Development, Administration of—*pub*	92512	9532
Community development groups: Grantmaking and Giving Services, Other—*serv*	813219	8399
Social Advocacy Organizations, Other—*serv*	813319	8399
Voluntary Health Organizations—*serv*	813212	8399
Community Food and Housing, and Emergency and Other Relief Services	**6242**	
Community Food Services	**62421**	**8322**
Community Housing Services	**62422**	
Community Housing Services, Other	**624229**	**8322**
Community membership clubs, other than amusement and recreation clubs: Civic and Social Organizations—*serv*	81341	8641
Community service employment training programs: Vocational Rehabilitation Services—*hlth*	62431	8331
Community theater productions: Theater Companies and Dinner Theaters—*arts*	71111	7922
Commutators, electric motor: Motor and Generator—*mfg*	335312	3621
Commutators, electronic: Electronic Component, Other—*mfg*	334419	3679
Motor Vehicle Electrical and Electronic Equipment, Other—*mfg*	336322	3679
Printed Circuit/Electronics Assembly—*mfg*	334418	3679
Radio and Television Broadcasting and Wireless Communications Equipment—*mfg*	33422	3679
Commuter bus operation: Bus and Motor Vehicle Transit Systems—*trans*	485113	4111
Commuter Rail Systems—*trans*	485112	4111
Mixed Mode Transit Systems—*trans*	485111	4111
Transit and Ground Passenger, All Other—*trans*	485999	4111
Urban Transit Systems, Other—*trans*	485119	4111
Commuter rail passenger operation: Bus and Motor Vehicle Transit Systems—*trans*	485113	4111
Commuter Rail Systems—*trans*	485112	4111
Mixed Mode Transit Systems—*trans*	485111	4111
Transit and Ground Passenger, All Other—*trans*	485999	4111
Urban Transit Systems, Other—*trans*	485119	4111
Commuter Rail Systems	**485112**	**4111**
Compact disc, prerecorded–except video: Integrated Record Production/Distribution—*info*	51222	3652
Prerecorded Compact Disc (except Software), Tape, and Record Reproducing—*mfg*	334612	3652
Compactors, soil–vibratory: Construction Machinery—*mfg*	33312	3531
Overhead Traveling Crane, Hoist and Monorail System—*mfg*	333923	3531
Railroad Rolling Stock—*mfg*	33651	3531
Compacts, except precious metal and solid leather: Costume Jewelry and Novelty—*mfg*	339914	3961
Compacts, precious metal: Jewelry (except Costume)—*mfg*	339911	3911
Compacts, solid leather: Personal Leather Good (except Women's Handbag and Purse)—*mfg*	316993	3172
Comparators (machinists' precision tools): Cutting Tool and Machine Tool Accessory—*mfg*	333515	3545
Hand and Edge Tool—*mfg*	332212	3545
Comparators, optical: Optical Instrument and Lens—*mfg*	333314	3827
Compasses, gyroscopic and magnetic except portable: Search, Detection, Navigation, Guidance, Aeronautical, and Nautical System and Instrument—*mfg*	334511	3812
Compasses, magnetic–portable type: Measuring and Controlling Device, Other—*mfg*	334519	3829
Surgical and Medical Instrument—*mfg*	339112	3829
Composite board products, wood-based: Building Material Dealers, Other—*retail*	44419	5031
Composition blocks for paving: Asphalt Paving Mixture and Block—*mfg*	324121	2951
Composition stone, plastics: Plastics Pipe and Pipe Fitting—*mfg*	326122	3089
Plastics Product, All Other—*mfg*	326199	3089
Unsupported Plastics Profile Shape—*mfg*	326121	3089
Composition, hand–for the printing trade: Prepress Services—*mfg*	323122	2791
Composition, machine–e.g., linotype, monotype-for the printing trade: Prepress Services—*mfg*	323122	2791
Compost: Fertilizer (Mixing Only)—*mfg*	325314	2875
Compounding of Purchased Resin, Custom	**325991**	**3087**
Compounds, dental: Dental Equipment and Supplies—*mfg*	339114	3843
Compressed gas cylinder valves: Industrial Valve—*mfg*	332911	3491
Compressors for refrigeration and air-conditioning: Air-Conditioning and Warm Air Heating Equipment and Commercial and Industrial Refrigeration Equipment—*mfg*	333415	3585
Motor Vehicle Air-Conditioning—*mfg*	336391	3585
Compressors, air and gas–for general industrial use: Air and Gas Compressor—*mfg*	333912	3563
Compressors, air-conditioning: Warm Air Heating and Air-Conditioning Equipment and Supplies—*whlse*	42173	5075
Compressors, except air-conditioning and refrigeration: Industrial Machinery and Equipment—*whlse*	42183	5084
Computer and Computer Peripheral Equipment and Software Wholesalers	**42143**	**5045**

ALPHABETICAL INDEX	NAICS	SIC
Computer and Electronic Product Manufacturing	**334**	
Computer and Office Machine Repair and Maintenance	**811212**	**7629**
Computer and Peripheral Equipment Manufacturing	**3341**	
Computer and Peripheral Equipment Manufacturing	**33411**	
Computer and peripheral equipment, mail-order: Electronic Shopping and Mail-Order Houses—*retail*	45411	5961
Computer and Software Stores	**44312**	**5734**
Computer code authors: Custom Computer Programming Services, Custom—*prof*	541511	7371
Computer consultants: Computer Related Services, Other—*prof*	541519	7379
Computer Systems Design Services—*prof*	541512	7379
Computer Facilities Management Services	**541513**	**7376**
Computer forms, manifold or continuous (excludes paper simply lined): Manifold Business Form Printing—*mfg*	323116	2761
Computer hardware rental or leasing, except finance leasing or by the manufacturer: Office Machinery and Equipment Rental and Leasing—*real*	53242	7377
Computer input-output service: Data Processing Services—*info*	51421	7374
Computer interface equipment for industrial process control: Instruments and Related Products for Measuring, Displaying, and Controlling Industrial Process Variables—*mfg*	334513	3823
Computer logic modules: Semiconductor and Related Device—*mfg*	334413	3674
Computer operator training: Computer Training—*educ*	61142	8243
Technical and Trade Schools, Other—*educ*	611519	8243
Computer output to microfilm units, computer peripheral equipment: Computer Peripheral Equipment, Other—*mfg*	334119	3577
Computer paper: Office Supplies and Stationery Stores—*retail*	45321	5112
Stationary and Office Supplies—*whlse*	42212	5112
Computer paper tape punchers and devices, computer peripheral equipment: Computer Peripheral Equipment, Other—*mfg*	334119	3577
Computer Peripheral Equipment Manufacturing, Other	**334119**	**3578**
Computer peripheral equipment repair and maintenance: Computer and Office Machine Repair and Maintenance—*serv*	811212	7378
Computer and Software Stores—*retail*	44312	7378
Computer peripheral equipment, rental and leasing: Office Machinery and Equipment Rental and Leasing—*real*	53242	7377
Computer photography or portraits: Personal Services, All Other—*serv*	81299	7299
Computer printer stores: Computer and Software Stores—*retail*	44312	5734
Computer programming services: Custom Computer Programming Services, Custom—*prof*	541511	7371
Computer programs or systems software development, custom: Custom Computer Programming Services, Custom—*prof*	541511	7371
Computer Related Services, Other	**541519**	**7379**
Computer repair and maintenance: Computer and Office Machine Repair and Maintenance—*serv*	811212	7378
Computer and Software Stores—*retail*	44312	7378

ALPHABETICAL INDEX	NAICS	SIC
Computer repair training: Computer Training—*educ*	61142	8243
Technical and Trade Schools, Other—*educ*	611519	8243
Computer software publishers, prepackaged: Publishers—*info*	51121	7372
Software Reproducing—*mfg*	334611	7372
Computer software stores: Computer and Software Stores—*retail*	44312	5734
Computer software systems analysis and design, custom: Custom Computer Programming Services, Custom—*prof*	541511	7371
Computer software tape and disks, blank–rigid and floppy: Magnetic and Optical Recording Media—*mfg*	334613	3695
Computer software training: Computer Training—*educ*	61142	8243
Technical and Trade Schools, Other—*educ*	611519	8243
Computer software writers, freelance: Custom Computer Programming Services, Custom—*prof*	541511	7371
Computer software, mail-order: Electronic Shopping and Mail-Order Houses—*retail*	45411	5961
Computer Storage Device Manufacturing	**334112**	**3572**
Computer storage units: Computer Storage Device—*mfg*	334112	3572
Computer stores: Computer and Software Stores—*retail*	44312	5734
Computer Systems Design and Related Services	**54151**	
Computer Systems Design and Related Services	**5415**	
Computer Systems Design Services	**541512**	**7379**
Computer Terminal Manufacturing	**334113**	**3575**
Computer terminals: Computer and Computer Peripheral Equipment and Software—*whlse*	42143	5045
Computer and Software Stores—*retail*	44312	5045
Computer Terminal—*mfg*	334113	3575
Computer time brokerage: Data Processing Services—*info*	51421	7374
Computer time sharing: Data Processing Services—*info*	51421	7374
Computer Training	**61142**	**8243**
Computer-aided design (CAD) systems services: Computer Systems Design Services—*prof*	541512	7373
Computer-aided engineering (CAE) systems services: Computer Systems Design Services—*prof*	541512	7373
Computer-aided manufacturing (CAM) systems services: Computer Systems Design Services—*prof*	541512	7373
Computerized axial tomography (CT/CAT scanner) apparatus: Electromedical and Electrotherapeutic Apparatus—*mfg*	334510	3845
Irradiation Apparatus—*mfg*	334517	3845
Computers: Computer and Computer Peripheral Equipment and Software—*whlse*	42143	5045
Computer and Software Stores—*retail*	44312	5045
Computers–digital, analog, and hybrid: Electronic Computer—*mfg*	334111	3571
Concentrates, drink–except frozen fruit: Flavoring Syrup and Concentrate—*mfg*	31193	2087
Food, All Other Miscellaneous—*mfg*	311999	2087
Spice and Extract—*mfg*	311942	2087
Concentrates, flavoring: Flavoring Syrup and Concentrate—*mfg*	31193	2087

Description	NAICS	SIC
Food, All Other Miscellaneous—*mfg*	311999	2087
Spice and Extract—*mfg*	311942	2087
Concentrates, frozen fruit juice: Frozen Fruit, Juice and Vegetable—*mfg*	311411	2037
Concentrates, metallic: Coal and Other Mineral and Ore—*whlse*	42152	5052
Concentrates, perfume: Soap and Other Detergent—*mfg*	325611	2844
Toilet Preparation—*mfg*	32562	2844
Concentration machinery (metallurgical and mining): Mining Machinery and Equipment—*mfg*	333131	3532
Concert artists: Independent Artists, Writers, and Performers—*arts*	71151	7929
Musical Groups and Artists—*arts*	71113	7929
Performing Arts Companies, Other—*arts*	71119	7929
Concert management service: Promoters of Performing Arts, Sports and Similar Events without Facilities—*arts*	71132	7922
Theater Companies and Dinner Theaters—*arts*	71111	7922
Concertinas and parts: Musical Instrument—*mfg*	339992	3931
Concession operators, amusement devices and rides: Amusement and Recreation Industries, All Other—*arts*	71399	7999
Concession stands, prepared food (e.g., in airports and sports arenas): Cafeterias—*accom*	722212	5812
Caterers—*accom*	72232	5812
Foodservice Contractors—*accom*	72231	5812
Full-Service Restaurants—*accom*	72211	5812
Limited-Service Restaurants—*accom*	722211	5812
Snack and Nonalcoholic Beverage Bars—*accom*	722213	5812
Theater Companies and Dinner Theaters—*arts*	71111	5812
Concrete additives: Chemical and Allied Products, Other—*whlse*	42269	5169
Concrete and cinder block: Brick, Stone and Related Material—*whlse*	42132	5032
Building Material Dealers, Other—*retail*	44419	5032
Concrete and cinder block dealers: Building Material Dealers, Other—*retail*	44419	5211
Home Centers—*retail*	44411	5211
Concrete and masonry drilling tools, power–portable: Power-Driven Hand Tool—*mfg*	333991	3546
Concrete articulated mattresses for river revetment: Concrete Pipe—*mfg*	327332	3272
Concrete Product, Other—*mfg*	32739	3272
Nonmetallic Mineral Product, All Other Miscellaneous—*mfg*	327999	3272
Concrete Block and Brick Manufacturing	**327331**	**3271**
Concrete block laying–contractors: Masonry and Stone Contractors—*const*	23541	1741
Concrete breaking for streets and highways–contractors: Wrecking and Demolition Contractors—*const*	23594	1795
Concrete buggies, powered: Construction Machinery—*mfg*	33312	3531
Overhead Traveling Crane, Hoist and Monorail System—*mfg*	333923	3531
Railroad Rolling Stock—*mfg*	33651	3531
Concrete building products: Brick, Stone and Related Material—*whlse*	42132	5032
Building Material Dealers, Other—*retail*	44419	5032
Concrete burial vaults and boxes: Cosmetics, Beauty Supplies and Perfume Stores—*retail*	44612	5087
Service Establishment Equipment and Supplies—*whlse*	42185	5087
Concrete construction–roads, highways, public sidewalks, and streets–contractors: Highway and Street—*const*	23411	1611
Concrete Contractors	**2357**	
Concrete Contractors	**23571**	**1771**
Concrete curing compounds blends of pigments, waxes, and resins): Basic Organic Chemical, All Other—*mfg*	325199	2899
Chemical Product, All Other Miscellaneous—*mfg*	325998	2899
Concrete finishers–contractors: Concrete Contractors—*const*	23571	1771
Drywall, Plastering, Acoustical and Insulation Contractors—*const*	23542	1771
Concrete forms, sheet metal: Metal Container, Other—*mfg*	332439	3444
Sheet Metal Work—*mfg*	332322	3444
Concrete grouting equipment: Construction Machinery—*mfg*	33312	3531
Overhead Traveling Crane, Hoist and Monorail System—*mfg*	333923	3531
Railroad Rolling Stock—*mfg*	33651	3531
Concrete gunning equipment: Construction Machinery—*mfg*	33312	3531
Overhead Traveling Crane, Hoist and Monorail System—*mfg*	333923	3531
Railroad Rolling Stock—*mfg*	33651	3531
Concrete hardening compounds: Basic Organic Chemical, All Other—*mfg*	325199	2899
Chemical Product, All Other Miscellaneous—*mfg*	325998	2899
Concrete mixers and finishing machinery: Construction Machinery—*mfg*	33312	3531
Overhead Traveling Crane, Hoist and Monorail System—*mfg*	333923	3531
Railroad Rolling Stock—*mfg*	33651	3531
Concrete mixtures: Brick, Stone and Related Material—*whlse*	42132	5032
Building Material Dealers, Other—*retail*	44419	5032
Concrete Pipe Manufacturing	**327332**	**3272**
Concrete Pipe, Brick and Block Manufacturing	**32733**	
Concrete plants: Construction Machinery—*mfg*	33312	3531
Overhead Traveling Crane, Hoist and Monorail System—*mfg*	333923	3531
Railroad Rolling Stock—*mfg*	33651	3531
Concrete processing equipment: Construction and (except Petroleum) Machinery and Equipment—*whlse*	42181	5082
Concrete Product Manufacturing, Other	**32739**	**3272**
Concrete products machinery: Industrial Machinery, All Other—*mfg*	333298	3559
Machinery, Other Commercial and Service Industry—*mfg*	333319	3559
Concrete products, precast–except block and brick: Concrete Pipe—*mfg*	327332	3272
Concrete Product, Other—*mfg*	32739	3272
Nonmetallic Mineral Product, All Other Miscellaneous—*mfg*	327999	3272
Concrete products, structural precast or prestressed–placing of–contractors: Structural Steel Erection Contractors—*const*	23591	1791
Concrete reinforcement, placing of–contractors: Structural Steel Erection Contractors—*const*	23591	1791
Concrete reinforcing bars: Metal Service Centers and Offices—*whlse*	42151	5051

ALPHABETICAL INDEX	NAICS	SIC
Concrete reinforcing mesh, made from purchased wire: Fabricated Wire Product, Other—*mfg*	332618	3496
Concrete reinforcing steel bars, fabricated: Fabricated Structural Metal—*mfg*	332312	3449
Metal Window and Door—*mfg*	332321	3449
Ornamental and Architectural Metal Work—*mfg*	332323	3449
Roll Forming, Custom—*mfg*	332114	3449
Concrete work, except paving–contractors: Concrete Contractors—*const*	23571	1771
Drywall, Plastering, Acoustical and Insulation Contractors—*const*	23542	1771
Concrete work–private driveways, sidewalks, and parking areas–contractors: Concrete Contractors—*const*	23571	1771
Drywall, Plastering, Acoustical and Insulation Contractors—*const*	23542	1771
Concrete, asphaltic–not made in petroleum refineries: Asphalt Paving Mixture and Block—*mfg*	324121	2951
Concrete, bituminous: Asphalt Paving Mixture and Block—*mfg*	324121	2951
Concrete, dry mixture: Concrete Pipe—*mfg*	327332	3272
Concrete Product, Other—*mfg*	32739	3272
Nonmetallic Mineral Product, All Other Miscellaneous—*mfg*	327999	3272
Condensate production, cycle (natural gas): Natural Gas Liquid Extraction—*mining*	211112	1321
Condensation plastics: Plastics Material and Resin—*mfg*	325211	2821
Condensed and evaporated milk: Dry, Condensed, and Evaporated Dairy Product—*mfg*	311514	2023
Condensed and evaporated milk machinery: Food Product Machinery—*mfg*	333294	3556
Condenser boxes, metal plate: Air-Conditioning and Warm Air Heating Equipment and Commercial and Industrial Refrigeration Equipment—*mfg*	333415	3443
Metal Tank (Heavy Gauge)—*mfg*	33242	3443
Plate Work—*mfg*	332313	3443
Power Boiler and Heat Exchanger—*mfg*	33241	3443
Condenser paper: Coated and Laminated Paper—*mfg*	322222	2672
Newsprint Mills—*mfg*	322122	2621
Paper (except Newsprint) Mills—*mfg*	322121	2621
Condensers and condensing units–refrigeration and air-conditioning: Air-Conditioning and Warm Air Heating Equipment and Commercial and Industrial Refrigeration Equipment—*mfg*	333415	3585
Motor Vehicle Air-Conditioning—*mfg*	336391	3585
Condensers for motors and generators: Electrical Equipment and Component, All Other Miscellaneous—*mfg*	335999	3629
Condensers, barometric: Air-Conditioning and Warm Air Heating Equipment and Commercial and Industrial Refrigeration Equipment—*mfg*	333415	3443
Metal Tank (Heavy Gauge)—*mfg*	33242	3443
Plate Work—*mfg*	332313	3443
Power Boiler and Heat Exchanger—*mfg*	33241	3443

ALPHABETICAL INDEX	NAICS	SIC
Condensers, electronic: Electronic Capacitor—*mfg*	334414	3675
Electronic Parts and Equipment, Other—*whlse*	42169	5065
Condensers, except electronic–fixed and variable: Electrical Equipment and Component, All Other Miscellaneous—*mfg*	335999	3629
Condensers, steam: Air-Conditioning and Warm Air Heating Equipment and Commercial and Industrial Refrigeration Equipment—*mfg*	333415	3443
Metal Tank (Heavy Gauge)—*mfg*	33242	3443
Plate Work—*mfg*	332313	3443
Power Boiler and Heat Exchanger—*mfg*	33241	3443
Condensers, synchronous–electric: Motor and Generator—*mfg*	335312	3621
Condensing units, air-conditioning: Warm Air Heating and Air-Conditioning Equipment and Supplies—*whlse*	42173	5075
Condensing units, refrigeration: Refrigeration Equipment and Supplies—*whlse*	42174	5078
Condominium developers on own account: Building, Commercial and Institutional—*const*	23332	1531
Manufacturing and Industrial Building—*const*	23331	1531
Multifamily Housing—*const*	23322	1531
Single Family Housing—*const*	23321	1531
Condominium managers: Nonresidential Property Managers—*real*	531312	6531
Residential Property Managers—*real*	531311	6531
Conductor connectors, solderless connectors, sleeves, or soldering lugs: Current-Carrying Wiring Device—*mfg*	335931	3643
Conduit construction–contractors: Power and Communication Transmission Line—*const*	23492	1623
Water, Sewer, and Pipeline—*const*	23491	1623
Conduit, vitrified clay: Structural Clay Product, Other—*mfg*	327123	3259
Conduit–welded, lock joint, and heavy riveted: Iron and Steel Pipes and Tubes from Purchased Steel—*mfg*	33121	3317
Conduits and fittings, electrical: Noncurrent-Carrying Wiring Device—*mfg*	335932	3644
Conduits and raceways: Building Material Dealers, Other—*retail*	44419	5063
Electrical Apparatus and Equipment, Wiring Supplies and Material—*whlse*	42161	5063
Conduits, asbestos cement: Motor Vehicle Brake System—*mfg*	33634	3292
Nonmetallic Mineral Product, All Other Miscellaneous—*mfg*	327999	3292
Conduits, concrete: Concrete Pipe—*mfg*	327332	3272
Concrete Product, Other—*mfg*	32739	3272
Nonmetallic Mineral Product, All Other Miscellaneous—*mfg*	327999	3272
Conduits, fiber (pressed pulp): Coated and Laminated Paper—*mfg*	322222	2679
Converted Paper Product, All Other—*mfg*	322298	2679
Die-Cut Paper and Paperboard Office Supplies—*mfg*	322231	2679
Non-Folding Sanitary Food Container—*mfg*	322215	2679
Cones, fiber–for winding yarn, string, ribbons, or cloth: Fiber Can, Tube, Drum, and Similar Products—*mfg*	322214	2655
Cones, ice cream: Bakeries, Commercial—*mfg*	311812	2052

Entry	NAICS	SIC
Cookie and Cracker—*mfg*	311821	2052
Snack Food, Other—*mfg*	311919	2052
Cones, pyrometric–earthenware: Vitreous China, Fine Earthenware and Other Pottery Product—*mfg*	327112	3269
Confectioners' colors: Flavoring Syrup and Concentrate—*mfg*	31193	2087
Food, All Other Miscellaneous—*mfg*	311999	2087
Spice and Extract—*mfg*	311942	2087
Confectionery: Confectionery—*whlse*	42245	5145
Confectionery from Purchased Chocolate—*mfg*	31133	2064
Non-Chocolate Confectionery—*mfg*	31134	2064
Confectionery and Nut Stores	**445292**	**5441**
Confectionery machinery: Food Product Machinery—*mfg*	333294	3556
Confectionery Manufacturing from Purchased Chocolate	**31133**	**2064**
Confectionery produced for direct sale on the premises: Confectionery and Nut Stores—*retail*	445292	5441
Confectionery stores: Confectionery and Nut Stores—*retail*	445292	5441
Confectionery Wholesalers	**42245**	**5145**
Confetti: Coated and Laminated Paper—*mfg*	322222	2679
Converted Paper Product, All Other—*mfg*	322298	2679
Die-Cut Paper and Paperboard Office Supplies—*mfg*	322231	2679
Non-Folding Sanitary Food Container—*mfg*	322215	2679
Congress: Legislative Bodies—*pub*	92112	9121
Connecting rods, motor vehicle–gasoline engine: Gasoline Engine and Engine Parts—*mfg*	336312	3714
Motor Vehicle Parts, All Other—*mfg*	336399	3714
Connectors and terminals for electrical devices: Current-Carrying Wiring Device—*mfg*	335931	3643
Connectors, conductor–solderless connectors, sleeves, or soldering lugs: Current-Carrying Wiring Device—*mfg*	335931	3643
Connectors, electric cord: Current-Carrying Wiring Device—*mfg*	335931	3643
Connectors, electronic: Electronic Parts and Equipment, Other—*whlse*	42169	5065
Connectors, electronic–e.g., coaxial, cylindrical, rack and panel, printed circuit: Electronic Connector—*mfg*	334417	3678
Connectors, power: Switchgear and Switchboard Apparatus—*mfg*	335313	3613
Connectors, solderless (wiring devices): Current-Carrying Wiring Device—*mfg*	335931	3643
Conservation and stabilization agencies: Land, Mineral, Wildlife, and Forest Conservation—*pub*	92412	9512
Console tables, wood: Nonupholstered Wood Household Furniture—*mfg*	337122	2511
Constant impedance transformers: Electronic Coil, Transformer, and Other Inductor—*mfg*	334416	3677
Construction	**23**	
Construction and Mining (except Petroleum) Machinery and Equipment Wholesalers	**42181**	**5082**
Construction and mining equipment forgings, ferrous–not made in rolling mills: Iron and Steel Forging—*mfg*	332111	3462

Entry	NAICS	SIC
Construction equipment operation schools: Apprenticeship Training—*educ*	611513	8249
Technical and Trade Schools, Other—*educ*	611519	8249
Construction equipment, heavy–rental and leasing: Construction, and Forestry Machinery and Equipment Rental and Leasing—*real*	532412	7353
Heavy, All Other—*const*	23499	7353
Construction machinery and equipment: Construction and (except Petroleum) Machinery and Equipment—*whlse*	42181	5082
Construction Machinery Manufacturing	**33312**	**3531**
Construction machinery, except mining: Construction Machinery—*mfg*	33312	3531
Overhead Traveling Crane, Hoist and Monorail System—*mfg*	333923	3531
Railroad Rolling Stock—*mfg*	33651	3531
Construction management: Office Administrative Services—*admin*	56111	8741
Construction Material Wholesalers, Other	**42139**	**5039**
Construction materials, electrical–interior and exterior: Building Material Dealers, Other—*retail*	44419	5063
Electrical Apparatus and Equipment, Wiring Supplies and Material—*whlse*	42161	5063
Construction paper: Newsprint Mills—*mfg*	322122	2621
Paper (except Newsprint) Mills—*mfg*	322121	2621
Construction Sand and Gravel Mining	**212321**	**1442**
Construction sand mining: Construction Sand and Gravel—*mining*	212321	1442
Construction, Mining and Forestry Machinery and Equipment Rental and Leasing	**532412**	**7359**
Construction, Transportation, Mining and Forestry Machinery and Equipment Rental and Leasing	**53241**	
Construction–bridges, tunnels, and elevated highways–general contractors: Bridge and Tunnel—*const*	23412	1622
Construction–water, sewer, pipeline, power line–general contractors: Power and Communication Transmission Line—*const*	23492	1623
Water, Sewer, and Pipeline—*const*	23491	1623
Consulates: International Affairs—*pub*	92812	9721
Consultants, nuclear–not connected with business service laboratories: Environmental Consulting Services—*prof*	54162	8999
Scientific and Technical Consulting Services, Other—*prof*	54169	8999
Consultants, tariff: Freight Arrangement—*trans*	48851	4731
Management Consulting Services, Other—*prof*	541618	4731
Consumer buying service: Personal Services, All Other—*serv*	81299	7299
Consumer credit reporting bureaus: Credit Bureaus—*admin*	56145	7323
Consumer electronic equipment stores: Automotive Parts and Accessories Stores—*retail*	44131	5731
Radio, Television and Other Electronics Stores—*retail*	443112	5731
Consumer Electronics and Appliances Rental	**53221**	**7359**
Consumer Electronics Repair and Maintenance	**811211**	**7629**
Consumer finance companies: Consumer Lending—*fin*	522291	6141
Credit Card Issuing—*fin*	52221	6141
Sales Financing—*fin*	52222	6141

ALPHABETICAL INDEX	NAICS	SIC
Consumer Goods Rental	**5322**	
Consumer Goods Rental, All Other	**532299**	**7359**
Consumer Goods Rental, Other	**53229**	
Consumer Lending	**522291**	**6141**
Consumer protection offices: General Economic Programs, Administration of—*pub*	92611	9611
Contact lens insurance: Direct Property and Casualty Insurance Carriers—*fin*	524126	6331
Insurance Funds, Other—*fin*	52519	6331
Reinsurance Carriers—*fin*	52413	6331
Contact lenses: Ophthalmic Goods—*mfg*	339115	3851
Ophthalmic Goods—*whlse*	42146	5048
Contacts, electrical–except carbon and graphite: Current-Carrying Wiring Device—*mfg*	335931	3643
Container board: Paperboard Mills—*mfg*	32213	2631
Containers for packing, bottling, and canning–glass: Glass Container—*mfg*	327213	3221
Containers made of staves: Wood Container and Pallet—*mfg*	32192	2449
Containers, air cargo–metal: Fabricated Metal Product, All Other Miscellaneous—*mfg*	332999	3537
Industrial Truck, Tractor, Trailer and Stacker Machinery—*mfg*	333924	3537
Metal Container, Other—*mfg*	332439	3537
Containers, corrugated and solid fiberboard: Corrugated and Solid Fiber Box—*mfg*	322211	2653
Containers, foil–for bakery goods and frozen goods: Fabricated Metal Product, All Other Miscellaneous—*mfg*	332999	3497
Laminated Aluminum Foil for Flexible Packaging Uses—*mfg*	322225	3497
Containers, food, sanitary–except folding: Non-Folding Sanitary Food Container—*mfg*	322215	2656
Containers, laminated phenolic and vulcanized fiber: Fiber Can, Tube, Drum, and Similar Products—*mfg*	322214	2655
Containers, liquid tight fiber (except sanitary food containers): Fiber Can, Tube, Drum, and Similar Products—*mfg*	322214	2655
Containers, metal–food, milk, oil, beer, general line: Metal Can—*mfg*	332431	3411
Containers, paper and disposable plastics: Industrial and Personal Service Paper—*whlse*	42213	5113
Containers, plastics–except foam, bottles, and bags: Plastics Pipe and Pipe Fitting—*mfg*	326122	3089
Plastics Product, All Other—*mfg*	326199	3089
Unsupported Plastics Profile Shape—*mfg*	326121	3089
Containers, shipping–barrels, kegs, drums, packages-liquid tight (metal): Metal Container, Other—*mfg*	332439	3412
Containers, shipping–metal plate (bombs, etc.) except missile casings: Air-Conditioning and Warm Air Heating Equipment and Commercial and Industrial Refrigeration Equipment—*mfg*	333415	3443
Metal Tank (Heavy Gauge)—*mfg*	33242	3443

ALPHABETICAL INDEX	NAICS	SIC
Plate Work—*mfg*	332313	3443
Power Boiler and Heat Exchanger—*mfg*	33241	3443
Containers, veneer and plywood–except nailed and lock corner boxes: Wood Container and Pallet—*mfg*	32192	2449
Continuing Care Retirement Communities	**623311**	**8052**
Continuing education programs: Schools and Instruction, All Other Miscellaneous—*educ*	611699	8299
Continuous forms, office and business–carbonized or multiple reproduction: Manifold Business Form Printing—*mfg*	323116	2761
Continuous towel supply service: Linen Supply—*serv*	812331	7213
Contour projectors: Optical Instrument and Lens—*mfg*	333314	3827
Contract feeding: Cafeterias—*accom*	722212	5812
Caterers—*accom*	72232	5812
Foodservice Contractors—*accom*	72231	5812
Full-Service Restaurants—*accom*	72211	5812
Limited-Service Restaurants—*accom*	722211	5812
Snack and Nonalcoholic Beverage Bars—*accom*	722213	5812
Theater Companies and Dinner Theaters—*arts*	71111	5812
Contractors' associations: Business Associations—*serv*	81391	8611
Contractors' disbursement control: Business Support Services, All Other—*admin*	561499	7389
Contrast media diagnostic products (e.g., iodine and barium): In-Vitro Diagnostic Substance—*mfg*	325413	2835
Pharmaceutical Preparation—*mfg*	325412	2835
Control circuit devices–magnet and solid-state: Relay and Industrial Control—*mfg*	335314	3625
Control circuit relays, industrial: Relay and Industrial Control—*mfg*	335314	3625
Control equipment for buses and trucks: Motor and Generator—*mfg*	335312	3621
Control equipment, electric: Relay and Industrial Control—*mfg*	335314	3625
Control equipment, motor vehicle–acceleration mechanisms and governors: Gasoline Engine and Engine Parts—*mfg*	336312	3714
Motor Vehicle Electrical and Electronic Equipment, Other—*mfg*	336322	3714
Motor Vehicle Parts, All Other—*mfg*	336399	3714
Control panels, electric power distribution: Switchgear and Switchboard Apparatus—*mfg*	335313	3613
Control rod drive mechanisms for use on nuclear reactors: Industrial Machinery, All Other—*mfg*	333298	3559
Machinery, Other Commercial and Service Industry—*mfg*	333319	3559
Control transformers: Power, Distribution and Specialty Transformer—*mfg*	335311	3612
Control valves, fluid power–metal: Fluid Power Valve and Hose Fitting—*mfg*	332912	3492
Controlled rectifiers, solid-state: Semiconductor and Related Device—*mfg*	334413	3674
Controllers for process variables–electric, electronic, and pneumatic: Instruments and Related Products for Measuring, Displaying, and Controlling Industrial Process Variables—*mfg*	334513	3823

Description	NAICS	SIC
Controllers' offices: Public Finance—*pub*	92113	9311
Controlling instruments and accessories, industrial: Industrial Machinery and Equipment—*whlse*	42183	5084
Controls and control accessories, industrial: Relay and Industrial Control—*mfg*	335314	3625
Controls for adjustable speed drives: Relay and Industrial Control—*mfg*	335314	3625
Controls, revolution and timing instruments: Totalizing Fluid Meter and Counting Device—*mfg*	334514	3824
Convalescent homes for psychiatric patients, with health care: Continuing Care Retirement Communities—*hlth*	623311	8059
Nursing Care Facilities—*hlth*	62311	8059
Convalescent homes with continuous nursing care: Continuing Care Retirement Communities—*hlth*	623311	8051
Nursing Care Facilities—*hlth*	62311	8051
Convalescent homes with health care: Continuing Care Retirement Communities—*hlth*	623311	8059
Nursing Care Facilities—*hlth*	62311	8059
Convection ovens, household–including portable: Household Cooking Appliance—*mfg*	335221	3631
Convectors: Building Material Dealers, Other—*retail*	44419	5074
Plumbing and Heating Equipment and Supplies (Hydronics)—*whlse*	42172	5074
Convenience food stores: Convenience Stores—*retail*	44512	5411
Gasoline Stations with Convenience Stores—*retail*	44711	5411
Supermarkets and Other Grocery (except Convenience) Stores—*retail*	44511	5411
Warehouse Clubs and Superstores—*retail*	45291	5411
Convenience outlets, electric: Current-Carrying Wiring Device—*mfg*	335931	3643
Convenience Stores	**44512**	**5411**
Convention and Trade Show Organizers	**56192**	**7389**
Convention and Visitors Bureaus	**561591**	**7389**
Convention bureaus: Convention and Trade Show Organizers—*admin*	56192	7389
Convention decorators: Convention and Trade Show Organizers—*admin*	56192	7389
Convention and Visitors Bureaus—*admin*	561591	7389
Convents: Religious Organizations—*serv*	81311	8661
Converted Paper Product Manufacturing	**3222**	
Converted Paper Product Manufacturing, All Other	**322298**	**2679**
Converted Paper Product Manufacturing, Other	**32229**	
Converters, phase and rotary–electrical equipment: Motor and Generator—*mfg*	335312	3621
Convertible sofas: Mattress—*mfg*	33791	2515
Upholstered Household Furniture—*mfg*	337121	2515
Convertors, leather: Leather and Hide Tanning and Finishing—*mfg*	31611	3111
Conveyor and Conveying Equipment Manufacturing	**333922**	**3535**
Conveyor belts, made from purchased wire: Fabricated Wire Product, Other—*mfg*	332618	3496
Conveyor system installation–contractors: Building Equipment and Other Machinery Installation Contractors—*const*	23595	1796
Conveyor systems: Industrial Machinery and Equipment—*whlse*	42183	5084
Conveyor systems for general industrial use: Conveyor and Conveying Equipment—*mfg*	333922	3535
Conveyors, farm (agricultural machinery): Conveyor and Conveying Equipment—*mfg*	333922	3523
Farm Machinery and Equipment—*mfg*	333111	3523
Cookers, pressure–stamped or drawn: Kitchen Utensil, Pot and Pan—*mfg*	332214	3469
Cookers, steam–restaurant type: Machinery, Other Commercial and Service Industry—*mfg*	333319	3589
Cookie and Cracker Manufacturing	**311821**	**2052**
Cookie stores: Baked Goods Stores—*retail*	445291	5461
Retail Bakeries—*mfg*	311811	5461
Snack and Nonalcoholic Beverage Bars—*accom*	722213	5461
Cookie, Cracker, and Pasta Manufacturing	**31182**	
Cookies: Bakeries, Commercial—*mfg*	311812	2052
Cookie and Cracker—*mfg*	311821	2052
Grocery and Related Products, Other—*whlse*	42249	5149
Snack Food, Other—*mfg*	311919	2052
Cooking appliances, household–electric, except convection and microwaveovens: Electric Housewares and Household Fan—*mfg*	335211	3634
Heating Equipment (except Electric and Warm Air Furnaces)—*mfg*	333414	3634
Cooking equipment, commercial: Equipment, Other Commercial—*whlse*	42144	5046
Machinery, Other Commercial and Service Industry—*mfg*	333319	3589
Cooking oils: Grocery and Related Products, Other—*whlse*	42249	5149
Cooking oils, vegetable–except corn oil-refined: Fats and Oils Refining and Blending—*mfg*	311225	2079
Oilseed Processing, Other—*mfg*	311223	2079
Soybean Processing—*mfg*	311222	2079
Cooking schools: Schools and Instruction, All Other Miscellaneous—*educ*	611699	8299
Cooking utensils, cast aluminum–except die-castings: Aluminum Foundries—*mfg*	331524	3365
Cooking utensils, cast iron: Iron Foundries—*mfg*	331511	3321
Cooking utensils, glass and glass ceramic: Pressed and Blown Glass and Glassware, Other—*mfg*	327212	3229
Cooking ware, china: Vitreous China, Fine Earthenware and Other Pottery Product—*mfg*	327112	3262
Cooking ware, fine earthenware: Vitreous China, Fine Earthenware and Other Pottery Product—*mfg*	327112	3263
Cooking ware, porcelain enameled: Kitchen Utensil, Pot and Pan—*mfg*	332214	3469
Cooking ware–stoneware, coarse earthen-ware, and pottery': Vitreous China, Fine Earthenware and Other Pottery Product—*mfg*	327112	3269

ALPHABETICAL INDEX	NAICS	SIC
Cookware: Home Furnishings Stores, All Other—*retail*	442299	5719
Window Treatment Stores—*retail*	442291	5719
Cooled air suppliers: Steam and Air-Conditioning Supply—*util*	22133	4961
Coolers, beverage and drinking water–mechanical: Refrigeration Equipment and Supplies—*whlse*	42174	5078
Coolers, milk and water–electric: Air-Conditioning and Warm Air Heating Equipment and Commercial and Industrial Refrigeration Equipment—*mfg*	333415	3585
Motor Vehicle Air-Conditioning—*mfg*	336391	3585
Coolers, portable–foamed plastics: Polystyrene Foam Product—*mfg*	32614	3086
Urethane and Other Foam Product (except Polystyrene)—*mfg*	32615	3086
Cooling of railroad cars: Air, Rail, and Water Equipment Rental and Leasing, Commercial—*real*	532411	4741
Rail Support Activities—*trans*	48821	4741
Cooling systems, aircraft engine: Aircraft Engine and Engine Parts—*mfg*	336412	3724
Cooling towers, metal plate: Air-Conditioning and Warm Air Heating Equipment and Commercial and Industrial Refrigeration Equipment—*mfg*	333415	3443
Metal Tank (Heavy Gauge)—*mfg*	33242	3443
Plate Work—*mfg*	332313	3443
Power Boiler and Heat Exchanger—*mfg*	33241	3443
Cooling towers, sheet metal: Metal Container, Other—*mfg*	332439	3444
Sheet Metal Work—*mfg*	332322	3444
Cooling towers, wood or wood and sheetmetal combination: Manufacturing, All Other Miscellaneous—*mfg*	339999	2499
Wood Container and Pallet—*mfg*	32192	2499
Wood Product, All Other Miscellaneous—*mfg*	321999	2499
Cooperage: Wood Container and Pallet—*mfg*	32192	2449
Cooperage stock: Industrial Machinery and Equipment—*whlse*	42183	5085
Industrial Supplies—*whlse*	42184	5085
Cooperage stock mills: Cut Stock, Resawing Lumber, and Planing—*mfg*	321912	2429
Sawmills—*mfg*	321113	2429
Wood Product, All Other Miscellaneous—*mfg*	321999	2429
Cooperage stock–staves, heading, and hoops-sawed or split: Cut Stock, Resawing Lumber, and Planing—*mfg*	321912	2429
Sawmills—*mfg*	321113	2429
Wood Product, All Other Miscellaneous—*mfg*	321999	2429
Cooperative apartment developers on own account: Building, Commercial and Institutional—*const*	23332	1531
Manufacturing and Industrial Building—*const*	23331	1531
Multifamily Housing—*const*	23322	1531
Single Family Housing—*const*	23321	1531
Cooperative apartment manager: Nonresidential Property Managers—*real*	531312	6531
Residential Property Managers—*real*	531311	6531

ALPHABETICAL INDEX	NAICS	SIC
Cooperative life insurance organizations: Direct Life Insurance Carriers—*fin*	524113	6311
Reinsurance Carriers—*fin*	52413	6311
Coopered tubs: Wood Container and Pallet—*mfg*	32192	2449
Coordinate sets–women's, children's, and infants': Women's, Children's, and Infants' and Accessories—*whlse*	42233	5137
Coping, wall–clay: Structural Clay Product, Other—*mfg*	327123	3259
Copings, concrete: Concrete Pipe—*mfg*	327332	3272
Concrete Product, Other—*mfg*	32739	3272
Nonmetallic Mineral Product, All Other Miscellaneous—*mfg*	327999	3272
Copolymers–butadiene-styrene, butadiene-acrylonitrile, over 50 percent butadiene: Synthetic Rubber—*mfg*	325212	2822
Copper and copper-base alloy castings, except die-castings: Copper Foundries—*mfg*	331525	3366
Copper and copper-base alloy foundries: Copper Foundries—*mfg*	331525	3366
Copper arsenate, formulated: Pesticide and Other Agricultural Chemical—*mfg*	32532	2879
Copper chloride: Basic Inorganic Chemical, All Other—*mfg*	325188	2819
Chemical Product, All Other Miscellaneous—*mfg*	325998	2819
Copper die-castings: Nonferrous (except Aluminum) Die-Castings—*mfg*	331522	3364
Copper foil, not made in rolling mills: Fabricated Metal Product, All Other Miscellaneous—*mfg*	332999	3497
Laminated Aluminum Foil for Flexible Packaging Uses—*mfg*	322225	3497
Copper Foundries	**331525**	**3366**
Copper foundries, except die-castings: Copper Foundries—*mfg*	331525	3366
Copper ingots and refinery bars, primary: Primary Smelting and Refining of Copper—*mfg*	331411	3331
Copper iodide and oxide: Basic Inorganic Chemical, All Other—*mfg*	325188	2819
Chemical Product, All Other Miscellaneous—*mfg*	325998	2819
Copper or: Coal and Other Mineral and Ore—*whlse*	42152	5052
Copper Ore and Nickel Ore Mining	**212234**	**1061**
Copper ore mining: Copper Ore and Nickel Ore—*mining*	212234	1021
Copper Rolling, Drawing and Extruding	**331421**	**3351**
Copper rolling, drawing, and extruding: Copper Rolling, Drawing and Extruding—*mfg*	331421	3351
Copper Rolling, Drawing, Extruding, and Alloying	**33142**	
Copper sheets, plates, bars, rods, pipes, etc.: Metal Service Centers and Offices—*whlse*	42151	5051
Copper smelting and refining, primary: Primary Smelting and Refining of Copper—*mfg*	331411	3331
Copper smelting and refining, secondary: Secondary Smelting and Alloying of Aluminum—*mfg*	331314	3341
Secondary Smelting, Refining, and Alloying of Copper—*mfg*	331423	3341
Copper sulfate: Basic Inorganic Chemical, All Other—*mfg*	325188	2819
Chemical Product, All Other Miscellaneous—*mfg*	325998	2819
Copper Wire (except Mechanical) Drawing	**331422**	**3357**

Item	NAICS	SIC
Copper, Nickel, Lead and Zinc Mining	**21223**	
Coppersmithing, in connection with construction work-contractors: Roofing, Siding and Sheet Metal Contractors—*const*	23561	1761
Copy holders, printers': Printing Machinery and Equipment—*mfg*	333293	3555
Copyright buying and licensing: Owners and Lessors of Other Non-Financial Assets—*real*	53311	6794
Copyright protection service: Legal Services, All Other—*prof*	541199	7389
Cord connectors, electric: Current-Carrying Wiring Device—*mfg*	335931	3643
Cord for reinforcing rubber tires, industrial belting, and fuel cells: Tire Cord and Tire Fabric Mills—*mfg*	314992	2296
Cord sets, flexible–made in wiredrawing plants: Aluminum Rolling and Drawing, Other—*mfg*	331319	3357
Communication and Energy Wire, Other—*mfg*	335929	3357
Copper Wire (except Mechanical) Drawing—*mfg*	331422	3357
Fiber Optic Cable—*mfg*	335921	3357
Nonferrous Metal (except Copper and Aluminum) Rolling, Drawing and Extruding—*mfg*	331491	3357
Cord, asbestos: Motor Vehicle Brake System—*mfg*	33634	3292
Nonmetallic Mineral Product, All Other Miscellaneous—*mfg*	327999	3292
Cord, braided: Rope, Cordage and Twine Mills—*mfg*	314991	2298
Cordage: Industrial Machinery and Equipment—*whlse*	42183	5085
Industrial Supplies—*whlse*	42184	5085
Cordage and rope machines: Textile Machinery—*mfg*	333292	3552
Cordage yarn, cotton: Yarn Spinning Mills—*mfg*	313111	2281
Cordage–abaca (Manila), sisal, henequen, hemp, jute, and other fibers: Rope, Cordage and Twine Mills—*mfg*	314991	2298
Cordeau detonant (explosives): Explosives—*mfg*	32592	2892
Cordials, alcoholic: Distilleries—*mfg*	31214	2085
Cordials, nonalcoholic: Flavoring Syrup and Concentrate—*mfg*	31193	2087
Food, All Other Miscellaneous—*mfg*	311999	2087
Spice and Extract—*mfg*	311942	2087
Cordite (explosives): Explosives—*mfg*	32592	2892
Cords, fabric: Narrow Fabric Mills—*mfg*	313221	2241
Corduroys, cotton: Broadwoven Fabric Mills—*mfg*	31321	2211
Cordwood: Durable Goods, Other Miscellaneous—*whlse*	42199	5099
Core baking and mold drying ovens: Industrial Process Furnace and Oven—*mfg*	333994	3567
Core drilling for building construction–contractors: Trade Contractors, All Other Special—*const*	23599	1799
Core drills: Mining Machinery and Equipment—*mfg*	333131	3532
Core oil and binders: Basic Organic Chemical, All Other—*mfg*	325199	2899
Chemical Product, All Other Miscellaneous—*mfg*	325998	2899
Core wash: Basic Organic Chemical, All Other—*mfg*	325199	2899
Chemical Product, All Other Miscellaneous—*mfg*	325998	2899
Core wax: Basic Organic Chemical, All Other—*mfg*	325199	2899
Chemical Product, All Other Miscellaneous—*mfg*	325998	2899
Cores, bullet–30 mm. (or 1.18 inch) or less: Small Arms Ammunition—*mfg*	332992	3482
Cores, fiber (metal-end or all-fiber): Fiber Can, Tube, Drum, and Similar Products—*mfg*	322214	2655
Cores, magnetic: Electronic Component, Other—*mfg*	334419	3679
Motor Vehicle Electrical and Electronic Equipment, Other—*mfg*	336322	3679
Printed Circuit/Electronics Assembly—*mfg*	334418	3679
Radio and Television Broadcasting and Wireless Communications Equipment—*mfg*	33422	3679
Cores, sand (foundry): Industrial Pattern—*mfg*	332997	3543
Cores, tire valve: Motor Vehicle Parts, All Other—*mfg*	336399	3714
Cork: Industrial Machinery and Equipment—*whlse*	42183	5085
Industrial Supplies—*whlse*	42184	5085
Cork products: Manufacturing, All Other Miscellaneous—*mfg*	339999	2499
Wood Container and Pallet—*mfg*	32192	2499
Wood Product, All Other Miscellaneous—*mfg*	321999	2499
Cork working machinery: Industrial Machinery, All Other—*mfg*	333298	3559
Machinery, Other Commercial and Service Industry—*mfg*	333319	3559
Corks, bottle: Manufacturing, All Other Miscellaneous—*mfg*	339999	2499
Wood Container and Pallet—*mfg*	32192	2499
Wood Product, All Other Miscellaneous—*mfg*	321999	2499
Corn: Grain and Field Bean—*whlse*	42251	5153
Corn chips: Confectionery—*whlse*	42245	5145
Corn chips and related corn snacks: Snack Food, Other—*mfg*	311919	2096
Corn cribs, prefabricated–wood: Prefabricated Wood Building—*mfg*	321992	2452
Corn drying: Postharvest Crop Activities (except Cotton Ginning)—*ag*	115114	723
Corn Farming	**11115**	**119**
Corn farms, except sweet corn or popcorn: Corn Farming—*ag*	11115	115
Corn farms, sweet: Vegetable (except Potato) and Melon Farming, Other—*ag*	111219	161
Corn flakes: Breakfast Cereal—*mfg*	31123	2043
Coffee and Tea—*mfg*	31192	2043
Corn grits and flakes for brewers' use: Flour Milling—*mfg*	311211	2041
Corn heads for combines: Farm Machinery and Equipment—*mfg*	333111	3523
Corn knives: Hand and Edge Tool—*mfg*	332212	3423
Corn meal and flour: Flour Milling—*mfg*	311211	2041
Corn oil cake and meal: Wet Corn Milling—*mfg*	311221	2046
Corn oil, crude and refined: Wet Corn Milling—*mfg*	311221	2046
Corn pickers and shellers, farm: Farm Machinery and Equipment—*mfg*	333111	3523
Corn poppers, electric: Electric Housewares and Household Fan—*mfg*	335211	3634
Heating Equipment (except Electric and Warm Air Furnaces)—*mfg*	333414	3634
Corn popping machines, commercial type: Machinery, Other Commercial and Service Industry—*mfg*	333319	3589
Corn popping machines, industrial type: Food Product Machinery—*mfg*	333294	3556
Corn remover and bunion pads: Surgical Appliance and Supplies—*mfg*	339113	3842

Description	NAICS	SIC
Cosmetology schools: Beauty Salons—*serv*	812112	7231
Cosmetology and Barber Schools—*educ*	611511	7231
Nail Salons—*serv*	812113	7231
Cosmetology shops or salons: Beauty Salons—*serv*	812112	7231
Cosmetology and Barber Schools—*educ*	611511	7231
Nail Salons—*serv*	812113	7231
Costume accessories–handbags, costume jewelry, gloves, etc.: Clothing Accessories Stores—*retail*	44815	5632
Clothing Stores, Other—*retail*	44819	5632
Costume Jewelry and Novelty Manufacturing	**339914**	**3499**
Costume jewelry stores: Clothing Accessories Stores—*retail*	44815	5632
Clothing Stores, Other—*retail*	44819	5632
Costume jewelry, except precious metal and precious or semiprecious stones: Costume Jewelry and Novelty—*mfg*	339914	3961
Costume rental: Formal Wear and Costume Rental—*real*	53222	7299
Costumes–e.g., lodge, masquerade, theatrical: Cut and Sew Apparel, All Other—*mfg*	315299	2389
Cot springs, assembled: Mattress—*mfg*	33791	2515
Upholstered Household Furniture—*mfg*	337121	2515
Cots, finger–rubber: Fabric Coating Mills—*mfg*	31332	3069
Rubber Product, All Other—*mfg*	326299	3069
Cots, household–metal: Metal Household Furniture—*mfg*	337124	2514
Cots, household–wood: Nonupholstered Wood Household Furniture—*mfg*	337122	2511
Cottage cheese, including pot, bakers', and farmers' cheese: Fluid Milk—*mfg*	311511	2026
Cottage sets (curtains): Curtain and Drapery Mills—*mfg*	314121	2391
Cotter pins, metal: Bolt, Nut, Screw, Rivet and Washer—*mfg*	332722	3452
Cotter pins, plastics: Plastics Pipe and Pipe Fitting—*mfg*	326122	3089
Plastics Product, All Other—*mfg*	326199	3089
Unsupported Plastics Profile Shape—*mfg*	326121	3089
Cotton balers and presses: Farm Machinery and Equipment—*mfg*	333111	3523
Cotton broadwoven fabric finishing: Broadwoven Fabric Finishing Mills—*mfg*	313311	2261
Cotton broadwoven goods: Broadwoven Fabric Mills—*mfg*	31321	2211
Cotton compresses and warehouses: Farm Product Warehousing and Storage Facilities—*trans*	49313	4221
Cotton Farming	**11192**	**131**
Cotton farms: Cotton Farming—*ag*	11192	131
Cotton fiber paper: Newsprint Mills—*mfg*	322122	2621
Paper (except Newsprint) Mills—*mfg*	322121	2621
Cotton Ginning	**115111**	**724**
Cotton ginning machinery: Industrial Machinery, All Other—*mfg*	333298	3559
Machinery, Other Commercial and Service Industry—*mfg*	333319	3559
Cotton merchants, not members of exchanges: Farm Product Raw Material, Other—*whlse*	42259	5159
Cotton narrow fabrics: Narrow Fabric Mills—*mfg*	313221	2241
Cotton picker and stripper harvesting machinery: Farm Machinery and Equipment—*mfg*	333111	3523
Cotton pickery: Cotton Ginning—*ag*	115111	724
Cotton piece goods: Broadwoven Fabric Finishing Mills—*mfg*	313311	5131
Piece Goods, Notions and Other Dry Goods—*whlse*	42231	5131
Textile and Fabric Finishing (except Broadwoven Fabric) Mills—*mfg*	313312	5131
Cotton seed delinting: Postharvest Crop Activities (except Cotton Ginning)—*ag*	115114	723
Cotton thread: Textile and Fabric Finishing (except Broadwoven Fabric) Mills—*mfg*	313312	2284
Thread Mills—*mfg*	313113	2284
Cotton yarn, spinning: Yarn Spinning Mills—*mfg*	313111	2281
Cotton yarns: Nondurable Goods, Other Miscellaneous—*whlse*	42299	5199
Cotton, absorbent–sterilized: Surgical Appliance and Supplies—*mfg*	339113	3842
Cotton, including cotton balls: Surgical Appliance and Supplies—*mfg*	339113	3842
Cotton, machine harvesting of: Crop Harvesting, Primarily by Machine—*ag*	115113	722
Cotton, raw: Farm Product Raw Material, Other—*whlse*	42259	5159
Cottonades: Broadwoven Fabric Mills—*mfg*	31321	2211
Cottonseed cooking and salad oil: Fats and Oils Refining and Blending—*mfg*	311225	2079
Oilseed Processing, Other—*mfg*	311223	2079
Soybean Processing—*mfg*	311222	2079
Cottonseed farms: Cotton Farming—*ag*	11192	131
Cottonseed oil, cake, and meal–made in cottonseed oil mills: Fats and Oils Refining and Blending—*mfg*	311225	2074
Oilseed Processing, Other—*mfg*	311223	2074
Cottonseed oil, deodorized: Fats and Oils Refining and Blending—*mfg*	311225	2074
Oilseed Processing, Other—*mfg*	311223	2074
Couch springs, assembled: Mattress—*mfg*	33791	2515
Upholstered Household Furniture—*mfg*	337121	2515
Couches, studio–on frames of any material: Mattress—*mfg*	33791	2515
Upholstered Household Furniture—*mfg*	337121	2515
Couches, upholstered on wood frames, except convertible beds: Upholstered Household Furniture—*mfg*	337121	2512
Cough drops, except pharmaceutical preparations: Confectionery from Purchased Chocolate—*mfg*	31133	2064
Non-Chocolate Confectionery—*mfg*	31134	2064
Cough medicines: Pharmaceutical Preparation—*mfg*	325412	2834
Coulometric analyzers, industrial process type: Instruments and Related Products for Measuring, Displaying, and Controlling Industrial Process Variables—*mfg*	334513	3823
Coulometric analyzers, laboratory type: Analytical Laboratory Instrument—*mfg*	334516	3826
Coumarin: Basic Organic Chemical, All Other—*mfg*	325199	2869
Coumarone-indene resins: Plastics Material and Resin—*mfg*	325211	2821
Councils for social agencies, exceptional children, and poverty: Grantmaking and Giving Services, Other—*serv*	813219	8399

ALPHABETICAL INDEX	NAICS	SIC
Social Advocacy Organizations, Other—*serv*	813319	8399
Voluntary Health Organizations—*serv*	813212	8399
Counseling centers: Child and Youth Services—*hlth*	62411	8322
Community Food Services—*hlth*	62421	8322
Community Housing Services, Other—*hlth*	624229	8322
Emergency and Other Relief Services—*hlth*	62423	8322
Individual and Family Services, Other—*hlth*	62419	8322
Parole Offices and Probation Offices—*pub*	92215	8322
Services for the Elderly and Persons with Disabilities—*hlth*	62412	8322
Temporary Shelters—*hlth*	624221	8322
Counselors at law: Lawyers, Offices Of—*prof*	54111	8111
Count rate meters, nuclear radiation: Measuring and Controlling Device, Other—*mfg*	334519	3829
Surgical and Medical Instrument—*mfg*	339112	3829
Counter coverings, plastics: Plastics Pipe and Pipe Fitting—*mfg*	326122	3089
Plastics Product, All Other—*mfg*	326199	3089
Unsupported Plastics Profile Shape—*mfg*	326121	3089
Counter top installation–contractors: Trade Contractors, All Other Special—*const*	23599	1799
Counter type registers: Totalizing Fluid Meter and Counting Device—*mfg*	334514	3824
Counterbores: Industrial Machinery and Equipment—*whlse*	42183	5084
Counterbores and countersinking bits, woodworking: Hand and Edge Tool—*mfg*	332212	3423
Counterbores, metalworking: Cutting Tool and Machine Tool Accessory—*mfg*	333515	3545
Hand and Edge Tool—*mfg*	332212	3545
Countermeasure dispensers, aircraft: Aircraft Part and Auxiliary Equipment, Other—*mfg*	336413	3728
Fluid Power Valve and Hose Fitting—*mfg*	332912	3728
Counters (shoe cut stock): Fastener, Button, Needle and Pin—*mfg*	339993	3131
Leather Good, All Other—*mfg*	316999	3131
Wood Product, All Other Miscellaneous—*mfg*	321999	3131
Counters and counter display cases, except refrigerated-wood: Architectural Woodwork and Millwork, Custom—*mfg*	337212	2541
Showcase, Partition, Shelving, and Locker—*mfg*	337215	2541
Wood Kitchen Cabinet and Counter Top—*mfg*	33711	2541
Counters and counter display cases, not refrigerated–except wood: Showcase, Partition, Shelving, and Locker—*mfg*	337215	2542
Counters and counter display cases, refrigerated: Air-Conditioning and Warm Air Heating Equipment and Commercial and Industrial Refrigeration Equipment—*mfg*	333415	3585
Motor Vehicle Air-Conditioning—*mfg*	336391	3585
Counters, revolution: Totalizing Fluid Meter and Counting Device—*mfg*	334514	3824
Counters–mechanical, electrical, and electronic totalizing: Totalizing Fluid Meter and Counting Device—*mfg*	334514	3824

ALPHABETICAL INDEX	NAICS	SIC
Countersinking machines: Machine Tool (Metal Cutting Types)—*mfg*	333512	3541
Countersinks: Hand and Edge Tool—*mfg*	332212	3423
Industrial Machinery and Equipment—*whlse*	42183	5084
Countersinks and countersink drill combinations (machine tool accessories): Cutting Tool and Machine Tool Accessory—*mfg*	333515	3545
Hand and Edge Tool—*mfg*	332212	3545
Country buyers of cotton or cotton linters: Farm Product Raw Material, Other—*whlse*	42259	5159
Country clubs, membership: Golf Courses and Country Clubs—*arts*	71391	7997
Country general stores: General Merchandise Stores, All Other—*retail*	45299	5399
Warehouse Clubs and Superstores—*retail*	45291	5399
County commissioners: Legislative Bodies—*pub*	92112	9121
County development agencies: Urban Planning and Community and Rural Development, Administration of—*pub*	92512	9532
County supervisors of education, except school boards: Education Programs, Administration of—*pub*	92311	9411
County supervisors' and executives' offices: Executive Offices—*pub*	92111	9111
Coupling transformers: Electronic Coil, Transformer, and Other Inductor—*mfg*	334416	3677
Couplings, hose: Other Metal Valve and Pipe Fitting, Other—*mfg*	332919	3429
Couplings, pipe–except pressure and soil pipe-metal: Fabricated Metal Product, All Other Miscellaneous—*mfg*	332999	3494
Other Metal Valve and Pipe Fitting, Other—*mfg*	332919	3494
Couplings, pipe–fabricated from purchased metal pipe: Fabricated Pipe and Pipe Fitting—*mfg*	332996	3498
Couplings, pipe–pressure and soil pipe-cast iron: Iron Foundries—*mfg*	331511	3321
Couplings, shaft–rigid, flexible, universal joint, etc.: Mechanical Power Transmission Equipment—*mfg*	333613	3568
Coupon distribution: Advertising Material Distribution Services—*prof*	54187	7319
Advertising, Other Services Related to—*prof*	54189	7319
Display Advertising—*prof*	54185	7319
Media Buying Agencies—*prof*	54183	7319
Nonscheduled Air, Other—*trans*	481219	7319
Coupon redemption service, except trading stamps: Advertising, Other Services Related to—*prof*	54189	7389
Business Support Services, All Other—*admin*	561499	7389
Coupon stores (redemption of trading stamps): Advertising, Other Services Related to—*prof*	54189	7389
Coupons, lithographed: Lithographic Printing, Commercial—*mfg*	323110	2752
Quick Printing—*mfg*	323114	2752
Coupons, printed–except lithographed or gravure: Digital Printing—*mfg*	323115	2759

Entry	NAICS	SIC
Flexographic Printing, Commercial—*mfg*	323112	2759
Printing, Other Commercial—*mfg*	323119	2759
Quick Printing—*mfg*	323114	2759
Coupons–gravure printing: Gravure Printing, Commercial—*mfg*	323111	2754
Courier services, air: Couriers—*trans*	49211	4513
Courier services, except by air: Couriers—*trans*	49211	4215
Local Messengers and Local Delivery—*trans*	49221	4215
Couriers	**4921**	
Couriers	**49211**	**4513**
Couriers and Messengers	**492**	
Court Reporting and Stenotype Services	**561492**	**7338**
Court reporting schools: Business and Secretarial Schools—*educ*	61141	8244
Court reporting service: Court Reporting and Stenotype Services—*admin*	561492	7338
Document Preparation Services—*admin*	56141	7338
Courts	**92211**	**9211**
Courts of law: Courts—*pub*	92211	9211
Courts, auto: Bed and Breakfast Inns—*accom*	721191	7011
Casino Hotels—*accom*	72112	7011
Hotels (except Casino Hotels) and Motels—*accom*	72111	7011
Traveler Accommodation, All Other—*accom*	721199	7011
Coutil, cotton: Broadwoven Fabric Mills—*mfg*	31321	2211
Cover paper: Newsprint Mills—*mfg*	322122	2621
Paper (except Newsprint) Mills—*mfg*	322121	2621
Coveralls, work: Men's and Boys' Cut and Sew Apparel Contractors—*mfg*	315211	2326
Men's and Boys' Cut and Sew Work Clothing—*mfg*	315225	2326
Covers, annealing: Air-Conditioning and Warm Air Heating Equipment and Commercial and Industrial Refrigeration Equipment—*mfg*	333415	3443
Metal Tank (Heavy Gauge)—*mfg*	33242	3443
Plate Work—*mfg*	332313	3443
Power Boiler and Heat Exchanger—*mfg*	33241	3443
Covers, automobile tire and seat: Motor Vehicle Fabric Accessories and Seat—*mfg*	33636	2399
Covers, bottle and demUohn–willow, rattan, and reed: Manufacturing, All Other Miscellaneous—*mfg*	339999	2499
Wood Container and Pallet—*mfg*	32192	2499
Wood Product, All Other Miscellaneous—*mfg*	321999	2499
Covers, catch basin–concrete: Concrete Pipe—*mfg*	327332	3272
Concrete Product, Other—*mfg*	32739	3272
Nonmetallic Mineral Product, All Other Miscellaneous—*mfg*	327999	3272
Covers, fabric: Canvas and Related Product Mills—*mfg*	314912	2394
Covers, floating–metal plate: Air-Conditioning and Warm Air Heating Equipment and Commercial and Industrial Refrigeration Equipment—*mfg*	333415	3443
Metal Tank (Heavy Gauge)—*mfg*	33242	3443
Plate Work—*mfg*	332313	3443
Power Boiler and Heat Exchanger—*mfg*	33241	3443
Covers, lace–chair, dresser, piano, andtable: Knit Fabric and Lace Mills, Other—*mfg*	313249	2258
Textile and Fabric Finishing (except Broadwoven Fabric) Mills—*mfg*	313312	2258
Coverts, cotton: Broadwoven Fabric Mills—*mfg*	31321	2211
Cowls or scoops, air (ship ventilators):sheet metal: Metal Container, Other—*mfg*	332439	3444
Sheet Metal Work—*mfg*	332322	3444
Cowpea farms: Grain Farming, All Other—*ag*	111199	119
CPA (certified public accountant): Accounting Services, Other—*prof*	541219	8721
Certified Public Accountants, Offices Of—*prof*	541211	8721
Payroll Services—*prof*	541214	8721
Crab traps, steel–except wire: Hardware—*mfg*	33251	3429
Other Metal Valve and Pipe Fitting, Other—*mfg*	332919	3429
Crabcakes, frozen: Fresh and Frozen Seafood Processing—*mfg*	311712	2092
Crabmeat picking: Fresh and Frozen Seafood Processing—*mfg*	311712	2092
Crabmeat, canned and cured: Seafood Canning—*mfg*	311711	2091
Crabmeat, fresh–packed in nonsealed containers: Fresh and Frozen Seafood Processing—*mfg*	311712	2092
Crabs, catching of: Shellfish Fishing—*ag*	114112	913
Cracker making machines: Food Product Machinery—*mfg*	333294	3556
Cracker meal and crumbs: Bakeries, Commercial—*mfg*	311812	2052
Cookie and Cracker—*mfg*	311821	2052
Snack Food, Other—*mfg*	311919	2052
Crackers: Grocery and Related Products, Other—*whlse*	42249	5149
Crackers–e.g., graham, soda: Bakeries, Commercial—*mfg*	311812	2052
Cookie and Cracker—*mfg*	311821	2052
Snack Food, Other—*mfg*	311919	2052
Cradle assemblies (wire making equipment): Other Metalworking Machinery, Other—*mfg*	333518	3549
Cradles, wood: Nonupholstered Wood Household Furniture—*mfg*	337122	2511
Craft and hobby kits and sets: Game, Toy, and Children's Vehicle—*mfg*	339932	3944
Craft kits: Toy and Hobby Goods and Supplies—*whlse*	42192	5092
Craft kits and supplies: Hobby, Toy and Game Stores—*retail*	45112	5945
Cranberry bogs: Berry (except Strawberry) Farming—*ag*	111334	171
Strawberry Farming—*ag*	111333	171
Crane and hoist controls, including metal mill: Relay and Industrial Control—*mfg*	335314	3625
Crane carriers: Construction Machinery—*mfg*	33312	3531
Overhead Traveling Crane, Hoist and Monorail System—*mfg*	333923	3531
Railroad Rolling Stock—*mfg*	33651	3531
Crane rental and leasing: Construction, and Forestry Machinery and Equipment Rental and Leasing—*real*	532412	7353
Heavy, All Other—*const*	23499	7353
Cranes, construction: Construction and (except Petroleum) Machinery and Equipment—*whlse*	42181	5082
Construction Machinery—*mfg*	33312	3531
Overhead Traveling Crane, Hoist and Monorail System—*mfg*	333923	3531

ALPHABETICAL INDEX	NAICS	SIC
Railroad Rolling Stock—*mfg*	33651	3531
Cranes, except industrial plant: Construction Machinery—*mfg*	33312	3531
Overhead Traveling Crane, Hoist and Monorail System—*mfg*	333923	3531
Railroad Rolling Stock—*mfg*	33651	3531
Cranes, industrial: Industrial Machinery and Equipment—*whlse*	42183	5084
Cranes, mobile industrial truck: Fabricated Metal Product, All Other Miscellaneous—*mfg*	332999	3537
Industrial Truck, Tractor, Trailer and Stacker Machinery—*mfg*	333924	3537
Metal Container, Other—*mfg*	332439	3537
Cranes, overhead traveling: Overhead Traveling Crane, Hoist and Monorail System—*mfg*	333923	3536
Crankshaft and camshaft machining: Fabricated Metal Product, All Other Miscellaneous—*mfg*	332999	3599
General Purpose Machinery , All Other—*mfg*	333999	3599
Machine Shops—*mfg*	33271	3599
Machinery, Other Commercial and Service Industry—*mfg*	333319	3599
Motor Vehicle Parts, All Other—*mfg*	336399	3599
Crankshaft assemblies, motor vehicle–gasoline engine: Gasoline Engine and Engine Parts—*mfg*	336312	3714
Motor Vehicle Parts, All Other—*mfg*	336399	3714
Crankshaft regrinding machines: Machine Tool (Metal Cutting Types)—*mfg*	333512	3541
Crankshafts, forged steel–not made in rolling mills: Iron and Steel Forging—*mfg*	332111	3462
Crash toweling, cotton: Broadwoven Fabric Mills—*mfg*	31321	2211
Crash, linen: Broadwoven Fabric Mills—*mfg*	31321	2299
Narrow Fabric Mills—*mfg*	313221	2299
Nonwoven Fabric Mills—*mfg*	31323	2299
Textile and Fabric Finishing (except Broadwoven Fabric) Mills—*mfg*	313312	2299
Textile Product Mills, All Other Miscellaneous—*mfg*	314999	2299
Thread Mills—*mfg*	313113	2299
Yarn Spinning Mills—*mfg*	313111	2299
Crates, except paper: Industrial Machinery and Equipment—*whlse*	42183	5085
Industrial Supplies—*whlse*	42184	5085
Crates–berry, butter, fruit, and vegetable-wood, wirebound: Wood Container and Pallet—*mfg*	32192	2449
Crating goods for shipping: Packing and Crating—*trans*	488991	4783
Crayfish, catching of: Shellfish Fishing—*ag*	114112	913
Crayons–chalk, gypsum, charcoal, fusains, pastel, and wax: Chemical Product, All Other Miscellaneous—*mfg*	325998	3952
Institutional Furniture—*mfg*	337127	3952
Lead Pencil and Art Good—*mfg*	339942	3952
Cream of tartar: Basic Organic Chemical, All Other—*mfg*	325199	2869
Cream separators, except farm: Industrial Machinery and Equipment—*whlse*	42183	5084

ALPHABETICAL INDEX	NAICS	SIC
Cream separators, farm: Farm and Garden Machinery and Equipment—*whlse*	42182	5083
Farm Machinery and Equipment—*mfg*	333111	3523
Outdoor Power Equipment Stores—*retail*	44421	5083
Cream separators, industrial: Food Product Machinery—*mfg*	333294	3556
Cream stations: Dairy Product (except Dried or Canned)—*whlse*	42243	5143
Cream substitutes: Dry, Condensed, and Evaporated Dairy Product—*mfg*	311514	2023
Cream, aerated: Fluid Milk—*mfg*	311511	2026
Cream, bottled: Fluid Milk—*mfg*	311511	2026
Cream, sour: Fluid Milk—*mfg*	311511	2026
Cream–dried, powdered, and canned: Dry, Condensed, and Evaporated Dairy Product—*mfg*	311514	2023
Creamery butter: Creamery Butter—*mfg*	311512	2021
Creamery Butter Manufacturing	**311512**	**2021**
Creams, cosmetic: Soap and Other Detergent—*mfg*	325611	2844
Toilet Preparation—*mfg*	32562	2844
Creams, shaving: Soap and Other Detergent—*mfg*	325611	2844
Toilet Preparation—*mfg*	32562	2844
Credit and other financial responsibilityinsurance: Direct Property and Casualty Insurance Carriers—*fin*	524126	6351
Reinsurance Carriers—*fin*	52413	6351
Credit Bureaus	**56145**	**7323**
Credit bureaus and agencies: Credit Bureaus—*admin*	56145	7323
Credit Card Issuing	**52221**	**6022**
Credit card service (collection by individual firms): Financial Transactions Processing, Reserve, and Clearing House Activities—*fin*	52232	7389
Credit card service, collection by centralagency: Financial Transactions Processing, Reserve, and Clearing House Activities—*fin*	52232	6153
Non-Depository Credit Intermediation, All Other—*fin*	522298	6153
Sales Financing—*fin*	52222	6153
Credit clearinghouses: Credit Bureaus—*admin*	56145	7323
Credit institutions, agricultural: International Trade Financing—*fin*	522293	6159
Non-Depository Credit Intermediation, All Other—*fin*	522298	6159
Sales Financing—*fin*	52222	6159
Credit Intermediation and Related Activities	**522**	
Credit Intermediation, Activities Related to	**5223**	
Credit Intermediation, Other Activities Related to	**52239**	**6162**
Credit investigation services: Credit Bureaus—*admin*	56145	7323
Credit Unions	**52213**	**6062**
Credit unions, Federal: Credit Unions—*fin*	52213	6061
Credit unions, State–not federally chartered: Credit Unions—*fin*	52213	6062
Creels, fish: Sporting and Athletic Goods—*mfg*	33992	3949
Creels, textile machinery: Textile Machinery—*mfg*	333292	3552
Cremating ovens: General Purpose Machinery , All Other—*mfg*	333999	3569

Entry	NAICS	SIC
Crematories: Cemeteries and Crematories—*serv*	81222	7261
Funeral Homes—*serv*	81221	7261
Creosote oil, made in chemical plants: Cyclic Crude and Intermediate—*mfg*	325192	2865
Petrochemical—*mfg*	32511	2865
Creosote, woed: Gum and Wood Chemical—*mfg*	325191	2861
Creosoting of wood: Wood Preservation—*mfg*	321114	2491
Crepe paper: Coated and Laminated Paper—*mfg*	322222	2679
Converted Paper Product, All Other—*mfg*	322298	2679
Die-Cut Paper and Paperboard Office Supplies—*mfg*	322231	2679
Non-Folding Sanitary Food Container—*mfg*	322215	2679
Crepe satins: Broadwoven Fabric Mills—*mfg*	31321	2221
Crepes, cotton: Broadwoven Fabric Mills—*mfg*	31321	2211
Cresol resins: Plastics Material and Resin—*mfg*	325211	2821
Cresol-furfural resins: Plastics Material and Resin—*mfg*	325211	2821
Cresols, made in chemical plants: Cyclic Crude and Intermediate—*mfg*	325192	2865
Petrochemical—*mfg*	32511	2865
Cresylic acid, made in chemical plants: Cyclic Crude and Intermediate—*mfg*	325192	2865
Petrochemical—*mfg*	32511	2865
Cretonne, cotton: Broadwoven Fabric Mills—*mfg*	31321	2211
Crew boats, building and repairing: Ship Building and Repairing—*mfg*	336611	3731
Crew leaders, farm labor–contract: Farm Labor Contractors and Crew Leaders—*ag*	115115	761
Crew socks: Hosiery and Sock Mills, Other—*mfg*	315119	2252
Sheer Hosiery Mills—*mfg*	315111	2252
Cribbing, concrete: Concrete Pipe—*mfg*	327332	3272
Concrete Product, Other—*mfg*	32739	3272
Nonmetallic Mineral Product, All Other Miscellaneous—*mfg*	327999	3272
Cribs, metal: Metal Household Furniture—*mfg*	337124	2514
Cribs, wood: Nonupholstered Wood Household Furniture—*mfg*	337122	2511
Cricket equipment. Sporting and Athletic Goods—*mfg*	33992	3949
Criminal justice statistics centers: Justice, Public Order, and Safety, All Other—*pub*	92219	9229
Crinoline: Broadwoven Fabric Mills—*mfg*	31321	2211
Crisis centers: Child and Youth Services—*hlth*	62411	8322
Community Food Services—*hlth*	62421	8322
Community Housing Services, Other—*hlth*	624229	8322
Emergency and Other Relief Services—*hlth*	62423	8322
Individual and Family Services, Other—*hlth*	62419	8322
Parole Offices and Probation Offices—*pub*	92215	8322
Services for the Elderly and Persons with Disabilities—*hlth*	62412	8322
Temporary Shelters—*hlth*	624221	8322
Crisis intervention centers: Child and Youth Services—*hlth*	62411	8322
Community Food Services—*hlth*	62421	8322
Community Housing Services, Other—*hlth*	624229	8322
Emergency and Other Relief Services—*hlth*	62423	8322
Individual and Family Services, Other—*hlth*	62419	8322
Parole Offices and Probation Offices—*pub*	92215	8322
Services for the Elderly and Persons with Disabilities—*hlth*	62412	8322
Temporary Shelters—*hlth*	624221	8322
Crochet thread–cotton, silk, manmade fibers, and wool: Textile and Fabric Finishing (except Broadwoven Fabric) Mills—*mfg*	313312	2284
Thread Mills—*mfg*	313113	2284
Crochet ware, machine-made: Men's and Boys' Cut and Sew Apparel Contractors—*mfg*	315211	2395
Textile Product Mills, All Other Miscellaneous—*mfg*	314999	2395
Women's and Girls' Cut and Sew Apparel Contractors—*mfg*	315212	2395
Crochet yarn–cotton, silk, wool, and manmade staple: Yarn Spinning Mills—*mfg*	313111	2281
Crock pots, electric: Electric Housewares and Household Fan—*mfg*	335211	3634
Heating Equipment (except Electric and Warm Air Furnaces)—*mfg*	333414	3634
Crockery: Home Furnishing—*whlse*	42122	5023
Vitreous China, Fine Earthenware and Other Pottery Product—*mfg*	327112	3269
Crockery stores: Home Furnishings Stores, All Other—*retail*	442299	5719
Window Treatment Stores—*retail*	442291	5719
Croissants, except frozen: Bakeries, Commercial—*mfg*	311812	2051
Croissants, frozen: Frozen Bakery Product—*mfg*	311813	2053
Crop driers, farm: Farm Machinery and Equipment—*mfg*	333111	3523
Crop dusting, with/without fertilizing: Nonscheduled Air, Other—*trans*	481219	721
Soil Preparation, Planting, and Cultivating—*ag*	115112	721
Crop Farming, All Other	**11199**	
Crop Farming, All Other Miscellaneous	**111998**	**191**
Crop Farming, Other	**1119**	
Crop farms, general: Crop Farming, All Other Miscellaneous—*ag*	111998	191
Crop Harvesting, Primarily by Machine	**115113**	**722**
Crop Production	**111**	
Crop Production Support Activities	**11511**	
Crop Production Support Activities	**1151**	
Crop spraying, with/without fertilizing: Nonscheduled Air, Other—*trans*	481219	721
Soil Preparation, Planting, and Cultivating—*ag*	115112	721
Crops, riding: Leather Good, All Other—*mfg*	316999	3199
Croquet sets: Sporting and Athletic Goods—*mfg*	33992	3949
Crossing slabs, concrete: Concrete Pipe—*mfg*	327332	3272
Concrete Product, Other—*mfg*	32739	3272
Nonmetallic Mineral Product, All Other Miscellaneous—*mfg*	327999	3272
Crossties, treated: Wood Preservation—*mfg*	321114	2491
Crown and Closure Manufacturing	**332115**	**3466**
Crowns and bridges made in dental laboratories to order for the profession: Dental Laboratories—*mfg*	339116	8072
Crowns and closures, metal: Industrial Machinery and Equipment—*whlse*	42183	5085

ALPHABETICAL INDEX	NAICS	SIC
Industrial Supplies—*whlse*	42184	5085
Crowns, jar–stamped metal: Crown and Closure—*mfg*	332115	3466
Crucibles, fire clay: Clay Refractory—*mfg*	327124	3255
Crucibles–graphite, magnesite, chrome, silica, or other nonclay materials: Nonclay Refractory—*mfg*	327125	3297
Crude oil production: Crude Petroleum and Natural Gas Extraction—*mining*	211111	1311
Crude oil, except bulk stations and terminals: Petroleum and Petroleum Products (except Bulk Stations and Terminals)—*whlse*	42272	5172
Crude Petroleum and Natural Gas Extraction	**211111**	**1311**
Crude petroleum pipelines: Pipeline of Crude Oil—*trans*	48611	4612
Crude petroleum productioii: Crude Petroleum and Natural Gas Extraction—*mining*	211111	1311
Cruising timber: Forestry Support Activities—*ag*	11531	851
Crullers, except frozen: Bakeries, Commercial—*mfg*	311812	2051
Crushed and Broken Granite Mining and Quarrying	**212313**	**1423**
Crushed and Broken Limestone Mining and Quarrying	**212312**	**1422**
Crushed and Broken Stone Mining and Quarrying, Other	**212319**	**1499**
Crushers, feed (agricultural machinery): Farm Machinery and Equipment—*mfg*	333111	3523
Crushers, ice–except household: General Purpose Machinery , All Other—*mfg*	333999	3569
Crushers, mineral–portable: Construction Machinery—*mfg*	33312	3531
Overhead Traveling Crane, Hoist and Monorail System—*mfg*	333923	3531
Railroad Rolling Stock—*mfg*	33651	3531
Crushers, mineral–stationary-rnfg: Mining Machinery and Equipment—*mfg*	333131	3532
Crushing machinery and equipment, industrial: Industrial Machinery and Equipment—*whlse*	42183	5084
Crushing plants, bituminous coal: Bituminous Coal and Lignite Surface—*mining*	212111	1221
Crushing, pulverizing and screening machinery for construction and mining: Construction and (except Petroleum) Machinery and Equipment—*whlse*	42181	5082
Crustacean farms: Animal Aquaculture, Other—*ag*	112519	273
Finfish Farming and Fish Hatcheries—*ag*	112511	273
Shellfish Farming—*ag*	112512	273
Crutches and walkers: Surgical Appliance and Supplies—*mfg*	339113	3842
Cryogenic cooling devices (e.g., cryostats)for infrared detectors and masers: Electronic Component, Other—*mfg*	334419	3679
Motor Vehicle Electrical and Electronic Equipment, Other—*mfg*	336322	3679
Printed Circuit/Electronics Assembly—*mfg*	334418	3679
Radio and Television Broadcasting and Wireless Communications Equipment—*mfg*	33422	3679

ALPHABETICAL INDEX	NAICS	SIC
Cryogenic tanks, for liquids and gases–metal plate: Air-Conditioning and Warm Air Heating Equipment and Commercial and Industrial Refrigeration Equipment—*mfg*	333415	3443
Metal Tank (Heavy Gauge)—*mfg*	33242	3443
Plate Work—*mfg*	332313	3443
Power Boiler and Heat Exchanger—*mfg*	33241	3443
Cryolite mining: Crushed and Broken Stone and Quarrying, Other—*mining*	212319	1499
Non-Metallic Mineral, All Other—*mining*	212399	1499
Crystallized fruits and fruit peel: Confectionery from Purchased Chocolate—*mfg*	31133	2064
Non-Chocolate Confectionery—*mfg*	31134	2064
Crystals and crystal assemblies, radio: Electronic Component, Other—*mfg*	334419	3679
Motor Vehicle Electrical and Electronic Equipment, Other—*mfg*	336322	3679
Printed Circuit/Electronics Assembly—*mfg*	334418	3679
Radio and Television Broadcasting and Wireless Communications Equipment—*mfg*	33422	3679
Crystals, watch–made from purchased glass: Glass Product Made of Purchased Glass—*mfg*	327215	3231
Cubicles (electric switchboard equipment): Switchgear and Switchboard Apparatus—*mfg*	335313	3613
Cucumber farms: Vegetable (except Potato) and Melon Farming, Other—*ag*	111219	161
Cues and cue tips, billiard and pool: Sporting and Athletic Goods—*mfg*	33992	3949
Cuff buttons, except precious metal and precious or semiprecious stones: Fastener, Button, Needle and Pin—*mfg*	339993	3965
Cuff buttons, precious metal and precious or semiprecious stones: Jewelry (except Costume)—*mfg*	339911	3911
Cuff links and studs, except precious metal and gems: Costume Jewelry and Novelty—*mfg*	339914	3961
Cuffs, leg–iron: Hardware—*mfg*	33251	3429
Culm bank recovery, anthracite–except on a contract basis: Anthracite—*mining*	212113	1231
Culm bank recovery, bituminous coal or lignite–except on a contract basis: Bituminous Coal and Lignite Surface—*mining*	212111	1221
Culm bank recovery–bituminous coal, anthracite, and lignite on a contract basis: Coal Support Activities—*mining*	213113	1241
Culottes: Apparel Accessories and Apparel, Other—*mfg*	315999	2339
Cut and Sew Apparel, All Other—*mfg*	315299	2339
Women's and Girls' Cut and Sew Apparel Contractors—*mfg*	315212	2339
Women's and Girls' Cut and Sew Other Outerwear—*mfg*	315238	2339
Cultivating machinery and equipment: Farm and Garden Machinery and Equipment—*whlse*	42182	5083
Outdoor Power Equipment Stores—*retail*	44421	5083

Entry	NAICS	SIC
Cultivation services, mechanical and flame: Nonscheduled Air, Other—*trans*	481219	721
Soil Preparation, Planting, and Cultivating—*ag*	115112	721
Cultivators garden tractor equipment): Hand and Edge Tool—*mfg*	332212	3524
Lawn and Garden Tractor and Home Lawn and Garden Equipment—*mfg*	333112	3524
Cultivators, agricultural field and row crop: Farm Machinery and Equipment—*mfg*	333111	3523
Culture cups, rubber: Fabric Coating Mills—*mfg*	31332	3069
Rubber Product, All Other—*mfg*	326299	3069
Culture media or concentrates, except in vitro and in vivo: Biological Product (except Diagnostic)—*mfg*	325414	2836
Cultured pearl production: Crop Farming, All Other Miscellaneous—*ag*	111998	919
Marine Fishing, Other—*ag*	114119	919
Culvert construction-contractors: Concrete Contractors—*const*	23571	1771
Drywall, Plastering, Acoustical and Insulation Contractors—*const*	23542	1771
Culvert pipe, concrete: Concrete Pipe—*mfg*	327332	3272
Concrete Product, Other—*mfg*	32739	3272
Nonmetallic Mineral Product, All Other Miscellaneous—*mfg*	327999	3272
Culverts, metal plate: Air-Conditioning and Warm Air Heating Equipment and Commercial and Industrial Refrigeration Equipment—*mfg*	333415	3443
Metal Tank (Heavy Gauge)—*mfg*	33242	3443
Plate Work—*mfg*	332313	3443
Power Boiler and Heat Exchanger—*mfg*	33241	3443
Culverts, sheet metal: Metal Container, Other—*mfg*	332439	3444
Sheet Metal Work—*mfg*	332322	3444
Cummerbunds: Apparel Accessories and Apparel, Other—*mfg*	315999	2389
Cupolas, metal plate: Air-Conditioning and Warm Air Heating Equipment and Commercial and Industrial Refrigeration Equipment—*mfg*	333415	3443
Metal Tank (Heavy Gauge)—*mfg*	33242	3443
Plate Work—*mfg*	332313	3443
Power Boiler and Heat Exchanger—*mfg*	33241	3443
Cuprammonium fibers: Cellulosic Organic Fiber—*mfg*	325221	2823
Cuprite mining: Copper Ore and Nickel Ore—*mining*	212234	1021
Cups, foamed plastics: Polystyrene Foam Product—*mfg*	32614	3086
Urethane and Other Foam Product (except Polystyrene)—*mfg*	32615	3086
Cups, oil and grease–metal: Fabricated Metal Product, All Other Miscellaneous—*mfg*	332999	3599
General Purpose Machinery , All Other—*mfg*	333999	3599
Machine Shops—*mfg*	33271	3599
Machinery, Other Commercial and Service Industry—*mfg*	333319	3599
Motor Vehicle Parts, All Other—*mfg*	336399	3599
Cups, paper and dispssable plastics: Industrial and Personal Service Paper—*whlse*	42213	5113
Cups, paper–except those made from pressed or molded pul: Non-Folding Sanitary Food Container—*mfg*	322215	2656
Cups, plastics–except foam: Plastics Pipe and Pipe Fitting—*mfg*	326122	3089
Plastics Product, All Other—*mfg*	326199	3089
Unsupported Plastics Profile Shape—*mfg*	326121	3089
Cups, pressed and molded pulp: Coated and Laminated Paper—*mfg*	322222	2679
Converted Paper Product, All Other—*mfg*	322298	2679
Die-Cut Paper and Paperboard Office Supplies—*mfg*	322231	2679
Non-Folding Sanitary Food Container—*mfg*	322215	2679
Cups, primer and cartridge–copper and copper alloy: Copper Rolling, Drawing and Extruding—*mfg*	331421	3351
Curb construction-contractors: Concrete Contractors—*const*	23571	1771
Drywall, Plastering, Acoustical and Insulation Contractors—*const*	23542	1771
Curbing, granite and stone: Cut Stone and Stone Product—*mfg*	327991	3281
Cured meats: Animal (except Poultry) Slaughtering—*mfg*	311611	2011
Cured meats–brined, dried, and salted: Meat Processed from Carcasses—*mfg*	311612	2013
Curers, tobacco: Farm Machinery and Equipment—*mfg*	333111	3523
Curin rods, poles, and flxtures: Blind and Shade—*mfg*	33792	2591
Curing compounds, concrete blends of pigments, waxes, and resins): Basic Organic Chemical, All Other—*mfg*	325199	2899
Chemical Product, All Other Miscellaneous—*mfg*	325998	2899
Curio shops: Gift, Novelty and Souvenir Stores—*retail*	45322	5947
Curios: Nondurable Goods, Other Miscellaneous—*whlse*	42299	5199
Curlers, hair–designed for beauty parlors: Fabricated Metal Product, All Other Miscellaneous—*mfg*	332999	3999
Plastics Product, All Other—*mfg*	326199	3999
Curlers, hair–except equipment designed for beauty parlor use: Fastener, Button, Needle and Pin—*mfg*	339993	3965
Curlers, hair–rubber: Fabric Coating Mills—*mfg*	31332	3069
Rubber Product, All Other—*mfg*	326299	3069
Curling irons, electric: Electric Housewares and Household Fan—*mfg*	335211	3634
Heating Equipment (except Electric and Warm Air Furnaces)—*mfg*	333414	3634
Currant farms: Berry (except Strawberry) Farming—*ag*	111334	171
Strawberry Farming—*ag*	111333	171
Currency, engraving of: Digital Printing—*mfg*	323115	2759
Flexographic Printing, Commercial—*mfg*	323112	2759
Printing, Other Commercial—*mfg*	323119	2759
Quick Printing—*mfg*	323114	2759
Current collector wheels for trolley rigging: Electrical Equipment and Component, All Other Miscellaneous—*mfg*	335999	3629
Current limiting reactors, electrical: Power, Distribution and Specialty Transformer—*mfg*	335311	3612
Current measuring equipment: Electronic Coil, Transformer, and Other Inductor—*mfg*	334416	3825
Instrument for Measuring and Testing Electricity and Electrical Signals—*mfg*	334515	3825
Current taps, attachment plug and screwshell types: Current-Carrying Wiring Device—*mfg*	335931	3643

ALPHABETICAL INDEX	NAICS	SIC
Current-Carrying Wiring Device Manufacturing	**335931**	**3643**
Curriculum development, educational: Educational Support Services—*educ*	61171	8299
Professional and Management Development Training—*educ*	61143	8299
Currying of leather: Leather and Hide Tanning and Finishing—*mfg*	31611	3111
Curtain and Drapery Mills	**314121**	**5714**
Curtain and Linen Mills	**31412**	
Curtain cleaning and repair: Drycleaning Plants—*serv*	812322	7216
Curtain stores: Curtain and Drapery Mills—*mfg*	314121	5714
Sewing, Needlework and Piece Goods Stores—*retail*	45113	5714
Window Treatment Stores—*retail*	442291	5714
Curtain stretchers, wood: Manufacturing, All Other Miscellaneous—*mfg*	339999	2499
Wood Container and Pallet—*mfg*	32192	2499
Wood Product, All Other Miscellaneous—*mfg*	321999	2499
Curtain wall installation-contractors: Structural Steel Erection Contractors—*const*	23591	1791
Curtain wall, metal: Fabricated Structural Metal—*mfg*	332312	3449
Metal Window and Door—*mfg*	332321	3449
Ornamental and Architectural Metal Work—*mfg*	332323	3449
Roll Forming, Custom—*mfg*	332114	3449
Curtains: Home Furnishing—*whlse*	42122	5023
Knit Fabric and Lace Mills, Other—*mfg*	313249	2259
Weft Knit Fabric Mills—*mfg*	313241	2259
Curtains and curtain fabrics, lace: Knit Fabric and Lace Mills, Other—*mfg*	313249	2258
Textile and Fabric Finishing (except Broadwoven Fabric) Mills—*mfg*	313312	2258
Curtains, shower: Household Textile Product Mills, Other—*mfg*	314129	2392
Curtains, window: Curtain and Drapery Mills—*mfg*	314121	2391
Curtains–dock and welding: Canvas and Related Product Mills—*mfg*	314912	2394
Cushion springs, assembled: Mattress—*mfg*	33791	2515
Upholstered Household Furniture—*mfg*	337121	2515
Cushions and burnishers, gilders': Chemical Product, All Other Miscellaneous—*mfg*	325998	3952
Institutional Furniture—*mfg*	337127	3952
Lead Pencil and Art Good—*mfg*	339942	3952
Cushions, carpet and rug–plastics foam: Polystyrene Foam Product—*mfg*	32614	3086
Urethane and Other Foam Product (except Polystyrene)—*mfg*	32615	3086
Cushions, except spring and carpet cushions: Household Textile Product Mills, Other—*mfg*	314129	2392
Cushions, spring: Mattress—*mfg*	33791	2515
Upholstered Household Furniture—*mfg*	337121	2515
Custard, froren: Ice Cream and Frozen Dessert—*mfg*	31152	2024
Custodians of schools on a contract or feebasis: Janitorial Services—*admin*	56172	7349

ALPHABETICAL INDEX	NAICS	SIC
Custodians of securities: Financial Investment Activities, Miscellaneous—*fin*	523999	6289
Trust, Fiduciary and Custody Activities—*fin*	523991	6289
Custom builders, industrial and warehouse–general contractors: Building, Commercial and Institutional—*const*	23332	1541
Manufacturing and Industrial Building—*const*	23331	1541
Custom builders, nonresidential–except industrial and warehouses-general con-tractors: Building, Commercial and Institutional—*const*	23332	1542
Custom builders, residential–except single-family–general contractors: Building, Commercial and Institutional—*const*	23332	1522
Multifamily Housing—*const*	23322	1522
Custom builders, singl-family houses–general contractors: Single Family Housing—*const*	23321	1521
Custom compounding of purchased resins: Compounding of Purchased Resin, Custom—*mfg*	325991	3087
Custom compounding of rubber materials: Fabric Coating Mills—*mfg*	31332	3069
Rubber Product, All Other—*mfg*	326299	3069
Custom Computer Programming Services, Custom	**541511**	**7371**
Custom roll formed products, metal: Fabricated Structural Metal—*mfg*	332312	3449
Metal Window and Door—*mfg*	332321	3449
Ornamental and Architectural Metal Work—*mfg*	332323	3449
Roll Forming, Custom—*mfg*	332114	3449
Custom sawmills: Cut Stock, Resawing Lumber, and Planing—*mfg*	321912	2421
Millwork (including Flooring), Other—*mfg*	321918	2421
Sawmills—*mfg*	321113	2421
Wood Product, All Other Miscellaneous—*mfg*	321999	2421
Custom tailors: Clothing Accessories Stores—*retail*	44815	5699
Clothing Stores, Other—*retail*	44819	5699
Customhouse brokers: Freight Arrangement—*trans*	48851	4731
Management Consulting Services, Other—*prof*	541618	4731
Customizing automobiles, trucks or vans–except on a factory basis: Automotive Body, Paint and Interior Repair and Maintenance—*serv*	811121	7532
Customs Bureaus: Public Finance—*pub*	92113	9311
Customs clearance of freight: Freight Arrangement—*trans*	48851	4731
Management Consulting Services, Other—*prof*	541618	4731
Cut and engraved glassware, made from purchased glass: Glass Product Made of Purchased Glass—*mfg*	327215	3231
Cut flowers: Florists—*retail*	45311	5992
Flower, Nursery Stock and Florists' Supplies—*whlse*	42293	5193
Nursery and Garden Centers—*retail*	44422	5193
Cut stock for boots and shoes: Fastener, Button, Needle and Pin—*mfg*	339993	3131
Leather Good, All Other—*mfg*	316999	3131

Description	NAICS	SIC
Wood Product, All Other Miscellaneous—*mfg*	321999	3131
Cut Stock, Resawing Lumber, and Planing	**321912**	**2426**
Cut stock, softwood: Cut Stock, Resawing Lumber, and Planing—*mfg*	321912	2421
Millwork (including Flooring), Other—*mfg*	321918	2421
Sawmills—*mfg*	321113	2421
Wood Product, All Other Miscellaneous—*mfg*	321999	2421
Cut Stone and Stone Product Manufacturing	**327991**	**3281**
Cut stone products: Cut Stone and Stone Product—*mfg*	327991	3281
Cutlery: Hardware—*whlse*	42171	5072
Cutlery and Flatware (except Precious) Manufacturing	**332211**	**3914**
Cutlery and Hand Tool Manufacturing	**33221**	
Cutlery and Hand Tool Manufacturing	**3322**	
Cutlery stores: Home Furnishings Stores, All Other—*retail*	442299	5719
Window Treatment Stores—*retail*	442291	5719
Cutlery, except table cutlery with handles of metal: Cutlery and Flatware (except Precious)—*mfg*	332211	3421
Cutlery, with metal handles and blades: Cutlery and Flatware (except Precious)—*mfg*	332211	3914
Silverware and Plated Ware—*mfg*	339912	3914
Cutoff machines (metalworking machinery): Machine Tool (Metal Cutting Types)—*mfg*	333512	3541
Cutouts and displays, window and lobby: Sign—*mfg*	33995	3993
Cutouts, distribution: Switchgear and Switchboard Apparatus—*mfg*	335313	3613
Cutouts, paper and paperboard–die-cut from purchased material: Converted Paper Product, All Other—*mfg*	322298	2675
Die-Cut Paper and Paperboard Office Supplies—*mfg*	322231	2675
Surface-Coated Paperboard—*mfg*	322292	2675
Cutouts, switch and fuse: Current-Carrying Wiring Device—*mfg*	335931	3643
Cutters, biscuit (machines): Food Product Machinery—*mfg*	333294	3556
Cutters, coal: Mining Machinery and Equipment—*mfg*	333131	3532
Cutters, ensilage: Farm Machinery and Equipment—*mfg*	333111	3523
Cutters, glass: Hand and Edge Tool—*mfg*	332212	3423
Cutters, milling: Cutting Tool and Machine Tool Accessory—*mfg*	333515	3545
Hand and Edge Tool—*mfg*	332212	3545
Cutting and folding machines, paper: Paper Industry Machinery—*mfg*	333291	3554
Cutting dies, for cutting metal: Die and Tool, Die Set, Jig and Fixture, Special—*mfg*	333514	3544
Industrial Mold—*mfg*	333511	3544
Cutting dies, paper industry: Hand and Edge Tool—*mfg*	332212	3423
Cutting dies–except metal cutting: Hand and Edge Tool—*mfg*	332212	3423
Cutting instruments, dental: Dental Equipment and Supplies—*mfg*	339114	3843
Cutting machines, pipe (machine tools): Machine Tool (Metal Cutting Types)—*mfg*	333512	3541
Cutting of cards: Converted Paper Product, All Other—*mfg*	322298	2675
Die-Cut Paper and Paperboard Office Supplies—*mfg*	322231	2675
Surface-Coated Paperboard—*mfg*	322292	2675
Cutting of leather: Leather and Hide Tanning and Finishing—*mfg*	31611	3111
Cutting oils, blending and compounding from purchased material: Petroleum Lubricating Oil and Grease—*mfg*	324191	2992
Cutting right-of-way–general contractors: Heavy, All Other—*const*	23499	1629
Industrial Nonbuilding Structure—*const*	23493	1629
Cutting Tool and Machine Tool Accessory Manufacturing	**333515**	**3545**
Cutting tools and bits for use on lathes, planers, shapers, etc.: Cutting Tool and Machine Tool Accessory—*mfg*	333515	3545
Hand and Edge Tool—*mfg*	332212	3545
Cutting up lines: Other Metalworking Machinery, Other—*mfg*	333518	3549
Cutware, made from purchased glass: Glass Product Made of Purchased Glass—*mfg*	327215	3231
Cyanides: Basic Inorganic Chemical, All Other—*mfg*	325188	2819
Chemical Product, All Other Miscellaneous—*mfg*	325998	2819
Cyanite mining: Clay and Ceramic and Refractory Minerals—*mining*	212325	1459
Cycle condensate production (natural gas): Natural Gas Liquid Extraction—*mining*	211112	1321
Cycles, sidewalk–children's: Game, Toy, and Children's Vehicle—*mfg*	339932	3944
Cyclic Crude and Intermediate Manufacturing	**325192**	**2865**
Cyclic crudes and intermediates: Chemical and Allied Products, Other—*whlse*	42269	5169
Cyclic crudes, coal tar–product of coal tar distillation: Cyclic Crude and Intermediate—*mfg*	325192	2865
Petrochemical—*mfg*	32511	2865
Cyclic intermediates, made in chemical plants: Cyclic Crude and Intermediate—*mfg*	325192	2865
Petrochemical—*mfg*	32511	2865
Cyclo rubbers, natural: Fabric Coating Mills—*mfg*	31332	3069
Rubber Product, All Other—*mfg*	326299	3069
Cyclo rubbers, synthetic: Synthetic Rubber—*mfg*	325212	2822
Cyclohexane: Cyclic Crude and Intermediate—*mfg*	325192	2865
Petrochemical—*mfg*	32511	2865
Cyclones, industrial–metal plate: Air-Conditioning and Warm Air Heating Equipment and Commercial and Industrial Refrigeration Equipment—*mfg*	333415	3443
Metal Tank (Heavy Gauge)—*mfg*	33242	3443
Plate Work—*mfg*	332313	3443
Power Boiler and Heat Exchanger—*mfg*	33241	3443
Cyclopropane: Basic Organic Chemical, All Other—*mfg*	325199	2869
Cyclopropane for anesthetic use (U.S.P. par N.F.), packaged: Pharmaceutical Preparation—*mfg*	325412	2834
Cyclotrons: Electrical Equipment and Component, All Other Miscellaneous—*mfg*	335999	3699
Machinery, Other Commercial and Service Industry—*mfg*	333319	3699
Cylinder heads, motor vehicle–gasoline engines: Gasoline Engine and Engine Parts—*mfg*	336312	3714
Motor Vehicle Parts, All Other—*mfg*	336399	3714
Cylinder pipe, prestressed concrete: Concrete Pipe—*mfg*	327332	3272
Concrete Product, Other—*mfg*	32739	3272

ALPHABETICAL INDEX	NAICS	SIC
Nonmetallic Mineral Product, All Othe: Miscellaneous—*mfg*	327999	3272
Cylinder pipe, pretensioned concrete: Concrete Pipe—*mfg*	327332	3272
Concrete Product, Other—*mfg*	32739	3272
Nonmetallic Mineral Product, All Other Miscellaneous—*mfg*	327999	3272
Cylinder reboring machines: Machine Tool (Metal Cutting Types)—*mfg*	333512	3541
Cylinder wire cloth, made from purchased wire: Fabricated Wire Product, Other—*mfg*	332618	3496
Cylinders and clips, gun–30 mm. (or 1.18 inch) or less: Small Arms—*mfg*	332994	3484
Cylinders, fluid power–hydraulic and pneumatic: Fluid Power Cylinder and Actuator—*mfg*	333995	3593
Cylinders, pressure–metal plate: Air-Conditioning and Warm Air Heating Equipment and Commercial and Industrial Refrigeration Equipment—*mfg*	333415	3443
Metal Tank (Heavy Gauge)—*mfg*	33242	3443
Plate Work—*mfg*	332313	3443
Power Boiler and Heat Exchanger—*mfg*	33241	3443
Cylinders, pump: Pump and Pumping Equipment—*mfg*	333911	3561
Cymbals and parts: Musical Instrument—*mfg*	339992	3931
Cystoscopes except electromedical: Surgical and Medical Instrument—*mfg*	339112	3841
Cystoscopes, electromedical: Electromedical and Electrotherapeutic Apparatus—*mfg*	334510	3845
Irradiation Apparatus—*mfg*	334517	3845
Cytology and histology diagnostic products: In-Vitro Diagnostic Substance—*mfg*	325413	2835
Pharmaceutical Preparation—*mfg*	325412	2835
Dairy Cattle and Milk Production	**11212**	**241**
Dairy depots: Dairy Product (except Dried or Canned)—*whlse*	42243	5143
Dairy equipment, farm: Farm Machinery and Equipment—*mfg*	333111	3523
Dairy farm machinery and equipment: Farm and Garden Machinery and Equipment—*whlse*	42182	5083
Outdoor Power Equipment Stores—*retail*	44421	5083
Dairy farms: Beef Cattle Ranching and Farming—*ag*	112111	241
Dairy Cattle and Milk Production—*ag*	11212	241
Dairy heifer replacement farms: Beef Cattle Ranching and Farming—*ag*	112111	241
Dairy Cattle and Milk Production—*ag*	11212	241
Dairy herd improvement associations: Animal Production Support Activities—*ag*	11521	751
Dairy Product (except Dried or Canned) Wholesalers	**42243**	**5143**
Dairy Product (except Frozen) Manufacturing	**31151**	
Dairy Product Manufacturing	**3115**	
Dairy products machinery and equipment: Food Product Machinery—*mfg*	333294	3556

ALPHABETICAL INDEX	NAICS	SIC
Dairy products manufacturing machinery: Industrial Machinery and Equipment—*whlse*	42183	5084
Dairy products stores: Food Stores, All Other Specialty—*retail*	445299	5451
Dairy products, dried or canned: Grocery and Related Products, Other—*whlse*	42249	5149
Dairy products, except dried or canned: Dairy Product (except Dried or Canned)—*whlse*	42243	5143
Dairy products, house-to-house: Direct Selling Establishments, Other—*retail*	45439	5963
Mobile Foodservices—*accom*	72233	5963
Dairybars: Cafeterias—*accom*	722212	5812
Caterers—*accom*	72232	5812
Foodservice Contractors—*accom*	72231	5812
Full-Service Restaurants—*accom*	72211	5812
Limited-Service Restaurants—*accom*	722211	5812
Snack and Nonalcoholic Beverage Bars—*accom*	722213	5812
Theater Companies and Dinner Theaters—*arts*	71111	5812
Dam construction–general contractors: Heavy, All Other—*const*	23499	1629
Industrial Nonbuilding Structure—*const*	23493	1629
Dam gates, metal plate: Fabricated Structural Metal—*mfg*	332312	3441
Damasks, cotton: Broadwoven Fabric Mills—*mfg*	31321	2211
Damper operators–pneumatic, thermostatic, and electric: Automatic Environmental Control for Residential, Commercial and Appliance Use—*mfg*	334512	3822
Dampers, sheet metal-m[g: Metal Container, Other—*mfg*	332439	3444
Sheet Metal Work—*mfg*	332322	3444
Dampproofing buildings-contractors: Trade Contractors, All Other Special—*const*	23599	1799
Dance bands: Independent Artists, Writers, and Performers—*arts*	71151	7929
Musical Groups and Artists—*arts*	71113	7929
Performing Arts Companies, Other—*arts*	71119	7929
Dance Companies	**71112**	**7922**
Dance hall operation: Amusement and Recreation Industries, All Other—*arts*	71399	7911
Fine Arts Schools—*educ*	61161	7911
Dance instructors: Amusement and Recreation Industries, All Other—*arts*	71399	7911
Fine Arts Schools—*educ*	61161	7911
Dance studios and schools: Amusement and Recreation Industries, All Other—*arts*	71399	7911
Fine Arts Schools—*educ*	61161	7911
Dancing schools, professional: Amusement and Recreation Industries, All Other—*arts*	71399	7911
Fine Arts Schools—*educ*	61161	7911
Darkroom apparatus: Photographic Equipment and Supplies—*whlse*	42141	5043
Darning thread–cotton, silk, manmade fibers, and wool: Textile and Fabric Finishing (except Broadwoven Fabric) Mills—*mfg*	313312	2284

Description	NAICS	SIC
Thread Mills—*mfg*	313113	2284
Darning yarn–cotton, silk, wool, and manmade staple: Yarn Spinning Mills—*mfg*	313111	2281
Darts and dart games: Game, Toy, and Children's Vehicle—*mfg*	339932	3944
Data base developers: Computer Related Services, Other—*prof*	541519	7379
Computer Systems Design Services—*prof*	541512	7379
Data base information retrieval services: On-Line Information Services—*info*	514191	7375
Data entry service: Data Processing Services—*info*	51421	7374
Data loggers, industrial process type: Instruments and Related Products for Measuring, Displaying, and Controlling Industrial Process Variables—*mfg*	334513	3823
Data processing consultants: Computer Related Services, Other—*prof*	541519	7379
Computer Systems Design Services—*prof*	541512	7379
Data processing schools: Computer Training—*educ*	61142	8243
Technical and Trade Schools, Other—*educ*	611519	8243
Data Processing Services	**5142**	
Data Processing Services	**51421**	**7374**
Data sets, telephone and telegraph: Electronic Coil, Transformer, and Other Inductor—*mfg*	334416	3661
Printed Circuit/Electronics Assembly—*mfg*	334418	3661
Telephone Apparatus—*mfg*	33421	3661
Data telephone communications: Telecommunications Resellers—*info*	51333	4813
Wired Telecommunications Carriers—*info*	51331	4813
Data verification service: Data Processing Services—*info*	51421	7374
Database and Directory Publishers	**51114**	**2741**
Date orchards and farms: Fruit and Tree Nut Combination Farming—*ag*	111336	179
Noncitrus Fruit Farming, Other—*ag*	111339	179
Date stamps, hand–with rubber or metal type: Marking Device—*mfg*	339943	3953
Dates, dried: Dried and Dehydrated Food—*mfg*	311423	2034
Flour Milling—*mfg*	311211	2034
Dates–chocolate covered, sugared, and stuffed: Confectionery from Purchased Chocolate—*mfg*	31133	2064
Non-Chocolate Confectionery—*mfg*	31134	2064
Dating devices and machines, except rubber stamps: Lead Pencil and Art Good—*mfg*	339942	3579
Office Machinery—*mfg*	333313	3579
Watch, Clock, and Part—*mfg*	334518	3579
Dating service: Personal Services, All Other—*serv*	81299	7299
Davits: Overhead Traveling Crane, Hoist and Monorail System—*mfg*	333923	3536
Day camps: Amusement and Recreation Industries, All Other—*arts*	71399	7999
Day care centers, adult and handicapped: Child and Youth Services—*hlth*	62411	8322
Community Food Services—*hlth*	62421	8322
Community Housing Services, Other—*hlth*	624229	8322
Emergency and Other Relief Services—*hlth*	62423	8322
Individual and Family Services, Other—*hlth*	62419	8322
Parole Offices and Probation Offices—*pub*	92215	8322
Services for the Elderly and Persons with Disabilities—*hlth*	62412	8322
Temporary Shelters—*hlth*	624221	8322
Day care centers, child: Child Day Care Services—*hlth*	62441	8351
DDT (insecticide), formulated: Pesticide and Other Agricultural Chemical—*mfg*	32532	2879
DDT, technical: Basic Organic Chemical, All Other—*mfg*	325199	2869
Dealers in dairy products: Dairy Product (except Dried or Canned)—*whlse*	42243	5143
Dealers in poultry and poultry products: Poultry and Poultry Product—*whlse*	42244	5144
Dealers in raw farm products, except grain, field beans, and livestock: Farm Product Raw Material, Other—*whlse*	42259	5159
Dealers, commodity contract: Commodity Brokerage—*fin*	52314	6221
Commodity Contracts Dealing—*fin*	52313	6221
Dealers, mineral royalties or leases: Financial Investment Activities, Miscellaneous—*fin*	523999	6211
Intermediation, Miscellaneous—*fin*	52391	6211
Investment Banking and Securities Dealing—*fin*	52311	6211
Securities Brokerage—*fin*	52312	6211
Dealers, security: Financial Investment Activities, Miscellaneous—*fin*	523999	6211
Intermediation, Miscellaneous—*fin*	52391	6211
Investment Banking and Securities Dealing—*fin*	52311	6211
Securities Brokerage—*fin*	52312	6211
Death Care Services	**8122**	
Debris removal, local carting only: General Freight Trucking, Local—*trans*	48411	4212
Hazardous Waste Collection—*admin*	562112	4212
Solid Waste Collection—*admin*	562111	4212
Waste Collection, Other—*admin*	562119	4212
Debt counseling or adjustment service to individuals: Personal Services, All Other—*serv*	81299	7299
Deburring machines: Machine Tool (Metal Cutting Types)—*mfg*	333512	3541
Decade boxes–capacitance, inductance, and resistance: Electronic Coil, Transformer, and Other Inductor—*mfg*	334416	3825
Instrument for Measuring and Testing Electricity and Electrical Signals—*mfg*	334515	3825
Decahydronaphthalene: Basic Organic Chemical, All Other—*mfg*	325199	2869
Decalcomania work on china and glass, for the trade: Vitreous China, Fine Earthenware and Other Pottery Product—*mfg*	327112	3269
Decalcomanias (dry transfers), lithographed: Lithographic Printing, Commercial—*mfg*	323110	2752
Quick Printing—*mfg*	323114	2752
Decalcomanias, printed–except lithographed or gravure: Digital Printing—*mfg*	323115	2759
Flexographic Printing, Commercial—*mfg*	323112	2759
Printing, Other Commercial—*mfg*	323119	2759

ALPHABETICAL INDEX	NAICS	SIC
Quick Printing—*mfg*	323114	2759
Deckling books, cards, and paper: Tradebinding and Related Work—*mfg*	323121	2789
Decoders, computer peripheral equipment: Computer Peripheral Equipment, Other—*mfg*	334119	3577
Decontaminating and cleaning of missile and satellite parts, for the trade: Electroplating, Plating, Polishing, Anodizing and Coloring—*mfg*	332813	3471
Decorated glassware–e.g., chipped, engraved, etched, sandblasted-made from purchased glass: Glass Product Made of Purchased Glass—*mfg*	327215	3231
Decorating china, for the trade: Vitreous China, Fine Earthenware and Other Pottery Product—*mfg*	327112	3269
Decoration service for special events: Design Services, Other Specialized—*prof*	54149	7389
Decorative area lighting fixtures, except residential: Lighting Equipment, Other—*mfg*	335129	3648
Decorative glassware–made in glassmaking establishments: Pressed and Blown Glass and Glassware, Other—*mfg*	327212	3229
Decorative plating and finishing of formed products, for the trade: Electroplating, Plating, Polishing, Anodizing and Coloring—*mfg*	332813	3471
Decorative stitching, for the trade: Men's and Boys' Cut and Sew Apparel Contractors—*mfg*	315211	2395
Textile Product Mills, All Other Miscellaneous—*mfg*	314999	2395
Women's and Girls' Cut and Sew Apparel Contractors—*mfg*	315212	2395
Decorators consulting service, interior-not painters or paperhangers: Design Services, Other Specialized—*prof*	54149	7389
Interior Design Services—*prof*	54141	7389
Decorticating flax: Postharvest Crop Activities (except Cotton Ginning)—*ag*	115114	723
Decoys, duck and other game birds: Sporting and Athletic Goods—*mfg*	33992	3949
Deep fat fryers, household–electric: Electric Housewares and Household Fan—*mfg*	335211	3634
Heating Equipment (except Electric and Warm Air Furnaces)—*mfg*	333414	3634
Deep sea foreign passenger transportation: Coastal and Great Lakes Passenger—*trans*	483114	4481
Deep Sea Passenger—*trans*	483112	4481
Deep sea foreign transportation of freight: Deep Sea Freight—*trans*	483111	4412
Deep Sea Freight Transportation	**483111**	**4412**
Deep Sea Passenger Transportation	**483112**	**4481**
Deep sea transportation of passengers: Coastal and Great Lakes Passenger—*trans*	483114	4481
Deep Sea Passenger—*trans*	483112	4481
Deep Sea, Coastal and Great Lakes Water Transportation	**4831**	

ALPHABETICAL INDEX	NAICS	SIC
Deep Sea, Coastal and Great Lakes Water Transportation	**48311**	
Defibrilators: Electromedical and Electrotherapeutic Apparatus—*mfg*	334510	3845
Irradiation Apparatus—*mfg*	334517	3845
Defluorinated phosphates: Phosphatic Fertilizer—*mfg*	325312	2874
Defoliants: Pesticide and Other Agricultural Chemical—*mfg*	32532	2879
Defrosters, motor vehicle: Motor Vehicle Electrical and Electronic Equipment, Other—*mfg*	336322	3714
Motor Vehicle Parts, All Other—*mfg*	336399	3714
Degreasing machines, automotive (garage equipment): Industrial Machinery, All Other—*mfg*	333298	3559
Machinery, Other Commercial and Service Industry—*mfg*	333319	3559
Degreasing machines, industrial: Industrial Machinery, All Other–-*mfg*	333298	3559
Machinery, Other Commercial and Service Industry—*mfg*	333319	3559
Degreasing solvent-m[g: Polish and Other Sanitation Good—*mfg*	325612	2842
Dehumidifiers, electric–portable: Electric Housewares and Household Fan—*mfg*	335211	3634
Heating Equipment (except Electric and Warm Air Furnaces)—*mfg*	333414	3634
Dehumidifiers, except portable–electric: Air-Conditioning and Warm Air Heating Equipment and Commercial and Industrial Refrigeration Equipment—*mfg*	333415	3585
Motor Vehicle Air-Conditioning—*mfg*	336391	3585
Dehydrated fruits, vegetables, and soups: Dried and Dehydrated Food—*mfg*	311423	2034
Flour Milling—*mfg*	311211	2034
Dehydrating equipment, food processing: Food Product Machinery—*mfg*	333294	3556
Deicing equipment, aircraft: Aircraft Part and Auxiliary Equipment, Other—*mfg*	336413	3728
Fluid Power Valve and Hose Fitting—*mfg*	332912	3728
Deicing fluid: Basic Organic Chemical, All Other—*mfg*	325199	2899
Chemical Product, All Other Miscellaneous—*mfg*	325998	2899
Deinking of newsprint: Paper (except Newsprint) Mills—*mfg*	322121	2611
Paperboard Mills—*mfg*	32213	2611
Pulp Mills—*mfg*	32211	2611
Delay lines: Electronic Component, Other—*mfg*	334419	3679
Motor Vehicle Electrical and Electronic Equipment, Other—*mfg*	336322	3679
Printed Circuit/Electronics Assembly—*mfg*	334418	3679
Radio and Television Broadcasting and Wireless Communications Equipment—*mfg*	33422	3679
Delivering advertising, private: Advertising Material Distribution Services—*prof*	54187	7319
Advertising, Other Services Related to—*prof*	54189	7319
Display Advertising—*prof*	54185	7319
Media Buying Agencies—*prof*	54183	7319
Nonscheduled Air, Other—*trans*	481219	7319

Entry	NAICS	SIC
Delivery cases, made from purchased wire: Fabricated Wire Product, Other—*mfg*	332618	3496
Demand meters, electric: Electronic Coil, Transformer, and Other Inductor—*mfg*	334416	3825
Instrument for Measuring and Testing Electricity and Electrical Signals—*mfg*	334515	3825
Demijohn covers–willow, rattan and reed: Manufacturing, All Other Miscellaneous—*mfg*	339999	2499
Wood Container and Pallet—*mfg*	32192	2499
Wood Product, All Other Miscellaneous—*mfg*	321999	2499
Demolition of buildings or other structures, except marine–contractors: Wrecking and Demolition Contractors—*const*	23594	1795
Demonstration service, separate from sale: Advertising, Other Services Related to—*prof*	54189	7389
Demountable cargo containers: Truck Trailer—*mfg*	336212	3715
Denatured alcohol, industrial (nonbeverage): Basic Organic Chemical, All Other—*mfg*	325199	2869
Ethyl Alcohol—*mfg*	325193	2869
Denims: Broadwoven Fabric Mills—*mfg*	31321	2211
Densitometers: Photographic and Photocopying Equipment—*mfg*	333315	3861
Photographic Film, Paper, Plate and Chemical—*mfg*	325992	3861
Densitometers, analytical: Analytical Laboratory Instrument—*mfg*	334516	3826
Density and specific gravity instruments, industrial process type: Instruments and Related Products for Measuring, Displaying, and Controlling Industrial Process Variables—*mfg*	334513	3823
Dental alloys for amalgams: Dental Equipment and Supplies—*mfg*	339114	3843
Dental associations: Professional Organizations—*serv*	81392	8621
Dental chairs: Dental Equipment and Supplies—*mfg*	339114	3843
Dental engines: Dental Equipment and Supplies—*mfg*	339114	3843
Dental equipment: Health and Personal Care Stores, All Other—*retail*	446199	5047
Medical, Dental and Hospital Equipment and Supplies—*whlse*	42145	5047
Dental equipment and supplies: Dental Equipment and Supplies—*mfg*	339114	3843
Dental Equipment and Supplies Manufacturing	**339114**	**3843**
Dental hand instruments, including forceps: Dental Equipment and Supplies—*mfg*	339114	3843
Dental hygienists, offices of: Health Practitioners, Offices Of Miscellaneous—*hlth*	621399	8049
Mental Health Practitioners (except Physicians), Offices Of—*hlth*	62133	8049
Physical, Occupational and Speech Therapists and Audiologists, Offices Of—*hlth*	62134	8049
Dental insurance (providing services by contracts with health facilities): Direct Health and Medical Insurance Carriers—*fin*	524114	6324
Insurance Funds, Other—*fin*	52519	6324
Reinsurance Carriers—*fin*	52413	6324
Dental Laboratories	**339116**	**8072**
Dental laboratories, except X-ray: Dental Laboratories—*mfg*	339116	8072
Dental laboratories, X-ray: Diagnostic Imaging Centers—*hlth*	621512	8071
Medical Laboratories—*hlth*	621511	8071
Dental laboratory equipment: Dental Equipment and Supplies—*mfg*	339114	3843
Health and Personal Care Stores, All Other—*retail*	446199	5047
Medical, Dental and Hospital Equipment and Supplies—*whlse*	42145	5047
Dental metal: Dental Equipment and Supplies—*mfg*	339114	3843
Dental surgeons, offices of: Dentists, Offices Of—*hlth*	62121	8021
Dentifrices: Soap and Other Detergent—*mfg*	325611	2844
Toilet Preparation—*mfg*	32562	2844
Dentists' professional supplies: Health and Personal Care Stores, All Other—*retail*	446199	5047
Medical, Dental and Hospital Equipment and Supplies—*whlse*	42145	5047
Dentists, offices and clinics of: Dentists, Offices Of—*hlth*	62121	8021
Dentists, Offices Of	**62121**	**8021**
Dentists, Offices Of	**6212**	
Denture cleaners: Soap and Other Detergent—*mfg*	325611	2844
Toilet Preparation—*mfg*	32562	2844
Denture materials: Dental Equipment and Supplies—*mfg*	339114	3843
Dentures made in dental laboratories to order for the profession: Dental Laboratories—*mfg*	339116	8072
Deodorant servicing of rest rooms: Exterminating and Pest Control Services—*admin*	56171	7342
Janitorial Services—*admin*	56172	7342
Deodorants, nonpersonal: Polish and Other Sanitation Good—*mfg*	325612	2842
Deodorants, personal: Soap and Other Detergent—*mfg*	325611	2844
Toilet Preparation—*mfg*	32562	2844
Depalishiag metal, for the trade: Electroplating, Plating, Polishing, Anodizing and Coloring—*mfg*	332813	3471
Department Stores	**45211**	**5311**
Department Stores	**4521**	
Depilatories, cosmetic: Soap and Other Detergent—*mfg*	325611	2844
Toilet Preparation—*mfg*	32562	2844
Depilatory salons: Personal Care Services, Other—*serv*	812199	7299
Deposit brokers: Commodity Contracts Dealing—*fin*	52313	6099
Credit Intermediation, Other Activities Related to—*fin*	52239	6099
Financial Investment Activities, Miscellaneous—*fin*	523999	6099
Financial Transactions Processing, Reserve, and Clearing House Activities—*fin*	52232	6099
Trust, Fiduciary and Custody Activities—*fin*	523991	6099
Deposit or share insurance: Direct Insurance (except Life, Health and Medical) Carriers, Other—*fin*	524128	6399
Depository Credit Intermediation	**5221**	
Depository Credit Intermediation, Other	**52219**	**6022**
Depressors, tongue: Surgical Appliance and Supplies—*mfg*	339113	3842
Depth charge release pistols and projectors: Ordnance and Accessories, Other—*mfg*	332995	3489
Depth charges and parts (ordnance): Ammunition (except Small Arms)—*mfg*	332993	3483
Dermatological preparations: Pharmaceutical Preparation—*mfg*	325412	2834

ALPHABETICAL INDEX	NAICS	SIC
Dermatologists, offices of: Freestanding Ambulatory Surgical and Emergency Centers—*hlth*	621493	8011
HMO Medical Centers—*hlth*	621491	8011
Physicians (except Mental Health Specialists), Offices Of—*hlth*	621111	8011
Physicians, Mental Health Specialists, Offices Of—*hlth*	621112	8011
Derrick buildihg, repairing, and dismantling–oil and gas on a contract basis: Oil and Gas Operations Support Activities—*mining*	213112	1389
Derricks: Industrial Machinery and Equipment—*whlse*	42183	5084
Derricks, except oil and gas field: Construction Machinery—*mfg*	33312	3531
Overhead Traveling Crane, Hoist and Monorail System—*mfg*	333923	3531
Railroad Rolling Stock—*mfg*	33651	3531
Derricks, oil and gas field: Oil and Gas Field Machinery and Equipment—*mfg*	333132	3533
Desalination equipment: Industrial Machinery, All Other—*mfg*	333298	3559
Machinery, Other Commercial and Service Industry—*mfg*	333319	3559
Desalter kits, sea water: Basic Organic Chemical, All Other—*mfg*	325199	2899
Chemical Product, All Other Miscellaneous—*mfg*	325998	2899
Desiccants, activated–clay: Ground or Treated Mineral and Earth—*mfg*	327992	3295
Desiccants, activated–silica gel: Basic Inorganic Chemical, All Other—*mfg*	325188	2819
Chemical Product, All Other Miscellaneous—*mfg*	325998	2819
Design Services, Other Specialized	**54149**	**7389**
Design Services, Specialized	**5414**	
Designing and erecting combined–single-family houses–general contractors: Single Family Housing—*const*	23321	1521
Designing and erecting, combined–commercial–general contractors: Building, Commercial and Institutional—*const*	23332	1542
Designing and erecting, combined–industrial–general contractors: Building, Commercial and Institutional—*const*	23332	1541
Manufacturing and Industrial Building—*const*	23331	1541
Designing and erecting, combined–residential, except single-family–general contractors: Building, Commercial and Institutional—*const*	23332	1522
Multifamily Housing—*const*	23322	1522
Designing–ship, boat, and machine: Engineering Services—*prof*	54133	8711
Desk fans, electric: Electric Housewares and Household Fan—*mfg*	335211	3634
Heating Equipment (except Electric and Warm Air Furnaces)—*mfg*	333414	3634
Desk lamps, commercial: Electric Lighting Fixture, Commercial, Industrial and Institutional—*mfg*	335122	3646
Desk lamps, residential: Residential Electric Lighting Fixture—*mfg*	335121	3645
Desk pads, paper: Stationery, Tablet, and Related Product—*mfg*	322233	2678
Desk set bases, onyx: Cut Stone and Stone Product—*mfg*	327991	3281
Desk sets, leather: Leather Good, All Other—*mfg*	316999	3199
Desks, household–wood: Nonupholstered Wood Household Furniture—*mfg*	337122	2511

ALPHABETICAL INDEX	NAICS	SIC
Desks, including school: Furniture—*whlse*	42121	5021
Furniture Stores—*retail*	44211	5021
Desks, office–except wood: Nonwood Office Furniture—*mfg*	337214	2522
Desks, office–wood: Wood Office Furniture—*mfg*	337211	2521
Dessert pops, frozen–flavored ice, fruit, pudding, and gelatin: Ice Cream and Frozen Dessert—*mfg*	31152	2024
Desserts, frozen–except bakery: Ice Cream and Frozen Dessert—*mfg*	31152	2024
Destroyer tenders, building and repairing: Ship Building and Repairing—*mfg*	336611	3731
Detailing (cleaning and polishing) newautos for dealers on a contract or feebasis: Car Washes—*serv*	811192	7542
Detasseling of corn: Nonscheduled Air, Other—*trans*	481219	721
Soil Preparation, Planting, and Cultivating—*ag*	115112	721
Detective agencies: Armored Car Services—*admin*	561613	7381
Investigation Services—*admin*	561611	7381
Security Guards and Patrol Services—*admin*	561612	7381
Detectors, scintillation: Measuring and Controlling Device, Other—*mfg*	334519	3829
Surgical and Medical Instrument—*mfg*	339112	3829
Detention centers: Correctional Institutions—*pub*	92214	9223
Detergents: Chemical and Allied Products, Other—*whlse*	42269	5169
Detergents, synthetic organic and inorganic alkaline: Soap and Other Detergent—*mfg*	325611	2841
Detinning of cans: Secondary Smelting and Alloying of Aluminum—*mfg*	331314	3341
Secondary Smelting, Refining, and Alloying of Nonferrous Metal (except Copper and Aluminum)—*mfg*	331492	3341
Detinning of scrap: Secondary Smelting and Alloying of Aluminum—*mfg*	331314	3341
Secondary Smelting, Refining, and Alloying of Nonferrous Metal (except Copper and Aluminum)—*mfg*	331492	3341
Detonating caps for safety fuses: Explosives—*mfg*	32592	2892
Detonators (explosive compounds): Explosives—*mfg*	32592	2892
Detonators for ammunition more than 30 mm. (or more than 1.18 inch): Ammunition (except Small Arms)—*mfg*	332993	3483
Detonators–mine, bomb, depth charge, and chemical warfare projectile: Ammunition (except Small Arms)—*mfg*	332993	3483
Detoxification centers, outpatient: Family Planning Centers—*hlth*	62141	8093
Outpatient Care Centers, All Other—*hlth*	621498	8093
Outpatient Mental Health and Substance Abuse Centers—*hlth*	62142	8093
Developers, prepared photographic–not made in chemical plants: Photographic and Photocopying Equipment—*mfg*	333315	3861
Photographic Film, Paper, Plate and Chemical—*mfg*	325992	3861
Developing and printing of commercial motion picture film: Independent Artists, Writers, and Performers—*arts*	71151	7819
Motion Picture and Video Industries, Other—*info*	512199	7819
Teleproduction and Other Post-Production Services—*info*	512191	7819

Description	NAICS	SIC
Developing and printing of film, except commercial motion picture film: One-Hour Photo Finishing—*serv*	812922	7384
Photo Finishing Laboratories (except One-Hour)—*serv*	812921	7384
Developing and processing of home movies: One-Hour Photo Finishing—*serv*	812922	7384
Photo Finishing Laboratories (except One-Hour)—*serv*	812921	7384
Developing apparatus, photographic: Photographic Equipment and Supplies—*whlse*	42141	5043
Developing machines and equipment, still or motion picture: Photographic and Photocopying Equipment—*mfg*	333315	3861
Photographic Film, Paper, Plate and Chemical—*mfg*	325992	3861
Dewatering–contractors: Trade Contractors, All Other Special—*const*	23599	1799
Dewberryfarms: Berry (except Strawberry) Farming—*ag*	111334	171
Strawberry Farming—*ag*	111333	171
Dextrine: Wet Corn Milling—*mfg*	311221	2046
Dextrine sizes: Basic Organic Chemical, All Other—*mfg*	325199	2899
Chemical Product, All Other Miscellaneous—*mfg*	325998	2899
Dextrose: Wet Corn Milling—*mfg*	311221	2046
Dextrose and sodium chloride injection, mixed: Pharmaceutical Preparation—*mfg*	325412	2834
Dextrose injection: Pharmaceutical Preparation—*mfg*	325412	2834
Diabase, crushed and broken: Crushed and Broken Stone and Quarrying, Other—*mining*	212319	1429
Diabase, dimension: Dimension Stone and Quarrying—*mining*	212311	1411
Diagnostic agents, biological: In-Vitro Diagnostic Substance—*mfg*	325413	2835
Pharmaceutical Preparation—*mfg*	325412	2835
Diagnostic apparatus, physicians': Surgical and Medical Instrument—*mfg*	339112	3841
Diagnostic centers, automotive: Automotive Oil Change and Lubrication Shops—*serv*	811191	7549
Automotive Repair and Maintenance, All Other—*serv*	811198	7549
Motor Vehicle Towing—*trans*	48841	7549
Diagnostic equipment, medical: Health and Personal Care Stores, All Other—*retail*	446199	5047
Medical, Dental and Hospital Equipment and Supplies—*whlse*	42145	5047
Diagnostic Imaging Centers	**621512**	**8071**
Dial light sockets, radio: Current-Carrying Wiring Device—*mfg*	335931	3643
Dialyzers, electromedical: Electromedical and Electrotherapeutic Apparatus—*mfg*	334510	3845
Irradiation Apparatus—*mfg*	334517	3845
Diammonium phosphates: Phosphatic Fertilizer—*mfg*	325312	2874
Diamond cloth, made from purchased wire: Fabricated Wire Product, Other—*mfg*	332618	3496
Diamond cutting and polishing: Jewelers' Material and Lapidary Work—*mfg*	339913	3915
Diamond cutting tools for turning, boring, burnishing, etc.: Cutting Tool and Machine Tool Accessory—*mfg*	333515	3545
Hand and Edge Tool—*mfg*	332212	3545
Diamond dies, metalworking: Die and Tool, Die Set, Jig and Fixture, Special—*mfg*	333514	3544
Industrial Mold—*mfg*	333511	3544
Diamond dressing and wheel crushing attachments: Cutting Tool and Machine Tool Accessory—*mfg*	333515	3545
Hand and Edge Tool—*mfg*	332212	3545
Diamond dressing wheels: Abrasive Product—*mfg*	32791	3291
Fabricated Metal Product, All Other Miscellaneous—*mfg*	332999	3291
Diamond drilling for building construction–contractors: Trade Contractors, All Other Special—*const*	23599	1799
Diamond mining, industrial: Crushed and Broken Stone and Quarrying, Other—*mining*	212319	1499
Non-Metallic Mineral, All Other—*mining*	212399	1499
Diamond points for phonograph needles: Jewelers' Material and Lapidary Work—*mfg*	339913	3915
Diamond powder: Abrasive Product—*mfg*	32791	3291
Fabricated Metal Product, All Other Miscellaneous—*mfg*	332999	3291
Diamonds (gems): Jewelry, Watch, Precious Stone and Precious Metal—*whlse*	42194	5094
Diamonds, industrial–natural and crude: Industrial Machinery and Equipment—*whlse*	42183	5085
Industrial Supplies—*whlse*	42184	5085
Diaper covers, waterproof–except vulcanized rubber: Apparel Accessories and Apparel, Other—*mfg*	315999	2385
Infants' Cut and Sew Apparel—*mfg*	315291	2385
Men's and Boys' Cut and Sew Apparel Contractors—*mfg*	315211	2385
Men's and Boys' Cut and Sew Other Outerwear—*mfg*	315228	2385
Men's and Boys' Cut and Sew Suit, Coat and Overcoat—*mfg*	315222	2385
Women's and Girls' Cut and Sew Apparel Contractors—*mfg*	315212	2385
Women's and Girls' Cut and Sew Other Outerwear—*mfg*	315238	2385
Women's and Girls' Cut and Sew Suit, Coat, Tailored Jacket and Skirt—*mfg*	315234	2385
Diaper fabrics: Broadwoven Fabric Mills—*mfg*	31321	2211
Diaper service: Linen Supply—*serv*	812331	7219
Diapers: Women's, Children's, and Infants' and Accessories—*whlse*	42233	5137
Diapers, disposable: Sanitary Paper Product—*mfg*	322291	2676
Diapers, except disposable: Textile Product Mills, All Other Miscellaneous—*mfg*	314999	2399
Diaphragms, rubber–separate and in kits: Fabric Coating Mills—*mfg*	31332	3069
Rubber Product, All Other—*mfg*	326299	3069
Diaries: Blankbook, Loose-leaf Binder and Device—*mfg*	323118	2782
Flexographic Printing, Commercial—*mfg*	323112	2782
Gravure Printing, Commercial—*mfg*	323111	2782
Lithographic Printing, Commercial—*mfg*	323110	2782
Printing, Other Commercial—*mfg*	323119	2782
Screen Printing, Commercial—*mfg*	323113	2782
Diaspore mining: Clay and Ceramic and Refractory Minerals—*mining*	212325	1459

ALPHABETICAL INDEX	NAICS	SIC
Diathermy apparatus, electromedical: Electromedical and Electrotherapeutic Apparatus—*mfg*	334510	3845
Irradiation Apparatus—*mfg*	334517	3845
Diathermy unit: Electromedical and Electrotherapeutic Apparatus—*mfg*	334510	3845
Irradiation Apparatus—*mfg*	334517	3845
Diatomaceous earth mining: Crushed and Broken Stone and Quarrying, Other—*mining*	212319	1499
Non-Metallic Mineral, All Other—*mining*	212399	1499
Diatomaceous earth, ground or otherwise treated: Ground or Treated Mineral and Earth—*mfg*	327992	3295
Diatomite mining: Crushed and Broken Stone and Quarrying, Other—*mining*	212319	1499
Non-Metallic Mineral, All Other—*mining*	212399	1499
Diazo (whiteprint) paper and cloth, sensitized: Photographic and Photocopying Equipment—*mfg*	333315	3861
Photographic Film, Paper, Plate and Chemical—*mfg*	325992	3861
Diazotype (whiteprint) reproduction ma-chines and equipment: Photographic and Photocopying Equipment—*mfg*	333315	3861
Photographic Film, Paper, Plate and Chemical—*mfg*	325992	3861
Dice and dice cups: Game, Toy, and Children's Vehicle—*mfg*	339932	3944
Dichlorodifluoromethane: Basic Organic Chemical, All Other—*mfg*	325199	2869
Dichromates: Basic Inorganic Chemical, All Other—*mfg*	325188	2819
Chemical Product, All Other Miscellaneous—*mfg*	325998	2819
Dickeys: Apparel Accessories and Apparel, Other—*mfg*	315999	2339
Cut and Sew Apparel, All Other—*mfg*	315299	2339
Women's and Girls' Cut and Sew Apparel Contractors—*mfg*	315212	2339
Women's and Girls' Cut and Sew Other Outerwear—*mfg*	315238	2339
Dictating machines, office types: Lead Pencil and Art Good—*mfg*	339942	3579
Office Machinery—*mfg*	333313	3579
Watch, Clock, and Part—*mfg*	334518	3579
Diction schools: Language Schools—*educ*	61163	8299
Dicyandiamine resins: Plastics Material and Resin—*mfg*	325211	2821
Die and hub cutting equipment jewelry: Industrial Machinery, All Other—*mfg*	333298	3559
Machinery, Other Commercial and Service Industry—*mfg*	333319	3559
Die and strip handlers: Fabricated Metal Product, All Other Miscellaneous—*mfg*	332999	3537
Industrial Truck, Tractor, Trailer and Stacker Machinery—*mfg*	333924	3537
Metal Container, Other—*mfg*	332439	3537
Die and Tool, Die Set, Jig and Fixture Manufacturing, Special	**333514**	**3544**
Die-casting machines: Machine Tool (Metal Forming Types)—*mfg*	333513	3542
Die-casting nonferrous metals, except aluminum: Nonferrous (except Aluminum) Die-Castings—*mfg*	331522	3364
Die-castings, aluminum: Aluminum Die-Castings—*mfg*	331521	3363
Die-cut paper and paperboard: Converted Paper Product, All Other—*mfg*	322298	2675
Die-Cut Paper and Paperboard Office Supplies—*mfg*	322231	2675
Surface-Coated Paperboard—*mfg*	322292	2675
Die-Cut Paper and Paperboard Office Supplies Manufacturing	**322231**	**2679**
Die-cutting and stamping machinery(paper converting machinery): Paper Industry Machinery—*mfg*	333291	3554
Die-cutting of leather: Leather and Hide Tanning and Finishing—*mfg*	31611	3111
Dielectric heating equipment: Industrial Process Furnace and Oven—*mfg*	333994	3567
Dies and die holders for metal diecastingand metal cutting and forming, exceptthreading: Die and Tool, Die Set, Jig and Fixture, Special—*mfg*	333514	3544
Industrial Mold—*mfg*	333511	3544
Dies, biscuit cutting: Food Product Machinery—*mfg*	333294	3556
Dies, cutting–except metal cutting: Hand and Edge Tool—*mfg*	332212	3423
Dies, diamond–metalworking: Die and Tool, Die Set, Jig and Fixture, Special—*mfg*	333514	3544
Industrial Mold—*mfg*	333511	3544
Dies, hand seal: Marking Device—*mfg*	339943	3953
Dies, metalworking: Industrial Machinery and Equipment—*whlse*	42183	5084
Dies, metalworking, except threading: Die and Tool, Die Set, Jig and Fixture, Special—*mfg*	333514	3544
Industrial Mold—*mfg*	333511	3544
Dies, plastics forming: Die and Tool, Die Set, Jig and Fixture, Special—*mfg*	333514	3544
Industrial Mold—*mfg*	333511	3544
Dies, steel rule': Die and Tool, Die Set, Jig and Fixture, Special—*mfg*	333514	3544
Industrial Mold—*mfg*	333511	3544
Dies, thread cutting: Cutting Tool and Machine Tool Accessory—*mfg*	333515	3545
Hand and Edge Tool—*mfg*	332212	3545
Diesel and semidiesel engines–for stationary, marine, traction, etc.: Engine Equipment, Other—*mfg*	333618	3519
Motor Vehicle Parts, All Other—*mfg*	336399	3519
Diesel engine parts: Engine Equipment, Other—*mfg*	333618	3519
Motor Vehicle Parts, All Other—*mfg*	336399	3519
Diesel engine repair, automotive: General Automotive Repair—*serv*	811111	7538
Diesel engines and engine parts, industrial: Industrial Machinery and Equipment—*whlse*	42183	5084
Diesets for metal stamping (presses): Die and Tool, Die Set, Jig and Fixture, Special—*mfg*	333514	3544
Industrial Mold—*mfg*	333511	3544
Diesinking machines: Machine Tool (Metal Cutting Types)—*mfg*	333512	3541
Diet and Weight Reducing Centers	**812191**	**7299**
Diet workshops: Diet and Weight Reducing Centers—*serv*	812191	7299
Personal Care Services, Other—*serv*	812199	7299
Dietary supplements, dairy and nondairy base: Dry, Condensed, and Evaporated Dairy Product—*mfg*	311514	2023

Description	NAICS	SIC
Dietetic food stores: Food (Health) Supplement Stores—*retail*	446191	5499
Food Stores, All Other Specialty—*retail*	445299	5499
Limited-Service Restaurants—*accom*	722211	5499
Meat Markets—*retail*	44521	5499
Diethylcyclohexane (mixed isomers): Basic Organic Chemical, All Other—*mfg*	325199	2869
Diethylene glycol ether: Basic Organic Chemical, All Other—*mfg*	325199	2869
Dieticians, offices of: Health Practitioners, Offices Of Miscellaneous—*hlth*	621399	8049
Mental Health Practitioners (except Physicians), Offices Of—*hlth*	62133	8049
Physical, Occupational and Speech Therapists and Audiologists, Offices Of—*hlth*	62134	8049
Differential pressure instruments, mdustrial process type: Instruments and Related Products for Measuring, Displaying, and Controlling Industrial Process Variables—*mfg*	334513	3823
Differential thermal analysis instruments: Analytical Laboratory Instrument—*mfg*	334516	3826
Differentials and parts, motor vehicle: Gasoline Engine and Engine Parts—*mfg*	336312	3714
Motor Vehicle Parts, All Other—*mfg*	336399	3714
Motor Vehicle Steering and Suspension Components (except Spring)—*mfg*	33633	3714
Motor Vehicle Transmission and Power Train Parts—*mfg*	33635	3714
Digesters, process–metal plate: Air-Conditioning and Warm Air Heating Equipment and Commercial and Industrial Refrigeration Equipment—*mfg*	333415	3443
Metal Tank (Heavy Gauge)—*mfg*	33242	3443
Plate Work—*mfg*	332313	3443
Power Boiler and Heat Exchanger—*mfg*	33241	3443
Digital displays of process variables: Instruments and Related Products for Measuring, Displaying, and Controlling Industrial Process Variables—*mfg*	334513	3823
Digital encoders: Radio and Television Broadcasting and Wireless Communications Equipment—*mfg*	33422	3663
Digital panel meters, electricity measuring: Electronic Coil, Transformer, and Other Inductor—*mfg*	334416	3825
Instrument for Measuring and Testing Electricity and Electrical Signals—*mfg*	334515	3825
Digital Printing	**323115**	**2759**
Digital test equipment, electronic and electrical circuits and equipment: Electronic Coil, Transformer, and Other Inductor—*mfg*	334416	3825
Instrument for Measuring and Testing Electricity and Electrical Signals—*mfg*	334515	3825
Digital-analog converters, electronic instrumentation type: Electronic Coil, Transformer, and Other Inductor—*mfg*	334416	3825
Instrument for Measuring and Testing Electricity and Electrical Signals—*mfg*	334515	3825
Digitalis pharmaceutical preparations: Pharmaceutical Preparation—*mfg*	325412	2834
Digitoxin: Medicinal and Botanical—*mfg*	325411	2833
Diisocyanate resins: Plastics Material and Resin—*mfg*	325211	2821
Dike construction–general contractors: Heavy, All Other—*const*	23499	1629
Industrial Nonbuilding Structure—*const*	23493	1629
Dimension stone for buildings: Cut Stone and Stone Product—*mfg*	327991	3281
Dimension Stone Mining and Quarrying	**212311**	**1411**
Dimension, hardwood: Cut Stock, Resawing Lumber, and Planing—*mfg*	321912	2426
Millwork (including Flooring), Other—*mfg*	321918	2426
Showcase, Partition, Shelving, and Locker—*mfg*	337215	2426
Wood Product, All Other Miscellaneous—*mfg*	321999	2426
Dimethyl divinyl acetylene (di-isopropenyl acetylene): Basic Organic Chemical, All Other—*mfg*	325199	2869
Industrial Gas—*mfg*	32512	2869
Dimethylhydrazine, unsymmetrical: Basic Organic Chemical, All Other—*mfg*	325199	2869
Dimities: Broadwoven Fabric Mills—*mfg*	31321	2211
Diners (eating places): Cafeterias—*accom*	722212	5812
Caterers—*accom*	72232	5812
Foodservice Contractors—*accom*	72231	5812
Full-Service Restaurants—*accom*	72211	5812
Limited-Service Restaurants—*accom*	722211	5812
Snack and Nonalcoholic Beverage Bars—*accom*	722213	5812
Theater Companies and Dinner Theaters—*arts*	71111	5812
Dinette sets, metal: Metal Household Furniture—*mfg*	337124	2514
Dinghies, building and repairing: Boat Building—*mfg*	336612	3732
Personal and Household Goods Repair and Maintenance, Other—*serv*	81149	3732
Dining car operations, not performed by line-haul railroad companies: Rail Support Activities—*trans*	48821	4789
Scenic and Sightseeing, Land—*trans*	48711	4789
Transportation, All Other Support Activities—*trans*	488999	4789
Dining cars and car equipment: Pump and Pumping Equipment—*mfg*	333911	3743
Railroad Rolling Stock—*mfg*	33651	3743
Dining room furniture, wood: Nonupholstered Wood Household Furniture—*mfg*	337122	2511
Dining rooms: Cafeterias—*accom*	722212	5812
Caterers—*accom*	72232	5812
Foodservice Contractors—*accom*	72231	5812
Full-Service Restaurants—*accom*	72211	5812
Limited-Service Restaurants—*accom*	722211	5812
Snack and Nonalcoholic Beverage Bars—*accom*	722213	5812
Theater Companies and Dinner Theaters—*arts*	71111	5812
Dinner theaters: Cafeterias—*accom*	722212	5812
Caterers—*accom*	72232	5812
Foodservice Contractors—*accom*	72231	5812
Full-Service Restaurants—*accom*	72211	5812

ALPHABETICAL INDEX	NAICS	SIC
Limited-Service Restaurants—*accom*	722211	5812
Snack and Nonalcoholic Beverage Bars—*accom*	722213	5812
Theater Companies and Dinner Theaters—*arts*	71111	5812
Dinners, frozen: Packaged Frozen Food—*whlse*	42242	5142
Dinners, frozen–packaged: Frozen Specialty Food—*mfg*	311412	2038
Dinnerware, plastics–except foam: Plastics Pipe and Pipe Fitting—*mfg*	326122	3089
Plastics Product, All Other—*mfg*	326199	3089
Unsupported Plastics Profile Shape—*mfg*	326121	3089
Diode and transistor testers: Electronic Coil, Transformer, and Other Inductor—*mfg*	334416	3825
Instrument for Measuring and Testing Electricity and Electrical Signals—*mfg*	334515	3825
Diodes: Electronic Parts and Equipment, Other—*whlse*	42169	5065
Diodes, solid-state (germanium, silicon, etc.): Semiconductor and Related Device—*mfg*	334413	3674
Diorite, crushed and broken: Crushed and Broken Granite and Quarrying—*mining*	212313	1423
Diorite, dimension: Dimension Stone and Quarrying—*mining*	212311	1411
Diphenylamine: Cyclic Crude and Intermediate—*mfg*	325192	2865
Petrochemical—*mfg*	32511	2865
Diphtheria toxin: Biological Product (except Diagnostic)—*mfg*	325414	2836
Diplomatic services: International Affairs—*pub*	92812	9721
Dippers, ice cream: Kitchen Utensil, Pot and Pan—*mfg*	332214	3469
Dipping metal in plastics solution as a preservative, for the trade: Costume Jewelry and Novelty—*mfg*	339914	3479
Jewelry (except Costume)—*mfg*	339911	3479
Metal Coating, Engraving (except Jewelry and Silverware), and Allied Services to Manufacturers—*mfg*	332812	3479
Silverware and Plated Ware—*mfg*	339912	3479
Dips, cattk and sheep: Pesticide and Other Agricultural Chemical—*mfg*	32532	2879
Dips, cheese-based: Cheese—*mfg*	311513	2022
Dips, except cheese and sour creambaeed: Food, All Other Miscellaneous—*mfg*	311999	2099
Dips, sour cream based: Fluid Milk—*mfg*	311511	2026
Direct broadcast satellite (DBS) services: Cable and Other Program Distribution—*info*	51322	4841
Cable Networks—*info*	51321	4841
Direct Health and Medical Insurance Carriers	**524114**	**6321**
Direct Insurance (except Life, Health and Medical) Carriers, Other	**524128**	**6399**
Direct Insurance (except Life, Health, and Medical) Carriers	**52412**	
Direct Life Insurance Carriers	**524113**	**6311**
Direct Life, Health and Medical Insurance Carriers	**52411**	
Direct Mail Advertising	**54186**	**7331**
Direct mail advertising service: Direct Mail Advertising—*prof*	54186	7331
Direct Property and Casualty Insurance Carriers	**524126**	**6351**
Direct Selling Establishments	**4543**	
Direct Selling Establishments, Other	**45439**	**5963**
Direct selling organizations (headquarters of door-to-door canvassers): Direct Selling Establishments, Other—*retail*	45439	5963
Mobile Foodservices—*accom*	72233	5963
Direct Title Insurance Carriers	**524127**	**6361**
Direct working capital financing: Financial Transactions Processing, Reserve, and Clearing House Activities—*fin*	52232	6153
Non-Depository Credit Intermediation, All Other—*fin*	522298	6153
Sales Financing—*fin*	52222	6153
Directional drilling of oil and gas wells ona contract basis: Drilling Oil and Gas Wells—*mining*	213111	1381
Directional signals, motor vehicle: Motor Vehicle Body—*mfg*	336211	3714
Motor Vehicle Electrical and Electronic Equipment, Other—*mfg*	336322	3714
Motor Vehicle Parts, All Other—*mfg*	336399	3714
Directories, printed–except lithographed or gravure (not publishing): Digital Printing—*mfg*	323115	2759
Flexographic Printing, Commercial—*mfg*	323112	2759
Printing, Other Commercial—*mfg*	323119	2759
Quick Printing—*mfg*	323114	2759
Directories–gravure printing (not publishing): Gravure Printing, Commercial—*mfg*	323111	2754
Directories–publishing and printing, orpublishing only: Database and Directory Publishers—*info*	51114	2741
Music Publishers—*info*	51223	2741
Publishers, All Other—*info*	511199	2741
Directors, motion picture–independent: Independent Artists, Writers, and Performers—*arts*	71151	7819
Motion Picture and Video Industries, Other—*info*	512199	7819
Dirigibles: Aircraft—*mfg*	336411	3721
Dirt moving–contractors: Excavation Contractors—*const*	23593	1794
Dirt sweeping units, industrial: Machinery, Other Commercial and Service Industry—*mfg*	333319	3589
Disability health insurance: Direct Health and Medical Insurance Carriers—*fin*	524114	6321
Insurance Funds, Other—*fin*	52519	6321
Reinsurance Carriers—*fin*	52413	6321
Disaster preparedness and management offices: Justice, Public Order, and Safety, All Other—*pub*	92219	9229
Disaster services: Child and Youth Services—*hlth*	62411	8322
Community Food Services—*hlth*	62421	8322
Community Housing Services, Other—*hlth*	624229	8322
Emergency and Other Relief Services—*hlth*	62423	8322
Individual and Family Services, Other—*hlth*	62419	8322
Parole Offices and Probation Offices—*pub*	92215	8322
Services for the Elderly and Persons with Disabilities—*hlth*	62412	8322

Temporary Shelters—*hlth*	624221	8322
Disc players, compact: Audio and Video Equipment—*mfg*	33431	3651
Discharging station construction, mine–general contractors: Heavy, All Other—*const*	23499	1629
Industrial Nonbuilding Structure—*const*	23493	1629
Discotheques, alcoholic beverage: Drinking Places (Alcoholic Beverages)—*accom*	72241	5813
Discotheques, except those serving alcoholic beverages: Amusement and Recreation Industries, All Other—*arts*	71399	7911
Fine Arts Schools—*educ*	61161	7911
Discs, laser–audio prerecorded: Integrated Record Production/Distribution—*info*	51222	3652
Prerecorded Compact Disc (except Software), Tape, and Record Reproducing—*mfg*	334612	3652
Disease control for crops, with or without fertilizing: Nonscheduled Air, Other—*trans*	481219	721
Soil Preparation, Planting, and Cultivating—*ag*	115112	721
Dish carts, restaurant: Institutional Furniture—*mfg*	337127	2599
Dishcloths: Knit Fabric and Lace Mills, Other—*mfg*	313249	2259
Weft Knit Fabric Mills—*mfg*	313241	2259
Dishcloths, nonwoven textile: Household Textile Product Mills, Other—*mfg*	314129	2392
Dishcloths, woven–made in weaving mills: Broadwoven Fabric Mills—*mfg*	31321	2211
Dishes, abrasive–dental: Dental Equipment and Supplies—*mfg*	339114	3843
Dishes, commercial and household–fine earthenware (whiteware): Vitreous China, Fine Earthenware and Other Pottery Product—*mfg*	327112	3263
Dishes, paper and disposable plastics: Industrial and Personal Service Paper—*whlse*	42213	5113
Dishes, paper–except those made from pressed or molded pulp: Non-Folding Sanitary Food Container—*mfg*	322215	2656
Dishes, plastics–except foam: Plastics Pipe and Pipe Fitting—*mfg*	326122	3089
Plastics Product, All Other—*mfg*	326199	3089
Unsupported Plastics Profile Shape—*mfg*	326121	3089
Dishes, pressed and molded pulp: Coated and Laminated Paper—*mfg*	322222	2679
Converted Paper Product, All Other—*mfg*	322298	2679
Die-Cut Paper and Paperboard Office Supplies—*mfg*	322231	2679
Non-Folding Sanitary Food Container—*mfg*	322215	2679
Dishes, toy: Game, Toy, and Children's Vehicle—*mfg*	339932	3944
Dishes, wood: Manufacturing, All Other Miscellaneous—*mfg*	339999	2499
Wood Container and Pallet—*mfg*	32192	2499
Wood Product, All Other Miscellaneous—*mfg*	321999	2499
Dishes–commercial and household-vitreous china: Vitreous China, Fine Earthenware and Other Pottery Product—*mfg*	327112	3262
Dishwashers, household–electric: Electrical Appliance, Television and Radio Set—*whlse*	42162	5064
Dishwashing compounds: Soap and Other Detergent—*mfg*	325611	2841
Dishwashing machines, commercial: Machinery, Other Commercial and Service Industry—*mfg*	333319	3589
Dishwashing machines, household: Major Household Appliance, Other—*mfg*	335228	3639
Disinfectants, agricultural: Pesticide and Other Agricultural Chemical—*mfg*	32532	2879
Disinfectants, household and industrial plant: Polish and Other Sanitation Good—*mfg*	325612	2842
Disinfecting service: Exterminating and Pest Control Services—*admin*	56171	7342
Janitorial Services—*admin*	56172	7342
Disk and diskette conversion services: Computer Related Services, Other—*prof*	541519	7379
Computer Systems Design Services—*prof*	541512	7379
Disk and diskette recertification services: Computer Related Services, Other—*prof*	541519	7379
Computer Systems Design Services—*prof*	541512	7379
Disk drives: Computer and Computer Peripheral Equipment and Software—*whlse*	42143	5045
Computer and Software Stores—*retail*	44312	5045
Disk drives, computer: Computer Storage Device—*mfg*	334112	3572
Disk pack inspectors, computer peripheral equipment: Computer Peripheral Equipment, Other—*mfg*	334119	3577
Diskettes: Electronic Parts and Equipment, Other—*whlse*	42169	5065
Disks, music and video: Prerecorded Tape, Compact Disc and Record Stores—*retail*	45122	5735
Dismantling of machinery and other industrial equipment–contractors: Building Equipment and Other Machinery Installation Contractors—*const*	23595	1796
Dismantling of oil well rigs (oil field service) on a contract basis: Oil and Gas Operations Support Activities—*mining*	213112	1389
Dismantling ships: Air, Rail, and Water Equipment Rental and Leasing, Commercial—*real*	532411	4499
Navigational Services to Shipping—*trans*	48833	4499
Port and Harbor Operations—*trans*	48831	4499
Water, Other Support Activities for—*trans*	48839	4499
Dismantling steel oil tanks, except oil field work–contractors: Wrecking and Demolition Contractors—*const*	23594	1795
Dispensers, soap: Fabricated Metal Product, All Other Miscellaneous—*mfg*	332999	3999
Plastics Product, All Other—*mfg*	326199	3999
Dispensers, tissue–plastics: Plastics Pipe and Pipe Fitting—*mfg*	326122	3089
Plastics Product, All Other—*mfg*	326199	3089
Unsupported Plastics Profile Shape—*mfg*	326121	3089
Dispensing and measuring pumps, gasoline and oil: Measuring and Dispensing Pump—*mfg*	333913	3586
Dispensing machine sale of products: Vending Machine Operators—*retail*	45421	5962

Description	NAICS	SIC
Ditchers, ladder–vertical boom or wheel: Construction Machinery—*mfg*	33312	3531
Overhead Traveling Crane, Hoist and Monorail System—*mfg*	333923	3531
Railroad Rolling Stock—*mfg*	33651	3531
Diuretics: Pharmaceutical Preparation—*mfg*	325412	2834
Dive brakes, aircraft: Aircraft Part and Auxiliary Equipment, Other—*mfg*	336413	3728
Fluid Power Valve and Hose Fitting—*mfg*	332912	3728
Dock construction–general contractors: Heavy, All Other—*const*	23499	1629
Industrial Nonbuilding Structure—*const*	23493	1629
Docking of ocean vessels: Coastal and Great Lakes Freight—*trans*	483113	4492
Inland Water Freight—*trans*	483211	4492
Navigational Services to Shipping—*trans*	48833	4492
Docks, building, prefabricated–metal: Prefabricated Metal Building and Component—*mfg*	332311	3448
Docks, including buildings and facilities–operation and maintenance: Marine Cargo Handling—*trans*	48832	4491
Port and Harbor Operations—*trans*	48831	4491
Docks, loading–portable, adjustable, and hydraulic: Fabricated Metal Product, All Other Miscellaneous—*mfg*	332999	3537
Industrial Truck, Tractor, Trailer and Stacker Machinery—*mfg*	333924	3537
Metal Container, Other—*mfg*	332439	3537
Document entry conversion devices, computer peripheral equipment: Computer Peripheral Equipment, Other—*mfg*	334119	3577
Document Preparation Services	**56141**	**7338**
Dog and cat food: Grocery and Related Products, Other—*whlse*	42249	5149
Dog and Cat Food Manufacturing	**311111**	**2047**
Dog farms: Animal Production, All Other—*ag*	11299	279
Apiculture—*ag*	11291	279
Dog food: Dog and Cat Food—*mfg*	311111	2047
Dog furnishings, leather–e.g., collars, leashes, harnesses, muzzles: Leather Good, All Other—*mfg*	316999	3199
Dog grooming: Animal Production Support Activities—*ag*	11521	752
Pet Care (except Veterinary) Services—*serv*	81291	752
Dog pounds: Animal Production Support Activities—*ag*	11521	752
Pet Care (except Veterinary) Services—*serv*	81291	752
Dog racing: Race Tracks—*arts*	711212	7948
Spectator Sports, Other—*arts*	711219	7948
Dogs: Nondurable Goods, Other Miscellaneous—*whlse*	42299	5199
Dogs, rental of–for protective service: Armored Car Services—*admin*	561613	7381
Investigation Services—*admin*	561611	7381
Security Guards and Patrol Services—*admin*	561612	7381
Doilies, paper: Coated and Laminated Paper—*mfg*	322222	2679
Converted Paper Product, All Other—*mfg*	322298	2679
Die-Cut Paper and Paperboard Office Supplies—*mfg*	322231	2679
Non-Folding Sanitary Food Container—*mfg*	322215	2679
Doll and Stuffed Toy Manufacturing	**339931**	**3942**
Doll carriages and carts: Game, Toy, and Children's Vehicle—*mfg*	339932	3944
Doll wigs: Plastics Product, All Other—*mfg*	326199	3999
Doll, Toy, and Game Manufacturing	**33993**	
Dollies (hand or power trucks), industrial–except mining: Fabricated Metal Product, All Other Miscellaneous—*mfg*	332999	3537
Industrial Truck, Tractor, Trailer and Stacker Machinery—*mfg*	333924	3537
Metal Container, Other—*mfg*	332439	3537
Dolls: Toy and Hobby Goods and Supplies—*whlse*	42192	5092
Dolls, doll parts, and doll clothing–except wigs: Doll and Stuffed Toy—*mfg*	339931	3942
Dolls, miniature–collectors': Doll and Stuffed Toy—*mfg*	339931	3942
Dolomite and dolomite-magnesite brick and shapes: Nonclay Refractory—*mfg*	327125	3297
Dolomite, crushed and broken: Crushed and Broken Limestone and Quarrying—*mining*	212312	1422
Dolomite, dead-burned: Lime—*mfg*	32741	3274
Dolomite, dimension: Dimension Stone and Quarrying—*mining*	212311	1411
Dolomitic lime: Lime—*mfg*	32741	3274
Dolomitic marble, crushed and broken: Crushed and Broken Stone and Quarrying, Other—*mining*	212319	1429
Dolomitic marble, dimension: Dimension Stone and Quarrying—*mining*	212311	1411
Dome construction–general contractors: Building, Commercial and Institutional—*const*	23332	1542
Dome lights, motor vehicle: Vehicular Lighting Equipment—*mfg*	336321	3647
Domestic forwarding: Freight Arrangement—*trans*	48851	4731
Management Consulting Services, Other—*prof*	541618	4731
Domestic freight transportation, deep sea: Coastal and Great Lakes Freight—*trans*	483113	4424
Domestic service (private households employing cooks, maids, etc.): Private Households—*serv*	81411	8811
Domestic water pumps: Pump and Pumping Equipment—*mfg*	333911	3561
Domiciliary care with health care: Continuing Care Retirement Communities—*hlth*	623311	8059
Nursing Care Facilities—*hlth*	62311	8059
Dominoes: Game, Toy, and Children's Vehicle—*mfg*	339932	3944
Donkey farms: Horse and Other Equine Production—*ag*	11292	272
Door and jamb assemblies, prefabricated–metal: Metal Window and Door—*mfg*	332321	3442
Door and window (prefabricated) installation-contractors: Carpentry Contractors—*const*	23551	1751
Door bolts and checks: Hardware—*mfg*	33251	3429
Door frames and sash, metal: Metal Window and Door—*mfg*	332321	3442
Door frames and sash, wood and covered wood: Millwork (including Flooring), Other—*mfg*	321918	2431
Wood Window and Door—*mfg*	321911	2431
Door frames, all materials: Building Material Dealers, Other—*retail*	44419	5031
Door frames, concrete: Concrete Pipe—*mfg*	327332	3272
Concrete Product, Other—*mfg*	32739	3272
Nonmetallic Mineral Product, All Other Miscellaneous—*mfg*	327999	3272
Door hoods, aluminum: Metal Container, Other—*mfg*	332439	3444

ALPHABETICAL INDEX	NAICS	SIC
Sheet Metal Work—*mfg*	332322	3444
Door jambs, wood: Millwork (including Flooring), Other—*mfg*	321918	2431
Wood Window and Door—*mfg*	321911	2431
Door locks and lock sets: Hardware—*mfg*	33251	3429
Hardware Stores—*retail*	44413	5251
Door mats, made from purchased wire: Fabricated Wire Product, Other—*mfg*	332618	3496
Door mats, rubber: Fabric Coating Mills—*mfg*	31332	3069
Rubber Product, All Other—*mfg*	326299	3069
Door mats–twisted paper, grass, reed, coir, sisal, jute, and rag: Carpet and Rug Mills—*mfg*	31411	2273
Door opening and closing devices, electrical: Electrical Equipment and Component, All Other Miscellaneous—*mfg*	335999	3699
Door opening and closing devices, except electrical: Hardware—*mfg*	33251	3429
Door screens, wood: Millwork (including Flooring), Other—*mfg*	321918	2431
Wood Window and Door—*mfg*	321911	2431
Door shutters, wood: Millwork (including Flooring), Other—*mfg*	321918	2431
Wood Window and Door—*mfg*	321911	2431
Door trim, wood: Millwork (including Flooring), Other—*mfg*	321918	2431
Wood Window and Door—*mfg*	321911	2431
Door units, prehung–wood and covered wood: Millwork (including Flooring), Other—*mfg*	321918	2431
Wood Window and Door—*mfg*	321911	2431
Doorbell transformers, electric: Power, Distribution and Specialty Transformer—*mfg*	335311	3612
Doors: Building Material Dealers, Other—*retail*	44419	5211
Home Centers—*retail*	44411	5211
Doors, combination screen–storm–wood: Millwork (including Flooring), Other—*mfg*	321918	2431
Wood Window and Door—*mfg*	321911	2431
Doors, folding–installation–contractors: Carpentry Contractors—*const*	23551	1751
Doors, folding–plastics or plastics coated fabric: Plastics Pipe and Pipe Fitting—*mfg*	326122	3089
Plastics Product, All Other—*mfg*	326199	3089
Unsupported Plastics Profile Shape—*mfg*	326121	3089
Doors, garage–installation or erection–contractors: Carpentry Contractors—*const*	23551	1751
Doors, louver–all metal or metal frame: Metal Window and Door—*mfg*	332321	3442
Doors, made from purchased glass: Glass Product Made of Purchased Glass—*mfg*	327215	3231
Doors, metal: Metal Window and Door—*mfg*	332321	3442
Doors, safe and vault–metal: Metal Container, Other—*mfg*	332439	3499
Doors, wood and covered wood: Millwork (including Flooring), Other—*mfg*	321918	2431
Wood Window and Door—*mfg*	321911	2431

ALPHABETICAL INDEX	NAICS	SIC
Dopes, paint: Paint and Coating—*mfg*	32551	2851
Dories, building and repairing: Boat Building—*mfg*	336612	3732
Personal and Household Goods Repair and Maintenance, Other—*serv*	81149	3732
Dormitories, commercially operated: Rooming and Boarding Houses—*accom*	72131	7021
Dormitory construction–general contractors: Building, Commercial and Institutional—*const*	23332	1522
Multifamily Housing—*const*	23322	1522
Dosimetry, radiation: Testing Laboratories—*prof*	54138	8734
Veterinary Services—*prof*	54194	8734
Doubling and twisting frames (textile machinery): Textile Machinery—*mfg*	333292	3552
Dough mixing machinery: Food Product Machinery—*mfg*	333294	3556
Dough, biscuit: Flour Milling—*mfg*	311211	2041
Flour Mixes and Dough from Purchased Flour—*mfg*	311822	2045
Doughnut mixes: Flour Mixes and Dough from Purchased Flour—*mfg*	311822	2045
Doughnut shops: Baked Goods Stores—*retail*	445291	5461
Retail Bakeries—*mfg*	311811	5461
Snack and Nonalcoholic Beverage Bars—*accom*	722213	5461
Doughnuts, except frozen: Bakeries, Commercial—*mfg*	311812	2051
Doughnuts, frozen: Frozen Bakery Product—*mfg*	311813	2053
Doughs, refrigerated or frozen: Flour Milling—*mfg*	311211	2041
Flour Mixes and Dough from Purchased Flour—*mfg*	311822	2045
Dovetailing machines (woodworking machinery): Sawmill and Woodworking Machinery—*mfg*	33321	3553
Dowel pins, metal: Bolt, Nut, Screw, Rivet and Washer—*mfg*	332722	3452
Dowels, wood: Manufacturing, All Other Miscellaneous—*mfg*	339999	2499
Wood Container and Pallet—*mfg*	32192	2499
Wood Product, All Other Miscellaneous—*mfg*	321999	2499
Down-filled clothing: Cut and Sew Apparel, All Other—*mfg*	315299	2329
Men's and Boys' Cut and Sew Apparel Contractors—*mfg*	315211	2329
Men's and Boys' Cut and Sew Other Outerwear—*mfg*	315228	2329
Down-filled coats, jackets, and vests: Apparel Accessories and Apparel, Other—*mfg*	315999	2339
Cut and Sew Apparel, All Other—*mfg*	315299	2339
Women's and Girls' Cut and Sew Apparel Contractors—*mfg*	315212	2339
Women's and Girls' Cut and Sew Other Outerwear—*mfg*	315238	2339
Downspout installation, metal-contractors: Roofing, Siding and Sheet Metal Contractors—*const*	23561	1761
Downspouts, plastics: Plastics Pipe and Pipe Fitting—*mfg*	326122	3089
Plastics Product, All Other—*mfg*	326199	3089
Unsupported Plastics Profile Shape—*mfg*	326121	3089
Downspouts, sheet metal: Metal Container, Other—*mfg*	332439	3444
Sheet Metal Work—*mfg*	332322	3444

ALPHABETICAL INDEX	NAICS	SIC
Drawing machinery and equipment, except wiredrawing dies: Other Metalworking Machinery, Other—*mfg*	333518	3549
Drawing tables and boards, artists': Chemical Product, All Other Miscellaneous—*mfg*	325998	3952
Institutional Furniture—*mfg*	337127	3952
Lead Pencil and Art Good—*mfg*	339942	3952
Drawknives: Hand and Edge Tool—*mfg*	332212	3423
Draying, local–without storage: Freight (except Used Goods) Trucking, Local Specialized—*trans*	48422	4212
General Freight Trucking, Local—*trans*	48411	4212
Dredges and draglines, except ships: Construction and (except Petroleum) Machinery and Equipment—*whlse*	42181	5082
Dredges, building and repairing: Ship Building and Repairing—*mfg*	336611	3731
Dredging machinery: Construction Machinery—*mfg*	33312	3531
Overhead Traveling Crane, Hoist and Monorail System—*mfg*	333923	3531
Railroad Rolling Stock—*mfg*	33651	3531
Dredging, anthracite: Anthracite—*mining*	212113	1231
Dredging–general contractors: Heavy, All Other—*const*	23499	1629
Industrial Nonbuilding Structure—*const*	23493	1629
Dres: Infants' Cut and Sew Apparel—*mfg*	315291	2361
Men's and Boys' Cut and Sew Apparel Contractors—*mfg*	315211	2361
Men's and Boys' Cut and Sew Shirt (except Work Shirt)—*mfg*	315223	2361
Women's and Girls' Cut and Sew Apparel Contractors—*mfg*	315212	2361
Women's and Girls' Cut and Sew Blouse and Shirt—*mfg*	315232	2361
Women's and Girls' Cut and Sew Dress—*mfg*	315233	2361
Dress and semidress gloves, knit: Outerwear Knitting Mills—*mfg*	315191	2259
Dress and semidress gloves, leather: Glove and Mitten—*mfg*	315992	3151
Dress fabrics, cotton: Broadwoven Fabric Mills—*mfg*	31321	2211
Dress fabrics, manmade fiber and silk: Broadwoven Fabric Mills—*mfg*	31321	2221
Dress linings: Apparel Accessories and Apparel, Other—*mfg*	315999	2396
Textile Product Mills, All Other Miscellaneous—*mfg*	314999	2396
Dress Manufacturing, Women's and Girls' Cut and Sew	**315233**	**2361**
Dress shields, vulcanized rubber and rubberized fabric: Fabric Coating Mills—*mfg*	31332	3069
Rubber Product, All Other—*mfg*	326299	3069
Dress shoes, men's: Men's Footwear (except Athletic)—*mfg*	316213	3143
Dress shops: Women's Clothing Stores—*retail*	44812	5621
Dress suit rental: Formal Wear and Costume Rental—*real*	53222	7299
Dress trimmings, fabric: Apparel Accessories and Apparel, Other—*mfg*	315999	2396
Textile Product Mills, All Other Miscellaneous—*mfg*	314999	2396
Dresser saarves: Household Textile Product Mills, Other—*mfg*	314129	2392
Dressers: Nonupholstered Wood Household Furniture—*mfg*	337122	2511
Dressers, abrasive wheel–diamond point and other: Cutting Tool and Machine Tool Accessory—*mfg*	333515	3545
Hand and Edge Tool—*mfg*	332212	3545

ALPHABETICAL INDEX	NAICS	SIC
Dresses: Outerwear Knitting Mills—*mfg*	315191	2253
Women's and Girls' Cut and Sew Apparel Contractors—*mfg*	315212	2335
Women's and Girls' Cut and Sew Dress—*mfg*	315233	2335
Women's, Children's, and Infants' and Accessories—*whlse*	42233	5137
Dresses made to order: Clothing Accessories Stores—*retail*	44815	5699
Clothing Stores, Other—*retail*	44819	5699
Dresses, doll: Doll and Stuffed Toy—*mfg*	339931	3942
Dresses, hand-knit: Outerwear Knitting Mills—*mfg*	315191	2253
Dresses, paper, cut and sewn: Women's and Girls' Cut and Sew Apparel Contractors—*mfg*	315212	2335
Women's and Girls' Cut and Sew Dress—*mfg*	315233	2335
Dressing gowns, men's and women's: Men's and Boys' Cut and Sew Apparel Contractors—*mfg*	315211	2384
Men's and Boys' Cut and Sew Underwear and Nightwear—*mfg*	315221	2384
Women's and Girls' Cut and Sew Apparel Contractors—*mfg*	315212	2384
Women's and Girls' Cut and Sew Lingerie, Loungewear and Nightwear—*mfg*	315231	2384
Dressing tables: Nonupholstered Wood Household Furniture—*mfg*	337122	2511
Dressings for fabricated leather and other materials: Polish and Other Sanitation Good—*mfg*	325612	2842
Dressings, cosmetic: Soap and Other Detergent—*mfg*	325611	2844
Toilet Preparation—*mfg*	32562	2844
Dressings, surgical: Surgical Appliance and Supplies—*mfg*	339113	3842
Dressmakers' shops, custom: Clothing Accessories Stores—*retail*	44815	5699
Clothing Stores, Other—*retail*	44819	5699
Dressmaking services on material ownedby individual customers: Personal and Household Goods Repair and Maintenance, Other—*serv*	81149	7219
Dried and Dehydrated Food Manufacturing	**311423**	**2099**
Dried beet pulp: Farm Product Raw Material, Other—*whlse*	42259	5159
Dried citrus pulp: Frozen Fruit, Juice and Vegetable—*mfg*	311411	2037
Dried fruits and vegetables: Dried and Dehydrated Food—*mfg*	311423	2034
Flour Milling—*mfg*	311211	2034
Dried meats: Animal (except Poultry) Slaughtering—*mfg*	311611	2011
Meat Processed from Carcasses—*mfg*	311612	2013
Driers and redriers, industrial process: Industrial Process Furnace and Oven—*mfg*	333994	3567
Driers and reel, firehose: General Purpose Machinery , All Other—*mfg*	333999	3569
Driers, paint: Paint and Coating—*mfg*	32551	2851
Driers, photographic: Photographic and Photocopying Equipment—*mfg*	333315	3861
Photographic Film, Paper, Plate and Chemical—*mfg*	325992	3861
Driers–grain, hay, and seed (agricultural implements): Farm Machinery and Equipment—*mfg*	333111	3523
Driers–hand, face, and hair-electric: Electric Housewares and Household Fan—*mfg*	335211	3634

Description	NAICS	SIC
Heating Equipment (except Electric and Warm Air Furnaces)—*mfg*	333414	3634
Driftmeters, aeronautical: Search, Detection, Navigation, Guidance, Aeronautical, and Nautical System and Instrument—*mfg*	334511	3812
Drill bits, metalworking: Cutting Tool and Machine Tool Accessory—*mfg*	333515	3545
Hand and Edge Tool—*mfg*	332212	3545
Drill bits, woodworking: Hand and Edge Tool—*mfg*	332212	3423
Drill bushings (drilling jig): Cutting Tool and Machine Tool Accessory—*mfg*	333515	3545
Hand and Edge Tool—*mfg*	332212	3545
Drill presses (machine tools): Machine Tool (Metal Cutting Types)—*mfg*	333512	3541
Drill rigs, all types: Oil and Gas Field Machinery and Equipment—*mfg*	333132	3533
Drill stands, metal: Fabricated Metal Product, All Other Miscellaneous—*mfg*	332999	3499
Drilling and production platforms, floating, oil and gas: Ship Building and Repairing—*mfg*	336611	3731
Drilling bits: Industrial Machinery and Equipment—*whlse*	42183	5084
Drilling for bituminous coal, anthracite, and lignite on a contract basis: Coal Support Activities—*mining*	213113	1241
Drilling for metal mining–on a contract basis: Geophysical Surveying and Mapping Services—*prof*	54136	1081
Metal Support Activities—*mining*	213114	1081
Drilling for nonmetallic minerals, except fuels–on a contract basis: Geophysical Surveying and Mapping Services—*prof*	54136	1481
Non-Metallic Minerals (except Fuels) Support Activities—*mining*	213115	1481
Drilling machine attachments and accessories (machine tool accessories): Cutting Tool and Machine Tool Accessory—*mfg*	333515	3545
Hand and Edge Tool—*mfg*	332212	3545
Drilling machine tools (metal cutting): Machine Tool (Metal Cutting Types)—*mfg*	333512	3541
Drilling mud: Basic Organic Chemical, All Other—*mfg*	325199	2899
Chemical and Allied Products, Other—*whlse*	42269	5169
Chemical Product, All Other Miscellaneous—*mfg*	325998	2899
Drilling of oil and gas wells–on a contract basis: Drilling Oil and Gas Wells—*mining*	213111	1381
Drilling of pearls: Jewelers' Material and Lapidary Work—*mfg*	339913	3915
Drilling Oil and Gas Wells	**213111**	**1381**
Drilling tools for gas, oil, or water wells: Oil and Gas Field Machinery and Equipment—*mfg*	333132	3533
Drilling tools, masonry and concrete–power (portable): Power-Driven Hand Tool—*mfg*	333991	3546
Drilling water intake wells–on a contractbasis: Drilling Oil and Gas Wells—*mining*	213111	1381
Drilling water wells–contractors: Water Well Drilling Contractors—*const*	23581	1781
Drilling, service well–on a contract basis: Drilling Oil and Gas Wells—*mining*	213111	1381
Drills (except rock drilling and coring), portable–electric and pneumatic: Power-Driven Hand Tool—*mfg*	333991	3546
Drills (machine tool accessories): Cutting Tool and Machine Tool Accessory—*mfg*	333515	3545
Hand and Edge Tool—*mfg*	332212	3545
Drills and drilling equipment, mining:except oil and gas field: Mining Machinery and Equipment—*mfg*	333131	3532
Drills, core: Mining Machinery and Equipment—*mfg*	333131	3532
Drills, cotton: Broadwoven Fabric Mills—*mfg*	31321	2211
Drills, dental: Dental Equipment and Supplies—*mfg*	339114	3843
Drills, hand–electric: Power-Driven Hand Tool—*mfg*	333991	3546
Drills, hand–except power: Hand and Edge Tool—*mfg*	332212	3423
Drills, rock–portable: Mining Machinery and Equipment—*mfg*	333131	3532
Drink powders and concentrates: Flavoring Syrup and Concentrate—*mfg*	31193	2087
Food, All Other Miscellaneous—*mfg*	311999	2087
Spice and Extract—*mfg*	311942	2087
Drinking cups, paper–except those made from pressed or molded pulp: Non-Folding Sanitary Food Container—*mfg*	322215	2656
Drinking fountains, except mechanically refrigerated–metal: Enameled Iron and Metal Sanitary Ware—*mfg*	332998	3431
Drinking fountains, except mechanically refrigerated–plastics: Plastics Plumbing Fixture—*mfg*	326191	3088
Drinking fountains, mechanically refrigerated: Air-Conditioning and Warm Air Heating Equipment and Commercial and Industrial Refrigeration Equipment—*mfg*	333415	3585
Motor Vehicle Air-Conditioning—*mfg*	336391	3585
Drinking fountains, vitreous china: Vitreous China Plumbing Fixture and China and Earthenware Fittings and Bathroom Accessories—*mfg*	327111	3261
Drinking Places (Alcoholic Beverages)	**7224**	
Drinking Places (Alcoholic Beverages)	**72241**	**5813**
Drinking places, alcoholic beverages: Drinking Places (Alcoholic Beverages)—*accom*	72241	5813
Drinking straws, except glass or plastics: Non-Folding Sanitary Food Container—*mfg*	322215	2656
Drinking straws, glass: Pressed and Blown Glass and Glassware, Other—*mfg*	327212	3229
Drinking water coolers, mechanical: Refrigeration Equipment and Supplies—*whlse*	42174	5078
Drinks, fruit–bottled, canned, or fresh: Bottled Water—*mfg*	312112	2086
Soft Drink—*mfg*	312111	2086
Drive chains, bicycle and motorcycle: Mechanical Power Transmission Equipment—*mfg*	333613	3568
Drive shafts, motor vehicle: Motor Vehicle Parts, All Other—*mfg*	336399	3714
Motor Vehicle Steering and Suspension Components (except Spring)—*mfg*	33633	3714

ALPHABETICAL INDEX	NAICS	SIC
Motor Vehicle Transmission and Power Train Parts—*mfg*	33635	3714
Drive-In Motion Picture Theaters	**512132**	**7833**
Drive-in restaurants: Cafeterias—*accom*	722212	5812
Caterers—*accom*	72232	5812
Foodservice Contractors—*accom*	72231	5812
Full-Service Restaurants—*accom*	72211	5812
Limited-Service Restaurants—*accom*	722211	5812
Snack and Nonalcoholic Beverage Bars—*accom*	722213	5812
Theater Companies and Dinner Theaters—*arts*	71111	5812
Drive-in theaters: Drive-In Motion Picture Theaters—*info*	512132	7833
Drivers, drill and cutters (machine tool accessories): Cutting Tool and Machine Tool Accessory—*mfg*	333515	3545
Hand and Edge Tool—*mfg*	332212	3545
Drives, computer–disk and drum: Computer Storage Device—*mfg*	334112	3572
Drives, high-speed industrial–except hydrostatic: Speed Changer, Industrial High-Speed Drive and Gear—*mfg*	333612	3566
Drives, hydrostatic transmissions: Fluid Power Pump and Motor—*mfg*	333996	3594
Driving piling–general contractors: Heavy, All Other—*const*	23499	1629
Industrial Nonbuilding Structure—*const*	23493	1629
Driving timber: Logging—*ag*	11331	2411
Drop cloths, fabric: Canvas and Related Product Mills—*mfg*	314912	2394
Drop forgings, iron and steel–not made in rolling mills: Iron and Steel Forging—*mfg*	332111	3462
Drop hammers, for forging and shaping metal: Machine Tool (Metal Forming Types)—*mfg*	333513	3542
Drug addiction rehabilitation hospitals: General Medical and Surgical Hospitals—*hlth*	62211	8069
Hospitals (except Psychiatric and Substance Abuse), Specialty—*hlth*	62231	8069
Psychiatric and Substance Abuse Hospitals—*hlth*	62221	8069
Drug dyes, synthetic: Petrochemical—*mfg*	32511	2865
Drug grading, grinding, and milling: Medicinal and Botanical—*mfg*	325411	2833
Drug proprietaries: Drug, Drug Proprietaries and Druggists' Sundries—*whlse*	42221	5122
Drug rehabilitation centers, residential–with health care incidental: Homes for the Elderly—*hlth*	623312	8361
Residential Care Facilities, Other—*hlth*	62399	8361
Residential Mental Health and Substance Abuse Facilities—*hlth*	62322	8361
Drug stores: Pharmacies and Drug Stores—*retail*	44611	5912
Drug treatment, outpatient clinics: Family Planning Centers—*hlth*	62141	8093
Outpatient Care Centers, All Other—*hlth*	621498	8093
Outpatient Mental Health and Substance Abuse Centers—*hlth*	62142	8093
Drug, Drug Proprietaries and Druggists' Sundries Wholesalers	**4222**	
Drug, Drug Proprietaries and Druggists' Sundries Wholesalers	**42221**	**5122**
Druggists' sundries: Drug, Drug Proprietaries and Druggists' Sundries—*whlse*	42221	5122

ALPHABETICAL INDEX	NAICS	SIC
Druggists' sundries, rubber: Fabric Coating Mills—*mfg*	31332	3069
Rubber Product, All Other—*mfg*	326299	3069
Drugs: Drug, Drug Proprietaries and Druggists' Sundries—*whlse*	42221	5122
Drum and bugle corps (drill teams): Independent Artists, Writers, and Performers—*arts*	71151	7929
Musical Groups and Artists—*arts*	71113	7929
Performing Arts Companies, Other—*arts*	71119	7929
Drum cradles: Fabricated Metal Product, All Other Miscellaneous—*mfg*	332999	3537
Industrial Truck, Tractor, Trailer and Stacker Machinery—*mfg*	333924	3537
Metal Container, Other—*mfg*	332439	3537
Drum drives, computer: Computer Storage Device—*mfg*	334112	3572
Drummers' traps: Musical Instrument—*mfg*	339992	3931
Drums, fiber (metal-end or all-fiber): Fiber Can, Tube, Drum, and Similar Products—*mfg*	322214	2655
Drums, new and reconditioned: Industrial Machinery and Equipment—*whlse*	42183	5085
Industrial Supplies—*whlse*	42184	5085
Drums, parts, and accessories (musical instruments): Musical Instrument—*mfg*	339992	3931
Drums, plastics (containers): Plastics Pipe and Pipe Fitting—*mfg*	326122	3089
Plastics Product, All Other—*mfg*	326199	3089
Unsupported Plastics Profile Shape—*mfg*	326121	3089
Drums, plywood: Wood Container and Pallet—*mfg*	32192	2449
Drums, shipping–metal: Metal Container, Other—*mfg*	332439	3412
Drums, shipping–wood-wirebound: Wood Container and Pallet—*mfg*	32192	2449
Drums, toy: Game, Toy, and Children's Vehicle—*mfg*	339932	3944
Dry and Wet Primary Battery Manufacturing	**335912**	**3692**
Dry cell batteries, single and multiplecell: Dry and Wet Primary Battery—*mfg*	335912	3692
Dry felts, except textile: Newsprint Mills—*mfg*	322122	2621
Paper (except Newsprint) Mills—*mfg*	322121	2621
Dry ice: Chemical and Allied Products, Other—*whlse*	42269	5169
Dry ice (solid carbon dioxide): Industrial Gas—*mfg*	32512	2813
Dry milk processing machinery: Food Product Machinery—*mfg*	333294	3556
Dry milk products–whole milk, nonfatmilk, buttermilk, whey, and cream: Dry, Condensed, and Evaporated Dairy Product—*mfg*	311514	2023
Dry Pea and Bean Farming	**11113**	**119**
Dry shavers (electric razors): Electric Housewares and Household Fan—*mfg*	335211	3634
Heating Equipment (except Electric and Warm Air Furnaces)—*mfg*	333414	3634
Dry well construction, cesspool–contractors: Plumbing, Heating and Air-Conditioning Contractors—*const*	23511	1711
Dry, Condensed, and Evaporated Dairy Product Manufacturing	**311514**	**2023**
Drycleaning and laundry machines, household–including coin-operated: Household Laundry Equipment—*mfg*	335224	3633

Entry	NAICS	SIC
Drycleaning and Laundry Services (except Coin-Operated)	**81232**	
Drycleaning equipment and machinery, commercial: Laundry, Drycleaning and Pressing Machine, Commercial—*mfg*	333312	3582
Drycleaning plant construction-generalcontractors: Building, Commercial and Institutional—*const*	23332	1541
Manufacturing and Industrial Building—*const*	23331	1541
Drycleaning plant equipment and supplies: Cosmetics, Beauty Supplies and Perfume Stores—*retail*	44612	5087
Service Establishment Equipment and Supplies—*whlse*	42185	5087
Drycleaning Plants	**812322**	**7216**
Drycleaning plants, except rug cleaning: Drycleaning Plants—*serv*	812322	7216
Drycleaning preparations: Polish and Other Sanitation Good—*mfg*	325612	2842
Drycleaning, coin-operated: Coin-Operated Laundries and Drycleaners—*serv*	81231	7215
Drydocks, floating: Ship Building and Repairing—*mfg*	336611	3731
Dryers, beauty shop: Cosmetics, Beauty Supplies and Perfume Stores—*retail*	44612	5087
Service Establishment Equipment and Supplies—*whlse*	42185	5087
Dryers, clothes (clothes horses)–wood: Manufacturing, All Other Miscellaneous—*mfg*	339999	2499
Wood Container and Pallet—*mfg*	32192	2499
Wood Product, All Other Miscellaneous—*mfg*	321999	2499
Dryers, clothes–electric or gas: Electrical Appliance, Television and Radio Set—*whlse*	42162	5064
Dryers, commercial laundry, including coin-operated: Laundry, Drycleaning and Pressing Machine, Commercial—*mfg*	333312	3582
Dryers, laundry–commercial, including coin-operated: Laundry, Drycleaning and Pressing Machine, Commercial—*mfg*	333312	3582
Dryers, laundry–household, including coin-operated: Household Laundry Equipment—*mfg*	335224	3633
Drying belts, made from purchased wire: Fabricated Wire Product, Other—*mfg*	332618	3496
Drying japans: Paint and Coating—*mfg*	32551	2851
Drying kilns, lumber: Industrial Machinery, All Other—*mfg*	333298	3559
Machinery, Other Commercial and Service Industry—*mfg*	333319	3559
Drying machines, textile–for stock, yarn, and cloth: Textile Machinery—*mfg*	333292	3552
Drying of corn, rice, hay, fruits, and vegetables: Postharvest Crop Activities (except Cotton Ginning)—*ag*	115114	723
Drywall construction–contractors: Drywall, Plastering, Acoustical and Insulation Contractors—*const*	23542	1742
Drywall, Plastering, Acoustical and Insulation Contractors	**23542**	**1743**
Dual Purpose Cattle Ranching and Farming	**11213**	
Duck farms: Poultry Production, Other—*ag*	11239	259
Duck pin centers: Bowling Centers—*arts*	71395	7933
Duck, cotton: Broadwoven Fabric Mills—*mfg*	31321	2211
Ducks, processed–fresh, frozen, canned, or cooked: Food, All Other Miscellaneous—*mfg*	311999	2015
Poultry Processing—*mfg*	311615	2015
Ducks–slaughtering and dressing: Food, All Other Miscellaneous—*mfg*	311999	2015
Poultry Processing—*mfg*	311615	2015
Duct work, sheet metal–contractors: Roofing, Siding and Sheet Metal Contractors—*const*	23561	1761
Ductile iron castings: Iron Foundries—*mfg*	331511	3321
Ducting, metal plate: Air-Conditioning and Warm Air Heating Equipment and Commercial and Industrial Refrigeration Equipment—*mfg*	333415	3443
Metal Tank (Heavy Gauge)—*mfg*	33242	3443
Plate Work—*mfg*	332313	3443
Power Boiler and Heat Exchanger—*mfg*	33241	3443
Ducts, asbestos cement: Motor Vehicle Brake System—*mfg*	33634	3292
Nonmetallic Mineral Product, All Other Miscellaneous—*mfg*	327999	3292
Ducts, sheet metal: Metal Container, Other—*mfg*	332439	3444
Sheet Metal Work—*mfg*	332322	3444
Dude ranches: Recreational and Vacation Camps—*accom*	721214	7032
Duffel bags, canvas: Textile Bag Mills—*mfg*	314911	2393
Dumbbells: Sporting and Athletic Goods—*mfg*	33992	3949
Dumbwaiter installation–contractors: Building Equipment and Other Machinery Installation Contractors—*const*	23595	1796
Dumbwaiters: Elevator and Moving Stairway—*mfg*	333921	3534
Dumortierite mining: Clay and Ceramic and Refractory Minerals—*mining*	212325	1459
Dumpers, car–mining: Mining Machinery and Equipment—*mfg*	333131	3532
Dumps, operation of: Hazardous Waste Collection—*admin*	562112	4953
Hazardous Waste Treatment and Disposal—*admin*	562211	4953
Materials Recovery Facilities—*admin*	56292	4953
Nonhazardous Waste Treatment and Disposal, Other—*admin*	562219	4953
Solid Waste Collection—*admin*	562111	4953
Solid Waste Combustors and Incinerators—*admin*	562213	4953
Solid Waste Landfill—*admin*	562212	4953
Waste Collection, Other—*admin*	562119	4953
Dumptruck lifting mechanisms: Motor Vehicle Parts, All Other—*mfg*	336399	3714
Dunebuggies: Motor Vehicle Dealers, All Other—*retail*	441229	5599
Dungarees: Men's and Boys' Cut and Sew Apparel Contractors—*mfg*	315211	2325
Men's and Boys' Cut and Sew Trouser, Slack and Jean—*mfg*	315224	2325
Dunnage (marine supplies): Transportation Equipment and Supplies (except Motor Vehicle)—*whlse*	42186	5088
Duplicating ink: Printing Ink—*mfg*	32591	2893
Duplicating machines: Lead Pencil and Art Good—*mfg*	339942	3579
Office Equipment—*whlse*	42142	5044
Office Machinery—*mfg*	333313	3579
Watch, Clock, and Part—*mfg*	334518	3579
Duplicating services, except printing: Business Service Centers (including Copy Shops), Other—*admin*	561439	7334
Duplicator, machine tools: Machine Tool (Metal Cutting Types)—*mfg*	333512	3541
Durable Goods Wholesalers, Miscellaneous	**4219**	

ALPHABETICAL INDEX	NAICS	SIC
Durable Goods Wholesalers, Other Miscellaneous	**42199**	**7822**
Durum flour: Flour Milling—*mfg*	311211	2041
Dust and fume collecting equipment, industrial: Air Purification Equipment—*mfg*	333411	3564
Industrial and Commercial Fan and Blower—*mfg*	333412	3564
Dust cloths: Household Textile Product Mills, Other—*mfg*	314129	2392
Dust collecting equipment installation–contractors: Building Equipment and Other Machinery Installation Contractors—*const*	23595	1796
Dust collection equipment: Air Purification Equipment—*mfg*	333411	3564
Industrial and Commercial Fan and Blower—*mfg*	333412	3564
Warm Air Heating and Air-Conditioning Equipment and Supplies—*whlse*	42173	5075
Dust mats, gelatin: Polish and Other Sanitation Good—*mfg*	325612	2842
Dust mops: Broom, Brush and Mop—*mfg*	339994	2392
Household Textile Product Mills, Other—*mfg*	314129	2392
Dusters (apparel): Men's and Boys' Cut and Sew Apparel Contractors—*mfg*	315211	2384
Men's and Boys' Cut and Sew Underwear and Nightwear—*mfg*	315221	2384
Women's and Girls' Cut and Sew Apparel Contractors—*mfg*	315212	2384
Women's and Girls' Cut and Sew Lingerie, Loungewear and Nightwear—*mfg*	315231	2384
Dusters, fabric: Broom, Brush and Mop—*mfg*	339994	2392
Household Textile Product Mills, Other—*mfg*	314129	2392
Dusters, mechanical–agricultural: Farm Machinery and Equipment—*mfg*	333111	3523
Dusting and spraying equipment, aircraft: Aircraft Part and Auxiliary Equipment, Other—*mfg*	336413	3728
Fluid Power Valve and Hose Fitting—*mfg*	332912	3728
Dusting cloths, chemically treated: Polish and Other Sanitation Good—*mfg*	325612	2842
Dusting cloths, plain: Household Textile Product Mills, Other—*mfg*	314129	2392
Dusting crops, with or without fertilizing: Nonscheduled Air, Other—*trans*	481219	721
Soil Preparation, Planting, and Cultivating—*ag*	115112	721
Dusting outfits for metal, paints, andchemicals (portable or vehicular): Air and Gas Compressor—*mfg*	333912	3563
Duvetyn, cotton: Broadwoven Fabric Mills—*mfg*	31321	2211
Duvetyn, manmade fiber and silk: Broadwoven Fabric Mills—*mfg*	31321	2221
Dwellings (four or fewer) housing units–operators of: Lessors of Residential Buildings and Dwellings—*real*	53111	6514
Dwellings, mobile: Manufactured Home (Mobile Home)—*mfg*	321991	2451
Dwellings, prefabricated–metal: Prefabricated Metal Building and Component—*mfg*	332311	3448
Dye (cyclic) intermediates: Petrochemical—*mfg*	32511	2865
Dye and Pigment Manufacturing	**32513**	

ALPHABETICAL INDEX	NAICS	SIC
Dye removing cream, petroleum base: Polish and Other Sanitation Good—*mfg*	325612	2842
Dye removing cream, soap base: Soap and Other Detergent—*mfg*	325611	2841
Dyeing and cleaning plants, except rugcleaning: Drycleaning Plants—*serv*	812322	7216
Dyeing and extract materials, natural: Gum and Wood Chemical—*mfg*	325191	2861
Dyeing and finishing circular knit fabrics: Textile and Fabric Finishing (except Broadwoven Fabric) Mills—*mfg*	313312	2257
Weft Knit Fabric Mills—*mfg*	313241	2257
Dyeing and finishing hosiery, except women's full-length and knee-length: Hosiery and Sock Mills, Other—*mfg*	315119	2252
Sheer Hosiery Mills—*mfg*	315111	2252
Dyeing and finishing knit gloves and mittens: Outerwear Knitting Mills—*mfg*	315191	2259
Dyeing and finishing knit outerwear, except hosiery, gloves, and nightwear: Outerwear Knitting Mills—*mfg*	315191	2253
Dyeing and finishing knit underwear: Underwear and Nightwear Knitting Mills—*mfg*	315192	2254
Dyeing and finishing lace goods: Knit Fabric and Lace Mills, Other—*mfg*	313249	2258
Textile and Fabric Finishing (except Broadwoven Fabric) Mills—*mfg*	313312	2258
Dyeing and finishing of rugs and carpets: Carpet and Rug Mills—*mfg*	31411	2273
Dyeing and finishing of wool and similar animal fibers–except knit: Broadwoven Fabric Finishing Mills—*mfg*	313311	2231
Broadwoven Fabric Mills—*mfg*	31321	2231
Textile and Fabric Finishing (except Broadwoven Fabric) Mills—*mfg*	313312	2231
Dyeing and finishing warp knit fabrics: Knit Fabric and Lace Mills, Other—*mfg*	313249	2258
Textile and Fabric Finishing (except Broadwoven Fabric) Mills—*mfg*	313312	2258
Dyeing and finishing weft knit fabrics: Textile and Fabric Finishing (except Broadwoven Fabric) Mills—*mfg*	313312	2257
Weft Knit Fabric Mills—*mfg*	313241	2257
Dyeing and finishing women's full-length and knee-length hosiery, except socks: Sheer Hosiery Mills—*mfg*	315111	2251
Dyeing cotton broadwoven fabrics: Broadwoven Fabric Finishing Mills—*mfg*	313311	2261
Dyeing gloves, woven or knit–for the trade: Glove and Mitten—*mfg*	315992	2381
Dyeing machinery, textile: Textile Machinery—*mfg*	333292	3552
Dyeing manmade fiber and silk broadwoven fabrics: Broadwoven Fabric Finishing Mills—*mfg*	313311	2262
Dyeing raw steck, yarn, and narrow fabrics–except knit and wool: Broadwoven Fabric Finishing Mills—*mfg*	313311	2269

Term	NAICS	SIC
Textile and Fabric Finishing (except Broadwoven Fabric) Mills—*mfg*	313312	2269
Dyes, food–synthetic: Organic Dye and Pigment—*mfg*	325132	2865
Petrochemical—*mfg*	32511	2865
Dyes, hair: Soap and Other Detergent—*mfg*	325611	2844
Toilet Preparation—*mfg*	32562	2844
Dyes, household: Basic Organic Chemical, All Other—*mfg*	325199	2899
Chemical Product, All Other Miscellaneous—*mfg*	325998	2899
Dyes, synthetic organic: Organic Dye and Pigment—*mfg*	325132	2865
Petrochemical—*mfg*	32511	2865
Dyestuffs: Chemical and Allied Products, Other—*whlse*	42269	5169
Dyestuffs, natural: Gum and Wood Chemical—*mfg*	325191	2861
Dynamite: Explosives—*mfg*	32592	2892
Dynamometer instruments: Measuring and Controlling Device, Other—*mfg*	334519	3829
Surgical and Medical Instrument—*mfg*	339112	3829
Dynamos, electric–except automotive: Motor and Generator—*mfg*	335312	3621
Dynamotors: Motor and Generator—*mfg*	335312	3621
Dynamotrons: Electrical Equipment and Component, All Other Miscellaneous—*mfg*	335999	3699
Machinery, Other Commercial and Service Industry—*mfg*	333319	3699
Dynetric balancing stands, aircraft: Aircraft Part and Auxiliary Equipment, Other—*mfg*	336413	3728
Fluid Power Valve and Hose Fitting—*mfg*	332912	3728
Dzus fasteners: Hardware—*mfg*	33251	3429
Ear stoppers: Surgical Appliance and Supplies—*mfg*	339113	3842
Earth moving equipment rental and leasing: Construction, and Forestry Machinery and Equipment Rental and Leasing—*real*	532412	7353
Heavy, All Other—*const*	23499	7353
Earth moving, not connected with building construction–general contractors: Heavy, All Other—*const*	23499	1629
Industrial Nonbuilding Structure—*const*	23493	1629
Earth moving-contractors: Excavation Contractors—*const*	23593	1794
Earthenware table and kitchen articles, coarse: Vitreous China, Fine Earthenware and Other Pottery Product—*mfg*	327112	3269
Earthenware–commercial and household–semivitreous: Vitreous China, Fine Earthenware and Other Pottery Product—*mfg*	327112	3263
Earthworm food and bedding: Animal Food, Other—*mfg*	311119	2048
Earthworm hatcheries: Animal Production, All Other—*ag*	11299	279
Apiculture—*ag*	11291	279
Easels, artists': Chemical Product, All Other Miscellaneous—*mfg*	325998	3952
Institutional Furniture—*mfg*	337127	3952
Lead Pencil and Art Good—*mfg*	339942	3952
Easter cards, except hand painted: Flexographic Printing, Commercial—*mfg*	323112	2771
Gravure Printing, Commercial—*mfg*	323111	2771
Greeting Card Publishers—*info*	511191	2771
Lithographic Printing, Commercial—*mfg*	323110	2771
Printing, Other Commercial—*mfg*	323119	2771
Screen Printing, Commercial—*mfg*	323113	2771
Eating utensils–forks, knives, spoons-disposable plastics: Industrial and Personal Service Paper—*whlse*	42213	5113
Eaves, sheet metal: Metal Container, Other—*mfg*	332439	3444
Sheet Metal Work—*mfg*	332322	3444
Ecclesiastical statuary, marble: Cut Stone and Stone Product—*mfg*	327991	3281
Ecclesiastical statuary–gypsum, clay, or papier-mache–factory production only: Gypsum and Gypsum Product—*mfg*	32742	3299
Nonmetallic Mineral Product, All Other Miscellaneous—*mfg*	327999	3299
Ecclesiastical ware–silver, nickel silver, pewter, and plated: Cutlery and Flatware (except Precious)—*mfg*	332211	3914
Silverware and Plated Ware—*mfg*	339912	3914
Economic consulting: Educational Support Services—*educ*	61171	8748
Management Consulting Services, Other—*prof*	541618	8748
Scientific and Technical Consulting Services, Other—*prof*	54169	8748
Economic development agencies: General Economic Programs, Administration of—*pub*	92611	9611
Economic Programs, Administration of	**9261**	
Economic Programs, Administration of	**926**	
Economic research, commercial: Marketing Research and Public Opinion Polling—*prof*	54191	8732
Research and Development in the Social Sciences and Humanities—*prof*	54173	8732
Economic research, noncommercial: Research and Development in the Life Sciences—*prof*	54172	8733
Research and Development in the Physical Sciences and Engineering Sciences—*prof*	54171	8733
Research and Development in the Social Sciences and Humanities—*prof*	54173	8733
Economizers (boilers): Air-Conditioning and Warm Air Heating Equipment and Commercial and Industrial Refrigeration Equipment—*mfg*	333415	3443
Metal Tank (Heavy Gauge)—*mfg*	33242	3443
Plate Work—*mfg*	332313	3443
Power Boiler and Heat Exchanger—*mfg*	33241	3443
Edge Act Corporations: International Trade Financing—*fin*	522293	6082
Edge tools for woodworking–augers, bits, gimlets, countersinks, etc.: Hand and Edge Tool—*mfg*	332212	3423
Edging books, cards, or paper: Tradebinding and Related Work—*mfg*	323121	2789
Edgings, lace: Knit Fabric and Lace Mills, Other—*mfg*	313249	2258
Textile and Fabric Finishing (except Broadwoven Fabric) Mills—*mfg*	313312	2258
Editing equipment, motion picture–rewinds, viewers, titlers, and splicers: Photographic and Photocopying Equipment—*mfg*	333315	3861
Photographic Film, Paper, Plate and Chemical—*mfg*	325992	3861
Editing of motion picture film: Independent Artists, Writers, and Performers—*arts*	71151	7819
Motion Picture and Video Industries, Other—*info*	512199	7819

ALPHABETICAL INDEX	NAICS	SIC
Prerecorded Compact Disc (except Software), Tape, and Record Reproducing—*mfg*	334612	7819
Teleproduction and Other Post-Production Services—*info*	512191	7819
Editing service: Court Reporting and Stenotype Services—*admin*	561492	7338
Document Preparation Services—*admin*	56141	7338
Education offices, nonoperating: Education Programs, Administration of—*pub*	92311	9411
Education Programs, Administration of	**92311**	**9411**
Education statistics centers: Education Programs, Administration of—*pub*	92311	9411
Educational consulting, except management: Educational Support Services—*educ*	61171	8748
Management Consulting Services, Other—*prof*	541618	8748
Scientific and Technical Consulting Services, Other—*prof*	54169	8748
Educational motion picture production: Motion Picture and Video Production—*info*	51211	7812
Educational research, commercial: Marketing Research and Public Opinion Polling—*prof*	54191	8732
Research and Development in the Social Sciences and Humanities—*prof*	54173	8732
Educational research, noncommercial: Research and Development in the Life Sciences—*prof*	54172	8733
Research and Development in the Physical Sciences and Engineering Sciences—*prof*	54171	8733
Research and Development in the Social Sciences and Humanities—*prof*	54173	8733
Educational Services	**611**	
Educational Services	**61**	
Educational Support Services	**6117**	
Educational Support Services	**61171**	**8748**
Educational trusts, management of: Grantmaking Foundations—*serv*	813211	6732
Eels, catching of: Finfish Fishing—*ag*	114111	912
Effervescent salts: Pharmaceutical Preparation—*mfg*	325412	2834
Egg albumen: Food, All Other Miscellaneous—*mfg*	311999	2015
Poultry Processing—*mfg*	311615	2015
Egg cartons, diecut paper and paperboard: Converted Paper Product, All Other—*mfg*	322298	2675
Die-Cut Paper and Paperboard Office Supplies—*mfg*	322231	2675
Surface-Coated Paperboard—*mfg*	322292	2675
Egg cartons, molded pulp: Coated and Laminated Paper—*mfg*	322222	2679
Converted Paper Product, All Other—*mfg*	322298	2679
Die-Cut Paper and Paperboard Office Supplies—*mfg*	322231	2679
Non-Folding Sanitary Food Container—*mfg*	322215	2679
Egg case filler flats, molded pulp: Coated and Laminated Paper—*mfg*	322222	2679
Converted Paper Product, All Other—*mfg*	322298	2679
Die-Cut Paper and Paperboard Office Supplies—*mfg*	322231	2679
Non-Folding Sanitary Food Container—*mfg*	322215	2679
Egg case fillers and flats, diecut from purchased paper or paperboard: Converted Paper Product, All Other—*mfg*	322298	2675
Die-Cut Paper and Paperboard Office Supplies—*mfg*	322231	2675
Surface-Coated Paperboard—*mfg*	322292	2675
Egg cases, wood: Wood Container and Pallet—*mfg*	32192	2441
Egg cookers, electric: Electric Housewares and Household Fan—*mfg*	335211	3634
Heating Equipment (except Electric and Warm Air Furnaces)—*mfg*	333414	3634
Egg dealers: Food (Health) Supplement Stores—*retail*	446191	5499
Food Stores, All Other Specialty—*retail*	445299	5499
Limited-Service Restaurants—*accom*	722211	5499
Meat Markets—*retail*	44521	5499
Egg farms, chicken: Chicken Egg Production—*ag*	11231	252
Egg farms, poultry–except chicken and turkey: Poultry Production, Other—*ag*	11239	259
Egg farms, turkey: Turkey Production—*ag*	11233	253
Egg hatcheries, poultry: Poultry Hatcheries—*ag*	11234	254
Egg substitutes made from eggs: Food, All Other Miscellaneous—*mfg*	311999	2015
Poultry Processing—*mfg*	311615	2015
Eggnog, alcoholic: Distilleries—*mfg*	31214	2085
Eggnog, canned–nonalcoholic: Dry, Condensed, and Evaporated Dairy Product—*mfg*	311514	2023
Eggnog, fresh–nonalcoholic: Fluid Milk—*mfg*	311511	2026
Eggs: Poultry and Poultry Product—*whlse*	42244	5144
Eggs–canned, dehydrated, desiccated, frozen, and processed: Food, All Other Miscellaneous—*mfg*	311999	2015
Poultry Processing—*mfg*	311615	2015
Eggs–cleaning, oil treating, packing, and grading: Poultry and Poultry Product—*whlse*	42244	5144
Eggs–drying, freezing, and breaking: Food, All Other Miscellaneous—*mfg*	311999	2015
Poultry Processing—*mfg*	311615	2015
Elapsed time meters, electronic: Electronic Coil, Transformer, and Other Inductor—*mfg*	334416	3825
Instrument for Measuring and Testing Electricity and Electrical Signals—*mfg*	334515	3825
Elastic fabrics, cotton–more than 12 inches in width: Broadwoven Fabric Mills—*mfg*	31321	2211
Elastic fabrics, manmade fiber and silk–more than 12 inches in width: Broadwoven Fabric Mills—*mfg*	31321	2221
Elastic girdle blanks: Underwear and Nightwear Knitting Mills—*mfg*	315192	2259
Elastic hosiery, orthopedic: Surgical Appliance and Supplies—*mfg*	339113	3842
Elastic membrane metal forming machines: Machine Tool (Metal Forming Types)—*mfg*	333513	3542
Elastic narrow fabrics, woven or braided: Narrow Fabric Mills—*mfg*	313221	2241
Elastic webbing: Narrow Fabric Mills—*mfg*	313221	2241

Description	NAICS	SIC
Elastomeric fibers: Noncellulosic Organic Fiber—*mfg*	325222	2824
Elastomers, nonvulcanizable (plastics): Plastics Material and Resin—*mfg*	325211	2821
Elastomers, vulcanizable (synthetic rubber): Synthetic Rubber—*mfg*	325212	2822
Elbows for conductor pipe, hot air ducts, and stovepipe–sheet metal: Metal Container, Other—*mfg*	332439	3444
Sheet Metal Work—*mfg*	332322	3444
Elbows, pipe–except pressure and soil pipe-metal: Fabricated Metal Product, All Other Miscellaneous—*mfg*	332999	3494
Other Metal Valve and Pipe Fitting, Other—*mfg*	332919	3494
Elbows, pipe–pressure and soil pipe-cast iron: Iron Foundries—*mfg*	331511	3321
Electric air cleaner controls, automatic: Automatic Environmental Control for Residential, Commercial and Appliance Use—*mfg*	334512	3822
Electric and electronic controllers, industrial process type: Instruments and Related Products for Measuring, Displaying, and Controlling Industrial Process Variables—*mfg*	334513	3823
Electric and other services combined (electric less than 95 percent of total): Electric Bulk Power Transmission and Control—*util*	221121	4931
Electric Power Distribution—*util*	221122	4931
Electric Power Generation, Other—*util*	221119	4931
Fossil Fuel Electric Power Generation—*util*	221112	4931
Hydroelectric Power Generation—*util*	221111	4931
Natural Gas Distribution—*util*	22121	4931
Nuclear Electric Power Generation—*util*	221113	4931
Electric appliance repair: Appliance Repair and Maintenance—*serv*	811412	7629
Consumer Electronics Repair and Maintenance—*serv*	811211	7629
Household Appliance Stores—*retail*	443111	7629
Electric appliances, household: Electrical Appliance, Television and Radio Set—*whlse*	42162	5064
Electric Bulk Power Transmission and Control	**221121**	**4931**
Electric comfort heating equipment: Air-Conditioning and Warm Air Heating Equipment and Commercial and Industrial Refrigeration Equipment—*mfg*	333415	3585
Motor Vehicle Air-Conditioning—*mfg*	336391	3585
Electric fence chargers: Electrical Equipment and Component, All Other Miscellaneous—*mfg*	335999	3699
Machinery, Other Commercial and Service Industry—*mfg*	333319	3699
Electric furnace transformers: Power, Distribution and Specialty Transformer—*mfg*	335311	3612
Electric heat proportioning controls, modulating controls: Automatic Environmental Control for Residential, Commercial and Appliance Use—*mfg*	334512	3822
Electric household appliance stores: Household Appliance Stores—*retail*	443111	5722
Electric Housewares and Household Fan Manufacturing	**335211**	**3634**
Electric housewares and household fans: Electrical Appliance, Television and Radio Set—*whlse*	42162	5064
Electric insulating tapes and braids, except plastic: Narrow Fabric Mills—*mfg*	313221	2241
Electric irons: Electrical Appliance, Television and Radio Set—*whlse*	42162	5064
Electric lamp (bulb) parts: Electric Lamp Bulb and Part—*mfg*	33511	3641
Electric Lamp Bulb and Part Manufacturing	**33511**	**3641**
Electric lamps: Electric Lamp Bulb and Part—*mfg*	33511	3641
Electric light bulbs, complete: Electric Lamp Bulb and Part—*mfg*	33511	3641
Electric Lighting Equipment Manufacturing	**3351**	
Electric Lighting Fixture Manufacturing, Commercial, Industrial and Institutional	**335122**	**3646**
Electric motor repair: Machinery and Equipment (except Automotive and Electronic) Repair and Maintenance, Commercial and Industrial—*serv*	81131	7694
Motor and Generator—*mfg*	335312	7694
Electric musical instruments: Musical Instrument—*mfg*	339992	3931
Electric Power Distribution	**221122**	**4931**
Electric Power Generation	**22111**	
Electric Power Generation, Other	**221119**	**4931**
Electric power generation, transmisalon, or distribution: Electric Bulk Power Transmission and Control—*util*	221121	4911
Electric Power Distribution—*util*	221122	4911
Electric Power Generation, Other—*util*	221119	4911
Fossil Fuel Electric Power Generation—*util*	221112	4911
Hydroelectric Power Generation—*util*	221111	4911
Nuclear Electric Power Generation—*util*	221113	4911
Electric Power Generation, Transmission and Distribution	**2211**	
Electric power line construction–general contractors: Power and Communication Transmission Line—*const*	23492	1623
Water, Sewer, and Pipeline—*const*	23491	1623
Electric Power Transmission, Control and Distribution	**22112**	
Electric railroads, line-haul operating: Line-Haul Railroads—*trans*	482111	4011
Electric ranges: Electrical Appliance, Television and Radio Set—*whlse*	42162	5064
Electric razor repair: Appliance Repair and Maintenance—*serv*	811412	7629
Household Appliance Stores—*retail*	443111	7629
Electric razor shops: Stores (except Tobacco Stores), All Other Miscellaneous—*retail*	453998	5999
Electric razors: Electrical Appliance, Television and Radio Set—*whlse*	42162	5064
Electric screening equipment: Industrial Machinery, All Other—*mfg*	333298	3559
Machinery, Other Commercial and Service Industry—*mfg*	333319	3559
Electric space heater controls, automatic: Automatic Environmental Control for Residential, Commercial and Appliance Use—*mfg*	334512	3822
Electric space heaters: Electric Housewares and Household Fan—*mfg*	335211	3634
Heating Equipment (except Electric and Warm Air Furnaces)—*mfg*	333414	3634
Electric tool repair: Appliance Repair and Maintenance—*serv*	811412	7629
Consumer Electronics Repair and Maintenance—*serv*	811211	7629

ALPHABETICAL INDEX	NAICS	SIC
Household Appliance Stores—*retail*	443111	7629
Electric warm air furnaces: Air-Conditioning and Warm Air Heating Equipment and Commercial and Industrial Refrigeration Equipment—*mfg*	333415	3585
Motor Vehicle Air-Conditioning—*mfg*	336391	3585
Electric washing machines: Electrical Appliance, Television and Radio Set—*whlse*	42162	5064
Electrical Apparatus and Equipment, Wiring Supplies and Construction Material Wholesalers	**42161**	**5063**
Electrical Appliance, Television and Radio Set Wholesalers	**42162**	**5064**
Electrical automobile engine testing equipment: Automotive Parts and Accessories Stores—*retail*	44131	5013
Motor Vehicle Supplies and New Part—*whlse*	42112	5013
Electrical construction materials: Building Material Dealers, Other—*retail*	44419	5063
Electrical Apparatus and Equipment, Wiring Supplies and Material—*whlse*	42161	5063
Electrical Contractors	**23531**	**1731**
Electrical Contractors	**2353**	
Electrical discharge erosion machines: Machine Tool (Metal Cutting Types)—*mfg*	333512	3541
Electrical discharge grinding machines: Machine Tool (Metal Cutting Types)—*mfg*	333512	3541
Electrical discharge machining (EDM): Fabricated Metal Product, All Other Miscellaneous—*mfg*	332999	3599
General Purpose Machinery , All Other—*mfg*	333999	3599
Machine Shops—*mfg*	33271	3599
Machinery, Other Commercial and Service Industry—*mfg*	333319	3599
Motor Vehicle Parts, All Other—*mfg*	336399	3599
Electrical Equipment and Component Manufacturing, All Other	**33599**	
Electrical Equipment and Component Manufacturing, All Other Miscellaneous	**335999**	**3699**
Electrical Equipment and Component Manufacturing, Other	**3359**	
Electrical Equipment Manufacturing	**33531**	
Electrical Equipment Manufacturing	**3353**	
Electrical Equipment, Appliance and Component Manufacturing	**335**	
Electrical generators: Building Material Dealers, Other—*retail*	44419	5063
Electrical Apparatus and Equipment, Wiring Supplies and Material—*whlse*	42161	5063
Electrical Goods Wholesalers	**4216**	
Electrical insulators, glass: Pressed and Blown Glass and Glassware, Other—*mfg*	327212	3229
Electrical insulators–pin, suspension, switch, and bus type-porcelain: Porcelain Electrical Supply—*mfg*	327113	3264
Electrical measuring instrument repair and calibration: Electronic and Precision Equipment Repair and Maintenance, Other—*serv*	811219	7629

ALPHABETICAL INDEX	NAICS	SIC
Electrical power measuring equipment: Electronic Coil, Transformer, and Other Inductor—*mfg*	334416	3825
Instrument for Measuring and Testing Electricity and Electrical Signals—*mfg*	334515	3825
Electrical repair at site of construction–contractors: Electrical Contractors—*const*	23531	1731
Security Systems Services (except Locksmiths)—*admin*	561621	1731
Electrical repair shops, except radio, television, and refrigerator repair: Appliance Repair and Maintenance—*serv*	811412	7629
Communication Equipment Repair and Maintenance—*serv*	811213	7629
Computer and Office Machine Repair and Maintenance—*serv*	811212	7629
Consumer Electronics Repair and Maintenance—*serv*	811211	7629
Electronic and Precision Equipment Repair and Maintenance, Other—*serv*	811219	7629
Household Appliance Stores—*retail*	443111	7629
Electrical service, automotive (battery and ignition repair): Automotive Mechanical and Electrical Repair and Maintenance, Other—*serv*	811118	7539
Electrical signs and advertising displays: Sign—*mfg*	33995	3993
Electrical work-contractors: Electrical Contractors—*const*	23531	1731
Security Systems Services (except Locksmiths)—*admin*	561621	1731
Electricians' gloves, rubber: Fabric Coating Mills—*mfg*	31332	3069
Rubber Product, All Other—*mfg*	326299	3069
Electrocardiographs: Electromedical and Electrotherapeutic Apparatus—*mfg*	334510	3845
Irradiation Apparatus—*mfg*	334517	3845
Electrocars for transporting golfers: Transportation Equipment, All Other—*mfg*	336999	3799
Electrochemical generators (fuel cells): Electrical Equipment and Component, All Other Miscellaneous—*mfg*	335999	3629
Electrochemical milling machines: Machine Tool (Metal Cutting Types)—*mfg*	333512	3541
Electrode holders for electric welding apparatus: Power, Distribution and Specialty Transformer—*mfg*	335311	3548
Welding and Soldering Equipment—*mfg*	333992	3548
Electrodes for thermal and electrolytic uses, carbon and graphite: Carbon and Graphite Product—*mfg*	335991	3624
Electrodes used in industrial process measurement: Instruments and Related Products for Measuring, Displaying, and Controlling Industrial Process Variables—*mfg*	334513	3823
Electrodes, cold cathode fluorescent lamp: Electric Lamp Bulb and Part—*mfg*	33511	3641
Electrodes, electric welding: Power, Distribution and Specialty Transformer—*mfg*	335311	3548
Welding and Soldering Equipment—*mfg*	333992	3548
Electroencephalographs: Electromedical and Electrotherapeutic Apparatus—*mfg*	334510	3845

Entry	NAICS	SIC
Irradiation Apparatus—*mfg*	334517	3845
Electroforming machines: Machine Tool (Metal Forming Types)—*mfg*	333513	3542
Electrogamma ray loggers: Measuring and Controlling Device, Other—*mfg*	334519	3829
Surgical and Medical Instrument—*mfg*	339112	3829
Electrogastrograph: Electromedical and Electrotherapeutic Apparatus—*mfg*	334510	3845
Irradiation Apparatus—*mfg*	334517	3845
Electrohydraulic servo valves, fluid power:metal: Fluid Power Valve and Hose Fitting—*mfg*	332912	3492
Electrolizing steel, for the trade: Electroplating, Plating, Polishing, Anodizing and Coloring—*mfg*	332813	3471
Electrolysis (hair removal): Personal Care Services, Other—*serv*	812199	7299
Electrolyte diagnostic reagents: In-Vitro Diagnostic Substance—*mfg*	325413	2835
Pharmaceutical Preparation—*mfg*	325412	2835
Electrolytic conductivity instruments, industrial process type: Instruments and Related Products for Measuring, Displaying, and Controlling Industrial Process Variables—*mfg*	334513	3823
Electrolytic conductivity instruments, laboratory type: Analytical Laboratory Instrument—*mfg*	334516	3826
Electrolytic metal cutting machine tools: Machine Tool (Metal Cutting Types)—*mfg*	333512	3541
Electromagnetic brakes and clutches: Relay and Industrial Control—*mfg*	335314	3625
Electromechanical counters: Totalizing Fluid Meter and Counting Device—*mfg*	334514	3824
Electromedical and Electrotherapeutic Apparatus Manufacturing	**334510**	**3845**
Electromedical apparatus: Electromedical and Electrotherapeutic Apparatus—*mfg*	334510	3845
Irradiation Apparatus—*mfg*	334517	3845
Electromedical equipment: Health and Personal Care Stores, All Other—*retail*	446199	5047
Medical, Dental and Hospital Equipment and Supplies—*whlse*	42145	5047
Electrometallurgical Ferroalloy Product Manufacturing	**331112**	**3312**
Electromyographs: Electromedical and Electrotherapeutic Apparatus—*mfg*	334510	3845
Irradiation Apparatus—*mfg*	334517	3845
Electron beam (beta ray) generator tubes: Electron Tube—*mfg*	334411	3671
Electron beam metal cutting, forming, and welding machines: Electrical Equipment and Component, All Other Miscellaneous—*mfg*	335999	3699
Machinery, Other Commercial and Service Industry—*mfg*	333319	3699
Electron linear accelerators: Electrical Equipment and Component, All Other Miscellaneous—*mfg*	335999	3699
Machinery, Other Commercial and Service Industry—*mfg*	333319	3699
Electron microprobes: Analytical Laboratory Instrument—*mfg*	334516	3826
Electron microscopes: Analytical Laboratory Instrument—*mfg*	334516	3826
Electron paramagnetic spin type apparatus: Analytical Laboratory Instrument—*mfg*	334516	3826
Electron tube making machinery: Industrial Machinery, All Other—*mfg*	333298	3559
Machinery, Other Commercial and Service Industry—*mfg*	333319	3559
Electron Tube Manufacturing	**334411**	**3671**
Electron tube parts, except glass blanks–bases, getters, and guns: Electron Tube—*mfg*	334411	3671
Electron tube test equipment: Electronic Coil, Transformer, and Other Inductor—*mfg*	334416	3825
Instrument for Measuring and Testing Electricity and Electrical Signals—*mfg*	334515	3825
Electron tubes: Electron Tube—*mfg*	334411	3671
Electron-discharge metal cutting machine tools: Machine Tool (Metal Cutting Types)—*mfg*	333512	3541
Electronic and Precision Equipment Repair and Maintenance	**81121**	
Electronic and Precision Equipment Repair and Maintenance	**8112**	
Electronic and Precision Equipment Repair and Maintenance, Other	**811219**	**7699**
Electronic Capacitor Manufacturing	**334414**	**3675**
Electronic Coil, Transformer, and Other Inductor Manufacturing	**334416**	**3677**
Electronic coils and transformers: Electronic Parts and Equipment, Other—*whlse*	42169	5065
Electronic Component Manufacturing, Other	**334419**	**3679**
Electronic Computer Manufacturing	**334111**	**3571**
Electronic computer subassembly for film reader and phototheodolite: Computer Peripheral Equipment, Other—*mfg*	334119	3577
Electronic Connector Manufacturing	**334417**	**3678**
Electronic connectors: Electronic Parts and Equipment, Other—*whlse*	42169	5065
Electronic control system installation–contractors: Electrical Contractors—*const*	23531	1731
Security Systems Services (except Locksmiths)—*admin*	561621	1731
Electronic enclosures–stamped or pressed: Metal Stamping—*mfg*	332116	3469
Electronic equipment rental and leasing, except medical and computer equipment: Consumer Electronics and Appliances Rental—*real*	53221	7359
Electronic equipment repair, except computers and computer peripheral equipment: Appliance Repair and Maintenance—*serv*	811412	7629
Communication Equipment Repair and Maintenance—*serv*	811213	7629
Computer and Office Machine Repair and Maintenance—*serv*	811212	7629
Consumer Electronics Repair and Maintenance—*serv*	811211	7629
Electronic and Precision Equipment Repair and Maintenance, Other—*serv*	811219	7629
Household Appliance Stores—*retail*	443111	7629
Electronic funds transfer networks, including switching: Commodity Contracts Dealing—*fin*	52313	6099

ALPHABETICAL INDEX	NAICS	SIC
Credit Intermediation, Other Activities Related to—*fin*	52239	6099
Financial Investment Activities, Miscellaneous—*fin*	523999	6099
Financial Transactions Processing, Reserve, and Clearing House Activities—*fin*	52232	6099
Trust, Fiduciary and Custody Activities—*fin*	523991	6099
Electronic game machines, except coin-operated: Game, Toy, and Children's Vehicle—*mfg*	339932	3944
Electronic kits for home assembly–radio and television receiving sets, and phonograph equipment: Audio and Video Equipment—*mfg*	33431	3651
Electronic mail services: Wired Telecommunications Carriers—*info*	51331	4822
Electronic musical instruments: Musical Instrument—*mfg*	339992	3931
Electronic parts: Electronic Parts and Equipment, Other—*whlse*	42169	5065
Electronic Parts and Equipment Wholesalers, Other	**42169**	**5065**
Electronic Resistor Manufacturing	**334415**	**3676**
Electronic Shopping and Mail-Order Houses	**45411**	**5961**
Electronic Shopping and Mail-Order Houses	**4541**	
Electronic test equipment for testing electrical characteristics: Electronic Coil, Transformer, and Other Inductor—*mfg*	334416	3825
Instrument for Measuring and Testing Electricity and Electrical Signals—*mfg*	334515	3825
Electronic totalizing counters: Totalizing Fluid Meter and Counting Device—*mfg*	334514	3824
Electronic toys: Game, Toy, and Children's Vehicle—*mfg*	339932	3944
Electronic tubes–receiving, transmitting, and industrial: Electronic Parts and Equipment, Other—*whlse*	42169	5065
Electronics and Appliance Stores	**4431**	
Electronics and Appliance Stores	**443**	
Electrophoresis instruments: Analytical Laboratory Instrument—*mfg*	334516	3826
Electroplating machinery and equipment, except rolling mill lines: Industrial Machinery, All Other—*mfg*	333298	3559
Machinery, Other Commercial and Service Industry—*mfg*	333319	3559
Electroplating of metals and formed products, for the trade: Electroplating, Plating, Polishing, Anodizing and Coloring—*mfg*	332813	3471
Electroplating, Plating, Polishing, Anodizing and Coloring	**332813**	**3471**
Electrostatic painting on site (including of lockers and fixtures)–contractors: Painting and Wall Covering Contractors—*const*	23521	1721
Electrostatic particle accelerators: Electrical Equipment and Component, All Other Miscellaneous—*mfg*	335999	3699
Machinery, Other Commercial and Service Industry—*mfg*	333319	3699
Electrostatic precipitators: Air Purification Equipment—*mfg*	333411	3564
Industrial and Commercial Fan and Blower—*mfg*	333412	3564
Electrotherapeutic lamp units for ultraviolet and infrared radiation: Electric Lamp Bulb and Part—*mfg*	33511	3641

ALPHABETICAL INDEX	NAICS	SIC
Electrotherapy unit: Electromedical and Electrotherapeutic Apparatus—*mfg*	334510	3845
Irradiation Apparatus—*mfg*	334517	3845
Electrotype plates: Prepress Services—*mfg*	323122	2796
Electrotyping for the trade: Prepress Services—*mfg*	323122	2796
Electrotyping machines: Printing Machinery and Equipment—*mfg*	333293	3555
Elemental analyzers (CHNOS): Analytical Laboratory Instrument—*mfg*	334516	3826
Elementary and Secondary Schools	**61111**	**8211**
Elementary and Secondary Schools	**6111**	
Elementary schools: Elementary and Secondary Schools—*educ*	61111	8211
Elements, minor or trace (agricultural chemicals): Pesticide and Other Agricultural Chemical—*mfg*	32532	2879
Elevated highway construction–general contractors: Bridge and Tunnel—*const*	23412	1622
Elevated railway operation: Bus and Motor Vehicle Transit Systems—*trans*	485113	4111
Commuter Rail Systems—*trans*	485112	4111
Mixed Mode Transit Systems—*trans*	485111	4111
Transit and Ground Passenger, All Other—*trans*	485999	4111
Urban Transit Systems, Other—*trans*	485119	4111
Elevator and Moving Stairway Manufacturing	**333921**	**3534**
Elevator front installation, metal-contractors: Structural Steel Erection Contractors—*const*	23591	1791
Elevator fronts: Elevator and Moving Stairway—*mfg*	333921	3534
Elevator guide rails, metal: Ornamental and Architectural Metal Work—*mfg*	332323	3446
Elevator installation, conversion, and repair–contractors: Building Equipment and Other Machinery Installation Contractors—*const*	23595	1796
Elevators: Industrial Machinery and Equipment—*whlse*	42183	5084
Elevators and elevator equipment, passenger and freight: Elevator and Moving Stairway—*mfg*	333921	3534
Elevators, aircraft: Aircraft Part and Auxiliary Equipment, Other—*mfg*	336413	3728
Fluid Power Valve and Hose Fitting—*mfg*	332912	3728
Elevators, farm: Farm Machinery and Equipment—*mfg*	333111	3523
Elevators, grain–storage only: Farm Product Warehousing and Storage Facilities—*trans*	49313	4221
Elevators, powered–nonfarm: Elevator and Moving Stairway—*mfg*	333921	3534
Embassies: International Affairs—*pub*	92812	9721
Emblems, embroidered: Men's and Boys' Cut and Sew Apparel Contractors—*mfg*	315211	2395
Textile Product Mills, All Other Miscellaneous—*mfg*	314999	2395
Women's and Girls' Cut and Sew Apparel Contractors—*mfg*	315212	2395
Emblems, made from fabrics: Textile Product Mills, All Other Miscellaneous—*mfg*	314999	2399

Description	NAICS	SIC
Embossed leather goods for the trade: Leather Good, All Other—*mfg*	316999	3199
Embossing cotton broadwoven fabrics: Broadwoven Fabric Finishing Mills—*mfg*	313311	2261
Embossing linen broadwoven fabrics: Broadwoven Fabric Finishing Mills—*mfg*	313311	2269
Textile and Fabric Finishing (except Broadwoven Fabric) Mills—*mfg*	313312	2269
Embossing machines for store and office use: Lead Pencil and Art Good—*mfg*	339942	3579
Office Machinery—*mfg*	333313	3579
Watch, Clock, and Part—*mfg*	334518	3579
Embossing manmade fiber and silk broad-woven fabrics: Broadwoven Fabric Finishing Mills—*mfg*	313311	2262
Embossing of books: Tradebinding and Related Work—*mfg*	323121	2789
Embossing of leather: Leather and Hide Tanning and Finishing—*mfg*	31611	3111
Embossing on paper: Digital Printing—*mfg*	323115	2759
Flexographic Printing, Commercial—*mfg*	323112	2759
Printing, Other Commercial—*mfg*	323119	2759
Quick Printing—*mfg*	323114	2759
Embossing plates for printing: Prepress Services—*mfg*	323122	2796
Embroideries, Schiffli machine: Schiffli Machine Embroidery—*mfg*	313222	2397
Embroideries–metallic, beaded, and sequined: Men's and Boys' Cut and Sew Apparel Contractors—*mfg*	315211	2395
Textile Product Mills, All Other Miscellaneous—*mfg*	314999	2395
Women's and Girls' Cut and Sew Apparel Contractors—*mfg*	315212	2395
Embroidering of advertising on shirts, etc.: Design Services, Other Specialized—*prof*	54149	7389
Embroidery machines: Textile Machinery—*mfg*	333292	3552
Embroidery products, except Schiffli machine: Men's and Boys' Cut and Sew Apparel Contractors—*mfg*	315211	2395
Textile Product Mills, All Other Miscellaneous—*mfg*	314999	2395
Women's and Girls' Cut and Sew Apparel Contractors—*mfg*	315212	2395
Embroidery thread–cotton, silk, manmade fibers, and wool: Textile and Fabric Finishing (except Broadwoven Fabric) Mills—*mfg*	313312	2284
Thread Mills—*mfg*	313113	2284
Embroidery yarn–cotton, silk, wool, and manmade staple: Yarn Spinning Mills—*mfg*	313111	2281
Emergency and Other Relief Services	**62423**	**8322**
Emergency management offices: Justice, Public Order, and Safety, All Other—*pub*	92219	9229
Emergency shelters: Child and Youth Services—*hlth*	62411	8322
Community Food Services—*hlth*	62421	8322
Community Housing Services, Other—*hlth*	624229	8322
Emergency and Other Relief Services—*hlth*	62423	8322
Individual and Family Services, Other—*hlth*	62419	8322
Parole Offices and Probation Offices—*pub*	92215	8322
Services for the Elderly and Persons with Disabilities—*hlth*	62412	8322
Temporary Shelters—*hlth*	624221	8322

Description	NAICS	SIC
Emery abrasives: Abrasive Product—*mfg*	32791	3291
Fabricated Metal Product, All Other Miscellaneous—*mfg*	332999	3291
Emery mining: Crushed and Broken Stone and Quarrying, Other—*mining*	212319	1499
Non-Metallic Mineral, All Other—*mining*	212399	1499
Emissions testing service, automotive–without repair: Automotive Oil Change and Lubrication Shops—*serv*	811191	7549
Automotive Repair and Maintenance, All Other—*serv*	811198	7549
Motor Vehicle Towing—*trans*	48841	7549
Empennage (tail) assemblies and parts, aircraft: Aircraft Part and Auxiliary Equipment, Other—*mfg*	336413	3728
Fluid Power Valve and Hose Fitting—*mfg*	332912	3728
Employee leasing service: Employee Leasing Services—*admin*	56133	7363
Temporary Help Services—*admin*	56132	7363
Employee Leasing Services	**56133**	**7363**
Employees' associations for improvement of wages and working conditions: Labor Unions and Similar Labor Organizations—*serv*	81393	8631
Employment agencies, except theatrical and motion picture: Employment Placement Agencies—*admin*	56131	7361
Human Resources and Executive Search Consulting Services—*prof*	541612	7361
Employment agencies, motion picture: Employment Placement Agencies—*admin*	56131	7819
Independent Artists, Writers, and Performers—*arts*	71151	7819
Motion Picture and Video Industries, Other—*info*	512199	7819
Employment agencies–theatrical, radio, and television-except motion picture: Employment Placement Agencies—*admin*	56131	7922
Employment Placement Agencies	**56131**	**7819**
Employment Services	**5613**	
Emulsifiers, except food and pharmaceutical: Surface Active Agent—*mfg*	325613	2843
Emulsifiers, fluorescent inspection: Pharmaceutical Preparation—*mfg*	325412	2834
Emulsifiers, food: Food, All Other Miscellaneous—*mfg*	311999	2099
Emulsions, pharmaceutical: Pharmaceutical Preparation—*mfg*	325412	2834
Enamel sand mining: Industrial Sand—*mining*	212322	1446
Enamel tile, floor and wall–clay: Ceramic Wall and Floor Tile—*mfg*	327122	3253
Enameled glass, made from purchased glass: Glass Product Made of Purchased Glass—*mfg*	327215	3231
Enameled Iron and Metal Sanitary Ware Manufacturing	**332998**	**3431**
Enameled paper: Coated and Laminated Paper—*mfg*	322222	2672
Enameled tileboard (hardboard): Building Material Dealers, Other—*retail*	44419	5031
Enameling (including porcelain) of metal products, for the trade: Costume Jewelry and Novelty—*mfg*	339914	3479
Jewelry (except Costume)—*mfg*	339911	3479
Metal Coating, Engraving (except Jewelry and Silverware), and Allied Services to Manufacturers—*mfg*	332812	3479

ALPHABETICAL INDEX	NAICS	SIC
Silverware and Plated Ware—*mfg*	339912	3479
Enameling ovens: Industrial Process Furnace and Oven—*mfg*	333994	3567
Enamels: Paint and Wallpaper Stores—*retail*	44412	5198
Paint, Varnish and Supplies—*whlse*	42295	5198
Enamels, china painting: Chemical Product, All Other Miscellaneous—*mfg*	325998	3952
Institutional Furniture—*mfg*	337127	3952
Lead Pencil and Art Good—*mfg*	339942	3952
Enamels, dentists': Dental Equipment and Supplies—*mfg*	339114	3843
Enamels, except dental and china painting: Paint and Coating—*mfg*	32551	2851
Enamelware stores: Home Furnishings Stores, All Other—*retail*	442299	5719
Window Treatment Stores—*retail*	442291	5719
Enchiladas, canned: Canning, Specialty—*mfg*	311422	2032
Food, All Other Miscellaneous—*mfg*	311999	2032
Encrusting gold, silver, or other metal on china, for the trade: Vitreous China, Fine Earthenware and Other Pottery Product—*mfg*	327112	3269
Encrusting gold, silver, or other metals on glass products–made from purchased glass: Glass Product Made of Purchased Glass—*mfg*	327215	3231
Encryption devices: Radio and Television Broadcasting and Wireless Communications Equipment—*mfg*	33422	3663
Encyclopedias, house-to-house selling: Direct Selling Establishments, Other—*retail*	45439	5963
Mobile Foodservices—*accom*	72233	5963
End tables, wood: Nonupholstered Wood Household Furniture—*mfg*	337122	2511
Endocrine products: Medicinal and Botanical—*mfg*	325411	2833
Endodontists, offices of: Dentists, Offices Of—*hlth*	62121	8021
Endoscopic equipment, electromedical:e.g., bronchoscopes, cystoscopes, and colonoscopes: Electromedical and Electrotherapeutic Apparatus—*mfg*	334510	3845
Irradiation Apparatus—*mfg*	334517	3845
Energy cutoff controls, residential and commercial types: Automatic Environmental Control for Residential, Commercial and Appliance Use—*mfg*	334512	3822
Energy development and conservation agencies-nonoperating: General Economic Programs, Administration of—*pub*	92611	9611
Energy measuring equipment, electrical: Electronic Coil, Transformer, and Other Inductor—*mfg*	334416	3825
Instrument for Measuring and Testing Electricity and Electrical Signals—*mfg*	334515	3825
Engine and turbine forgings, nonferrous–not made in hot-rolling mills: Nonferrous Forging—*mfg*	332112	3463
Engine electrical equipment, automotive: Automotive Parts and Accessories Stores—*retail*	44131	5013
Motor Vehicle Supplies and New Part—*whlse*	42112	5013
Engine Equipment Manufacturing, Other	**333618**	**3699**

ALPHABETICAL INDEX	NAICS	SIC
Engine forgings, ferrous–not made in rollmg mills: Iron and Steel Forging—*mfg*	332111	3462
Engine heaters, aircraft: Aircraft Engine and Engine Parts—*mfg*	336412	3724
Engine mount parts, aircraft: Aircraft Engine and Engine Parts—*mfg*	336412	3724
Engine pumps, aircraft: Aircraft Engine and Engine Parts—*mfg*	336412	3724
Engine repair, automotive: General Automotive Repair—*serv*	811111	7538
Engine repair, except automotive: Home and Garden Equipment Repair and Maintenance—*serv*	811411	7699
Machinery and Equipment (except Automotive and Electronic) Repair and Maintenance, Commercial and Industrial—*serv*	81131	7699
Engine repair, truck–except industrial: General Automotive Repair—*serv*	811111	7538
Engine stands and racks, metal: Fabricated Metal Product, All Other Miscellaneous—*mfg*	332999	3537
Industrial Truck, Tractor, Trailer and Stacker Machinery—*mfg*	333924	3537
Metal Container, Other—*mfg*	332439	3537
Engine testing equipment, automobile–electrical: Automotive Parts and Accessories Stores—*retail*	44131	5013
Motor Vehicle Supplies and New Part—*whlse*	42112	5013
Engine, Turbine and Power Transmission Equipment Manufacturing	**33361**	
Engine, Turbine, and Power Transmission Equipment Manufacturing	**3336**	
Engineered Wood Member (except Truss) Manufacturing	**321213**	**2439**
Engineering associations: Professional Organizations—*serv*	81392	8621
Engineering job shops (temporary employees): Employee Leasing Services—*admin*	56133	7363
Temporary Help Services—*admin*	56132	7363
Engineering laboratories, commercial research–except testing: Research and Development in the Life Sciences—*prof*	54172	8731
Research and Development in the Physical Sciences and Engineering Sciences—*prof*	54171	8731
Engineering Services	**54133**	**8711**
Engineering services–architectural: Architectural Services—*prof*	54131	8712
Engineering services–industrial, civil, electrical, mechanical, petroleum, marine, and design: Engineering Services—*prof*	54133	8711
Engineering services–photogrammetric: Geophysical Surveying and Mapping Services—*prof*	54136	8713
Surveying and Mapping (except Geophysical) Services—*prof*	54137	8713
Engineers' equipment and supplies: Office Supplies and Stationery Stores—*retail*	45321	5049
Professional Equipment and Supplies, Other—*whlse*	42149	5049
Engines and engine parts, aircraft–internal combustion and jet propulsion: Aircraft Engine and Engine Parts—*mfg*	336412	3724
Engines and engine parts, guided missile: Guided Missile and Space Vehicle Propulsion Unit and Propulsion Unit Parts—*mfg*	336415	3764

Description	NAICS	SIC
Engines and engine parts, internal combustion- military tank: Engine Equipment, Other—*mfg*	333618	3519
Motor Vehicle Parts, All Other—*mfg*	336399	3519
Engines and parts, diesel: Industrial Machinery and Equipment—*whlse*	42183	5084
Engines and parts, except diesel–motor vehicle: Gasoline Engine and Engine Parts—*mfg*	336312	3714
Motor Vehicle Parts, All Other—*mfg*	336399	3714
Engines, internal combustion–except air-craft and nondiesel automotive: Engine Equipment, Other—*mfg*	333618	3519
Motor Vehicle Parts, All Other—*mfg*	336399	3519
Engines, miniature: Game, Toy, and Children's Vehicle—*mfg*	339932	3944
Engines, steam (1ocomotives): Pump and Pumping Equipment—*mfg*	333911	3743
Railroad Rolling Stock—*mfg*	33651	3743
Engines, steam–except locomotives: Turbine and Turbine Generator Set Unit—*mfg*	333611	3511
Engines–diesel and semidiesel and dual fuel except aircraft: Engine Equipment, Other—*mfg*	333618	3519
Motor Vehicle Parts, All Other—*mfg*	336399	3519
English pea farms: Vegetable (except Potato) and Melon Farming, Other—*ag*	111219	161
Engraved glassware: Glass Product Made of Purchased Glass—*mfg*	327215	3231
Engravers' tools, hand: Hand and Edge Tool—*mfg*	332212	3423
Engraving jewelry, silverware, and metal for the trade–except printing: Costume Jewelry and Novelty—*mfg*	339914	3479
Jewelry (except Costume)—*mfg*	339911	3479
Metal Coating, Engraving (except Jewelry and Silverware), and Allied Services to Manufacturers—*mfg*	332812	3479
Silverware and Plated Ware—*mfg*	339912	3479
Engraving machinery and equipment(printing trades machinery): Printing Machinery and Equipment—*mfg*	333293	3555
Engraving of cards, except greeting cards: Digital Printing—*mfg*	323115	2759
Flexographic Printing, Commercial—*mfg*	323112	2759
Printing, Other Commercial—*mfg*	323119	2759
Quick Printing—*mfg*	323114	2759
Engraving of plastics: Plastics Pipe and Pipe Fitting—*mfg*	326122	3089
Plastics Product, All Other—*mfg*	326199	3089
Unsupported Plastics Profile Shape—*mfg*	326121	3089
Engraving on copper, steel, wood, or rubber plates for printing purposes: Prepress Services—*mfg*	323122	2796
Engraving on textile printing plates and cylinders: Prepress Services—*mfg*	323122	2796
Engraving, steel line–for printing purposes: Prepress Services—*mfg*	323122	2796
Enlargers, photographic: Photographic and Photocopying Equipment—*mfg*	333315	3861
Photographic Film, Paper, Plate and Chemical—*mfg*	325992	3861
Ensemble dresses: Women's and Girls' Cut and Sew Apparel Contractors—*mfg*	315212	2335
Women's and Girls' Cut and Sew Dress—*mfg*	315233	2335
Ensilage blowers and cutters: Farm Machinery and Equipment—*mfg*	333111	3523
Hand and Edge Tool—*mfg*	332212	3523
Entertainers: Independent Artists, Writers, and Performers—*arts*	71151	7929
Musical Groups and Artists—*arts*	71113	7929
Performing Arts Companies, Other—*arts*	71119	7929
Entertainment groups: Independent Artists, Writers, and Performers—*arts*	71151	7929
Musical Groups and Artists—*arts*	71113	7929
Performing Arts Companies, Other—*arts*	71119	7929
Entomological service, agricultural: Nonscheduled Air, Other—*trans*	481219	721
Soil Preparation, Planting, and Cultivating—*ag*	115112	721
Entomologists, consulting–not with business service laboratories: Environmental Consulting Services—*prof*	54162	8999
Scientific and Technical Consulting Services, Other—*prof*	54169	8999
Envalope stuffing, sealing, and addressing machines: Lead Pencil and Art Good—*mfg*	339942	3579
Office Machinery—*mfg*	333313	3579
Watch, Clock, and Part—*mfg*	334518	3579
Envelope Manufacturing	**322232**	**2677**
Envelope printing presses: Printing Machinery and Equipment—*mfg*	333293	3555
Envelopes: Office Supplies and Stationery Stores—*retail*	45321	5112
Stationary and Office Supplies—*whlse*	42212	5112
Envelopes, printed or unprinted–paper, glassine, cellophane, and pliofilm: Envelope—*mfg*	322232	2677
Envelopes, printed–except lithographed or gravure: Digital Printing—*mfg*	323115	2759
Flexographic Printing, Commercial—*mfg*	323112	2759
Printing, Other Commercial—*mfg*	323119	2759
Quick Printing—*mfg*	323114	2759
Envelopes–gravure printing: Gravure Printing, Commercial—*mfg*	323111	2754
Environment, Conservation and Wildlife Organizations	**813312**	**8699**
Environmental Consulting Services	**54162**	**8999**
Environmental health programs: Public Health Programs, Administration of—*pub*	92312	9431
Environmental protection agencies: Air and Water Resource and Solid Waste Management—*pub*	92411	9511
Environmental quality and control agencies: Air and Water Resource and Solid Waste Management—*pub*	92411	9511
Environmental Quality Programs, Administration of	**924**	
Environmental Quality Programs, Administration of	**9241**	
Enzyme and isoenzyme diagnostic reagents: In-Vitro Diagnostic Substance—*mfg*	325413	2835
Pharmaceutical Preparation—*mfg*	325412	2835
Enzymes, except diagnostic substances: Basic Organic Chemical, All Other—*mfg*	325199	2869
Eosine toners: Petrochemical—*mfg*	32511	2865
EPDM polymers: Synthetic Rubber—*mfg*	325212	2822
Ephedrine and derivatives: Medicinal and Botanical—*mfg*	325411	2833
Epichlorohydrin bisphenol: Plastics Material and Resin—*mfg*	325211	2821

ALPHABETICAL INDEX	NAICS	SIC
Epichlorohydrin diphenol: Plastics Material and Resin—*mfg*	325211	2821
Epichlorohydrin elastomem: Synthetic Rubber—*mfg*	325212	2822
Epoxy adhesives: Adhesive—*mfg*	32552	2891
Epoxy application–contractors: Trade Contractors, All Other Special—*const*	23599	1799
Epoxy coatings, made from purchased resin: Paint and Coating—*mfg*	32551	2851
Epoxy resins: Plastics Material and Resin—*mfg*	325211	2821
Equal employment opportunity offices: Social, Human Resource and Income Maintenance Programs, Administration of—*pub*	92313	9441
Equipment Wholesalers, Other Commercial	**42144**	**5046**
Eraser guides and shields: Chemical Product, All Other Miscellaneous—*mfg*	325998	3952
Institutional Furniture—*mfg*	337127	3952
Lead Pencil and Art Good—*mfg*	339942	3952
Erasers–rubber, or rubber and abrasive combined: Fabric Coating Mills—*mfg*	31332	3069
Rubber Product, All Other—*mfg*	326299	3069
Erecting lease tanks, oil and gas field–on a contract basis: Oil and Gas Operations Support Activities—*mining*	213112	1389
Erection and dismantling of forms for poured concrete–contractors: Trade Contractors, All Other Special—*const*	23599	1799
Erector sets, toy: Game, Toy, and Children's Vehicle—*mfg*	339932	3944
Ergot alkaloids: Medicinal and Botanical—*mfg*	325411	2833
Escalators, passenger and freight: Elevator and Moving Stairway—*mfg*	333921	3534
Escort service: Personal Services, All Other—*serv*	81299	7299
Escrow agents, real estate: Real Estate, Other Activities Related to—*real*	53139	6531
Escrow institutions other than real estate: Commodity Contracts Dealing—*fin*	52313	6099
Credit Intermediation, Other Activities Related to—*fin*	52239	6099
Financial Investment Activities, Miscellaneous—*fin*	523999	6099
Financial Transactions Processing, Reserve, and Clearing House Activities—*fin*	52232	6099
Trust, Fiduciary and Custody Activities—*fin*	523991	6099
Essential oils: Basic Organic Chemical, All Other—*mfg*	325199	2899
Chemical and Allied Products, Other—*whlse*	42269	5169
Chemical Product, All Other Miscellaneous—*mfg*	325998	2899
Spice and Extract—*mfg*	311942	2899
Estane: Synthetic Rubber—*mfg*	325212	2822
Estates, private: Private Households—*serv*	81411	8811
Ester gum: Plastics Material and Resin—*mfg*	325211	2821
Esters of phosphoric, adipic, lauric, oleic, sebacic, and stearic acjds: Basic Organic Chemical, All Other—*mfg*	325199	2869
Esters of phthalic anhydride: Basic Organic Chemical, All Other—*mfg*	325199	2869

ALPHABETICAL INDEX	NAICS	SIC
Esters of polyhydric alcohols: Basic Organic Chemical, All Other—*mfg*	325199	2869
Estimating timber: Forestry Support Activities—*ag*	11531	851
Etching machines (printing trades machinery): Printing Machinery and Equipment—*mfg*	333293	3555
Etching on copper, steel, wood, or rubber plates for printing purposes: Prepress Services—*mfg*	323122	2796
Etching on metals for purposes other than printing: Costume Jewelry and Novelty—*mfg*	339914	3479
Jewelry (except Costume)—*mfg*	339911	3479
Metal Coating, Engraving (except Jewelry and Silverware), and Allied Services to Manufacturers—*mfg*	332812	3479
Silverware and Plated Ware—*mfg*	339912	3479
Etching–photochemical, for the trade: Costume Jewelry and Novelty—*mfg*	339914	3479
Jewelry (except Costume)—*mfg*	339911	3479
Metal Coating, Engraving (except Jewelry and Silverware), and Allied Services to Manufacturers—*mfg*	332812	3479
Silverware and Plated Ware—*mfg*	339912	3479
Ethane (natural) production: Natural Gas Liquid Extraction—*mining*	211112	1321
Ethanol, industrial: Basic Organic Chemical, All Other—*mfg*	325199	2869
Ethyl Alcohol—*mfg*	325193	2869
Ether: Basic Organic Chemical, All Other—*mfg*	325199	2869
Ethyl acetate, natural: Gum and Wood Chemical—*mfg*	325191	2861
Ethyl acetate, synthetic: Basic Organic Chemical, All Other—*mfg*	325199	2869
Ethyl alcohol for medicinal and beverage purposes: Distilleries—*mfg*	31214	2085
Ethyl Alcohol Manufacturing	**325193**	**2869**
Ethyl alcohol, industrial (nonbeverage): Basic Organic Chemical, All Other—*mfg*	325199	2869
Ethyl Alcohol—*mfg*	325193	2869
Ethyl butyrate: Basic Organic Chemical, All Other—*mfg*	325199	2869
Ethyl cellulose plastics: Plastics Material and Resin—*mfg*	325211	2821
Ethyl cellulose, unplasticized: Basic Organic Chemical, All Other—*mfg*	325199	2869
Ethyl chloride: Basic Organic Chemical, All Other—*mfg*	325199	2869
Ethyl ether: Basic Organic Chemical, All Other—*mfg*	325199	2869
Ethyl formate: Basic Organic Chemical, All Other—*mfg*	325199	2869
Ethyl nitrite: Basic Organic Chemical, All Other—*mfg*	325199	2869
Ethyl perhydrophenanthrene: Basic Organic Chemical, All Other—*mfg*	325199	2869
Ethylbenzene: Cyclic Crude and Intermediate—*mfg*	325192	2865
Petrochemical—*mfg*	32511	2865
Ethylene glycol: Basic Organic Chemical, All Other—*mfg*	325199	2869
Ethylene glycol antifreeze preparations: Basic Organic Chemical, All Other—*mfg*	325199	2899
Chemical Product, All Other Miscellaneous—*mfg*	325998	2899
Ethylene glycol ether: Basic Organic Chemical, All Other—*mfg*	325199	2869

Description	NAICS	SIC
Ethylene glycol, inhibited: Basic Organic Chemical, All Other—*mfg*	325199	2869
Ethylene oxide: Basic Organic Chemical, All Other—*mfg*	325199	2869
Ethylene, made in chemical plants: Basic Organic Chemical, All Other—*mfg*	325199	2869
Ethylene, produced in petroleum refineries: Petroleum Refineries—*mfg*	32411	2911
Ethylene-propylene rubbers: Synthetic Rubber—*mfg*	325212	2822
Ethylene-vinyl acetate resins: Plastics Material and Resin—*mfg*	325211	2821
Eucalyptus oil: Spice and Extract—*mfg*	311942	2899
Evaporated milk: Dry, Condensed, and Evaporated Dairy Product—*mfg*	311514	2023
Evaporation meters: Measuring and Controlling Device, Other—*mfg*	334519	3829
Surgical and Medical Instrument—*mfg*	339112	3829
Evaporative condensers (heat transfer equipment): Air-Conditioning and Warm Air Heating Equipment and Commercial and Industrial Refrigeration Equipment—*mfg*	333415	3585
Motor Vehicle Air-Conditioning—*mfg*	336391	3585
Evaporators (process vessels), metal plate: Air-Conditioning and Warm Air Heating Equipment and Commercial and Industrial Refrigeration Equipment—*mfg*	333415	3443
Metal Tank (Heavy Gauge)—*mfg*	33242	3443
Plate Work—*mfg*	332313	3443
Power Boiler and Heat Exchanger—*mfg*	33241	3443
Exam Preparation and Tutoring	**611691**	**8299**
Excavating machinery and equipment: Construction and (except Petroleum) Machinery and Equipment—*whlse*	42181	5082
Excavating slush pits and cellars on a contract basis: Oil and Gas Operations Support Activities—*mining*	213112	1389
Excavation Contractors	**23593**	**1794**
Excavation work-contractors: Excavation Contractors—*const*	23593	1794
Excavators–e.g., cable, clamshell, crane, derrick, dragline, power shovel: Construction Machinery—*mfg*	33312	3531
Overhead Traveling Crane, Hoist and Monorail System—*mfg*	333923	3531
Railroad Rolling Stock—*mfg*	33651	3531
Excelsior, including pads and wrappers–wood: Cut Stock, Resawing Lumber, and Planing—*mfg*	321912	2429
Sawmills—*mfg*	321113	2429
Wood Product, All Other Miscellaneous—*mfg*	321999	2429
Excelsior, paper: Coated and Laminated Paper—*mfg*	322222	2679
Converted Paper Product, All Other—*mfg*	322298	2679
Die-Cut Paper and Paperboard Office Supplies—*mfg*	322231	2679
Non-Folding Sanitary Food Container—*mfg*	322215	2679
Exchange clearinghouses, commodity: Financial Investment Activities, Miscellaneous—*fin*	523999	6289
Trust, Fiduciary and Custody Activities—*fin*	523991	6289
Exchange clearinghouses, security: Financial Investment Activities, Miscellaneous—*fin*	523999	6289
Trust, Fiduciary and Custody Activities—*fin*	523991	6289
Exchangers, heat–industrial, scientific, and nuclear: Air-Conditioning and Warm Air Heating Equipment and Commercial and Industrial Refrigeration Equipment—*mfg*	333415	3443
Metal Tank (Heavy Gauge)—*mfg*	33242	3443
Plate Work—*mfg*	332313	3443
Power Boiler and Heat Exchanger—*mfg*	33241	3443
Exchanges, commodity contract: Securities and Commodity Exchanges—*fin*	52321	6231
Exchanges, security: Securities and Commodity Exchanges—*fin*	52321	6231
Exciter assemblies, motor and generator: Motor and Generator—*mfg*	335312	3621
Excursion boat operations: Inland Water Passenger—*trans*	483212	4489
Scenic and Sightseeing, Water—*trans*	48721	4489
Executive and Legislative Offices, Combined	**92114**	**9131**
Executive Offices	**92111**	**9111**
Executive placing services: Employment Placement Agencies—*admin*	56131	7361
Human Resources and Executive Search Consulting Services—*prof*	541612	7361
Executive, Legislative, Public Finance and General Government	**9211**	
Executive, Legislative, Public Finance and General Government	**921**	
Exercise apparatus: Sporting Goods Stores—*retail*	45111	5941
Exercise cycles: Sporting and Athletic Goods—*mfg*	33992	3949
Exercise salons: Fitness and Recreational Sports Centers—*arts*	71394	7991
Exercising machines: Sporting and Athletic Goods—*mfg*	33992	3949
Exhaust fans, except household and kitchen: Air Purification Equipment—*mfg*	333411	3564
Industrial and Commercial Fan and Blower—*mfg*	333412	3564
Exhaust system services, automotive: Automotive Exhaust System Repair—*serv*	811112	7533
Exhaust systems and parts, motor vehicle: Gasoline Engine and Engine Parts—*mfg*	336312	3714
Motor Vehicle Parts, All Other—*mfg*	336399	3714
Exhaust systems, aircraft: Aircraft Engine and Engine Parts—*mfg*	336412	3724
Exhibition operation: Amusement and Recreation Industries, All Other—*arts*	71399	7999
Exhibits, building of–by industrial contractors: Advertising, Other Services Related to—*prof*	54189	7389
Exothermics for metal industries: Basic Organic Chemical, All Other—*mfg*	325199	2899
Chemical Product, All Other Miscellaneous—*mfg*	325998	2899
Exotic leather: Leather and Hide Tanning and Finishing—*mfg*	31611	3111
Expansion joints (structural shapes)–iron and steel: Fabricated Structural Metal—*mfg*	332312	3441
Exploration for metal mining–on a con-tract basis: Geophysical Surveying and Mapping Services—*prof*	54136	1081
Metal Support Activities—*mining*	213114	1081
Exploration for nonmetallic minerals, except fuels–on a contract basis: Geophysical Surveying and Mapping Services—*prof*	54136	1481
Non-Metallic Minerals (except Fuels) Support Activities—*mining*	213115	1481

ALPHABETICAL INDEX	NAICS	SIC
Exploration, oil and gas field–on a contract basis: Geophysical Surveying and Mapping Services—*prof*	54136	1382
Oil and Gas Operations Support Activities—*mining*	213112	1382
Explosive cartridges for concussion forming of metal: Explosives—*mfg*	32592	2892
Explosive compounds: Explosives—*mfg*	32592	2892
Explosives: Explosives—*mfg*	32592	2892
Explosives Manufacturing	**32592**	**2892**
Explosives, all kinds except ammunition and fireworks: Chemical and Allied Products, Other—*whlse*	42269	5169
Export-Import Bank: International Trade Financing—*fin*	522293	6111
Non-Depository Credit Intermediation, All Other—*fin*	522298	6111
Secondary Market Financing—*fin*	522294	6111
Exposition operation: Amusement and Recreation Industries, All Other—*arts*	71399	7999
Exposure meters, photographic: Photographic and Photocopying Equipment—*mfg*	333315	3861
Photographic Film, Paper, Plate and Chemical—*mfg*	325992	3861
Expresi stripes, cotton: Broadwoven Fabric Mills—*mfg*	31321	2211
Express wagons, children's: Game, Toy, and Children's Vehicle—*mfg*	339932	3944
Extended care facilities: Continuing Care Retirement Communities—*hlth*	623311	8051
Nursing Care Facilities—*hlth*	62311	8051
Extension cords, made from purchaeed insulated wire: Electrical Equipment and Component, All Other Miscellaneous—*mfg*	335999	3699
Machinery, Other Commercial and Service Industry—*mfg*	333319	3699
Extension planks, wood: Manufacturing, All Other Miscellaneous—*mfg*	339999	2499
Wood Container and Pallet—*mfg*	32192	2499
Wood Product, All Other Miscellaneous—*mfg*	321999	2499
Extension shoes, orthopedic: Surgical Appliance and Supplies—*mfg*	339113	3842
Exterminating and Pest Control Services	**56171**	**7342**
Exterminating products, for household and industrial use: Pesticide and Other Agricultural Chemical—*mfg*	32532	2879
Exterminating service: Exterminating and Pest Control Services—*admin*	56171	7342
Janitorial Services—*admin*	56172	7342
External power units, aircraft–for hand-inertia starters': Aircraft Engine and Engine Parts—*mfg*	336412	3724
Extract, malt: Breweries—*mfg*	31212	2082
Extractors and driers, commercial laundry: Laundry, Drycleaning and Pressing Machine, Commercial—*mfg*	333312	3582
Extractors, piling: Construction Machinery—*mfg*	33312	3531
Overhead Traveling Crane, Hoist and Monorail System—*mfg*	333923	3531
Railroad Rolling Stock—*mfg*	33651	3531
Extracts of botanicals–powdered, pilular, solid, and fluid, except diagnostics: Pharmaceutical Preparation—*mfg*	325412	2834

ALPHABETICAL INDEX	NAICS	SIC
Extracts, dyeing and tanning–natural: Gum and Wood Chemical—*mfg*	325191	2861
Extruded shapes, aluminum: Aluminum Extruded Product—*mfg*	331316	3354
Extruded shapes, copper and copper alloy: Copper Rolling, Drawing and Extruding—*mfg*	331421	3351
Extruded shapes, nonferrous metals and alloys, except copper and aluminum: Nonferrous Metal (except Copper and Aluminum) Rolling, Drawing and Extruding—*mfg*	331491	3356
Extruding machines (machine tools), metal: Machine Tool (Metal Forming Types)—*mfg*	333513	3542
Extrusion dies: Die and Tool, Die Set, Jig and Fixture, Special—*mfg*	333514	3544
Industrial Mold—*mfg*	333511	3544
Extrusion ingot, aluminum–made in rollmg mills: Aluminum Rolling and Drawing, Other—*mfg*	331319	3355
Extrusion ingot, aluminum–primary: Primary Aluminum Production—*mfg*	331312	3334
Eye examin'ng instruments and apparatus: Surgical and Medical Instrument—*mfg*	339112	3841
Eye, ear, nose, and throat hospitals–in-patient: General Medical and Surgical Hospitals—*hlth*	62211	8069
Hospitals (except Psychiatric and Substance Abuse), Specialty—*hlth*	62231	8069
Psychiatric and Substance Abuse Hospitals—*hlth*	62221	8069
Eyeglass cases, regardless of material: Personal Leather Good (except Women's Handbag and Purse)—*mfg*	316993	3172
Eyeglasses, lenses, and frames: Ophthalmic Goods—*mfg*	339115	3851
Eyelet making, for the trade: Men's and Boys' Cut and Sew Apparel Contractors—*mfg*	315211	2395
Textile Product Mills, All Other Miscellaneous—*mfg*	314999	2395
Women's and Girls' Cut and Sew Apparel Contractors—*mfg*	315212	2395
Eyelets, metal–for clothing, fabrics, boots and shces, and paper: Fastener, Button, Needle and Pin—*mfg*	339993	3965
Eyes, glass and plastics: Ophthalmic Goods—*mfg*	339115	3851
Fabric Coating Mills	**31332**	**3069**
Fabric finishing of wool, mohair, and similar animal fibers–except knit: Broadwoven Fabric Finishing Mills—*mfg*	313311	2231
Broadwoven Fabric Mills—*mfg*	31321	2231
Textile and Fabric Finishing (except Broadwoven Fabric) Mills—*mfg*	313312	2231
Fabric finishing, cotton broadwoven fabrics: Broadwoven Fabric Finishing Mills—*mfg*	313311	2261
Fabric finishing, manmade fiber and silk broadwoven: Broadwoven Fabric Finishing Mills—*mfg*	313311	2262
Fabric finishing, warp knit: Knit Fabric and Lace Mills, Other—*mfg*	313249	2258
Textile and Fabric Finishing (except Broadwoven Fabric) Mills—*mfg*	313312	2258
Fabric Mills	**3132**	

Description	NAICS	SIC
Fabric shops: Sewing, Needlework and Piece Goods Stores—*retail*	45113	5949
Fabric softeners: Polish and Other Sanitation Good—*mfg*	325612	2842
Fabricated Metal Product Manufacturing	**332**	
Fabricated Metal Product Manufacturing, All Other	**33299**	
Fabricated Metal Product Manufacturing, All Other Miscellaneous	**332999**	**3432**
Fabricated Metal Product Manufacturing, Other	**3329**	
Fabricated pipe and fittings–threading, bending, etc.-of purchased pipe: Fabricated Pipe and Pipe Fitting—*mfg*	332996	3498
Fabricated Pipe and Pipe Fitting Manufacturing	**332996**	**3498**
Fabricated Structural Metal Manufacturing	**332312**	**3449**
Fabricated structural steel: Fabricated Structural Metal—*mfg*	332312	3441
Fabricated Wire Product Manufacturing, Other	**332618**	**3399**
Fabrics for reinforcing rubber tires, industrial belting, and fuel cells: Tire Cord and Tire Fabric Mills—*mfg*	314992	2296
Fabrics, animal fiber–broadwoven wool, mohair, and similar animal fibers: Broadwoven Fabric Finishing Mills—*mfg*	313311	2231
Broadwoven Fabric Mills—*mfg*	31321	2231
Textile and Fabric Finishing (except Broadwoven Fabric) Mills—*mfg*	313312	2231
Fabrics, animal fiber–narrow woven: Narrow Fabric Mills—*mfg*	313221	2241
Fabrics, bonded fiber–except felt: Nonwoven Fabric Mills—*mfg*	31323	2297
Fabrics, broadwoven–cotton: Broadwoven Fabric Mills—*mfg*	31321	2211
Fabrics, broadwoven–manmade fiber and silk: Broadwoven Fabric Mills—*mfg*	31321	2221
Fabrics, broadwoven–wool, mohair, and similar animal fibers: Broadwoven Fabric Finishing Mills—*mfg*	313311	2231
Broadwoven Fabric Mills—*mfg*	31321	2231
Textile and Fabric Finishing (except Broadwoven Fabric) Mills—*mfg*	313312	2231
Fabrics, circular knit: Textile and Fabric Finishing (except Broadwoven Fabric) Mills—*mfg*	313312	2257
Weft Knit Fabric Mills—*mfg*	313241	2257
Fabrics, coated and impregnated–except rubberized: Fabric Coating Mills—*mfg*	31332	2295
Fabrics, nonwoven–except felts: Nonwoven Fabric Mills—*mfg*	31323	2297
Fabrics, roofing–asphalt or tar saturated: Asphalt Shingle and Coating Materials—*mfg*	324122	2952
Fabrics, rubberized: Fabric Coating Mills—*mfg*	31332	3069
Rubber Product, All Other—*mfg*	326299	3069
Fabrics, warp knit: Knit Fabric and Lace Mills, Other—*mfg*	313249	2258
Textile and Fabric Finishing (except Broadwoven Fabric) Mills—*mfg*	313312	2258
Fabrics, weft knit: Textile and Fabric Finishing (except Broadwoven Fabric) Mills—*mfg*	313312	2257
Weft Knit Fabric Mills—*mfg*	313241	2257
Fabrics, woven wire–made from purchased wire: Fabricated Wire Product, Other—*mfg*	332618	3496
Fabrics–linen, jute, hemp, ramie: Broadwoven Fabric Mills—*mfg*	31321	2299
Narrow Fabric Mills—*mfg*	313221	2299
Nonwoven Fabric Mills—*mfg*	31323	2299
Textile and Fabric Finishing (except Broadwoven Fabric) Mills—*mfg*	313312	2299
Textile Product Mills, All Other Miscellaneous—*mfg*	314999	2299
Thread Mills—*mfg*	313113	2299
Yarn Spinning Mills—*mfg*	313111	2299
Face creams and lotions: Soap and Other Detergent—*mfg*	325611	2844
Toilet Preparation—*mfg*	32562	2844
Face plates (wiring devices): Noncurrent-Carrying Wiring Device—*mfg*	335932	3644
Face powders: Soap and Other Detergent—*mfg*	325611	2844
Toilet Preparation—*mfg*	32562	2844
Face-amount certificate issuing: Financial Vehicles, Other—*fin*	52599	6726
Facial salons: Beauty Salons—*serv*	812112	7231
Cosmetology and Barber Schools—*educ*	611511	7231
Nail Salons—*serv*	812113	7231
Facial tissue stock: Newsprint Mills—*mfg*	322122	2621
Paper (except Newsprint) Mills—*mfg*	322121	2621
Facial tissues: Sanitary Paper Product—*mfg*	322291	2676
Facilities management services, computer: Computer Facilities Management Services—*prof*	541513	7376
Facilities management, except computer: Facilities Support Services—*admin*	56121	8744
Facilities Support Services	**56121**	**8744**
Facilities Support Services	**5612**	
Facilities support services, except computer: Facilities Support Services—*admin*	56121	8744
Facing machines: Machine Tool (Metal Cutting Types)—*mfg*	333512	3541
Facing tile, clay: Brick and Structural Clay Tile—*mfg*	327121	3251
Facings (chemical foundry supplies): Basic Organic Chemical, All Other—*mfg*	325199	2899
Chemical Product, All Other Miscellaneous—*mfg*	325998	2899
Facsimile equipment: Electronic Coil, Transformer, and Other Inductor—*mfg*	334416	3661
Printed Circuit/Electronics Assembly—*mfg*	334418	3661
Telephone Apparatus—*mfg*	33421	3661
Facsimile letters–gravure printing: Gravure Printing, Commercial—*mfg*	323111	2754
Facsimile transmission services: Wired Telecommunications Carriers—*info*	51331	4822
Factors of commercial paper: Financial Transactions Processing, Reserve, and Clearing House Activities—*fin*	52232	6153
Non-Depository Credit Intermediation, All Other—*fin*	522298	6153
Sales Financing—*fin*	52222	6153
Factory construction–general contractors: Building, Commercial and Institutional—*const*	23332	1541
Manufacturing and Industrial Building—*const*	23331	1541

ALPHABETICAL INDEX	NAICS	SIC
Factory furniture–stools, work benches, tool stands, and cabinets:		
Institutional Furniture—*mfg*	337127	2599
Faience tile: Ceramic Wall and Floor Tile—*mfg*	327122	3253
Failles: Broadwoven Fabric Mills—*mfg*	31321	2221
Fairs, agricultural–operation of: Amusement and Recreation Industries, All Other—*arts*	71399	7999
False faces, papier mache: Coated and Laminated Paper—*mfg*	322222	2679
Converted Paper Product, All Other—*mfg*	322298	2679
Die-Cut Paper and Paperboard Office Supplies—*mfg*	322231	2679
Non-Folding Sanitary Food Container—*mfg*	322215	2679
Family Clothing Stores	**44814**	**5651**
Family counseling services: Child and Youth Services—*hlth*	62411	8322
Community Food Services—*hlth*	62421	8322
Community Housing Services, Other—*hlth*	624229	8322
Emergency and Other Relief Services—*hlth*	62423	8322
Individual and Family Services, Other—*hlth*	62419	8322
Parole Offices and Probation Offices—*pub*	92215	8322
Services for the Elderly and Persons with Disabilities—*hlth*	62412	8322
Temporary Shelters—*hlth*	624221	8322
Family location services: Child and Youth Services—*hlth*	62411	8322
Community Food Services—*hlth*	62421	8322
Community Housing Services, Other—*hlth*	624229	8322
Emergency and Other Relief Services—*hlth*	62423	8322
Individual and Family Services, Other—*hlth*	62419	8322
Parole Offices and Probation Offices—*pub*	92215	8322
Services for the Elderly and Persons with Disabilities—*hlth*	62412	8322
Temporary Shelters—*hlth*	624221	8322
Family Planning Centers	**62141**	**8099**
Family service agencies: Child and Youth Services—*hlth*	62411	8322
Community Food Services—*hlth*	62421	8322
Community Housing Services, Other—*hlth*	624229	8322
Emergency and Other Relief Services—*hlth*	62423	8322
Individual and Family Services, Other—*hlth*	62419	8322
Parole Offices and Probation Offices—*pub*	92215	8322
Services for the Elderly and Persons with Disabilities—*hlth*	62412	8322
Temporary Shelters—*hlth*	624221	8322
Fan control, temperature responsive: Automatic Environmental Control for Residential, Commercial and Appliance Use—*mfg*	334512	3822
Fan forges: Fabricated Metal Product, All Other Miscellaneous—*mfg*	332999	3599
General Purpose Machinery , All Other—*mfg*	333999	3599
Machine Shops—*mfg*	33271	3599
Machinery, Other Commercial and Service Industry—*mfg*	333319	3599
Fancy leathers: Leather and Hide Tanning and Finishing—*mfg*	31611	3111
Fancy paper, coated and glared–except for packaging: Coated and Laminated Paper—*mfg*	322222	2672
Fanfold forms: Manifold Business Form Printing—*mfg*	323116	2761

ALPHABETICAL INDEX	NAICS	SIC
Fans, except household: Air Purification Equipment—*mfg*	333411	3564
Industrial and Commercial Fan and Blower—*mfg*	333412	3564
Fans, household–electric, except attic fans: Electric Housewares and Household Fan—*mfg*	335211	3634
Heating Equipment (except Electric and Warm Air Furnaces)—*mfg*	333414	3634
Fans, household–kitchen–except attic: Electric Housewares and Household Fan—*mfg*	335211	3634
Heating Equipment (except Electric and Warm Air Furnaces)—*mfg*	333414	3634
Fans, industrial: Industrial Machinery and Equipment—*whlse*	42183	5084
Fare registers–e.g., for streetcars and buses: Measuring and Controlling Device, Other—*mfg*	334519	3829
Surgical and Medical Instrument—*mfg*	339112	3829
Farina, cereal breakfast food: Breakfast Cereal—*mfg*	31123	2043
Coffee and Tea—*mfg*	31192	2043
Farina, except breakfast foed: Flour Milling—*mfg*	311211	2041
Farm and Garden Machinery and Equipment Wholesalers	**42182**	**5083**
Farm building construction, except residential–general contractors: Building, Commercial and Institutional—*const*	23332	1542
Farm buildings, prefabricated or portable–wood: Prefabricated Wood Building—*mfg*	321992	2452
Farm buildings, prefabricated–metal: Prefabricated Metal Building and Component—*mfg*	332311	3448
Farm bureaus: Business Associations—*serv*	81391	8699
Farm elevators: Farm Machinery and Equipment—*mfg*	333111	3523
Farm granges: Business Associations—*serv*	81391	8699
Farm homes, noncommercial: Private Households—*serv*	81411	8811
Farm labor contractors: Farm Labor Contractors and Crew Leaders—*ag*	115115	761
Farm Labor Contractors and Crew Leaders	**115115**	**761**
Farm machinery and equipment: Conveyor and Conveying Equipment—*mfg*	333922	3523
Farm and Garden Machinery and Equipment—*whlse*	42182	5083
Farm Machinery and Equipment—*mfg*	333111	3523
Outdoor Power Equipment Stores—*retail*	44421	5083
Farm Machinery and Equipment Manufacturing	**333111**	**3523**
Farm machinery repair: Machinery and Equipment (except Automotive and Electronic) Repair and Maintenance, Commercial and Industrial—*serv*	81131	7699
Farm Management Services	**115116**	**762**
Farm mortgage companies: International Trade Financing—*fin*	522293	6159
Non-Depository Credit Intermediation, All Other—*fin*	522298	6159
Sales Financing—*fin*	52222	6159
Farm Product Raw Material Wholesalers	**4225**	
Farm Product Raw Material Wholesalers, Other	**42259**	**5159**
Farm Product Warehousing and Storage Facilities	**49313**	**4221**

Entry	NAICS	SIC
Farm product warehousing and storage, other than cold storage: Farm Product Warehousing and Storage Facilities—*trans*	49313	4221
Farm storage tanks, metal plate: Air-Conditioning and Warm Air Heating Equipment and Commercial and Industrial Refrigeration Equipment—*mfg*	333415	3443
Metal Tank (Heavy Gauge)—*mfg*	33242	3443
Plate Work—*mfg*	332313	3443
Power Boiler and Heat Exchanger—*mfg*	33241	3443
Farm supplies: Farm Supplies—*whlse*	42291	5191
Nursery and Garden Centers—*retail*	44422	5191
Farm Supplies Wholesalers	**42291**	**5191**
Farm to market hauling: Freight (except Used Goods) Trucking, Local Specialized—*trans*	48422	4212
General Freight Trucking, Local—*trans*	48411	4212
Farm tractors: Farm Machinery and Equipment—*mfg*	333111	3523
Farm wagons: Farm Machinery and Equipment—*mfg*	333111	3523
Farmers Home Administration: International Trade Financing—*fin*	522293	6111
Non-Depository Credit Intermediation, All Other—*fin*	522298	6111
Secondary Market Financing—*fin*	522294	6111
Farms, residential–noncommercial: Private Households—*serv*	81411	8811
Farriers (blacksmith shops): Animal Production Support Activities—*ag*	11521	7699
Fascia, plastics (siding): Plastics Pipe and Pipe Fitting—*mfg*	326122	3089
Plastics Product, All Other—*mfg*	326199	3089
Unsupported Plastics Profile Shape—*mfg*	326121	3089
Fashion plates, lithographed: Lithographic Printing, Commercial—*mfg*	323110	2752
Quick Printing—*mfg*	323114	2752
Fashion plates, printed–except lithographed or gravure: Digital Printing—*mfg*	323115	2759
Flexographic Printing, Commercial—*mfg*	323112	2759
Printing, Other Commercial—*mfg*	323119	2759
Quick Printing—*mfg*	323114	2759
Fashion plates–gravure printing: Gravure Printing, Commercial—*mfg*	323111	2754
Fashion show model supply service: Employee Leasing Services—*admin*	56133	7363
Temporary Help Services—*admin*	56132	7363
Fast food restaurants: Cafeterias—*accom*	722212	5812
Caterers—*accom*	72232	5812
Foodservice Contractors—*accom*	72231	5812
Full-Service Restaurants—*accom*	72211	5812
Limited-Service Restaurants—*accom*	722211	5812
Snack and Nonalcoholic Beverage Bars—*accom*	722213	5812
Theater Companies and Dinner Theaters—*arts*	71111	5812
Fast food stores (prepared food): Cafeterias—*accom*	722212	5812
Caterers—*accom*	72232	5812
Foodservice Contractors—*accom*	72231	5812
Full-Service Restaurants—*accom*	72211	5812
Limited-Service Restaurants—*accom*	722211	5812
Snack and Nonalcoholic Beverage Bars—*accom*	722213	5812
Theater Companies and Dinner Theaters—*arts*	71111	5812
Fastener, Button, Needle and Pin Manufacturing	**339993**	**3131**
Fasteners, hardware: Hardware—*whlse*	42171	5072
Fasteners–glove, slide, snap, and hook-and-eye: Fastener, Button, Needle and Pin—*mfg*	339993	3965
Fathometers: Search, Detection, Navigation, Guidance, Aeronautical, and Nautical System and Instrument—*mfg*	334511	3812
Fatigue testing machines, industrial–mechanical: Measuring and Controlling Device, Other—*mfg*	334519	3829
Surgical and Medical Instrument—*mfg*	339112	3829
Fats and Oils Refining and Blending	**311225**	**2074**
Fats, sulfonated: Surface Active Agent—*mfg*	325613	2843
Fatty acid esters and amines: Basic Organic Chemical, All Other—*mfg*	325199	2869
Fatty acids–margaric, oleic, and stearic: Basic Organic Chemical, All Other—*mfg*	325199	2899
Chemical Product, All Other Miscellaneous—*mfg*	325998	2899
Faucet handles, vitreous china and earthenware: Vitreous China Plumbing Fixture and China and Earthenware Fittings and Bathroom Accessories—*mfg*	327111	3261
Faucets, metal and plastics: Fabricated Metal Product, All Other Miscellaneous—*mfg*	332999	3432
Plumbing Fixture Fitting and Trim—*mfg*	332913	3432
Faucets, wood: Manufacturing, All Other Miscellaneous—*mfg*	339999	2499
Wood Container and Pallet—*mfg*	32192	2499
Wood Product, All Other Miscellaneous—*mfg*	321999	2499
Feather cleaning and sterilizing machinery: Laundry, Drycleaning and Pressing Machine, Commercial—*mfg*	333312	3582
Feather meal: Fats and Oils Refining and Blending—*mfg*	311225	2077
Fresh and Frozen Seafood Processing—*mfg*	311712	2077
Rendering and Meat By-product Processing—*mfg*	311613	2077
Seafood Canning—*mfg*	311711	2077
Feather-filled clothing: Cut and Sew Apparel, All Other—*mfg*	315299	2329
Men's and Boys' Cut and Sew Apparel Contractors—*mfg*	315211	2329
Men's and Boys' Cut and Sew Other Outerwear—*mfg*	315228	2329
Feather-filled coats, jackets, and vests: Apparel Accessories and Apparel, Other—*mfg*	315999	2339
Cut and Sew Apparel, All Other—*mfg*	315299	2339
Women's and Girls' Cut and Sew Apparel Contractors—*mfg*	315212	2339
Women's and Girls' Cut and Sew Other Outerwear—*mfg*	315238	2339
Feathers: Farm Product Raw Material, Other—*whlse*	42259	5159
Federal credit unions: Credit Unions—*fin*	52213	6061
Federal Crop Insurance Corporation: Direct Property and Casualty Insurance Carriers—*fin*	524126	6331
Insurance Funds, Other—*fin*	52519	6331
Reinsurance Carriers—*fin*	52413	6331
Federal Deposit Insurance Corporation: Direct Insurance (except Life, Health and Medical) Carriers, Other—*fin*	524128	6399

ALPHABETICAL INDEX	NAICS	SIC
Federal Eeserve branches: Monetary Authcrities - Central Bank—*fin*	52111	6011
Federal Home Loan Banks: Financial Transactions Processing, Reserve, and Clearing House Activities—*fin*	52232	6019
Federal Home Loan Mortgage Corporation: International Trade Financing—*fin*	522293	6111
Non-Depository Credit Intermediation, All Other—*fin*	522298	6111
Secondary Market Financing—*fin*	522294	6111
Federal Intermediate Credit Bank: International Trade Financing—*fin*	522293	6111
Non-Depository Credit Intermediation, All Other—*fin*	522298	6111
Secondary Market Financing—*fin*	522294	6111
Federal Land Banks: International Trade Financing—*fin*	522293	6111
Non-Depository Credit Intermediation, All Other—*fin*	522298	6111
Secondary Market Financing—*fin*	522294	6111
Federal National Mortgage Association: International Trade Financing—*fin*	522293	6111
Non-Depository Credit Intermediation, All Other—*fin*	522298	6111
Secondary Market Financing—*fin*	522294	6111
Federal Reserve banks: Monetary Authorities - Central Bank—*fin*	52111	6011
Federal savings and loan associations: Savings Institutions—*fin*	52212	6035
Federal Savings and Loan Insurance Corporation: Direct Insurance (except Life, Health and Medical) Carriers, Other—*fin*	524128	6399
Federal savings banks: Savings Institutions—*fin*	52212	6035
Feed additives, animal: Farm Supplies—*whlse*	42291	5191
Nursery and Garden Centers—*retail*	44422	5191
Feed bags for horses: Leather Good, All Other—*mfg*	316999	3199
Feed concentrates: Animal Food, Other—*mfg*	311119	2048
Feed grinders, crushers, and mixers (agricultural machinery): Farm Machinery and Equipment—*mfg*	333111	3523
Feed grinders-mixers: Farm Machinery and Equipment—*mfg*	333111	3523
Feed mixers, except agricultural machinery: Food Product Machinery—*mfg*	333294	3556
Feed premixes: Animal Food, Other—*mfg*	311119	2048
Feed supplements: Animal Food, Other—*mfg*	311119	2048
Feed, except unmixed grain: Farm Supplies—*whlse*	42291	5191
Nursery and Garden Centers—*retail*	44422	5191
Feed, gluten: Wet Corn Milling—*mfg*	311221	2046
Feeder voltage regulators and boosters (electric transformers): Power, Distribution and Specialty Transformer—*mfg*	335311	3612
Feeders, chicken: Farm Machinery and Equipment—*mfg*	333111	3523
Feeders, ore and aggregate: Mining Machinery and Equipment—*mfg*	333131	3532
Feedlots, cattle: Cattle Feedlots—*ag*	112112	211
Feedlots, hog: Hog and Pig Farming—*ag*	11221	213
Feedlots, lamb: Goat Farming—*ag*	11242	214
Sheep Farming—*ag*	11241	214
Feeds, prepared (including mineral)–for animals and fowls-except dogs and cats: Animal Food, Other—*mfg*	311119	2048

ALPHABETICAL INDEX	NAICS	SIC
Feeds, specialty–mice, guinea pigs, minks, etc.: Animal Food, Other—*mfg*	311119	2048
Feeds, stock–dry: Animal Food, Other—*mfg*	311119	2048
Feldspar mining: Clay and Ceramic and Refractory Minerals—*mining*	212325	1459
Feldspar, ground or otherwise treated: Ground or Treated Mineral and Earth—*mfg*	327992	3295
Fellies, wood: Manufacturing, All Other Miscellaneous—*mfg*	339999	2499
Wood Container and Pallet—*mfg*	32192	2499
Wood Product, All Other Miscellaneous—*mfg*	321999	2499
Felt: Nondurable Goods, Other Miscellaneous—*whlse*	42299	5199
Felt goods, except woven felts and hats–wool, hair, jute, or other fiber: Broadwoven Fabric Mills—*mfg*	31321	2299
Narrow Fabric Mills—*mfg*	313221	2299
Nonwoven Fabric Mills—*mfg*	31323	2299
Textile and Fabric Finishing (except Broadwoven Fabric) Mills—*mfg*	313312	2299
Textile Product Mills, All Other Miscellaneous—*mfg*	314999	2299
Thread Mills—*mfg*	313113	2299
Felt roll roofing, asbestos: Motor Vehicle Brake System—*mfg*	33634	3292
Nonmetallic Mineral Product, All Other Miscellaneous—*mfg*	327999	3292
Felt tip markers: Pen and Mechanical Pencil—*mfg*	339941	3951
Felt, woven amosite–asbestos: Motor Vehicle Brake System—*mfg*	33634	3292
Nonmetallic Mineral Product, All Other Miscellaneous—*mfg*	327999	3292
Felts, building: Newsprint Mills—*mfg*	322122	2621
Paper (except Newsprint) Mills—*mfg*	322121	2621
Felts, pressed or needle loom: Broadwoven Fabric Mills—*mfg*	31321	2299
Narrow Fabric Mills—*mfg*	313221	2299
Nonwoven Fabric Mills—*mfg*	31323	2299
Textile and Fabric Finishing (except Broadwoven Fabric) Mills—*mfg*	313312	2299
Textile Product Mills, All Other Miscellaneous—*mfg*	314999	2299
Thread Mills—*mfg*	313113	2299
Felts, roofing–asphalt saturated and tar-saturated–roll or shingle: Asphalt Shingle and Coating Materials—*mfg*	324122	2952
Felts, tarred: Roofing, Siding and Insulation Material—*whlse*	42133	5033
Felts–wool, mohair, and similar animal fibers–woven: Broadwoven Fabric Finishing Mills—*mfg*	313311	2231
Broadwoven Fabric Mills—*mfg*	31321	2231
Textile and Fabric Finishing (except Broadwoven Fabric) Mills—*mfg*	313312	2231
Fence chargers, electric: Machinery, Other Commercial and Service Industry—*mfg*	333319	3699
Fence construction–contractors: Trade Contractors, All Other Special—*const*	23599	1799
Fence gates posts, and fittings–steel-made in wiredrawing plants: Fabricated Wire Product, Other—*mfg*	332618	3315

Description	NAICS	SIC
Steel Wire Drawing—*mfg*	331222	3315
Fence gates, made from purchased wire: Fabricated Wire Product, Other—*mfg*	332618	3496
Fence posts, iron and steel–made in steel works or rolling mills: Iron and Steel Mills—*mfg*	331111	3312
Petroleum and Coal Productsa, All Other—*mfg*	324199	3312
Fence stretchers (handtools): Hand and Edge Tool—*mfg*	332212	3423
Fences and posts, ornamental iron and steel: Ornamental and Architectural Metal Work—*mfg*	332323	3446
Fencing and accessories, wire: Building Material Dealers, Other—*retail*	44419	5039
Construction Material, Other—*whlse*	42139	5039
Fencing dealers: Building Material Dealers, Other—*retail*	44419	5211
Home Centers—*retail*	44411	5211
Fencing equipment (sporting goods): Sporting and Athletic Goods—*mfg*	33992	3949
Fencing, made from purchased wire: Fabricated Wire Product, Other—*mfg*	332618	3496
Fencing, wood: Building Material Dealers, Other—*retail*	44419	5031
Fencing, wood except rough pickets, poles, and rails: Manufacturing, All Other Miscellaneous—*mfg*	339999	2499
Wood Container and Pallet—*mfg*	32192	2499
Wood Product, All Other Miscellaneous—*mfg*	321999	2499
Fenders, stamped and pressed: Motor Vehicle Metal Stamping—*mfg*	33637	3465
Ferberite mining: Copper Ore and Nickel Ore—*mining*	212234	1061
Metal Ore, All Other—*mining*	212299	1061
Fermenters (process vessels), metal plate: Air-Conditioning and Warm Air Heating Equipment and Commercial and Industrial Refrigeration Equipment—*mfg*	333415	3443
Metal Tank (Heavy Gauge)—*mfg*	33242	3443
Plate Work—*mfg*	332313	3443
Power Boiler and Heat Exchanger—*mfg*	33241	3443
Ferric ammonium oxalate: Basic Organic Chemical, All Other—*mfg*	325199	2869
Ferric chloride: Basic Inorganic Chemical, All Other—*mfg*	325188	2819
Chemical Product, All Other Miscellaneous—*mfg*	325998	2819
Ferric oxide pigments: Carbon Black—*mfg*	325182	2816
Inorganic Dye and Pigment—*mfg*	325131	2816
Ferric oxides, except pigments: Basic Inorganic Chemical, All Other—*mfg*	325188	2819
Chemical Product, All Other Miscellaneous—*mfg*	325998	2819
Ferries operation of: Coastal and Great Lakes Passenger—*trans*	483114	4482
Inland Water Passenger—*trans*	483212	4482
Ferris wheels: Fabricated Metal Product, All Other Miscellaneous—*mfg*	332999	3599
General Purpose Machinery , All Other—*mfg*	333999	3599
Machine Shops—*mfg*	33271	3599
Machinery, Other Commercial and Service Industry—*mfg*	333319	3599
Ferrite: Porcelain Electrical Supply—*mfg*	327113	3264
Ferroalloys: Metal Service Centers and Offices—*whlse*	42151	5051
Ferroalloys (including high percentage): Electrometallurgical Ferroalloy Product—*mfg*	331112	3313
Secondary Smelting, Refining, and Alloying of Nonferrous Metal (except Copper and Aluminum)—*mfg*	331492	3313
Ferrochromium: Electrometallurgical Ferroalloy Product—*mfg*	331112	3313
Secondary Smelting, Refining, and Alloying of Nonferrous Metal (except Copper and Aluminum)—*mfg*	331492	3313
Ferrocyanides: Basic Inorganic Chemical, All Other—*mfg*	325188	2819
Chemical Product, All Other Miscellaneous—*mfg*	325998	2819
Ferromanganese: Electrometallurgical Ferroalloy Product—*mfg*	331112	3313
Secondary Smelting, Refining, and Alloying of Nonferrous Metal (except Copper and Aluminum)—*mfg*	331492	3313
Ferromolybdenum: Electrometallurgical Ferroalloy Product—*mfg*	331112	3313
Secondary Smelting, Refining, and Alloying of Nonferrous Metal (except Copper and Aluminum)—*mfg*	331492	3313
Ferrophosphorus: Electrometallurgical Ferroalloy Product—*mfg*	331112	3313
Secondary Smelting, Refining, and Alloying of Nonferrous Metal (except Copper and Aluminum)—*mfg*	331492	3313
Ferrosilicon: Electrometallurgical Ferroalloy Product—*mfg*	331112	3313
Secondary Smelting, Refining, and Alloying of Nonferrous Metal (except Copper and Aluminum)—*mfg*	331492	3313
Ferrotitanium: Electrometallurgical Ferroalloy Product—*mfg*	331112	3313
Secondary Smelting, Refining, and Alloying of Nonferrous Metal (except Copper and Aluminum)—*mfg*	331492	3313
Ferrotungsten: Electrometallurgical Ferroalloy Product—*mfg*	331112	3313
Secondary Smelting, Refining, and Alloying of Nonferrous Metal (except Copper and Aluminum)—*mfg*	331492	3313
Ferrous and nonferrous mill equipment, auxiliary: Rolling Mill Machinery and Equipment—*mfg*	333516	3547
Ferrous Metal Foundries	**33151**	
Ferrovanadium: Electrometallurgical Ferroalloy Product—*mfg*	331112	3313
Secondary Smelting, Refining, and Alloying of Nonferrous Metal (except Copper and Aluminum)—*mfg*	331492	3313
Ferrules, metal: Fabricated Metal Product, All Other Miscellaneous—*mfg*	332999	3499
Ferryboats, building and repairing: Ship Building and Repairing—*mfg*	336611	3731
Fertilizer (Mixing Only) Manufacturing	**325314**	**2875**
Fertilizer and fertilizer materials: Farm Supplies—*whlse*	42291	5191
Nursery and Garden Centers—*retail*	44422	5191
Fertilizer application for crops: Soil Preparation, Planting, and Cultivating—*ag*	115112	711
Fertilizer Manufacturing	**32531**	
Fertilizer materials–muriate and sulfate of potash, not produced at mines: Basic Inorganic Chemical, All Other—*mfg*	325188	2819
Chemical Product, All Other Miscellaneous—*mfg*	325998	2819
Fertilizers, mixed–made in plants not manufacturing fertilizer materials: Fertilizer (Mixing Only)—*mfg*	325314	2875

ALPHABETICAL INDEX	NAICS	SIC
Fertilizers, mixed–made in plants producing nitrogenous fertilizer materials-mA: Nitrogenous Fertilizer—*mfg*	325311	2873
Fertilizers–natural (organic), except compost: Nitrogenous Fertilizer—*mfg*	325311	2873
Fertilizing machinery, farm: Farm Machinery and Equipment—*mfg*	333111	3523
Fever remedies: Pharmaceutical Preparation—*mfg*	325412	2834
Fiber Can, Tube, Drum, and Similar Products Manufacturing	**322214**	**2655**
Fiber cans and drums: Industrial and Personal Service Paper—*whlse*	42213	5113
Fiber furniture, household: Household Furniture (except Wood and Metal)—*mfg*	337125	2519
Fiber optic cable: Aluminum Rolling and Drawing, Other—*mfg*	331319	3357
Communication and Energy Wire, Other—*mfg*	335929	3357
Copper Wire (except Mechanical) Drawing—*mfg*	331422	3357
Fiber Optic Cable—*mfg*	335921	3357
Nonferrous Metal (except Copper and Aluminum) Rolling, Drawing and Extruding—*mfg*	331491	3357
Fiber Optic Cable Manufacturing	**335921**	**3357**
Fiber optics strands: Pressed and Blown Glass and Glassware, Other—*mfg*	327212	3229
Fiber pulp–made from wood, rags, waste paper, linters, straw, and bagasse: Paper (except Newsprint) Mills—*mfg*	322121	2611
Paperboard Mills—*mfg*	32213	2611
Pulp Mills—*mfg*	32211	2611
Fiber, Yarn, and Thread Mills	**31311**	
Fiber, Yarn, and Thread Mills	**3131**	
Fiberglass fabrics: Broadwoven Fabric Finishing Mills—*mfg*	313311	5131
Broadwoven Fabric Mills—*mfg*	31321	2221
Piece Goods, Notions and Other Dry Goods—*whlse*	42231	5131
Textile and Fabric Finishing (except Broadwoven Fabric) Mills—*mfg*	313312	5131
Fiberglass insulation: Mineral Wool—*mfg*	327993	3296
Fiberglass insulation materials: Roofing, Siding and Insulation Material—*whlse*	42133	5033
Fibers, carbon and graphite: Carbon and Graphite Product—*mfg*	335991	3624
Fibers, cellulose manmade: Cellulosic Organic Fiber—*mfg*	325221	2823
Fibers, glass, textile: Pressed and Blown Glass and Glassware, Other—*mfg*	327212	3229
Fibers, manmade–except cellulosic: Noncellulosic Organic Fiber—*mfg*	325222	2824
Fibers, rayon: Cellulosic Organic Fiber—*mfg*	325221	2823
Fibers, textile–recovery from textile mill waste and rags: Broadwoven Fabric Mills—*mfg*	31321	2299
Narrow Fabric Mills—*mfg*	313221	2299
Nonwoven Fabric Mills—*mfg*	31323	2299
Textile and Fabric Finishing (except Broadwoven Fabric) Mills—*mfg*	313312	2299
Textile Product Mills, All Other Miscellaneous—*mfg*	314999	2299
Thread Mills—*mfg*	313113	2299
Yarn Spinning Mills—*mfg*	313111	2299
Fibers, vegetable: Farm Product Raw Material, Other—*whlse*	42259	5159
Fibers, viscose: Cellulosic Organic Fiber—*mfg*	325221	2823
Fidelity insurance: Direct Property and Casualty Insurance Carriers—*fin*	524126	6351
Reinsurance Carriers—*fin*	52413	6351
Fiduciaries, real estate: Real Estate, Other Activities Related to—*real*	53139	6531
Fiduciary agencies other than real estate or trust: Commodity Contracts Dealing—*fin*	52313	6099
Credit Intermediation, Other Activities Related to—*fin*	52239	6099
Financial Investment Activities, Miscellaneous—*fin*	523999	6099
Financial Transactions Processing, Reserve, and Clearing House Activities—*fin*	52232	6099
Trust, Fiduciary and Custody Activities—*fin*	523991	6099
Field artillery: Ordnance and Accessories, Other—*mfg*	332995	3489
Field jackets, military: Cut and Sew Apparel, All Other—*mfg*	315299	2329
Men's and Boys' Cut and Sew Apparel Contractors—*mfg*	315211	2329
Men's and Boys' Cut and Sew Other Outerwear—*mfg*	315228	2329
Field nurseries–growing of flowers and shrubbery, except forest shrubbery: Floriculture Production—*ag*	111422	181
Nursery and Tree Production—*ag*	111421	181
Field strength and intensity measuring equipment, electrical: Electronic Coil, Transformer, and Other Inductor—*mfg*	334416	3825
Instrument for Measuring and Testing Electricity and Electrical Signals—*mfg*	334515	3825
Field type rotary tillers (agricultural machinery): Farm Machinery and Equipment—*mfg*	333111	3523
Field warehousing, not public warehousing: Business Support Services, All Other—*admin*	561499	7389
Fifth wheels: Motor Vehicle Parts, All Other—*mfg*	336399	3714
Motor Vehicle Steering and Suspension Components (except Spring)—*mfg*	33633	3714
Fig orchards and farms: Fruit and Tree Nut Combination Farming—*ag*	111336	179
Noncitrus Fruit Farming, Other—*ag*	111339	179
Figures (marking devices), metal: Marking Device—*mfg*	339943	3953
Figures, pottery–china, earthenware, and stoneware: Vitreous China, Fine Earthenware and Other Pottery Product—*mfg*	327112	3269
Filaments for electric lamps: Electric Lamp Bulb and Part—*mfg*	33511	3641
Filbert groves and farms: Tree Nut Farming—*ag*	111335	173
Filbert hulling and shelling: Postharvest Crop Activities (except Cotton Ginning)—*ag*	115114	723
File cards: Office Supplies and Stationery Stores—*retail*	45321	5112
Stationary and Office Supplies—*whlse*	42212	5112
File drawer frames–except weed: Nonwood Office Furniture—*mfg*	337214	2522
File folders: Office Supplies and Stationery Stores—*retail*	45321	5112

Description	NAICS	SIC
Stationary and Office Supplies—*whlse*	42212	5112
Files, including recutting and resharpening: Hand and Edge Tool—*mfg*	332212	3423
Files, machine tool: Cutting Tool and Machine Tool Accessory—*mfg*	333515	3545
Hand and Edge Tool—*mfg*	332212	3545
Filing boxes, cabinets, and cases–except wood: Nonwood Office Furniture—*mfg*	337214	2522
Filing boxes, cabinets, and cases–weed: Wood Office Furniture—*mfg*	337211	2521
Filing boxes, paperboard: Setup Paperboard Box—*mfg*	322213	2652
Filing folders: Converted Paper Product, All Other—*mfg*	322298	2675
Die-Cut Paper and Paperboard Office Supplies—*mfg*	322231	2675
Surface-Coated Paperboard—*mfg*	322292	2675
Filing machines, metal (machine tools): Machine Tool (Metal Cutting Types)—*mfg*	333512	3541
Fill dirt pits: Crushed and Broken Stone and Quarrying, Other—*mining*	212319	1499
Non-Metallic Mineral, All Other—*mining*	212399	1499
Fillers and flats, egg case–die-cut from purchased paper or paperboard: Converted Paper Product, All Other—*mfg*	322298	2675
Die-Cut Paper and Paperboard Office Supplies—*mfg*	322231	2675
Surface-Coated Paperboard—*mfg*	322292	2675
Fillers and forms, looseleaf–pen ruled or printed only: Blankbook, Loose-leaf Binder and Device—*mfg*	323118	2782
Flexographic Printing, Commercial—*mfg*	323112	2782
Gravure Printing, Commercial—*mfg*	323111	2782
Lithographic Printing, Commercial—*mfg*	323110	2782
Printing, Other Commercial—*mfg*	323119	2782
Screen Printing, Commercial—*mfg*	323113	2782
Fillers for looseleaf devices, except printed forms: Stationery, Tablet, and Related Product—*mfg*	322233	2678
Fillers, wood–dry, liquid, and paste: Paint and Coating—*mfg*	32551	2851
Fillets, lish: Fresh and Frozen Seafood Processing—*mfg*	311712	2092
Filling pressure containers (aerosol) with hair spray, insecticides, etc.: Packaging and Labeling Services—*admin*	56191	7389
Filling stations, gasoline: Gasoline Stations with Convenience Stores—*retail*	44711	5541
Gasoline Stations, Other—*retail*	44719	5541
Filling, upholstery–textile: Broadwoven Fabric Mills—*mfg*	31321	2299
Narrow Fabric Mills—*mfg*	313221	2299
Nonwoven Fabric Mills—*mfg*	31323	2299
Textile and Fabric Finishing (except Broadwoven Fabric) Mills—*mfg*	313312	2299
Textile Product Mills, All Other Miscellaneous—*mfg*	314999	2299
Thread Mills—*mfg*	313113	2299
Yarn Spinning Mills—*mfg*	313111	2299
Fills, insulating–paper: Coated and Laminated Paper—*mfg*	322222	2679
Converted Paper Product, All Other—*mfg*	322298	2679
Die-Cut Paper and Paperboard Office Supplies—*mfg*	322231	2679
Non-Folding Sanitary Food Container—*mfg*	322215	2679

Description	NAICS	SIC
Film badge service (radiation detection): Testing Laboratories—*prof*	54138	8734
Veterinary Services—*prof*	54194	8734
Film delivery, motion picture: Motion Picture and Video Distribution—*info*	51212	7829
Motion Picture and Video Industries, Other—*info*	512199	7829
Film exchanges, motion picture: Durable Goods, Other Miscellaneous—*whlse*	42199	7822
Motion Picture and Video Distribution—*info*	51212	7822
Film libraries, motion picture: Motion Picture and Video Distribution—*info*	51212	7829
Motion Picture and Video Industries, Other—*info*	512199	7829
Film libraries, stock footage: Independent Artists, Writers, and Performers—*arts*	71151	7819
Motion Picture and Video Industries, Other—*info*	512199	7819
Prerecorded Compact Disc (except Software), Tape, and Record Reproducing—*mfg*	334612	7819
Teleproduction and Other Post-Production Services—*info*	512191	7819
Film processing, except for the motion pic ture industry: One-Hour Photo Finishing—*serv*	812922	7384
Photo Finishing Laboratories (except One-Hour)—*serv*	812921	7384
Film processing, motion picture: Independent Artists, Writers, and Performers—*arts*	71151	7819
Motion Picture and Video Industries, Other—*info*	512199	7819
Prerecorded Compact Disc (except Software), Tape, and Record Reproducing—*mfg*	334612	7819
Teleproduction and Other Post-Production Services—*info*	512191	7819
Film purchasing agencies, motion picture: Motion Picture and Video Distribution—*info*	51212	7829
Motion Picture and Video Industries, Other—*info*	512199	7829
Film strip and slide producers: Graphic Design Services—*prof*	54143	7336
Film, photographic: Photographic Equipment and Supplies—*whlse*	42141	5043
Film, plastics–unsupported: Unsupported Plastics Film and Sheet (except Packaging)—*mfg*	326113	3081
Film, rubber: Fabric Coating Mills—*mfg*	31332	3069
Rubber Product, All Other—*mfg*	326299	3069
Film, sensitized–motion picture, X-ray, still camera, and special purpose: Photographic and Photocopying Equipment—*mfg*	333315	3861
Photographic Film, Paper, Plate and Chemical—*mfg*	325992	3861
Filter cloth, cotton: Broadwoven Fabric Mills—*mfg*	31321	2211
Filter elements, fluid–hydraulic line: General Purpose Machinery , All Other—*mfg*	333999	3569
Filter paper: Newsprint Mills—*mfg*	322122	2621
Paper (except Newsprint) Mills—*mfg*	322121	2621
Filter paper, converted: Coated and Laminated Paper—*mfg*	322222	2679
Converted Paper Product, All Other—*mfg*	322298	2679
Die-Cut Paper and Paperboard Office Supplies—*mfg*	322231	2679
Non-Folding Sanitary Food Container—*mfg*	322215	2679
Filtering clays, treated purchased materials: Ground or Treated Mineral and Earth—*mfg*	327992	3295

ALPHABETICAL INDEX	NAICS	SIC
Filtering media, pottery: Vitreous China, Fine Earthenware and Other Pottery Product—*mfg*	327112	3269
Filters, air–for furnaces and air-conditioning equipment: Pump and Pumping Equipment—*mfg*	333911	3561
Filters, fluid, general line industrial–except internal combustion engine: General Purpose Machinery , All Other—*mfg*	333999	3569
Filters, internal combustion engine–oil, gasoline, air intake, except motor vehicle engine: Fabricated Metal Product, All Other Miscellaneous—*mfg*	332999	3599
General Purpose Machinery , All Other—*mfg*	333999	3599
Machine Shops—*mfg*	33271	3599
Machinery, Other Commercial and Service Industry—*mfg*	333319	3599
Filters, pipeline: General Purpose Machinery , All Other—*mfg*	333999	3569
Filters–oil, fuel, and air-motor vehicle: Automobile—*mfg*	336111	3711
Heavy Duty Truck—*mfg*	33612	3711
Light Truck and Utility Vehicle—*mfg*	336112	3711
Military Armored Vehicle, Tank and Tank Component—*mfg*	336992	3711
Motor Vehicle Body—*mfg*	336211	3711
Filtration sand mining: Industrial Sand—*mining*	212322	1446
Fin assemblies, mortar–more than 30 mm.(or more than 1.18 inch): Ammunition (except Small Arms)—*mfg*	332993	3483
Finance and Insurance	**52**	
Finance leasing of automobiles, trucks and machinery: International Trade Financing—*fin*	522293	6159
Non-Depository Credit Intermediation, All Other—*fin*	522298	6159
Sales Financing—*fin*	52222	6159
Finance leasing of equipment and vehicles: International Trade Financing—*fin*	522293	6159
Non-Depository Credit Intermediation, All Other—*fin*	522298	6159
Sales Financing—*fin*	52222	6159
Financial advice, investment: Investment Advice—*fin*	52393	6282
Portfolio Management—*fin*	52392	6282
Financial Investment Activities, All Other	**52399**	
Financial Investment Activities, Miscellaneous	**523999**	**6211**
Financial Investment Activities, Other	**5239**	
Financial reporting: Financial Investment Activities, Miscellaneous—*fin*	523999	6289
Trust, Fiduciary and Custody Activities—*fin*	523991	6289
Financial responsibility insurance: Direct Property and Casualty Insurance Carriers—*fin*	524126	6351
Reinsurance Carriers—*fin*	52413	6351
Financial Transactions Processing, Reserve, and Clearing House Activities	**52232**	**6099**
Financial Vehicles, Other	**52599**	**6726**
Financing of automobiles, furniture, appliances, personal airplanes, etc.–not engaged in deposit banking: Consumer Lending—*fin*	522291	6141
Credit Card Issuing—*fin*	52221	6141
Sales Financing—*fin*	52222	6141
Financing of dealers by motor vehicle manufacturers' organizations: Financial Transactions Processing, Reserve, and Clearing House Activities—*fin*	52232	6153
Non-Depository Credit Intermediation, All Other—*fin*	522298	6153
Sales Financing—*fin*	52222	6153
Findings, boot and shoe: Fastener, Button, Needle and Pin—*mfg*	339993	3131
Leather Good, All Other—*mfg*	316999	3131
Wood Product, All Other Miscellaneous—*mfg*	321999	3131
Findings, jewelers: Jewelers' Material and Lapidary Work—*mfg*	339913	3915
Findings, shoe repair: Cosmetics, Beauty Supplies and Perfume Stores—*retail*	44612	5087
Service Establishment Equipment and Supplies—*whlse*	42185	5087
Findings, suit and coat–e.g., coat fronts, pockets: Apparel Accessories and Apparel, Other—*mfg*	315999	2396
Textile Product Mills, All Other Miscellaneous—*mfg*	314999	2396
Fine Arts Schools	**61161**	**7911**
Finfish Farming and Fish Hatcheries	**112511**	**921**
Finfish farms: Animal Aquaculture, Other—*ag*	112519	273
Finfish Farming and Fish Hatcheries—*ag*	112511	273
Shellfish Farming—*ag*	112512	273
Finfish Fishing	**114111**	**912**
Finfish, catching of: Finfish Fishing—*ag*	114111	912
Finger cots, rubber: Fabric Coating Mills—*mfg*	31332	3069
Rubber Product, All Other—*mfg*	326299	3069
Fingerprint service: Armored Car Services—*admin*	561613	7381
Investigation Services—*admin*	561611	7381
Security Guards and Patrol Services—*admin*	561612	7381
Finishers and spreaders, construction: Construction Machinery—*mfg*	33312	3531
Overhead Traveling Crane, Hoist and Monorail System—*mfg*	333923	3531
Railroad Rolling Stock—*mfg*	33651	3531
Finishers of tufted carpets and rugs: Carpet and Rug Mills—*mfg*	31411	2273
Finishers, concrete and bituminous–powered: Construction Machinery—*mfg*	33312	3531
Overhead Traveling Crane, Hoist and Monorail System—*mfg*	333923	3531
Railroad Rolling Stock—*mfg*	33651	3531
Finishing agents, textile and leather: Surface Active Agent—*mfg*	325613	2843
Finishing equipment, rolling mill: Rolling Mill Machinery and Equipment—*mfg*	333516	3547
Finishing machinery, textile: Textile Machinery—*mfg*	333292	3552
Finishing metal products and formed products, for the trade: Electroplating, Plating, Polishing, Anodizing and Coloring—*mfg*	332813	3471
Finishing of circular knit fabrics: Textile and Fabric Finishing (except Broadwoven Fabric) Mills—*mfg*	313312	2257
Weft Knit Fabric Mills—*mfg*	313241	2257

Description	NAICS	SIC
Finishing of cotton broadwoven fabrics: Broadwoven Fabric Finishing Mills—*mfg*	313311	2261
Finishing of leather: Leather and Hide Tanning and Finishing—*mfg*	31611	3111
Finishing of manmade fiber and silk broadwoven fabrics: Broadwoven Fabric Finishing Mills—*mfg*	313311	2262
Finishing of raw stock, yarn, and narrow fabrics–except knit and wool: Broadwoven Fabric Finishing Mills—*mfg*	313311	2269
Textile and Fabric Finishing (except Broadwoven Fabric) Mills—*mfg*	313312	2269
Finishing of warp knit fabrics: Knit Fabric and Lace Mills, Other—*mfg*	313249	2258
Textile and Fabric Finishing (except Broadwoven Fabric) Mills—*mfg*	313312	2258
Finishing of wool, mohair, and similar animal fiber fabrics–except knit: Broadwoven Fabric Finishing Mills—*mfg*	313311	2231
Broadwoven Fabric Mills—*mfg*	31321	2231
Textile and Fabric Finishing (except Broadwoven Fabric) Mills—*mfg*	313312	2231
Finishing schools, charm and modeling: Schools and Instruction, All Other Miscellaneous—*educ*	611699	8299
Finishing schools, secondary: Elementary and Secondary Schools—*educ*	61111	8211
Finnan haddie (smoked haddock): Seafood Canning—*mfg*	311711	2091
Fins, aircraft: Aircraft Part and Auxiliary Equipment, Other—*mfg*	336413	3728
Fluid Power Valve and Hose Fitting—*mfg*	332912	3728
Fins, tube–stamped metal: Metal Stamping—*mfg*	332116	3469
Fire alarm apparatus, electric: Communications Equipment, Other—*mfg*	33429	3669
Fire alarm installation–contractors: Electrical Contractors—*const*	23531	1731
Security Systems Services (except Locksmiths)—*admin*	561621	1731
Fire alarm monitoring and maintenance: Security Systems Services (except Locksmiths)—*admin*	561621	7382
Fire clay blocks, bricks, tile, and special shapes: Clay Refractory—*mfg*	327124	3255
Fire clay mining: Clay and Ceramic and Refractory Minerals—*mining*	212325	1459
Fire control (military) equipment repair: Machinery and Equipment (except Automotive and Electronic) Repair and Maintenance, Commercial and Industrial—*serv*	81131	7699
Fire department vehicles (motor vehicles): Automobile—*mfg*	336111	3711
Heavy Duty Truck—*mfg*	33612	3711
Light Truck and Utility Vehicle—*mfg*	336112	3711
Military Armored Vehicle, Tank and Tank Component—*mfg*	336992	3711
Motor Vehicle Body—*mfg*	336211	3711
Fire departments, including volunteer: Fire Protection—*pub*	92216	9224
Fire detection systems, electric: Communications Equipment, Other—*mfg*	33429	3669
Fire detector systems, nonelectric: Measuring and Controlling Device, Other—*mfg*	334519	3829
Surgical and Medical Instrument—*mfg*	339112	3829
Fire doors, metal: Metal Window and Door—*mfg*	332321	3442
Fire escape installation-contractors: Trade Contractors, All Other Special—*const*	23599	1799
Fire escapes, metal: Ornamental and Architectural Metal Work—*mfg*	332323	3446
Fire extinguisher charges: Basic Organic Chemical, All Other—*mfg*	325199	2899
Chemical Product, All Other Miscellaneous—*mfg*	325998	2899
Fire extinguishers: Durable Goods, Other Miscellaneous—*whlse*	42199	5099
Fire extinguishers, portable: Fabricated Metal Product, All Other Miscellaneous—*mfg*	332999	3999
Fire extinguishers, service of: Building Inspection Services—*prof*	54135	7389
Fire hydrant valves: Industrial Valve—*mfg*	332911	3491
Fire Insurance Underwriters' Laboratories: Claims Adjusters—*fin*	524291	6411
Insurance Agencies and Brokerages—*fin*	52421	6411
Insurance Related Activities, All Other—*fin*	524298	6411
Third Party Administration for Insurance and Pension Funds—*fin*	524292	6411
Fire loss appraisal: Claims Adjusters—*fin*	524291	6411
Insurance Agencies and Brokerages—*fin*	52421	6411
Insurance Related Activities, All Other—*fin*	524298	6411
Third Party Administration for Insurance and Pension Funds—*fin*	524292	6411
Fire marshals' offices: Fire Protection—*pub*	92216	9224
Fire prevention offices: Fire Protection—*pub*	92216	9224
Fire prevention, forest: Forestry Support Activities—*ag*	11531	851
Fire Protection	**92216**	**9224**
Fire resistance finishing of cotton broad-woven fabrics: Broadwoven Fabric Finishing Mills—*mfg*	313311	2261
Fire resistance finishing of manmade fiber and silk broadwoven fabrics: Broadwoven Fabric Finishing Mills—*mfg*	313311	2262
Fire retardant chemical preparations: Basic Organic Chemical, All Other—*mfg*	325199	2899
Chemical Product, All Other Miscellaneous—*mfg*	325998	2899
Fire station construction–general contractors: Building, Commercial and Institutional—*const*	23332	1542
Firearms: Sporting Goods Stores—*retail*	45111	5941
Firearms, 30 mm (or 1.18 inch) or less: Small Arms—*mfg*	332994	3484
Firearms, except sporting: Durable Goods, Other Miscellaneous—*whlse*	42199	5099
Firearms, sporting: Sporting and Recreational Goods and Supplies—*whlse*	42191	5091
Fireboats, building and repairing: Ship Building and Repairing—*mfg*	336611	3731
Firebrick, clay: Clay Refractory—*mfg*	327124	3255
Firefighters' dress uniforms, men's: Men's and Boys' Cut and Sew Apparel Contractors—*mfg*	315211	2311
Men's and Boys' Cut and Sew Suit, Coat and Overcoat—*mfg*	315222	2311
Firefighting apparatus, except automotive and chemical: General Purpose Machinery , All Other—*mfg*	333999	3569
Firefighting equipment: Cosmetics, Beauty Supplies and Perfume Stores—*retail*	44612	5087
Service Establishment Equipment and Supplies—*whlse*	42185	5087

ALPHABETICAL INDEX	NAICS	SIC
Firefighting service, other than forestry or public: Business Support Services, All Other—*admin*	561499	7389
Firefighting, forest: Forestry Support Activities—*ag*	11531	851
Firehose, except rubber: General Purpose Machinery , All Other—*mfg*	333999	3569
Firehose, rubber: Rubber and Plastics Hoses and Belting—*mfg*	32622	3052
Fireplace equipment (hardware): Hardware—*mfg*	33251	3429
Fireplace inserts: Heating Equipment (except Electric and Warm Air Furnaces)—*mfg*	333414	3433
Fireplace logs, made from coal: Petroleum and Coal Productsa, All Other—*mfg*	324199	2999
Fireplace screens and accessories: Home Furnishings Stores, All Other—*retail*	442299	5719
Window Treatment Stores—*retail*	442291	5719
Fireplace stores: Home Furnishings Stores, All Other—*retail*	442299	5719
Window Treatment Stores—*retail*	442291	5719
Fireplaces, concrete: Concrete Pipe—*mfg*	327332	3272
Concrete Product, Other—*mfg*	32739	3272
Nonmetallic Mineral Product, All Other Miscellaneous—*mfg*	327999	3272
Fireplaces, prefabricated: Building Material Dealers, Other—*retail*	44419	5074
Plumbing and Heating Equipment and Supplies (Hydronics)—*whlse*	42172	5074
Fireproof flooring construction–contractors: Floor Laying and Other Floor Contractors—*const*	23552	1752
Fireproofing buildings–contractors: Trade Contractors, All Other Special—*const*	23599	1799
Fireproofing tile, clay: Brick and Structural Clay Tile—*mfg*	327121	3251
Firewood: Durable Goods, Other Miscellaneous—*whlse*	42199	5099
Firewood and fuel wood containing fuel binder: Manufacturing, All Other Miscellaneous—*mfg*	339999	2499
Wood Container and Pallet—*mfg*	32192	2499
Wood Product, All Other Miscellaneous—*mfg*	321999	2499
Fireworks: Basic Organic Chemical, All Other—*mfg*	325199	2899
Chemical Product, All Other Miscellaneous—*mfg*	325998	2899
Stores (except Tobacco Stores), All Other Miscellaneous—*retail*	453998	5999
Toy and Hobby Goods and Supplies—*whlse*	42192	5092
Fireworks display service: Amusement and Recreation Industries, All Other—*arts*	71399	7999
Firing china, for the trade: Vitreous China, Fine Earthenware and Other Pottery Product—*mfg*	327112	3269
Firkins and kits, wood–coopered: Wood Container and Pallet—*mfg*	32192	2449
First aid, snake bite, and burn kits: Surgical Appliance and Supplies—*mfg*	339113	3842
Fish and seafood cakes, frozen: Fresh and Frozen Seafood Processing—*mfg*	311712	2092
Fish and seafood cakes–canned: Seafood Canning—*mfg*	311711	2091
Fish and Seafood Markets	**44522**	**5421**

ALPHABETICAL INDEX	NAICS	SIC
Fish and Seafood Wholesalers	**42246**	**5146**
Fish and shellfish processing machinery: Food Product Machinery—*mfg*	333294	3556
Fish and wildlife preservation: Land, Mineral, Wildlife, and Forest Conservation—*pub*	92412	9512
Fish egg bait, canned: Seafood Canning—*mfg*	311711	2091
Fish farms, except hatcheries: Animal Aquaculture, Other—*ag*	112519	273
Finfish Farming and Fish Hatcheries—*ag*	112511	273
Shellfish Farming—*ag*	112512	273
Fish fillets: Fresh and Frozen Seafood Processing—*mfg*	311712	2092
Fish food: Animal Food, Other—*mfg*	311119	2048
Fish hatcheries: Finfish Farming and Fish Hatcheries—*ag*	112511	921
Shellfish Farming—*ag*	112512	921
Fish liver oils, crude: Fats and Oils Refining and Blending—*mfg*	311225	2077
Fresh and Frozen Seafood Processing—*mfg*	311712	2077
Rendering and Meat By-product Processing—*mfg*	311613	2077
Seafood Canning—*mfg*	311711	2077
Fish liver oils, refined and concentrated for medicinal use: Medicinal and Botanical—*mfg*	325411	2833
Fish markets: Direct Selling Establishments, Other—*retail*	45439	5421
Fish and Seafood Markets—*retail*	44522	5421
Meat Markets—*retail*	44521	5421
Fish meal: Fats and Oils Refining and Blending—*mfg*	311225	2077
Fresh and Frozen Seafood Processing—*mfg*	311712	2077
Rendering and Meat By-product Processing—*mfg*	311613	2077
Seafood Canning—*mfg*	311711	2077
Fish nets and seines, made in cordage or twine mills: Rope, Cordage and Twine Mills—*mfg*	314991	2298
Fish oU and fish oil meal: Fats and Oils Refining and Blending—*mfg*	311225	2077
Fresh and Frozen Seafood Processing—*mfg*	311712	2077
Rendering and Meat By-product Processing—*mfg*	311613	2077
Seafood Canning—*mfg*	311711	2077
Fish sticks: Fresh and Frozen Seafood Processing—*mfg*	311712	2092
Fish wire (electrical wiring tool): Noncurrent-Carrying Wiring Device—*mfg*	335932	3644
Fish, canned and cured: Seafood Canning—*mfg*	311711	2091
Fish, cured: Fish and Seafood—*whlse*	42246	5146
Fish, fresh: Fish and Seafood—*whlse*	42246	5146
Fish, frozen–except packaged: Fish and Seafood—*whlse*	42246	5146
Fish, frozen–packaged: Packaged Frozen Food—*whlse*	42242	5142
Fish, tropical: Nondurable Goods, Other Miscellaneous—*whlse*	42299	5199
Fish–cured, dried, pickled, salted, andsmoked: Seafood Canning—*mfg*	311711	2091
Fish–fresh and frozen, prepared: Fresh and Frozen Seafood Processing—*mfg*	311712	2092
Fisheries, finfish: Finfish Fishing—*ag*	114111	912
Fisheries, shellfish: Shellfish Fishing—*ag*	114112	913

Description	NAICS	SIC
Fishing	**11411**	
Fishing	**1141**	
Fishing boats, small: Boat Building—*mfg*	336612	3732
Personal and Household Goods Repair and Maintenance, Other—*serv*	81149	3732
Fishing camps: Recreational and Vacation Camps—*accom*	721214	7032
Fishing equipment: Sporting Goods Stores—*retail*	45111	5941
Fishing for tools, oil and gas field–on a contract basis: Oil and Gas Operations Support Activities—*mining*	213112	1389
Fishing knives: Cutlery and Flatware (except Precious)—*mfg*	332211	3421
Fishing lines, nets, seines–made in cordage or twine mills: Rope, Cordage and Twine Mills—*mfg*	314991	2298
Fishing nets: Textile Product Mills, All Other Miscellaneous—*mfg*	314999	2399
Fishing preserves: Finfish Farming and Fish Hatcheries—*ag*	112511	921
Shellfish Farming—*ag*	112512	921
Fishing tackie (except lines, nets, andseines): Sporting and Athletic Goods—*mfg*	33992	3949
Fishing vessels, large–seiners and trawlers-building and repairing: Ship Building and Repairing—*mfg*	336611	3731
Fishing, Hunting and Trapping	**114**	
Fissionable material production: Basic Inorganic Chemical, All Other—*mfg*	325188	2819
Chemical Product, All Other Miscellaneous—*mfg*	325998	2819
Fitness and Recreational Sports Centers	**71394**	**7997**
Fitness salons: Fitness and Recreational Sports Centers—*arts*	71394	7991
Fittings for pipe, plastics: Plastics Pipe and Pipe Fitting—*mfg*	326122	3089
Plastics Product, All Other—*mfg*	326199	3089
Unsupported Plastics Profile Shape—*mfg*	326121	3089
Fittings, plastics: Plastics Pipe and Pipe Fitting—*mfg*	326122	3089
Plastics Product, All Other—*mfg*	326199	3089
Unsupported Plastics Profile Shape—*mfg*	326121	3089
Fittings, plumbers': Building Material Dealers, Other—*retail*	44419	5074
Plumbing and Heating Equipment and Supplies (Hydronics)—*whlse*	42172	5074
Fittings, soil and pressure pipe–cast iron: Iron Foundries—*mfg*	331511	3321
Fiuoroscopes: Irradiation Apparatus—*mfg*	334517	3844
Fixation appliances, internal: Surgical and Medical Instrument—*mfg*	339112	3841
Fixers, prepared photographic–not made in chemical plants: Photographic and Photocopying Equipment—*mfg*	333315	3861
Photographic Film, Paper, Plate and Chemical—*mfg*	325992	3861
Fixture tops, plastics laminated: Architectural Woodwork and Millwork, Custom—*mfg*	337212	2541
Showcase, Partition, Shelving, and Locker—*mfg*	337215	2541
Wood Kitchen Cabinet and Counter Top—*mfg*	33711	2541
Fixtures, curtain and drapery: Blind and Shade—*mfg*	33792	2591
Fixtures, display–office and store-except wood: Showcase, Partition, Shelving, and Locker—*mfg*	337215	2542
Fixtures, display–office and store-weed: Architectural Woodwork and Millwork, Custom—*mfg*	337212	2541
Showcase, Partition, Shelving, and Locker—*mfg*	337215	2541
Wood Kitchen Cabinet and Counter Top—*mfg*	33711	2541
Fixtures, office and store–except wood: Showcase, Partition, Shelving, and Locker—*mfg*	337215	2542
Fixtures, refrigerated: Refrigeration Equipment and Supplies—*whlse*	42174	5078
Fixtures, store, not refrigerated: Equipment, Other Commercial—*whlse*	42144	5046
Flag shops: Stores (except Tobacco Stores), All Other Miscellaneous—*retail*	453998	5999
Flagging service (traffic control): Business Support Services, All Other—*admin*	561499	7389
Flagpoles, metal: Ornamental and Architectural Metal Work—*mfg*	332323	3446
Flagpoles, weed: Manufacturing, All Other Miscellaneous—*mfg*	339999	2499
Wood Container and Pallet—*mfg*	32192	2499
Wood Product, All Other Miscellaneous—*mfg*	321999	2499
Flags, fabric: Textile Product Mills, All Other Miscellaneous—*mfg*	314999	2399
Flagstone mining: Dimension Stone and Quarrying—*mining*	212311	1411
Flagstones: Cut Stone and Stone Product—*mfg*	327991	3281
Flakeboard: Reconstituted Wood Product—*mfg*	321219	2493
Flakes, metal: Electroplating, Plating, Polishing, Anodizing and Coloring—*mfg*	332813	3399
Iron and Steel Mills—*mfg*	331111	3399
Secondary Smelting and Alloying of Aluminum—*mfg*	331314	3399
Secondary Smelting, Refining, and Alloying of Copper—*mfg*	331423	3399
Secondary Smelting, Refining, and Alloying of Nonferrous Metal (except Copper and Aluminum)—*mfg*	331492	3399
Flame and heat resistant clothing supply service: Industrial Launderers—*serv*	812332	7218
Flame photometers: Analytical Laboratory Instrument—*mfg*	334516	3826
Flame safety controls for furnaces and boilers: Automatic Environmental Control for Residential, Commercial and Appliance Use—*mfg*	334512	3822
Flame throwers (ordnance): Ordnance and Accessories, Other—*mfg*	332995	3489
Flameware, glass and glass ceramic: Pressed and Blown Glass and Glassware, Other—*mfg*	327212	3229
Flange facing machines: Machine Tool (Metal Cutting Types)—*mfg*	333512	3541
Flange units for ball or roller bearings: Ball and Roller Bearing—*mfg*	332991	3562
Flange, valve and pipe fitting forgings, nonferrous–not made in hot-rolling mills: Nonferrous Forging—*mfg*	332112	3463
Flange, valve, and pipe fitting forgings, ferrous–not made in rolling mills: Iron and Steel Forging—*mfg*	332111	3462
Flanges and flange unions, pipe–metal: Fabricated Metal Product, All Other Miscellaneous—*mfg*	332999	3494
Other Metal Valve and Pipe Fitting, Other—*mfg*	332919	3494
Flannel shirts, except work shirts: Men's and Boys' Cut and Sew Apparel Contractors—*mfg*	315211	2321
Men's and Boys' Cut and Sew Shirt (except Work Shirt)—*mfg*	315223	2321
Flannelette: Broadwoven Fabric Mills—*mfg*	31321	2211
Flannels, cotton: Broadwoven Fabric Mills—*mfg*	31321	2211

ALPHABETICAL INDEX	NAICS	SIC
Flannels–wool, mohair, and similar animal fibers: Broadwoven Fabric Finishing Mills—*mfg*	313311	2231
Broadwoven Fabric Mills—*mfg*	31321	2231
Textile and Fabric Finishing (except Broadwoven Fabric) Mills—*mfg*	313312	2231
Flaps, aircraft wing: Aircraft Part and Auxiliary Equipment, Other—*mfg*	336413	3728
Fluid Power Valve and Hose Fitting—*mfg*	332912	3728
Flares: Basic Organic Chemical, All Other—*mfg*	325199	2899
Chemical Product, All Other Miscellaneous—*mfg*	325998	2899
Flasher lights, automobile: Vehicular Lighting Equipment—*mfg*	336321	3647
Flashlight apparatus for photographers, except bulbs: Photographic and Photocopying Equipment—*mfg*	333315	3861
Photographic Film, Paper, Plate and Chemical—*mfg*	325992	3861
Flashlight bombs (pyrotechnics): Basic Organic Chemical, All Other—*mfg*	325199	2899
Chemical Product, All Other Miscellaneous—*mfg*	325998	2899
Flashlight bulhs, photographic: Electric Lamp Bulb and Part—*mfg*	33511	3641
Flashlights: Building Material Dealers, Other—*retail*	44419	5063
Electrical Apparatus and Equipment, Wiring Supplies and Material—*whlse*	42161	5063
Lighting Equipment, Other—*mfg*	335129	3648
Flat bright steel strip, cold-rolled–not made in hot-rolling mills: Cold-Rolled Steel Shape—*mfg*	331221	3316
Flat crepes: Broadwoven Fabric Mills—*mfg*	31321	2221
Flat Glass Manufacturing	**327211**	**3211**
Flat panels, plastics: Plastics Pipe and Pipe Fitting—*mfg*	326122	3089
Plastics Product, All Other—*mfg*	326199	3089
Unsupported Plastics Profile Shape—*mfg*	326121	3089
Flat springs, sheet or strip stock: Steel Spring (except Wire)—*mfg*	332611	3493
Flats, iron and steel–made in steel works or hot-rolling mills: Iron and Steel Mills—*mfg*	331111	3312
Petroleum and Coal Productsa, All Other—*mfg*	324199	3312
Flats, wood–greenhouse: Wood Container and Pallet—*mfg*	32192	2441
Flatware, table–with metal handles and blades: Cutlery and Flatware (except Precious)—*mfg*	332211	3914
Silverware and Plated Ware—*mfg*	339912	3914
Flavored milk drinks: Fluid Milk—*mfg*	311511	2026
Flavoring concentrates: Flavoring Syrup and Concentrate—*mfg*	31193	2087
Food, All Other Miscellaneous—*mfg*	311999	2087
Spice and Extract—*mfg*	311942	2087
Flavoring extract, except for fountain use: Grocery and Related Products, Other—*whlse*	42249	5149
Flavoring extracts, pastes, powders, and syrups: Flavoring Syrup and Concentrate—*mfg*	31193	2087
Food, All Other Miscellaneous—*mfg*	311999	2087
Spice and Extract—*mfg*	311942	2087
Flavoring Syrup and Concentrate Manufacturing	**31193**	**2087**
Flavors and flavoring materials, synthetic: Basic Organic Chemical, All Other—*mfg*	325199	2869
Flax decorticating and retting: Postharvest Crop Activities (except Cotton Ginning)—*ag*	115114	723
Flax yarns and roving: Broadwoven Fabric Mills—*mfg*	31321	2299
Narrow Fabric Mills—*mfg*	313221	2299
Nonwoven Fabric Mills—*mfg*	31323	2299
Textile and Fabric Finishing (except Broadwoven Fabric) Mills—*mfg*	313312	2299
Textile Product Mills, All Other Miscellaneous—*mfg*	314999	2299
Thread Mills—*mfg*	313113	2299
Yarn Spinning Mills—*mfg*	313111	2299
Flaxseed farms: Grain Farming, All Other—*ag*	111199	119
Fleshers, leather (flesh side of split leather): Leather and Hide Tanning and Finishing—*mfg*	31611	3111
Flexible shaft metalworking machines, portable: Power-Driven Hand Tool—*mfg*	333991	3546
Flexographic ink: Printing Ink—*mfg*	32591	2893
Flexographic plates, preparation of: Prepress Services—*mfg*	323122	2796
Flexographic Printing, Commercial	**323112**	**2771**
Flies, artificial–for fishing: Sporting and Athletic Goods—*mfg*	33992	3949
Flight instruments, aeronautical: Search, Detection, Navigation, Guidance, Aeronautical, and Nautical System and Instrument—*mfg*	334511	3812
Flight simulators (training aids), electronic: Electrical Equipment and Component, All Other Miscellaneous—*mfg*	335999	3699
Machinery, Other Commercial and Service Industry—*mfg*	333319	3699
Flight Training	**611512**	**8299**
Flint clay mining: Clay and Ceramic and Refractory Minerals—*mining*	212325	1459
Flint, ground or otherwise treated: Ground or Treated Mineral and Earth—*mfg*	327992	3295
Flitches (veneer stock), made in sawmills: Cut Stock, Resawing Lumber, and Planing—*mfg*	321912	2421
Millwork (including Flooring), Other—*mfg*	321918	2421
Sawmills—*mfg*	321113	2421
Wood Product, All Other Miscellaneous—*mfg*	321999	2421
Float controls, residential and commercial types: Automatic Environmental Control for Residential, Commercial and Appliance Use—*mfg*	334512	3822
Float glass: Flat Glass—*mfg*	327211	3211
Floaters, glasshouse–clay: Clay Refractory—*mfg*	327124	3255
Floating covers, metal plate: Air-Conditioning and Warm Air Heating Equipment and Commercial and Industrial Refrigeration Equipment—*mfg*	333415	3443
Metal Tank (Heavy Gauge)—*mfg*	33242	3443

Plate Work—*mfg*	332313	3443
Power Boiler and Heat Exchanger—*mfg*	33241	3443
Floats for fish lines: Sporting and Athletic Goods—*mfg*	33992	3949
Floats, decoration of: Design Services, Other Specialized—*prof*	54149	7389
Flock (recovered textile fibers): Broadwoven Fabric Mills—*mfg*	31321	2299
Narrow Fabric Mills—*mfg*	313221	2299
Nonwoven Fabric Mills—*mfg*	31323	2299
Textile and Fabric Finishing (except Broadwoven Fabric) Mills—*mfg*	313312	2299
Textile Product Mills, All Other Miscellaneous—*mfg*	314999	2299
Thread Mills—*mfg*	313113	2299
Yarn Spinning Mills—*mfg*	313111	2299
Flock printing of cotton broadwoven fabrics: Broadwoven Fabric Finishing Mills—*mfg*	313311	2261
Flock printing of manmade fiber and silk broadwoven fabrics: Broadwoven Fabric Finishing Mills—*mfg*	313311	2262
Flock printing of narrow fabrics, except wool: Broadwoven Fabric Finishing Mills—*mfg*	313311	2269
Textile and Fabric Finishing (except Broadwoven Fabric) Mills—*mfg*	313312	2269
Flocking metal products for the trade: Fabricated Metal Product, All Other Miscellaneous—*mfg*	332999	3999
Flocking of cotton broadwoven fabrics: Broadwoven Fabric Finishing Mills—*mfg*	313311	2261
Flocking of manmade fiber and silk broad-woven fabrics: Broadwoven Fabric Finishing Mills—*mfg*	313311	2262
Flood control project construction–general contractors: Heavy, All Other—*const*	23499	1629
Industrial Nonbuilding Structure—*const*	23493	1629
Floodlights: Lighting Equipment, Other—*mfg*	335129	3648
Floor arch tile, clay: Brick and Structural Clay Tile—*mfg*	327121	3251
Floor baseboards, wood: Millwork (including Flooring), Other—*mfg*	321918	2431
Wood Window and Door—*mfg*	321911	2431
Floor composition, magnesite: Gypsum and Gypsum Product—*mfg*	32742	3299
Nonmetallic Mineral Product, All Other Miscellaneous—*mfg*	327999	3299
Floor composition, mastic–hot and cold: Asphalt Paving Mixture and Block—*mfg*	324121	2951
Floor Covering Stores	**44221**	**5713**
Floor coverings: Floor Covering Stores—*retail*	44221	5023
Floor coverings, asphalted-felt-base (linoleum): Resilient Floor Covering—*mfg*	326192	3996
Floor coverings, plastics: Plastics Pipe and Pipe Fitting—*mfg*	326122	3089
Plastics Product, All Other—*mfg*	326199	3089
Unsupported Plastics Profile Shape—*mfg*	326121	3089
Floor coverings, textile fiber: Carpet and Rug Mills—*mfg*	31411	2273
Floor coverings, tufted: Carpet and Rug Mills—*mfg*	31411	2273
Floor coverings–twisted paper, grass, rood, coir, sisal, jute, and rag: Carpet and Rug Mills—*mfg*	31411	2273
Floor fans, electric: Electric Housewares and Household Fan—*mfg*	335211	3634
Heating Equipment (except Electric and Warm Air Furnaces)—*mfg*	333414	3634
Floor filler tiles, concrete: Concrete Pipe—*mfg*	327332	3272
Concrete Product, Other—*mfg*	32739	3272
Nonmetallic Mineral Product, All Other Miscellaneous—*mfg*	327999	3272
Floor jacks, metal: Fabricated Structural Metal—*mfg*	332312	3441
Floor lamps: Residential Electric Lighting Fixture—*mfg*	335121	3645
Floor Laying and Other Floor Contractors	**23552**	**1752**
Floor laying, scraping, finishing, and refinishing–contractors: Floor Laying and Other Floor Contractors—*const*	23552	1752
Floor mops: Broom, Brush and Mop—*mfg*	339994	2392
Household Textile Product Mills, Other—*mfg*	314129	2392
Floor posts, adjustable–metal: Fabricated Structural Metal—*mfg*	332312	3441
Floor sanding, washing, and polishing machines–commercial type: Machinery, Other Commercial and Service Industry—*mfg*	333319	3589
Floor slabs, precast concrete: Concrete Pipe—*mfg*	327332	3272
Concrete Product, Other—*mfg*	32739	3272
Nonmetallic Mineral Product, All Other Miscellaneous—*mfg*	327999	3272
Floor tile stores: Floor Covering Stores—*retail*	44221	5713
Floor tile, asphalt: Motor Vehicle Brake System—*mfg*	33634	3292
Nonmetallic Mineral Product, All Other Miscellaneous—*mfg*	327999	3292
Floor tile, ceramic: Ceramic Wall and Floor Tile—*mfg*	327122	3253
Floor tile, precast terrazzo: Concrete Pipe—*mfg*	327332	3272
Concrete Product, Other—*mfg*	32739	3272
Nonmetallic Mineral Product, All Other Miscellaneous—*mfg*	327999	3272
Floor tile, stamped metal: Metal Stamping—*mfg*	332116	3469
Floor traders, commodity contract: Commodity Brokerage—*fin*	52314	6221
Commodity Contracts Dealing—*fin*	52313	6221
Floor traders, security: Financial Investment Activities, Miscellaneous—*fin*	523999	6211
Intermediation, Miscellaneous—*fin*	52391	6211
Investment Banking and Securities Dealing—*fin*	52311	6211
Securities Brokerage—*fin*	52312	6211
Floor wax emulsion: Polish and Other Sanitation Good—*mfg*	325612	2842
Floor waxers and polishers, household–electric: Major Household Appliance, Other—*mfg*	335228	3639
Floor waxes: Polish and Other Sanitation Good—*mfg*	325612	2842
Floor waxing service: Janitorial Services—*admin*	56172	7349
Flooring (dressed lumber), softwood: Cut Stock, Resawing Lumber, and Planing—*mfg*	321912	2421
Millwork (including Flooring), Other—*mfg*	321918	2421
Sawmills—*mfg*	321113	2421
Wood Product, All Other Miscellaneous—*mfg*	321999	2421
Flooring brick, clay: Brick and Structural Clay Tile—*mfg*	327121	3251
Flooring, cellular steel: Metal Container, Other—*mfg*	332439	3444
Sheet Metal Work—*mfg*	332322	3444
Flooring, hardwood: Cut Stock, Resawing Lumber, and Planing—*mfg*	321912	2426
Millwork (including Flooring), Other—*mfg*	321918	2426

ALPHABETICAL INDEX	NAICS	SIC
Showcase, Partition, Shelving, and Locker—*mfg*	337215	2426
Wood Product, All Other Miscellaneous—*mfg*	321999	2426
Flooring, open steel (grating): Ornamental and Architectural Metal Work—*mfg*	332323	3446
Flooring, rubber–tile or sheet: Fabric Coating Mills—*mfg*	31332	3069
Resilient Floor Covering—*mfg*	326192	3069
Rubber Product, All Other—*mfg*	326299	3069
Flooring, wood: Building Material Dealers, Other—*retail*	44419	5211
Home Centers—*retail*	44411	5211
Flooring, wood block–treated: Wood Preservation—*mfg*	321114	2491
Flooring, wood–contractors: Floor Laying and Other Floor Contractors—*const*	23552	1752
Floors, prefabricated–wood: Prefabricated Wood Building—*mfg*	321992	2452
Floriculture Production	**111422**	**181**
Florists	**4531**	
Florists	**45311**	**5992**
Flower, Nursery Stock and Florists' Supplies—*whlse*	42293	5193
Nursery and Garden Centers—*retail*	44422	5193
Florists' articles, red earthenware: Vitreous China, Fine Earthenware and Other Pottery Product—*mfg*	327112	3269
Florists' designs, made from purchased wire: Fabricated Wire Product, Other—*mfg*	332618	3496
Florists' greens, cultivated–growing of: Floriculture Production—*ag*	111422	181
Nursery and Tree Production—*ag*	111421	181
Flotation companies, security: Financial Investment Activities, Miscellaneous—*fin*	523999	6211
Intermediation, Miscellaneous—*fin*	52391	6211
Investment Banking and Securities Dealing—*fin*	52311	6211
Securities Brokerage—*fin*	52312	6211
Flotation machinery (mining machinery): Mining Machinery and Equipment—*mfg*	333131	3532
Flouncings, lace: Knit Fabric and Lace Mills, Other—*mfg*	313249	2258
Textile and Fabric Finishing (except Broadwoven Fabric) Mills—*mfg*	313312	2258
Flour: Grocery and Related Products, Other—*whlse*	42249	5149
Flour bags, except fabric: Plastics, Foil, and Coated Paper Bag—*mfg*	322223	2673
Unsupported Plastics Bag—*mfg*	326111	2673
Flour bass, fabric: Textile Bag Mills—*mfg*	314911	2393
Flour mill machinery: Food Product Machinery—*mfg*	333294	3556
Flour Milling	**311211**	**2041**
Flour Milling and Malt Manufacturing	**31121**	
Flour mills, cercals–except rice: Flour Milling—*mfg*	311211	2041
Flour mixes: Flour Milling—*mfg*	311211	2041
Flour Mixes and Dough Manufacturing from Purchased Flour	**311822**	**2045**
Flour, rice: Rice Milling—*mfg*	311212	2044
Flour, wood: Manufacturing, All Other Miscellaneous—*mfg*	339999	2499
Wood Container and Pallet—*mfg*	32192	2499

ALPHABETICAL INDEX	NAICS	SIC
Wood Product, All Other Miscellaneous—*mfg*	321999	2499
Flour–blended or self-rising: Flour Mixes and Dough from Purchased Flour—*mfg*	311822	2045
Flour–blended, prepared, or self-rising: Flour Milling—*mfg*	311211	2041
Flour–buckwheat, corn, graham, rye, and wheat: Flour Milling—*mfg*	311211	2041
Flow actuated electrical switches: Relay and Industrial Control—*mfg*	335314	3625
Flow instruments, industrial proess type: Instruments and Related Products for Measuring, Displaying, and Controlling Industrial Process Variables—*mfg*	334513	3823
Flower and field bulbs: Farm Supplies—*whlse*	42291	5191
Nursery and Garden Centers—*retail*	44422	5191
Flower boxes, plaster of paris–factory production only: Gypsum and Gypsum Product—*mfg*	32742	3299
Nonmetallic Mineral Product, All Other Miscellaneous—*mfg*	327999	3299
Flower bulbs: Nursery and Garden Centers—*retail*	44422	5261
Outdoor Power Equipment Stores—*retail*	44421	5261
Stores (except Tobacco Stores), All Other Miscellaneous—*retail*	453998	5261
Flower pots, plastics: Plastics Pipe and Pipe Fitting—*mfg*	326122	3089
Plastics Product, All Other—*mfg*	326199	3089
Unsupported Plastics Profile Shape—*mfg*	326121	3089
Flower pots, red earthenware: Vitreous China, Fine Earthenware and Other Pottery Product—*mfg*	327112	3269
Flower, Nursery Stock and Florists' Supplies Wholesalers	**42293**	**5193**
Flowers and florists' supplies: Flower, Nursery Stock and Florists' Supplies—*whlse*	42293	5193
Nursery and Garden Centers—*retail*	44422	5193
Flowers, artificial: Flower, Nursery Stock and Florists' Supplies—*whlse*	42293	5193
Nursery and Garden Centers—*retail*	44422	5193
Stores (except Tobacco Stores), All Other Miscellaneous—*retail*	453998	5999
Flowers, artificial, except glass: Plastics Product, All Other—*mfg*	326199	3999
Flowers, foliage, fruits and vines–artificial glass-made from purchased glass: Glass Product Made of Purchased Glass—*mfg*	327215	3231
Flowers, fresh: Florists—*retail*	45311	5992
Flower, Nursery Stock and Florists' Supplies—*whlse*	42293	5193
Nursery and Garden Centers—*retail*	44422	5193
Flowers, growing of: Floriculture Production—*ag*	111422	181
Nursery and Tree Production—*ag*	111421	181
Flowers, made from purchased glass: Glass Product Made of Purchased Glass—*mfg*	327215	3231
Flue lining, clay: Structural Clay Product, Other—*mfg*	327123	3259
Flues, stove and furnace–sheet metal: Metal Container, Other—*mfg*	332439	3444
Sheet Metal Work—*mfg*	332322	3444
Fluid Milk Manufacturing	**311511**	**2026**
Fluid milk shipping containers, metal: Metal Container, Other—*mfg*	332439	3412

Description	NAICS	SIC
Fluid power actuators, hydraulic and pneumatic: Fluid Power Cylinder and Actuator—*mfg*	333995	3593
Fluid Power Cylinder and Actuator Manufacturing	**333995**	**3593**
Fluid power cylinders, hydraulic and pneumatic: Fluid Power Cylinder and Actuator—*mfg*	333995	3593
Fluid power motors: Fluid Power Cylinder and Actuator—*mfg*	333995	3593
Fluid Power Pump and Motor Manufacturing	**333996**	**3594**
Fluid power pumps and motors: Fluid Power Pump and Motor—*mfg*	333996	3594
Fluid Power Valve and Hose Fitting Manufacturing	**332912**	**3728**
Fluid power valves and fittings: Fluid Power Valve and Hose Fitting—*mfg*	332912	3492
Fluidic devices, circuits, and systems forprocess control: Instruments and Related Products for Measuring, Displaying, and Controlling Industrial Process Variables—*mfg*	334513	3823
Fluidifier (retarder) for concrete: Basic Organic Chemical, All Other—*mfg*	325199	2899
Chemical Product, All Other Miscellaneous—*mfg*	325998	2899
Flumes, metal plate: Air-Conditioning and Warm Air Heating Equipment and Commercial and Industrial Refrigeration Equipment—*mfg*	333415	3443
Metal Tank (Heavy Gauge)—*mfg*	33242	3443
Plate Work—*mfg*	332313	3443
Power Boiler and Heat Exchanger—*mfg*	33241	3443
Flumes, sheet metal: Metal Container, Other—*mfg*	332439	3444
Sheet Metal Work—*mfg*	332322	3444
Fluorescent ballasts (transformers): Power, Distribution and Specialty Transformer—*mfg*	335311	3612
Fluorescent inspection oil: Basic Organic Chemical, All Other—*mfg*	325199	2899
Chemical Product, All Other Miscellaneous—*mfg*	325998	2899
Fluorescent lamp electrodes, cold cathode: Electric Lamp Bulb and Part—*mfg*	33511	3641
Fluorescent lamps, electric: Electric Lamp Bulb and Part—*mfg*	33511	3641
Fluorescent lighting fixtures, commercial: Electric Lighting Fixture, Commercial, Industrial and Institutional—*mfg*	335122	3646
Fluorescent lighting fixtures, residential: Residential Electric Lighting Fixture—*mfg*	335121	3645
Fluorescent lighting transformers: Power, Distribution and Specialty Transformer—*mfg*	335311	3612
Fluorescent starters: Current-Carrying Wiring Device—*mfg*	335931	3643
Fluorinated hydrocarbon gaees: Basic Organic Chemical, All Other—*mfg*	325199	2869
Fluorine, elemental: Basic Inorganic Chemical, All Other—*mfg*	325188	2819
Chemical Product, All Other Miscellaneous—*mfg*	325998	2819
Fluorite mining: Chemical and Fertilizer Mineral, Other—*mining*	212393	1479
Fluoro rubbers: Synthetic Rubber—*mfg*	325212	2822
Fluorocarbon derivative rubbers: Synthetic Rubber—*mfg*	325212	2822
Fluorocarbon fibers: Noncellulosic Organic Fiber—*mfg*	325222	2824
Fluorohydrocarbon resins: Plastics Material and Resin—*mfg*	325211	2821
Fluoroscopic X-ray apparatus and tubes: Irradiation Apparatus—*mfg*	334517	3844
Fluorspar mining: Chemical and Fertilizer Mineral, Other—*mining*	212393	1479
Fluorspar, ground or otherwise treated: Chemical and Fertilizer Mineral, Other—*mining*	212393	1479
Flush tanks, metal: Enameled Iron and Metal Sanitary Ware—*mfg*	332998	3431
Flush tanks, plastics: Plastics Plumbing Fixture—*mfg*	326191	3088
Flush tanks, vitreous china: Vitreous China Plumbing Fixture and China and Earthenware Fittings and Bathroom Accessories—*mfg*	327111	3261
Flush valves: Fabricated Metal Product, All Other Miscellaneous—*mfg*	332999	3432
Plumbing Fixture Fitting and Trim—*mfg*	332913	3432
Flushers, street (motor vehicles): Automobile—*mfg*	336111	3711
Heavy Duty Truck—*mfg*	33612	3711
Light Truck and Utility Vehicle—*mfg*	336112	3711
Military Armored Vehicle, Tank and Tank Component—*mfg*	336992	3711
Motor Vehicle Body—*mfg*	336211	3711
Flutes and parts: Musical Instrument—*mfg*	339992	3931
Fluxes–brazing, soldering, galvanising, and welding: Basic Organic Chemical, All Other—*mfg*	325199	2899
Chemical Product, All Other Miscellaneous—*mfg*	325998	2899
Fly nets (11arness): Leather Good, All Other—*mfg*	316999	3199
Fly screening, made from purchased wire: Fabricated Wire Product, Other—*mfg*	332618	3496
Fly sprays: Pesticide and Other Agricultural Chemical—*mfg*	32532	2879
Fly swatters: Fabricated Metal Product, All Other Miscellaneous—*mfg*	332999	3999
Plastics Product, All Other—*mfg*	326199	3999
Flyback transformers: Electronic Coil, Transformer, and Other Inductor—*mfg*	334416	3677
Flying charter services: Ambulance Services—*hlth*	62191	4522
Nonscheduled Chartered Freight Air—*trans*	481212	4522
Nonscheduled Chartered Passenger Air—*trans*	481211	4522
Scenic and Sightseeing, Other—*trans*	48799	4522
Flying fields maintained by aviation clubs: Amusement and Recreation Industries, All Other—*arts*	71399	7997
Flying fields, except those maintained by aviation clubs: Airport Operations, Other—*trans*	488119	4581
Flying instruction: Flight Training—*educ*	611512	8299
Flypaper: Coated and Laminated Paper—*mfg*	322222	2672
Flytraps, electrical: Electrical Equipment and Component, All Other Miscellaneous—*mfg*	335999	3699
FM and AM tuners: Audio and Video Equipment—*mfg*	33431	3651
Foam charge mixtures: Basic Organic Chemical, All Other—*mfg*	325199	2899
Chemical Product, All Other Miscellaneous—*mfg*	325998	2899
Foam rubber: Fabric Coating Mills—*mfg*	31332	3069
Nondurable Goods, Other Miscellaneous—*whlse*	42299	5199
Resilient Floor Covering—*mfg*	326192	3069
Rubber Product, All Other—*mfg*	326299	3069
Foamed plastics products: Polystyrene Foam Product—*mfg*	32614	3086

ALPHABETICAL INDEX	NAICS	SIC
Urethane and Other Foam Product (except Polystyrene)—*mfg*	32615	3086
Fog lights, motor vehicle: Vehicular Lighting Equipment—*mfg*	336321	3647
Foil board: Coated and Laminated Paper—*mfg*	322222	2679
Converted Paper Product, All Other—*mfg*	322298	2679
Die-Cut Paper and Paperboard Office Supplies—*mfg*	322231	2679
Non-Folding Sanitary Food Container—*mfg*	322215	2679
Foil containers for bakery goods and frozen foods, except bags and liners: Fabricated Metal Product, All Other Miscellaneous—*mfg*	332999	3497
Laminated Aluminum Foil for Flexible Packaging Uses—*mfg*	322225	3497
Foil, except aluminum–not made in rolling mills: Fabricated Metal Product, All Other Miscellaneous—*mfg*	332999	3497
Laminated Aluminum Foil for Flexible Packaging Uses—*mfg*	322225	3497
Foil, laminated to paper or other materials: Fabricated Metal Product, All Other Miscellaneous—*mfg*	332999	3497
Laminated Aluminum Foil for Flexible Packaging Uses—*mfg*	322225	3497
Foil, plain aluminum: Aluminum Sheet, Plate and Foil—*mfg*	331315	3353
Folding and refolding service–textiles and apparel: Business Support Services, All Other—*admin*	561499	7389
Folding boxboards: Paperboard Mills—*mfg*	32213	2631
Folding cartons, except milk cartons–paperboard: Folding Paperboard Box—*mfg*	322212	2657
Folding door installation-contractors: Carpentry Contractors—*const*	23551	1751
Folding doors–plastic or plastic coated fabric, metal frame: Plastics Pipe and Pipe Fitting—*mfg*	326122	3089
Plastics Product, All Other—*mfg*	326199	3089
Unsupported Plastics Profile Shape—*mfg*	326121	3089
Folding machines, paper–except office machines: Paper Industry Machinery—*mfg*	333291	3554
Folding Paperboard Box Manufacturing	**322212**	**2657**
Folding paperboard boxes: Industrial and Personal Service Paper—*whlse*	42213	5113
Foliage, artificial and preserved–except glass: Plastics Product, All Other—*mfg*	326199	3999
Foliage, growing of: Floriculture Production—*ag*	111422	181
Nursery and Tree Production—*ag*	111421	181
Foliage, made from purchased glass: Glass Product Made of Purchased Glass—*mfg*	327215	3231
Food (Health) Supplement Stores	**446191**	**5499**
Food additives, chemical: Chemical and Allied Products, Other—*whlse*	42269	5169
Food and Beverage Stores	**445**	
Food and freezer plans, meat: Direct Selling Establishments, Other—*retail*	45439	5421
Fish and Seafood Markets—*retail*	44522	5421
Meat Markets—*retail*	44521	5421
Food brokers, general line: General Line Grocery—*whlse*	42241	5141
Food casings, plastics: Plastics Pipe and Pipe Fitting—*mfg*	326122	3089
Plastics Product, All Other—*mfg*	326199	3089
Unsupported Plastics Profile Shape—*mfg*	326121	3089
Food choppers, grinders, mixers, and slicers–commercial type: Food Product Machinery—*mfg*	333294	3556
Food colorings, except synthetic: Flavoring Syrup and Concentrate—*mfg*	31193	2087
Food, All Other Miscellaneous—*mfg*	311999	2087
Spice and Extract—*mfg*	311942	2087
Food containers, metal: Metal Can—*mfg*	332431	3411
Food containers, nonfolding paperboard, sanitary: Non-Folding Sanitary Food Container—*mfg*	322215	2656
Food containers, sanitary–except folding: Non-Folding Sanitary Food Container—*mfg*	322215	2656
Food contamination testing and screening kits: Basic Organic Chemical, All Other—*mfg*	325199	2899
Chemical Product, All Other Miscellaneous—*mfg*	325998	2899
Food Crops Grown Under Cover	**11141**	
Food Crops Grown Under Cover, Other	**111419**	**182**
Food dyes and colors, synthetic: Organic Dye and Pigment—*mfg*	325132	2865
Petrochemical—*mfg*	32511	2865
Food glace, for glazing foods: Flavoring Syrup and Concentrate—*mfg*	31193	2087
Food, All Other Miscellaneous—*mfg*	311999	2087
Spice and Extract—*mfg*	311942	2087
Food inspection agencies: Agricultural Marketing and Commodities, Regulation of—*pub*	92614	9641
Food lockers, rental: Refrigerated Warehousing and Storage Facilities—*trans*	49312	4222
Food Manufacturing	**311**	
Food Manufacturing, All Other	**31199**	
Food Manufacturing, All Other Miscellaneous	**311999**	**2032**
Food Manufacturing, Other	**3119**	
Food markets: Convenience Stores—*retail*	44512	5411
Gasoline Stations with Convenience Stores—*retail*	44711	5411
Supermarkets and Other Grocery (except Convenience) Stores—*retail*	44511	5411
Warehouse Clubs and Superstores—*retail*	45291	5411
Food mixers, household–electric: Electric Housewares and Household Fan—*mfg*	335211	3634
Heating Equipment (except Electric and Warm Air Furnaces)—*mfg*	333414	3634
Food Product Machinery Manufacturing	**333294**	**3556**
Food product manufacturing machinery: Industrial Machinery and Equipment—*whlse*	42183	5084
Food products manufacturing or packing plant construction–general contractors: Building, Commercial and Institutional—*const*	23332	1541

Manufacturing and Industrial Building—*const*	23331	1541
Food research, commercial: Research and Development in the Life Sciences—*prof*	54172	8731
Research and Development in the Physical Sciences and Engineering Sciences—*prof*	54171	8731
Food service, institutional: Cafeterias—*accom*	722212	5812
Caterers—*accom*	72232	5812
Foodservice Contractors—*accom*	72231	5812
Full-Service Restaurants—*accom*	72211	5812
Limited-Service Restaurants—*accom*	722211	5812
Snack and Nonalcoholic Beverage Bars—*accom*	722213	5812
Theater Companies and Dinner Theaters—*arts*	71111	5812
Food service, mobile: Direct Selling Establishments, Other—*retail*	45439	5963
Mobile Foodservices—*accom*	72233	5963
Food specialties, canned: Canning, Specialty—*mfg*	311422	2032
Food, All Other Miscellaneous—*mfg*	311999	2032
Food Stores, All Other Specialty	**445299**	**5451**
Food Stores, Other Specialty	**44529**	
Food Stores, Specialty	**4452**	
Food testing services: Testing Laboratories—*prof*	54138	8734
Veterinary Services—*prof*	54194	8734
Food trucks, restaurant: Institutional Furniture—*mfg*	337127	2599
Food wagons, restaurant: Institutional Furniture—*mfg*	337127	2599
Food warming equipment, commercial: Equipment, Other Commercial—*whlse*	42144	5046
Machinery, Other Commercial and Service Industry—*mfg*	333319	3589
Food waste disposal units, household: Major Household Appliance, Other—*mfg*	335228	3639
Food, mail-order: Electronic Shopping and Mail-Order Houses—*retail*	45411	5961
Foodbars: Cafeterias—*accom*	722212	5812
Caterers—*accom*	72232	5812
Foodservice Contractors—*accom*	72231	5812
Full-Service Restaurants—*accom*	72211	5812
Limited-Service Restaurants—*accom*	722211	5812
Snack and Nonalcoholic Beverage Bars—*accom*	722213	5812
Theater Companies and Dinner Theaters—*arts*	71111	5812
Foodservice Contractors	**72231**	**5812**
Foodservices and Drinking Places	**722**	
Foodservices, Special	**7223**	
Foot appliances, orthopedic: Surgical Appliance and Supplies—*mfg*	339113	3842
Football clubs, except professional and semiprofessional: Fitness and Recreational Sports Centers—*arts*	71394	7997
Football clubs, professional or semiprofessional: Agents and Managers for Artists, Athletes, Entertainers and Other Public Figures—*arts*	71141	7941
Promoters of Performing Arts, Sports and Similar Events with Facilities—*arts*	71131	7941
Promoters of Performing Arts, Sports and Similar Events without Facilities—*arts*	71132	7941
Spectator Sports, Other—*arts*	711219	7941
Sports Teams and Clubs—*arts*	711211	7941
Footballs and football equipment and supplies, except uniforms and footwear: Sporting and Athletic Goods—*mfg*	33992	3949
Footholds, rubber: Rubber and Plastics Footwear—*mfg*	316211	3021
Footlets: Apparel Accessories and Apparel, Other—*mfg*	315999	2389
Footwear: Footwear—*whlse*	42234	5139
Footwear and Leather Goods Repair	**81143**	**7699**
Footwear Manufacturing	**3162**	
Footwear Manufacturing	**31621**	
Footwear Manufacturing, Other	**316219**	**3149**
Footwear stores: Shoe Stores—*retail*	44821	5661
Footwear Wholesalers	**42234**	**5139**
Footwear, children's–house slippers and vulcanized rubber footwear: Footwear, Other—*mfg*	316219	3149
Footwear, children's–leather or vinyl with molded or vulcanized shoes: Footwear, Other—*mfg*	316219	3149
Footwear, men's–except house slippers, athletic, and vulcanized rubber footwear: Men's Footwear (except Athletic)—*mfg*	316213	3143
Footwear, men's–leather or vinyl with molded or vukanized soles: Men's Footwear (except Athletic)—*mfg*	316213	3143
Footwear, rubber or rubber soled fabric: Rubber and Plastics Footwear—*mfg*	316211	3021
Footwear, women's–except house slippers, athletic, and vulcanized rubber footwear: Women's Footwear (except Athletic)—*mfg*	316214	3144
Footwear, women's–leather or vinyl with molded or vulcanized soles: Women's Footwear (except Athletic)—*mfg*	316214	3144
Forage blowers: Farm Machinery and Equipment—*mfg*	333111	3523
Hand and Edge Tool—*mfg*	332212	3523
Forage harvesters: Farm Machinery and Equipment—*mfg*	333111	3523
Forceps, dental: Dental Equipment and Supplies—*mfg*	339114	3843
Forceps, surgical: Surgical and Medical Instrument—*mfg*	339112	3841
Foreign currency exchanges: Commodity Contracts Dealing—*fin*	52313	6099
Credit Intermediation, Other Activities Related to—*fin*	52239	6099
Financial Investment Activities, Miscellaneous—*fin*	523999	6099
Financial Transactions Processing, Reserve, and Clearing House Activities—*fin*	52232	6099
Trust, Fiduciary and Custody Activities—*fin*	523991	6099
Foreign forwarding: Freight Arrangement—*trans*	48851	4731
Management Consulting Services, Other—*prof*	541618	4731
Foreign missions: International Affairs—*pub*	92812	9721
Foreign trade zone warehousing, and storage: General Warehousing and Storage Facilities—*trans*	49311	4226
Refrigerated Warehousing and Storage Facilities—*trans*	49312	4226
Warehousing and Storage Facilities, Other—*trans*	49319	4226
Forensic laboratories: Testing Laboratories—*prof*	54138	8734
Veterinary Services—*prof*	54194	8734

ALPHABETICAL INDEX	NAICS	SIC
Forest management plans, preparation of: Forestry Support Activities—*ag*	11531	851
Forest nurseries: Crop Farming, All Other Miscellaneous—*ag*	111998	831
Forest Nurseries and Gathering of Forest Products—*ag*	11321	831
Forest Nurseries and Gathering of Forest Products	**11321**	**831**
Forest Nurseries and Gathering of Forest Products	**1132**	
Forest properties, lessors of: Lessors of Other Real Estate Property—*real*	53119	6519
Forestry and Logging	**113**	
Forestry equipment: Construction and (except Petroleum) Machinery and Equipment—*whlse*	42181	5082
Forestry services: Forestry Support Activities—*ag*	11531	851
Forestry Support Activities	**11531**	**851**
Forestry Support Activities	**1153**	
Forges, fan: Fabricated Metal Product, All Other Miscellaneous—*mfg*	332999	3599
General Purpose Machinery , All Other—*mfg*	333999	3599
Machine Shops—*mfg*	33271	3599
Machinery, Other Commercial and Service Industry—*mfg*	333319	3599
Forging and Stamping	**3321**	
Forging and Stamping	**33211**	
Forging machinery and hammers: Machine Tool (Metal Forming Types)—*mfg*	333513	3542
Forgings, ferrous: Metal Service Centers and Offices—*whlse*	42151	5051
Forgings, iron and steel–made in steelworks or rolling mills: Iron and Steel Mills—*mfg*	331111	3312
Petroleum and Coal Productsa, All Other—*mfg*	324199	3312
Forgings, iron and steel–not made in rolling mills: Iron and Steel Forging—*mfg*	332111	3462
Forgings, nonferrous metal–not made inhot rolling mills: Nonferrous Forging—*mfg*	332112	3463
Forgings, projectile–machined-for ammunition more than 30 mm. (or more than 1.18 inch): Ammunition (except Small Arms)—*mfg*	332993	3483
Forklift trucks: Fabricated Metal Product, All Other Miscellaneous—*mfg*	332999	3537
Industrial Truck, Tractor, Trailer and Stacker Machinery—*mfg*	333924	3537
Metal Container, Other—*mfg*	332439	3537
Forks, table–all metal: Cutlery and Flatware (except Precious)—*mfg*	332211	3914
Silverware and Plated Ware—*mfg*	339912	3914
Forks, table–except all metal: Cutlery and Flatware (except Precious)—*mfg*	332211	3421
Forks–garden, hay and manure, stone and ballast: Hand and Edge Tool—*mfg*	332212	3423
Form ties, made in wiredrawing plants: Fabricated Wire Product, Other—*mfg*	332618	3315
Steel Wire Drawing—*mfg*	331222	3315

ALPHABETICAL INDEX	NAICS	SIC
Formal jackets: Men's and Boys' Cut and Sew Apparel Contractors—*mfg*	315211	2311
Men's and Boys' Cut and Sew Suit, Coat and Overcoat—*mfg*	315222	2311
Formal Wear and Costume Rental	**53222**	**7819**
Formaldehyde (formalin): Basic Organic Chemical, All Other—*mfg*	325199	2869
Formalin: Basic Organic Chemical, All Other—*mfg*	325199	2869
Formic acid and metallic salts: Basic Organic Chemical, All Other—*mfg*	325199	2869
Forming machine work for the trade, except stampings–sheet metal: Metal Container, Other—*mfg*	332439	3444
Sheet Metal Work—*mfg*	332322	3444
Forming machines: Machine Tool (Metal Forming Types)—*mfg*	333513	3542
Forms and fillers, looseleaf–pen ruled or printed only: Blankbook, Loose-leaf Binder and Device—*mfg*	323118	2782
Flexographic Printing, Commercial—*mfg*	323112	2782
Gravure Printing, Commercial—*mfg*	323111	2782
Lithographic Printing, Commercial—*mfg*	323110	2782
Printing, Other Commercial—*mfg*	323119	2782
Screen Printing, Commercial—*mfg*	323113	2782
Forms for concrete, sheet metal: Metal Container, Other—*mfg*	332439	3444
Sheet Metal Work—*mfg*	332322	3444
Forms for dipped rubber products, pottery: Vitreous China, Fine Earthenware and Other Pottery Product—*mfg*	327112	3269
Forms for poured concrete, erection and dismantling-contractors: Trade Contractors, All Other Special—*const*	23599	1799
Forms handling equipment for store and office use: Lead Pencil and Art Good—*mfg*	339942	3579
Office Machinery—*mfg*	333313	3579
Watch, Clock, and Part—*mfg*	334518	3579
Forms, business–manifold or continuous: Manifold Business Form Printing—*mfg*	323116	2761
Forms, collapsible–for tunnels: Air-Conditioning and Warm Air Heating Equipment and Commercial and Industrial Refrigeration Equipment—*mfg*	333415	3443
Metal Tank (Heavy Gauge)—*mfg*	33242	3443
Plate Work—*mfg*	332313	3443
Power Boiler and Heat Exchanger—*mfg*	33241	3443
Forms, concrete construction–steel: Metal Service Centers and Offices—*whlse*	42151	5051
Forms, display–for hoots and shoes-regardless of material: Manufacturing, All Other Miscellaneous—*mfg*	339999	2499
Wood Container and Pallet—*mfg*	32192	2499
Wood Product, All Other Miscellaneous—*mfg*	321999	2499
Forms, metal (molds)–for foundry and plastics working machinery: Die and Tool, Die Set, Jig and Fixture, Special—*mfg*	333514	3544
Industrial Mold—*mfg*	333511	3544

Forms–display, dress, and show-except shoe display forms:		
Fabricated Metal Product, All Other Miscellaneous—*mfg*	332999	3999
Wood Product, All Other Miscellaneous—*mfg*	321999	3999
Forwarding, domestic: Freight Arrangement—*trans*	48851	4731
Management Consulting Services, Other—*prof*	541618	4731
Forwarding, foreign: Freight Arrangement—*trans*	48851	4731
Management Consulting Services, Other—*prof*	541618	4731
Fossil Fuel Electric Power Generation	**221112**	**4931**
Foster homes, group: Homes for the Elderly—*hlth*	623312	8361
Residential Care Facilities, Other—*hlth*	62399	8361
Residential Mental Health and Substance Abuse Facilities—*hlth*	62322	8361
Foundation digging (excavation)-contractors: Excavation Contractors—*const*	23593	1794
Foundation garments: Clothing Accessories Stores—*retail*	44815	5632
Clothing Stores, Other—*retail*	44819	5632
Women's and Girls' Cut and Sew Apparel Contractors—*mfg*	315212	2342
Women's and Girls' Cut and Sew Lingerie, Loungewear and Nightwear—*mfg*	315231	2342
Foundations, bed–spring, foam, and platform: Mattress—*mfg*	33791	2515
Upholstered Household Furniture—*mfg*	337121	2515
Foundations, building of–block, stone, or brick-contractors: Masonry and Stone Contractors—*const*	23541	1741
Foundations, building of–poured concrete–contractors: Concrete Contractors—*const*	23571	1771
Drywall, Plastering, Acoustical and Insulation Contractors—*const*	23542	1771
Foundations, cardboard: Converted Paper Product, All Other—*mfg*	322298	2675
Die-Cut Paper and Paperboard Office Supplies—*mfg*	322231	2675
Surface-Coated Paperboard—*mfg*	322292	2675
Foundries	**3315**	
Foundries, aluminum–except die-castings: Aluminum Foundries—*mfg*	331524	3365
Foundries, gray iron and semisteel: Iron Foundries—*mfg*	331511	3321
Foundries, malleable iron: Iron Foundries—*mfg*	331511	3322
Foundries, steel–except investment: Steel Foundries, (except Investment)—*mfg*	331513	3325
Foundries–brass, bronze, copper, and copper-base alloy-except die-castings: Copper Foundries—*mfg*	331525	3366
Foundry cores: Industrial Pattern—*mfg*	332997	3543
Foundry facings, ground or otherwise treated: Ground or Treated Mineral and Earth—*mfg*	327992	3295
Foundry machinery and equipment: Industrial Machinery, All Other—*mfg*	333298	3559
Machinery, Other Commercial and Service Industry—*mfg*	333319	3559
Foundry patternmaking: Industrial Pattern—*mfg*	332997	3543
Foundry products: Metal Service Centers and Offices—*whlse*	42151	5051
Foundry refractories, clay: Clay Refractory—*mfg*	327124	3255
Foundry sand mining: Industrial Sand—*mining*	212322	1446
Foundry supplies, chemical preparations: Basic Organic Chemical, All Other—*mfg*	325199	2899

Chemical Product, All Other Miscellaneous—*mfg*	325998	2899
Foundry type for printing: Printing Machinery and Equipment—*mfg*	333293	3555
Fountain fruits and syrups: Confectionery—*whlse*	42245	5145
Fountain lighting fixtures: Lighting Equipment, Other—*mfg*	335129	3648
Fountain pens and fountain pen desksets: Pen and Mechanical Pencil—*mfg*	339941	3951
Fountain syringes, rubber: Fabric Coating Mills—*mfg*	31332	3069
Rubber Product, All Other—*mfg*	326299	3069
Fountain syrup dispensing equipment: Air-Conditioning and Warm Air Heating Equipment and Commercial and Industrial Refrigeration Equipment—*mfg*	333415	3585
Motor Vehicle Air-Conditioning—*mfg*	336391	3585
Fountains, concrete: Concrete Pipe—*mfg*	327332	3272
Concrete Product, Other—*mfg*	32739	3272
Nonmetallic Mineral Product, All Other Miscellaneous—*mfg*	327999	3272
Fountains, drinking–except mechanically refrigerated: Enameled Iron and Metal Sanitary Ware—*mfg*	332998	3431
Fountains, drinking–mechanically refrigerated: Air-Conditioning and Warm Air Heating Equipment and Commercial and Industrial Refrigeration Equipment—*mfg*	333415	3585
Motor Vehicle Air-Conditioning—*mfg*	336391	3585
Fountains, metal (except drinking): Fabricated Metal Product, All Other Miscellaneous—*mfg*	332999	3499
Fountains, plaster of paris–factory production only: Gypsum and Gypsum Product—*mfg*	32742	3299
Nonmetallic Mineral Product, All Other Miscellaneous—*mfg*	327999	3299
Fountains, wash–precast terraszo: Concrete Pipe—*mfg*	327332	3272
Concrete Product, Other—*mfg*	32739	3272
Nonmetallic Mineral Product, All Other Miscellaneous—*mfg*	327999	3272
Fourdrinier machines (paper manufacturmg machinery): Paper Industry Machinery—*mfg*	333291	3554
Fourdrinier wire cloth, made from purchased wire: Fabricated Wire Product, Other—*mfg*	332618	3496
Fox farms: Fur-Bearing Animal and Rabbit Production—*ag*	11293	271
Fractionating columns, metal plate: Air-Conditioning and Warm Air Heating Equipment and Commercial and Industrial Refrigeration Equipment—*mfg*	333415	3443
Metal Tank (Heavy Gauge)—*mfg*	33242	3443
Plate Work—*mfg*	332313	3443
Power Boiler and Heat Exchanger—*mfg*	33241	3443
Fractionating natural gas liquids: Natural Gas Liquid Extraction—*mining*	211112	1321
Fractionating towers, metal plate: Air-Conditioning and Warm Air Heating Equipment and Commercial and Industrial Refrigeration Equipment—*mfg*	333415	3443
Metal Tank (Heavy Gauge)—*mfg*	33242	3443
Plate Work—*mfg*	332313	3443
Power Boiler and Heat Exchanger—*mfg*	33241	3443

ALPHABETICAL INDEX	NAICS	SIC
Fractionation products of crude petroleum, produced in petroleum refineries: Petroleum Refineries—*mfg*	32411	2911
Fracture appliances, surgical: Surgical Appliance and Supplies—*mfg*	339113	3842
Frame repair shops, automotive: Automotive Mechanical and Electrical Repair and Maintenance, Other—*serv*	811118	7539
Frame straighteners, automotive (garage equipment): Industrial Machinery, All Other—*mfg*	333298	3559
Machinery, Other Commercial and Service Industry—*mfg*	333319	3559
Frames and handles, handbag and luggage–except precious metal: Plastics Product, All Other—*mfg*	326199	3999
Wood Product, All Other Miscellaneous—*mfg*	321999	3999
Frames and parts, eyeglass and spectacle: Ophthalmic Goods—*mfg*	339115	3851
Frames for artists' canvases: Chemical Product, All Other Miscellaneous—*mfg*	325998	3952
Institutional Furniture—*mfg*	337127	3952
Lead Pencil and Art Good—*mfg*	339942	3952
Frames for box springs or bedsprings, metal: Metal Household Furniture—*mfg*	337124	2514
Frames for box springs, bedsprings, or water beds–wood: Nonupholstered Wood Household Furniture—*mfg*	337122	2511
Frames for upholstered furniture, weed: Cut Stock, Resawing Lumber, and Planing—*mfg*	321912	2426
Millwork (including Flooring), Other—*mfg*	321918	2426
Showcase, Partition, Shelving, and Locker—*mfg*	337215	2426
Wood Product, All Other Miscellaneous—*mfg*	321999	2426
Frames, chair–metal: Fabricated Metal Product, All Other Miscellaneous—*mfg*	332999	3499
Frames, clothes drying–wood: Manufacturing, All Other Miscellaneous—*mfg*	339999	2499
Wood Container and Pallet—*mfg*	32192	2499
Wood Product, All Other Miscellaneous—*mfg*	321999	2499
Frames, door and window–metal: Metal Window and Door—*mfg*	332321	3442
Frames, door and window–wood: Millwork (including Flooring), Other—*mfg*	321918	2431
Wood Window and Door—*mfg*	321911	2431
Frames, doubling and twisting (textile machinery): Textile Machinery—*mfg*	333292	3552
Frames, lamp shade: Fabricated Metal Product, All Other Miscellaneous—*mfg*	332999	3999
Plastics Product, All Other—*mfg*	326199	3999
Residential Electric Lighting Fixture—*mfg*	335121	3999
Frames, motor vehicle: Motor Vehicle Parts, All Other—*mfg*	336399	3714
Frames, motorcycle and bicycle: Motorcycle, Bicycle and Parts—*mfg*	336991	3751
Frames, ophthalmic: Ophthalmic Goods—*whlse*	42146	5048
Frames, piano-back: Musical Instrument—*mfg*	339992	3931
Frames, umbrella and parasol: Fabricated Metal Product, All Other Miscellaneous—*mfg*	332999	3999

ALPHABETICAL INDEX	NAICS	SIC
Plastics Product, All Other—*mfg*	326199	3999
Wood Product, All Other Miscellaneous—*mfg*	321999	3999
Frames–medallion, mirror, photograph, and picture-wood or metal: Manufacturing, All Other Miscellaneous—*mfg*	339999	2499
Wood Container and Pallet—*mfg*	32192	2499
Wood Product, All Other Miscellaneous—*mfg*	321999	2499
Framing-contractors: Carpentry Contractors—*const*	23551	1751
Franchises, selling or licensing: Owners and Lessors of Other Non-Financial Assets—*real*	53311	6794
Frankfurter (hot dog) stands: Cafeterias—*accom*	722212	5812
Caterers—*accom*	72232	5812
Foodservice Contractors—*accom*	72231	5812
Full-Service Restaurants—*accom*	72211	5812
Limited-Service Restaurants—*accom*	722211	5812
Snack and Nonalcoholic Beverage Bars—*accom*	722213	5812
Theater Companies and Dinner Theaters—*arts*	71111	5812
Frankfurters, except poultry: Animal (except Poultry) Slaughtering—*mfg*	311611	2011
Meat Processed from Carcasses—*mfg*	311612	2013
Frankfurters, poultry: Food, All Other Miscellaneous—*mfg*	311999	2015
Poultry Processing—*mfg*	311615	2015
Fraternal accident and health insurance organizations: Direct Health and Medical Insurance Carriers—*fin*	524114	6321
Insurance Funds, Other—*fin*	52519	6321
Reinsurance Carriers—*fin*	52413	6321
Fraternal associations, other than insurance offices: Civic and Social Organizations—*serv*	81341	8641
Fraternal life insurance organizations: Direct Life Insurance Carriers—*fin*	524113	6311
Reinsurance Carriers—*fin*	52413	6311
Fraternal lodges: Civic and Social Organizations—*serv*	81341	8641
Fraternal protective associations: Direct Life Insurance Carriers—*fin*	524113	6311
Reinsurance Carriers—*fin*	52413	6311
Fraternities and sororities, except residential: Child and Youth Services—*hlth*	62411	8641
Fraternity residential houses: Hotels (except Casino Hotels) and Motels—*accom*	72111	7041
Rooming and Boarding Houses—*accom*	72131	7041
Freestanding Ambulatory Surgical and Emergency Centers	**621493**	**8011**
Freestanding emergency medical (M.D.) centers: Freestanding Ambulatory Surgical and Emergency Centers—*hlth*	621493	8011
HMO Medical Centers—*hlth*	621491	8011
Physicians (except Mental Health Specialists), Offices Of—*hlth*	621111	8011
Physicians, Mental Health Specialists, Offices Of—*hlth*	621112	8011
Freeze-dried coffee: Coffee and Tea—*mfg*	31192	2095
Spice and Extract—*mfg*	311942	2095

Freezer food plans, meat: Direct Selling Establishments, Other—*retail*	45439	5421
Fish and Seafood Markets—*retail*	44522	5421
Meat Markets—*retail*	44521	5421
Freezer provisioners, meat: Direct Selling Establishments, Other—*retail*	45439	5421
Fish and Seafood Markets—*retail*	44522	5421
Meat Markets—*retail*	44521	5421
Freezers, home and farm: Household Refrigerator and Home Freezer—*mfg*	335222	3632
Freezers, household: Electrical Appliance, Television and Radio Set—*whlse*	42162	5064
Household Appliance Stores—*retail*	443111	5722
Freezers, ice cream–commercial: Food Product Machinery—*mfg*	333294	3556
Freezers, ice cream–household-metal: Fabricated Metal Product, All Other Miscellaneous—*mfg*	332999	3499
Freight (except Used Goods) Trucking, Local Specialized	**48422**	**4214**
Freight (except Used Goods) Trucking, Long-Distance, Specialized	**48423**	**4213**
Freight agencies, railroad–not operated by railroad companies: Freight Arrangement—*trans*	48851	4731
Management Consulting Services, Other—*prof*	541618	4731
Freight car loading and unloading, not trucking: Rail Support Activities—*trans*	48821	4789
Scenic and Sightseeing, Land—*trans*	48711	4789
Transportation, All Other Support Activities—*trans*	488999	4789
Freight cars and car equipment: Pump and Pumping Equipment—*mfg*	333911	3743
Railroad Rolling Stock—*mfg*	33651	3743
Freight consolidation: Freight Arrangement—*trans*	48851	4731
Management Consulting Services, Other—*prof*	541618	4731
Freight forwarding: Freight Arrangement—*trans*	48851	4731
Management Consulting Services, Other—*prof*	541618	4731
Freight packing and crating: Packing and Crating—*trans*	488991	4783
Freight rate auditors: Freight Arrangement—*trans*	48851	4731
Management Consulting Services, Other—*prof*	541618	4731
Freight rate information service: Freight Arrangement—*trans*	48851	4731
Management Consulting Services, Other—*prof*	541618	4731
Freight Transportation Arrangement	**48851**	**4731**
Freight Transportation Arrangement	**4885**	
Freight trucking terminals, with or with-out maintenance facilities: Road, Other Support Activities for—*trans*	48849	4231
Freight Trucking, Specialized	**4842**	
French crepes: Broadwoven Fabric Mills—*mfg*	31321	2221
French dressing: Fruit and Vegetable Canning—*mfg*	311421	2035
Mayonnaise, Dressing and Other Prepared Sauce—*mfg*	311941	2035
French toast, frozen: Frozen Specialty Food—*mfg*	311412	2038
Frequency converters (electric generators): Motor and Generator—*mfg*	335312	3621
Frequency meters–electrical, mechanical, and electronic: Electronic Coil, Transformer, and Other Inductor—*mfg*	334416	3825
Instrument for Measuring and Testing Electricity and Electrical Signals—*mfg*	334515	3825
Frequency synthesizers: Electronic Coil, Transformer, and Other Inductor—*mfg*	334416	3825
Instrument for Measuring and Testing Electricity and Electrical Signals—*mfg*	334515	3825
Fresco work-contractors: Drywall, Plastering, Acoustical and Insulation Contractors—*const*	23542	1743
Tile, Marble, Terrazzo and Mosaic Contractors—*const*	23543	1743
Fresh and Frozen Seafood Processing	**311712**	**2092**
Fresh Fruit and Vegetable Wholesalers	**42248**	**5148**
Fretted instruments and parts: Musical Instrument—*mfg*	339992	3931
Friction material, made from powdered metal: Fabricated Metal Product, All Other Miscellaneous—*mfg*	332999	3499
Friction materials, asbestos–woven: Motor Vehicle Brake System—*mfg*	33634	3292
Nonmetallic Mineral Product, All Other Miscellaneous—*mfg*	327999	3292
Friction tape, rubber: Fabric Coating Mills—*mfg*	31332	3069
Rubber Product, All Other—*mfg*	326299	3069
Fringes, weaving: Narrow Fabric Mills—*mfg*	313221	2241
Frisket paper (artists' material): Chemical Product, All Other Miscellaneous—*mfg*	325998	3952
Institutional Furniture—*mfg*	337127	3952
Lead Pencil and Art Good—*mfg*	339942	3952
Frit: Basic Organic Chemical, All Other—*mfg*	325199	2899
Chemical Product, All Other Miscellaneous—*mfg*	325998	2899
Frog farms: Animal Production, All Other—*ag*	11299	279
Apiculture—*ag*	11291	279
Frogs, catching of: Crop Farming, All Other Miscellaneous—*ag*	111998	919
Marine Fishing, Other—*ag*	114119	919
Frogs, iron and steel–made in steel works or rolling mills: Iron and Steel Mills—*mfg*	331111	3312
Petroleum and Coal Productsa, All Other—*mfg*	324199	3312
Frogs, railroad–forgings not made in rolling mills: Iron and Steel Forging—*mfg*	332111	3462
Front end repair, automotive: Automotive Mechanical and Electrical Repair and Maintenance, Other—*serv*	811118	7539
Front-end loaders: Construction and (except Petroleum) Machinery and Equipment—*whlse*	42181	5082
Fronts and temples, ophthalmic: Ophthalmic Goods—*mfg*	339115	3851
Fronts, store–prefabricated-wood: Architectural Woodwork and Millwork, Custom—*mfg*	337212	2541
Showcase, Partition, Shelving, and Locker—*mfg*	337215	2541
Wood Kitchen Cabinet and Counter Top—*mfg*	33711	2541
Frosting, prepared: Food, All Other Miscellaneous—*mfg*	311999	2099
Frozen Bakery Product Manufacturing	**311813**	**2053**
Frozen bread and bread-type rolls: Bakeries, Commercial—*mfg*	311812	2051

Entry	NAICS	SIC
Fruit, mail-order: Electronic Shopping and Mail-Order Houses—*retail*	45411	5961
Fruit, vegetable, berry, and grape harvestmg machines: Farm Machinery and Equipment—*mfg*	333111	3523
Fruits grown under cover: Food Crops Grown Under Cover, Other—*ag*	111419	182
Mushroom Production—*ag*	111411	182
Fruits, artificial and preserved–except glass: Plastics Product, All Other—*mfg*	326199	3999
Fruits, artificial, except glass: Plastics Product, All Other—*mfg*	326199	3999
Fruits, canned: Fruit and Vegetable Canning—*mfg*	311421	2033
Fruits, crushed–for soda fountain use: Flavoring Syrup and Concentrate—*mfg*	31193	2087
Food, All Other Miscellaneous—*mfg*	311999	2087
Spice and Extract—*mfg*	311942	2087
Fruits, dried: Grocery and Related Products, Other—*whlse*	42249	5149
Fruits, dried or dehydrated: Dried and Dehydrated Food—*mfg*	311423	2034
Flour Milling—*mfg*	311211	2034
Fruits, fountain: Confectionery—*whlse*	42245	5145
Fruits, fresh: Fresh Fruit and Vegetable—*whlse*	42248	5148
Fruit and Vegetable Markets—*retail*	44523	5431
Fruits, frozen: Packaged Frozen Food—*whlse*	42242	5142
Fruits, machine harvesting of: Crop Harvesting, Primarily by Machine—*ag*	115113	722
Fruits, pickled and brined: Fruit and Vegetable Canning—*mfg*	311421	2035
Mayonnaise, Dressing and Other Prepared Sauce—*mfg*	311941	2035
Fruits, quick frozen and cold-pack (frozen): Frozen Fruit, Juice and Vegetable—*mfg*	311411	2037
Fruits, sulphured: Dried and Dehydrated Food—*mfg*	311423	2034
Flour Milling—*mfg*	311211	2034
Fruits–candied, glazed, and crystallized: Confectionery from Purchased Chocolate—*mfg*	31133	2064
Non-Chocolate Confectionery—*mfg*	31134	2064
Fryers, commercial: Machinery, Other Commercial and Service Industry—*mfg*	333319	3589
Fryers, household–electric: Electric Housewares and Household Fan—*mfg*	335211	3634
Heating Equipment (except Electric and Warm Air Furnaces)—*mfg*	333414	3634
Frying chickens, raising of: Broilers and Other Meat Type Chicken Production—*ag*	11232	251
Frying pans, glass and glass ceramic: Pressed and Blown Glass and Glassware, Other—*mfg*	327212	3229
Fudge (candy): Confectionery from Purchased Chocolate—*mfg*	31133	2064
Non-Chocolate Confectionery—*mfg*	31134	2064
Fuel additives: Chemical and Allied Products, Other—*whlse*	42269	5169
Fuel briquettes or boulets, made with petroleum binder: Petroleum and Coal Productsa, All Other—*mfg*	324199	2999
Fuel cell forms, cardboard: Coated and Laminated Paper—*mfg*	322222	2679
Converted Paper Product, All Other—*mfg*	322298	2679
Die-Cut Paper and Paperboard Office Supplies—*mfg*	322231	2679
Non-Folding Sanitary Food Container—*mfg*	322215	2679
Fuel cell reinforcement, cord and fabric: Tire Cord and Tire Fabric Mills—*mfg*	314992	2296
Fuel cells, electrochemical generators: Electrical Equipment and Component, All Other Miscellaneous—*mfg*	335999	3629
Fuel cells, rubber: Fabric Coating Mills—*mfg*	31332	3069
Rubber Product, All Other—*mfg*	326299	3069
Fuel cells, solid-state: Semiconductor and Related Device—*mfg*	334413	3674
Fuel Dealers	**45431**	
Fuel dealers, bottled liquefied petroleum gas: Liquefied Petroleum Gas (Bottled Gas) Dealers—*retail*	454312	5984
Fuel Dealers, Other	**454319**	**5989**
Fuel densitometers, aircraft engine: Measuring and Controlling Device, Other—*mfg*	334519	3829
Surgical and Medical Instrument—*mfg*	339112	3829
Fuel mixture indicators, aircraft engine: Measuring and Controlling Device, Other—*mfg*	334519	3829
Surgical and Medical Instrument—*mfg*	339112	3829
Fuel oil burner installation and servicing-contractors: Plumbing, Heating and Air-Conditioning Contractors—*const*	23511	1711
Fuel oil dealers: Heating Oil Dealers—*retail*	454311	5983
Fuel oil, except bulk stations and terminals: Petroleum and Petroleum Products (except Bulk Stations and Terminals)—*whlse*	42272	5172
Fuel propellants, solid–inorganic: Basic Inorganic Chemical, All Other—*mfg*	325188	2819
Chemical Product, All Other Miscellaneous—*mfg*	325998	2819
Fuel propellants, solid–organic: Basic Organic Chemical, All Other—*mfg*	325199	2869
Fuel pumps, motor vehicle: Gasoline Engine and Engine Parts—*mfg*	336312	3714
Motor Vehicle Parts, All Other—*mfg*	336399	3714
Fuel system conversion, automotive: Automotive Mechanical and Electrical Repair and Maintenance, Other—*serv*	811118	7539
Fuel system instruments, aircraft: Measuring and Controlling Device, Other—*mfg*	334519	3829
Surgical and Medical Instrument—*mfg*	339112	3829
Fuel system repair, automotive: Automotive Mechanical and Electrical Repair and Maintenance, Other—*serv*	811118	7539
Fuel systems and parts, motor vehicle: Gasoline Engine and Engine Parts—*mfg*	336312	3714
Motor Vehicle Parts, All Other—*mfg*	336399	3714
Fuel tank and engine cleaning chemicals, automotive and aircraft: Basic Organic Chemical, All Other—*mfg*	325199	2899
Chemical Product, All Other Miscellaneous—*mfg*	325998	2899
Fuel tanks, aircraft–including self-sealing: Aircraft Part and Auxiliary Equipment, Other—*mfg*	336413	3728
Fluid Power Valve and Hose Fitting—*mfg*	332912	3728
Fuel tanks, collapsible–rubberized fabric: Fabric Coating Mills—*mfg*	31332	3069

ALPHABETICAL INDEX	NAICS	SIC
Rubber Product, All Other—*mfg*	326299	3069
Fuel tanks, metal plate: Air-Conditioning and Warm Air Heating Equipment and Commercial and Industrial Refrigeration Equipment—*mfg*	333415	3443
Metal Tank (Heavy Gauge)—*mfg*	33242	3443
Plate Work—*mfg*	332313	3443
Power Boiler and Heat Exchanger—*mfg*	33241	3443
Fuel totalizers, aircraft engine: Measuring and Controlling Device, Other—*mfg*	334519	3829
Surgical and Medical Instrument—*mfg*	339112	3829
Fuel wood: Fuel Dealers, Other—*retail*	454319	5989
Fuel wood harvesting: Logging—*ag*	11331	2411
Fuel–coal and coke-wbolesale: Coal and Other Mineral and Ore—*whlse*	42152	5052
Fueling services, aircraft: Petroleum and Petroleum Products (except Bulk Stations and Terminals)—*whlse*	42272	5172
Fuels, high energy–inorganic: Basic Inorganic Chemical, All Other—*mfg*	325188	2819
Chemical Product, All Other Miscellaneous—*mfg*	325998	2819
Fuels, high energy–organic: Basic Organic Chemical, All Other—*mfg*	325199	2869
Fuels, jet: Petroleum Refineries—*mfg*	32411	2911
Fuelwood, from mill waste: Cut Stock, Resawing Lumber, and Planing—*mfg*	321912	2421
Millwork (including Flooring), Other—*mfg*	321918	2421
Sawmills—*mfg*	321113	2421
Wood Product, All Other Miscellaneous—*mfg*	321999	2421
Full-Service Restaurants	**7221**	
Full-Service Restaurants	**72211**	**5812**
Fuller's earth mining: Clay and Ceramic and Refractory Minerals—*mining*	212325	1459
Fuller's earth, ground or otherwise treated: Ground or Treated Mineral and Earth—*mfg*	327992	3295
Fulminate of mercury (explosive compounds): Explosives—*mfg*	32592	2892
Fumigating chambers, metal plate: Air-Conditioning and Warm Air Heating Equipment and Commercial and Industrial Refrigeration Equipment—*mfg*	333415	3443
Metal Tank (Heavy Gauge)—*mfg*	33242	3443
Plate Work—*mfg*	332313	3443
Power Boiler and Heat Exchanger—*mfg*	33241	3443
Fumigating service: Exterminating and Pest Control Services—*admin*	56171	7342
Janitorial Services—*admin*	56172	7342
Function generators: Electronic Coil, Transformer, and Other Inductor—*mfg*	334416	3825
Instrument for Measuring and Testing Electricity and Electrical Signals—*mfg*	334515	3825

ALPHABETICAL INDEX	NAICS	SIC
Fundraising on a contract or fee basis: Telemarketing Bureaus—*admin*	561422	7389
Fundraising organizations, except on a contract or fee basis: Environment, Conservation and Wildlife Organizations—*serv*	813312	8399
Fundraising organizations, except on acontract or fee basis: Grantmaking and Giving Services, Other—*serv*	813219	8399
Human Rights Organizations—*serv*	813311	8399
Social Advocacy Organizations, Other—*serv*	813319	8399
Voluntary Health Organizations—*serv*	813212	8399
Funds transfer devices: Computer Peripheral Equipment, Other—*mfg*	334119	3578
Office Machinery—*mfg*	333313	3578
Funds, Trusts and Other Financial Vehicles (U.S. Only)	**525**	
Funeral directors: Cemeteries and Crematories—*serv*	81222	7261
Funeral Homes—*serv*	81221	7261
Funeral Homes	**81221**	**7261**
Funeral homes or parlors: Cemeteries and Crematories—*serv*	81222	7261
Funeral Homes—*serv*	81221	7261
Funeral insurance: Direct Life Insurance Carriers—*fin*	524113	6311
Reinsurance Carriers—*fin*	52413	6311
Fungicides: Pesticide and Other Agricultural Chemical—*mfg*	32532	2879
Funnels, rubber: Fabric Coating Mills—*mfg*	31332	3069
Rubber Product, All Other—*mfg*	326299	3069
Fur and Leather Apparel Manufacturing	**315292**	**2386**
Fur apparel made to custom order: Clothing Accessories Stores—*retail*	44815	5632
Clothing Stores, Other—*retail*	44819	5632
Fur apparel–capes, coats, hats, jackets, and neckpieces: Fur and Leather Apparel—*mfg*	315292	2371
Fur clothing: Women's, Children's, and Infants' and Accessories—*whlse*	42233	5137
Fur cuttings and scraps: Recyclable Material—*whlse*	42193	5093
Fur farms: Fur-Bearing Animal and Rabbit Production—*ag*	11293	271
Fur finishers and liners for the fur goodstrade–buttonhole making: Fur and Leather Apparel—*mfg*	315292	2371
Fur garments–cleaning, repairing, andstorage: Personal and Household Goods Repair and Maintenance, Other—*serv*	81149	7219
Fur plates and trimmings: Fur and Leather Apparel—*mfg*	315292	2371
Fur sewing machines: Industrial Machinery, All Other—*mfg*	333298	3559
Machinery, Other Commercial and Service Industry—*mfg*	333319	3559
Fur shops: Clothing Accessories Stores—*retail*	44815	5632
Clothing Stores, Other—*retail*	44819	5632
Fur storage for the trade: General Warehousing and Storage Facilities—*trans*	49311	4226
Refrigerated Warehousing and Storage Facilities—*trans*	49312	4226
Warehousing and Storage Facilities, Other—*trans*	49319	4226
Fur stripping: Leather and Hide Tanning and Finishing—*mfg*	31611	3999

Description	NAICS	SIC
Fur-Bearing Animal and Rabbit Production	**11293**	**271**
Fur-type fabrics, manmade fiber: Broadwoven Fabric Mills—*mfg*	31321	2221
Furnace black: Carbon Black—*mfg*	325182	2895
Furnace blowers (blower filter units): Air Purification Equipment—*mfg*	333411	3564
Industrial and Commercial Fan and Blower—*mfg*	333412	3564
Furnace casings, sheet metal: Metal Container, Other—*mfg*	332439	3444
Sheet Metal Work—*mfg*	332322	3444
Furnace construction for industrial plants–general contractors: Heavy, All Other—*const*	23499	1629
Industrial Nonbuilding Structure—*const*	23493	1629
Furnace flues, sheet metal: Metal Container, Other—*mfg*	332439	3444
Sheet Metal Work—*mfg*	332322	3444
Furnace repair–contractors: Plumbing, Heating and Air-Conditioning Contractors—*const*	23511	1711
Furnaces, domestic–steam or hot water: Heating Equipment (except Electric and Warm Air Furnaces)—*mfg*	333414	3433
Furnaces, except electric and warm air: Building Material Dealers, Other—*retail*	44419	5074
Plumbing and Heating Equipment and Supplies (Hydronics)—*whlse*	42172	5074
Furnaces, heating–electric: Warm Air Heating and Air-Conditioning Equipment and Supplies—*whlse*	42173	5075
Furnaces, industrial process: Industrial Process Furnace and Oven—*mfg*	333994	3567
Furnaces, laboratory–dental: Dental Equipment and Supplies—*mfg*	339114	3843
Furnaces, warm air: Warm Air Heating and Air-Conditioning Equipment and Supplies—*whlse*	42173	5075
Furnaces–gravity air flow: Air-Conditioning and Warm Air Heating Equipment and Commercial and Industrial Refrigeration Equipment—*mfg*	333415	3585
Motor Vehicle Air-Conditioning—*mfg*	336391	3585
Furnished rooms, rental of: Rooming and Boarding Houses—*accom*	72131	7021
Furnishings, clothing except shoes–women's, children's, and infants': Women's, Children's, and Infants' and Accessories—*whlse*	42233	5137
Furnishings, except shoes–men's and boys': Men's and Boys' Clothing and Furnishings—*whlse*	42232	5136
Furniture and Home Furnishing Wholesalers	**4212**	
Furniture and Home Furnishings Stores	**442**	
Furniture and Related Product Manufacturing	**337**	
Furniture cleaning on customers' premises: Carpet and Upholstery Cleaning Services—*admin*	56174	7217
Furniture components, porcelain enameled: Kitchen Utensil, Pot and Pan—*mfg*	332214	3469
Metal Stamping—*mfg*	332116	3469
Furniture denim: Broadwoven Fabric Mills—*mfg*	31321	2211
Furniture dimension stock, hardwood: Cut Stock, Resawing Lumber, and Planing—*mfg*	321912	2426
Millwork (including Flooring), Other—*mfg*	321918	2426
Showcase, Partition, Shelving, and Locker—*mfg*	337215	2426
Wood Product, All Other Miscellaneous—*mfg*	321999	2426
Furniture dimension stock, softwood: Cut Stock, Resawing Lumber, and Planing—*mfg*	321912	2421
Millwork (including Flooring), Other—*mfg*	321918	2421
Sawmills—*mfg*	321113	2421
Wood Product, All Other Miscellaneous—*mfg*	321999	2421
Furniture frames for upholstering, wood: Cut Stock, Resawing Lumber, and Planing—*mfg*	321912	2426
Millwork (including Flooring), Other—*mfg*	321918	2426
Showcase, Partition, Shelving, and Locker—*mfg*	337215	2426
Wood Product, All Other Miscellaneous—*mfg*	321999	2426
Furniture hardware, including casters: Hardware—*mfg*	33251	3429
Furniture inlays (veneers): Manufacturing, All Other Miscellaneous—*mfg*	339999	2499
Wood Container and Pallet—*mfg*	32192	2499
Wood Product, All Other Miscellaneous—*mfg*	321999	2499
Furniture made on a custom basis to individual order: Furniture Stores—*retail*	44211	5712
Nonupholstered Wood Household Furniture—*mfg*	337122	5712
Upholstered Household Furniture—*mfg*	337121	5712
Wood Kitchen Cabinet and Counter Top—*mfg*	33711	5712
Furniture makers' machinery (woodworking): Sawmill and Woodworking Machinery—*mfg*	33321	3553
Furniture moving, local–combined with storage: Freight (except Used Goods) Trucking, Local Specialized—*trans*	48422	4214
General Freight Trucking, Local—*trans*	48411	4214
Used Household and Office Goods Moving—*trans*	48421	4214
Furniture moving, local–without storage: Freight (except Used Goods) Trucking, Local Specialized—*trans*	48422	4212
General Freight Trucking, Local—*trans*	48411	4212
Used Household and Office Goods Moving—*trans*	48421	4212
Furniture parts, metal: Fabricated Metal Product, All Other Miscellaneous—*mfg*	332999	3499
Furniture polish and wax: Polish and Other Sanitation Good—*mfg*	325612	2842
Furniture refinishing: Reupholstery and Furniture Repair—*serv*	81142	7641
Furniture Related Product Manufacturing, Other	**3379**	
Furniture rental and leasing: Consumer Electronics and Appliances Rental—*real*	53221	7359
Consumer Goods Rental, All Other—*real*	532299	7359
Furniture repairing, redecorating, and remodeling shops: Reupholstery and Furniture Repair—*serv*	81142	7641
Furniture restoration, antique: Reupholstery and Furniture Repair—*serv*	81142	7641
Furniture springs, unassembled–made from purchased wire: Watch, Clock, and Part—*mfg*	334518	3495
Wire Spring—*mfg*	332612	3495
Furniture squares, hardwood: Cut Stock, Resawing Lumber, and Planing—*mfg*	321912	2426

ALPHABETICAL INDEX	NAICS	SIC
Millwork (including Fiooring), Other—*mfg*	321918	2426
Showcase, Partition, Shelving, and Locker—*mfg*	337215	2426
Wood Product, All Other Miscellaneous—*mfg*	321999	2426
Furniture storage, without local trucking: General Warehousing and Storage Facilities—*trans*	49311	4226
Refrigerated Warehousing and Storage Facilities—*trans*	49312	4226
Warehousing and Storage Facilities, Other—*trans*	49319	4226
Furniture Stores	**4421**	
Furniture Stores	**44211**	**5712**
Furniture stores, household: Furniture Stores—*retail*	44211	5712
Nonupholstered Wood Household Furniture—*mfg*	337122	5712
Upholstered Household Furniture—*mfg*	337121	5712
Wood Kitchen Cabinet and Counter Top—*mfg*	33711	5712
Furniture stores, secondhand: Non-Depository Credit Intermediation, All Other—*fin*	522298	5932
Used Merchandise Stores—*retail*	45331	5932
Furniture tops, glass–cut, beveled, and polished: Glass Product Made of Purchased Glass—*mfg*	327215	3231
Furniture trimmings, fabric: Apparel Accessories and Apparel, Other—*mfg*	315999	2396
Textile Product Mills, All Other Miscellaneous—*mfg*	314999	2396
Furniture turnings and carvings, wood: Cut Stock, Resawing Lumber, and Planing—*mfg*	321912	2426
Millwork (including Flooring), Other—*mfg*	321918	2426
Showcase, Partition, Shelving, and Locker—*mfg*	337215	2426
Wood Product, All Other Miscellaneous—*mfg*	321999	2426
Furniture Wholesalers	**42121**	**5021**
Furniture, antique: Non-Depository Credit Intermediation, All Other—*fin*	522298	5932
Used Merchandise Stores—*retail*	45331	5932
Furniture, beauty shop and barber shop: Fabricated Metal Product, All Other Miscellaneous—*mfg*	332999	3999
Furniture, clubroom–metal: Metal Household Furniture—*mfg*	337124	2514
Furniture, custom made: Furniture Stores—*retail*	44211	5712
Nonupholstered Wood Household Furniture—*mfg*	337122	5712
Upholstered Household Furniture—*mfg*	337121	5712
Wood Kitchen Cabinet and Counter Top—*mfg*	33711	5712
Furniture, cut stone: Cut Stone and Stone Product—*mfg*	327991	3281
Furniture, factory–stools, work benches, tool stands, and cabinets: Institutional Furniture—*mfg*	337127	2599
Furniture, garden–concrete: Concrete Pipe—*mfg*	327332	3272
Concrete Product, Other—*mfg*	32739	3272
Nonmetallic Mineral Product, All Other Miscellaneous—*mfg*	327999	3272
Furniture, household, with or without furnishings and appliances: Furniture Stores—*retail*	44211	5712
Nonupholstered Wood Household Furniture—*mfg*	337122	5712
Upholstered Household Furniture—*mfg*	337121	5712

ALPHABETICAL INDEX	NAICS	SIC
Wood Kitchen Cabinet and Counter Top—*mfg*	33711	5712
Furniture, household, wood–porch, lawn, garden, and beach: Nonupholstered Wood Household Furniture—*mfg*	337122	2511
Furniture, household, wood–unassembled or knock-down: Nonupholstered Wood Household Furniture—*mfg*	337122	2511
Furniture, household, wood–unfinished: Nonupholstered Wood Household Furniture—*mfg*	337122	2511
Furniture, household–glass and plastics(including fiberglass): Household Furniture (except Wood and Metal)—*mfg*	337125	2519
Furniture, household–metal: Metal Household Furniture—*mfg*	337124	2514
Furniture, household–rattan, reed, malacca, fiber, willow, and wicker: Household Furniture (except Wood and Metal)—*mfg*	337125	2519
Furniture, household–upholstered on metal frames, except dual-purpose sleepfurniture: Metal Household Furniture—*mfg*	337124	2514
Furniture, household–upholstered on woodframes, except convertible beds: Upholstered Household Furniture—*mfg*	337121	2512
Furniture, juvenile: Furniture—*whlse*	42121	5021
Furniture Stores—*retail*	44211	5021
Furniture, office–except wood: Nonwood Office Furniture—*mfg*	337214	2522
Furniture, office–wood: Wood Office Furniture—*mfg*	337211	2521
Furniture, restaurant: Institutional Furniture—*mfg*	337127	2599
Furniture, unfinished: Furniture—*whlse*	42121	5021
Furniture Stores—*retail*	44211	5021
Furniture–church, library, school, theater, and other public buildings: Institutional Furniture—*mfg*	337127	2531
Furniture–household, clubroom, novelty-wood, except upholstered: Nonupholstered Wood Household Furniture—*mfg*	337122	2511
Furniture–household, office, restaurant, and public building: Furniture—*whlse*	42121	5021
Furniture Stores—*retail*	44211	5021
Furriers: Clothing Accessories Stores—*retail*	44815	5632
Clothing Stores, Other—*retail*	44819	5632
Furring channels: Ornamental and Architectural Metal Work—*mfg*	332323	3446
Furring tile, clay: Brick and Structural Clay Tile—*mfg*	327121	3251
Furs, dressed: Nondurable Goods, Other Miscellaneous—*whlse*	42299	5199
Furs, dressed–bleached, curried, scraped, tanned, and dyed: Leather and Hide Tanning and Finishing—*mfg*	31611	3999
Furs, raw: Farm Product Raw Material, Other—*whlse*	42259	5159
Fuse clips and blocks, electric: Switchgear and Switchboard Apparatus—*mfg*	335313	3613
Fuse cutouts: Current-Carrying Wiring Device—*mfg*	335931	3643
Fuse devices, power–600 volts and over: Switchgear and Switchboard Apparatus—*mfg*	335313	3613
Fuse mountings, electric power: Switchgear and Switchboard Apparatus—*mfg*	335313	3613
Fuse powder: Explosives—*mfg*	32592	2892

Fuse setters (fire control equipment): Optical Instrument and Lens—*mfg*	333314	3827
Fusees–highway, marine, and railroad: Basic Organic Chemical, All Other—*mfg*	325199	2899
Chemical Product, All Other Miscellaneous—*mfg*	325998	2899
Fuselage assemblies, aircraft: Aircraft Part and Auxiliary Equipment, Other—*mfg*	336413	3728
Fluid Power Valve and Hose Fitting—*mfg*	332912	3728
Fuses and accessories: Building Material Dealers, Other—*retail*	44419	5063
Electrical Apparatus and Equipment, Wiring Supplies and Material—*whlse*	42161	5063
Fuses for ammunition more than 30 mm.(or more than 1.18 inch): Ammunition (except Small Arms)—*mfg*	332993	3483
Fuses, electric: Switchgear and Switchboard Apparatus—*mfg*	335313	3613
Fuses, safety: Explosives—*mfg*	32592	2892
Fuses–mine, torpedo, bomb, depth charge, and chemical warfare projectile: Ammunition (except Small Arms)—*mfg*	332993	3483
Fustic wood extract: Gum and Wood Chemical—*mfg*	325191	2861
Futures advisory service: Investment Advice—*fin*	52393	6282
Portfolio Management—*fin*	52392	6282
Futures brokers, commodity: Commodity Brokerage—*fin*	52314	6221
Commodity Contracts Dealing—*fin*	52313	6221
Futures dealers, commodity: Commodity Brokerage—*fin*	52314	6221
Commodity Contracts Dealing—*fin*	52313	6221
Futures exchanges, contract: Securities and Commodity Exchanges—*fin*	52321	6231
Gabardine, cotton: Broadwoven Fabric Mills—*mfg*	31321	2211
Gabbro, crushed and broken: Crushed and Broken Stone and Quarrying, Other—*mining*	212319	1429
Gabbro, dimension: Dimension Stone and Quarrying—*mining*	212311	1411
Gaiters, rubber or rubber soled fabric: Rubber and Plastics Footwear—*mfg*	316211	3021
Galatea, cotton: Broadwoven Fabric Mills—*mfg*	31321	2211
Galena mining: Lead Ore and Zinc Ore—*mining*	212231	1031
Galenical preparations: Pharmaceutical Preparation—*mfg*	325412	2834
Galleys and chases, printers': Printing Machinery and Equipment—*mfg*	333293	3555
Galloons, lace: Knit Fabric and Lace Mills, Other—*mfg*	313249	2258
Textile and Fabric Finishing (except Broadwoven Fabric) Mills—*mfg*	313312	2258
Galoshes, plastics: Rubber and Plastics Footwear—*mfg*	316211	3021
Galoshes, rubber or rubber soled fabric: Rubber and Plastics Footwear—*mfg*	316211	3021
Galvanized hoops, pipes, plates, sheets, and strips–iron and steel: Iron and Steel Mills—*mfg*	331111	3312
Petroleum and Coal Productsa, All Other—*mfg*	324199	3312
Galvanizing fluxes: Basic Organic Chemical, All Other—*mfg*	325199	2899
Chemical Product, All Other Miscellaneous—*mfg*	325998	2899
Galvanizing lines (rolling mill equipment): Rolling Mill Machinery and Equipment—*mfg*	333516	3547
Galvanizing of iron and steel and end formed products, for the trade: Costume Jewelry and Novelty—*mfg*	339914	3479
Jewelry (except Costume)—*mfg*	339911	3479
Metal Coating, Engraving (except Jewelry and Silverware), and Allied Services to Manufacturers—*mfg*	332812	3479
Silverware and Plated Ware—*mfg*	339912	3479
Galvanometers, except geophysical: Electronic Coil, Transformer, and Other Inductor—*mfg*	334416	3825
Instrument for Measuring and Testing Electricity and Electrical Signals—*mfg*	334515	3825
Gambier extract: Gum and Wood Chemical—*mfg*	325191	2861
Gambling control boards: Public Finance—*pub*	92113	9311
Gambling establishments not primarily operating coin-operated machines: Gambling Industries, Other—*arts*	71329	7999
Gambling establishments primarily operating coin-operated machines: Amusement and Recreation Industries, All Other—*arts*	71399	7993
Amusement Arcades—*arts*	71312	7993
Gambling Industries, Other—*arts*	71329	7993
Gambling Industries	**7132**	
Gambling Industries, Other	**71329**	**7999**
Gambling machines, coin-operated–operation of: Amusement and Recreation Industries, All Other—*arts*	71399	7993
Amusement Arcades—*arts*	71312	7993
Gambling Industries, Other—*arts*	71329	7993
Gambling machines, except coin-operated:operation of: Gambling Industries, Other—*arts*	71329	7999
Game and inland fish agencies: Land, Mineral, Wildlife, and Forest Conservation—*pub*	92412	9512
Game calls: Sporting and Athletic Goods—*mfg*	33992	3949
Game farms (fur-bearing animals): Fur-Bearing Animal and Rabbit Production—*ag*	11293	271
Game machines, coin-operated: Durable Goods, Other Miscellaneous—*whlse*	42199	5099
Game management: Hunting and Trapping—*ag*	11421	971
Game parlors, except coin-operated: Gambling Industries, Other—*arts*	71329	7999
Game preserves: Hunting and Trapping—*ag*	11421	971
Game propagation: Hunting and Trapping—*ag*	11421	971
Game retreats, operation of: Hunting and Trapping—*ag*	11421	971
Game shops: Hobby, Toy and Game Stores—*retail*	45112	5945
Game, small–fresh, frozen, canned, or cooked: Food, All Other Miscellaneous—*mfg*	311999	2015
Poultry Processing—*mfg*	311615	2015
Game, small–slaughtering and dressing: Food, All Other Miscellaneous—*mfg*	311999	2015
Poultry Processing—*mfg*	311615	2015

ALPHABETICAL INDEX	NAICS	SIC
Game, Toy, and Children's Vehicle Manufacturing	**339932**	**3944**
Games (including electronic), except coin-operated: Toy and Hobby Goods and Supplies—*whlse*	42192	5092
Games for children and adults–puzzles, bingo, marbles, poker chips, and chess: Game, Toy, and Children's Vehicle—*mfg*	339932	3944
Games, coin-operated–pinball and other: Fabricated Metal Product, All Other Miscellaneous—*mfg*	332999	3999
Games, computer software–prepackaged: Publishers—*info*	51121	7372
Software Reproducing—*mfg*	334611	7372
Games, teaching of: Gambling Industries, Other—*arts*	71329	7999
Sports and Recreation Instruction—*educ*	61162	7999
Gamma ray irradiation equipment: Irradiation Apparatus—*mfg*	334517	3844
Ganister, crushed and broken: Crushed and Broken Stone and Quarrying, Other—*mining*	212319	1429
Garage construction–general contractors: Building, Commercial and Institutional—*const*	23332	1542
Garage door installation-contractors: Carpentry Contractors—*const*	23551	1751
Garage doors: Building Material Dealers, Other—*retail*	44419	5211
Home Centers—*retail*	44411	5211
Garage doors, overhead–metal: Metal Window and Door—*mfg*	332321	3442
Garage doors, overhead–wood: Millwork (including Flooring), Other—*mfg*	321918	2431
Wood Window and Door—*mfg*	321911	2431
Garage service equipment: Automotive Parts and Accessories Stores—*retail*	44131	5013
Motor Vehicle Supplies and New Part—*whlse*	42112	5013
Garages, automobile parking: Parking Lots and Garages—*serv*	81293	7521
Garages, do-it-yourself: Automotive Oil Change and Lubrication Shops—*serv*	811191	7549
Automotive Repair and Maintenance, All Other—*serv*	811198	7549
Motor Vehicle Towing—*trans*	48841	7549
Garages, general automotive repair andservice: General Automotive Repair—*serv*	811111	7538
Garages, prefabricated–metal: Prefabricated Metal Building and Component—*mfg*	332311	3448
Garbage boxes, concrete: Concrete Pipe—*mfg*	327332	3272
Concrete Product, Other—*mfg*	32739	3272
Nonmetallic Mineral Product, All Other Miscellaneous—*mfg*	327999	3272
Garbage containers, plastics: Plastics Pipe and Pipe Fitting—*mfg*	326122	3089
Plastics Product, All Other—*mfg*	326199	3089
Unsupported Plastics Profile Shape—*mfg*	326121	3089
Garbage disposal units, household: Major Household Appliance, Other—*mfg*	335228	3639
Garbage disposals, electric: Electrical Appliance, Television and Radio Set—*whlse*	42162	5064
Garbage disposers, commercial: Machinery, Other Commercial and Service Industry—*mfg*	333319	3589

ALPHABETICAL INDEX	NAICS	SIC
Garbage disposers, electric: Household Appliance Stores—*retail*	443111	5722
Garbage, local collecting and transporting–without disposal: General Freight Trucking, Local—*trans*	48411	4212
Hazardous Waste Collection—*admin*	562112	4212
Solid Waste Collection—*admin*	562111	4212
Waste Collection, Other—*admin*	562119	4212
Garbage–collecting, destroying, and processing: Hazardous Waste Collection—*admin*	562112	4953
Hazardous Waste Treatment and Disposal—*admin*	562211	4953
Materials Recovery Facilities—*admin*	56292	4953
Nonhazardous Waste Treatment and Disposal, Other—*admin*	562219	4953
Solid Waste Collection—*admin*	562111	4953
Solid Waste Combustors and Incinerators—*admin*	562213	4953
Solid Waste Landfill—*admin*	562212	4953
Waste Collection, Other—*admin*	562119	4953
Garden furniture, metal: Metal Household Furniture—*mfg*	337124	2514
Garden furniture, wood: Nonupholstered Wood Household Furniture—*mfg*	337122	2511
Garden furniture–except wood, metal, stone, and concrete: Household Furniture (except Wood and Metal)—*mfg*	337125	2519
Garden handtools: Hand and Edge Tool—*mfg*	332212	3423
Garden hose, plastics or rubber: Rubber and Plastics Hoses and Belting—*mfg*	32622	3052
Garden machinery and equipment: Farm and Garden Machinery and Equipment—*whlse*	42182	5083
Outdoor Power Equipment Stores—*retail*	44421	5083
Garden maintenance: Landscaping Services—*admin*	56173	782
Garden planning: Landscape Architectural Services—*prof*	54132	781
Scientific and Technical Consulting Services, Other—*prof*	54169	781
Garden planting: Landscaping Services—*admin*	56173	782
Garden pottery: Vitreous China, Fine Earthenware and Other Pottery Product—*mfg*	327112	3269
Garden supplies and tools: Nursery and Garden Centers—*retail*	44422	5261
Outdoor Power Equipment Stores—*retail*	44421	5261
Stores (except Tobacco Stores), All Other Miscellaneous—*retail*	453998	5261
Garden umbrellas: Fabricated Metal Product, All Other Miscellaneous—*mfg*	332999	3999
Plastics Product, All Other—*mfg*	326199	3999
Garlands, wreaths and sprays; made from tree boughs, cones, etc.: Plastics Product, All Other—*mfg*	326199	3999
Garment alteration and repair shops: Personal and Household Goods Repair and Maintenance, Other—*serv*	81149	7219
Garment hangers, made from purchased wire: Fabricated Wire Product, Other—*mfg*	332618	3496
Garment hangers, wood: Manufacturing, All Other Miscellaneous—*mfg*	339999	2499
Wood Container and Pallet—*mfg*	32192	2499

Wood Product, All Other Miscellaneous—*mfg*	321999	2499
Garment leather: Leather and Hide Tanning and Finishing—*mfg*	31611	3111
Garment pressing shops: Garment Pressing, and Agents for Laundries—*serv*	812391	7212
Garment Pressing, and Agents for Laundries	**812391**	**7212**
Garment racks, except wood: Showcase, Partition, Shelving, and Locker—*mfg*	337215	2542
Garment racks, wood: Architectural Woodwork and Millwork, Custom—*mfg*	337212	2541
Showcase, Partition, Shelving, and Locker—*mfg*	337215	2541
Wood Kitchen Cabinet and Counter Top—*mfg*	33711	2541
Garment storage bags made of materials, except paper or plastics film: Household Textile Product Mills, Other—*mfg*	314129	2392
Textile Bag Mills—*mfg*	314911	2392
Garment storage bags, coated paper or plastics film: Plastics, Foil, and Coated Paper Bag—*mfg*	322223	2673
Unsupported Plastics Bag—*mfg*	326111	2673
Garments, leather or sheep-lined: Fur and Leather Apparel—*mfg*	315292	2386
Garnet abrasives: Abrasive Product—*mfg*	32791	3291
Fabricated Metal Product, All Other Miscellaneous—*mfg*	332999	3291
Garnet mining: Crushed and Broken Stone and Quarrying, Other—*mining*	212319	1499
Non-Metallic Mineral, All Other—*mining*	212399	1499
Garnet paper: Abrasive Product—*mfg*	32791	3291
Fabricated Metal Product, All Other Miscellaneous—*mfg*	332999	3291
Garnetting machines, textile: Textile Machinery—*mfg*	333292	3552
Garnetting of textile waste and rags: Broadwoven Fabric Mills—*mfg*	31321	2299
Narrow Fabric Mills—*mfg*	313221	2299
Nonwoven Fabric Mills—*mfg*	31323	2299
Textile and Fabric Finishing (except Broadwoven Fabric) Mills—*mfg*	313312	2299
Textile Product Mills, All Other Miscellaneous—*mfg*	314999	2299
Thread Mills—*mfg*	313113	2299
Yarn Spinning Mills—*mfg*	313111	2299
Garter belts: Women's and Girls' Cut and Sew Lingerie, Loungewear and Nightwear—*mfg*	315231	2389
Garters: Apparel Accessories and Apparel, Other—*mfg*	315999	2389
Women's and Girls' Cut and Sew Lingerie, Loungewear and Nightwear—*mfg*	315231	2389
Gas (natural) compressing station construction–general contractors: Power and Communication Transmission Line—*const*	23492	1623
Water, Sewer, and Pipeline—*const*	23491	1623
Gas (natural) production: Crude Petroleum and Natural Gas Extraction—*mining*	211111	1311
Gas absorbers: Air-Conditioning and Warm Air Heating Equipment and Commercial and Industrial Refrigeration Equipment—*mfg*	333415	3443
Metal Tank (Heavy Gauge)—*mfg*	33242	3443
Plate Work—*mfg*	332313	3443
Power Boiler and Heat Exchanger—*mfg*	33241	3443
Gas analyzers, laboratory type: Analytical Laboratory Instrument—*mfg*	334516	3826
Gas and diesel engine rebuilding, on a factory basis: Engine Equipment, Other—*mfg*	333618	3519
Motor Vehicle Parts, All Other—*mfg*	336399	3519
Gas and liquid analysis instruments, industrial process type: Instruments and Related Products for Measuring, Displaying, and Controlling Industrial Process Variables—*mfg*	334513	3823
Gas and other services combined (gas less than 95 percent of total): Natural Gas Distribution—*util*	22121	4932
Gas and vapor tubes: Electron Tube—*mfg*	334411	3671
Gas burner automatic controls, except valves: Automatic Environmental Control for Residential, Commercial and Appliance Use—*mfg*	334512	3822
Gas burners, domestic: Heating Equipment (except Electric and Warm Air Furnaces)—*mfg*	333414	3433
Gas capes (cold climate individual protective covers): Surgical Appliance and Supplies—*mfg*	339113	3842
Gas chromatographic instruments, laboratory type: Analytical Laboratory Instrument—*mfg*	334516	3826
Gas compressing, natural gas at the field on a contract basis: Oil and Gas Operations Support Activities—*mining*	213112	1389
Gas field exploration–on a contract basis: Geophysical Surveying and Mapping Services—*prof*	54136	1382
Oil and Gas Operations Support Activities—*mining*	213112	1382
Gas flow computers, industrial process type: Instruments and Related Products for Measuring, Displaying, and Controlling Industrial Process Variables—*mfg*	334513	3823
Gas heaters, room: Heating Equipment (except Electric and Warm Air Furnaces)—*mfg*	333414	3433
Gas holders, metal plate: Air-Conditioning and Warm Air Heating Equipment and Commercial and Industrial Refrigeration Equipment—*mfg*	333415	3443
Metal Tank (Heavy Gauge)—*mfg*	33242	3443
Plate Work—*mfg*	332313	3443
Power Boiler and Heat Exchanger—*mfg*	33241	3443
Gas household appliance stores: Household Appliance Stores—*retail*	443111	5722
Gas infrared heating units: Heating Equipment (except Electric and Warm Air Furnaces)—*mfg*	333414	3433
Gas leakage detection–contractors: Trade Contractors, All Other Special—*const*	23599	1799
Gas lighting fixtures: Durable Goods, Other Miscellaneous—*whlse*	42199	5099
Lighting Equipment, Other—*mfg*	335129	3648
Gas main construction–general contractors: Power and Communication Transmission Line—*const*	23492	1623
Water, Sewer, and Pipeline—*const*	23491	1623
Gas masks: Surgical Appliance and Supplies—*mfg*	339113	3842
Gas pipe, cast iron: Iron Foundries—*mfg*	331511	3321

ALPHABETICAL INDEX	NAICS	SIC
Gas producers (machinery): General Purpose Machinery , All Other—*mfg*	333999	3569
Gas ranges, domestic: Household Cooking Appliance—*mfg*	335221	3631
Gas separators (machinery): General Purpose Machinery , All Other—*mfg*	333999	3569
Gas tanks, metal plate: Air-Conditioning and Warm Air Heating Equipment and Commercial and Industrial Refrigeration Equipment—*mfg*	333415	3443
Metal Tank (Heavy Gauge)—*mfg*	33242	3443
Plate Work—*mfg*	332313	3443
Power Boiler and Heat Exchanger—*mfg*	33241	3443
Gas tanks, motor vehicle: Gasoline Engine and Engine Parts—*mfg*	336312	3714
Motor Vehicle Parts, All Other—*mfg*	336399	3714
Gas turbine generator set units, complete: Turbine and Turbine Generator Set Unit—*mfg*	333611	3511
Gas turbines and parts, except aircraft type: Turbine and Turbine Generator Set Unit—*mfg*	333611	3511
Gas turbines, mechanical drive: Turbine and Turbine Generator Set Unit—*mfg*	333611	3511
Gas valves and parts, industrial: Industrial Valve—*mfg*	332911	3491
Gas welding equipment: Power, Distribution and Specialty Transformer—*mfg*	335311	3548
Welding and Soldering Equipment—*mfg*	333992	3548
Gas welding rods, made from purchased wire: Fabricated Wire Product, Other—*mfg*	332618	3496
Gas well drilling–on a contract basis: Drilling Oil and Gas Wells—*mining*	213111	1381
Gas well machinery and equipment: Oil and Gas Field Machinery and Equipment—*mfg*	333132	3533
Gas well rig building, repairing, and dismantling on a contract basis: Oil and Gas Operations Support Activities—*mining*	213112	1389
Gas, coal–derived from chemical recovery coke ovens: Iron and Steel Mills—*mfg*	331111	3312
Petroleum and Coal Productsa, All Other—*mfg*	324199	3312
Gas, liquefied petroleum–bottled: Liquefied Petroleum Gas (Bottled Gas) Dealers—*retail*	454312	5984
Gas, liquefied petroleum–distribution through mains: Natural Gas Distribution—*util*	22121	4925
Gas, manufactured–production and distribution: Natural Gas Distribution—*util*	22121	4925
Gas, mixed natural and manufactured–production and distribution: Natural Gas Distribution—*util*	22121	4925
Gas, natural–distribution: Natural Gas Distribution—*util*	22121	4924
Gas, natural–transmission: Pipeline of Natural Gas—*trans*	48621	4922
Gas, natural–transmission and distribution: Natural Gas Distribution—*util*	22121	4923
Pipeline of Natural Gas—*trans*	48621	4923

ALPHABETICAL INDEX	NAICS	SIC
Gas, refinery or still oil–produced in petroleum refineries: Petroleum Refineries—*mfg*	32411	2911
Gas-oil burners, combination: Heating Equipment (except Electric and Warm Air Furnaces)—*mfg*	333414	3433
Gases, chemical warfare: Basic Organic Chemical, All Other—*mfg*	325199	2869
Gases, compressed and liquefied–except liquefied petroleum gas: Chemical and Allied Products, Other—*whlse*	42269	5169
Gases, fluorinated hydrocarbon: Basic Organic Chemical, All Other—*mfg*	325199	2869
Gases, industrial–compressed, liquefied, or solid: Industrial Gas—*mfg*	32512	2813
Gases, liquefied petroleum--except bulkstations and terminals: Petroleum and Petroleum Products (except Bulk Stations an Terminals)—*whlse*	42272	5172
Gases, liquefied petroleum–produced in petroleum refineries: Petroleum Refineries—*mfg*	32411	2911
Gasket, Packing, and Sealing Device Manufacturing	**339991**	**3053**
Gaskets: Industrial Machinery and Equipment—*whlse*	42183	5085
Industrial Supplies—*whlse*	42184	5085
Gaskets, regardless of mate rial: Gasket, Packing, and Sealing Device—*mfg*	339991	3053
Gasline hookup–contractors: Plumbing, Heating and Air-Conditioning Contractors—*const*	23511	1711
Gasmeters–domestic, large capacity, and industrial: Totalizing Fluid Meter and Counting Device—*mfg*	334514	3824
Gasoline (natural) production: Natural Gas Liquid Extraction—*mining*	211112	1321
Gasoline and oil: Gasoline Stations with Convenience Stores—*retail*	44711	5541
Gasoline Stations, Other—*retail*	44719	5541
Gasoline blending plants: Petroleum Refineries—*mfg*	32411	2911
Gasoline dispensing meters (except pumps): Totalizing Fluid Meter and Counting Device—*mfg*	334514	3824
Gasoline Engine and Engine Parts Manufacturing	**336312**	**3714**
Gasoline filling stations: Gasoline Stations with Convenience Stores—*retail*	44711	5541
Gasoline Stations, Other—*retail*	44719	5541
Gasoline filters, internal combustion engine–except motor vehicle: Fabricated Metal Product, All Other Miscellaneous—*mfg*	332999	3599
General Purpose Machinery , All Other—*mfg*	333999	3599
Machine Shops—*mfg*	33271	3599
Machinery, Other Commercial and Service Industry—*mfg*	333319	3599
Gasoline measuring and dispensing pumps: Measuring and Dispensing Pump—*mfg*	333913	3586
Gasoline pipelines, common carriers: Pipeline of Refined—*trans*	48691	4613
Gasoline pump installation–contractors: Trade Contractors, All Other Special—*const*	23599	1799
Gasoline Stations	**4471**	

Description	NAICS	SIC
Gasoline Stations	**447**	
Gasoline Stations with Convenience Stores	**44711**	**5411**
Gasoline Stations, Other	**44719**	**5541**
Gasoline, except bulk stations and terminals: Petroleum and Petroleum Products (except Bulk Stations and Terminals)—*whlse*	42272	5172
Gasoline, except natural gasoline: Petroleum Refineries—*mfg*	32411	2911
Gasoline–buying in bulk and selling to farmers: Petroleum and Petroleum Products (except Bulk Stations and Terminals)—*whlse*	42272	5172
Gassing yarn: Broadwoven Fabric Finishing Mills—*mfg*	313311	2269
Textile and Fabric Finishing (except Broadwoven Fabric) Mills—*mfg*	313312	2269
Gastroscopes, electromedical: Electromedical and Electrotherapeutic Apparatus—*mfg*	334510	3845
Irradiation Apparatus—*mfg*	334517	3845
Gastroscopes, except electromedical: Surgical and Medical Instrument—*mfg*	339112	3841
Gate and bridge machinery, hydraulic: General Purpose Machinery , All Other—*mfg*	333999	3569
Gate hooks: Bolt, Nut, Screw, Rivet and Washer—*mfg*	332722	3452
Gate hooks, plastics: Plastics Pipe and Pipe Fitting—*mfg*	326122	3089
Plastics Product, All Other—*mfg*	326199	3089
Unsupported Plastics Profile Shape—*mfg*	326121	3089
Gates and accessories, wire: Building Material Dealers, Other—*retail*	44419	5039
Construction Material, Other—*whlse*	42139	5039
Gates, dam–metal plate: Fabricated Structural Metal—*mfg*	332312	3441
Gates, fence–made from purchased wire: Fabricated Wire Product, Other—*mfg*	332618	3496
Gates, holding (farm equipment): Farm Machinery and Equipment—*mfg*	333111	3523
Gates, ornamental metal: Ornamental and Architectural Metal Work—*mfg*	332323	3446
Gathering of forest products–(e.g., gums, barks, seeds): Crop Farming, All Other Miscellaneous—*ag*	111998	831
Forest Nurseries and Gathering of Forest Products—*ag*	11321	831
Gathering, extracting, and selling of tree seeds: Crop Farming, All Other Miscellaneous—*ag*	111998	831
Forest Nurseries and Gathering of Forest Products—*ag*	11321	831
Gauge blocks: Cutting Tool and Machine Tool Accessory—*mfg*	333515	3545
Hand and Edge Tool—*mfg*	332212	3545
Gauges except electric, motor vehicle–oil pressure and water temperature: Measuring and Controlling Device, Other—*mfg*	334519	3829
Surgical and Medical Instrument—*mfg*	339112	3829
Gauges for computing pressure-temperature corrections: Totalizing Fluid Meter and Counting Device—*mfg*	334514	3824
Gauges, except optical (machine tool accessories): Cutting Tool and Machine Tool Accessory—*mfg*	333515	3545
Hand and Edge Tool—*mfg*	332212	3545

Description	NAICS	SIC
Gauging instruments, thickness–ultrasonic: Measuring and Controlling Device, Other—*mfg*	334519	3829
Surgical and Medical Instrument—*mfg*	339112	3829
Gauze: Broadwoven Fabric Mills—*mfg*	31321	2211
Gauze, surgical–not made in weaving mills: Surgical Appliance and Supplies—*mfg*	339113	3842
Gavels, wood: Manufacturing, All Other Miscellaneous—*mfg*	339999	2499
Wood Container and Pallet—*mfg*	32192	2499
Wood Product, All Other Miscellaneous—*mfg*	321999	2499
Gear chamfering machines (machine tools): Machine Tool (Metal Cutting Types)—*mfg*	333512	3541
Gear cutting and finishing machines: Machine Tool (Metal Cutting Types)—*mfg*	333512	3541
Gear pullers, handtools: Hand and Edge Tool—*mfg*	332212	3423
Gear rolling machines: Machine Tool (Metal Forming Types)—*mfg*	333513	3542
Gear tooth grinding machines (machine tools): Machine Tool (Metal Cutting Types)—*mfg*	333512	3541
Gearmotors (power transmission equipment): Speed Changer, Industrial High-Speed Drive and Gear—*mfg*	333612	3566
Gears: Industrial Machinery and Equipment—*whlse*	42183	5085
Industrial Supplies—*whlse*	42184	5085
Gears, forged steel–not made in rolling mills: Iron and Steel Forging—*mfg*	332111	3462
Gears, motor vehicle: Gasoline Engine and Engine Parts—*mfg*	336312	3714
Motor Vehicle Parts, All Other—*mfg*	336399	3714
Motor Vehicle Steering and Suspension Components (except Spring)—*mfg*	33633	3714
Gears, motorcycle and bicycle: Motorcycle, Bicycle and Parts—*mfg*	336991	3751
Gears, power transmission–aircraft: Aircraft Part and Auxiliary Equipment, Other—*mfg*	336413	3728
Fluid Power Valve and Hose Fitting—*mfg*	332912	3728
Gears, power transmission–except motor vehicle and aircraft: Speed Changer, Industrial High-Speed Drive and Gear—*mfg*	333612	3566
Geese farms: Poultry Production, Other—*ag*	11239	259
Geese, processed–fresh, frozen, canned, or cooked: Food, All Other Miscellaneous—*mfg*	311999	2015
Poultry Processing—*mfg*	311615	2015
Geese–slaughtering and dressing: Food, All Other Miscellaneous—*mfg*	311999	2015
Poultry Processing—*mfg*	311615	2015
Geiger counters: Measuring and Controlling Device, Other—*mfg*	334519	3829
Surgical and Medical Instrument—*mfg*	339112	3829
Geiger Mueller tubes: Electron Tube—*mfg*	334411	3671
Gelatin: Chemical and Allied Products, Other—*whlse*	42269	5169
Gelatin capsules, empty: Basic Organic Chemical, All Other—*mfg*	325199	2899
Chemical Product, All Other Miscellaneous—*mfg*	325998	2899
Gelatin dessert preparations: Food, All Other Miscellaneous—*mfg*	311999	2099
Gelatin rolls used in printing: Printing Machinery and Equipment—*mfg*	333293	3555

ALPHABETICAL INDEX	NAICS	SIC
Gelatin, vegetable (agar-agar): Medicinal and Botanical—*mfg*	325411	2833
Gelatin–edible, technical, photographic, and pharmaceutical: Basic Organic Chemical, All Other—*mfg*	325199	2899
Chemical Product, All Other Miscellaneous—*mfg*	325998	2899
Gem stone mining: Crushed and Broken Stone and Quarrying, Other—*mining*	212319	1499
Non-Metallic Mineral, All Other—*mining*	212399	1499
Gem stones: Jewelry, Watch, Precious Stone and Precious Metal—*whlse*	42194	5094
Gem stones, rough: Jewelry Stores—*retail*	44831	5999
Gems, real and imitation–preparation for setting: Jewelers' Material and Lapidary Work—*mfg*	339913	3915
Genealogical investigation service: Personal Services, All Other—*serv*	81299	7299
General Warehousing and Storage Facilities	**49311**	**4226**
General accounting offices: General Government, All Other—*pub*	92119	9199
General and industrial loan institutions: International Trade Financing—*fin*	522293	6159
Non-Depository Credit Intermediation, All Other—*fin*	522298	6159
Sales Financing—*fin*	52222	6159
General Automotive Repair	**811111**	**7538**
General Economic Programs, Administration of	**92611**	**9611**
General economic statistics agencies: General Economic Programs, Administration of—*pub*	92611	9611
General Freight Trucking	**4841**	
General Freight Trucking, Local	**48411**	**4214**
General Freight Trucking, Long-Distance	**48412**	
General Freight Trucking, Long-Distance, Less Than Truckload	**484122**	**4213**
General Freight Trucking, Long-Distance, Truckload	**484121**	**4213**
General Government, All Other	**92119**	**9199**
General line cans, metal: Metal Can—*mfg*	332431	3411
General Line Grocery Wholesalers	**42241**	**5141**
General management consultants: Administrative Management and General Management Consulting Services—*prof*	541611	8742
Human Resources and Executive Search Consulting Services—*prof*	541612	8742
Marketing Consulting Services—*prof*	541613	8742
Process, Physical, Distribution and Logistics Consulting Services—*prof*	541614	8742
General Medical and Surgical Hospitals	**62211**	**8069**
General Medical and Surgical Hospitals	**6221**	
General medical and surgical hospitals: General Medical and Surgical Hospitals—*hlth*	62211	8062
General Merchandise Stores	**452**	
General merchandise stores: General Merchandise Stores, All Other—*retail*	45299	5399
Warehouse Clubs and Superstores—*retail*	45291	5399
General Merchandise Stores, All Other	**45299**	**5331**
General Merchandise Stores, Other	**4529**	
General Purpose Machinery Manufacturing, All Other	**333999**	**3569**
General Purpose Machinery Manufacturing, All Other	**33399**	
General Purpose Machinery Manufacturing, Other	**3339**	
General Rental Centers	**5323**	
General Rental Centers	**53231**	**7359**
General services departments: General Government, All Other—*pub*	92119	9199
General stores: General Merchandise Stores, All Other—*retail*	45299	5399
Warehouse Clubs and Superstores—*retail*	45291	5399
General warehousing and storage: General Warehousing and Storage Facilities—*trans*	49311	4225
Lessors of Miniwarehouses and Self Storage Units—*real*	53113	4225
Generating apparatus and parts, electrical–except internal combustion engineand arc-welding: Motor and Generator—*mfg*	335312	3621
Generation of electric power: Electric Bulk Power Transmission and Control—*util*	221121	4911
Electric Power Distribution—*util*	221122	4911
Electric Power Generation, Other—*util*	221119	4911
Fossil Fuel Electric Power Generation—*util*	221112	4911
Hydroelectric Power Generation—*util*	221111	4911
Nuclear Electric Power Generation—*util*	221113	4911
Generator and starter repair, automotive: Automotive Mechanical and Electrical Repair and Maintenance, Other—*serv*	811118	7539
Generator control and metering panels: Switchgear and Switchboard Apparatus—*mfg*	335313	3613
Generator set units, turbine–complete-steam, gas, and hydraulic: Turbine and Turbine Generator Set Unit—*mfg*	333611	3511
Generator sets–gasoline, diesel, and dual fuel: Motor and Generator—*mfg*	335312	3621
Generator voltage regulators, electric induction and step type: Power, Distribution and Specialty Transformer—*mfg*	335311	3612
Generators (separate) for arc-welders: Power, Distribution and Specialty Transformer—*mfg*	335311	3548
Welding and Soldering Equipment—*mfg*	333992	3548
Generators and sets, electric–except internal combustion engine, welding, andturbogenerators: Motor and Generator—*mfg*	335312	3621
Generators for gas-electric and oil-electric vehicles: Motor and Generator—*mfg*	335312	3621
Generators for storage battery chargers, except internal combustion engine and aircraft: Motor and Generator—*mfg*	335312	3621
Generators, aircraft and motor vehicle: Motor Vehicle Electrical and Electronic Equipment, Other—*mfg*	336322	3694
Generators, electrical: Building Material Dealers, Other—*retail*	44419	5063
Electrical Apparatus and Equipment, Wiring Supplies and Material—*whlse*	42161	5063
Generators, gas: General Purpose Machinery , All Other—*mfg*	333999	3569

Generators, smoke (ordnance): Ordnance and Accessories, Other—*mfg*	332995	3489
Generators, X-ray: Irradiation Apparatus—*mfg*	334517	3844
Generators–steam, liquid oxygen, and nitrogen: General Purpose Machinery , All Other—*mfg*	333999	3569
Geodesic domes, prefabricated–wood: Prefabricated Wood Building—*mfg*	321992	2452
Geological exploration, oil and gas field–on a contract basis: Geophysical Surveying and Mapping Services—*prof*	54136	1382
Oil and Gas Operations Support Activities—*mining*	213112	1382
Geologists, consulting–not connected with business service laboratories: Environmental Consulting Services—*prof*	54162	8999
Scientific and Technical Consulting Services, Other—*prof*	54169	8999
Geophysical exploration services, for metal mining–on a contract basis: Geophysical Surveying and Mapping Services—*prof*	54136	1081
Metal Support Activities—*mining*	213114	1081
Geophysical exploration services, for nonmetallic minerals, except fuels–on a contract basis: Geophysical Surveying and Mapping Services—*prof*	54136	1481
Non-Metallic Minerals (except Fuels) Support Activities—*mining*	213115	1481
Geophysical exploration, oil and gas field–on a contract basis: Geophysical Surveying and Mapping Services—*prof*	54136	1382
Oil and Gas Operations Support Activities—*mining*	213112	1382
Geophysical Surveying and Mapping Services	**54136**	**1081**
Georgettes: Broadwoven Fabric Mills—*mfg*	31321	2221
Geothermal drilling-contractors: Water Well Drilling Contractors—*const*	23581	1781
Geothermal steam production: Steam and Air-Conditioning Supply—*util*	22133	4961
Geraniol, synthetic: Basic Organic Chemical, All Other—*mfg*	325199	2869
Germanium refining, primary: Primary Smelting and Refining of Nonferrous Metal (except Copper and Aluminum)—*mfg*	331419	3339
Germanium refining, secondary: Secondary Smelting and Alloying of Aluminum—*mfg*	331314	3341
Secondary Smelting, Refining, and Alloying of Nonferrous Metal (except Copper and Aluminum)—*mfg*	331492	3341
Ghost writing: Independent Artists, Writers, and Performers—*arts*	71151	8999
Gift shops: Gift, Novelty and Souvenir Stores—*retail*	45322	5947
Gift wrap paper: Coated and Laminated Paper—*mfg*	322222	2679
Converted Paper Product, All Other—*mfg*	322298	2679
Die-Cut Paper and Paperboard Office Supplies—*mfg*	322231	2679
Non-Folding Sanitary Food Container—*mfg*	322215	2679
Gift, Novelty and Souvenir Stores	**45322**	**5947**
Gifts and novelties: Nondurable Goods, Other Miscellaneous—*whlse*	42299	5199
Gilding hooks, cards, or pa per-rn fg: Tradebinding and Related Work—*mfg*	323121	2789
Gilsonite mining: Crushed and Broken Stone and Quarrying, Other—*mining*	212319	1499
Non-Metallic Mineral, All Other—*mining*	212399	1499
Gimlets (edge tools): Hand and Edge Tool—*mfg*	332212	3423
Gimps: Narrow Fabric Mills—*mfg*	313221	2241
Gin (alcoholic beverage): Distilleries—*mfg*	31214	2085
Ginger ale, bottled or canned: Bottled Water—*mfg*	312112	2086
Soft Drink—*mfg*	312111	2086
Gingerbread mixes: Flour Mixes and Dough from Purchased Flour—*mfg*	311822	2045
Ginghams: Broadwoven Fabric Mills—*mfg*	31321	2211
Ginning cotton: Cotton Ginning—*ag*	115111	724
Ginning machines, cotton: Industrial Machinery, All Other—*mfg*	333298	3559
Machinery, Other Commercial and Service Industry—*mfg*	333319	3559
Ginning moss: Postharvest Crop Activities (except Cotton Ginning)—*ag*	115114	723
Gins, cotton–operation of: Cotton Ginning—*ag*	115111	724
Ginseng, gathering of: Crop Farming, All Other Miscellaneous—*ag*	111998	831
Forest Nurseries and Gathering of Forest Products—*ag*	11321	831
Girdle blanks, elastic: Underwear and Nightwear Knitting Mills—*mfg*	315192	2259
Girdles: Women's and Girls' Cut and Sew Apparel Contractors—*mfg*	315212	2342
Women's and Girls' Cut and Sew Lingerie, Loungewear and Nightwear—*mfg*	315231	2342
Girdles (elastic) and other foundation garments: Underwear and Nightwear Knitting Mills—*mfg*	315192	2259
Girls' camps: Recreational and Vacation Camps—*accom*	721214	7032
Girls' hosiery: Hosiery and Sock Mills, Other—*mfg*	315119	2252
Sheer Hosiery Mills—*mfg*	315111	2252
Glace fruits and nuts: Confectionery from Purchased Chocolate—*mfg*	31133	2064
Non-Chocolate Confectionery—*mfg*	31134	2064
Gland derivatives–bulk, uncompounded: Medicinal and Botanical—*mfg*	325411	2833
Glass and Glass Product Manufacturing	**3272**	
Glass and Glass Product Manufacturing	**32721**	
Glass and glassware made in glassmaking establishments–for industrial, scientific, and technical use: Pressed and Blown Glass and Glassware, Other—*mfg*	327212	3229
Glass and Glazing Contractors	**23592**	**1799**
Glass blanks for electric light bulbs: Pressed and Blown Glass and Glassware, Other—*mfg*	327212	3229
Glass bottles: Industrial Machinery and Equipment—*whlse*	42183	5085
Industrial Supplies—*whlse*	42184	5085
Glass brick: Pressed and Blown Glass and Glassware, Other—*mfg*	327212	3229
Glass broadwoven fabrics: Broadwoven Fabric Mills—*mfg*	31321	2221
Glass Container Manufacturing	**327213**	**3221**
Glass eyes: Ophthalmic Goods—*mfg*	339115	3851
Glass installation, except automotive–contractors: Glass and Glazing Contractors—*const*	23592	1793
Glass making machinery–blowing, molding, forming, grinding, etc.: Industrial Machinery, All Other—*mfg*	333298	3559

ALPHABETICAL INDEX	NAICS	SIC
Machinery, Other Commercial and Service Industry—*mfg*	333319	3559
Glass narrow fabrics: Narrow Fabric Mills—*mfg*	313221	2241
Glass Product Manufacturing Made of Purchased Glass	**327215**	**3231**
Glass replacement and repair, automotive: Automotive Glass Replacement Shops—*serv*	811122	7536
Glass sand mining: Industrial Sand—*mining*	212322	1446
Glass stores: Building Material Dealers, Other—*retail*	44419	5231
Paint and Wallpaper Stores—*retail*	44412	5231
Paint, Varnish and Supplies—*whlse*	42295	5231
Glass tire cord and tire cord fabrics: Tire Cord and Tire Fabric Mills—*mfg*	314992	2296
Glass toweling, cotton: Broadwoven Fabric Mills—*mfg*	31321	2211
Glass window cleaning preparations: Polish and Other Sanitation Good—*mfg*	325612	2842
Glass wool: Mineral Wool—*mfg*	327993	3296
Glass work, except automotive-contractors: Glass and Glazing Contractors—*const*	23592	1793
Glass, colored–cathedral and antique: Flat Glass—*mfg*	327211	3211
Glass, flat: Flat Glass—*mfg*	327211	3211
Glass, flat–except automotive: Building Material Dealers, Other—*retail*	44419	5039
Construction Material, Other—*whlse*	42139	5039
Glass, medical: Drug, Drug Proprietaries and Druggists' Sundries—*whlse*	42221	5122
Glass, scientific apparatus–for druggists', hospitals, laboratories-made from purchased glass: Glass Product Made of Purchased Glass—*mfg*	327215	3231
Glass, sheet–bent-made from purchased glass: Glass Product Made of Purchased Glass—*mfg*	327215	3231
Glass–cut, ground, leaded, laminated, ornamented, and tinted: Glass Product Made of Purchased Glass—*mfg*	327215	3231
Glasses, field or opera: Optical Instrument and Lens—*mfg*	333314	3827
Glasses, sun or glare: Ophthalmic Goods—*mfg*	339115	3851
Glasshouse refractories: Clay Refractory—*mfg*	327124	3255
Glassine bags, uncoated paper: Uncoated Paper and Multiwall Bag—*mfg*	322224	2674
Glassine wrapping paper: Newsprint Mills—*mfg*	322122	2621
Paper (except Newsprint) Mills—*mfg*	322121	2621
Glassware for packing, bottling and homecanning: Glass Container—*mfg*	327213	3221
Glassware stores: Home Furnishings Stores, All Other—*retail*	442299	5719
Window Treatment Stores—*retail*	442291	5719
Glassware, antique: Non-Depository Credit Intermediation, All Other—*fin*	522298	5932
Used Merchandise Stores—*retail*	45331	5932
Glassware, cut and engraved-made from purchased glass: Glass Product Made of Purchased Glass—*mfg*	327215	3231

ALPHABETICAL INDEX	NAICS	SIC
Glassware, cutting and engraving: Glass Product Made of Purchased Glass—*mfg*	327215	3231
Glassware, decorated–e.g., chipped, en-graved, sand-blasted, etched-made from purchased glass: Glass Product Made of Purchased Glass—*mfg*	327215	3231
Glassware, except glass containers for packing, bottling, and canning: Pressed and Blown Glass and Glassware, Other—*mfg*	327212	3229
Glassware, household: Home Furnishing—*whlse*	42122	5023
Glassware, novelty: Nondurable Goods, Other Miscellaneous—*whlse*	42299	5199
Glassware–art, decorative, and novelty: Pressed and Blown Glass and Glassware, Other—*mfg*	327212	3229
Glauber's salt: Basic Inorganic Chemical, All Other—*mfg*	325188	2819
Chemical Product, All Other Miscellaneous—*mfg*	325998	2819
Glauber's salt mining: Potash, Soda, and Borate Mineral—*mining*	212391	1474
Glazing furs: Fur and Leather Apparel—*mfg*	315292	2371
Glazing of concrete surfaces–contractors: Glass and Glazing Contractors—*const*	23592	1799
Glazing panels, plastics: Plastics Pipe and Pipe Fitting—*mfg*	326122	3089
Plastics Product, All Other—*mfg*	326199	3089
Unsupported Plastics Profile Shape—*mfg*	326121	3089
Glazing work-contractors: Glass and Glazing Contractors—*const*	23592	1793
Glide slope instrumentation: Search, Detection, Navigation, Guidance, Aeronautical, and Nautical System and Instrument—*mfg*	334511	3812
Gliders (aircraft): Aircraft—*mfg*	336411	3721
Gliders (furniture), metal: Metal Household Furniture—*mfg*	337124	2514
Globe covers (maps)–publishing and printing, or publishing only: Database and Directory Publishers—*info*	51114	2741
Music Publishers—*info*	51223	2741
Publishers, All Other—*info*	511199	2741
Globes, geographical: Plastics Product, All Other—*mfg*	326199	3999
Glove and Mitten Manufacturing	**315992**	**3151**
Glove fabrics, cotton: Broadwoven Fabric Mills—*mfg*	31321	2211
Glove leather: Leather and Hide Tanning and Finishing—*mfg*	31611	3111
Glove lining fabrics: Narrow Fabric Mills—*mfg*	313221	2241
Glove linings, except fur: Glove and Mitten—*mfg*	315992	2381
Glove linings, fur: Fur and Leather Apparel—*mfg*	315292	2371
Glove mending on factory basis: Apparel Accessories and Apparel, Other—*mfg*	315999	2399
Gloves: Outerwear Knitting Mills—*mfg*	315191	2259
Gloves (all materials), men's and boys': Men's and Boys' Clothing and Furnishings—*whlse*	42232	5136
Gloves and mittens, plastics: Plastics Pipe and Pipe Fitting—*mfg*	326122	3089
Plastics Product, All Other—*mfg*	326199	3089
Unsupported Plastics Profile Shape—*mfg*	326121	3089
Gloves and mittens, woven or knit: Glove and Mitten—*mfg*	315992	2381

Gloves, (all materials)–women's, children's, and infants': Women's, Children's, and Infants' and Accessories—*whlse*	42233	5137
Gloves, leather: Glove and Mitten—*mfg*	315992	3151
Gloves, safety–all material: Surgical Appliance and Supplies—*mfg*	339113	3842
Gloves, sport and athletic–e.g., boxing, baseball, racketball, handball: Sporting and Athletic Goods—*mfg*	33992	3949
Gloves–e.g., surgeons', electricians', household-rubber: Fabric Coating Mills—*mfg*	31332	3069
Rubber Product, All Other—*mfg*	326299	3069
Glow lamp bulbs: Electric Lamp Bulb and Part—*mfg*	33511	3641
Glucose: Wet Corn Milling—*mfg*	311221	2046
Glue: Chemical and Allied Products, Other—*whlse*	42269	5169
Glue size: Basic Organic Chemical, All Other—*mfg*	325199	2899
Chemical Product, All Other Miscellaneous—*mfg*	325998	2899
Glue, dental: Dental Equipment and Supplies—*mfg*	339114	3843
Glue, except dental–animal, vegetable, fish, casein, and synthetic resin: Adhesive—*mfg*	32552	2891
Gluten feed: Wet Corn Milling—*mfg*	311221	2046
Gluten meal: Wet Corn Milling—*mfg*	311221	2046
Glycerin, crude and refined–from fats-except synthetic: Soap and Other Detergent—*mfg*	325611	2841
Glycerin, except from fats (synthetic): Basic Organic Chemical, All Other—*mfg*	325199	2869
Glycosides: Medicinal and Botanical—*mfg*	325411	2833
Gneiss, crushed and broken: Crushed and Broken Granite and Quarrying—*mining*	212313	1423
Gneiss, dimension: Dimension Stone and Quarrying—*mining*	212311	1411
Goat Farming	**11242**	**214**
Goat farms: Goat Farming—*ag*	11242	214
Sheep Farming—*ag*	11241	214
Goats: Livestock—*whlse*	42252	5154
Goats' milk production: Goat Farming—*ag*	11242	214
Sheep Farming—*ag*	11241	214
Goblets, glass: Pressed and Blown Glass and Glassware, Other—*mfg*	327212	3229
Gocart raceway operation: Amusement and Recreation Industries, All Other—*arts*	71399	7999
Gocart rentals: Recreational Goods Rental—*real*	532292	7999
Gocarts: Motor Vehicle Dealers, All Other—*retail*	441229	5599
Sporting and Recreational Goods and Supplies—*whlse*	42191	5091
Gocarts, children's: Game, Toy, and Children's Vehicle—*mfg*	339932	3944
Gocarts, except children's: Transportation Equipment, All Other—*mfg*	336999	3799
Goggles–sun, safety, industrial, and underwater: Ophthalmic Goods—*mfg*	339115	3851
Gold and gold alloy bars, sheets, strip, and tubing: Nonferrous Metal (except Copper and Aluminum) Rolling, Drawing and Extruding—*mfg*	331491	3356
Gold beating (manufacturing of gold leaf and foil): Fabricated Metal Product, All Other Miscellaneous—*mfg*	332999	3497

Laminated Aluminum Foil for Flexible Packaging Uses—*mfg*	322225	3497
Gold foil and leaf, not made in rolling mills: Fabricated Metal Product, All Other Miscellaneous—*mfg*	332999	3497
Laminated Aluminum Foil for Flexible Packaging Uses—*mfg*	322225	3497
Gold ink: Printing Ink—*mfg*	32591	2893
Gold lode mining: Gold Ore—*mining*	212221	1041
Gold or bronze mixtures, powders, paints, and sizes–artists': Chemical Product, All Other Miscellaneous—*mfg*	325998	3952
Institutional Furniture—*mfg*	337127	3952
Lead Pencil and Art Good—*mfg*	339942	3952
Gold ore: Coal and Other Mineral and Ore—*whlse*	42152	5052
Gold Ore and Silver Ore Mining	**21222**	
Gold Ore Mining	**212221**	**1041**
Gold placer mining: Gold Ore—*mining*	212221	1041
Gold plating, ior the trade: Electroplating, Plating, Polishing, Anodizing and Coloring—*mfg*	332813	3471
Gold refining, primary: Primary Smelting and Refining of Nonferrous Metal (except Copper and Aluminum)—*mfg*	331419	3339
Gold rolling and drawing: Nonferrous Metal (except Copper and Aluminum) Rolling, Drawing and Extruding—*mfg*	331491	3356
Gold smelting and refining, secondary: Secondary Smelting and Alloying of Aluminum—*mfg*	331314	3341
Secondary Smelting, Refining, and Alloying of Copper—*mfg*	331423	3341
Secondary Smelting, Refining, and Alloying of Nonferrous Metal (except Copper and Aluminum)—*mfg*	331492	3341
Gold stamping on books: Tradebinding and Related Work—*mfg*	323121	2789
Gold, dental: Dental Equipment and Supplies—*mfg*	339114	3843
Goldfish farms: Animal Aquaculture, Other—*ag*	112519	273
Finfish Farming and Fish Hatcheries—*ag*	112511	273
Shellfish Farming—*ag*	112512	273
Golf carts, except self-propelled-whole-sale: Sporting and Recreational Goods and Supplies—*whlse*	42191	5091
Golf carts, hand: Sporting and Athletic Goods—*mfg*	33992	3949
Golf carts, powered: Transportation Equipment, All Other—*mfg*	336999	3799
Golf carts, self-propelled: Transportation Equipment and Supplies (except Motor Vehicle)—*whlse*	42186	5088
Golf clubs, membership: Golf Courses and Country Clubs—*arts*	71391	7997
Golf clubs, non membership: Golf Courses and Country Clubs—*arts*	71391	7992
Golf course construction–general contractors: Heavy, All Other—*const*	23499	1629
Industrial Nonbuilding Structure—*const*	23493	1629
Golf Courses and Country Clubs	**71391**	**7997**
Golf courses, miniature–operation of: Amusement and Recreation Industries, All Other—*arts*	71399	7999
Golf courses, public–operation of: Golf Courses and Country Clubs—*arts*	71391	7992
Golf driving ranges: Amusement and Recreation Industries, All Other—*arts*	71399	7999

ALPHABETICAL INDEX	NAICS	SIC
Golf equipment: Sporting and Recreational Goods and Supplies—*whlse*	42191	5091
Golf goods and equipment: Sporting Goods Stores—*retail*	45111	5941
Golf professionals operating retail stores: Sporting Goods Stores—*retail*	45111	5941
Golf, pitch-n-putt: Amusement and Recreation Industries, All Other—*arts*	71399	7999
Golfing equipment–e.g., caddy carts and bags, clubs, tees, balls: Sporting and Athletic Goods—*mfg*	33992	3949
Gongs, electric: Electrical Equipment and Component, All Other Miscellaneous—*mfg*	335999	3699
Gouges, woodworking: Hand and Edge Tool—*mfg*	332212	3423
Government National Mortgage Association: International Trade Financing—*fin*	522293	6111
Non-Depository Credit Intermediation, All Other—*fin*	522298	6111
Secondary Market Financing—*fin*	522294	6111
Government National Mortgage Association (GNMA) pools: Financial Vehicles, Other—*fin*	52599	6726
Governors' offices: Executive Offices—*pub*	92111	9111
Governors, aircraft propeller feathering: Aircraft Part and Auxiliary Equipment, Other—*mfg*	336413	3728
Fluid Power Valve and Hose Fitting—*mfg*	332912	3728
Governors, diesel engine: Engine Equipment, Other—*mfg*	333618	3519
Motor Vehicle Parts, All Other—*mfg*	336399	3519
Governors, motor vehicle: Gasoline Engine and Engine Parts—*mfg*	336312	3714
Motor Vehicle Parts, All Other—*mfg*	336399	3714
Governors, pump–for gas engines: Engine Equipment, Other—*mfg*	333618	3519
Motor Vehicle Parts, All Other—*mfg*	336399	3519
Governors, steam: Turbine and Turbine Generator Set Unit—*mfg*	333611	3511
Gown supply service, uniform: Linen Supply—*serv*	812331	7213
Gowns, formal: Women's and Girls' Cut and Sew Apparel Contractors—*mfg*	315212	2335
Women's and Girls' Cut and Sew Dress—*mfg*	315233	2335
Gowns, hospital–surgical and patient: Cut and Sew Apparel, All Other—*mfg*	315299	2389
Gowns, night: Underwear and Nightwear Knitting Mills—*mfg*	315192	2254
Gowns, wedding: Women's and Girls' Cut and Sew Apparel Contractors—*mfg*	315212	2335
Women's and Girls' Cut and Sew Dress—*mfg*	315233	2335
Gowns–academic, choir, clerical: Cut and Sew Apparel, All Other—*mfg*	315299	2389
Grader attachments, elevating: Construction Machinery—*mfg*	33312	3531
Overhead Traveling Crane, Hoist and Monorail System—*mfg*	333923	3531
Railroad Rolling Stock—*mfg*	33651	3531
Graders, motor: Construction and (except Petroleum) Machinery and Equipment—*whlse*	42181	5082
Graders, road (construction machinery): Construction Machinery—*mfg*	33312	3531
Overhead Traveling Crane, Hoist and Monorail System—*mfg*	333923	3531
Railroad Rolling Stock—*mfg*	33651	3531
Grading for highways, streets, and airport runways–contractors: Highway and Street—*const*	23411	1611
Grading of drugs and herbs: Medicinal and Botanical—*mfg*	325411	2833
Grading oil and gas well foundations on a contract basis: Oil and Gas Operations Support Activities—*mining*	213112	1389
Grading, cleaning, and sorting machines–fruit, grain, and vegetable: Farm Machinery and Equipment—*mfg*	333111	3523
Grading–except for highways, streets, and airport runways–contractors: Excavation Contractors—*const*	23593	1794
Gradual switches, pneumatic: Automatic Environmental Control for Residential, Commercial and Appliance Use—*mfg*	334512	3822
Grafts, artificial–for surgery-made of braided or mesh artificial fibers: Surgical Appliance and Supplies—*mfg*	339113	3842
Graham flour: Flour Milling—*mfg*	311211	2041
Grahamite mining: Crushed and Broken Stone and Quarrying, Other—*mining*	212319	1499
Non-Metallic Mineral, All Other—*mining*	212399	1499
Grain: Grain and Field Bean—*whlse*	42251	5153
Grain alcohol for medicinal and beverage purposes: Distilleries—*mfg*	31214	2085
Grain alcohol, industrial (nonbeverage): Basic Organic Chemical, All Other—*mfg*	325199	2869
Ethyl Alcohol—*mfg*	325193	2869
Grain and Field Bean Wholesalers	**42251**	**5153**
Grain and Oilseed Milling	**3112**	
Grain cereals, cracked: Flour Milling—*mfg*	311211	2041
Grain cleaning: Postharvest Crop Activities (except Cotton Ginning)—*ag*	115114	723
Grain drills, including legume planters(agricultural machinery): Farm Machinery and Equipment—*mfg*	333111	3523
Grain elevator construction–general contractors: Building, Commercial and Institutional—*const*	23332	1541
Manufacturing and Industrial Building—*const*	23331	1541
Grain elevators, except storage only: Grain and Field Bean—*whlse*	42251	5153
Grain elevators, storage only: Farm Product Warehousing and Storage Facilities—*trans*	49313	4221
Grain Farming, All Other	**111199**	**119**
Grain Farming, Other	**11119**	
Grain farms–except wheat, rice, corn, and soybeans: Grain Farming, All Other—*ag*	111199	119
Grain fumigation: Postharvest Crop Activities (except Cotton Ginning)—*ag*	115114	723
Grain grading, cleaning, and sorting machines: Farm Machinery and Equipment—*mfg*	333111	3523

Description	NAICS	SIC
Grain grinding, custom: Postharvest Crop Activities (except Cotton Ginning)—*ag*	115114	723
Grain leveling in railroad cars: Air, Rail, and Water Equipment Rental and Leasing, Commercial—*real*	532411	4741
Rail Support Activities—*trans*	48821	4741
Grain measures, wood–turned and shaped: Manufacturing, All Other Miscellaneous—*mfg*	339999	2499
Wood Container and Pallet—*mfg*	32192	2499
Wood Product, All Other Miscellaneous—*mfg*	321999	2499
Grain mill machinery: Food Product Machinery—*mfg*	333294	3556
Grain stackers: Farm Machinery and Equipment—*mfg*	333111	3523
Grain storage bins: Building Material Dealers, Other—*retail*	44419	5039
Construction Material, Other—*whlse*	42139	5039
Grain trimming service for railroad shipment: Air, Rail, and Water Equipment Rental and Leasing, Commercial—*real*	532411	4741
Rail Support Activities—*trans*	48821	4741
Grain, brewers': Breweries—*mfg*	31212	2082
Grain, machine harvesting of: Crop Harvesting, Primarily by Machine—*ag*	115113	722
Grains, abrasive–natural and artificial: Abrasive Product—*mfg*	32791	3291
Fabricated Metal Product, All Other Miscellaneous—*mfg*	332999	3291
Granite building stone: Brick, Stone and Related Material—*whlse*	42132	5032
Building Material Dealers, Other—*retail*	44419	5032
Granite, crushed and broken: Crushed and Broken Granite and Quarrying—*mining*	212313	1423
Granite, cut and shaped: Cut Stone and Stone Product—*mfg*	327991	3281
Granite, dimension: Dimension Stone and Quarrying—*mining*	212311	1411
Granola bars and clusters: Confectionery from Purchased Chocolate—*mfg*	31133	2064
Non-Chocolate Confectionery—*mfg*	31134	2064
Granola, except bars and clusters: Breakfast Cereal—*mfg*	31123	2043
Coffee and Tea—*mfg*	31192	2043
Grantmaking and Giving Services	**8132**	
Grantmaking and Giving Services	**81321**	
Grantmaking and Giving Services, Other	**813219**	**8399**
Grantmaking Foundations	**813211**	**6732**
Granular wheat flour: Flour Milling—*mfg*	311211	2041
Granulated beet sugar: Beet Sugar—*mfg*	311313	2063
Grape farms: Grape Vineyards—*ag*	111332	172
Grape Vineyards	**111332**	**172**
Grapefruit groves and farms: Citrus (except Orange) Groves—*ag*	11132	174
Orange Groves—*ag*	11131	174
Grapefruit oil: Chemical Product, All Other Miscellaneous—*mfg*	325998	2899
Spice and Extract—*mfg*	311942	2899
Graph paper, ruled: Blankbook, Loose-leaf Binder and Device—*mfg*	323118	2782
Flexographic Printing, Commercial—*mfg*	323112	2782
Gravure Printing, Commercial—*mfg*	323111	2782
Lithographic Printing, Commercial—*mfg*	323110	2782
Printing, Other Commercial—*mfg*	323119	2782
Screen Printing, Commercial—*mfg*	323113	2782
Graphic arts and related design: Graphic Design Services—*prof*	54143	7336
Graphic arts plates, sensitized: Photographic and Photocopying Equipment—*mfg*	333315	3861
Photographic Film, Paper, Plate and Chemical—*mfg*	325992	3861
Graphic Design Services	**54143**	**8099**
Graphic displays, except graphic terminals–computer peripheral equipment: Computer Peripheral Equipment, Other—*mfg*	334119	3577
Graphic recording meters-electric: Electronic Coil, Transformer, and Other Inductor—*mfg*	334416	3825
Instrument for Measuring and Testing Electricity and Electrical Signals—*mfg*	334515	3825
Graphite electrodes and contacts, electric: Carbon and Graphite Product—*mfg*	335991	3624
Graphite mining: Crushed and Broken Stone and Quarrying, Other—*mining*	212319	1499
Non-Metallic Mineral, All Other—*mining*	212399	1499
Graphite, natural–ground, pulverized, refined, or blended: Ground or Treated Mineral and Earth—*mfg*	327992	3295
Grapples–rock, wood, etc.: Construction Machinery—*mfg*	33312	3531
Overhead Traveling Crane, Hoist and Monorail System—*mfg*	333923	3531
Railroad Rolling Stock—*mfg*	33651	3531
Grass catchers, lawnmower: Hand and Edge Tool—*mfg*	332212	3524
Lawn and Garden Tractor and Home Lawn and Garden Equipment—*mfg*	333112	3524
Grass hooks: Hand and Edge Tool—*mfg*	332212	3423
Grass seed farms: Crop Farming, All Other Miscellaneous—*ag*	111998	139
Hay Farming—*ag*	11194	139
Peanut Farming—*ag*	111992	139
Vegetable (except Potato) and Melon Farming, Other—*ag*	111219	139
Grasses, artificial and preserved–except glass: Plastics Product, All Other—*mfg*	326199	3999
Grasses, artificial–made from purchased glass: Glass Product Made of Purchased Glass—*mfg*	327215	3231
Gratings (open steel flooring): Ornamental and Architectural Metal Work—*mfg*	332323	3446
Gratings, diffraction: Optical Instrument and Lens—*mfg*	333314	3827
Gratings, tread–fabricated metal: Ornamental and Architectural Metal Work—*mfg*	332323	3446
Grave excavation–contractors: Trade Contractors, All Other Special—*const*	23599	1799
Grave markers, concrete: Concrete Pipe—*mfg*	327332	3272
Concrete Product, Other—*mfg*	32739	3272
Nonmetallic Mineral Product, All Other Miscellaneous—*mfg*	327999	3272
Grave vaults, concrete: Concrete Pipe—*mfg*	327332	3272
Concrete Product, Other—*mfg*	32739	3272
Nonmetallic Mineral Product, All Other Miscellaneous—*mfg*	327999	3272
Grave vaults, metal: Burial Casket—*mfg*	339995	3995
Gravel: Brick, Stone and Related Material—*whlse*	42132	5032

Dozers, tractor mounted–material moving: Construction Machinery—*mfg*	33312	3531
Overhead Traveling Crane, Hoist and Monorail System—*mfg*	333923	3531
Railroad Rolling Stock—*mfg*	33651	3531
Draft gauges, industrial process type: Instruments and Related Products for Measuring, Displaying, and Controlling Industrial Process Variables—*mfg*	334513	3823
Drafting instrument repair: Electronic and Precision Equipment Repair and Maintenance, Other—*serv*	811219	7699
Drafting instruments and machines: Measuring and Controlling Device, Other—*mfg*	334519	3829
Surgical and Medical Instrument—*mfg*	339112	3829
Drafting instruments and tables: Office Supplies and Stationery Stores—*retail*	45321	5049
Professional Equipment and Supplies, Other—*whlse*	42149	5049
Drafting materials, except instruments: Chemical Product, All Other Miscellaneous—*mfg*	325998	3952
Institutional Furniture—*mfg*	337127	3952
Lead Pencil and Art Good—*mfg*	339942	3952
Drafting service (temporary employees): Employee Leasing Services—*admin*	56133	7363
Temporary Help Services—*admin*	56132	7363
Drafting service, except temporary help: Surveying and Mapping (except Geophysical) Services—*prof*	54137	7389
Drafting Services	**54134**	**7389**
Draglines, powered: Construction Machinery—*mfg*	33312	3531
Overhead Traveling Crane, Hoist and Monorail System—*mfg*	333923	3531
Railroad Rolling Stock—*mfg*	33651	3531
Dragon's blood: Gum and Wood Chemical—*mfg*	325191	2861
Drags (agricultural equipment): Farm Machinery and Equipment—*mfg*	333111	3523
Drags, road (construction and road maintenance equipment): Construction Machinery—*mfg*	33312	3531
Overhead Traveling Crane, Hoist and Monorail System—*mfg*	333923	3531
Railroad Rolling Stock—*mfg*	33651	3531
Dragstrip operation: Race Tracks—*arts*	711212	7948
Spectator Sports, Other—*arts*	711219	7948
Drain cocks: Fabricated Metal Product, All Other Miscellaneous—*mfg*	332999	3432
Plumbing Fixture Fitting and Trim—*mfg*	332913	3432
Drain pipe solvents and cleaners: Polish and Other Sanitation Good—*mfg*	325612	2842
Drain plugs, magnetic–metal: Fabricated Metal Product, All Other Miscellaneous—*mfg*	332999	3499
Drain tile, clay: Structural Clay Product, Other—*mfg*	327123	3259
Drain tile, concrete: Concrete Pipe—*mfg*	327332	3272
Concrete Product, Other—*mfg*	32739	3272
Nonmetallic Mineral Product, All Other Miscellaneous—*mfg*	327999	3272

Drainage project construction–general contractors: Heavy, All Other—*const*	23499	1629
Industrial Nonbuilding Structure—*const*	23493	1629
Drainage system installation, cesspool and septic tank-contractors: Plumbing, Heating and Air-Conditioning Contractors—*const*	23511	1711
Drainboards, plastics laminated: Architectural Woodwork and Millwork, Custom—*mfg*	337212	2541
Showcase, Partition, Shelving, and Locker—*mfg*	337215	2541
Wood Kitchen Cabinet and Counter Top—*mfg*	33711	2541
Draining or pumping of bituminous coal, anthracite, or lignite mines on a con-tract basis: Coal Support Activities—*mining*	213113	1241
Draining or pumping of metal mines–on a contract basis: Geophysical Surveying and Mapping Services—*prof*	54136	1081
Metal Support Activities—*mining*	213114	1081
Draining or pumping of nonmetallic minerals mines, except fuels–on a contract basis: Geophysical Surveying and Mapping Services—*prof*	54136	1481
Non-Metallic Minerals (except Fuels) Support Activities—*mining*	213115	1481
Drains, plumbers': Fabricated Metal Product, All Other Miscellaneous—*mfg*	332999	3432
Plumbing Fixture Fitting and Trim—*mfg*	332913	3432
Drama schools: Fine Arts Schools—*educ*	61161	8299
Language Schools—*educ*	61163	8299
Draperies: Home Furnishing—*whlse*	42122	5023
Draperies and drapery fabrics, cotton: Broadwoven Fabric Mills—*mfg*	31321	2211
Draperies and drapery fabrics, manmade fiber and silk: Broadwoven Fabric Mills—*mfg*	31321	2221
Draperies, plastics and textile: Curtain and Drapery Mills—*mfg*	314121	2391
Drapery drycleaning plants: Drycleaning Plants—*serv*	812322	7216
Drapery material: Broadwoven Fabric Finishing Mills—*mfg*	313311	5131
Piece Goods, Notions and Other Dry Goods—*whlse*	42231	5131
Textile and Fabric Finishing (except Broadwoven Fabric) Mills—*mfg*	313312	5131
Drapery rods, poles, and fixtures: Blind and Shade—*mfg*	33792	2591
Drapery stores: Curtain and Drapery Mills—*mfg*	314121	5714
Sewing, Needlework and Piece Goods Stores—*retail*	45113	5714
Window Treatment Stores—*retail*	442291	5714
Drapes, surgical–cotton: Surgical Appliance and Supplies—*mfg*	339113	3842
Draw benches: Other Metalworking Machinery, Other—*mfg*	333518	3549
Drawers: Men's and Boys' Cut and Sew Apparel Contractors—*mfg*	315211	2322
Men's and Boys' Cut and Sew Underwear and Nightwear—*mfg*	315221	2322
Drawers, apparel: Underwear and Nightwear Knitting Mills—*mfg*	315192	2254
Drawing frames, textile: Textile Machinery—*mfg*	333292	3552
Drawing inks, blacks and colored: Chemical Product, All Other Miscellaneous—*mfg*	325998	3952
Institutional Furniture—*mfg*	337127	3952
Lead Pencil and Art Good—*mfg*	339942	3952

ALPHABETICAL INDEX	NAICS	SIC
Building Material Dealers, Other—*retail*	44419	5032
Gravel mining: Construction Sand and Gravel—*mining*	212321	1442
Gravel painting: Gypsum and Gypsum Product—*mfg*	32742	3299
Nonmetallic Mineral Product, All Other Miscellaneous—*mfg*	327999	3299
Gravestones, finished: Stores (except Tobacco Stores), All Other Miscellaneous—*retail*	453998	5999
Gravure ink: Printing Ink—*mfg*	32591	2893
Gravure plates and cylinders, preparation of: Prepress Services—*mfg*	323122	2796
Gravure presses: Printing Machinery and Equipment—*mfg*	333293	3555
Gravure printing: Gravure Printing, Commercial—*mfg*	323111	2754
Gravure Printing, Commercial	**323111**	**2771**
Gravy mixes, dry: Dried and Dehydrated Food—*mfg*	311423	2099
Gray iron castings: Iron Foundries—*mfg*	331511	3321
Gray iron foundries: Iron Foundries—*mfg*	331511	3321
Grease cups, metal: Fabricated Metal Product, All Other Miscellaneous—*mfg*	332999	3599
General Purpose Machinery , All Other—*mfg*	333999	3599
Machine Shops—*mfg*	33271	3599
Machinery, Other Commercial and Service Industry—*mfg*	333319	3599
Motor Vehicle Parts, All Other—*mfg*	336399	3599
Grease guns (lubricators): Measuring and Dispensing Pump—*mfg*	333913	3586
Grease rendering, inedible: Fats and Oils Refining and Blending—*mfg*	311225	2077
Fresh and Frozen Seafood Processing—*mfg*	311712	2077
Rendering and Meat By-product Processing—*mfg*	311613	2077
Seafood Canning—*mfg*	311711	2077
Grease retainers, leather: Gasket, Packing, and Sealing Device—*mfg*	339991	3053
Grease seals, asbestos: Gasket, Packing, and Sealing Device—*mfg*	339991	3053
Grease traps, concrete: Concrete Pipe—*mfg*	327332	3272
Concrete Product, Other—*mfg*	32739	3272
Nonmetallic Mineral Product, All Other Miscellaneous—*mfg*	327999	3272
Grease, wool: Broadwoven Fabric Mills—*mfg*	31321	2299
Narrow Fabric Mills—*mfg*	313221	2299
Nonwoven Fabric Mills—*mfg*	31323	2299
Textile and Fabric Finishing (except Broadwoven Fabric) Mills—*mfg*	313312	2299
Textile Product Mills, All Other Miscellaneous—*mfg*	314999	2299
Thread Mills—*mfg*	313113	2299
Yarn Spinning Mills—*mfg*	313111	2299
Greaseproof wrapping paper: Newsprint Mills—*mfg*	322122	2621
Paper (except Newsprint) Mills—*mfg*	322121	2621
Greases, animal and vegetable: Nondurable Goods, Other Miscellaneous—*whlse*	42299	5199
Greases, lubricating: Petroleum Lubricating Oil and Grease—*mfg*	324191	2992
Greases, lubricating–produced in petroleuum refineries: Petroleum Refineries—*mfg*	32411	2911
Greases, sulfonated: Surface Active Agent—*mfg*	325613	2843
Great Lakes and St. Lawrence Seaway freight transportation: Coastal and Great Lakes Freight—*trans*	483113	4432
Green lima bean farms: Vegetable (except Potato) and Melon Farming, Other—*ag*	111219	161
Green pea farms: Vegetable (except Potato) and Melon Farming, Other—*ag*	111219	161
Greenhouse, Nursery and Floriculture Production	**1114**	
Greenhouses for floral products: Floriculture Production—*ag*	111422	181
Nursery and Tree Production—*ag*	111421	181
Greenhouses for food crops: Food Crops Grown Under Cover, Other—*ag*	111419	182
Mushroom Production—*ag*	111411	182
Greenhouses, prefabricated–metal: Prefabricated Metal Building and Component—*mfg*	332311	3448
Greens mowing equipment: Farm Machinery and Equipment—*mfg*	333111	3523
Greensand mining: Crushed and Broken Stone and Quarrying, Other—*mining*	212319	1499
Non-Metallic Mineral, All Other—*mining*	212399	1499
Greenstone, dimension: Dimension Stone and Quarrying—*mining*	212311	1411
Greeting Card Publishers	**511191**	**2771**
Greeting card shops: Gift, Novelty and Souvenir Stores—*retail*	45322	5947
Greeting cards: Office Supplies and Stationery Stores—*retail*	45321	5112
Stationary and Office Supplies—*whlse*	42212	5112
Greeting cards, except hand painted: Flexographic Printing, Commercial—*mfg*	323112	2771
Gravure Printing, Commercial—*mfg*	323111	2771
Greeting Card Publishers—*info*	511191	2771
Lithographic Printing, Commercial—*mfg*	323110	2771
Printing, Other Commercial—*mfg*	323119	2771
Screen Printing, Commercial—*mfg*	323113	2771
Grenade launchers: Small Arms—*mfg*	332994	3484
Grenades and parts: Ammunition (except Small Arms)—*mfg*	332993	3483
Grenades, hand (fire extinguishers): Fabricated Metal Product, All Other Miscellaneous—*mfg*	332999	3999
Hand and Edge Tool—*mfg*	332212	3999
Griddles and grills, household–electric: Electric Housewares and Household Fan—*mfg*	335211	3634
Heating Equipment (except Electric and Warm Air Furnaces)—*mfg*	333414	3634
Grids, electric: Electrical Equipment and Component, All Other Miscellaneous—*mfg*	335999	3699
Lighting Equipment, Other—*mfg*	335129	3699
Machinery, Other Commercial and Service Industry—*mfg*	333319	3699
Grilles and grillework, woven wire–made from purchased wire: Fabricated Wire Product, Other—*mfg*	332618	3496
Grillework, ornamental metal: Ornamental and Architectural Metal Work—*mfg*	332323	3446

Grills (eating places): Cafeterias—*accom*	722212	5812
Caterers—*accom*	72232	5812
Foodservice Contractors—*accom*	72231	5812
Full-Service Restaurants—*accom*	72211	5812
Limited-Service Restaurants—*accom*	722211	5812
Snack and Nonalcoholic Beverage Bars—*accom*	722213	5812
Theater Companies and Dinner Theaters—*arts*	71111	5812
Grinders and crushers, feed (agricultural machinery): Farm Machinery and Equipment—*mfg*	333111	3523
Grinders, food–commercial types: Food Product Machinery—*mfg*	333294	3556
Grinders, pneumatic and electric–portable (metalworking machinery): Power-Driven Hand Tool—*mfg*	333991	3546
Grinders, snagging: Power-Driven Hand Tool—*mfg*	333991	3546
Grinders, stone–portable: Construction Machinery—*mfg*	33312	3531
Overhead Traveling Crane, Hoist and Monorail System—*mfg*	333923	3531
Railroad Rolling Stock—*mfg*	33651	3531
Grinders, stone–stationary: Mining Machinery and Equipment—*mfg*	333131	3532
Grinding balls, ceramic: Abrasive Product—*mfg*	32791	3291
Fabricated Metal Product, All Other Miscellaneous—*mfg*	332999	3291
Grinding castings for the trade: Fabricated Metal Product, All Other Miscellaneous—*mfg*	332999	3599
General Purpose Machinery , All Other—*mfg*	333999	3599
Machine Shops—*mfg*	33271	3599
Machinery, Other Commercial and Service Industry—*mfg*	333319	3599
Grinding machines, metalworking: Machine Tool (Metal Cutting Types)—*mfg*	333512	3541
Grinding media, pottery: Vitreous China, Fine Earthenware and Other Pottery Product—*mfg*	327112	3269
Grinding of drugs and herbs: Medicinal and Botanical—*mfg*	325411	2833
Grinding peat: Crushed and Broken Stone and Quarrying, Other—*mining*	212319	1499
Non-Metallic Mineral, All Other—*mining*	212399	1499
Grinding sand mining: Industrial Sand—*mining*	212322	1446
Grindstone quarrying: Crushed and Broken Stone and Quarrying, Other—*mining*	212319	1499
Non-Metallic Mineral, All Other—*mining*	212399	1499
Grindstones, artificial: Abrasive Product—*mfg*	32791	3291
Fabricated Metal Product, All Other Miscellaneous—*mfg*	332999	3291
Grips and handles, rubber: Fabric Coating Mills—*mfg*	31332	3069
Rubber Product, All Other—*mfg*	326299	3069
Grit, steel: Abrasive Product—*mfg*	32791	3291
Fabricated Metal Product, All Other Miscellaneous—*mfg*	332999	3291
Grits and flakes, corn–for brewers' use: Flour Milling—*mfg*	311211	2041
Grits mining (crushed stone): Crushed and Broken Stone and Quarrying, Other—*mining*	212319	1429
Groceries, general line: General Line Grocery—*whlse*	42241	5141
Grocers' bags and sacks, uncoated paper: Uncoated Paper and Multiwall Bag—*mfg*	322224	2674
Grocery Stores	**4451**	
Grocery and Related Product Wholesalers	**4224**	
Grocery and Related Products Wholesalers, Other	**42249**	**5149**
Grocery carts, made from purchased wire: Fabricated Wire Product, Other—*mfg*	332618	3496
Grocery stores, with or without fresh meat: Convenience Stores—*retail*	44512	5411
Gasoline Stations with Convenience Stores—*retail*	44711	5411
Supermarkets and Other Grocery (except Convenience) Stores—*retail*	44511	5411
Warehouse Clubs and Superstores—*retail*	45291	5411
Grommets: Industrial Machinery and Equipment—*whlse*	42183	5085
Industrial Supplies—*whlse*	42184	5085
Grommets, rubber: Fabric Coating Mills—*mfg*	31332	3069
Rubber Product, All Other—*mfg*	326299	3069
Grooving machines (machine tools): Machine Tool (Metal Cutting Types)—*mfg*	333512	3541
Grosgrain, cotton: Broadwoven Fabric Mills—*mfg*	31321	2211
Ground clamps (electric wiring devices): Current-Carrying Wiring Device—*mfg*	335931	3643
Ground glass, made from purchased glass: Glass Product Made of Purchased Glass—*mfg*	327215	3231
Ground or Treated Mineral and Earth Manufacturing	**327992**	**3295**
Grounds mowing equipment: Farm Machinery and Equipment—*mfg*	333111	3523
Groundwood paper: Newsprint Mills—*mfg*	322122	2621
Paper (except Newsprint) Mills—*mfg*	322121	2621
Group day care centers, child: Child Day Care Services—*hlth*	62441	8351
Group foster homes: Homes for the Elderly—*hlth*	623312	8361
Residential Care Facilities, Other—*hlth*	62399	8361
Residential Mental Health and Substance Abuse Facilities—*hlth*	62322	8361
Group hospitalization plans: Direct Health and Medical Insurance Carriers—*fin*	524114	6324
Insurance Funds, Other—*fin*	52519	6324
Reinsurance Carriers—*fin*	52413	6324
Grouting material (concrete mending compound): Basic Organic Chemical, All Other—*mfg*	325199	2899
Chemical Product, All Other Miscellaneous—*mfg*	325998	2899
Grouting work-contractors: Concrete Contractors—*const*	23571	1771
Drywall, Plastering, Acoustical and Insulation Contractors—*const*	23542	1771
Grower pots, plastics: Plastics Pipe and Pipe Fitting—*mfg*	326122	3089
Plastics Product, All Other—*mfg*	326199	3089
Unsupported Plastics Profile Shape—*mfg*	326121	3089
Growers' associations, not engaged in contract buying or selling: Business Associations—*serv*	81391	8611
Growers' marketing advisory services: Business Associations—*serv*	81391	8611
Growth regulants, agricultural: Pesticide and Other Agricultural Chemical—*mfg*	32532	2879
Guano mining: Chemical and Fertilizer Mineral, Other—*mining*	212393	1479
Guaranty of titles: Direct Title Insurance Carriers—*fin*	524127	6361
Reinsurance Carriers—*fin*	52413	6361

ALPHABETICAL INDEX	NAICS	SIC
Guard service: Armored Car Services—*admin*	561613	7381
Investigation Services—*admin*	561611	7381
Security Guards and Patrol Services—*admin*	561612	7381
Guardrail construction on highways-contractors: Highway and Street—*const*	23411	1611
Guardrails, highway–sheet metal: Metal Container, Other—*mfg*	332439	3444
Sheet Metal Work—*mfg*	332322	3444
Guards, bannisters, railings, etc.–made from metal pipe: Ornamental and Architectural Metal Work—*mfg*	332323	3446
Guards, made from purchased wire: Fabricated Wire Product, Other—*mfg*	332618	3496
Guards–e.g., football, basketball, soccer, lacrosse: Sporting and Athletic Goods—*mfg*	33992	3949
Guided Missile and Space Vehicle Manufacturing	**336414**	**3761**
Guided Missile and Space Vehicle Parts and Auxiliary Equipment Manufacturing, Other	**336419**	**3769**
Guided Missile and Space Vehicle Propulsion Unit and Propulsion Unit Parts Manufacturing	**336415**	**3764**
Guided missiles and space vehicles: Transportation Equipment and Supplies (except Motor Vehicle)—*whlse*	42186	5088
Guided missiles, complete: Guided Missile and Space Vehicle—*mfg*	336414	3761
Guides, hunting: Sports and Recreation Instruction—*educ*	61162	7999
Guides–publishing and printing, or publishing only: Database and Directory Publishers—*info*	51114	2741
Music Publishers—*info*	51223	2741
Publishers, All Other—*info*	511199	2741
Guitars and parts, electric and nonelectric: Musical Instrument—*mfg*	339992	3931
Gum and Wood Chemical Manufacturing	**325191**	**2861**
Gum and wood chemicals: Chemical and Allied Products, Other—*whlse*	42269	5169
Gum naval stores, processing but not gathering or warehousing: Gum and Wood Chemical—*mfg*	325191	2861
Gum sizes: Basic Organic Chemical, All Other—*mfg*	325199	2899
Chemical Product, All Other Miscellaneous—*mfg*	325998	2899
Gummed labels and seals, printed–except lithographed or gravure: Digital Printing—*mfg*	323115	2759
Flexographic Printing, Commercial—*mfg*	323112	2759
Printing, Other Commercial—*mfg*	323119	2759
Quick Printing—*mfg*	323114	2759
Gummed paper: Coated and Laminated Paper—*mfg*	322222	2672
Gummed tape moisteners for store and office use: Lead Pencil and Art Good—*mfg*	339942	3579
Office Machinery—*mfg*	333313	3579
Watch, Clock, and Part—*mfg*	334518	3579
Gummed tape, cloth and paper base: Coated and Laminated Paper—*mfg*	322222	2672
Gums, gathering of: Crop Farming, All Other Miscellaneous—*ag*	111998	831

ALPHABETICAL INDEX	NAICS	SIC
Forest Nurseries and Gathering of Forest Products—*ag*	11321	831
Gun barrels, 30 mm. (or 1.18 inch) or less: Small Arms—*mfg*	332994	3484
Gun cases (sporting equipment): Sporting and Athletic Goods—*mfg*	33992	3949
Gun clubs, membership: Fitness and Recreational Sports Centers—*arts*	71394	7997
Gun forgings, iron and steel–made in steelworks or rolling mills: Iron and Steel Mills—*mfg*	331111	3312
Petroleum and Coal Productsa, All Other—*mfg*	324199	3312
Gun limbers: Ordnance and Accessories, Other—*mfg*	332995	3489
Gun magazines, 30 mm. (or 1.18 inch) or less: Small Arms—*mfg*	332994	3484
Gun sights, except optical–30 mm. (or 1.18 inch) or less: Small Arms—*mfg*	332994	3484
Gun sights, optical: Optical Instrument and Lens—*mfg*	333314	3827
Gun slushing compounds: Basic Organic Chemical, All Other—*mfg*	325199	2899
Chemical Product, All Other Miscellaneous—*mfg*	325998	2899
Gun springs, precision–made from purchased wire: Watch, Clock, and Part—*mfg*	334518	3495
Wire Spring—*mfg*	332612	3495
Gun stocks, wood: Cut Stock, Resawing Lumber, and Planing—*mfg*	321912	2426
Millwork (including Flooring), Other—*mfg*	321918	2426
Showcase, Partition, Shelving, and Locker—*mfg*	337215	2426
Wood Product, All Other Miscellaneous—*mfg*	321999	2426
Gun trigger locks: Hardware—*mfg*	33251	3429
Gun turrets and parts for artillery morethan 30 mm. (or more than 1.18 inch): Ordnance and Accessories, Other—*mfg*	332995	3489
Gunite work–contractors: Concrete Contractors—*const*	23571	1771
Drywall, Plastering, Acoustical and Insulation Contractors—*const*	23542	1771
Gunn effect devices: Semiconductor and Related Device—*mfg*	334413	3674
Gunning mixes, nonclay: Nonclay Refractory—*mfg*	327125	3297
Gunpowder: Explosives—*mfg*	32592	2892
Guns, 30 mm. (or 1.18 inch) or less: Small Arms—*mfg*	332994	3484
Guns, catapult: Ordnance and Accessories, Other—*mfg*	332995	3489
Guns, caulking: Hand and Edge Tool—*mfg*	332212	3423
Guns, dart–except toy: Small Arms—*mfg*	332994	3484
Guns, grease (lubricators): Measuring and Dispensing Pump—*mfg*	333913	3586
Guns, more than 30 mm. (or more than 1.18 inch): Ordnance and Accessories, Other—*mfg*	332995	3489
Guns, pneumatic–chip removal: Power-Driven Hand Tool—*mfg*	333991	3546
Guns, toy: Game, Toy, and Children's Vehicle—*mfg*	339932	3944
Guns–BB and pellet: Small Arms—*mfg*	332994	3484
Gunsmith shops: Sporting Goods Stores—*retail*	45111	7699
Gut sutures, surgical: Surgical Appliance and Supplies—*mfg*	339113	3842
Gutta percha compounds: Fabric Coating Mills—*mfg*	31332	3069
Rubber Product, All Other—*mfg*	326299	3069
Gutter installation, metal–contractors: Roofing, Siding and Sheet Metal Contractors—*const*	23561	1761

Description	NAICS	SIC
Gutters, plastics–glass fiber reinforced: Plastics Pipe and Pipe Fitting—*mfg*	326122	3089
Plastics Product, All Other—*mfg*	326199	3089
Unsupported Plastics Profile Shape—*mfg*	326121	3089
Gutters, sheet metal: Metal Container, Other—*mfg*	332439	3444
Sheet Metal Work—*mfg*	332322	3444
Gymnasium and playground equipment: Sporting and Athletic Goods—*mfg*	33992	3949
Gymnasium clothing: Cut and Sew Apparel, All Other—*mfg*	315299	2329
Gymnasium equipment: Sporting Goods Stores—*retail*	45111	5941
Gymnasiums: Fitness and Recreational Sports Centers—*arts*	71394	7991
Gymnastics instruction: Sports and Recreation Instruction—*educ*	61162	7999
Gynecological supplies and appliances: Surgical Appliance and Supplies—*mfg*	339113	3842
Gynecologists, offices of: Freestanding Ambulatory Surgical and Emergency Centers—*hlth*	621493	8011
HMO Medical Centers—*hlth*	621491	8011
Physicians (except Mental Health Specialists), Offices Of—*hlth*	621111	8011
Physicians, Mental Health Specialists, Offices Of—*hlth*	621112	8011
Gypsite mining: Crushed and Broken Stone and Quarrying, Other—*mining*	212319	1499
Non-Metallic Mineral, All Other—*mining*	212399	1499
Gypsum and Gypsum Product Manufacturing	**32742**	**3299**
Gypsum mining: Crushed and Broken Stone and Quarrying, Other—*mining*	212319	1499
Non-Metallic Mineral, All Other—*mining*	212399	1499
Gypsum products–e.g., block, board, plaster, lath, rock, tile: Gypsum and Gypsum Product—*mfg*	32742	3275
Gyrocompasses: Search, Detection, Navigation, Guidance, Aeronautical, and Nautical System and Instrument—*mfg*	334511	3812
Gyrogimbals: Search, Detection, Navigation, Guidance, Aeronautical, and Nautical System and Instrument—*mfg*	334511	3812
Gyropilots: Search, Detection, Navigation, Guidance, Aeronautical, and Nautical System and Instrument—*mfg*	334511	3812
Gyroscopes: Search, Detection, Navigation, Guidance, Aeronautical, and Nautical System and Instrument—*mfg*	334511	3812
Haberdashery stores: Clothing Accessories Stores—*retail*	44815	5611
Men's Clothing Stores—*retail*	44811	5611
Haddock, catching of: Finfish Fishing—*ag*	114111	912
Hair accessories: Broadwoven Fabric Finishing Mills—*mfg*	313311	5131
Piece Goods, Notions and Other Dry Goods—*whlse*	42231	5131
Textile and Fabric Finishing (except Broadwoven Fabric) Mills—*mfg*	313312	5131
Hair clippers for animal use, hand and electric: Farm Machinery and Equipment—*mfg*	333111	3523
Hair clippers for human use, hand and electric: Hand and Edge Tool—*mfg*	332212	3999
Hair coloring preparations: Soap and Other Detergent—*mfg*	325611	2844
Toilet Preparation—*mfg*	32562	2844
Hair curlers, electric-mig: Electric Housewares and Household Fan—*mfg*	335211	3634
Heating Equipment (except Electric and Warm Air Furnaces)—*mfg*	333414	3634
Hair curlers, except equipment designed for beauty parlor use: Fastener, Button, Needle and Pin—*mfg*	339993	3965
Hair curlers, rubber: Fabric Coating Mills—*mfg*	31332	3069
Rubber Product, All Other—*mfg*	326299	3069
Hair dryers, electric–except equipment designed for beauty parlor use: Electric Housewares and Household Fan—*mfg*	335211	3634
Heating Equipment (except Electric and Warm Air Furnaces)—*mfg*	333414	3634
Hair pencils (artists' brushes): Broom, Brush and Mop—*mfg*	339994	3991
Hair preparations: Drug, Drug Proprietaries and Druggists' Sundries—*whlse*	42221	5122
Hair preparations–dressings, rinses, tonics, and scalp conditioners: Soap and Other Detergent—*mfg*	325611	2844
Toilet Preparation—*mfg*	32562	2844
Hair removal (electrolysis): Personal Care Services, Other—*serv*	812199	7299
Hair stylists, men's: Barber Shops—*serv*	812111	7241
Cosmetology and Barber Schools—*educ*	611511	7241
Hair weaving or replacement service: Personal Care Services, Other—*serv*	812199	7299
Hair, animal: Farm Product Raw Material, Other—*whlse*	42259	5159
Hair, curled–for upholstery, pillow, and quilt filling: Broadwoven Fabric Mills—*mfg*	31321	2299
Narrow Fabric Mills—*mfg*	313221	2299
Nonwoven Fabric Mills—*mfg*	31323	2299
Textile and Fabric Finishing (except Broadwoven Fabric) Mills—*mfg*	313312	2299
Textile Product Mills, All Other Miscellaneous—*mfg*	314999	2299
Thread Mills—*mfg*	313113	2299
Yarn Spinning Mills—*mfg*	313111	2299
Hair, Nail, and Skin Care Services	**81211**	
Hairbrushes: Nondurable Goods, Other Miscellaneous—*whlse*	42299	5199
Hairdoth–wool, mohair, and similar animal fibers: Broadwoven Fabric Finishing Mills—*mfg*	313311	2231
Broadwoven Fabric Mills—*mfg*	31321	2231
Textile and Fabric Finishing (except Broadwoven Fabric) Mills—*mfg*	313312	2231
Hairdressers: Beauty Salons—*serv*	812112	7231
Cosmetology and Barber Schools—*educ*	611511	7231
Nail Salons—*serv*	812113	7231
Hairdressings, dyes, bleaches, tonics, and removers: Soap and Other Detergent—*mfg*	325611	2844
Toilet Preparation—*mfg*	32562	2844
Hairpins, except rubber: Fastener, Button, Needle and Pin—*mfg*	339993	3965
Hairpins, rubber: Fabric Coating Mills—*mfg*	31332	3069
Rubber Product, All Other—*mfg*	326299	3069

ALPHABETICAL INDEX	NAICS	SIC
Hairsprings, made from purchased wire: Watch, Clock, and Part—*mfg*	334518	3495
Wire Spring—*mfg*	332612	3495
Half and half: Fluid Milk—*mfg*	311511	2026
Halftones, engraved-m[g: Digital Printing—*mfg*	323115	2759
Flexographic Printing, Commercial—*mfg*	323112	2759
Printing, Other Commercial—*mfg*	323119	2759
Quick Printing—*mfg*	323114	2759
Halfway group homes for persons with social or personal problems: Homes for the Elderly—*hlth*	623312	8361
Residential Care Facilities, Other—*hlth*	62399	8361
Residential Mental Health and Substance Abuse Facilities—*hlth*	62322	8361
Halfway homes for delinquents and offenders: Homes for the Elderly—*hlth*	623312	8361
Residential Care Facilities, Other—*hlth*	62399	8361
Residential Mental Health and Substance Abuse Facilities—*hlth*	62322	8361
Hall effect devices: Semiconductor and Related Device—*mfg*	334413	3674
Halloween lanterns, papier-mache: Coated and Laminated Paper—*mfg*	322222	2679
Converted Paper Product, All Other—*mfg*	322298	2679
Die-Cut Paper and Paperboard Office Supplies—*mfg*	322231	2679
Non-Folding Sanitary Food Container—*mfg*	322215	2679
Halters (harness): Leather Good, All Other—*mfg*	316999	3199
Halvah (candy): Confectionery from Purchased Chocolate—*mfg*	31133	2064
Non-Chocolate Confectionery—*mfg*	31134	2064
Ham, poultry: Food, All Other Miscellaneous—*mfg*	311999	2015
Poultry Processing—*mfg*	311615	2015
Hamburger stands: Cafeterias—*accom*	722212	5812
Caterers—*accom*	72232	5812
Foodservice Contractors—*accom*	72231	5812
Full-Service Restaurants—*accom*	72211	5812
Limited-Service Restaurants—*accom*	722211	5812
Snack and Nonalcoholic Beverage Bars—*accom*	722213	5812
Theater Companies and Dinner Theaters—*arts*	71111	5812
Hammer and roughage mills (agricultural machinery): Farm Machinery and Equipment—*mfg*	333111	3523
Hammer forgings, not made in rolling mills: Iron and Steel Forging—*mfg*	332111	3462
Hammer mills (rock and ore crushing ma-chines), stationary: Mining Machinery and Equipment—*mfg*	333131	3532
Hammer mills (rock and ore crushing machines), portable: Construction Machinery—*mfg*	33312	3531
Overhead Traveling Crane, Hoist and Monorail System—*mfg*	333923	3531
Railroad Rolling Stock—*mfg*	33651	3531
Hammers (handtools): Hand and Edge Tool—*mfg*	332212	3423
Hammers, drop–for forging and shaping metal: Machine Tool (Metal Forming Types)—*mfg*	333513	3542

ALPHABETICAL INDEX	NAICS	SIC
Hammers, meat–wood: Manufacturing, All Other Miscellaneous—*mfg*	339999	2499
Wood Container and Pallet—*mfg*	32192	2499
Wood Product, All Other Miscellaneous—*mfg*	321999	2499
Hammers, piano: Musical Instrument—*mfg*	339992	3931
Hammers, pile driving: Construction Machinery—*mfg*	33312	3531
Overhead Traveling Crane, Hoist and Monorail System—*mfg*	333923	3531
Railroad Rolling Stock—*mfg*	33651	3531
Hammers, power (forging machinery): Machine Tool (Metal Forming Types)—*mfg*	333513	3542
Hammers–portable electric and pneumatic–e.g., chipping, riveting, caulking: Power-Driven Hand Tool—*mfg*	333991	3546
Hammocks, fabric: Textile Product Mills, All Other Miscellaneous—*mfg*	314999	2399
Hammocks, metal or fabric and metal combination: Metal Household Furniture—*mfg*	337124	2514
Hampers, fruit and vegetable–veneer and splint: Wood Container and Pallet—*mfg*	32192	2449
Hampers, laundry–rattan, reed, splint, veneer, and willow: Manufacturing, All Other Miscellaneous—*mfg*	339999	2499
Wood Container and Pallet—*mfg*	32192	2499
Wood Product, All Other Miscellaneous—*mfg*	321999	2499
Hampers, laundry–sheet metal: Metal Container, Other—*mfg*	332439	3444
Sheet Metal Work—*mfg*	332322	3444
Hampers, shipping–paperboard and solid fiber: Corrugated and Solid Fiber Box—*mfg*	322211	2653
Hampers, shipping–vulcanized fiber: Fiber Can, Tube, Drum, and Similar Products—*mfg*	322214	2655
Hams, except poultry: Animal (except Poultry) Slaughtering—*mfg*	311611	2011
Meat Processed from Carcasses—*mfg*	311612	2013
Hand and Edge Tool Manufacturing	**332212**	**3523**
Hand laundries: Laundry Services, All Other—*serv*	812399	7219
Hand pieces and parts, dental: Dental Equipment and Supplies—*mfg*	339114	3843
Hand stamps, stencils, and brands: Marking Device—*mfg*	339943	3953
Hand-knitting thread–cotton, silk, manmade fibers, and wool: Textile and Fabric Finishing (except Broadwoven Fabric) Mills—*mfg*	313312	2284
Thread Mills—*mfg*	313113	2284
Handbag frames: Fabricated Metal Product, All Other Miscellaneous—*mfg*	332999	3999
Handbag leather: Leather and Hide Tanning and Finishing—*mfg*	31611	3111
Handbag stores: Clothing Accessories Stores—*retail*	44815	5632
Clothing Stores, Other—*retail*	44819	5632
Handbags: Women's, Children's, and Infants' and Accessories—*whlse*	42233	5137
Handbags, men's–regardless of material: Personal Leather Good (except Women's Handbag and Purse)—*mfg*	316993	3172
Handbags, precious metal: Jewelry (except Costume)—*mfg*	339911	3911

Description	NAICS	SIC
Handbags, women's–of all materials, except precious metal: Women's Handbag and Purse—*mfg*	316992	3171
Handball clubs, membership: Fitness and Recreational Sports Centers—*arts*	71394	7997
Handball courts, except membership clubs: Fitness and Recreational Sports Centers—*arts*	71394	7999
Handbill distribution service: Advertising Material Distribution Services—*prof*	54187	7319
Advertising, Other Services Related to—*prof*	54189	7319
Display Advertising—*prof*	54185	7319
Media Buying Agencies—*prof*	54183	7319
Nonscheduled Air, Other—*trans*	481219	7319
Handcuffs: Hardware—*mfg*	33251	3429
Handkerchief fabrics, cotton: Broadwoven Fabric Mills—*mfg*	31321	2211
Handkerchiefs, except paper: Apparel Accessories and Apparel, Other—*mfg*	315999	2389
Handkerchiefs, men's and boys': Men's and Boys' Clothing and Furnishings—*whlse*	42232	5136
Handkerchiefs, paper: Sanitary Paper Product—*mfg*	322291	2676
Handkerchiefs–women's and children's: Women's, Children's, and Infants' and Accessories—*whlse*	42233	5137
Handle bars, motorcycle and bicycle: Motorcycle, Bicycle and Parts—*mfg*	336991	3751
Handle blanks, wood: Cut Stock, Resawing Lumber, and Planing—*mfg*	321912	2426
Millwork (including Flooring), Other—*mfg*	321918	2426
Showcase, Partition, Shelving, and Locker—*mfg*	337215	2426
Wood Product, All Other Miscellaneous—*mfg*	321999	2426
Handle bolts, wood–hewn: Logging—*ag*	11331	2411
Handle stock, sawed or planed: Cut Stock, Resawing Lumber, and Planing—*mfg*	321912	2426
Millwork (including Flooring), Other—*mfg*	321918	2426
Showcase, Partition, Shelving, and Locker—*mfg*	337215	2426
Wood Product, All Other Miscellaneous—*mfg*	321999	2426
Handles, brush and tool–plastics: Plastics Pipe and Pipe Fitting—*mfg*	326122	3089
Plastics Product, All Other—*mfg*	326199	3089
Unsupported Plastics Profile Shape—*mfg*	326121	3089
Handles, faucet–vitreous china and earthenware: Vitreous China Plumbing Fixture and China and Earthenware Fittings and Bathroom Accessories—*mfg*	327111	3261
Handles, rubber: Fabric Coating Mills—*mfg*	31332	3069
Rubber Product, All Other—*mfg*	326299	3069
Handles, umbrella and parasol–except precious metal: Fabricated Metal Product, All Other Miscellaneous—*mfg*	332999	3999
Wood Product, All Other Miscellaneous—*mfg*	321999	3999
Handles, umbrella and parasol–gold and silver: Jewelry (except Costume)—*mfg*	339911	3911
Handles, whip and luggage–leather: Leather Good, All Other—*mfg*	316999	3199
Handles, wood–turned and shaped: Manufacturing, All Other Miscellaneous—*mfg*	339999	2499
Wood Container and Pallet—*mfg*	32192	2499
Wood Product, All Other Miscellaneous—*mfg*	321999	2499
Handsaws: Hardware—*whlse*	42171	5072
Handtool designers: Industrial Design Services—*prof*	54142	7389
Handtools: Hardware Stores—*retail*	44413	5251
Handtools, except automotive and machinists' precision: Hardware—*whlse*	42171	5072
Handtools, powerdriven–woodworking or metalworking: Power-Driven Hand Tool—*mfg*	333991	3546
Handwoven fabrics: Broadwoven Fabric Mills—*mfg*	31321	2299
Narrow Fabric Mills—*mfg*	313221	2299
Nonwoven Fabric Mills—*mfg*	31323	2299
Textile and Fabric Finishing (except Broadwoven Fabric) Mills—*mfg*	313312	2299
Textile Product Mills, All Other Miscellaneous—*mfg*	314999	2299
Thread Mills—*mfg*	313113	2299
Yarn Spinning Mills—*mfg*	313111	2299
Hang gliders: Aircraft—*mfg*	336411	3721
Hangar doors, sheet metal: Metal Window and Door—*mfg*	332321	3442
Hangar operation: Airport Operations, Other—*trans*	488119	4581
Hangers, garment–made from purchased wire: Fabricated Wire Product, Other—*mfg*	332618	3496
Hangers, garment–wood: Manufacturing, All Other Miscellaneous—*mfg*	339999	2499
Wood Container and Pallet—*mfg*	32192	2499
Wood Product, All Other Miscellaneous—*mfg*	321999	2499
Hangers–photographic film, plate, andpaper: Photographic and Photocopying Equipment—*mfg*	333315	3861
Photographic Film, Paper, Plate and Chemical—*mfg*	325992	3861
Hanging and fastening devices, electrical: Building Material Dealers, Other—*retail*	44419	5063
Electrical Apparatus and Equipment, Wiring Supplies and Material—*whlse*	42161	5063
Hanging paper (wallpaper stock): Newsprint Mills—*mfg*	322122	2621
Paper (except Newsprint) Mills—*mfg*	322121	2621
Harbor construction–general contractors: Heavy, All Other—*const*	23499	1629
Industrial Nonbuilding Structure—*const*	23493	1629
Hard banding service–on a contract basis: Oil and Gas Operations Support Activities—*mining*	213112	1389
Hard coal surface mining, except Pennsylvania anthracite: Bituminous Coal and Lignite Surface—*mining*	212111	1221
Hard coal underground mining, except Pennsylvania anthracite: Bituminous Coal Underground—*mining*	212112	1222
Hard fiber cordage and twine: Rope, Cordage and Twine Mills—*mfg*	314991	2298
Hard rubber products: Fabric Coating Mills—*mfg*	31332	3069
Rubber Product, All Other—*mfg*	326299	3069
Hard surface floor coverings–rubber: Fabric Coating Mills—*mfg*	31332	3069

ALPHABETICAL INDEX	NAICS	SIC
Rubber Product, All Other—*mfg*	326299	3069
Hard surfaced floor coverings, exceptrubber and cork: Resilient Floor Covering—*mfg*	326192	3996
Hardboard: Building Material Dealers, Other—*retail*	44419	5031
Reconstituted Wood Product—*mfg*	321219	2493
Hardening compounds, concrete: Basic Organic Chemical, All Other—*mfg*	325199	2899
Chemical Product, All Other Miscellaneous—*mfg*	325998	2899
Hardening of metal for the trade: Metal Heat Treating—*mfg*	332811	3398
Hardness testing equipment: Measuring and Controlling Device, Other—*mfg*	334519	3829
Surgical and Medical Instrument—*mfg*	339112	3829
Hardware cloth, woven wire–made from purchased wire: Fabricated Wire Product, Other—*mfg*	332618	3496
Hardware Manufacturing	**3325**	
Hardware Manufacturing	**33251**	**3499**
Hardware Stores	**44413**	**5251**
Hardware Wholesalers	**42171**	**5072**
Hardware, and Plumbing and Heating Equipment and Supplies Wholesalers	**4217**	
Hardware, automotive: Automotive Parts and Accessories Stores—*retail*	44131	5013
Motor Vehicle Supplies and New Part—*whlse*	42112	5013
Hardware, heavy: Hardware—*whlse*	42171	5072
Hardware, plastics: Plastics Pipe and Pipe Fitting—*mfg*	326122	3089
Plastics Product, All Other—*mfg*	326199	3089
Unsupported Plastics Profile Shape—*mfg*	326121	3089
Hardware, pole line: Building Material Dealers, Other—*retail*	44419	5063
Electrical Apparatus and Equipment, Wiring Supplies and Material—*whlse*	42161	5063
Noncurrent-Carrying Wiring Device—*mfg*	335932	3644
Hardware, shelf or light: Hardware—*whlse*	42171	5072
Hardware, stage: Fabricated Metal Product, All Other Miscellaneous—*mfg*	332999	3999
Wood Product, All Other Miscellaneous—*mfg*	321999	3999
Hardwood dimension: Cut Stock, Resawing Lumber, and Planing—*mfg*	321912	2426
Millwork (including Flooring), Other—*mfg*	321918	2426
Showcase, Partition, Shelving, and Locker—*mfg*	337215	2426
Wood Product, All Other Miscellaneous—*mfg*	321999	2426
Hardwood distillates: Gum and Wood Chemical—*mfg*	325191	2861
Hardwood flooring–contractors: Floor Laying and Other Floor Contractors—*const*	23552	1752
Hardwood plywood composites: Hardwood Veneer and Plywood—*mfg*	321211	2435
Hardwood Veneer and Plywood Manufacturing	**321211**	**2435**
Hardwood veneer or plywood: Hardwood Veneer and Plywood—*mfg*	321211	2435

ALPHABETICAL INDEX	NAICS	SIC
Harmonicas: Musical Instrument—*mfg*	339992	3931
Harness assemblies for electronic use–wire and cable: Electronic Component, Other—*mfg*	334419	3679
Motor Vehicle Electrical and Electronic Equipment, Other—*mfg*	336322	3679
Printed Circuit/Electronics Assembly—*mfg*	334418	3679
Radio and Television Broadcasting and Wireless Communications Equipment—*mfg*	33422	3679
Harness dressing: Polish and Other Sanitation Good—*mfg*	325612	2842
Harness equipment: Farm Supplies—*whlse*	42291	5191
Nursery and Garden Centers—*retail*	44422	5191
Harness hardware: Hardware—*mfg*	33251	3429
Harness leather: Leather and Hide Tanning and Finishing—*mfg*	31611	3111
Harness made to individual order: Farm Supplies—*whlse*	42291	5191
Nursery and Garden Centers—*retail*	44422	5191
Harness repair shops: Animal Production Support Activities—*ag*	11521	7699
Footwear and Leather Goods Repair—*serv*	81143	7699
Harness wiring sets for internal combustion engines: Motor Vehicle Electrical and Electronic Equipment, Other—*mfg*	336322	3694
Harness, dog: Leather Good, All Other—*mfg*	316999	3199
Harnesses and harness parts: Leather Good, All Other—*mfg*	316999	3199
Harps and parts: Musical Instrument—*mfg*	339992	3931
Harpsichords: Musical Instrument—*mfg*	339992	3931
Harrows–disc, spring, and tine: Farm Machinery and Equipment—*mfg*	333111	3523
Harvest hats, straw: Hat, Cap and Millinery—*mfg*	315991	2353
Harvesting machinery and equipment: Farm and Garden Machinery and Equipment—*whlse*	42182	5083
Outdoor Power Equipment Stores—*retail*	44421	5083
Harvesting machines: Farm Machinery and Equipment—*mfg*	333111	3523
Hassock fans, electric: Electric Housewares and Household Fan—*mfg*	335211	3634
Heating Equipment (except Electric and Warm Air Furnaces)—*mfg*	333414	·3634
Hassocks, textile: Household Textile Product Mills, Other—*mfg*	314129	2392
Hat and cap material: Broadwoven Fabric Finishing Mills—*mfg*	313311	5131
Piece Goods, Notions and Other Dry Goods—*whlse*	42231	5131
Textile and Fabric Finishing (except Broadwoven Fabric) Mills—*mfg*	313312	5131
Hat band fabrics: Narrow Fabric Mills—*mfg*	313221	2241
Hat blocks and display forms: Fabricated Metal Product, All Other Miscellaneous—*mfg*	332999	3999
Wood Product, All Other Miscellaneous—*mfg*	321999	3999
Hat bodies–fur-felt, straw, and wool-felt: Hat, Cap and Millinery—*mfg*	315991	2353
Hat boxes, except paper or paperboard: Luggage—*mfg*	316991	3161
Hat findings: Apparel Accessories and Apparel, Other—*mfg*	315999	2396
Textile Product Mills, All Other Miscellaneous—*mfg*	314999	2396

Hat linings and trimmings: Apparel Accessories and Apparel, Other—*mfg*	315999	2396
Textile Product Mills, All Other Miscellaneous—*mfg*	314999	2396
Hat making and hat renovating machinery: Industrial Machinery, All Other—*mfg*	333298	3559
Machinery, Other Commercial and Service Industry—*mfg*	333319	3559
Hat stores, men's and boys': Clothing Accessories Stores—*retail*	44815	5611
Men's Clothing Stores—*retail*	44811	5611
Hat, Cap and Millinery Manufacturing	**315991**	**2353**
Hatcheries, fish: Finfish Farming and Fish Hatcheries—*ag*	112511	921
Shellfish Farming—*ag*	112512	921
Hatcheries, poultry: Poultry Hatcheries—*ag*	11234	254
Hatchets: Hand and Edge Tool—*mfg*	332212	3423
Hatcleaning and blocking shops: Footwear and Leather Goods Repair—*serv*	81143	7251
Hats: Outerwear Knitting Mills—*mfg*	315191	2253
Hats, doll: Doll and Stuffed Toy—*mfg*	339931	3942
Hats, fur: Fur and Leather Apparel—*mfg*	315292	2371
Hats, leather: Fur and Leather Apparel—*mfg*	315292	2386
Hats, men's and boys': Men's and Boys' Clothing and Furnishings—*whlse*	42232	5136
Hats, paper: Coated and Laminated Paper—*mfg*	322222	2679
Converted Paper Product, All Other—*mfg*	322298	2679
Die-Cut Paper and Paperboard Office Supplies—*mfg*	322231	2679
Non-Folding Sanitary Food Container—*mfg*	322215	2679
Hats, trimmed: Hat, Cap and Millinery—*mfg*	315991	2353
Hats–fur-felt, straw, and wool-felt: Hat, Cap and Millinery—*mfg*	315991	2353
Hats–textiles, straw, fur-felt, and woolfelt: Hat, Cap and Millinery—*mfg*	315991	2353
Hats–women's, children's, and infants': Women's, Children's, and Infants' and Accessories—*whlse*	42233	5137
Hatters' fur: Apparel Accessories and Apparel, Other—*mfg*	315999	2396
Textile Product Mills, All Other Miscellaneous—*mfg*	314999	2396
Hauling live animals, local: Freight (except Used Goods) Trucking, Local Specialized—*trans*	48422	4212
General Freight Trucking, Local—*trans*	48411	4212
Hauling, by dump truck: Freight (except Used Goods) Trucking, Local Specialized—*trans*	48422	4212
General Freight Trucking, Local—*trans*	48411	4212
Hauling, farm to market: Freight (except Used Goods) Trucking, Local Specialized—*trans*	48422	4212
General Freight Trucking, Local—*trans*	48411	4212
Hay: Farm Supplies—*whlse*	42291	5191
Nursery and Garden Centers—*retail*	44422	5191
Hay balers and presses, farm: Farm Machinery and Equipment—*mfg*	333111	3523
Hay Farming	**11194**	**139**
Hay farms: Crop Farming, All Other Miscellaneous—*ag*	111998	139
Hay Farming—*ag*	11194	139
Peanut Farming—*ag*	111992	139
Vegetable (except Potato) and Melon Farming, Other—*ag*	111219	139
Hay forks: Hand and Edge Tool—*mfg*	332212	3423
Hay knives: Hand and Edge Tool—*mfg*	332212	3423
Hay mowing, raking, baling, and chopping: Crop Harvesting, Primarily by Machine—*ag*	115113	722
Hay, cubed: Animal Food, Other—*mfg*	311119	2048
Haying machinery: Farm and Garden Machinery and Equipment—*whlse*	42182	5083
Outdoor Power Equipment Stores—*retail*	44421	5083
Haying machines–mowers, rakes, loaders, stockers, balers, presses, etc.: Conveyor and Conveying Equipment—*mfg*	333922	3523
Farm Machinery and Equipment—*mfg*	333111	3523
Hazardous Waste Collection	**562112**	**4953**
Hazardous waste material disposal sites: Hazardous Waste Collection—*admin*	562112	4953
Hazardous Waste Treatment and Disposal—*admin*	562211	4953
Materials Recovery Facilities—*admin*	56292	4953
Nonhazardous Waste Treatment and Disposal, Other—*admin*	562219	4953
Solid Waste Collection—*admin*	562111	4953
Solid Waste Combustors and Incinerators—*admin*	562213	4953
Solid Waste Landfill—*admin*	562212	4953
Waste Collection, Other—*admin*	562119	4953
Hazardous Waste Treatment and Disposal	**562211**	**4953**
Head rice: Rice Milling—*mfg*	311212	2044
Head Start centers, except in conjunction with schools: Child Day Care Services—*hlth*	62441	8351
Headboards, wood: Nonupholstered Wood Household Furniture—*mfg*	337122	2511
Headcheese: Meat Processed from Carcasses—*mfg*	311612	2013
Headers: Machine Tool (Metal Forming Types)—*mfg*	333513	3542
Heading bolts, wood–hewn: Logging—*ag*	11331	2411
Heading, barrel (cooperage stock)–sawed or split: Cut Stock, Resawing Lumber, and Planing—*mfg*	321912	2429
Sawmills—*mfg*	321113	2429
Wood Product, All Other Miscellaneous—*mfg*	321999	2429
Headlights (fixtures), vehicular: Vehicular Lighting Equipment—*mfg*	336321	3647
Headphones, radio: Electronic Component, Other—*mfg*	334419	3679
Motor Vehicle Electrical and Electronic Equipment, Other—*mfg*	336322	3679
Printed Circuit/Electronics Assembly—*mfg*	334418	3679
Radio and Television Broadcasting and Wireless Communications Equipment—*mfg*	33422	3679
Heads, banjo and drum: Musical Instrument—*mfg*	339992	3931
Heads, recording for speech and musical equipment: Electronic Component, Other—*mfg*	334419	3679
Motor Vehicle Electrical and Electronic Equipment, Other—*mfg*	336322	3679
Printed Circuit/Electronics Assembly—*mfg*	334418	3679
Radio and Television Broadcasting and Wireless Communications Equipment—*mfg*	33422	3679

ALPHABETICAL INDEX	NAICS	SIC
Heads-up display (HUD) systems, aeronautical: Search, Detection, Navigation, Guidance, Aeronautical, and Nautical System and Instrument—*mfg*	334511	3812
Headsets, telephone: Electronic Coil, Transformer, and Other Inductor—*mfg*	334416	3661
Printed Circuit/Electronics Assembly—*mfg*	334418	3661
Telephone Apparatus—*mfg*	33421	3661
Headwear: Outerwear Knitting Mills—*mfg*	315191	2253
Health and accident insurance: Direct Health and Medical Insurance Carriers—*fin*	524114	6321
Insurance Funds, Other—*fin*	52519	6321
Reinsurance Carriers—*fin*	52413	6321
Health and Personal Care Stores	**4461**	
Health and Personal Care Stores	**446**	
Health and Personal Care Stores, All Other	**446199**	**5999**
Health and Personal Care Stores, Other	**44619**	
Health and welfare councils: Grantmaking and Giving Services, Other—*serv*	813219	8399
Social Advocacy Organizations, Other—*serv*	813319	8399
Voluntary Health Organizations—*serv*	813212	8399
Health and Welfare Funds	**52512**	**6371**
Health Care and Social Assistance	**62**	
Health food stores: Food (Health) Supplement Stores—*retail*	446191	5499
Food Stores, All Other Specialty—*retail*	445299	5499
Limited-Service Restaurants—*accom*	722211	5499
Meat Markets—*retail*	44521	5499
Health foods: Grocery and Related Products, Other—*whlse*	42249	5149
Health insurance coverage consulting service: Claims Adjusters—*fin*	524291	6411
Insurance Agencies and Brokerages—*fin*	52421	6411
Insurance Related Activities, All Other—*fin*	524298	6411
Third Party Administration for Insurance and Pension Funds—*fin*	524292	6411
Health insurance for pets: Direct Insurance (except Life, Health and Medical) Carriers, Other—*fin*	524128	6399
Health insurance, indemnity plans–except medical service: Direct Health and Medical Insurance Carriers—*fin*	524114	6321
Insurance Funds, Other—*fin*	52519	6321
Reinsurance Carriers—*fin*	52413	6321
Health lamps, infrared and ultraviolet-radiation: Electric Lamp Bulb and Part—*mfg*	33511	3641
Health Practitioners, Offices Of	**62139**	
Health Practitioners, Offices Of Miscellaneous	**621399**	**8049**
Health screening service: Ambulatory Health Care Services, All Other Miscellaneous—*hlth*	621999	8099
Health statistics centers: Public Health Programs, Administration of—*pub*	92312	9431
Health systems agencies: Grantmaking and Giving Services, Other—*serv*	813219	8399

ALPHABETICAL INDEX	NAICS	SIC
Social Advocacy Organizations, Other—*serv*	813319	8399
Voluntary Health Organizations—*serv*	813212	8399
Hearing aid repair: Appliance Repair and Maintenance—*serv*	811412	7629
Consumer Electronics Repair and Maintenance—*serv*	811211	7629
Electronic and Precision Equipment Repair and Maintenance, Other—*serv*	811219	7629
Household Appliance Stores—*retail*	443111	7629
Hearing aids: Electromedical and Electrotherapeutic Apparatus—*mfg*	334510	3842
Health and Personal Care Stores, All Other—*retail*	446199	5047
Health and Personal Care Stores, All Other—*retail*	446199	5999
Medical, Dental and Hospital Equipment and Supplies—*whlse*	42145	5047
Hearing testing service: Ambulatory Health Care Services, All Other Miscellaneous—*hlth*	621999	8099
Hearse bodies: Motor Vehicle Body—*mfg*	336211	3713
Hearse rental with drivers: Limousine Service—*trans*	48532	4119
Transportation, Special Needs—*trans*	485991	4119
Hearse rental, without drivers: Passenger Car Rental—*real*	532111	7514
Hearses (motor vehicles): Automobile—*mfg*	336111	3711
Heavy Duty Truck—*mfg*	33612	3711
Light Truck and Utility Vehicle—*mfg*	336112	3711
Military Armored Vehicle, Tank and Tank Component—*mfg*	336992	3711
Motor Vehicle Body—*mfg*	336211	3711
Hearses and limousines, rental without drivers: Passenger Car Rental—*real*	532111	7514
Heart-lung machine: Electromedical and Electrotherapeutic Apparatus—*mfg*	334510	3845
Irradiation Apparatus—*mfg*	334517	3845
Heat exchange equipment, industrial: Industrial Machinery and Equipment—*whlse*	42183	5084
Heat exchangers–industrial, scientific, and nuclear: Air-Conditioning and Warm Air Heating Equipment and Commercial and Industrial Refrigeration Equipment—*mfg*	333415	3443
Metal Tank (Heavy Gauge)—*mfg*	33242	3443
Plate Work—*mfg*	332313	3443
Power Boiler and Heat Exchanger—*mfg*	33241	3443
Heat insulating compounds: Basic Organic Chemical, All Other—*mfg*	325199	2899
Chemical Product, All Other Miscellaneous—*mfg*	325998	2899
Heat insulating materials except felt–for covering boilers, pipes, etc.: Motor Vehicle Brake System—*mfg*	33634	3292
Nonmetallic Mineral Product, All Other Miscellaneous—*mfg*	327999	3292
Heat pumps, electric: Air-Conditioning and Warm Air Heating Equipment and Commercial and Industrial Refrigeration Equipment—*mfg*	333415	3585
Motor Vehicle Air-Conditioning—*mfg*	336391	3585
Heat sensitized paper made from purchased paper: Photographic and Photocopying Equipment—*mfg*	333315	3861

Photographic Film, Paper, Plate and Chemical—*mfg*	325992	3861
Heat transfer drives (finned tubing): Air-Conditioning and Warm Air Heating Equipment and Commercial and Industrial Refrigeration Equipment—*mfg*	333415	3443
Metal Tank (Heavy Gauge)—*mfg*	33242	3443
Plate Work—*mfg*	332313	3443
Power Boiler and Heat Exchanger—*mfg*	33241	3443
Heat treating of metal for the trade: Metal Heat Treating—*mfg*	332811	3398
Heat treating ovens: Industrial Process Furnace and Oven—*mfg*	333994	3567
Heat treating salts: Basic Organic Chemical, All Other—*mfg*	325199	2899
Chemical Product, All Other Miscellaneous—*mfg*	325998	2899
Heater hose, plastics or rubber: Rubber and Plastics Hoses and Belting—*mfg*	32622	3052
Heater parts, pottery: Vitreous China, Fine Earthenware and Other Pottery Product—*mfg*	327112	3269
Heater radiants, clay: Clay Refractory—*mfg*	327124	3255
Heaters, immersion–household-electric: Electric Housewares and Household Fan—*mfg*	335211	3634
Heating Equipment (except Electric and Warm Air Furnaces)—*mfg*	333414	3634
Heaters, motor vehicle: Motor Vehicle Parts, All Other—*mfg*	336399	3714
Heaters, space–electric: Electric Housewares and Household Fan—*mfg*	335211	3634
Heating Equipment (except Electric and Warm Air Furnaces)—*mfg*	333414	3634
Heaters, space–except electric: Heating Equipment (except Electric and Warm Air Furnaces)—*mfg*	333414	3433
Heaters, swimming pool–electric: General Purpose Machinery , All Other—*mfg*	333999	3569
Heaters, swimming pool–oil or gas: Heating Equipment (except Electric and Warm Air Furnaces)—*mfg*	333414	3433
Heaters, tape: Electric Housewares and Household Fan—*mfg*	335211	3634
Heating Equipment (except Electric and Warm Air Furnaces)—*mfg*	333414	3634
Heating and air-conditioning combination units: Air-Conditioning and Warm Air Heating Equipment and Commercial and Industrial Refrigeration Equipment—*mfg*	333415	3585
Motor Vehicle Air-Conditioning—*mfg*	336391	3585
Heating apparatus, except electric or warm air: Heating Equipment (except Electric and Warm Air Furnaces)—*mfg*	333414	3433
Heating Equipment (except Electric and Warm Air Furnaces) Manufacturing	**333414**	**3634**
Heating equipment installation–contractors: Plumbing, Heating and Air-Conditioning Contractors—*const*	23511	1711
Heating equipment, induction: Industrial Process Furnace and Oven—*mfg*	333994	3567
Heating of railroad cars: Air, Rail, and Water Equipment Rental and Leasing, Commercial—*real*	532411	4741
Rail Support Activities—*trans*	48821	4741

Heating Oil Dealers	**454311**	**5983**
Heating pads, electric: Electric Housewares and Household Fan—*mfg*	335211	3634
Heating Equipment (except Electric and Warm Air Furnaces)—*mfg*	333414	3634
Heating systems, steam (suppliers of heat): Steam and Air-Conditioning Supply—*util*	22133	4961
Heating units and devices, industrial–electric: Industrial Process Furnace and Oven—*mfg*	333994	3567
Heating units for electric appliances: Electric Housewares and Household Fan—*mfg*	335211	3634
Heating Equipment (except Electric and Warm Air Furnaces)—*mfg*	333414	3634
Heating units, baseboard or wail–electric (radiant heating element): Electric Housewares and Household Fan—*mfg*	335211	3634
Heating Equipment (except Electric and Warm Air Furnaces)—*mfg*	333414	3634
Heating, with or without sheet metalwork-contractors: Plumbing, Heating and Air-Conditioning Contractors—*const*	23511	1711
Heavy Construction	**234**	
Heavy Construction, All Other	**23499**	**7353**
Heavy Construction, Other	**2349**	
Heavy Duty Truck Manufacturing	**33612**	**3711**
Heavy water: Basic Inorganic Chemical, All Other—*mfg*	325188	2819
Chemical Product, All Other Miscellaneous—*mfg*	325998	2819
Heddles for loom harnesses, wire: Textile Machinery—*mfg*	333292	3552
Hedge shears and trimmers, except power: Cutlery and Flatware (except Precious)—*mfg*	332211	3421
Hedge trimmers, power: Hand and Edge Tool—*mfg*	332212	3524
Lawn and Garden Tractor and Home Lawn and Garden Equipment—*mfg*	333112	3524
Heel caps, leather or metal: Fastener, Button, Needle and Pin—*mfg*	339993	3131
Leather Good, All Other—*mfg*	316999	3131
Wood Product, All Other Miscellaneous—*mfg*	321999	3131
Heel lifts, leather: Fastener, Button, Needle and Pin—*mfg*	339993	3131
Leather Good, All Other—*mfg*	316999	3131
Wood Product, All Other Miscellaneous—*mfg*	321999	3131
Heels, boot and shce–finished wood orleather: Fastener, Button, Needle and Pin—*mfg*	339993	3131
Leather Good, All Other—*mfg*	316999	3131
Wood Product, All Other Miscellaneous—*mfg*	321999	3131
Heels, boot and shce–plastics: Plastics Pipe and Pipe Fitting—*mfg*	326122	3089
Plastics Product, All Other—*mfg*	326199	3089
Unsupported Plastics Profile Shape—*mfg*	326121	3089
Heels, hoot and shee–rubber, composition, and fiber: Fabric Coating Mills—*mfg*	31332	3069
Rubber Product, All Other—*mfg*	326299	3069
Helical springs, hot wound–for railroad equipment and vehicles: Steel Spring (except Wire)—*mfg*	332611	3493

ALPHABETICAL INDEX	NAICS	SIC
Helicopter carriers: Ambulance Services—*hlth*	62191	4522
Nonscheduled Chartered Freight Air—*trans*	481212	4522
Nonscheduled Chartered Passenger Air—*trans*	481211	4522
Scenic and Sightseeing, Other—*trans*	48799	4522
Helicopters: Aircraft—*mfg*	336411	3721
Helium: Industrial Gas—*mfg*	32512	2813
Helmets, athletic: Sporting and Athletic Goods—*mfg*	33992	3949
Helmets, except athletic–leather: Leather Good, All Other—*mfg*	316999	3199
Helmets, jungle-cloth–wool-lined: Hat, Cap and Millinery—*mfg*	315991	2353
Helmets, space: Electromedical and Electrotherapeutic Apparatus—*mfg*	334510	3842
Helmets, steel: Metal Stamping—*mfg*	332116	3469
Help supply service: Employee Leasing Services—*admin*	56133	7363
Temporary Help Services—*admin*	56132	7363
Helping hand services: Child and Youth Services—*hlth*	62411	8322
Community Food Services—*hlth*	62421	8322
Community Housing Services, Other—*hlth*	624229	8322
Emergency and Other Relief Services—*hlth*	62423	8322
Individual and Family Services, Other—*hlth*	62419	8322
Parole Offices and Probation Offices—*pub*	92215	8322
Services for the Elderly and Persons with Disabilities—*hlth*	62412	8322
Temporary Shelters—*hlth*	624221	8322
Hematite mining: Iron Ore—*mining*	21221	1011
Hematology diagnostic reagents: In-Vitro Diagnostic Substance—*mfg*	325413	2835
Pharmaceutical Preparation—*mfg*	325412	2835
Hematology products, except in vitro andin vivo reagents: Biological Product (except Diagnostic)—*mfg*	325414	2836
Hemlock extract: Gum and Wood Chemical—*mfg*	325191	2861
Hemlock gum, gathering of: Crop Farming, All Other Miscellaneous—*ag*	111998	831
Forest Nurseries and Gathering of Forest Products—*ag*	11321	831
Hemodialysis apparatus: Surgical and Medical Instrument—*mfg*	339112	3841
Hemp yarn, thread, roving, and textiles: Broadwoven Fabric Mills—*mfg*	31321	2299
Narrow Fabric Mills—*mfg*	313221	2299
Nonwoven Fabric Mills—*mfg*	31323	2299
Textile and Fabric Finishing (except Broadwoven Fabric) Mills—*mfg*	313312	2299
Textile Product Mills, All Other Miscellaneous—*mfg*	314999	2299
Thread Mills—*mfg*	313113	2299
Yarn Spinning Mills—*mfg*	313111	2299
Hemstitching, for the trade: Men's and Boys' Cut and Sew Apparel Contractors—*mfg*	315211	2395
Textile Product Mills, All Other Miscellaneous—*mfg*	314999	2395
Women's and Girls' Cut and Sew Apparel Contractors—*mfg*	315212	2395
Herb grinding, grading, and milling: Medicinal and Botanical—*mfg*	325411	2833

ALPHABETICAL INDEX	NAICS	SIC
Herbicides: Pesticide and Other Agricultural Chemical—*mfg*	32532	2879
Hermetic seals for electronic equipment: Electronic Component, Other—*mfg*	334419	3679
Motor Vehicle Electrical and Electronic Equipment, Other—*mfg*	336322	3679
Printed Circuit/Electronics Assembly—*mfg*	334418	3679
Radio and Television Broadcasting and Wireless Communications Equipment—*mfg*	33422	3679
Hermetics repair: Machinery and Equipment (except Automotive and Electronic) Repair and Maintenance, Commercial and Industrial—*serv*	81131	7694
Motor and Generator—*mfg*	335312	7694
Herring–smoked, salted, dried, and pickled: Seafood Canning—*mfg*	311711	2091
Hexamethylenediamine: Basic Organic Chemical, All Other—*mfg*	325199	2869
Hexamethylenetetramine: Basic Organic Chemical, All Other—*mfg*	325199	2869
Hickory stripes, cotton: Broadwoven Fabric Mills—*mfg*	31321	2211
Hides (may include curing): Farm Product Raw Material, Other—*whlse*	42259	5159
Hides and skins, cured or uncured: Animal (except Poultry) Slaughtering—*mfg*	311611	2011
Hides–tanning, currying, and finishing: Leather and Hide Tanning and Finishing—*mfg*	31611	3111
High chairs, children's–wood: Nonupholstered Wood Household Furniture—*mfg*	337122	2511
High energy rate metal forming machines: Machine Tool (Metal Forming Types)—*mfg*	333513	3542
High explosives: Explosives—*mfg*	32592	2892
High fidelity (hi-fi) equipment: Automotive Parts and Accessories Stores—*retail*	44131	5731
Electrical Appliance, Television and Radio Set—*whlse*	42162	5064
Radio, Television and Other Electronics Stores—*retail*	443112	5731
High fructose syrup: Wet Corn Milling—*mfg*	311221	2046
High percentage ferroalloys: Electrometallurgical Ferroalloy Product—*mfg*	331112	3313
Secondary Smelting, Refining, and Alloying of Nonferrous Metal (except Copper and Aluminum)—*mfg*	331492	3313
High percentage nonferrous additive alloys, except copper: Electrometallurgical Ferroalloy Product—*mfg*	331112	3313
Secondary Smelting, Refining, and Alloying of Nonferrous Metal (except Copper and Aluminum)—*mfg*	331492	3313
High purity grade chemicals, inorganic–refined from technical grades: Basic Inorganic Chemical, All Other—*mfg*	325188	2819
Chemical Product, All Other Miscellaneous—*mfg*	325998	2819
High purity grade chemicals, organic–refined from technical grades: Basic Organic Chemical, All Other—*mfg*	325199	2869
High schools: Elementary and Secondary Schools—*educ*	61111	8211
High temperature mortar, nonclay: Nonclay Refractory—*mfg*	327125	3297

Entry	NAICS	SIC
High vacuum coaters, metal plate: Air-Conditioning and Warm Air Heating Equipment and Commercial and Industrial Refrigeration Equipment—*mfg*	333415	3443
Metal Tank (Heavy Gauge)—*mfg*	33242	3443
Plate Work—*mfg*	332313	3443
Power Boiler and Heat Exchanger—*mfg*	33241	3443
Highway and Street Construction	**23411**	**1611**
Highway bridge sections, prefabricated metal: Fabricated Structural Metal—*mfg*	332312	3441
Highway bridges, operation of: Road, Other Support Activities for—*trans*	48849	4785
Water, Other Support Activities for—*trans*	48839	4785
Highway construction, elevated–general contractors: Bridge and Tunnel—*const*	23412	1622
Highway construction, except elevated–general contractors: Highway and Street—*const*	23411	1611
Highway fusees: Basic Organic Chemical, All Other—*mfg*	325199	2899
Chemical Product, All Other Miscellaneous—*mfg*	325998	2899
Highway guardrails, sheet metal: Metal Container, Other—*mfg*	332439	3444
Sheet Metal Work—*mfg*	332322	3444
Highway lighting and electrical signal construction–contractors: Electrical Contractors—*const*	23531	1731
Security Systems Services (except Locksmiths)—*admin*	561621	1731
Highway patrols: Police Protection—*pub*	92212	9221
Highway signals, electric: Communications Equipment, Other—*mfg*	33429	3669
Highway signs, installation of–contractors: Highway and Street—*const*	23411	1611
Highway, Street, Bridge and Tunnel Construction	**2341**	
Hinge tubes: Hardware—*mfg*	33251	3429
Hinges: Hardware—*mfg*	33251	3429
Historical clubs, other than professional: Civic and Social Organizations—*serv*	81341	8699
Historical Sites	**71212**	**8412**
Hitches, trailer: Transportation Equipment, All Other—*mfg*	336999	3799
HMO Medical Centers	**621491**	**8011**
Hobby kits: Toy and Hobby Goods and Supplies—*whlse*	42192	5092
Hobby shops: Hobby, Toy and Game Stores—*retail*	45112	5945
Hobby, Toy and Game Stores	**45112**	**5945**
Hobbyhorses: Game, Toy, and Children's Vehicle—*mfg*	339932	3944
Hobs: Cutting Tool and Machine Tool Accessory—*mfg*	333515	3545
Hand and Edge Tool—*mfg*	332212	3545
Industrial Machinery and Equipment—*whlse*	42183	5084
Hockey clubs, except professional and semiprofessional: Fitness and Recreational Sports Centers—*arts*	71394	7997
Hockey equipment, except uniforms and footwear: Sporting and Athletic Goods—*mfg*	33992	3949
Hoeing: Nonscheduled Air, Other—*trans*	481219	721
Soil Preparation, Planting, and Cultivating—*ag*	115112	721
Hoes, garden and masons': Hand and Edge Tool—*mfg*	332212	3423
Hog and Pig Farming	**1122**	
Hog and Pig Farming	**11221**	**213**
Hog farms: Hog and Pig Farming—*ag*	11221	213
Hog feeding, handling, and watering equipment: Farm Machinery and Equipment—*mfg*	333111	3523
Hog rings, made from purchased wire: Fabricated Wire Product, Other—*mfg*	332618	3496
Hog slaughtering plants: Animal (except Poultry) Slaughtering—*mfg*	311611	2011
Hogs: Livestock—*whlse*	42252	5154
Hogsheads, wood–coopered: Wood Container and Pallet—*mfg*	32192	2449
Hoists: Industrial Machinery and Equipment—*whlse*	42183	5084
Hoists, aircraft loading: Fabricated Metal Product, All Other Miscellaneous—*mfg*	332999	3537
Industrial Truck, Tractor, Trailer and Stacker Machinery—*mfg*	333924	3537
Metal Container, Other—*mfg*	332439	3537
Hoists, except aircraft loading and automobile wrecker hoists: Overhead Traveling Crane, Hoist and Monorail System—*mfg*	333923	3536
Hoists, hand: Overhead Traveling Crane, Hoist and Monorail System—*mfg*	333923	3536
Hoists, overhead: Overhead Traveling Crane, Hoist and Monorail System—*mfg*	333923	3536
Holders, cigar and cigarette: Plastics Product, All Other—*mfg*	326199	3999
Wood Product, All Other Miscellaneous—*mfg*	321999	3999
Holders, pencil: Chemical Product, All Other Miscellaneous—*mfg*	325998	3952
Institutional Furniture—*mfg*	337127	3952
Lead Pencil and Art Good—*mfg*	339942	3952
Holders, plastics–papertowel, grocery bag, dust mop and broom: Plastics Pipe and Pipe Fitting—*mfg*	326122	3089
Plastics Product, All Other—*mfg*	326199	3089
Unsupported Plastics Profile Shape—*mfg*	326121	3089
Holders, surgical needle: Surgical and Medical Instrument—*mfg*	339112	3841
Holders–photographic film, plate, andpaper: Photographic and Photocopying Equipment—*mfg*	333315	3861
Photographic Film, Paper, Plate and Chemical—*mfg*	325992	3861
Holding companies, except bank: Other Holding Companies, Offices Of—*manag*	551112	6719
Hollowware, silver, nickel silver, pewter, stainless steel, and plated: Cutlery and Flatware (except Precious)—*mfg*	332211	3914
Silverware and Plated Ware—*mfg*	339912	3914
Holsters, leather: Leather Good, All Other—*mfg*	316999	3199
Home and Garden Equipment and Appliance Repair and Maintenance	**81141**	
Home and Garden Equipment Repair and Maintenance	**811411**	**7699**
Home Centers	**44411**	**5211**
Home Furnishing Wholesalers	**42122**	**5023**
Home Furnishings Stores	**4422**	
Home Furnishings Stores, All Other	**442299**	**5719**
Home Furnishings Stores, Other	**44229**	
Home Health Care Services	**6216**	

ALPHABETICAL INDEX	NAICS	SIC
Home Health Care Services	**62161**	**8082**
Home Health Equipment Rental	**532291**	**7352**
Home improvements, residential–except single-family–general contractors: Building, Commercial and Institutional—*const*	23332	1522
Multifamily Housing—*const*	23322	1522
Home improvements, single-family–general contractors: Single Family Housing—*const*	23321	1521
Home permanent kits: Soap and Other Detergent—*mfg*	325611	2844
Toilet Preparation—*mfg*	32562	2844
Home photographers: Photography Studios, Portrait—*prof*	541921	7221
Home tape recorders–cassette, cartridge, and reel: Audio and Video Equipment—*mfg*	33431	3651
Home workshop machine teols, metalworking: Machine Tool (Metal Cutting Types)—*mfg*	333512	3541
Homefurnishing stores, secondhand: Non-Depository Credit Intermediation, All Other—*fin*	522298	5932
Used Merchandise Stores—*retail*	45331	5932
Homefurnishings: Home Furnishing—*whlse*	42122	5023
Homefurnishings, antique: Non-Depository Credit Intermediation, All Other—*fin*	522298	5932
Used Merchandise Stores—*retail*	45331	5932
Homemaker's service, primarily nonmedical: Child and Youth Services—*hlth*	62411	8322
Community Food Services—*hlth*	62421	8322
Community Housing Services, Other—*hlth*	624229	8322
Emergency and Other Relief Services—*hlth*	62423	8322
Individual and Family Services, Other—*hlth*	62419	8322
Parole Offices and Probation Offices—*pub*	92215	8322
Services for the Elderly and Persons with Disabilities—*hlth*	62412	8322
Temporary Shelters—*hlth*	624221	8322
Homeowner associations, except property management: Civic and Social Organizations—*serv*	81341	8641
Organizations, Other Similar—*serv*	81399	8641
Homes for children, with health care incidental: Homes for the Elderly—*hlth*	623312	8361
Residential Care Facilities, Other—*hlth*	62399	8361
Residential Mental Health and Substance Abuse Facilities—*hlth*	62322	8361
Homes for destitute men and women: Homes for the Elderly—*hlth*	623312	8361
Residential Care Facilities, Other—*hlth*	62399	8361
Residential Mental Health and Substance Abuse Facilities—*hlth*	62322	8361
Homes for the aged, with health care incidental: Homes for the Elderly—*hlth*	623312	8361
Residential Care Facilities, Other—*hlth*	62399	8361
Residential Mental Health and Substance Abuse Facilities—*hlth*	62322	8361
Homes for the deaf or blind, with healthcare incidental: Homes for the Elderly—*hlth*	623312	8361
Residential Care Facilities, Other—*hlth*	62399	8361

ALPHABETICAL INDEX	NAICS	SIC
Residential Mental Health and Substance Abuse Facilities—*hlth*	62322	8361
Homes for the Elderly	**623312**	**8361**
Homes for the emotionally disturbed, with health care incidental: Homes for the Elderly—*hlth*	623312	8361
Residential Care Facilities, Other—*hlth*	62399	8361
Residential Mental Health and Substance Abuse Facilities—*hlth*	62322	8361
Homes for the mentally handicapped, with health care incidental: Homes for the Elderly—*hlth*	623312	8361
Residential Care Facilities, Other—*hlth*	62399	8361
Residential Mental Health and Substance Abuse Facilities—*hlth*	62322	8361
Homes for the mentally retarded with health care, except skilled and intermediate care facilities: Continuing Care Retirement Communities—*hlth*	623311	8059
Nursing Care Facilities—*hlth*	62311	8059
Homes for the physically handicapped, with health care incidental: Homes for the Elderly—*hlth*	623312	8361
Residential Care Facilities, Other—*hlth*	62399	8361
Residential Mental Health and Substance Abuse Facilities—*hlth*	62322	8361
Hominy grits prepared as cereal breakfast food: Breakfast Cereal—*mfg*	31123	2043
Coffee and Tea—*mfg*	31192	2043
Hominy grits, except breakfast food: Flour Milling—*mfg*	311211	2041
Hominy, canned: Fruit and Vegetable Canning—*mfg*	311421	2033
Homogenizing machinery–dairy, fruit, vegetable, and other foods: Food Product Machinery—*mfg*	333294	3556
Hones: Abrasive Product—*mfg*	32791	3291
Fabricated Metal Product, All Other Miscellaneous—*mfg*	332999	3291
Honey: Grocery and Related Products, Other—*whlse*	42249	5149
Honey production: Animal Production, All Other—*ag*	11299	279
Apiculture—*ag*	11291	279
Honey straining on the farm: Animal Production Support Activities—*ag*	11521	752
Pet Care (except Veterinary) Services—*serv*	81291	752
Honey, strained and bottled: Food, All Other Miscellaneous—*mfg*	311999	2099
Honeycomb core and board: Coated and Laminated Paper—*mfg*	322222	2679
Converted Paper Product, All Other—*mfg*	322298	2679
Die-Cut Paper and Paperboard Office Supplies—*mfg*	322231	2679
Non-Folding Sanitary Food Container—*mfg*	322215	2679
Honeycomb foundations (beekeepers' supplies): Wood Product, All Other Miscellaneous—*mfg*	321999	3999
Honeycombed metal: Metal Stamping—*mfg*	332116	3469
Honing and lapping machines: Machine Tool (Metal Cutting Types)—*mfg*	333512	3541
Honing heads: Cutting Tool and Machine Tool Accessory—*mfg*	333515	3545
Hand and Edge Tool—*mfg*	332212	3545
Honor camps: Correctional Institutions—*pub*	92214	9223

Description	NAICS	SIC
Hoods, industrial–metal plate: Air-Conditioning and Warm Air Heating Equipment and Commercial and Industrial Refrigeration Equipment—*mfg*	333415	3443
Metal Tank (Heavy Gauge)—*mfg*	33242	3443
Plate Work—*mfg*	332313	3443
Power Boiler and Heat Exchanger—*mfg*	33241	3443
Hoods, motor vehicle: Motor Vehicle Body—*mfg*	336211	3714
Motor Vehicle Parts, All Other—*mfg*	336399	3714
Hoods, range–sheet metal: Metal Container, Other—*mfg*	332439	3444
Sheet Metal Work—*mfg*	332322	3444
Hooked rugs: Carpet and Rug Mills—*mfg*	31411	2273
Hooks and eyes: Fastener, Button, Needle and Pin—*mfg*	339993	3965
Hooks, crane–laminated plate: Air-Conditioning and Warm Air Heating Equipment and Commercial and Industrial Refrigeration Equipment—*mfg*	333415	3443
Metal Tank (Heavy Gauge)—*mfg*	33242	3443
Plate Work—*mfg*	332313	3443
Power Boiler and Heat Exchanger—*mfg*	33241	3443
Hooks, crochet: Fastener, Button, Needle and Pin—*mfg*	339993	3965
Hooks, fishing: Sporting and Athletic Goods—*mfg*	33992	3949
Hooks, gatc: Bolt, Nut, Screw, Rivet and Washer—*mfg*	332722	3452
Hooks, screw: Bolt, Nut, Screw, Rivet and Washer—*mfg*	332722	3452
Hooks–bush, grass, baling, and husking: Hand and Edge Tool—*mfg*	332212	3423
Hoops, galvanized iron and steel: Iron and Steel Mills—*mfg*	331111	3312
Petroleum and Coal Productsa, All Other—*mfg*	324199	3312
Hoops, iron and steel–made in steel works or hot-rolling mills: Iron and Steel Mills—*mfg*	331111	3312
Petroleum and Coal Productsa, All Other—*mfg*	324199	3312
Hoops, metal–other than wire: Fabricated Metal Product, All Other Miscellaneous—*mfg*	332999	3499
Hoops, wood–for tight or slack cooper-age-sawed or split: Cut Stock, Resawing Lumber, and Planing—*mfg*	321912	2429
Sawmills—*mfg*	321113	2429
Wood Product, All Other Miscellaneous—*mfg*	321999	2429
Hop extract: Grocery and Related Products, Other—*whlse*	42249	5149
Hop farms: Crop Farming, All Other Miscellaneous—*ag*	111998	139
Hay Farming—*ag*	11194	139
Peanut Farming—*ag*	111992	139
Vegetable (except Potato) and Melon Farming, Other—*ag*	111219	139
Hopper feed devices: Cutting Tool and Machine Tool Accessory—*mfg*	333515	3545
Hand and Edge Tool—*mfg*	332212	3545
Hoppers, end dump: Fabricated Metal Product, All Other Miscellaneous—*mfg*	332999	3537
Industrial Truck, Tractor, Trailer and Stacker Machinery—*mfg*	333924	3537
Metal Container, Other—*mfg*	332439	3537
Hoppers, metal plate: Air-Conditioning and Warm Air Heating Equipment and Commercial and Industrial Refrigeration Equipment—*mfg*	333415	3443
Metal Tank (Heavy Gauge)—*mfg*	33242	3443
Plate Work—*mfg*	332313	3443
Power Boiler and Heat Exchanger—*mfg*	33241	3443
Hoppers, sheet metal: Metal Container, Other—*mfg*	332439	3444
Sheet Metal Work—*mfg*	332322	3444
Hops: Farm Product Raw Material, Other—*whlse*	42259	5159
Horizon situation instrumentation: Search, Detection, Navigation, Guidance, Aeronautical, and Nautical System and Instrument—*mfg*	334511	3812
Hormone preparations, except diagnostics: Pharmaceutical Preparation—*mfg*	325412	2834
Hormones and derivatives: Medicinal and Botanical—*mfg*	325411	2833
Hormones, plant: Pesticide and Other Agricultural Chemical—*mfg*	32532	2879
Horns, motor vehicle: Motor Vehicle Electrical and Electronic Equipment, Other—*mfg*	336322	3714
Motor Vehicle Parts, All Other—*mfg*	336399	3714
Horns, toy: Game, Toy, and Children's Vehicle—*mfg*	339932	3944
Horse and Other Equine Production	**11292**	**272**
Horse bits: Hardware—*mfg*	33251	3429
Horse blankets: Textile Product Mills, All Other Miscellaneous—*mfg*	314999	2399
Horse farms: Horse and Other Equine Production—*ag*	11292	272
Horse hoots and muzzles: Leather Good, All Other—*mfg*	316999	3199
Horsehair, artificial–nylon: Noncellulosic Organic Fiber—*mfg*	325222	2824
Horsehair, artificial–rayon: Cellulosic Organic Fiber—*mfg*	325221	2823
Horsemeat for human consumption: Animal (except Poultry) Slaughtering—*mfg*	311611	2011
Horsemeat, except for human consumption: Animal (except Poultry) Slaughtering—*mfg*	311611	2048
Animal Food, Other—*mfg*	311119	2048
Horseradish, prepared: Fruit and Vegetable Canning—*mfg*	311421	2035
Mayonnaise, Dressing and Other Prepared Sauce—*mfg*	311941	2035
Horses: Farm Product Raw Material, Other—*whlse*	42259	5159
Horses, boarding or training (except race horses): Animal Production Support Activities—*ag*	11521	752
Pet Care (except Veterinary) Services—*serv*	81291	752
Horses, race–owners of: Race Tracks—*arts*	711212	7948
Spectator Sports, Other—*arts*	711219	7948
Horses, race–training: Race Tracks—*arts*	711212	7948
Spectator Sports, Other—*arts*	711219	7948
Horses, racing of: Race Tracks—*arts*	711212	7948
Spectator Sports, Other—*arts*	711219	7948
Horseshoe calks, forged–not made in rolling mills: Iron and Steel Forging—*mfg*	332111	3462
Horseshoe nails: Fabricated Wire Product, Other—*mfg*	332618	3315
Steel Wire Drawing—*mfg*	331222	3315
Horseshoeing: Animal Production Support Activities—*ag*	11521	7699
Horseshoes, not made in rolling mills: Iron and Steel Forging—*mfg*	332111	3462
Horticultural advisory or counseling services: Landscape Architectural Services—*prof*	54132	781

ALPHABETICAL INDEX	NAICS	SIC
Scientific and Technical Consulting Services, Other—*prof*	54169	781
Hose clamps: Other Metal Valve and Pipe Fitting, Other—*mfg*	332919	3429
Hose couplings: Other Metal Valve and Pipe Fitting, Other—*mfg*	332919	3429
Hose fabrics, tubular: Narrow Fabric Mills—*mfg*	313221	2241
Hose fittings and assemblies, fluid power–metal: Fluid Power Valve and Hose Fitting—*mfg*	332912	3492
Hose, belting, and packing–industrial: Industrial Machinery and Equipment—*whlse*	42183	5085
Industrial Supplies—*whlse*	42184	5085
Hose, fire–except rubber: General Purpose Machinery , All Other—*mfg*	333999	3569
Hose, flexible metallic: Fabricated Metal Product, All Other Miscellaneous—*mfg*	332999	3599
General Purpose Machinery , All Other—*mfg*	333999	3599
Machine Shops—*mfg*	33271	3599
Machinery, Other Commercial and Service Industry—*mfg*	333319	3599
Hose, plastics or rubber: Rubber and Plastics Hoses and Belting—*mfg*	32622	3052
Hose–cotton fabric, rubber lined: Rubber and Plastics Hoses and Belting—*mfg*	32622	3052
Hosiery and Sock Mills	**31511**	
Hosiery and Sock Mills, Other	**315119**	**2252**
Hosiery machines: Textile Machinery—*mfg*	333292	3552
Hosiery stores: Clothing Accessories Stores—*retail*	44815	5632
Clothing Stores, Other—*retail*	44819	5632
Hosiery, elastic–orthopedic: Surgical Appliance and Supplies—*mfg*	339113	3842
Hosiery, except women's and misses' full-length and knee-length: Hosiery and Sock Mills, Other—*mfg*	315119	2252
Sheer Hosiery Mills—*mfg*	315111	2252
Hosiery, men's and boys': Men's and Boys' Clothing and Furnishings—*whlse*	42232	5136
Hosiery, support: Surgical Appliance and Supplies—*mfg*	339113	3842
Hosiery, women's full-length and knee-length, except socks: Sheer Hosiery Mills—*mfg*	315111	2251
Hosiery–women's, children's, and infants': Women's, Children's, and Infants' and Accessories—*whlse*	42233	5137
Hospital and medical service plans: Direct Health and Medical Insurance Carriers—*fin*	524114	6324
Insurance Funds, Other—*fin*	52519	6324
Reinsurance Carriers—*fin*	52413	6324
Hospital beds: Institutional Furniture—*mfg*	337127	2599
Surgical Appliance and Supplies—*mfg*	339113	2599
Hospital construction–general contractors: Building, Commercial and Institutional—*const*	23332	1542
Hospital dollies: Fabricated Metal Product, All Other Miscellaneous—*mfg*	332999	3537
Industrial Truck, Tractor, Trailer and Stacker Machinery—*mfg*	333924	3537

ALPHABETICAL INDEX	NAICS	SIC
Metal Container, Other—*mfg*	332439	3537
Hospital equipment: Health and Personal Care Stores, All Other—*retail*	446199	5047
Medical, Dental and Hospital Equipment and Supplies—*whlse*	42145	5047
Hospital furniture: Health and Personal Care Stores, All Other—*retail*	446199	5047
Medical, Dental and Hospital Equipment and Supplies—*whlse*	42145	5047
Hospital gowns–women's and children's: Women's, Children's, and Infants' and Accessories—*whlse*	42233	5137
Hospital service apparel, washable: Men's and Boys' Cut and Sew Apparel Contractors—*mfg*	315211	2326
Men's and Boys' Cut and Sew Work Clothing—*mfg*	315225	2326
Hospital sheets, nonwoven textiles: Household Textile Product Mills, Other—*mfg*	314129	2392
Hospital utensils, cast aluminum–except die-castings: Aluminum Foundries—*mfg*	331524	3365
Hospital utensils, porcelain enameled: Kitchen Utensil, Pot and Pan—*mfg*	332214	3469
Hospitals	**622**	
Hospitals (except Psychiatric and Substance Abuse), Specialty	**6223**	
Hospitals (except Psychiatric and Substance Abuse), Specialty	**62231**	**8069**
Hospitals, specialty–except psychiatric: General Medical and Surgical Hospitals—*hlth*	62211	8069
Hospitals (except Psychiatric and Substance Abuse), Specialty—*hlth*	62231	8069
Psychiatric and Substance Abuse Hospitals—*hlth*	62221	8069
Hospitalware, plastics–except foam: Plastics Pipe and Pipe Fitting—*mfg*	326122	3089
Plastics Product, All Other—*mfg*	326199	3089
Unsupported Plastics Profile Shape—*mfg*	326121	3089
Hostels: Bed and Breakfast Inns—*accom*	721191	7011
Casino Hotels—*accom*	72112	7011
Hotels (except Casino Hotels) and Motels—*accom*	72111	7011
Traveler Accommodation, All Other—*accom*	721199	7011
Hot dip coating of metals and formed products, for the trade: Costume Jewelry and Novelty—*mfg*	339914	3479
Jewelry (except Costume)—*mfg*	339911	3479
Metal Coating, Engraving (except Jewelry and Silverware), and Allied Services to Manufacturers—*mfg*	332812	3479
Silverware and Plated Ware—*mfg*	339912	3479
Hot dog (frankfurter) stands: Cafeterias—*accom*	722212	5812
Caterers—*accom*	72232	5812
Foodservice Contractors—*accom*	72231	5812
Full-Service Restaurants—*accom*	72211	5812
Limited-Service Restaurants—*accom*	722211	5812
Snack and Nonalcoholic Beverage Bars—*accom*	722213	5812
Theater Companies and Dinner Theaters—*arts*	71111	5812

Description	NAICS	SIC
Hot oil treating of oil field tanks–on a contract basis: Oil and Gas Operations Support Activities—*mining*	213112	1389
Hot shot service–on a contract basis: Oil and Gas Operations Support Activities—*mining*	213112	1389
Hot strip mill machinery: Rolling Mill Machinery and Equipment—*mfg*	333516	3547
Hot top refractories, clay: Clay Refractory—*mfg*	327124	3255
Hot top refractories, nonclay: Nonclay Refractory—*mfg*	327125	3297
Hot tubs: Sporting and Recreational Goods and Supplies—*whlse*	42191	5091
Stores (except Tobacco Stores), All Other Miscellaneous—*retail*	453998	5999
Hot tubs, coopered: Wood Container and Pallet—*mfg*	32192	2449
Hot tubs, plastics or fiberglass: Plastics Plumbing Fixture—*mfg*	326191	3088
Hot water heaters, household–including nonelectric: Major Household Appliance, Other—*mfg*	335228	3639
Hot wound springs, except wire springs: Steel Spring (except Wire)—*mfg*	332611	3493
Hot-rolled iron and steel products: Iron and Steel Mills—*mfg*	331111	3312
Petroleum and Coal Productsa, All Other—*mfg*	324199	3312
Hotel construction–general contractors: Building, Commercial and Institutional—*const*	23332	1522
Multifamily Housing—*const*	23322	1522
Hotel reservation service: Travel Arrangement and Reservation Services, All Other—*admin*	561599	7389
Hotel tableware and kitchen articles, vitreous china: Vitreous China, Fine Earthenware and Other Pottery Product—*mfg*	327112	3262
Hotels (except Casino Hotels) and Motels	**72111**	**7041**
Hotels operated by organizations for members only: Hotels (except Casino Hotels) and Motels—*accom*	72111	7041
Rooming and Boarding Houses—*accom*	72131	7041
Hotels, except residential: Bed and Breakfast Inns—*accom*	721191	7011
Casino Hotels—*accom*	72112	7011
Hotels (except Casino Hotels) and Motels—*accom*	72111	7011
Traveler Accommodation, All Other—*accom*	721199	7011
Hotels, residential–operators: Lessors of Residential Buildings and Dwellings—*real*	53111	6513
Hotels, seasonal: Bed and Breakfast Inns—*accom*	721191	7011
Casino Hotels—*accom*	72112	7011
Hotels (except Casino Hotels) and Motels—*accom*	72111	7011
Traveler Accommodation, All Other—*accom*	721199	7011
Hotlines: Child and Youth Services—*hlth*	62411	8322
Community Food Services—*hlth*	62421	8322
Community Housing Services, Other—*hlth*	624229	8322
Emergency and Other Relief Services—*hlth*	62423	8322
Individual and Family Services, Other—*hlth*	62419	8322
Parole Offices and Probation Offices—*pub*	92215	8322
Services for the Elderly and Persons with Disabilities—*hlth*	62412	8322
Temporary Shelters—*hlth*	624221	8322
Hotplates, electric: Electric Housewares and Household Fan—*mfg*	335211	3634
Heating Equipment (except Electric and Warm Air Furnaces)—*mfg*	333414	3634
House construction, single-family–general contractors: Single Family Housing—*const*	23321	1521
House delivery of purchased milk: Direct Selling Establishments, Other—*retail*	45439	5963
Mobile Foodservices—*accom*	72233	5963
House designers: Architectural Services—*prof*	54131	8712
House moving–contractors: Trade Contractors, All Other Special—*const*	23599	1799
House painting–contractors: Painting and Wall Covering Contractors—*const*	23521	1721
House Slipper Manufacturing	**316212**	**3142**
House slippers: House Slipper—*mfg*	316212	3142
House trailer rental: Truck, Utility Trailer, and RV (Recreational Vehicle) Rental and Leasing—*real*	53212	7519
House–shell erection, single-family–general contractors: Single Family Housing—*const*	23321	1521
House-to-house selling of coffee, soda, beer, bottled water, or other products: Direct Selling Establishments, Other—*retail*	45439	5963
Mobile Foodservices—*accom*	72233	5963
Houseboat rentals: Recreational Goods Rental—*real*	532292	7999
Houseboats, building and repairing: Boat Building—*mfg*	336612	3732
Personal and Household Goods Repair and Maintenance, Other—*serv*	81149	3732
Housecoats: Men's and Boys' Cut and Sew Apparel Contractors—*mfg*	315211	2384
Men's and Boys' Cut and Sew Underwear and Nightwear—*mfg*	315221	2384
Outerwear Knitting Mills—*mfg*	315191	2253
Women's and Girls' Cut and Sew Apparel Contractors—*mfg*	315212	2384
Women's and Girls' Cut and Sew Lingerie, Loungewear and Nightwear—*mfg*	315231	2384
Housedresses: Women's and Girls' Cut and Sew Apparel Contractors—*mfg*	315212	2335
Women's and Girls' Cut and Sew Dress—*mfg*	315233	2335
Housefurnishings, except curtains and draperies: Household Textile Product Mills, Other—*mfg*	314129	2392
Household and Institutional Furniture and Kitchen Cabinet Manufacturing	**3371**	
Household and Institutional Furniture Manufacturing	**33712**	
Household Appliance Manufacturing	**3352**	
Household Appliance Stores	**443111**	**5999**
Household appliance stores, electric orgas: Household Appliance Stores—*retail*	443111	5722
Household bleaches, dry or liquid: Polish and Other Sanitation Good—*mfg*	325612	2842
Household brooms and brushes: Broom, Brush and Mop—*mfg*	339994	3991
Household Cooking Appliance Manufacturing	**335221**	**3631**
Household earthenware, semivitreous: Vitreous China, Fine Earthenware and Other Pottery Product—*mfg*	327112	3263

ALPHABETICAL INDEX	NAICS	SIC
Household furniture: Furniture—*whlse*	42121	5021
Furniture Stores—*retail*	44211	5021
Furniture Stores—*retail*	44211	5712
Nonupholstered Wood Household Furniture—*mfg*	337122	5712
Upholstered Household Furniture—*mfg*	337121	5712
Wood Kitchen Cabinet and Counter Top—*mfg*	33711	5712
Household Furniture (except Wood and Metal) Manufacturing	**337125**	**2519**
Household furniture upholstered on woodframes, except dual-purpose sleep furniture: Upholstered Household Furniture—*mfg*	337121	2512
Household furniture, glass and plastics: Household Furniture (except Wood and Metal)—*mfg*	337125	2519
Household furniture, wood–except upholstered: Nonupholstered Wood Household Furniture—*mfg*	337122	2511
Household furniture–rattan, reed, malacca, fiber, willow, and wicker: Household Furniture (except Wood and Metal)—*mfg*	337125	2519
Household gloves, rubber: Fabric Coating Mills—*mfg*	31332	3069
Rubber Product, All Other—*mfg*	326299	3069
Household goods moving, local–combined with storage: Freight (except Used Goods) Trucking, Local Specialized—*trans*	48422	4214
General Freight Trucking, Local—*trans*	48411	4214
Used Household and Office Goods Moving—*trans*	48421	4214
Household goods warehousing and storage, without local trucking: General Warehousing and Storage Facilities—*trans*	49311	4226
Refrigerated Warehousing and Storage Facilities—*trans*	49312	4226
Warehousing and Storage Facilities, Other—*trans*	49319	4226
Household insecticides: Pesticide and Other Agricultural Chemical—*mfg*	32532	2879
Household Laundry Equipment Manufacturing	**335224**	**3633**
Household Refrigerator and Home Freezer Manufacturing	**335222**	**3632**
Household tableware and kitchen articles, vitreous china: Vitreous China, Fine Earthenware and Other Pottery Product—*mfg*	327112	3262
Household Textile Product Mills, Other	**314129**	**2392**
Household tints and dyes: Basic Organic Chemical, All Other—*mfg*	325199	2899
Chemical Product, All Other Miscellaneous—*mfg*	325998	2899
Household utensils, cast aluminum–except die-castings: Aluminum Foundries—*mfg*	331524	3365
Household utensils, porcelain enameled: Kitchen Utensil, Pot and Pan—*mfg*	332214	3469
Household utensils, stamped and pressed metal: Kitchen Utensil, Pot and Pan—*mfg*	332214	3469
Household Vacuum Cleaner Manufacturing	**335212**	**3639**
Household woodenware: Manufacturing, All Other Miscellaneous—*mfg*	339999	2499
Wood Container and Pallet—*mfg*	32192	2499
Wood Product, All Other Miscellaneous—*mfg*	321999	2499
Households, private–employing cooks, maids, chauffeurs, gardeners, etc.: Private Households—*serv*	81411	8811
Housekeeping (cleaning service) on a contract or fee basis: Janitorial Services—*admin*	56172	7349
Houses of correction: Correctional Institutions—*pub*	92214	9223
Houses, portable–prefabricated wood-except mobile homes: Prefabricated Wood Building—*mfg*	321992	2452
Houses, prefabricated–metal: Prefabricated Metal Building and Component—*mfg*	332311	3448
Housetrailers, except as permanent dwellings: Travel Trailer and Camper—*mfg*	336214	3792
Housewares stores: Home Furnishings Stores, All Other—*retail*	442299	5719
Window Treatment Stores—*retail*	442291	5719
Housewares–house-tohouse, telephone or party plan selling: Direct Selling Establishments, Other—*retail*	45439	5963
Mobile Foodservices—*accom*	72233	5963
Housing agencies, nonoperating: Housing Programs, Administration of—*pub*	92511	9531
Housing authorities, nonoperating-govemment: Housing Programs, Administration of—*pub*	92511	9531
Housing authorities, operating: Real Estate, Other Activities Related to—*real*	53139	6531
Housing cabinets for radium, metal plate: Air-Conditioning and Warm Air Heating Equipment and Commercial and Industrial Refrigeration Equipment—*mfg*	333415	3443
Metal Tank (Heavy Gauge)—*mfg*	33242	3443
Plate Work—*mfg*	332313	3443
Power Boiler and Heat Exchanger—*mfg*	33241	3443
Housing components, prefabricated–concrete: Concrete Pipe—*mfg*	327332	3272
Concrete Product, Other—*mfg*	32739	3272
Nonmetallic Mineral Product, All Other Miscellaneous—*mfg*	327999	3272
Housing Programs, Administration of	**92511**	**9531**
Housing Programs, Urban Planning, and Community Development, Administration of	**9251**	
Housing Programs, Urban Planning, and Community Development, Administration of	**925**	
Housings for business machines, sheet metal–except stamped: Metal Container, Other—*mfg*	332439	3444
Sheet Metal Work—*mfg*	332322	3444
Housings, pressure: Air-Conditioning and Warm Air Heating Equipment and Commercial and Industrial Refrigeration Equipment—*mfg*	333415	3443
Metal Tank (Heavy Gauge)—*mfg*	33242	3443
Plate Work—*mfg*	332313	3443
Power Boiler and Heat Exchanger—*mfg*	33241	3443
Howitzers, more than 30 mm. (or more than 1.18 inch): Ordnance and Accessories, Other—*mfg*	332995	3489

Description	NAICS	SIC
Hub and diecutting machines (jewelers): Industrial Machinery, All Other—*mfg*	333298	3559
Machinery, Other Commercial and Service Industry—*mfg*	333319	3559
Hub caps, automotive: stamped: Motor Vehicle Metal Stamping—*mfg*	33637	3465
Hubs, aircraft propeller: Aircraft Part and Auxiliary Equipment, Other—*mfg*	336413	3728
Fluid Power Valve and Hose Fitting—*mfg*	332912	3728
Hubs, wood: Manufacturing, All Other Miscellaneous—*mfg*	339999	2499
Wood Container and Pallet—*mfg*	32192	2499
Wood Product, All Other Miscellaneous—*mfg*	321999	2499
Huck toweling: Broadwoven Fabric Mills—*mfg*	31321	2211
Huckleberry greens, gathering of: Crop Farming, All Other Miscellaneous—*ag*	111998	831
Forest Nurseries and Gathering of Forest Products—*ag*	11321	831
Hucksters: Direct Selling Establishments, Other—*retail*	45439	5963
Mobile Foodservices—*accom*	72233	5963
Huebnerite mining: Copper Ore and Nickel Ore—*mining*	212234	1061
Metal Ore, All Other—*mining*	212299	1061
Hulling and shelling of tree nuts: Postharvest Crop Activities (except Cotton Ginning)—*ag*	115114	723
Hulling machinery, agricultural: Farm Machinery and Equipment—*mfg*	333111	3523
Human resource consultants: Administrative Management and General Management Consulting Services—*prof*	541611	8742
Human Resources and Executive Search Consulting Services—*prof*	541612	8742
Marketing Consulting Services—*prof*	541613	8742
Process, Physical, Distribution and Logistics Consulting Services—*prof*	541614	8742
Human Resource Programs, Administration of	**9231**	
Human Resource Programs, Administration of	**923**	
Human Resources and Executive Search Consulting Services	**541612**	**7361**
Human Rights Organizations	**813311**	**8399**
Humane societies, animal: Environment, Conservation and Wildlife Organizations—*serv*	813312	8699
Humidifiers and dehumidifiers, except portable: Warm Air Heating and Air-Conditioning Equipment and Supplies—*whlse*	42173	5075
Humidifiers and dehumidifiers, portable: Electrical Appliance, Television and Radio Set—*whlse*	42162	5064
Humidifiers, electric: portable: Electric Housewares and Household Fan—*mfg*	335211	3634
Heating Equipment (except Electric and Warm Air Furnaces)—*mfg*	333414	3634
Humidifying equipment, except portable: Air-Conditioning and Warm Air Heating Equipment and Commercial and Industrial Refrigeration Equipment—*mfg*	333415	3585
Motor Vehicle Air-Conditioning—*mfg*	336391	3585
Humidistats: wall, duct, and skeleton: Automatic Environmental Control for Residential, Commercial and Appliance Use—*mfg*	334512	3822
Humidity controls, air-conditioning types: Automatic Environmental Control for Residential, Commercial and Appliance Use—*mfg*	334512	3822
Humidity instruments, except industrial process and airconditioning type: Measuring and Controlling Device, Other—*mfg*	334519	3829
Surgical and Medical Instrument—*mfg*	339112	3829
Humidity instruments, industrial processtype: Instruments and Related Products for Measuring, Displaying, and Controlling Industrial Process Variables—*mfg*	334513	3823
Hunt clubs, membership: Fitness and Recreational Sports Centers—*arts*	71394	7997
Hunters' equipment: Sporting Goods Stores—*retail*	45111	5941
Hunting and Trapping	**1142**	
Hunting and Trapping	**11421**	**971**
Hunting camps: Recreational and Vacation Camps—*accom*	721214	7032
Hunting carried on as a business enterprise: Hunting and Trapping—*ag*	11421	971
Hunting coats and vests: Cut and Sew Apparel, All Other—*mfg*	315299	2329
Hunting knives: Cutlery and Flatware (except Precious)—*mfg*	332211	3421
Hunting preserves, operation of: Hunting and Trapping—*ag*	11421	971
Husking hooks: Hand and Edge Tool—*mfg*	332212	3423
Hybrid integrated circuits: Semiconductor and Related Device—*mfg*	334413	3674
Hydranine-mfg: Basic Inorganic Chemical, All Other—*mfg*	325188	2819
Chemical Product, All Other Miscellaneous—*mfg*	325998	2819
Hydrated alumina silicate powder: Alumina Refining—*mfg*	331311	2819
Hydrated lime: Lime—*mfg*	32741	3274
Hydraulic and pneumatic pistons and valves: Industrial Machinery and Equipment—*whlse*	42183	5085
Industrial Supplies—*whlse*	42184	5085
Hydraulic cylinders, fluid power: Fluid Power Cylinder and Actuator—*mfg*	333995	3593
Hydraulic fluid power pumps for automotive steering mechanisms: Motor Vehicle Parts, All Other—*mfg*	336399	3714
Motor Vehicle Steering and Suspension Components (except Spring)—*mfg*	33633	3714
Hydraulic fluids, synthetic base: Basic Organic Chemical, All Other—*mfg*	325199	2869
Hydraulic fluids-mfg: Petroleum Lubricating Oil and Grease—*mfg*	324191	2992
Hydraulic fracturing wells on a contract basis: Oil and Gas Operations Support Activities—*mining*	213112	1389
Hydraulic hose assemblies: Fluid Power Valve and Hose Fitting—*mfg*	332912	3492
Hydraulic pumps, aircraft: Fluid Power Pump and Motor—*mfg*	333996	3594
Hydraulic turbine generator set units, complete: Turbine and Turbine Generator Set Unit—*mfg*	333611	3511
Hydraulic turbines: Turbine and Turbine Generator Set Unit—*mfg*	333611	3511

ALPHABETICAL INDEX	NAICS	SIC
Hydraulic valves, including aircraft: fluidpower–metal: Fluid Power Valve and Hose Fitting—*mfg*	332912	3492
Hydrocarbon fluid, produced in petroleum refineries: Petroleum Refineries—*mfg*	32411	2911
Hydrocarbon gases, fluorinated-mfg: Basic Organic Chemical, All Other—*mfg*	325199	2869
Hydrochloric acid: Basic Inorganic Chemical, All Other—*mfg*	325188	2819
Chemical Product, All Other Miscellaneous—*mfg*	325998	2819
Hydrocyanic acid: Basic Inorganic Chemical, All Other—*mfg*	325188	2819
Chemical Product, All Other Miscellaneous—*mfg*	325998	2819
Hydroelectric plant construction–general contractors: Heavy, All Other—*const*	23499	1629
Industrial Nonbuilding Structure—*const*	23493	1629
Hydroelectric Power Generation	**221111**	**4931**
Hydrofluoric acid: Basic Inorganic Chemical, All Other—*mfg*	325188	2819
Chemical Product, All Other Miscellaneous—*mfg*	325998	2819
Hydrofluoric acid compound, for etching and polishing glass: Basic Organic Chemical, All Other—*mfg*	325199	2899
Chemical Product, All Other Miscellaneous—*mfg*	325998	2899
Hydrofoil boats: Boat Building—*mfg*	336612	3732
Personal and Household Goods Repair and Maintenance, Other—*serv*	81149	3732
Hydrofoil vessels: Ship Building and Repairing—*mfg*	336611	3731
Hydrogen: Industrial Gas—*mfg*	32512	2813
Hydrogen peroxide: Basic Inorganic Chemical, All Other—*mfg*	325188	2819
Chemical Product, All Other Miscellaneous—*mfg*	325998	2819
Hydrogen sulfide: Basic Inorganic Chemical, All Other—*mfg*	325188	2819
Chemical Product, All Other Miscellaneous—*mfg*	325998	2819
Hydrojet marine engine units: Pump and Pumping Equipment—*mfg*	333911	3561
Hydrol: Wet Corn Milling—*mfg*	311221	2046
Hydrometers, except industrial process type: Measuring and Controlling Device, Other—*mfg*	334519	3829
Surgical and Medical Instrument—*mfg*	339112	3829
Hydrometers, industrial process type: Instruments and Related Products for Measuring, Displaying, and Controlling Industrial Process Variables—*mfg*	334513	3823
Hydronic circulator control, automatic: Automatic Environmental Control for Residential, Commercial and Appliance Use—*mfg*	334512	3822
Hydronic heating equipment and supplies: Building Material Dealers, Other—*retail*	44419	5074
Plumbing and Heating Equipment and Supplies (Hydronics)—*whlse*	42172	5074
Hydronic limit control: Automatic Environmental Control for Residential, Commercial and Appliance Use—*mfg*	334512	3822

ALPHABETICAL INDEX	NAICS	SIC
Hydronic pressure and temperature controls: Automatic Environmental Control for Residential, Commercial and Appliance Use—*mfg*	334512	3822
Hydrophones-mfg: Search, Detection, Navigation, Guidance, Aeronautical, and Nautical System and Instrument—*mfg*	334511	3812
Hydropneumatic tanks, metal plate: Air-Conditioning and Warm Air Heating Equipment and Commercial and Industrial Refrigeration Equipment—*mfg*	333415	3443
Metal Tank (Heavy Gauge)—*mfg*	33242	3443
Plate Work—*mfg*	332313	3443
Power Boiler and Heat Exchanger—*mfg*	33241	3443
Hydroponic crops, grown under cover: Food Crops Grown Under Cover, Other—*ag*	111419	182
Mushroom Production—*ag*	111411	182
Hydroquinone: Cyclic Crude and Intermediate—*mfg*	325192	2865
Petrochemical—*mfg*	32511	2865
Hydrostatic drives (transmissions): Fluid Power Pump and Motor—*mfg*	333996	3594
Hydrostatic testing laboratories: Testing Laboratories—*prof*	54138	8734
Veterinary Services—*prof*	54194	8734
Hydrostatic transmissions-mfg: Fluid Power Pump and Motor—*mfg*	333996	3594
Hydrosulfites-mfg: Basic Inorganic Chemical, All Other—*mfg*	325188	2819
Chemical Product, All Other Miscellaneous—*mfg*	325998	2819
Hydrotherapy equipment: Electromedical and Electrotherapeutic Apparatus—*mfg*	334510	3842
Hygrometers, except industrial process type: Measuring and Controlling Device, Other—*mfg*	334519	3829
Surgical and Medical Instrument—*mfg*	339112	3829
Hygrothermographs-mfg: Measuring and Controlling Device, Other—*mfg*	334519	3829
Surgical and Medical Instrument—*mfg*	339112	3829
Hypalon: Synthetic Rubber—*mfg*	325212	2822
Hypnosis schools: Schools and Instruction, All Other Miscellaneous—*educ*	611699	8299
Hypnotists, offices of: Health Practitioners, Offices Of Miscellaneous—*hlth*	621399	8049
Mental Health Practitioners (except Physicians), Offices Of—*hlth*	62133	8049
Physical, Occupational and Speech Therapists and Audiologists, Offices Of—*hlth*	62134	8049
Hypodermic needles and syringes: Surgical and Medical Instrument—*mfg*	339112	3841
Hypophosphites: Basic Inorganic Chemical, All Other—*mfg*	325188	2819
Chemical Product, All Other Miscellaneous—*mfg*	325998	2819
Ice bags, rubber or rubberized fabric: Fabric Coating Mills—*mfg*	31332	3069
Rubber Product, All Other—*mfg*	326299	3069
Ice bank controls-mfg: Automatic Environmental Control for Residential, Commercial and Appliance Use—*mfg*	334512	3822

Description	NAICS	SIC
Ice boxes, household: Household Refrigerator and Home Freezer—*mfg*	335222	3632
Ice boxes, industrial: Air-Conditioning and Warm Air Heating Equipment and Commercial and Industrial Refrigeration Equipment—*mfg*	333415	3585
Motor Vehicle Air-Conditioning—*mfg*	336391	3585
Ice buckets, plastics: except foam: Plastics Pipe and Pipe Fitting—*mfg*	326122	3089
Plastics Product, All Other—*mfg*	326199	3089
Unsupported Plastics Profile Shape—*mfg*	326121	3089
Ice chests or coolers, portable, except insulated foam plastics: Metal Container, Other—*mfg*	332439	3429
Ice chests or coolers, portable, plastics–except insulated or foam plastics: Plastics Pipe and Pipe Fitting—*mfg*	326122	3089
Plastics Product, All Other—*mfg*	326199	3089
Unsupported Plastics Profile Shape—*mfg*	326121	3089
Ice chests or coolers, portable–foamed plastics: Polystyrene Foam Product—*mfg*	32614	3086
Urethane and Other Foam Product (except Polystyrene)—*mfg*	32615	3086
Ice cream (packaged) stores: Food Stores, All Other Specialty—*retail*	445299	5451
Ice Cream and Frozen Dessert Manufacturing	**31152**	**2024**
Ice cream and ices: Dairy Product (except Dried or Canned)—*whlse*	42243	5143
Ice cream cabinets: Refrigeration Equipment and Supplies—*whlse*	42174	5078
Ice cream cans, metal: Metal Can—*mfg*	332431	3411
Ice cream cones and wafers: Bakeries, Commercial—*mfg*	311812	2052
Cookie and Cracker—*mfg*	311821	2052
Snack Food, Other—*mfg*	311919	2052
Ice cream containers, folding paperboard: Folding Paperboard Box—*mfg*	322212	2657
Ice cream containers, nonfolding paperboard: Non-Folding Sanitary Food Container—*mfg*	322215	2656
Ice cream freezers, household, nonelectric–metal: Fabricated Metal Product. All Other Miscellaneous—*mfg*	332999	3499
Ice cream manufacturing machinery: Food Product Machinery—*mfg*	333294	3556
Ice cream mix, unfrozen–liquid or dry: Dry, Condensed, and Evaporated Dairy Product—*mfg*	311514	2023
Ice cream stands: Cafeterias—*accom*	722212	5812
Caterers—*accom*	72232	5812
Foodservice Contractors—*accom*	72231	5812
Full-Service Restaurants—*accom*	72211	5812
Limited-Service Restaurants—*accom*	722211	5812
Snack and Nonalcoholic Beverage Bars—*accom*	722213	5812
Theater Companies and Dinner Theaters—*arts*	71111	5812
Ice cream wagons: Direct Selling Establishments, Other—*retail*	45439	5963
Mobile Foodservices—*accom*	72233	5963
Ice cream–e.g., bulk, packaged, molded, on sticks: Ice Cream and Frozen Dessert—*mfg*	31152	2024
Ice crushers, electric: Electric Housewares and Household Fan—*mfg*	335211	3634
Heating Equipment (except Electric and Warm Air Furnaces)—*mfg*	333414	3634
Ice crushers, except household: General Purpose Machinery , All Other—*mfg*	333999	3569
Ice cubes: Ice—*mfg*	312113	2097
Ice dealers: Stores (except Tobacco Stores), All Other Miscellaneous—*retail*	453998	5999
Ice hockey clubs, professional or semiprofessional: Agents and Managers for Artists, Athletes, Entertainers and Other Public Figures—*arts*	71141	7941
Promoters of Performing Arts, Sports and Similar Events with Facilities—*arts*	71131	7941
Promoters of Performing Arts, Sports and Similar Events without Facilities—*arts*	71132	7941
Spectator Sports, Other—*arts*	711219	7941
Sports Teams and Clubs—*arts*	711211	7941
Ice maker controls: Automatic Environmental Control for Residential, Commercial and Appliance Use—*mfg*	334512	3822
Ice making machinerv: Air-Conditioning and Warm Air Heating Equipment and Commercial and Industrial Refrigeration Equipment—*mfg*	333415	3585
Motor Vehicle Air-Conditioning—*mfg*	336391	3585
Ice making machines: Refrigeration Equipment and Supplies—*whlse*	42174	5078
Ice Manufacturing	**312113**	**2097**
Ice milk mix, unfrozen–liquid or dry: Dry, Condensed, and Evaporated Dairy Product—*mfg*	311514	2023
Ice milk–e.g., bulk, packaged, molded, on sticks: Ice Cream and Frozen Dessert—*mfg*	31152	2024
Ice plants, operated by public utilities: Ice—*mfg*	312113	2097
Ice skates: Sporting and Athletic Goods—*mfg*	33992	3949
Ice, manufactured or artificial–except dry ice: Ice—*mfg*	312113	2097
Ice, manufactured or natural: Nondurable Goods, Other Miscellaneous—*whlse*	42299	5199
Iced tea, bottled or canned: Bottled Water—*mfg*	312112	2086
Soft Drink—*mfg*	312111	2086
Iceland spar mining (optical grade calcite): Crushed and Broken Stone and Quarrying, Other—*mining*	212319	1499
Non-Metallic Mineral, All Other—*mining*	212399	1499
Ices and sherbets: Ice Cream and Frozen Dessert—*mfg*	31152	2024
Icing of railroad cars: Air, Rail, and Water Equipment Rental and Leasing, Commercial—*real*	532411	4741
Rail Support Activities—*trans*	48821	4741
Identification plates: Fabricated Metal Product, All Other Miscellaneous—*mfg*	332999	3999
Identification tags, except paper: Fabricated Metal Product, All Other Miscellaneous—*mfg*	332999	3999
Identity recorders for photographing checks and fingerprints: Photographic Equipment and Supplies—*whlse*	42141	5043

ALPHABETICAL INDEX	NAICS	SIC
Igniter grains, boron potassium nitrate: Basic Organic Chemical, All Other—*mfg*	325199	2899
Chemical Product, All Other Miscellaneous—*mfg*	325998	2899
Igniters, tracer–for ammunition morethan 30 mm. (or more than 1.18 inch): Ammunition (except Small Arms)—*mfg*	332993	3483
Ignition apparatus for internal combustion engines: Motor Vehicle Electrical and Electronic Equipment, Other—*mfg*	336322	3694
Ignition cable sets or wire assemblies for internal combustion engines: Motor Vehicle Electrical and Electronic Equipment, Other—*mfg*	336322	3694
Ignition controls for gas appliances and furnaces, automatic: Automatic Environmental Control for Residential, Commercial and Appliance Use—*mfg*	334512	3822
Ignition service, automotive: Automotive Mechanical and Electrical Repair and Maintenance, Other—*serv*	811118	7539
Ignition systems, high frequency: Motor Vehicle Electrical and Electronic Equipment, Other—*mfg*	336322	3694
Ignition testing instruments: Electronic Coil, Transformer, and Other Inductor—*mfg*	334416	3825
Instrument for Measuring and Testing Electricity and Electrical Signals—*mfg*	334515	3825
Ignition transformers: Power, Distribution and Specialty Transformer—*mfg*	335311	3612
Illuminating glass–light shades, reflectors, lamp chimneys, and globes: Pressed and Blown Glass and Glassware, Other—*mfg*	327212	3229
Illuminating oil, produced in petroleum refineries: Petroleum Refineries—*mfg*	32411	2911
Ilmenite mining: Metal Ore, All Other—*mining*	212299	1099
Images, small–gypsum, clay, or papier mache-factory production only: Gypsum and Gypsum Product—*mfg*	32742	3299
Nonmetallic Mineral Product, All Other Miscellaneous—*mfg*	327999	3299
Immersion heaters, household–electric: Electric Housewares and Household Fan—*mfg*	335211	3634
Heating Equipment (except Electric and Warm Air Furnaces)—*mfg*	333414	3634
Immigration services: International Affairs—*pub*	92812	9721
Immunization program administration: Public Health Programs, Administration of—*pub*	92312	9431
Impedance conversion units, high frequency: Electronic Component, Other—*mfg*	334419	3679
Motor Vehicle Electrical and Electronic Equipment, Other—*mfg*	336322	3679
Printed Circuit/Electronics Assembly—*mfg*	334418	3679
Radio and Television Broadcasting and Wireless Communications Equipment—*mfg*	33422	3679
Impedance measuring equipment: Electronic Coil, Transformer, and Other Inductor—*mfg*	334416	3825
Instrument for Measuring and Testing Electricity and Electrical Signals—*mfg*	334515	3825
Impeller and counter driven flow meters: Totalizing Fluid Meter and Counting Device—*mfg*	334514	3824
Implants, surgical: Electromedical and Electrotherapeutic Apparatus—*mfg*	334510	3842
Surgical Appliance and Supplies—*mfg*	339113	3842
Impounding and storing salt water in connection with petroleum production: Oil and Gas Operations Support Activities—*mining*	213112	1389
Impounding reservoirs, irrigation: Water Supply and Irrigation Systems—*util*	..2131	4971
Impregnating and coating of fabrics, except rubberizing: Fabric Coating Mills—*mfg*	31332	2295
Impression material, dental: Dental Equipment and Supplies—*mfg*	339114	3843
Imprinting, except lithographed or gravure: Digital Printing—*mfg*	323115	2759
Flexographic Printing, Commercial—*mfg*	323112	2759
Printing, Other Commercial—*mfg*	323119	2759
Quick Printing—*mfg*	323114	2759
Imprinting–gravure: Gravure Printing, Commercial—*mfg*	323111	2754
In vitro diagnostics: In-Vitro Diagnostic Substance—*mfg*	325413	2835
Pharmaceutical Preparation—*mfg*	325412	2835
In vivo diagnostics: In-Vitro Diagnostic Substance—*mfg*	325413	2835
Pharmaceutical Preparation—*mfg*	325412	2835
In vivo radioactive reagents: In-Vitro Diagnostic Substance—*mfg*	325413	2835
Pharmaceutical Preparation—*mfg*	325412	2835
In-built thermostats, filled system and bimetal types: Automatic Environmental Control for Residential, Commercial and Appliance Use—*mfg*	334512	3822
In-Vitro Diagnostic Substance Manufacturing	**325413**	**2835**
Incandescent filament lamp bulbs, complete: Electric Lamp Bulb and Part—*mfg*	33511	3641
Incandescent lamp making machinery: Industrial Machinery, All Other—*mfg*	333298	3559
Machinery, Other Commercial and Service Industry—*mfg*	333319	3559
Incense: Basic Organic Chemical, All Other—*mfg*	325199	2899
Chemical Product, All Other Miscellaneous—*mfg*	325998	2899
Incinerator control systems, residential and commercial type: Automatic Environmental Control for Residential, Commercial and Appliance Use—*mfg*	334512	3822
Incinerator installation, small–contractors: Building Equipment and Other Machinery Installation Contractors—*const*	23595	1796
Incinerator operation: Hazardous Waste Collection—*admin*	562112	4953
Hazardous Waste Treatment and Disposal—*admin*	562211	4953
Materials Recovery Facilities—*admin*	56292	4953
Nonhazardous Waste Treatment and Disposal, Other—*admin*	562219	4953
Solid Waste Collection—*admin*	562111	4953

Description	NAICS	SIC
Solid Waste Combustors and Incinerators—*admin*	562213	4953
Solid Waste Landfill—*admin*	562212	4953
Waste Collection, Other—*admin*	562119	4953
Incinerators, concrete: Concrete Pipe—*mfg*	327332	3272
Concrete Product, Other—*mfg*	32739	3272
Nonmetallic Mineral Product, All Other Miscellaneous—*mfg*	327999	3272
Incinerators, metal–domestic and commercial: Industrial Process Furnace and Oven—*mfg*	333994	3567
Income tax return preparation services without accounting, auditing, or book-keeping services: Tax Preparation Services—*prof*	541213	7291
Incubators, except laboratory and infant: Farm Machinery and Equipment—*mfg*	333111	3523
Incubators, infant: Surgical Appliance and Supplies—*mfg*	339113	3842
Independent Artists, Writers, and Performers	**71151**	**7929**
Independent Artists, Writers, and Performers	**7115**	
Index and other cut cards: Converted Paper Product, All Other—*mfg*	322298	2675
Die-Cut Paper and Paperboard Office Supplies—*mfg*	322231	2675
Surface-Coated Paperboard—*mfg*	322292	2675
India ink: Chemical Product, All Other Miscellaneous—*mfg*	325998	3952
Institutional Furniture—*mfg*	337127	3952
Lead Pencil and Art Good—*mfg*	339942	3952
Indian clubs: Sporting and Athletic Goods—*mfg*	33992	3949
Indicating instruments and accessories: Industrial Machinery and Equipment—*whlse*	42183	5084
Indicating instruments, electric: Electronic Coil, Transformer, and Other Inductor—*mfg*	334416	3825
Instrument for Measuring and Testing Electricity and Electrical Signals—*mfg*	334515	3825
Indicator testers, turntable: Measuring and Controlling Device, Other—*mfg*	334519	3829
Surgical and Medical Instrument—*mfg*	339112	3829
Indicators, chemical: Cyclic Crude and Intermediate—*mfg*	325192	2865
Petrochemical—*mfg*	32511	2865
Indium chloride: Basic Inorganic Chemical, All Other—*mfg*	325188	2819
Chemical Product, All Other Miscellaneous—*mfg*	325998	2819
Individual and Family Services	**6241**	
Individual and Family Services, Other	**62419**	**8322**
Induction heating equipment: Industrial Process Furnace and Oven—*mfg*	333994	3567
Inductors, electronic: Electronic Coil, Transformer, and Other Inductor—*mfg*	334416	3677
Industrial alcohol denatured (nonbeverage): Basic Organic Chemical, All Other—*mfg*	325199	2869
Ethyl Alcohol—*mfg*	325193	2869
Industrial and commercial buildings, operators of: Lessors of Nonresidential Buildings (except Miniwarehouses)—*real*	53112	6512
Promoters of Performing Arts, Sports and Similar Events with Facilities—*arts*	71131	6512
Industrial and Commercial Fan and Blower Manufacturing	**333412**	**3564**

Description	NAICS	SIC
Industrial and Personal Service Paper Wholesalers	**42213**	**5113**
Industrial belting reinforcement, cord and fabric: Tire Cord and Tire Fabric Mills—*mfg*	314992	2296
Industrial brooms and brushes: Broom, Brush and Mop—*mfg*	339994	3991
Industrial building construction–general contractors: Building, Commercial and Institutional—*const*	23332	1541
Manufacturing and Industrial Building—*const*	23331	1541
Industrial chemicals: Chemical and Allied Products, Other—*whlse*	42269	5169
Industrial controls–push button, selector switches, and pilot: Relay and Industrial Control—*mfg*	335314	3625
Industrial Design Services	**54142**	**7389**
Industrial development planning service, commercial: Educational Support Services—*educ*	61171	8748
Management Consulting Services, Other—*prof*	541618	8748
Scientific and Technical Consulting Services, Other—*prof*	54169	8748
Industrial equipment installation-con-tractors: Building Equipment and Other Machinery Installation Contractors—*const*	23595	1796
Industrial feeding: Cafeterias—*accom*	722212	5812
Caterers—*accom*	72232	5812
Foodservice Contractors—*accom*	72231	5812
Full-Service Restaurants—*accom*	72211	5812
Limited-Service Restaurants—*accom*	722211	5812
Snack and Nonalcoholic Beverage Bars—*accom*	722213	5812
Theater Companies and Dinner Theaters—*arts*	71111	5812
Industrial fittings: Industrial Machinery and Equipment—*whlse*	42183	5085
Industrial Supplies—*whlse*	42184	5085
Industrial garments: Men's and Boys' Cut and Sew Apparel Contractors—*mfg*	315211	2326
Men's and Boys' Cut and Sew Work Clothing—*mfg*	315225	2326
Industrial Gas Manufacturing	**32512**	**2869**
Industrial gases: Chemical and Allied Products, Other—*whlse*	42269	5169
Industrial glassware and glass products, pressed or blown: Pressed and Blown Glass and Glassware, Other—*mfg*	327212	3229
Industrial glassware, made from purchased glass: Glass Product Made of Purchased Glass—*mfg*	327215	3231
Industrial incinerator construction–general contractors: Heavy, All Other—*const*	23499	1629
Industrial Nonbuilding Structure—*const*	23493	1629
Industrial laboratories, commercial research–except testing: Research and Development in the Life Sciences—*prof*	54172	8731
Research and Development in the Physical Sciences and Engineering Sciences—*prof*	54171	8731
Industrial Launderers	**812332**	**7218**
Industrial lighting fixtures: Electric Lighting Fixture, Commercial, Industrial and Institutional—*mfg*	335122	3646
Industrial loan companies, not engaged in deposit banking: Consumer Lending—*fin*	522291	6141
Credit Card Issuing—*fin*	52221	6141
Sales Financing—*fin*	52222	6141

ALPHABETICAL INDEX	NAICS	SIC
Industrial locomotives and parts: Pump and Pumping Equipment—*mfg*	333911	3743
Railroad Rolling Stock—*mfg*	33651	3743
Industrial Machinery and Equipment Wholesalers	**42183**	**5085**
Industrial Machinery Manufacturing	**3332**	
Industrial Machinery Manufacturing, All Other	**333298**	**3639**
Industrial Machinery Manufacturing, Other	**33329**	
Industrial mercury' lighting fixtures: Electric Lighting Fixture, Commercial, Industrial and Institutional—*mfg*	335122	3646
Industrial Mold Manufacturing	**333511**	**3544**
Industrial molds: Die and Tool, Die Set, Jig and Fixture, Special—*mfg*	333514	3544
Industrial Mold—*mfg*	333511	3544
Industrial motion picture production: Motion Picture and Video Production—*info*	51211	7812
Industrial motor controls: Building Material Dealers, Other—*retail*	44419	5063
Electrical Apparatus and Equipment, Wiring Supplies and Material—*whlse*	42161	5063
Industrial Nonbuilding Structure Construction	**23493**	**1629**
Industrial organic cyclic compounds: Basic Organic Chemical, All Other—*mfg*	325199	2869
Industrial Pattern Manufacturing	**332997**	**3543**
Industrial plant appurtenance construction–general contractors: Heavy, All Other—*const*	23499	1629
Industrial Nonbuilding Structure—*const*	23493	1629
Industrial plant construction–general contractors: Building, Commercial and Institutional—*const*	23332	1541
Manufacturing and Industrial Building—*const*	23331	1541
Industrial plant disinfectants and deodorants: Polish and Other Sanitation Good—*mfg*	325612	2842
Industrial process control instruments: Instruments and Related Products for Measuring, Displaying, and Controlling Industrial Process Variables—*mfg*	334513	3823
Industrial Process Furnace and Oven Manufacturing	**333994**	**3567**
Industrial process furnaces and ovens, except bakery ovens: Industrial Process Furnace and Oven—*mfg*	333994	3567
Industrial safety devices–first-aid kits, face and eye masks: Health and Personal Care Stores, All Other—*retail*	446199	5047
Medical, Dental and Hospital Equipment and Supplies—*whlse*	42145	5047
Industrial salts: Chemical and Allied Products, Other—*whlse*	42269	5169
Industrial Sand Mining	**212322**	**1446**
Industrial scales: Scale and Balance (except Laboratory)—*mfg*	333997	3596
Industrial sewing thread: Industrial Machinery and Equipment—*whlse*	42183	5085
Industrial Supplies—*whlse*	42184	5085
Industrial sizes: Basic Organic Chemical, All Other—*mfg*	325199	2899
Chemical Product, All Other Miscellaneous—*mfg*	325998	2899

ALPHABETICAL INDEX	NAICS	SIC
Industrial standards committees: Business Associations—*serv*	81391	8611
Industrial Supplies Wholesalers	**42184**	**5085**
Industrial truck cranes: Fabricated Metal Product, All Other Miscellaneous—*mfg*	332999	3537
Industrial Truck, Tractor, Trailer and Stacker Machinery—*mfg*	333924	3537
Metal Container, Other—*mfg*	332439	3537
Industrial truck rental and leasing: Construction, and Forestry Machinery and Equipment Rental and Leasing—*real*	532412	7359
Machinery and Equipment Rental and Leasing, Other Commercial and Industrial—*real*	53249	7359
Industrial truck repair: Machinery and Equipment (except Automotive and Electronic) Repair and Maintenance, Commercial and Industrial—*serv*	81131	7699
Industrial Truck, Tractor, Trailer and Stacker Machinery Manufacturing	**333924**	**3537**
Industrial trucks and tractors: Fabricated Metal Product, All Other Miscellaneous—*mfg*	332999	3537
Industrial Truck, Tractor, Trailer and Stacker Machinery—*mfg*	333924	3537
Metal Container, Other—*mfg*	332439	3537
Industrial uniform supply service: Industrial Launderers—*serv*	812332	7218
Industrial Valve Manufacturing	**332911**	**3491**
Industrial wheels: Industrial Machinery and Equipment—*whlse*	42183	5085
Industrial Supplies—*whlse*	42184	5085
Industrial yarn: Nondurable Goods, Other Miscellaneous—*whlse*	42299	5199
Inertial navigation systems, aeronautical: Search, Detection, Navigation, Guidance, Aeronautical, and Nautical System and Instrument—*mfg*	334511	3812
Infant incubators: Surgical Appliance and Supplies—*mfg*	339113	3842
Infants' foods, cereal type: Breakfast Cereal—*mfg*	31123	2043
Coffee and Tea—*mfg*	31192	2043
Infants' wear: Women's, Children's, and Infants' and Accessories—*whlse*	42233	5137
Infants' wear stores: Children's and Infants' Clothing Stores—*retail*	44813	5641
Information	**51**	
Information retrieval services, on-line: On-Line Information Services—*info*	514191	7375
Information service, freight rate: Freight Arrangement—*trans*	48851	4731
Management Consulting Services, Other—*prof*	541618	4731
Information Services	**5141**	
Information Services and Data Processing Services	**514**	
Information Services, All Other	**514199**	**8999**
Information Services, Other	**51419**	
Infrared homing systems, aeronautical: Search, Detection, Navigation, Guidance, Aeronautical, and Nautical System and Instrument—*mfg*	334511	3812

Description	NAICS	SIC
Infrared instruments, industrial process type: Instruments and Related Products for Measuring, Displaying, and Controlling Industrial Process Variables—*mfg*	334513	3823
Infrared lamp bulbs: Electric Lamp Bulb and Part—*mfg*	33511	3641
Infrared lamp fixtures: Lighting Equipment, Other—*mfg*	335129	3648
Infrared ovens, industrial: Industrial Process Furnace and Oven—*mfg*	333994	3567
Infrared sensors, solid-state: Semiconductor and Related Device—*mfg*	334413	3674
Infrared type analytical instruments, laboratory type: Analytical Laboratory Instrument—*mfg*	334516	3826
Ingot molds and stools: Iron Foundries—*mfg*	331511	3321
Ingot, aluminum–made in rolling mills: Aluminum Rolling and Drawing, Other—*mfg*	331319	3355
Ingots: Metal Service Centers and Offices—*whlse*	42151	5051
Ingots, aluminum–primary: Primary Aluminum Production—*mfg*	331312	3334
Ingots, copper–primary: Primary Smelting and Refining of Copper—*mfg*	331411	3331
Ingots, lead: Primary Smelting and Refining of Nonferrous Metal (except Copper and Aluminum)—*mfg*	331419	3339
Ingots, nonferrous–smelting and refining-secondary: Secondary Smelting and Alloying of Aluminum—*mfg*	331314	3341
Secondary Smelting, Refining, and Alloying of Copper—*mfg*	331423	3341
Secondary Smelting, Refining, and Alloying of Nonferrous Metal (except Copper and Aluminum)—*mfg*	331492	3341
Ingots, primary–nonferrous metals, except copper and aluminum: Primary Smelting and Refining of Nonferrous Metal (except Copper and Aluminum)—*mfg*	331419	3339
Ingots, steel: Iron and Steel Mills—*mfg*	331111	3312
Petroleum and Coal Productsa, All Other—*mfg*	324199	3312
Inhalation therapists, registered: Health Practitioners, Offices Of Miscellaneous—*hlth*	621399	8049
Mental Health Practitioners (except Physicians), Offices Of—*hlth*	62133	8049
Physical, Occupational and Speech Therapists and Audiologists, Offices Of—*hlth*	62134	8049
Inhalation therapy equipment: Surgical and Medical Instrument—*mfg*	339112	3841
Inhalators, surgical and medical: Surgical and Medical Instrument—*mfg*	339112	3841
Ink and writing fluids, except printing and drawing: Basic Organic Chemical, All Other—*mfg*	325199	2899
Chemical Product, All Other Miscellaneous—*mfg*	325998	2899
Ink eradicators: Polish and Other Sanitation Good—*mfg*	325612	2842
Ink, burnishing: Polish and Other Sanitation Good—*mfg*	325612	2842
Ink, drawing–black and colored: Chemical Product, All Other Miscellaneous—*mfg*	325998	3952
Institutional Furniture—*mfg*	337127	3952
Lead Pencil and Art Good—*mfg*	339942	3952
Ink, duplicating: Printing Ink—*mfg*	32591	2893
Ink, indelible: Basic Organic Chemical, All Other—*mfg*	325199	2899
Chemical Product, All Other Miscellaneous—*mfg*	325998	2899
Ink, printers': Industrial Machinery and Equipment—*whlse*	42183	5085
Industrial Supplies—*whlse*	42184	5085
Ink, printing–base or finished: Printing Ink—*mfg*	32591	2893
Ink, stamp pad: Basic Organic Chemical, All Other—*mfg*	325199	2899
Chemical Product, All Other Miscellaneous—*mfg*	325998	2899
Ink, writing: Office Supplies and Stationery Stores—*retail*	45321	5112
Stationary and Office Supplies—*whlse*	42212	5112
Inked ribbons: Office Supplies and Stationery Stores—*retail*	45321	5112
Stationary and Office Supplies—*whlse*	42212	5112
Inkwells, glass: Pressed and Blown Glass and Glassware, Other—*mfg*	327212	3229
Inland Water Freight Transportation	**483211**	**4492**
Inland Water Passenger Transportation	**483212**	**4489**
Inland Water Transportation	**48321**	
Inland Water Transportation	**4832**	
Inlays for furniture (veneers): Manufacturing, All Other Miscellaneous—*mfg*	339999	2499
Wood Container and Pallet—*mfg*	32192	2499
Wood Product, All Other Miscellaneous—*mfg*	321999	2499
Inner soles, leather: Fastener, Button, Needle and Pin—*mfg*	339993	3131
Leather Good, All Other—*mfg*	316999	3131
Wood Product, All Other Miscellaneous—*mfg*	321999	3131
Inner tubes–airplane, automobile, bicycle, motorcycle, and tractor: Tire (except Retreading)—*mfg*	326211	3011
Inns, furnishing food and lodging: Bed and Breakfast Inns—*accom*	721191	7011
Casino Hotels—*accom*	72112	7011
Hotels (except Casino Hotels) and Motels—*accom*	72111	7011
Traveler Accommodation, All Other—*accom*	721199	7011
Inorganic acids, except nitric or phosphoric: Basic Inorganic Chemical, All Other—*mfg*	325188	2819
Chemical Product, All Other Miscellaneous—*mfg*	325998	2819
Inorganic Dye and Pigment Manufacturing	**325131**	**2819**
Inorganic medicinal chemicals–bulk, uncompounded: Medicinal and Botanical—*mfg*	325411	2833
Inorganic pigments: Carbon Black—*mfg*	325182	2816
Inorganic Dye and Pigment—*mfg*	325131	2816
Input/output equipment, computer–except terminals: Computer Peripheral Equipment, Other—*mfg*	334119	3577
Insect control for crops, with or without fertilizing: Nonscheduled Air, Other—*trans*	481219	721
Soil Preparation, Planting, and Cultivating—*ag*	115112	721
Insect powder, household: Pesticide and Other Agricultural Chemical—*mfg*	32532	2879
Insect screening, woven wire–made from purchased wire: Fabricated Wire Product, Other—*mfg*	332618	3496
Insecticides: Farm Supplies—*whlse*	42291	5191
Nursery and Garden Centers—*retail*	44422	5191
Insecticides, agricultural: Pesticide and Other Agricultural Chemical—*mfg*	32532	2879

ALPHABETICAL INDEX	NAICS	SIC
Insecticides, household: Pesticide and Other Agricultural Chemical—*mfg*	32532	2879
Inserts, cutting tool: Cutting Tool and Machine Tool Accessory—*mfg*	333515	3545
Hand and Edge Tool—*mfg*	332212	3545
Insignia, military–except textile: Fabricated Metal Product, All Other Miscellaneous—*mfg*	332999	3999
Insignia, military–textile: Apparel Accessories and Apparel, Other—*mfg*	315999	2399
Inspection for labor standards: Regulation, Licensing, and Inspection of Miscellaneous Commercial Sectors—*pub*	92615	9651
Inspection oil, fluorescent: Basic Organic Chemical, All Other—*mfg*	325199	2899
Chemical Product, All Other Miscellaneous—*mfg*	325998	2899
Inspection service, automotive: Automotive Oil Change and Lubrication Shops—*serv*	811191	7549
Automotive Repair and Maintenance, All Other—*serv*	811198	7549
Motor Vehicle Towing—*trans*	48841	7549
Inspection services connected with transportation: Road, Other Support Activities for—*trans*	48849	4785
Water, Other Support Activities for—*trans*	48839	4785
Installation of machinery and other industrial equipment-contractors: Building Equipment and Other Machinery Installation Contractors—*const*	23595	1796
Installment notes, buying of: Financial Transactions Processing, Reserve, and Clearing House Activities—*fin*	52232	6153
Non-Depository Credit Intermediation, All Other—*fin*	522298	6153
Sales Financing—*fin*	52222	6153
Installment paper dealer: Financial Transactions Processing, Reserve, and Clearing House Activities—*fin*	52232	6153
Non-Depository Credit Intermediation, All Other—*fin*	522298	6153
Sales Financing—*fin*	52222	6153
Installment sales finance, other than banks: Consumer Lending—*fin*	522291	6141
Credit Card Issuing—*fin*	52221	6141
Sales Financing—*fin*	52222	6141
Instant coffee: Coffee and Tea—*mfg*	31192	2095
Spice and Extract—*mfg*	311942	2095
Instant printing, except photocopy service: Lithographic Printing, Commercial—*mfg*	323110	2752
Quick Printing—*mfg*	323114	2752
Institutional building construction, nonresidential–general contractors: Building, Commercial and Institutional—*const*	23332	1542
Institutional Furniture Manufacturing	**337127**	**2599**
Institutional lighting fixtures: Electric Lighting Fixture, Commercial, Industrial and Institutional—*mfg*	335122	3646
Instrument beard assemblies, motor vehicle: Motor Vehicle Electrical and Electronic Equipment, Other—*mfg*	336322	3714
Motor Vehicle Parts, All Other—*mfg*	336399	3714

ALPHABETICAL INDEX	NAICS	SIC
Instrument landing system instrumentation, airborne or airport: Search, Detection, Navigation, Guidance, Aeronautical, and Nautical System and Instrument—*mfg*	334511	3812
Instrument lenses: Optical Instrument and Lens—*mfg*	333314	3827
Instrument Manufacturing for Measuring and Testing Electricity and Electrical Signals	**334515**	**3825**
Instrument panel mockups–aircraft training units: Aircraft Part and Auxiliary Equipment, Other—*mfg*	336413	3728
Fluid Power Valve and Hose Fitting—*mfg*	332912	3728
Instrument relays, all types: Electronic Coil, Transformer, and Other Inductor—*mfg*	334416	3825
Instrument for Measuring and Testing Electricity and Electrical Signals—*mfg*	334515	3825
Instrument shunts: Electronic Coil, Transformer, and Other Inductor—*mfg*	334416	3825
Instrument for Measuring and Testing Electricity and Electrical Signals—*mfg*	334515	3825
Instrument springs, precision–made from purchased wire: Watch, Clock, and Part—*mfg*	334518	3495
Wire Spring—*mfg*	332612	3495
Instrument transformers, except portable: Power, Distribution and Specialty Transformer—*mfg*	335311	3612
Instrumentation for reactor controls, auxiliary: Measuring and Controlling Device, Other—*mfg*	334519	3829
Surgical and Medical Instrument—*mfg*	339112	3829
Instrumentation type tape, blank: Magnetic and Optical Recording Media—*mfg*	334613	3695
Instruments and apparatus, except electromedical–medical, surgical, ophthalmic, and veterinary: Surgical and Medical Instrument—*mfg*	339112	3841
Instruments and Related Products Manufacturing for Measuring, Displaying, and Controlling Industrial Process Variables	**334513**	**3823**
Instruments for industrial process control: Instruments and Related Products for Measuring, Displaying, and Controlling Industrial Process Variables—*mfg*	334513	3823
Instruments for measuring electrical quantities: Electronic Coil, Transformer, and Other Inductor—*mfg*	334416	3825
Instrument for Measuring and Testing Electricity and Electrical Signals—*mfg*	334515	3825
Instruments, electric–for testing electrical characteristics: Electronic Coil, Transformer, and Other Inductor—*mfg*	334416	3825
Instrument for Measuring and Testing Electricity and Electrical Signals—*mfg*	334515	3825
Instruments, lettering–artists': Chemical Product, All Other Miscellaneous—*mfg*	325998	3952
Institutional Furniture—*mfg*	337127	3952
Lead Pencil and Art Good—*mfg*	339942	3952

Description	NAICS	SIC
Instruments, microsurgical–except electromedical: Surgical and Medical Instrument—*mfg*	339112	3841
Instruments, musical: Musical Instrument—*mfg*	339992	3931
Instruments, photographic: Photographic and Photocopying Equipment—*mfg*	333315	3861
Photographic Film, Paper, Plate and Chemical—*mfg*	325992	3861
Insulated wire and cable, nonferrous: Aluminum Rolling and Drawing, Other—*mfg*	331319	3357
Communication and Energy Wire, Other—*mfg*	335929	3357
Copper Wire (except Mechanical) Drawing—*mfg*	331422	3357
Fiber Optic Cable—*mfg*	335921	3357
Nonferrous Metal (except Copper and Aluminum) Rolling, Drawing and Extruding—*mfg*	331491	3357
Insulating batts, fills, and blankets–paper: Coated and Laminated Paper—*mfg*	322222	2679
Converted Paper Product, All Other—*mfg*	322298	2679
Die-Cut Paper and Paperboard Office Supplies—*mfg*	322231	2679
Non-Folding Sanitary Food Container—*mfg*	322215	2679
Insulating compounds: Basic Organic Chemical, All Other—*mfg*	325199	2899
Chemical Product, All Other Miscellaneous—*mfg*	325998	2899
Insulating firebrick and shapes, clay: Clay Refractory—*mfg*	327124	3255
Insulating glass, sealed units: Flat Glass—*mfg*	327211	3211
Insulating materials for covering boilers and pipes: Motor Vehicle Brake System—*mfg*	33634	3292
Nonmetallic Mineral Product, All Other Miscellaneous—*mfg*	327999	3292
Insulating materials, cork: Manufacturing, All Other Miscellaneous—*mfg*	339999	2499
Wood Container and Pallet—*mfg*	32192	2499
Wood Product, All Other Miscellaneous—*mfg*	321999	2499
Insulating plaster, gypsum: Gypsum and Gypsum Product—*mfg*	32742	3275
Insulating siding, board: Reconstituted Wood Product—*mfg*	321219	2493
Insulating siding, impregnated: Asphalt Shingle and Coating Materials—*mfg*	324122	2952
Insulating tapes and braids, electric, except plastics: Narrow Fabric Mills—*mfg*	313221	2241
Insulation and cushioning–foamed plastics: Polystyrene Foam Product—*mfg*	32614	3086
Urethane and Other Foam Product (except Polystyrene)—*mfg*	32615	3086
Insulation board, cellular fiber or hard pressed (without gypsum): Reconstituted Wood Product—*mfg*	321219	2493
Insulation installation, buildings-contractors: Drywall, Plastering, Acoustical and Insulation Contractors—*const*	23542	1742
Insulation material, building: Building Material Dealers, Other—*retail*	44419	5211
Home Centers—*retail*	44411	5211
Insulation of pipes and boilers–contractors: Trade Contractors, All Other Special—*const*	23599	1799
Insulation, cellulose: Coated and Laminated Paper—*mfg*	322222	2679
Converted Paper Product, All Other—*mfg*	322298	2679
Die-Cut Paper and Paperboard Office Supplies—*mfg*	322231	2679
Non-Folding Sanitary Food Container—*mfg*	322215	2679
Insulation, molded asbestos: Motor Vehicle Brake System—*mfg*	33634	3292
Nonmetallic Mineral Product, All Other Miscellaneous—*mfg*	327999	3292
Insulation, thermal: Roofing, Siding and Insulation Material—*whlse*	42133	5033
Insulation–rock wool, fiberglass, slag, and silica minerals: Mineral Wool—*mfg*	327993	3296
Insulator pads, cordage: Rope, Cordage and Twine Mills—*mfg*	314991	2298
Insulators, electrical: Building Material Dealers, Other—*retail*	44419	5063
Electrical Apparatus and Equipment, Wiring Supplies and Material—*whlse*	42161	5063
Insulators, electrical–except glass and ceramic: Noncurrent-Carrying Wiring Device—*mfg*	335932	3644
Insulators, electrical–glass: Pressed and Blown Glass and Glassware, Other—*mfg*	327212	3229
Insulators, porcelain: Porcelain Electrical Supply—*mfg*	327113	3264
Insulin preparations: Pharmaceutical Preparation—*mfg*	325412	2834
Insulin–bulk, uncompounded: Medicinal and Botanical—*mfg*	325411	2833
Insulsleeves (foundry materials): Gypsum and Gypsum Product—*mfg*	32742	3299
Nonmetallic Mineral Product, All Other Miscellaneous—*mfg*	327999	3299
Insurance adjusters: Claims Adjusters—*fin*	524291	6411
Insurance Agencies and Brokerages—*fin*	52421	6411
Insurance Related Activities, All Other—*fin*	524298	6411
Third Party Administration for Insurance and Pension Funds—*fin*	524292	6411
Insurance advisory services: Claims Adjusters—*fin*	524291	6411
Insurance Agencies and Brokerages—*fin*	52421	6411
Insurance Related Activities, All Other—*fin*	524298	6411
Third Party Administration for Insurance and Pension Funds—*fin*	524292	6411
Insurance Agencies and Brokerages	**52421**	**6411**
Insurance Agencies, Brokerages and Other Insurance Related Activities	**5242**	
Insurance agents: Claims Adjusters—*fin*	524291	6411
Insurance Agencies and Brokerages—*fin*	52421	6411
Insurance Related Activities, All Other—*fin*	524298	6411
Third Party Administration for Insurance and Pension Funds—*fin*	524292	6411
Insurance and Employee Benefit Funds	**5251**	
Insurance brokers: Claims Adjusters—*fin*	524291	6411
Insurance Agencies and Brokerages—*fin*	52421	6411
Insurance Related Activities, All Other—*fin*	524298	6411
Third Party Administration for Insurance and Pension Funds—*fin*	524292	6411
Insurance buildings, operation of: Lessors of Nonresidential Buildings (except Miniwarehouses)—*real*	53112	6512
Promoters of Performing Arts, Sports and Similar Events with Facilities—*arts*	71131	6512
Insurance Carriers	**5241**	
Insurance Carriers and Related Activities	**524**	
Insurance carriers, accident: Direct Health and Medical Insurance Carriers—*fin*	524114	6321
Insurance Funds, Other—*fin*	52519	6321

ALPHABETICAL INDEX	NAICS	SIC
Reinsurance Carriers—*fin*	52413	6321
Insurance carriers, health: Direct Health and Medical Insurance Carriers—*fin*	524114	6321
Insurance Funds, Other—*fin*	52519	6321
Reinsurance Carriers—*fin*	52413	6321
Insurance carriers, life: Direct Life Insurance Carriers—*fin*	524113	6311
Reinsurance Carriers—*fin*	52413	6311
Insurance carriers–fire, marine, and casualty: Direct Property and Casualty Insurance Carriers—*fin*	524126	6331
Insurance Funds, Other—*fin*	52519	6331
Reinsurance Carriers—*fin*	52413	6331
Insurance claim adjusters, not employed by insurance companies: Claims Adjusters—*fin*	524291	6411
Insurance Agencies and Brokerages—*fin*	52421	6411
Insurance Related Activities, All Other—*fin*	524298	6411
Third Party Administration for Insurance and Pension Funds—*fin*	524292	6411
Insurance commissions: Regulation, Licensing, and Inspection of Miscellaneous Commercial Sectors—*pub*	92615	9651
Insurance educational services: Claims Adjusters—*fin*	524291	6411
Insurance Agencies and Brokerages—*fin*	52421	6411
Insurance Related Activities, All Other—*fin*	524298	6411
Third Party Administration for Insurance and Pension Funds—*fin*	524292	6411
Insurance Funds, Other	**52519**	**6324**
Insurance information bureaus: Claims Adjusters—*fin*	524291	6411
Insurance Agencies and Brokerages—*fin*	52421	6411
Insurance Related Activities, All Other—*fin*	524298	6411
Third Party Administration for Insurance and Pension Funds—*fin*	524292	6411
Insurance inspection and investigation services: Claims Adjusters—*fin*	524291	6411
Insurance Agencies and Brokerages—*fin*	52421	6411
Insurance Related Activities, All Other—*fin*	524298	6411
Third Party Administration for Insurance and Pension Funds—*fin*	524292	6411
Insurance loss prevention services: Claims Adjusters—*fin*	524291	6411
Insurance Agencies and Brokerages—*fin*	52421	6411
Insurance Related Activities, All Other—*fin*	524298	6411
Third Party Administration for Insurance and Pension Funds—*fin*	524292	6411
Insurance patrol services: Claims Adjusters—*fin*	524291	6411
Insurance Agencies and Brokerages—*fin*	52421	6411
Insurance Related Activities, All Other—*fin*	524298	6411
Third Party Administration for Insurance and Pension Funds—*fin*	524292	6411
Insurance physical examination service, except by physicians: Ambulatory Health Care Services, All Other Miscellaneous—*hlth*	621999	8099
Insurance professional standards services: Claims Adjusters—*fin*	524291	6411
Insurance Agencies and Brokerages—*fin*	52421	6411
Insurance Related Activities, All Other—*fin*	524298	6411
Third Party Administration for Insurance and Pension Funds—*fin*	524292	6411

ALPHABETICAL INDEX	NAICS	SIC
Insurance rate making services: Claims Adjusters—*fin*	524291	6411
Insurance Agencies and Brokerages—*fin*	52421	6411
Insurance Related Activities, All Other—*fin*	524298	6411
Third Party Administration for Insurance and Pension Funds—*fin*	524292	6411
Insurance Related Activities, All Other	**524298**	**6411**
Insurance Related Activities, Other	**52429**	
Insurance reporting services: Claims Adjusters—*fin*	524291	6411
Insurance Agencies and Brokerages—*fin*	52421	6411
Insurance Related Activities, All Other—*fin*	524298	6411
Third Party Administration for Insurance and Pension Funds—*fin*	524292	6411
Insurance research services: Claims Adjusters—*fin*	524291	6411
Insurance Agencies and Brokerages—*fin*	52421	6411
Insurance Related Activities, All Other—*fin*	524298	6411
Third Party Administration for Insurance and Pension Funds—*fin*	524292	6411
Insurance services: Claims Adjusters—*fin*	524291	6411
Insurance Agencies and Brokerages—*fin*	52421	6411
Insurance Related Activities, All Other—*fin*	524298	6411
Third Party Administration for Insurance and Pension Funds—*fin*	524292	6411
Insurance, accident and health: Direct Health and Medical Insurance Carriers—*fin*	524114	6321
Insurance Funds, Other—*fin*	52519	6321
Reinsurance Carriers—*fin*	52413	6321
Insurance, bank deposit or share: Direct Insurance (except Life, Health and Medical) Carriers, Other—*fin*	524128	6399
Insurance, credit or other financial responsibility: Direct Property and Casualty Insurance Carriers—*fin*	524126	6351
Reinsurance Carriers—*fin*	52413	6351
Insurance, fidelity: Direct Property and Casualty Insurance Carriers—*fin*	524126	6351
Reinsurance Carriers—*fin*	52413	6351
Insurance, life: Direct Life Insurance Carriers—*fin*	524113	6311
Reinsurance Carriers—*fin*	52413	6311
Insurance, surety: Direct Property and Casualty Insurance Carriers—*fin*	524126	6351
Reinsurance Carriers—*fin*	52413	6351
Insurance, title protection: Direct Title Insurance Carriers—*fin*	524127	6361
Reinsurance Carriers—*fin*	52413	6361
Insurance–fire, marine, and casualty: Direct Property and Casualty Insurance Carriers—*fin*	524126	6331
Insurance Funds, Other—*fin*	52519	6331
Reinsurance Carriers—*fin*	52413	6331
Intaglio ink vehicle: Paint and Coating—*mfg*	32551	2851
Intaglio printing: Gravure Printing, Commercial—*mfg*	323111	2754
Integrated microcircuits: Semiconductor and Related Device—*mfg*	334413	3674
Integrated Record Production/Distribution	**51222**	**3652**
Integrated-circuit testers: Electronic Coil, Transformer, and Other Inductor—*mfg*	334416	3825

Description	NAICS	SIC
Instrument for Measuring and Testing Electricity and Electrical Signals—*mfg*	334515	3825
Integrating electricity meters: Electronic Coil, Transformer, and Other Inductor—*mfg*	334416	3825
Instrument for Measuring and Testing Electricity and Electrical Signals—*mfg*	334515	3825
Integrating meters, nonelectric: Totalizing Fluid Meter and Counting Device—*mfg*	334514	3824
Interceptors, plumbers': Fabricated Metal Product, All Other Miscellaneous—*mfg*	332999	3432
Plumbing Fixture Fitting and Trim—*mfg*	332913	3432
Intercity bus lines: Interurban and Rural Bus—*trans*	48521	4131
Intercoastal transportation of freight: Coastal and Great Lakes Freight—*trans*	483113	4424
Intercommunications equipment installation–contractors: Electrical Contractors—*const*	23531	1731
Security Systems Services (except Locksmiths)—*admin*	561621	1731
Intercommunications equipment repair: Communication Equipment Repair and Maintenance—*serv*	811213	7622
Consumer Electronics Repair and Maintenance—*serv*	811211	7622
Radio, Television and Other Electronics Stores—*retail*	443112	7622
Intercommunications equipment, electronic: Communications Equipment, Other—*mfg*	33429	3669
Electronic Parts and Equipment, Other—*whlse*	42169	5065
Intercooler shells: Air-Conditioning and Warm Air Heating Equipment and Commercial and Industrial Refrigeration Equipment—*mfg*	333415	3443
Metal Tank (Heavy Gauge)—*mfg*	33242	3443
Plate Work—*mfg*	332313	3443
Power Boiler and Heat Exchanger—*mfg*	33241	3443
Interferometers: Optical Instrument and Lens—*mfg*	333314	3827
Interior decorating consulting service, except painters and paperhangers: Interior Design Services—*prof*	54141	7389
Interior Design Services	**54141**	**7389**
Interior designing service, except painters and paperhangers: Interior Design Services—*prof*	54141	7389
Interlining material, cotton: Broadwoven Fabric Mills—*mfg*	31321	2211
Interlinings, pockets, belt loops, etc.: Apparel Accessories and Apparel, Other—*mfg*	315999	2396
Textile Product Mills, All Other Miscellaneous—*mfg*	314999	2396
Interlinings–for suits and coats: Apparel Accessories and Apparel, Other—*mfg*	315999	2396
Textile Product Mills, All Other Miscellaneous—*mfg*	314999	2396
Intermediate care facilities: Continuing Care Retirement Communities—*hlth*	623311	8052
Nursing Care Facilities—*hlth*	62311	8052
Residential Mental Retardation Facilities—*hlth*	62321	8052
Intermediates, cyclic (coal tar): Cyclic Crude and Intermediate—*mfg*	325192	2865
Petrochemical—*mfg*	32511	2865
Intermediation, Miscellaneous	**52391**	**6799**
Internal combustion engine (stationary and mobile) forgings, ferrous–not made in rolling mills: Iron and Steel Forging—*mfg*	332111	3462
Internal combustion engine analyzers, to test electrical characteristics: Electronic Coil, Transformer, and Other Inductor—*mfg*	334416	3825
Instrument for Measuring and Testing Electricity and Electrical Signals—*mfg*	334515	3825
Internal combustion engines, except aircraft and nondiesel automotive: Engine Equipment, Other—*mfg*	333618	3519
Motor Vehicle Parts, All Other—*mfg*	336399	3519
International Affairs	**92812**	**9721**
International Trade Financing	**522293**	**6082**
Interstate bus lines: Interurban and Rural Bus—*trans*	48521	4131
Intertype machines: Printing Machinery and Equipment—*mfg*	333293	3555
Interurban and Rural Bus Transportation	**4852**	
Interurban and Rural Bus Transportation	**48521**	**4131**
Interurban bus lines: Interurban and Rural Bus—*trans*	48521	4131
Interurban cars and car equipment: Pump and Pumping Equipment—*mfg*	333911	3743
Railroad Rolling Stock—*mfg*	33651	3743
Interurban railways: Line-Haul Railroads—*trans*	482111	4011
Intra ocular lenses: Ophthalmic Goods—*mfg*	339115	3851
Intracoastal freight transportation: Inland Water Freight—*trans*	483211	4449
Intrauterine devices: Surgical Appliance and Supplies—*mfg*	339113	3842
Intravenous solutions: Pharmaceutical Preparation—*mfg*	325412	2834
Invalid supplies rental and leasing: Home Health Equipment Rental—*real*	532291	7352
Machinery and Equipment Rental and Leasing, Other Commercial and Industrial—*real*	53249	7352
Inventors: Scientific and Technical Consulting Services, Other—*prof*	54169	8999
Inventory blankbooks: Blankbook, Loose-leaf Binder and Device—*mfg*	323118	2782
Flexographic Printing, Commercial—*mfg*	323112	2782
Gravure Printing, Commercial—*mfg*	323111	2782
Lithographic Printing, Commercial—*mfg*	323110	2782
Printing, Other Commercial—*mfg*	323119	2782
Screen Printing, Commercial—*mfg*	323113	2782
Inventory computing service: Business Support Services, All Other—*admin*	561499	7389
Invert sugar: Cane Sugar Refining—*mfg*	311312	2062
Inverters, nonrotating: electrical: Electrical Equipment and Component, All Other Miscellaneous—*mfg*	335999	3629
Inverters, rotating: electrical: Motor and Generator—*mfg*	335312	3621
Investigation and Security Services	**5616**	
Investigation Services	**561611**	**7381**
Investigation, Guard and Armored Car Services	**56161**	
Investigators, private: Armored Car Services—*admin*	561613	7381

ALPHABETICAL INDEX	NAICS	SIC
Investigation Services—*admin*	561611	7381
Security Guards and Patrol Services—*admin*	561612	7381
Investment Advice	**52393**	**6282**
Investment advisory service: Investment Advice—*fin*	52393	6282
Portfolio Management—*fin*	52392	6282
Investment bankers: Financial Investment Activities, Miscellaneous—*fin*	523999	6211
Intermediation, Miscellaneous—*fin*	52391	6211
Investment Banking and Securities Dealing—*fin*	52311	6211
Securities Brokerage—*fin*	52312	6211
Investment Banking and Securities Dealing	**52311**	**6211**
Investment castings, steel: Steel Investment Foundries—*mfg*	331512	3324
Investment certificates, sale of: Financial Investment Activities, Miscellaneous—*fin*	523999	6211
Intermediation, Miscellaneous—*fin*	52391	6211
Investment Banking and Securities Dealing—*fin*	52311	6211
Securities Brokerage—*fin*	52312	6211
Investment clubs: Commodity Contracts Dealing—*fin*	52313	6799
Financial Investment Activities, Miscellaneous—*fin*	523999	6799
Intermediation, Miscellaneous—*fin*	52391	6799
Portfolio Management—*fin*	52392	6799
Investment companies, small business: International Trade Financing—*fin*	522293	6159
Non-Depository Credit Intermediation, All Other—*fin*	522298	6159
Sales Financing—*fin*	52222	6159
Investment counselors: Investment Advice—*fin*	52393	6282
Portfolio Management—*fin*	52392	6282
Investment firm-general brokerage: Financial Investment Activities, Miscellaneous—*fin*	523999	6211
Intermediation, Miscellaneous—*fin*	52391	6211
Investment Banking and Securities Dealing—*fin*	52311	6211
Securities Brokerage—*fin*	52312	6211
Investment funds (management) open-end: Open-End Investment Funds—*fin*	52591	6722
Investment funds, closed-end: management of: Financial Vehicles, Other—*fin*	52599	6726
Investment holding companies, except bank: Other Holding Companies, Offices Of—*manag*	551112	6719
Investment material, dental: Dental Equipment and Supplies—*mfg*	339114	3843
Investment Pools and Funds, Other	**5259**	
Investment research: Investment Advice—*fin*	52393	6282
Portfolio Management—*fin*	52392	6282
Investment trusts, unit: Financial Vehicles, Other—*fin*	52599	6726
Investors' syndicates: Financial Vehicles, Other—*fin*	52599	6726
Invitations, engraved-mfg: Digital Printing—*mfg*	323115	2759
Flexographic Printing, Commercial—*mfg*	323112	2759
Printing, Other Commercial—*mfg*	323119	2759
Quick Printing—*mfg*	323114	2759
Iodides-mfg: Basic Inorganic Chemical, All Other—*mfg*	325188	2819
Chemical Product, All Other Miscellaneous—*mfg*	325998	2819
Iodine, elemental-mfg: Basic Inorganic Chemical, All Other—*mfg*	325188	2819
Chemical Product, All Other Miscellaneous—*mfg*	325998	2819
Iodine, resubh'med-mfg: Basic Inorganic Chemical, All Other—*mfg*	325188	2819
Chemical Product, All Other Miscellaneous—*mfg*	325998	2819
Iodine, tincture of: Pharmaceutical Preparation—*mfg*	325412	2834
Ion chambers-mfg: Measuring and Controlling Device, Other—*mfg*	334519	3829
Surgical and Medical Instrument—*mfg*	339112	3829
Ion exchange resins: Plastics Material and Resin—*mfg*	325211	2821
Ionone: Basic Organic Chemical, All Other—*mfg*	325199	2869
Iridium ore mining: Metal Ore, All Other—*mining*	212299	1099
Iridium refining, primary: Primary Smelting and Refining of Nonferrous Metal (except Copper and Aluminum)—*mfg*	331419	3339
Iridium smelting and refining, secondary: Secondary Smelting and Alloying of Aluminum—*mfg*	331314	3341
Secondary Smelting, Refining, and Alloying of Nonferrous Metal (except Copper and Aluminum)—*mfg*	331492	3341
Irish potato farms: Potato Farming—*ag*	111211	134
Iron agglomerate and pellet production: Iron Ore—*mining*	21221	1011
Iron and steel flat products: Metal Service Centers and Offices—*whlse*	42151	5051
Iron and Steel Forging	**332111**	**3462**
Iron and Steel Mills	**331111**	**3399**
Iron and Steel Mills and Ferroalloy Manufacturing	**3311**	
Iron and Steel Mills and Ferroalloy Manufacturing	**33111**	
Iron and Steel Pipes and Tubes Manufacturing from Purchased Steel	**33121**	**3317**
Iron and steel scrap: Recyclable Material—*whlse*	42193	5093
Iron and steel semifinished products: Metal Service Centers and Offices—*whlse*	42151	5051
Iron blue pigments: Carbon Black—*mfg*	325182	2816
Inorganic Dye and Pigment—*mfg*	325131	2816
Iron castings, ductile and nodular-mfg: Iron Foundries—*mfg*	331511	3321
Iron cement, household-mfg: Adhesive—*mfg*	32552	2891
Iron colors: Carbon Black—*mfg*	325182	2816
Inorganic Dye and Pigment—*mfg*	325131	2816
Iron Foundries	**331511**	**3322**
Iron lungs: Surgical Appliance and Supplies—*mfg*	339113	3842
Iron ore: Coal and Other Mineral and Ore—*whlse*	42152	5052
Iron ore dressing (beneficiation) plants: Iron Ore—*mining*	21221	1011
Iron Ore Mining	**21221**	**1011**
Iron ore, blocked: mining: Iron Ore—*mining*	21221	1011
Iron ore, recovery from open hearth slag: Iron and Steel Mills—*mfg*	331111	3399
Secondary Smelting, Refining, and Alloying of Nonferrous Metal (except Copper and Aluminum)—*mfg*	331492	3399

Description	NAICS	SIC
Iron oxide, black: Carbon Black—*mfg*	325182	2816
Inorganic Dye and Pigment—*mfg*	325131	2816
Iron oxide, yellow: Carbon Black—*mfg*	325182	2816
Inorganic Dye and Pigment—*mfg*	325131	2816
Iron oxide. magnetic: Carbon Black—*mfg*	325182	2816
Iron sinter, made in steel mills: Iron and Steel Mills—*mfg*	331111	3312
Petroleum and Coal Productsa, All Other—*mfg*	324199	3312
Iron sulphate: Basic Inorganic Chemical, All Other—*mfg*	325188	2819
Chemical Product, All Other Miscellaneous—*mfg*	325998	2819
Iron work, ornamental-contractors: Trade Contractors, All Other Special—*const*	23599	1799
Iron work, structural-contractors: Structural Steel Erection Contractors—*const*	23591	1791
Iron, pig: Iron and Steel Mills—*mfg*	331111	3312
Metal Service Centers and Offices—*whlse*	42151	5051
Petroleum and Coal Productsa, All Other—*mfg*	324199	3312
Iron, powdered: Electroplating, Plating, Polishing, Anodizing and Coloring—*mfg*	332813	3399
Iron and Steel Mills—*mfg*	331111	3399
Secondary Smelting, Refining, and Alloying of Nonferrous Metal (except Copper and Aluminum)—*mfg*	331492	3399
Ironer parts, porcelain enameled: Kitchen Utensil, Pot and Pan—*mfg*	332214	3469
Ironers and mangles, household, except portable irons: Household Laundry Equipment—*mfg*	335224	3633
Ironers, commercial laundry and drycleaning: Laundry, Drycleaning and Pressing Machine, Commercial—*mfg*	333312	3582
Ironers, household: electric: Electrical Appliance, Television and Radio Set—*whlse*	42162	5064
Ironing board pads: Household Textile Product Mills, Other—*mfg*	314129	2392
Ironing boards, wood: Manufacturing, All Other Miscellaneous—*mfg*	339999	2499
Wood Container and Pallet—*mfg*	32192	2499
Wood Product, All Other Miscellaneous—*mfg*	321999	2499
Ironing hoards, metal: Fabricated Metal Product, All Other Miscellaneous—*mfg*	332999	3499
Irons, domestic: electric: Electric Housewares and Household Fan—*mfg*	335211	3634
Heating Equipment (except Electric and Warm Air Furnaces)—*mfg*	333414	3634
Irons, marking or branding: Marking Device—*mfg*	339943	3953
Ironworkers' handtools: Hand and Edge Tool—*mfg*	332212	3423
Irradiation Apparatus Manufacturing	**334517**	**3845**
Irradiation equipment: Irradiation Apparatus—*mfg*	334517	3844
Irrigation districts-nonoperating: Communications, Electric, Gas, and Other Utilities, Regulation and Administration of—*pub*	92613	9631
Irrigation equipment: Farm and Garden Machinery and Equipment—*whlse*	42182	5083
Outdoor Power Equipment Stores—*retail*	44421	5083
Irrigation equipment, self-propelled: Farm Machinery and Equipment—*mfg*	333111	3523
Irrigation pipe, concrete: Concrete Pipe—*mfg*	327332	3272
Concrete Product, Other—*mfg*	32739	3272
Nonmetallic Mineral Product, All Other Miscellaneous—*mfg*	327999	3272
Irrigation pipe, sheet metal: Metal Container, Other—*mfg*	332439	3444
Sheet Metal Work—*mfg*	332322	3444
Irrigation prolects construction–general contractors: Heavy, All Other—*const*	23499	1629
Industrial Nonbuilding Structure—*const*	23493	1629
Irrigation system operation: Water Supply and Irrigation Systems—*util*	22131	4971
Irrigation system operation services (not providing water): Nonscheduled Air, Other—*trans*	481219	721
Soil Preparation, Planting, and Cultivating—*ag*	115112	721
Isobutane (natural) production: Natural Gas Liquid Extraction—*mining*	211112	1321
Isobutylene polymers: Plastics Material and Resin—*mfg*	325211	2821
Isobutylene-isoprene rubbers: Synthetic Rubber—*mfg*	325212	2822
Isocyanate type rubber: Synthetic Rubber—*mfg*	325212	2822
Isocyanates: Cyclic Crude and Intermediate—*mfg*	325192	2865
Petrochemical—*mfg*	32511	2865
Isolation transformers: Power, Distribution and Specialty Transformer—*mfg*	335311	3612
Isoprene rubbers, synthetic: Synthetic Rubber—*mfg*	325212	2822
Isopropyl alcohol: Basic Organic Chemical, All Other—*mfg*	325199	2869
Ethyl Alcohol—*mfg*	325193	2869
Isotopes, radioactive: Basic Inorganic Chemical, All Other—*mfg*	325188	2819
Chemical Product, All Other Miscellaneous—*mfg*	325998	2819
Issuing of face amount installment certificates: Financial Vehicles, Other—*fin*	52599	6726
Italian foods, canned: Canning, Specialty—*mfg*	311422	2032
Food, All Other Miscellaneous—*mfg*	311999	2032
IV transfusion apparatus-mfg: Surgical and Medical Instrument—*mfg*	339112	3841
Jack screws: General Purpose Machinery , All Other—*mfg*	333999	3569
Jackets: Outerwear Knitting Mills—*mfg*	315191	2253
Jackets, bullet: 30 mm. (or 1.18 inch) or less: Small Arms Ammunition—*mfg*	332992	3482
Jackets, fur: Fur and Leather Apparel—*mfg*	315292	2371
Jackets, industrial: metal plate: Air-Conditioning and Warm Air Heating Equipment and Commercial and Industrial Refrigeration Equipment—*mfg*	333415	3443
Metal Tank (Heavy Gauge)—*mfg*	33242	3443
Plate Work—*mfg*	332313	3443
Power Boiler and Heat Exchanger—*mfg*	33241	3443
Jackets, leather (except welders') or sheep-lined: Fur and Leather Apparel—*mfg*	315292	2386
Jackets, nontailored except work: Cut and Sew Apparel, All Other—*mfg*	315299	2329
Men's and Boys' Cut and Sew Apparel Contractors—*mfg*	315211	2329
Men's and Boys' Cut and Sew Other Outerwear—*mfg*	315228	2329

ALPHABETICAL INDEX	NAICS	SIC
Jackets, not tailored: Apparel Accessories and Apparel, Other—*mfg*	315999	2339
Cut and Sew Apparel, All Other—*mfg*	315299	2339
Women's and Girls' Cut and Sew Apparel Contractors—*mfg*	315212	2339
Women's and Girls' Cut and Sew Other Outerwear—*mfg*	315238	2339
Jackets, overall and work: Men's and Boys' Cut and Sew Apparel Contractors—*mfg*	315211	2326
Men's and Boys' Cut and Sew Work Clothing—*mfg*	315225	2326
Jackets, service apparel (e.g., medical and lab): Apparel Accessories and Apparel, Other—*mfg*	315999	2339
Cut and Sew Apparel, All Other—*mfg*	315299	2339
Women's and Girls' Cut and Sew Apparel Contractors—*mfg*	315212	2339
Women's and Girls' Cut and Sew Other Outerwear—*mfg*	315238	2339
Jackets, ski: Apparel Accessories and Apparel, Other—*mfg*	315999	2339
Cut and Sew Apparel, All Other—*mfg*	315299	2339
Women's and Girls' Cut and Sew Apparel Contractors—*mfg*	315212	2339
Women's and Girls' Cut and Sew Other Outerwear—*mfg*	315238	2339
Jackets, smoking: Men's and Boys' Cut and Sew Apparel Contractors—*mfg*	315211	2384
Men's and Boys' Cut and Sew Underwear and Nightwear—*mfg*	315221	2384
Women's and Girls' Cut and Sew Apparel Contractors—*mfg*	315212	2384
Women's and Girls' Cut and Sew Lingerie, Loungewear and Nightwear—*mfg*	315231	2384
Jackets, sport, nontailored: Cut and Sew Apparel, All Other—*mfg*	315299	2329
Men's and Boys' Cut and Sew Apparel Contractors—*mfg*	315211	2329
Men's and Boys' Cut and Sew Other Outerwear—*mfg*	315228	2329
Jackets, tailored suit-type: Men's and Boys' Cut and Sew Apparel Contractors—*mfg*	315211	2311
Men's and Boys' Cut and Sew Suit, Coat and Overcoat—*mfg*	315222	2311
Jackets, tailored, except fur, sheep-lined, and leather: Women's and Girls' Cut and Sew Apparel Contractors—*mfg*	315212	2337
Women's and Girls' Cut and Sew Suit, Coat, Tailored Jacket and Skirt—*mfg*	315234	2337
Jackets, welders'–leather: Leather Good, All Other—*mfg*	316999	3199
Jacks, hydraulic–for general industrial use: General Purpose Machinery , All Other—*mfg*	333999	3569
Jacks, ladder–wood: Manufacturing, All Other Miscellaneous—*mfg*	339999	2499
Wood Container and Pallet—*mfg*	32192	2499
Wood Product, All Other Miscellaneous—*mfg*	321999	2499
Jacks, mud: Construction Machinery—*mfg*	33312	3531
Overhead Traveling Crane, Hoist and Monorail System—*mfg*	333923	3531
Railroad Rolling Stock—*mfg*	33651	3531
Jacks–lifting, screw, and ratchet (handtools): Hand and Edge Tool—*mfg*	332212	3423
Jacquard card cutting machines: Textile Machinery—*mfg*	333292	3552
Jacquard cards: Converted Paper Product, All Other—*mfg*	322298	2675
Die-Cut Paper and Paperboard Office Supplies—*mfg*	322231	2675
Surface-Coated Paperboard—*mfg*	322292	2675

ALPHABETICAL INDEX	NAICS	SIC
Jacquard loom parts and attachments: Textile Machinery—*mfg*	333292	3552
Jacquard woven fabrics, cotton: Broadwoven Fabric Mills—*mfg*	31321	2211
Jacquard woven fabrics, manmade fiber and silk: Broadwoven Fabric Mills—*mfg*	31321	2221
Jade mining: Crushed and Broken Stone and Quarrying, Other—*mining*	212319	1499
Non-Metallic Mineral, All Other—*mining*	212399	1499
Jails: Correctional Institutions—*pub*	92214	9223
Jails, privately operated: Facilities Support Services—*admin*	56121	8744
Jalousies, all metal or metal frame: Metal Window and Door—*mfg*	332321	3442
Jalousies, glass–wood frame: Millwork (including Flooring), Other—*mfg*	321918	2431
Wood Window and Door—*mfg*	321911	2431
Jams, including imitation: Fruit and Vegetable Canning—*mfg*	311421	2033
Janitorial service on airplanes: Airport Operations, Other—*trans*	488119	4581
Janitorial Services—*admin*	56172	4581
Janitorial Services	**56172**	**4581**
Janitorial services on a contract or fee basis: Janitorial Services—*admin*	56172	7349
Janitors' carts: Machinery, Other Commercial and Service Industry—*mfg*	333319	3589
Janitors' supplies: Cosmetics, Beauty Supplies and Perfume Stores—*retail*	44612	5087
Service Establishment Equipment and Supplies—*whlse*	42185	5087
Japanning of leather: Leather and Hide Tanning and Finishing—*mfg*	31611	3111
Japanning of metal: Costume Jewelry and Novelty—*mfg*	339914	3479
Jewelry (except Costume)—*mfg*	339911	3479
Metal Coating, Engraving (except Jewelry and Silverware), and Allied Services to Manufacturers—*mfg*	332812	3479
Silverware and Plated Ware—*mfg*	339912	3479
Japanning ovens: Industrial Process Furnace and Oven—*mfg*	333994	3567
Japans, baking and drying: Paint and Coating—*mfg*	32551	2851
Jar crowns and tops, stamped metal: Crown and Closure—*mfg*	332115	3466
Jar rings, rubber: Fabric Coating Mills—*mfg*	31332	3069
Rubber Product, All Other—*mfg*	326299	3069
Jars for packing, bottling, and canning–glass: Glass Container—*mfg*	327213	3221
Jars, battery–hard rubber: Fabric Coating Mills—*mfg*	31332	3069
Rubber Product, All Other—*mfg*	326299	3069
Jars, plastics: Plastics Pipe and Pipe Fitting—*mfg*	326122	3089
Plastics Product, All Other—*mfg*	326199	3089
Unsupported Plastics Profile Shape—*mfg*	326121	3089
Jazz music groups or artists: Independent Artists, Writers, and Performers—*arts*	71151	7929
Musical Groups and Artists—*arts*	71113	7929
Performing Arts Companies, Other—*arts*	71119	7929
Jean fabrics, cotton: Broadwoven Fabric Mills—*mfg*	31321	2211
Jean-cut casual slacks: Apparel Accessories and Apparel, Other—*mfg*	315999	2339

Description	NAICS	SIC
Cut and Sew Apparel, All Other—*mfg*	315299	2339
Men's and Boys' Cut and Sew Apparel Contractors—*mfg*	315211	2325
Men's and Boys' Cut and Sew Trouser, Slack and Jean—*mfg*	315224	2325
Women's and Girls' Cut and Sew Apparel Contractors—*mfg*	315212	2339
Women's and Girls' Cut and Sew Other Outerwear—*mfg*	315238	2339
Jeans: Apparel Accessories and Apparel, Other—*mfg*	315999	2339
Cut and Sew Apparel, All Other—*mfg*	315299	2339
Men's and Boys' Cut and Sew Apparel Contractors—*mfg*	315211	2325
Men's and Boys' Cut and Sew Trouser, Slack and Jean—*mfg*	315224	2325
Women's and Girls' Cut and Sew Apparel Contractors—*mfg*	315212	2339
Women's and Girls' Cut and Sew Other Outerwear—*mfg*	315238	2339
Jeans stores: Family Clothing Stores—*retail*	44814	5651
Jellies, edible–including imitation: Fruit and Vegetable Canning—*mfg*	311421	2033
Jelly, corncob (gelatin): Food, All Other Miscellaneous—*mfg*	311999	2099
Jersey fabrics: Textile and Fabric Finishing (except Broadwoven Fabric) Mills—*mfg*	313312	2257
Weft Knit Fabric Mills—*mfg*	313241	2257
Jerseys and sweaters: Outerwear Knitting Mills—*mfg*	315191	2253
Jet assisted takeoff devices (JATO): Aircraft Engine and Engine Parts—*mfg*	336412	3724
Jet fuel igniters: Basic Organic Chemical, All Other—*mfg*	325199	2899
Chemical Product, All Other Miscellaneous—*mfg*	325998	2899
Jet fuels: Petroleum Refineries—*mfg*	32411	2911
Jet propulsion and internal combustion engines and parts, aircraft: Aircraft Engine and Engine Parts—*mfg*	336412	3724
Jet propulsion projectiles, complete: Ammunition (except Small Arms)—*mfg*	332993	3483
Jetty construction–general contractors: Heavy, All Other—*const*	23499	1629
Industrial Nonbuilding Structure—*const*	23493	1629
Jewel bearings, synthetic: Jewelers' Material and Lapidary Work—*mfg*	339913	3915
Jewel cutting, drilling, polishing, recutting, or setting: Jewelers' Material and Lapidary Work—*mfg*	339913	3915
Jewel preparing–for instruments, tools, watches, and jewelry: Jewelers' Material and Lapidary Work—*mfg*	339913	3915
Jewel settings and mountings, precious metal: Jewelry (except Costume)—*mfg*	339911	3911
Jewelers' cards: Converted Paper Product, All Other—*mfg*	322298	2675
Die-Cut Paper and Paperboard Office Supplies—*mfg*	322231	2675
Surface-Coated Paperboard—*mfg*	322292	2675
Jewelers' findings: Jewelry, Watch, Precious Stone and Precious Metal—*whlse*	42194	5094
Jewelers' findings and materials: Jewelers' Material and Lapidary Work—*mfg*	339913	3915
Jewelers' handtools: Hand and Edge Tool—*mfg*	332212	3423
Jewelers' machines: Industrial Machinery, All Other—*mfg*	333298	3559
Machinery, Other Commercial and Service Industry—*mfg*	333319	3559
Jewelers' Material and Lapidary Work Manufacturing	**339913**	**3915**
Jewelry: Jewelry, Watch, Precious Stone and Precious Metal—*whlse*	42194	5094
Jewelry (except Costume) Manufacturing	**339911**	**3479**
Jewelry and Silverware Manufacturing	**33991**	
Jewelry boxes: Nondurable Goods, Other Miscellaneous—*whlse*	42299	5199
Jewelry enameling, for the trade: Costume Jewelry and Novelty—*mfg*	339914	3479
Jewelry (except Costume)—*mfg*	339911	3479
Metal Coating, Engraving (except Jewelry and Silverware), and Allied Services to Manufacturers—*mfg*	332812	3479
Silverware and Plated Ware—*mfg*	339912	3479
Jewelry parts, unassembled: Jewelers' Material and Lapidary Work—*mfg*	339913	3915
Jewelry polishing for the trade: Jewelers' Material and Lapidary Work—*mfg*	339913	3915
Jewelry repair shops: Personal and Household Goods Repair and Maintenance, Other—*serv*	81149	7631
Jewelry soldering for the trade: Jewelers' Material and Lapidary Work—*mfg*	339913	3915
Jewelry Stores	**44831**	**5944**
Jewelry stores, costume: Clothing Accessories Stores—*retail*	44815	5632
Clothing Stores, Other—*retail*	44819	5632
Jewelry stores, except costume: Jewelry Stores—*retail*	44831	5944
Jewelry, costume–except precious metal and precious or semiprecious stone: Costume Jewelry and Novelty—*mfg*	339914	3961
Jewelry, Luggage, and Leather Goods Stores	**4483**	
Jewelry, made of precious metal or precious or semiprecious stones: Jewelry (except Costume)—*mfg*	339911	3911
Jewelry, mail-order: Electronic Shopping and Mail-Order Houses—*retail*	45411	5961
Jewelry, natural or cultured pearls-rafg: Jewelry (except Costume)—*mfg*	339911	3911
Jewelry, precious stones and precious metals–including custom made: Jewelry Stores—*retail*	44831	5944
Jewelry, Watch, Precious Stone and Precious Metal Wholesalers	**42194**	**5094**
Jig boring machines: Machine Tool (Metal Cutting Types)—*mfg*	333512	3541
Jig grinding machines: Machine Tool (Metal Cutting Types)—*mfg*	333512	3541
Jigs: Industrial Machinery and Equipment—*whlse*	42183	5084
Jigs and fixtures (metalworking machin ery accessories): Die and Tool, Die Set, Jig and Fixture, Special—*mfg*	333514	3544
Industrial Mold—*mfg*	333511	3544
Jigs–inspection, gauging, and checking: Die and Tool, Die Set, Jig and Fixture, Special—*mfg*	333514	3544
Industrial Mold—*mfg*	333511	3544
Job counseling: Vocational Rehabilitation Services—*hlth*	62431	8331
Job printing and newspaper publishing combined: Newspaper Publishers—*info*	51111	2711
Job printing, except lithographic or gravure: Digital Printing—*mfg*	323115	2759
Flexographic Printing, Commercial—*mfg*	323112	2759
Printing, Other Commercial—*mfg*	323119	2759
Quick Printing—*mfg*	323114	2759

ALPHABETICAL INDEX	NAICS	SIC
Job printing, gravure: Gravure Printing, Commercial—*mfg*	323111	2754
Job printing, lithographic: Lithographic Printing, Commercial—*mfg*	323110	2752
Quick Printing—*mfg*	323114	2752
Job printing, offset: Lithographic Printing, Commercial—*mfg*	323110	2752
Quick Printing—*mfg*	323114	2752
Job training: Vocational Rehabilitation Services—*hlth*	62431	8331
Jockeys, horseracing: Race Tracks—*arts*	711212	7948
Spectator Sports, Other—*arts*	711219	7948
Jogging machines: Sporting and Athletic Goods—*mfg*	33992	3949
Jogging suits: Apparel Accessories and Apparel, Other—*mfg*	315999	2339
Cut and Sew Apparel, All Other—*mfg*	315299	2329
Cut and Sew Apparel, All Other—*mfg*	315299	2339
Outerwear Knitting Mills—*mfg*	315191	2253
Women's and Girls' Cut and Sew Apparel Contractors—*mfg*	315212	2339
Women's and Girls' Cut and Sew Other Outerwear—*mfg*	315238	2339
Joinery, ship–contractors: Carpentry Contractors—*const*	23551	1751
Joint compounds: Adhesive—*mfg*	32552	2891
Jointers (woodworking machines): Sawmill and Woodworking Machinery—*mfg*	33321	3553
Joints, swivel–except motor vehicle and aircraft: Mechanical Power Transmission Equipment—*mfg*	333613	3568
Joints, universal–except motor vehicle: Mechanical Power Transmission Equipment—*mfg*	333613	3568
Joists, concrete: Concrete Pipe—*mfg*	327332	3272
Concrete Product, Other—*mfg*	32739	3272
Nonmetallic Mineral Product, All Other Miscellaneous—*mfg*	327999	3272
Joists, fabricated bar: Fabricated Structural Metal—*mfg*	332312	3449
Metal Window and Door—*mfg*	332321	3449
Ornamental and Architectural Metal Work—*mfg*	332323	3449
Roll Forming, Custom—*mfg*	332114	3449
Joists, open web steel–long-span series: Fabricated Structural Metal—*mfg*	332312	3441
Joists, sheet metal: Metal Container, Other—*mfg*	332439	3444
Sheet Metal Work—*mfg*	332322	3444
Judo instruction: Sports and Recreation Instruction—*educ*	61162	7999
Jugs for packing, bottling, and canning–glass: Glass Container—*mfg*	327213	3221
Jugs, vacuum: Metal Container, Other—*mfg*	332439	3429
Juice extractors, electric: Electric Housewares and Household Fan—*mfg*	335211	3634
Heating Equipment (except Electric and Warm Air Furnaces)—*mfg*	333414	3634
Juice extractors, fruit and vegetable–commercial type: Food Product Machinery—*mfg*	333294	3556
Juice pops, frozen: Ice Cream and Frozen Dessert—*mfg*	31152	2024
Juice, fruit–concentrated-hot pack: Fruit and Vegetable Canning—*mfg*	311421	2033
Juices, fresh–fruit or vegetable: Fruit and Vegetable Canning—*mfg*	311421	2033

ALPHABETICAL INDEX	NAICS	SIC
Juices, fruit and vegetable–canned or fresh: Fruit and Vegetable Canning—*mfg*	311421	2033
Juke boxes: Audio and Video Equipment—*mfg*	33431	3651
Juke boxes, operation of: Amusement and Recreation Industries, All Other—*arts*	71399	7993
Amusement Arcades—*arts*	71312	7993
Gambling Industries, Other—*arts*	71329	7993
Jumpsuits: Women's and Girls' Cut and Sew Apparel Contractors—*mfg*	315212	2337
Women's and Girls' Cut and Sew Suit, Coat, Tailored Jacket and Skirt—*mfg*	315234	2337
Junior Chambers of Commerce: Business Associations—*serv*	81391	8611
Junior Colleges	**6112**	
Junior Colleges	**61121**	**8222**
Junk and scrap, general line: Recyclable Material—*whlse*	42193	5093
Justice, Public Order, and Safety	**9221**	
Justice, Public Order, and Safety	**922**	
Justice, Public Order, and Safety, All Other	**92219**	**9229**
Jute liner board: Paperboard Mills—*mfg*	32213	2631
Jute piece goods: Broadwoven Fabric Finishing Mills—*mfg*	313311	5131
Piece Goods, Notions and Other Dry Goods—*whlse*	42231	5131
Textile and Fabric Finishing (except Broadwoven Fabric) Mills—*mfg*	313312	5131
Juvenile correctional homes: Homes for the Elderly—*hlth*	623312	8361
Residential Care Facilities, Other—*hlth*	62399	8361
Residential Mental Health and Substance Abuse Facilities—*hlth*	62322	8361
Juvenile furniture: Furniture Stores—*retail*	44211	5712
Nonupholstered Wood Household Furniture—*mfg*	337122	5712
Upholstered Household Furniture—*mfg*	337121	5712
Wood Kitchen Cabinet and Counter Top—*mfg*	33711	5712
Juvenile furniture, metal: Metal Household Furniture—*mfg*	337124	2514
Juvenile furniture, rattan and reed: Household Furniture (except Wood and Metal)—*mfg*	337125	2519
Juvenile furniture, upholstered on wood frames, except convertible beds: Upholstered Household Furniture—*mfg*	337121	2512
Juvenile furniture, wood–except upholstered: Nonupholstered Wood Household Furniture—*mfg*	337122	2511
Kalsomines, dry or paste: Paint and Coating—*mfg*	32551	2851
Kaolin and Ball Clay Mining	**212324**	**1455**
Kaolin mining: Kaolin and Ball Clay—*mining*	212324	1455
Kaolin, ground or otherwise treated-rnfg: Ground or Treated Mineral and Earth—*mfg*	327992	3295
Karate instruction: Sports and Recreation Instruction—*educ*	61162	7999
Karate uniforms–women's and children's: Women's, Children's, and Infants' and Accessories—*whlse*	42233	5137
Kayaks, building and repairing: Boat Building—*mfg*	336612	3732

Personal and Household Goods Repair and Maintenance, Other—*serv*	81149	3732
Keene's cement: Gypsum and Gypsum Product—*mfg*	32742	3275
Kegs, wood–coopered: Wood Container and Pallet—*mfg*	32192	2449
Kelp meal and pellets: Animal Food, Other—*mfg*	311119	2048
Kelp plants: Medicinal and Botanical—*mfg*	325411	2833
Kelvin bridges (electrical measuring instruments): Electronic Coil, Transformer, and Other Inductor—*mfg*	334416	3825
Instrument for Measuring and Testing Electricity and Electrical Signals—*mfg*	334515	3825
Kennels, boarding: Animal Production Support Activities—*ag*	11521	752
Pet Care (except Veterinary) Services—*serv*	81291	752
Kennels, breeding and raising own stock: Animal Production, All Other—*ag*	11299	279
Apiculture—*ag*	11291	279
Kennels, dogracing: Race Tracks—*arts*	711212	7948
Spectator Sports, Other—*arts*	711219	7948
Kernite mining: Potash, Soda, and Borate Mineral—*mining*	212391	1474
Kerogen processing: Crude Petroleum and Natural Gas Extraction—*mining*	211111	1311
Kerosene: Petroleum and Petroleum Products (except Bulk Stations and Terminals)—*whlse*	42272	5172
Petroleum Refineries—*mfg*	32411	2911
Kerosene space heaters: Heating Equipment (except Electric and Warm Air Furnaces)—*mfg*	333414	3433
Ketchup: Fruit and Vegetable Canning—*mfg*	311421	2033
Ketone, methyl ethyl: Basic Organic Chemical, All Other—*mfg*	325199	2869
Ketone, methyl isobutyl: Basic Organic Chemical, All Other—*mfg*	325199	2869
Kettles (process vessels), metal plate: Air-Conditioning and Warm Air Heating Equipment and Commercial and Industrial Refrigeration Equipment—*mfg*	333415	3443
Metal Tank (Heavy Gauge)—*mfg*	33242	3443
Plate Work—*mfg*	332313	3443
Power Boiler and Heat Exchanger—*mfg*	33241	3443
Key blanks: Hardware—*mfg*	33251	3429
Key cases, regardless of material: Personal Leather Good (except Women's Handbag and Purse)—*mfg*	316993	3172
Key rings, made from purchased wire: Fabricated Wire Product, Other—*mfg*	332618	3496
Key to tape or disk devices: Computer Storage Device—*mfg*	334112	3572
Key-tape equipment–reel, cassette, or cartridge: Computer Peripheral Equipment, Other—*mfg*	334119	3577
Keyboards, piano or organ: Musical Instrument—*mfg*	339992	3931
Keydisk or diskette equipment, computer peripheral equipment: Computer Peripheral Equipment, Other—*mfg*	334119	3577
Keying equipment: Computer and Computer Peripheral Equipment and Software—*whlse*	42143	5045
Computer and Software Stores—*retail*	44312	5045
Keying equipment, computer peripheral equipment: Computer Peripheral Equipment, Other—*mfg*	334119	3577
Keypunch service: Data Processing Services—*info*	51421	7374
Keypunch/verify cards, computer peripheral equipment: Computer Peripheral Equipment, Other—*mfg*	334119	3577
Keys: Hardware—*mfg*	33251	3429
Keys, can–made from purchased wire: Fabricated Wire Product, Other—*mfg*	332618	3496
Keyseating machines (machine tools): Machine Tool (Metal Cutting Types)—*mfg*	333512	3541
Kiddie parks: Amusement and Theme Parks—*arts*	71311	7996
Kidney Dialysis Centers	**621492**	**8092**
Kier bleaching, continuous machine: Broadwoven Fabric Finishing Mills—*mfg*	313311	2261
Kiln construction–general contractors: Heavy, All Other—*const*	23499	1629
Industrial Nonbuilding Structure—*const*	23493	1629
Kiln drying of lumber: Cut Stock, Resawing Lumber, and Planing—*mfg*	321912	2421
Millwork (including Flooring), Other—*mfg*	321918	2421
Sawmills—*mfg*	321113	2421
Wood Product, All Other Miscellaneous—*mfg*	321999	2421
Kiln furniture, clay: Clay Refractory—*mfg*	327124	3255
Kilns–cement, wood, and chemical: Industrial Machinery, All Other—*mfg*	333298	3559
Machinery, Other Commercial and Service Industry—*mfg*	333319	3559
Kilns–except cement, chemical, and wood: Industrial Process Furnace and Oven—*mfg*	333994	3567
Kindergartens: Elementary and Secondary Schools—*educ*	61111	8211
Kinematic test and measuring equipment: Measuring and Controlling Device, Other—*mfg*	334519	3829
Surgical and Medical Instrument—*mfg*	339112	3829
Kitchen articles, coarse earthenware: Vitreous China, Fine Earthenware and Other Pottery Product—*mfg*	327112	3269
Kitchen cabinets to be built in: Building Material Dealers, Other—*retail*	44419	5031
Kitchen cabinets, metal: Metal Household Furniture—*mfg*	337124	2514
Kitchen cabinets, wood–to be installed: Wood Kitchen Cabinet and Counter Top—*mfg*	33711	2434
Kitchen cutlery: Cutlery and Flatware (except Precious)—*mfg*	332211	3421
Kitchen tools and utensils, except precious metal flatware: Home Furnishing—*whlse*	42122	5023
Kitchen Utensil, Pot and Pan Manufacturing	**332214**	**3469**
Kitchen utensils stamped and pressed metal: Kitchen Utensil, Pot and Pan—*mfg*	332214	3469
Kitchen utensils, cast aluminum–except die-castings: Aluminum Foundries—*mfg*	331524	3365
Kitchen utensils, porcelain enameled: Kitchen Utensil, Pot and Pan—*mfg*	332214	3469

ALPHABETICAL INDEX	NAICS	SIC
Kitchen wire goods, made from purchased wire: Fabricated Wire Product, Other—*mfg*	332618	3496
Kitchen woodenware: Manufacturing, All Other Miscellaneous—*mfg*	339999	2499
Wood Container and Pallet—*mfg*	32192	2499
Wood Product, All Other Miscellaneous—*mfg*	321999	2499
Kitchens, complete (sinks, cabinets, etc.): Household Appliance Stores—*retail*	443111	5722
Kitchenware stores: Home Furnishings Stores, All Other—*retail*	442299	5719
Window Treatment Stores—*retail*	442291	5719
Kitchenware, plastics–except foam: Plastics Pipe and Pipe Fitting—*mfg*	326122	3089
Plastics Product, All Other—*mfg*	326199	3089
Unsupported Plastics Profile Shape—*mfg*	326121	3089
Kitchenware, semivitreous earthenware: Vitreous China, Fine Earthenware and Other Pottery Product—*mfg*	327112	3263
Kitchenware–commercial and household-vitreous china: Vitreous China, Fine Earthenware and Other Pottery Product—*mfg*	327112	3262
Kite (toy) stores: Hobby, Toy and Game Stores—*retail*	45112	5945
Kites: Game, Toy, and Children's Vehicle—*mfg*	339932	3944
Kits, hosiery–sewing and mending: Fabricated Metal Product, All Other Miscellaneous—*mfg*	332999	3999
Kits, wood–coopered: Wood Container and Pallet—*mfg*	32192	2449
Kiwi fruit farms: Fruit and Tree Nut Combination Farming—*ag*	111336	179
Noncitrus Fruit Farming, Other—*ag*	111339	179
Klystron tubes: Electron Tube—*mfg*	334411	3671
Knapsacks, canvas: Textile Bag Mills—*mfg*	314911	2393
Kneecap supporters, orthopedic: Surgical Appliance and Supplies—*mfg*	339113	3842
Kneeling pads, rubber: Fabric Coating Mills—*mfg*	31332	3069
Rubber Product, All Other—*mfg*	326299	3069
Knickers: Apparel Accessories and Apparel, Other—*mfg*	315999	2339
Cut and Sew Apparel, All Other—*mfg*	315299	2339
Women's and Girls' Cut and Sew Apparel Contractors—*mfg*	315212	2339
Women's and Girls' Cut and Sew Other Outerwear—*mfg*	315238	2339
Knickers, dress (separate): Cut and Sew Apparel, All Other—*mfg*	315299	2329
Men's and Boys' Cut and Sew Apparel Contractors—*mfg*	315211	2329
Men's and Boys' Cut and Sew Other Outerwear—*mfg*	315228	2329
Knife blades: Cutlery and Flatware (except Precious)—*mfg*	332211	3421
Knife blanks: Cutlery and Flatware (except Precious)—*mfg*	332211	3421
Knife switches, electric: Switchgear and Switchboard Apparatus—*mfg*	335313	3613
Knishes, except frozen: Bakeries, Commercial—*mfg*	311812	2051
Knit Fabric and Lace Mills, Other	**313249**	**2259**
Knit Fabric Mills	**31324**	
Knit fabrics: Broadwoven Fabric Finishing Mills—*mfg*	313311	5131
Piece Goods, Notions and Other Dry Goods—*whlse*	42231	5131
Textile and Fabric Finishing (except Broadwoven Fabric) Mills—*mfg*	313312	5131
Knit fabrics, warp–knitting, dyeing, or finishing: Knit Fabric and Lace Mills, Other—*mfg*	313249	2258
Textile and Fabric Finishing (except Broadwoven Fabric) Mills—*mfg*	313312	2258
Knit fabrics, weft (circular)–knitting, dyeing, or finishing: Textile and Fabric Finishing (except Broadwoven Fabric) Mills—*mfg*	313312	2257
Weft Knit Fabric Mills—*mfg*	313241	2257
Knit fabrics, weft knit–knitting, dyeing, or finishing: Textile and Fabric Finishing (except Broadwoven Fabric) Mills—*mfg*	313312	2257
Weft Knit Fabric Mills—*mfg*	313241	2257
Knit gloves: Glove and Mitten—*mfg*	315992	2381
Knitting hand thread–cotton, silk, and manmade fibers: Textile and Fabric Finishing (except Broadwoven Fabric) Mills—*mfg*	313312	2284
Thread Mills—*mfg*	313113	2284
Knitting machines: Textile Machinery—*mfg*	333292	3552
Knitting yarn shops: Sewing, Needlework and Piece Goods Stores—*retail*	45113	5949
Knitting yarn–cotton, silk, wool, and manmade staple: Yarn Spinning Mills—*mfg*	313111	2281
Knives, agricultural and industrial: Hand and Edge Tool—*mfg*	332212	3423
Knives, electric: Electric Housewares and Household Fan—*mfg*	335211	3634
Heating Equipment (except Electric and Warm Air Furnaces)—*mfg*	333414	3634
Knives, machine; except metal cutting: Hand and Edge Tool—*mfg*	332212	3423
Knives, shear: Cutting Tool and Machine Tool Accessory—*mfg*	333515	3545
Hand and Edge Tool—*mfg*	332212	3545
Knives, surgical: Surgical and Medical Instrument—*mfg*	339112	3841
Knives, table–metal, except all metal: Cutlery and Flatware (except Precious)—*mfg*	332211	3421
Knives–butchers', hunting, pocket, table-except all metal table and electric: Cutlery and Flatware (except Precious)—*mfg*	332211	3421
Knives–silver, silver-plated, and stainless steel: Cutlery and Flatware (except Precious)—*mfg*	332211	3914
Silverware and Plated Ware—*mfg*	339912	3914
Knobs, organ: Musical Instrument—*mfg*	339992	3931
Knobs, porcelain: Porcelain Electrical Supply—*mfg*	327113	3264
Knobs, wood: Manufacturing, All Other Miscellaneous—*mfg*	339999	2499
Wood Container and Pallet—*mfg*	32192	2499
Wood Product, All Other Miscellaneous—*mfg*	321999	2499
Knockouts, free water–metal plate: Air-Conditioning and Warm Air Heating Equipment and Commercial and Industrial Refrigeration Equipment—*mfg*	333415	3443
Metal Tank (Heavy Gauge)—*mfg*	33242	3443
Plate Work—*mfg*	332313	3443

Description	NAICS	SIC
Power Boiler and Heat Exchanger—*mfg*	33241	3443
Knot tying machines (textile machinery): Textile Machinery—*mfg*	333292	3552
Knurling machines: Machine Tool (Metal Forming Types)—*mfg*	333513	3542
Kraft liner board: Paperboard Mills—*mfg*	32213	2631
Kraft sheathing paper: Newsprint Mills—*mfg*	322122	2621
Paper (except Newsprint) Mills—*mfg*	322121	2621
Kraft wrapping paper: Newsprint Mills—*mfg*	322122	2621
Paper (except Newsprint) Mills—*mfg*	322121	2621
Kyanite mining: Clay and Ceramic and Refractory Minerals—*mining*	212325	1459
Label moisteners, industrial type: Packaging Machinery—*mfg*	333993	3565
Labeling bottles, cans, cartons, etc. for the trade–not printing: Packaging and Labeling Services—*admin*	56191	7389
Labeling machinery, industrial type: Packaging Machinery—*mfg*	333993	3565
Labeling machines, address: Lead Pencil and Art Good—*mfg*	339942	3579
Office Machinery—*mfg*	333313	3579
Watch, Clock, and Part—*mfg*	334518	3579
Labels, cotton–printed: Broadwoven Fabric Finishing Mills—*mfg*	313311	2269
Textile and Fabric Finishing (except Broadwoven Fabric) Mills—*mfg*	313312	2269
Labels, lithographed: Lithographic Printing, Commercial—*mfg*	323110	2752
Quick Printing—*mfg*	323114	2752
Labels, printed–except lithographed or gravure: Digital Printing—*mfg*	323115	2759
Flexographic Printing, Commercial—*mfg*	323112	2759
Printing, Other Commercial—*mfg*	323119	2759
Quick Printing—*mfg*	323114	2759
Labels, woven: Broadwoven Fabric Finishing Mills—*mfg*	313311	5131
Narrow Fabric Mills—*mfg*	313221	2241
Piece Goods, Notions and Other Dry Goods—*whlse*	42231	5131
Textile and Fabric Finishing (except Broadwoven Fabric) Mills—*mfg*	313312	5131
Labels–gravure printing: Gravure Printing, Commercial—*mfg*	323111	2754
Labor contractors (employment agencies), except farm labor: Employment Placement Agencies—*admin*	56131	7361
Human Resources and Executive Search Consulting Services—*prof*	541612	7361
Labor organizations: Labor Unions and Similar Labor Organizations—*serv*	81393	8631
Labor pools: Employee Leasing Services—*admin*	56133	7363
Temporary Help Services—*admin*	56132	7363
Labor unions: Labor Unions and Similar Labor Organizations—*serv*	81393	8631
Labor Unions and Similar Labor Organizations	**81393**	**8631**
Labor-management negotiations boards: Regulation, Licensing, and Inspection of Miscellaneous Commercial Sectors—*pub*	92615	9651
Laboratories, dental-X-ray: Diagnostic Imaging Centers—*hlth*	621512	8071
Medical Laboratories—*hlth*	621511	8071
Laboratories, industrial–commercial research, except testing: Research and Development in the Life Sciences—*prof*	54172	8731
Research and Development in the Physical Sciences and Engineering Sciences—*prof*	54171	8731
Laboratories, motion picture: Independent Artists, Writers, and Performers—*arts*	71151	7819
Motion Picture and Video Industries, Other—*info*	512199	7819
Prerecorded Compact Disc (except Software), Tape, and Record Reproducing—*mfg*	334612	7819
Teleproduction and Other Post-Production Services—*info*	512191	7819
Laboratories, product testing–not manufacturing auxiliaries: Testing Laboratories—*prof*	54138	8734
Veterinary Services—*prof*	54194	8734
Laboratories, research–commercial: Research and Development in the Life Sciences—*prof*	54172	8731
Research and Development in the Physical Sciences and Engineering Sciences—*prof*	54171	8731
Laboratories–biological, medical, and Xray (picture and treatment): Diagnostic Imaging Centers—*hlth*	621512	8071
Medical Laboratories—*hlth*	621511	8071
Laboratory (physical) research and development: Research and Development in the Life Sciences—*prof*	54172	8731
Research and Development in the Physical Sciences and Engineering Sciences—*prof*	54171	8731
Laboratory animal farms (e.g., rats, mice, guinea pigs): Animal Production, All Other—*ag*	11299	279
Apiculture—*ag*	11291	279
Laboratory Apparatus and Furniture Manufacturing	**339111**	**3829**
Laboratory chemicals, inorganic: Basic Inorganic Chemical, All Other—*mfg*	325188	2819
Chemical Product, All Other Miscellaneous—*mfg*	325998	2819
Laboratory chemicals, organic: Basic Organic Chemical, All Other—*mfg*	325199	2869
Laboratory coats: Men's and Boys' Cut and Sew Apparel Contractors—*mfg*	315211	2326
Men's and Boys' Cut and Sew Work Clothing—*mfg*	315225	2326
Laboratory equipment, dental and medical: Health and Personal Care Stores, All Other—*retail*	446199	5047
Medical, Dental and Hospital Equipment and Supplies—*whlse*	42145	5047
Laboratory equipment, except medical ordental: Office Supplies and Stationery Stores—*retail*	45321	5049
Professional Equipment and Supplies, Other—*whlse*	42149	5049
Laboratory glassware, made from purchased glass: Glass Product Made of Purchased Glass—*mfg*	327215	3231
Laboratory instrument repair, except electric: Electronic and Precision Equipment Repair and Maintenance, Other—*serv*	811219	7699
Laboratory standards, electric–resistance, inductance, and capacitance: Electronic Coil, Transformer, and Other Inductor—*mfg*	334416	3825
Instrument for Measuring and Testing Electricity and Electrical Signals—*mfg*	334515	3825

ALPHABETICAL INDEX	NAICS	SIC
Laboratory sundries–e.g., cases, covers, funnels, cups, bottles-rubber:		
Fabric Coating Mills—*mfg*	31332	3069
Rubber Product, All Other—*mfg*	326299	3069
Laboratoryware, plastics: Plastics Pipe and Pipe Fitting—*mfg*	326122	3089
Plastics Product, All Other—*mfg*	326199	3089
Unsupported Plastics Profile Shape—*mfg*	326121	3089
Lac production: Crop Farming, All Other Miscellaneous—*ag*	111998	831
Forest Nurseries and Gathering of Forest Products—*ag*	11321	831
Lace and net machines: Textile Machinery—*mfg*	333292	3552
Lace fabrics: Broadwoven Fabric Finishing Mills—*mfg*	313311	5131
Piece Goods, Notions and Other Dry Goods—*whlse*	42231	5131
Textile and Fabric Finishing (except Broadwoven Fabric) Mills—*mfg*	313312	5131
Lace goods–curtains, bedspreads, tablecovers, flouncings, and insertions: Knit Fabric and Lace Mills, Other—*mfg*	313249	2258
Textile and Fabric Finishing (except Broadwoven Fabric) Mills—*mfg*	313312	2258
Lace leather: Leather and Hide Tanning and Finishing—*mfg*	31611	3111
Lace machine bobbins, wood or metal: Textile Machinery—*mfg*	333292	3552
Lace, auto wind: Narrow Fabric Mills—*mfg*	313221	2241
Lace, burnt-out: Men's and Boys' Cut and Sew Apparel Contractors—*mfg*	315211	2395
Textile Product Mills, All Other Miscellaneous—*mfg*	314999	2395
Women's and Girls' Cut and Sew Apparel Contractors—*mfg*	315212	2395
Lace, knit: Knit Fabric and Lace Mills, Other—*mfg*	313249	2258
Textile and Fabric Finishing (except Broadwoven Fabric) Mills—*mfg*	313312	2258
Lace, paper–die-cut from purchased materials: Converted Paper Product, All Other—*mfg*	322298	2675
Die-Cut Paper and Paperboard Office Supplies—*mfg*	322231	2675
Surface-Coated Paperboard—*mfg*	322292	2675
Laces, boot and shoe–leather: Fastener, Button, Needle and Pin—*mfg*	339993	3131
Leather Good, All Other—*mfg*	316999	3131
Wood Product, All Other Miscellaneous—*mfg*	321999	3131
Laces, corset and shoe–textile: Narrow Fabric Mills—*mfg*	313221	2241
Laces–Barmen, bobbinet, levers, and Nottingham: Knit Fabric and Lace Mills, Other—*mfg*	313249	2258
Textile and Fabric Finishing (except Broadwoven Fabric) Mills—*mfg*	313312	2258
Lacings: Narrow Fabric Mills—*mfg*	313221	2241
Lacquer bases and dopes: Paint and Coating—*mfg*	32551	2851
Lacquer thinner: Paint and Coating—*mfg*	32551	2851
Lacquer, clear and pigmented: Paint and Coating—*mfg*	32551	2851
Lacquering of metal products, for the trade: Costume Jewelry and Novelty—*mfg*	339914	3479
Jewelry (except Costume)—*mfg*	339911	3479

ALPHABETICAL INDEX	NAICS	SIC
Metal Coating, Engraving (except Jewelry and Silverware), and Allied Services to Manufacturers—*mfg*	332812	3479
Silverware and Plated Ware—*mfg*	339912	3479
Lacquering ovens: Industrial Process Furnace and Oven—*mfg*	333994	3567
Lacquers: Paint and Wallpaper Stores—*retail*	44412	5198
Paint, Varnish and Supplies—*whlse*	42295	5198
Lacquers, plastics: Paint and Coating—*mfg*	32551	2851
Lacrosse equipment: Sporting and Athletic Goods—*mfg*	33992	3949
Lactose, edible: Dry, Condensed, and Evaporated Dairy Product—*mfg*	311514	2023
Ladder assemblies, combination work-stand–metal: Fabricated Metal Product, All Other Miscellaneous—*mfg*	332999	3499
Ladder ditchers, vertical boom or wheel: Construction Machinery—*mfg*	33312	3531
Overhead Traveling Crane, Hoist and Monorail System—*mfg*	333923	3531
Railroad Rolling Stock—*mfg*	33651	3531
Ladder jacks, metal: Hardware—*mfg*	33251	3429
Ladder jacks, wood: Manufacturing, All Other Miscellaneous—*mfg*	339999	2499
Wood Container and Pallet—*mfg*	32192	2499
Wood Product, All Other Miscellaneous—*mfg*	321999	2499
Ladder round: Cut Stock, Resawing Lumber, and Planing—*mfg*	321912	2426
Millwork (including Flooring), Other—*mfg*	321918	2426
Showcase, Partition, Shelving, and Locker—*mfg*	337215	2426
Wood Product, All Other Miscellaneous—*mfg*	321999	2426
Ladder rounds or rungs, hardwood: Cut Stock, Resawing Lumber, and Planing—*mfg*	321912	2426
Millwork (including Flooring), Other—*mfg*	321918	2426
Showcase, Partition, Shelving, and Locker—*mfg*	337215	2426
Wood Product, All Other Miscellaneous—*mfg*	321999	2426
Ladders: Industrial Machinery and Equipment—*whlse*	42183	5084
Ladders, chain–metal: Ornamental and Architectural Metal Work—*mfg*	332323	3446
Ladders, for permanent installation–metal: Ornamental and Architectural Metal Work—*mfg*	332323	3446
Ladders, metal–portable: Fabricated Metal Product, All Other Miscellaneous—*mfg*	332999	3499
Ladders, plastics: Plastics Pipe and Pipe Fitting—*mfg*	326122	3089
Plastics Product, All Other—*mfg*	326199	3089
Unsupported Plastics Profile Shape—*mfg*	326121	3089
Ladders, wood: Manufacturing, All Other Miscellaneous—*mfg*	339999	2499
Wood Container and Pallet—*mfg*	32192	2499
Wood Product, All Other Miscellaneous—*mfg*	321999	2499
Ladies' handkerchiefs: Women's, Children's, and Infants' and Accessories—*whlse*	42233	5137
Ladies' purses: Women's, Children's, and Infants' and Accessories—*whlse*	42233	5137

Description	NAICS	SIC
Ladle bails: Air-Conditioning and Warm Air Heating Equipment and Commercial and Industrial Refrigeration Equipment—*mfg*	333415	3443
Metal Tank (Heavy Gauge)—*mfg*	33242	3443
Plate Work—*mfg*	332313	3443
Power Boiler and Heat Exchanger—*mfg*	33241	3443
Ladle brick, clay: Clay Refractory—*mfg*	327124	3255
Ladles, metal plate: Air-Conditioning and Warm Air Heating Equipment and Commercial and Industrial Refrigeration Equipment—*mfg*	333415	3443
Metal Tank (Heavy Gauge)—*mfg*	33242	3443
Plate Work—*mfg*	332313	3443
Power Boiler and Heat Exchanger—*mfg*	33241	3443
Lake freight transportation, except on the Great Lakes: Inland Water Freight—*trans*	483211	4449
Lake red C toners: Organic Dye and Pigment—*mfg*	325132	2865
Petrochemical—*mfg*	32511	2865
Lakes, color: Organic Dye and Pigment—*mfg*	325132	2865
Petrochemical—*mfg*	32511	2865
Lamb: Animal (except Poultry) Slaughtering—*mfg*	311611	2011
Lamb stew: Meat Processed from Carcasses—*mfg*	311612	2013
Laminated Aluminum Foil Manufacturing for Flexible Packaging Uses	**322225**	**3497**
Laminated building paper: Coated and Laminated Paper—*mfg*	322222	2679
Converted Paper Product, All Other—*mfg*	322298	2679
Die-Cut Paper and Paperboard Office Supplies—*mfg*	322231	2679
Non-Folding Sanitary Food Container—*mfg*	322215	2679
Laminated cardboard: Converted Paper Product, All Other—*mfg*	322298	2675
Die-Cut Paper and Paperboard Office Supplies—*mfg*	322231	2675
Surface-Coated Paperboard—*mfg*	322292	2675
Laminated glass, made from glass produced in the same establishment: Flat Glass—*mfg*	327211	3211
Laminated glass, made from purchased glass: Glass Product Made of Purchased Glass—*mfg*	327215	3231
Laminated plastics plate, rods, and tube sand sheet, except flexible packaging: Laminated Plastics Plate, Sheet and Shape—*mfg*	32613	3083
Laminated Plastics Plate, Sheet and Shape Manufacturing	**32613**	**3083**
Laminating compounds: Adhesive—*mfg*	32552	2891
Laminating of fabrics: Fabric Coating Mills—*mfg*	31332	2295
Laminating of photographs (coating photographs with plastics): Business Service Centers (including Copy Shops), Other—*admin*	561439	7389
Laminating steel for the trade: Electroplating, Plating, Polishing, Anodizing and Coloring—*mfg*	332813	3399
Iron and Steel Mills—*mfg*	331111	3399
Secondary Smelting, Refining, and Alloying of Nonferrous Metal (except Copper and Aluminum)—*mfg*	331492	3399
Lamp (bulb) parts, electric: Electric Lamp Bulb and Part—*mfg*	33511	3641
Lamp and shade shops: Home Furnishings Stores, All Other—*retail*	442299	5719
Window Treatment Stores—*retail*	442291	5719
Lamp bases, onyx: Cut Stone and Stone Product—*mfg*	327991	3281
Lamp bases, plastics: Plastics Pipe and Pipe Fitting—*mfg*	326122	3089
Plastics Product, All Other—*mfg*	326199	3089
Unsupported Plastics Profile Shape—*mfg*	326121	3089
Lamp bases, pottery: Vitreous China, Fine Earthenware and Other Pottery Product—*mfg*	327112	3269
Lamp black: Carbon Black—*mfg*	325182	2816
Inorganic Dye and Pigment—*mfg*	325131	2816
Lamp bulbs: Building Material Dealers, Other—*retail*	44419	5063
Electrical Apparatus and Equipment, Wiring Supplies and Material—*whlse*	42161	5063
Lamp bulbs and tubes, electric–incandescent filament, fluorescent, and vapor: Electric Lamp Bulb and Part—*mfg*	33511	3641
Lamp bulbs and tubes, health–infrared and ultraviolet radiation: Electric Lamp Bulb and Part—*mfg*	33511	3641
Lamp fixtures, infrared: Lighting Equipment, Other—*mfg*	335129	3648
Lamp frames, wire–made from purchased wire: Fabricated Wire Product, Other—*mfg*	332618	3496
Lamp making machinery, incandescent: Industrial Machinery, All Other—*mfg*	333298	3559
Machinery, Other Commercial and Service Industry—*mfg*	333319	3559
Lamp parts, glass: Pressed and Blown Glass and Glassware, Other—*mfg*	327212	3229
Lamp posts, metal: Ornamental and Architectural Metal Work—*mfg*	332323	3446
Lamp shade frames: Fabricated Metal Product, All Other Miscellaneous—*mfg*	332999	3999
Residential Electric Lighting Fixture—*mfg*	335121	3999
Lamp shades, glass: Pressed and Blown Glass and Glassware, Other—*mfg*	327212	3229
Lamp shades, metal: Residential Electric Lighting Fixture—*mfg*	335121	3645
Lamp shades, plastics: Plastics Pipe and Pipe Fitting—*mfg*	326122	3089
Plastics Product, All Other—*mfg*	326199	3089
Unsupported Plastics Profile Shape—*mfg*	326121	3089
Lamp shades–except metal and glass: Residential Electric Lighting Fixture—*mfg*	335121	3999
Lamp sockets and receptacles (electric wiring devices): Current-Carrying Wiring Device—*mfg*	335931	3643
Lamps (lighting fixtures), residential–electric: Residential Electric Lighting Fixture—*mfg*	335121	3645
Lamps, glow: Electric Lamp Bulb and Part—*mfg*	33511	3641
Lamps, insect–electric: Lighting Equipment, Other—*mfg*	335129	3699
Lamps, marker and clearance–motor vehicle: Vehicular Lighting Equipment—*mfg*	336321	3647
Lamps, sealed beam: Electric Lamp Bulb and Part—*mfg*	33511	3641
Lamps, slit (ophthalmic goods): Surgical and Medical Instrument—*mfg*	339112	3841
Lamps, X-ray: Irradiation Apparatus—*mfg*	334517	3844
Lamps–floor, boudoir, desk: Home Furnishing—*whlse*	42122	5023
Land clearing–contractors: Heavy, All Other—*const*	23499	1629

ALPHABETICAL INDEX	NAICS	SIC
Industrial Nonbuilding Structure—*const*	23493	1629
Land drainage–contractors: Heavy, All Other—*const*	23499	1629
Industrial Nonbuilding Structure—*const*	23493	1629
Land leveling (irrigation)–contractors: Heavy, All Other—*const*	23499	1629
Industrial Nonbuilding Structure—*const*	23493	1629
Land management agencies: Land, Mineral, Wildlife, and Forest Conservation—*pub*	92412	9512
Land preparation machinery, agricultural: Farm and Garden Machinery and Equipment—*whlse*	42182	5083
Outdoor Power Equipment Stores—*retail*	44421	5083
Land reclamation–contractors: Heavy, All Other—*const*	23499	1629
Industrial Nonbuilding Structure—*const*	23493	1629
Land rollers and levelers (agricultural machinery): Farm Machinery and Equipment—*mfg*	333111	3523
Land Subdivision and Land Development	**2331**	
Land Subdivision and Land Development	**23311**	**6552**
Land surveying: Geophysical Surveying and Mapping Services—*prof*	54136	8713
Surveying and Mapping (except Geophysical) Services—*prof*	54137	8713
Land, Mineral, Wildlife, and Forest Conservation	**92412**	**9512**
Landfill, sanitary–operation of: Hazardous Waste Collection—*admin*	562112	4953
Hazardous Waste Treatment and Disposal—*admin*	562211	4953
Materials Recovery Facilities—*admin*	56292	4953
Nonhazardous Waste Treatment and Disposal, Other—*admin*	562219	4953
Solid Waste Collection—*admin*	562111	4953
Solid Waste Combustors and Incinerators—*admin*	562213	4953
Solid Waste Landfill—*admin*	562212	4953
Waste Collection, Other—*admin*	562119	4953
Landholding offices: Lessors of Other Real Estate Property—*real*	53119	6519
Landing gear, aircraft: Aircraft Part and Auxiliary Equipment, Other—*mfg*	336413	3728
Fluid Power Valve and Hose Fitting—*mfg*	332912	3728
Landing mats, aircraft–metal: Fabricated Structural Metal—*mfg*	332312	3449
Metal Window and Door—*mfg*	332321	3449
Ornamental and Architectural Metal Work—*mfg*	332323	3449
Roll Forming, Custom—*mfg*	332114	3449
Landing ships, building and repairing: Ship Building and Repairing—*mfg*	336611	3731
Landing skis and tracks, aircraft: Aircraft Part and Auxiliary Equipment, Other—*mfg*	336413	3728
Fluid Power Valve and Hose Fitting—*mfg*	332912	3728
Landscape architects: Landscape Architectural Services—*prof*	54132	781
Scientific and Technical Consulting Services, Other—*prof*	54169	781
Landscape Architectural Services	**54132**	**781**
Landscape counseling: Landscape Architectural Services—*prof*	54132	781
Scientific and Technical Consulting Services, Other—*prof*	54169	781
Landscape planning: Landscape Architectural Services—*prof*	54132	781
Scientific and Technical Consulting Services, Other—*prof*	54169	781

ALPHABETICAL INDEX	NAICS	SIC
Landscaping Services	**56173**	**783**
Language Schools	**61163**	**8299**
Language schools: Fine Arts Schools—*educ*	61161	8299
Lantern globes, glass–pressed or blown: Pressed and Blown Glass and Glassware, Other—*mfg*	327212	3229
Lantern slide plates, sensitized: Photographic and Photocopying Equipment—*mfg*	333315	3861
Photographic Film, Paper, Plate and Chemical—*mfg*	325992	3861
Lanterns, halloween–papier mache: Coated and Laminated Paper—*mfg*	322222	2679
Converted Paper Product, All Other—*mfg*	322298	2679
Die-Cut Paper and Paperboard Office Supplies—*mfg*	322231	2679
Non-Folding Sanitary Food Container—*mfg*	322215	2679
Lanterns–electric, gas, carbide, kerosene, and gasoline: Lighting Equipment, Other—*mfg*	335129	3648
Lapidary equipment: Industrial Machinery and Equipment—*whlse*	42183	5085
Industrial Supplies—*whlse*	42184	5085
Lapidary work, contract and other: Jewelers' Material and Lapidary Work—*mfg*	339913	3915
Lapping machines: Machine Tool (Metal Cutting Types)—*mfg*	333512	3541
Lard: Animal (except Poultry) Slaughtering—*mfg*	311611	2011
Meat and Meat Product—*whlse*	42247	5147
Meat Processed from Carcasses—*mfg*	311612	2013
Meat Processed from Carcasses—*mfg*	311612	5147
Laser diodes: Semiconductor and Related Device—*mfg*	334413	3674
Laser Systems and equipment, medical: Electromedical and Electrotherapeutic Apparatus—*mfg*	334510	3845
Irradiation Apparatus—*mfg*	334517	3845
Laser welding, drilling and cutting equipment: Electrical Equipment and Component, All Other Miscellaneous—*mfg*	335999	3699
Machinery, Other Commercial and Service Industry—*mfg*	333319	3699
Lashes (whips): Leather Good, All Other—*mfg*	316999	3199
Last blocks, wood–hewn or riven: Logging—*ag*	11331	2411
Last sole patterns, regardless of material: Manufacturing, All Other Miscellaneous—*mfg*	339999	2499
Wood Container and Pallet—*mfg*	32192	2499
Wood Product, All Other Miscellaneous—*mfg*	321999	2499
Lasts, boot and shoe–regardless of material: Manufacturing, All Other Miscellaneous—*mfg*	339999	2499
Wood Container and Pallet—*mfg*	32192	2499
Wood Product, All Other Miscellaneous—*mfg*	321999	2499
Latex, foamed: Fabric Coating Mills—*mfg*	31332	3069
Rubber Product, All Other—*mfg*	326299	3069
Lath, expanded metal: Fabricated Structural Metal—*mfg*	332312	3449
Metal Window and Door—*mfg*	332321	3449
Ornamental and Architectural Metal Work—*mfg*	332323	3449
Roll Forming, Custom—*mfg*	332114	3449

Lath, fiber: Reconstituted Wood Product—*mfg*	321219	2493
Lath, gypsum: Gypsum and Gypsum Product—*mfg*	32742	3275
Lath, made in sawmills and lathmills: Cut Stock, Resawing Lumber, and Planing—*mfg*	321912	2421
Millwork (including Flooring), Other—*mfg*	321918	2421
Sawmills—*mfg*	321113	2421
Wood Product, All Other Miscellaneous—*mfg*	321999	2421
Lath, woven wire–made from purchased wire: Fabricated Wire Product, Other—*mfg*	332618	3496
Lathe attachments and cutting tools (machine tool accessories): Cutting Tool and Machine Tool Accessory—*mfg*	333515	3545
Hand and Edge Tool—*mfg*	332212	3545
Lathes, metal cutting: Machine Tool (Metal Cutting Types)—*mfg*	333512	3541
Lathes, metal polishing: Machine Tool (Metal Cutting Types)—*mfg*	333512	3541
Lathes, spinning: Machine Tool (Metal Forming Types)—*mfg*	333513	3542
Lathes, wood turning–including accessories: Sawmill and Woodworking Machinery—*mfg*	33321	3553
Lathing–contractors: Drywall, Plastering, Acoustical and Insulation Contractors—*const*	23542	1742
Latigo leather: Leather and Hide Tanning and Finishing—*mfg*	31611	3111
Laundered mat and rug supply service: Industrial Launderers—*serv*	812332	7218
Launderers, industrial: Industrial Launderers—*serv*	812332	7218
Launderettes: Coin-Operated Laundries and Drycleaners—*serv*	81231	7215
Laundries, automotive: Car Washes—*serv*	811192	7542
Laundries, except power and coin-operated: Laundry Services, All Other—*serv*	812399	7219
Laundries, Family and Commercial	**812321**	**7211**
Laundries, power–family and commercial: Laundries, Family and Commercial—*serv*	812321	7211
Laundromats: Coin-Operated Laundries and Drycleaners—*serv*	81231	7215
Laundry collecting and distributing outlets operated by power laundries: Laundries, Family and Commercial—*serv*	812321	7211
Laundry containers on wheels: Fabricated Metal Product, All Other Miscellaneous—*mfg*	332999	3537
Industrial Truck, Tractor, Trailer and Stacker Machinery—*mfg*	333924	3537
Metal Container, Other—*mfg*	332439	3537
Laundry equipment and supplies: Cosmetics, Beauty Supplies and Perfume Stores—*retail*	44612	5087
Service Establishment Equipment and Supplies—*whlse*	42185	5087
Laundry fabrics, cotton: Broadwoven Fabric Mills—*mfg*	31321	2211
Laundry hampers, sheet metal: Metal Container, Other—*mfg*	332439	3444
Sheet Metal Work—*mfg*	332322	3444
Laundry machine routes, coin-operated: Coin-Operated Laundries and Drycleaners—*serv*	81231	7215
Laundry machinery and equipment, commercial, including coin-operated: Laundry, Drycleaning and Pressing Machine, Commercial—*mfg*	333312	3582
Laundry machinery, household, including coin-operated: Household Laundry Equipment—*mfg*	335224	3633
Laundry nets: Broadwoven Fabric Mills—*mfg*	31321	2211
Laundry Services	**8123**	
Laundry Services, All Other	**812399**	**7219**
Laundry Services, Other	**81239**	
Laundry soap, chips, and powder-whole-sale: Chemical and Allied Products, Other—*whlse*	42269	5169
Laundry sours: Basic Organic Chemical, All Other—*mfg*	325199	2899
Chemical Product, All Other Miscellaneous—*mfg*	325998	2899
Laundry trays, concrete: Concrete Pipe—*mfg*	327332	3272
Concrete Product, Other—*mfg*	32739	3272
Nonmetallic Mineral Product, All Other Miscellaneous—*mfg*	327999	3272
Laundry trays, vitreous china: Vitreous China Plumbing Fixture and China and Earthenware Fittings and Bathroom Accessories—*mfg*	327111	3261
Laundry tubs, enameled iron and other metal: Enameled Iron and Metal Sanitary Ware—*mfg*	332998	3431
Laundry tubs, plastics: Plastics Plumbing Fixture—*mfg*	326191	3088
Laundry, Drycleaning and Pressing Machine Manufacturing, Commercial	**333312**	**3582**
Lauric acid esters: Basic Organic Chemical, All Other—*mfg*	325199	2869
Lavatories enameled iron and other metal: Enameled Iron and Metal Sanitary Ware—*mfg*	332998	3431
Lavatories, plastics: Plastics Plumbing Fixture—*mfg*	326191	3088
Lavatories, vitreous china: Vitreous China Plumbing Fixture and China and Earthenware Fittings and Bathroom Accessories—*mfg*	327111	3261
Law enforcement statistics centers: Justice, Public Order, and Safety, All Other—*pub*	92219	9229
Law offices: Lawyers, Offices Of—*prof*	54111	8111
Lawn and Garden Equipment and Supplies Stores	**4442**	
Lawn and Garden Tractor and Home Lawn and Garden Equipment Manufacturing	**333112**	**3524**
Lawn care: Landscaping Services—*admin*	56173	782
Lawn edgers, power: Hand and Edge Tool—*mfg*	332212	3524
Lawn and Garden Tractor and Home Lawn and Garden Equipment—*mfg*	333112	3524
Lawn fertilizing services: Landscaping Services—*admin*	56173	782
Lawn furniture: Furniture—*whlse*	42121	5021
Furniture Stores—*retail*	44211	5021
Lawn furniture, metal: Metal Household Furniture—*mfg*	337124	2514
Lawn furniture–except wood, metal, stone, and concrete: Household Furniture (except Wood and Metal)—*mfg*	337125	2519
Lawn machinery and equipment: Farm and Garden Machinery and Equipment—*whlse*	42182	5083
Outdoor Power Equipment Stores—*retail*	44421	5083
Lawn mowing services: Landscaping Services—*admin*	56173	782
Lawn mulching services: Landscaping Services—*admin*	56173	782
Lawn rollers, residential: Hand and Edge Tool—*mfg*	332212	3524

ALPHABETICAL INDEX	NAICS	SIC
Lawn and Garden Tractor and Home Lawn and Garden Equipment—*mfg*	333112	3524
Lawn seeding services: Landscaping Services—*admin*	56173	782
Lawn spraying services: Landscaping Services—*admin*	56173	782
Lawn sprigging services: Landscaping Services—*admin*	56173	782
Lawn sprinkler system installation–contractors: Plumbing, Heating and Air-Conditioning Contractors—*const*	23511	1711
Lawnmower repair shops: Home and Garden Equipment Repair and Maintenance—*serv*	811411	7699
Machinery and Equipment (except Automotive and Electronic) Repair and Maintenance, Commercial and Industrial—*serv*	81131	7699
Lawnmowers: Nursery and Garden Centers—*retail*	44422	5261
Outdoor Power Equipment Stores—*retail*	44421	5261
Stores (except Tobacco Stores), All Other Miscellaneous—*retail*	453998	5261
Lawnmowers, hand and power–residential: Hand and Edge Tool—*mfg*	332212	3524
Lawn and Garden Tractor and Home Lawn and Garden Equipment—*mfg*	333112	3524
Lawns, cotton: Broadwoven Fabric Mills—*mfg*	31321	2211
Lawyers: Lawyers, Offices Of—*prof*	54111	8111
Lawyers, Offices Of	**54111**	**8111**
Laxatives: Pharmaceutical Preparation—*mfg*	325412	2834
Leaching of uranium, radium or vanadium ores at mine site: Uranium-Radium-Vanadium Ore—*mining*	212291	1094
Lead: Metal Service Centers and Offices—*whlse*	42151	5051
Lead acid batteries (storage batteries): Storage Battery—*mfg*	335911	3691
Lead and lead alloy bars, pipe, plates, rods, sheets, strip, and tubing: Nonferrous Metal (except Copper and Aluminum) Rolling, Drawing and Extruding—*mfg*	331491	3356
Lead arsenate, formulated: Pesticide and Other Agricultural Chemical—*mfg*	32532	2879
Lead azide (explosives): Explosives—*mfg*	32592	2892
Lead burning–contractors: Trade Contractors, All Other Special—*const*	23599	1799
Lead die-castings: Nonferrous (except Aluminum) Die-Castings—*mfg*	331522	3364
Lead foil, not made in rolling mills: Fabricated Metal Product, All Other Miscellaneous—*mfg*	332999	3497
Laminated Aluminum Foil for Flexible Packaging Uses—*mfg*	322225	3497
Lead ore: Coal and Other Mineral and Ore—*whlse*	42152	5052
Lead Ore and Zinc Ore Mining	**212231**	**1031**
Lead ore mining: Lead Ore and Zinc Ore—*mining*	212231	1031
Lead oxide pigments: Carbon Black—*mfg*	325182	2816
Inorganic Dye and Pigment—*mfg*	325131	2816
Lead oxides, other than pigments: Basic Inorganic Chemical, All Other—*mfg*	325188	2819
Chemical Product, All Other Miscellaneous—*mfg*	325998	2819
Lead Pencil and Art Good Manufacturing	**339942**	**3579**
Lead pigments: Carbon Black—*mfg*	325182	2816
Inorganic Dye and Pigment—*mfg*	325131	2816
Lead pigs, blocks, ingots, and refinery shapes–primary: Primary Smelting and Refining of Nonferrous Metal (except Copper and Aluminum)—*mfg*	331419	3339
Lead rolling, drawing, and extruding: Nonferrous Metal (except Copper and Aluminum) Rolling, Drawing and Extruding—*mfg*	331491	3356
Lead silicate: Basic Inorganic Chemical, All Other—*mfg*	325188	2819
Chemical Product, All Other Miscellaneous—*mfg*	325998	2819
Lead smelting and refining, primary: Primary Smelting and Refining of Nonferrous Metal (except Copper and Aluminum)—*mfg*	331419	3339
Lead smelting and refining, secondary: Secondary Smelting and Alloying of Aluminum—*mfg*	331314	3341
Secondary Smelting, Refining, and Alloying of Nonferrous Metal (except Copper and Aluminum)—*mfg*	331492	3341
Lead, black (natural graphite)–ground, refined, or blended: Ground or Treated Mineral and Earth—*mfg*	327992	3295
Lead-in oil paints: Paint and Coating—*mfg*	32551	2851
Lead-in wires, electric lamp–made from purchased wire: Electric Lamp Bulb and Part—*mfg*	33511	3641
Lead-zinc ore mining: Lead Ore and Zinc Ore—*mining*	212231	1031
Leaded glass, made from purchased glass: Glass Product Made of Purchased Glass—*mfg*	327215	3231
Leads, printers': Printing Machinery and Equipment—*mfg*	333293	3555
Leaf skimmers and swimming pool rakes: Hand and Edge Tool—*mfg*	332212	3423
Leaf springs–automobile, locomotive, and other vehicle: Steel Spring (except Wire)—*mfg*	332611	3493
Leaf, metal: Fabricated Metal Product, All Other Miscellaneous—*mfg*	332999	3497
Laminated Aluminum Foil for Flexible Packaging Uses—*mfg*	322225	3497
Leak detectors, water: Fabricated Metal Product, All Other Miscellaneous—*mfg*	332999	3599
General Purpose Machinery , All Other—*mfg*	333999	3599
Machine Shops—*mfg*	33271	3599
Machinery, Other Commercial and Service Industry—*mfg*	333319	3599
Lease tanks, oil and gas field–erecting, cleaning, and repairing-on a contractbasis: Oil and Gas Operations Support Activities—*mining*	213112	1389
Leasing of computer time: Data Processing Services—*info*	51421	7374
Leasing of computers, except finance leasing or by the manufacturer: Office Machinery and Equipment Rental and Leasing—*real*	53242	7377
Leather and Allied Product Manufacturing	**316**	
Leather and Allied Product Manufacturing, Other	**3169**	
Leather and Allied Product Manufacturing, Other	**31699**	

Leather and cut stock: Nondurable Goods, Other Miscellaneous—*whlse*	42299	5199
Leather and Hide Tanning and Finishing	**31611**	**3999**
Leather and Hide Tanning and Finishing	**3161**	
Leather and sheep-lined clothing, men's and boys': Men's and Boys' Clothing and Furnishings—*whlse*	42232	5136
Leather and sheep-lined clothing–women and children's: Women's, Children's, and Infants' and Accessories—*whlse*	42233	5137
Leather belting for machinery–flat, solid, twisted, and built-up: Leather Good, All Other—*mfg*	316999	3199
Leather belting, packing: Industrial Machinery and Equipment—*whlse*	42183	5085
Industrial Supplies—*whlse*	42184	5085
Leather coloring, cutting, embossing, japanning, and welting: Leather and Hide Tanning and Finishing—*mfg*	31611	3111
Leather converters: Leather and Hide Tanning and Finishing—*mfg*	31611	3111
Leather dressings and finishes: Polish and Other Sanitation Good—*mfg*	325612	2842
Leather dyes and stains, synthetic: Organic Dye and Pigment—*mfg*	325132	2865
Petrochemical—*mfg*	32511	2865
Leather finishing agents: Surface Active Agent—*mfg*	325613	2843
Leather gloves or mittens: Glove and Mitten—*mfg*	315992	3151
Leather Good Manufacturing, All Other	**316999**	**3199**
Leather goods repair shops: Footwear and Leather Goods Repair—*serv*	81143	7699
Leather goods, except footwear, gloves, luggage, and belting: Nondurable Goods, Other Miscellaneous—*whlse*	42299	5199
Leather goods, including goods made to individual order: Luggage and Leather Goods Stores—*retail*	44832	5948
Leather goods, small–personal: Personal Leather Good (except Women's Handbag and Purse)—*mfg*	316993	3172
Leather welting: Fastener, Button, Needle and Pin—*mfg*	339993	3131
Leather Good, All Other—*mfg*	316999	3131
Wood Product, All Other Miscellaneous—*mfg*	321999	3131
Leather working machinery: Industrial Machinery, All Other—*mfg*	333298	3559
Machinery, Other Commercial and Service Industry—*mfg*	333319	3559
Leather, artificial or imitation: Fabric Coating Mills—*mfg*	31332	2295
Leather–tanning, currying, and finishing: Leather and Hide Tanning and Finishing—*mfg*	31611	3111
Leatherboard: Paperboard Mills—*mfg*	32213	2631
Leavening compounds, prepared: Food, All Other Miscellaneous—*mfg*	311999	2099
Lecithin, cottonseed: Fats and Oils Refining and Blending—*mfg*	311225	2074
Oilseed Processing, Other—*mfg*	311223	2074
Lecithin, soybean: Fats and Oils Refining and Blending—*mfg*	311225	2075
Soybean Processing—*mfg*	311222	2075
Lecturers: Independent Artists, Writers, and Performers—*arts*	71151	8999
Ledgers and ledger sheets: Blankbook, Loose-leaf Binder and Device—*mfg*	323118	2782
Flexographic Printing, Commercial—*mfg*	323112	2782
Gravure Printing, Commercial—*mfg*	323111	2782
Lithographic Printing, Commercial—*mfg*	323110	2782
Printing, Other Commercial—*mfg*	323119	2782
Screen Printing, Commercial—*mfg*	323113	2782
Leeks and lock sets–except safe, vault, and coin-operated: Hardware—*mfg*	33251	3429
Leeks, trigger, for guns: Hardware—*mfg*	33251	3429
Leg warmers: Hosiery and Sock Mills, Other—*mfg*	315119	2252
Sheer Hosiery Mills—*mfg*	315111	2252
Legal aid services: Lawyers, Offices Of—*prof*	54111	8111
Legal Counsel and Prosecution	**92213**	**9222**
Legal counsel offices: Legal Counsel and Prosecution—*pub*	92213	9222
Legal reserve life insurance: Direct Life Insurance Carriers—*fin*	524113	6311
Reinsurance Carriers—*fin*	52413	6311
Legal Services	**5411**	
Legal services: Lawyers, Offices Of—*prof*	54111	8111
Legal Services, All Other	**541199**	**7389**
Legal Services, Other	**54119**	
Leggings, welders'–leather: Leather Good, All Other—*mfg*	316999	3199
Legislative and executive office combinations: Executive and Legislative Offices, Combined—*pub*	92114	9131
Legislative assemblies: Legislative Bodies—*pub*	92112	9121
Legislative Bodies	**92112**	**9121**
Legitimate theater producers: Promoters of Performing Arts, Sports and Similar Events without Facilities—*arts*	71132	7922
Lemon groves and farms: Citrus (except Orange) Groves—*ag*	11132	174
Orange Groves—*ag*	11131	174
Lemon oil: Spice and Extract—*mfg*	311942	2899
Lemonade–bottled, canned, or fresh: Bottled Water—*mfg*	312112	2086
Soft Drink—*mfg*	312111	2086
Lending libraries: Libraries and Archives—*info*	51412	8231
Leno fabrics, cotton: Broadwoven Fabric Mills—*mfg*	31321	2211
Leno fabrics, manmade fiber and silk: Broadwoven Fabric Mills—*mfg*	31321	2221
Lens blanks, optical and ophthalmic: Pressed and Blown Glass and Glassware, Other—*mfg*	327212	3229
Lens coating: Optical Instrument and Lens—*mfg*	333314	3827
Lens coating, ophthalmic: Ophthalmic Goods—*mfg*	339115	3851
Lens grinding, except ophthalmic: Optical Instrument and Lens—*mfg*	333314	3827
Lens grinding, ophthalmic, except prescription: Ophthalmic Goods—*mfg*	339115	3851
Lens mounts: Optical Instrument and Lens—*mfg*	333314	3827
Lens shades, camera: Photographic and Photocopying Equipment—*mfg*	333315	3861
Photographic Film, Paper, Plate and Chemical—*mfg*	325992	3861
Lenses, glass–for lanterns, flashlights, headlights, and searchlights: Pressed and Blown Glass and Glassware, Other—*mfg*	327212	3229
Lenses, ophthalmic: Ophthalmic Goods—*mfg*	339115	3851

ALPHABETICAL INDEX	NAICS	SIC
Ophthalmic Goods—*whlse*	42146	5048
Lenses, optical–photographic, magnifying, projection, and instrument: Optical Instrument and Lens—*mfg*	333314	3827
Lenses, plastics–except ophthalmic or optical: Plastics Pipe and Pipe Fitting—*mfg*	326122	3089
Plastics Product, All Other—*mfg*	326199	3089
Unsupported Plastics Profile Shape—*mfg*	326121	3089
Lentil farms: Grain Farming, All Other—*ag*	111199	119
Leotards: Apparel Accessories and Apparel, Other—*mfg*	315999	2339
Cut and Sew Apparel, All Other—*mfg*	315299	2339
Outerwear Knitting Mills—*mfg*	315191	2253
Women's and Girls' Cut and Sew Apparel Contractors—*mfg*	315212	2339
Women's and Girls' Cut and Sew Other Outerwear—*mfg*	315238	2339
Lepidolite mining: Chemical and Fertilizer Mineral, Other—*mining*	212393	1479
Lergnettes: Ophthalmic Goods—*mfg*	339115	3851
Lessors of Miniwarehouses and Self Storage Units	**53113**	**4225**
Lessors of Nonresidential Buildings (except Miniwarehouses)	**53112**	**6512**
Lessors of Other Real Estate Property	**53119**	**6517**
Lessors of piers, docks, and associated buildings and facilities: Lessors of Nonresidential Buildings (except Miniwarehouses)—*real*	53112	6512
Promoters of Performing Arts, Sports and Similar Events with Facilities—*arts*	71131	6512
Lessors of property, except railroad, buildings, or mobile home sites: Lessors of Other Real Estate Property—*real*	53119	6519
Lessors of railroad property: Lessors of Other Real Estate Property—*real*	53119	6517
Lessors of Real Estate	**5311**	
Lessors of Residential Buildings and Dwellings	**53111**	**6514**
Letter delivery, private–air: Couriers—*trans*	49211	4513
Letter delivery, private–except air: Couriers—*trans*	49211	4215
Local Messengers and Local Delivery—*trans*	49221	4215
Letter folding, stuffing, and sealing machines: Lead Pencil and Art Good—*mfg*	339942	3579
Office Machinery—*mfg*	333313	3579
Watch, Clock, and Part—*mfg*	334518	3579
Letter pins (gauging and measuring): Cutting Tool and Machine Tool Accessory—*mfg*	333515	3545
Hand and Edge Tool—*mfg*	332212	3545
Letter writing service: Court Reporting and Stenotype Services—*admin*	561492	7338
Document Preparation Services—*admin*	56141	7338
Lettering instruments, artists': Chemical Product, All Other Miscellaneous—*mfg*	325998	3952
Institutional Furniture—*mfg*	337127	3952
Lead Pencil and Art Good—*mfg*	339942	3952

ALPHABETICAL INDEX	NAICS	SIC
Lettering service: Business Service Centers (including Copy Shops), Other—*admin*	561439	7389
Letterpress ink: Printing Ink—*mfg*	32591	2893
Letterpress plates, preparation of: Prepress Services—*mfg*	323122	2796
Letterpress printing: Digital Printing—*mfg*	323115	2759
Flexographic Printing, Commercial—*mfg*	323112	2759
Printing, Other Commercial—*mfg*	323119	2759
Quick Printing—*mfg*	323114	2759
Letters (marking devices), metal: Marking Device—*mfg*	339943	3953
Letters for signs, metal: Sign—*mfg*	33995	3993
Letters, cardboard: Converted Paper Product, All Other—*mfg*	322298	2675
Die-Cut Paper and Paperboard Office Supplies—*mfg*	322231	2675
Surface-Coated Paperboard—*mfg*	322292	2675
Letters, circular and form–except lithographed or gravure printed: Digital Printing—*mfg*	323115	2759
Flexographic Printing, Commercial—*mfg*	323112	2759
Printing, Other Commercial—*mfg*	323119	2759
Quick Printing—*mfg*	323114	2759
Letters, circular and form–gravure printing: Gravure Printing, Commercial—*mfg*	323111	2754
Letters, circular and form–lithographed: Lithographic Printing, Commercial—*mfg*	323110	2752
Quick Printing—*mfg*	323114	2752
Letters, wood: Manufacturing, All Other Miscellaneous—*mfg*	339999	2499
Wood Container and Pallet—*mfg*	32192	2499
Wood Product, All Other Miscellaneous—*mfg*	321999	2499
Lettuce farms: Vegetable (except Potato) and Melon Farming, Other—*ag*	111219	161
Levee construction–general contractors: Heavy, All Other—*const*	23499	1629
Industrial Nonbuilding Structure—*const*	23493	1629
Level and bulk measuring instruments, industrial process type: Instruments and Related Products for Measuring, Displaying, and Controlling Industrial Process Variables—*mfg*	334513	3823
Level gauges, radiation type: Measuring and Controlling Device, Other—*mfg*	334519	3829
Surgical and Medical Instrument—*mfg*	339112	3829
Level vials for instruments, glass: Pressed and Blown Glass and Glassware, Other—*mfg*	327212	3229
Levelers, roller (rolling mill equipment): Rolling Mill Machinery and Equipment—*mfg*	333516	3547
Levels and tapes, surveying: Measuring and Controlling Device, Other—*mfg*	334519	3829
Surgical and Medical Instrument—*mfg*	339112	3829
Levels, carpenters': Hand and Edge Tool—*mfg*	332212	3423
Liability insurance: Direct Property and Casualty Insurance Carriers—*fin*	524126	6351
Reinsurance Carriers—*fin*	52413	6351

Libraries and Archives	**51412**	**8231**
Libraries, except motion picture film: Libraries and Archives—*info*	51412	8231
Libraries, printed matter: Libraries and Archives—*info*	51412	8231
Library binders, looseleaf: Blankbook, Loose-leaf Binder and Device—*mfg*	323118	2782
Flexographic Printing, Commercial—*mfg*	323112	2782
Gravure Printing, Commercial—*mfg*	323111	2782
Lithographic Printing, Commercial—*mfg*	323110	2782
Printing, Other Commercial—*mfg*	323119	2782
Screen Printing, Commercial—*mfg*	323113	2782
Library' cards, paperboard: Converted Paper Product, All Other—*mfg*	322298	2675
Die-Cut Paper and Paperboard Office Supplies—*mfg*	322231	2675
Surface-Coated Paperboard—*mfg*	322292	2675
Licensing and inspection of transportation facilities and services: Air Traffic Control—*trans*	488111	9621
Transportation Programs, Regulation and Administration of—*pub*	92612	9621
Licensing and inspection of utilities: Regulation and Administration of Communications, Electric, Gas, and Other Utilities—*pub*	92613	9631
Licensing and permit for professional occupations: Regulation, Licensing, and Inspection of Miscellaneous Commercial Sectors—*pub*	92615	9651
Licensing and permit for retail trade: Regulation, Licensing, and Inspection of Miscellaneous Commercial Sectors—*pub*	92615	9651
Licorice candy: Confectionery from Purchased Chocolate—*mfg*	31133	2064
Non-Chocolate Confectionery—*mfg*	31134	2064
Lie detection service: Armored Car Services—*admin*	561613	7381
Investigation Services—*admin*	561611	7381
Security Guards and Patrol Services—*admin*	561612	7381
Life insurance: Direct Life Insurance Carriers—*fin*	524113	6311
Reinsurance Carriers—*fin*	52413	6311
Life insurance agents: Claims Adjusters—*fin*	524291	6411
Insurance Agencies and Brokerages—*fin*	52421	6411
Insurance Related Activities, All Other—*fin*	524298	6411
Third Party Administration for Insurance and Pension Funds—*fin*	524292	6411
Life insurance funds, savings bank: Direct Life Insurance Carriers—*fin*	524113	6311
Reinsurance Carriers—*fin*	52413	6311
Life preservers, cork: Manufacturing, All Other Miscellaneous—*mfg*	339999	2499
Wood Container and Pallet—*mfg*	32192	2499
Wood Product, All Other Miscellaneous—*mfg*	321999	2499
Life preservers, except cork and inflatable: Surgical Appliance and Supplies—*mfg*	339113	3842
Life reinsurance: Direct Life Insurance Carriers—*fin*	524113	6311
Reinsurance Carriers—*fin*	52413	6311
Lifeboats, building and repairing: Boat Building—*mfg*	336612	3732
Personal and Household Goods Repair and Maintenance, Other—*serv*	81149	3732
Lifejackets, plastics: Plastics Pipe and Pipe Fitting—*mfg*	326122	3089
Plastics Product, All Other—*mfg*	326199	3089
Unsupported Plastics Profile Shape—*mfg*	326121	3089
Lifejackets–inflatable rubberized fabric: Fabric Coating Mills—*mfg*	31332	3069
Rubber Product, All Other—*mfg*	326299	3069
Liferafts, except inflatable (rubber andplastics): Boat Building—*mfg*	336612	3732
Personal and Household Goods Repair and Maintenance, Other—*serv*	81149	3732
Liferafts, nonrigid–plastics: Plastics Pipe and Pipe Fitting—*mfg*	326122	3089
Plastics Product, All Other—*mfg*	326199	3089
Unsupported Plastics Profile Shape—*mfg*	326121	3089
Liferafts, rubber: Fabric Coating Mills—*mfg*	31332	3069
Rubber Product, All Other—*mfg*	326299	3069
Lift trucks: Industrial Machinery and Equipment—*whlse*	42183	5084
Lift trucks, industrial–fork, platform, straddle, etc.: Fabricated Metal Product, All Other Miscellaneous—*mfg*	332999	3537
Industrial Truck, Tractor, Trailer and Stacker Machinery—*mfg*	333924	3537
Metal Container, Other—*mfg*	332439	3537
Lifts (elevators), passenger and freight: Elevator and Moving Stairway—*mfg*	333921	3534
Lifts, heel–leather: Fastener, Button, Needle and Pin—*mfg*	339993	3131
Leather Good, All Other—*mfg*	316999	3131
Wood Product, All Other Miscellaneous—*mfg*	321999	3131
Ligatures, medical: Surgical Appliance and Supplies—*mfg*	339113	3842
Light and power plant construction–general contractors: Heavy, All Other—*const*	23499	1629
Industrial Nonbuilding Structure—*const*	23493	1629
Light bulbs, electric: Building Material Dealers, Other—*retail*	44419	5063
Electrical Apparatus and Equipment, Wiring Supplies and Material—*whlse*	42161	5063
Light bulbs, electric–complete: Electric Lamp Bulb and Part—*mfg*	33511	3641
Light communications equipment: Radio and Television Broadcasting and Wireless Communications Equipment—*mfg*	33422	3663
Light emitting diodes: Semiconductor and Related Device—*mfg*	334413	3674
Light meters, photographic: Photographic and Photocopying Equipment—*mfg*	333315	3861
Photographic Film, Paper, Plate and Chemical—*mfg*	325992	3861
Light reconnaissance and surveilance systems and equipment: Search, Detection, Navigation, Guidance, Aeronautical, and Nautical System and Instrument—*mfg*	334511	3812
Light sensing and emitting tubes: Electron Tube—*mfg*	334411	3671
Light sensitive devices, solid-state: Semiconductor and Related Device—*mfg*	334413	3674
Light shades, glass–pressed or blown: Pressed and Blown Glass and Glassware, Other—*mfg*	327212	3229
Light shades, metal: Residential Electric Lighting Fixture—*mfg*	335121	3645
Light sources, standard: Optical Instrument and Lens—*mfg*	333314	3827
Light Truck and Utility Vehicle Manufacturing	**336112**	**3711**
Lighter fluid: Basic Organic Chemical, All Other—*mfg*	325199	2899
Chemical Product, All Other Miscellaneous—*mfg*	325998	2899

ALPHABETICAL INDEX	NAICS	SIC
Lighterage: Air, Rail, and Water Equipment Rental and Leasing, Commercial—*real*	532411	4499
Navigational Services to Shipping—*trans*	48833	4499
Port and Harbor Operations—*trans*	48831	4499
Water, Other Support Activities for—*trans*	48839	4499
Lighters, cigar and cigarette: Nondurable Goods, Other Miscellaneous—*whlse*	42299	5199
Lighters, cigar and cigarette–except precious metal and electric: Fabricated Metal Product, All Other Miscellaneous—*mfg*	332999	3999
Lighters, marine–building and repairing: Ship Building and Repairing—*mfg*	336611	3731
Lighthouse tenders, building and repairing: Ship Building and Repairing—*mfg*	336611	3731
Lighting carbons: Carbon and Graphite Product—*mfg*	335991	3624
Lighting Equipment Manufacturing, Other	**335129**	**3699**
Lighting Fixture Manufacturing	**33512**	
Lighting fixtures, airport–runway, approach, taxi, and ramp: Lighting Equipment, Other—*mfg*	335129	3648
Lighting fixtures, commercial: Electric Lighting Fixture, Commercial, Industrial and Institutional—*mfg*	335122	3646
Lighting fixtures, motor vehicle: Vehicular Lighting Equipment—*mfg*	336321	3647
Lighting fixtures, residential, electric–e.g., garden, patio, walkway, yard: Residential Electric Lighting Fixture—*mfg*	335121	3645
Lighting fixtures, residential, except electric: Lighting Equipment, Other—*mfg*	335129	3648
Lighting fixtures, vehicular: Vehicular Lighting Equipment—*mfg*	336321	3647
Lighting fixtures–residential, commercial, and industrial: Building Material Dealers, Other—*retail*	44419	5063
Electrical Apparatus and Equipment, Wiring Supplies and Material—*whlse*	42161	5063
Lighting glassware, pressed or blown: Pressed and Blown Glass and Glassware, Other—*mfg*	327212	3229
Lighting maintenance service (1)ulb replacement and cleaning): Janitorial Services—*admin*	56172	7349
Lighting transformers, fluorescent: Power, Distribution and Specialty Transformer—*mfg*	335311	3612
Lighting transformers, street and airport: Power, Distribution and Specialty Transformer—*mfg*	335311	3612
Lightning arrestors and coils: Current-Carrying Wiring Device—*mfg*	335931	3643
Lightning conductor erection–contractors: Trade Contractors, All Other Special—*const*	23599	1799
Lightning protection equipment: Current-Carrying Wiring Device—*mfg*	335931	3643
Lights, yard–electric: Residential Electric Lighting Fixture—*mfg*	335121	3645
Lignin plastics: Plastics Material and Resin—*mfg*	325211	2821
Lignite mining: Bituminous Coal and Lignite Surface—*mining*	212111	1221

ALPHABETICAL INDEX	NAICS	SIC
Lignite mining services on a contract basis: Coal Support Activities—*mining*	213113	1241
Limbers, gun and caisson: Ordnance and Accessories, Other—*mfg*	332995	3489
Limbs, artificial: Surgical Appliance and Supplies—*mfg*	339113	3842
Lime and plaster dealers: Building Material Dealers, Other—*retail*	44419	5211
Home Centers—*retail*	44411	5211
Lime bleaching compounds: Basic Inorganic Chemical, All Other—*mfg*	325188	2819
Chemical Product, All Other Miscellaneous—*mfg*	325998	2819
Lime citrate: Basic Organic Chemical, All Other—*mfg*	325199	2869
Lime groves and farms: Citrus (except Orange) Groves—*ag*	11132	174
Orange Groves—*ag*	11131	174
Lime Manufacturing	**32741**	**3274**
Lime plaster: Lime—*mfg*	32741	3274
Lime rock, ground: Crushed and Broken Limestone and Quarrying—*mining*	212312	1422
Lime spreading for crops: Soil Preparation, Planting, and Cultivating—*ag*	115112	711
Lime, agricultural: Farm Supplies—*whlse*	42291	5191
Nursery and Garden Centers—*retail*	44422	5191
Lime, except agricultural: Brick, Stone and Related Material—*whlse*	42132	5032
Building Material Dealers, Other—*retail*	44419	5032
Lime, Gypsum and Gypsum Product Manufacturing	**3274**	
Limestone: Brick, Stone and Related Material—*whlse*	42132	5032
Building Material Dealers, Other—*retail*	44419	5032
Limestone, cut and shaped: Cut Stone and Stone Product—*mfg*	327991	3281
Limestone, dimension: Dimension Stone and Quarrying—*mining*	212311	1411
Limestone, except bituminous–crushed and broken: Crushed and Broken Limestone and Quarrying—*mining*	212312	1422
Limesullur, dry and solution: Pesticide and Other Agricultural Chemical—*mfg*	32532	2879
Limit controls, residential and commercial heating types: Automatic Environmental Control for Residential, Commercial and Appliance Use—*mfg*	334512	3822
Limited price variety stores: General Merchandise Stores, All Other—*retail*	45299	5331
Limited-Service Eating Places	**7222**	
Limited-Service Eating Places	**72221**	
Limited-Service Restaurants	**722211**	**5499**
Limonite mining: Iron Ore—*mining*	21221	1011
Limousine rental with drivers: Limousine Service—*trans*	48532	4119
Transit and Ground Passenger, All Other—*trans*	485999	4119
Transportation, Special Needs—*trans*	485991	4119
Limousine rental, without drivers: Passenger Car Rental—*real*	532111	7514
Limousine Service	**48532**	**4119**
Lindane, formulated: Pesticide and Other Agricultural Chemical—*mfg*	32532	2879

Description	NAICS	SIC
Line markers, self-propelled: Construction Machinery—*mfg*	33312	3531
Overhead Traveling Crane, Hoist and Monorail System—*mfg*	333923	3531
Railroad Rolling Stock—*mfg*	33651	3531
Line or limit control for electric heat: Automatic Environmental Control for Residential, Commercial and Appliance Use—*mfg*	334512	3822
Line strainers, for use in piping systems-metal: Fabricated Metal Product, All Other Miscellaneous—*mfg*	332999	3494
Other Metal Valve and Pipe Fitting, Other—*mfg*	332919	3494
Line voltage regulators: Power, Distribution and Specialty Transformer—*mfg*	335311	3612
Line-Haul Railroads	**482111**	**4011**
Linear accelerators: Electrical Equipment and Component, All Other Miscellaneous—*mfg*	335999	3699
Machinery, Other Commercial and Service Industry—*mfg*	333319	3699
Linear counters: Totalizing Fluid Meter and Counting Device—*mfg*	334514	3824
Linear esters fibers: Noncellulosic Organic Fiber—*mfg*	325222	2824
Linecuts: Prepress Services—*mfg*	323122	2796
Linemen's safety belts: Surgical Appliance and Supplies—*mfg*	339113	3842
Linen and Uniform Supply	**81233**	
Linen fabrics–dyeing, finishing, and printing: Broadwoven Fabric Finishing Mills—*mfg*	313311	2269
Textile and Fabric Finishing (except Broadwoven Fabric) Mills—*mfg*	313312	2269
Linen piece goods: Broadwoven Fabric Finishing Mills—*mfg*	313311	5131
Piece Goods, Notions and Other Dry Goods—*whlse*	42231	5131
Textile and Fabric Finishing (except Broadwoven Fabric) Mills—*mfg*	313312	5131
Linen shops: Home Furnishings Stores, All Other—*retail*	442299	5719
Window Treatment Stores—*retail*	442291	5719
Linen Supply	**812331**	**7219**
Linen supply service: Linen Supply—*serv*	812331	7213
Linens: Home Furnishing—*whlse*	42122	5023
Liner board, kraft and jute: Paperboard Mills—*mfg*	32213	2631
Liner brick and plates, for lining sewers, tanks, etc.–vitrified clay: Structural Clay Product, Other—*mfg*	327123	3259
Liner strips, rubber: Fabric Coating Mills—*mfg*	31332	3069
Rubber Product, All Other—*mfg*	326299	3069
Liners and covers, fabric–pond, pit, andlandfill: Canvas and Related Product Mills—*mfg*	314912	2394
Liners for freight car doors–reinforced with metal strip: Converted Paper Product, All Other—*mfg*	322298	2675
Die-Cut Paper and Paperboard Office Supplies—*mfg*	322231	2675
Surface-Coated Paperboard—*mfg*	322292	2675
Liners, industrial–metal plate: Air-Conditioning and Warm Air Heating Equipment and Commercial and Industrial Refrigeration Equipment—*mfg*	333415	3443
Metal Tank (Heavy Gauge)—*mfg*	33242	3443
Plate Work—*mfg*	332313	3443

Description	NAICS	SIC
Power Boiler and Heat Exchanger—*mfg*	33241	3443
Lingerie: Women's, Children's, and Infants' and Accessories—*whlse*	42233	5137
Lingerie stores: Clothing Accessories Stores—*retail*	44815	5632
Clothing Stores, Other—*retail*	44819	5632
Lingerie, Loungewear and Nightwear Manufacturing, Women's and Girls' Cut and Sew	**315231**	**2342**
Liniments: Pharmaceutical Preparation—*mfg*	325412	2834
Lining fabrics, manmade fiber and silk–except glove lining fabrics: Broadwoven Fabric Mills—*mfg*	31321	2221
Lining leather: Leather and Hide Tanning and Finishing—*mfg*	31611	3111
Lining paper: Newsprint Mills—*mfg*	322122	2621
Paper (except Newsprint) Mills—*mfg*	322121	2621
Lining, stove and flue–clay: Structural Clay Product, Other—*mfg*	327123	3259
Linings, boot and shoe–leather: Fastener, Button, Needle and Pin—*mfg*	339993	3131
Leather Good, All Other—*mfg*	316999	3131
Wood Product, All Other Miscellaneous—*mfg*	321999	3131
Linings, carpet–felt except woven: Broadwoven Fabric Mills—*mfg*	31321	2299
Narrow Fabric Mills—*mfg*	313221	2299
Nonwoven Fabric Mills—*mfg*	31323	2299
Textile and Fabric Finishing (except Broadwoven Fabric) Mills—*mfg*	313312	2299
Textile Product Mills, All Other Miscellaneous—*mfg*	314999	2299
Thread Mills—*mfg*	313113	2299
Yarn Spinning Mills—*mfg*	313111	2299
Linings, carpet–textile, except felt: Household Textile Product Mills, Other—*mfg*	314129	2392
Linings, handbag or pocketbook: Apparel Accessories and Apparel, Other—*mfg*	315999	2396
Textile Product Mills, All Other Miscellaneous—*mfg*	314999	2396
Linings, hat: Apparel Accessories and Apparel, Other—*mfg*	315999	2396
Textile Product Mills, All Other Miscellaneous—*mfg*	314999	2396
Linings, luggage: Apparel Accessories and Apparel, Other—*mfg*	315999	2396
Textile Product Mills, All Other Miscellaneous—*mfg*	314999	2396
Linings, rayon or silk: Broadwoven Fabric Mills—*mfg*	31321	2221
Linings, safe and vault–metal: Metal Container, Other—*mfg*	332439	3499
Linings, shoe: Knit Fabric and Lace Mills, Other—*mfg*	313249	2259
Weft Knit Fabric Mills—*mfg*	313241	2259
Linings, vulcanizable elastomeric–rubber: Fabric Coating Mills—*mfg*	31332	3069
Rubber Product, All Other—*mfg*	326299	3069
Linings–e.g., suit, coat, shirt, skirt, dress, necktie, millinery: Apparel Accessories and Apparel, Other—*mfg*	315999	2396
Textile Product Mills, All Other Miscellaneous—*mfg*	314999	2396
Link trainers (aircraft training mechanisms): Aircraft Part and Auxiliary Equipment, Other—*mfg*	336413	3728
Fluid Power Valve and Hose Fitting—*mfg*	332912	3728
Links for ammunition more than 30 mm. (or more than 1.18 inch): Ordnance and Accessories, Other—*mfg*	332995	3489

ALPHABETICAL INDEX	NAICS	SIC
Links, for ammunition 30 mm. (or 1.18 inch) or less: Small Arms—*mfg*	332994	3484
Linoleates, paint driers: Paint and Coating—*mfg*	32551	2851
Linoleum: Floor Covering Stores—*retail*	44221	5023
Resilient Floor Covering—*mfg*	326192	3996
Linoleum installation–contractors: Floor Laying and Other Floor Contractors—*const*	23552	1752
Linoleum stores: Floor Covering Stores—*retail*	44221	5713
Linotype machines: Printing Machinery and Equipment—*mfg*	333293	3555
Linseed oil: Nondurable Goods, Other Miscellaneous—*whlse*	42299	5199
Linseed oil, cake, and meal: Fats and Oils Refining and Blending—*mfg*	311225	2076
Oilseed Processing, Other—*mfg*	311223	2076
Lintels, concrete: Concrete Pipe—*mfg*	327332	3272
Concrete Product, Other—*mfg*	32739	3272
Nonmetallic Mineral Product, All Other Miscellaneous—*mfg*	327999	3272
Lintels, light gauge steel: Ornamental and Architectural Metal Work—*mfg*	332323	3446
Lip balms: Pharmaceutical Preparation—*mfg*	325412	2834
Lipsticks: Soap and Other Detergent—*mfg*	325611	2844
Toilet Preparation—*mfg*	32562	2844
Liquefied petroleum (LP) gas delivered to customers' premises: Liquefied Petroleum Gas (Bottled Gas) Dealers—*retail*	454312	5984
Liquefied petroleum (LP) gas, distribution through mains: Natural Gas Distribution—*util*	22121	4925
Liquefied Petroleum Gas (Bottled Gas) Dealers	**454312**	**5984**
Liquefied petroleum gases (natural) production: Natural Gas Liquid Extraction—*mining*	211112	1321
Liquid analysis instruments, industrial process type: Instruments and Related Products for Measuring, Displaying, and Controlling Industrial Process Variables—*mfg*	334513	3823
Liquid chromatographic instruments, laboratory type: Analytical Laboratory Instrument—*mfg*	334516	3826
Liquid concentration instruments, industrial process type: Instruments and Related Products for Measuring, Displaying, and Controlling Industrial Process Variables—*mfg*	334513	3823
Liquid crystal displays: Electronic Component, Other—*mfg*	334419	3679
Motor Vehicle Electrical and Electronic Equipment, Other—*mfg*	336322	3679
Printed Circuit/Electronics Assembly—*mfg*	334418	3679
Radio and Television Broadcasting and Wireless Communications Equipment—*mfg*	33422	3679
Liquid level controls, residential and commercial heating types: Automatic Environmental Control for Residential, Commercial and Appliance Use—*mfg*	334512	3822
Liquid level instruments, industrial process type: Instruments and Related Products for Measuring, Displaying, and Controlling Industrial Process Variables—*mfg*	334513	3823

ALPHABETICAL INDEX	NAICS	SIC
Liquid oxygen tanks, metal plate: Air-Conditioning and Warm Air Heating Equipment and Commercial and Industrial Refrigeration Equipment—*mfg*	333415	3443
Metal Tank (Heavy Gauge)—*mfg*	33242	3443
Plate Work—*mfg*	332313	3443
Power Boiler and Heat Exchanger—*mfg*	33241	3443
Liquidators of merchandise on a contract or fee basis: Repossession Services—*admin*	561491	7389
Liquor. packaged: Beer, Wine and Liquor Stores—*retail*	44531	5921
Liquors, distilled: Wine and Distilled Alcoholic Beverage—*whlse*	42282	5182
Liquors, malt: Breweries—*mfg*	31212	2082
Liquors–distilled and blended-except brandy: Distilleries—*mfg*	31214	2085
List finders, automatic: Lead Pencil and Art Good—*mfg*	339942	3579
Office Machinery—*mfg*	333313	3579
Watch, Clock, and Part—*mfg*	334518	3579
Listers: Farm Machinery and Equipment—*mfg*	333111	3523
Listing service, real estate: Real Estate, Other Activities Related to—*real*	53139	6531
Litharge: Carbon Black—*mfg*	325182	2816
Lithium compounds: Basic Inorganic Chemical, All Other—*mfg*	325188	2819
Chemical Product, All Other Miscellaneous—*mfg*	325998	2819
Lithium metal: Basic Inorganic Chemical, All Other—*mfg*	325188	2819
Chemical Product, All Other Miscellaneous—*mfg*	325998	2819
Lithium mineral mining: Chemical and Fertilizer Mineral, Other—*mining*	212393	1479
Lithograph paper: Newsprint Mills—*mfg*	322122	2621
Paper (except Newsprint) Mills—*mfg*	322121	2621
Lithographic ink: Printing Ink—*mfg*	32591	2893
Lithographic plates, positives or negatives–preparation of: Prepress Services—*mfg*	323122	2796
Lithographic Printing, Commercial	**323110**	**2771**
Lithographic stones: Printing Machinery and Equipment—*mfg*	333293	3555
Lithographic varnishes: Paint and Coating—*mfg*	32551	2851
Lithographing on metal or paper: Lithographic Printing, Commercial—*mfg*	323110	2752
Quick Printing—*mfg*	323114	2752
Lithol rubine lakes and toners: Organic Dye and Pigment—*mfg*	325132	2865
Petrochemical—*mfg*	32511	2865
Lithopone: Carbon Black—*mfg*	325182	2816
Lithotripters: Electromedical and Electrotherapeutic Apparatus—*mfg*	334510	3845
Irradiation Apparatus—*mfg*	334517	3845
Litmus paper: Coated and Laminated Paper—*mfg*	322222	2672
Livens projectors (ordnance): Ordnance and Accessories, Other—*mfg*	332995	3489
Livestock and animal specialty farms, general: Animal Production, All Other—*ag*	11299	291
Livestock breeding services: Animal Production Support Activities—*ag*	11521	751

Description	NAICS	SIC
Livestock loan companies: International Trade Financing—*fin*	522293	6159
Non-Depository Credit Intermediation, All Other—*fin*	522298	6159
Sales Financing—*fin*	52222	6159
Livestock Wholesalers	**42252**	**5154**
Livestock, except horses and mules: Livestock—*whlse*	42252	5154
Living room furniture, upholstered on wood frames, except convertible beds: Upholstered Household Furniture—*mfg*	337121	2512
Loaders (garden tractor equipment): Hand and Edge Tool—*mfg*	332212	3524
Lawn and Garden Tractor and Home Lawn and Garden Equipment—*mfg*	333112	3524
Loaders, farm type (general utility): Conveyor and Conveying Equipment—*mfg*	333922	3523
Farm Machinery and Equipment—*mfg*	333111	3523
Loaders, shovel: Construction Machinery—*mfg*	33312	3531
Overhead Traveling Crane, Hoist and Monorail System—*mfg*	333923	3531
Railroad Rolling Stock—*mfg*	33651	3531
Loading and assembling bombs, powder bags, and shells–more than 30 mm. (or more than 1.18 inch): Ammunition (except Small Arms)—*mfg*	332993	3483
Loading machines, underground–mobile: Mining Machinery and Equipment—*mfg*	333131	3532
Loading station construction, mine–general contractors: Heavy, All Other—*const*	23499	1629
Industrial Nonbuilding Structure—*const*	23493	1629
Loading vessels: Marine Cargo Handling—*trans*	48832	4491
Port and Harbor Operations—*trans*	48831	4491
Loads, electronic: Electronic Component, Other—*mfg*	334419	3679
Motor Vehicle Electrical and Electronic Equipment, Other—*mfg*	336322	3679
Printed Circuit/Electronics Assembly—*mfg*	334418	3679
Radio and Television Broadcasting and Wireless Communications Equipment—*mfg*	33422	3679
Loan agents: Mortgage and Other Loan Brokers—*fin*	52231	6163
Loan brokers: Mortgage and Other Loan Brokers—*fin*	52231	6163
Loan companies, small–licensed: Consumer Lending—*fin*	522291	6141
Credit Card Issuing—*fin*	52221	6141
Sales Financing—*fin*	52222	6141
Loan correspondents: Credit Intermediation, Other Activities Related to—*fin*	52239	6162
Real Estate Credit—*fin*	522292	6162
Loan institutions, general and industrial: International Trade Financing—*fin*	522293	6159
Non-Depository Credit Intermediation, All Other—*fin*	522298	6159
Sales Financing—*fin*	52222	6159
Loan societies, remedial: Consumer Lending—*fin*	522291	6141
Credit Card Issuing—*fin*	52221	6141
Sales Financing—*fin*	52222	6141
Lobbyists: Public Relations Agencies—*prof*	54182	8743
Lobsters, catching of: Shellfish Fishing—*ag*	114112	913
Local area network (LAN) system integrators: Computer Systems Design Services—*prof*	541512	7373
Local Messengers and Local Delivery	**49221**	**4215**
Local Messengers and Local Delivery	**4922**	
Local railway passenger operation: Bus and Motor Vehicle Transit Systems—*trans*	485113	4111
Commuter Rail Systems—*trans*	485112	4111
Mixed Mode Transit Systems—*trans*	485111	4111
Transit and Ground Passenger, All Other—*trans*	485999	4111
Urban Transit Systems, Other—*trans*	485119	4111
Local telephone communications, except radio telephone: Telecommunications Resellers—*info*	51333	4813
Wired Telecommunications Carriers—*info*	51331	4813
Local trucking, without storage: Freight (except Used Goods) Trucking, Local Specialized—*trans*	48422	4212
General Freight Trucking, Local—*trans*	48411	4212
Used Household and Office Goods Moving—*trans*	48421	4212
Lock and waterway construction–general contractors: Heavy, All Other—*const*	23499	1629
Industrial Nonbuilding Structure—*const*	23493	1629
Lock parts made to individual order: Locksmiths—*admin*	561622	7699
Lock washers: Bolt, Nut, Screw, Rivet and Washer—*mfg*	332722	3452
Lock washers, plastics: Plastics Pipe and Pipe Fitting—*mfg*	326122	3089
Plastics Product, All Other—*mfg*	326199	3089
Unsupported Plastics Profile Shape—*mfg*	326121	3089
Locker rental, except cold storage: Personal Services, All Other—*serv*	81299	7299
Lockers, not refrigerated: Equipment, Other Commercial—*whlse*	42144	5046
Lockers, not refrigerated–except wood: Showcase, Partition, Shelving, and Locker—*mfg*	337215	2542
Lockers, not refrigerated–wood: Architectural Woodwork and Millwork, Custom—*mfg*	337212	2541
Showcase, Partition, Shelving, and Locker—*mfg*	337215	2541
Wood Kitchen Cabinet and Counter Top—*mfg*	33711	2541
Lockers, refrigerated: Air-Conditioning and Warm Air Heating Equipment and Commercial and Industrial Refrigeration Equipment—*mfg*	333415	3585
Motor Vehicle Air-Conditioning—*mfg*	336391	3585
Locks and related materials: Hardware—*whlse*	42171	5072
Locks, coin-operated: Automatic Vending Machine—*mfg*	333311	3581
Locksmith shops: Locksmiths—*admin*	561622	7699
Locksmiths	**561622**	**7699**
Locomotive and railroad car lights: Vehicular Lighting Equipment—*mfg*	336321	3647
Locomotive cranes: Construction Machinery—*mfg*	33312	3531
Overhead Traveling Crane, Hoist and Monorail System—*mfg*	333923	3531
Railroad Rolling Stock—*mfg*	33651	3531
Locomotive wheels, forged–not made in rolling mills: Iron and Steel Forging—*mfg*	332111	3462

ALPHABETICAL INDEX	NAICS	SIC
Locomotives, locomotive frames, and parts: Pump and Pumping Equipment—*mfg*	333911	3743
Railroad Rolling Stock—*mfg*	33651	3743
Lode gold mining: Gold Ore—*mining*	212221	1041
Lodging houses operated by organizations for members only: Hotels (except Casino Hotels) and Motels—*accom*	72111	7041
Rooming and Boarding Houses—*accom*	72131	7041
Lodging houses, except organization: Rooming and Boarding Houses—*accom*	72131	7021
Iodinated diagnostic agents: In-Vitro Diagnostic Substance—*mfg*	325413	2835
Pharmaceutical Preparation—*mfg*	325412	2835
Log cabins, prefabricated–wood: Prefabricated Wood Building—*mfg*	321992	2452
Log rafting and towing: Inland Water Freight—*trans*	483211	4449
Log splitters: Construction Machinery—*mfg*	33312	3531
Overhead Traveling Crane, Hoist and Monorail System—*mfg*	333923	3531
Railroad Rolling Stock—*mfg*	33651	3531
Log trucking: Freight (except Used Goods) Trucking, Local Specialized—*trans*	48422	4212
General Freight Trucking, Local—*trans*	48411	4212
Loganberry farms: Berry (except Strawberry) Farming—*ag*	111334	171
Strawberry Farming—*ag*	111333	171
Logging	**1133**	
Logging	**11331**	**2411**
Logging contractors: Logging—*ag*	11331	2411
Logging equipment: Construction and (except Petroleum) Machinery and Equipment—*whlse*	42181	5082
Construction Machinery—*mfg*	33312	3531
Overhead Traveling Crane, Hoist and Monorail System—*mfg*	333923	3531
Railroad Rolling Stock—*mfg*	33651	3531
Logging railroads: Rail Support Activities—*trans*	48821	4013
Short Line Railroads—*trans*	482112	4013
Logging wells on a contract basis: Oil and Gas Operations Support Activities—*mining*	213112	1389
Logic circuit testers: Electronic Coil, Transformer, and Other Inductor—*mfg*	334416	3825
Instrument for Measuring and Testing Electricity and Electrical Signals—*mfg*	334515	3825
Logs: Logging—*ag*	11331	2411
Logs, fireplace–electric: Electrical Equipment and Component, All Other Miscellaneous—*mfg*	335999	3699
Logs, fireplace–gas: Heating Equipment (except Electric and Warm Air Furnaces)—*mfg*	333414	3433
Logs, hewn ties, posts, and poles: Durable Goods, Other Miscellaneous—*whlse*	42199	5099
Logwood extract: Gum and Wood Chemical—*mfg*	325191	2861
Long cloth, cotton: Broadwoven Fabric Mills—*mfg*	31321	2211

ALPHABETICAL INDEX	NAICS	SIC
Long distance telephone communications: Telecommunications Resellers—*info*	51333	4813
Wired Telecommunications Carriers—*info*	51331	4813
Long-distance trucking: Freight (except Used Goods) Trucking, Long-Distance, Specialized—*trans*	48423	4213
General Freight Trucking, Long-Distance, Less Than Truckload—*trans*	484122	4213
General Freight Trucking, Long-Distance, Truckload—*trans*	484121	4213
Used Household and Office Goods Moving—*trans*	48421	4213
Ionomer resins: Plastics Material and Resin—*mfg*	325211	2821
Loom bobbins, wood or metal: Textile Machinery—*mfg*	333292	3552
Looms (textile machinery): Textile Machinery—*mfg*	333292	3552
Loopers (textile machinery): Textile Machinery—*mfg*	333292	3552
Looping, for the trade: Men's and Boys' Cut and Sew Apparel Contractors—*mfg*	315211	2395
Textile Product Mills, All Other Miscellaneous—*mfg*	314999	2395
Women's and Girls' Cut and Sew Apparel Contractors—*mfg*	315212	2395
Looseleaf binders: Office Supplies and Stationery Stores—*retail*	45321	5112
Stationary and Office Supplies—*whlse*	42212	5112
Looseleaf devices and binders: Blankbook, Loose-leaf Binder and Device—*mfg*	323118	2782
Flexographic Printing, Commercial—*mfg*	323112	2782
Gravure Printing, Commercial—*mfg*	323111	2782
Lithographic Printing, Commercial—*mfg*	323110	2782
Printing, Other Commercial—*mfg*	323119	2782
Screen Printing, Commercial—*mfg*	323113	2782
Looseleaf fillers and ream paper in filler sizes, except printed: Stationery, Tablet, and Related Product—*mfg*	322233	2678
Looseleaf forms and fillers, pen ruled or printed only: Blankbook, Loose-leaf Binder and Device—*mfg*	323118	2782
Flexographic Printing, Commercial—*mfg*	323112	2782
Gravure Printing, Commercial—*mfg*	323111	2782
Lithographic Printing, Commercial—*mfg*	323110	2782
Printing, Other Commercial—*mfg*	323119	2782
Screen Printing, Commercial—*mfg*	323113	2782
Lotteries, operation of: Gambling Industries, Other—*arts*	71329	7999
Lottery clubs and ticket sales to individuals: Gambling Industries, Other—*arts*	71329	7999
Lottery control boards: Public Finance—*pub*	92113	9311
Loudspeakers, electredynamic and magnetic: Audio and Video Equipment—*mfg*	33431	3651
Lounges, cocktail: Drinking Places (Alcoholic Beverages)—*accom*	72241	5813
Lounging robes: Outerwear Knitting Mills—*mfg*	315191	2253
Lounging robes and dressing gowns: Men's and Boys' Cut and Sew Apparel Contractors—*mfg*	315211	2384
Men's and Boys' Cut and Sew Underwear and Nightwear—*mfg*	315221	2384
Women's and Girls' Cut and Sew Apparel Contractors—*mfg*	315212	2384

Women's and Girls' Cut and Sew Lingerie, Loungewear and Nightwear—*mfg*	315231	2384
Louver windows and doors, glass with wood frame: Millwork (including Flooring), Other—*mfg*	321918	2431
Wood Window and Door—*mfg*	321911	2431
Louver windows, all metal or metalframe: Metal Window and Door—*mfg*	332321	3442
Louvers, sheet metal: Metal Container, Other—*mfg*	332439	3444
Sheet Metal Work—*mfg*	332322	3444
Loving cups, silver, nickel silver, pewter, and plated: Cutlery and Flatware (except Precious)—*mfg*	332211	3914
Silverware and Plated Ware—*mfg*	339912	3914
Lozenges, candy–nonmedicated: Confectionery from Purchased Chocolate—*mfg*	31133	2064
Non-Chocolate Confectionery—*mfg*	31134	2064
Lozenges, pharmaceutical: Pharmaceutical Preparation—*mfg*	325412	2834
Lubricating greases and oils: Petroleum Lubricating Oil and Grease—*mfg*	324191	2992
Lubricating oils and greases: Petroleum and Petroleum Products (except Bulk Stations and Terminals)—*whlse*	42272	5172
Lubricating oils, refining: Petroleum Lubricating Oil and Grease—*mfg*	324191	2992
Lubricating service, automotive: Automotive Oil Change and Lubrication Shops—*serv*	811191	7549
Automotive Repair and Maintenance, All Other—*serv*	811198	7549
Motor Vehicle Towing—*trans*	48841	7549
Lubricating systems, aircraft: Aircraft Engine and Engine Parts—*mfg*	336412	3724
Lubricating systems, centralized: General Purpose Machinery , All Other—*mfg*	333999	3569
Lubrication equipment, industrial: General Purpose Machinery , All Other—*mfg*	333999	3569
Lubrication machinery, automatic: General Purpose Machinery , All Other—*mfg*	333999	3569
Lubrication systems and parts, motor vehicle: Gasoline Engine and Engine Parts—*mfg*	336312	3714
Motor Vehicle Parts, All Other—*mfg*	336399	3714
Lubrication systems, locomotive: Pump and Pumping Equipment—*mfg*	333911	3743
Railroad Rolling Stock—*mfg*	33651	3743
Luggage: Durable Goods, Other Miscellaneous—*whlse*	42199	5099
Luggage and Leather Goods Stores	**44832**	**5948**
Luggage fabrics, cotton: Broadwoven Fabric Mills—*mfg*	31321	2211
Luggage hardware: Hardware—*mfg*	33251	3429
Luggage linings: Apparel Accessories and Apparel, Other—*mfg*	315999	2396
Luggage Manufacturing	**316991**	**3161**
Luggage repair shops: Footwear and Leather Goods Repair—*serv*	81143	7699
Luggage, regardless of material: Luggage—*mfg*	316991	3161
Lugs and connectors, electrical: Building Material Dealers, Other—*retail*	44419	5063
Electrical Apparatus and Equipment, Wiring Supplies and Material—*whlse*	42161	5063
Lumber and building materials dealers: Building Material Dealers, Other—*retail*	44419	5211
Home Centers—*retail*	44411	5211
Lumber and Other Construction Materials Wholesalers	**4213**	
Lumber and planing mill product dealers: Building Material Dealers, Other—*retail*	44419	5211
Home Centers—*retail*	44411	5211
Lumber stacking or sticking: Cut Stock, Resawing Lumber, and Planing—*mfg*	321912	2421
Millwork (including Flooring), Other—*mfg*	321918	2421
Sawmills—*mfg*	321113	2421
Wood Product, All Other Miscellaneous—*mfg*	321999	2421
Lumber terminals, storage for hire: General Warehousing and Storage Facilities—*trans*	49311	4226
Refrigerated Warehousing and Storage Facilities—*trans*	49312	4226
Warehousing and Storage Facilities, Other—*trans*	49319	4226
Lumber, hardwood dimension-m[g: Cut Stock, Resawing Lumber, and Planing—*mfg*	321912	2426
Millwork (including Flooring), Other—*mfg*	321918	2426
Showcase, Partition, Shelving, and Locker—*mfg*	337215	2426
Wood Product, All Other Miscellaneous—*mfg*	321999	2426
Lumber, kiln drying of: Cut Stock, Resawing Lumber, and Planing—*mfg*	321912	2421
Millwork (including Flooring), Other—*mfg*	321918	2421
Sawmills—*mfg*	321113	2421
Wood Product, All Other Miscellaneous—*mfg*	321999	2421
Lumber, Plywood, Millwork and Wood Panel Wholesalers	**42131**	**5031**
Lumber–rough, dressed, and finished: Building Material Dealers, Other—*retail*	44419	5031
Lumber–rough, sawed, or planed: Cut Stock, Resawing Lumber, and Planing—*mfg*	321912	2421
Millwork (including Flooring), Other—*mfg*	321918	2421
Sawmills—*mfg*	321113	2421
Wood Product, All Other Miscellaneous—*mfg*	321999	2421
Lumberjackets: Cut and Sew Apparel, All Other—*mfg*	315299	2329
Men's and Boys' Cut and Sew Apparel Contractors—*mfg*	315211	2329
Men's and Boys' Cut and Sew Other Outerwear—*mfg*	315228	2329
Luminous compounds, radium: Basic Inorganic Chemical, All Other—*mfg*	325188	2819
Chemical Product, All Other Miscellaneous—*mfg*	325998	2819
Luminous panel ceilings: Electric Lighting Fixture, Commercial, Industrial and Institutional—*mfg*	335122	3646
Luminous tube transformers: Power, Distribution and Specialty Transformer—*mfg*	335311	3612
Lunch bars: Cafeterias—*accom*	722212	5812
Caterers—*accom*	72232	5812
Foodservice Contractors—*accom*	72231	5812

ALPHABETICAL INDEX	NAICS	SIC
Full-Service Restaurants—*accom*	72211	5812
Limited-Service Restaurants—*accom*	722211	5812
Snack and Nonalcoholic Beverage Bars—*accom*	722213	5812
Theater Companies and Dinner Theaters—*arts*	71111	5812
Lunch boxes, stamped metal: Metal Stamping—*mfg*	332116	3469
Lunch cloths: Household Textile Product Mills, Other—*mfg*	314129	2392
Lunch counters: Cafeterias—*accom*	722212	5812
Caterers—*accom*	72232	5812
Foodservice Contractors—*accom*	72231	5812
Full-Service Restaurants—*accom*	72211	5812
Limited-Service Restaurants—*accom*	722211	5812
Snack and Nonalcoholic Beverage Bars—*accom*	722213	5812
Theater Companies and Dinner Theaters—*arts*	71111	5812
Lunch wagons, mobile: Direct Selling Establishments, Other—*retail*	45439	5963
Mobile Foodservices—*accom*	72233	5963
Luncheon meat, except poultry: Animal (except Poultry) Slaughtering—*mfg*	311611	2011
Meat Processed from Carcasses—*mfg*	311612	2013
Luncheon meat, poultry: Food, All Other Miscellaneous—*mfg*	311999	2015
Poultry Processing—*mfg*	311615	2015
Luncheonettes: Cafeterias—*accom*	722212	5812
Caterers—*accom*	72232	5812
Foodservice Contractors—*accom*	72231	5812
Full-Service Restaurants—*accom*	72211	5812
Limited-Service Restaurants—*accom*	722211	5812
Snack and Nonalcoholic Beverage Bars—*accom*	722213	5812
Theater Companies and Dinner Theaters—*arts*	71111	5812
Lunchroom fixtures, except wood: Showcase, Partition, Shelving, and Locker—*mfg*	337215	2542
Lunchroom fixtures, wood: Architectural Woodwork and Millwork, Custom—*mfg*	337212	2541
Showcase, Partition, Shelving, and Locker—*mfg*	337215	2541
Wood Kitchen Cabinet and Counter Top—*mfg*	33711	2541
Lunchrooms: Cafeterias—*accom*	722212	5812
Caterers—*accom*	72232	5812
Foodservice Contractors—*accom*	72231	5812
Full-Service Restaurants—*accom*	72211	5812
Limited-Service Restaurants—*accom*	722211	5812
Snack and Nonalcoholic Beverage Bars—*accom*	722213	5812
Theater Companies and Dinner Theaters—*arts*	71111	5812
Lupes magnifying instruments, optical: Optical Instrument and Lens—*mfg*	333314	3827
Lye, household: Polish and Other Sanitation Good—*mfg*	325612	2842
Macadamia groves and farms: Tree Nut Farming—*ag*	111335	173
Macaroni: Grocery and Related Products, Other—*whlse*	42249	5149
Macaroni and products, dry–e.g., alpha-bets, rings, seashells: Pasta—*mfg*	311823	2098

ALPHABETICAL INDEX	NAICS	SIC
Macaroni machinery–for making macaroni, spaghetti, and noodles: Food Product Machinery—*mfg*	333294	3556
Macaroni, canned: Canning, Specialty—*mfg*	311422	2032
Food, All Other Miscellaneous—*mfg*	311999	2032
Machetes: Hand and Edge Tool—*mfg*	332212	3423
Machine bases, metal: Fabricated Metal Product, All Other Miscellaneous—*mfg*	332999	3499
Machine chain, platinum or karat gold: Jewelers' Material and Lapidary Work—*mfg*	339913	3915
Machine guards, sheet metal: Metal Container, Other—*mfg*	332439	3444
Sheet Metal Work—*mfg*	332322	3444
Machine gun belts, metallic–30 mm. (or 1.18: Small Arms—*mfg*	332994	3484
Machine guns: Durable Goods, Other Miscellaneous—*whlse*	42199	5099
Machine guns and parts, 30 mm. (or 1.18 inch) or less: Small Arms—*mfg*	332994	3484
Machine guns, more than 30 mm. (or more than 1.18 inch): Ordnance and Accessories, Other—*mfg*	332995	3489
Machine keys: Bolt, Nut, Screw, Rivet and Washer—*mfg*	332722	3452
Machine knives, except metal cutting: Hand and Edge Tool—*mfg*	332212	3423
Machine knives, metalworking: Cutting Tool and Machine Tool Accessory—*mfg*	333515	3545
Hand and Edge Tool—*mfg*	332212	3545
Machine nuts, plastics: Plastics Pipe and Pipe Fitting—*mfg*	326122	3089
Plastics Product, All Other—*mfg*	326199	3089
Unsupported Plastics Profile Shape—*mfg*	326121	3089
Machine parts, stamped and pressed metal-rnfg: Metal Stamping—*mfg*	332116	3469
Machine rigging–contractors: Building Equipment and Other Machinery Installation Contractors—*const*	23595	1796
Machine Shops	**33271**	**3599**
Machine shops, jobbing and repair: Fabricated Metal Product, All Other Miscellaneous—*mfg*	332999	3599
General Purpose Machinery , All Other—*mfg*	333999	3599
Machine Shops—*mfg*	33271	3599
Machinery, Other Commercial and Service Industry—*mfg*	333319	3599
Machine Shops, Turned Product, and Screw, Nut and Bolt Manufacturing	**3327**	
Machine Tool (Metal Cutting Types) Manufacturing	**333512**	**3541**
Machine Tool (Metal Forming Types) Manufacturing	**333513**	**3542**
Machine tool accessories: Industrial Machinery and Equipment—*whlse*	42183	5084
Machine tool attachments and accessories: Cutting Tool and Machine Tool Accessory—*mfg*	333515	3545
Hand and Edge Tool—*mfg*	332212	3545
Machine tool designers: Engineering Services—*prof*	54133	8711
Machine tool replacement and repair parts, metal cutting types: Machine Tool (Metal Cutting Types)—*mfg*	333512	3541

Description	NAICS	SIC
Machine tool transformers: Power, Distribution and Specialty Transformer—*mfg*	335311	3612
Machine tools: Industrial Machinery and Equipment—*whlse*	42183	5084
Machine tools, metal cutting–e.g., exotic, chemical, explosive: Machine Tool (Metal Cutting Types)—*mfg*	333512	3541
Machine tools, metal forming types–including rebuilding: Machine Tool (Metal Forming Types)—*mfg*	333513	3542
Machinery and Equipment (except Automotive and Electronic) Repair and Maintenance, Commercial and Industrial	**8113**	
Machinery and Equipment (except Automotive and Electronic) Repair and Maintenance, Commercial and Industrial	**81131**	**7623**
Machinery and equipment finance leasing: International Trade Financing—*fin*	522293	6159
Non-Depository Credit Intermediation, All Other—*fin*	522298	6159
Sales Financing—*fin*	52222	6159
Machinery and Equipment Rental and Leasing, Commercial and Industrial	**5324**	
Machinery and Equipment Rental and Leasing, Other Commercial and Industrial	**53249**	**7359**
Machinery castings brass, copper, and copper-base alloy -except diecastings: Copper Foundries—*mfg*	331525	3366
Machinery castings, aluminum–except die-castings: Aluminum Foundries—*mfg*	331524	3365
Machinery castings, nonferrous–except aluminum, copper, copper alloys, and die-castings- mig: Nonferrous Foundries, Other—*mfg*	331528	3369
Machinery cleaning: Machinery and Equipment (except Automotive and Electronic) Repair and Maintenance, Commercial and Industrial—*serv*	81131	7699
Machinery forgings, ferrous–not made in rolling mills: Iron and Steel Forging—*mfg*	332111	3462
Machinery forgings, nonferrous–not made in hot-rolling mills: Nonferrous Forging—*mfg*	332112	3463
Machinery Manu:acturing	**333**	
Machinery Manufacturing, Commercial and Service Industry	**3333**	
Machinery Manufacturing, Commercial and Service Industry	**33331**	
Machinery Manufacturing, Other Commercial and Service Industry	**333319**	**3589**
Machinery, Equipment and Supplies Wholesalers	**4218**	
Machinists' precision measuring tools: Industrial Machinery and Equipment—*whlse*	42183	5084
Machmeters: Search, Detection, Navigation, Guidance, Aeronautical, and Nautical System and Instrument—*mfg*	334511	3812
Mackerel, catching of: Finfish Fishing—*ag*	114111	912
Mackerel–smoked, salted, dried, and pickled: Seafood Canning—*mfg*	311711	2091
Mackinaws: Cut and Sew Apparel, All Other—*mfg*	315299	2329
Men's and Boys' Cut and Sew Apparel Contractors—*mfg*	315211	2329
Men's and Boys' Cut and Sew Other Outerwear—*mfg*	315228	2329
Magazine racks, wood: Nonupholstered Wood Household Furniture—*mfg*	337122	2511
Magazine stands: News Dealers and Newsstands—*retail*	451212	5994
Magazine subscription sales, except mail-order: Direct Selling Establishments, Other—*retail*	45439	5963
Mobile Foodservices—*accom*	72233	5963
Magazines: Book, Periodical and Newspaper—*whlse*	42292	5192
Magazines, binding only: Tradebinding and Related Work—*mfg*	323121	2789
Magazines, gim–30 mm. (or 1.18 inch) or less: Small Arms—*mfg*	332994	3484
Magazines, house-to-house selling: Direct Selling Establishments, Other—*retail*	45439	5963
Mobile Foodservices—*accom*	72233	5963
Magazines, mail-order: Electronic Shopping and Mail-Order Houses—*retail*	45411	5961
Magazines, printed–except lithographed or gravure (not publishing): Digital Printing—*mfg*	323115	2759
Flexographic Printing, Commercial—*mfg*	323112	2759
Printing, Other Commercial—*mfg*	323119	2759
Quick Printing—*mfg*	323114	2759
Magazines–gravure printing (not publishing): Gravure Printing, Commercial—*mfg*	323111	2754
Magazines–publishing and printing, or publishing only: Periodical Publishers—*info*	51112	2721
Magic lanterns (toys): Game, Toy, and Children's Vehicle—*mfg*	339932	3944
Magicians: Independent Artists, Writers, and Performers—*arts*	71151	7929
Musical Groups and Artists—*arts*	71113	7929
Performing Arts Companies, Other—*arts*	71119	7929
Magnesite mining: Clay and Ceramic and Refractory Minerals—*mining*	212325	1459
Magnesite, crude–ground, calcined, or dead-burned: Ground or Treated Mineral and Earth—*mfg*	327992	3295
Magnesium and magnesium alloy bars, rods, shapes, sheets', strip, and tubing: Nonferrous Metal (except Copper and Aluminum) Rolling, Drawing and Extruding—*mfg*	331491	3356
Magnesium and magnesium base alloy foil, not made in rolling mills: Fabricated Metal Product, All Other Miscellaneous—*mfg*	332999	3497
Laminated Aluminum Foil for Flexible Packaging Uses—*mfg*	322225	3497
Magnesium carbonate: Basic Inorganic Chemical, All Other—*mfg*	325188	2819
Chemical Product, All Other Miscellaneous—*mfg*	325998	2819
Magnesium castings, except die-castings: Nonferrous Foundries, Other—*mfg*	331528	3369
Magnesium chloride: Basic Inorganic Chemical, All Other—*mfg*	325188	2819
Chemical Product, All Other Miscellaneous—*mfg*	325998	2819
Magnesium compounds, inorganic: Basic Inorganic Chemical, All Other—*mfg*	325188	2819
Chemical Product, All Other Miscellaneous—*mfg*	325998	2819
Magnesium die-castings: Nonferrous (except Aluminum) Die-Castings—*mfg*	331522	3364

ALPHABETICAL INDEX	NAICS	SIC
Magnesium refining, primary: Primary Smelting and Refining of Nonferrous Metal (except Copper and Aluminum)—*mfg*	331419	3339
Magnesium rolling, drawing, and extruding: Nonferrous Metal (except Copper and Aluminum) Rolling, Drawing and Extruding—*mfg*	331491	3356
Magnesium smelting and refining, secondary: Secondary Smelting and Alloying of Aluminum—*mfg*	331314	3341
Secondary Smelting, Refining, and Alloying of Nonferrous Metal (except Copper and Aluminum)—*mfg*	331492	3341
Magnet wire, insulatod: Aluminum Rolling and Drawing, Other—*mfg*	331319	3357
Communication and Energy Wire, Other—*mfg*	335929	3357
Copper Wire (except Mechanical) Drawing—*mfg*	331422	3357
Fiber Optic Cable—*mfg*	335921	3357
Nonferrous Metal (except Copper and Aluminum) Rolling, Drawing and Extruding—*mfg*	331491	3357
Magnetic and Optical Recording Media Manufacturing	**334613**	**3695**
Magnetic bubble memory device: Semiconductor and Related Device—*mfg*	334413	3674
Magnetic counters: Totalizing Fluid Meter and Counting Device—*mfg*	334514	3824
Magnetic flow meters, industrial process type: Instruments and Related Products for Measuring, Displaying, and Controlling Industrial Process Variables—*mfg*	334513	3823
Magnetic forming machines: Machine Tool (Metal Forming Types)—*mfg*	333513	3542
Magnetic ink recognition devices, computer peripheral equipment: Computer Peripheral Equipment, Other—*mfg*	334119	3577
Magnetic inspection oil and powder: Basic Organic Chemical, All Other—*mfg*	325199	2899
Chemical Product, All Other Miscellaneous—*mfg*	325998	2899
Magnetic recording tape: Electronic Parts and Equipment, Other—*whlse*	42169	5065
Magnetic recording tape, blank–reels, cassettes, and disks: Magnetic and Optical Recording Media—*mfg*	334613	3695
Magnetic resonance imaging device (diagnostic), nuclear: Electromedical and Electrotherapeutic Apparatus—*mfg*	334510	3845
Irradiation Apparatus—*mfg*	334517	3845
Magnetic resonance imaging type apparatus, except diagnostic: Analytical Laboratory Instrument—*mfg*	334516	3826
Magnetic storage devices for computers: Computer Storage Device—*mfg*	334112	3572
Magnetic tape, audio–prerecorded: Integrated Record Production/Distribution—*info*	51222	3652
Prerecorded Compact Disc (except Software), Tape, and Record Reproducing—*mfg*	334612	3652
Magnetite mining: Iron Ore—*mining*	21221	1011

ALPHABETICAL INDEX	NAICS	SIC
Magnetohydrodynamic (MHD) devices: Semiconductor and Related Device—*mfg*	334413	3674
Magnetometers: Measuring and Controlling Device, Other—*mfg*	334519	3829
Surgical and Medical Instrument—*mfg*	339112	3829
Magnetron tubes: Electron Tube—*mfg*	334411	3671
Magnets, permanent–ceramic or ferrite: Porcelain Electrical Supply—*mfg*	327113	3264
Magnets, permanent–metallic: Fabricated Metal Product, All Other Miscellaneous—*mfg*	332999	3499
Magnifiers (readers and simple magnifiers): Ophthalmic Goods—*mfg*	339115	3851
Magnifying instruments, optical: Optical Instrument and Lens—*mfg*	333314	3827
MaH pouch racks, except wood: Showcase, Partition, Shelving, and Locker—*mfg*	337215	2542
Maid registries: Employment Placement Agencies—*admin*	56131	7361
Human Resources and Executive Search Consulting Services—*prof*	541612	7361
Maid service on a contract or fee basis: Janitorial Services—*admin*	56172	7349
Mail advertising service: Direct Mail Advertising—*prof*	54186	7331
Mail boxes, except collection boxes: Metal Stamping—*mfg*	332116	3469
Mail carriers, bulk, contract–local: Freight (except Used Goods) Trucking, Local Specialized—*trans*	48422	4212
General Freight Trucking, Local—*trans*	48411	4212
Mail chutes, sheet metal: Metal Container, Other—*mfg*	332439	3444
Sheet Metal Work—*mfg*	332322	3444
Mail collection or storage boxes, sheetmetal: Metal Container, Other—*mfg*	332439	3444
Sheet Metal Work—*mfg*	332322	3444
Mail delivery, private–except air: Couriers—*trans*	49211	4215
Local Messengers and Local Delivery—*trans*	49221	4215
Mail tying (bundling) machines: Lead Pencil and Art Good—*mfg*	339942	3579
Office Machinery—*mfg*	333313	3579
Watch, Clock, and Part—*mfg*	334518	3579
Mail-order houses-retail (not including retail outlets): Electronic Shopping and Mail-Order Houses—*retail*	45411	5961
Mailgram services: Wired Telecommunications Carriers—*info*	51331	4822
Mailing cases and tubes, paper fiber(metal-end or all-fiber): Fiber Can, Tube, Drum, and Similar Products—*mfg*	322214	2655
Mailing list compilers: Direct Mail Advertising—*prof*	54186	7331
Mailing machines: Lead Pencil and Art Good—*mfg*	339942	3579
Office Equipment—*whlse*	42142	5044
Office Machinery—*mfg*	333313	3579
Watch, Clock, and Part—*mfg*	334518	3579
Mailing racks, postal service–except wood: Showcase, Partition, Shelving, and Locker—*mfg*	337215	2542
Mailing service: Direct Mail Advertising—*prof*	54186	7331
Mainframe computers: Electronic Computer—*mfg*	334111	3571

Term	NAICS	SIC
Maintenance facilities for motor vehicle passenger transportation: Road, Other Support Activities for—*trans*	48849	4173
Maintenance, building–except repairs: Janitorial Services—*admin*	56172	7349
Major Appliance Manufacturing	**33522**	
Major Household Appliance Manufacturing, Other	**335228**	**3639**
Malacca furniture: Household Furniture (except Wood and Metal)—*mfg*	337125	2519
Malaria control: Airport Operations, Other—*trans*	488119	4959
Exterminating and Pest Control Services—*admin*	56171	4959
Remediation Services—*admin*	56291	4959
Waste Management Services, All Other Miscellaneous—*admin*	562998	4959
Maleic anhydride: Cyclic Crude and Intermediate—*mfg*	325192	2865
Petrochemical—*mfg*	32511	2865
Mallets, printers': Hand and Edge Tool—*mfg*	332212	3423
Mallets, rubber: Fabric Coating Mills—*mfg*	31332	3069
Rubber Product, All Other—*mfg*	326299	3069
Mallets, sports–e.g., polo, croquet: Sporting and Athletic Goods—*mfg*	33992	3949
Mallets, wood: Manufacturing, All Other Miscellaneous—*mfg*	339999	2499
Wood Container and Pallet—*mfg*	32192	2499
Wood Product, All Other Miscellaneous—*mfg*	321999	2499
Malononitrile, technical grade: Basic Organic Chemical, All Other—*mfg*	325199	2869
Malt: Grocery and Related Products, Other—*whlse*	42249	5149
Malt byproducts: Malt—*mfg*	311213	2083
Malt extract: Grocery and Related Products, Other—*whlse*	42249	5149
Malt extract, liquors, and syrups: Breweries—*mfg*	31212	2082
Malt Manufacturing	**311213**	**2083**
Malt mills: Food Product Machinery—*mfg*	333294	3556
Malt–barley, rye, wheat, and corn: Malt—*mfg*	311213	2083
Malted milk: Dry, Condensed, and Evaporated Dairy Product—*mfg*	311514	2023
Malthouses: Malt—*mfg*	311213	2083
Management Consulting Services	**54161**	
Management Consulting Services, Other	**541618**	**8748**
Management engineering consultants: Administrative Management and General Management Consulting Services—*prof*	541611	8742
Human Resources and Executive Search Consulting Services—*prof*	541612	8742
Marketing Consulting Services—*prof*	541613	8742
Process, Physical, Distribution and Logistics Consulting Services—*prof*	541614	8742
Management information systems consultants: Administrative Management and General Management Consulting Services—*prof*	541611	8742
Human Resources and Executive Search Consulting Services—*prof*	541612	8742
Marketing Consulting Services—*prof*	541613	8742
Process, Physical, Distribution and Logistics Consulting Services—*prof*	541614	8742

Term	NAICS	SIC
Management investment funds, closedend: Financial Vehicles, Other—*fin*	52599	6726
Management investment funds, openend: Open-End Investment Funds—*fin*	52591	6722
Management of Companies and Enterprises	**55111**	
Management of Companies and Enterprises	**55**	
Management of Companies and Enterprises	**551**	
Management of Companies and Enterprises	**5511**	
Management services, farm: Farm Management Services—*ag*	115116	762
Management, Scientific and Technical Consulting Services	**5416**	
Manager of mutual funds, contract or feebasis: Investment Advice—*fin*	52393	6282
Portfolio Management—*fin*	52392	6282
Managers of individual professional athletes: Agents and Managers for Artists, Athletes, Entertainers and Other Public Figures—*arts*	71141	7941
Promoters of Performing Arts, Sports and Similar Events with Facilities—*arts*	71131	7941
Promoters of Performing Arts, Sports and Similar Events without Facilities—*arts*	71132	7941
Spectator Sports, Other—*arts*	711219	7941
Sports Teams and Clubs—*arts*	711211	7941
Managers or agents dddfor mutual funds: Financial Investment Activities, Miscellaneous—*fin*	523999	6211
Intermediation, Miscellaneous—*fin*	52391	6211
Investment Banking and Securities Dealing—*fin*	52311	6211
Securities Brokerage—*fin*	52312	6211
Managers, real estate: Nonresidential Property Managers—*real*	531312	6531
Residential Property Managers—*real*	531311	6531
Mandolins and parts: Musical Instrument—*mfg*	339992	3931
Mandrels: Cutting Tool and Machine Tool Accessory—*mfg*	333515	3545
Hand and Edge Tool—*mfg*	332212	3545
Manganese dioxide powder, synthetic: Basic Inorganic Chemical, All Other—*mfg*	325188	2819
Chemical Product, All Other Miscellaneous—*mfg*	325998	2819
Manganese metal: Electrometallurgical Ferroalloy Product—*mfg*	331112	3313
Secondary Smelting, Refining, and Alloying of Nonferrous Metal (except Copper and Aluminum)—*mfg*	331492	3313
Manganese ore mining: Copper Ore and Nickel Ore—*mining*	212234	1061
Metal Ore, All Other—*mining*	212299	1061
Manganiferous ore mining, valued chiefly for iron content: Iron Ore—*mining*	21221	1011
Manganite miningS: Copper Ore and Nickel Ore—*mining*	212234	1061
Metal Ore, All Other—*mining*	212299	1061
Mangrove extract: Gum and Wood Chemical—*mfg*	325191	2861
Manhole construction–contractors: Power and Communication Transmission Line—*const*	23492	1623
Water, Sewer, and Pipeline—*const*	23491	1623
Manhole covers and frames, concrete: Concrete Pipe—*mfg*	327332	3272

ALPHABETICAL INDEX	NAICS	SIC
Concrete Product, Other—*mfg*	32739	3272
Nonmetallic Mineral Product, All Other Miscellaneous—*mfg*	327999	3272
Manhole covers, metal: Iron Foundries—*mfg*	331511	3321
Manicure and pedicure salons: Beauty Salons—*serv*	812112	7231
Cosmetology and Barber Schools—*educ*	611511	7231
Nail Salons—*serv*	812113	7231
Manicure preparations: Soap and Other Detergent—*mfg*	325611	2844
Toilet Preparation—*mfg*	32562	2844
Manifold Business Form Printing	**323116**	**2761**
Manifold business forms: Office Supplies and Stationery Stores—*retail*	45321	5112
Stationary and Office Supplies—*whlse*	42212	5112
Manifolds, motor vehicle–gasoline engine: Gasoline Engine and Engine Parts—*mfg*	336312	3714
Motor Vehicle Parts, All Other—*mfg*	336399	3714
Manifolds, pipe–fabricated from purchased metal pipe: Fabricated Pipe and Pipe Fitting—*mfg*	332996	3498
Manila folders: Converted Paper Product, All Other—*mfg*	322298	2675
Die-Cut Paper and Paperboard Office Supplies—*mfg*	322231	2675
Surface-Coated Paperboard—*mfg*	322292	2675
Manila lined board: Paperboard Mills—*mfg*	32213	2631
Manila wrapping paper: Newsprint Mills—*mfg*	322122	2621
Paper (except Newsprint) Mills—*mfg*	322121	2621
Manmade fiber thread: Textile and Fabric Finishing (except Broadwoven Fabric) Mills—*mfg*	313312	2284
Thread Mills—*mfg*	313113	2284
Manmade fibers: Chemical and Allied Products, Other—*whlse*	42269	5169
Manmade staple fiber yarn, spun: Yarn Spinning Mills—*mfg*	313111	2281
Mannequin decorating service: Design Services, Other Specialized—*prof*	54149	7389
Mannequins: Equipment, Other Commercial—*whlse*	42144	5046
Mannikins and display forms: Wood Product, All Other Miscellaneous—*mfg*	321999	3999
Manometers, industrial process type: Instruments and Related Products for Measuring, Displaying, and Controlling Industrial Process Variables—*mfg*	334513	3823
Manpower pools: Employee Leasing Services—*admin*	56133	7363
Temporary Help Services—*admin*	56132	7363
Manpower training: Vocational Rehabilitation Services—*hlth*	62431	8331
Mantel work–contractors: Drywall, Plastering, Acoustical and Insulation Contractors—*const*	23542	1743
Tile, Marble, Terrazzo and Mosaic Contractors—*const*	23543	1743
Mantels, concrete: Concrete Pipe—*mfg*	327332	3272
Concrete Product, Other—*mfg*	32739	3272
Nonmetallic Mineral Product, All Other Miscellaneous—*mfg*	327999	3272
Manufactured (Mobile) Home Dealers	**45393**	**5271**

ALPHABETICAL INDEX	NAICS	SIC
Manufactured gas production and distribution: Natural Gas Distribution—*util*	22121	4925
Manufactured Home (Mobile Home) Manufacturing	**321991**	**2451**
Manufacturers' institutes: Business Associations—*serv*	81391	8611
Manufacturing	**31-33**	
Manufacturing and Industrial Building Construction	**23331**	**1541**
Manufacturing and Reproducing Magnetic and Optical Media	**3346**	
Manufacturing and Reproducing Magnetic and Optical Media	**33461**	
Manufacturing management consultants: Administrative Management and General Management Consulting Services—*prof*	541611	8742
Human Resources and Executive Search Consulting Services—*prof*	541612	8742
Marketing Consulting Services—*prof*	541613	8742
Process, Physical, Distribution and Logistics Consulting Services—*prof*	541614	8742
Manufacturing, All Other Miscellaneous	**33999**	
Manufacturing, All Other Miscellaneous	**339999**	**3999**
Manufacturing, Miscellaneous	**339**	
Manufacturing, Other Miscellaneous	**3399**	
Manuscripts, rare: Non-Depository Credit Intermediation, All Other—*fin*	522298	5932
Used Merchandise Stores—*retail*	45331	5932
Map drafting service: Surveying and Mapping (except Geophysical) Services—*prof*	54137	7389
Map plotting instruments: Measuring and Controlling Device, Other—*mfg*	334519	3829
Surgical and Medical Instrument—*mfg*	339112	3829
Maple sap, gathering of: Crop Farming, All Other Miscellaneous—*ag*	111998	831
Forest Nurseries and Gathering of Forest Products—*ag*	11321	831
Mapmaking, including aerial: Surveying and Mapping (except Geophysical) Services—*prof*	54137	7389
Maps, engraved: Digital Printing—*mfg*	323115	2759
Flexographic Printing, Commercial—*mfg*	323112	2759
Printing, Other Commercial—*mfg*	323119	2759
Quick Printing—*mfg*	323114	2759
Maps, lithographed: Lithographic Printing, Commercial—*mfg*	323110	2752
Quick Printing—*mfg*	323114	2752
Maps, printed–except lithographed or gravure (not publishing): Digital Printing—*mfg*	323115	2759
Flexographic Printing, Commercial—*mfg*	323112	2759
Printing, Other Commercial—*mfg*	323119	2759
Quick Printing—*mfg*	323114	2759
Maps–gravure printing (not publishing): Gravure Printing, Commercial—*mfg*	323111	2754
Maps–publishing and printing, or publishing only: Database and Directory Publishers—*info*	51114	2741

Description	NAICS	SIC
Music Publishers—*info*	51223	2741
Publishers, All Other—*info*	511199	2741
Marble building stone: Brick, Stone and Related Material—*whlse*	42132	5032
Building Material Dealers, Other—*retail*	44419	5032
Marble installation, interior–including finishing–contractors: Drywall, Plastering, Acoustical and Insulation Contractors—*const*	23542	1743
Tile, Marble, Terrazzo and Mosaic Contractors—*const*	23543	1743
Marble work, exterior construction–contractors: Masonry and Stone Contractors—*const*	23541	1741
Marble, building–cut and shaped: Cut Stone and Stone Product—*mfg*	327991	3281
Marble, crushed and broken: Crushed and Broken Stone and Quarrying, Other—*mining*	212319	1429
Marble, dimension: Dimension Stone and Quarrying—*mining*	212311	1411
Marcasite mining: Chemical and Fertilizer Mineral, Other—*mining*	212393	1479
Margaric acid: Basic Organic Chemical, All Other—*mfg*	325199	2899
Chemical Product, All Other Miscellaneous—*mfg*	325998	2899
Margarine: Grocery and Related Products, Other—*whlse*	42249	5149
Margarine oil, except corn: Fats and Oils Refining and Blending—*mfg*	311225	2079
Oilseed Processing, Other—*mfg*	311223	2079
Soybean Processing—*mfg*	311222	2079
Margarine, including imitation: Fats and Oils Refining and Blending—*mfg*	311225	2079
Oilseed Processing, Other—*mfg*	311223	2079
Soybean Processing—*mfg*	311222	2079
Margarine-butter blend: Fats and Oils Refining and Blending—*mfg*	311225	2079
Oilseed Processing, Other—*mfg*	311223	2079
Soybean Processing—*mfg*	311222	2079
Marimbas: Musical Instrument—*mfg*	339992	3931
Marinas	**71393**	**4493**
Marinas, prefabricated–wood: Prefabricated Wood Building—*mfg*	321992	2452
Marine and navy auxiliary controls: Relay and Industrial Control—*mfg*	335314	3625
Marine basins, operation of: Marinas—*arts*	71393	4493
Marine Cargo Handling	**48832**	**4491**
Marine cargo handling: Port and Harbor Operations—*trans*	48831	4491
Marine construction–general contractors: Heavy, All Other—*const*	23499	1629
Industrial Nonbuilding Structure—*const*	23493	1629
Marine Corps: National Security—*pub*	92811	9711
Marine engineering services: Engineering Services—*prof*	54133	8711
Marine engines–diesel, semidiesel, and other internal combustion: Engine Equipment, Other—*mfg*	333618	3519
Motor Vehicle Parts, All Other—*mfg*	336399	3519
Marine Fishing, Other	**114119**	**919**
Marine hardware: Hardware—*mfg*	33251	3429
Marine horns, compressed air or steam–metal: Fabricated Metal Product, All Other Miscellaneous—*mfg*	332999	3499
Marine horns, electric: Communications Equipment, Other—*mfg*	33429	3669
Marine paints: Paint and Coating—*mfg*	32551	2851
Marine propulsion machinery and equipment: Transportation Equipment and Supplies (except Motor Vehicle)—*whlse*	42186	5088
Marine radio communications equipment: Radio and Television Broadcasting and Wireless Communications Equipment—*mfg*	33422	3663
Marine railways for drydocking, operationof: Air, Rail, and Water Equipment Rental and Leasing, Commercial—*real*	532411	4499
Navigational Services to Shipping—*trans*	48833	4499
Port and Harbor Operations—*trans*	48831	4499
Water, Other Support Activities for—*trans*	48839	4499
Marine rigging: Ship Building and Repairing—*mfg*	336611	3731
Marine salvaging: Air, Rail, and Water Equipment Rental and Leasing, Commercial—*real*	532411	4499
Navigational Services to Shipping—*trans*	48833	4499
Port and Harbor Operations—*trans*	48831	4499
Water, Other Support Activities for—*trans*	48839	4499
Marine service stations: Gasoline Stations with Convenience Stores—*retail*	44711	5541
Gasoline Stations, Other—*retail*	44719	5541
Marine supplies (dunnage): Transportation Equipment and Supplies (except Motor Vehicle)—*whlse*	42186	5088
Marine supply dealers: Boat Dealers—*retail*	441222	5551
Marine surveyors, except cargo: Air, Rail, and Water Equipment Rental and Leasing, Commercial—*real*	532411	4499
Navigational Services to Shipping—*trans*	48833	4499
Port and Harbor Operations—*trans*	48831	4499
Water, Other Support Activities for—*trans*	48839	4499
Marine towing: Coastal and Great Lakes Freight—*trans*	483113	4492
Inland Water Freight—*trans*	483211	4492
Navigational Services to Shipping—*trans*	48833	4492
Marine wrecking–ships for scrap: Air, Rail, and Water Equipment Rental and Leasing, Commercial—*real*	532411	4499
Navigational Services to Shipping—*trans*	48833	4499
Port and Harbor Operations—*trans*	48831	4499
Water, Other Support Activities for—*trans*	48839	4499
Marionettes (puppets): Wood Product, All Other Miscellaneous—*mfg*	321999	3999
Marker lamps, motor vehicle: Vehicular Lighting Equipment—*mfg*	336321	3647
Markers, soft tip–e.g., felt, fabric, plastics: Pen and Mechanical Pencil—*mfg*	339941	3951
Market baskets, except fruit and vegetdble–veneer and splint-rnfg: Manufacturing, All Other Miscellaneous—*mfg*	339999	2499
Wood Container and Pallet—*mfg*	32192	2499
Wood Product, All Other Miscellaneous—*mfg*	321999	2499
Market baskets, fruit and vegetable:veneer and splint: Wood Container and Pallet—*mfg*	32192	2449
Market gardens: Vegetable (except Potato) and Melon Farming, Other—*ag*	111219	161

ALPHABETICAL INDEX	NAICS	SIC
Market research, commercial: Marketing Research and Public Opinion Polling—*prof*	54191	8732
Research and Development in the Social Sciences and Humanities—*prof*	54173	8732
Marketing and consumer services: Agricultural Marketing and Commodities, Regulation of—*pub*	92614	9641
Marketing consultants: Administrative Management and General Management Consulting Services—*prof*	541611	8742
Human Resources and Executive Search Consulting Services—*prof*	541612	8742
Marketing Consulting Services—*prof*	541613	8742
Process, Physical, Distribution and Logistics Consulting Services—*prof*	541614	8742
Marketing Consulting Services	**541613**	**8742**
Marketing Research and Public Opinion Polling	**54191**	**8732**
Marking Device Manufacturing	**339943**	**3953**
Marking devices: Office Supplies and Stationery Stores—*retail*	45321	5112
Stationary and Office Supplies—*whlse*	42212	5112
Marking machines, metalworking: Other Metalworking Machinery, Other—*mfg*	333518	3549
Marl, crushed and broken: Crushed and Broken Limestone and Quarrying—*mining*	212312	1422
Marmalade: Fruit and Vegetable Canning—*mfg*	311421	2033
Marquetry, wood: Manufacturing, All Other Miscellaneous—*mfg*	339999	2499
Wood Container and Pallet—*mfg*	32192	2499
Wood Product, All Other Miscellaneous—*mfg*	321999	2499
Marquisettes, cotton: Broadwoven Fabric Mills—*mfg*	31321	2211
Marquisettes, manmade fiber: Broadwoven Fabric Mills—*mfg*	31321	2221
Marriage bureaus: Personal Services, All Other—*serv*	81299	7299
Marriage counseling services: Child and Youth Services—*hlth*	62411	8322
Community Food Services—*hlth*	62421	8322
Community Housing Services, Other—*hlth*	624229	8322
Emergency and Other Relief Services—*hlth*	62423	8322
Individual and Family Services, Other—*hlth*	62419	8322
Parole Offices and Probation Offices—*pub*	92215	8322
Services for the Elderly and Persons with Disabilities—*hlth*	62412	8322
Temporary Shelters—*hlth*	624221	8322
Marshals' offices, police: Police Protection—*pub*	92212	9221
Marshmallow creme: Food, All Other Miscellaneous—*mfg*	311999	2099
Marshmallows: Confectionery from Purchased Chocolate—*mfg*	31133	2064
Non-Chocolate Confectionery—*mfg*	31134	2064
Marzipan (candy): Confectionery from Purchased Chocolate—*mfg*	31133	2064
Non-Chocolate Confectionery—*mfg*	31134	2064
Maser amplifiers: Electrical Equipment and Component, All Other Miscellaneous—*mfg*	335999	3699
Machinery, Other Commercial and Service Industry—*mfg*	333319	3699

ALPHABETICAL INDEX	NAICS	SIC
Mashers, potato–wood: Manufacturing, All Other Miscellaneous—*mfg*	339999	2499
Wood Container and Pallet—*mfg*	32192	2499
Wood Product, All Other Miscellaneous—*mfg*	321999	2499
Masking tape: Coated and Laminated Paper—*mfg*	322222	2672
Masks, papier-mache: Coated and Laminated Paper—*mfg*	322222	2679
Converted Paper Product, All Other—*mfg*	322298	2679
Die-Cut Paper and Paperboard Office Supplies—*mfg*	322231	2679
Non-Folding Sanitary Food Container—*mfg*	322215	2679
Masks, sports–e.g., baseball, fencing, hockey: Sporting and Athletic Goods—*mfg*	33992	3949
Masonry and concrete drilling tools, power–portable: Power-Driven Hand Tool—*mfg*	333991	3546
Masonry and Stone Contractors	**23541**	**1741**
Masonry, Drywall, Insulation, and Tile Contractors	**2354**	
Masonry–contractors: Masonry and Stone Contractors—*const*	23541	1741
Masons' handtools: Hand and Edge Tool—*mfg*	332212	3423
Masons' lime: Lime—*mfg*	32741	3274
Masons' materials: Brick, Stone and Related Material—*whlse*	42132	5032
Building Material Dealers, Other—*retail*	44419	5032
Mass spectrometers: Analytical Laboratory Instrument—*mfg*	334516	3826
Mass spectroscopy instrumentation: Analytical Laboratory Instrument—*mfg*	334516	3826
Massage machines, electric–designed for beauty and barber shops: Hand and Edge Tool—*mfg*	332212	3999
Massage machines, electric–except designed for beauty and barber shop: Electric Housewares and Household Fan—*mfg*	335211	3634
Heating Equipment (except Electric and Warm Air Furnaces)—*mfg*	333414	3634
Massage parlors: Personal Care Services, Other—*serv*	812199	7299
Mastic floor composition, hot and cold: Asphalt Paving Mixture and Block—*mfg*	324121	2951
Mastic roofing composition: Asphalt Shingle and Coating Materials—*mfg*	324122	2952
Masts, wood: Manufacturing, All Other Miscellaneous—*mfg*	339999	2499
Wood Container and Pallet—*mfg*	32192	2499
Wood Product, All Other Miscellaneous—*mfg*	321999	2499
Matches: Nondurable Goods, Other Miscellaneous—*whlse*	42299	5199
Matches and match books: Chemical Product, All Other Miscellaneous—*mfg*	325998	3999
Wood Product, All Other Miscellaneous—*mfg*	321999	3999
Matelasse, cotton: Broadwoven Fabric Mills—*mfg*	31321	2211
Material Handling Equipment Manufacturing	**33392**	
Materials handling equipment: Industrial Machinery and Equipment—*whlse*	42183	5084
Materials Recovery Facilities	**56292**	**4953**

Description	NAICS	SIC
Maternity and child health program administration: Public Health Programs, Administration of—*pub*	92312	9431
Maternity bras and corsets: Women's and Girls' Cut and Sew Apparel Contractors—*mfg*	315212	2342
Women's and Girls' Cut and Sew Lingerie, Loungewear and Nightwear—*mfg*	315231	2342
Maternity hospitals: General Medical and Surgical Hospitals—*hlth*	62211	8069
Hospitals (except Psychiatric and Substance Abuse), Specialty—*hlth*	62231	8069
Psychiatric and Substance Abuse Hospitals—*hlth*	62221	8069
Maternity shops: Women's Clothing Stores—*retail*	44812	5621
Matrix board: Paperboard Mills—*mfg*	32213	2631
Matrix paper: Newsprint Mills—*mfg*	322122	2621
Paper (except Newsprint) Mills—*mfg*	322121	2621
Mats and matting, made from purchased wire: Fabricated Wire Product, Other—*mfg*	332618	3496
Mats and matting, textile: Carpet and Rug Mills—*mfg*	31411	2273
Mats and matting–e.g., bath, door-rubber: Fabric Coating Mills—*mfg*	31332	3069
Rubber Product, All Other—*mfg*	326299	3069
Mats and matting–twisted paper, grass, reed, coir, sisal, jute, and rag: Carpet and Rug Mills—*mfg*	31411	2273
Mats, advertising and newspaper (matrices): Printing Machinery and Equipment—*mfg*	333293	3555
Mats, felt–except woven: Broadwoven Fabric Mills—*mfg*	31321	2299
Narrow Fabric Mills—*mfg*	313221	2299
Nonwoven Fabric Mills—*mfg*	31323	2299
Textile and Fabric Finishing (except Broadwoven Fabric) Mills—*mfg*	313312	2299
Textile Product Mills, All Other Miscellaneous—*mfg*	314999	2299
Thread Mills—*mfg*	313113	2299
Yarn Spinning Mills—*mfg*	313111	2299
Mats, preseeded–soil erosion-growing of: Floriculture Production—*ag*	111422	181
Nursery and Tree Production—*ag*	111421	181
Mats, varnished glass: Fabric Coating Mills—*mfg*	31332	2295
Mattocks (handtools): Hand and Edge Tool—*mfg*	332212	3423
Mattress Manufacturing	**33791**	**2515**
Mattress pads: Household Textile Product Mills, Other—*mfg*	314129	2392
Mattress protectors, except rubber: Household Textile Product Mills, Other—*mfg*	314129	2392
Mattress protectors, rubber: Fabric Coating Mills—*mfg*	31332	3069
Rubber Product, All Other—*mfg*	326299	3069
Mattress renovating and repair shops: Personal and Household Goods Repair and Maintenance, Other—*serv*	81149	7699
Mattress stores, including custom made: Furniture Stores—*retail*	44211	5712
Nonupholstered Wood Household Furniture—*mfg*	337122	5712
Upholstered Household Furniture—*mfg*	337121	5712
Wood Kitchen Cabinet and Counter Top—*mfg*	33711	5712
Mattresses: Furniture—*whlse*	42121	5021
Furniture Stores—*retail*	44211	5021
Mattresses for river revetment, concrete articulated: Concrete Pipe—*mfg*	327332	3272
Concrete Product, Other—*mfg*	32739	3272
Nonmetallic Mineral Product, All Other Miscellaneous—*mfg*	327999	3272
Mattresses, asbestos: Motor Vehicle Brake System—*mfg*	33634	3292
Nonmetallic Mineral Product, All Other Miscellaneous—*mfg*	327999	3292
Mattresses, containing felt, foam rubber, urethane, etc.: Mattress—*mfg*	33791	2515
Upholstered Household Furniture—*mfg*	337121	2515
Mattresses, pneumatic–fabric coated withrubber: Fabric Coating Mills—*mfg*	31332	3069
Rubber Product, All Other—*mfg*	326299	3069
Mattresses–innerspring, box spring, and noninnerspring: Mattress—*mfg*	33791	2515
Upholstered Household Furniture—*mfg*	337121	2515
Matzoths: Bakeries, Commercial—*mfg*	311812	2052
Cookie and Cracker—*mfg*	311821	2052
Snack Food, Other—*mfg*	311919	2052
Mauls, metal (handtools): Hand and Edge Tool—*mfg*	332212	3423
Mauls, wood: Manufacturing, All Other Miscellaneous—*mfg*	339999	2499
Wood Container and Pallet—*mfg*	32192	2499
Wood Product, All Other Miscellaneous—*mfg*	321999	2499
Maulsticks, artists': Chemical Product, All Other Miscellaneous—*mfg*	325998	3952
Institutional Furniture—*mfg*	337127	3952
Lead Pencil and Art Good—*mfg*	339942	3952
Mausoleum construction–general contractors: Building, Commercial and Institutional—*const*	23332	1542
Mausoleum operation: Cemeteries and Crematories—*serv*	81222	6553
Mayonnaise: Fruit and Vegetable Canning—*mfg*	311421	2035
Mayonnaise, Dressing and Other Prepared Sauce—*mfg*	311941	2035
Mayonnaise, Dressing and Other Prepared Sauce Manufacturing	**311941**	**2099**
Mayors' offices: Executive Offices—*pub*	92111	9111
MDF (Medium density fiberboard): Building Material Dealers, Other—*retail*	44419	5031
MDF (medium density fiberboard): Reconstituted Wood Product—*mfg*	321219	2493
Meal delivery programs: Child and Youth Services—*hlth*	62411	8322
Community Food Services—*hlth*	62421	8322
Community Housing Services, Other—*hlth*	624229	8322
Emergency and Other Relief Services—*hlth*	62423	8322
Individual and Family Services, Other—*hlth*	62419	8322
Parole Offices and Probation Offices—*pub*	92215	8322
Services for the Elderly and Persons with Disabilities—*hlth*	62412	8322
Temporary Shelters—*hlth*	624221	8322
Meal, blood: Fats and Oils Refining and Blending—*mfg*	311225	2077
Fresh and Frozen Seafood Processing—*mfg*	311712	2077
Rendering and Meat By-product Processing—*mfg*	311613	2077

ALPHABETICAL INDEX	NAICS	SIC
Seafood Canning—*mfg*	311711	2077
Meal, bone–prepared as feed for animals and fowls: Animal (except Poultry) Slaughtering—*mfg*	311611	2048
Animal Food, Other—*mfg*	311119	2048
Meal, corn: Flour Milling—*mfg*	311211	2041
Meal, gluten: Wet Corn Milling—*mfg*	311221	2046
Meal, meat and bone–not prepared as feed: Fats and Oils Refining and Blending—*mfg*	311225	2077
Fresh and Frozen Seafood Processing—*mfg*	311712	2077
Rendering and Meat By-product Processing—*mfg*	311613	2077
Seafood Canning—*mfg*	311711	2077
Meals, frozen: Frozen Specialty Food—*mfg*	311412	2038
Measuring and Controlling Device Manufacturing, Other	**334519**	**3829**
Measuring and controlling instrument repair, mechanical: Electronic and Precision Equipment Repair and Maintenance, Other—*serv*	811219	7699
Measuring and Dispensing Pump Manufacturing	**333913**	**3586**
Measuring and testing equipment, electrical, except automotive: Industrial Machinery and Equipment—*whlse*	42183	5084
Measuring equipment for electronic and electrical circuits and equipment: Electronic Coil, Transformer, and Other Inductor—*mfg*	334416	3825
Instrument for Measuring and Testing Electricity and Electrical Signals—*mfg*	334515	3825
Measuring instruments and meters, electric: Electronic Coil, Transformer, and Other Inductor—*mfg*	334416	3825
Instrument for Measuring and Testing Electricity and Electrical Signals—*mfg*	334515	3825
Measuring tools and machines, machinists' metalworking type: Cutting Tool and Machine Tool Accessory—*mfg*	333515	3545
Hand and Edge Tool—*mfg*	332212	3545
Measuring wheels: Totalizing Fluid Meter and Counting Device—*mfg*	334514	3824
Meat: Animal (except Poultry) Slaughtering—*mfg*	311611	2011
Meat and bone meal and tankage: Fats and Oils Refining and Blending—*mfg*	311225	2077
Fresh and Frozen Seafood Processing—*mfg*	311712	2077
Rendering and Meat By-product Processing—*mfg*	311613	2077
Seafood Canning—*mfg*	311711	2077
Meat and Meat Product Wholesalers	**42247**	**5147**
Meat and poultry processing machinery: Food Product Machinery—*mfg*	333294	3556
Meat bagging: Knit Fabric and Lace Mills, Other—*mfg*	313249	2259
Weft Knit Fabric Mills—*mfg*	313241	2259
Meat extracts: Animal (except Poultry) Slaughtering—*mfg*	311611	2011
Meat Processed from Carcasses—*mfg*	311612	2013
Meat grinders: Food Product Machinery—*mfg*	333294	3556

ALPHABETICAL INDEX	NAICS	SIC
Meat Markets	**44521**	**5499**
Meat markets: Direct Selling Establishments, Other—*retail*	45439	5421
Fish and Seafood Markets—*retail*	44522	5421
Meat Markets—*retail*	44521	5421
Meat packing plants: Animal (except Poultry) Slaughtering—*mfg*	311611	2011
Meat pies, frozen: Packaged Frozen Food—*whlse*	42242	5142
Meat Processed from Carcasses	**311612**	**5147**
Meat Product Manufacturing	**3116**	
Meat products–cooked, cured, frozen, smoked, and spiced: Meat Processed from Carcasses—*mfg*	311612	2013
Meat, frozen–packaged: Packaged Frozen Food—*whlse*	42242	5142
Meats, cured or smoked: Meat and Meat Product—*whlse*	42247	5147
Meat Processed from Carcasses—*mfg*	311612	5147
Meats, fresh: Meat and Meat Product—*whlse*	42247	5147
Meat Processed from Carcasses—*mfg*	311612	5147
Mechanical contractors: Plumbing, Heating and Air-Conditioning Contractors—*const*	23511	1711
Mechanical games, coin-operated–operation of: Amusement and Recreation Industries, All Other—*arts*	71399	7993
Amusement Arcades—*arts*	71312	7993
Gambling Industries, Other—*arts*	71329	7993
Mechanical leather: Leather and Hide Tanning and Finishing—*mfg*	31611	3111
Mechanical Power Transmission Equipment Manufacturing	**333613**	**3568**
Mechanical power transmission forgings, ferrous–not made in rolling mills: Iron and Steel Forging—*mfg*	332111	3462
Mechanical power transmission forgings, nonferrous–not made in hot-rolling mills: Nonferrous Forging—*mfg*	332112	3463
Mechanical rubber goods–molded, extruded, and lathe-cut: Rubber Product for Mechanical Use—*mfg*	326291	3061
Mechanical springs, precision–made from purchased wire: Watch, Clock, and Part—*mfg*	334518	3495
Wire Spring—*mfg*	332612	3495
Mechanical-pneumatic or hydraulic metal forming machines: Machine Tool (Metal Forming Types)—*mfg*	333513	3542
Mechanics' handtools: Hand and Edge Tool—*mfg*	332212	3423
Mechanics' paste: Nonupholstered Wood Household Furniture—*mfg*	337122	2511
Mechanisms for clockwork operated de vices: Watch, Clock, and Part—*mfg*	334518	3873
Mechanisms for coin-operated machines: Automatic Vending Machine—*mfg*	333311	3581
Medallions: Jewelry, Watch, Precious Stone and Precious Metal—*whlse*	42194	5094
Medals of precious or semiprecious metals: Jewelry (except Costume)—*mfg*	339911	3911
Media Buying Agencies	**54183**	**7319**
Media buying service: Advertising Material Distribution Services—*prof*	54187	7319

Advertising, Other Services Related to—*prof*	54189	7319
Display Advertising—*prof*	54185	7319
Media Buying Agencies—*prof*	54183	7319
Nonscheduled Air, Other—*trans*	481219	7319
Media Representatives	**54184**	**7313**
Media-to-media data conversion equipment, computer peripheral equipment: Computer Peripheral Equipment, Other—*mfg*	334119	3577
Medical and Diagnostic Laboratories	**6215**	
Medical and Diagnostic Laboratories	**62151**	
Medical assistance program administration: Social, Human Resource and Income Maintenance Programs, Administration of—*pub*	92313	9441
Medical associations: Professional Organizations—*serv*	81392	8621
Medical equipment: Health and Personal Care Stores, All Other—*retail*	446199	5047
Medical, Dental and Hospital Equipment and Supplies—*whlse*	42145	5047
Medical Equipment and Supplies Manufacturing	**33911**	
Medical Equipment and Supplies Manufacturing	**3391**	
Medical equipment rental and leasing: Home Health Equipment Rental—*real*	532291	7352
Machinery and Equipment Rental and Leasing, Other Commercial and Industrial—*real*	53249	7352
Medical equipment repair, electrical: Appliance Repair and Maintenance—*serv*	811412	7629
Electronic and Precision Equipment Repair and Maintenance, Other—*serv*	811219	7629
Medical glass: Health and Personal Care Stores, All Other—*retail*	446199	5047
Medical, Dental and Hospital Equipment and Supplies—*whlse*	42145	5047
Medical insurance claims, processing of–contract or fee basis: Claims Adjusters—*fin*	524291	6411
Insurance Agencies and Brokerages—*fin*	52421	6411
Insurance Related Activities, All Other—*fin*	524298	6411
Third Party Administration for Insurance and Pension Funds—*fin*	524292	6411
Medical Laboratories	**621511**	**8071**
Medical laboratories, clinical: Diagnostic Imaging Centers—*hlth*	621512	8071
Medical Laboratories—*hlth*	621511	8071
Medical photography and art: Graphic Design Services—*prof*	54143	8099
Medical research, noncommercial: Research and Development in the Life Sciences—*prof*	54172	8733
Research and Development in the Physical Sciences and Engineering Sciences—*prof*	54171	8733
Mechanical springs, precision–made from purchased wire: Watch, Clock, and Part—*mfg*	334518	3495
Wire Spring—*mfg*	332612	3495
Mechanical-pneumatic or hydraulic metal forming machines: Machine Tool (Metal Forming Types)—*mfg*	333513	3542
Mechanics' handtools: Hand and Edge Tool—*mfg*	332212	3423
Mechanics' paste: Nonupholstered Wood Household Furniture—*mfg*	337122	2511
Mechanisms for clockwork operated de vices: Watch, Clock, and Part—*mfg*	334518	3873
Mechanisms for coin-operated machines: Automatic Vending Machine—*mfg*	333311	3581
Medallions: Jewelry, Watch, Precious Stone and Precious Metal—*whlse*	42194	5094
Medals of precious or semiprecious metals: Jewelry (except Costume)—*mfg*	339911	3911
Media Buying Agencies	**54183**	**7319**
Media buying service: Advertising Material Distribution Services—*prof*	54187	7319

Advertising, Other Services Related to—*prof*	54189	7319
Display Advertising—*prof*	54185	7319
Media Buying Agencies—*prof*	54183	7319
Nonscheduled Air, Other—*trans*	481219	7319
Media Representatives	**54184**	**7313**
Media-to-media data conversion equipment, computer peripheral equipment: Computer Peripheral Equipment, Other—*mfg*	334119	3577
Medical and Diagnostic Laboratories	**6215**	
Medical and Diagnostic Laboratories	**62151**	
Medical assistance program administration: Social, Human Resource and Income Maintenance Programs, Administration of—*pub*	92313	9441
Medical associations: Professional Organizations—*serv*	81392	8621
Medical equipment: Health and Personal Care Stores, All Other—*retail*	446199	5047
Medical, Dental and Hospital Equipment and Supplies—*whlse*	42145	5047
Medical Equipment and Supplies Manufacturing	**33911**	
Medical Equipment and Supplies Manufacturing	**3391**	
Medical equipment rental and leasing: Home Health Equipment Rental—*real*	532291	7352
Machinery and Equipment Rental and Leasing, Other Commercial and Industrial—*real*	53249	7352
Medical equipment repair, electrical: Appliance Repair and Maintenance—*serv*	811412	7629
Electronic and Precision Equipment Repair and Maintenance, Other—*serv*	811219	7629
Medical glass: Health and Personal Care Stores, All Other—*retail*	446199	5047
Medical, Dental and Hospital Equipment and Supplies—*whlse*	42145	5047
Medical insurance claims, processing of–contract or fee basis: Claims Adjusters—*fin*	524291	6411
Insurance Agencies and Brokerages—*fin*	52421	6411
Insurance Related Activities, All Other—*fin*	524298	6411
Third Party Administration for Insurance and Pension Funds—*fin*	524292	6411
Medical Laboratories	**621511**	**8071**
Medical laboratories, clinical: Diagnostic Imaging Centers—*hlth*	621512	8071
Medical Laboratories—*hlth*	621511	8071
Medical photography and art: Graphic Design Services—*prof*	54143	8099
Medical research, noncommercial: Research and Development in the Life Sciences—*prof*	54172	8733
Research and Development in the Physical Sciences and Engineering Sciences—*prof*	54171	8733

ALPHABETICAL INDEX	NAICS	SIC
Research and Development in the Social Sciences and Humanities—*prof*	54173	8733
Medical rubber goods: Drug, Drug Proprietaries and Druggists' Sundries—*whlse*	42221	5122
Medical service plans: Direct Health and Medical Insurance Carriers—*fin*	524114	6324
Insurance Funds, Other—*fin*	52519	6324
Reinsurance Carriers—*fin*	52413	6324
Medical sundries, rubber: Fabric Coating Mills—*mfg*	31332	3069
Rubber Product, All Other—*mfg*	326299	3069
Medical uniforms: Men's and Boys' Cut and Sew Apparel Contractors—*mfg*	315211	2326
Men's and Boys' Cut and Sew Work Clothing—*mfg*	315225	2326
Medical, Dental and Hospital Equipment and Supplies Wholesalers	**42145**	**5047**
Medicinal and Botanical Manufacturing	**325411**	**2833**
Medicinals and botanicals: Drug, Drug Proprietaries and Druggists' Sundries—*whlse*	42221	5122
Medicine bottles, glass: Glass Container—*mfg*	327213	3221
Medicine cabinet sundries: Drug, Drug Proprietaries and Druggists' Sundries—*whlse*	42221	5122
Medicine droppers, made from purchased glass: Glass Product Made of Purchased Glass—*mfg*	327215	3231
Medicines, capsuled or ampuled: Pharmaceutical Preparation—*mfg*	325412	2834
Medium density fiberboard: Building Material Dealers, Other—*retail*	44419	5031
Medium density fiberboard (MDF): Reconstituted Wood Product—*mfg*	321219	2493
Meerschaum mining or quarrying: Crushed and Broken Stone and Quarrying, Other—*mining*	212319	1499
Non-Metallic Mineral, All Other—*mining*	212399	1499
Melamine resins: Plastics Material and Resin—*mfg*	325211	2821
Mellorine: Ice Cream and Frozen Dessert—*mfg*	31152	2024
Melon farms: Vegetable (except Potato) and Melon Farming, Other—*ag*	111219	161
Melting pots, for metal: Air-Conditioning and Warm Air Heating Equipment and Commercial and Industrial Refrigeration Equipment—*mfg*	333415	3443
Metal Tank (Heavy Gauge)—*mfg*	33242	3443
Plate Work—*mfg*	332313	3443
Power Boiler and Heat Exchanger—*mfg*	33241	3443
Melting pots, glasshouse–clay: Clay Refractory—*mfg*	327124	3255
Melton jackets: Cut and Sew Apparel, All Other—*mfg*	315299	2329
Men's and Boys' Cut and Sew Apparel Contractors—*mfg*	315211	2329
Men's and Boys' Cut and Sew Other Outerwear—*mfg*	315228	2329
Memorandum books, except printed: Stationery, Tablet, and Related Product—*mfg*	322233	2678

ALPHABETICAL INDEX	NAICS	SIC
Memorandum books, printed: Blankbook, Loose-leaf Binder and Device—*mfg*	323118	2782
Flexographic Printing, Commercial—*mfg*	323112	2782
Gravure Printing, Commercial—*mfg*	323111	2782
Lithographic Printing, Commercial—*mfg*	323110	2782
Printing, Other Commercial—*mfg*	323119	2782
Screen Printing, Commercial—*mfg*	323113	2782
Memories, solid-state: Semiconductor and Related Device—*mfg*	334413	3674
Men's and Boys' Clothing and Furnishings Wholesalers	**42232**	**5136**
Men's Clothing Stores	**44811**	**5611**
Men's Footwear (except Athletic) Manufacturing	**316213**	**3143**
Men's hosiery: Hosiery and Sock Mills, Other—*mfg*	315119	2252
Sheer Hosiery Mills—*mfg*	315111	2252
Men's wearing apparel: Clothing Accessories Stores—*retail*	44815	5611
Men's Clothing Stores—*retail*	44811	5611
Menhaden, catching of: Finfish Fishing—*ag*	114111	912
Mental health agencies: Public Health Programs, Administration of—*pub*	92312	9431
Mental Health Practitioners (except Physicians), Offices Of	**62133**	**8049**
Mental hospitals, except for the mentally retarded: Psychiatric and Substance Abuse Hospitals—*hlth*	62221	8063
Mental retardation hospitals: Continuing Care Retirement Communities—*hlth*	623311	8051
Nursing Care Facilities—*hlth*	62311	8051
Menus, except lithographed or gravure printed: Digital Printing—*mfg*	323115	2759
Flexographic Printing, Commercial—*mfg*	323112	2759
Printing, Other Commercial—*mfg*	323119	2759
Quick Printing—*mfg*	323114	2759
Menus, lithographed: Lithographic Printing, Commercial—*mfg*	323110	2752
Quick Printing—*mfg*	323114	2752
Menus–gravure printing: Gravure Printing, Commercial—*mfg*	323111	2754
Mercantile credit reporting bureaus: Credit Bureaus—*admin*	56145	7323
Mercantile financing: Financial Transactions Processing, Reserve, and Clearing House Activities—*fin*	52232	6153
Non-Depository Credit Intermediation, All Other—*fin*	522298	6153
Sales Financing—*fin*	52222	6153
Mercerizing cotton broadwoven fabric: Broadwoven Fabric Finishing Mills—*mfg*	313311	2261
Mercerizing machinery: Textile Machinery—*mfg*	333292	3552
Mercerizing yarn, braided goods, narrow fabrics–except knit and wool: Broadwoven Fabric Finishing Mills—*mfg*	313311	2269
Textile and Fabric Finishing (except Broadwoven Fabric) Mills—*mfg*	313312	2269
Merchandise bags, plastics: Plastics, Foil, and Coated Paper Bag—*mfg*	322223	2673
Unsupported Plastics Bag—*mfg*	326111	2673

Description	NAICS	SIC
Merchandise bags, uncoated paper: Uncoated Paper and Multiwall Bag—*mfg*	322224	2674
Merchandising machines, automatic: Automatic Vending Machine—*mfg*	333311	3581
Equipment, Other Commercial—*whlse*	42144	5046
Merchandising, automatic (sale of products through vending machines): Vending Machine Operators—*retail*	45421	5962
Merchant tailors: Clothing Accessories Stores—*retail*	44815	5699
Clothing Stores, Other—*retail*	44819	5699
Merchants of raw farm products, except grain, field beans, and livestock: Farm Product Raw Material, Other—*whlse*	42259	5159
Merchants' associations, not engaged in credit investigations: Business Associations—*serv*	81391	8611
Mercury: Metal Service Centers and Offices—*whlse*	42151	5051
Mercury arc rectifiers (electrical apparatus): Electrical Equipment and Component, All Other Miscellaneous—*mfg*	335999	3629
Mercury azide (explosives): Explosives—*mfg*	32592	2892
Mercury chlorides (calomel, corrosive sublimate), except U.S.P.: Basic Inorganic Chemical, All Other—*mfg*	325188	2819
Chemical Product, All Other Miscellaneous—*mfg*	325998	2819
Mercury chlorides, U.S.P.: Medicinal and Botanical—*mfg*	325411	2833
Mercury compounds, inorganic: Basic Inorganic Chemical, All Other—*mfg*	325188	2819
Chemical Product, All Other Miscellaneous—*mfg*	325998	2819
Mercury compounds, medicinal–organic and inorganic: Medicinal and Botanical—*mfg*	325411	2833
Mercury ore mining: Metal Ore, All Other—*mining*	212299	1099
Mercury oxides: Basic Inorganic Chemical, All Other—*mfg*	325188	2819
Chemical Product, All Other Miscellaneous—*mfg*	325998	2819
Mercury, redistilled: Basic Inorganic Chemical, All Other—*mfg*	325188	2819
Chemical Product, All Other Miscellaneous—*mfg*	325998	2819
Mesh, made from purchased wire: Fabricated Wire Product, Other—*mfg*	332618	3496
Message concentrators: Electronic Coil, Transformer, and Other Inductor—*mfg*	334416	3661
Printed Circuit/Electronics Assembly—*mfg*	334418	3661
Telephone Apparatus—*mfg*	33421	3661
Metabolism apparatus: Surgical and Medical Instrument—*mfg*	339112	3841
Metabolite diagnostic reagents: In-Vitro Diagnostic Substance—*mfg*	325413	2835
Pharmaceutical Preparation—*mfg*	325412	2835
Metal and Mineral (except Petroleum) Wholesalers	**4215**	
Metal buildings: Building Material Dealers, Other—*retail*	44419	5039
Construction Material, Other—*whlse*	42139	5039
Metal Can Manufacturing	**332431**	**3411**
Metal Can, Box, and Other Metal Container (Light Gauge) Manufacturing	**33243**	
Metal Coating, Engraving (except Jewelry and Silverware), and Allied Services to Manufacturers	**332812**	**3479**
Metal Container Manufacturing, Other	**332439**	**3429**
Metal cyanides: Chemical and Allied Products, Other—*whlse*	42269	5169
Metal deposit forming machines: Machine Tool (Metal Forming Types)—*mfg*	333513	3542
Metal doors, sash and trim: Building Material Dealers, Other—*retail*	44419	5031
Metal drawing compound lubricants: Basic Organic Chemical, All Other—*mfg*	325199	2899
Chemical Product, All Other Miscellaneous—*mfg*	325998	2899
Metal fasteners, spring and cold-rolled steel, not made in rolling mills: Hardware—*mfg*	33251	3429
Metal finishing equipment for plating, except rolling mill lines: Industrial Machinery, All Other—*mfg*	333298	3559
Machinery, Other Commercial and Service Industry—*mfg*	333319	3559
Metal furring–contractors: Structural Steel Erection Contractors—*const*	23591	1791
Metal Heat Treating	**332811**	**3398**
Metal Household Furniture Manufacturing	**337124**	**2514**
Metal melting furnaces, industrial: Industrial Process Furnace and Oven—*mfg*	333994	3567
Metal Mining Support Activities	**213114**	**1081**
Metal Ore Mining	**2122**	
Metal Ore Mining, All Other	**212299**	**1099**
Metal oxide silicon (MOS) devices: Semiconductor and Related Device—*mfg*	334413	3674
Metal pickling equipment, except rolling mill lines: Industrial Machinery, All Other—*mfg*	333298	3559
Machinery, Other Commercial and Service Industry—*mfg*	333319	3559
Metal polishes: Chemical and Allied Products, Other—*whlse*	42269	5169
Metal polishing lathes: Machine Tool (Metal Cutting Types)—*mfg*	333512	3541
Metal refining machinery and equipment: Industrial Machinery and Equipment—*whlse*	42183	5084
Metal salts: Chemical and Allied Products, Other—*whlse*	42269	5169
Metal sanitary ware: Building Material Dealers, Other—*retail*	44419	5074
Plumbing and Heating Equipment and Supplies (Hydronics)—*whlse*	42172	5074
Metal Service Centers and Offices	**42151**	**5051**
Metal smelting and refining machinery, except furnaces and ovens: Industrial Machinery, All Other—*mfg*	333298	3559
Machinery, Other Commercial and Service Industry—*mfg*	333319	3559
Metal Stamping	**332116**	**3469**
Metal Tank (Heavy Gauge) Manufacturing	**33242**	**3443**
Metal treating compounds: Basic Organic Chemical, All Other—*mfg*	325199	2899
Chemical Product, All Other Miscellaneous—*mfg*	325998	2899
Metal Valve Manufacturing	**33291**	
Metal waste and scrap: Recyclable Material—*whlse*	42193	5093
Metal Window and Door Manufacturing	**332321**	**3449**
Metallic abrasives: Abrasive Product—*mfg*	32791	3291
Fabricated Metal Product, All Other Miscellaneous—*mfg*	332999	3291
Metallic concentrates: Coal and Other Mineral and Ore—*whlse*	42152	5052

ALPHABETICAL INDEX	NAICS	SIC
Metallic covered paper for packaging: Coated and Laminated Packaging Paper and Plastics Film—*mfg*	322221	2671
Unsupported Plastics Packaging Film and Sheet—*mfg*	326112	2671
Metallic covered paper, except for packaging: Coated and Laminated Paper—*mfg*	322222	2672
Metallic emulsion sensitized paper and cloth, photographic: Photographic and Photocopying Equipment—*mfg*	333315	3861
Photographic Film, Paper, Plate and Chemical—*mfg*	325992	3861
Metallic ores: Coal and Other Mineral and Ore—*whlse*	42152	5052
Metallic pigments, inorganic: Inorganic Dye and Pigment—*mfg*	325131	2816
Metallic pignients, inorganic: Carbon Black—*mfg*	325182	2816
Metallic salts of acyclic organic chemicals: Basic Organic Chemical, All Other—*mfg*	325199	2869
Metallic stearate: Basic Organic Chemical, All Other—*mfg*	325199	2869
Metallizing of fabrics: Fabric Coating Mills—*mfg*	31332	2295
Metallographs: Optical Instrument and Lens—*mfg*	333314	3827
Metallurgical testing laboratories: Testing Laboratories—*prof*	54138	8734
Veterinary Services—*prof*	54194	8734
Metals, except precious: Metal Service Centers and Offices—*whlse*	42151	5051
Metals, liquid: Basic Inorganic Chemical, All Other—*mfg*	325188	2819
Chemical Product, All Other Miscellaneous—*mfg*	325998	2819
Metals, precious: Jewelry, Watch, Precious Stone and Precious Metal—*whlse*	42194	5094
Metalware stores: Home Furnishings Stores, All Other—*retail*	442299	5719
Window Treatment Stores—*retail*	442291	5719
Metalworking machinery: Industrial Machinery and Equipment—*whlse*	42183	5084
Metalworking Machinery Manufacturing	**3335**	
Metalworking Machinery Manufacturing	**33351**	
Metalworking tools–drills, taps, dies, grinding wheels, and files: Industrial Machinery and Equipment—*whlse*	42183	5084
Meteorogic tracking systems: Measuring and Controlling Device, Other—*mfg*	334519	3829
Surgical and Medical Instrument—*mfg*	339112	3829
Meteorological instrument repair: Electronic and Precision Equipment Repair and Maintenance, Other—*serv*	811219	7699
Meteorological instruments: Measuring and Controlling Device, Other—*mfg*	334519	3829
Surgical and Medical Instrument—*mfg*	339112	3829
Meter boxes, concrete: Concrete Pipe—*mfg*	327332	3272
Concrete Product, Other—*mfg*	32739	3272
Nonmetallic Mineral Product, All Other Miscellaneous—*mfg*	327999	3272
Meter pens: Pen and Mechanical Pencil—*mfg*	339941	3951
Metering panels, electric: Switchgear and Switchboard Apparatus—*mfg*	335313	3613
Meters, electric–pocket, portable, panel-board, and graphic recording: Electronic Coil, Transformer, and Other Inductor—*mfg*	334416	3825
Instrument for Measuring and Testing Electricity and Electrical Signals—*mfg*	334515	3825
Meters, power factor and phase angle: Electronic Coil, Transformer, and Other Inductor—*mfg*	334416	3825
Instrument for Measuring and Testing Electricity and Electrical Signals—*mfg*	334515	3825
Meters–gas, liquid, tallying, and mechanical measuring-except electrical: Totalizing Fluid Meter and Counting Device—*mfg*	334514	3824
Methanol, natural (wood alcohol): Gum and Wood Chemical—*mfg*	325191	2861
Methanol, synthetic (methyl alcohol): Basic Organic Chemical, All Other—*mfg*	325199	2869
Ethyl Alcohol—*mfg*	325193	2869
Methyl acetone: Gum and Wood Chemical—*mfg*	325191	2861
Methyl acrylate resins: Plastics Material and Resin—*mfg*	325211	2821
Methyl alcohol, natural (wood alcohol): Gum and Wood Chemical—*mfg*	325191	2861
Methyl cellulose plastics: Plastics Material and Resin—*mfg*	325211	2821
Methyl chloride: Basic Organic Chemical, All Other—*mfg*	325199	2869
Methyl methacrylate resins: Plastics Material and Resin—*mfg*	325211	2821
Methyl perhydrofluorine: Basic Organic Chemical, All Other—*mfg*	325199	2869
Methyl salicylate: Basic Organic Chemical, All Other—*mfg*	325199	2869
Methyl violet toners: Cyclic Crude and Intermediate—*mfg*	325192	2865
Petrochemical—*mfg*	32511	2865
Methylamine: Basic Organic Chemical, All Other—*mfg*	325199	2869
Methylene chloride: Basic Organic Chemical, All Other—*mfg*	325199	2869
Mexican foods, canned: Canning, Specialty—*mfg*	311422	2032
Food, All Other Miscellaneous—*mfg*	311999	2032
Mica mining: Crushed and Broken Stone and Quarrying, Other—*mining*	212319	1499
Non-Metallic Mineral, All Other—*mining*	212399	1499
Mica products, built-up and sheet, except radio parts: Gypsum and Gypsum Product—*mfg*	32742	3299
Nonmetallic Mineral Product, All Other Miscellaneous—*mfg*	327999	3299
Mica schist, crushed and broken-quarrymg: Crushed and Broken Stone and Quarrying, Other—*mining*	212319	1429
Mica schist, dimension: Dimension Stone and Quarrying—*mining*	212311	1411
Mica splitting: Gypsum and Gypsum Product—*mfg*	32742	3299
Nonmetallic Mineral Product, All Other Miscellaneous—*mfg*	327999	3299
Mica, ground or otherwise treated: Ground or Treated Mineral and Earth—*mfg*	327992	3295
Mica, laminated: Gypsum and Gypsum Product—*mfg*	32742	3299
Nonmetallic Mineral Product, All Other Miscellaneous—*mfg*	327999	3299
Microbiology, virology, and serology and diagnostic products: In-Vitro Diagnostic Substance—*mfg*	325413	2835

Pharmaceutical Preparation—*mfg*	325412	2835
Microcircuits, integrated (semiconductor): Semiconductor and Related Device—*mfg*	334413	3674
Microcomputers: Electronic Computer—*mfg*	334111	3571
Microfiche cameras: Photographic and Photocopying Equipment—*mfg*	333315	3861
Photographic Film, Paper, Plate and Chemical—*mfg*	325992	3861
Microfiche readers and reader printers: Photographic and Photocopying Equipment—*mfg*	333315	3861
Photographic Film, Paper, Plate and Chemical—*mfg*	325992	3861
Microfilm equipment–cameras, projectors, and readers: Photographic and Photocopying Equipment—*mfg*	333315	3861
Photographic Film, Paper, Plate and Chemical—*mfg*	325992	3861
Microfilming equipment: Office Equipment—*whlse*	42142	5044
Microlite mining: Metal Ore, All Other—*mining*	212299	1099
Micrometers: Cutting Tool and Machine Tool Accessory—*mfg*	333515	3545
Hand and Edge Tool—*mfg*	332212	3545
Microphones: Audio and Video Equipment—*mfg*	33431	3651
Microprobes–electron, ion, laser, X-ray: Analytical Laboratory Instrument—*mfg*	334516	3826
Microprocessors: Semiconductor and Related Device—*mfg*	334413	3674
Microprojectors: Optical Instrument and Lens—*mfg*	333314	3827
Micropublishing: Database and Directory Publishers—*info*	51114	2741
Music Publishers—*info*	51223	2741
Publishers, All Other—*info*	511199	2741
Microscopes, electron and proton: Analytical Laboratory Instrument—*mfg*	334516	3826
Microscopes, except electron, proton, andcorneal: Optical Instrument and Lens—*mfg*	333314	3827
Microwave communications equipment: Radio and Television Broadcasting and Wireless Communications Equipment—*mfg*	33422	3663
Microwave components: Electronic Component, Other—*mfg*	334419	3679
Motor Vehicle Electrical and Electronic Equipment, Other—*mfg*	336322	3679
Printed Circuit/Electronics Assembly—*mfg*	334418	3679
Radio and Television Broadcasting and Wireless Communications Equipment—*mfg*	33422	3679
Microwave ovens, household: Electrical Appliance, Television and Radio Set—*whlse*	42162	5064
Microwave ovens, household–including portable: Household Cooking Appliance—*mfg*	335221	3631
Microwave test equipment: Electronic Coil, Transformer, and Other Inductor—*mfg*	334416	3825
Instrument for Measuring and Testing Electricity and Electrical Signals—*mfg*	334515	3825
Microwaveware, plastics: Plastics Pipe and Pipe Fitting—*mfg*	326122	3089
Plastics Product, All Other—*mfg*	326199	3089
Unsupported Plastics Profile Shape—*mfg*	326121	3089
Middies: Infants' Cut and Sew Apparel—*mfg*	315291	2361
Men's and Boys' Cut and Sew Apparel Contractors—*mfg*	315211	2361
Men's and Boys' Cut and Sew Shirt (except Work Shirt)—*mfg*	315223	2361
Women's and Girls' Cut and Sew Apparel Contractors—*mfg*	315212	2361
Women's and Girls' Cut and Sew Blouse and Shirt—*mfg*	315232	2361
Women's and Girls' Cut and Sew Dress—*mfg*	315233	2361
Midwives, offices of: Health Practitioners, Offices Of Miscellaneous—*hlth*	621399	8049
Mental Health Practitioners (except Physicians), Offices Of—*hlth*	62133	8049
Physical, Occupational and Speech Therapists and Audiologists, Offices Of—*hlth*	62134	8049
Mildew proofing cotton broadwoven fabrics: Broadwoven Fabric Finishing Mills—*mfg*	313311	2261
Mildew proofing manmade fiber and silk broadwoven fabrics: Broadwoven Fabric Finishing Mills—*mfg*	313311	2262
Military academies, elementary and secondary level: Elementary and Secondary Schools—*educ*	61111	8211
Military Armored Vehicle, Tank and Tank Component Manufacturing	**336992**	**3795**
Military insignia, except textile: Fabricated Metal Product, All Other Miscellaneous—*mfg*	332999	3999
Military pyrotechnics: Basic Organic Chemical, All Other—*mfg*	325199	2899
Chemical Product, All Other Miscellaneous—*mfg*	325998	2899
Military training schools: National Security—*pub*	92811	9711
Military uniforms, tailored: Men's and Boys' Cut and Sew Apparel Contractors—*mfg*	315211	2311
Men's and Boys' Cut and Sew Suit, Coat and Overcoat—*mfg*	315222	2311
Milk (fluid) shipping containers, metal: Metal Container, Other—*mfg*	332439	3412
Milk and cream, fluid: Dairy Product (except Dried or Canned)—*whlse*	42243	5143
Milk and other dairy products stores: Food Stores, All Other Specialty—*retail*	445299	5451
Milk bottles, glass: Glass Container—*mfg*	327213	3221
Milk cans, metal: Metal Can—*mfg*	332431	3411
Milk carton board: Paperboard Mills—*mfg*	32213	2631
Milk cartons, paperboard: Non-Folding Sanitary Food Container—*mfg*	322215	2656
Milk cooling stations, operated by farm assemblers: Dairy Product (except Dried or Canned)—*whlse*	42243	5143
Milk delivery and sale of purchased milk, without processing: Direct Selling Establishments, Other—*retail*	45439	5963
Mobile Foodservices—*accom*	72233	5963
Milk depots: Dairy Product (except Dried or Canned)—*whlse*	42243	5143
Milk filter disks: Newsprint Mills—*mfg*	322122	2621
Paper (except Newsprint) Mills—*mfg*	322121	2621
Milk filter disks, diecut from purchased paper: Converted Paper Product, All Other—*mfg*	322298	2675
Die-Cut Paper and Paperboard Office Supplies—*mfg*	322231	2675
Surface-Coated Paperboard—*mfg*	322292	2675

ALPHABETICAL INDEX	NAICS	SIC
Milk processing (pasteurizing, homogenizing, vitaminizing, bottling): Fluid Milk—*mfg*	311511	2026
Milk processing machinery: Food Product Machinery—*mfg*	333294	3556
Milk production, dairy cattle farm: Beef Cattle Ranching and Farming—*ag*	112111	241
Dairy Cattle and Milk Production—*ag*	11212	241
Milk production, except farm: Fluid Milk—*mfg*	311511	2026
Milk production, goat farm: Goat Farming—*ag*	11242	214
Sheep Farming—*ag*	11241	214
Milk products manufacturing machinery and equipment: Industrial Machinery and Equipment—*whlse*	42183	5084
Milk testing for butterfat: Animal Production Support Activities—*ag*	11521	751
Milk, acidophilus: Fluid Milk—*mfg*	311511	2026
Milk, bottled: Fluid Milk—*mfg*	311511	2026
Milk, canned or dried: Grocery and Related Products, Other—*whlse*	42249	5149
Milk, flavored: Fluid Milk—*mfg*	311511	2026
Milk, reconstituted: Fluid Milk—*mfg*	311511	2026
Milk, ultra-high temperature: Fluid Milk—*mfg*	311511	2026
Milk, whole–canned: Dry, Condensed, and Evaporated Dairy Product—*mfg*	311514	2023
Milk–concentrated, condensed, dried, evaporated, and powdered: Dry, Condensed, and Evaporated Dairy Product—*mfg*	311514	2023
Milking machinery and equipment: Farm and Garden Machinery and Equipment—*whlse*	42182	5083
Outdoor Power Equipment Stores—*retail*	44421	5083
Milking machines: Farm Machinery and Equipment—*mfg*	333111	3523
Milkshake mix: Dry, Condensed, and Evaporated Dairy Product—*mfg*	311514	2023
Mill end store: Sewing, Needlework and Piece Goods Stores—*retail*	45113	5949
Mill enders, contract–cotton, silk, and manmade fiber: Broadwoven Fabric Finishing Mills—*mfg*	313311	2269
Textile and Fabric Finishing (except Broadwoven Fabric) Mills—*mfg*	313312	2269
Mill menders, contract–wool, mohair, and similar animal fibers: Broadwoven Fabric Finishing Mills—*mfg*	313311	2231
Broadwoven Fabric Mills—*mfg*	31321	2231
Textile and Fabric Finishing (except Broadwoven Fabric) Mills—*mfg*	313312	2231
Mill strapping for textile mills, leather: Leather Good, All Other—*mfg*	316999	3199
Mill supplies: Industrial Machinery and Equipment—*whlse*	42183	5085
Industrial Supplies—*whlse*	42184	5085
Mill tables (rolling mill equipment): Rolling Mill Machinery and Equipment—*mfg*	333516	3547
Millboard, asbestos: Motor Vehicle Brake System—*mfg*	33634	3292
Nonmetallic Mineral Product, All Other Miscellaneous—*mfg*	327999	3292
Millinery: Hat, Cap and Millinery—*mfg*	315991	2353

ALPHABETICAL INDEX	NAICS	SIC
Women's, Children's, and Infants' and Accessories—*whlse*	42233	5137
Millinery stores: Clothing Accessories Stores—*retail*	44815	5632
Clothing Stores, Other—*retail*	44819	5632
Millinery supplies: Broadwoven Fabric Finishing Mills—*mfg*	313311	5131
Piece Goods, Notions and Other Dry Goods—*whlse*	42231	5131
Textile and Fabric Finishing (except Broadwoven Fabric) Mills—*mfg*	313312	5131
Millinery trimmings: Apparel Accessories and Apparel, Other—*mfg*	315999	2396
Milling machine attachments (machinetool accessories): Cutting Tool and Machine Tool Accessory—*mfg*	333515	3545
Hand and Edge Tool—*mfg*	332212	3545
Milling machines (machine tools): Machine Tool (Metal Cutting Types)—*mfg*	333512	3541
Milling of grains, dry, except rice: Flour Milling—*mfg*	311211	2041
Milling of rice-rnfg: Rice Milling—*mfg*	311212	2044
Mills and presses–beet, eider, and sugarcane: Food Product Machinery—*mfg*	333294	3556
Millstone quarrying: Crushed and Broken Stone and Quarrying, Other—*mining*	212319	1499
Non-Metallic Mineral, All Other—*mining*	212399	1499
Millwork	**32191**	
Building Material Dealers, Other—*retail*	44419	5031
Millwork (including Flooring), Other	**321918**	**2421**
Millwork and lumbei- dealers: Building Material Dealers, Other—*retail*	44419	5211
Home Centers—*retail*	44411	5211
Millwork products: Millwork (including Flooring), Other—*mfg*	321918	2431
Wood Window and Door—*mfg*	321911	2431
Millwork, treated: Wood Preservation—*mfg*	321114	2491
Millwrights: Building Equipment and Other Machinery Installation Contractors—*const*	23595	1796
Milo farms: Grain Farming, All Other—*ag*	111199	119
Mimeograph equipment: Office Equipment—*whlse*	42142	5044
Mimeograph paper: Office Supplies and Stationery Stores—*retail*	45321	5112
Stationary and Office Supplies—*whlse*	42212	5112
Mimeographing service: Business Service Centers (including Copy Shops), Other—*admin*	561439	7334
Mincemeat, canned: Canning, Specialty—*mfg*	311422	2032
Food, All Other Miscellaneous—*mfg*	311999	2032
Mine conveyors-rnfg: Conveyor and Conveying Equipment—*mfg*	333922	3535
Mine development for metal mining–on acontract basis: Geophysical Surveying and Mapping Services—*prof*	54136	1081
Metal Support Activities—*mining*	213114	1081
Mine development for nonmetallic minerals, except fuels–on a contract basis: Geophysical Surveying and Mapping Services—*prof*	54136	1481
Non-Metallic Minerals (except Fuels) Support Activities—*mining*	213115	1481

Mine loading and discharging station con struction–general contractors: Heavy, All Other—*const*	23499	1629
Industrial Nonbuilding Structure—*const*	23493	1629
Mine props, treated: Wood Preservation—*mfg*	321114	2491
Mine ties, wood–treated: Wood Preservation—*mfg*	321114	2491
Mine timbers, hewn: Logging—*ag*	11331	2411
Mineral beneficiation machinery: Construction and (except Petroleum) Machinery and Equipment—*whlse*	42181	5082
Mineral colors and pigments: Carbon Black—*mfg*	325182	2816
Inorganic Dye and Pigment—*mfg*	325131	2816
Mineral feed supplements: Animal Food, Other—*mfg*	311119	2048
Mineral jelly, produced in petroleum refineries: Petroleum Refineries—*mfg*	32411	2911
Mineral leases, dealers in: Financial Investment Activities, Miscellaneous—*fin*	523999	6211
Intermediation, Miscellaneous—*fin*	52391	6211
Investment Banking and Securities Dealing—*fin*	52311	6211
Securities Brokerage—*fin*	52312	6211
Mineral oils, natural–produced in petroleum refineries: Petroleum Refineries—*mfg*	32411	2911
Mineral pigment mining: Chemical and Fertilizer Mineral, Other—*mining*	212393	1479
Mineral royalties, dealers in: Financial Investment Activities, Miscellaneous—*fin*	523999	6211
Intermediation, Miscellaneous—*fin*	52391	6211
Investment Banking and Securities Dealing—*fin*	52311	6211
Securities Brokerage—*fin*	52312	6211
Mineral supplements, animal: Farm Supplies—*whlse*	42291	5191
Nursery and Garden Centers—*retail*	44422	5191
Mineral water, carbonated–bottled orcanned: Bottled Water—*mfg*	312112	2086
Soft Drink—*mfg*	312111	2086
Mineral waxes, natural–produced in petroleum refineries: Petroleum Refineries—*mfg*	32411	2911
Mineral wool insulation materials-whole-sale: Roofing, Siding and Insulation Material—*whlse*	42133	5033
Mineral Wool Manufacturing	**327993**	**3296**
Mineral wool roofing mats: Mineral Wool—*mfg*	327993	3296
Miners' lamps: Lighting Equipment, Other—*mfg*	335129	3648
Mines and parts (ordnance): Ammunition (except Small Arms)—*mfg*	332993	3483
Minicomputers: Electronic Computer—*mfg*	334111	3571
Minimum wage program administration: Regulation, Licensing, and Inspection of Miscellaneous Commercial Sectors—*pub*	92615	9651
Mining	**21**	
Mining (except Oil and Gas)	**212**	
Mining and Oil and Gas Field Machinery Manufacturing	**33313**	
Mining appurtenance construction–general contractors: Heavy, All Other—*const*	23499	1629
Industrial Nonbuilding Structure—*const*	23493	1629
Mining cars and trucks (dollies): Mining Machinery and Equipment—*mfg*	333131	3532
Mining equipment, except oil and gasfield–rebuilding on a factory basis: Mining Machinery and Equipment—*mfg*	333131	3532
Mining locomotives and parts: Pump and Pumping Equipment—*mfg*	333911	3743
Railroad Rolling Stock—*mfg*	33651	3743
Mining Machinery and Equipment Manufacturing	**333131**	**3532**
Mining machinery and equipment, except oil and gas field: Mining Machinery and Equipment—*mfg*	333131	3532
Mining machinery and equipment, except petroleum: Construction and (except Petroleum) Machinery and Equipment—*whlse*	42181	5082
Mining Support Activities	**213**	
Mining Support Activities	**2131**	
Mining Support Activities	**21311**	
Minium (pigments): Carbon Black—*mfg*	325182	2816
Inorganic Dye and Pigment—*mfg*	325131	2816
Miniwarehouse warehousing: General Warehousing and Storage Facilities—*trans*	49311	4225
Lessors of Miniwarehouses and Self Storage Units—*real*	53113	4225
Mink farms: Fur-Bearing Animal and Rabbit Production—*ag*	11293	271
Minnow farms: Animal Aquaculture, Other—*ag*	112519	273
Finfish Farming and Fish Hatcheries—*ag*	112511	273
Shellfish Farming—*ag*	112512	273
Mint farms: Crop Farming, All Other Miscellaneous—*ag*	111998	139
Hay Farming—*ag*	11194	139
Peanut Farming—*ag*	111992	139
Vegetable (except Potato) and Melon Farming, Other—*ag*	111219	139
Mirrors: Home Furnishings Stores, All Other—*retail*	442299	5719
Window Treatment Stores—*retail*	442291	5719
Mirrors, framed or unframed–made from purchased glass: Glass Product Made of Purchased Glass—*mfg*	327215	3231
Mirrors, optical: Optical Instrument and Lens—*mfg*	333314	3827
Mirrors, transportation equipment–made from purchased glass: Glass Product Made of Purchased Glass—*mfg*	327215	3231
Missile facilities construction–general contractors: Heavy, All Other—*const*	23499	1629
Industrial Nonbuilding Structure—*const*	23493	1629
Missile forgings, ferrous–not made in rolling mills: Iron and Steel Forging—*mfg*	332111	3462
Missile forgings, nonferrous–not made in hot-rolling mills: Nonferrous Forging—*mfg*	332112	3463
Missile guidance systems and equipment: Search, Detection, Navigation, Guidance, Aeronautical, and Nautical System and Instrument—*mfg*	334511	3812
Missile silos and components, metal plate: Air-Conditioning and Warm Air Heating Equipment and Commercial and Industrial Refrigeration Equipment—*mfg*	333415	3443
Metal Tank (Heavy Gauge)—*mfg*	33242	3443
Plate Work—*mfg*	332313	3443

ALPHABETICAL INDEX	NAICS	SIC
Power Boiler and Heat Exchanger—*mfg*	33241	3443
Missile warheads: Ammunition (except Small Arms)—*mfg*	332993	3483
Mitre boxes, metal: Hand and Edge Tool—*mfg*	332212	3423
Mitten flannel, cotton: Broadwoven Fabric Mills—*mfg*	31321	2211
Mittens: Outerwear Knitting Mills—*mfg*	315191	2259
Mittens, leather: Glove and Mitten—*mfg*	315992	3151
Mittens, men's and boys': Men's and Boys' Clothing and Furnishings—*whlse*	42232	5136
Mittens, rubber: Fabric Coating Mills—*mfg*	31332	3069
Rubber Product, All Other—*mfg*	326299	3069
Mittens–women's, children's, and infants': Women's, Children's, and Infants' and Accessories—*whlse*	42233	5137
Mixed acid: Basic Inorganic Chemical, All Other—*mfg*	325188	2819
Chemical Product, All Other Miscellaneous—*mfg*	325998	2819
Mixed Mode Transit Systems	**485111**	**4111**
Mixers and whippers, electric–for food manufacturing industries: Food Product Machinery—*mfg*	333294	3556
Mixers for hot metal: Air-Conditioning and Warm Air Heating Equipment and Commercial and Industrial Refrigeration Equipment—*mfg*	333415	3443
Metal Tank (Heavy Gauge)—*mfg*	33242	3443
Plate Work—*mfg*	332313	3443
Power Boiler and Heat Exchanger—*mfg*	33241	3443
Mixers, construction and mining: Construction and (except Petroleum) Machinery and Equipment—*whlse*	42181	5082
Mixers, feed–except agricultural machinery: Food Product Machinery—*mfg*	333294	3556
Mixers, food–commercial types: Food Product Machinery—*mfg*	333294	3556
Mixers–e.g., concrete, ore, sand, slag, plaster, mortar, bituminous: Construction Machinery—*mfg*	33312	3531
Overhead Traveling Crane, Hoist and Monorail System—*mfg*	333923	3531
Railroad Rolling Stock—*mfg*	33651	3531
Mixes, flour–e.g., pancake, cake, biscuit, doughnut: Flour Milling—*mfg*	311211	2041
Flour Mixes and Dough from Purchased Flour—*mfg*	311822	2045
Mobile buildings for commercial use (e.g., offices, banks): Manufactured Home (Mobile Home)—*mfg*	321991	2451
Mobile classrooms: Manufactured Home (Mobile Home)—*mfg*	321991	2451
Mobile communications equipment: Radio and Television Broadcasting and Wireless Communications Equipment—*mfg*	33422	3663
Mobile dwellings: Manufactured Home (Mobile Home)—*mfg*	321991	2451
Mobile Foodservices	**72233**	**5963**
Mobile home equipment: Manufactured (Mobile) Home Dealers—*retail*	45393	5271
Mobile home parts and accessories: Manufactured (Mobile) Home Dealers—*retail*	45393	5271

ALPHABETICAL INDEX	NAICS	SIC
Mobile home rental, except on site: Truck, Utility Trailer, and RV (Recreational Vehicle) Rental and Leasing—*real*	53212	7519
Mobile home repair, on site–general contractors: Single Family Housing—*const*	23321	1521
Mobile home site setup and tie down–contractors: Trade Contractors, All Other Special—*const*	23599	1799
Mobile homes: Building Material Dealers, Other—*retail*	44419	5039
Construction Material, Other—*whlse*	42139	5039
Mobile homes, except recreational: Manufactured Home (Mobile Home)—*mfg*	321991	2451
Mobile homes, new and used: Manufactured (Mobile) Home Dealers—*retail*	45393	5271
Mobile lounges (motor vehicle): Automobile—*mfg*	336111	3711
Heavy Duty Truck—*mfg*	33612	3711
Light Truck and Utility Vehicle—*mfg*	336112	3711
Military Armored Vehicle, Tank and Tank Component—*mfg*	336992	3711
Motor Vehicle Body—*mfg*	336211	3711
Mobile straddle carriers: Fabricated Metal Product, All Other Miscellaneous—*mfg*	332999	3537
Industrial Truck, Tractor, Trailer and Stacker Machinery—*mfg*	333924	3537
Metal Container, Other—*mfg*	332439	3537
Moccasins: Footwear, Other—*mfg*	316219	3149
Modacrylic broadwoven fabrics: Broadwoven Fabric Mills—*mfg*	31321	2221
Modacrylic fibers: Noncellulosic Organic Fiber—*mfg*	325222	2824
Modacrylic yarn, made from purchased staple–spun: Yarn Spinning Mills—*mfg*	313111	2281
Model kits: Toy and Hobby Goods and Supplies—*whlse*	42192	5092
Model registries: Employment Placement Agencies—*admin*	56131	7361
Human Resources and Executive Search Consulting Services—*prof*	541612	7361
Modeling clay: Chemical Product, All Other Miscellaneous—*mfg*	325998	3952
Institutional Furniture—*mfg*	337127	3952
Lead Pencil and Art Good—*mfg*	339942	3952
Modeling schools, clothes: Schools and Instruction, All Other Miscellaneous—*educ*	611699	8299
Modeling service: Employee Leasing Services—*admin*	56133	7363
Temporary Help Services—*admin*	56132	7363
Models, anatomical: Surgical Appliance and Supplies—*mfg*	339113	3842
Models, except toy and hobby: Fabricated Metal Product, All Other Miscellaneous—*mfg*	332999	3999
Plastics Product, All Other—*mfg*	326199	3999
Wood Product, All Other Miscellaneous—*mfg*	321999	3999
Models, toy and hobby–e.g., airplane, boat, ship, railroad equipment: Game, Toy, and Children's Vehicle—*mfg*	339932	3944
Modems: Electronic Coil, Transformer, and Other Inductor—*mfg*	334416	3661
Electronic Parts and Equipment, Other—*whlse*	42169	5065
Printed Circuit/Electronics Assembly—*mfg*	334418	3661

Term	NAICS	SIC
Telephone Apparatus—*mfg*	33421	3661
Modular furniture systems, office, wood: Wood Office Furniture—*mfg*	337211	2521
Modular furniture systems, office–exceptwood: Nonwood Office Furniture—*mfg*	337214	2522
Modular housing, single-family (assembledon site)–general contractors: Single Family Housing—*const*	23321	1521
Modules, solid-state: Semiconductor and Related Device—*mfg*	334413	3674
Mohair production: Goat Farming—*ag*	11242	214
Sheep Farming—*ag*	11241	214
Mohair yarn–twisting, winding, or spooling: Textile and Fabric Finishing (except Broadwoven Fabric) Mills—*mfg*	313312	2282
Yarn Texturing, Throwing and Twisting Mills—*mfg*	313112	2282
Mohair, raw: Farm Product Raw Material, Other—*whlse*	42259	5159
Moisteners, gummed tape–for store and office use: Lead Pencil and Art Good—*mfg*	339942	3579
Office Machinery—*mfg*	333313	3579
Watch, Clock, and Part—*mfg*	334518	3579
Moisture analysers, laboratory type: Analytical Laboratory Instrument—*mfg*	334516	3826
Moisture meters, industrial process type: Instruments and Related Products for Measuring, Displaying, and Controlling Industrial Process Variables—*mfg*	334513	3823
Molasses beet pulp: Beet Sugar—*mfg*	311313	2063
Molasses, blackstrap–made from purchased raw cane sugar or sugar syrup: Cane Sugar Refining—*mfg*	311312	2062
Molasses, blackstrap–made from sugarcane: Sugarcane Mills—*mfg*	311311	2061
Molasses, industrial: Grocery and Related Products, Other—*whlse*	42249	5149
Molasses, made from sugar beets: Beet Sugar—*mfg*	311313	2063
Molasses, made from sugarcane: Sugarcane Mills—*mfg*	311311	2061
Molasses, mixed or blended: Food, All Other Miscellaneous—*mfg*	311999	2099
Molding compounds, plastics: Plastics Material and Resin—*mfg*	325211	2821
Molding of plastics for the trade, except foam: Plastics Pipe and Pipe Fitting—*mfg*	326122	3089
Plastics Product, All Other—*mfg*	326199	3089
Unsupported Plastics Profile Shape—*mfg*	326121	3089
Molding primary plastics for the trade, except foam: Plastics Pipe and Pipe Fitting—*mfg*	326122	3089
Plastics Product, All Other—*mfg*	326199	3089
Unsupported Plastics Profile Shape—*mfg*	326121	3089
Molding sand mining: Industrial Sand—*mining*	212322	1446
Molding, all materials: Building Material Dealers, Other—*retail*	44419	5031
Moldings and trim, automotive–stamped: Motor Vehicle Metal Stamping—*mfg*	33637	3465
Moldings and trim, metal–except automobile: Metal Window and Door—*mfg*	332321	3442
Moldings, architectural–plaster of paris-factory production only: Gypsum and Gypsum Product—*mfg*	32742	3299
Nonmetallic Mineral Product, All Other Miscellaneous—*mfg*	327999	3299
Moldings, picture frame–finished: Manufacturing, All Other Miscellaneous—*mfg*	339999	2499
Wood Container and Pallet—*mfg*	32192	2499
Wood Product, All Other Miscellaneous—*mfg*	321999	2499
Moldings, wood and covered wood–unfinished and prefinished: Millwork (including Flooring), Other—*mfg*	321918	2431
Wood Window and Door—*mfg*	321911	2431
Molds, industrial: Die and Tool, Die Set, Jig and Fixture, Special—*mfg*	333514	3544
Industrial Mold—*mfg*	333511	3544
Molecular devices, solid-state: Semiconductor and Related Device—*mfg*	334413	3674
Moleskins: Broadwoven Fabric Mills—*mfg*	31321	2211
Mollusk farms: Animal Aquaculture, Other—*ag*	112519	273
Finfish Farming and Fish Hatcheries—*ag*	112511	273
Shellfish Farming—*ag*	112512	273
Molybdenite mining: Copper Ore and Nickel Ore—*mining*	212234	1061
Metal Ore, All Other—*mining*	212299	1061
Molybdenum ore mining: Copper Ore and Nickel Ore—*mining*	212234	1061
Metal Ore, All Other—*mining*	212299	1061
Molybdenum silicon: Electrometallurgical Ferroalloy Product—*mfg*	331112	3313
Secondary Smelting, Refining, and Alloying of Nonferrous Metal (except Copper and Aluminum)—*mfg*	331492	3313
Molybdite mining: Copper Ore and Nickel Ore—*mining*	212234	1061
Metal Ore, All Other—*mining*	212299	1061
Momie crepe, cotton: Broadwoven Fabric Mills—*mfg*	31321	2211
Monasteries: Religious Organizations—*serv*	81311	8661
Monazite mining: Metal Ore, All Other—*mining*	212299	1099
Monetary Authorities - Central Bank	**52111**	**6011**
Monetary Authorities - Central Bank	**521**	
Monetary Authorities - Central Bank	**5211**	
Money chests, metal: Metal Container, Other—*mfg*	332439	3499
Money market mutual funds: Open-End Investment Funds—*fin*	52591	6722
Money order issuance: Commodity Contracts Dealing—*fin*	52313	6099
Credit Intermediation, Other Activities Related to—*fin*	52239	6099
Financial Investment Activities, Miscellaneous—*fin*	523999	6099
Financial Transactions Processing, Reserve, and Clearing House Activities—*fin*	52232	6099
Trust, Fiduciary and Custody Activities—*fin*	523991	6099
Monochlorodifluoromethane: Basic Organic Chemical, All Other—*mfg*	325199	2869
Monochrometers, laboratory type: Analytical Laboratory Instrument—*mfg*	334516	3826
Monofilaments, plastics–not suited for textile use: Plastics Pipe and Pipe Fitting—*mfg*	326122	3089
Plastics Product, All Other—*mfg*	326199	3089
Unsupported Plastics Profile Shape—*mfg*	326121	3089
Monolithic integrated circuits (solid-state): Semiconductor and Related Device—*mfg*	334413	3674

Description	NAICS	SIC
Casino Hotels—*accom*	72112	7011
Hotels (except Casino Hotels) and Motels—*accom*	72111	7011
Traveler Accommodation, All Other—*accom*	721199	7011
Moth repellants: Pesticide and Other Agricultural Chemical—*mfg*	32532	2879
Motion Picture and Sound Recording Industries	**512**	
Motion Picture and Video Distribution	**51212**	**7829**
Motion Picture and Video Exhibition	**51213**	
Motion Picture and Video Industries	**5121**	
Motion Picture and Video Industries, Other	**512199**	**7829**
Motion Picture and Video Production	**51211**	**7812**
Motion picture apparatus and equipment: Photographic and Photocopying Equipment—*mfg*	333315	3861
Photographic Film, Paper, Plate and Chemical—*mfg*	325992	3861
Motion picture camera equipment, and supplies: Photographic Equipment and Supplies—*whlse*	42141	5043
Motion picture consultants: Independent Artists, Writers, and Performers—*arts*	71151	7819
Motion Picture and Video Industries, Other—*info*	512199	7819
Motion picture distribution, exclusive of production: Durable Goods, Other Miscellaneous—*whlse*	42199	7822
Motion Picture and Video Distribution—*info*	51212	7822
Motion picture exhibitors for airlines: Motion Picture Theaters, Except Drive-Ins.—*info*	512131	7832
Motion picture exhibitors, itinerant: Motion Picture Theaters, Except Drive-Ins.—*info*	512131	7832
Motion picture film: Photographic and Photocopying Equipment—*mfg*	333315	3861
Photographic Film, Paper, Plate and Chemical—*mfg*	325992	3861
Motion picture film or tape rental to the general public: Video Tape and Disc Rental—*real*	53223	7841
Motion picture production and distribution: Motion Picture and Video Production—*info*	51211	7812
Motion picture reproduction: Independent Artists, Writers, and Performers—*arts*	71151	7819
Motion Picture and Video Industries, Other—*info*	512199	7819
Prerecorded Compact Disc (except Software), Tape, and Record Reproducing—*mfg*	334612	7819
Teleproduction and Other Post-Production Services—*info*	512191	7819
Motion picture studio and theater equipment: Photographic Equipment and Supplies—*whlse*	42141	5043
Motion picture theaters, drive-in: Drive-In Motion Picture Theaters—*info*	512132	7833
Motion Picture Theaters, Except Drive-Ins.	**512131**	**7832**
Motor and Generator Manufacturing	**335312**	**7694**
Motor buses, except trackless trolley: Automobile—*mfg*	336111	3711
Heavy Duty Truck—*mfg*	33612	3711
Light Truck and Utility Vehicle—*mfg*	336112	3711
Military Armored Vehicle, Tank and Tank Component—*mfg*	336992	3711
Motor Vehicle Body—*mfg*	336211	3711
Motor carrier licensing and inspection offices: Air Traffic Control—*trans*	488111	9621
Transportation Programs, Regulation and Administration of—*pub*	92612	9621
Motor control accessories, including over load relays-rnfg: Relay and Industrial Control—*mfg*	335314	3625
Motor control centers: Relay and Industrial Control—*mfg*	335314	3625
Motor controls, electric: Building Material Dealers, Other—*retail*	44419	5063
Electrical Apparatus and Equipment, Wiring Supplies and Material—*whlse*	42161	5063
Relay and Industrial Control—*mfg*	335314	3625
Motor generator sets, except automotive and turbogenerators: Motor and Generator—*mfg*	335312	3621
Motor home dealers: Recreational Vehicle Dealers—*retail*	44121	5561
Motor Home Manufacturing	**336213**	**3716**
Motor home rental: Truck, Utility Trailer, and RV (Recreational Vehicle) Rental and Leasing—*real*	53212	7519
Motor homes: Automobile and Other Motor Vehicle—*whlse*	42111	5012
Motor homes, self-contained: Automobile—*mfg*	336111	3711
Heavy Duty Truck—*mfg*	33612	3711
Light Truck and Utility Vehicle—*mfg*	336112	3711
Military Armored Vehicle, Tank and Tank Component—*mfg*	336992	3711
Motor Vehicle Body—*mfg*	336211	3711
Motor homes, self-contained–made on purchased chassis: Motor Home—*mfg*	336213	3716
Motor housings: Motor and Generator—*mfg*	335312	3621
Motor repair, automotive: General Automotive Repair—*serv*	811111	7538
Motor scooters: Automobile and Other Motor Vehicle—*whlse*	42111	5012
Motorcycle Dealers—*retail*	441221	5571
Motor scooters and parts-rnfg: Motorcycle, Bicycle and Parts—*mfg*	336991	3751
Motor starters, contactors, and controllers, industrial: Relay and Industrial Control—*mfg*	335314	3625
Motor truck scales: Scale and Balance (except Laboratory)—*mfg*	333997	3596
Motor truck trailers: Truck Trailer—*mfg*	336212	3715
Motor trucks, except off-highway: Automobile—*mfg*	336111	3711
Heavy Duty Truck—*mfg*	33612	3711
Light Truck and Utility Vehicle—*mfg*	336112	3711
Military Armored Vehicle, Tank and Tank Component—*mfg*	336992	3711
Motor Vehicle Body—*mfg*	336211	3711
Motor Vehicle Air-Conditioning Manufacturing	**336391**	**3585**
Motor Vehicle and Motor Vehicle Part and Supplies Wholesalers	**4211**	
Motor Vehicle and Parts Dealers	**441**	
Motor Vehicle Body and Trailer Manufacturing	**3362**	
Motor Vehicle Body and Trailer Manufacturing	**33621**	
Motor Vehicle Body Manufacturing	**336211**	**3713**
Motor Vehicle Brake System Manufacturing	**33634**	**3714**
Motor vehicle dealers new and used cars: New Car Dealers—*retail*	44111	5511
Motor Vehicle Dealers, All Other	**441229**	**5599**
Motor Vehicle Dealers, Other	**4412**	

ALPHABETICAL INDEX	NAICS	SIC
Motor vehicle dealers, used cars only- retail: Used Car Dealers—*retail*	44112	5521
Motor Vehicle Electrical and Electronic Equipment Manufacturing	**33632**	
Motor Vehicle Electrical and Electronic Equipment Manufacturing, Other	**336322**	**3694**
Motor Vehicle Fabric Accessories and Seat Manufacturing	**33636**	**2399**
Motor Vehicle Gasoline Engine and Engine Parts Manufacturing	**33631**	
Motor vehicle gasoline engine rebuildingon a factory basis: Gasoline Engine and Engine Parts—*mfg*	336312	3714
Motor Vehicle Parts, All Other—*mfg*	336399	3714
Motor vehicle hardware: Hardware—*mfg*	33251	3429
Motor vehicle licensing and inspection offices: Air Traffic Control—*trans*	488111	9621
Transportation Programs, Regulation and Administration of—*pub*	92612	9621
Motor Vehicle Manufacturing	**3361**	
Motor Vehicle Metal Stamping	**33637**	**3465**
Motor Vehicle Part (Used) Wholesalers	**42114**	**5015**
Motor vehicle parts and accessories, except motor vehicle stampings: Gasoline Engine and Engine Parts—*mfg*	336312	3714
Motor Vehicle Body—*mfg*	336211	3714
Motor Vehicle Brake System—*mfg*	33634	3714
Motor Vehicle Parts, All Other—*mfg*	336399	3714
Motor Vehicle Steering and Suspension Components (except Spring)—*mfg*	33633	3714
Motor Vehicle Transmission and Power Train Parts—*mfg*	33635	3714
Motor Vehicle Parts Manufacturing	**3363**	
Motor Vehicle Parts Manufacturing, All Other	**336399**	**3599**
Motor Vehicle Parts Manufacturing, Other	**33639**	
Motor vehicle parts, used-wholesale or retail: Motor Vehicle Part (Used)—*whlse*	42114	5015
Motor vehicle radios: Electrical Appliance, Television and Radio Set—*whlse*	42162	5064
Motor Vehicle Steering and Suspension Components (except Spring) Manufacturing	**33633**	**3714**
Motor Vehicle Supplies and New Part Wholesalers	**42112**	**5013**
Motor vehicle tires and tubes: Tire and Tube—*whlse*	42113	5014
Tire Dealers—*retail*	44132	5014
Motor Vehicle Towing	**48841**	**7549**
Motor Vehicle Transmission and Power Train Parts Manufacturing	**33635**	**3714**
Motor vehicle-commercial: Automobile and Other Motor Vehicle—*whlse*	42111	5012
Motor vehicle-including amphibian: Automobile—*mfg*	336111	3711
Heavy Duty Truck—*mfg*	33612	3711
Light Truck and Utility Vehicle—*mfg*	336112	3711
Military Armored Vehicle, Tank and Tank Component—*mfg*	336992	3711

ALPHABETICAL INDEX	NAICS	SIC
Motor Vehicle Body—*mfg*	336211	3711
Motorbikes and parts: Motorcycle, Bicycle and Parts—*mfg*	336991	3751
Motorboat dealers: Boat Dealers—*retail*	441222	5551
Motorboat inboard and outboard–build ing and repairing: Boat Building—*mfg*	336612	3732
Personal and Household Goods Repair and Maintenance, Other—*serv*	81149	3732
Motorcycle Dealers	**441221**	**5571**
Motorcycle lamps: Vehicular Lighting Equipment—*mfg*	336321	3647
Motorcycle parts: Automotive Parts and Accessories Stores—*retail*	44131	5013
Motor Vehicle Supplies and New Part—*whlse*	42112	5013
Motorcycle Dealers—*retail*	441221	5571
Motorcycle racing: Race Tracks—*arts*	711212	7948
Spectator Sports, Other—*arts*	711219	7948
Motorcycle repair service: Machinery and Equipment (except Automotive and Electronic) Repair and Maintenance, Commercial and Industrial—*serv*	81131	7699
Motorcycle, Bicycle and Parts Manufacturing	**336991**	**3751**
Motorcycle, Boat and Other Motor Vehicle Dealers	**44122**	
Motorcycles: Automobile and Other Motor Vehicle—*whlse*	42111	5012
Motorcycles and parts: Motorcycle, Bicycle and Parts—*mfg*	336991	3751
Motors, air or hydraulic (fluid power): Fluid Power Pump and Motor—*mfg*	333996	3594
Motors, air or hydraulic fluid power: Fluid Power Pump and Motor—*mfg*	333996	3594
Motors, electric: Building Material Dealers, Other—*retail*	44419	5063
Electrical Apparatus and Equipment, Wiring Supplies and Material—*whlse*	42161	5063
Motors, electric–except engine starting motors and gear motors: Motor and Generator—*mfg*	335312	3621
Motors, gear: Speed Changer, Industrial High-Speed Drive and Gear—*mfg*	333612	3566
Motors, pneumatic: Fluid Power Pump and Motor—*mfg*	333996	3594
Motors, starting–motor vehicle and aircraft: Motor Vehicle Electrical and Electronic Equipment, Other—*mfg*	336322	3694
Mounting heads on fur neckpieces: Fur and Leather Apparel—*mfg*	315292	2371
Mounting of maps and samples, for the trade: Tradebinding and Related Work—*mfg*	323121	2789
Mountings, comb and hairpin except precious metal: Fabricated Metal Product, All Other Miscellaneous—*mfg*	332999	3999
Wood Product, All Other Miscellaneous—*mfg*	321999	3999
Mountings, eyeglass and spectacle: Ophthalmic Goods—*mfg*	339115	3851
Mountings, gold and silver–for pens, leather goods, and umbrellas: Jewelry (except Costume)—*mfg*	339911	3911
Mounts for guns, 30 mm. (or 1.18 inch or less): Small Arms—*mfg*	332994	3484
Mouthpiece for pipes and cigarette hold ers, rubber: Fabric Coating Mills—*mfg*	31332	3069

Entry	NAICS	SIC
Rubber Product, All Other—*mfg*	326299	3069
Mouthpieces for musical instruments: Musical Instrument—*mfg*	339992	3931
Mouthwashes: Soap and Other Detergent—*mfg*	325611	2844
Toilet Preparation—*mfg*	32562	2844
Movements, watch or clock: Watch, Clock, and Part—*mfg*	334518	3873
Mowers and mower-conditioners, hay: Farm Machinery and Equipment—*mfg*	333111	3523
Mowers power: Farm and Garden Machinery and Equipment—*whlse*	42182	5083
Outdoor Power Equipment Stores—*retail*	44421	5083
Mowing highway center strips and edges: Landscaping Services—*admin*	56173	782
Mucilage: Adhesive—*mfg*	32552	2891
Mud jacks: Construction Machinery—*mfg*	33312	3531
Overhead Traveling Crane, Hoist and Monorail System—*mfg*	333923	3531
Railroad Rolling Stock—*mfg*	33651	3531
Mud service, oil field drilling–on a contract basis: Oil and Gas Operations Support Activities—*mining*	213112	1389
Mufflers: Men's and Boys' Neckwear—*mfg*	315993	2323
Outerwear Knitting Mills—*mfg*	315191	2253
Mufflers, automotive–installation, repair, or sales and installation: Automotive Exhaust System Repair—*serv*	811112	7533
Mufflers, exhaust–motor vehicle: Gasoline Engine and Engine Parts—*mfg*	336312	3714
Motor Vehicle Parts, All Other—*mfg*	336399	3714
Mufflers, men's and boys': Men's and Boys' Clothing and Furnishings—*whlse*	42232	5136
Mulchers, residential lawn and garden: Hand and Edge Tool—*mfg*	332212	3524
Lawn and Garden Tractor and Home Lawn and Garden Equipment—*mfg*	333112	3524
Mule farms: Horse and Other Equine Production—*ag*	11292	272
Mules: Farm Product Raw Material, Other—*whlse*	42259	5159
Multifamily Housing Construction	**23322**	**1531**
Multigraphing service: Business Service Centers (including Copy Shops), Other—*admin*	561439	7334
Multilithing service: Business Service Centers (including Copy Shops), Other—*admin*	561439	7334
Multimedia educational kits–publishing and printing, or publishing only: Database and Directory Publishers—*info*	51114	2741
Music Publishers—*info*	51223	2741
Publishers, All Other—*info*	511199	2741
Multimeters: Electronic Coil, Transformer, and Other Inductor—*mfg*	334416	3825
Instrument for Measuring and Testing Electricity and Electrical Signals—*mfg*	334515	3825
Multiple listing services, real estate: Real Estate, Other Activities Related to—*real*	53139	6531
Multiple-glazed insulating units: Flat Glass—*mfg*	327211	3211
Multiple-glazed insulating units, made from purchased glass: Glass Product Made of Purchased Glass—*mfg*	327215	3231
Multiplex equipment, radio: Radio and Television Broadcasting and Wireless Communications Equipment—*mfg*	33422	3663
Multiplex equipment, telephone and telegraph: Electronic Coil, Transformer, and Other Inductor—*mfg*	334416	3661
Printed Circuit/Electronics Assembly—*mfg*	334418	3661
Telephone Apparatus—*mfg*	33421	3661
Multipoint distribution systems (MDS) services: Cable and Other Program Distribution—*info*	51322	4841
Cable Networks—*info*	51321	4841
Multiservice centers, neighborhood: Child and Youth Services—*hlth*	62411	8322
Community Food Services—*hlth*	62421	8322
Community Housing Services, Other—*hlth*	624229	8322
Emergency and Other Relief Services—*hlth*	62423	8322
Individual and Family Services, Other—*hlth*	62419	8322
Parole Offices and Probation Offices—*pub*	92215	8322
Services for the Elderly and Persons with Disabilities—*hlth*	62412	8322
Temporary Shelters—*hlth*	624221	8322
Multistation CRT/teleprinters: Computer Terminal—*mfg*	334113	3575
Multiwall bags, paper: Uncoated Paper and Multiwall Bag—*mfg*	322224	2674
Muriate of potash, not produced at mines: Basic Inorganic Chemical, All Other—*mfg*	325188	2819
Chemical Product, All Other Miscellaneous—*mfg*	325998	2819
Muscle exercise apparatus, ophthalmic: Surgical and Medical Instrument—*mfg*	339112	3841
Muscovite mining: Crushed and Broken Stone and Quarrying, Other—*mining*	212319	1499
Non-Metallic Mineral, All Other—*mining*	212399	1499
Museum construction–general contractors: Building, Commercial and Institutional—*const*	23332	1542
Museums	**71211**	**8412**
Historical Sites—*arts*	71212	8412
Museums, Historical Sites and Similar Institutions	**7121**	
Museums, Historical Sites and Similar Institutions	**712**	
Mushroom Production	**111411**	**182**
Mushroom spawn, production of: Food Crops Grown Under Cover, Other—*ag*	111419	182
Mushroom Production—*ag*	111411	182
Mushrooms , growing of: Food Crops Grown Under Cover, Other—*ag*	111419	182
Mushroom Production—*ag*	111411	182
Mushrooms, canned: Fruit and Vegetable Canning—*mfg*	311421	2033
Music arrangers: Music Publishers—*info*	51223	8999
Record Production—*info*	51221	8999
Music books–printing or printing and binding, not publishing: Book Printing—*mfg*	323117	2732
Music books–publishing and printing, or publishing only: Book Publishers—*info*	51113	2731
Music Publishers—*info*	51223	2731

ALPHABETICAL INDEX	NAICS	SIC
Music boxes: Fabricated Metal Product, All Other Miscellaneous—*mfg*	332999	3999
Wood Product, All Other Miscellaneous—*mfg*	321999	3999
Music distribution apparatus, except records or tape: Audio and Video Equipment—*mfg*	33431	3651
Music distribution systems, coin-operated: Amusement and Recreation Industries, All Other—*arts*	71399	7993
Amusement Arcades—*arts*	71312	7993
Gambling Industries, Other—*arts*	71329	7993
Music licensing to radio stations: Owners and Lessors of Other Non-Financial Assets—*real*	53311	6794
Music Publishers	**51223**	**2741**
Music rolls, perforated: Musical Instrument—*mfg*	339992	3931
Music royalties, sheet and record: Owners and Lessors of Other Non-Financial Assets—*real*	53311	6794
Music schools: Fine Arts Schools—*educ*	61161	8299
Music stands: Musical Instrument—*mfg*	339992	3931
Music video production: Motion Picture and Video Production—*info*	51211	7812
Music, sheet–except lithographed or gravure (not publishing): Digital Printing—*mfg*	323115	2759
Flexographic Printing, Commercial—*mfg*	323112	2759
Printing, Other Commercial—*mfg*	323119	2759
Quick Printing—*mfg*	323114	2759
Music, sheet–gravure printing (not publishing): Gravure Printing, Commercial—*mfg*	323111	2754
Music, sheet–publishing and printing, or publishing only: Database and Directory Publishers—*info*	51114	2741
Music Publishers—*info*	51223	2741
Publishers, All Other—*info*	511199	2741
Musical chests: Fabricated Metal Product, All Other Miscellaneous—*mfg*	332999	3999
Wood Product, All Other Miscellaneous—*mfg*	321999	3999
Musical Groups and Artists	**71113**	**7929**
Musical instrument accessories–e.g., reeds, mouthpieces, stands, traps: Musical Instrument—*mfg*	339992	3931
Musical instrument amplifiers: Audio and Video Equipment—*mfg*	33431	3651
Musical Instrument and Supplies Stores	**45114**	**5736**
Musical instrument cases: Luggage—*mfg*	316991	3161
Musical Instrument Manufacturing	**339992**	**3931**
Musical instrument repair shops: Personal and Household Goods Repair and Maintenance, Other—*serv*	81149	7699
Musical instrument stores: Musical Instrument and Supplies Stores—*retail*	45114	5736
Musical instrument stores, secondhand: Non-Depository Credit Intermediation, All Other—*fin*	522298	5932
Used Merchandise Stores—*retail*	45331	5932
Musical instruments: Durable Goods, Other Miscellaneous—*whlse*	42199	5099

ALPHABETICAL INDEX	NAICS	SIC
Musical instruments, including electric and electronic: Musical Instrument—*mfg*	339992	3931
Musical instruments, toy: Game, Toy, and Children's Vehicle—*mfg*	339932	3944
Musicians: Independent Artists, Writers, and Performers—*arts*	71151	7929
Musical Groups and Artists—*arts*	71113	7929
Performing Arts Companies, Other—*arts*	71119	7929
Muslin, cotton: Broadwoven Fabric Mills—*mfg*	31321	2211
Mussels, taking of: Shellfish Fishing—*ag*	114112	913
Mustard gas: Basic Organic Chemical, All Other—*mfg*	325199	2869
Mustard seed farms: Grain Farming, All Other—*ag*	111199	119
Mustard, prepared (wet): Fruit and Vegetable Canning—*mfg*	311421	2035
Mayonnaise, Dressing and Other Prepared Sauce—*mfg*	311941	2035
Mutton: Animal (except Poultry) Slaughtering—*mfg*	311611	2011
Mutual accident associations: Direct Health and Medical Insurance Carriers—*fin*	524114	6321
Insurance Funds, Other—*fin*	52519	6321
Reinsurance Carriers—*fin*	52413	6321
Mutual benefit associations: Consumer Lending—*fin*	522291	6141
Credit Card Issuing—*fin*	52221	6141
Sales Financing—*fin*	52222	6141
Mutual fire, marine, and casualty insurance: Direct Property and Casualty Insurance Carriers—*fin*	524126	6331
Insurance Funds, Other—*fin*	52519	6331
Reinsurance Carriers—*fin*	52413	6331
Mutual fund agents: Financial Investment Activities, Miscellaneous—*fin*	523999	6211
Intermediation, Miscellaneous—*fin*	52391	6211
Investment Banking and Securities Dealing—*fin*	52311	6211
Securities Brokerage—*fin*	52312	6211
Mutual fund sales on own account: Open-End Investment Funds—*fin*	52591	6722
Mutual funds, selling by independent salesperson: Financial Investment Activities, Miscellaneous—*fin*	523999	6211
Intermediation, Miscellaneous—*fin*	52391	6211
Investment Banking and Securities Dealing—*fin*	52311	6211
Securities Brokerage—*fin*	52312	6211
Myrobalans extract: Gum and Wood Chemical—*mfg*	325191	2861
N-methylpiperazine: Medicinal and Botanical—*mfg*	325411	2833
N-type rubber: Synthetic Rubber—*mfg*	325212	2822
Nacelles, aircraft: Aircraft Part and Auxiliary Equipment, Other—*mfg*	336413	3728
Fluid Power Valve and Hose Fitting—*mfg*	332912	3728
Nail heading machines: Machine Tool (Metal Forming Types)—*mfg*	333513	3542
Nail Salons	**812113**	**7231**
Nails: Metal Service Centers and Offices—*whlse*	42151	5051
Nails, nonferrous metal (including wire): Iron and Steel Mills—*mfg*	331111	3399
Secondary Smelting and Alloying of Aluminum—*mfg*	331314	3399
Secondary Smelting, Refining, and Alloying of Copper—*mfg*	331423	3399

Description	NAICS	SIC
Secondary Smelting, Refining, and Alloying of Nonferrous Metal (except Copper and Aluminum)—*mfg*	331492	3399
Nails, steel–wire or cut: Fabricated Wire Product, Other—*mfg*	332618	3315
Steel Wire Drawing—*mfg*	331222	3315
Nainsook, cotton: Broadwoven Fabric Mills—*mfg*	31321	2211
Nameplates, metal–except e.g., engraved, etched, chased: Sign—*mfg*	33995	3993
Nameplates–engraved and etched: Costume Jewelry and Novelty—*mfg*	339914	3479
Jewelry (except Costume)—*mfg*	339911	3479
Metal Coating, Engraving (except Jewelry and Silverware), and Allied Services to Manufacturers—*mfg*	332812	3479
Silverware and Plated Ware—*mfg*	339912	3479
Napalm: Basic Organic Chemical, All Other—*mfg*	325199	2899
Chemical Product, All Other Miscellaneous—*mfg*	325998	2899
Naphtha, except bulk stations and terminals: Petroleum and Petroleum Products (except Bulk Stations and Terminals)—*whlse*	42272	5172
Naphtha, produced in petroleum refineries: Petroleum Refineries—*mfg*	32411	2911
Naphtha, solvent–made in chemicalplants: Cyclic Crude and Intermediate—*mfg*	325192	2865
Petrochemical—*mfg*	32511	2865
Naphthalene chips and flakes: Cyclic Crude and Intermediate—*mfg*	325192	2865
Petrochemical—*mfg*	32511	2865
Naphthalene sulfonic acid condensates: Basic Organic Chemical, All Other—*mfg*	325199	2869
Naphthalene, made in chemical plants: Cyclic Crude and Intermediate—*mfg*	325192	2865
Petrochemical—*mfg*	32511	2865
Naphthanate driers: Paint and Coating—*mfg*	32551	2851
Naphthenic acid soaps: Basic Organic Chemical, All Other—*mfg*	325199	2869
Naphthenic acids, produced in petroleum refineries: Petroleum Refineries—*mfg*	32411	2911
Naphthol, alpha and beta: Cyclic Crude and Intermediate—*mfg*	325192	2865
Petrochemical—*mfg*	32511	2865
Naphtholsulfonic acids: Cyclic Crude and Intermediate—*mfg*	325192	2865
Petrochemical—*mfg*	32511	2865
Napkin stock, paper: Newsprint Mills—*mfg*	322122	2621
Paper (except Newsprint) Mills—*mfg*	322121	2621
Napkins, fabric and nonwoven textiles: Household Textile Product Mills, Other—*mfg*	314129	2392
Napkins, paper: Industrial and Personal Service Paper—*whlse*	42213	5113
Sanitary Paper Product—*mfg*	322291	2676
Napkins, sanitary: Sanitary Paper Product—*mfg*	322291	2676
Napping machines (textile machinery): Textile Machinery—*mfg*	333292	3552
Napping of cotton broadwoven fabrics: Broadwoven Fabric Finishing Mills—*mfg*	313311	2261
Napping of manmade fiber and silk broad-woven fabrics: Broadwoven Fabric Finishing Mills—*mfg*	313311	2262
Napping of wool, mohair, and similaranimal fiber fabrics: Broadwoven Fabric Finishing Mills—*mfg*	313311	2231
Broadwoven Fabric Mills—*mfg*	31321	2231
Textile and Fabric Finishing (except Broadwoven Fabric) Mills—*mfg*	313312	2231
Narrow Fabric Mills	**313221**	**2299**
Narrow Fabric Mills and Schiffli Machine Embroidery	**31322**	
Narrow fabrics: Broadwoven Fabric Finishing Mills—*mfg*	313311	5131
Piece Goods, Notions and Other Dry Goods—*whlse*	42231	5131
Textile and Fabric Finishing (except Broadwoven Fabric) Mills—*mfg*	313312	5131
Narrow fabrics, dyeing and finishing:wool, mohair, and similar animal fibers: Broadwoven Fabric Finishing Mills—*mfg*	313311	2231
Broadwoven Fabric Mills—*mfg*	31321	2231
Textile and Fabric Finishing (except Broadwoven Fabric) Mills—*mfg*	313312	2231
Narrow fabrics, elastic–woven or braided: Narrow Fabric Mills—*mfg*	313221	2241
Narrow fabrics, except knit and wool–bleaching, dyeing, and finishing: Broadwoven Fabric Finishing Mills—*mfg*	313311	2269
Textile and Fabric Finishing (except Broadwoven Fabric) Mills—*mfg*	313312	2269
Narrow woven fabrics–cotton, rayon, wool, silk, glass, and manmade fiber: Narrow Fabric Mills—*mfg*	313221	2241
Narrow woven fabrics–linen, jute, hemp, and ramie: Broadwoven Fabric Mills—*mfg*	31321	2299
Narrow Fabric Mills—*mfg*	313221	2299
Nonwoven Fabric Mills—*mfg*	31323	2299
Textile and Fabric Finishing (except Broadwoven Fabric) Mills—*mfg*	313312	2299
Textile Product Mills, All Other Miscellaneous—*mfg*	314999	2299
Thread Mills—*mfg*	313113	2299
Yarn Spinning Mills—*mfg*	313111	2299
National banks, commercial: Banking, Commercial—*fin*	52211	6021
Credit Card Issuing—*fin*	52221	6021
Trust, Fiduciary and Custody Activities—*fin*	523991	6021
National Consumer Cooperative Bank: International Trade Financing—*fin*	522293	6111
Non-Depository Credit Intermediation, All Other—*fin*	522298	6111
Secondary Market Financing—*fin*	522294	6111
National Credit Union Administration(NCUA): Financial Transactions Processing, Reserve, and Clearing House Activities—*fin*	52232	6019
National Guard: National Security—*pub*	92811	9711
National Security	**92811**	**9711**
National Security and International Affairs	**928**	
National Security and International Affairs	**9281**	
Nationality specialty foods, canned: Canning, Specialty—*mfg*	311422	2032
Food, All Other Miscellaneous—*mfg*	311999	2032
Native foods, canned: Canning, Specialty—*mfg*	311422	2032

ALPHABETICAL INDEX	NAICS	SIC
Food, All Other Miscellaneous—*mfg*	311999	2032
Native foods, frozen: Frozen Specialty Food—*mfg*	311412	2038
Natural abrasives mining (except sand): Crushed and Broken Stone and Quarrying, Other—*mining*	212319	1499
Non-Metallic Mineral, All Other—*mining*	212399	1499
Natural gas compressing station construction–general contractors: Power and Communication Transmission Line—*const*	23492	1623
Water, Sewer, and Pipeline—*const*	23491	1623
Natural Gas Distribution	**22121**	**4924**
Natural Gas Distribution	**2212**	
Natural Gas Liquid Extraction	**211112**	**1321**
Natural gas liquids production: Natural Gas Liquid Extraction—*mining*	211112	1321
Natural gas production: Crude Petroleum and Natural Gas Extraction—*mining*	211111	1311
Natural gas storage: Pipeline of Natural Gas—*trans*	48621	4922
Natural gas transmission: Pipeline of Natural Gas—*trans*	48621	4922
Natural gas transmission and distribution: Natural Gas Distribution—*util*	22121	4923
Pipeline of Natural Gas—*trans*	48621	4923
Natural gasoline production: Natural Gas Liquid Extraction—*mining*	211112	1321
Natural wonders, tourist attraction–commercial: Nature Parks and Other Similar Institutions—*arts*	71219	7999
Nature Parks and Other Similar Institutions	**71219**	**8422**
Naturopaths, offices of: Health Practitioners, Offices Of Miscellaneous—*hlth*	621399	8049
Mental Health Practitioners (except Physicians), Offices Of—*hlth*	62133	8049
Physical, Occupational and Speech Therapists and Audiologists, Offices Of—*hlth*	62134	8049
Nautical and navigational instrumentrepair, except electric: Electronic and Precision Equipment Repair and Maintenance, Other—*serv*	811219	7699
Nautical instruments: Search, Detection, Navigation, Guidance, Aeronautical, and Nautical System and Instrument—*mfg*	334511	3812
Naval artillery: Ordnance and Accessories, Other—*mfg*	332995	3489
Naval ships, building and repairing: Ship Building and Repairing—*mfg*	336611	3731
Naval stores: Chemical and Allied Products, Other—*whlse*	42269	5169
Naval stores, gum–processing but notgathering or warehousing: Gum and Wood Chemical—*mfg*	325191	2861
Naval stores, wood: Gum and Wood Chemical—*mfg*	325191	2861
Navigational instruments: Search, Detection, Navigation, Guidance, Aeronautical, and Nautical System and Instrument—*mfg*	334511	3812
Navigational Services to Shipping	**48833**	**4499**
Navigational, Measuring, Medical, and Control Instruments Manufacturing	**33451**	

ALPHABETICAL INDEX	NAICS	SIC
Navigational, Measuring, Medical, and Control Instruments Manufacturing	**3345**	
Navy: National Security—*pub*	92811	9711
Near beer: Breweries—*mfg*	31212	2082
Neckpieces, fur: Fur and Leather Apparel—*mfg*	315292	2371
Necktie fabrics, manmade fiber and silk–broadwoven: Broadwoven Fabric Mills—*mfg*	31321	2221
Necktie linings, cutting of: Apparel Accessories and Apparel, Other—*mfg*	315999	2396
Neckties: Men's and Boys' Neckwear—*mfg*	315993	2323
Outerwear Knitting Mills—*mfg*	315191	2253
Neckwear: Apparel Accessories and Apparel, Other—*mfg*	315999	2339
Cut and Sew Apparel, All Other—*mfg*	315299	2339
Men's and Boys' Neckwear—*mfg*	315993	2323
Women's and Girls' Cut and Sew Apparel Contractors—*mfg*	315212	2339
Women's and Girls' Cut and Sew Other Outerwear—*mfg*	315238	2339
Neckwear Manufacturing, Men's and Boys'	**315993**	**2323**
Neckwear–men's and boys': Men's and Boys' Clothing and Furnishings—*whlse*	42232	5136
Nectarine orchards and farms: Apple Orchards—*ag*	111331	175
Noncitrus Fruit Farming, Other—*ag*	111339	175
Nectars, fruit: Fruit and Vegetable Canning—*mfg*	311421	2033
Needle holders, surgical: Surgical and Medical Instrument—*mfg*	339112	3841
Needles, hand and machine: Fastener, Button, Needle and Pin—*mfg*	339993	3965
Needles, hypodermic: Surgical and Medical Instrument—*mfg*	339112	3841
Needles, suture: Surgical and Medical Instrument—*mfg*	339112	3841
Needlework stores: Sewing, Needlework and Piece Goods Stores—*retail*	45113	5949
Needlework, art: Men's and Boys' Cut and Sew Apparel Contractors—*mfg*	315211	2395
Textile Product Mills, All Other Miscellaneous—*mfg*	314999	2395
Women's and Girls' Cut and Sew Apparel Contractors—*mfg*	315212	2395
Negligees: Infants' Cut and Sew Apparel—*mfg*	315291	2341
Underwear and Nightwear Knitting Mills—*mfg*	315192	2254
Women's and Girls' Cut and Sew Apparel Contractors—*mfg*	315212	2341
Women's and Girls' Cut and Sew Lingerie, Loungewear and Nightwear—*mfg*	315231	2341
Neighborhood centers: Child and Youth Services—*hlth*	62411	8322
Community Food Services—*hlth*	62421	8322
Community Housing Services, Other—*hlth*	624229	8322
Emergency and Other Relief Services—*hlth*	62423	8322
Individual and Family Services, Other—*hlth*	62419	8322
Parole Offices and Probation Offices—*pub*	92215	8322
Services for the Elderly and Persons with Disabilities—*hlth*	62412	8322
Temporary Shelters—*hlth*	624221	8322
Neon: Industrial Gas—*mfg*	32512	2813
Neon signs: Equipment, Other Commercial—*whlse*	42144	5046

Description	NAICS	SIC
Sign—*mfg*	33995	3993
Neoprene: Synthetic Rubber—*mfg*	325212	2822
Nepheline syenite quarrying: Clay and Ceramic and Refractory Minerals—*mining*	212325	1459
Nephelometers, except meteorological: Analytical Laboratory Instrument—*mfg*	334516	3826
Nephoscopes: Measuring and Controlling Device, Other—*mfg*	334519	3829
Surgical and Medical Instrument—*mfg*	339112	3829
Net and lace machines: Textile Machinery—*mfg*	333292	3552
Net goods: Broadwoven Fabric Finishing Mills—*mfg*	313311	5131
Piece Goods, Notions and Other Dry Goods—*whlse*	42231	5131
Textile and Fabric Finishing (except Broadwoven Fabric) Mills—*mfg*	313312	5131
Nets and nettings: Broadwoven Fabric Mills—*mfg*	31321	2211
Nets, fishing: Textile Product Mills, All Other Miscellaneous—*mfg*	314999	2399
Nets, launderers' and dyers': Textile Product Mills, All Other Miscellaneous—*mfg*	314999	2399
Nets, rope: Rope, Cordage and Twine Mills—*mfg*	314991	2298
Nets–e.g., badminton, basketball, tennis-not made in weaving mills: Sporting and Athletic Goods—*mfg*	33992	3949
Netting made on a lace or net machine: Knit Fabric and Lace Mills, Other—*mfg*	313249	2258
Textile and Fabric Finishing (except Broadwoven Fabric) Mills—*mfg*	313312	2258
Netting, knit: Knit Fabric and Lace Mills, Other—*mfg*	313249	2258
Textile and Fabric Finishing (except Broadwoven Fabric) Mills—*mfg*	313312	2258
Netting, plastics: Plastics Pipe and Pipe Fitting—*mfg*	326122	3089
Plastics Product, All Other—*mfg*	326199	3089
Unsupported Plastics Profile Shape—*mfg*	326121	3089
Netting, woven wire–made from purchased wire: Fabricated Wire Product, Other—*mfg*	332618	3496
Network analyzers: Electronic Coil, Transformer, and Other Inductor—*mfg*	334416	3825
Instrument for Measuring and Testing Electricity and Electrical Signals—*mfg*	334515	3825
Network systems integration, computer: Computer Systems Design Services—*prof*	541512	7373
Neurologists, offices of: Freestanding Ambulatory Surgical and Emergency Centers—*hlth*	621493	8011
HMO Medical Centers—*hlth*	621491	8011
Physicians (except Mental Health Specialists), Offices Of—*hlth*	621111	8011
Physicians, Mental Health Specialists, Offices Of—*hlth*	621112	8011
Neutral fruit spirits and neutral brandy: Wineries—*mfg*	31213	2084
Neutral spirits: Wine and Distilled Alcoholic Beverage—*whlse*	42282	5182
Neutral spirits for beverage purletees, except fruit: Distilleries—*mfg*	31214	2085
Neutron activation analysis instruments: Analytical Laboratory Instrument—*mfg*	334516	3826
New Car Dealers	**44111**	**5511**
Newel posts, wood: Millwork (including Flooring), Other—*mfg*	321918	2431
Wood Window and Door—*mfg*	321911	2431
News correspondents, independent: News Syndicates—*info*	51411	7383
News dealers: News Dealers and Newsstands—*retail*	451212	5994
News Dealers and Newsstands	**451212**	**5994**
News feature syndicates: News Syndicates—*info*	51411	7383
News pictures, gathering and distributing: News Syndicates—*info*	51411	7383
News reporting services for newspapers and periodicals: News Syndicates—*info*	51411	7383
News Syndicates	**51411**	**7383**
News tablet paper: Newsprint Mills—*mfg*	322122	2621
Paper (except Newsprint) Mills—*mfg*	322121	2621
News ticker services: News Syndicates—*info*	51411	7383
Newsboard: Paperboard Mills—*mfg*	32213	2631
Newsboard, pasted: Converted Paper Product, All Other—*mfg*	322298	2675
Die-Cut Paper and Paperboard Office Supplies—*mfg*	322231	2675
Surface-Coated Paperboard—*mfg*	322292	2675
Newspaper advertising representatives, not auxiliary to publishing: Media Representatives—*prof*	54184	7313
Newspaper agencies: Book, Periodical and Newspaper—*whlse*	42292	5192
Newspaper branch offices, editorial and advertising: Newspaper Publishers—*info*	51111	2711
Newspaper columnists: Independent Artists, Writers, and Performers—*arts*	71151	8999
Newspaper Publishers	**51111**	**2711**
Newspaper, Periodical, Book and Database Publishers	**5111**	
Newspapers, home delivery–except by newspaper printers or publishers: Direct Selling Establishments, Other—*retail*	45439	5963
Mobile Foodservices—*accom*	72233	5963
Newspapers, lithographed–not published: Lithographic Printing, Commercial—*mfg*	323110	2752
Quick Printing—*mfg*	323114	2752
Newspapers, printed–except lithographed or gravure (not publishing): Digital Printing—*mfg*	323115	2759
Flexographic Printing, Commercial—*mfg*	323112	2759
Printing, Other Commercial—*mfg*	323119	2759
Quick Printing—*mfg*	323114	2759
Newspapers–gravure printing (not publishing): Gravure Printing, Commercial—*mfg*	323111	2754
Newspapers–publishing and printing, or publishing only: Newspaper Publishers—*info*	51111	2711
Newsprint: Newsprint Mills—*mfg*	322122	2621
Paper (except Newsprint) Mills—*mfg*	322121	2621
Newsprint Mills	**322122**	**2621**
Newsprint tablets and pads: Stationery, Tablet, and Related Product—*mfg*	322233	2678
Newsstands: News Dealers and Newsstands—*retail*	451212	5994
Nibs (pen points)–gold, steel, or other metal: Pen and Mechanical Pencil—*mfg*	339941	3951

ALPHABETICAL INDEX	NAICS	SIC
Nickel ammonium sulfate: Basic Inorganic Chemical, All Other—*mfg*	325188	2819
Chemical Product, All Other Miscellaneous—*mfg*	325998	2819
Nickel and nickel alloy pipe, plates, sheets, strips, and tubing: Nonferrous Metal (except Copper and Aluminum) Rolling, Drawing and Extruding—*mfg*	331491	3356
Nickel cadmium storage batteries: Storage Battery—*mfg*	335911	3691
Nickel carbonate: Basic Inorganic Chemical, All Other—*mfg*	325188	2819
Chemical Product, All Other Miscellaneous—*mfg*	325998	2819
Nickel compounds, inorganic: Basic Inorganic Chemical, All Other—*mfg*	325188	2819
Chemical Product, All Other Miscellaneous—*mfg*	325998	2819
Nickel foil, not made in rolling mills: Fabricated Metal Product, All Other Miscellaneous—*mfg*	332999	3497
Laminated Aluminum Foil for Flexible Packaging Uses—*mfg*	322225	3497
Nickel ore mining: Copper Ore and Nickel Ore—*mining*	212234	1061
Metal Ore, All Other—*mining*	212299	1061
Nickel refining, primary: Primary Smelting and Refining of Nonferrous Metal (except Copper and Aluminum)—*mfg*	331419	3339
Nickel smelting and refining, secondary: Secondary Smelting and Alloying of Aluminum—*mfg*	331314	3341
Secondary Smelting, Refining, and Alloying of Nonferrous Metal (except Copper and Aluminum)—*mfg*	331492	3341
Nickel sulfate: Basic Inorganic Chemical, All Other—*mfg*	325188	2819
Chemical Product, All Other Miscellaneous—*mfg*	325998	2819
Nicotine and salts: Pesticide and Other Agricultural Chemical—*mfg*	32532	2879
Nicotine bearing insecticides: Pesticide and Other Agricultural Chemical—*mfg*	32532	2879
Nigbtshirts: Men's and Boys' Cut and Sew Apparel Contractors—*mfg*	315211	2322
Men's and Boys' Cut and Sew Underwear and Nightwear—*mfg*	315221	2322
Night clubs: Drinking Places (Alcoholic Beverages)—*accom*	72241	5813
Nightgowns: Infants' Cut and Sew Apparel—*mfg*	315291	2341
Underwear and Nightwear Knitting Mills—*mfg*	315192	2254
Women's and Girls' Cut and Sew Apparel Contractors—*mfg*	315212	2341
Women's and Girls' Cut and Sew Lingerie, Loungewear and Nightwear—*mfg*	315231	2341
Nightwear: Infants' Cut and Sew Apparel—*mfg*	315291	2341
Men's and Boys' Cut and Sew Apparel Contractors—*mfg*	315211	2322
Men's and Boys' Cut and Sew Underwear and Nightwear—*mfg*	315221	2322
Underwear and Nightwear Knitting Mills—*mfg*	315192	2254
Women's and Girls' Cut and Sew Apparel Contractors—*mfg*	315212	2341
Women's and Girls' Cut and Sew Lingerię, Loungewear and Nightwear—*mfg*	315231	2341
Nightwear, men's and boys': Men's and Boys' Clothing and Furnishings—*whlse*	42232	5136
Nightwear–women's, children's, and infants': Women's, Children's, and Infants' and Accessories—*whlse*	42233	5137

ALPHABETICAL INDEX	NAICS	SIC
Nipples, metal pipe–except pressure andsoil pipe: Fabricated Pipe and Pipe Fitting—*mfg*	332996	3498
Nipples, pipe–pressure and soil pipecacastiron: Iron Foundries—*mfg*	331511	3321
Nipples, rubber: Fabric Coating Mills—*mfg*	31332	3069
Rubber Product, All Other—*mfg*	326299	3069
Nitrate resins–cellulose: Plastics Material and Resin—*mfg*	325211	2821
Nitrated carbohydrates (explosives): Explosives—*mfg*	32592	2892
Nitric acid: Nitrogenous Fertilizer—*mfg*	325311	2873
Nitrile type rubber: Synthetic Rubber—*mfg*	325212	2822
Nitrile-butadiene rubbers: Synthetic Rubber—*mfg*	325212	2822
Nitrile-chloroprene rubbers: Synthetic Rubber—*mfg*	325212	2822
Nitro dyes: Petrochemical—*mfg*	32511	2865
Nitroaniline: Cyclic Crude and Intermediate—*mfg*	325192	2865
Petrochemical—*mfg*	32511	2865
Nitrobenzene: Cyclic Crude and Intermediate—*mfg*	325192	2865
Petrochemical—*mfg*	32511	2865
Nitrocellulose fibers: Cellulosic Organic Fiber—*mfg*	325221	2823
Nitrocellulose plastics (pyroxylin): Plastics Material and Resin—*mfg*	325211	2821
Nitrocellulose powder (explosives): Explosives—*mfg*	32592	2892
Nitrofuran preparations: Pharmaceutical Preparation—*mfg*	325412	2834
Nitrogen: Industrial Gas—*mfg*	32512	2813
Nitrogen solutions (fertilizer): Nitrogenous Fertilizer—*mfg*	325311	2873
Nitrogenous Fertilizer Manufacturing	**325311**	**2873**
Nitroglycerin (explosives): Explosives—*mfg*	32592	2892
Nitromannitol (explosives): Explosives—*mfg*	32592	2892
Nitrophenol: Cyclic Crude and Intermediate—*mfg*	325192	2865
Petrochemical—*mfg*	32511	2865
Nitroso dyes: Petrochemical—*mfg*	32511	2865
Nitrostarch (explosives): Explosives—*mfg*	32592	2892
Nitrosugars (explosives): Explosives—*mfg*	32592	2892
Nitrous ether: Basic Organic Chemical, All Other—*mfg*	325199	2869
Nitrous oxide: Industrial Gas—*mfg*	32512	2813
Nodular iron castings: Iron Foundries—*mfg*	331511	3321
Noils, wool: Farm Product Raw Material, Other—*whlse*	42259	5159
Noils, wool and mohair: Broadwoven Fabric Mills—*mfg*	31321	2299
Narrow Fabric Mills—*mfg*	313221	2299
Nonwoven Fabric Mills—*mfg*	31323	2299
Textile and Fabric Finishing (except Broadwoven Fabric) Mills—*mfg*	313312	2299
Textile Product Mills, All Other Miscellaneous—*mfg*	314999	2299
Thread Mills—*mfg*	313113	2299
Yarn Spinning Mills—*mfg*	313111	2299
Noise protectors, personal: Surgical Appliance and Supplies—*mfg*	339113	3842
Non-Chocolate Confectionery Manufacturing	**31134**	**2067**
Non-Depository Credit Intermediation	**5222**	
Non-Depository Credit Intermediation, All Other	**522298**	**6081**
Non-Depository Credit Intermediation, Other	**52229**	

Entry	NAICS	SIC
Non-Folding Sanitary Food Container Manufacturing	**322215**	**2679**
Non-Metallic Mineral Mining and Quarrying	**2123**	
Non-Metallic Mineral Mining and Quarrying, Other	**21239**	
Non-Metallic Mineral Mining, All Other	**212399**	**1499**
Non-Metallic Minerals (except Fuels) Support Activities	**213115**	**1481**
Noncellulosic Organic Fiber Manufacturing	**325222**	**2824**
Noncitrus Fruit and Tree Nut Farming	**11133**	
Noncitrus Fruit Farming, Other	**111339**	**179**
Nonclay refractories: Nonclay Refractory—*mfg*	327125	3297
Nonclay Refractory Manufacturing	**327125**	**3297**
Noncurrent-Carrying Wiring Device Manufacturing	**335932**	**3644**
Nondeposit trust companies: Trust, Fiduciary and Custody Activities—*fin*	523991	6091
Nondurable Goods Wholesalers, Miscellaneous	**4229**	
Nondurable Goods Wholesalers, Other Miscellaneous	**42299**	**5199**
Nonferrous (except Aluminum) Die-Castings	**331522**	**3364**
Nonferrous additive alloys, high percentage–except copper: Electrometallurgical Ferroalloy Product—*mfg*	331112	3313
Secondary Smelting, Refining, and Alloying of Nonferrous Metal (except Copper and Aluminum)—*mfg*	331492	3313
Nonferrous Forging	**332112**	**3463**
Nonferrous forgings, not made in hot-rolling mills: Nonferrous Forging—*mfg*	332112	3463
Nonferrous Foundries, Other	**331528**	**3369**
Nonferrous foundries–brass, bronze, copper, and copper base alloy: Copper Foundries—*mfg*	331525	3366
Nonferrous foundries–except aluminum, copper, and copper alloys: Nonferrous Foundries, Other—*mfg*	331528	3369
Nonferrous Metal (except Aluminum) Production and Processing	**3314**	
Nonferrous Metal (except Aluminum) Smelting and Refining	**33141**	
Nonferrous Metal (except Copper and Aluminum) Rolling, Drawing and Extruding	**331491**	**3357**
Nonferrous Metal Foundries	**33152**	
Nonferrous metal foundries, except aluminum, copper, and die-castings: Nonferrous Foundries, Other—*mfg*	331528	3369
Nonferrous metal machinery castings–except aluminum, copper, and die-castings: Nonferrous Foundries, Other—*mfg*	331528	3369
Nonferrous metal smelting and refining, secondary: Secondary Smelting and Alloying of Aluminum—*mfg*	331314	3341
Secondary Smelting, Refining, and Alloying of Copper—*mfg*	331423	3341
Secondary Smelting, Refining, and Alloying of Nonferrous Metal (except Copper and Aluminum)—*mfg*	331492	3341
Nonferrous metal, except precious–e.g., sheets, bars, rods: Metal Service Centers and Offices—*whlse*	42151	5051
Nonferrous Metals (except Copper and Aluminum) Rolling, Drawing, Extruding and Alloying	**33149**	
Nonferrous metals scrap: Recyclable Material—*whlse*	42193	5093
Nonferrous refining, primary–except copper and aluminum: Primary Smelting and Refining of Nonferrous Metal (except Copper and Aluminum)—*mfg*	331419	3339
Nonferrous rolling, drawing, and extruding–except copper and aluminum: Nonferrous Metal (except Copper and Aluminum) Rolling, Drawing and Extruding—*mfg*	331491	3356
Nonferrous smelting, primary–except copper and aluminum: Primary Smelting and Refining of Nonferrous Metal (except Copper and Aluminum)—*mfg*	331419	3339
Nonhazardous Waste Treatment and Disposal, Other	**562219**	**4953**
Nonmetallic Mineral Product Manufacturing	**327**	
Nonmetallic Mineral Product Manufacturing, All Other	**32799**	
Nonmetallic Mineral Product Manufacturing, All Other Miscellaneous	**327999**	**3292**
Nonmetallic Mineral Product Manufacturing, Other	**3279**	
Nonmetallic minerals and concentrates, crude–except petroleum: Coal and Other Mineral and Ore—*whlse*	42152	5052
Nonresidential Building Construction	**2333**	
Nonresidential buildings, operators of: Lessors of Nonresidential Buildings (except Miniwarehouses)—*real*	53112	6512
Promoters of Performing Arts, Sports and Similar Events with Facilities—*arts*	71131	6512
Nonresidential Property Managers	**531312**	**6531**
Nonscheduled Air Transportation	**48121**	
Nonscheduled Air Transportation	**4812**	
Nonscheduled Air Transportation, Other	**481219**	**721**
Nonscheduled Chartered Freight Air Transportation	**481212**	**4522**
Nonscheduled Chartered Passenger Air Transportation	**481211**	**4522**
Nonstore Retailers	**454**	
Nontheatrical motion picture production: Motion Picture and Video Production—*info*	51211	7812
Nonupholstered Wood Household Furniture Manufacturing	**337122**	**5712**
Nonwood Office Furniture Manufacturing	**337214**	**2522**
Nonwoven Fabric Mills	**31323**	**2299**
Nonwoven fabrics, except felt: Nonwoven Fabric Mills—*mfg*	31323	2297
Noodles, fried (e.g., Chinese): Food, All Other Miscellaneous—*mfg*	311999	2099
Noodles, uncooked–packaged with other ingredients: Food, All Other Miscellaneous—*mfg*	311999	2099
Noodles–egg, plain, and water: Pasta—*mfg*	311823	2098
Normal hexyl decalin: Basic Organic Chemical, All Other—*mfg*	325199	2869
Nose cones, guided missile: Guided Missile and Space Vehicle Parts and Auxiliary Equipment, Other—*mfg*	336419	3769
Nose plugs: Surgical Appliance and Supplies—*mfg*	339113	3842
Notaries public: Legal Services, All Other—*prof*	541199	7389
Notaries, Offices Of	**54112**	
Note brokers: Financial Investment Activities, Miscellaneous—*fin*	523999	6211
Intermediation, Miscellaneous—*fin*	52391	6211
Investment Banking and Securities Dealing—*fin*	52311	6211
Securities Brokerage—*fin*	52312	6211

ALPHABETICAL INDEX	NAICS	SIC
Notebooks, including mechanically bound by wire, plastics, etc.: Stationery, Tablet, and Related Product—*mfg*	322233	2678
Notion stores: Sewing, Needlework and Piece Goods Stores—*retail*	45113	5949
Notions: Broadwoven Fabric Finishing Mills—*mfg*	313311	5131
Piece Goods, Notions and Other Dry Goods—*whlse*	42231	5131
Textile and Fabric Finishing (except Broadwoven Fabric) Mills—*mfg*	313312	5131
Nottingham lace: Knit Fabric and Lace Mills, Other—*mfg*	313249	2258
Textile and Fabric Finishing (except Broadwoven Fabric) Mills—*mfg*	313312	2258
Novelties and specialties, metal–except advertising novelties: Fabricated Metal Product, All Other Miscellaneous—*mfg*	332999	3499
Metal Container, Other—*mfg*	332439	3499
Novelties, advertising: Sign—*mfg*	33995	3993
Novelties, costume–except precious metal and gems: Costume Jewelry and Novelty—*mfg*	339914	3961
Novelties, glass–e.g., fruit, foliage, flowers, animals, made from purchased glass: Glass Product Made of Purchased Glass—*mfg*	327215	3231
Novelties, leather: Leather Good, All Other—*mfg*	316999	3199
Novelties, paper: Coated and Laminated Paper—*mfg*	322222	2679
Converted Paper Product, All Other—*mfg*	322298	2679
Die-Cut Paper and Paperboard Office Supplies—*mfg*	322231	2679
Non-Folding Sanitary Food Container—*mfg*	322215	2679
Nondurable Goods, Other Miscellaneous—*whlse*	42299	5199
Novelties, wood fiber: Manufacturing, All Other Miscellaneous—*mfg*	339999	2499
Wood Container and Pallet—*mfg*	32192	2499
Wood Product, All Other Miscellaneous—*mfg*	321999	2499
Novelty furniture, metal: Metal Household Furniture—*mfg*	337124	2514
Novelty glassware–made in glassmaking plants: Pressed and Blown Glass and Glassware, Other—*mfg*	327212	3229
Novelty merchandise, mail-order: Electronic Shopping and Mail-Order Houses—*retail*	45411	5961
Novelty shops: Gift, Novelty and Souvenir Stores—*retail*	45322	5947
Novelty stitching, for the trade: Men's and Boys' Cut and Sew Apparel Contractors—*mfg*	315211	2395
Textile Product Mills, All Other Miscellaneous—*mfg*	314999	2395
Women's and Girls' Cut and Sew Apparel Contractors—*mfg*	315212	2395
Nozzles, fire fighting: Other Metal Valve and Pipe Fitting, Other—*mfg*	332919	3429
Nozzles, lawn hose: Fabricated Metal Product, All Other Miscellaneous—*mfg*	332999	3432
Plumbing Fixture Fitting and Trim—*mfg*	332913	3432
Nozzles, plumbers': Fabricated Metal Product, All Other Miscellaneous—*mfg*	332999	3432
Plumbing Fixture Fitting and Trim—*mfg*	332913	3432

ALPHABETICAL INDEX	NAICS	SIC
Nozzles, spray–aerosol paint, and insecticides: Other Metal Valve and Pipe Fitting, Other—*mfg*	332919	3499
Nuclear core structurals, metal plate: Air-Conditioning and Warm Air Heating Equipment and Commercial and Industrial Refrigeration Equipment—*mfg*	333415	3443
Metal Tank (Heavy Gauge)—*mfg*	33242	3443
Plate Work—*mfg*	332313	3443
Power Boiler and Heat Exchanger—*mfg*	33241	3443
Nuclear cores, inorganic: Basic Inorganic Chemical, All Other—*mfg*	325188	2819
Chemical Product, All Other Miscellaneous—*mfg*	325998	2819
Nuclear Electric Power Generation	**221113**	**4931**
Nuclear energy inspection and regulation offices: Regulation and Administration of Communications, Electric, Gas, and Other Utilities—*pub*	92613	9631
Nuclear fuel reactor cores, inorganic: Basic Inorganic Chemical, All Other—*mfg*	325188	2819
Chemical Product, All Other Miscellaneous—*mfg*	325998	2819
Nuclear fuel scrap reprocessing: Basic Inorganic Chemical, All Other—*mfg*	325188	2819
Chemical Product, All Other Miscellaneous—*mfg*	325998	2819
Nuclear fuels, organic: Basic Organic Chemical, All Other—*mfg*	325199	2869
Nuclear instrument modules: Measuring and Controlling Device, Other—*mfg*	334519	3829
Surgical and Medical Instrument—*mfg*	339112	3829
Nuclear irradiation equipment: Irradiation Apparatus—*mfg*	334517	3844
Nuclear power plant forgings, ferrous–not made in rolling mills: Iron and Steel Forging—*mfg*	332111	3462
Nuclear radiation detection and monitoring instruments: Measuring and Controlling Device, Other—*mfg*	334519	3829
Surgical and Medical Instrument—*mfg*	339112	3829
Nuclear reactor containment structureconstruction–general contractors: Heavy, All Other—*const*	23499	1629
Industrial Nonbuilding Structure—*const*	23493	1629
Nuclear reactor control rod drive mechanisms: Industrial Machinery, All Other—*mfg*	333298	3559
Machinery, Other Commercial and Service Industry—*mfg*	333319	3559
Nuclear reactor controls: Instruments and Related Products for Measuring, Displaying, and Controlling Industrial Process Variables—*mfg*	334513	3823
Nuclear reactors, military and industrial: Air-Conditioning and Warm Air Heating Equipment and Commercial and Industrial Refrigeration Equipment—*mfg*	333415	3443
Metal Tank (Heavy Gauge)—*mfg*	33242	3443
Plate Work—*mfg*	332313	3443
Power Boiler and Heat Exchanger—*mfg*	33241	3443

Nuclear shielding, metal plate: Air-Conditioning and Warm Air Heating Equipment and Commercial and Industrial Refrigeration Equipment—*mfg*	333415	3443
Metal Tank (Heavy Gauge)—*mfg*	33242	3443
Plate Work—*mfg*	332313	3443
Power Boiler and Heat Exchanger—*mfg*	33241	3443
Nudist camps: Recreational and Vacation Camps—*accom*	721214	7032
Numbering machines, office and store–mechanical: Lead Pencil and Art Good—*mfg*	339942	3579
Office Machinery—*mfg*	333313	3579
Watch, Clock, and Part—*mfg*	334518	3579
Numbering stamps, with rubber type:hand: Marking Device—*mfg*	339943	3953
Numerical controls: Relay and Industrial Control—*mfg*	335314	3625
Numerically controlled metal cutting machine tools: Machine Tool (Metal Cutting Types)—*mfg*	333512	3541
Numismatist shops: Stores (except Tobacco Stores), All Other Miscellaneous—*retail*	453998	5999
Nurseries, forest: Crop Farming, All Other Miscellaneous—*ag*	111998	831
Forest Nurseries and Gathering of Forest Products—*ag*	11321	831
Nursery and Floriculture Production	**11142**	
Nursery and Garden Centers	**44422**	**5193**
Nursery and Tree Production	**111421**	**811**
Nursery furniture, metal: Metal Household Furniture—*mfg*	337124	2514
Nursery furniture, wood: Nonupholstered Wood Household Furniture—*mfg*	337122	2511
Nursery schools: Child Day Care Services—*hlth*	62441	8351
Nursery stock: Flower, Nursery Stock and Florists' Supplies—*whlse*	42293	5193
Nursery and Garden Centers—*retail*	44422	5193
Nursery stock, growing of: Floriculture Production—*ag*	111422	181
Nursery and Tree Production—*ag*	111421	181
Nursery stock, seeds and bulbs: Nursery and Garden Centers—*retail*	44422	5261
Outdoor Power Equipment Stores—*retail*	44421	5261
Stores (except Tobacco Stores), All Other Miscellaneous—*retail*	453998	5261
Nurses' registries: Employment Placement Agencies—*admin*	56131	7361
Human Resources and Executive Search Consulting Services—*prof*	541612	7361
Nurses, registered and practical–offices of, except home health care services: Health Practitioners, Offices Of Miscellaneous—*hlth*	621399	8049
Mental Health Practitioners (except Physicians), Offices Of—*hlth*	62133	8049
Physical, Occupational and Speech Therapists and Audiologists, Offices Of—*hlth*	62134	8049
Nursing and Residential Care Facilities	**623**	
Nursing Care Facilities	**6231**	
Nursing Care Facilities	**62311**	**8052**
Nursing homes except skilled and intermediate care facilities: Continuing Care Retirement Communities—*hlth*	623311	8059
Nursing Care Facilities—*hlth*	62311	8059
Nursing homes, intermediate care: Continuing Care Retirement Communities—*hlth*	623311	8052
Nursing Care Facilities—*hlth*	62311	8052
Residential Mental Retardation Facilities—*hlth*	62321	8052
Nursing homes, skilled: Continuing Care Retirement Communities—*hlth*	623311	8051
Nursing Care Facilities—*hlth*	62311	8051
Nursing schools, practical: Apprenticeship Training—*educ*	611513	8249
Technical and Trade Schools, Other—*educ*	611519	8249
Nut (tree) groves and farms: Tree Nut Farming—*ag*	111335	173
Nut crackers and pickers, metal: Hardware—*mfg*	33251	3429
Nut hulling and shelling: Postharvest Crop Activities (except Cotton Ginning)—*ag*	115114	723
Nut margarine: Fats and Oils Refining and Blending—*mfg*	311225	2079
Oilseed Processing, Other—*mfg*	311223	2079
Soybean Processing—*mfg*	311222	2079
Nut rods, iron and steel: made in steelworks or rolling mills: Iron and Steel Mills—*mfg*	331111	3312
Petroleum and Coal Productsa, All Other—*mfg*	324199	3312
Nut shellers (agricultural machinery): Farm Machinery and Equipment—*mfg*	333111	3523
Nut stores: Confectionery and Nut Stores—*retail*	445292	5441
Nutritionists, offices of: Health Practitioners, Offices Of Miscellaneous—*hlth*	621399	8049
Mental Health Practitioners (except Physicians), Offices Of—*hlth*	62133	8049
Physical, Occupational and Speech Therapists and Audiologists, Offices Of—*hlth*	62134	8049
Nuts, candy covered: Confectionery from Purchased Chocolate—*mfg*	31133	2064
Non-Chocolate Confectionery—*mfg*	31134	2064
Nuts, dehydrated or dried: Roasted Nuts and Peanut Butter—*mfg*	311911	2068
Nuts, glace: Confectionery from Purchased Chocolate—*mfg*	31133	2064
Non-Chocolate Confectionery—*mfg*	31134	2064
Nuts, machine harvesting of: Crop Harvesting, Primarily by Machine—*ag*	115113	722
Nuts, metal: Bolt, Nut, Screw, Rivet and Washer—*mfg*	332722	3452
Nuts, plastics: Plastics Pipe and Pipe Fitting—*mfg*	326122	3089
Plastics Product, All Other—*mfg*	326199	3089
Unsupported Plastics Profile Shape—*mfg*	326121	3089
Nuts, salted or roasted: Confectionery—*whlse*	42245	5145
Nuts, unprocessed or shelled only: Farm Product Raw Material, Other—*whlse*	42259	5159
Nuts: salted, roasted, cooked, or canned: Roasted Nuts and Peanut Butter—*mfg*	311911	2068
Nylon broadwoven fabrics: Broadwoven Fabric Mills—*mfg*	31321	2221
Nylon fibers and bristles: Noncellulosic Organic Fiber—*mfg*	325222	2824
Nylon piece goods: Broadwoven Fabric Finishing Mills—*mfg*	313311	5131
Piece Goods, Notions and Other Dry Goods—*whlse*	42231	5131

Showcase, Partition, Shelving, and Locker—*mfg*	337215	2541
Wood Kitchen Cabinet and Counter Top—*mfg*	33711	2541
Office furniture: Furniture—*whlse*	42121	5021
Furniture Stores—*retail*	44211	5021
Office Furniture (including Fixtures) Manufacturing	**3372**	
Office Furniture (including Fixtures) Manufacturing	**33721**	
Office furniture, except wood: Nonwood Office Furniture—*mfg*	337214	2522
Office furniture, wood: Wood Office Furniture—*mfg*	337211	2521
Office help supply service: Employee Leasing Services—*admin*	56133	7363
Temporary Help Services—*admin*	56132	7363
Office machine rental and leasing, except computers: Consumer Electronics and Appliances Rental—*real*	53221	7359
Office Machinery and Equipment Rental and Leasing—*real*	53242	7359
Office machine repair, electrical: except typewriters, computers, and computer peripheral equipment: Computer and Office Machine Repair and Maintenance—*serv*	811212	7629
Office Machinery and Equipment Rental and Leasing	**53242**	**7377**
Office Machinery Manufacturing	**333313**	**3579**
Office management services: Office Administrative Services—*admin*	56111	8741
Office supplies: Office Supplies and Stationery Stores—*retail*	45321	5112
Stationary and Office Supplies—*whlse*	42212	5112
Office Supplies (except Paper) Manufacturing	**33994**	
Office Supplies and Stationery Stores	**45321**	**5112**
Office Supplies, Stationery and Gift Stores	**4532**	
Offset ink: Printing Ink—*mfg*	32591	2893
Offset paper: Newsprint Mills—*mfg*	322122	2621
Paper (except Newsprint) Mills—*mfg*	322121	2621
Offset plates, positives or negatives: preparation of: Prepress Services—*mfg*	323122	2796
Offset printing: Lithographic Printing, Commercial—*mfg*	323110	2752
Quick Printing—*mfg*	323114	2752
offshore supply boats, building and repairing: Ship Building and Repairing—*mfg*	336611	3731
Ohmmeters: Electronic Coil, Transformer, and Other Inductor—*mfg*	334416	3825
Instrument for Measuring and Testing Electricity and Electrical Signals—*mfg*	334515	3825
Oil (crude) production: Crude Petroleum and Natural Gas Extraction—*mining*	211111	1311
Oil additives: Chemical and Allied Products, Other—*whlse*	42269	5169
Oil and Gas Extraction	**21111**	
Oil and Gas Extraction	**211**	
Oil and Gas Extraction	**2111**	
Oil and gas field machinery and equipment: Oil and Gas Field Machinery and Equipment—*mfg*	333132	3533
Oil and Gas Field Machinery and Equipment Manufacturing	**333132**	**3533**
Oil and gas field machinery and equipment mechanical rubber goods: molded, extruded, and lathe-cut: Rubber Product for Mechanical Use—*mfg*	326291	3061
Oil and gas lease brokers: Financial Investment Activities, Miscellaneous—*fin*	523999	6211
Intermediation, Miscellaneous—*fin*	52391	6211
Investment Banking and Securities Dealing—*fin*	52311	6211
Securities Brokerage—*fin*	52312	6211
Oil and Gas Operations Support Activities	**213112**	**1389**
Oil and gasoline storage caverns for hire: General Warehousing and Storage Facilities—*trans*	49311	4226
Refrigerated Warehousing and Storage Facilities—*trans*	49312	4226
Warehousing and Storage Facilities, Other—*trans*	49319	4226
Oil and meal, fish: Fats and Oils Refining and Blending—*mfg*	311225	2077
Fresh and Frozen Seafood Processing—*mfg*	311712	2077
Rendering and Meat By-product Processing—*mfg*	311613	2077
Seafood Canning—*mfg*	311711	2077
Oil burners: Building Material Dealers, Other—*retail*	44419	5074
Plumbing and Heating Equipment and Supplies (Hydronics)—*whlse*	42172	5074
Oil burners, domestic and industrial: Heating Equipment (except Electric and Warm Air Furnaces)—*mfg*	333414	3433
Oil cans, metal: Metal Can—*mfg*	332431	3411
Oil cups, metal: Fabricated Metal Product, All Other Miscellaneous—*mfg*	332999	3599
General Purpose Machinery , All Other—*mfg*	333999	3599
Machine Shops—*mfg*	33271	3599
Machinery, Other Commercial and Service Industry—*mfg*	333319	3599
Motor Vehicle Parts, All Other—*mfg*	336399	3599
Oil drilling muds: Chemical and Allied Products, Other—*whlse*	42269	5169
Oil field equipment rental and leasing: Machinery and Equipment Rental and Leasing, Other Commercial and Industrial—*real*	53249	7359
Oil field exploration: on a contract basis: Geophysical Surveying and Mapping Services—*prof*	54136	1382
Oil and Gas Operations Support Activities—*mining*	213112	1382
Oil filters, internal combustion engine: except motor vehicle: Fabricated Metal Product, All Other Miscellaneous—*mfg*	332999	3599
General Purpose Machinery , All Other—*mfg*	333999	3599
Machine Shops—*mfg*	33271	3599
Machinery, Other Commercial and Service Industry—*mfg*	333319	3599
Oil filters, motor vehicle: Gasoline Engine and Engine Parts—*mfg*	336312	3714
Motor Vehicle Parts, All Other—*mfg*	336399	3714
Oil kernels: Farm Product Raw Material, Other—*whlse*	42259	5159
Oil leases, buying and selling on own account: Financial Investment Activities, Miscellaneous—*fin*	523999	6792
Owners and Lessors of Other Non-Financial Assets—*real*	53311	6792
Oil measuring and dispensing pumps: Measuring and Dispensing Pump—*mfg*	333913	3586
Oil nuts: Farm Product Raw Material, Other—*whlse*	42259	5159
Oil paints: Paint and Coating—*mfg*	32551	2851
Oil pressure gauges, motor vehicle: Measuring and Controlling Device, Other—*mfg*	334519	3829

ALPHABETICAL INDEX	NAICS	SIC
Surgical and Medical Instrument—*mfg*	339112	3829
Oil properties, lessors of: Lessors of Other Real Estate Property—*real*	53119	6519
Oil refinery construction-general contractor: Heavy, All Other—*const*	23499	1629
Industrial Nonbuilding Structure—*const*	23493	1629
Oil refining machinery, equipment, and supplies: Industrial Machinery and Equipment—*whlse*	42183	5084
Oil royalties, dealers in: Financial Investment Activities, Miscellaneous—*fin*	523999	6211
Intermediation, Miscellaneous—*fin*	52391	6211
Investment Banking and Securities Dealing—*fin*	52311	6211
Securities Brokerage—*fin*	52312	6211
Oil royalty companies: Financial Investment Activities, Miscellaneous—*fin*	523999	6792
Owners and Lessors of Other Non-Financial Assets—*real*	53311	6792
Oil sampling service for oil companies on a contract basis: Oil and Gas Operations Support Activities—*mining*	213112	1389
Oil sand mining: Crude Petroleum and Natural Gas Extraction—*mining*	211111	1311
Oil seals, asbestos: Gasket, Packing, and Sealing Device—*mfg*	339991	3053
Oil seals, leather: Gasket, Packing, and Sealing Device—*mfg*	339991	3053
Oil seals, rubber: Gasket, Packing, and Sealing Device—*mfg*	339991	3053
Oil shale mining: Crude Petroleum and Natural Gas Extraction—*mining*	211111	1311
Oil spill cleanup: Airport Operations, Other—*trans*	488119	4959
Exterminating and Pest Control Services—*admin*	56171	4959
Remediation Services—*admin*	56291	4959
Waste Management Services, All Other Miscellaneous—*admin*	562998	4959
Oil stains: Paint and Coating—*mfg*	32551	2851
Oil still gas, produced in petroleum refineries: Petroleum Refineries—*mfg*	32411	2911
Oil storage tanks, metal plate: Air-Conditioning and Warm Air Heating Equipment and Commercial and Industrial Refrigeration Equipment—*mfg*	333415	3443
Metal Tank (Heavy Gauge)—*mfg*	33242	3443
Plate Work—*mfg*	332313	3443
Power Boiler and Heat Exchanger—*mfg*	33241	3443
Oil treating compounds: Basic Organic Chemical, All Other—*mfg*	325199	2899
Chemical Product, All Other Miscellaneous—*mfg*	325998	2899
Oil well drilling equipment rental and leasing: Machinery and Equipment Rental and Leasing, Other Commercial and Industrial—*real*	53249	7359
Oil well drilling–on a contract basis: Drilling Oil and Gas Wells—*mining*	213111	1381
Oil well logging on a contract basis: Oil and Gas Operations Support Activities—*mining*	213112	1389

ALPHABETICAL INDEX	NAICS	SIC
Oil well machinery, equipment, and supplies: Industrial Machinery and Equipment—*whlse*	42183	5084
Oil well rig building, repairing, and dis-mantling–on a contract basis: Oil and Gas Operations Support Activities—*mining*	213112	1389
Oil well supply houses: Industrial Machinery and Equipment—*whlse*	42183	5084
Oil, acid–produced in petroleum refineries: Petroleum Refineries—*mfg*	32411	2911
Oil, aniline: Cyclic Crude and Intermediate—*mfg*	325192	2865
Petrochemical—*mfg*	32511	2865
Oil, corn–crude and refined: Wet Corn Milling—*mfg*	311221	2046
Oil, cottonseed: Fats and Oils Refining and Blending—*mfg*	311225	2074
Oilseed Processing, Other—*mfg*	311223	2074
Oil, creosote–product of coal tar distillation: Cyclic Crude and Intermediate—*mfg*	325192	2865
Petrochemical—*mfg*	32511	2865
Oil, hydrogenated–edible: Fats and Oils Refining and Blending—*mfg*	311225	2079
Oilseed Processing, Other—*mfg*	311223	2079
Soybean Processing—*mfg*	311222	2079
Oil, olive: Fats and Oils Refining and Blending—*mfg*	311225	2079
Oilseed Processing, Other—*mfg*	311223	2079
Soybean Processing—*mfg*	311222	2079
Oil, partially hydrogenated–edible: Fats and Oils Refining and Blending—*mfg*	311225	2079
Oilseed Processing, Other—*mfg*	311223	2079
Soybean Processing—*mfg*	311222	2079
Oil, pine–produced by distillation of pine gum or pine wood: Gum and Wood Chemical—*mfg*	325191	2861
Oil, red (oleic acid): Basic Organic Chemical, All Other—*mfg*	325199	2899
Chemical Product, All Other Miscellaneous—*mfg*	325998	2899
Oil, soybean: Fats and Oils Refining and Blending—*mfg*	311225	2075
Soybean Processing—*mfg*	311222	2075
Oil, turkey red: Surface Active Agent—*mfg*	325613	2843
Oil, vegetable winter stearin: Fats and Oils Refining and Blending—*mfg*	311225	2079
Oilseed Processing, Other—*mfg*	311223	2079
Soybean Processing—*mfg*	311222	2079
Oil, waste: Recyclable Material—*whlse*	42193	5093
Oilcloth: Fabric Coating Mills—*mfg*	31332	2295
Oiled paper: Coated and Laminated Paper—*mfg*	322222	2672
Oils, animal: Fats and Oils Refining and Blending—*mfg*	311225	2077
Fresh and Frozen Seafood Processing—*mfg*	311712	2077
Rendering and Meat By-product Processing—*mfg*	311613	2077
Seafood Canning—*mfg*	311711	2077
Oils, cosmetic: Soap and Other Detergent—*mfg*	325611	2844
Toilet Preparation—*mfg*	32562	2844
Oils, essential: Basic Organic Chemical, All Other—*mfg*	325199	2899
Chemical Product, All Other Miscellaneous—*mfg*	325998	2899

Description	NAICS	SIC
Oils, except cooking–animal and vegetable: Nondurable Goods, Other Miscellaneous—*whlse*	42299	5199
Oils, fish and manne animal–herring, menhaden, whale (refined), sardine: Fats and Oils Refining and Blending—*mfg*	311225	2077
Fresh and Frozen Seafood Processing—*mfg*	311712	2077
Rendering and Meat By-product Processing—*mfg*	311613	2077
Seafood Canning—*mfg*	311711	2077
Oils, fish and marine animal–e.g., herring, menhaden, whale (refined), sardine: Fats and Oils Refining and Blending—*mfg*	311225	2077
Fresh and Frozen Seafood Processing—*mfg*	311712	2077
Rendering and Meat By-product Processing—*mfg*	311613	2077
Seafood Canning—*mfg*	311711	2077
Oils, lubricating: Petroleum Lubricating Oil and Grease—*mfg*	324191	2992
Oils, lubricating–refining: Petroleum Lubricating Oil and Grease—*mfg*	324191	2992
Oils, partly refined–sold for rerunning-produced in petroleum refineries: Petroleum Refineries—*mfg*	32411	2911
Oils, soluble (textile assistants): Surface Active Agent—*mfg*	325613	2843
Oils, sulfonated: Surface Active Agent—*mfg*	325613	2843
Oils, vegetable (except corn oil) refined–cooking and salad: Fats and Oils Refining and Blending—*mfg*	311225	2079
Oilseed Processing, Other—*mfg*	311223	2079
Soybean Processing—*mfg*	311222	2079
Oils, vegetable and animal–medicinal grade–refined and concentrated: Medicinal and Botanical—*mfg*	325411	2833
Oils, vegetable–except corn, cottonseed, and soybean: Fats and Oils Refining and Blending—*mfg*	311225	2076
Oilseed Processing, Other—*mfg*	311223	2076
Oils, wood–product of hardwood distillation: Gum and Wood Chemical—*mfg*	325191	2861
Oils–fuel, lubricating, and illuminating-produced in petroleum refineries: Petroleum Refineries—*mfg*	32411	2911
Oils–light, medium, and heavy–made in chemical plants: Cyclic Crude and Intermediate—*mfg*	325192	2865
Petrochemical—*mfg*	32511	2865
Oilseed (except Soybean) Farming	**11112**	**119**
Oilseed and Grain Combination Farming	**111191**	**119**
Oilseed and Grain Farming	**1111**	
Oilseed crushing and extracting machinery: Food Product Machinery—*mfg*	333294	3556
Oilseed Processing, Other	**311223**	**2076**
Ointments: Pharmaceutical Preparation—*mfg*	325412	2834
Oiticica oil: Fats and Oils Refining and Blending—*mfg*	311225	2076
Oilseed Processing, Other—*mfg*	311223	2076
Old age assistance: Child and Youth Services—*hlth*	62411	8322
Community Food Services—*hlth*	62421	8322
Community Housing Services, Other—*hlth*	624229	8322
Emergency and Other Relief Services—*hlth*	62423	8322
Individual and Family Services, Other—*hlth*	62419	8322
Parole Offices and Probation Offices—*pub*	92215	8322
Services for the Elderly and Persons with Disabilities—*hlth*	62412	8322
Temporary Shelters—*hlth*	624221	8322
Old soldiers' homes: Homes for the Elderly—*hlth*	623312	8361
Residential Care Facilities, Other—*hlth*	62399	8361
Residential Mental Health and Substance Abuse Facilities—*hlth*	62322	8361
Oleate driers: Paint and Coating—*mfg*	32551	2851
Olefin fibers: Noncellulosic Organic Fiber—*mfg*	325222	2824
Oleic acid (red oil): Basic Organic Chemical, All Other—*mfg*	325199	2899
Chemical Product, All Other Miscellaneous—*mfg*	325998	2899
Oleic acid esters: Basic Organic Chemical, All Other—*mfg*	325199	2869
Oleo struts, aircraft: Aircraft Part and Auxiliary Equipment, Other—*mfg*	336413	3728
Fluid Power Valve and Hose Fitting—*mfg*	332912	3728
Oleum (fuming sulfuric acid): Basic Inorganic Chemical, All Other—*mfg*	325188	2819
Chemical Product, All Other Miscellaneous—*mfg*	325998	2819
Olive groves and farms: Fruit and Tree Nut Combination Farming—*ag*	111336	179
Noncitrus Fruit Farming, Other—*ag*	111339	179
Olive oil: Fats and Oils Refining and Blending—*mfg*	311225	2079
Oilseed Processing, Other—*mfg*	311223	2079
Soybean Processing—*mfg*	311222	2079
Olives, brined–bulk: Fruit and Vegetable Canning—*mfg*	311421	2035
Mayonnaise, Dressing and Other Prepared Sauce—*mfg*	311941	2035
Olives, dried: Dried and Dehydrated Food—*mfg*	311423	2034
Flour Milling—*mfg*	311211	2034
Olives, including stuffed–canned: Fruit and Vegetable Canning—*mfg*	311421	2033
Olivine (nongem) mining: Clay and Ceramic and Refractory Minerals—*mining*	212325	1459
Omnibearing instrumentation: Search, Detection, Navigation, Guidance, Aeronautical, and Nautical System and Instrument—*mfg*	334511	3812
On-line data base information retrieval services: On-Line Information Services—*info*	514191	7375
On-Line Information Services	**514191**	**7375**
One-family house construction–general contractors: Single Family Housing—*const*	23321	1521
One-Hour Photo Finishing	**812922**	**7384**
Onion farms: Vegetable (except Potato) and Melon Farming, Other—*ag*	111219	161
Onions, pickled: Fruit and Vegetable Canning—*mfg*	311421	2035
Mayonnaise, Dressing and Other Prepared Sauce—*mfg*	311941	2035
Onyx marble, crushed and broken: Crushed and Broken Stone and Quarrying, Other—*mining*	212319	1429
Onyx marble, dimension: Dimension Stone and Quarrying—*mining*	212311	1411
Opalescent flat glass: Flat Glass—*mfg*	327211	3211
Opaline, cotton: Broadwoven Fabric Mills—*mfg*	31321	2211

ALPHABETICAL INDEX	NAICS	SIC
Open air motion picture theaters: Drive-In Motion Picture Theaters—*info*	512132	7833
Open-End Investment Funds	**52591**	**6722**
Openers, bottle–made from purchased wire: Fabricated Wire Product, Other—*mfg*	332618	3496
Opera companies: Theater Companies and Dinner Theaters—*arts*	71111	7922
Opera glasses: Optical Instrument and Lens—*mfg*	333314	3827
Opera hats: Hat, Cap and Millinery—*mfg*	315991	2353
Operating systems software, computer–prepackaged: Publishers—*info*	51121	7372
Software Reproducing—*mfg*	334611	7372
Operating tables: Surgical and Medical Instrument—*mfg*	339112	3841
Operations research consultants: Administrative Management and General Management Consulting Services—*prof*	541611	8742
Human Resources and Executive Search Consulting Services—*prof*	541612	8742
Marketing Consulting Services—*prof*	541613	8742
Process, Physical, Distribution and Logistics Consulting Services—*prof*	541614	8742
Operations research, computer systems design: Computer Systems Design Services—*prof*	541512	7373
Operative builders on own account: Building, Commercial and Institutional—*const*	23332	1531
Manufacturing and Industrial Building—*const*	23331	1531
Multifamily Housing—*const*	23322	1531
Single Family Housing—*const*	23321	1531
Operators of apartment buildings (five or more housing units): Lessors of Residential Buildings and Dwellings—*real*	53111	6513
Operators of apartment hotels: Lessors of Residential Buildings and Dwellings—*real*	53111	6513
Operators of commercial and industrial buildings: Lessors of Nonresidential Buildings (except Miniwarehouses)—*real*	53112	6512
Promoters of Performing Arts, Sports and Similar Events with Facilities—*arts*	71131	6512
Operators of dwellings (four or fewer housing units): Lessors of Residential Buildings and Dwellings—*real*	53111	6514
Operators of mobile home sites: Lessors of Other Real Estate Property—*real*	53119	6515
Operators of nonresidential buildings: Lessors of Nonresidential Buildings (except Miniwarehouses)—*real*	53112	6512
Promoters of Performing Arts, Sports and Similar Events with Facilities—*arts*	71131	6512
Operators of residential buildings (four or fewer housing units): Lessors of Residential Buildings and Dwellings—*real*	53111	6514
Operators of residential hotels: Lessors of Residential Buildings and Dwellings—*real*	53111	6513

ALPHABETICAL INDEX	NAICS	SIC
Operators of retirement hotels: Lessors of Residential Buildings and Dwellings—*real*	53111	6513
Ophthalmic glass, except flat: Pressed and Blown Glass and Glassware, Other—*mfg*	327212	3229
Ophthalmic glass, flat: Flat Glass—*mfg*	327211	3211
Ophthalmic goods: Ophthalmic Goods—*whlse*	42146	5048
Ophthalmic Goods Manufacturing	**339115**	**5995**
Ophthalmic Goods Wholesalers	**42146**	**5048**
Ophthalmic instruments and apparatus: Surgical and Medical Instrument—*mfg*	339112	3841
Ophthalmic lens blanks: Pressed and Blown Glass and Glassware, Other—*mfg*	327212	3229
Ophthalmic lens grinding, except prescription: Ophthalmic Goods—*mfg*	339115	3851
Ophthalmologists, offices of: Freestanding Ambulatory Surgical and Emergency Centers—*hlth*	621493	8011
HMO Medical Centers—*hlth*	621491	8011
Physicians (except Mental Health Specialists), Offices Of—*hlth*	621111	8011
Physicians, Mental Health Specialists, Offices Of—*hlth*	621112	8011
Ophthalmometers and ophthalmoscopes: Surgical and Medical Instrument—*mfg*	339112	3841
Opinion research, commercial: Marketing Research and Public Opinion Polling—*prof*	54191	8732
Research and Development in the Social Sciences and Humanities—*prof*	54173	8732
Opium derivatives: Medicinal and Botanical—*mfg*	325411	2833
Optical alignment and display instruments, except photographic: Optical Instrument and Lens—*mfg*	333314	3827
Optical comparators: Optical Instrument and Lens—*mfg*	333314	3827
Optical disks and tape, blank: Magnetic and Optical Recording Media—*mfg*	334613	3695
Optical glass blanks: Pressed and Blown Glass and Glassware, Other—*mfg*	327212	3229
Optical glass, flat: Flat Glass—*mfg*	327211	3211
Optical goods: Ophthalmic Goods—*mfg*	339115	5995
Optical Goods Stores—*retail*	44613	5995
Optical Goods Stores	**44613**	**5995**
Optical grinding service for the trade: Ophthalmic Goods—*mfg*	339115	3851
Optical Instrument and Lens Manufacturing	**333314**	**3827**
Optical isolators: Semiconductor and Related Device—*mfg*	334413	3674
Optical lens blanks: Pressed and Blown Glass and Glassware, Other—*mfg*	327212	3229
Optical lens machinery: Industrial Machinery, All Other—*mfg*	333298	3559
Machinery, Other Commercial and Service Industry—*mfg*	333319	3559
Rubber and Plastics Industry Machinery—*mfg*	33322	3559
Optical readers and scanners: Computer Peripheral Equipment, Other—*mfg*	334119	3577

Description	NAICS	SIC
Optical scanning data service: Data Processing Services—*info*	51421	7374
Optical scanning devices, computer peripheral equipment: Computer Peripheral Equipment, Other—*mfg*	334119	3577
Optical storage devices for computers: Computer Storage Device—*mfg*	334112	3572
Optical test and inspection equipment: Optical Instrument and Lens—*mfg*	333314	3827
Opticians: Ophthalmic Goods—*mfg*	339115	5995
Optical Goods Stores—*retail*	44613	5995
Option dealers, stock: Financial Investment Activities, Miscellaneous—*fin*	523999	6211
Intermediation, Miscellaneous—*fin*	52391	6211
Investment Banking and Securities Dealing—*fin*	52311	6211
Securities Brokerage—*fin*	52312	6211
Option exchanges, stock: Securities and Commodity Exchanges—*fin*	52321	6231
Optometers: Surgical and Medical Instrument—*mfg*	339112	3841
Optometric equipment and supplies- wholesale: Ophthalmic Goods—*whlse*	42146	5048
Optometrists, offices and clinics of: Optometrists, Offices Of—*hlth*	62132	8042
Optometrists, Offices Of	**62132**	**8042**
Oral pathologists, offices of: Dentists, Offices Of—*hlth*	62121	8021
Orange Groves	**11131**	**174**
Orange groves and farms: Citrus (except Orange) Groves—*ag*	11132	174
Orange Groves—*ag*	11131	174
Orange oil: Spice and Extract—*mfg*	311942	2899
Orchard cultivation services: Nonscheduled Air, Other—*trans*	481219	721
Soil Preparation, Planting, and Cultivating—*ag*	115112	721
Orchard management and maintenance, with or without crop services: Farm Management Services—*ag*	115116	762
Orchestras: Independent Artists, Writers, and Performers—*arts*	71151	7929
Musical Groups and Artists—*arts*	71113	7929
Performing Arts Companies, Other—*arts*	71119	7929
Order taking offices of mail-order houses- retail: Electronic Shopping and Mail-Order Houses—*retail*	45411	5961
Ordnance and Accessories Manufacturing, Other	**332995**	**3489**
Ordnance forgings, ferrous–not made in rolling mills: Iron and Steel Forging—*mfg*	332111	3462
Ordnance forgings, nonferrous–not made in hot-rolling mills: Nonferrous Forging—*mfg*	332112	3463
Ordnance testing chambers: General Purpose Machinery , All Other—*mfg*	333999	3569
Ore and aggregate feeders: Mining Machinery and Equipment—*mfg*	333131	3532
Ore crushing, washing, screening, and loading machinery: Mining Machinery and Equipment—*mfg*	333131	3532
Organ hardware: Hardware—*mfg*	33251	3429
Organ parts and materials, except organ hardware: Musical Instrument—*mfg*	339992	3931
Organ tuning and repair: Electronic and Precision Equipment Repair and Maintenance, Other—*serv*	811219	7699
Personal and Household Goods Repair and Maintenance, Other—*serv*	81149	7699
Organdy, cotton: Broadwoven Fabric Mills—*mfg*	31321	2211
Organic acid esters: Basic Organic Chemical, All Other—*mfg*	325199	2869
Organic chemicals, acyclic: Basic Organic Chemical, All Other—*mfg*	325199	2869
Organic chemicals, synthetic: Chemical and Allied Products, Other—*whlse*	42269	5169
Organic colors, full strength: Petrochemical—*mfg*	32511	2865
Organic Dye and Pigment Manufacturing	**325132**	**2865**
Organic fibers, synthetic–except cellulosic: Noncellulosic Organic Fiber—*mfg*	325222	2824
Organic medicinal chemicals–bulk: Medicinal and Botanical—*mfg*	325411	2833
Organic pigments (lakes and toners): Organic Dye and Pigment—*mfg*	325132	2865
Petrochemical—*mfg*	32511	2865
Organizations, Other Similar	**81399**	**8641**
Organizers for closets, drawers, and shelves–plastics: Plastics Pipe and Pipe Fitting—*mfg*	326122	3089
Plastics Product, All Other—*mfg*	326199	3089
Unsupported Plastics Profile Shape—*mfg*	326121	3089
Organs, all types–e.g., pipe, reed, hand, street, barrel, electronic, player: Musical Instrument—*mfg*	339992	3931
Oriented strandboard: Reconstituted Wood Product—*mfg*	321219	2493
Ornamental and Architectural Metal Products Manufacturing	**33232**	
Ornamental and Architectural Metal Work Manufacturing	**332323**	**3449**
Ornamental and architectural metalwork: Ornamental and Architectural Metal Work—*mfg*	332323	3446
Ornamental and architectural plasterwork–e.g., mantels and columns: Gypsum and Gypsum Product—*mfg*	32742	3299
Nonmetallic Mineral Product, All Other Miscellaneous—*mfg*	327999	3299
Ornamental bush planting, pruning, bracing, spraying, removal, and surgery: Landscaping Services—*admin*	56173	783
Ornamental metal work–contractors: Trade Contractors, All Other Special—*const*	23599	1799
Ornamental tree planting, pruning, bracing, spraying, removal, and surgery: Landscaping Services—*admin*	56173	783
Ornamental woodwork–e.g., cornices andmantels: Millwork (including Flooring), Other—*mfg*	321918	2431
Wood Window and Door—*mfg*	321911	2431
Ornamented glass, made from purchasedglass: Glass Product Made of Purchased Glass—*mfg*	327215	3231
Ornaments, Christmas tree–electric: Lighting Equipment, Other—*mfg*	335129	3699
Ornaments, Christmas tree–except glassand electric: Fabricated Metal Product, All Other Miscellaneous—*mfg*	332999	3999
Plastics Product, All Other—*mfg*	326199	3999
Wood Product, All Other Miscellaneous—*mfg*	321999	3999
Ornaments, Christmas tree–glass: Pressed and Blown Glass and Glassware, Other—*mfg*	327212	3229

ALPHABETICAL INDEX	NAICS	SIC
Ornaments, Christmas tree–made frompurchased glass: Glass Product Made of Purchased Glass—*mfg*	327215	3231
Ornaments, costume–except precious metal and gems: Costume Jewelry and Novelty—*mfg*	339914	3961
Ornaments, shoe: Fastener, Button, Needle and Pin—*mfg*	339993	3131
Leather Good, All Other—*mfg*	316999	3131
Wood Product, All Other Miscellaneous—*mfg*	321999	3131
Orphanages: Homes for the Elderly—*hlth*	623312	8361
Residential Care Facilities, Other—*hlth*	62399	8361
Residential Mental Health and Substance Abuse Facilities—*hlth*	62322	8361
Orris oil: Basic Organic Chemical, All Other—*mfg*	325199	2899
Chemical Product, All Other Miscellaneous—*mfg*	325998	2899
Orthodichlorobenzene: Cyclic Crude and Intermediate—*mfg*	325192	2865
Petrochemical—*mfg*	32511	2865
Orthodontic appliances: Dental Equipment and Supplies—*mfg*	339114	3843
Orthodontic appliances made in dental laboratories to order for the profession: Dental Laboratories—*mfg*	339116	8072
Orthodontists, offices of: Dentists, Offices Of—*hlth*	62121	8021
Orthopedic and artificial limb stores: Health and Personal Care Stores, All Other—*retail*	446199	5999
Orthopedic devices and materials: Surgical Appliance and Supplies—*mfg*	339113	3842
Orthopedic equipment: Health and Personal Care Stores, All Other—*retail*	446199	5047
Medical, Dental and Hospital Equipment and Supplies—*whlse*	42145	5047
Orthopedic hosiery, elastic: Surgical Appliance and Supplies—*mfg*	339113	3842
Orthopedic hospitals: General Medical and Surgical Hospitals—*hlth*	62211	8069
Hospitals (except Psychiatric and Substance Abuse), Specialty—*hlth*	62231	8069
Psychiatric and Substance Abuse Hospitals—*hlth*	62221	8069
Orthopedic physicians, offices of: Freestanding Ambulatory Surgical and Emergency Centers—*hlth*	621493	8011
HMO Medical Centers—*hlth*	621491	8011
Physicians (except Mental Health Specialists), Offices Of—*hlth*	621111	8011
Physicians, Mental Health Specialists, Offices Of—*hlth*	621112	8011
Orthopedic plaster, gypsum: Gypsum and Gypsum Product—*mfg*	32742	3275
Orthopedic shoes, children's–except extension shoes: Footwear, Other—*mfg*	316219	3149
Orthopedic shoes, extension: Surgical Appliance and Supplies—*mfg*	339113	3842
Orthopedic shoes, men's–except extension shoes: Men's Footwear (except Athletic)—*mfg*	316213	3143
Orthopedic shoes, women's–except extension shoes: Women's Footwear (except Athletic)—*mfg*	316214	3144
Orthopedic sundries, molded rubber: Fabric Coating Mills—*mfg*	31332	3069
Rubber Product, All Other—*mfg*	326299	3069
Oscillators, audiofrequency and radiofrequency (instrument types): Electronic Coil, Transformer, and Other Inductor—*mfg*	334416	3825

ALPHABETICAL INDEX	NAICS	SIC
Instrument for Measuring and Testing Electricity and Electrical Signals—*mfg*	334515	3825
Oscillators, except laboratory type: Electronic Component, Other—*mfg*	334419	3679
Motor Vehicle Electrical and Electronic Equipment, Other—*mfg*	336322	3679
Printed Circuit/Electronics Assembly—*mfg*	334418	3679
Radio and Television Broadcasting and Wireless Communications Equipment—*mfg*	33422	3679
Oscillographs and oscilloscopes: Electronic Coil, Transformer, and Other Inductor—*mfg*	334416	3825
Instrument for Measuring and Testing Electricity and Electrical Signals—*mfg*	334515	3825
Osmium ore mining: Metal Ore, All Other—*mining*	212299	1099
Osmometers: Analytical Laboratory Instrument—*mfg*	334516	3826
Osnaburgs: Broadwoven Fabric Mills—*mfg*	31321	2211
Ossein: Basic Organic Chemical, All Other—*mfg*	325199	2899
Chemical Product, All Other Miscellaneous—*mfg*	325998	2899
Osteopathic physicians, offices and clinics of: Physicians (except Mental Health Specialists), Offices Of—*hlth*	621111	8031
Physicians, Mental Health Specialists, Offices Of—*hlth*	621112	8031
Osteoperosis centers: Ambulatory Health Care Services, All Other Miscellaneous—*hlth*	621999	8099
Other Health Practitioners, Offices Of	**6213**	
Other Holding Companies, Offices Of	**551112**	**6719**
Other Metal Ore Mining, Other	**21229**	
Other Metal Valve and Pipe Fitting Manufacturing, Other	**332919**	**3494**
Other Metalworking Machinery Manufacturing, Other	**333518**	**3549**
Otoscopes, electromedical: Electromedical and Electrotherapeutic Apparatus—*mfg*	334510	3845
Irradiation Apparatus—*mfg*	334517	3845
Otoscopes, except electromedical: Surgical and Medical Instrument—*mfg*	339112	3841
Ouseed cake and meal: Nondurable Goods, Other Miscellaneous—*whlse*	42299	5199
Ouseeds: Farm Product Raw Material, Other—*whlse*	42259	5159
Oustone quarrying: Crushed and Broken Stone and Quarrying, Other—*mining*	212319	1499
Non-Metallic Mineral, All Other—*mining*	212399	1499
Oustones, artificial: Abrasive Product—*mfg*	32791	3291
Fabricated Metal Product, All Other Miscellaneous—*mfg*	332999	3291
Outboard motor dealers: Boat Dealers—*retail*	441222	5551
Outboard motors: Sporting and Recreational Goods and Supplies—*whlse*	42191	5091
Outboard motors, electric: Electrical Equipment and Component, All Other Miscellaneous—*mfg*	335999	3699
Engine Equipment, Other—*mfg*	333618	3699
Machinery, Other Commercial and Service Industry—*mfg*	333319	3699

Outboard motors, except electric: Engine Equipment, Other—*mfg*	333618	3519
Motor Vehicle Parts, All Other—*mfg*	336399	3519
Outdoor advertising service: Display Advertising—*prof*	54185	7312
Outdoor furniture: Furniture Stores—*retail*	44211	5712
Nonupholstered Wood Household Furniture—*mfg*	337122	5712
Upholstered Household Furniture—*mfg*	337121	5712
Wood Kitchen Cabinet and Counter Top—*mfg*	33711	5712
Outdoor Power Equipment Stores	**44421**	**5261**
Outerwear handknitted–for the trade: Outerwear Knitting Mills—*mfg*	315191	2253
Outerwear Knitting Mills	**315191**	**2259**
Outerwear Manufacturing, Men's and Boys' Cut and Sew, Other	**315228**	**2369**
Outerwear Manufacturing, Women's and Girls' Cut and Sew, Other	**315238**	**2369**
Outerwear, men's and boys': Men's and Boys' Clothing and Furnishings—*whlse*	42232	5136
Outerwear–women's, children's, and infants': Women's, Children's, and Infants' and Accessories—*whlse*	42233	5137
Outing flannel, cotton: Broadwoven Fabric Mills—*mfg*	31321	2211
Outlet boxes (electric wiring devices): Noncurrent-Carrying Wiring Device—*mfg*	335932	3644
Outlets, convenience–electric: Current-Carrying Wiring Device—*mfg*	335931	3643
Outpatient Care Centers	**6214**	
Outpatient Care Centers, All Other	**621498**	**8093**
Outpatient Care Centers, Other	**62149**	
Outpatient detoxification centers: Family Planning Centers—*hlth*	62141	8093
Outpatient Care Centers, All Other—*hlth*	621498	8093
Outpatient Mental Health and Substance Abuse Centers—*hlth*	62142	8093
Outpatient Mental Health and Substance Abuse Centers	**62142**	**8093**
Outpatient mental health clinics: Family Planning Centers—*hlth*	62141	8093
Outpatient Care Centers, All Other—*hlth*	621498	8093
Outpatient Mental Health and Substance Abuse Centers—*hlth*	62142	8093
Outpatient treatment clinics for alcoholism and drug addiction: Family Planning Centers—*hlth*	62141	8093
Outpatient Care Centers, All Other—*hlth*	621498	8093
Outpatient Mental Health and Substance Abuse Centers—*hlth*	62142	8093
Outreach programs: Child and Youth Services—*hlth*	62411	8322
Community Food Services—*hlth*	62421	8322
Community Housing Services, Other—*hlth*	624229	8322
Emergency and Other Relief Services—*hlth*	62423	8322
Individual and Family Services, Other—*hlth*	62419	8322
Parole Offices and Probation Offices—*pub*	92215	8322
Services for the Elderly and Persons with Disabilities—*hlth*	62412	8322
Temporary Shelters—*hlth*	624221	8322
Oven construction for industrial plants–general contractors: Heavy, All Other—*const*	23499	1629
Industrial Nonbuilding Structure—*const*	23493	1629
Oven construction, bakers'–general contractors: Heavy, All Other—*const*	23499	1629
Industrial Nonbuilding Structure—*const*	23493	1629
Oven temperature controls, nonindustrial: Automatic Environmental Control for Residential, Commercial and Appliance Use—*mfg*	334512	3822
Ovens, bakery: Food Product Machinery—*mfg*	333294	3556
Ovens, cafeteria food warming–portable: Machinery, Other Commercial and Service Industry—*mfg*	333319	3589
Ovens, household–excluding portable appliances other than microwave and convection: Household Cooking Appliance—*mfg*	335221	3631
Ovens, household–portable–except microwave and convection ovens: Electric Housewares and Household Fan—*mfg*	335211	3634
Heating Equipment (except Electric and Warm Air Furnaces)—*mfg*	333414	3634
Ovens, industrial process–except bakery: Industrial Process Furnace and Oven—*mfg*	333994	3567
Ovens, microwave cooking equipment):commercial: Machinery, Other Commercial and Service Industry—*mfg*	333319	3589
Ovens, microwave–commercial: Equipment, Other Commercial—*whlse*	42144	5046
Ovens, microwave–household: Electrical Appliance, Television and Radio Set—*whlse*	42162	5064
Ovens, sherardizing: Industrial Process Furnace and Oven—*mfg*	333994	3567
Ovens, surveillance–for aging and testing powder: General Purpose Machinery , All Other—*mfg*	333999	3569
Ovenware, glass: Pressed and Blown Glass and Glassware, Other—*mfg*	327212	3229
Ovenware, plastics-rnfg: Plastics Pipe and Pipe Fitting—*mfg*	326122	3089
Plastics Product, All Other—*mfg*	326199	3089
Unsupported Plastics Profile Shape—*mfg*	326121	3089
Over-the-road trucking: Freight (except Used Goods) Trucking, Long-Distance, Specialized—*trans*	48423	4213
General Freight Trucking, Long-Distance, Less Than Truckload—*trans*	484122	4213
General Freight Trucking, Long-Distance, Truckload—*trans*	484121	4213
Used Household and Office Goods Moving—*trans*	48421	4213
Overall jackets: Men's and Boys' Cut and Sew Apparel Contractors—*mfg*	315211	2326
Men's and Boys' Cut and Sew Work Clothing—*mfg*	315225	2326
Overalls, work: Men's and Boys' Cut and Sew Apparel Contractors—*mfg*	315211	2326
Men's and Boys' Cut and Sew Work Clothing—*mfg*	315225	2326
Overburden removal for bituminous coal, anthracite, and lignite on a contractbasis: Coal Support Activities—*mining*	213113	1241
Overburden removal for metal mining–ona contract basis: Geophysical Surveying and Mapping Services—*prof*	54136	1081
Metal Support Activities—*mining*	213114	1081
Overburden removal for nonmetallic minerals, except fuels–on a contract basis: Geophysical Surveying and Mapping Services—*prof*	54136	1481

ALPHABETICAL INDEX	NAICS	SIC
Non-Metallic Minerals (except Fuels) Support Activities—*mining*	213115	1481
Overcoatings–Wool, mohair, and similar animal fibers: Broadwoven Fabric Finishing Mills—*mfg*	313311	2231
Broadwoven Fabric Mills—*mfg*	31321	2231
Textile and Fabric Finishing (except Broadwoven Fabric) Mills—*mfg*	313312	2231
Overcoats: Men's and Boys' Cut and Sew Apparel Contractors—*mfg*	315211	2311
Men's and Boys' Cut and Sew Suit, Coat and Overcoat—*mfg*	315222	2311
Overcoats, men's and boys': Men's and Boys' Clothing and Furnishings—*whlse*	42232	5136
Overhead conveyor systems for general industrial use: Conveyor and Conveying Equipment—*mfg*	333922	3535
Overhead Traveling Crane, Hoist and Monorail System Manufacturing	**333923**	**3531**
Overpass construction–general contractors: Bridge and Tunnel—*const*	23412	1622
Overprinting manmade fiber and silk broadwoven fabric: Broadwoven Fabric Finishing Mills—*mfg*	313311	2262
Overshoes, plastics: Rubber and Plastics Footwear—*mfg*	316211	3021
Overshoes, rubber or rubber soled fabric: Rubber and Plastics Footwear—*mfg*	316211	3021
Owners and Lessors of Other Non-Financial Assets	**53311**	**6794**
Owners and Lessors of Other Non-Financial Assets	**5331**	
Owners and Lessors of Other Non-Financial Assets	**533**	
Ox bile salts and derivatives–bulk, uncompounded: Medicinal and Botanical—*mfg*	325411	2833
Oxalates: Basic Organic Chemical, All Other—*mfg*	325199	2869
Oxalic acid and metallic salts: Basic Organic Chemical, All Other—*mfg*	325199	2869
Oxfords (cotton fabrics): Broadwoven Fabric Mills—*mfg*	31321	2211
Oxidation catalyst made from porcelain: Basic Inorganic Chemical, All Other—*mfg*	325188	2819
Chemical Product, All Other Miscellaneous—*mfg*	325998	2819
Oxidizers, inorganic: Basic Organic Chemical, All Other—*mfg*	325199	2899
Chemical Product, All Other Miscellaneous—*mfg*	325998	2899
Oxygen systems for aircraft: Aircraft Part and Auxiliary Equipment, Other—*mfg*	336413	3728
Fluid Power Valve and Hose Fitting—*mfg*	332912	3728
Oxygen tent service: Ambulatory Health Care Services, All Other Miscellaneous—*hlth*	621999	8099
Oxygen tents: Surgical and Medical Instrument—*mfg*	339112	3841
Oxygen, compressed and liquefied: Industrial Gas—*mfg*	32512	2813
Oyster bars: Cafeterias—*accom*	722212	5812
Caterers—*accom*	72232	5812
Foodservice Contractors—*accom*	72231	5812
Full-Service Restaurants—*accom*	72211	5812
Limited-Service Restaurants—*accom*	722211	5812

ALPHABETICAL INDEX	NAICS	SIC
Snack and Nonalcoholic Beverage Bars—*accom*	722213	5812
Theater Companies and Dinner Theaters—*arts*	71111	5812
Oyster beds: Shellfish Fishing—*ag*	114112	913
Oyster shells, ground–used as feed for animals and fowls: Animal Food, Other—*mfg*	311119	2048
Oysters, canned and cured: Seafood Canning—*mfg*	311711	2091
Oysters, dredging or tonging of: Shellfish Fishing—*ag*	114112	913
Oysters, fresh–shucking and packing in nonsealed containers: Fresh and Frozen Seafood Processing—*mfg*	311712	2092
Ozokerite mining: Crushed and Broken Stone and Quarrying, Other—*mining*	212319	1499
Non-Metallic Mineral, All Other—*mining*	212399	1499
Ozone machines: Industrial Machinery, All Other—*mfg*	333298	3559
Machinery, Other Commercial and Service Industry—*mfg*	333319	3559
Pacemakers: Electromedical and Electrotherapeutic Apparatus- -*mfg*	334510	3845
Irradiation Apparatus—*mfg*	334517	3845
Pacifiers, rubber: Fabric Coating Mills—*mfg*	31332	3069
Rubber Product, All Other—*mfg*	326299	3069
Pack trains for amusement: Amusement and Recreation Industries, All Other—*arts*	71399	7999
Package delivery, private–air: Couriers—*trans*	49211	4513
Package delivery, private–except air: Couriers—*trans*	49211	4215
Local Messengers and Local Delivery—*trans*	49221	4215
Packaged Frozen Food Wholesalers	**42242**	**5142**
Packaging and labeling service (not packing and crating): Packaging and Labeling Services—*admin*	56191	7389
Packaging and Labeling Services	**56191**	**7389**
Packaging foamed plastics: Polystyrene Foam Product—*mfg*	32614	3086
Urethane and Other Foam Product (except Polystyrene)—*mfg*	32615	3086
Packaging fresh or farm-dried fruits and vegetables: Postharvest Crop Activities (except Cotton Ginning)—*ag*	115114	723
Packaging machinery: Packaging Machinery—*mfg*	333993	3565
Packaging Machinery Manufacturing	**333993**	**3565**
Packers' cans, metal: Metal Can—*mfg*	332431	3411
Packers' salt: Basic Organic Chemical, All Other—*mfg*	325199	2899
Chemical Product, All Other Miscellaneous—*mfg*	325998	2899
Packers' ware (containers), glass: Glass Container—*mfg*	327213	3221
Packing and Crating	**488991**	**4783**
Packing cases, wood–nailed or lockcorner: Wood Container and Pallet—*mfg*	32192	2441
Packing for steam engines, pipe joints, air compressors, etc.: Gasket, Packing, and Sealing Device—*mfg*	339991	3053
Packing fruits and vegetables: Postharvest Crop Activities (except Cotton Ginning)—*ag*	115114	723
Packing goods for shipping: Packing and Crating—*trans*	488991	4783
Packing machinery and equipment: Industrial Machinery and Equipment—*whlse*	42183	5084

Description	NAICS	SIC
Packing, hose, and belting–industrial: Industrial Machinery and Equipment—*whlse*	42183	5085
Industrial Supplies—*whlse*	42184	5085
Packing, metallic: Gasket, Packing, and Sealing Device—*mfg*	339991	3053
Packing, rubber: Gasket, Packing, and Sealing Device—*mfg*	339991	3053
Packing, twisted jute: Broadwoven Fabric Mills—*mfg*	31321	2299
Narrow Fabric Mills—*mfg*	313221	2299
Nonwoven Fabric Mills—*mfg*	31323	2299
Textile and Fabric Finishing (except Broadwoven Fabric) Mills—*mfg*	313312	2299
Textile Product Mills, All Other Miscellaneous—*mfg*	314999	2299
Thread Mills—*mfg*	313113	2299
Yarn Spinning Mills—*mfg*	313111	2299
Packing–cup, U-valve, etc.-leather: Gasket, Packing, and Sealing Device—*mfg*	339991	3053
Packup assemblies (wheel overhaul): Industrial Machinery, All Other—*mfg*	333298	3559
Machinery, Other Commercial and Service Industry—*mfg*	333319	3559
Pacs, rubber or rubber soled fabric: Rubber and Plastics Footwear—*mfg*	316211	3021
Padding and wadding, textile: Broadwoven Fabric Mills—*mfg*	31321	2299
Narrow Fabric Mills—*mfg*	313221	2299
Nonwoven Fabric Mills—*mfg*	31323	2299
Textile and Fabric Finishing (except Broadwoven Fabric) Mills—*mfg*	313312	2299
Textile Product Mills, All Other Miscellaneous—*mfg*	314999	2299
Thread Mills—*mfg*	313113	2299
Yarn Spinning Mills—*mfg*	313111	2299
Padlocks: Hardware—*mfg*	33251	3429
Pads and padding, felt–except woven: Broadwoven Fabric Mills—*mfg*	31321	2299
Narrow Fabric Mills—*mfg*	313221	2299
Nonwoven Fabric Mills—*mfg*	31323	2299
Textile and Fabric Finishing (except Broadwoven Fabric) Mills—*mfg*	313312	2299
Textile Product Mills, All Other Miscellaneous—*mfg*	314999	2299
Thread Mills—*mfg*	313113	2299
Yarn Spinning Mills—*mfg*	313111	2299
Pads and padding, table–except asbestos, felt, rattan, rood, and willow: Household Textile Product Mills, Other—*mfg*	314129	2392
Pads, athletic–e.g., football, basketball, soccer, lacrosse: Sporting and Athletic Goods—*mfg*	33992	3949
Pads, corrugated and solid fiberboard: Corrugated and Solid Fiber Box—*mfg*	322211	2653
Pads, desk–paper: Stationery, Tablet, and Related Product—*mfg*	322233	2678
Pads, excelsior–wood: Cut Stock, Resawing Lumber, and Planing—*mfg*	321912	2429
Sawmills—*mfg*	321113	2429
Wood Product, All Other Miscellaneous—*mfg*	321999	2429
Pads, fiber–henequen, sisal, istle: Broadwoven Fabric Mills—*mfg*	31321	2299
Narrow Fabric Mills—*mfg*	313221	2299
Nonwoven Fabric Mills—*mfg*	31323	2299
Textile and Fabric Finishing (except Broadwoven Fabric) Mills—*mfg*	313312	2299
Textile Product Mills, All Other Miscellaneous—*mfg*	314999	2299
Thread Mills—*mfg*	313113	2299
Yarn Spinning Mills—*mfg*	313111	2299
Pads, incontinent and bed: Surgical Appliance and Supplies—*mfg*	339113	3842
Pads, inking and stamping: Marking Device—*mfg*	339943	3953
Pads, kneeling–rubber: Fabric Coating Mills—*mfg*	31332	3069
Rubber Product, All Other—*mfg*	326299	3069
Pads, scouring–soap impregnated: Abrasive Product—*mfg*	32791	3291
Fabricated Metal Product, All Other Miscellaneous—*mfg*	332999	3291
Pads, shoulder–e.g., for coats and suits: Apparel Accessories and Apparel, Other—*mfg*	315999	2396
Textile Product Mills, All Other Miscellaneous—*mfg*	314999	2396
Pads, table–rattan, reed, and willow: Manufacturing, All Other Miscellaneous—*mfg*	339999	2499
Wood Container and Pallet—*mfg*	32192	2499
Wood Product, All Other Miscellaneous—*mfg*	321999	2499
Pagers (one-way): Radio and Television Broadcasting and Wireless Communications Equipment—*mfg*	33422	3663
Paging	**513321**	**4812**
Paging services–radiotelephone: Cellular and Other Wireless Telecommunications—*info*	513322	4812
Paging—*info*	513321	4812
Telecommunications Resellers—*info*	51333	4812
Pail mills: Other Metalworking Machinery, Other—*mfg*	333518	3549
Pails, except shipping and stamped–metal: Metal Can—*mfg*	332431	3411
Pails, folding sanitary food–paperboard: Folding Paperboard Box—*mfg*	322212	2657
Pails, metal: Industrial Machinery and Equipment—*whlse*	42183	5085
Industrial Supplies—*whlse*	42184	5085
Pails, plastics: Plastics Pipe and Pipe Fitting—*mfg*	326122	3089
Plastics Product, All Other—*mfg*	326199	3089
Unsupported Plastics Profile Shape—*mfg*	326121	3089
Pails, plywood: Wood Container and Pallet—*mfg*	32192	2449
Pails, shipping–metal-except tinned: Metal Container, Other—*mfg*	332439	3412
Pails, stamped and pressed metal–except tinned and shipping type: Kitchen Utensil, Pot and Pan—*mfg*	332214	3469
Pails, wood–coopered: Wood Container and Pallet—*mfg*	32192	2449
Paint and Coating Manufacturing	**32551**	**2899**
Paint and wallpaper cleaners: Polish and Other Sanitation Good—*mfg*	325612	2842
Paint and Wallpaper Stores	**44412**	**5231**
Paint and wallpaper stripping–contractors: Painting and Wall Covering Contractors—*const*	23521	1799

ALPHABETICAL INDEX	NAICS	SIC
Paint baking and drying ovens: Industrial Process Furnace and Oven—*mfg*	333994	3567
Paint brushes, rollers, and sprayers: Paint and Wallpaper Stores—*retail*	44412	5198
Paint, Varnish and Supplies—*whlse*	42295	5198
Paint driers: Paint and Coating—*mfg*	32551	2851
Paint makiug machinery: Industrial Machinery, All Other—*mfg*	333298	3559
Machinery, Other Commercial and Service Industry—*mfg*	333319	3559
Paint pignients, inorgaaic: Carbon Black—*mfg*	325182	2816
Paint pignients, inorganic: Inorganic Dye and Pigment—*mfg*	325131	2816
Paint pignients, organic: Organic Dye and Pigment—*mfg*	325132	2865
Petrochemical—*mfg*	32511	2865
Paint primers: Paint and Coating—*mfg*	32551	2851
Paint removers: Paint and Coating—*mfg*	32551	2851
Paint rollers: Broom, Brush and Mop—*mfg*	339994	3991
Paint sets, children's: Game, Toy, and Children's Vehicle—*mfg*	339932	3944
Paint shops, automotive: Automotive Body, Paint and Interior Repair and Maintenance—*serv*	811121	7532
Paint spray equipment, industrial: Industrial Machinery and Equipment—*whlse*	42183	5084
Paint sprayers: Air and Gas Compressor—*mfg*	333912	3563
Paint sticks, wood: Manufacturing, All Other Miscellaneous—*mfg*	339999	2499
Wood Container and Pallet—*mfg*	32192	2499
Wood Product, All Other Miscellaneous—*mfg*	321999	2499
Paint stores: Building Material Dealers, Other—*retail*	44419	5231
Paint and Wallpaper Stores—*retail*	44412	5231
Paint, Varnish and Supplies—*whlse*	42295	5231
Paint, Coating, Adhesive, and Sealant Manufacturing	**3255**	
Paint, gold or bronze: Chemical Product, All Other Miscellaneous—*mfg*	325998	3952
Institutional Furniture—*mfg*	337127	3952
Lead Pencil and Art Good—*mfg*	339942	3952
Paint, Varnish and Supplies Wholesalers	**42295**	**5231**
Paintbrush cleaners: Paint and Coating—*mfg*	32551	2851
Paintbrushes: Broom, Brush and Mop—*mfg*	339994	3991
Painting (enameling aud varnishing) of metal products, for the trade: Costume Jewelry and Novelty—*mfg*	339914	3479
Jewelry (except Costume)—*mfg*	339911	3479
Metal Coating, Engraving (except Jewelry and Silverware), and Allied Services to Manufacturers—*mfg*	332812	3479
Silverware and Plated Ware—*mfg*	339912	3479
Painting and Wall Covering Contractors	**23521**	**1799**
Painting and Wall Covering Contractors	**2352**	
Painting instrument dials, for the trade: Fabricated Metal Product, All Other Miscellaneous—*mfg*	332999	3999
Painting of buildings and other structures, except roofs–contractors: Painting and Wall Covering Contractors—*const*	23521	1721

ALPHABETICAL INDEX	NAICS	SIC
Painting ships–contractors: Painting and Wall Covering Contractors—*const*	23521	1721
Painting traffic lanes–contractors: Painting and Wall Covering Contractors—*const*	23521	1721
Paints: Paint and Wallpaper Stores—*retail*	44412	5198
Paint, Varnish and Supplies—*whlse*	42295	5198
Paints for burnt wood or leather work, platinum: Chemical Product, All Other Miscellaneous—*mfg*	325998	3952
Institutional Furniture—*mfg*	337127	3952
Lead Pencil and Art Good—*mfg*	339942	3952
Paints for china painting: Chemical Product, All Other Miscellaneous—*mfg*	325998	3952
Institutional Furniture—*mfg*	337127	3952
Lead Pencil and Art Good—*mfg*	339942	3952
Paints, artists,: Chemical Product, All Other Miscellaneous—*mfg*	325998	3952
Institutional Furniture—*mfg*	337127	3952
Lead Pencil and Art Good—*mfg*	339942	3952
Paints, asphalt and bituminous: Paint and Coating—*mfg*	32551	2851
Paints, plastics texture–paste and dry: Paint and Coating—*mfg*	32551	2851
Paints, waterproof: Paint and Coating—*mfg*	32551	2851
Paints–oil and alkyd vehicle, and water thinned: Paint and Coating—*mfg*	32551	2851
Pajama checks, toxtile: Broadwoven Fabric Mills—*mfg*	31321	2211
Pajamas: Infants' Cut and Sew Apparel—*mfg*	315291	2341
Men's and Boys' Cut and Sew Apparel Contractors—*mfg*	315211	2322
Men's and Boys' Cut and Sew Underwear and Nightwear—*mfg*	315221	2322
Underwear and Nightwear Knitting Mills—*mfg*	315192	2254
Women's and Girls' Cut and Sew Apparel Contractors—*mfg*	315212	2341
Women's and Girls' Cut and Sew Lingerie, Loungewear and Nightwear—*mfg*	315231	2341
Palettes, artists': Chemical Product, All Other Miscellaneous—*mfg*	325998	3952
Institutional Furniture—*mfg*	337127	3952
Lead Pencil and Art Good—*mfg*	339942	3952
Palladium ore mining: Metal Ore, All Other—*mining*	212299	1099
Pallet assemblies for landing mats: Fabricated Metal Product, All Other Miscellaneous—*mfg*	332999	3537
Industrial Truck, Tractor, Trailer and Stacker Machinery—*mfg*	333924	3537
Metal Container, Other—*mfg*	332439	3537
Pallet containors, wood or wood and metal combination: Wood Container and Pallet—*mfg*	32192	2448
Pallet loaders and unloaders: Fabricated Metal Product, All Other Miscellaneous—*mfg*	332999	3537
Industrial Truck, Tractor, Trailer and Stacker Machinery—*mfg*	333924	3537
Metal Container, Other—*mfg*	332439	3537
Pallet racks, except wood: Showcase, Partition, Shelving, and Locker—*mfg*	337215	2542
Pallet spacers, fiber: Coated and Laminated Paper—*mfg*	322222	2679

Description	NAICS	SIC
Converted Paper Product, All Other—*mfg*	322298	2679
Die-Cut Paper and Paperboard Office Supplies—*mfg*	322231	2679
Non-Folding Sanitary Food Container—*mfg*	322215	2679
Palletizers and depalletizers: Fabricated Metal Product, All Other Miscellaneous—*mfg*	332999	3537
Industrial Truck, Tractor, Trailer and Stacker Machinery—*mfg*	333924	3537
Metal Container, Other—*mfg*	332439	3537
Pallets, corrugated and solid fiberboard: Corrugated and Solid Fiber Box—*mfg*	322211	2653
Pallets, metal: Fabricated Metal Product, All Other Miscellaneous—*mfg*	332999	3537
Industrial Truck, Tractor, Trailer and Stacker Machinery—*mfg*	333924	3537
Metal Container, Other—*mfg*	332439	3537
Pallets, wood or wood and metal combination: Wood Container and Pallet—*mfg*	32192	2448
Palm kernel oil: Fats and Oils Refining and Blending—*mfg*	311225	2076
Oilseed Processing, Other—*mfg*	311223	2076
Pamphlets, binding only: Tradebinding and Related Work—*mfg*	323121	2789
Pamphlets–printing or printing and binding, not publishing: Book Printing—*mfg*	323117	2732
Pamphlets–publishing and printing, or publishing only: Book Publishers—*info*	51113	2731
Music Publishers—*info*	51223	2731
Pan glazing, for the trade: Costume Jewelry and Novelty—*mfg*	339914	3479
Jewelry (except Costume)—*mfg*	339911	3479
Metal Coating, Engraving (except Jewelry and Silverware), and Allied Services to Manufacturers—*mfg*	332812	3479
Silverware and Plated Ware—*mfg*	339912	3479
Panama hats: Hat, Cap and Millinery—*mfg*	315991	2353
Pancake batter, refrigerated or frozen: Flour Milling—*mfg*	311211	2041
Flour Mixes and Dough from Purchased Flour—*mfg*	311822	2045
Pancake mixes: Flour Mixes and Dough from Purchased Flour—*mfg*	311822	2045
Pancake syrup, blended and mixed: Food, All Other Miscellaneous—*mfg*	311999	2099
Panel assemblies Ihydromatic propellertest stands), aircraft: Aircraft Part and Auxiliary Equipment, Other—*mfg*	336413	3728
Fluid Power Valve and Hose Fitting—*mfg*	332912	3728
Panel furniture systems, office, wood: Wood Office Furniture—*mfg*	337211	2521
Panel furniture systems, office–exceptwood: Nonwood Office Furniture—*mfg*	337214	2522
Panel work, wood: Millwork (including Flooring), Other—*mfg*	321918	2431
Wood Window and Door—*mfg*	321911	2431
Panelboard indicators, recorders and controllers–receiver type: Instruments and Related Products for Measuring, Displaying, and Controlling Industrial Process Variables—*mfg*	334513	3823
Panelboards: Building Material Dealers, Other—*retail*	44419	5063
Electrical Apparatus and Equipment, Wiring Supplies and Material—*whlse*	42161	5063

Description	NAICS	SIC
Panelboards and distribution boards, electric: Switchgear and Switchboard Apparatus—*mfg*	335313	3613
Paneling: Building Material Dealers, Other—*retail*	44419	5211
Home Centers—*retail*	44411	5211
Paneling, wood: Building Material Dealers, Other—*retail*	44419	5031
Panels and sections, prefabricated–concrete: Concrete Pipe—*mfg*	327332	3272
Concrete Product, Other—*mfg*	32739	3272
Nonmetallic Mineral Product, All Other Miscellaneous—*mfg*	327999	3272
Panels for prefabricated metal buildings: Prefabricated Metal Building and Component—*mfg*	332311	3448
Panels for prefabricated wood buildings: Prefabricated Wood Building—*mfg*	321992	2452
Panels, cardboard–nifpm: Converted Paper Product, All Other—*mfg*	322298	2675
Die-Cut Paper and Paperboard Office Supplies—*mfg*	322231	2675
Surface-Coated Paperboard—*mfg*	322292	2675
Panels, electric control and metering: Switchgear and Switchboard Apparatus—*mfg*	335313	3613
Panels, hardwood plywood: Hardwood Veneer and Plywood—*mfg*	321211	2435
Panels, papier-mache or plaster of paris: Gypsum and Gypsum Product—*mfg*	32742	3299
Nonmetallic Mineral Product, All Other Miscellaneous—*mfg*	327999	3299
Panels, plaster–gypsum: Gypsum and Gypsum Product—*mfg*	32742	3275
Panels, softwood plywood: Softwood Veneer and Plywood—*mfg*	321212	2436
Panoramic telescopes: Optical Instrument and Lens—*mfg*	333314	3827
Pans and voids, fiber or cardboard: Fiber Can, Tube, Drum, and Similar Products—*mfg*	322214	2655
Pans, stamped and pressed metal–except tinned: Kitchen Utensil, Pot and Pan—*mfg*	332214	3469
Pans, tinned: Metal Can—*mfg*	332431	3411
Panties: Infants' Cut and Sew Apparel—*mfg*	315291	2341
Underwear and Nightwear Knitting Mills—*mfg*	315192	2254
Women's and Girls' Cut and Sew Apparel Contractors—*mfg*	315212	2341
Women's and Girls' Cut and Sew Lingerie, Loungewear and Nightwear—*mfg*	315231	2341
Pantings–wool, mohair, and similar animal fibers: Broadwoven Fabric Finishing Mills—*mfg*	313311	2231
Broadwoven Fabric Mills—*mfg*	31321	2231
Textile and Fabric Finishing (except Broadwoven Fabric) Mills—*mfg*	313312	2231
Pantographs for drafting: Chemical Product, All Other Miscellaneous—*mfg*	325998	3952
Institutional Furniture—*mfg*	337127	3952
Lead Pencil and Art Good—*mfg*	339942	3952
Pants outfits, except pantsuits: Apparel Accessories and Apparel, Other—*mfg*	315999	2339
Cut and Sew Apparel, All Other—*mfg*	315299	2339
Women's and Girls' Cut and Sew Apparel Contractors—*mfg*	315212	2339
Women's and Girls' Cut and Sew Other Outerwear—*mfg*	315238	2339

ALPHABETICAL INDEX	NAICS	SIC
Pants, athletic and gymnasium: Cut and Sew Apparel, All Other—*mfg*	315299	2329
Pants, baby–vulcanized rubber and rubberized fabric: Fabric Coating Mills—*mfg*	31332	3069
Rubber Product, All Other—*mfg*	326299	3069
Pants, dress (separate): Men's and Boys' Cut and Sew Apparel Contractors—*mfg*	315211	2325
Men's and Boys' Cut and Sew Trouser, Slack and Jean—*mfg*	315224	2325
Pants, leather: Fur and Leather Apparel—*mfg*	315292	2386
Pants, outerwear: Outerwear Knitting Mills—*mfg*	315191	2253
Pants, ski: Apparel Accessories and Apparel, Other—*mfg*	315999	2339
Cut and Sew Apparel, All Other—*mfg*	315299	2339
Women's and Girls' Cut and Sew Apparel Contractors—*mfg*	315212	2339
Women's and Girls' Cut and Sew Other Outerwear—*mfg*	315238	2339
Pants, sweat: Apparel Accessories and Apparel, Other—*mfg*	315999	2339
Cut and Sew Apparel, All Other—*mfg*	315299	2339
Women's and Girls' Cut and Sew Apparel Contractors—*mfg*	315212	2339
Women's and Girls' Cut and Sew Other Outerwear—*mfg*	315238	2339
Pants, waterproof: Apparel Accessories and Apparel, Other—*mfg*	315999	2385
Infants' Cut and Sew Apparel—*mfg*	315291	2385
Men's and Boys' Cut and Sew Apparel Contractors—*mfg*	315211	2385
Men's and Boys' Cut and Sew Other Outerwear—*mfg*	315228	2385
Men's and Boys' Cut and Sew Suit, Coat and Overcoat—*mfg*	315222	2385
Women's and Girls' Cut and Sew Apparel Contractors—*mfg*	315212	2385
Women's and Girls' Cut and Sew Other Outerwear—*mfg*	315238	2385
Women's and Girls' Cut and Sew Suit, Coat, Tailored Jacket and Skirt—*mfg*	315234	2385
Pants, work, except jeans and dungarees: Men's and Boys' Cut and Sew Apparel Contractors—*mfg*	315211	2326
Men's and Boys' Cut and Sew Work Clothing—*mfg*	315225	2326
Pants–sweat, athletic, gymnasium, ski, and snow: Cut and Sew Apparel, All Other—*mfg*	315299	2329
Pantsuits: Women's and Girls' Cut and Sew Apparel Contractors—*mfg*	315212	2337
Women's and Girls' Cut and Sew Suit, Coat, Tailored Jacket and Skirt—*mfg*	315234	2337
Panty girdles: Women's and Girls' Cut and Sew Apparel Contractors—*mfg*	315212	2342
Women's and Girls' Cut and Sew Lingerie, Loungewear and Nightwear—*mfg*	315231	2342
Panty hose, women's: Sheer Hosiery Mills—*mfg*	315111	2251
Paper: Newsprint Mills—*mfg*	322122	2621
Paper (except Newsprint) Mills—*mfg*	322121	2621
Paper (except Newsprint) Mills	**322121**	**2621**
Paper and Paper Product Wholesalers	**4221**	
Paper and plastics bags: Industrial and Personal Service Paper—*whlse*	42213	5113

ALPHABETICAL INDEX	NAICS	SIC
Paper and products, wrapping or coarse: Industrial and Personal Service Paper—*whlse*	42213	5113
Paper Bag and Coated and Treated Paper Manufacturing	**32222**	
Paper boxes: Industrial and Personal Service Paper—*whlse*	42213	5113
Paper broadwoven fabrics: Broadwoven Fabric Mills—*mfg*	31321	2221
Paper bronzing, gilding, edging, and deckling: Tradebinding and Related Work—*mfg*	323121	2789
Paper clay mining: Kaolin and Ball Clay—*mining*	212324	1455
Paper clips and fasteners, made from purchased wire: Fabricated Wire Product, Other—*mfg*	332618	3496
Paper clips, steel–made in wire drawing plants: Fabricated Wire Product, Other—*mfg*	332618	3315
Steel Wire Drawing—*mfg*	331222	3315
Paper cups, dishes, napkins, towels and patterns: Industrial and Personal Service Paper—*whlse*	42213	5113
Paper cutters and trimmers (hand office equipment): Lead Pencil and Art Good—*mfg*	339942	3579
Office Machinery—*mfg*	333313	3579
Watch, Clock, and Part—*mfg*	334518	3579
Paper cutting, except die-cutting: Tradebinding and Related Work—*mfg*	323121	2789
Paper die-cut, from purchased materials: Converted Paper Product, All Other—*mfg*	322298	2675
Die-Cut Paper and Paperboard Office Supplies—*mfg*	322231	2675
Surface-Coated Paperboard—*mfg*	322292	2675
Paper dresses, cut and sewn: Women's and Girls' Cut and Sew Apparel Contractors—*mfg*	315212	2335
Women's and Girls' Cut and Sew Dress—*mfg*	315233	2335
Paper hanging-contractors: Painting and Wall Covering Contractors—*const*	23521	1721
Paper Industry Machinery Manufacturing	**333291**	**3554**
Paper machine wire cloth, made from purchased wire: Fabricated Wire Product, Other—*mfg*	332618	3496
Paper Manufacturing	**322**	
Paper manufacturing machinery: Industrial Machinery and Equipment—*whlse*	42183	5084
Paper mill machinery–e.g., plating, slitting, waxing: Paper Industry Machinery—*mfg*	333291	3554
Paper Mills	**32212**	
Paper mills: Newsprint Mills—*mfg*	322122	2621
Paper (except Newsprint) Mills—*mfg*	322121	2621
Paper napkins: Sanitary Paper Product—*mfg*	322291	2676
Paper product machines, except printing machines: Paper Industry Machinery—*mfg*	333291	3554
Paper pulp mill construction–general contractors: Building, Commercial and Institutional—*const*	23332	1541
Manufacturing and Industrial Building—*const*	23331	1541

Entry	NAICS	SIC
Paper punches, hand: Lead Pencil and Art Good—*mfg*	339942	3579
Office Machinery—*mfg*	333313	3579
Watch, Clock, and Part—*mfg*	334518	3579
Paper ruling: Blankbook, Loose-leaf Binder and Device—*mfg*	323118	2782
Flexographic Printing, Commercial—*mfg*	323112	2782
Gravure Printing, Commercial—*mfg*	323111	2782
Lithographic Printing, Commercial—*mfg*	323110	2782
Printing, Other Commercial—*mfg*	323119	2782
Screen Printing, Commercial—*mfg*	323113	2782
Paper ruling and sewing machines (book-binders' machinery): Printing Machinery and Equipment—*mfg*	333293	3555
Paper shells, 30 mm. (or 1.18 inch) or less: Small Arms Ammunition—*mfg*	332992	3482
Paper stencils: Marking Device—*mfg*	339943	3953
Paper, abrasive: Abrasive Product—*mfg*	32791	3291
Fabricated Metal Product, All Other Miscellaneous—*mfg*	332999	3291
Paper, building: Newsprint Mills—*mfg*	322122	2621
Paper (except Newsprint) Mills—*mfg*	322121	2621
Paper, building–laminated: Coated and Laminated Paper—*mfg*	322222	2679
Converted Paper Product, All Other—*mfg*	322298	2679
Die-Cut Paper and Paperboard Office Supplies—*mfg*	322231	2679
Non-Folding Sanitary Food Container—*mfg*	322215	2679
Paper, carbon–for typewriters, sales books, etc.: Carbon Paper and Inked Ribbon—*mfg*	339944	3955
Paper, chart and graph–ruled: Blankbook, Loose-leaf Binder and Device—*mfg*	323118	2782
Flexographic Printing, Commercial—*mfg*	323112	2782
Gravure Printing, Commercial—*mfg*	323111	2782
Lithographic Printing, Commercial—*mfg*	323110	2782
Printing, Other Commercial—*mfg*	323119	2782
Screen Printing, Commercial—*mfg*	323113	2782
Paper, coated and laminated–except for packaging: Coated and Laminated Paper—*mfg*	322222	2672
Paper, coated or laminated–for packaging: Coated and Laminated Packaging Paper and Plastics Film—*mfg*	322221	2671
Unsupported Plastics Packaging Film and Sheet—*mfg*	326112	2671
Paper, corrugated: Coated and Laminated Paper—*mfg*	322222	2679
Converted Paper Product, All Other—*mfg*	322298	2679
Die-Cut Paper and Paperboard Office Supplies—*mfg*	322231	2679
Non-Folding Sanitary Food Container—*mfg*	322215	2679
Paper, crepe and crepe paper products: Coated and Laminated Paper—*mfg*	322222	2679
Converted Paper Product, All Other—*mfg*	322298	2679
Die-Cut Paper and Paperboard Office Supplies—*mfg*	322231	2679
Non-Folding Sanitary Food Container—*mfg*	322215	2679
Paper, except printing or writing and office supplies: Industrial and Personal Service Paper—*whlse*	42213	5113
Paper, fine or printing and writing: Printing and Writing Paper—*whlse*	42211	5111
Paper, frisket (artists' material): Chemical Product, All Other Miscellaneous—*mfg*	325998	3952
Institutional Furniture—*mfg*	337127	3952
Lead Pencil and Art Good—*mfg*	339942	3952
Paper, heat sensitized–made from purchased paper: Photographic and Photocopying Equipment—*mfg*	333315	3861
Photographic Film, Paper, Plate and Chemical—*mfg*	325992	3861
Paper, photographic–sensitized: Photographic and Photocopying Equipment—*mfg*	333315	3861
Photographic Film, Paper, Plate and Chemical—*mfg*	325992	3861
Paper, waste: Recyclable Material—*whlse*	42193	5093
Paper–garnet, emery, aluminum oxide, and silicon carbide coated: Abrasive Product—*mfg*	32791	3291
Fabricated Metal Product, All Other Miscellaneous—*mfg*	332999	3291
Paperboard and products, except office supplies: Industrial and Personal Service Paper—*whlse*	42213	5113
Paperboard backs for blister or skin packages: Folding Paperboard Box—*mfg*	322212	2657
Paperboard Container Manufacturing	**32221**	
Paperboard die-cut, from purchased materials: Converted Paper Product, All Other—*mfg*	322298	2675
Die-Cut Paper and Paperboard Office Supplies—*mfg*	322231	2675
Surface-Coated Paperboard—*mfg*	322292	2675
Paperboard Mills	**32213**	**2631**
Paperboard mills, except building boardmills: Paperboard Mills—*mfg*	32213	2631
Paperboard, except building board: Paperboard Mills—*mfg*	32213	2631
Paperboard–pasted, lined, laminated, or surface coated: Converted Paper Product, All Other—*mfg*	322298	2675
Die-Cut Paper and Paperboard Office Supplies—*mfg*	322231	2675
Surface-Coated Paperboard—*mfg*	322292	2675
Papermakers' felts, woven–wool, mohair, and similar animal fibers: Broadwoven Fabric Finishing Mills—*mfg*	313311	2231
Broadwoven Fabric Mills—*mfg*	31321	2231
Textile and Fabric Finishing (except Broadwoven Fabric) Mills—*mfg*	313312	2231
Papeteries: Stationery, Tablet, and Related Product—*mfg*	322233	2678
Papier-mache articles, except statuary and art goods: Coated and Laminated Paper—*mfg*	322222	2679
Converted Paper Product, All Other—*mfg*	322298	2679
Die-Cut Paper and Paperboard Office Supplies—*mfg*	322231	2679
Non-Folding Sanitary Food Container—*mfg*	322215	2679
Parachute fabrics: Broadwoven Fabric Mills—*mfg*	31321	2221
Parachute hardware: Hardware—*mfg*	33251	3429
Parachute training for pleasure: Sports and Recreation Instruction—*educ*	61162	7999
Parachutes: Textile Product Mills, All Other Miscellaneous—*mfg*	314999	2399
Paraffin wax, produced in petroleum refineries: Petroleum Refineries—*mfg*	32411	2911

ALPHABETICAL INDEX	NAICS	SIC
Paralegal service: Legal Services, All Other—*prof*	541199	7389
Paramedics, offices of: Health Practitioners, Offices Of Miscellaneous—*hlth*	621399	8049
Mental Health Practitioners (except Physicians), Offices Of—*hlth*	62133	8049
Physical, Occupational and Speech Therapists and Audiologists, Offices Of—*hlth*	62134	8049
Parametric amplifiers: Electronic Component, Other—*mfg*	334419	3679
Motor Vehicle Electrical and Electronic Equipment, Other—*mfg*	336322	3679
Printed Circuit/Electronics Assembly—*mfg*	334418	3679
Radio and Television Broadcasting and Wireless Communications Equipment—*mfg*	33422	3679
Parametric diodes: Semiconductor and Related Device—*mfg*	334413	3674
Parcel delivery, private–air: Couriers—*trans*	49211	4513
Parcel delivery, private–except air: Couriers—*trans*	49211	4215
Local Messengers and Local Delivery—*trans*	49221	4215
Parcel packing service (packaging): Packaging and Labeling Services—*admin*	56191	7389
Parchment leather: Leather and Hide Tanning and Finishing—*mfg*	31611	3111
Parchment paper: Newsprint Mills—*mfg*	322122	2621
Paper (except Newsprint) Mills—*mfg*	322121	2621
Parent-teacher associations: Civic and Social Organizations—*serv*	81341	8641
Parenteral solutions: Pharmaceutical Preparation—*mfg*	325412	2834
Parfait: Ice Cream and Frozen Dessert—*mfg*	31152	2024
Pari-mutuel totalizator equipment finance leasing and maintenance: International Trade Financing—*fin*	522293	6159
Non-Depository Credit Intermediation, All Other—*fin*	522298	6159
Sales Financing—*fin*	52222	6159
Paris green (insecticide): Pesticide and Other Agricultural Chemical—*mfg*	32532	2879
Parkerizing, for the trade: Costume Jewelry and Novelty—*mfg*	339914	3479
Jewelry (except Costume)—*mfg*	339911	3479
Metal Coating, Engraving (except Jewelry and Silverware), and Allied Services to Manufacturers—*mfg*	332812	3479
Silverware and Plated Ware—*mfg*	339912	3479
Parking lights, automotive: Vehicular Lighting Equipment—*mfg*	336321	3647
Parking lot construction–contractors: Concrete Contractors—*const*	23571	1771
Drywall, Plastering, Acoustical and Insulation Contractors—*const*	23542	1771
Parking lots: Parking Lots and Garages—*serv*	81293	7521
Parking Lots and Garages	**81293**	**7521**
Parking meters: Totalizing Fluid Meter and Counting Device—*mfg*	334514	3824
Parking structures: Parking Lots and Garages—*serv*	81293	7521
Parking, valet: Personal Services, All Other—*serv*	81299	7299
Parkway construction–general contractors: Highway and Street—*const*	23411	1611
Parlor car operations, not performed by line-haul railroad companies: Rail Support Activities—*trans*	48821	4789
Scenic and Sightseeing, Land—*trans*	48711	4789

ALPHABETICAL INDEX	NAICS	SIC
Transportation, All Other Support Activities—*trans*	488999	4789
Parochial schools, elementary and secondary: Elementary and Secondary Schools—*educ*	61111	8211
Parole offices: Child and Youth Services—*hlth*	62411	8322
Community Food Services—*hlth*	62421	8322
Community Housing Services, Other—*hlth*	624229	8322
Emergency and Other Relief Services—*hlth*	62423	8322
Individual and Family Services, Other—*hlth*	62419	8322
Parole Offices and Probation Offices—*pub*	92215	8322
Services for the Elderly and Persons with Disabilities—*hlth*	62412	8322
Temporary Shelters—*hlth*	624221	8322
Parole Offices and Probation Offices	**92215**	**8322**
Parquet flooring, hardwood: Cut Stock, Resawing Lumber, and Planing—*mfg*	321912	2426
Millwork (including Flooring), Other—*mfg*	321918	2426
Showcase, Partition, Shelving, and Locker—*mfg*	337215	2426
Wood Product, All Other Miscellaneous—*mfg*	321999	2426
Parquet flooring–contractors: Floor Laying and Other Floor Contractors—*const*	23552	1752
Particle accelerators, high voltage: Electrical Equipment and Component, All Other Miscellaneous—*mfg*	335999	3699
Machinery, Other Commercial and Service Industry—*mfg*	333319	3699
Particle size analyzers: Analytical Laboratory Instrument—*mfg*	334516	3826
Particleboard: Building Material Dealers, Other—*retail*	44419	5031
Reconstituted Wood Product—*mfg*	321219	2493
Parting compounds (chemical foundry supplies): Basic Organic Chemical, All Other—*mfg*	325199	2899
Chemical Product, All Other Miscellaneous—*mfg*	325998	2899
Partition tile, clay: Brick and Structural Clay Tile—*mfg*	327121	3251
Partitions: Equipment, Other Commercial—*whlse*	42144	5046
Partitions and grillework, made from purchased wire: Fabricated Wire Product, Other—*mfg*	332618	3496
Partitions and grillework, ornamental metal: Ornamental and Architectural Metal Work—*mfg*	332323	3446
Partitions, corrugated and solid fiberboard: Corrugated and Solid Fiber Box—*mfg*	322211	2653
Partitions, office–not for floor attachment-except wood: Nonwood Office Furniture—*mfg*	337214	2522
Partitions, office–not for floor attachment-wood: Wood Office Furniture—*mfg*	337211	2521
Partitions, prefabricated–except wood and free-standing: Showcase, Partition, Shelving, and Locker—*mfg*	337215	2542
Partitions, prefabricated–wood-for floor attachment: Architectural Woodwork and Millwork, Custom—*mfg*	337212	2541
Showcase, Partition, Shelving, and Locker—*mfg*	337215	2541
Wood Kitchen Cabinet and Counter Top—*mfg*	33711	2541

Description	NAICS	SIC
Party supplies rental and leasing: Consumer Goods Rental, All Other—*real*	532299	7359
Party-plan merchandising: Direct Selling Establishments, Other—*retail*	45439	5963
Mobile Foodservices—*accom*	72233	5963
Passbooks: Blankbook, Loose-leaf Binder and Device—*mfg*	323118	2782
Flexographic Printing, Commercial—*mfg*	323112	2782
Gravure Printing, Commercial—*mfg*	323111	2782
Lithographic Printing, Commercial—*mfg*	323110	2782
Printing, Other Commercial—*mfg*	323119	2782
Screen Printing, Commercial—*mfg*	323113	2782
Passementeries: Apparel Accessories and Apparel, Other—*mfg*	315999	2396
Passenger and freight terminal building construction–general contractors: Building, Commercial and Institutional—*const*	23332	1542
Passenger automobile bodies: Automobile—*mfg*	336111	3711
Heavy Duty Truck—*mfg*	33612	3711
Light Truck and Utility Vehicle—*mfg*	336112	3711
Military Armored Vehicle, Tank and Tank Component—*mfg*	336992	3711
Motor Vehicle Body—*mfg*	336211	3711
Passenger baggage belt loaders: Conveyor and Conveying Equipment—*mfg*	333922	3535
Passenger Car Leasing	**532112**	**7515**
Passenger car leasing, except finance leasing–without drivers: Passenger Car Leasing—*real*	532112	7515
Passenger Car Rental	**532111**	**7514**
Passenger Car Rental and Leasing	**53211**	
Passenger car rental, without drivers: Passenger Car Rental—*real*	532111	7514
Passenger cargo vessels, building and repairing: Ship Building and Repairing—*mfg*	336611	3731
Passenger transportation, regular route, road or rail–between airports and terminals: Bus and Motor Vehicle Transit Systems—*trans*	485113	4111
Commuter Rail Systems—*trans*	485112	4111
Mixed Mode Transit Systems—*trans*	485111	4111
Transit and Ground Passenger, All Other—*trans*	485999	4111
Urban Transit Systems, Other—*trans*	485119	4111
Passenger water transportation on rivers and canals: Inland Water Passenger—*trans*	483212	4489
Scenic and Sightseeing, Water—*trans*	48721	4489
Passive repeaters: Electronic Component, Other—*mfg*	334419	3679
Motor Vehicle Electrical and Electronic Equipment, Other—*mfg*	336322	3679
Printed Circuit/Electronics Assembly—*mfg*	334418	3679
Radio and Television Broadcasting and Wireless Communications Equipment—*mfg*	33422	3679
Passport photographers: Photography Studios, Portrait—*prof*	541921	7221
Pasta Manufacturing	**311823**	**2098**
Pasta, canned: Canning, Specialty—*mfg*	311422	2032
Food, All Other Miscellaneous—*mfg*	311999	2032
Pasta, uncooked–packaged with other ingredients: Food, All Other Miscellaneous—*mfg*	311999	2099
Paste, adhesive: Adhesive—*mfg*	32552	2891
Paste, metal: Electroplating, Plating, Polishing, Anodizing and Coloring—*mfg*	332813	3399
Iron and Steel Mills—*mfg*	331111	3399
Secondary Smelting and Alloying of Aluminum—*mfg*	331314	3399
Secondary Smelting, Refining, and Alloying of Copper—*mfg*	331423	3399
Secondary Smelting, Refining, and Alloying of Nonferrous Metal (except Copper and Aluminum)—*mfg*	331492	3399
Pastels, artists': Chemical Product, All Other Miscellaneous—*mfg*	325998	3952
Institutional Furniture—*mfg*	337127	3952
Lead Pencil and Art Good—*mfg*	339942	3952
Pastes, almond: Roasted Nuts and Peanut Butter—*mfg*	311911	2099
Pastes, fruit and vegetable: Fruit and Vegetable Canning—*mfg*	311421	2033
Pasteurizing equipment, dairy and other food: Food Product Machinery—*mfg*	333294	3556
Pastrami: Meat Processed from Carcasses—*mfg*	311612	2013
Pastries, except frozen–e.g., Danish, French: Bakeries, Commercial—*mfg*	311812	2051
Pastry boards, wood: Manufacturing, All Other Miscellaneous—*mfg*	339999	2499
Wood Container and Pallet—*mfg*	32192	2499
Wood Product, All Other Miscellaneous—*mfg*	321999	2499
Patching plaster, household: Basic Organic Chemical, All Other—*mfg*	325199	2899
Chemical Product, All Other Miscellaneous—*mfg*	325998	2899
Patent brokers: Legal Services, All Other—*prof*	541199	7389
Patent buying and licensing: Owners and Lessors of Other Non-Financial Assets—*real*	53311	6794
Patent coated paperboard: Paperboard Mills—*mfg*	32213	2631
Patent leasing: Owners and Lessors of Other Non-Financial Assets—*real*	53311	6794
Patent leather: Leather and Hide Tanning and Finishing—*mfg*	31611	3111
Patent medicines: Drug, Drug Proprietaries and Druggists' Sundries—*whlse*	42221	5122
Patent solicitors' offices: Lawyers, Offices Of—*prof*	54111	8111
Pathological laboratories: Diagnostic Imaging Centers—*hlth*	621512	8071
Medical Laboratories—*hlth*	621511	8071
Pathologists (M.D.), offices of: Freestanding Ambulatory Surgical and Emergency Centers—*hlth*	621493	8011
HMO Medical Centers—*hlth*	621491	8011
Physicians (except Mental Health Specialists), Offices Of—*hlth*	621111	8011
Physicians, Mental Health Specialists, Offices Of—*hlth*	621112	8011
Pathologists, oral–offices of: Dentists, Offices Of—*hlth*	62121	8021
Patient monitoring equipment: Health and Personal Care Stores, All Other—*retail*	446199	5047
Medical, Dental and Hospital Equipment and Supplies—*whlse*	42145	5047
Patient monitoring equipment–intensive care/coronary care unit: Electromedical and Electrotherapeutic Apparatus—*mfg*	334510	3845

ALPHABETICAL INDEX	NAICS	SIC
Irradiation Apparatus—*mfg*	334517	3845
Patio construction, concrete–contractors: Concrete Contractors—*const*	23571	1771
Drywall, Plastering, Acoustical and Insulation Contractors—*const*	23542	1771
Patrol boats, building and repairing: Ship Building and Repairing—*mfg*	336611	3731
Patrol wagons (motor vehicles): Automobile—*mfg*	336111	3711
Heavy Duty Truck—*mfg*	33612	3711
Light Truck and Utility Vehicle—*mfg*	336112	3711
Military Armored Vehicle, Tank and Tank Component—*mfg*	336992	3711
Motor Vehicle Body—*mfg*	336211	3711
Pattern makers' machinery (woodworking): Sawmill and Woodworking Machinery—*mfg*	33321	3553
Patterns on metal: Metal Stamping—*mfg*	332116	3469
Patterns, industrial: Industrial Pattern—*mfg*	332997	3543
Patterns, last sole–regardless of material: Manufacturing, All Other Miscellaneous—*mfg*	339999	2499
Wood Container and Pallet—*mfg*	32192	2499
Wood Product, All Other Miscellaneous—*mfg*	321999	2499
Patterns, paper: Industrial and Personal Service Paper—*whlse*	42213	5113
Patterns, paper, including clothing patterns–publishing and printing, or publishing only: Database and Directory Publishers—*info*	51114	2741
Music Publishers—*info*	51223	2741
Publishers, All Other—*info*	511199	2741
Pavers: Construction and (except Petroleum) Machinery and Equipment—*whlse*	42181	5082
Construction Machinery—*mfg*	33312	3531
Overhead Traveling Crane, Hoist and Monorail System—*mfg*	333923	3531
Railroad Rolling Stock—*mfg*	33651	3531
Paving blocks and mixtures (except brick, concrete, and cut stone): Asphalt Paving Mixture and Block—*mfg*	324121	2951
Paving blocks, concrete: Concrete Block and Brick—*mfg*	327331	3271
Paving blocks, cut stone: Cut Stone and Stone Product—*mfg*	327991	3281
Paving breakers: Construction Machinery—*mfg*	33312	3531
Overhead Traveling Crane, Hoist and Monorail System—*mfg*	333923	3531
Railroad Rolling Stock—*mfg*	33651	3531
Paving brick, clay: Brick and Structural Clay Tile—*mfg*	327121	3251
Paving construction–contractors: Highway and Street—*const*	23411	1611
Paving materials, prefabricated concrete, except blocks: Concrete Pipe—*mfg*	327332	3272
Concrete Product, Other—*mfg*	32739	3272
Nonmetallic Mineral Product, All Other Miscellaneous—*mfg*	327999	3272
Paving mixtures: Brick, Stone and Related Material—*whlse*	42132	5032
Building Material Dealers, Other—*retail*	44419	5032
Pawnshops: Non-Depository Credit Intermediation, All Other—*fin*	522298	5932
Used Merchandise Stores—*retail*	45331	5932
Payroll accounting service: Accounting Services, Other—*prof*	541219	8721

ALPHABETICAL INDEX	NAICS	SIC
Certified Public Accountants, Offices Of—*prof*	541211	8721
Payroll Services—*prof*	541214	8721
Payroll Services	**541214**	**8721**
PBX equipment, manual and automatic: Electronic Coil, Transformer, and Other Inductor—*mfg*	334416	3661
Printed Circuit/Electronics Assembly—*mfg*	334418	3661
Telephone Apparatus—*mfg*	33421	3661
PCV valves: Gasoline Engine and Engine Parts—*mfg*	336312	3714
Motor Vehicle Parts, All Other—*mfg*	336399	3714
Pea farms, dry field and seed: Dry Pea and Bean Farming—*ag*	11113	119
Grain Farming, All Other—*ag*	111199	119
Pea farms, except dry peas: Vegetable (except Potato) and Melon Farming, Other—*ag*	111219	161
Peach orchards and farms: Apple Orchards—*ag*	111331	175
Noncitrus Fruit Farming, Other—*ag*	111339	175
Peacock blue lake: Organic Dye and Pigment—*mfg*	325132	2865
Petrochemical—*mfg*	32511	2865
Peanut butter: Roasted Nuts and Peanut Butter—*mfg*	311911	2099
Peanut combines, diggers, packers, and threshers (agricultural equipment): Farm Machinery and Equipment—*mfg*	333111	3523
Peanut cooking and salad oil: Fats and Oils Refining and Blending—*mfg*	311225	2079
Oilseed Processing, Other—*mfg*	311223	2079
Soybean Processing—*mfg*	311222	2079
Peanut Farming	**111992**	**139**
Peanut farms: Crop Farming, All Other Miscellaneous—*ag*	111998	139
Hay Farming—*ag*	11194	139
Peanut Farming—*ag*	111992	139
Vegetable (except Potato) and Melon Farming, Other—*ag*	111219	139
Peanut oil, cake, and meal: Fats and Oils Refining and Blending—*mfg*	311225	2076
Oilseed Processing, Other—*mfg*	311223	2076
Peanut roasting machines: Food Product Machinery—*mfg*	333294	3556
Peanut shelling, custom: Postharvest Crop Activities (except Cotton Ginning)—*ag*	115114	723
Peanuts, bulk–unprocessed or shelled only: Farm Product Raw Material, Other—*whlse*	42259	5159
Peanuts, machine harvesting of: Crop Harvesting, Primarily by Machine—*ag*	115113	722
Pear: Apple Orchards—*ag*	111331	175
Noncitrus Fruit Farming, Other—*ag*	111339	175
Pearl essence: Carbon Black—*mfg*	325182	2816
Inorganic Dye and Pigment—*mfg*	325131	2816
Pearl restringing for the trade: Personal and Household Goods Repair and Maintenance, Other—*serv*	81149	7631
Pearlitic castings, malleable iron: Iron Foundries—*mfg*	331511	3322
Pearls: Jewelry, Watch, Precious Stone and Precious Metal—*whlse*	42194	5094

Pearls, artificial: Costume Jewelry and Novelty—*mfg*	339914	3961
Pearls, cultured–production of: Crop Farming, All Other Miscellaneous—*ag*	111998	919
Marine Fishing, Other—*ag*	114119	919
Pearls–drilling, sawing, or peeling of: Jewelers' Material and Lapidary Work—*mfg*	339913	3915
Peat: Crushed and Broken Stone and Quarrying, Other—*mining*	212319	1499
Non-Metallic Mineral, All Other—*mining*	212399	1499
Peavies (handtools): Hand and Edge Tool—*mfg*	332212	3423
Pebble mining: Crushed and Broken Limestone and Quarrying—*mining*	212312	1422
Pecan: Farm Product Raw Material, Other—*whlse*	42259	5159
Pecan groves and farms: Tree Nut Farming—*ag*	111335	173
Pecan hulling and shelling: Postharvest Crop Activities (except Cotton Ginning)—*ag*	115114	723
Pectin: Spice and Extract—*mfg*	311942	2099
Pedestals, marble: Cut Stone and Stone Product—*mfg*	327991	3281
Pedestals, statuary–plaster of paris or papier-mache-factory production only: Gypsum and Gypsum Product—*mfg*	32742	3299
Nonmetallic Mineral Product, All Other Miscellaneous—*mfg*	327999	3299
Pedestals, statuary–wood: Architectural Woodwork and Millwork, Custom—*mfg*	337212	2541
Showcase, Partition, Shelving, and Locker—*mfg*	337215	2541
Wood Kitchen Cabinet and Counter Top—*mfg*	33711	2541
Pedestrian traffic control equipment: Communications Equipment, Other—*mfg*	33429	3669
Pediatricians, offices of: Freestanding Ambulatory Surgical and Emergency Centers—*hlth*	621493	8011
HMO Medical Centers—*hlth*	621491	8011
Physicians (except Mental Health Specialists), Offices Of—*hlth*	621111	8011
Physicians, Mental Health Specialists, Offices Of—*hlth*	621112	8011
Pedigree record services for cattle, hogs, sheep, goats, and poultry: Animal Production Support Activities—*ag*	11521	751
Pedigree record services for pets and other animal specialties: Animal Production Support Activities—*ag*	11521	752
Pet Care (except Veterinary) Services—*serv*	81291	752
Pedometers: Totalizing Fluid Meter and Counting Device—*mfg*	334514	3824
Peeler logs: Logging—*ag*	11331	2411
Pegmatite (feldspar) mining: Clay and Ceramic and Refractory Minerals—*mining*	212325	1459
Pegs, shoe: Fastener, Button, Needle and Pin—*mfg*	339993	3131
Leather Good, All Other—*mfg*	316999	3131
Wood Product, All Other Miscellaneous—*mfg*	321999	3131
Pellet mills (mining machinery): Mining Machinery and Equipment—*mfg*	333131	3532
Pellet powder (explosives): Explosives—*mfg*	32592	2892
Pellets, ammunition–pistol and air rifle: Small Arms Ammunition—*mfg*	332992	3482
Pelts: Farm Product Raw Material, Other—*whlse*	42259	5159
Pelvimeters: Surgical and Medical Instrument—*mfg*	339112	3841
Pen and Mechanical Pencil Manufacturing	**339941**	**3951**
Pen and pencil shops: Office Supplies and Stationery Stores—*retail*	45321	5943
Pencil holders: Chemical Product, All Other Miscellaneous—*mfg*	325998	3952
Institutional Furniture—*mfg*	337127	3952
Lead Pencil and Art Good—*mfg*	339942	3952
Pencil lead–black, indelible, or colored: Chemical Product, All Other Miscellaneous—*mfg*	325998	3952
Institutional Furniture—*mfg*	337127	3952
Lead Pencil and Art Good—*mfg*	339942	3952
Pencil sharpeners: Lead Pencil and Art Good—*mfg*	339942	3579
Office Machinery—*mfg*	333313	3579
Watch, Clock, and Part—*mfg*	334518	3579
Pencil slats: Manufacturing, All Other Miscellaneous—*mfg*	339999	2499
Wood Container and Pallet—*mfg*	32192	2499
Wood Product, All Other Miscellaneous—*mfg*	321999	2499
Pencils: Office Supplies and Stationery Stores—*retail*	45321	5112
Stationary and Office Supplies—*whlse*	42212	5112
Pencils and pencil parts, mechanical: Pen and Mechanical Pencil—*mfg*	339941	3951
Pencils, except mechanical: Chemical Product, All Other Miscellaneous—*mfg*	325998	3952
Institutional Furniture—*mfg*	337127	3952
Lead Pencil and Art Good—*mfg*	339942	3952
Pencils, hair (artists' brushes): Broom, Brush and Mop—*mfg*	339994	3991
Pendant lamps–commercial, industrial, and institutional: Electric Lighting Fixture, Commercial, Industrial and Institutional—*mfg*	335122	3646
Penetrants: Surface Active Agent—*mfg*	325613	2843
Penetrants, inspection: Basic Organic Chemical, All Other—*mfg*	325199	2899
Chemical Product, All Other Miscellaneous—*mfg*	325998	2899
Penholders and parts: Pen and Mechanical Pencil—*mfg*	339941	3951
Penicillin preparations: Pharmaceutical Preparation—*mfg*	325412	2834
Penicillin–bulk, uncompounded: Medicinal and Botanical—*mfg*	325411	2833
Penitentiaries: Correctional Institutions—*pub*	92214	9223
Pennants: Textile Product Mills, All Other Miscellaneous—*mfg*	314999	2399
Penpoints–gold, steel, or other metal: Pen and Mechanical Pencil—*mfg*	339941	3951
Pens and pen parts–fountain, stylographic, and ballpoint: Pen and Mechanical Pencil—*mfg*	339941	3951
Pens, writing: Office Supplies and Stationery Stores—*retail*	45321	5112
Stationary and Office Supplies—*whlse*	42212	5112
Pension and retirement plan consultants: Claims Adjusters—*fin*	524291	6411
Insurance Agencies and Brokerages—*fin*	52421	6411
Insurance Related Activities, All Other—*fin*	524298	6411
Third Party Administration for Insurance and Pension Funds—*fin*	524292	6411
Pension Funds	**52511**	**6371**
Pension funds: Health and Welfare Funds—*fin*	52512	6371
Portfolio Management—*fin*	52392	6371

ALPHABETICAL INDEX	NAICS	SIC
Third Party Administration for Insurance and Pension Funds—*fin*	524292	6371
Penstocks, metal plate: Air-Conditioning and Warm Air Heating Equipment and Commercial and Industrial Refrigeration Equipment—*mfg*	333415	3443
Metal Tank (Heavy Gauge)—*mfg*	33242	3443
Plate Work—*mfg*	332313	3443
Power Boiler and Heat Exchanger—*mfg*	33241	3443
Pentachlorophenol: Cyclic Crude and Intermediate—*mfg*	325192	2865
Petrochemical—*mfg*	32511	2865
Pentaerythritol: Basic Organic Chemical, All Other—*mfg*	325199	2869
Pentolite (explosives): Explosives—*mfg*	32592	2892
Pepper: Spice and Extract—*mfg*	311942	2099
Pepper farms, sweet and hot (vegetables): Vegetable (except Potato) and Melon Farming, Other—*ag*	111219	161
Peppermint oil: Spice and Extract—*mfg*	311942	2899
Percale: Broadwoven Fabric Mills—*mfg*	31321	2211
Percaline, cotton: Broadwoven Fabric Mills—*mfg*	31321	2211
Percentage correctors: Optical Instrument and Lens—*mfg*	333314	3827
Perchloric acid: Basic Inorganic Chemical, All Other—*mfg*	325188	2819
Chemical Product, All Other Miscellaneous—*mfg*	325998	2819
Perchloroethylene: Basic Organic Chemical, All Other—*mfg*	325199	2869
Percolators, electric: Electric Housewares and Household Fan—*mfg*	335211	3634
Electrical Appliance, Television and Radio Set—*whlse*	42162	5064
Heating Equipment (except Electric and Warm Air Furnaces)—*mfg*	333414	3634
Percussion caps, for ammunition of 30 mm. (or 1.18 inch) or less: Small Arms Ammunition—*mfg*	332992	3482
Percussion musical instruments: Musical Instrument—*mfg*	339992	3931
Perforated metal, stamped: Metal Stamping—*mfg*	332116	3469
Perforating on heavy metal: Air-Conditioning and Warm Air Heating Equipment and Commercial and Industrial Refrigeration Equipment—*mfg*	333415	3443
Metal Tank (Heavy Gauge)—*mfg*	33242	3443
Plate Work—*mfg*	332313	3443
Power Boiler and Heat Exchanger—*mfg*	33241	3443
Perforating on light metal: Metal Stamping—*mfg*	332116	3469
Perforating well casings on a contract basis: Oil and Gas Operations Support Activities—*mining*	213112	1389
Perforators (office machines): Lead Pencil and Art Good—*mfg*	339942	3579
Office Machinery—*mfg*	333313	3579
Watch, Clock, and Part—*mfg*	334518	3579
Performance rights, publishing and licensing of: Owners and Lessors of Other Non-Financial Assets—*real*	53311	6794
Performing artists: Independent Artists, Writers, and Performers—*arts*	71151	7929
Musical Groups and Artists—*arts*	71113	7929
Performing Arts Companies, Other—*arts*	71119	7929

ALPHABETICAL INDEX	NAICS	SIC
Performing arts center productions: Promoters of Performing Arts, Sports and Similar Events with Facilities—*arts*	71131	7922
Performing Arts Companies	**7111**	
Performing Arts Companies, Other	**71119**	**7999**
Performing Arts, Spectator Sports and Related Industries	**711**	
Perfume bases, blending and compounding: Soap and Other Detergent—*mfg*	325611	2844
Toilet Preparation—*mfg*	32562	2844
Perfume materials, synthetic: Basic Organic Chemical, All Other—*mfg*	325199	2869
Perfumes: Drug, Drug Proprietaries and Druggists' Sundries—*whlse*	42221	5122
Perfumes, natural and synthetic: Soap and Other Detergent—*mfg*	325611	2844
Toilet Preparation—*mfg*	32562	2844
Periodical Publishers	**51112**	**2721**
Periodicals: Book, Periodical and Newspaper—*whlse*	42292	5192
Periodicals, lithographed–not published: Lithographic Printing, Commercial—*mfg*	323110	2752
Quick Printing—*mfg*	323114	2752
Periodicals, printed–except lithographed or gravure (not publishing): Digital Printing—*mfg*	323115	2759
Flexographic Printing, Commercial—*mfg*	323112	2759
Printing, Other Commercial—*mfg*	323119	2759
Quick Printing—*mfg*	323114	2759
Periodicals–gravure printing (not publishing): Gravure Printing, Commercial—*mfg*	323111	2754
Periodicals–publishing and printing, or publishing only: Periodical Publishers—*info*	51112	2721
Periodontists, offices of: Dentists, Offices Of—*hlth*	62121	8021
Peripheral equipment, computer: Computer and Computer Peripheral Equipment and Software—*whlse*	42143	5045
Computer and Software Stores—*retail*	44312	5045
Peripheral equipment, computer stores: Computer and Software Stores—*retail*	44312	5734
Periscopes: Optical Instrument and Lens—*mfg*	333314	3827
Perishable Prepared Food Manufacturing	**311991**	**2099**
Perlite aggregate: Ground or Treated Mineral and Earth—*mfg*	327992	3295
Perlite mining: Crushed and Broken Stone and Quarrying, Other—*mining*	212319	1499
Non-Metallic Mineral, All Other—*mining*	212399	1499
Perlite, expanded: Ground or Treated Mineral and Earth—*mfg*	327992	3295
Permanent pleating and pressing, for the trade: Men's and Boys' Cut and Sew Apparel Contractors—*mfg*	315211	2395
Textile Product Mills, All Other Miscellaneous—*mfg*	314999	2395
Women's and Girls' Cut and Sew Apparel Contractors—*mfg*	315212	2395
Permissible explosives: Explosives—*mfg*	32592	2892
Peroxides, inorganic: Basic Inorganic Chemical, All Other—*mfg*	325188	2819
Chemical Product, All Other Miscellaneous—*mfg*	325998	2819

Entry	NAICS	SIC
Persian orange lake: Organic Dye and Pigment—*mfg*	325132	2865
Petrochemical—*mfg*	32511	2865
Persimmon orchards and farms: Apple Orchards—*ag*	111331	175
Noncitrus Fruit Farming, Other—*ag*	111339	175
Personal affairs management: Private Households—*serv*	81411	8811
Personal and Household Goods Repair and Maintenance	**8114**	
Personal and Household Goods Repair and Maintenance, Other	**81149**	**7219**
Personal and Laundry Services	**812**	
Personal care facilities with health care: Continuing Care Retirement Communities—*hlth*	623311	8059
Nursing Care Facilities—*hlth*	62311	8059
Personal care homes with health care: Continuing Care Retirement Communities—*hlth*	623311	8059
Nursing Care Facilities—*hlth*	62311	8059
Personal Care Services	**8121**	
Personal Care Services, Other	**812199**	**7299**
Personal Care Services, Other	**81219**	
Personal computers: Electronic Computer—*mfg*	334111	3571
Personal development schools: Professional and Management Development Training—*educ*	61143	8299
Personal finance companies, small loan–licensed: Consumer Lending—*fin*	522291	6141
Credit Card Issuing—*fin*	52221	6141
Sales Financing—*fin*	52222	6141
Personal holding companies, except bank: Other Holding Companies, Offices Of—*manag*	551112	6719
Personal investment trusts, management of: Insurance Funds, Other—*fin*	52519	6733
Portfolio Management—*fin*	52392	6733
Trust, Fiduciary and Custody Activities—*fin*	523991	6733
Trusts, Estates, and Agency Accounts—*fin*	52592	6733
Personal Leather Good (except Women's Handbag and Purse) Manufacturing	**316993**	**3172**
Personal leather goods, small: Personal Leather Good (except Women's Handbag and Purse)—*mfg*	316993	3172
Personal safety appliances and equipment: Electromedical and Electrotherapeutic Apparatus—*mfg*	334510	3842
Surgical Appliance and Supplies—*mfg*	339113	3842
Personal Services, All Other	**81299**	**7389**
Personal Services, Other	**8129**	
Personal shopping service: Personal Services, All Other—*serv*	81299	7299
Personnel agencies: General Government, All Other—*pub*	92119	9199
Personnel carriers, for highway use: Automobile—*mfg*	336111	3711
Heavy Duty Truck—*mfg*	33612	3711
Light Truck and Utility Vehicle—*mfg*	336112	3711
Military Armored Vehicle, Tank and Tank Component—*mfg*	336992	3711
Motor Vehicle Body—*mfg*	336211	3711
Personnel dosimetry devices: Measuring and Controlling Device, Other—*mfg*	334519	3829
Surgical and Medical Instrument—*mfg*	339112	3829
Personnel management consultants, except employment service: Administrative Management and General Management Consulting Services—*prof*	541611	8742
Human Resources and Executive Search Consulting Services—*prof*	541612	8742
Marketing Consulting Services—*prof*	541613	8742
Process, Physical, Distribution and Logistics Consulting Services—*prof*	541614	8742
Pest control in structures: Exterminating and Pest Control Services—*admin*	56171	7342
Janitorial Services—*admin*	56172	7342
Pest control, forest: Forestry Support Activities—*ag*	11531	851
Pesticide and Other Agricultural Chemical Manufacturing	**32532**	**2879**
Pesticide, Fertilizer and Other Agricultural Chemical Manufacturing	**3253**	
Pesticides: Farm Supplies—*whlse*	42291	5191
Nursery and Garden Centers—*retail*	44422	5191
Pesticides, agricultural: Pesticide and Other Agricultural Chemical—*mfg*	32532	2879
Pesticides, household: Pesticide and Other Agricultural Chemical—*mfg*	32532	2879
Pet and Pet Supplies Stores	**45391**	**5999**
Pet Care (except Veterinary) Services	**81291**	**752**
Pet food: Grocery and Related Products, Other—*whlse*	42249	5149
Pet food stores: Pet and Pet Supplies Stores—*retail*	45391	5999
Stores (except Tobacco Stores), All Other Miscellaneous—*retail*	453998	5999
Pet food, except dog and cat–canned, frozen, and dry: Animal Food, Other—*mfg*	311119	2048
Pet hospitals: Veterinary Services—*prof*	54194	742
Pet shops: Stores (except Tobacco Stores), All Other Miscellaneous—*retail*	453998	5999
Pet supplies, except pet food: Nondurable Goods, Other Miscellaneous—*whlse*	42299	5199
Petrochemical Manufacturing	**32511**	**2869**
Petrochemical plant construction–general contractors: Heavy, All Other—*const*	23499	1629
Industrial Nonbuilding Structure—*const*	23493	1629
Petrolatums, produced in petroleum refineries: Petroleum Refineries—*mfg*	32411	2911
Petroleum and chemical bulk stations and terminals for hire: General Warehousing and Storage Facilities—*trans*	49311	4226
Refrigerated Warehousing and Storage Facilities—*trans*	49312	4226
Warehousing and Storage Facilities, Other—*trans*	49319	4226
Petroleum and Coal Products Manufacturing	**3241**	
Petroleum and Coal Products Manufacturing	**324**	
Petroleum and Coal Products Manufacturing, Other	**32419**	
Petroleum and Coal Products Manufacturinga, All Other	**324199**	**2999**

ALPHABETICAL INDEX	NAICS	SIC
Petroleum and its products, except bulk stations and terminals: Petroleum and Petroleum Products (except Bulk Stations and Terminals)—*whlse*	42272	5172
Petroleum and Petroleum Products (except Bulk Stations and Terminals) Wholesalers	**42272**	**5172**
Petroleum and Petroleum Products Wholesalers	**4227**	
Petroleum brokers: Petroleum and Petroleum Products (except Bulk Stations and Terminals)—*whlse*	42272	5172
Petroleum Bulk Stations and Terminals	**42271**	**5171**
Petroleum bulk stations and terminals: Heating Oil Dealers—*retail*	454311	5171
Liquefied Petroleum Gas (Bottled Gas) Dealers—*retail*	454312	5171
Petroleum coke, produced in petroleum refineries: Petroleum Refineries—*mfg*	32411	2911
Petroleum engineering services: Engineering Services—*prof*	54133	8711
Petroleum Lubricating Oil and Grease Manufacturing	**324191**	**2992**
Petroleum pipelines, crude: Pipeline of Crude Oil—*trans*	48611	4612
Petroleum pipelines, refined: Pipeline of Refined—*trans*	48691	4613
Petroleum polymer resins: Plastics Material and Resin—*mfg*	325211	2821
Petroleum production-crude: Crude Petroleum and Natural Gas Extraction—*mining*	211111	1311
Petroleum Refineries	**32411**	**2911**
Petroleum refinery construction–general contractors: Heavy, All Other—*const*	23499	1629
Industrial Nonbuilding Structure—*const*	23493	1629
Petroleum refinery equipment: Industrial Machinery, All Other—*mfg*	333298	3559
Machinery, Other Commercial and Service Industry—*mfg*	333319	3559
Petroleum refining: Petroleum Refineries—*mfg*	32411	2911
Pews, church: Institutional Furniture—*mfg*	337127	2531
Pewter ware: Cutlery and Flatware (except Precious)—*mfg*	332211	3914
Silverware and Plated Ware—*mfg*	339912	3914
PH instruments, industrial process type: Instruments and Related Products for Measuring, Displaying, and Controlling Industrial Process Variables—*mfg*	334513	3823
PH measuring equipment: Analytical Laboratory Instrument—*mfg*	334516	3826
Pharmaceutical and Medicine Manufacturing	**3254**	
Pharmaceutical and Medicine Manufacturing	**32541**	
Pharmaceutical machinery: Industrial Machinery, All Other—*mfg*	333298	3559
Machinery, Other Commercial and Service Industry—*mfg*	333319	3559
Pharmaceutical manufacturing plant construction–general contractors: Building, Commercial and Institutional—*const*	23332	1541
Manufacturing and Industrial Building—*const*	23331	1541
Pharmaceutical Preparation Manufacturing	**325412**	**2835**
Pharmaceuticals: Drug, Drug Proprietaries and Druggists' Sundries—*whlse*	42221	5122
Pharmaceutical Preparation—*mfg*	325412	2834
Pharmacies: Pharmacies and Drug Stores—*retail*	44611	5912
Pharmacies and Drug Stores	**44611**	**5912**

ALPHABETICAL INDEX	NAICS	SIC
Phase angle meters: Electronic Coil, Transformer, and Other Inductor—*mfg*	334416	3825
Instrument for Measuring and Testing Electricity and Electrical Signals—*mfg*	334515	3825
Phase converters (electrical equipment): Motor and Generator—*mfg*	335312	3621
Pheasant farms: Poultry Production, Other—*ag*	11239	259
Phenol: Cyclic Crude and Intermediate—*mfg*	325192	2865
Petrochemical—*mfg*	32511	2865
Phenol formaldehyde coatings, baking and air curing: Paint and Coating—*mfg*	32551	2851
Phenol-furfural resins: Plastics Material and Resin—*mfg*	325211	2821
Phenolic resins: Plastics Material and Resin—*mfg*	325211	2821
Phenoxy resins: Plastics Material and Resin—*mfg*	325211	2821
Philatelist and autograph retail: Stores (except Tobacco Stores), All Other Miscellaneous—*retail*	453998	5999
Phlogopite mining: Crushed and Broken Stone and Quarrying, Other—*mining*	212319	1499
Non-Metallic Mineral, All Other—*mining*	212399	1499
Phloxine toners: Petrochemical—*mfg*	32511	2865
Phonocardiographs: Electromedical and Electrotherapeutic Apparatus—*mfg*	334510	3845
Irradiation Apparatus—*mfg*	334517	3845
Phonograph and phonograph stores, secondhand-retail supply stores-record: Non-Depository Credit Intermediation, All Other—*fin*	522298	5932
Used Merchandise Stores—*retail*	45331	5932
Phonograph and radio combinations: Audio and Video Equipment—*mfg*	33431	3651
Phonograph cabinets and cases, wood: Wood Television, Radio, and Sewing Machine Cabinet—*mfg*	337129	2517
Phonograph needle cartridges: Electronic Component, Other—*mfg*	334419	3679
Motor Vehicle Electrical and Electronic Equipment, Other—*mfg*	336322	3679
Printed Circuit/Electronics Assembly—*mfg*	334418	3679
Radio and Television Broadcasting and Wireless Communications Equipment—*mfg*	33422	3679
Phonograph needles: Electronic Component, Other—*mfg*	334419	3679
Motor Vehicle Electrical and Electronic Equipment, Other—*mfg*	336322	3679
Printed Circuit/Electronics Assembly—*mfg*	334418	3679
Radio and Television Broadcasting and Wireless Communications Equipment—*mfg*	33422	3679
Phonograph record blanks: Integrated Record Production/Distribution—*info*	51222	3652
Prerecorded Compact Disc (except Software), Tape, and Record Reproducing—*mfg*	334612	3652
Phonograph record stores: Prerecorded Tape, Compact Disc and Record Stores—*retail*	45122	5735
Phonograph records: Durable Goods, Other Miscellaneous—*whlse*	42199	5099

Description	NAICS	SIC
Phonograph records (including preparation of the master): Integrated Record Production/Distribution—*info*	51222	3652
Prerecorded Compact Disc (except Software), Tape, and Record Reproducing—*mfg*	334612	3652
Phonograph repair–stereo, hi-fi, and tape recorder: Communication Equipment Repair and Maintenance—*serv*	811213	7622
Consumer Electronics Repair and Maintenance—*serv*	811211	7622
Radio, Television and Other Electronics Stores—*retail*	443112	7622
Phonograph stores: Automotive Parts and Accessories Stores—*retail*	44131	5731
Radio, Television and Other Electronics Stores—*retail*	443112	5731
Phonograph turntables: Audio and Video Equipment—*mfg*	33431	3651
Phonographs, coin-operated: Equipment, Other Commercial—*whlse*	42144	5046
Phonographs, except coin-operated: Electrical Appliance, Television and Radio Set—*whlse*	42162	5064
Phonographs, including coin-operated: Audio and Video Equipment—*mfg*	33431	3651
Phosgene: Basic Organic Chemical, All Other—*mfg*	325199	2869
Phosphate coating of metal and metal products, for the trade: Costume Jewelry and Novelty—*mfg*	339914	3479
Jewelry (except Costume)—*mfg*	339911	3479
Metal Coating, Engraving (except Jewelry and Silverware), and Allied Services to Manufacturers—*mfg*	332812	3479
Silverware and Plated Ware—*mfg*	339912	3479
Phosphate Rock Mining	**212392**	**1475**
Phosphate rock, ground: Farm Supplies—*whlse*	42291	5191
Nursery and Garden Centers—*retail*	44422	5191
Phosphates, except defluorinated and ammoniated: Basic Inorganic Chemical, All Other—*mfg*	325188	2819
Chemical Product, All Other Miscellaneous—*mfg*	325998	2819
Phosphatic Fertilizer Manufacturing	**325312**	**2874**
Phosphomolybdic acid lakes and toners: Organic Dye and Pigment—*mfg*	325132	2865
Petrochemical—*mfg*	32511	2865
Phosphoric acid: Phosphatic Fertilizer—*mfg*	325312	2874
Phosphoric acid esters: Basic Organic Chemical, All Other—*mfg*	325199	2869
Phosphorus and phosphorus oxychloride: Basic Inorganic Chemical, All Other—*mfg*	325188	2819
Chemical Product, All Other Miscellaneous—*mfg*	325998	2819
Phosphotungstic acid lakes and toners: Organic Dye and Pigment—*mfg*	325132	2865
Petrochemical—*mfg*	32511	2865
Photo Finishing	**81292**	
Photo Finishing Laboratories (except One-Hour)	**812921**	**7384**
Photo-offset printing: Lithographic Printing, Commercial—*mfg*	323110	2752
Quick Printing—*mfg*	323114	2752
Photocomposition: Prepress Services—*mfg*	323122	2791
Photoconductive cells: Semiconductor and Related Device—*mfg*	334413	3674
Photocopy machines: Office Equipment—*whlse*	42142	5044
Photographic and Photocopying Equipment—*mfg*	333315	3861
Photographic Film, Paper, Plate and Chemical—*mfg*	325992	3861
Photocopying service: Business Service Centers (including Copy Shops), Other—*admin*	561439	7334
Photocopying supplies: Office Supplies and Stationery Stores—*retail*	45321	5112
Stationary and Office Supplies—*whlse*	42212	5112
Photoelectric cells, solid-state (electronic eye): Semiconductor and Related Device—*mfg*	334413	3674
Photoelectric magnetic devices: Semiconductor and Related Device—*mfg*	334413	3674
Photoengraving for the trade: Prepress Services—*mfg*	323122	2796
Photoengraving machines: Printing Machinery and Equipment—*mfg*	333293	3555
Photoengraving plates (halftones and line cuts): Prepress Services—*mfg*	323122	2796
Photofinishing laboratories, except for the motion picture industry: One-Hour Photo Finishing—*serv*	812922	7384
Photo Finishing Laboratories (except One-Hour)—*serv*	812921	7384
Photoflash and photoflood lamp bulbs and tubes: Electric Lamp Bulb and Part—*mfg*	33511	3641
Photoflash equipment, except lamp bulbs: Photographic and Photocopying Equipment—*mfg*	333315	3861
Photographic Film, Paper, Plate and Chemical—*mfg*	325992	3861
Photogrammetric engineering: Geophysical Surveying and Mapping Services—*prof*	54136	8713
Surveying and Mapping (except Geophysical) Services—*prof*	54137	8713
Photogrammetric mapping service (not professional engineers): Surveying and Mapping (except Geophysical) Services—*prof*	54137	7389
Photogrammetrical instruments: Measuring and Controlling Device, Other—*mfg*	334519	3829
Surgical and Medical Instrument—*mfg*	339112	3829
Photograph developing and retouching: One-Hour Photo Finishing—*serv*	812922	7384
Photo Finishing Laboratories (except One-Hour)—*serv*	812921	7384
Photograph folders, mats, and mounts: Converted Paper Product, All Other—*mfg*	322298	2675
Die-Cut Paper and Paperboard Office Supplies—*mfg*	322231	2675
Surface-Coated Paperboard—*mfg*	322292	2675
Photograph frames, wood or metal: Manufacturing, All Other Miscellaneous—*mfg*	339999	2499
Wood Container and Pallet—*mfg*	32192	2499
Wood Product, All Other Miscellaneous—*mfg*	321999	2499
Photograph transmission services: Wired Telecommunications Carriers—*info*	51331	4822
Photographers, portrait–still or video: Photography Studios, Portrait—*prof*	541921	7221
Photographers, school: Photography Studios, Portrait—*prof*	541921	7221
Photographic and Photocopying Equipment Manufacturing	**333315**	**3861**
Photographic cameras, projectors, equipment and supplies: Photographic Equipment and Supplies—*whlse*	42141	5043

ALPHABETICAL INDEX	NAICS	SIC
Photographic chemicals, packaged: Photographic and Photocopying Equipment—*mfg*	333315	3861
Photographic Film, Paper, Plate and Chemical—*mfg*	325992	3861
Photographic equipment and accessories: Photographic and Photocopying Equipment—*mfg*	333315	3861
Photographic Film, Paper, Plate and Chemical—*mfg*	325992	3861
Photographic Equipment and Supplies Wholesalers	**42141**	**5043**
Photographic Film, Paper, Plate and Chemical Manufacturing	**325992**	**3861**
Photographic instruments, electronic: Photographic and Photocopying Equipment—*mfg*	333315	3861
Photographic Film, Paper, Plate and Chemical—*mfg*	325992	3861
Photographic laboratories, except for the motion picture industry: One-Hour Photo Finishing—*serv*	812922	7384
Photo Finishing Laboratories (except One-Hour)—*serv*	812921	7384
Photographic lenses: Optical Instrument and Lens—*mfg*	333314	3827
Photographic paper and cloth, sensitized: Photographic and Photocopying Equipment—*mfg*	333315	3861
Photographic Film, Paper, Plate and Chemical—*mfg*	325992	3861
Photographic sensitized goods: Photographic and Photocopying Equipment—*mfg*	333315	3861
Photographic Film, Paper, Plate and Chemical—*mfg*	325992	3861
Photographic Services	**54192**	
Photographic studios, commercial: Nonscheduled Air, Other—*trans*	481219	7335
Photography, Commercial—*prof*	541922	7335
Photographic studios, portrait: Photography Studios, Portrait—*prof*	541921	7221
Photographic supply stores: Camera and Photographic Supplies Stores—*retail*	44313	5946
Photographic, micrographic, and X-ray plastics, sheet, and film–unsupported: Unsupported Plastics Film and Sheet (except Packaging)—*mfg*	326113	3081
Photography Studios, Portrait	**541921**	**7221**
Photography, aerial–except map making: Graphic Design Services—*prof*	54143	7336
Photography, Commercial	**541922**	**8099**
Photography, commercial: Nonscheduled Air, Other—*trans*	481219	7335
Photogravure printing: Gravure Printing, Commercial—*mfg*	323111	2754
Photolithographing: Lithographic Printing, Commercial—*mfg*	323110	2752
Quick Printing—*mfg*	323114	2752
Photomask blanks, glass: Pressed and Blown Glass and Glassware, Other—*mfg*	327212	3229
Photometers, except photographic exposure meters: Analytical Laboratory Instrument—*mfg*	334516	3826
Photomultiplier tubes: Electron Tube—*mfg*	334411	3671
Photopitometers: Measuring and Controlling Device, Other—*mfg*	334519	3829
Surgical and Medical Instrument—*mfg*	339112	3829
Photoreconnaissance systems: Photographic and Photocopying Equipment—*mfg*	333315	3861

ALPHABETICAL INDEX	NAICS	SIC
Photographic Film, Paper, Plate and Chemical—*mfg*	325992	3861
Photosensitized paper: Photographic and Photocopying Equipment—*mfg*	333315	3861
Photographic Film, Paper, Plate and Chemical—*mfg*	325992	3861
Phototheodolites: Optical Instrument and Lens—*mfg*	333314	3827
Phototransmission equipment: Radio and Television Broadcasting and Wireless Communications Equipment—*mfg*	33422	3663
Phototypesetting: Prepress Services—*mfg*	323122	2791
Photovoltaic devices, solid-state: Semiconductor and Related Device—*mfg*	334413	3674
Phthalates: Basic Organic Chemical, All Other—*mfg*	325199	2869
Phthalic alkyd resins: Plastics Material and Resin—*mfg*	325211	2821
Phthalic anhydride: Cyclic Crude and Intermediate—*mfg*	325192	2865
Petrochemical—*mfg*	32511	2865
Phthalic anhydride resins: Plastics Material and Resin—*mfg*	325211	2821
Phthalocyanine toners: Organic Dye and Pigment—*mfg*	325132	2865
Petrochemical—*mfg*	32511	2865
Physical distribution consultants: Administrative Management and General Management Consulting Services—*prof*	541611	8742
Human Resources and Executive Search Consulting Services—*prof*	541612	8742
Marketing Consulting Services—*prof*	541613	8742
Process, Physical, Distribution and Logistics Consulting Services—*prof*	541614	8742
Physical examination service, except by physicians: Ambulatory Health Care Services, All Other Miscellaneous—*hlth*	621999	8099
Physical fitness centers: Fitness and Recreational Sports Centers—*arts*	71394	7991
Physical properties testing and inspection equipment: Measuring and Controlling Device, Other—*mfg*	334519	3829
Surgical and Medical Instrument—*mfg*	339112	3829
Physical research, commercial: Research and Development in the Life Sciences—*prof*	54172	8731
Research and Development in the Physical Sciences and Engineering Sciences—*prof*	54171	8731
Physical research, noncommercial: Research and Development in the Life Sciences—*prof*	54172	8733
Research and Development in the Physical Sciences and Engineering Sciences—*prof*	54171	8733
Research and Development in the Social Sciences and Humanities—*prof*	54173	8733
Physical therapists, offices of: Health Practitioners, Offices Of Miscellaneous—*hlth*	621399	8049
Mental Health Practitioners (except Physicians), Offices Of—*hlth*	62133	8049
Physical, Occupational and Speech Therapists and Audiologists, Offices Of—*hlth*	62134	8049

Description	NAICS	SIC
Physical, Occupational and Speech Therapists and Audiologists, Offices Of	**62134**	**8049**
Physicians (except Mental Health Specialists), Offices Of	**621111**	**8031**
Physicians (M.D.), including specialists–offices and clinics of: Freestanding Ambulatory Surgical and Emergency Centers—*hlth*	621493	8011
HMO Medical Centers—*hlth*	621491	8011
Physicians (except Mental Health Specialists), Offices Of—*hlth*	621111	8011
Physicians, Mental Health Specialists, Offices Of—*hlth*	621112	8011
Physicians' assistants, offices of: Health Practitioners, Offices Of Miscellaneous—*hlth*	621399	8049
Mental Health Practitioners (except Physicians), Offices Of—*hlth*	62133	8049
Physical, Occupational and Speech Therapists and Audiologists, Offices Of—*hlth*	62134	8049
Physicians' equipment: Health and Personal Care Stores, All Other—*retail*	446199	5047
Medical, Dental and Hospital Equipment and Supplies—*whlse*	42145	5047
Physicians' supplies: Health and Personal Care Stores, All Other—*retail*	446199	5047
Medical, Dental and Hospital Equipment and Supplies—*whlse*	42145	5047
Physicians, Mental Health Specialists, Offices Of	**621112**	**8031**
Physicians, Offices Of	**6211**	
Physicians, Offices Of	**62111**	
Physicians, osteopathic–offices and clinics of: Physicians (except Mental Health Specialists), Offices Of—*hlth*	621111	8031
Physicians, Mental Health Specialists, Offices Of—*hlth*	621112	8031
Physicists, consulting–not connected with business service laboratories: Scientific and Technical Consulting Services, Other—*prof*	54169	8999
Physiotherapy equipment, electrical: Surgical and Medical Instrument—*mfg*	339112	3841
Physostigmine and derivatives: Medicinal and Botanical—*mfg*	325411	2833
Phytoactin: Pesticide and Other Agricultural Chemical—*mfg*	32532	2879
Piano hardware: Hardware—*mfg*	33251	3429
Piano parts and materials, except piano hardware: Musical Instrument—*mfg*	339992	3931
Piano rental and leasing: Consumer Goods Rental, All Other—*real*	532299	7359
Piano stores: Musical Instrument and Supplies Stores—*retail*	45114	5736
Piano tuning and repair: Electronic and Precision Equipment Repair and Maintenance, Other—*serv*	811219	7699
Personal and Household Goods Repair and Maintenance, Other—*serv*	81149	7699
Pianos, all types–e.g., vertical, grand, spinet, player, coin-operated: Musical Instrument—*mfg*	339992	3931
Piccolos and parts: Musical Instrument—*mfg*	339992	3931
Picker machines (textile machinery): Textile Machinery—*mfg*	333292	3552
Picker stick blanks: Cut Stock, Resawing Lumber, and Planing—*mfg*	321912	2426
Millwork (including Flooring), Other—*mfg*	321918	2426
Showcase, Partition, Shelving, and Locker—*mfg*	337215	2426
Wood Product, All Other Miscellaneous—*mfg*	321999	2426
Picker sticks for looms: Textile Machinery—*mfg*	333292	3552
Pickets and paling–round or split: Logging—*ag*	11331	2411
Picking of crab meat: Fresh and Frozen Seafood Processing—*mfg*	311712	2092
Picklers and pickling lines, sheet and strip(rolling mill equipment): Rolling Mill Machinery and Equipment—*mfg*	333516	3547
Pickles and pickle salting: Fruit and Vegetable Canning—*mfg*	311421	2035
Mayonnaise, Dressing and Other Prepared Sauce—*mfg*	311941	2035
Pickles, preserves, jellies, jams, and sauces: Grocery and Related Products, Other—*whlse*	42249	5149
Picks (handtools): Hand and Edge Tool—*mfg*	332212	3423
Pickup and delivery station laundry not operated by laundries: Garment Pressing, and Agents for Laundries—*serv*	812391	7212
Pickup coaches (campers), for mounting on pickup trucks: Travel Trailer and Camper—*mfg*	336214	3792
Pickup covers, canopies or caps: Travel Trailer and Camper—*mfg*	336214	3792
Pickup heads, phonograph: Audio and Video Equipment—*mfg*	33431	3651
Pickups and vans, new and used: New Car Dealers—*retail*	44111	5511
Pickups and vans, used only: Used Car Dealers—*retail*	44112	5521
Picnic grounds operation: Amusement and Recreation Industries, All Other—*arts*	71399	7999
Picnic jugs, plastics: Plastics Pipe and Pipe Fitting—*mfg*	326122	3089
Plastics Product, All Other—*mfg*	326199	3089
Unsupported Plastics Profile Shape—*mfg*	326121	3089
Picric acid (explosives): Explosives—*mfg*	32592	2892
Pictorial situation instrumentation: Search, Detection, Navigation, Guidance, Aeronautical, and Nautical System and Instrument—*mfg*	334511	3812
Picture frame moldings, finished: Manufacturing, All Other Miscellaneous—*mfg*	339999	2499
Wood Container and Pallet—*mfg*	32192	2499
Wood Product, All Other Miscellaneous—*mfg*	321999	2499
Picture frames, ready-made: Stores (except Tobacco Stores), All Other Miscellaneous—*retail*	453998	5999
Picture frames, wood or metal: Manufacturing, All Other Miscellaneous—*mfg*	339999	2499
Wood Container and Pallet—*mfg*	32192	2499
Wood Product, All Other Miscellaneous—*mfg*	321999	2499
Picture framing to individual order, not connected with retail art stores: Personal and Household Goods Repair and Maintenance, Other—*serv*	81149	7699
Picture framing, custom: Personal and Household Goods Repair and Maintenance, Other—*serv*	81149	7699
Picture glass: Flat Glass—*mfg*	327211	3211
Picture post cards–except lithographed or gravure: Digital Printing—*mfg*	323115	2759
Flexographic Printing, Commercial—*mfg*	323112	2759
Printing, Other Commercial—*mfg*	323119	2759
Quick Printing—*mfg*	323114	2759

ALPHABETICAL INDEX	NAICS	SIC
Picture postcards, lithographed: Lithographic Printing, Commercial—*mfg*	323110	2752
Quick Printing—*mfg*	323114	2752
Picture tube reprocessing: Electron Tube—*mfg*	334411	3671
Pie fillings, except fruits, vegetables and meat: Food, All Other Miscellaneous—*mfg*	311999	2099
Piece goods: Broadwoven Fabric Finishing Mills—*mfg*	313311	5131
Piece Goods, Notions and Other Dry Goods—*whlse*	42231	5131
Sewing, Needlework and Piece Goods Stores—*retail*	45113	5949
Textile and Fabric Finishing (except Broadwoven Fabric) Mills—*mfg*	313312	5131
Piece Goods, Notions and Other Dry Goods Wholesalers	**42231**	**5131**
Pier construction–general contractors: Heavy, All Other—*const*	23499	1629
Industrial Nonbuilding Structure—*const*	23493	1629
Pier footings, prefabricated concrete: Concrete Pipe—*mfg*	327332	3272
Concrete Product, Other—*mfg*	32739	3272
Nonmetallic Mineral Product, All Other Miscellaneous—*mfg*	327999	3272
Piers, amusement: Amusement and Theme Parks—*arts*	71311	7996
Piers, including buildings and facilities–operation and maintenance: Marine Cargo Handling—*trans*	48832	4491
Port and Harbor Operations—*trans*	48831	4491
Pies, bakery, except frozen: Bakeries, Commercial—*mfg*	311812	2051
Pies, bakery, frozen: Frozen Bakery Product—*mfg*	311813	2053
Pies, fruit–frozen: Packaged Frozen Food—*whlse*	42242	5142
Pies, meat–canned: Canning, Specialty—*mfg*	311422	2032
Food, All Other Miscellaneous—*mfg*	311999	2032
Piezoelectric crystals: Electronic Component, Other—*mfg*	334419	3679
Motor Vehicle Electrical and Electronic Equipment, Other—*mfg*	336322	3679
Printed Circuit/Electronics Assembly—*mfg*	334418	3679
Radio and Television Broadcasting and Wireless Communications Equipment—*mfg*	33422	3679
Pig iron: Iron and Steel Mills—*mfg*	331111	3312
Metal Service Centers and Offices—*whlse*	42151	5051
Petroleum and Coal Productsa, All Other—*mfg*	324199	3312
Pigeon farms: Poultry Production, Other—*ag*	11239	259
Pigeons, clay (targets): Sporting and Athletic Goods—*mfg*	33992	3949
Pigment scarlet lake: Organic Dye and Pigment—*mfg*	325132	2865
Petrochemical—*mfg*	32511	2865
Pigments and colors: Paint and Wallpaper Stores—*retail*	44412	5198
Paint, Varnish and Supplies—*whlse*	42295	5198
Pigments, inorganic: Carbon Black—*mfg*	325182	2816
Inorganic Dye and Pigment—*mfg*	325131	2816
Pigments, organic–except animal black and bone black: Organic Dye and Pigment—*mfg*	325132	2865
Petrochemical—*mfg*	32511	2865
Pigs' feet, cooked and pickled: Meat Processed from Carcasses—*mfg*	311612	2013
Pigs, aluminum: Primary Aluminum Production—*mfg*	331312	3334

ALPHABETICAL INDEX	NAICS	SIC
Pigs, copper: Primary Smelting and Refining of Copper—*mfg*	331411	3331
Pigs, lead: Primary Smelting and Refining of Nonferrous Metal (except Copper and Aluminum)—*mfg*	331419	3339
Pigs, primary–nonferrous metals, except copper and aluminum: Primary Smelting and Refining of Nonferrous Metal (except Copper and Aluminum)—*mfg*	331419	3339
Pilchard, catching of: Finfish Fishing—*ag*	114111	912
Pile driving–contractors: Heavy, All Other—*const*	23499	1629
Industrial Nonbuilding Structure—*const*	23493	1629
Pile fabrics, circular knit: Textile and Fabric Finishing (except Broadwoven Fabric) Mills—*mfg*	313312	2257
Weft Knit Fabric Mills—*mfg*	313241	2257
Pile fabrics, cotton: Broadwoven Fabric Mills—*mfg*	31321	2211
Pile fabrics, manmade fiber and silk: Broadwoven Fabric Mills—*mfg*	31321	2221
Pile fabrics, warp knit: Knit Fabric and Lace Mills, Other—*mfg*	313249	2258
Textile and Fabric Finishing (except Broadwoven Fabric) Mills—*mfg*	313312	2258
Pile shells, metal plate: Air-Conditioning and Warm Air Heating Equipment and Commercial and Industrial Refrigeration Equipment—*mfg*	333415	3443
Metal Tank (Heavy Gauge)—*mfg*	33242	3443
Plate Work—*mfg*	332313	3443
Power Boiler and Heat Exchanger—*mfg*	33241	3443
Pile shells, sheet metal: Metal Container, Other—*mfg*	332439	3444
Sheet Metal Work—*mfg*	332322	3444
Piledriving equipment-rnfg: Construction Machinery—*mfg*	33312	3531
Overhead Traveling Crane, Hoist and Monorail System—*mfg*	333923	3531
Railroad Rolling Stock—*mfg*	33651	3531
Piles, foundation and marine construction–treated: Wood Preservation—*mfg*	321114	2491
Piling extractors: Construction Machinery—*mfg*	33312	3531
Overhead Traveling Crane, Hoist and Monorail System—*mfg*	333923	3531
Railroad Rolling Stock—*mfg*	33651	3531
Piling, driving–general contractors: Heavy, All Other—*const*	23499	1629
Industrial Nonbuilding Structure—*const*	23493	1629
Piling, iron and steel: Metal Service Centers and Offices—*whlse*	42151	5051
Piling, prefabricated concrete: Concrete Pipe—*mfg*	327332	3272
Concrete Product, Other—*mfg*	32739	3272
Nonmetallic Mineral Product, All Other Miscellaneous—*mfg*	327999	3272
Piling, wood–treated: Wood Preservation—*mfg*	321114	2491
Piling, wood–untreated-rnfg: Logging—*ag*	11331	2411
Pilings, sheet, plain–iron arid steel: Iron and Steel Mills—*mfg*	331111	3312
Petroleum and Coal Productsa, All Other—*mfg*	324199	3312
Pillow block units for ball or roller bearings: Ball and Roller Bearing—*mfg*	332991	3562
Pillow blocks, with bail or roller bearings: Ball and Roller Bearing—*mfg*	332991	3562

Description	NAICS	SIC
Pillow blocks, with plain bearings: Mechanical Power Transmission Equipment—*mfg*	333613	3568
Pillow cleaning and renovating: Laundry Services, All Other—*serv*	812399	7219
Pillow filling–curled ha ir (e.g., cotton waste, moss, hemp tow, kapok): Broadwoven Fabric Mills—*mfg*	31321	2299
Narrow Fabric Mills—*mfg*	313221	2299
Nonwoven Fabric Mills—*mfg*	31323	2299
Textile and Fabric Finishing (except Broadwoven Fabric) Mills—*mfg*	313312	2299
Textile Product Mills, All Other Miscellaneous—*mfg*	314999	2299
Thread Mills—*mfg*	313113	2299
Yarn Spinning Mills—*mfg*	313111	2299
Pillow tubing: Broadwoven Fabric Mills—*mfg*	31321	2211
Pillowcases: Broadwoven Fabric Mills—*mfg*	31321	2211
Home Furnishing—*whlse*	42122	5023
Household Textile Product Mills, Other—*mfg*	314129	2392
Pillows, bed: Household Textile Product Mills, Other—*mfg*	314129	2392
Pillows, sponge rubber: Fabric Coating Mills—*mfg*	31332	3069
Rubber Product, All Other—*mfg*	326299	3069
Pillows, stereo: Audio and Video Equipment—*mfg*	33431	3651
Pills, pharmaceutical: Pharmaceutical Preparation—*mfg*	325412	2834
Piloting vessels in and out of harbors: Air, Rail, and Water Equipment Rental and Leasing, Commercial—*real*	532411	4499
Navigational Services to Shipping—*trans*	48833	4499
Port and Harbor Operations—*trans*	48831	4499
Water, Other Support Activities for—*trans*	48839	4499
Pilots, automatic, aircraft: Search, Detection, Navigation, Guidance, Aeronautical, and Nautical System and Instrument—*mfg*	334511	3812
Pin checks, cotton: Broadwoven Fabric Mills—*mfg*	31321	2211
Pin stems jewelry findings): Jewelers' Material and Lapidary Work—*mfg*	339913	3915
Pin stripes, cotton: Broadwoven Fabric Mills—*mfg*	31321	2211
Pin tickets, paper: Coated and Laminated Paper—*mfg*	322222	2679
Converted Paper Product, All Other—*mfg*	322298	2679
Die-Cut Paper and Paperboard Office Supplies—*mfg*	322231	2679
Non-Folding Sanitary Food Container—*mfg*	322215	2679
Pinball machines, operation of: Amusement and Recreation Industries, All Other—*arts*	71399	7993
Amusement Arcades—*arts*	71312	7993
Gambling Industries, Other—*arts*	71329	7993
Pine gum, extraction of: Crop Farming, All Other Miscellaneous—*ag*	111998	831
Forest Nurseries and Gathering of Forest Products—*ag*	11321	831
Pine oil, produced by distillation of pine gum or pine wood: Gum and Wood Chemical—*mfg*	325191	2861
Pineapple farms: Fruit and Tree Nut Combination Farming—*ag*	111336	179
Noncitrus Fruit Farming, Other—*ag*	111339	179
Ping pong parlors: Amusement and Recreation Industries, All Other—*arts*	71399	7999
Pinite mining: Clay and Ceramic and Refractory Minerals—*mining*	212325	1459
Pins, costume jewelry–except precious metal and gems: Costume Jewelry and Novelty—*mfg*	339914	3961
Pins, except jewelry–toilet, safety, hatpins, and hairpins-steel or brass: Fastener, Button, Needle and Pin—*mfg*	339993	3965
Pins, precious metal: Jewelry (except Costume)—*mfg*	339911	3911
Pinsetters for bowling, automatic: Sporting and Athletic Goods—*mfg*	33992	3949
Pipe and boiler covering: Building Material Dealers, Other—*retail*	44419	5074
Plumbing and Heating Equipment and Supplies (Hydronics)—*whlse*	42172	5074
Pipe and boiler covering, except felt: Motor Vehicle Brake System—*mfg*	33634	3292
Nonmetallic Mineral Product, All Other Miscellaneous—*mfg*	327999	3292
Pipe and boiler covering, felt: Broadwoven Fabric Mills—*mfg*	31321	2299
Narrow Fabric Mills—*mfg*	313221	2299
Nonwoven Fabric Mills—*mfg*	31323	2299
Textile and Fabric Finishing (except Broadwoven Fabric) Mills—*mfg*	313312	2299
Textile Product Mills, All Other Miscellaneous—*mfg*	314999	2299
Thread Mills—*mfg*	313113	2299
Yarn Spinning Mills—*mfg*	313111	2299
Pipe and boilers, insulation of contractors: Trade Contractors, All Other Special—*const*	23599	1799
Pipe and fittings, fabricated from purchased metal pipe: Fabricated Pipe and Pipe Fitting—*mfg*	332996	3498
Pipe and fittings, molded pulp: Coated and Laminated Paper—*mfg*	322222	2679
Converted Paper Product, All Other—*mfg*	322298	2679
Die-Cut Paper and Paperboard Office Supplies—*mfg*	322231	2679
Non-Folding Sanitary Food Container—*mfg*	322215	2679
Pipe and fittings, soil and pressure–cast iron: Iron Foundries—*mfg*	331511	3321
Pipe and tube mills: Rolling Mill Machinery and Equipment—*mfg*	333516	3547
Pipe and tubing, steel: Metal Service Centers and Offices—*whlse*	42151	5051
Pipe bannisters, railings, and guards: Ornamental and Architectural Metal Work—*mfg*	332323	3446
Pipe couplings–fabricated from purchased metal pipe: Fabricated Pipe and Pipe Fitting—*mfg*	332996	3498
Pipe covering (insulation), laminated asbestos paper: Motor Vehicle Brake System—*mfg*	33634	3292
Nonmetallic Mineral Product, All Other Miscellaneous—*mfg*	327999	3292
Pipe covering–contractors: Trade Contractors, All Other Special—*const*	23599	1799
Pipe cutting and threading machines (machine tools)-rnfg: Machine Tool (Metal Cutting Types)—*mfg*	333512	3541
Pipe fittings, except plumbers' brass goods:metal: Fabricated Metal Product, All Other Miscellaneous—*mfg*	332999	3494
Other Metal Valve and Pipe Fitting, Other—*mfg*	332919	3494
Pipe hangers, metal: Fabricated Metal Product, All Other Miscellaneous—*mfg*	332999	3494
Other'Metal Valve and Pipe Fitting, Other—*mfg*	332919	3494

ALPHABETICAL INDEX	NAICS	SIC
Pipe headers, welded–fabricated from purchased metal pipe:		
Fabricated Pipe and Pipe Fitting—*mfg*	332996	3498
Pipe mouthpieces, molded rubber: Fabric Coating Mills—*mfg*	31332	3069
Rubber Product, All Other—*mfg*	326299	3069
Pipe sealing compounds: Adhesive—*mfg*	32552	2891
Pipe stems and bits, tobacco–hard rubber: Fabric Coating Mills—*mfg*	31332	3069
Rubber Product, All Other—*mfg*	326299	3069
Pipe testing service, oil and gas field–on a contract basis: Oil and Gas		
Operations Support Activities—*mining*	213112	1389
Pipe, aluminum–extruded: Aluminum Extruded Product—*mfg*	331316	3354
Pipe, cast iron: Metal Service Centers and Offices—*whlse*	42151	5051
Pipe, chimney–clay-mig: Structural Clay Product, Other—*mfg*	327123	3259
Pipe, concrete: Concrete Pipe—*mfg*	327332	3272
Concrete Product, Other—*mfg*	32739	3272
Nonmetallic Mineral Product, All Other Miscellaneous—*mfg*	327999	3272
Pipe, extruded and drawn–brass, bronze, and copper: Copper		
Rolling, Drawing and Extruding—*mfg*	331421	3351
Pipe, fabricated from purchased metal pipe: Fabricated Pipe and Pipe		
Fitting—*mfg*	332996	3498
Pipe, iron and steel–made in steel works or rolling mills: Iron and		
Steel Mills—*mfg*	331111	3312
Petroleum and Coal Productsa, All Other—*mfg*	324199	3312
Pipe, large diameter–metal plate-made by plate fabricators:		
Air-Conditioning and Warm Air Heating Equipment and		
Commercial and Industrial Refrigeration Equipment—*mfg*	333415	3443
Metal Tank (Heavy Gauge)—*mfg*	33242	3443
Plate Work—*mfg*	332313	3443
Power Boiler and Heat Exchanger—*mfg*	33241	3443
Pipe, lined with concrete: Concrete Pipe—*mfg*	327332	3272
Concrete Product, Other—*mfg*	32739	3272
Nonmetallic Mineral Product, All Other Miscellaneous—*mfg*	327999	3272
Pipe, plastics: Plastics Pipe and Pipe Fitting—*mfg*	326122	3084
Pipe, pressure–asbestos cement: Motor Vehicle Brake System—*mfg*	33634	3292
Nonmetallic Mineral Product, All Other Miscellaneous—*mfg*	327999	3292
Pipe, seamless steel: Iron and Steel Pipes and Tubes from Purchased		
Steel—*mfg*	33121	3317
Pipe, sewer–clay: Structural Clay Product, Other—*mfg*	327123	3259
Pipe, sheet metal: Metal Container, Other—*mfg*	332439	3444
Sheet Metal Work—*mfg*	332322	3444
Pipe, wrought–welded, lock joint, and heavy riveted: Iron and Steel		
Pipes and Tubes from Purchased Steel—*mfg*	33121	3317
Pipe–lead, magnesium, nickel, tin, zinc, and their alloys: Nonferrous		
Metal (except Copper and Aluminum) Rolling, Drawing and		
Extruding—*mfg*	331491	3356
Pipelaying–general contractors: Power and Communication		
Transmission Line—*const*	23492	1623
Water, Sewer, and Pipeline—*const*	23491	1623

ALPHABETICAL INDEX	NAICS	SIC
Pipeline construction–general contractors: Power and		
Communication Transmission Line—*const*	23492	1623
Water, Sewer, and Pipeline—*const*	23491	1623
Pipeline operation, except petroleum and natural gas pipelines:		
Pipeline, All Other—*trans*	48699	4619
Pipeline terminal facilities independently operated: Rail Support		
Activities—*trans*	48821	4789
Scenic and Sightseeing, Land—*trans*	48711	4789
Transportation, All Other Support Activities—*trans*	488999	4789
Pipeline Transportation	**486**	
Pipeline Transportation of Crude Oil	**48611**	**4612**
Pipeline Transportation of Crude Oil	**4861**	
Pipeline Transportation of Natural Gas	**4862**	
Pipeline Transportation of Natural Gas	**48621**	**4923**
Pipeline Transportation of Refined	**48691**	**4613**
Pipeline Transportation, All Other	**48699**	**4619**
Pipeline Transportation, Other	**4869**	
Pipeline wrapping–contractors: Power and Communication		
Transmission Line—*const*	23492	1623
Water, Sewer, and Pipeline—*const*	23491	1623
Pipelines (common carriers), gasoline: Pipeline of Refined—*trans*	48691	4613
Pipelines, crude petroleum: Pipeline of Crude Oil—*trans*	48611	4612
Pipelines, natural gas: Pipeline of Natural Gas—*trans*	48621	4922
Pipelines, refined petroleum: Pipeline of Refined—*trans*	48691	4613
Pipes, fuel–motor vehicle: Gasoline Engine and Engine Parts—*mfg*	336312	3714
Motor Vehicle Parts, All Other—*mfg*	336399	3714
Pipes, organ: Musical Instrument—*mfg*	339992	3931
Pipes, smokers': Nondurable Goods, Other Miscellaneous—*whlse*	42299	5199
Pipestone mining: Crushed and Broken Stone and Quarrying,		
Other—*mining*	212319	1499
Non-Metallic Mineral, All Other—*mining*	212399	1499
Piping systems, metal–for pulp, paper, and chemical industries:		
Fabricated Pipe and Pipe Fitting—*mfg*	332996	3498
Piping, plumbing–contractors: Plumbing, Heating and		
Air-Conditioning Contractors—*const*	23511	1711
Piques, cotton: Broadwoven Fabric Mills—*mfg*	31321	2211
Pistachio groves and farms: Tree Nut Farming—*ag*	111335	173
Pistols and parts, except toy: Small Arms—*mfg*	332994	3484
Pistols, depth charge release: Ordnance and Accessories, Other—*mfg*	332995	3489
Pistols, toy: Game, Toy, and Children's Vehicle—*mfg*	339932	3944
Pistons and piston rings: Carburetor, Piston, Piston Ring and		
Valve—*mfg*	336311	3592
Pistons and valves, industrial: Industrial Machinery and		
Equipment—*whlse*	42183	5085
Industrial Supplies—*whlse*	42184	5085
Pit charcoal: Gum and Wood Chemical—*mfg*	325191	2861

Pitch, product of coal tar distillation: Cyclic Crude and Intermediate—*mfg*	325192	2865
Petrochemical—*mfg*	32511	2865
Pitch, roofing: Asphalt Shingle and Coating Materials—*mfg*	324122	2952
Pitch, wood: Gum and Wood Chemical—*mfg*	325191	2861
Pitchblende mining: Uranium-Radium-Vanadium Ore—*mining*	212291	1094
Pitometers: Measuring and Controlling Device, Other—*mfg*	334519	3829
Surgical and Medical Instrument—*mfg*	339112	3829
Pituitary gland derivatives–bulk, uncompounded: Medicinal and Botanical—*mfg*	325411	2833
Pituitary gland pharmaceutical preparations: Pharmaceutical Preparation—*mfg*	325412	2834
Pivots, power transmission: Mechanical Power Transmission Equipment—*mfg*	333613	3568
Pizza mixes and doughs: Flour Mixes and Dough from Purchased Flour—*mfg*	311822	2045
Pizza mixes and prepared dough: Flour Milling—*mfg*	311211	2041
Pizza parlors: Cafeterias—*accom*	722212	5812
Caterers—*accom*	72232	5812
Foodservice Contractors—*accom*	72231	5812
Full-Service Restaurants—*accom*	72211	5812
Limited-Service Restaurants—*accom*	722211	5812
Snack and Nonalcoholic Beverage Bars—*accom*	722213	5812
Theater Companies and Dinner Theaters—*arts*	71111	5812
Pizza, frozen: Frozen Specialty Food—*mfg*	311412	2038
Pizza, refrigerated–not frozen: Food, All Other Miscellaneous—*mfg*	311999	2099
Pizzerias: Cafeterias—*accom*	722212	5812
Caterers—*accom*	72232	5812
Foodservice Contractors—*accom*	72231	5812
Full-Service Restaurants—*accom*	72211	5812
Limited-Service Restaurants—*accom*	722211	5812
Snack and Nonalcoholic Beverage Bars—*accom*	722213	5812
Theater Companies and Dinner Theaters—*arts*	71111	5812
Placemats, plastics and textiles: Household Textile Product Mills, Other—*mfg*	314129	2392
Placer gold mining: Gold Ore—*mining*	212221	1041
Plaids, cotton: Broadwoven Fabric Mills—*mfg*	31321	2211
Planar triode tubes: Electron Tube—*mfg*	334411	3671
Planers, bituminous: Construction Machinery—*mfg*	33312	3531
Overhead Traveling Crane, Hoist and Monorail System—*mfg*	333923	3531
Railroad Rolling Stock—*mfg*	33651	3531
Planers, metal cutting: Machine Tool (Metal Cutting Types)—*mfg*	333512	3541
Planers, woodworking: Sawmill and Woodworking Machinery—*mfg*	33321	3553
Planes, pnnters': Printing Machinery and Equipment—*mfg*	333293	3555
Planes, woodworking–hand: Hand and Edge Tool—*mfg*	332212	3423
Planetaria: Historical Sites—*arts*	71212	8412
Museums—*arts*	71211	8412
Planing mill machinery-mig: Sawmill and Woodworking Machinery—*mfg*	33321	3553
Planing mill products and lumber dealers: Building Material Dealers, Other—*retail*	44419	5211
Home Centers—*retail*	44411	5211
Planing mills, independent–except millwork: Cut Stock, Resawing Lumber, and Planing—*mfg*	321912	2421
Millwork (including Flooring), Other—*mfg*	321918	2421
Sawmills—*mfg*	321113	2421
Wood Product, All Other Miscellaneous—*mfg*	321999	2421
Planing mills, millwork: Millwork (including Flooring), Other—*mfg*	321918	2431
Wood Window and Door—*mfg*	321911	2431
Planning and development of housing programs: Housing Programs, Administration of—*pub*	92511	9531
Planographing: Lithographic Printing, Commercial—*mfg*	323110	2752
Quick Printing—*mfg*	323114	2752
Plant food: Nondurable Goods, Other Miscellaneous—*whlse*	42299	5199
Plant foods, mixed–made in plants producing nitrogenous fertilizer materials: Nitrogenous Fertilizer—*mfg*	325311	2873
Plant foods, mixed–made in plants producing phosphatic fertilizer materials: Phosphatic Fertilizer—*mfg*	325312	2874
Plant hormones: Pesticide and Other Agricultural Chemical—*mfg*	32532	2879
Plantain farms: Fruit and Tree Nut Combination Farming—*ag*	111336	179
Noncitrus Fruit Farming, Other—*ag*	111339	179
Planters, plastics: Plastics Pipe and Pipe Fitting—*mfg*	326122	3089
Plastics Product, All Other—*mfg*	326199	3089
Unsupported Plastics Profile Shape—*mfg*	326121	3089
Planting crops, with or without fertilizing: Nonscheduled Air, Other—*trans*	481219	721
Soil Preparation, Planting, and Cultivating—*ag*	115112	721
Planting machinery and equipment: Farm and Garden Machinery and Equipment—*whlse*	42182	5083
Outdoor Power Equipment Stores—*retail*	44421	5083
Planting machines, agricultural: Farm Machinery and Equipment—*mfg*	333111	3523
Plants and foliage, artificial–made from purchased glass: Glass Product Made of Purchased Glass—*mfg*	327215	3231
Plants, live–rental and leasing: Consumer Goods Rental, All Other—*real*	532299	7359
Plants, ornamental–growing of: Floriculture Production—*ag*	111422	181
Nursery and Tree Production—*ag*	111421	181
Plants, potted: Florists—*retail*	45311	5992
Flower, Nursery Stock and Florists' Supplies—*whlse*	42293	5193
Nursery and Garden Centers—*retail*	44422	5193
Plants, potted–growing of: Floriculture Production—*ag*	111422	181
Nursery and Tree Production—*ag*	111421	181
Plaques, picture–laminated: Wood Product, All Other Miscellaneous—*mfg*	321999	3999
Plaques–clay, plaster, or papier-mache factory production only: Gypsum and Gypsum Product—*mfg*	32742	3299
Nonmetallic Mineral Product, All Other Miscellaneous—*mfg*	327999	3299

ALPHABETICAL INDEX	NAICS	SIC
Plasma jet spray metal forming machines: Machine Tool (Metal Forming Types)—*mfg*	333513	3542
Plasma process metal cutting machines, except welding machines: Machine Tool (Metal Cutting Types)—*mfg*	333512	3541
Plasmapheresis centers: Blood and Organ Banks—*hlth*	621991	8099
Plasmas: Biological Product (except Diagnostic)—*mfg*	325414	2836
Plaster: Brick, Stone and Related Material—*whlse*	42132	5032
Building Material Dealers, Other—*retail*	44419	5032
Plaster and plasterboard, gypsum: Gypsum and Gypsum Product—*mfg*	32742	3275
Plaster mixers: Construction Machinery—*mfg*	33312	3531
Overhead Traveling Crane, Hoist and Monorail System—*mfg*	333923	3531
Railroad Rolling Stock—*mfg*	33651	3531
Plaster of paris: Gypsum and Gypsum Product—*mfg*	32742	3275
Plaster work, ornamental and architectural: Gypsum and Gypsum Product—*mfg*	32742	3299
Nonmetallic Mineral Product, All Other Miscellaneous—*mfg*	327999	3299
Plaster, dental: Dental Equipment and Supplies—*mfg*	339114	3843
Plaster, gypsum: Gypsum and Gypsum Product—*mfg*	32742	3275
Plaster, patching–household: Basic Organic Chemical, All Other—*mfg*	325199	2899
Chemical Product, All Other Miscellaneous—*mfg*	325998	2899
Plastering accessories, metal: Fabricated Structural Metal—*mfg*	332312	3449
Metal Window and Door—*mfg*	332321	3449
Ornamental and Architectural Metal Work—*mfg*	332323	3449
Roll Forming, Custom—*mfg*	332114	3449
Plastering, plain or ornamental–contractors: Drywall, Plastering, Acoustical and Insulation Contractors—*const*	23542	1742
Plasters, adhesive–medicated or nonmedicated: Surgical Appliance and Supplies—*mfg*	339113	3842
Plastic coating of metals for the trade: Costume Jewelry and Novelty—*mfg*	339914	3479
Jewelry (except Costume)—*mfg*	339911	3479
Metal Coating, Engraving (except Jewelry and Silverware), and Allied Services to Manufacturers—*mfg*	332812	3479
Silverware and Plated Ware—*mfg*	339912	3479
Plastic fire clay mining: Clay and Ceramic and Refractory Minerals—*mining*	212325	1459
Plastic surgeons, offices of: Freestanding Ambulatory Surgical and Emergency Centers—*hlth*	621493	8011
HMO Medical Centers—*hlth*	621491	8011
Physicians (except Mental Health Specialists), Offices Of—*hlth*	621111	8011
Physicians, Mental Health Specialists, Offices Of—*hlth*	621112	8011
Plasticizers, organic–cyclic and acyclic: Basic Organic Chemical, All Other—*mfg*	325199	2869
Plastics and Rubber Products Manufacturing	**326**	
Plastics base paints and varnishes: Paint and Coating—*mfg*	32551	2851
Plastics basic shapes: Plastics Materials and Basic Forms and Shapes—*whlse*	42261	5162
Plastics Bottle Manufacturing	**32616**	**3085**
Plastics casting, for the trade: Plastics Pipe and Pipe Fitting—*mfg*	326122	3089
Plastics Product, All Other—*mfg*	326199	3089
Unsupported Plastics Profile Shape—*mfg*	326121	3089
Plastics coated fabrics: Fabric Coating Mills—*mfg*	31332	2295
Plastics film: Plastics Materials and Basic Forms and Shapes—*whlse*	42261	5162
Plastics film and sheet, unsupported: Unsupported Plastics Film and Sheet (except Packaging)—*mfg*	326113	3081
Plastics film, coated or laminated–for packaging: Coated and Laminated Packaging Paper and Plastics Film—*mfg*	322221	2671
Unsupported Plastics Packaging Film and Sheet—*mfg*	326112	2671
Plastics fire clay bricks: Clay Refractory—*mfg*	327124	3255
Plastics foam: Nondurable Goods, Other Miscellaneous—*whlse*	42299	5199
Plastics gowns: Apparel Accessories and Apparel, Other—*mfg*	315999	2385
Infants' Cut and Sew Apparel—*mfg*	315291	2385
Men's and Boys' Cut and Sew Apparel Contractors—*mfg*	315211	2385
Men's and Boys' Cut and Sew Other Outerwear—*mfg*	315228	2385
Men's and Boys' Cut and Sew Suit, Coat and Overcoat—*mfg*	315222	2385
Women's and Girls' Cut and Sew Apparel Contractors—*mfg*	315212	2385
Women's and Girls' Cut and Sew Other Outerwear—*mfg*	315238	2385
Women's and Girls' Cut and Sew Suit, Coat, Tailored Jacket and Skirt—*mfg*	315234	2385
Plastics laminated over particleboard (fixture tops): Architectural Woodwork and Millwork, Custom—*mfg*	337212	2541
Showcase, Partition, Shelving, and Locker—*mfg*	337215	2541
Wood Kitchen Cabinet and Counter Top—*mfg*	33711	2541
Plastics Material and Resin Manufacturing	**325211**	**2821**
Plastics materials: Plastics Materials and Basic Forms and Shapes—*whlse*	42261	5162
Plastics Materials and Basic Forms and Shapes Wholesalers	**42261**	**5162**
Plastics molding, for the trade: Plastics Pipe and Pipe Fitting—*mfg*	326122	3089
Plastics Product, All Other—*mfg*	326199	3089
Unsupported Plastics Profile Shape—*mfg*	326121	3089
Plastics Pipe and Pipe Fitting Manufacturing	**326122**	**3089**
Plastics Pipe, Pipe Fitting, and Unsupported Profile Shape Manufacturing	**32612**	
Plastics Plumbing Fixture Manufacturing	**326191**	**3088**
Plastics Product Manufacturing	**3261**	
Plastics Product Manufacturing, All Other	**326199**	**3999**
Plastics Product Manufacturing, Other	**32619**	
Plastics refractories, clay: Clay Refractory—*mfg*	327124	3255
Plastics refractories, nonclay: Nonclay Refractory—*mfg*	327125	3297
Plastics resins: Plastics Materials and Basic Forms and Shapes—*whlse*	42261	5162

Description	NAICS	SIC
Plastics resins, custom compounding of: Compounding of Purchased Resin, Custom—*mfg*	325991	3087
Plastics scrap: Recyclable Material—*whlse*	42193	5093
Plastics sheet and rods: Plastics Materials and Basic Forms and Shapes—*whlse*	42261	5162
Plastics wall tile installation-contractors: Trade Contractors, All Other Special—*const*	23599	1799
Plastics working machinery: Industrial Machinery, All Other—*mfg*	333298	3559
Machinery, Other Commercial and Service Industry—*mfg*	333319	3559
Rubber and Plastics Industry Machinery—*mfg*	33322	3559
Plastics, Foil, and Coated Paper Bag Manufacturing	**322223**	**2673**
Plastics, laminated–plate, rods, tubes, profiles and sheet, except flexible packaging: Laminated Plastics Plate, Sheet and Shape—*mfg*	32613	3083
Plastisol coating compound: Paint and Coating—*mfg*	32551	2851
Plate glass: Building Material Dealers, Other—*retail*	44419	5039
Construction Material, Other—*whlse*	42139	5039
Plate glass blanks for optical or ophthalmic uses: Flat Glass—*mfg*	327211	3211
Plate glass insurance: Direct Property and Casualty Insurance Carriers—*fin*	524126	6331
Insurance Funds, Other—*fin*	52519	6331
Reinsurance Carriers—*fin*	52413	6331
Plate glass, polished and rough: Flat Glass—*mfg*	327211	3211
Plate holders, photographic: Photographic and Photocopying Equipment—*mfg*	333315	3861
Photographic Film, Paper, Plate and Chemical—*mfg*	325992	3861
Plate printing: Digital Printing—*mfg*	323115	2759
Flexographic Printing, Commercial—*mfg*	323112	2759
Printing, Other Commercial—*mfg*	323119	2759
Quick Printing—*mfg*	323114	2759
Plate rolling mill machinery: Rolling Mill Machinery and Equipment—*mfg*	333516	3547
Plate Work and Fabricated Structural Product Manufacturing	**33231**	
Plate Work Manufacturing	**332313**	**3443**
Plate work, fabricated–cutting, punching, bending, and shaping: Air-Conditioning and Warm Air Heating Equipment and Commercial and Industrial Refrigeration Equipment—*mfg*	333415	3443
Metal Tank (Heavy Gauge)—*mfg*	33242	3443
Plate Work—*mfg*	332313	3443
Power Boiler and Heat Exchanger—*mfg*	33241	3443
Plate, laminated plastics: Laminated Plastics Plate, Sheet and Shape—*mfg*	32613	3083
Plated ware–flatware, hollow ware, toiletware, ecclesiastical ware, etc: Cutlery and Flatware (except Precious)—*mfg*	332211	3914
Silverware and Plated Ware—*mfg*	339912	3914
Plateless engraving: Digital Printing—*mfg*	323115	2759
Flexographic Printing, Commercial—*mfg*	323112	2759
Printing, Other Commercial—*mfg*	323119	2759
Quick Printing—*mfg*	323114	2759
Platens, except printers'–solid or covered rubber: Fabric Coating Mills—*mfg*	31332	3069
Rubber Product, All Other—*mfg*	326299	3069
Plates and cylinders, rotogravure printing–preparation of: Prepress Services—*mfg*	323122	2796
Plates for printing, embossing of: Prepress Services—*mfg*	323122	2796
Plates, addressing: Lead Pencil and Art Good—*mfg*	339942	3579
Office Machinery—*mfg*	333313	3579
Watch, Clock, and Part—*mfg*	334518	3579
Plates, aluminum: Aluminum Sheet, Plate and Foil—*mfg*	331315	3353
Plates, bone: Surgical and Medical Instrument—*mfg*	339112	3841
Plates, copper and copper alloy: Copper Rolling, Drawing and Extruding—*mfg*	331421	3351
Plates, dinnerware, plastics–except foam: Plastics Pipe and Pipe Fitting—*mfg*	326122	3089
Plastics Product, All Other—*mfg*	326199	3089
Unsupported Plastics Profile Shape—*mfg*	326121	3089
Plates, face (wiring devices): Noncurrent-Carrying Wiring Device—*mfg*	335932	3644
Plates, foamed plastics: Polystyrene Foam Product—*mfg*	32614	3086
Urethane and Other Foam Product (except Polystyrene)—*mfg*	32615	3086
Plates, lithographic–preparation of: Prepress Services—*mfg*	323122	2796
Plates, made in steel works or rolling mills: Iron and Steel Mills—*mfg*	331111	3312
Petroleum and Coal Productsa, All Other—*mfg*	324199	3312
Plates, metal: Metal Service Centers and Offices—*whlse*	42151	5051
Plates, metal–engravers': Printing Machinery and Equipment—*mfg*	333293	3555
Plates, paper–except those made from pressed or molded pulp: Non-Folding Sanitary Food Container—*mfg*	322215	2656
Plates, photoengraving: Prepress Services—*mfg*	323122	2796
Plates, photographic–sensitieed: Photographic and Photocopying Equipment—*mfg*	333315	3861
Photographic Film, Paper, Plate and Chemical—*mfg*	325992	3861
Plates, pressed and molded pulp: Coated and Laminated Paper—*mfg*	322222	2679
Converted Paper Product, All Other—*mfg*	322298	2679
Die-Cut Paper and Paperboard Office Supplies—*mfg*	322231	2679
Non-Folding Sanitary Food Container—*mfg*	322215	2679
Plates, printers'–of all materials: Printing Machinery and Equipment—*mfg*	333293	3555
Plates, printing–preparation of: Prepress Services—*mfg*	323122	2796
Plates–lead, magnesium, nickel, zinc, and their alloys: Nonferrous Metal (except Copper and Aluminum) Rolling, Drawing and Extruding—*mfg*	331491	3356
Platforms, cargo–metal: Fabricated Metal Product, All Other Miscellaneous—*mfg*	332999	3537
Industrial Truck, Tractor, Trailer and Stacker Machinery—*mfg*	333924	3537
Metal Container, Other—*mfg*	332439	3537
Plating compounds: Basic Organic Chemical, All Other—*mfg*	325199	2899
Chemical Product, All Other Miscellaneous—*mfg*	325998	2899

ALPHABETICAL INDEX	NAICS	SIC
Plating of metals and formed products, for the trade: Electroplating, Plating, Polishing, Anodizing and Coloring—*mfg*	332813	3471
Platinum and platinum alloy sheets and tubing: Nonferrous Metal (except Copper and Aluminum) Rolling, Drawing and Extruding—*mfg*	331491	3356
Platinum and platinum base alloy foil: Fabricated Metal Product, All Other Miscellaneous—*mfg*	332999	3497
Laminated Aluminum Foil for Flexible Packaging Uses—*mfg*	322225	3497
Platinum group ore mining: Metal Ore, All Other—*mining*	212299	1099
Platinum-group metals refining, primary: Primary Smelting and Refining of Nonferrous Metal (except Copper and Aluminum)—*mfg*	331419	3339
Platinum-group metals rolling, drawing, and extruding: Nonferrous Metal (except Copper and Aluminum) Rolling, Drawing and Extruding—*mfg*	331491	3356
Platinum-group metals smelting and refining, secondary: Secondary Smelting and Alloying of Aluminum—*mfg*	331314	3341
Secondary Smelting, Refining, and Alloying of Nonferrous Metal (except Copper and Aluminum)—*mfg*	331492	3341
Playground equipment: Sporting and Athletic Goods—*mfg*	33992	3949
Sporting Goods Stores—*retail*	45111	5941
Playing cards: Toy and Hobby Goods and Supplies—*whlse*	42192	5092
Playing cards, lithographed: Lithographic Printing, Commercial—*mfg*	323110	2752
Quick Printing—*mfg*	323114	2752
Playing cards, printed–except lithographed or gravure: Digital Printing—*mfg*	323115	2759
Flexographic Printing, Commercial—*mfg*	323112	2759
Printing, Other Commercial—*mfg*	323119	2759
Quick Printing—*mfg*	323114	2759
Playing cards–gravure printing: Gravure Printing, Commercial—*mfg*	323111	2754
Playpens, children's–metal: Metal Household Furniture—*mfg*	337124	2514
Playpens, children's–wood: Nonupholstered Wood Household Furniture—*mfg*	337122	2511
Plays (road companies and stock companies): Theater Companies and Dinner Theaters—*arts*	71111	7922
Playsuits: Apparel Accessories and Apparel, Other—*mfg*	315999	2339
Cut and Sew Apparel, All Other—*mfg*	315299	2339
Women's and Girls' Cut and Sew Apparel Contractors—*mfg*	315212	2339
Women's and Girls' Cut and Sew Other Outerwear—*mfg*	315238	2339
Pleating, for the trade: Men's and Boys' Cut and Sew Apparel Contractors—*mfg*	315211	2395
Textile Product Mills, All Other Miscellaneous—*mfg*	314999	2395
Women's and Girls' Cut and Sew Apparel Contractors—*mfg*	315212	2395
Pliers (handtools): Hand and Edge Tool—*mfg*	332212	3423
Pliers, dental: Dental Equipment and Supplies—*mfg*	339114	3843
Plinth blocks, precast terrazzo: Concrete Block and Brick—*mfg*	327331	3271

ALPHABETICAL INDEX	NAICS	SIC
Plioflim bags: Plastics, Foil, and Coated Paper Bag—*mfg*	322223	2673
Unsupported Plastics Bag—*mfg*	326111	2673
Plisse crepe, cotton: Broadwoven Fabric Mills—*mfg*	31321	2211
Plisse printing of cotton broadwoven fabrics: Broadwoven Fabric Finishing Mills—*mfg*	313311	2261
Plisse printing of manmade fiber and silk broadwoven fabrics: Broadwoven Fabric Finishing Mills—*mfg*	313311	2262
Plotter controllers, computer peripheral equipment: Computer Peripheral Equipment, Other—*mfg*	334119	3577
Plotters, computer: Computer Peripheral Equipment, Other—*mfg*	334119	3577
Plotting boards (sighting and fire control equipment): Optical Instrument and Lens—*mfg*	333314	3827
Plowing: Soil Preparation, Planting, and Cultivating—*ag*	115112	711
Plows (garden tractor equipment): Hand and Edge Tool—*mfg*	332212	3524
Lawn and Garden Tractor and Home Lawn and Garden Equipment—*mfg*	333112	3524
Plows, agricultural–disc, moldboard, chisel, etc.: Farm Machinery and Equipment—*mfg*	333111	3523
Plows, coal: Mining Machinery and Equipment—*mfg*	333131	3532
Plows, construction–excavating and grading: Construction Machinery—*mfg*	33312	3531
Overhead Traveling Crane, Hoist and Monorail System—*mfg*	333923	3531
Railroad Rolling Stock—*mfg*	33651	3531
Plows, snow (motor vehicles): Automobile—*mfg*	336111	3711
Heavy Duty Truck—*mfg*	33612	3711
Light Truck and Utility Vehicle—*mfg*	336112	3711
Military Armored Vehicle, Tank and Tank Component—*mfg*	336992	3711
Motor Vehicle Body—*mfg*	336211	3711
Plugging and abandoning wells on a contract basis: Oil and Gas Operations Support Activities—*mining*	213112	1389
Plugs, drain–magnetic-metal: Fabricated Metal Product, All Other Miscellaneous—*mfg*	332999	3499
Plugs, ear and nose: Surgical Appliance and Supplies—*mfg*	339113	3842
Plugs, electric: Current-Carrying Wiring Device—*mfg*	335931	3643
Plugs, wood: Manufacturing, All Other Miscellaneous—*mfg*	339999	2499
Wood Container and Pallet—*mfg*	32192	2499
Wood Product, All Other Miscellaneous—*mfg*	321999	2499
Plum orchards and farms: Apple Orchards—*ag*	111331	175
Noncitrus Fruit Farming, Other—*ag*	111339	175
Plum pudding: Canning, Specialty—*mfg*	311422	2032
Food, All Other Miscellaneous—*mfg*	311999	2032
Plumbago–ground, refined, or blended: Ground or Treated Mineral and Earth—*mfg*	327992	3295
Plumbers' brass goeds: Fabricated Metal Product, All Other Miscellaneous—*mfg*	332999	3432
Plumbing Fixture Fitting and Trim—*mfg*	332913	3432

Description	NAICS	SIC
Plumbers' brass goods, fittings, and valves: Building Material Dealers, Other—*retail*	44419	5074
Plumbing and Heating Equipment and Supplies (Hydronics)—*whlse*	42172	5074
Plumbers' handtools: Hand and Edge Tool—*mfg*	332212	3423
Plumbers' rubber goods: Fabric Coating Mills—*mfg*	31332	3069
Rubber Product, All Other—*mfg*	326299	3069
Plumbing and Heating Equipment and Supplies (Hydronics) Wholesalers	**42172**	**5074**
Plumbing and heating valves: Building Material Dealers, Other—*retail*	44419	5074
Plumbing and Heating Equipment and Supplies (Hydronics)—*whlse*	42172	5074
Plumbing and heating valves, metal: Fabricated Metal Product, All Other Miscellaneous—*mfg*	332999	3494
Other Metal Valve and Pipe Fitting, Other—*mfg*	332919	3494
Plumbing and heating–contractors: Plumbing, Heating and Air-Conditioning Contractors—*const*	23511	1711
Plumbing Fixture Fitting and Trim Manufacturing	**332913**	**3432**
Plumbing fixture fittings and trim: Fabricated Metal Product, All Other Miscellaneous—*mfg*	332999	3432
Plumbing Fixture Fitting and Trim—*mfg*	332913	3432
Plumbing fixture forgings, nonferrous–not made in hot-rolling mills: Nonferrous Forging—*mfg*	332112	3463
Plumbing fixtures, equipment, and supplies: Building Material Dealers, Other—*retail*	44419	5074
Plumbing and Heating Equipment and Supplies (Hydronics)—*whlse*	42172	5074
Plumbing fixtures, plastics: Plastics Plumbing Fixture—*mfg*	326191	3088
Plumbing fixtures, vitreous china: Vitreous China Plumbing Fixture and China and Earthenware Fittings and Bathroom Accessories—*mfg*	327111	3261
Plumbing fixtures–enameled iron, cast iron, and pressed metal: Enameled Iron and Metal Sanitary Ware—*mfg*	332998	3431
Plumbing repair–contractors: Plumbing, Heating and Air-Conditioning Contractors—*const*	23511	1711
Plumbing, Heating and Air-Conditioning Contractors	**2351**	
Plumbing, Heating and Air-Conditioning Contractors	**23511**	**1711**
Plumbing, with or without sheet metalwork–contractors: Plumbing, Heating and Air-Conditioning Contractors—*const*	23511	1711
Plushes, cotton: Broadwoven Fabric Mills—*mfg*	31321	2211
Plushes, manmade fiber and silk: Broadwoven Fabric Mills—*mfg*	31321	2221
Plywood: Building Material Dealers, Other—*retail*	44419	5031
Plywood, hardwood or hardwood faced: Hardwood Veneer and Plywood—*mfg*	321211	2435
Plywood, softwood: Softwood Veneer and Plywood—*mfg*	321212	2436
Pneumatic casings (rubber tires): Tire (except Retreading)—*mfg*	326211	3011
Pneumatic controllers, industrial process type: Instruments and Related Products for Measuring, Displaying, and Controlling Industrial Process Variables—*mfg*	334513	3823
Pneumatic cylinders, fluid power: Fluid Power Cylinder and Actuator—*mfg*	333995	3593
Pneumatic hose assemblies: Fluid Power Valve and Hose Fitting—*mfg*	332912	3492
Pneumatic hose, rubber or rubberized fabric–e.g., air brake and air line: Rubber and Plastics Hoses and Belting—*mfg*	32622	3052
Pneumatic mattresses: Canvas and Related Product Mills—*mfg*	314912	2394
Pneumatic relays, air-conditioning type: Automatic Environmental Control for Residential, Commercial and Appliance Use—*mfg*	334512	3822
Pneumatic tube conveyor systems for general industrial use: Conveyor and Conveying Equipment—*mfg*	333922	3535
Pneumatic tube system installation–contractors: Building Equipment and Other Machinery Installation Contractors—*const*	23595	1796
Pneumatic valves, including aircraft–fluidpower-metal: Fluid Power Valve and Hose Fitting—*mfg*	332912	3492
Pocket knives: Cutlery and Flatware (except Precious)—*mfg*	332211	3421
Pocketbook linings: Apparel Accessories and Apparel, Other—*mfg*	315999	2396
Textile Product Mills, All Other Miscellaneous—*mfg*	314999	2396
Pocketbook repair shops: Personal and Household Goods Repair and Maintenance, Other—*serv*	81149	7699
Pocketbooks, men's–regardless of material: Personal Leather Good (except Women's Handbag and Purse)—*mfg*	316993	3172
Pocketbooks, women's–of all materials, except precious metal: Women's Handbag and Purse—*mfg*	316992	3171
Pocketing twill, cotton: Broadwoven Fabric Mills—*mfg*	31321	2211
Pockets for men's suits and coats: Apparel Accessories and Apparel, Other—*mfg*	315999	2396
Podiatrists, offices and clinics of: Podiatrists, Offices Of—*hlth*	621391	8043
Podiatrists, Offices Of	**621391**	**8043**
Poetry associations: Civic and Social Organizations—*serv*	81341	8699
Point-of-sale devices: Computer Peripheral Equipment, Other—*mfg*	334119	3578
Office Machinery—*mfg*	333313	3578
Pointing furs: Fur and Leather Apparel—*mfg*	315292	2371
Pointing, chamfering, and burring machines: Machine Tool (Metal Cutting Types)—*mfg*	333512	3541
Points, abrasive–dental: Dental Equipment and Supplies—*mfg*	339114	3843
Poison–ant, rat, roach, and rodent-household: Pesticide and Other Agricultural Chemical—*mfg*	32532	2879
Poker chips: Game, Toy, and Children's Vehicle—*mfg*	339932	3944
Polariscopes: Analytical Laboratory Instrument—*mfg*	334516	3826
Polarizens: Analytical Laboratory Instrument—*mfg*	334516	3826
Polarographic equipment: Analytical Laboratory Instrument—*mfg*	334516	3826
Pole cutting contractors: Logging—*ag*	11331	2411
Pole line construction–general contractors: Power and Communication Transmission Line—*const*	23492	1623

ALPHABETICAL INDEX	NAICS	SIC
Water, Sewer, and Pipeline—*const*	23491	1623
Pole line hardware: Building Material Dealers, Other—*retail*	44419	5063
Electrical Apparatus and Equipment, Wiring Supplies and Material—*whlse*	42161	5063
Noncurrent-Carrying Wiring Device—*mfg*	335932	3644
Pole line hardware forgings, ferrous–not made in rolling mills: Iron and Steel Forging—*mfg*	332111	3462
Pole line hardware forgings, nonferrous–not made in hot-rolling mills: Nonferrous Forging—*mfg*	332112	3463
Poles and pole crossarms, treated: Wood Preservation—*mfg*	321114	2491
Poles, concrete: Concrete Pipe—*mfg*	327332	3272
Concrete Product, Other—*mfg*	32739	3272
Nonmetallic Mineral Product, All Other Miscellaneous—*mfg*	327999	3272
Poles, curtain and drapery: Blind and Shade—*mfg*	33792	2591
Poles, cutting and preserving: Wood Preservation—*mfg*	321114	2491
Poles, wood–e.g., clothesline, tent, flag: Manufacturing, All Other Miscellaneous—*mfg*	339999	2499
Wood Container and Pallet—*mfg*	32192	2499
Wood Product, All Other Miscellaneous—*mfg*	321999	2499
Poles, wood–untreated: Logging—*ag*	11331	2411
Police departments: Police Protection—*pub*	92212	9221
Police hats and caps, except protective head gear: Hat, Cap and Millinery—*mfg*	315991	2353
Police officer's clubs, wood: Manufacturing, All Other Miscellaneous—*mfg*	339999	2499
Wood Container and Pallet—*mfg*	32192	2499
Wood Product, All Other Miscellaneous—*mfg*	321999	2499
Police Protection	**92212**	**9221**
Police supply stores: Stores (except Tobacco Stores), All Other Miscellaneous—*retail*	453998	5999
Police uniforms: Men's and Boys' Cut and Sew Apparel Contractors—*mfg*	315211	2311
Men's and Boys' Cut and Sew Suit, Coat and Overcoat—*mfg*	315222	2311
Policyholders' consulting service: Claims Adjusters—*fin*	524291	6411
Insurance Agencies and Brokerages—*fin*	52421	6411
Insurance Related Activities, All Other—*fin*	524298	6411
Third Party Administration for Insurance and Pension Funds—*fin*	524292	6411
Polish and Other Sanitation Good Manufacturing	**325612**	**2842**
Polishes–furniture, automobile, metal, shoe, and stove: Polish and Other Sanitation Good—*mfg*	325612	2842
Polishes–furniture, automobile, metal, shoe, etc.: Chemical and Allied Products, Other—*whlse*	42269	5169
Polishing and buffing machines (machine tools): Machine Tool (Metal Cutting Types)—*mfg*	333512	3541
Polishing and cleaning preparations: Polish and Other Sanitation Good—*mfg*	325612	2842
Polishing cloths, chemically treated: Polish and Other Sanitation Good—*mfg*	325612	2842
Polishing cloths, plain: Household Textile Product Mills, Other—*mfg*	314129	2392
Polishing felts, except woven: Broadwoven Fabric Mills—*mfg*	31321	2299
Narrow Fabric Mills—*mfg*	313221	2299
Nonwoven Fabric Mills—*mfg*	31323	2299
Textile and Fabric Finishing (except Broadwoven Fabric) Mills—*mfg*	313312	2299
Textile Product Mills, All Other Miscellaneous—*mfg*	314999	2299
Thread Mills—*mfg*	313113	2299
Yarn Spinning Mills—*mfg*	313111	2299
Polishing machines (machine tools): Machine Tool (Metal Cutting Types)—*mfg*	333512	3541
Polishing of metals and formed products, for the trade: Electroplating, Plating, Polishing, Anodizing and Coloring—*mfg*	332813	3471
Polishing of rice: Rice Milling—*mfg*	311212	2044
Polishing rouge (abrasive): Abrasive Product—*mfg*	32791	3291
Fabricated Metal Product, All Other Miscellaneous—*mfg*	332999	3291
Polishing wheels: Abrasive Product—*mfg*	32791	3291
Fabricated Metal Product, All Other Miscellaneous—*mfg*	332999	3291
Political Action Committees (PACs): Political Organizations—*serv*	81394	8651
Political campaign organizations: Political Organizations—*serv*	81394	8651
Political fund-raising, except on a contract or fee basis: Political Organizations—*serv*	81394	8651
Political Organizations	**81394**	**8651**
Political organizations and clubs: Political Organizations—*serv*	81394	8651
Pollack, catching of: Finfish Fishing—*ag*	114111	912
Pollen extracts, except in vitro and in vivo: Biological Product (except Diagnostic)—*mfg*	325414	2836
Pollinating: Nonscheduled Air, Other—*trans*	481219	721
Soil Preparation, Planting, and Cultivating—*ag*	115112	721
Pollution control agencies: Air and Water Resource and Solid Waste Management—*pub*	92411	9511
Pollution testing, except automotive emissions testing: Testing Laboratories—*prof*	54138	8734
Veterinary Services—*prof*	54194	8734
Polo equipment, except apparel and footwear: Sporting and Athletic Goods—*mfg*	33992	3949
Polo shirts: Men's and Boys' Cut and Sew Apparel Contractors—*mfg*	315211	2321
Men's and Boys' Cut and Sew Shirt (except Work Shirt)—*mfg*	315223	2321
Outerwear Knitting Mills—*mfg*	315191	2253
Polvisobutylenes: Plastics Material and Resin—*mfg*	325211	2821
Polyacrylonitrile resins: Plastics Material and Resin—*mfg*	325211	2821
Polyamide resins: Plastics Material and Resin—*mfg*	325211	2821
Polybutadienes: Synthetic Rubber—*mfg*	325212	2822

Description	NAICS	SIC
Polycarbonate resins: Plastics Material and Resin—*mfg*	325211	2821
Polyester broadwoven fabrics: Broadwoven Fabric Mills—*mfg*	31321	2221
Polyester fibers: Noncellulosic Organic Fiber—*mfg*	325222	2824
Polyester filament yarn–throwing, twisting, winding, or spooling: Textile and Fabric Finishing (except Broadwoven Fabric) Mills—*mfg*	313312	2282
Yarn Texturing, Throwing and Twisting Mills—*mfg*	313112	2282
Polyester film and sheet, unsupported: Unsupported Plastics Film and Sheet (except Packaging)—*mfg*	326113	3081
Polyester thread: Textile and Fabric Finishing (except Broadwoven Fabric) Mills—*mfg*	313312	2284
Thread Mills—*mfg*	313113	2284
Polyester yarn, made from purchased staple–spun: Yarn Spinning Mills—*mfg*	313111	2281
Polyesters: Plastics Material and Resin—*mfg*	325211	2821
Polyethylene broadwoven fabrics: Broadwoven Fabric Mills—*mfg*	31321	2221
Polyethylene film and sheet, unsupported: Unsupported Plastics Film and Sheet (except Packaging)—*mfg*	326113	3081
Polyethylene resins: Plastics Material and Resin—*mfg*	325211	2821
Polyethylenes, chlorosulfonated: Synthetic Rubber—*mfg*	325212	2822
Polygraph service: Armored Car Services—*admin*	561613	7381
Investigation Services—*admin*	561611	7381
Security Guards and Patrol Services—*admin*	561612	7381
Polyhexamethylenediamine adipamide resins: Plastics Material and Resin—*mfg*	325211	2821
Polyhydric alcohol esters and amines: Basic Organic Chemical, All Other—*mfg*	325199	2869
Ethyl Alcohol—*mfg*	325193	2869
Polyhydric alcohols: Basic Organic Chemical, All Other—*mfg*	325199	2869
Ethyl Alcohol—*mfg*	325193	2869
Polyisobutylene (synthetic rubber): Synthetic Rubber—*mfg*	325212	2822
Polyisobutylene-isoprene elastomers: Synthetic Rubber—*mfg*	325212	2822
Polymerization plastics, except fibers: Plastics Material and Resin—*mfg*	325211	2821
Polymethylene rubbers: Synthetic Rubber—*mfg*	325212	2822
Polypropylene broadwoven fabrics: Broadwoven Fabric Mills—*mfg*	31321	2221
Polypropylene filament yarn–throwing, twisting, winding, or spooling: Textile and Fabric Finishing (except Broadwoven Fabric) Mills—*mfg*	313312	2282
Yarn Texturing, Throwing and Twisting Mills—*mfg*	313112	2282
Polypropylene film and sheet, unsupported: Unsupported Plastics Film and Sheet (except Packaging)—*mfg*	326113	3081
Polypropylene resins: Plastics Material and Resin—*mfg*	325211	2821
Polypropylene yarn, made from purchased staple–spun: Yarn Spinning Mills—*mfg*	313111	2281
Polystyrene Foam Product Manufacturing	**32614**	**3086**
Polystyrene resins: Plastics Material and Resin—*mfg*	325211	2821
Polysulfides: Synthetic Rubber—*mfg*	325212	2822
Polyurethane coatings: Paint and Coating—*mfg*	32551	2851
Polyurethane resins: Plastics Material and Resin—*mfg*	325211	2821
Polyvinyl alcohol resins: Plastics Material and Resin—*mfg*	325211	2821
Polyvinyl chloride resins: Plastics Material and Resin—*mfg*	325211	2821
Polyvinyl ester fibers: Noncellulosic Organic Fiber—*mfg*	325222	2824
Polyvinyl film and sheet, unsupported: Unsupported Plastics Film and Sheet (except Packaging)—*mfg*	326113	3081
Polyvinyl halide resins: Plastics Material and Resin—*mfg*	325211	2821
Polyvinyl resins: Plastics Material and Resin—*mfg*	325211	2821
Polyvinylidene chloride fibers: Noncellulosic Organic Fiber—*mfg*	325222	2824
Pomegranate orchards and farms: Apple Orchards—*ag*	111331	175
Noncitrus Fruit Farming, Other—*ag*	111339	175
Pond construction–general contractors: Heavy, All Other—*const*	23499	1629
Industrial Nonbuilding Structure—*const*	23493	1629
Pongee, cotton: Broadwoven Fabric Mills—*mfg*	31321	2211
Pongee, manmade fiber and silk: Broadwoven Fabric Mills—*mfg*	31321	2221
Pontoens, aircraft: Aircraft Part and Auxiliary Equipment, Other—*mfg*	336413	3728
Fluid Power Valve and Hose Fitting—*mfg*	332912	3728
Pontoons, except aircraft and inflatable(rubber and plastics): Boat Building—*mfg*	336612	3732
Personal and Household Goods Repair and Maintenance, Other—*serv*	81149	3732
Pontoons, nonrigid–plastics: Plastics Pipe and Pipe Fitting—*mfg*	326122	3089
Plastics Product, All Other—*mfg*	326199	3089
Unsupported Plastics Profile Shape—*mfg*	326121	3089
Pontoons, rubber: Fabric Coating Mills—*mfg*	31332	3069
Rubber Product, All Other—*mfg*	326299	3069
Pony farms: Horse and Other Equine Production—*ag*	11292	272
Pool and billiards table stores: Sporting Goods Stores—*retail*	45111	5941
Pool balls, pockets, tables, and equipment: Sporting and Athletic Goods—*mfg*	33992	3949
Pool equipment and supplies: Sporting and Recreational Goods and Supplies—*whlse*	42191	5091
Pool parlors: Fitness and Recreational Sports Centers—*arts*	71394	7999
Pop safety valves, over 15 lbs. w.s.p.: Industrial Valve—*mfg*	332911	3491
Popcorn: Confectionery—*whlse*	42245	5145
Popcorn balls and candy covered popcorn products: Confectionery from Purchased Chocolate—*mfg*	31133	2064
Non-Chocolate Confectionery—*mfg*	31134	2064
Popcorn farms: Grain Farming, All Other—*ag*	111199	119
Popcorn poppers for home use–electric: Electric Housewares and Household Fan—*mfg*	335211	3634
Heating Equipment (except Electric and Warm Air Furnaces)—*mfg*	333414	3634
Popcorn stands: Confectionery and Nut Stores—*retail*	445292	5441
Popcorn, popped–except candy covered: Snack Food, Other—*mfg*	311919	2096
Poplin, cotton: Broadwoven Fabric Mills—*mfg*	31321	2211
Poplin,, manmade fiber: Broadwoven Fabric Mills—*mfg*	31321	2221

ALPHABETICAL INDEX	NAICS	SIC
Pops, dessert–frozen-flavored ice, fruit, pudding and gelatin: Ice Cream and Frozen Dessert—*mfg*	31152	2024
Popular music groups or artists: Independent Artists, Writers, and Performers—*arts*	71151	7929
Musical Groups and Artists—*arts*	71113	7929
Performing Arts Companies, Other—*arts*	71119	7929
Popup camper rental: Truck, Utility Trailer, and RV (Recreational Vehicle) Rental and Leasing—*real*	53212	7519
Popup campers: Automobile and Other Motor Vehicle—*whlse*	42111	5012
Porcelain cement, household: Adhesive—*mfg*	32552	2891
Porcelain Electrical Supply Manufacturing	**327113**	**3264**
Porcelain parts, molded–for electrical and electronic devices: Porcelain Electrical Supply—*mfg*	327113	3264
Porcelain, chemical: Vitreous China, Fine Earthenware and Other Pottery Product—*mfg*	327112	3269
Porch columns, wood: Millwork (including Flooring), Other—*mfg*	321918	2431
Wood Window and Door—*mfg*	321911	2431
Porch shades, wood slat: Blind and Shade—*mfg*	33792	2591
Porch swings, metal: Metal Household Furniture—*mfg*	337124	2514
Porch swings, wood: Nonupholstered Wood Household Furniture—*mfg*	337122	2511
Porch work, wood: Millwork (including Flooring), Other—*mfg*	321918	2431
Wood Window and Door—*mfg*	321911	2431
Pork: Animal (except Poultry) Slaughtering—*mfg*	311611	2011
Pork and beans, canned: Canning, Specialty—*mfg*	311422	2032
Food, All Other Miscellaneous—*mfg*	311999	2032
Pork rinds: Snack Food, Other—*mfg*	311919	2096
Pork–pickled, cured, salted, or smoked: Meat Processed from Carcasses—*mfg*	311612	2013
Port and Harbor Operations	**48831**	**4499**
Port authorities and districts-nonoperating: Air Traffic Control—*trans*	488111	9621
Transportation Programs, Regulation and Administration of—*pub*	92612	9621
Portable buildings, prefabricated metal: Prefabricated Metal Building and Component—*mfg*	332311	3448
Portable buildings, prefabricated wood: Prefabricated Wood Building—*mfg*	321992	2452
Portable chemical toilets (metal): Enameled Iron and Metal Sanitary Ware—*mfg*	332998	3431
Portable chemical toilets, plastics: Plastics Plumbing Fixture—*mfg*	326191	3088
Portable test meters: Electronic Coil, Transformer, and Other Inductor—*mfg*	334416	3825
Instrument for Measuring and Testing Electricity and Electrical Signals—*mfg*	334515	3825
Porter: Beer and Ale—*whlse*	42281	5181
Porter (alcoholic beverage): Breweries—*mfg*	31212	2082
Porter service: Personal Services, All Other—*serv*	81299	7299

ALPHABETICAL INDEX	NAICS	SIC
Portfolio Management	**52392**	**6371**
Portland cement: Cement—*mfg*	32731	3241
Portrait photographers: Photography Studios, Portrait—*prof*	541921	7221
Portraits: Durable Goods, Other Miscellaneous—*whlse*	42199	5099
Position emission tomography (PET scanner): Electromedical and Electrotherapeutic Apparatus—*mfg*	334510	3845
Irradiation Apparatus—*mfg*	334517	3845
Position indicators, airframe equipment–e.g., for landing gear, stabilizers: Search, Detection, Navigation, Guidance, Aeronautical, and Nautical System and Instrument—*mfg*	334511	3812
Positive displacement meters: Totalizing Fluid Meter and Counting Device—*mfg*	334514	3824
Post hole diggers, hand: Hand and Edge Tool—*mfg*	332212	3423
Post hole diggers, powered: Construction Machinery—*mfg*	33312	3531
Overhead Traveling Crane, Hoist and Monorail System—*mfg*	333923	3531
Railroad Rolling Stock—*mfg*	33651	3531
Post office collection boxes: Metal Container, Other—*mfg*	332439	3444
Sheet Metal Work—*mfg*	332322	3444
Post office construction–general contractors: Building, Commercial and Institutional—*const*	23332	1542
Post office contract stations: Private Mail Centers—*admin*	561431	7389
Post Production and Other Motion Picture and Video Industries	**51219**	
Postage meters: Lead Pencil and Art Good—*mfg*	339942	3579
Office Machinery—*mfg*	333313	3579
Watch, Clock, and Part—*mfg*	334518	3579
Postal screen wire equipment: Fabricated Wire Product, Other—*mfg*	332618	3496
Postal Service	**4911**	
Postal Service	**491**	
Postal Service	**49111**	**4311**
Postal service lock boxes, except wood: Showcase, Partition, Shelving, and Locker—*mfg*	337215	2542
Postal Service, U.S.: Postal Service—*trans*	49111	4311
Postcards, picture–except lithographed or gravure printed: Digital Printing—*mfg*	323115	2759
Flexographic Printing, Commercial—*mfg*	323112	2759
Printing, Other Commercial—*mfg*	323119	2759
Quick Printing—*mfg*	323114	2759
Postcards, picture–gravure printing: Gravure Printing, Commercial—*mfg*	323111	2754
Postcards, picture–lithographed: Lithographic Printing, Commercial—*mfg*	323110	2752
Quick Printing—*mfg*	323114	2752
Poster advertising service, outdoor: Display Advertising—*prof*	54185	7312
Poster advertising services, except outdoor: Advertising Material Distribution Services—*prof*	54187	7319
Advertising, Other Services Related to—*prof*	54189	7319
Display Advertising—*prof*	54185	7319

Description	NAICS	SIC
Media Buying Agencies—*prof*	54183	7319
Nonscheduled Air, Other—*trans*	481219	7319
Poster paper: Newsprint Mills—*mfg*	322122	2621
Paper (except Newsprint) Mills—*mfg*	322121	2621
Posters, including billboard–except lithographed or gravure: Digital Printing—*mfg*	323115	2759
Flexographic Printing, Commercial—*mfg*	323112	2759
Printing, Other Commercial—*mfg*	323119	2759
Quick Printing—*mfg*	323114	2759
Posters, lithographed: Lithographic Printing, Commercial—*mfg*	323110	2752
Quick Printing—*mfg*	323114	2752
Posters–gravure printing: Gravure Printing, Commercial—*mfg*	323111	2754
Postharvest Crop Activities (except Cotton Ginning)	**115114**	**723**
Posthole digging-contractors: Trade Contractors, All Other Special—*const*	23599	1799
Posts, bumping–railroad-forged (not made in rolling mills): Iron and Steel Forging—*mfg*	332111	3462
Posts, concrete: Concrete Pipe—*mfg*	327332	3272
Concrete Product, Other—*mfg*	32739	3272
Nonmetallic Mineral Product, All Other Miscellaneous—*mfg*	327999	3272
Posts, wood–hewn, round, or split: Logging—*ag*	11331	2411
Posts, wood–treated: Wood Preservation—*mfg*	321114	2491
Pot cheese: Fluid Milk—*mfg*	311511	2026
Potash alum: Basic Inorganic Chemical, All Other—*mfg*	325188	2819
Chemical Product, All Other Miscellaneous—*mfg*	325998	2819
Potash mining: Potash, Soda, and Borate Mineral—*mining*	212391	1474
Potash, caustic: Alkalies and Chlorine—*mfg*	325181	2812
Potash, Soda, and Borate Mineral Mining	**212391**	**1474**
Potassium aluminum sulfate: Basic Inorganic Chemical, All Other—*mfg*	325188	2819
Chemical Product, All Other Miscellaneous—*mfg*	325998	2819
Potassium bichromate and chromate: Basic Inorganic Chemical, All Other—*mfg*	325188	2819
Chemical Product, All Other Miscellaneous—*mfg*	325998	2819
Potassium bitartrate: Basic Organic Chemical, All Other—*mfg*	325199	2869
Ethyl Alcohol—*mfg*	325193	2869
Potassium bromide: Basic Inorganic Chemical, All Other—*mfg*	325188	2819
Chemical Product, All Other Miscellaneous—*mfg*	325998	2819
Potassium carbonate: Alkalies and Chlorine—*mfg*	325181	2812
Potassium chlorate: Basic Inorganic Chemical, All Other—*mfg*	325188	2819
Chemical Product, All Other Miscellaneous—*mfg*	325998	2819
Potassium chloride: Basic Inorganic Chemical, All Other—*mfg*	325188	2819
Chemical Product, All Other Miscellaneous—*mfg*	325998	2819
Potassium compounds mining: Potash, Soda, and Borate Mineral—*mining*	212391	1474
Potassium compounds, inorganic–except potassium hydroxide and carbonate: Basic Inorganic Chemical, All Other—*mfg*	325188	2819
Chemical Product, All Other Miscellaneous—*mfg*	325998	2819
Potassium cyanide: Basic Inorganic Chemical, All Other—*mfg*	325188	2819
Chemical Product, All Other Miscellaneous—*mfg*	325998	2819
Potassium hydroxide: Alkalies and Chlorine—*mfg*	325181	2812
Potassium hypochlorate: Basic Inorganic Chemical, All Other—*mfg*	325188	2819
Chemical Product, All Other Miscellaneous—*mfg*	325998	2819
Potassium iodide: Basic Inorganic Chemical, All Other—*mfg*	325188	2819
Chemical Product, All Other Miscellaneous—*mfg*	325998	2819
Potassium metal: Basic Inorganic Chemical, All Other—*mfg*	325188	2819
Chemical Product, All Other Miscellaneous—*mfg*	325998	2819
Potassium nitrate and sulfate: Basic Inorganic Chemical, All Other—*mfg*	325188	2819
Chemical Product, All Other Miscellaneous—*mfg*	325998	2819
Potassium permanganate: Basic Inorganic Chemical, All Other—*mfg*	325188	2819
Chemical Product, All Other Miscellaneous—*mfg*	325998	2819
Potato cellars: Farm Product Warehousing and Storage Facilities—*trans*	49313	4221
Potato chips: Confectionery—*whlse*	42245	5145
Potato chips and related corn snacks: Snack Food, Other—*mfg*	311919	2096
Potato curing: Postharvest Crop Activities (except Cotton Ginning)—*ag*	115114	723
Potato diggers, harvesters, and planters (agricultural machinery): Farm Machinery and Equipment—*mfg*	333111	3523
Potato Farming	**111211**	**134**
Potato farms, except sweet potato and yam: Potato Farming—*ag*	111211	134
Potato farms, Irish: Potato Farming—*ag*	111211	134
Potato farms, sweet: Crop Farming, All Other Miscellaneous—*ag*	111998	139
Hay Farming—*ag*	11194	139
Peanut Farming—*ag*	111992	139
Vegetable (except Potato) and Melon Farming, Other—*ag*	111219	139
Potato farms, yam: Crop Farming, All Other Miscellaneous—*ag*	111998	139
Hay Farming—*ag*	11194	139
Peanut Farming—*ag*	111992	139
Vegetable (except Potato) and Melon Farming, Other—*ag*	111219	139
Potato flakes, granules, and other dehydrated potato products: Dried and Dehydrated Food—*mfg*	311423	2034
Flour Milling—*mfg*	311211	2034
Potato mashers, made from purchased wire: Fabricated Wire Product, Other—*mfg*	332618	3496
Potato mashers, wood: Manufacturing, All Other Miscellaneous—*mfg*	339999	2499
Wood Container and Pallet—*mfg*	32192	2499
Wood Product, All Other Miscellaneous—*mfg*	321999	2499
Potato peelers, electric: Food Product Machinery—*mfg*	333294	3556
Potato peelers, hand: Cutlery and Flatware (except Precious)—*mfg*	332211	3421
Potato starch: Wet Corn Milling—*mfg*	311221	2046
Potato sticks: Snack Food, Other—*mfg*	311919	2096
Potatoes, dried–packaged with other ingredients: Dried and Dehydrated Food—*mfg*	311423	2099
Potatoes, fresh: Fresh Fruit and Vegetable—*whlse*	42248	5148
Potatoes, peeled for the trade: Perishable Prepared Food—*mfg*	311991	2099

ALPHABETICAL INDEX	NAICS	SIC
Potentiometric instruments, except industrial process type: Electronic Coil, Transformer, and Other Inductor—*mfg*	334416	3825
Instrument for Measuring and Testing Electricity and Electrical Signals—*mfg*	334515	3825
Potentiometric self-balancing instruments, except X-Y plotters: Instruments and Related Products for Measuring, Displaying, and Controlling Industrial Process Variables—*mfg*	334513	3823
Pots, melting–glass house-clay: Clay Refractory—*mfg*	327124	3255
Pots–annealing, melting, and smelting: Air-Conditioning and Warm Air Heating Equipment and Commercial and Industrial Refrigeration Equipment—*mfg*	333415	3443
Metal Tank (Heavy Gauge)—*mfg*	33242	3443
Plate Work—*mfg*	332313	3443
Power Boiler and Heat Exchanger—*mfg*	33241	3443
Potted meats: Meat Processed from Carcasses—*mfg*	311612	2013
Potted plants: Florists—*retail*	45311	5992
Pottery making machinery: Industrial Machinery, All Other—*mfg*	333298	3559
Machinery, Other Commercial and Service Industry—*mfg*	333319	3559
Pottery stores: Home Furnishings Stores, All Other—*retail*	442299	5719
Window Treatment Stores—*retail*	442291	5719
Pottery, Ceramics, and Plumbing Fixture Manufacturing	**32711**	
Pottery–art, garden, decorative, industrial, and laboratory: Vitreous China, Fine Earthenware and Other Pottery Product—*mfg*	327112	3269
Potting soil, mixed: Fertilizer (Mixing Only)—*mfg*	325314	2875
Pouches, tobacco–regardless of material: Personal Leather Good (except Women's Handbag and Purse)—*mfg*	316993	3172
Poultry and animal remedies: Pharmaceutical Preparation—*mfg*	325412	2834
Poultry and egg dealers: Food (Health) Supplement Stores—*retail*	446191	5499
Food Stores, All Other Specialty—*retail*	445299	5499
Limited-Service Restaurants—*accom*	722211	5499
Meat Markets—*retail*	44521	5499
Poultry and Egg Production	**1123**	
Poultry and Poultry Product Wholesalers	**42244**	**5144**
Poultry brooders, feeders, and waterers: Farm Machinery and Equipment—*mfg*	333111	3523
Poultry dealers: Food (Health) Supplement Stores—*retail*	446191	5499
Food Stores, All Other Specialty—*retail*	445299	5499
Limited-Service Restaurants—*accom*	722211	5499
Meat Markets—*retail*	44521	5499
Poultry equipment: Farm and Garden Machinery and Equipment—*whlse*	42182	5083
Outdoor Power Equipment Stores—*retail*	44421	5083
Poultry feeds, supplements, and concentrates: Animal Food, Other—*mfg*	311119	2048
Poultry Hatcheries	**11234**	**254**
Poultry netting, made from purchased wire: Fabricated Wire Product, Other—*mfg*	332618	3496
Poultry pies, frozen: Packaged Frozen Food—*whlse*	42242	5142
Poultry Processing	**311615**	**2015**
Poultry Production, Other	**11239**	**259**
Poultry products: Poultry and Poultry Product—*whlse*	42244	5144
Poultry vision control devices: Farm Machinery and Equipment—*mfg*	333111	3523
Poultry, frozen–packaged: Packaged Frozen Food—*whlse*	42242	5142
Poultry, processed–fresh, frozen, canned, or cooked: Food, All Other Miscellaneous—*mfg*	311999	2015
Poultry Processing—*mfg*	311615	2015
Poultry–live, dressed, or frozen (except packaged): Poultry and Poultry Product—*whlse*	42244	5144
Poultry–slaughtering and dressing: Food, All Other Miscellaneous—*mfg*	311999	2015
Poultry Processing—*mfg*	311615	2015
Powder bag loading: Ammunition (except Small Arms)—*mfg*	332993	3483
Powder metal products, custom molding: Fabricated Metal Product, All Other Miscellaneous—*mfg*	332999	3499
Powder Metallurgy Part Manufacturing	**332117**	**3499**
Powder testing chambers: General Purpose Machinery , All Other—*mfg*	333999	3569
Powder, blasting: Explosives—*mfg*	32592	2892
Powder, explosive–pellet, smokeless, and sporting: Explosives—*mfg*	32592	2892
Powder, metal–except artists' materials: Electroplating, Plating, Polishing, Anodizing and Coloring—*mfg*	332813	3399
Iron and Steel Mills—*mfg*	331111	3399
Secondary Smelting and Alloying of Aluminum—*mfg*	331314	3399
Secondary Smelting, Refining, and Alloying of Copper—*mfg*	331423	3399
Secondary Smelting, Refining, and Alloying of Nonferrous Metal (except Copper and Aluminum)—*mfg*	331492	3399
Powder–baby, face, talcum, and toilet: Soap and Other Detergent—*mfg*	325611	2844
Toilet Preparation—*mfg*	32562	2844
Powder-actuated hand tools: Power-Driven Hand Tool—*mfg*	333991	3546
Powders, drink: Flavoring Syrup and Concentrate—*mfg*	31193	2087
Food, All Other Miscellaneous—*mfg*	311999	2087
Spice and Extract—*mfg*	311942	2087
Powders, pharmaceutical: Pharmaceutical Preparation—*mfg*	325412	2834
Power and Communication Transmission Line Construction	**23492**	**1623**
Power Boiler and Heat Exchanger Manufacturing	**33241**	**3443**
Power boilers, industrial and marine: Air-Conditioning and Warm Air Heating Equipment and Commercial and Industrial Refrigeration Equipment—*mfg*	333415	3443
Metal Tank (Heavy Gauge)—*mfg*	33242	3443
Plate Work—*mfg*	332313	3443
Power Boiler and Heat Exchanger—*mfg*	33241	3443
Power circuit breakers: Switchgear and Switchboard Apparatus—*mfg*	335313	3613

Entry	NAICS	SIC
Power connectors: Switchgear and Switchboard Apparatus—*mfg*	335313	3613
Power conversion units, a.c to d.c.–static-electric: Electrical Equipment and Component, All Other Miscellaneous—*mfg*	335999	3629
Power cranes, draglines, and shovels: Construction Machinery—*mfg*	33312	3531
Overhead Traveling Crane, Hoist and Monorail System—*mfg*	333923	3531
Railroad Rolling Stock—*mfg*	33651	3531
Power factor meters: Electronic Coil, Transformer, and Other Inductor—*mfg*	334416	3825
Instrument for Measuring and Testing Electricity and Electrical Signals—*mfg*	334515	3825
Power fuses devices, 600 volts and over: Switchgear and Switchboard Apparatus—*mfg*	335313	3613
Power generating equipment installation–contractors: Building Equipment and Other Machinery Installation Contractors—*const*	23595	1796
Power generators: Motor and Generator—*mfg*	335312	3621
Power handtools: Hardware—*whlse*	42171	5072
Power laundries, family and commercial: Laundries, Family and Commercial—*serv*	812321	7211
Power line construction–general contractors: Power and Communication Transmission Line—*const*	23492	1623
Water, Sewer, and Pipeline—*const*	23491	1623
Power measuring equipment, electrical: Electronic Coil, Transformer, and Other Inductor—*mfg*	334416	3825
Instrument for Measuring and Testing Electricity and Electrical Signals—*mfg*	334515	3825
Power mowers: Nursery and Garden Centers—*retail*	44422	5261
Outdoor Power Equipment Stores—*retail*	44421	5261
Stores (except Tobacco Stores), All Other Miscellaneous—*retail*	453998	5261
Power plant construction–general contractors: Heavy, All Other—*const*	23499	1629
Industrial Nonbuilding Structure—*const*	23493	1629
Power plant machinery, except electrical: Industrial Machinery and Equipment—*whlse*	42183	5084
Power supplies, static, and variable frequency: Electronic Component, Other—*mfg*	334419	3679
Motor Vehicle Electrical and Electronic Equipment, Other—*mfg*	336322	3679
Printed Circuit/Electronics Assembly—*mfg*	334418	3679
Radio and Television Broadcasting and Wireless Communications Equipment—*mfg*	33422	3679
Power switchboards: Switchgear and Switchboard Apparatus—*mfg*	335313	3613
Power switching equipment: Switchgear and Switchboard Apparatus—*mfg*	335313	3613
Power tools: Hardware Stores—*retail*	44413	5251
Power transformers, electric: Power, Distribution and Specialty Transformer—*mfg*	335311	3612
Power transmission equipment, aircraft: Aircraft Part and Auxiliary Equipment, Other—*mfg*	336413	3728
Fluid Power Valve and Hose Fitting—*mfg*	332912	3728
Power transmission equipment, electric: Building Material Dealers, Other—*retail*	44419	5063
Electrical Apparatus and Equipment, Wiring Supplies and Material—*whlse*	42161	5063
Power transmission equipment, motor vehicle: Motor Vehicle Parts, All Other—*mfg*	336399	3714
Motor Vehicle Steering and Suspension Components (except Spring)—*mfg*	33633	3714
Motor Vehicle Transmission and Power Train Parts—*mfg*	33635	3714
Power transmission supplies, mechanical: Industrial Machinery and Equipment—*whlse*	42183	5085
Industrial Supplies—*whlse*	42184	5085
Power, Distribution and Specialty Transformer Manufacturing	**335311**	**3612**
Power, electric–generation transmission, or distribution: Electric Bulk Power Transmission and Control—*util*	221121	4911
Electric Power Distribution—*util*	221122	4911
Electric Power Generation, Other—*util*	221119	4911
Fossil Fuel Electric Power Generation—*util*	221112	4911
Hydroelectric Power Generation—*util*	221111	4911
Nuclear Electric Power Generation—*util*	221113	4911
Power-Driven Hand Tool Manufacturing	**333991**	**3546**
Pozzolana cement: Cement—*mfg*	32731	3241
Pozzolana mining: Crushed and Broken Stone and Quarrying, Other—*mining*	212319	1499
Non-Metallic Mineral, All Other—*mining*	212399	1499
Prayer shawls: Apparel Accessories and Apparel, Other—*mfg*	315999	2389
Precious metal mill shapes: Jewelry, Watch, Precious Stone and Precious Metal—*whlse*	42194	5094
Precious metal refining, primary: Primary Smelting and Refining of Nonferrous Metal (except Copper and Aluminum)—*mfg*	331419	3339
Precious metal smelting and refining, secondary: Secondary Smelting and Alloying of Aluminum—*mfg*	331314	3341
Secondary Smelting, Refining, and Alloying of Nonferrous Metal (except Copper and Aluminum)—*mfg*	331492	3341
Precious metals: Jewelry, Watch, Precious Stone and Precious Metal—*whlse*	42194	5094
Precious stones (gems): Jewelry, Watch, Precious Stone and Precious Metal—*whlse*	42194	5094
Precious stones mining: Crushed and Broken Stone and Quarrying, Other—*mining*	212319	1499
Non-Metallic Mineral, All Other—*mining*	212399	1499
Precipitators (process vessels), metal plate: Air-Conditioning and Warm Air Heating Equipment and Commercial and Industrial Refrigeration Equipment—*mfg*	333415	3443
Metal Tank (Heavy Gauge)—*mfg*	33242	3443
Plate Work—*mfg*	332313	3443
Power Boiler and Heat Exchanger—*mfg*	33241	3443
Precipitators, electrostatic: Air Purification Equipment—*mfg*	333411	3564
Industrial and Commercial Fan and Blower—*mfg*	333412	3564

Yarn Spinning Mills—*mfg*	313111	2299
Pressed logs of sawdust and other wood particles, nonpetroleum binder: Manufacturing, All Other Miscellaneous—*mfg*	339999	2499
Wood Container and Pallet—*mfg*	32192	2499
Wood Product, All Other Miscellaneous—*mfg*	321999	2499
Pressed metal products (stampings): Metal Stamping—*mfg*	332116	3469
Pressed products from wood pulp: Coated and Laminated Paper—*mfg*	322222	2679
Converted Paper Product, All Other—*mfg*	322298	2679
Die-Cut Paper and Paperboard Office Supplies—*mfg*	322231	2679
Non-Folding Sanitary Food Container—*mfg*	322215	2679
Presses and balers, farm–hay, cotton, etc.: Farm Machinery and Equipment—*mfg*	333111	3523
Presses, arbor: Machine Tool (Metal Forming Types)—*mfg*	333513	3542
Presses, finishing–commercial laundry and drycleaning: Laundry, Drycleaning and Pressing Machine, Commercial—*mfg*	333312	3582
Presses, metal baling: General Purpose Machinery , All Other—*mfg*	333999	3569
Presses, printing: Printing Machinery and Equipment—*mfg*	333293	3555
Presses, woodworking–particleboard, hard-hoard, medium density fiberboard(MDF), and plywood: Sawmill and Woodworking Machinery—*mfg*	33321	3553
Presses–cheese, beet, cider, and sugarcane: Food Product Machinery—*mfg*	333294	3556
Presses–forming, stamping, punching, andshearing (machine tools): Machine Tool (Metal Forming Types)—*mfg*	333513	3542
Presses–hydraulic and pneumatic, mechanical and manual: Machine Tool (Metal Forming Types)—*mfg*	333513	3542
Pressing blocks, tailors'–wood: Manufacturing, All Other Miscellaneous—*mfg*	339999	2499
Wood Container and Pallet—*mfg*	32192	2499
Wood Product, All Other Miscellaneous—*mfg*	321999	2499
Pressing machines, commercial laundry and drycleaning: Laundry, Drycleaning and Pressing Machine, Commercial—*mfg*	333312	3582
Pressure and vacuum indicators, aircraft engine: Measuring and Controlling Device, Other—*mfg*	334519	3829
Surgical and Medical Instrument—*mfg*	339112	3829
Pressure control valves, fluid power–metal: Fluid Power Valve and Hose Fitting—*mfg*	332912	3492
Pressure controllers, air-conditioning system type: Automatic Environmental Control for Residential, Commercial and Appliance Use—*mfg*	334512	3822
Pressure cookers, domestic–cast aluminum, except die-castings: Aluminum Foundries—*mfg*	331524	3365
Pressure cookers, stamped or drawn: Kitchen Utensil, Pot and Pan—*mfg*	332214	3469
Pressure cookers, steam–commercial: Machinery, Other Commercial and Service Industry—*mfg*	333319	3589
Pressure gauges, dial and digital: Instruments and Related Products for Measuring, Displaying, and Controlling Industrial Process Variables—*mfg*	334513	3823
Pressure instruments, industrial process type: Instruments and Related Products for Measuring, Displaying, and Controlling Industrial Process Variables—*mfg*	334513	3823
Pressure pipe, cast iron: Iron Foundries—*mfg*	331511	3321
Pressure pipe, reinforced concrete: Concrete Pipe—*mfg*	327332	3272
Concrete Product, Other—*mfg*	32739	3272
Nonmetallic Mineral Product, All Other Miscellaneous—*mfg*	327999	3272
Pressure sensitive paper and tape, except rubber backed: Coated and Laminated Paper—*mfg*	322222	2672
Pressure sensitive tape: Industrial and Personal Service Paper—*whlse*	42213	5113
Pressure transducers: Measuring and Controlling Device, Other—*mfg*	334519	3829
Surgical and Medical Instrument—*mfg*	339112	3829
Pressure valves, industrial–except power transfer: Industrial Valve—*mfg*	332911	3491
Pressure vessels, industrial–metal plate-made in boiler shops: Air-Conditioning and Warm Air Heating Equipment and Commercial and Industrial Refrigeration Equipment—*mfg*	333415	3443
Metal Tank (Heavy Gauge)—*mfg*	33242	3443
Plate Work—*mfg*	332313	3443
Power Boiler and Heat Exchanger—*mfg*	33241	3443
Pressurizers and auxiliary equipment, nuclear–metal plate: Air-Conditioning and Warm Air Heating Equipment and Commercial and Industrial Refrigeration Equipment—*mfg*	333415	3443
Metal Tank (Heavy Gauge)—*mfg*	33242	3443
Plate Work—*mfg*	332313	3443
Power Boiler and Heat Exchanger—*mfg*	33241	3443
Prestressed concrete products: Concrete Pipe—*mfg*	327332	3272
Concrete Product, Other—*mfg*	32739	3272
Nonmetallic Mineral Product, All Other Miscellaneous—*mfg*	327999	3272
Pretzel stores and stands: Baked Goods Stores—*retail*	445291	5461
Retail Bakeries—*mfg*	311811	5461
Snack and Nonalcoholic Beverage Bars—*accom*	722213	5461
Pretzels: Bakeries, Commercial—*mfg*	311812	2052
Cookie and Cracker—*mfg*	311821	2052
Grocery and Related Products, Other—*whlse*	42249	5149
Snack Food, Other—*mfg*	311919	2052
Price control agencies: Regulation, Licensing, and Inspection of Miscellaneous Commercial Sectors—*pub*	92615	9651
Primary Aluminum Production	**331312**	**3334**
Primary batteries, dry and wet: Dry and Wet Primary Battery—*mfg*	335912	3692
Primary care medical (M.D.) clinics: Freestanding Ambulatory Surgical and Emergency Centers—*hlth*	621493	8011
HMO Medical Centers—*hlth*	621491	8011
Physicians (except Mental Health Specialists), Offices Of—*hlth*	621111	8011
Physicians, Mental Health Specialists, Offices Of—*hlth*	621112	8011

ALPHABETICAL INDEX	NAICS	SIC
Primary elements for process flow measurement–orifice plates: Instruments and Related Products for Measuring, Displaying, and Controlling Industrial Process Variables—*mfg*	334513	3823
Primary Metal Manufacturing	**331**	
Primary oil burner controls, including stack controls and cadmium cells: Automatic Environmental Control for Residential, Commercial and Appliance Use—*mfg*	334512	3822
Primary production of aluminum: Primary Aluminum Production—*mfg*	331312	3334
Primary refining of nonferrous metal–except copper and aluminum: Primary Smelting and Refining of Nonferrous Metal (except Copper and Aluminum)—*mfg*	331419	3339
Primary Smelting and Refining of Copper	**331411**	**3331**
Primary Smelting and Refining of Nonferrous Metal (except Copper and Aluminum)	**331419**	**3339**
Primary smelting of nonferrous metal–except copper and aluminum: Primary Smelting and Refining of Nonferrous Metal (except Copper and Aluminum)—*mfg*	331419	3339
Primer cups, copper and copper alloy: Copper Rolling, Drawing and Extruding—*mfg*	331421	3351
Primers for ammunition, more than 30 mm. (or more than 1.18 inch): Ammunition (except Small Arms)—*mfg*	332993	3483
Primers, paint: Paint and Coating—*mfg*	32551	2851
Print cloths, cotton: Broadwoven Fabric Mills—*mfg*	31321	2211
Printed Circuit Board Manufacturing	**334412**	**3672**
Printed circuit boards: Printed Circuit Board—*mfg*	334412	3672
Printed Circuit/Electronics Assembly Manufacturing	**334418**	**3661**
Printed circuitry graphic layout: Industrial Design Services—*prof*	54142	7389
Printed circuits: Printed Circuit Board—*mfg*	334412	3672
Printer acoustic covers, plastics: Plastics Pipe and Pipe Fitting—*mfg*	326122	3089
Plastics Product, All Other—*mfg*	326199	3089
Unsupported Plastics Profile Shape—*mfg*	326121	3089
Printers' blankets, rubber: Fabric Coating Mills—*mfg*	31332	3069
Rubber Product, All Other—*mfg*	326299	3069
Printers' machines and equipment: Printing Machinery and Equipment—*mfg*	333293	3555
Printers' rolls, rubber: Fabric Coating Mills—*mfg*	31332	3069
Rubber Product, All Other—*mfg*	326299	3069
Printers, computer: Computer and Computer Peripheral Equipment and Software—*whlse*	42143	5045
Computer and Software Stores—*retail*	44312	5045
Computer Peripheral Equipment, Other—*mfg*	334119	3577
Printers, including strip (computer peripheral equipment): Computer Peripheral Equipment, Other—*mfg*	334119	3577
Printing	**32311**	
Printing and embossing on fabric articles: Apparel Accessories and Apparel, Other—*mfg*	315999	2396
Screen Printing, Commercial—*mfg*	323113	2396
Printing and finishing of cotton broadwoven fabrics: Broadwoven Fabric Finishing Mills—*mfg*	313311	2261
Printing and publishing, books and pamphlets: Book Publishers—*info*	51113	2731
Music Publishers—*info*	51223	2731
Printing and Related Support Activities	**323**	
Printing and Related Support Activities	**3231**	
Printing and Writing Paper Wholesalers	**42211**	**5111**
Printing apparatus, photographic: Photographic Equipment and Supplies—*whlse*	42141	5043
Printing dies, rubber: Marking Device—*mfg*	339943	3953
Printing equipment, photographic: Photographic and Photocopying Equipment—*mfg*	333315	3861
Photographic Film, Paper, Plate and Chemical—*mfg*	325992	3861
Printing frames, photographic: Photographic and Photocopying Equipment—*mfg*	333315	3861
Photographic Film, Paper, Plate and Chemical—*mfg*	325992	3861
Printing from engraved and etched plates: Digital Printing—*mfg*	323115	2759
Flexographic Printing, Commercial—*mfg*	323112	2759
Printing, Other Commercial—*mfg*	323119	2759
Quick Printing—*mfg*	323114	2759
Printing from lithographic or offset plates: Lithographic Printing, Commercial—*mfg*	323110	2752
Quick Printing—*mfg*	323114	2752
Printing Ink Manufacturing	**32591**	**2893**
Printing ink–base or finished: Printing Ink—*mfg*	32591	2893
Printing Machinery and Equipment Manufacturing	**333293**	**3555**
Printing machinery, textile: Textile Machinery—*mfg*	333292	3552
Printing manmade fiber and silk broadwoven fabrics: Broadwoven Fabric Finishing Mills—*mfg*	313311	2262
Printing narrow fabrics, except knit and wool: Broadwoven Fabric Finishing Mills—*mfg*	313311	2269
Textile and Fabric Finishing (except Broadwoven Fabric) Mills—*mfg*	313312	2269
Printing on fabric articles: Apparel Accessories and Apparel, Other—*mfg*	315999	2396
Screen Printing, Commercial—*mfg*	323113	2396
Printing only, books and pamphlets: Book Printing—*mfg*	323117	2732
Printing paper: Newsprint Mills—*mfg*	322122	2621
Paper (except Newsprint) Mills—*mfg*	322121	2621
Printing and Writing Paper—*whlse*	42211	5111
Printing paper, coated: Coated and Laminated Paper—*mfg*	322222	2672
Printing plates and cylinders, rotogravure–preparation of: Prepress Services—*mfg*	323122	2796
Printing presses: Printing Machinery and Equipment—*mfg*	333293	3555
Printing Support Activities	**32312**	

Description	NAICS	SIC
Printing trades machinery, equipment, and supplies: Industrial Machinery and Equipment—*whlse*	42183	5084
Printing, commercial or job–engraved plate: Digital Printing—*mfg*	323115	2759
Flexographic Printing, Commercial—*mfg*	323112	2759
Printing, Other Commercial—*mfg*	323119	2759
Quick Printing—*mfg*	323114	2759
Printing, commercial or job–except lithographic or gravure: Digital Printing—*mfg*	323115	2759
Flexographic Printing, Commercial—*mfg*	323112	2759
Printing, Other Commercial—*mfg*	323119	2759
Quick Printing—*mfg*	323114	2759
Printing, commercial or job–gravure: Gravure Printing, Commercial—*mfg*	323111	2754
Printing, commercial or job–lithographic and offset: Lithographic Printing, Commercial—*mfg*	323110	2752
Quick Printing—*mfg*	323114	2752
Printing, lithographic: Lithographic Printing, Commercial—*mfg*	323110	2752
Quick Printing—*mfg*	323114	2752
Printing, Other Commercial	**323119**	**2771**
Printing, photooffset: Lithographic Printing, Commercial—*mfg*	323110	2752
Quick Printing—*mfg*	323114	2752
Printing–gravure, photogravure, rotary photogravure, and rotogravure: Gravure Printing, Commercial—*mfg*	323111	2754
Prisms, optical: Optical Instrument and Lens—*mfg*	333314	3827
Prison farms: Correctional Institutions—*pub*	92214	9223
Prisons: Correctional Institutions—*pub*	92214	9223
Private Households	**81411**	**8811**
Private Households	**8141**	
Private Households	**814**	
Private Mail Centers	**561431**	**7389**
Probation offices: Child and Youth Services—*hlth*	62411	8322
Community Food Services—*hlth*	62421	8322
Community Housing Services, Other—*hlth*	624229	8322
Emergency and Other Relief Services—*hlth*	62423	8322
Individual and Family Services, Other—*hlth*	62419	8322
Parole Offices and Probation Offices—*pub*	92215	8322
Services for the Elderly and Persons with Disabilities—*hlth*	62412	8322
Temporary Shelters—*hlth*	624221	8322
Probe, electric, medical: Electromedical and Electrotherapeutic Apparatus—*mfg*	334510	3845
Irradiation Apparatus—*mfg*	334517	3845
Probertite mining: Potash, Soda, and Borate Mineral—*mining*	212391	1474
Probes, surgical: Surgical and Medical Instrument—*mfg*	339112	3841
Procaine and derivatives–bulk, uncompounded: Medicinal and Botanical—*mfg*	325411	2833
Procaine pharmaceutical preparations: Pharmaceutical Preparation—*mfg*	325412	2834

Description	NAICS	SIC
Process control instruments, industrial: Instruments and Related Products for Measuring, Displaying, and Controlling Industrial Process Variables—*mfg*	334513	3823
Process serving service: Legal Services, All Other—*prof*	541199	7389
Process vessels, industrial–metal plate: Air-Conditioning and Warm Air Heating Equipment and Commercial and Industrial Refrigeration Equipment—*mfg*	333415	3443
Metal Tank (Heavy Gauge)—*mfg*	33242	3443
Plate Work—*mfg*	332313	3443
Power Boiler and Heat Exchanger—*mfg*	33241	3443
Process, Physical, Distribution and Logistics Consulting Services	**541614**	**8742**
Processed butter: Food, All Other Miscellaneous—*mfg*	311999	2099
Processed cheese: Cheese—*mfg*	311513	2022
Processing equipment, photographic: Photographic and Photocopying Equipment—*mfg*	333315	3861
Photographic Film, Paper, Plate and Chemical—*mfg*	325992	3861
Processing of textile mill waste and recovering fibers: Broadwoven Fabric Mills—*mfg*	31321	2299
Narrow Fabric Mills—*mfg*	313221	2299
Nonwoven Fabric Mills—*mfg*	31323	2299
Textile and Fabric Finishing (except Broadwoven Fabric) Mills—*mfg*	313312	2299
Textile Product Mills, All Other Miscellaneous—*mfg*	314999	2299
Thread Mills—*mfg*	313113	2299
Yarn Spinning Mills—*mfg*	313111	2299
Produce markets and stands: Fruit and Vegetable Markets—*retail*	44523	5431
Producers, gas (machinery): General Purpose Machinery , All Other—*mfg*	333999	3569
Product testing services: Testing Laboratories—*prof*	54138	8734
Veterinary Services—*prof*	54194	8734
Production counters: Totalizing Fluid Meter and Counting Device—*mfg*	334514	3824
Production credit association, agricultural: International Trade Financing—*fin*	522293	6159
Non-Depository Credit Intermediation, All Other—*fin*	522298	6159
Sales Financing—*fin*	52222	6159
Professional and Commercial Equipment and Supplies Wholesalers	**4214**	
Professional and Management Development Training	**61143**	**8299**
Professional dancing schools: Amusement and Recreation Industries, All Other—*arts*	71399	7911
Fine Arts Schools—*educ*	61161	7911
Professional Equipment and Supplies Wholesalers, Other	**42149**	**5049**
Professional membership organizations: Professional Organizations—*serv*	81392	8621
Professional or semiprofessional sportsclubs: Agents and Managers for Artists, Athletes, Entertainers and Other Public Figures—*arts*	71141	7941

ALPHABETICAL INDEX	NAICS	SIC
Promoters of Performing Arts, Sports and Similar Events with Facilities—*arts*	71131	7941
Promoters of Performing Arts, Sports and Similar Events without Facilities—*arts*	71132	7941
Spectator Sports, Other—*arts*	711219	7941
Sports Teams and Clubs—*arts*	711211	7941
Professional Organizations	**81392**	**8621**
Professional schools–e.g., dental, engineering, law, medical: Colleges, Universities and Professional Schools—*educ*	61131	8221
Professional service apparel, washable: Men's and Boys' Cut and Sew Apparel Contractors—*mfg*	315211	2326
Men's and Boys' Cut and Sew Work Clothing—*mfg*	315225	2326
Professional sports instructors for golf, skiing, and swimming: Sports and Recreation Instruction—*educ*	61162	7999
Professional standards review boards: Professional Organizations—*serv*	81392	8621
Professional, Scientific and Technical Services	**54**	
Professional, Scientific and Technical Services	**541**	
Professional, Scientific and Technical Services, All Other	**54199**	**7389**
Professional, Scientific and Technical Services, Other	**5419**	
Profiles, unsupported plastics: Unsupported Plastics Profile Shape—*mfg*	326121	3082
Programmers, process type: Instruments and Related Products for Measuring, Displaying, and Controlling Industrial Process Variables—*mfg*	334513	3823
Programming services, computer–custom: Custom Computer Programming Services, Custom—*prof*	541511	7371
Projectile forgings, machined–for ammunition more than 30 mm. (or more than1.18 inch): Ammunition (except Small Arms)—*mfg*	332993	3483
Projectiles, chemical warfare: Ammunition (except Small Arms)—*mfg*	332993	3483
Projectiles, jet propulsion–complete: Ammunition (except Small Arms)—*mfg*	332993	3483
Projection apparatus, motion picture andslide–photographic: Photographic Equipment and Supplies—*whlse*	42141	5043
Projection lenses: Optical Instrument and Lens—*mfg*	333314	3827
Projectors, microfilm: Photographic and Photocopying Equipment—*mfg*	333315	3861
Photographic Film, Paper, Plate and Chemical—*mfg*	325992	3861
Projectors, still and motion picture–silent and sound: Photographic and Photocopying Equipment—*mfg*	333315	3861
Photographic Film, Paper, Plate and Chemical—*mfg*	325992	3861
Projectors–antisub, depth charge release, grenade, livens, and rocket: Ordnance and Accessories, Other—*mfg*	332995	3489
Promenade tile, clay: Ceramic Wall and Floor Tile—*mfg*	327122	3253

ALPHABETICAL INDEX	NAICS	SIC
Promoters of home shows and flowershows: Convention and Trade Show Organizers—*admin*	56192	7389
Promoters of Performing Arts, Sports and Similar Events	**7113**	
Promoters of Performing Arts, Sports and Similar Events with Facilities	**71131**	**7922**
Promoters of Performing Arts, Sports and Similar Events without Facilities	**71132**	**7941**
Promoters, sports events: Agents and Managers for Artists, Athletes, Entertainers and Other Public Figures—*arts*	71141	7941
Promoters of Performing Arts, Sports and Similar Events with Facilities—*arts*	71131	7941
Promoters of Performing Arts, Sports and Similar Events without Facilities—*arts*	71132	7941
Spectator Sports, Other—*arts*	711219	7941
Sports Teams and Clubs—*arts*	711211	7941
Proofreading service: Court Reporting and Stenotype Services—*admin*	561492	7338
Document Preparation Services—*admin*	56141	7338
Propane (natural) production: Natural Gas Liquid Extraction—*mining*	211112	1321
Propane gas, bottled: Liquefied Petroleum Gas (Bottled Gas) Dealers—*retail*	454312	5984
PropeHer fans, window type (household): Electric Housewares and Household Fan—*mfg*	335211	3634
Heating Equipment (except Electric and Warm Air Furnaces)—*mfg*	333414	3634
Propellants for missiles, solid–inorganic: Basic Inorganic Chemical, All Other—*mfg*	325188	2819
Chemical Product, All Other Miscellaneous—*mfg*	325998	2819
Propellants for missiles, solid–organic: Basic Organic Chemical, All Other—*mfg*	325199	2869
Propeller adapter assemblies, hydromatic: Aircraft Part and Auxiliary Equipment, Other—*mfg*	336413	3728
Fluid Power Valve and Hose Fitting—*mfg*	332912	3728
Propeller alming tables: Aircraft Part and Auxiliary Equipment, Other—*mfg*	336413	3728
Fluid Power Valve and Hose Fitting—*mfg*	332912	3728
Propeller straightening presses: Other Metalworking Machinery, Other—*mfg*	333518	3549
Propeller type meters with registers: Totalizing Fluid Meter and Counting Device—*mfg*	334514	3824
Propellers, ship and boat–machined: Fabricated Metal Product, All Other Miscellaneous—*mfg*	332999	3599
General Purpose Machinery , All Other—*mfg*	333999	3599
Machine Shops—*mfg*	33271	3599
Machinery, Other Commercial and Service Industry—*mfg*	333319	3599

Entry	NAICS	SIC
Propellers, ship and screw–cast brass, bronze, copper, and copper-base-except die-castings: Copper Foundries—*mfg*	331525	3366
Propellers, variable and fixed pitch and parts-aircraft: Aircraft Part and Auxiliary Equipment, Other—*mfg*	336413	3728
Fluid Power Valve and Hose Fitting—*mfg*	332912	3728
Property damage insurance: Direct Property and Casualty Insurance Carriers—*fin*	524126	6331
Insurance Funds, Other—*fin*	52519	6331
Reinsurance Carriers—*fin*	52413	6331
Property tax assessors' offices: Public Finance—*pub*	92113	9311
Prophylactics, rubber: Fabric Coating Mills—*mfg*	31332	3069
Rubber Product, All Other—*mfg*	326299	3069
Proprietary (nonprescripcion medicines)stores: Pharmacies and Drug Stores—*retail*	44611	5912
Proprietary (patent) medicines: Drug, Drug Proprietaries and Druggists' Sundries—*whlse*	42221	5122
Proprietary drug products: Pharmaceutical Preparation—*mfg*	325412	2834
Propulsion units for guided missiles and space vehicles: Guided Missile and Space Vehicle Propulsion Unit and Propulsion Unit Parts—*mfg*	336415	3764
Propylene glycol: Basic Organic Chemical, All Other—*mfg*	325199	2869
Propylene, made in chemical plants: Basic Organic Chemical, All Other—*mfg*	325199	2869
Propylene, produced in petroleum refineries: Petroleum Refineries—*mfg*	32411	2911
Prospect drilling for metal mining–on a contract basis: Geophysical Surveying and Mapping Services—*prof*	54136	1081
Metal Support Activities—*mining*	213114	1081
Prospect drilling for nonmetallic minerals except fuels–on a contract basis: Geophysical Surveying and Mapping Services—*prof*	54136	1481
Non-Metallic Minerals (except Fuels) Support Activities—*mining*	213115	1481
Prosthetic appliances and supplies: Surgical Appliance and Supplies—*mfg*	339113	3842
Prosthodontists, offices of: Dentists, Offices Of—*hlth*	62121	8021
Protective committees, security holders: Financial Investment Activities, Miscellaneous—*fin*	523999	6289
Trust, Fiduciary and Custody Activities—*fin*	523991	6289
Protective service, guard: Armored Car Services—*admin*	561613	7381
Investigation Services—*admin*	561611	7381
Security Guards and Patrol Services—*admin*	561612	7381
Protectors, check (machine): Lead Pencil and Art Good—*mfg*	339942	3579
Office Machinery—*mfg*	333313	3579
Watch, Clock, and Part—*mfg*	334518	3579
Protectors, eye: Ophthalmic Goods—*mfg*	339115	3851
Protectors, sports–e.g., baseball, basketball, hockey: Sporting and Athletic Goods—*mfg*	33992	3949
Protein analyzers, laboratory type: Analytical Laboratory Instrument—*mfg*	334516	3826
Protein fibers: Noncellulosic Organic Fiber—*mfg*	325222	2824
Protein plastics: Plastics Material and Resin—*mfg*	325211	2821
Prune orchards and farms: Apple Orchards—*ag*	111331	175
Noncitrus Fruit Farming, Other—*ag*	111339	175
Prunes, dried: Dried and Dehydrated Food—*mfg*	311423	2034
Flour Milling—*mfg*	311211	2034
Pruning of orchard trees and vines: Nonscheduled Air, Other—*trans*	481219	721
Soil Preparation, Planting, and Cultivating—*ag*	115112	721
Pruning tools: Hand and Edge Tool—*mfg*	332212	3423
Prussian blue pigtnents: Carbon Black—*mfg*	325182	2816
Inorganic Dye and Pigment—*mfg*	325131	2816
Prying bars (handtools): Hand and Edge Tool—*mfg*	332212	3423
Psilomelane mining: Copper Ore and Nickel Ore—*mining*	212234	1061
Metal Ore, All Other—*mining*	212299	1061
Psychiatric and Substance Abuse Hospitals	**6222**	
Psychiatric and Substance Abuse Hospitals	**62221**	**8069**
Psychiatric hospitals: Psychiatric and Substance Abuse Hospitals—*hlth*	62221	8063
Psychiatric patient's convalescent homes: Continuing Care Retirement Communities—*hlth*	623311	8059
Nursing Care Facilities—*hlth*	62311	8059
Psychiatric social workers, offices of: Health Practitioners, Offices Of Miscellaneous—*hlth*	621399	8049
Mental Health Practitioners (except Physicians), Offices Of—*hlth*	62133	8049
Physical, Occupational and Speech Therapists and Audiologists, Offices Of—*hlth*	62134	8049
Psychiatrists, offices of: Freestanding Ambulatory Surgical and Emergency Centers—*hlth*	621493	8011
HMO Medical Centers—*hlth*	621491	8011
Physicians (except Mental Health Specialists), Offices Of—*hlth*	621111	8011
Physicians, Mental Health Specialists, Offices Of—*hlth*	621112	8011
Psychoanalysts, offices of: Freestanding Ambulatory Surgical and Emergency Centers—*hlth*	621493	8011
HMO Medical Centers—*hlth*	621491	8011
Physicians (except Mental Health Specialists), Offices Of—*hlth*	621111	8011
Physicians, Mental Health Specialists, Offices Of—*hlth*	621112	8011
Psychologists, clinical–offices of: Health Practitioners, Offices Of Miscellaneous—*hlth*	621399	8049
Mental Health Practitioners (except Physicians), Offices Of—*hlth*	62133	8049
Physical, Occupational and Speech Therapists and Audiologists, Offices Of—*hlth*	62134	8049
Psychologists, industrial: Scientific and Technical Consulting Services, Other—*prof*	54169	8999
Psychotherapists, except M.D.–offices of: Health Practitioners, Offices Of Miscellaneous—*hlth*	621399	8049
Mental Health Practitioners (except Physicians), Offices Of—*hlth*	62133	8049
Physical, Occupational and Speech Therapists and Audiologists, Offices Of—*hlth*	62134	8049
Public accountants, certified: Accounting Services, Other—*prof*	541219	8721
Certified Public Accountants, Offices Of—*prof*	541211	8721

ALPHABETICAL INDEX	NAICS	SIC
Payroll Services—*prof*	541214	8721
Public address equipment: Electronic Parts and Equipment, Other—*whlse*	42169	5065
Public address system repair: Communication Equipment Repair and Maintenance—*serv*	811213	7622
Consumer Electronics Repair and Maintenance—*serv*	811211	7622
Radio, Television and Other Electronics Stores—*retail*	443112	7622
Public address systems: Audio and Video Equipment—*mfg*	33431	3651
Public Administration	**92**	
Public building fixtures: Institutional Furniture—*mfg*	337127	2531
Public building furniture: Furniture—*whlse*	42121	5021
Furniture Stores—*retail*	44211	5021
Public defenders' offices: Legal Counsel and Prosecution—*pub*	92213	9222
Public Finance	**92113**	**9311**
Public health agencies-nonoperating: Public Health Programs, Administration of—*pub*	92312	9431
Public Health Programs, Administration of	**92312**	**9431**
Public opinion research: Marketing Research and Public Opinion Polling—*prof*	54191	8732
Research and Development in the Social Sciences and Humanities—*prof*	54173	8732
Public prosecutors' offices: Legal Counsel and Prosecution—*pub*	92213	9222
Public Relations Agencies	**54182**	**8743**
Public relations services: Public Relations Agencies—*prof*	54182	8743
Public safety bureaus: Justice, Public Order, and Safety, All Other—*pub*	92219	9229
Public safety statistics centers: Justice, Public Order, and Safety, All Other—*pub*	92219	9229
Public service commissions, except transportation: Regulation and Administration of Communications, Electric, Gas, and Other Utilities—*pub*	92613	9631
Public speaking schools: Language Schools—*educ*	61163	8299
Public utility associations: Business Associations—*serv*	81391	8611
Public utility commissions: Regulation and Administration of Communications, Electric, Gas, and Other Utilities—*pub*	92613	9631
Public utility holding companies: Other Holding Companies, Offices Of—*manag*	551112	6719
Public utility property, lessors of: Lessors of Other Real Estate Property—*real*	53119	6519
Public welfare administration, nonoperating: Social, Human Resource and Income Maintenance Programs, Administration of—*pub*	92313	9441
Public welfare centers, offices of: Child and Youth Services—*hlth*	62411	8322
Community Food Services—*hlth*	62421	8322
Community Housing Services, Other—*hlth*	624229	8322
Emergency and Other Relief Services—*hlth*	62423	8322
Individual and Family Services, Other—*hlth*	62419	8322

ALPHABETICAL INDEX	NAICS	SIC
Parole Offices and Probation Offices—*pub*	92215	8322
Services for the Elderly and Persons with Disabilities—*hlth*	62412	8322
Temporary Shelters—*hlth*	624221	8322
Publication paper: Newsprint Mills—*mfg*	322122	2621
Paper (except Newsprint) Mills—*mfg*	322121	2621
Publishers	**51121**	**7372**
Publishers' representatives, advertising: Media Representatives—*prof*	54184	7313
Publishers, All Other	**511199**	**2741**
Publishers, Other	**51119**	
Publishing and printing maps, guides, directories, atlases, and sheet music: Database and Directory Publishers—*info*	1114	2741
Music Publishers—*info*	51223	2741
Publishers, All Other—*info*	511199	2741
Publishing and printing, books and pamphlets: Book Publishers—*info*	51113	2731
Music Publishers—*info*	51223	2731
Publishing and printing, or publishing only–newspapers: Newspaper Publishers—*info*	51111	2711
Publishing and printing, or publishing only–periodicals: Periodical Publishers—*info*	51112	2721
Publishing Industries	**511**	
Publishing only, books and pamphlets: Book Publishers—*info*	51113	2731
Music Publishers—*info*	51223	2731
Publishing without printing–maps: Database and Directory Publishers—*info*	51114	2741
Music Publishers—*info*	51223	2741
Publishers, All Other—*info*	511199	2741
Pudding pops, frozen: Ice Cream and Frozen Dessert—*mfg*	31152	2024
Puddings, except meat–canned: Canning, Specialty—*mfg*	311422	2032
Food, All Other Miscellaneous—*mfg*	311999	2032
Puddings, meat: Meat Processed from Carcasses—*mfg*	311612	2013
Pullers–wheel, gear, and bearing (handtools): Hand and Edge Tool—*mfg*	332212	3423
Pulleys, power transmission: Mechanical Power Transmission Equipment—*mfg*	333613	3568
Pulleys, wood: Manufacturing, All Other Miscellaneous—*mfg*	339999	2499
Wood Container and Pallet—*mfg*	32192	2499
Wood Product, All Other Miscellaneous—*mfg*	321999	2499
Pulling oil well casing–on a contract basis: Oil and Gas Operations Support Activities—*mining*	213112	1389
Pulp (wood) manufacturing machinery: Industrial Machinery and Equipment—*whlse*	42183	5084
Pulp colors, organic: Organic Dye and Pigment—*mfg*	325132	2865
Petrochemical—*mfg*	32511	2865
Pulp mill machinery: Paper Industry Machinery—*mfg*	333291	3554
Pulp Mills	**32211**	**2611**
Pulp mills: Paper (except Newsprint) Mills—*mfg*	322121	2611

Description	NAICS	SIC
Paperboard Mills—*mfg*	32213	2611
Pulp products, pressed and molded–except statuary: Coated and Laminated Paper—*mfg*	322222	2679
Converted Paper Product, All Other—*mfg*	322298	2679
Die-Cut Paper and Paperboard Office Supplies—*mfg*	322231	2679
Non-Folding Sanitary Food Container—*mfg*	322215	2679
Pulp, fiber–made from wood, rags, waste paper, linters, straw, and bagasse: Paper (except Newsprint) Mills—*mfg*	322121	2611
Paperboard Mills—*mfg*	32213	2611
Pulp Mills—*mfg*	32211	2611
Pulp, Paper, and Paperboard Mills	**3221**	
Pulp–soda, sulfate, sulfite, groundwood, rayon, and semichemical: Paper (except Newsprint) Mills—*mfg*	322121	2611
Paperboard Mills—*mfg*	32213	2611
Pulp Mills—*mfg*	32211	2611
Pulpits, cut stone: Cut Stone and Stone Product—*mfg*	327991	3281
Pulpits, except stone: Institutional Furniture—*mfg*	337127	2531
Pulpstone quarrying: Crushed and Broken Stone and Quarrying, Other—*mining*	212319	1499
Non-Metallic Mineral, All Other—*mining*	212399	1499
Pulpwood: Durable Goods, Other Miscellaneous—*whlse*	42199	5099
Pulpwood camps: Logging—*ag*	11331	2411
Pulpwood contractors engaged in cutting: Logging—*ag*	11331	2411
Pulse (signal) generators: Electronic Coil, Transformer, and Other Inductor—*mfg*	334416	3825
Instrument for Measuring and Testing Electricity and Electrical Signals—*mfg*	334515	3825
Pulse analyzers, nuclear monitoring: Measuring and Controlling Device, Other—*mfg*	334519	3829
Surgical and Medical Instrument—*mfg*	339112	3829
Pulse forming networks: Electronic Component, Other—*mfg*	334419	3679
Motor Vehicle Electrical and Electronic Equipment, Other—*mfg*	336322	3679
Printed Circuit/Electronics Assembly—*mfg*	334418	3679
Radio and Television Broadcasting and Wireless Communications Equipment—*mfg*	33422	3679
Pulverized earth: Ground or Treated Mineral and Earth—*mfg*	327992	3295
Pulverizers, soil (agricultural machinery): Farm Machinery and Equipment—*mfg*	333111	3523
Pulverizers, stone–portable: Construction Machinery—*mfg*	33312	3531
Overhead Traveling Crane, Hoist and Monorail System—*mfg*	333923	3531
Railroad Rolling Stock—*mfg*	33651	3531
Pulverizers, stone–stationary: Mining Machinery and Equipment—*mfg*	333131	3532
Pulverizing machinery and equipment, industrial: Industrial Machinery and Equipment—*whlse*	42183	5084
Pumice and pumicite abrasives: Abrasive Product—*mfg*	32791	3291
Fabricated Metal Product, All Other Miscellaneous—*mfg*	332999	3291
Pumice mining: Crushed and Broken Stone and Quarrying, Other—*mining*	212319	1499
Non-Metallic Mineral, All Other—*mining*	212399	1499
Pumice, ground or otherwise treated: Ground or Treated Mineral and Earth—*mfg*	327992	3295
Pumicite mining: Crushed and Broken Stone and Quarrying, Other—*mining*	212319	1499
Non-Metallic Mineral, All Other—*mining*	212399	1499
Pump and compressor forgings, ferrous–not made in rolling mills: Iron and Steel Forging—*mfg*	332111	3462
Pump and compressor forgings, nonferrous–not made in hot-rolling mills: Nonferrous Forging—*mfg*	332112	3463
Pump and Compressor Manufacturing	**33391**	
Pump and Pumping Equipment Manufacturing	**333911**	**3743**
Pump jacks: Pump and Pumping Equipment—*mfg*	333911	3561
Pump sleeves, rubber: Fabric Coating Mills—*mfg*	31332	3069
Rubber Product, All Other—*mfg*	326299	3069
Pumping of oil and gas wells on a contract basis: Oil and Gas Operations Support Activities—*mining*	213112	1389
Pumping or draining of anthracite mines–on a contract basis: Coal Support Activities—*mining*	213113	1241
Pumping or draining of bituminous coal or lignite mines–on a contract basis: Coal Support Activities—*mining*	213113	1241
Pumping or draining of metal mines–on a contract basis: Geophysical Surveying and Mapping Services—*prof*	54136	1081
Metal Support Activities—*mining*	213114	1081
Pumping or draining of nonmetallic mineral (except fuels) mines–on a contract basis: Geophysical Surveying and Mapping Services—*prof*	54136	1481
Non-Metallic Minerals (except Fuels) Support Activities—*mining*	213115	1481
Pumping station construction–general contractors: Power and Communication Transmission Line—*const*	23492	1623
Water, Sewer, and Pipeline—*const*	23491	1623
Pumps (shoes): Women's Footwear (except Athletic)—*mfg*	316214	3144
Pumps and pumping equipment, industrial: Industrial Machinery and Equipment—*whlse*	42183	5084
Pumps for fluid power systems: Fluid Power Pump and Motor—*mfg*	333996	3594
Pumps, aircraft engine: Aircraft Engine and Engine Parts—*mfg*	336412	3724
Pumps, domestic–water or sump: Pump and Pumping Equipment—*mfg*	333911	3561
Pumps, general industrial type: Pump and Pumping Equipment—*mfg*	333911	3561
Pumps, hydraulic fluid power–for automotive steering mechanisms: Motor Vehicle Parts, All Other—*mfg*	336399	3714
Motor Vehicle Steering and Suspension Components (except Spring)—*mfg*	33633	3714
Pumps, hydraulic power transfer: Fluid Power Pump and Motor—*mfg*	333996	3594
Pumps, measuring and dispensing–gasoline and oil: Automotive Parts and Accessories Stores—*retail*	44131	5013
Measuring and Dispensing Pump—*mfg*	333913	3586
Motor Vehicle Supplies and New Part—*whlse*	42112	5013

ALPHABETICAL INDEX	NAICS	SIC
Pumps, motor vehicle–oil, water, fuel, and power steering: Gasoline Engine and Engine Parts—*mfg*	336312	3714
Motor Vehicle Parts, All Other—*mfg*	336399	3714
Motor Vehicle Steering and Suspension Components (except Spring)—*mfg*	33633	3714
Pumps, oil well and oil field: Pump and Pumping Equipment—*mfg*	333911	3561
Pumps, propeller feathering: Aircraft Part and Auxiliary Equipment, Other—*mfg*	336413	3728
Fluid Power Valve and Hose Fitting—*mfg*	332912	3728
Punch card equipment–card readers, tabulators, collators, sorters, and interpreters: Computer Peripheral Equipment, Other—*mfg*	334119	3577
Punch card services, punching and processing: Data Processing Services—*info*	51421	7374
Punched card readers, sorters, and tabulators: Computer Peripheral Equipment, Other—*mfg*	334119	3577
Punched felts: Broadwoven Fabric Mills—*mfg*	31321	2299
Narrow Fabric Mills—*mfg*	313221	2299
Nonwoven Fabric Mills—*mfg*	31323	2299
Textile and Fabric Finishing (except Broadwoven Fabric) Mills—*mfg*	313312	2299
Textile Product Mills, All Other Miscellaneous—*mfg*	314999	2299
Thread Mills—*mfg*	313113	2299
Yarn Spinning Mills—*mfg*	313111	2299
Punches (handtools): Hand and Edge Tool—*mfg*	332212	3423
Punches, forming and stamping: Die and Tool, Die Set, Jig and Fixture, Special—*mfg*	333514	3544
Industrial Mold—*mfg*	333511	3544
Punches, paper–hand: Lead Pencil and Art Good—*mfg*	339942	3579
Office Machinery—*mfg*	333313	3579
Watch, Clock, and Part—*mfg*	334518	3579
Punching and shearing machines: Machine Tool (Metal Forming Types)—*mfg*	333513	3542
Punching machines, card: Computer Peripheral Equipment, Other—*mfg*	334119	3577
Puppets: Wood Product, All Other Miscellaneous—*mfg*	321999	3999
Purchasers of accounts receivable and commercial paper: Financial Transactions Processing, Reserve, and Clearing House Activities—*fin*	52232	6153
Non-Depository Credit Intermediation, All Other—*fin*	522298	6153
Sales Financing—*fin*	52222	6153
Purchasing and supply agencies: General Government, All Other—*pub*	92119	9199
Purees, fruit and vegetable: Fruit and Vegetable Canning—*mfg*	311421	2033
Purifiers, centrifugal: General Purpose Machinery , All Other—*mfg*	333999	3569
Purlins, light gauge steel: Ornamental and Architectural Metal Work—*mfg*	332323	3446

ALPHABETICAL INDEX	NAICS	SIC
Purses, men's–regardless of material: Personal Leather Good (except Women's Handbag and Purse)—*mfg*	316993	3172
Purses, women's–of all materials, except precious metal: Women's Handbag and Purse—*mfg*	316992	3171
Purses–women s and children's: Women's, Children's, and Infants' and Accessories—*whlse*	42233	5137
Push brooms: Broom, Brush and Mop—*mfg*	339994	3991
Pushcarts: Transportation Equipment, All Other—*mfg*	336999	3799
Pushers: Cutting Tool and Machine Tool Accessory—*mfg*	333515	3545
Hand and Edge Tool—*mfg*	332212	3545
Puttees, canvas and leather: Leather Good, All Other—*mfg*	316999	3199
Putty: Paint and Coating—*mfg*	32551	2851
Putty knives: Hand and Edge Tool—*mfg*	332212	3423
Pyrethrin bearing preparations: Pesticide and Other Agricultural Chemical—*mfg*	32532	2879
Pyrethrin concentrates: Pesticide and Other Agricultural Chemical—*mfg*	32532	2879
Pyrheliometers: Measuring and Controlling Device, Other—*mfg*	334519	3829
Surgical and Medical Instrument—*mfg*	339112	3829
Pyridine-butadiene copolymers: Synthetic Rubber—*mfg*	325212	2822
Pyridine-butadiene rubbers: Synthetic Rubber—*mfg*	325212	2822
Pyrites mining: Chemical and Fertilizer Mineral, Other—*mining*	212393	1479
Pyrography materials: Chemical Product, All Other Miscellaneous—*mfg*	325998	3952
Institutional Furniture—*mfg*	337127	3952
Lead Pencil and Art Good—*mfg*	339942	3952
Pyroligreous acid: Gum and Wood Chemical—*mfg*	325191	2861
Pyrolusite mining: Copper Ore and Nickel Ore—*mining*	212234	1061
Metal Ore, All Other—*mining*	212299	1061
Pyrolytic graphite: Nonclay Refractory—*mfg*	327125	3297
Pyrometer tubes: Vitreous China, Fine Earthenware and Other Pottery Product—*mfg*	327112	3269
Pyrometers, industrial process type: Instruments and Related Products for Measuring, Displaying, and Controlling Industrial Process Variables—*mfg*	334513	3823
Pyrometric cones–earthenware: Vitreous China, Fine Earthenware and Other Pottery Product—*mfg*	327112	3269
Pyrophyllite mining: Crushed and Broken Stone and Quarrying, Other—*mining*	212319	1499
Non-Metallic Mineral, All Other—*mining*	212399	1499
Pyrophyllite, ground or otherwise treated: Ground or Treated Mineral and Earth—*mfg*	327992	3295
Pyrotechnic ammunition–flares, signals, flashlight bombs, and rockets: Basic Organic Chemical, All Other—*mfg*	325199	2899
Chemical Product, All Other Miscellaneous—*mfg*	325998	2899
Pyrotechnic pistols and projectors: Small Arms—*mfg*	332994	3484
Pyroxylin: Plastics Material and Resin—*mfg*	325211	2821

Description	NAICS	SIC
Pyroxylin coated fabrics: Fabric Coating Mills—*mfg*	31332	2295
Pyrrhotite mining: Chemical and Fertilizer Mineral, Other—*mining*	212393	1479
Quail farms: Poultry Production, Other—*ag*	11239	259
Quarry tile, clay: Ceramic Wall and Floor Tile—*mfg*	327122	3253
Quarrying machinery and equipment: Construction and (except Petroleum) Machinery and Equipment—*whlse*	42181	5082
Quarters (shoe cut stock): Fastener, Button, Needle and Pin—*mfg*	339993	3131
Leather Good, All Other—*mfg*	316999	3131
Wood Product, All Other Miscellaneous—*mfg*	321999	3131
Quartz crystal mining (pure): Crushed and Broken Stone and Quarrying, Other—*mining*	212319	1499
Non-Metallic Mineral, All Other—*mining*	212399	1499
Quartz crystals for electronic application: Electronic Component, Other—*mfg*	334419	3679
Motor Vehicle Electrical and Electronic Equipment, Other—*mfg*	336322	3679
Printed Circuit/Electronics Assembly—*mfg*	334418	3679
Radio and Television Broadcasting and Wireless Communications Equipment—*mfg*	33422	3679
Quartzite, crushed and broken: Crushed and Broken Stone and Quarrying, Other—*mining*	212319	1429
Quartzite, dimension: Dimension Stone and Quarrying—*mining*	212311	1411
Quebracho extract: Gum and Wood Chemical—*mfg*	325191	2861
Quercitron extract: Gum and Wood Chemical—*mfg*	325191	2861
Quick Printing	**323114**	**2759**
Quick printing, except photocopy service: Lithographic Printing, Commercial—*mfg*	323110	2752
Quick Printing—*mfg*	323114	2752
Quicklime: Lime—*mfg*	32741	3274
Quicksilver (mercury) ore mining: Metal Ore, All Other—*mining*	212299	1099
Quilt filling–curled hair (e.g., cottonwaste, moss, hemp tow, kapok): Broadwoven Fabric Mills—*mfg*	31321	2299
Narrow Fabric Mills—*mfg*	313221	2299
Nonwoven Fabric Mills—*mfg*	31323	2299
Textile and Fabric Finishing (except Broadwoven Fabric) Mills—*mfg*	313312	2299
Textile Product Mills, All Other Miscellaneous—*mfg*	314999	2299
Thread Mills—*mfg*	313113	2299
Yarn Spinning Mills—*mfg*	313111	2299
Quilted fabrics or cloth: Men's and Boys' Cut and Sew Apparel Contractors—*mfg*	315211	2395
Textile Product Mills, All Other Miscellaneous—*mfg*	314999	2395
Women's and Girls' Cut and Sew Apparel Contractors—*mfg*	315212	2395
Quilting for individuals: Personal Services, All Other—*serv*	81299	7299
Quilting materials and supplies: Sewing, Needlework and Piece Goods Stores—*retail*	45113	5949
Quilting, for the trade: Men's and Boys' Cut and Sew Apparel Contractors—*mfg*	315211	2395
Textile Product Mills, All Other Miscellaneous—*mfg*	314999	2395
Women's and Girls' Cut and Sew Apparel Contractors—*mfg*	315212	2395
Quilts: Household Textile Product Mills, Other—*mfg*	314129	2392
Quilts, manmade fiber and silk: Broadwoven Fabric Mills—*mfg*	31321	2221
Quince orchards and farms: Apple Orchards—*ag*	111331	175
Noncitrus Fruit Farming, Other—*ag*	111339	175
Quinine and derivatives: Medicinal and Botanical—*mfg*	325411	2833
Quinoline dyes: Organic Dye and Pigment—*mfg*	325132	2865
Petrochemical—*mfg*	32511	2865
Quinuclidinol ester of benzylic acid: Basic Organic Chemical, All Other—*mfg*	325199	2869
Quotation service, stock: Financial Investment Activities, Miscellaneous—*fin*	523999	6289
Trust, Fiduciary and Custody Activities—*fin*	523991	6289
Rabbit farms: Fur-Bearing Animal and Rabbit Production—*ag*	11293	271
Rabbits, processed–fresh, frozen, canned, or cooked: Food, All Other Miscellaneous—*mfg*	311999	2015
Poultry Processing—*mfg*	311615	2015
Rabbits, slaughtering and dressing: Food, All Other Miscellaneous—*mfg*	311999	2015
Poultry Processing—*mfg*	311615	2015
Race car drivers and owners: Race Tracks—*arts*	711212	7948
Spectator Sports, Other—*arts*	711219	7948
Race track programs–publishing andprinting, or publishing only: Database and Directory Publishers—*info*	51114	2741
Music Publishers—*info*	51223	2741
Publishers, All Other—*info*	511199	2741
Race Tracks	**711212**	**7948**
Races, ball and roller bearing: Ball and Roller Bearing—*mfg*	332991	3562
Racetrack operation–e.g., horse, dog, auto: Race Tracks—*arts*	711212	7948
Spectator Sports, Other—*arts*	711219	7948
Raceways: Noncurrent-Carrying Wiring Device—*mfg*	335932	3644
Racing forms–publishing and printing, orpublishing only: Database and Directory Publishers—*info*	51114	2741
Music Publishers—*info*	51223	2741
Publishers, All Other—*info*	511199	2741
Racing stables, operation of: Race Tracks—*arts*	711212	7948
Spectator Sports, Other—*arts*	711219	7948
Rackets and frames, sports–e.g., tennis, badminton, squash, racketball, lacrosse: Sporting and Athletic Goods—*mfg*	33992	3949
Racks without rigid framework, madefrom purchased wire: Fabricated Wire Product, Other—*mfg*	332618	3496
Racks, book and magazine–woed: Nonupholstered Wood Household Furniture—*mfg*	337122	2511
Racks, for drying clothes–wood: Manufacturing, All Other Miscellaneous—*mfg*	339999	2499
Wood Container and Pallet—*mfg*	32192	2499
Wood Product, All Other Miscellaneous—*mfg*	321999	2499
Racks, merchandise display and storage:except wood: Showcase, Partition, Shelving, and Locker—*mfg*	337215	2542

ALPHABETICAL INDEX	NAICS	SIC
Racks, merchandise display–wood: Architectural Woodwork and Millwork, Custom—*mfg*	337212	2541
Showcase, Partition, Shelving, and Locker—*mfg*	337215	2541
Wood Kitchen Cabinet and Counter Top—*mfg*	33711	2541
Racks, trash–metal plate: Air-Conditioning and Warm Air Heating Equipment and Commercial and Industrial Refrigeration Equipment—*mfg*	333415	3443
Metal Tank (Heavy Gauge)—*mfg*	33242	3443
Plate Work—*mfg*	332313	3443
Power Boiler and Heat Exchanger—*mfg*	33241	3443
Racks–mail pouch, mailing, mail sorting, etc., except wood: Showcase, Partition, Shelving, and Locker—*mfg*	337215	2542
Racquetball clubs, membership: Fitness and Recreational Sports Centers—*arts*	71394	7997
Racquetball courts, except membership clubs: Fitness and Recreational Sports Centers—*arts*	71394	7999
Radar station operation: Cellular and Other Wireless Telecommunications—*info*	513322	4899
Satellite Telecommunications—*info*	51334	4899
Telecommunications, Other—*info*	51339	4899
Radar Systems and equipment: Search, Detection, Navigation, Guidance, Aeronautical, and Nautical System and Instrument—*mfg*	334511	3812
Radar testing instruments, electric: Electronic Coil, Transformer, and Other Inductor—*mfg*	334416	3825
Instrument for Measuring and Testing Electricity and Electrical Signals—*mfg*	334515	3825
Radar towers, floating: Ship Building and Repairing—*mfg*	336611	3731
Radiac equipment (radiation measuring and detecting): Measuring and Controlling Device, Other—*mfg*	334519	3829
Surgical and Medical Instrument—*mfg*	339112	3829
Radiant heating systems, industrial process–e.g., dryers, cookers': Industrial Process Furnace and Oven—*mfg*	333994	3567
Radiation dosimetry laboratories: Testing Laboratories—*prof*	54138	8734
Veterinary Services—*prof*	54194	8734
Radiation measuring and detecting (radiac) equipment: Measuring and Controlling Device, Other—*mfg*	334519	3829
Surgical and Medical Instrument—*mfg*	339112	3829
Radio and Television Broadcasting	**5131**	
Radio and Television Broadcasting and Wireless Communications Equipment Manufacturing	**33422**	**3679**
Radio Broadcasting	**51311**	
Radio Networks	**513111**	**4832**
Radio Stations	**513112**	**4832**
Radio, Television and Other Electronics Stores	**443112**	**5999**
Rail Transportation	**4821**	
Rail Transportation	**48211**	
Rail Transportation	**482**	
Rail Transportation Support Activities	**4882**	
Rail Transportation Support Activities	**48821**	**4741**
Railroad equipment springs: Steel Spring (except Wire)—*mfg*	332611	3493
Railroad ferries: Coastal and Great Lakes Passenger—*trans*	483114	4482
Inland Water Passenger—*trans*	483212	4482
Railroad freight agencies, not operated byrailroad companies: Freight Arrangement—*trans*	48851	4731
Management Consulting Services, Other—*prof*	541618	4731
Railroad fusees: Basic Organic Chemical, All Other—*mfg*	325199	2899
Chemical Product, All Other Miscellaneous—*mfg*	325998	2899
Railroad hardware: Hardware—*mfg*	33251	3429
Railroad locomotives and parts: Pump and Pumping Equipment—*mfg*	333911	3743
Railroad Rolling Stock—*mfg*	33651	3743
Railroad models, except toy and hobbymodels: Plastics Product, All Other—*mfg*	326199	3999
Wood Product, All Other Miscellaneous—*mfg*	321999	3999
Railroad models–toy and hobby: Game, Toy, and Children's Vehicle—*mfg*	339932	3944
Railroad property, lessors of: Lessors of Other Real Estate Property—*real*	53119	6517
Railroad Rolling Stock Manufacturing	**3365**	
Railroad Rolling Stock Manufacturing	**33651**	**3743**
Railroad seats: Motor Vehicle Fabric Accessories and Seat—*mfg*	33636	2531
Railroad signaling devices, electric: Communications Equipment, Other—*mfg*	33429	3669
Railroad switching: Rail Support Activities—*trans*	48821	4013
Short Line Railroads—*trans*	482112	4013
Railroad terminals: Rail Support Activities—*trans*	48821	4013
Short Line Railroads—*trans*	482112	4013
Railroad ticket offices, not operated bytransportation companies: Transportation, All Other Support Activities—*trans*	488999	4729
Travel Arrangement and Reservation Services, All Other—*admin*	561599	4729
Railroad ties, sawed: Cut Stock, Resawing Lumber, and Planing—*mfg*	321912	2421
Millwork (including Flooring), Other—*mfg*	321918	2421
Sawmills—*mfg*	321113	2421
Wood Product, All Other Miscellaneous—*mfg*	321999	2421
Railroad torpedoes: Basic Organic Chemical, All Other—*mfg*	325199	2899
Chemical Product, All Other Miscellaneous—*mfg*	325998	2899
Railroad track scales: Scale and Balance (except Laboratory)—*mfg*	333997	3596
Railroad wheels, axles, frogs, and related equipment–forged: Iron and Steel Forging—*mfg*	332111	3462
Railroads, belt line: Rail Support Activities—*trans*	48821	4013
Short Line Railroads—*trans*	482112	4013
Railroads, electric–line-haul: Line-Haul Railroads—*trans*	482111	4011

Entry	NAICS	SIC
Railroads, line-haul operating: Line-Haul Railroads—*trans*	482111	4011
Railroads, logging: Rail Support Activities—*trans*	48821	4013
Short Line Railroads—*trans*	482112	4013
Rails and accessories: Metal Service Centers and Offices—*whlse*	42151	5051
Rails, aluminum–rolled and drawn: Aluminum Rolling and Drawing, Other—*mfg*	331319	3355
Rails, fence–round or split: Logging—*ag*	11331	2411
Rails, iron and steel: Iron and Steel Mills—*mfg*	331111	3312
Petroleum and Coal Productsa, All Other—*mfg*	324199	3312
Rails, rerolled or renewed: Iron and Steel Mills—*mfg*	331111	3312
Petroleum and Coal Productsa, All Other—*mfg*	324199	3312
Rails, rolled and drawn–brass, bronze, and copper: Copper Rolling, Drawing and Extruding—*mfg*	331421	3351
Railway bridge sections, prefabricated metal: Fabricated Structural Metal—*mfg*	332312	3441
Railway crossties, wood–treated: Wood Preservation—*mfg*	321114	2491
Railway maintenance cars: Pump and Pumping Equipment—*mfg*	333911	3743
Railroad Rolling Stock—*mfg*	33651	3743
Railway motor cars: Pump and Pumping Equipment—*mfg*	333911	3743
Railroad Rolling Stock—*mfg*	33651	3743
Railway motors and control equipment, electric: Motor and Generator—*mfg*	335312	3621
Railway operation, local: Bus and Motor Vehicle Transit Systems—*trans*	485113	4111
Commuter Rail Systems—*trans*	485112	4111
Mixed Mode Transit Systems—*trans*	485111	4111
Transit and Ground Passenger, All Other—*trans*	485999	4111
Urban Transit Systems, Other—*trans*	485119	4111
Railway roadbed construction–general contractors: Heavy, All Other—*const*	23499	1629
Industrial Nonbuilding Structure—*const*	23493	1629
Railway track equipment–e.g., rail layers, ballast distributors: Construction Machinery—*mfg*	33312	3531
Overhead Traveling Crane, Hoist and Monorail System—*mfg*	333923	3531
Railroad Rolling Stock—*mfg*	33651	3531
Railways, interurban: Line-Haul Railroads—*trans*	482111	4011
Rain gauges: Measuring and Controlling Device, Other—*mfg*	334519	3829
Surgical and Medical Instrument—*mfg*	339112	3829
Raincoat stores: Clothing Accessories Stores—*retail*	44815	5699
Clothing Stores, Other—*retail*	44819	5699
Raincoats, except vulcanized rubber: Apparel Accessories and Apparel, Other—*mfg*	315999	2385
Infants' Cut and Sew Apparel—*mfg*	315291	2385
Men's and Boys' Cut and Sew Apparel Contractors—*mfg*	315211	2385
Men's and Boys' Cut and Sew Other Outerwear—*mfg*	315228	2385
Men's and Boys' Cut and Sew Suit, Coat and Overcoat—*mfg*	315222	2385
Women's and Girls' Cut and Sew Apparel Contractors—*mfg*	315212	2385
Women's and Girls' Cut and Sew Other Outerwear—*mfg*	315238	2385
Women's and Girls' Cut and Sew Suit, Coat, Tailored Jacket and Skirt—*mfg*	315234	2385
Raincoats, men's and boys': Men's and Boys' Clothing and Furnishings—*whlse*	42232	5136
Raincoats–women's and children's: Women's, Children's, and Infants' and Accessories—*whlse*	42233	5137
Raisins: Dried and Dehydrated Food—*mfg*	311423	2034
Flour Milling—*mfg*	311211	2034
Rakes, handtools: Hand and Edge Tool—*mfg*	332212	3423
Rakes, hay (agricultural machinery): Farm Machinery and Equipment—*mfg*	333111	3523
Rakes, land clearing–mechanical: Construction Machinery—*mfg*	33312	3531
Overhead Traveling Crane, Hoist and Monorail System—*mfg*	333923	3531
Railroad Rolling Stock—*mfg*	33651	3531
Ramie yarn, thread, roving, and textiles: Broadwoven Fabric Mills—*mfg*	31321	2299
Narrow Fabric Mills—*mfg*	313221	2299
Nonwoven Fabric Mills—*mfg*	31323	2299
Textile and Fabric Finishing (except Broadwoven Fabric) Mills—*mfg*	313312	2299
Textile Product Mills, All Other Miscellaneous—*mfg*	314999	2299
Thread Mills—*mfg*	313113	2299
Yarn Spinning Mills—*mfg*	313111	2299
Ramming mixes, nonclay: Nonclay Refractory—*mfg*	327125	3297
Ramps, aircraft-loading: Fabricated Metal Product, All Other Miscellaneous—*mfg*	332999	3537
Industrial Truck, Tractor, Trailer and Stacker Machinery—*mfg*	333924	3537
Metal Container, Other—*mfg*	332439	3537
Ramps, loading–portable, adjustable, and hydraulic: Fabricated Metal Product, All Other Miscellaneous—*mfg*	332999	3537
Industrial Truck, Tractor, Trailer and Stacker Machinery—*mfg*	333924	3537
Metal Container, Other—*mfg*	332439	3537
Ramps, prefabricated–metal: Prefabricated Metal Building and Component—*mfg*	332311	3448
Random access memories (RAMS): Semiconductor and Related Device—*mfg*	334413	3674
Rands (shoe cut stock): Fastener, Button, Needle and Pin—*mfg*	339993	3131
Leather Good, All Other—*mfg*	316999	3131
Wood Product, All Other Miscellaneous—*mfg*	321999	3131
Range boilers, galvanized iron and nonferrous metal: Heating Equipment (except Electric and Warm Air Furnaces)—*mfg*	333414	3433
Range finders, photographic: Photographic and Photocopying Equipment—*mfg*	333315	3861
Photographic Film, Paper, Plate and Chemical—*mfg*	325992	3861
Ranges, cooking–commercial: Machinery, Other Commercial and Service Industry—*mfg*	333319	3589
Ranges, cooking–household: Household Cooking Appliance—*mfg*	335221	3631
Ranges, electric: Electrical Appliance, Television and Radio Set—*whlse*	42162	5064

ALPHABETICAL INDEX	NAICS	SIC
Ranges, except electric: Building Material Dealers, Other—*retail*	44419	5074
Plumbing and Heating Equipment and Supplies (Hydronics)—*whlse*	42172	5074
Ranges, gas and electric: Household Appliance Stores—*retail*	443111	5722
Ranges, household cooking–electric and gas: Household Cooking Appliance—*mfg*	335221	3631
Rapid transit cars and equipment: Pump and Pumping Equipment—*mfg*	333911	3743
Railroad Rolling Stock—*mfg*	33651	3743
Rare book stores: Non-Depository Credit Intermediation, All Other—*fin*	522298	5932
Used Merchandise Stores—*retail*	45331	5932
Rare earth metal salts: Basic Inorganic Chemical, All Other—*mfg*	325188	2819
Chemical Product, All Other Miscellaneous—*mfg*	325998	2819
Rare-earths ore mining: Metal Ore, All Other—*mining*	212299	1099
Raspberry farms: Berry (except Strawberry) Farming—*ag*	111334	171
Strawberry Farming—*ag*	111333	171
Rasps, including recutting and resharpening: Hand and Edge Tool—*mfg*	332212	3423
Rat poisons: Pesticide and Other Agricultural Chemical—*mfg*	32532	2879
Rate making organizations, insurance: Claims Adjusters—*fin*	524291	6411
Insurance Agencies and Brokerages—*fin*	52421	6411
Insurance Related Activities, All Other—*fin*	524298	6411
Third Party Administration for Insurance and Pension Funds—*fin*	524292	6411
Rate services, transportation: Freight Arrangement—*trans*	48851	4731
Management Consulting Services, Other—*prof*	541618	4731
Rateofclimb instrumentation: Search, Detection, Navigation, Guidance, Aeronautical, and Nautical System and Instrument—*mfg*	334511	3812
Ratine, cotton: Broadwoven Fabric Mills—*mfg*	31321	2211
Ratio transformers: Power, Distribution and Specialty Transformer—*mfg*	335311	3612
Rattan ware, except furniture: Manufacturing, All Other Miscellaneous—*mfg*	339999	2499
Wood Container and Pallet—*mfg*	32192	2499
Wood Product, All Other Miscellaneous—*mfg*	321999	2499
Rattlesnake farms: Animal Production, All Other—*ag*	11299	279
Apiculture—*ag*	11291	279
Ravioli, canned: Canning, Specialty—*mfg*	311422	2032
Food, All Other Miscellaneous—*mfg*	311999	2032
Raw stock dyeing and finishing–wool, mohair, and similar animal fibers: Broadwoven Fabric Finishing Mills—*mfg*	313311	2231
Broadwoven Fabric Mills—*mfg*	31321	2231
Textile and Fabric Finishing (except Broadwoven Fabric) Mills—*mfg*	313312	2231
Raw stock dyeing and other finishing, except wool: Broadwoven Fabric Finishing Mills—*mfg*	313311	2269

ALPHABETICAL INDEX	NAICS	SIC
Textile and Fabric Finishing (except Broadwoven Fabric) Mills—*mfg*	313312	2269
Rawhide: Leather and Hide Tanning and Finishing—*mfg*	31611	3111
Rayon broadwoven fabrics: Broadwoven Fabric Mills—*mfg*	31321	2221
Rayon piece goods: Broadwoven Fabric Finishing Mills—*mfg*	313311	5131
Piece Goods, Notions and Other Dry Goods—*whlse*	42231	5131
Textile and Fabric Finishing (except Broadwoven Fabric) Mills—*mfg*	313312	5131
Rayon primary products–fibers, straw, strips, and yarn: Cellulosic Organic Fiber—*mfg*	325221	2823
Rayon pulp: Paper (except Newsprint) Mills—*mfg*	322121	2611
Paperboard Mills—*mfg*	32213	2611
Pulp Mills—*mfg*	32211	2611
Rayon thread: Textile and Fabric Finishing (except Broadwoven Fabric) Mills—*mfg*	313312	2284
Thread Mills—*mfg*	313113	2284
Rayon tops, combing and converting: Broadwoven Fabric Mills—*mfg*	31321	2299
Narrow Fabric Mills—*mfg*	313221	2299
Nonwoven Fabric Mills—*mfg*	31323	2299
Textile and Fabric Finishing (except Broadwoven Fabric) Mills—*mfg*	313312	2299
Textile Product Mills, All Other Miscellaneous—*mfg*	314999	2299
Thread Mills—*mfg*	313113	2299
Yarn Spinning Mills—*mfg*	313111	2299
Rayon yarn, filament–throwing, twisting, winding: Textile and Fabric Finishing (except Broadwoven Fabric) Mills—*mfg*	313312	2282
Yarn Texturing, Throwing and Twisting Mills—*mfg*	313112	2282
Rayon yarn, made from purchased staple:spun: Yarn Spinning Mills—*mfg*	313111	2281
Rayon yarn, made in chemical plants: Cellulosic Organic Fiber—*mfg*	325221	2823
Rayon yarns: Nondurable Goods, Other Miscellaneous—*whlse*	42299	5199
Rays, catching of: Finfish Fishing—*ag*	114111	912
Razor blade strip steel, cold-rolled–not made in hot-rolling mills: Cold-Rolled Steel Shape—*mfg*	331221	3316
Razor blades: Cutlery and Flatware (except Precious)—*mfg*	332211	3421
Drug, Drug Proprietaries and Druggists' Sundries—*whlse*	42221	5122
Razor strops: Leather Good, All Other—*mfg*	316999	3199
Razors, electric: Electric Housewares and Household Fan—*mfg*	335211	3634
Electrical Appliance, Television and Radio Set—*whlse*	42162	5064
Heating Equipment (except Electric and Warm Air Furnaces)—*mfg*	333414	3634
Razors, nonelectric: Drug, Drug Proprietaries and Druggists' Sundries—*whlse*	42221	5122
Razors–safety and straight: Cutlery and Flatware (except Precious)—*mfg*	332211	3421
RDX (explosives): Explosives—*mfg*	32592	2892

Description	NAICS	SIC
Re-refining drycleaning fluid: Polish and Other Sanitation Good—*mfg*	325612	2842
Reactor containment vessels, metal plate: Air-Conditioning and Warm Air Heating Equipment and Commercial and Industrial Refrigeration Equipment—*mfg*	333415	3443
Metal Tank (Heavy Gauge)—*mfg*	33242	3443
Plate Work—*mfg*	332313	3443
Power Boiler and Heat Exchanger—*mfg*	33241	3443
Reactors, current limiting: Power, Distribution and Specialty Transformer—*mfg*	335311	3612
Reactors, nuclear–military and industrial: Air-Conditioning and Warm Air Heating Equipment and Commercial and Industrial Refrigeration Equipment—*mfg*	333415	3443
Metal Tank (Heavy Gauge)—*mfg*	33242	3443
Plate Work—*mfg*	332313	3443
Power Boiler and Heat Exchanger—*mfg*	33241	3443
Read only memories (ROMS): Semiconductor and Related Device—*mfg*	334413	3674
Readers, microfilm: Photographic and Photocopying Equipment—*mfg*	333315	3861
Photographic Film, Paper, Plate and Chemical—*mfg*	325992	3861
Reading rooms, religious materials: Civic and Social Organizations—*serv*	81341	8699
Reading schools: Language Schools—*educ*	61163	8299
Ready-Mix Concrete Manufacturing	**32732**	**3273**
Ready-mixed concrete, production and distribution: Ready-Mix Concrete—*mfg*	32732	3273
Ready-to-wear stores, women's: Women's Clothing Stores—*retail*	44812	5621
Reagent grade chemicals, inorganic–refined from technical grades: Basic Inorganic Chemical, All Other—*mfg*	325188	2819
Chemical Product, All Other Miscellaneous—*mfg*	325998	2819
Reagent grade chemicals, organic–refined from technical grades, except diagnostic and substances: Basic Organic Chemical, All Other—*mfg*	325199	2869
Real Estate	**531**	
Real Estate Agents and Brokers, Offices Of	**5312**	
Real Estate Agents and Brokers, Offices Of	**53121**	**6531**
Real estate agents, brokers and managers: Real Estate Agents and Brokers, Offices Of—*real*	53121	6531
Real Estate and Rental and Leasing	**53**	
Real estate appraisers: Real Estate Appraisers, Offices Of—*real*	53132	6531
Real Estate Appraisers, Offices Of	**53132**	**6531**
Real estate auctions: Real Estate Agents and Brokers, Offices Of—*real*	53121	6531
Real Estate, Other Activities Related to—*real*	53139	6531
Real Estate Credit	**522292**	**6162**
Real estate hoards: Business Associations—*serv*	81391	8611
Real Estate Investment Trusts	**52593**	**6798**
Real estate investment trusts (REIT'S): Real Estate Investment Trusts—*fin*	52593	6798
Real Estate Property Managers	**53131**	
Real estate schools: Apprenticeship Training—*educ*	611513	8249
Technical and Trade Schools, Other—*educ*	611519	8249
Real estate title insurance: Direct Title Insurance Carriers—*fin*	524127	6361
Reinsurance Carriers—*fin*	52413	6361
Real Estate, Activities Related to	**5313**	
Real Estate, Other Activities Related to	**53139**	**6531**
Real property subdividers and developers, cemetery lots only: Cemeteries and Crematories—*serv*	81222	6553
Real property subdividers and developers, except of cemetery lots: Land Subdivision and Land Development—*const*	23311	6552
Realty investment trusts: Real Estate Investment Trusts—*fin*	52593	6798
Realty trusts: Real Estate Investment Trusts—*fin*	52593	6798
Reamers: Industrial Machinery and Equipment—*whlse*	42183	5084
Reamers, machine tool: Cutting Tool and Machine Tool Accessory—*mfg*	333515	3545
Hand and Edge Tool—*mfg*	332212	3545
Reaming machines: Machine Tool (Metal Cutting Types)—*mfg*	333512	3541
Rear axle housings, motor vehicle: Motor Vehicle Parts, All Other—*mfg*	336399	3714
Motor Vehicle Steering and Suspension Components (except Spring)—*mfg*	33633	3714
Motor Vehicle Transmission and Power Train Parts—*mfg*	33635	3714
Rebabbitting: Personal and Household Goods Repair and Maintenance, Other—*serv*	81149	7699
Rebinding books, magazines, or pamphlets: Tradebinding and Related Work—*mfg*	323121	2789
Rebuilding and retreading tires for the trade: Automotive Repair and Maintenance, All Other—*serv*	811198	7534
Tire Retreading—*mfg*	326212	7534
Rebuilding motor vehicle gasoline engines and transmissions on a factory basis: Gasoline Engine and Engine Parts—*mfg*	336312	3714
Motor Vehicle Parts, All Other—*mfg*	336399	3714
Rebuilding motors, other than automotive: Machinery and Equipment (except Automotive and Electronic) Repair and Maintenance, Commercial and Industrial—*serv*	81131	7694
Motor and Generator—*mfg*	335312	7694
Rebuilding tires: Automotive Repair and Maintenance, All Other—*serv*	811198	7534
Tire Retreading—*mfg*	326212	7534
Rebuilt machine tools, metal cutting types: Machine Tool (Metal Cutting Types)—*mfg*	333512	3541
Rebuilt machine tools, metal forming types: Machine Tool (Metal Forming Types)—*mfg*	333513	3542
Recapping machinery for tires: Industrial Machinery and Equipment—*whlse*	42183	5084

ALPHABETICAL INDEX	NAICS	SIC
Recapping tires: Automotive Repair and Maintenance, All Other—*serv*	811198	7534
Tire Retreading—*mfg*	326212	7534
Receipt books: Blankbook, Loose-leaf Binder and Device—*mfg*	323118	2782
Flexographic Printing, Commercial—*mfg*	323112	2782
Gravure Printing, Commercial—*mfg*	323111	2782
Lithographic Printing, Commercial—*mfg*	323110	2782
Printing, Other Commercial—*mfg*	323119	2782
Screen Printing, Commercial—*mfg*	323113	2782
Receiver4ransmitter units (transceivers): Radio and Television Broadcasting and Wireless Communications Equipment—*mfg*	33422	3663
Receivers, radio communications: Radio and Television Broadcasting and Wireless Communications Equipment—*mfg*	33422	3663
Receiving sets, radio and television–household: Audio and Video Equipment—*mfg*	33431	3651
Receiving type electron tubes: Electron Tube—*mfg*	334411	3671
Receptacles, electrical: Building Material Dealers, Other—*retail*	44419	5063
Electrical Apparatus and Equipment, Wiring Supplies and Material—*whlse*	42161	5063
Rechroming auto bumpers, for the trade: Electroplating, Plating, Polishing, Anodizing and Coloring—*mfg*	332813	3471
Reciprocal interinsurance exchanges, accident and health insurance: Direct Health and Medical Insurance Carriers—*fin*	524114	6321
Insurance Funds, Other—*fin*	52519	6321
Reinsurance Carriers—*fin*	52413	6321
Reciprocal interinsurance exchanges, surety and fidelity insurance: Direct Property and Casualty Insurance Carriers—*fin*	524126	6351
Reinsurance Carriers—*fin*	52413	6351
Reciprocal interinsurance exchanges–fire, marine, and casualty insurance: Direct Property and Casualty Insurance Carriers—*fin*	524126	6331
Insurance Funds, Other—*fin*	52519	6331
Reinsurance Carriers—*fin*	52413	6331
Reck crushing machinery, portable: Construction Machinery—*mfg*	33312	3531
Overhead Traveling Crane, Hoist and Monorail System—*mfg*	333923	3531
Railroad Rolling Stock—*mfg*	33651	3531
Reclaimed rubber (reworked by manufacturing processes): Fabric Coating Mills—*mfg*	31332	3069
Rubber Product, All Other—*mfg*	326299	3069
Reclaiming ferrous metals from clay: Iron and Steel Mills—*mfg*	331111	3399
Secondary Smelting and Alloying of Aluminum—*mfg*	331314	3399
Secondary Smelting, Refining, and Alloying of Copper—*mfg*	331423	3399
Secondary Smelting, Refining, and Alloying of Nonferrous Metal (except Copper and Aluminum)—*mfg*	331492	3399
Reclaiming iron and steel scrap fromslag: Recyclable Material—*whlse*	42193	5093

ALPHABETICAL INDEX	NAICS	SIC
Reclamation projects construction–general contractors: Heavy, All Other—*const*	23499	1629
Industrial Nonbuilding Structure—*const*	23493	1629
Recliners, upholstered on wood frames: Upholstered Household Furniture—*mfg*	337121	2512
Recoil mechanisms for guns more than 30 mm. (or more than 1.18 inch): Ordnance and Accessories, Other—*mfg*	332995	3489
Recoil mechanisms for guns, 30 mm. (or 1.18 inch) or less: Small Arms—*mfg*	332994	3484
Recoilless rifles: Ordnance and Accessories, Other—*mfg*	332995	3489
Reconstituted wood panels: Reconstituted Wood Product—*mfg*	321219	2493
Reconstituted Wood Product Manufacturing	**321219**	**2493**
Record albums: Blankbook, Loose-leaf Binder and Device—*mfg*	323118	2782
Flexographic Printing, Commercial—*mfg*	323112	2782
Gravure Printing, Commercial—*mfg*	323111	2782
Lithographic Printing, Commercial—*mfg*	323110	2782
Printing, Other Commercial—*mfg*	323119	2782
Screen Printing, Commercial—*mfg*	323113	2782
Record blanks, phonograph: Integrated Record Production/Distribution—*info*	51222	3652
Prerecorded Compact Disc (except Software), Tape, and Record Reproducing—*mfg*	334612	3652
Record clubs, mailorder: Electronic Shopping and Mail-Order Houses—*retail*	45411	5961
Record Production	**51221**	**8999**
Record stores: Prerecorded Tape, Compact Disc and Record Stores—*retail*	45122	5735
Recorders, home tape–cassette, cartridge, and reel: Audio and Video Equipment—*mfg*	33431	3651
Recorders, oscillographic: Electronic Coil, Transformer, and Other Inductor—*mfg*	334416	3825
Instrument for Measuring and Testing Electricity and Electrical Signals—*mfg*	334515	3825
Recorders, tape–for computers: Computer Storage Device—*mfg*	334112	3572
Recording and playback heads, magnetic: Electronic Component, Other—*mfg*	334419	3679
Motor Vehicle Electrical and Electronic Equipment, Other—*mfg*	336322	3679
Printed Circuit/Electronics Assembly—*mfg*	334418	3679
Radio and Television Broadcasting and Wireless Communications Equipment—*mfg*	33422	3679
Recording heads for speech and musical equipment: Electronic Component, Other—*mfg*	334419	3679
Motor Vehicle Electrical and Electronic Equipment, Other—*mfg*	336322	3679
Printed Circuit/Electronics Assembly—*mfg*	334418	3679
Radio and Television Broadcasting and Wireless Communications Equipment—*mfg*	33422	3679

Description	NAICS	SIC
Recording instruments and accessories: Industrial Machinery and Equipment—*whlse*	42183	5084
Recording machines, music and speech–except dictation and telephone answering machines: Audio and Video Equipment—*mfg*	33431	3651
Recording studios on a contract or feebasis: Sound Recording Studios—*info*	51224	7389
Records, phonograph: Integrated Record Production/Distribution—*info*	51222	3652
Prerecorded Compact Disc (except Software), Tape, and Record Reproducing—*mfg*	334612	3652
Recovering and refining of nonferrous metals: Secondary Smelting and Alloying of Aluminum—*mfg*	331314	3341
Secondary Smelting, Refining, and Alloying of Copper—*mfg*	331423	3341
Secondary Smelting, Refining, and Alloying of Nonferrous Metal (except Copper and Aluminum)—*mfg*	331492	3341
Recovering textile fibers from clippings and rags: Broadwoven Fabric Mills—*mfg*	31321	2299
Narrow Fabric Mills—*mfg*	313221	2299
Nonwoven Fabric Mills—*mfg*	31323	2299
Textile and Fabric Finishing (except Broadwoven Fabric) Mills—*mfg*	313312	2299
Textile Product Mills, All Other Miscellaneous—*mfg*	314999	2299
Thread Mills—*mfg*	313113	2299
Yarn Spinning Mills—*mfg*	313111	2299
Recovery of iron ore from open hearth slag: Iron and Steel Mills—*mfg*	331111	3399
Secondary Smelting, Refining, and Alloying of Nonferrous Metal (except Copper and Aluminum)—*mfg*	331492	3399
Recovery of silver from used photographic film: Secondary Smelting and Alloying of Aluminum—*mfg*	331314	3341
Secondary Smelting, Refining, and Alloying of Nonferrous Metal (except Copper and Aluminum)—*mfg*	331492	3341
Recreation and sports clubs, membership–except physical fitness: Amusement and Recreation Industries, All Other—*arts*	71399	7997
Recreational and Vacation Camps	**721214**	**7032**
Recreational camps: Recreational and Vacation Camps—*accom*	721214	7032
Recreational Goods Rental	**532292**	**7999**
Recreational hotels: Bed and Breakfast Inns—*accom*	721191	7011
Casino Hotels—*accom*	72112	7011
Hotels (except Casino Hotels) and Motels—*accom*	72111	7011
Traveler Accommodation, All Other—*accom*	721199	7011
Recreational program administration: Land, Mineral, Wildlife, and Forest Conservation—*pub*	92412	9512
Recreational Vehicle Dealers	**44121**	**5561**
Recreational vehicle parks: RV (Recreational Vehicle) Parks and Campgrounds—*accom*	721211	7033
Recreational vehicle parts and accessories: Recreational Vehicle Dealers—*retail*	44121	5561
Recreational vehicles: Automobile and Other Motor Vehicle—*whlse*	42111	5012
Rectifier transformers: Power, Distribution and Specialty Transformer—*mfg*	335311	3612
Rectifiers (electrical apparatus): Electrical Equipment and Component, All Other Miscellaneous—*mfg*	335999	3629
Rectifiers, electronic: Electronic Parts and Equipment, Other—*whlse*	42169	5065
Rectifiers, electronic–except solid-state: Electronic Component, Other—*mfg*	334419	3679
Motor Vehicle Electrical and Electronic Equipment, Other—*mfg*	336322	3679
Printed Circuit/Electronics Assembly—*mfg*	334418	3679
Radio and Television Broadcasting and Wireless Communications Equipment—*mfg*	33422	3679
Rectifiers, solid-state: Semiconductor and Related Device—*mfg*	334413	3674
Recyclable Material Wholesalers	**42193**	**5093**
Red lead pigments: Carbon Black—*mfg*	325182	2816
Inorganic Dye and Pigment—*mfg*	325131	2816
Red oil (oleic acid): Basic Organic Chemical, All Other—*mfg*	325199	2899
Chemical Product, All Other Miscellaneous—*mfg*	325998	2899
Redevelopment land agencies: Urban Planning and Community and Rural Development, Administration of—*pub*	92512	9532
Redox (oxidation-reduction potential) instruments: Analytical Laboratory Instrument—*mfg*	334516	3826
Redrilling oil and gas wells on a contract basis: Drilling Oil and Gas Wells—*mining*	213111	1381
Redrying and stemming of tobacco: Tobacco Product, Other—*mfg*	312229	2141
Tobacco Stemming and Redrying—*mfg*	31221	2141
Reducer returns, pipe–metal: Fabricated Metal Product, All Other Miscellaneous—*mfg*	332999	3494
Other Metal Valve and Pipe Fitting, Other—*mfg*	332919	3494
Reducers, speed: Speed Changer, Industrial High-Speed Drive and Gear—*mfg*	333612	3566
Reducing facilities, physical fitness, without lodging: Fitness and Recreational Sports Centers—*arts*	71394	7991
Reduction gears and gear units for turbines, except automotive and aircraft: Speed Changer, Industrial High-Speed Drive and Gear—*mfg*	333612	3566
Reed furniture: Household Furniture (except Wood and Metal)—*mfg*	337125	2519
Reed peat mining: Crushed and Broken Stone and Quarrying, Other—*mining*	212319	1499
Non-Metallic Mineral, All Other—*mining*	212399	1499
Reed ware, except furniture: Manufacturing, All Other Miscellaneous—*mfg*	339999	2499
Wood Container and Pallet—*mfg*	32192	2499
Wood Product, All Other Miscellaneous—*mfg*	321999	2499
Reedboards, organ: Musical Instrument—*mfg*	339992	3931
Reeds for musical instruments: Musical Instrument—*mfg*	339992	3931
Reeds, loom: Textile Machinery—*mfg*	333292	3552
Reels and racks, firehose: General Purpose Machinery , All Other—*mfg*	333999	3569

ALPHABETICAL INDEX	NAICS	SIC
Reels, cable–metal: Fabricated Metal Product, All Other Miscellaneous—*mfg*	332999	3499
Reels, cloth winding–wood: Manufacturing, All Other Miscellaneous—*mfg*	339999	2499
Wood Container and Pallet—*mfg*	32192	2499
Wood Product, All Other Miscellaneous—*mfg*	321999	2499
Reels, film: Photographic and Photocopying Equipment—*mfg*	333315	3861
Photographic Film, Paper, Plate and Chemical—*mfg*	325992	3861
Reels, fishing: Sporting and Athletic Goods—*mfg*	33992	3949
Reels, for drying clothes–wood: Manufacturing, All Other Miscellaneous—*mfg*	339999	2499
Wood Container and Pallet—*mfg*	32192	2499
Wood Product, All Other Miscellaneous—*mfg*	321999	2499
Reels, plywood: Manufacturing, All Other Miscellaneous—*mfg*	339999	2499
Wood Container and Pallet—*mfg*	32192	2499
Wood Product, All Other Miscellaneous—*mfg*	321999	2499
Reels, textile–fiber: Fiber Can, Tube, Drum, and Similar Products—*mfg*	322214	2655
Refactory brick construction–contractors: Masonry and Stone Contractors—*const*	23541	1741
Referees in bankruptcy: Lawyers, Offices Of—*prof*	54111	8111
Referral services for personal and social problems: Child and Youth Services—*hlth*	62411	8322
Community Food Services—*hlth*	62421	8322
Community Housing Services, Other—*hlth*	624229	8322
Emergency and Other Relief Services—*hlth*	62423	8322
Individual and Family Services, Other—*hlth*	62419	8322
Parole Offices and Probation Offices—*pub*	92215	8322
Services for the Elderly and Persons with Disabilities—*hlth*	62412	8322
Temporary Shelters—*hlth*	624221	8322
Refined petroleum pipelines: Pipeline of Refined—*trans*	48691	4613
Refineries, cane sugar: Cane Sugar Refining—*mfg*	311312	2062
Refineries, petroleum: Petroleum Refineries—*mfg*	32411	2911
Refinery gas produced in petroleum refineries: Petroleum Refineries—*mfg*	32411	2911
Refining of lead, primary: Primary Smelting and Refining of Nonferrous Metal (except Copper and Aluminum)—*mfg*	331419	3339
Refining of nonferrous metal, primary–except copper and aluminurn: Primary Smelting and Refining of Nonferrous Metal (except Copper and Aluminum)—*mfg*	331419	3339
Refining of nonferrous metals and alloys, secondary: Secondary Smelting and Alloying of Aluminum—*mfg*	331314	3341
Secondary Smelting, Refining, and Alloying of Copper—*mfg*	331423	3341
Secondary Smelting, Refining, and Alloying of Nonferrous Metal (except Copper and Aluminum)—*mfg*	331492	3341
Refining of zinc, primary: Primary Smelting and Refining of Nonferrous Metal (except Copper and Aluminum)—*mfg*	331419	3339

ALPHABETICAL INDEX	NAICS	SIC
Refinishing and sponging cloths–wool, mohair, and similar animal fibers, forthe trade: Broadwoven Fabric Finishing Mills—*mfg*	313311	2231
Broadwoven Fabric Mills—*mfg*	31321	2231
Textile and Fabric Finishing (except Broadwoven Fabric) Mills—*mfg*	313312	2231
Refinishing and sponging cotton broadwoven fabrics for the trade: Broadwoven Fabric Finishing Mills—*mfg*	313311	2261
Refinishing of manmade fiber and silk broadwoven fabrics: Broadwoven Fabric Finishing Mills—*mfg*	313311	2262
Reflectometers, sliding sborts: Electronic Coil, Transformer, and Other Inductor—*mfg*	334416	3825
Instrument for Measuring and Testing Electricity and Electrical Signals—*mfg*	334515	3825
Reflector glass beads, for highway signs and other reflectors–made from purchased glass: Glass Product Made of Purchased Glass—*mfg*	327215	3231
Reflectors for lighting equipment, glass–pressed or blown: Pressed and Blown Glass and Glassware, Other—*mfg*	327212	3229
Reflectors for lighting equipment–metal: Lighting Equipment, Other—*mfg*	335129	3648
Reflectors, clearance–vehicular: Vehicular Lighting Equipment—*mfg*	336321	3647
Reflectors, optical: Optical Instrument and Lens—*mfg*	333314	3827
Reflectors, searchlight: Optical Instrument and Lens—*mfg*	333314	3827
Reforestation: Forestry Support Activities—*ag*	11531	851
Reformatories: Correctional Institutions—*pub*	92214	9223
Refractometers, industrial process type: Instruments and Related Products for Measuring, Displaying, and Controlling Industrial Process Variables—*mfg*	334513	3823
Refractometers, laboratory: Analytical Laboratory Instrument—*mfg*	334516	3826
Refractories, castable–nonclay: Nonclay Refractory—*mfg*	327125	3297
Refractories, clay: Clay Refractory—*mfg*	327124	3255
Refractories, graphite–carbon bond or ceramic bond: Nonclay Refractory—*mfg*	327125	3297
Refractories, nonclay: Nonclay Refractory—*mfg*	327125	3297
Refractory cement and mortars, clay: Clay Refractory—*mfg*	327124	3255
Refractory cement, nonclay: Nonclay Refractory—*mfg*	327125	3297
Refractory material: Industrial Machinery and Equipment—*whlse*	42183	5085
Industrial Supplies—*whlse*	42184	5085
Refreshment stands: Cafeterias—*accom*	722212	5812
Caterers—*accom*	72232	5812
Foodservice Contractors—*accom*	72231	5812
Full-Service Restaurants—*accom*	72211	5812
Limited-Service Restaurants—*accom*	722211	5812
Snack and Nonalcoholic Beverage Bars—*accom*	722213	5812
Theater Companies and Dinner Theaters—*arts*	71111	5812

Refrigerated warehousing: Refrigerated Warehousing and Storage Facilities—*trans*	49312	4222
Refrigerated Warehousing and Storage Facilities	**49312**	**4226**
Refrigeration and freezer work–contractors: Plumbing, Heating and Air-Conditioning Contractors—*const*	23511	1711
Refrigeration compressors: Air-Conditioning and Warm Air Heating Equipment and Commercial and Industrial Refrigeration Equipment—*mfg*	333415	3585
Motor Vehicle Air-Conditioning—*mfg*	336391	3585
Refrigeration controls, pressure: Automatic Environmental Control for Residential, Commercial and Appliance Use—*mfg*	334512	3822
Refrigeration Equipment and Supplies Wholesalers	**42174**	**5078**
Refrigeration machinery and equipment, industrial: Air-Conditioning and Warm Air Heating Equipment and Commercial and Industrial Refrigeration Equipment—*mfg*	333415	3585
Motor Vehicle Air-Conditioning—*mfg*	336391	3585
Refrigeration repair service, electric: Appliance Repair and Maintenance—*serv*	811412	7623
Household Appliance Stores—*retail*	443111	7623
Machinery and Equipment (except Automotive and Electronic) Repair and Maintenance, Commercial and Industrial—*serv*	81131	7623
Refrigeration thermostats: Automatic Environmental Control for Residential, Commercial and Appliance Use—*mfg*	334512	3822
Refrigeration/air-conditioning defrost controls: Automatic Environmental Control for Residential, Commercial and Appliance Use—*mfg*	334512	3822
Refrigerator cabinets, household: Household Refrigerator and Home Freezer—*mfg*	335222	3632
Refrigerator dishes and jars, glass: Pressed and Blown Glass and Glassware, Other—*mfg*	327212	3229
Refrigerator parts, porcelain enameled: Kitchen Utensil, Pot and Pan—*mfg*	332214	3469
Refrigerator repair service, electric: Appliance Repair and Maintenance—*serv*	811412	7623
Household Appliance Stores—*retail*	443111	7623
Machinery and Equipment (except Automotive and Electronic) Repair and Maintenance, Commercial and Industrial—*serv*	81131	7623
Refrigerators and related electric and gas appliances: Household Appliance Stores—*retail*	443111	5722
Refrigerators, commercial–reach-in and walk-in: Refrigeration Equipment and Supplies—*whlse*	42174	5078
Refrigerators, household–electric and gas: Electrical Appliance, Television and Radio Set—*whlse*	42162	5064
Refrigerators, mechanical and absorption–household: Household Refrigerator and Home Freezer—*mfg*	335222	3632
Refueling equipment, airplane–for use in flight: Aircraft Part and Auxiliary Equipment, Other—*mfg*	336413	3728
Fluid Power Valve and Hose Fitting—*mfg*	332912	3728
Refugee services: Child and Youth Services—*hlth*	62411	8322
Community Food Services—*hlth*	62421	8322
Community Housing Services, Other—*hlth*	624229	8322
Emergency and Other Relief Services—*hlth*	62423	8322
Individual and Family Services, Other—*hlth*	62419	8322
Parole Offices and Probation Offices—*pub*	92215	8322
Services for the Elderly and Persons with Disabilities—*hlth*	62412	8322
Temporary Shelters—*hlth*	624221	8322
Refuse systems: Hazardous Waste Collection—*admin*	562112	4953
Hazardous Waste Treatment and Disposal—*admin*	562211	4953
Materials Recovery Facilities—*admin*	56292	4953
Nonhazardous Waste Treatment and Disposal, Other—*admin*	562219	4953
Solid Waste Collection—*admin*	562111	4953
Solid Waste Combustors and Incinerators—*admin*	562213	4953
Solid Waste Landfill—*admin*	562212	4953
Waste Collection, Other—*admin*	562119	4953
Refuse, local collecting and transporting–without disposal: General Freight Trucking, Local—*trans*	48411	4212
Hazardous Waste Collection—*admin*	562112	4212
Solid Waste Collection—*admin*	562111	4212
Waste Collection, Other—*admin*	562119	4212
Regalia: Cut and Sew Apparel, All Other—*mfg*	315299	2389
Regenerated cellulose fibers: Cellulosic Organic Fiber—*mfg*	325221	2823
Regional clearinghouse associations: Commodity Contracts Dealing—*fin*	52313	6099
Credit Intermediation, Other Activities Related to—*fin*	52239	6099
Financial Investment Activities, Miscellaneous—*fin*	523999	6099
Financial Transactions Processing, Reserve, and Clearing House Activities—*fin*	52232	6099
Trust, Fiduciary and Custody Activities—*fin*	523991	6099
Regional planning organizations, for social services: Grantmaking and Giving Services, Other—*serv*	813219	8399
Social Advocacy Organizations, Other—*serv*	813319	8399
Voluntary Health Organizations—*serv*	813212	8399
Registered nurses, offices of–except home care services: Health Practitioners, Offices Of Miscellaneous—*hlth*	621399	8049
Mental Health Practitioners (except Physicians), Offices Of—*hlth*	62133	8049
Physical, Occupational and Speech Therapists and Audiologists, Offices Of—*hlth*	62134	8049
Registers, air–metal: Ornamental and Architectural Metal Work—*mfg*	332323	3446
Registers, autographic: Lead Pencil and Art Good—*mfg*	339942	3579
Office Machinery—*mfg*	333313	3579
Watch, Clock, and Part—*mfg*	334518	3579
Registers, credit account: Computer Peripheral Equipment, Other—*mfg*	334119	3578
Office Machinery—*mfg*	333313	3578
Registers, fare–for streetcars, buses, etc.: Measuring and Controlling Device, Other—*mfg*	334519	3829
Surgical and Medical Instrument—*mfg*	339112	3829

ALPHABETICAL INDEX	NAICS	SIC
Registers, linear tallying: Totalizing Fluid Meter and Counting Device—*mfg*	334514	3824
Registries, nurses: Employment Placement Agencies—*admin*	56131	7361
Human Resources and Executive Search Consulting Services—*prof*	541612	7361
Regrinding machines, crankshaft: Machine Tool (Metal Cutting Types)—*mfg*	333512	3541
Regulation and Administration of Communications, Electric, Gas, and Other Utilities	**92613**	**9631**
Regulation and Administration of Transportation Programs	**92612**	**9621**
Regulation and inspection of agricultural products: Agricultural Marketing and Commodities, Regulation of—*pub*	92614	9641
Regulation of Agricultural Marketing and Commodities	**92614**	**9641**
Regulation of utilities: Regulation and Administration of Communications, Electric, Gas, and Other Utilities—*pub*	92613	9631
Regulation, Licensing, and Inspection of Miscellaneous Commercial Sectors	**92615**	**9651**
Regulators, feeder voltage (electric transformers): Power, Distribution and Specialty Transformer—*mfg*	335311	3612
Regulators, power: Switchgear and Switchboard Apparatus—*mfg*	335313	3613
Regulators, transmission and distribution voltage: Power, Distribution and Specialty Transformer—*mfg*	335311	3612
Regulators, voltage–motor vehicle: Motor Vehicle Electrical and Electronic Equipment, Other—*mfg*	336322	3694
Rehabilitation centers, outpatient (medical treatment): Family Planning Centers—*hlth*	62141	8093
Outpatient Care Centers, All Other—*hlth*	621498	8093
Outpatient Mental Health and Substance Abuse Centers—*hlth*	62142	8093
Rehabilitation centers, residential–with health care incidental: Homes for the Elderly—*hlth*	623312	8361
Residential Care Facilities, Other—*hlth*	62399	8361
Residential Mental Health and Substance Abuse Facilities—*hlth*	62322	8361
Rehabilitation counseling and training, vocational: Vocational Rehabilitation Services—*hlth*	62431	8331
Rehabilitation hospitals–drug addiction and alcoholism: General Medical and Surgical Hospitals—*hlth*	62211	8069
Hospitals (except Psychiatric and Substance Abuse), Specialty—*hlth*	62231	8069
Psychiatric and Substance Abuse Hospitals—*hlth*	62221	8069
Reinforcement mesh, wire: Metal Service Centers and Offices—*whlse*	42151	5051
Reinforcing mesh concrete–made from purchased wire: Fabricated Wire Product, Other—*mfg*	332618	3496
Reinsurance Carriers	**52413**	**6321**
Reinsurance carriers, accident and health: Direct Health and Medical Insurance Carriers—*fin*	524114	6321
Insurance Funds, Other—*fin*	52519	6321

ALPHABETICAL INDEX	NAICS	SIC
Reinsurance Carriers—*fin*	52413	6321
Reinsurance carriers, life: Direct Life Insurance Carriers—*fin*	524113	6311
Reinsurance Carriers—*fin*	52413	6311
Reinsurance, life: Direct Life Insurance Carriers—*fin*	524113	6311
Reinsurance Carriers—*fin*	52413	6311
Relay and Industrial Control Manufacturing	**335314**	**3625**
Relays: Building Material Dealers, Other—*retail*	44419	5063
Electrical Apparatus and Equipment, Wiring Supplies and Material—*whlse*	42161	5063
Relay and Industrial Control—*mfg*	335314	3625
Relays, instrument–all types: Electronic Coil, Transformer, and Other Inductor—*mfg*	334416	3825
Instrument for Measuring and Testing Electricity and Electrical Signals—*mfg*	334515	3825
Relief services, temporary: Child and Youth Services—*hlth*	62411	8322
Community Food Services—*hlth*	62421	8322
Community Housing Services, Other—*hlth*	624229	8322
Emergency and Other Relief Services—*hlth*	62423	8322
Individual and Family Services, Other—*hlth*	62419	8322
Parole Offices and Probation Offices—*pub*	92215	8322
Services for the Elderly and Persons with Disabilities—*hlth*	62412	8322
Temporary Shelters—*hlth*	624221	8322
Religious book stores: Book Stores—*retail*	451211	5942
Religious goods stores (other than books): Stores (except Tobacco Stores), All Other Miscellaneous—*retail*	453998	5999
Religious instruction, provided by religious organizations: Religious Organizations—*serv*	81311	8661
Religious motion picture production: Motion Picture and Video Production—*info*	51211	7812
Religious Organizations	**8131**	
Religious Organizations	**81311**	**8661**
Religious trusts, management of: Grantmaking Foundations—*serv*	813211	6732
Religious, Grantmaking, Civic, and Professional and Similar Organizations	**813**	
Relishes, fruit and vegetable: Fruit and Vegetable Canning—*mfg*	311421	2035
Mayonnaise, Dressing and Other Prepared Sauce—*mfg*	311941	2035
Remediation and Other Waste Management Services	**5629**	
Remediation Services	**56291**	**4959**
Remedies, human and animal: Pharmaceutical Preparation—*mfg*	325412	2834
Remnant stores: Sewing, Needlework and Piece Goods Stores—*retail*	45113	5949
Remodeling buildings, industrial and warehouse–general contractors: Building, Commercial and Institutional—*const*	23332	1541
Manufacturing and Industrial Building—*const*	23331	1541
Remodeling buildings, nonresidential–except industrial and warehouses–general contractors: Building, Commercial and Institutional—*const*	23332	1542

Description	NAICS	SIC
Remodeling buildings, residential–except single-family–general contractors: Building, Commercial and Institutional—*const*	23332	1522
Multifamily Housing—*const*	23322	1522
Remodeling buildings, single-family–general contractors: Single Family Housing—*const*	23321	1521
Remote data base information retrieval services: On-Line Information Services—*info*	514191	7375
Removal of condensate gasoline from field gathering lines–on a contract basis: Oil and Gas Operations Support Activities—*mining*	213112	1389
Removal of overburden for anthracite–on a contract basis: Coal Support Activities—*mining*	213113	1241
Removal of overburden for bituminous coal–on a contract basis: Coal Support Activities—*mining*	213113	1241
Removal of overburden for metal mining:on a contract basis: Geophysical Surveying and Mapping Services—*prof*	54136	1081
Metal Support Activities—*mining*	213114	1081
Removal of overburden for nonmetallic minerals except fuels–on a contract basis: Geophysical Surveying and Mapping Services—*prof*	54136	1481
Non-Metallic Minerals (except Fuels) Support Activities—*mining*	213115	1481
Rendering and Meat By-product Processing	**311613**	**2077**
Rendering plants, inedible grease andtallow: Fats and Oils Refining and Blending—*mfg*	311225	2077
Fresh and Frozen Seafood Processing—*mfg*	311712	2077
Rendering and Meat By-product Processing—*mfg*	311613	2077
Seafood Canning—*mfg*	311711	2077
Reneedling work: Personal and Household Goods Repair and Maintenance, Other—*serv*	81149	7699
Rennet: Nondurable Goods, Other Miscellaneous—*whlse*	42299	5199
Renovating buildings, industrial and warehouse–general contractors: Building, Commercial and Institutional—*const*	23332	1541
Manufacturing and Industrial Building—*const*	23331	1541
Renovating buildings, nonresidential–except industrial and warehouses–general contractors: Building, Commercial and Institutional—*const*	23332	1542
Renovating buildings, residential–except single-family–general contractors: Building, Commercial and Institutional—*const*	23332	1522
Multifamily Housing—*const*	23322	1522
Renovating buildings, single-family–general contractors: Single Family Housing—*const*	23321	1521
Rent control agencies: Regulation, Licensing, and Inspection of Miscellaneous Commercial Sectors—*pub*	92615	9651
Rental agents for real estate: Real Estate Agents and Brokers, Offices Of—*real*	53121	6531
Residential Property Managers—*real*	531311	6531
Rental and leasing of dishes, silverware, and tables: Consumer Goods Rental, All Other—*real*	532299	7359
Rental and Leasing Services	**532**	
Rental and servicing of electronic equipment, except computers: Consumer Electronics and Appliances Rental—*real*	53221	7359
Machinery and Equipment Rental and Leasing, Other Commercial and Industrial—*real*	53249	7359
Office Machinery and Equipment Rental and Leasing—*real*	53242	7359
Rental of automobiles, without drivers: Passenger Car Rental—*real*	532111	7514
Rental of beach chairs and accessories: Recreational Goods Rental—*real*	532292	7999
Rental of bicycles: Recreational Goods Rental—*real*	532292	7999
Rental of books: Libraries and Archives—*info*	51412	8231
Rental of coin-operated machines: Machinery and Equipment Rental and Leasing, Other Commercial and Industrial—*real*	53249	7359
Rental of cold storage lockers: Refrigerated Warehousing and Storage Facilities—*trans*	49312	4222
Rental of computer time: Data Processing Services—*info*	51421	7374
Rental of computers, except finance leasing or by the manufacturer: Office Machinery and Equipment Rental and Leasing—*real*	53242	7377
Rental of construction equipment: Construction, and Forestry Machinery and Equipment Rental and Leasing—*real*	532412	7353
Heavy, All Other—*const*	23499	7353
Rental of furnished rooms: Rooming and Boarding Houses—*accom*	72131	7021
Rental of furniture: Consumer Goods Rental, All Other—*real*	532299	7359
Rental of golf carts: Recreational Goods Rental—*real*	532292	7999
Rental of hearses and limousines, with drivers: Limousine Service—*trans*	48532	4119
Rental of motion picture equipment: Independent Artists, Writers, and Performers—*arts*	71151	7819
Machinery and Equipment Rental and Leasing, Other Commercial and Industrial—*real*	53249	7819
Motion Picture and Video Industries, Other—*info*	512199	7819
Rental of motion picture film: Durable Goods, Other Miscellaneous—*whlse*	42199	7822
Motion Picture and Video Distribution—*info*	51212	7822
Rental of oil field equipment: Machinery and Equipment Rental and Leasing, Other Commercial and Industrial—*real*	53249	7359
Rental of passenger automobiles, with drivers: Limousine Service—*trans*	48532	4119
Transportation, Special Needs—*trans*	485991	4119
Rental of railroad cars: Air, Rail, and Water Equipment Rental and Leasing, Commercial—*real*	532411	4741
Rail Support Activities—*trans*	48821	4741
Rental of rowboats and canoes: Recreational Goods Rental—*real*	532292	7999
Rental of saddle horses: Recreational Goods Rental—*real*	532292	7999
Rental of theatrical scenery: Machinery and Equipment Rental and Leasing, Other Commercial and Industrial—*real*	53249	7922
Rental of tools: Consumer Goods Rental, All Other—*real*	532299	7359
Rental of trailers: Truck, Utility Trailer, and RV (Recreational Vehicle) Rental and Leasing—*real*	53212	7519

ALPHABETICAL INDEX	NAICS	SIC
Rental of trucks with drivers: Freight (except Used Goods) Trucking, Local Specialized—*trans*	48422	4212
General Freight Trucking, Local—*trans*	48411	4212
Used Household and Office Goods Moving—*trans*	48421	4212
Rental of trucks, without drivers: Truck, Utility Trailer, and RV (Recreational Vehicle) Rental and Leasing—*real*	53212	7513
Renting automobile utility trailers: Truck, Utility Trailer, and RV (Recreational Vehicle) Rental and Leasing—*real*	53212	7519
Renting travel, camping, or recreational trailers: Truck, Utility Trailer, and RV (Recreational Vehicle) Rental and Leasing—*real*	53212	7519
Rep, cotton: Broadwoven Fabric Mills—*mfg*	31321	2211
Repair and Maintenance	**811**	
Repair materials, tire and tube: Tire and Tube—*whlse*	42113	5014
Tire Dealers—*retail*	44132	5014
Repair of cracked castings (welding service): Personal and Household Goods Repair and Maintenance, Other—*serv*	81149	7692
Repair of furniture upholstery: Reupholstery and Furniture Repair—*serv*	81142	7641
Repair of furs and other garments for individuals: Personal and Household Goods Repair and Maintenance, Other—*serv*	81149	7219
Repair of optical instruments: Electronic and Precision Equipment Repair and Maintenance, Other—*serv*	811219	7699
Repair of photographic equipment: Electronic and Precision Equipment Repair and Maintenance, Other—*serv*	811219	7699
Repair of roofs-contractors: Roofing, Siding and Sheet Metal Contractors—*const*	23561	1761
Repair of service station equipment: Machinery and Equipment (except Automotive and Electronic) Repair and Maintenance, Commercial and Industrial—*serv*	81131	7699
Repair shops, automotive–general: General Automotive Repair—*serv*	811111	7538
Repairing and cleaning plants, rug and carpet: Carpet and Upholstery Cleaning Services—*admin*	56174	7217
Repairing books (bookbinding): Tradebinding and Related Work—*mfg*	323121	2789
Repairing buildings, industrial and warehouse–general contractors: Building, Commercial and Institutional—*const*	23332	1541
Manufacturing and Industrial Building—*const*	23331	1541
Repairing buildings, nonresidential–except industrial and warehouses–general contractors: Building, Commercial and Institutional—*const*	23332	1542
Repairing buildings, residential–except single-family–general contractors: Building, Commercial and Institutional—*const*	23332	1522
Multifamily Housing—*const*	23322	1522
Repairing buildings, single-family–general contractors: Single Family Housing—*const*	23321	1521

ALPHABETICAL INDEX	NAICS	SIC
Repairing lease tanks, oil field–on a contract basis: Oil and Gas Operations Support Activities—*mining*	213112	1389
Repeater equipment, telephone and telegraph: Electronic Coil, Transformer, and Other Inductor—*mfg*	334416	3661
Printed Circuit/Electronics Assembly—*mfg*	334418	3661
Telephone Apparatus—*mfg*	33421	3661
Repertory or stock companies, theatrical: Theater Companies and Dinner Theaters—*arts*	71111	7922
Replacement parts, electronic: Electronic Parts and Equipment, Other—*whlse*	42169	5065
Repossession Services	**561491**	**7389**
Representative offices of foreign banks, excluding agents and branches: Commodity Contracts Dealing—*fin*	52313	6099
Credit Intermediation, Other Activities Related to—*fin*	52239	6099
Financial Investment Activities, Miscellaneous—*fin*	523999	6099
Financial Transactions Processing, Reserve, and Clearing House Activities—*fin*	52232	6099
Trust, Fiduciary and Custody Activities—*fin*	523991	6099
Reptile exhibits: Nature Parks and Other Similar Institutions—*arts*	71219	8422
Zoos and Botanical Gardens—*arts*	71213	8422
Requirements analysis, computer hardware: Computer Related Services, Other—*prof*	541519	7379
Computer Systems Design Services—*prof*	541512	7379
Rerefining lubricating oils and greases: Petroleum Lubricating Oil and Grease—*mfg*	324191	2992
Resawing lumber into smaller dimensions: Cut Stock, Resawing Lumber, and Planing—*mfg*	321912	2421
Millwork (including Flooring), Other—*mfg*	321918	2421
Sawmills—*mfg*	321113	2421
Wood Product, All Other Miscellaneous—*mfg*	321999	2421
Research and Development in the Life Sciences	**54172**	**8733**
Research and Development in the Physical Sciences and Engineering Sciences	**54171**	**8733**
Research and Development in the Social Sciences and Humanities	**54173**	**8733**
Research and development of computerand related hardware: Research and Development in the Life Sciences—*prof*	54172	8731
Research and Development in the Physical Sciences and Engineering Sciences—*prof*	54171	8731
Research and development on aircraft bythe manufacturer: Aircraft—*mfg*	336411	3721
Research and development on aircraft engines and engine parts by the manufacturer: Aircraft Engine and Engine Parts—*mfg*	336412	3724
Research and development on aircraft parts and auxiliary equipment by themanufacturer: Aircraft Part and Auxiliary Equipment, Other—*mfg*	336413	3728
Fluid Power Valve and Hose Fitting—*mfg*	332912	3728

Entry	NAICS	SIC
Research and development on guided missile and space vehicle components, bythe manufacturer: Guided Missile and Space Vehicle Parts and Auxiliary Equipment, Other—*mfg*	336419	3769
Guided Missile and Space Vehicle Propulsion Unit and Propulsion Unit Parts—*mfg*	336415	3764
Research and development on guided missiles and space vehicles, by the manufacturer: Guided Missile and Space Vehicle—*mfg*	336414	3761
Research and development, physical and biological–commercial: Research and Development in the Life Sciences—*prof*	54172	8731
Research and Development in the Physical Sciences and Engineering Sciences—*prof*	54171	8731
Research, noncommercial: Research and Development in the Life Sciences—*prof*	54172	8733
Research and Development in the Physical Sciences and Engineering Sciences—*prof*	54171	8733
Research and Development in the Social Sciences and Humanities—*prof*	54173	8733
Research–economic, sociological, and educational-commercial: Marketing Research and Public Opinion Polling—*prof*	54191	8732
Research and Development in the Social Sciences and Humanities—*prof*	54173	8732
Reserpines: Medicinal and Botanical—*mfg*	325411	2833
Reservation service, hotel: Travel Arrangement and Reservation Services, All Other—*admin*	561599	7389
Reservoir construction–general contractors: Heavy, All Other—*const*	23499	1629
Industrial Nonbuilding Structure—*const*	23493	1629
Residence clubs operated by organizations for members only: Hotels (except Casino Hotels) and Motels—*accom*	72111	7041
Rooming and Boarding Houses—*accom*	72131	7041
Residential Building Construction	**2332**	
Residential building, operators of (four orfewer housing units): Lessors of Residential Buildings and Dwellings—*real*	53111	6514
Residential Care Facilities, Other	**6239**	
Residential Care Facilities, Other	**62399**	**8361**
Residential construction, except single-family–general contractors: Building, Commercial and Institutional—*const*	23332	1522
Multifamily Housing—*const*	23322	1522
Residential construction, single-family–general contractors: Single Family Housing—*const*	23321	1521
Residential Electric Lighting Fixture Manufacturing	**335121**	**3999**
Residential farms, noncommercial: Private Households—*serv*	81411	8811
Residential hotels, operators of: Lessors of Residential Buildings and Dwellings—*real*	53111	6513
Residential Mental Health and Substance Abuse Facilities	**62322**	**8361**
Residential Mental Retardation Facilities	**62321**	**8052**
Residential Mental Retardation, Mental Health and Substance Abuse Facilities	**6232**	
Residential Property Managers	**531311**	**6531**
Resilient Floor Covering Manufacturing	**326192**	**3996**
Resilient floor laying–contractors: Floor Laying and Other Floor Contractors—*const*	23552	1752
Resin and Synthetic Rubber Manufacturing	**32521**	
Resin coated fabrics: Fabric Coating Mills—*mfg*	31332	2295
Resin modified resins: Plastics Material and Resin—*mfg*	325211	2821
Resin, Synthetic Rubber, and Artificial and Synthetic Fibers and Filaments Manufacturing	**3252**	
Resinate driers: Paint and Coating—*mfg*	32551	2851
Resinous impregnated paper for packag-ing: Coated and Laminated Packaging Paper and Plastics Film—*mfg*	322221	2671
Unsupported Plastics Packaging Film and Sheet—*mfg*	326112	2671
Resinous impregnated paper, except forpackaging: Coated and Laminated Paper—*mfg*	322222	2672
Resins, phenolic: Plastics Material and Resin—*mfg*	325211	2821
Resins, plastics: Plastics Materials and Basic Forms and Shapes—*whlse*	42261	5162
Resins, synthetic: Plastics Material and Resin—*mfg*	325211	2821
Resins, synthetic rubber: Chemical and Allied Products, Other—*whlse*	42269	5169
Resins, synthetic–except rubber: Plastics Materials and Basic Forms and Shapes—*whlse*	42261	5162
Resistance measuring equipment: Electronic Coil, Transformer, and Other Inductor—*mfg*	334416	3825
Instrument for Measuring and Testing Electricity and Electrical Signals—*mfg*	334515	3825
Resistance thermometers and bulbs, industrial process type: Instruments and Related Products for Measuring, Displaying, and Controlling Industrial Process Variables—*mfg*	334513	3823
Resistance welders, electric: Power, Distribution and Specialty Transformer—*mfg*	335311	3548
Welding and Soldering Equipment—*mfg*	333992	3548
Resistor networks: Electronic Resistor—*mfg*	334415	3676
Resistors, electronic: Electronic Parts and Equipment, Other—*whlse*	42169	5065
Electronic Resistor—*mfg*	334415	3676
Resolvers: Motor and Generator—*mfg*	335312	3621
Resonant reed devices, electronic: Electronic Component, Other—*mfg*	334419	3679
Motor Vehicle Electrical and Electronic Equipment, Other—*mfg*	336322	3679
Printed Circuit/Electronics Assembly—*mfg*	334418	3679
Radio and Television Broadcasting and Wireless Communications Equipment—*mfg*	33422	3679
Resorcinol: Cyclic Crude and Intermediate—*mfg*	325192	2865
Petrochemical—*mfg*	32511	2865
Resort hotels: Bed and Breakfast Inns—*accom*	721191	7011
Casino Hotels—*accom*	72112	7011
Hotels (except Casino Hotels) and Motels—*accom*	72111	7011
Traveler Accommodation, All Other—*accom*	721199	7011
Respirators: Surgical Appliance and Supplies—*mfg*	339113	3842

ALPHABETICAL INDEX	NAICS	SIC
Respiratory analysis equipment, electromedical: Electromedical and Electrotherapeutic Apparatus—*mfg*	334510	3845
Irradiation Apparatus—*mfg*	334517	3845
Respiratory protection equipment, personal: Surgical Appliance and Supplies—*mfg*	339113	3842
Respiratory therapy clinics: Family Planning Centers—*hlth*	62141	8093
Outpatient Care Centers, All Other—*hlth*	621498	8093
Outpatient Mental Health and Substance Abuse Centers—*hlth*	62142	8093
Rest homes with health care: Continuing Care Retirement Communities—*hlth*	623311	8059
Nursing Care Facilities—*hlth*	62311	8059
Rest homes, with health care incidental: Homes for the Elderly—*hlth*	623312	8361
Residential Care Facilities, Other—*hlth*	62399	8361
Residential Mental Health and Substance Abuse Facilities—*hlth*	62322	8361
Rest room cleaning service: Exterminating and Pest Control Services—*admin*	56171	7342
Janitorial Services—*admin*	56172	7342
Rest room operation: Personal Services, All Other—*serv*	81299	7299
Restaurant construction–general contractors: Building, Commercial and Institutional—*const*	23332	1542
Restaurant furniture: Institutional Furniture—*mfg*	337127	2599
Restaurant operation schools: Apprenticeship Training—*educ*	611513	8249
Technical and Trade Schools, Other—*educ*	611519	8249
Restaurant sheet metalwork: Metal Container, Other—*mfg*	332439	3444
Sheet Metal Work—*mfg*	332322	3444
Restaurants: Cafeterias—*accom*	722212	5812
Caterers—*accom*	72232	5812
Foodservice Contractors—*accom*	72231	5812
Full-Service Restaurants—*accom*	72211	5812
Limited-Service Restaurants—*accom*	722211	5812
Snack and Nonalcoholic Beverage Bars—*accom*	722213	5812
Theater Companies and Dinner Theaters—*arts*	71111	5812
Restaurants, carry-out: Cafeterias—*accom*	722212	5812
Caterers—*accom*	72232	5812
Foodservice Contractors—*accom*	72231	5812
Full-Service Restaurants—*accom*	72211	5812
Limited-Service Restaurants—*accom*	722211	5812
Snack and Nonalcoholic Beverage Bars—*accom*	722213	5812
Theater Companies and Dinner Theaters—*arts*	71111	5812
Restaurants, fast food: Cafeterias—*accom*	722212	5812
Caterers—*accom*	72232	5812
Foodservice Contractors—*accom*	72231	5812
Full-Service Restaurants—*accom*	72211	5812
Limited-Service Restaurants—*accom*	722211	5812
Snack and Nonalcoholic Beverage Bars—*accom*	722213	5812
Theater Companies and Dinner Theaters—*arts*	71111	5812

ALPHABETICAL INDEX	NAICS	SIC
Restitution apparatus, photogrammetrical: Measuring and Controlling Device, Other—*mfg*	334519	3829
Surgical and Medical Instrument—*mfg*	339112	3829
Restoration and repair of antique furniture: Reupholstery and Furniture Repair—*serv*	81142	7641
Restoration and repair of antiques, except furniture and automobiles: Personal and Household Goods Repair and Maintenance, Other—*serv*	81149	7699
Restraints, patient: Surgical Appliance and Supplies—*mfg*	339113	3842
Resume writing service: Court Reporting and Stenotype Services—*admin*	561492	7338
Document Preparation Services—*admin*	56141	7338
Resurfacing streets and highways-contractors: Highway and Street—*const*	23411	1611
Retail Bakeries	**311811**	**5461**
Retail establishments, property operation only: Lessors of Nonresidential Buildings (except Miniwarehouses)—*real*	53112	6512
Promoters of Performing Arts, Sports and Similar Events with Facilities—*arts*	71131	6512
Retail Trade	**44-45**	
Retaining wall construction–block, stone, or brick-contractors: Masonry and Stone Contractors—*const*	23541	1741
Retinning of cans and utensils, not done in rolling mills: Costume Jewelry and Novelty—*mfg*	339914	3479
Jewelry (except Costume)—*mfg*	339911	3479
Metal Coating, Engraving (except Jewelry and Silverware), and Allied Services to Manufacturers—*mfg*	332812	3479
Silverware and Plated Ware—*mfg*	339912	3479
Retinoscopes, electromedical: Electromedical and Electrotherapeutic Apparatus—*mfg*	334510	3845
Irradiation Apparatus—*mfg*	334517	3845
Retinoscopes, except electromedical: Surgical and Medical Instrument—*mfg*	339112	3841
Retirement hotels, operators of: Lessors of Residential Buildings and Dwellings—*real*	53111	6513
Retorts, graphite: Nonclay Refractory—*mfg*	327125	3297
Retorts, industrial: Air-Conditioning and Warm Air Heating Equipment and Commercial and Industrial Refrigeration Equipment—*mfg*	333415	3443
Metal Tank (Heavy Gauge)—*mfg*	33242	3443
Plate Work—*mfg*	332313	3443
Power Boiler and Heat Exchanger—*mfg*	33241	3443
Retorts, smelting: Air-Conditioning and Warm Air Heating Equipment and Commercial and Industrial Refrigeration Equipment—*mfg*	333415	3443
Metal Tank (Heavy Gauge)—*mfg*	33242	3443
Plate Work—*mfg*	332313	3443

Description	NAICS	SIC
Power Boiler and Heat Exchanger—*mfg*	33241	3443
Retractors: Surgical and Medical Instrument—*mfg*	339112	3841
Retreading materials, tire: Tire (except Retreading)—*mfg*	326211	3011
Retreading tires: Automotive Repair and Maintenance, All Other—*serv*	811198	7534
Tire Retreading—*mfg*	326212	7534
Retting flax: Postharvest Crop Activities (except Cotton Ginning)—*ag*	115114	723
Reupholstery and Furniture Repair	**81142**	**7641**
Reupholstery shops: Reupholstery and Furniture Repair—*serv*	81142	7641
Revetment construction–general contractors: Heavy, All Other—*const*	23499	1629
Industrial Nonbuilding Structure—*const*	23493	1629
Revolvers and parts: Small Arms—*mfg*	332994	3484
Revolving door installation-contractors: Building Equipment and Other Machinery Installation Contractors—*const*	23595	1796
Reweaving textiles (mending service): Personal and Household Goods Repair and Maintenance, Other—*serv*	81149	7219
Rewinding of yarn: Textile and Fabric Finishing (except Broadwoven Fabric) Mills—*mfg*	313312	2282
Yarn Texturing, Throwing and Twisting Mills—*mfg*	313112	2282
Rewinding stators: Machinery and Equipment (except Automotive and Electronic) Repair and Maintenance, Commercial and Industrial—*serv*	81131	7694
Motor and Generator—*mfg*	335312	7694
Rewinds, motion picture film: Photographic and Photocopying Equipment—*mfg*	333315	3861
Photographic Film, Paper, Plate and Chemical—*mfg*	325992	3861
Reworking oil and gas wells on a contract basis: Drilling Oil and Gas Wells—*mining*	213111	1381
RF power amplifiers, and IF amplifiers–sold separately: Radio and Television Broadcasting and Wireless Communications Equipment—*mfg*	33422	3663
Rhenium refining, primary: Primary Smelting and Refining of Nonferrous Metal (except Copper and Aluminum)—*mfg*	331419	3339
Rheostats, electronic: Electronic Component, Other—*mfg*	334419	3679
Motor Vehicle Electrical and Electronic Equipment, Other—*mfg*	336322	3679
Printed Circuit/Electronics Assembly—*mfg*	334418	3679
Radio and Television Broadcasting and Wireless Communications Equipment—*mfg*	33422	3679
Rheostats, industrial control: Relay and Industrial Control—*mfg*	335314	3625
Rhodium ore mining: Metal Ore, All Other—*mining*	212299	1099
Rhodochrosite mining: Copper Ore and Nickel Ore—*mining*	212234	1061
Metal Ore, All Other—*mining*	212299	1061
Rhubarb grown under cover: Food Crops Grown Under Cover, Other—*ag*	111419	182
Mushroom Production—*ag*	111411	182
Ribbon blocks, fiber: Fiber Can, Tube, Drum, and Similar Products—*mfg*	322214	2655
Ribbon, nonwoven (yarn bonded by plastics): Nonwoven Fabric Mills—*mfg*	31323	2297
Ribbon, textile: Broadwoven Fabric Finishing Mills—*mfg*	313311	5131
Piece Goods, Notions and Other Dry Goods—*whlse*	42231	5131
Textile and Fabric Finishing (except Broadwoven Fabric) Mills—*mfg*	313312	5131
Ribbons: Narrow Fabric Mills—*mfg*	313221	2241
Ribbons and bows, cut and sewed: Apparel Accessories and Apparel, Other—*mfg*	315999	2396
Ribbons, inked: Office Supplies and Stationery Stores—*retail*	45321	5112
Stationary and Office Supplies—*whlse*	42212	5112
Ribbons, inked–e.g., typewriter, adding machine, cash register: Carbon Paper and Inked Ribbon—*mfg*	339944	3955
Rice bran, flour, and meal: Rice Milling—*mfg*	311212	2044
Rice breakfast foods: Breakfast Cereal—*mfg*	31123	2043
Coffee and Tea—*mfg*	31192	2043
Rice cleaning and polishing: Rice Milling—*mfg*	311212	2044
Rice drying: Postharvest Crop Activities (except Cotton Ginning)—*ag*	115114	723
Rice Farming	**11116**	**112**
Rice farms: Rice Farming—*ag*	11116	112
Rice Milling	**311212**	**2044**
Rice polish: Rice Milling—*mfg*	311212	2044
Rice starch: Wet Corn Milling—*mfg*	311221	2046
Rice, brewers': Rice Milling—*mfg*	311212	2044
Rice, brown: Rice Milling—*mfg*	311212	2044
Rice, polished: Grocery and Related Products, Other—*whlse*	42249	5149
Rice, unpolished: Grain and Field Bean—*whlse*	42251	5153
Rice, vitamin and mineral enriched: Rice Milling—*mfg*	311212	2044
Rickrack braid: Narrow Fabric Mills—*mfg*	313221	2241
Riddles, sand (hand sifting or screening apparatus): Fabricated Metal Product, All Other Miscellaneous—*mfg*	332999	3599
General Purpose Machinery , All Other—*mfg*	333999	3599
Machine Shops—*mfg*	33271	3599
Machinery, Other Commercial and Service Industry—*mfg*	333319	3599
Riding academies and schools: Fitness and Recreational Sports Centers—*arts*	71394	7999
Sports and Recreation Instruction—*educ*	61162	7999
Riding apparel stores: Clothing Accessories Stores—*retail*	44815	5699
Clothing Stores, Other—*retail*	44819	5699
Riding clothes: Cut and Sew Apparel, All Other—*mfg*	315299	2329
Riding clubs, membership: Fitness and Recreational Sports Centers—*arts*	71394	7997
Riding crops: Leather Good, All Other—*mfg*	316999	3199
Riding goods and equipment: Sporting Goods Stores—*retail*	45111	5941
Riding habits: Apparel Accessories and Apparel, Other—*mfg*	315999	2339
Cut and Sew Apparel, All Other—*mfg*	315299	2339
Women's and Girls' Cut and Sew Apparel Contractors—*mfg*	315212	2339
Women's and Girls' Cut and Sew Other Outerwear—*mfg*	315238	2339

ALPHABETICAL INDEX	NAICS	SIC
Rifle bore cleaning compounds: Basic Organic Chemical, All Other—*mfg*	325199	2899
Chemical Product, All Other Miscellaneous—*mfg*	325998	2899
Rifle working machines (machine tools): Machine Tool (Metal Cutting Types)—*mfg*	333512	3541
Rifles and parts, 30 mm. (or 1.18 inch) orless: Small Arms—*mfg*	332994	3484
Rifles for propelling hypodermics into animals: Surgical and Medical Instrument—*mfg*	339112	3841
Rifles, high compression pneumatic–30 mm. (or 1.18 inch) or less: Small Arms—*mfg*	332994	3484
Rifles, recoilless: Ordnance and Accessories, Other—*mfg*	332995	3489
Rifles, toy: Game, Toy, and Children's Vehicle—*mfg*	339932	3944
Rifles–BB and pellet: Small Arms—*mfg*	332994	3484
Rifles–pneumatic, spring loaded, and compressed air-except toy: Small Arms—*mfg*	332994	3484
Rig building, repairing, and dismantling:on a contract basis: Oil and Gas Operations Support Activities—*mining*	213112	1389
Rigidizing metal: Metal Stamping—*mfg*	332116	3469
Rims, wheel–motor vehicle: Motor Vehicle Body—*mfg*	336211	3714
Motor Vehicle Parts, All Other—*mfg*	336399	3714
Motor Vehicle Steering and Suspension Components (except Spring)—*mfg*	33633	3714
Rings, finger–gold-plated wire: Costume Jewelry and Novelty—*mfg*	339914	3961
Rings, glasshouse–clay: Clay Refractory—*mfg*	327124	3255
Rings, piston: Carburetor, Piston, Piston Ring and Valve—*mfg*	336311	3592
Rings, precious metal: Jewelry (except Costume)—*mfg*	339911	3911
Riprap quarrying, except limestone orgranite: Crushed and Broken Stone and Quarrying, Other—*mining*	212319	1429
River freight transportation, except on the St. Lawrence Seaway: Inland Water Freight—*trans*	483211	4449
River rafting, operation of: Amusement and Recreation Industries. All Other—*arts*	71399	7999
Riveting hammers: Power-Driven Hand Tool—*mfg*	333991	3546
Riveting machines: Machine Tool (Metal Forming Types)—*mfg*	333513	3542
Rivets, metal: Bolt, Nut, Screw, Rivet and Washer—*mfg*	332722	3452
Rivets, plastics: Plastics Pipe and Pipe Fitting—*mfg*	326122	3089
Plastics Product, All Other—*mfg*	326199	3089
Unsupported Plastics Profile Shape—*mfg*	326121	3089
Roach poisons: Pesticide and Other Agricultural Chemical—*mfg*	32532	2879
Road companies, theatrical: Theater Companies and Dinner Theaters—*arts*	71111	7922
Road construction and maintenance machinery: Construction and (except Petroleum) Machinery and Equipment—*whlse*	42181	5082
Construction Machinery—*mfg*	33312	3531
Overhead Traveling Crane, Hoist and Monorail System—*mfg*	333923	3531
Railroad Rolling Stock—*mfg*	33651	3531

ALPHABETICAL INDEX	NAICS	SIC
Road construction, except elevated–general contractors: Highway and Street—*const*	23411	1611
Road materials, bituminous–not made in petroleum refineries: Asphalt Paving Mixture and Block—*mfg*	324121	2951
Road materials, bituminous–produced in petroleum refineries: Petroleum Refineries—*mfg*	32411	2911
Road oilers (motor vehicles): Automobile—*mfg*	336111	3711
Heavy Duty Truck—*mfg*	33612	3711
Light Truck and Utility Vehicle—*mfg*	336112	3711
Military Armored Vehicle, Tank and Tank Component—*mfg*	336992	3711
Motor Vehicle Body—*mfg*	336211	3711
Road oils, produced in petroleum refineries: Petroleum Refineries—*mfg*	32411	2911
Road service, automotive: Automotive Oil Change and Lubrication Shops—*serv*	811191	7549
Automotive Repair and Maintenance, All Other—*serv*	811198	7549
Motor Vehicle Towing—*trans*	48841	7549
Road Transportation Support Activities	**4884**	
Road Transportation, Other Support Activities for	**48849**	**4231**
Roads, toll–operation of: Road, Other Support Activities for—*trans*	48849	4785
Water, Other Support Activities for—*trans*	48839	4785
Roasted Nuts and Peanut Butter Manufacturing	**311911**	**2099**
Roasters, electric: Electric Housewares and Household Fan—*mfg*	335211	3634
Heating Equipment (except Electric and Warm Air Furnaces)—*mfg*	333414	3634
Roasting chickens, raising of: Broilers and Other Meat Type Chicken Production—*ag*	11232	251
Roasting machinery–coffee, peanut, etc.: Food Product Machinery—*mfg*	333294	3556
Robes and gowns–women s and children's: Women's, Children's, and Infants' and Accessories—*whlse*	42233	5137
Robes, lounging: Men's and Boys' Cut and Sew Apparel Contractors—*mfg*	315211	2384
Men's and Boys' Cut and Sew Underwear and Nightwear—*mfg*	315221	2384
Outerwear Knitting Mills—*mfg*	315191	2253
Women's and Girls' Cut and Sew Apparel Contractors—*mfg*	315212	2384
Women's and Girls' Cut and Sew Lingerie, Loungewear and Nightwear—*mfg*	315231	2384
Robes, men's and hoys': Men's and Boys' Clothing and Furnishings—*whlse*	42232	5136
Robotic conveyors for general industrial use: Conveyor and Conveying Equipment—*mfg*	333922	3535
Robots for drilling and cutting-machinetype, metalworking: Machine Tool (Metal Cutting Types)—*mfg*	333512	3541
Robots for general industrial use: General Purpose Machinery , All Other—*mfg*	333999	3569

Description	NAICS	SIC
Robots for grinding, polishing, and deburring-metalworking: Machine Tool (Metal Cutting Types)—*mfg*	333512	3541
Robots for metal forming–e.g., pressing, hammering, extruding: Machine Tool (Metal Forming Types)—*mfg*	333513	3542
Robots for spraying, painting-industrial: Air and Gas Compressor—*mfg*	333912	3563
Robots for welding, soldering, or brazing: Power, Distribution and Specialty Transformer—*mfg*	335311	3548
Welding and Soldering Equipment—*mfg*	333992	3548
Robots, plastics–for molding and forming: Industrial Machinery, All Other—*mfg*	333298	3559
Machinery, Other Commercial and Service Industry—*mfg*	333319	3559
Rubber and Plastics Industry Machinery—*mfg*	33322	3559
Rock and stone specimens: Jewelry Stores—*retail*	44831	5999
Stores (except Tobacco Stores), All Other Miscellaneous—*retail*	453998	5999
Rock crushing machinery, stationary: Mining Machinery and Equipment—*mfg*	333131	3532
Rock drills, portable: Mining Machinery and Equipment—*mfg*	333131	3532
Rock removal, underwater–contractors: Heavy, All Other—*const*	23499	1629
Industrial Nonbuilding Structure—*const*	23493	1629
Rock salt mining: Chemical and Fertilizer Mineral, Other—*mining*	212393	1479
Rock, gypsum: Gypsum and Gypsum Product—*mfg*	32742	3275
Rockers, upholstered on wood frames: Upholstered Household Furniture—*mfg*	337121	2512
Rockers, wood–except upholstered: Nonupholstered Wood Household Furniture—*mfg*	337122	2511
Rocket engine fuel, organic: Basic Organic Chemical, All Other—*mfg*	325199	2869
Rocket launchers, hand-held: Ordnance and Accessories, Other—*mfg*	332995	3489
Rocket motors, aircraft: Aircraft Engine and Engine Parts—*mfg*	336412	3724
Rocket motors, guided missile: Guided Missile and Space Vehicle Propulsion Unit and Propulsion Unit Parts—*mfg*	336415	3764
Rocket transportation casings: Air-Conditioning and Warm Air Heating Equipment and Commercial and Industrial Refrigeration Equipment—*mfg*	333415	3443
Metal Tank (Heavy Gauge)—*mfg*	33242	3443
Plate Work—*mfg*	332313	3443
Power Boiler and Heat Exchanger—*mfg*	33241	3443
Rockets (ammunition): Ammunition (except Small Arms)—*mfg*	332993	3483
Rockets (guided missiles), space and military–complete: Guided Missile and Space Vehicle—*mfg*	336414	3761
Rockets, pyrotechnic: Basic Organic Chemical, All Other—*mfg*	325199	2899
Chemical Product, All Other Miscellaneous—*mfg*	325998	2899
Rocking horses: Game, Toy, and Children's Vehicle—*mfg*	339932	3944
Rockingham earthenware: Vitreous China, Fine Earthenware and Other Pottery Product—*mfg*	327112	3269
Rod mills (rolling mill equipment): Rolling Mill Machinery and Equipment—*mfg*	333516	3547
Rodent poisons: Pesticide and Other Agricultural Chemical—*mfg*	32532	2879
Rodenticides: Pesticide and Other Agricultural Chemical—*mfg*	32532	2879
Rodeo animal rental: Amusement and Recreation Industries, All Other—*arts*	71399	7999
Recreational Goods Rental—*real*	532292	7999
Rodeos, operation of: Amusement and Recreation Industries, All Other—*arts*	71399	7999
Rods and rod parts, fishing: Sporting and Athletic Goods—*mfg*	33992	3949
Rods, aluminum–extruded: Aluminum Extruded Product—*mfg*	331316	3354
Rods, aluminum–rolled: Aluminum Rolling and Drawing, Other—*mfg*	331319	3355
Rods, copper and copper alloy: Copper Rolling, Drawing and Extruding—*mfg*	331421	3351
Rods, curtain and drapery: Blind and Shade—*mfg*	33792	2591
Rods, gas welding–made from purchased wire: Fabricated Wire Product, Other—*mfg*	332618	3496
Rods, hard rubber: Fabric Coating Mills—*mfg*	31332	3069
Rubber Product, All Other—*mfg*	326299	3069
Rods, iron and steel–made in steel worksor rolling mills: Iron and Steel Mills—*mfg*	331111	3312
Petroleum and Coal Productsa, All Other—*mfg*	324199	3312
Rods, laminated plastics: Laminated Plastics Plate, Sheet and Shape—*mfg*	32613	3083
Rods, metal: Metal Service Centers and Offices—*whlse*	42151	5051
Rods, surveyors': Measuring and Controlling Device, Other—*mfg*	334519	3829
Surgical and Medical Instrument—*mfg*	339112	3829
Rods, unsupported plastics: Unsupported Plastics Profile Shape—*mfg*	326121	3082
Rods–lead, magnesium, nickel, tin, titanium, and their alloys: Nonferrous Metal (except Copper and Aluminum) Rolling, Drawing and Extruding—*mfg*	331491	3356
Rolling doors for industrial buildings and warehouses, metal: Metal Window and Door—*mfg*	332321	3442
Roll coverings–rubber for papermill; industrial, steelmills, printers': Fabric Coating Mills—*mfg*	31332	3069
Rubber Product, All Other—*mfg*	326299	3069
Roll Forming, Custom	**332114**	**3449**
Roller bearings and parts: Ball and Roller Bearing—*mfg*	332991	3562
Roller covers, printers'–rubber: Fabric Coating Mills—*mfg*	31332	3069
Rubber Product, All Other—*mfg*	326299	3069
Roller leather: Leather and Hide Tanning and Finishing—*mfg*	31611	3111
Roller levelers (rolling mill machinery): Rolling Mill Machinery and Equipment—*mfg*	333516	3547
Roller printing of cotton broadwoven fabrics: Broadwoven Fabric Finishing Mills—*mfg*	313311	2261
Roller printing of manmade fiber and silk broadwoven fabrics: Broadwoven Fabric Finishing Mills—*mfg*	313311	2262
Roller skates: Sporting and Athletic Goods—*mfg*	33992	3949
Roller skating rink operation: Fitness and Recreational Sports Centers—*arts*	71394	7999

ALPHABETICAL INDEX	NAICS	SIC
Rollers and fittings, window shade: Blind and Shade—*mfg*	33792	2591
Rollers and levelers, land (agricultural machinery): Farm Machinery and Equipment—*mfg*	333111	3523
Rollers, paint: Broom, Brush and Mop—*mfg*	339994	3991
Rollers, road: Construction Machinery—*mfg*	33312	3531
Overhead Traveling Crane, Hoist and Monorail System—*mfg*	333923	3531
Railroad Rolling Stock—*mfg*	33651	3531
Rollers, sheepsfoot and vibratory: Construction Machinery—*mfg*	33312	3531
Overhead Traveling Crane, Hoist and Monorail System—*mfg*	333923	3531
Railroad Rolling Stock—*mfg*	33651	3531
Rollers, wood: Manufacturing, All Other Miscellaneous—*mfg*	339999	2499
Wood Container and Pallet—*mfg*	32192	2499
Wood Product, All Other Miscellaneous—*mfg*	321999	2499
Rolling and Drawing of Purchased Steel	**33122**	
Rolling machines, thread and spline: Machine Tool (Metal Forming Types)—*mfg*	333513	3542
Rolling mill machinery and equipment: Rolling Mill Machinery and Equipment—*mfg*	333516	3547
Rolling Mill Machinery and Equipment Manufacturing	**333516**	**3547**
Rolling mill rolls, iron–not machined: Iron Foundries—*mfg*	331511	3321
Rolling mill rolls, steel–not machined: Steel Foundries, (except Investment)—*mfg*	331513	3325
Rolling pins, wood: Manufacturing, All Other Miscellaneous—*mfg*	339999	2499
Wood Container and Pallet—*mfg*	32192	2499
Wood Product, All Other Miscellaneous—*mfg*	321999	2499
Rolling, drawing, and extruding of copper and copper alloys: Copper Rolling, Drawing and Extruding—*mfg*	331421	3351
Rolls for rolling mill machinery, machined: Rolling Mill Machinery and Equipment—*mfg*	333516	3547
Rolls, bread4ype, including frozen: Bakeries, Commercial—*mfg*	311812	2051
Rolls, paper–adding machine, telegraphtape, etc.: Coated and Laminated Paper—*mfg*	322222	2679
Converted Paper Product, All Other—*mfg*	322298	2679
Die-Cut Paper and Paperboard Office Supplies—*mfg*	322231	2679
Non-Folding Sanitary Food Container—*mfg*	322215	2679
Rolls, rolling mill–iron-not machined: Iron Foundries—*mfg*	331511	3321
Rolls, rolling mill–steel-not machined: Steel Foundries, (except Investment)—*mfg*	331513	3325
Rolls, solid or covered rubber: Fabric Coating Mills—*mfg*	31332	3069
Rubber Product, All Other—*mfg*	326299	3069
Rolls, sweet, except frozen: Bakeries, Commercial—*mfg*	311812	2051
Romaine farms: Vegetable (except Potato) and Melon Farming, Other—*ag*	111219	161
Rongeurs, bone: Surgical and Medical Instrument—*mfg*	339112	3841
Roof cement–asphalt, fibrous, and plastics: Asphalt Shingle and Coating Materials—*mfg*	324122	2952

ALPHABETICAL INDEX	NAICS	SIC
Roof coatings and cements–liquid and plastics: Asphalt Shingle and Coating Materials—*mfg*	324122	2952
Roof deck, sheet metal: Metal Container, Other—*mfg*	332439	3444
Sheet Metal Work—*mfg*	332322	3444
Roof spraying, painting, or coating–contractors: Roofing, Siding and Sheet Metal Contractors—*const*	23561	1761
Roof trusses, wood: Cut Stock, Resawing Lumber, and Planing—*mfg*	321912	2439
Engineered Wood Member (except Truss)—*mfg*	321213	2439
Truss—*mfg*	321214	2439
Roofing felt stock: Newsprint Mills—*mfg*	322122	2621
Paper (except Newsprint) Mills—*mfg*	322121	2621
Roofing felts, cements, and coatings–asphalt, tar, and composition: Asphalt Shingle and Coating Materials—*mfg*	324122	2952
Roofing granules: Ground or Treated Mineral and Earth—*mfg*	327992	3295
Roofing material dealers: Building Material Dealers, Other—*retail*	44419	5211
Home Centers—*retail*	44411	5211
Roofing pitch, coal tar–not made in byproduct coke ovens: Asphalt Shingle and Coating Materials—*mfg*	324122	2952
Roofing tile and slabs, concrete: Concrete Pipe—*mfg*	327332	3272
Concrete Product, Other—*mfg*	32739	3272
Nonmetallic Mineral Product, All Other Miscellaneous—*mfg*	327999	3272
Roofing tile, clay: Structural Clay Product, Other—*mfg*	327123	3259
Roofing work, including repairing–contractors: Roofing, Siding and Sheet Metal Contractors—*const*	23561	1761
Roofing, asbestos felt roll: Motor Vehicle Brake System—*mfg*	33634	3292
Nonmetallic Mineral Product, All Other Miscellaneous—*mfg*	327999	3292
Roofing, asphalt and sheet metal: Roofing, Siding and Insulation Material—*whlse*	42133	5033
Roofing, asphalt or tar saturated felt–built-up, roll, and shingle: Asphalt Shingle and Coating Materials—*mfg*	324122	2952
Roofing, sheet metal: Metal Container, Other—*mfg*	332439	3444
Sheet Metal Work—*mfg*	332322	3444
Roofing, Siding and Insulation Material Wholesalers	**42133**	**5033**
Roofing, Siding and Sheet Metal Contractors	**23561**	**1761**
Roofing, Siding and Sheet Metal Contractors	**2356**	
Roofing, single ply membrane–rubber: Fabric Coating Mills—*mfg*	31332	3069
Rubber Product, All Other—*mfg*	326299	3069
Roofing, slate: Cut Stone and Stone Product—*mfg*	327991	3281
Room coolers, portable: Air-Conditioning and Warm Air Heating Equipment and Commercial and Industrial Refrigeration Equipment—*mfg*	333415	3585
Motor Vehicle Air-Conditioning—*mfg*	336391	3585
Room dividers, household–wood: Nonupholstered Wood Household Furniture—*mfg*	337122	2511
Room heaters, except electric: Heating Equipment (except Electric and Warm Air Furnaces)—*mfg*	333414	3433

Description	NAICS	SIC
Room heaters, space–electric: Electric Housewares and Household Fan—*mfg*	335211	3634
Heating Equipment (except Electric and Warm Air Furnaces)—*mfg*	333414	3634
Room thermostats: Automatic Environmental Control for Residential, Commercial and Appliance Use—*mfg*	334512	3822
Rooming and Boarding Houses	**7213**	
Rooming and Boarding Houses	**72131**	**7041**
Rooming houses operated by organizations for members only: Hotels (except Casino Hotels) and Motels—*accom*	72111	7041
Rooming and Boarding Houses—*accom*	72131	7041
Rooming houses, except organization: Rooming and Boarding Houses—*accom*	72131	7021
Rooming houses, fraternity and sorority: Hotels (except Casino Hotels) and Motels—*accom*	72111	7041
Rooming and Boarding Houses—*accom*	72131	7041
Root beer, bottled or canned: Bottled Water—*mfg*	312112	2086
Soft Drink—*mfg*	312111	2086
Root starch, edible: Wet Corn Milling—*mfg*	311221	2046
Rope and cordage machines: Textile Machinery—*mfg*	333292	3552
Rope and jute wrapping paper: Newsprint Mills—*mfg*	322122	2621
Paper (except Newsprint) Mills—*mfg*	322121	2621
Rope fittings: Hardware—*mfg*	33251	3429
Rope, asbestos: Motor Vehicle Brake System—*mfg*	33634	3292
Nonmetallic Mineral Product, All Other Miscellaneous—*mfg*	327999	3292
Rope, Cordage and Twine Mills	**314991**	**2298**
Rope, except asbestos and wire: Rope, Cordage and Twine Mills—*mfg*	314991	2298
Rope, except wire rope: Industrial Machinery and Equipment—*whlse*	42183	5085
Industrial Supplies—*whlse*	42184	5085
Rope, uninsulated wire–made from purchased wire: Fabricated Wire Product, Other—*mfg*	332618	3496
Rope, wire–not insulated: Metal Service Centers and Offices—*whlse*	42151	5051
Rosaries and other small religious articles, except precious metal: Costume Jewelry and Novelty—*mfg*	339914	3961
Rosaries and other small religious articles, precious metal: Jewelry (except Costume)—*mfg*	339911	3911
Roscoelite (vanadium hydromica) mining: Uranium-Radium-Vanadium Ore—*mining*	212291	1094
Rose growers: Floriculture Production—*ag*	111422	181
Nursery and Tree Production—*ag*	111421	181
Rosin: Chemical and Allied Products, Other—*whlse*	42269	5169
Rosin sizes: Basic Organic Chemical, All Other—*mfg*	325199	2899
Chemical Product, All Other Miscellaneous—*mfg*	325998	2899
Rosin, produced by distillation of pine gum or pine wood: Gum and Wood Chemical—*mfg*	325191	2861
Rotary converters (electrical equipment): Motor and Generator—*mfg*	335312	3621
Rotary hoes (agricultural machinery): Farm Machinery and Equipment—*mfg*	333111	3523

Description	NAICS	SIC
Rotary photogravure printing: Gravure Printing, Commercial—*mfg*	323111	2754
Rotary slitters (metalworking machines): Other Metalworking Machinery, Other—*mfg*	333518	3549
Rotary tables, indexing: Cutting Tool and Machine Tool Accessory—*mfg*	333515	3545
Hand and Edge Tool—*mfg*	332212	3545
Rotary type meters, consumption registering: Totalizing Fluid Meter and Counting Device—*mfg*	334514	3824
Rotating bands, copper and copper alloy: Copper Rolling, Drawing and Extruding—*mfg*	331421	3351
Rotenone concentrates: Pesticide and Other Agricultural Chemical—*mfg*	32532	2879
Rotenone hearing preparations: Pesticide and Other Agricultural Chemical—*mfg*	32532	2879
Roto-blades for helicopters: Aircraft Part and Auxiliary Equipment, Other—*mfg*	336413	3728
Fluid Power Valve and Hose Fitting—*mfg*	332912	3728
Rotogravure paper: Newsprint Mills—*mfg*	322122	2621
Paper (except Newsprint) Mills—*mfg*	322121	2621
Rotogravure printing: Gravure Printing, Commercial—*mfg*	323111	2754
Rotogravure printing plates and cylinders: Prepress Services—*mfg*	323122	2796
Rotor retainers and housings: Motor and Generator—*mfg*	335312	3621
Rotors for motors: Motor and Generator—*mfg*	335312	3621
Rototillers (garden machinery): Hand and Edge Tool—*mfg*	332212	3524
Lawn and Garden Tractor and Home Lawn and Garden Equipment—*mfg*	333112	3524
Rouge, cosmetic: Soap and Other Detergent—*mfg*	325611	2844
Toilet Preparation—*mfg*	32562	2844
Rouge, polishing: Abrasive Product—*mfg*	32791	3291
Fabricated Metal Product, All Other Miscellaneous—*mfg*	332999	3291
Roughage mills (agricultural machinery): Farm Machinery and Equipment—*mfg*	333111	3523
Round stave baskets, for fruits and vegetables: Wood Container and Pallet—*mfg*	32192	2449
Rounds or rungs, ladder and furniture–hardwood: Cut Stock, Resawing Lumber, and Planing—*mfg*	321912	2426
Millwork (including Flooring), Other—*mfg*	321918	2426
Showcase, Partition, Shelving, and Locker—*mfg*	337215	2426
Wood Product, All Other Miscellaneous—*mfg*	321999	2426
Rounds, tube: Iron and Steel Mills—*mfg*	331111	3312
Petroleum and Coal Productsa, All Other—*mfg*	324199	3312
Roundwood: Durable Goods, Other Miscellaneous—*whlse*	42199	5099
Roustabout service–on a contract basis: Oil and Gas Operations Support Activities—*mining*	213112	1389
Routing machines, woodworking: Sawmill and Woodworking Machinery—*mfg*	33321	3553
Roves, flax and jute: Broadwoven Fabric Mills—*mfg*	31321	2299
Narrow Fabric Mills—*mfg*	313221	2299
Nonwoven Fabric Mills—*mfg*	31323	2299

ALPHABETICAL INDEX	NAICS	SIC
Textile and Fabric Finishing (except Broadwoven Fabric) Mills—*mfg*	313312	2299
Textile Product Mills, All Other Miscellaneous—*mfg*	314999	2299
Thread Mills—*mfg*	313113	2299
Yarn Spinning Mills—*mfg*	313111	2299
Roving machines (textile machinery): Textile Machinery—*mfg*	333292	3552
Rowboats, building and repairing: Boat Building—*mfg*	336612	3732
Personal and Household Goods Repair and Maintenance, Other—*serv*	81149	3732
Rowhouse (single-family) construction–general contractors: Single Family Housing—*const*	23321	1521
Rowing machines: Sporting and Athletic Goods—*mfg*	33992	3949
Royalty companies, oil: Financial Investment Activities, Miscellaneous—*fin*	523999	6792
Owners and Lessors of Other Non-Financial Assets—*real*	53311	6792
Royalty owners protective associations: Financial Investment Activities, Miscellaneous—*fin*	523999	6289
Trust, Fiduciary and Custody Activities—*fin*	523991	6289
Rubber and Plastics Footwear Manufacturing	**316211**	**3021**
Rubber and Plastics Hoses and Belting Manufacturing	**32622**	**3052**
Rubber and Plastics Industry Machinery Manufacturing	**33322**	**3559**
Rubber cement: Adhesive—*mfg*	32552	2891
Rubber clay mining: Kaolin and Ball Clay—*mining*	212324	1455
Rubber curing ovens: Industrial Process Furnace and Oven—*mfg*	333994	3567
Rubber goods, mechanical: Industrial Machinery and Equipment—*whlse*	42183	5085
Industrial Supplies—*whlse*	42184	5085
Rubber goods, mechanical–molded, extruded, and lathe-cut: Rubber Product for Mechanical Use—*mfg*	326291	3061
Rubber goods, medical: Drug, Drug Proprietaries and Druggists' Sundries—*whlse*	42221	5122
Rubber heels, soles, and soling strips: Fabric Coating Mills—*mfg*	31332	3069
Rubber Product, All Other—*mfg*	326299	3069
Rubber plantations: Crop Farming, All Other Miscellaneous—*ag*	111998	831
Forest Nurseries and Gathering of Forest Products—*ag*	11321	831
Rubber processing chemicals, organic–accelerators and antioxidants: Basic Organic Chemical, All Other—*mfg*	325199	2869
Rubber processing preparations: Basic Organic Chemical, All Other—*mfg*	325199	2899
Chemical Product, All Other Miscellaneous—*mfg*	325998	2899
Rubber Product Manufacturing	**3262**	
Rubber Product Manufacturing for Mechanical Use	**326291**	**3061**
Rubber Product Manufacturing, All Other	**326299**	**3069**
Rubber Product Manufacturing, Other	**32629**	
Rubber products machinery: Industrial Machinery, All Other—*mfg*	333298	3559
Machinery, Other Commercial and Service Industry—*mfg*	333319	3559
Rubber and Plastics Industry Machinery—*mfg*	33322	3559
Rubber scrap: Recyclable Material—*whlse*	42193	5093
Rubber sealing compounds, synthetic: Adhesive—*mfg*	32552	2891
Rubber stamp stores: Stores (except Tobacco Stores), All Other Miscellaneous—*retail*	453998	5999
Rubber thread and yarns, fabric covered: Narrow Fabric Mills—*mfg*	313221	2241
Rubber working machinery: Industrial Machinery, All Other—*mfg*	333298	3559
Machinery, Other Commercial and Service Industry—*mfg*	333319	3559
Rubber and Plastics Industry Machinery—*mfg*	33322	3559
Rubber, crude: Nondurable Goods, Other Miscellaneous—*whlse*	42299	5199
Rubber, reclaimed and reworked by manufacturing processes: Fabric Coating Mills—*mfg*	31332	3069
Rubber Product, All Other—*mfg*	326299	3069
Rubber, synthetic: Synthetic Rubber—*mfg*	325212	2822
Rubber-covered motor mounting rings (rubber bonded): Fabric Coating Mills—*mfg*	31332	3069
Rubber Product, All Other—*mfg*	326299	3069
Rubberbands: Fabric Coating Mills—*mfg*	31332	3069
Rubber Product, All Other—*mfg*	326299	3069
Rubberized fabrics: Fabric Coating Mills—*mfg*	31332	3069
Rubber Product, All Other—*mfg*	326299	3069
Rubbing stone quarrying: Crushed and Broken Stone and Quarrying, Other—*mining*	212319	1499
Non-Metallic Mineral, All Other—*mining*	212399	1499
Rubbing stones, artificial: Abrasive Product—*mfg*	32791	3291
Fabricated Metal Product, All Other Miscellaneous—*mfg*	332999	3291
Rubbish collection and disposal: Hazardous Waste Collection—*admin*	562112	4953
Hazardous Waste Treatment and Disposal—*admin*	562211	4953
Materials Recovery Facilities—*admin*	56292	4953
Nonhazardous Waste Treatment and Disposal, Other—*admin*	562219	4953
Solid Waste Collection—*admin*	562111	4953
Solid Waste Combustors and Incinerators—*admin*	562213	4953
Solid Waste Landfill—*admin*	562212	4953
Waste Collection, Other—*admin*	562119	4953
Rubble mining: Dimension Stone and Quarrying—*mining*	212311	1411
Rubidium metal: Basic Inorganic Chemical, All Other—*mfg*	325188	2819
Chemical Product, All Other Miscellaneous—*mfg*	325998	2819
Ruby mining: Crushed and Broken Stone and Quarrying, Other—*mining*	212319	1499
Non-Metallic Mineral, All Other—*mining*	212399	1499
Rudders, aircraft: Aircraft Part and Auxiliary Equipment, Other—*mfg*	336413	3728
Fluid Power Valve and Hose Fitting—*mfg*	332912	3728
Ruffling, for the trade: Men's and Boys' Cut and Sew Apparel Contractors—*mfg*	315211	2395
Textile Product Mills, All Other Miscellaneous—*mfg*	314999	2395
Women's and Girls' Cut and Sew Apparel Contractors—*mfg*	315212	2395
Rug backing compounds, latex: Fabric Coating Mills—*mfg*	31332	3069

Entry	NAICS	SIC
Rubber Product, All Other—*mfg*	326299	3069
Rug cleaning, drying, and napping machines–commercial laundry: Laundry, Drycleaning and Pressing Machine, Commercial—*mfg*	333312	3582
Rug cleaning, dyeing, and repairing plants: Carpet and Upholstery Cleaning Services—*admin*	56174	7217
Rug repair shops, not combined with cleaning: Personal and Household Goods Repair and Maintenance, Other—*serv*	81149	7699
Rug stores: Floor Covering Stores—*retail*	44221	5713
Rug, upholstery, and drycleaning detergents and spotters: Polish and Other Sanitation Good—*mfg*	325612	2842
Rugbacking, jute or other fiber: Broadwoven Fabric Mills—*mfg*	31321	2299
Narrow Fabric Mills—*mfg*	313221	2299
Nonwoven Fabric Mills—*mfg*	31323	2299
Textile and Fabric Finishing (except Broadwoven Fabric) Mills—*mfg*	313312	2299
Textile Product Mills, All Other Miscellaneous—*mfg*	314999	2299
Thread Mills—*mfg*	313113	2299
Yarn Spinning Mills—*mfg*	313111	2299
Rugs: Home Furnishing—*whlse*	42122	5023
Rugs, except rubber or plastics: Carpet and Rug Mills—*mfg*	31411	2273
Rules and rulers–metal, except slide: Hand and Edge Tool—*mfg*	332212	3423
Rules and rulers–wood, except slide: Manufacturing, All Other Miscellaneous—*mfg*	339999	2499
Wood Container and Pallet—*mfg*	32192	2499
Wood Product, All Other Miscellaneous—*mfg*	321999	2499
Rules, printers': Printing Machinery and Equipment—*mfg*	333293	3555
Rules, slide: Measuring and Controlling Device, Other—*mfg*	334519	3829
Surgical and Medical Instrument—*mfg*	339112	3829
Ruling of paper: Blankbook, Loose-leaf Binder and Device—*mfg*	323118	2782
Flexographic Printing, Commercial—*mfg*	323112	2782
Gravure Printing, Commercial—*mfg*	323111	2782
Lithographic Printing, Commercial—*mfg*	323110	2782
Printing, Other Commercial—*mfg*	323119	2782
Screen Printing, Commercial—*mfg*	323113	2782
Rum: Distilleries—*mfg*	31214	2085
Running, cutting, and pulling casings, tubes, and rods–oil and gas field: Oil and Gas Operations Support Activities—*mining*	213112	1389
Rural Electrification Administration: International Trade Financing—*fin*	522293	6111
Non-Depository Credit Intermediation, All Other—*fin*	522298	6111
Secondary Market Financing—*fin*	522294	6111
Rusk: Bakeries, Commercial—*mfg*	311812	2052
Cookie and Cracker—*mfg*	311821	2052
Snack Food, Other—*mfg*	311919	2052
Russian dressing: Fruit and Vegetable Canning—*mfg*	311421	2035
Mayonnaise, Dressing and Other Prepared Sauce—*mfg*	311941	2035
Rust arresting compounds, animal and vegetable oil base: Petroleum Lubricating Oil and Grease—*mfg*	324191	2992
Rust proofing (hot dipping) of metals and formed products, for the trade: Costume Jewelry and Novelty—*mfg*	339914	3479
Jewelry (except Costume)—*mfg*	339911	3479
Metal Coating, Engraving (except Jewelry and Silverware), and Allied Services to Manufacturers—*mfg*	332812	3479
Silverware and Plated Ware—*mfg*	339912	3479
Rust removers: Polish and Other Sanitation Good—*mfg*	325612	2842
Rust resisting compounds: Basic Organic Chemical, All Other—*mfg*	325199	2899
Chemical Product, All Other Miscellaneous—*mfg*	325998	2899
Rustproofing chemicals: Chemical and Allied Products, Other—*whlse*	42269	5169
Rustproofing service, automotive: Automotive Oil Change and Lubrication Shops—*serv*	811191	7549
Automotive Repair and Maintenance, All Other—*serv*	811198	7549
Motor Vehicle Towing—*trans*	48841	7549
Ruthenium ore mining: Metal Ore, All Other—*mining*	212299	1099
Rutile mining: Metal Ore, All Other—*mining*	212299	1099
RV (Recreational Vehicle) Parks and Campgrounds	**721211**	**7033**
RV (Recreational Vehicle) Parks and Recreational Camps	**7212**	
RV (Recreational Vehicle) Parks and Recreational Camps	**72121**	
Rye farms: Grain Farming, All Other—*ag*	111199	119
Rye flour: Flour Milling—*mfg*	311211	2041
S-type rubber: Synthetic Rubber—*mfg*	325212	2822
Saccharin: Basic Organic Chemical, All Other—*mfg*	325199	2869
Sachet: Soap and Other Detergent—*mfg*	325611	2844
Toilet Preparation—*mfg*	32562	2844
Sacks, multiwall or heavy-duty shipping sack: Uncoated Paper and Multiwall Bag—*mfg*	322224	2674
Saddle cloths: Textile Product Mills, All Other Miscellaneous—*mfg*	314999	2399
Saddle soap: Polish and Other Sanitation Good—*mfg*	325612	2842
Saddle trees, wood: Manufacturing, All Other Miscellaneous—*mfg*	339999	2499
Wood Container and Pallet—*mfg*	32192	2499
Wood Product, All Other Miscellaneous—*mfg*	321999	2499
Saddlery hardware: Hardware—*mfg*	33251	3429
Saddlery leather: Leather and Hide Tanning and Finishing—*mfg*	31611	3111
Saddlery repair shops: Animal Production Support Activities—*ag*	11521	7699
Footwear and Leather Goods Repair—*serv*	81143	7699
Saddlery stores: Sporting Goods Stores—*retail*	45111	5941
Saddles and parts: Leather Good, All Other—*mfg*	316999	3199
Saddles, motorcycle and bicycle: Motorcycle, Bicycle and Parts—*mfg*	336991	3751
Safe deposit boxes and chests, metal: Metal Container, Other—*mfg*	332439	3499
Safe deposit companies: Commodity Contracts Dealing—*fin*	52313	6099
Credit Intermediation, Other Activities Related to—*fin*	52239	6099
Financial Investment Activities, Miscellaneous—*fin*	523999	6099
Financial Transactions Processing, Reserve, and Clearing House Activities—*fin*	52232	6099
Trust, Fiduciary and Custody Activities—*fin*	523991	6099
Safe doors and linings, metal: Metal Container, Other—*mfg*	332439	3499

ALPHABETICAL INDEX	NAICS	SIC
Safe moving, local: Freight (except Used Goods) Trucking, Local Specialized—*trans*	48422	4212
General Freight Trucking, Local—*trans*	48411	4212
Used Household and Office Goods Moving—*trans*	48421	4212
Safes, metal: Metal Container, Other—*mfg*	332439	3499
Safety appliances and equipment, personal: Surgical Appliance and Supplies—*mfg*	339113	3842
Safety belts, leather: Leather Good, All Other—*mfg*	316999	3199
Safety fuses: Explosives—*mfg*	32592	2892
Safety glass, made from purchased glass: Glass Product Made of Purchased Glass—*mfg*	327215	3231
Safety glove supply service: Industrial Launderers—*serv*	812332	7218
Safety gloves, all materials: Surgical Appliance and Supplies—*mfg*	339113	3842
Safety inspection service, except automotive: Building Inspection Services—*prof*	54135	7389
Safety pins: Fastener, Button, Needle and Pin—*mfg*	339993	3965
Safety razor blades: Cutlery and Flatware (except Precious)—*mfg*	332211	3421
Safety razors: Cutlery and Flatware (except Precious)—*mfg*	332211	3421
Safety strap assemblies, automobile–except leather: Motor Vehicle Fabric Accessories and Seat—*mfg*	33636	2399
Safety switches: Building Material Dealers, Other—*retail*	44419	5063
Electrical Apparatus and Equipment, Wiring Supplies and Material—*whlse*	42161	5063
Safflower farms: Oilseed (except Soybean) Farming—*ag*	11112	119
Safflower oil: Fats and Oils Refining and Blending—*mfg*	311225	2076
Oilseed Processing, Other—*mfg*	311223	2076
Saggers: Clay Refractory—*mfg*	327124	3255
Sailboats: Sporting and Recreational Goods and Supplies—*whlse*	42191	5091
Sailboats, building and repairing: Boat Building—*mfg*	336612	3732
Personal and Household Goods Repair and Maintenance, Other—*serv*	81149	3732
Sailcloth: Broadwoven Fabric Mills—*mfg*	31321	2211
Sailhoards: Sporting and Athletic Goods—*mfg*	33992	3949
Sailing vessels, commercial–building and repairing: Ship Building and Repairing—*mfg*	336611	3731
Sails: Canvas and Related Product Mills—*mfg*	314912	2394
Sal soda (washing soda): Alkalies and Chlorine—*mfg*	325181	2812
Salad dressing: Grocery and Related Products, Other—*whlse*	42249	5149
Salad dressings, except dry mixes: Fruit and Vegetable Canning—*mfg*	311421	2035
Mayonnaise, Dressing and Other Prepared Sauce—*mfg*	311941	2035
Salad oils, vegetable–except corn oil-refined: Fats and Oils Refining and Blending—*mfg*	311225	2079
Oilseed Processing, Other—*mfg*	311223	2079
Soybean Processing—*mfg*	311222	2079
Salamanders, coke and gas burning: Heating Equipment (except Electric and Warm Air Furnaces)—*mfg*	333414	3433

ALPHABETICAL INDEX	NAICS	SIC
Sale of partnership shares in real estate syndicates: Financial Investment Activities, Miscellaneous—*fin*	523999	6211
Intermediation, Miscellaneous—*fin*	52391	6211
Investment Banking and Securities Dealing—*fin*	52311	6211
Securities Brokerage—*fin*	52312	6211
Sales and receipt books: Office Supplies and Stationery Stores—*retail*	45321	5112
Stationary and Office Supplies—*whlse*	42212	5112
Sales barns: Stores (except Tobacco Stores), All Other Miscellaneous—*retail*	453998	5999
Sales books: Manifold Business Form Printing—*mfg*	323116	2761
Sales Financing	**52222**	**6153**
Salicylic acid derivatives, medicinal grade: Medicinal and Botanical—*mfg*	325411	2833
Salines mining, except common salt: Potash, Soda, and Borate Mineral—*mining*	212391	1474
Salmon, catching of: Finfish Fishing—*ag*	114111	912
Salmon–smoked, salted, dried, canned, and pickled: Seafood Canning—*mfg*	311711	2091
Saloons (drinking places): Drinking Places (Alcoholic Beverages)—*accom*	72241	5813
Salt: Basic Organic Chemical, All Other—*mfg*	325199	2899
Chemical Product, All Other Miscellaneous—*mfg*	325998	2899
Salt cake (sodium sulfate): Basic Inorganic Chemical, All Other—*mfg*	325188	2819
Chemical Product, All Other Miscellaneous—*mfg*	325998	2819
Salt mining, common: Chemical and Fertilizer Mineral, Other—*mining*	212393	1479
Salt water, impounding (in connection with petroleum products): Oil and Gas Operations Support Activities—*mining*	213112	1389
Salt, evaporated: Grocery and Related Products, Other—*whlse*	42249	5149
Salted nuts: Confectionery—*whlse*	42245	5145
Saltines: Bakeries, Commercial—*mfg*	311812	2052
Cookie and Cracker—*mfg*	311821	2052
Snack Food, Other—*mfg*	311919	2052
Salts of rare earth metals: Basic Inorganic Chemical, All Other—*mfg*	325188	2819
Chemical Product, All Other Miscellaneous—*mfg*	325998	2819
Salts, effervescent: Pharmaceutical Preparation—*mfg*	325412	2834
Salts, heat treating: Basic Organic Chemical, All Other—*mfg*	325199	2899
Chemical Product, All Other Miscellaneous—*mfg*	325998	2899
Salts, industrial: Chemical and Allied Products, Other—*whlse*	42269	5169
Salts, metal: Chemical and Allied Products, Other—*whlse*	42269	5169
Sample Books: Blankbook, Loose-leaf Binder and Device—*mfg*	323118	2782
Flexographic Printing, Commercial—*mfg*	323112	2782
Gravure Printing, Commercial—*mfg*	323111	2782
Lithographic Printing, Commercial—*mfg*	323110	2782
Printing, Other Commercial—*mfg*	323119	2782

Screen Printing, Commercial—*mfg*	323113	2782
Sample cases, regardless of material: Luggage—*mfg*	316991	3161
Sample changers, nuclear radiation: Measuring and Controlling Device, Other—*mfg*	334519	3829
Surgical and Medical Instrument—*mfg*	339112	3829
Sample mounting for the trade: Tradebinding and Related Work—*mfg*	323121	2789
Samples, distribution of: Advertising Material Distribution Services—*prof*	54187	7319
Advertising, Other Services Related to—*prof*	54189	7319
Display Advertising—*prof*	54185	7319
Media Buying Agencies—*prof*	54183	7319
Nonscheduled Air, Other—*trans*	481219	7319
Sand and gravel dealers: Building Material Dealers, Other—*retail*	44419	5211
Home Centers—*retail*	44411	5211
Sand mixers: Construction Machinery—*mfg*	33312	3531
Overhead Traveling Crane, Hoist and Monorail System—*mfg*	333923	3531
Railroad Rolling Stock—*mfg*	33651	3531
Sand riddles (hand sifting or screening apparatus): Fabricated Metal Product, All Other Miscellaneous—*mfg*	332999	3599
General Purpose Machinery , All Other—*mfg*	333999	3599
Machine Shops—*mfg*	33271	3599
Machinery, Other Commercial and Service Industry—*mfg*	333319	3599
Sand, construction: Brick, Stone and Related Material—*whlse*	42132	5032
Building Material Dealers, Other—*retail*	44419	5032
Sand, Gravel, Clay, and Ceramic and Refractory Minerals Mining and Quarrying	**21232**	
Sandals, children's–except rubber: Footwear, Other—*mfg*	316219	3149
Sandals, rubber: Rubber and Plastics Footwear—*mfg*	316211	3021
Sandblasting of building exteriors–contractors: Trade Contractors, All Other Special—*const*	23599	1799
Sandblasting of metal parts, for thetrade: Electroplating, Plating, Polishing, Anodizing and Coloring—*mfg*	332813	3471
Sanders, hand–electric: Power-Driven Hand Tool—*mfg*	333991	3546
Sanders, motor vehicle safety: Motor Vehicle Parts, All Other—*mfg*	336399	3714
Sanding machines, except portable floor sanders (woodworking machinery): Sawmill and Woodworking Machinery—*mfg*	33321	3553
Sanding machines, floor: Machinery, Other Commercial and Service Industry—*mfg*	333319	3589
Sandpaper: Abrasive Product—*mfg*	32791	3291
Fabricated Metal Product, All Other Miscellaneous—*mfg*	332999	3291
Sandpaper manufacturing machines: Paper Industry Machinery—*mfg*	333291	3554
Sandstone, bituminous: Crushed and Broken Stone and Quarrying, Other—*mining*	212319	1499
Sandstone, dimension: Dimension Stone and Quarrying—*mining*	212311	1411
Sandstone, except bituminous–crushed and broken: Crushed and Broken Stone and Quarrying, Other—*mining*	212319	1429
Sandwich bars or shops: Cafeterias—*accom*	722212	5812
Caterers—*accom*	72232	5812
Foodservice Contractors—*accom*	72231	5812
Full-Service Restaurants—*accom*	72211	5812
Limited-Service Restaurants—*accom*	722211	5812
Snack and Nonalcoholic Beverage Bars—*accom*	722213	5812
Theater Companies and Dinner Theaters—*arts*	71111	5812
Sandwich spreads, cheese: Cheese—*mfg*	311513	2022
Sandwich spreads, meat: Meat Processed from Carcasses—*mfg*	311612	2013
Sandwich spreads, salad dressing base: Fruit and Vegetable Canning—*mfg*	311421	2035
Mayonnaise, Dressing and Other Prepared Sauce—*mfg*	311941	2035
Sandwich toasters and grills, household–electric: Electric Housewares and Household Fan—*mfg*	335211	3634
Heating Equipment (except Electric and Warm Air Furnaces)—*mfg*	333414	3634
Sandwiches: Grocery and Related Products, Other—*whlse*	42249	5149
Sanitary aprons: Surgical Appliance and Supplies—*mfg*	339113	3842
Sanitary districts-nonoperating: Regulation and Administration of Communications, Electric, Gas, and Other Utilities—*pub*	92613	9631
Sanitary engineering agencies: Air and Water Resource and Solid Waste Management—*pub*	92411	9511
Sanitary food containers–paper, paper-board, and disposable plastics: Industrial and Personal Service Paper—*whlse*	42213	5113
Sanitary napkins: Sanitary Paper Product—*mfg*	322291	2676
Sanitary paper food containers, liquid tight: Non-Folding Sanitary Food Container—*mfg*	322215	2656
Sanitary Paper Product Manufacturing	**322291**	**2676**
Sanitary pipe fittings: Fabricated Metal Product, All Other Miscellaneous—*mfg*	332999	3432
Plumbing Fixture Fitting and Trim—*mfg*	332913	3432
Sanitary ware, china or enameled iron: Building Material Dealers, Other—*retail*	44419	5074
Plumbing and Heating Equipment and Supplies (Hydronics)—*whlse*	42172	5074
Sanitary ware–bathtubs, lavoratories, and sinks-metal: Enameled Iron and Metal Sanitary Ware—*mfg*	332998	3431
Sanitation preparations: Chemical and Allied Products, Other—*whlse*	42269	5169
Polish and Other Sanitation Good—*mfg*	325612	2842
Sapphire mining: Crushed and Broken Stone and Quarrying, Other—*mining*	212319	1499
Non-Metallic Mineral, All Other—*mining*	212399	1499
Saran broadwoven fabrics: Broadwoven Fabric Mills—*mfg*	31321	2221
Saran fibers: Noncellulosic Organic Fiber—*mfg*	325222	2824
Sardine oil: Fats and Oils Refining and Blending—*mfg*	311225	2077
Fresh and Frozen Seafood Processing—*mfg*	311712	2077
Rendering and Meat By-product Processing—*mfg*	311613	2077
Seafood Canning—*mfg*	311711	2077
Sardines, canned: Seafood Canning—*mfg*	311711	2091
Sash balances, cast iron: Iron Foundries—*mfg*	331511	3321
Sash balances, spring: Watch, Clock, and Part—*mfg*	334518	3495

Description	NAICS	SIC
Sawmill and Woodworking Machinery Manufacturing	**33321**	**3553**
Sawmill machines: Sawmill and Woodworking Machinery—*mfg*	33321	3553
Sawmills	**321113**	**2429**
Sawmills and Wood Preservation	**32111**	
Sawmills and Wood Preservation	**3211**	
Sawmills, custom: Cut Stock, Resawing Lumber, and Planing—*mfg*	321912	2421
Millwork (including Flooring), Other—*mfg*	321918	2421
Sawmills—*mfg*	321113	2421
Wood Product, All Other Miscellaneous—*mfg*	321999	2421
Sawmills, except special product mills: Cut Stock, Resawing Lumber, and Planing—*mfg*	321912	2421
Millwork (including Flooring), Other—*mfg*	321918	2421
Sawmills—*mfg*	321113	2421
Wood Product, All Other Miscellaneous—*mfg*	321999	2421
Sawmills, special product–except lumber and veneer mills: Cut Stock, Resawing Lumber, and Planing—*mfg*	321912	2429
Sawmills—*mfg*	321113	2429
Wood Product, All Other Miscellaneous—*mfg*	321999	2429
Saws, hand–metalworking or woodworking: Saw Blade and Handsaw—*mfg*	332213	3425
Saws, portable hand held–power-driven-woodworking or metalworking: Power-Driven Hand Tool—*mfg*	333991	3546
Saws, power–bench and table (woodworking machinery)-except portable: Sawmill and Woodworking Machinery—*mfg*	33321	3553
Saws, power–metal cutting: Machine Tool (Metal Cutting Types)—*mfg*	333512	3541
Saws, surgical: Surgical and Medical Instrument—*mfg*	339112	3841
Saxophones and parts: Musical Instrument—*mfg*	339992	3931
Scaffolding: Construction and (except Petroleum) Machinery and Equipment—*whlse*	42181	5082
Scaffolding construction–contractors: Trade Contractors, All Other Special—*const*	23599	1799
Scaffolds, metal (mobile or stationary): Ornamental and Architectural Metal Work—*mfg*	332323	3446
Scaffolds, wood: Manufacturing, All Other Miscellaneous—*mfg*	339999	2499
Wood Container and Pallet—*mfg*	32192	2499
Wood Product, All Other Miscellaneous—*mfg*	321999	2499
Scale and Balance (except Laboratory) Manufacturing	**333997**	**3596**
Scalers for gummed tape–hand: Lead Pencil and Art Good—*mfg*	339942	3579
Office Machinery—*mfg*	333313	3579
Watch, Clock, and Part—*mfg*	334518	3579
Scalers, nuclear radiation: Measuring and Controlling Device, Other—*mfg*	334519	3829
Surgical and Medical Instrument—*mfg*	339112	3829
Scales, coin-operated–operation of: Personal Services, All Other—*serv*	81299	7299
Scales, except laboratory: Equipment, Other Commercial—*whlse*	42144	5046
Scale and Balance (except Laboratory)—*mfg*	333997	3596
Scales, measuring (machinists' precision tools): Cutting Tool and Machine Tool Accessory—*mfg*	333515	3545
Hand and Edge Tool—*mfg*	332212	3545
Scalloping, for the trade: Men's and Boys' Cut and Sew Apparel Contractors—*mfg*	315211	2395
Textile Product Mills, All Other Miscellaneous—*mfg*	314999	2395
Women's and Girls' Cut and Sew Apparel Contractors—*mfg*	315212	2395
Scalp treatment service: Personal Care Services, Other—*serv*	812199	7299
Scandium: Basic Inorganic Chemical, All Other—*mfg*	325188	2819
Chemical Product, All Other Miscellaneous—*mfg*	325998	2819
Scarfing machines (woodworking machinery): Sawmill and Woodworking Machinery—*mfg*	33321	3553
Scarfs: Outerwear Knitting Mills—*mfg*	315191	2253
Scarifiers, road: Construction Machinery—*mfg*	33312	3531
Overhead Traveling Crane, Hoist and Monorail System—*mfg*	333923	3531
Railroad Rolling Stock—*mfg*	33651	3531
Scarlet 2 R lake: Petrochemical—*mfg*	32511	2865
Scarves: Men's and Boys' Neckwear—*mfg*	315993	2323
Scarves, hoods, and headbands: Apparel Accessories and Apparel, Other—*mfg*	315999	2339
Cut and Sew Apparel, All Other—*mfg*	315299	2339
Women's and Girls' Cut and Sew Apparel Contractors—*mfg*	315212	2339
Women's and Girls' Cut and Sew Other Outerwear—*mfg*	315238	2339
Scarves, men's and boys': Men's and Boys' Clothing and Furnishings—*whlse*	42232	5136
Scarves–e.g., table, dresser: Household Textile Product Mills, Other—*mfg*	314129	2392
Scarves–women's, children's and infant's: Women's, Children's, and Infants' and Accessories—*whlse*	42233	5137
Scatter rugs, except rubber or plastics: Carpet and Rug Mills—*mfg*	31411	2273
Scavengering: Recyclable Material—*whlse*	42193	5093
Scenery, rental–theatrical: Machinery and Equipment Rental and Leasing, Other Commercial and Industrial—*real*	53249	7922
Scenic and Sightseeing Transportation	**487**	
Scenic and Sightseeing Transportation, Land	**4871**	
Scenic and Sightseeing Transportation, Land	**48711**	**4789**
Scenic and Sightseeing Transportation, Other	**48799**	**7999**
Scenic and Sightseeing Transportation, Other	**4879**	
Scenic and Sightseeing Transportation, Water	**48721**	**7999**
Scenic and Sightseeing Transportation, Water	**4872**	
Scenic railroads for amusement: Scenic and Sightseeing, Land—*trans*	48711	7999
Scenic and Sightseeing, Other—*trans*	48799	7999
Scheduled Air Transportation	**48111**	
Scheduled Air Transportation	**4811**	
Scheduled Freight Air Transportation	**481112**	**4512**
Scheduled Passenger Air Transportation	**481111**	**4512**
Schedules, transportation–except lithographed or gravure: Digital Printing—*mfg*	323115	2759

ALPHABETICAL INDEX	NAICS	SIC
Flexographic Printing, Commercial—*mfg*	323112	2759
Printing, Other Commercial—*mfg*	323119	2759
Quick Printing—*mfg*	323114	2759
Schedules, transportation–gravure printing: Gravure Printing, Commercial—*mfg*	323111	2754
Schedules, transportation–lithographed: Lithographic Printing, Commercial—*mfg*	323110	2752
Quick Printing—*mfg*	323114	2752
Scheelite mining: Copper Ore and Nickel Ore—*mining*	212234	1061
Metal Ore, All Other—*mining*	212299	1061
Schiffli machine embroideries: Schiffli Machine Embroidery—*mfg*	313222	2397
Schiffli Machine Embroidery	**313222**	**2397**
Schist, dimension: Dimension Stone and Quarrying—*mining*	212311	1411
School and Employee Bus Transportation	**4854**	
School and Employee Bus Transportation	**48541**	**4119**
School building construction–general contractors: Building, Commercial and Institutional—*const*	23332	1542
School buses: School and Employee Bus—*trans*	48541	4151
School desks: Furniture—*whlse*	42121	5021
Furniture Stores—*retail*	44211	5021
School furniture: Institutional Furniture—*mfg*	337127	2531
School furniture, except stone and concrete: Institutional Furniture—*mfg*	337127	2531
School photographers: Photography Studios, Portrait—*prof*	541921	7221
School supplies: Office Supplies and Stationery Stores—*retail*	45321	5943
Schools and camps, sports instructional: Sports and Recreation Instruction—*educ*	61162	7999
Schools and Instruction, All Other	**61169**	
Schools and Instruction, All Other Miscellaneous	**611699**	**8299**
Schools and Instruction, Other	**6116**	
Schools for the physically handicapped, elementary and secondary: Elementary and Secondary Schools—*educ*	61111	8211
Schools for the retarded: Elementary and Secondary Schools—*educ*	61111	8211
Schools, correspondence–including branch offices and solicitors: Apprenticeship Training—*educ*	611513	8249
Technical and Trade Schools, Other—*educ*	611519	8249
Schools, dance–including children's, and professionals': Amusement and Recreation Industries, All Other—*arts*	71399	7911
Fine Arts Schools—*educ*	61161	7911
Schools, elementary and secondary: Elementary and Secondary Schools—*educ*	61111	8211
Schools, vocational, except high schools, data processing, or business: Apprenticeship Training—*educ*	611513	8249
Technical and Trade Schools, Other—*educ*	611519	8249
Schottky diodes: Semiconductor and Related Device—*mfg*	334413	3674
Science kits–microscopes, chemistry sets, and natural science sets: Game, Toy, and Children's Vehicle—*mfg*	339932	3944
Scientific and Technical Consulting Services, Other	**54169**	**8748**
Scientific apparatus glass, made from purchased glass: Glass Product Made of Purchased Glass—*mfg*	327215	3231
Scientific glassware, made from purchased glass: Glass Product Made of Purchased Glass—*mfg*	327215	3231
Scientific glassware, pressed or blown–made in glassmaking plants: Pressed and Blown Glass and Glassware, Other—*mfg*	327212	3229
Scientific instrument repair, except electric: Electronic and Precision Equipment Repair and Maintenance, Other—*serv*	811219	7699
Scientific instruments: Office Supplies and Stationery Stores—*retail*	45321	5049
Professional Equipment and Supplies, Other—*whlse*	42149	5049
Scientific membership associations: Professional Organizations—*serv*	81392	8621
Scientific Research and Development Services	**5417**	
Scientific research, noncommercial: Research and Development in the Life Sciences—*prof*	54172	8733
Research and Development in the Physical Sciences and Engineering Sciences—*prof*	54171	8733
Research and Development in the Social Sciences and Humanities—*prof*	54173	8733
Scintillation detectors: Measuring and Controlling Device, Other—*mfg*	334519	3829
Surgical and Medical Instrument—*mfg*	339112	3829
Scissors, electric: Electric Housewares and Household Fan—*mfg*	335211	3634
Heating Equipment (except Electric and Warm Air Furnaces)—*mfg*	333414	3634
Scissors, hand: Cutlery and Flatware (except Precious)—*mfg*	332211	3421
Scissors–barbers', manicure, pedicure, tailors' and household: Cutlery and Flatware (except Precious)—*mfg*	332211	3421
Scoops, crab and fish: Sporting and Athletic Goods—*mfg*	33992	3949
Scoops, hand–metal: Hand and Edge Tool—*mfg*	332212	3423
Scoops, wood: Manufacturing, All Other Miscellaneous—*mfg*	339999	2499
Wood Container and Pallet—*mfg*	32192	2499
Wood Product, All Other Miscellaneous—*mfg*	321999	2499
Scooters, children's: Game, Toy, and Children's Vehicle—*mfg*	339932	3944
Scoreboards, electric: Sign—*mfg*	33995	3993
Scoria mining: Crushed and Broken Stone and Quarrying, Other—*mining*	212319	1499
Non-Metallic Mineral, All Other—*mining*	212399	1499
Scouring compounds: Soap and Other Detergent—*mfg*	325611	2841
Scouring machines, tannery: Industrial Machinery, All Other—*mfg*	333298	3559
Machinery, Other Commercial and Service Industry—*mfg*	333319	3559
Scouring of wool, mohair, and similar fibers: Broadwoven Fabric Mills—*mfg*	31321	2299
Narrow Fabric Mills—*mfg*	313221	2299
Nonwoven Fabric Mills—*mfg*	31323	2299

Description	NAICS	SIC
Textile and Fabric Finishing (except Broadwoven Fabric) Mills—*mfg*	313312	2299
Textile Product Mills, All Other Miscellaneous—*mfg*	314999	2299
Thread Mills—*mfg*	313113	2299
Yarn Spinning Mills—*mfg*	313111	2299
Scouring pads, soap impregnated: Abrasive Product—*mfg*	32791	3291
Fabricated Metal Product, All Other Miscellaneous—*mfg*	332999	3291
Scows, building and repairing: Ship Building and Repairing—*mfg*	336611	3731
Scrap and waste materials: Recyclable Material—*whlse*	42193	5093
Scrap, rubber: Recyclable Material—*whlse*	42193	5093
Scrapbooks: Blankbook, Loose-leaf Binder and Device—*mfg*	323118	2782
Flexographic Printing, Commercial—*mfg*	323112	2782
Gravure Printing, Commercial—*mfg*	323111	2782
Lithographic Printing, Commercial—*mfg*	323110	2782
Office Supplies and Stationery Stores—*retail*	45321	5112
Printing, Other Commercial—*mfg*	323119	2782
Screen Printing, Commercial—*mfg*	323113	2782
Stationary and Office Supplies—*whlse*	42212	5112
Scraper loaders, underground: Mining Machinery and Equipment—*mfg*	333131	3532
Scrapers, construction: Construction Machinery—*mfg*	33312	3531
Overhead Traveling Crane, Hoist and Monorail System—*mfg*	333923	3531
Railroad Rolling Stock—*mfg*	33651	3531
Scrapers, woodworking–hand: Hand and Edge Tool—*mfg*	332212	3423
Scrapple: Meat Processed from Carcasses—*mfg*	311612	2013
Screeds and screeding machines: Construction Machinery—*mfg*	33312	3531
Overhead Traveling Crane, Hoist and Monorail System—*mfg*	333923	3531
Railroad Rolling Stock—*mfg*	33651	3531
Screen doors, metal: Metal Window and Door—*mfg*	332321	3442
Screen printing of cotton broadwoven fabrics: Broadwoven Fabric Finishing Mills—*mfg*	313311	2261
Screen printing of manmade fiber and silk broadwoven fabrics: Broadwoven Fabric Finishing Mills—*mfg*	313311	2262
Screen Printing, Commercial	**323113**	**2759**
Screen process ink: Printing Ink—*mfg*	32591	2893
Screeners, portable: Construction Machinery—*mfg*	33312	3531
Overhead Traveling Crane, Hoist and Monorail System—*mfg*	333923	3531
Railroad Rolling Stock—*mfg*	33651	3531
Screeners, stationary: Mining Machinery and Equipment—*mfg*	333131	3532
Screening and sifting machines for general industrial use: General Purpose Machinery , All Other—*mfg*	333999	3569
Screening machinery and equipment, industrial: Industrial Machinery and Equipment—*whlse*	42183	5084
Screening peat: Crushed and Broken Stone and Quarrying, Other—*mining*	212319	1499
Non-Metallic Mineral, All Other—*mining*	212399	1499
Screening plants, anthracite: Anthracite—*mining*	212113	1231
Screening plants, bituminous coal: Bituminous Coal and Lignite Surface—*mining*	212111	1221
Screening, window–plastics: Plastics Pipe and Pipe Fitting—*mfg*	326122	3089
Plastics Product, All Other—*mfg*	326199	3089
Unsupported Plastics Profile Shape—*mfg*	326121	3089
Screening, woven wire–made from purchased wire: Fabricated Wire Product, Other—*mfg*	332618	3496
Screens, door and window–metal frame: Metal Window and Door—*mfg*	332321	3442
Screens, door and window–wood: Millwork (including Flooring), Other—*mfg*	321918	2431
Wood Window and Door—*mfg*	321911	2431
Screens, privacy–wood: Nonupholstered Wood Household Furniture—*mfg*	337122	2511
Screens, projection: Photographic and Photocopying Equipment—*mfg*	333315	3861
Photographic Film, Paper, Plate and Chemical—*mfg*	325992	3861
Screens, textile printing: Marking Device—*mfg*	339943	3953
Screw and nut slotting machines: Machine Tool (Metal Cutting Types)—*mfg*	333512	3541
Screw drivers: Hand and Edge Tool—*mfg*	332212	3423
Screw eyes, metal: Bolt, Nut, Screw, Rivet and Washer—*mfg*	332722	3452
Screw eyes, plastics: Plastics Pipe and Pipe Fitting—*mfg*	326122	3089
Plastics Product, All Other—*mfg*	326199	3089
Unsupported Plastics Profile Shape—*mfg*	326121	3089
Screw hooks: Bolt, Nut, Screw, Rivet and Washer—*mfg*	332722	3452
Screw machine products–produced on a job or order basis: Precision Turned Product—*mfg*	332721	3451
Screw machines, automatic: Machine Tool (Metal Cutting Types)—*mfg*	333512	3541
Screw propellers–cast brass, bronze, copper, and copper base: Copper Foundries—*mfg*	331525	3366
Screwdowns and boxes: Other Metalworking Machinery, Other—*mfg*	333518	3549
Screwdriving machines: Other Metalworking Machinery, Other—*mfg*	333518	3549
Screws, bone: Surgical and Medical Instrument—*mfg*	339112	3841
Screws, jack: General Purpose Machinery , All Other—*mfg*	333999	3569
Screws, metal: Bolt, Nut, Screw, Rivet and Washer—*mfg*	332722	3452
Scrim, cotton: Broadwoven Fabric Mills—*mfg*	31321	2211
Scroll casings: Air-Conditioning and Warm Air Heating Equipment and Commercial and Industrial Refrigeration Equipment—*mfg*	333415	3443
Metal Tank (Heavy Gauge)—*mfg*	33242	3443
Plate Work—*mfg*	332313	3443
Power Boiler and Heat Exchanger—*mfg*	33241	3443
Scrub cloths: Broadwoven Fabric Mills—*mfg*	31321	2211
Scrubbing machines: Machinery, Other Commercial and Service Industry—*mfg*	333319	3589
Scrubbing pads, plastics: Plastics Pipe and Pipe Fitting—*mfg*	326122	3089
Plastics Product, All Other—*mfg*	326199	3089
Unsupported Plastics Profile Shape—*mfg*	326121	3089

ALPHABETICAL INDEX	NAICS	SIC
Scuba and skin diving instruction: Sports and Recreation Instruction—*educ*	61162	7999
Scuba diving equipment, except clothing: Sporting and Athletic Goods—*mfg*	33992	3949
Sculptors' studios: Independent Artists, Writers, and Performers—*arts*	71151	8999
Sculptures, architectural–gypsum, clay, or papier-mache-factory production only: Gypsum and Gypsum Product—*mfg*	32742	3299
Nonmetallic Mineral Product, All Other Miscellaneous—*mfg*	327999	3299
Scythes: Hand and Edge Tool—*mfg*	332212	3423
Scythestone quarrying: Crushed and Broken Stone and Quarrying, Other—*mining*	212319	1499
Non-Metallic Mineral, All Other—*mining*	212399	1499
Scythestones, artificial: Abrasive Product—*mfg*	32791	3291
Fabricated Metal Product, All Other Miscellaneous—*mfg*	332999	3291
Sea herring, catching of: Finfish Fishing—*ag*	114111	912
Sea urchins, catching of: Crop Farming, All Other Miscellaneous—*ag*	111998	919
Marine Fishing, Other—*ag*	114119	919
Seafood Canning	**311711**	**2091**
Seafood markets: Direct Selling Establishments, Other—*retail*	45439	5421
Fish and Seafood Markets—*retail*	44522	5421
Meat Markets—*retail*	44521	5421
Seafood Product Preparation and Packaging	**31171**	
Seafood Product Preparation and Packaging	**3117**	
Seafood products, canned and cured: Seafood Canning—*mfg*	311711	2091
Seafoods, fresh and frozen: Fresh and Frozen Seafood Processing—*mfg*	311712	2092
Seafoods, frozen–packaged: Packaged Frozen Food—*whlse*	42242	5142
Seafoods, not canned or frozen packaged: Fish and Seafood—*whlse*	42246	5146
Seal presses, notary, hand: Marking Device—*mfg*	339943	3953
Sealants: Chemical and Allied Products, Other—*whlse*	42269	5169
Sealers, wood: Paint and Coating—*mfg*	32551	2851
Sealing compounds for pipe threads and joints: Adhesive—*mfg*	32552	2891
Sealing compounds, synthetic rubber and plastics: Adhesive—*mfg*	32552	2891
Sealing or insulating tape for pipe, fiberglass coated with tar or asphalt: Fabric Coating Mills—*mfg*	31332	2295
Sealing wax: Adhesive—*mfg*	32552	2891
Seals, corporation: Marking Device—*mfg*	339943	3953
Seals, gaskets, and packing: Industrial Machinery and Equipment—*whlse*	42183	5085
Industrial Supplies—*whlse*	42184	5085
Seals, hand (dies): Marking Device—*mfg*	339943	3953
Seals, hermetic–for electronic equipment: Electronic Component, Other—*mfg*	334419	3679
Motor Vehicle Electrical and Electronic Equipment, Other—*mfg*	336322	3679
Printed Circuit/Electronics Assembly—*mfg*	334418	3679

ALPHABETICAL INDEX	NAICS	SIC
Radio and Television Broadcasting and Wireless Communications Equipment—*mfg*	33422	3679
Seals, lithographed: Lithographic Printing, Commercial—*mfg*	323110	2752
Quick Printing—*mfg*	323114	2752
Seals–gravure printing: Gravure Printing, Commercial—*mfg*	323111	2754
Seals–printing except lithographic or gravure: Digital Printing—*mfg*	323115	2759
Flexographic Printing, Commercial—*mfg*	323112	2759
Printing, Other Commercial—*mfg*	323119	2759
Quick Printing—*mfg*	323114	2759
Seam welding apparatus, gas and electric: Power, Distribution and Specialty Transformer—*mfg*	335311	3548
Welding and Soldering Equipment—*mfg*	333992	3548
Search, Detection, Navigation, Guidance, Aeronautical, and Nautical System and Instrument Manufacturing	**334511**	**3812**
Searchlight mirrors and reflectors: Optical Instrument and Lens—*mfg*	333314	3827
Searchlights: Lighting Equipment, Other—*mfg*	335129	3648
Seasonal hotels: Bed and Breakfast Inns—*accom*	721191	7011
Casino Hotels—*accom*	72112	7011
Hotels (except Casino Hotels) and Motels—*accom*	72111	7011
Traveler Accommodation, All Other—*accom*	721199	7011
Seasoning and Dressing Manufacturing	**31194**	
Seasonings (prepared sauces), tomato: Fruit and Vegetable Canning—*mfg*	311421	2033
Seasonings (prepared sauces), vegetable:except tomato and dry: Fruit and Vegetable Canning—*mfg*	311421	2035
Mayonnaise, Dressing and Other Prepared Sauce—*mfg*	311941	2035
Seat cover cloth, automobile–cotton: Broadwoven Fabric Mills—*mfg*	31321	2211
Seat covers, automobile: Motor Vehicle Fabric Accessories and Seat—*mfg*	33636	2399
Seat covers, automotive: Automotive Parts and Accessories Stores—*retail*	44131	5013
Motor Vehicle Supplies and New Part—*whlse*	42112	5013
Seat covers, rattan: Manufacturing, All Other Miscellaneous—*mfg*	339999	2499
Wood Container and Pallet—*mfg*	32192	2499
Wood Product, All Other Miscellaneous—*mfg*	321999	2499
Seat ejector devices, aircraft: Aircraft Part and Auxiliary Equipment, Other—*mfg*	336413	3728
Fluid Power Valve and Hose Fitting—*mfg*	332912	3728
Seat posts, motorcycle and bicycle: Motorcycle, Bicycle and Parts—*mfg*	336991	3751
Seatbelts, automobile and aircraft–exceptleather: Motor Vehicle Fabric Accessories and Seat—*mfg*	33636	2399
Seatbelts, automotive: Automotive Parts and Accessories Stores—*retail*	44131	5013
Motor Vehicle Supplies and New Part—*whlse*	42112	5013
Seatbelts, leather: Leather Good, All Other—*mfg*	316999	3199

Entry	NAICS	SIC
Seats for metal household furniture: Metal Household Furniture—*mfg*	337124	2514
Seats, chair–hardwood: Cut Stock, Resawing Lumber, and Planing—*mfg*	321912	2426
Millwork (including Flooring), Other—*mfg*	321918	2426
Showcase, Partition, Shelving, and Locker—*mfg*	337215	2426
Wood Product, All Other Miscellaneous—*mfg*	321999	2426
Seats, railroad: Motor Vehicle Fabric Accessories and Seat—*mfg*	33636	2531
Seats, toilet–wood: Manufacturing, All Other Miscellaneous—*mfg*	339999	2499
Wood Container and Pallet—*mfg*	32192	2499
Wood Product, All Other Miscellaneous—*mfg*	321999	2499
Seats–automobile, vans, aircraft, railroad, and other public conveyances: Motor Vehicle Fabric Accessories and Seat—*mfg*	33636	2531
Seaweed grown under cover: Food Crops Grown Under Cover, Other—*ag*	111419	182
Mushroom Production—*ag*	111411	182
Seaweed, gathering of: Crop Farming, All Other Miscellaneous—*ag*	111998	919
Marine Fishing, Other—*ag*	114119	919
Sebacic acid: Basic Organic Chemical, All Other—*mfg*	325199	2869
Sebacic acid esters: Basic Organic Chemical, All Other—*mfg*	325199	2869
Secondary Market Financing	**522294**	**6111**
Secondary refining and smelting of nonferrous metals: Secondary Smelting and Alloying of Aluminum—*mfg*	331314	3341
Secondary Smelting, Refining, and Alloying of Copper—*mfg*	331423	3341
Secondary Smelting, Refining, and Alloying of Nonferrous Metal (except Copper and Aluminum)—*mfg*	331492	3341
Secondary schools: Elementary and Secondary Schools—*educ*	61111	8211
Secondary Smelting and Alloying of Aluminum	**331314**	**3399**
Secondary Smelting, Refining, and Alloying of Copper	**331423**	**3399**
Secondary Smelting, Refining, and Alloying of Nonferrous Metal (except Copper and Aluminum)	**331492**	**3341**
Secondhand book stores: Non-Depository Credit Intermediation, All Other—*fin*	522298	5932
Used Merchandise Stores—*retail*	45331	5932
Secondhand clothing and shoe stores: Non-Depository Credit Intermediation, All Other—*fin*	522298	5932
Used Merchandise Stores—*retail*	45331	5932
Secondhand furniture stores: Non-Depository Credit Intermediation, All Other—*fin*	522298	5932
Used Merchandise Stores—*retail*	45331	5932
Secretarial schools: Business and Secretarial Schools—*educ*	61141	8244
Secretarial service: Court Reporting and Stenotype Services—*admin*	561492	7338
Document Preparation Services—*admin*	56141	7338
Secretaries, household–wood: Nonupholstered Wood Household Furniture—*mfg*	337122	2511
Sections for prefabricated metal buildings: Prefabricated Metal Building and Component—*mfg*	332311	3448
Sections for prefabricated wood buildings: Prefabricated Wood Building—*mfg*	321992	2452
Sections, pipe–fabricated from purchasedmetal pipe: Fabricated Pipe and Pipe Fitting—*mfg*	332996	3498
Securities and Commodity Contracts Intermediation and Brokerage	**5231**	
Securities and Commodity Exchanges	**52321**	**6231**
Securities and Commodity Exchanges	**5232**	
Securities Brokerage	**52312**	**6211**
Securities regulation commissions: Regulation, Licensing, and Inspection of Miscellaneous Commercial Sectors—*pub*	92615	9651
Securities, Commodity Contracts and Other Intermediation and Related Activities	**523**	
Security brokers: Financial Investment Activities, Miscellaneous—*fin*	523999	6211
Intermediation, Miscellaneous—*fin*	52391	6211
Investment Banking and Securities Dealing—*fin*	52311	6211
Securities Brokerage—*fin*	52312	6211
Security certificates, engraved: Digital Printing—*mfg*	323115	2759
Flexographic Printing, Commercial—*mfg*	323112	2759
Printing, Other Commercial—*mfg*	323119	2759
Quick Printing—*mfg*	323114	2759
Security custodians: Financial Investment Activities, Miscellaneous—*fin*	523999	6289
Trust, Fiduciary and Custody Activities—*fin*	523991	6289
Security dealers: Financial Investment Activities, Miscellaneous—*fin*	523999	6211
Intermediation, Miscellaneous—*fin*	52391	6211
Investment Banking and Securities Dealing—*fin*	52311	6211
Securities Brokerage—*fin*	52312	6211
Security exchanges: Securities and Commodity Exchanges—*fin*	52321	6231
Security flotation companies: Financial Investment Activities, Miscellaneous—*fin*	523999	6211
Intermediation, Miscellaneous—*fin*	52391	6211
Investment Banking and Securities Dealing—*fin*	52311	6211
Securities Brokerage—*fin*	52312	6211
Security guard service: Armored Car Services—*admin*	561613	7381
Investigation Services—*admin*	561611	7381
Security Guards and Patrol Services—*admin*	561612	7381
Security Guards and Patrol Services	**561612**	**7381**
Security holders protective committees: Financial Investment Activities, Miscellaneous—*fin*	523999	6289
Trust, Fiduciary and Custody Activities—*fin*	523991	6289
Security speculators for own account: Commodity Contracts Dealing—*fin*	52313	6799
Financial Investment Activities, Miscellaneous—*fin*	523999	6799
Intermediation, Miscellaneous—*fin*	52391	6799
Portfolio Management—*fin*	52392	6799
Security systems devices, burglar and firealarm–monitoring and maintenance: Security Systems Services (except Locksmiths)—*admin*	561621	7382

Description	NAICS	SIC
Semibituminous coal underground mining: Bituminous Coal Underground—*mining*	212112	1222
Semiconductor and Other Electronic Component Manufacturing	**33441**	
Semiconductor and Other Electronic Component Manufacturing	**3344**	
Semiconductor and Related Device Manufacturing	**334413**	**3674**
Semiconductor circuit networks (solid-state integrated circuits): Semiconductor and Related Device—*mfg*	334413	3674
Semiconductor devices: Electronic Parts and Equipment, Other—*whlse*	42169	5065
Semiconductor and Related Device—*mfg*	334413	3674
Semiconductor Machinery Manufacturing	**333295**	**3559**
Semiconductor manufacturing machinery: Industrial Machinery, All Other—*mfg*	333298	3559
Machinery, Other Commercial and Service Industry—*mfg*	333319	3559
Semiconductor test equipment: Electronic Coil, Transformer, and Other Inductor—*mfg*	334416	3825
Instrument for Measuring and Testing Electricity and Electrical Signals—*mfg*	334515	3825
Semidiesel engines for stationary, marine, traction, or other uses: Engine Equipment, Other—*mfg*	333618	3519
Motor Vehicle Parts, All Other—*mfg*	336399	3519
Seminaries, below university grade: Elementary and Secondary Schools—*educ*	61111	8211
Seminaries, theological: Colleges, Universities and Professional Schools—*educ*	61131	8221
Semiprecious stones mining: Crushed and Broken Stone and Quarrying, Other—*mining*	212319	1499
Non-Metallic Mineral, All Other—*mining*	212399	1499
Semisteel castings: Iron Foundries—*mfg*	331511	3321
Semisteel foundries: Iron Foundries—*mfg*	331511	3321
Semitrailers for missile transportation: Truck Trailer—*mfg*	336212	3715
Semitrailers for truck tractors: Truck Trailer—*mfg*	336212	3715
Semolina (flour): Flour Milling—*mfg*	311211	2041
Senior citizens associations: Child and Youth Services—*hlth*	62411	8322
Community Food Services—*hlth*	62421	8322
Community Housing Services, Other—*hlth*	624229	8322
Emergency and Other Relief Services—*hlth*	62423	8322
Individual and Family Services, Other—*hlth*	62419	8322
Parole Offices and Probation Offices—*pub*	92215	8322
Services for the Elderly and Persons with Disabilities—*hlth*	62412	8322
Temporary Shelters—*hlth*	624221	8322
Sensitometers, photographic: Photographic and Photocopying Equipment—*mfg*	333315	3861
Photographic Film, Paper, Plate and Chemical—*mfg*	325992	3861
Sentinel, cardiac: Electromedical and Electrotherapeutic Apparatus—*mfg*	334510	3845
Irradiation Apparatus—*mfg*	334517	3845
Separating machinery, mineral: Mining Machinery and Equipment—*mfg*	333131	3532
Separators for steam, gas, vapor, and air (machinery): General Purpose Machinery , All Other—*mfg*	333999	3569
Separators, battery–rubber: Fabric Coating Mills—*mfg*	31332	3069
Rubber Product, All Other—*mfg*	326299	3069
Separators, battery–wood: Manufacturing, All Other Miscellaneous—*mfg*	339999	2499
Wood Container and Pallet—*mfg*	32192	2499
Wood Product, All Other Miscellaneous—*mfg*	321999	2499
Separators, cream–farm: Farm Machinery and Equipment—*mfg*	333111	3523
Separators, cream–industrial: Food Product Machinery—*mfg*	333294	3556
Separators, grain and berry–farm: Farm Machinery and Equipment—*mfg*	333111	3523
Separators, industrial process–metal plate: Air-Conditioning and Warm Air Heating Equipment and Commercial and Industrial Refrigeration Equipment—*mfg*	333415	3443
Metal Tank (Heavy Gauge)—*mfg*	33242	3443
Plate Work—*mfg*	332313	3443
Power Boiler and Heat Exchanger—*mfg*	33241	3443
Septic Tank and Related Services	**562991**	**7699**
Septic tank installation-contractors: Plumbing, Heating and Air-Conditioning Contractors—*const*	23511	1711
Septic tanks: Building Material Dealers, Other—*retail*	44419	5039
Construction Material, Other—*whlse*	42139	5039
Septic tanks, concrete: Concrete Pipe—*mfg*	327332	3272
Concrete Product, Other—*mfg*	32739	3272
Nonmetallic Mineral Product, All Other Miscellaneous—*mfg*	327999	3272
Septic tanks, metal plate: Air-Conditioning and Warm Air Heating Equipment and Commercial and Industrial Refrigeration Equipment—*mfg*	333415	3443
Metal Tank (Heavy Gauge)—*mfg*	33242	3443
Plate Work—*mfg*	332313	3443
Power Boiler and Heat Exchanger—*mfg*	33241	3443
Septic tanks, plastics: Plastics Pipe and Pipe Fitting—*mfg*	326122	3089
Plastics Product, All Other—*mfg*	326199	3089
Unsupported Plastics Profile Shape—*mfg*	326121	3089
Sequencing controls for electric heat: Automatic Environmental Control for Residential, Commercial and Appliance Use—*mfg*	334512	3822
Serges of wool, mohair, and similar animal fibers: Broadwoven Fabric Finishing Mills—*mfg*	313311	2231
Broadwoven Fabric Mills—*mfg*	31321	2231
Textile and Fabric Finishing (except Broadwoven Fabric) Mills—*mfg*	313312	2231
Serges, manmade fiber: Broadwoven Fabric Mills—*mfg*	31321	2221
Series capacitors, except electronic: Electrical Equipment and Component, All Other Miscellaneous—*mfg*	335999	3629
Serobacterins: Biological Product (except Diagnostic)—*mfg*	325414	2836
Serpentine, crushed and broken: Crushed and Broken Stone and Quarrying, Other—*mining*	212319	1429

ALPHABETICAL INDEX	NAICS	SIC
Serpentine, dimension: Dimension Stone and Quarrying—*mining*	212311	1411
Serums, except in vitro and in vivo: Biological Product (except Diagnostic)—*mfg*	325414	2836
Service academies (college): Colleges, Universities and Professional Schools—*educ*	61131	8221
Service and repair of broadcasting stations-contractors: Trade Contractors, All Other Special—*const*	23599	1799
Service apparel, washable: Men's and Boys' Cut and Sew Apparel Contractors—*mfg*	315211	2326
Men's and Boys' Cut and Sew Work Clothing—*mfg*	315225	2326
Service apparel, washable–e.g., nurses, maids', waitresses', laboratory uniforms: Apparel Accessories and Apparel, Other—*mfg*	315999	2339
Cut and Sew Apparel, All Other—*mfg*	315299	2339
Women's and Girls' Cut and Sew Apparel Contractors—*mfg*	315212	2339
Women's and Girls' Cut and Sew Other Outerwear—*mfg*	315238	2339
Service bureaus, computer: Data Processing Services—*info*	51421	7374
Service entrance equipment, electrical: Building Material Dealers, Other—*retail*	44419	5063
Electrical Apparatus and Equipment, Wiring Supplies and Material—*whlse*	42161	5063
Service Establishment Equipment and Supplies Wholesalers	**42185**	**5087**
Service leagues: Child and Youth Services—*hlth*	62411	8322
Community Food Services—*hlth*	62421	8322
Community Housing Services, Other—*hlth*	624229	8322
Emergency and Other Relief Services—*hlth*	62423	8322
Individual and Family Services, Other—*hlth*	62419	8322
Parole Offices and Probation Offices—*pub*	92215	8322
Services for the Elderly and Persons with Disabilities—*hlth*	62412	8322
Temporary Shelters—*hlth*	624221	8322
Service machine operation coin-operated: Personal Services, All Other—*serv*	81299	7299
Service station cleaning and degreasing service: Janitorial Services—*admin*	56172	7349
Service station construction–general contractors: Building, Commercial and Institutional—*const*	23332	1542
Service station equipment installation, maintenance, and repair–contractors: Trade Contractors, All Other Special—*const*	23599	1799
Service station equipment, automobile: Automotive Parts and Accessories Stores—*retail*	44131	5013
Motor Vehicle Supplies and New Part—*whlse*	42112	5013
Service stations, gasoline: Gasoline Stations with Convenience Stores—*retail*	44711	5541
Gasoline Stations, Other—*retail*	44719	5541
Service well drilling–on a contract basis: Drilling Oil and Gas Wells—*mining*	213111	1381
Services (except Public Administration), Other	**81**	

ALPHABETICAL INDEX	NAICS	SIC
Services for the Elderly and Persons with Disabilities	**62412**	**8322**
Services to Buildings and Dwellings	**5617**	
Servicing machines, coin-operated–except drycleaning and laundry: Machinery, Other Commercial and Service Industry—*mfg*	333319	3589
Servicing oil and gas wells on a contract basis: Oil and Gas Operations Support Activities—*mining*	213112	1389
Servicing water wells-contractors: Water Well Drilling Contractors—*const*	23581	1781
Serving carts, household–metal: Metal Household Furniture—*mfg*	337124	2514
Servomotors: Motor and Generator—*mfg*	335312	3621
Settlement houses: Child and Youth Services—*hlth*	62411	8322
Community Food Services—*hlth*	62421	8322
Community Housing Services, Other—*hlth*	624229	8322
Emergency and Other Relief Services—*hlth*	62423	8322
Individual and Family Services, Other—*hlth*	62419	8322
Parole Offices and Probation Offices—*pub*	92215	8322
Services for the Elderly and Persons with Disabilities—*hlth*	62412	8322
Temporary Shelters—*hlth*	624221	8322
Setup boxboard: Paperboard Mills—*mfg*	32213	2631
Setup Paperboard Box Manufacturing	**322213**	**2652**
Setup paperboard boxes: Industrial and Personal Service Paper—*whlse*	42213	5113
Sewage collection and disposal line construction–general contractors: Power and Communication Transmission Line—*const*	23492	1623
Water, Sewer, and Pipeline—*const*	23491	1623
Sewage treatment equipment: Machinery, Other Commercial and Service Industry—*mfg*	333319	3589
Sewage Treatment Facilities	**22132**	**4952**
Sewage treatment plant construction-general oontractors: Heavy, All Other—*const*	23499	1629
Industrial Nonbuilding Structure—*const*	23493	1629
Sewer cleaning equipment, power: Machinery, Other Commercial and Service Industry—*mfg*	333319	3589
Sewer construction–general contractors: Power and Communication Transmission Line—*const*	23492	1623
Water, Sewer, and Pipeline—*const*	23491	1623
Sewer hookups and connections for buildings-contractors: Plumbing, Heating and Air-Conditioning Contractors—*const*	23511	1711
Sewer liner brick, vitrified clay: Structural Clay Product, Other—*mfg*	327123	3259
Sewer pipe and fittings, clay: Structural Clay Product, Other—*mfg*	327123	3259
Sewer pipe, cast iron: Iron Foundries—*mfg*	331511	3321
Sewer pipe, clay: Brick, Stone and Related Material—*whlse*	42132	5032
Building Material Dealers, Other—*retail*	44419	5032
Sewer pipe, concrete: Concrete Pipe—*mfg*	327332	3272
Concrete Product, Other—*mfg*	32739	3272
Nonmetallic Mineral Product, All Other Miscellaneous—*mfg*	327999	3272
Sewerage systems: Sewage Treatment Facilities—*util*	22132	4952

Entry	NAICS	SIC
Sewing accessories: Broadwoven Fabric Finishing Mills—*mfg*	313311	5131
Piece Goods, Notions and Other Dry Goods—*whlse*	42231	5131
Textile and Fabric Finishing (except Broadwoven Fabric) Mills—*mfg*	313312	5131
Sewing cases, regardless of material: Personal Leather Good (except Women's Handbag and Purse)—*mfg*	316993	3172
Sewing machine cabinets and cases, wood: Wood Television, Radio, and Sewing Machine Cabinet—*mfg*	337129	2517
Sewing machine repair shops: Machinery and Equipment (except Automotive and Electronic) Repair and Maintenance, Commercial and Industrial—*serv*	81131	7699
Sewing machine stores: Household Appliance Stores—*retail*	443111	5722
Sewing machines and attachments, household: Major Household Appliance, Other—*mfg*	335228	3639
Sewing machines and attachments, industrial: Industrial Machinery, All Other—*mfg*	333298	3559
Machinery, Other Commercial and Service Industry—*mfg*	333319	3559
Sewing machines, household–electric: Electrical Appliance, Television and Radio Set—*whlse*	42162	5064
Sewing machines, industrial: Industrial Machinery and Equipment—*whlse*	42183	5084
Sewing supplies: Sewing, Needlework and Piece Goods Stores—*retail*	45113	5949
Sewing thread, except industrial: Broadwoven Fabric Finishing Mills—*mfg*	313311	5131
Piece Goods, Notions and Other Dry Goods—*whlse*	42231	5131
Textile and Fabric Finishing (except Broadwoven Fabric) Mills—*mfg*	313312	5131
Sewing thread–cotton, silk, manmade fibers, and wool: Textile and Fabric Finishing (except Broadwoven Fabric) Mills—*mfg*	313312	2284
Thread Mills—*mfg*	313113	2284
Sewing, Needlework and Piece Goods Stores	**45113**	**5949**
Sextants, except surveying: Search, Detection, Navigation, Guidance, Aeronautical, and Nautical System and Instrument—*mfg*	334511	3812
Sextants, surveying: Measuring and Controlling Device, Other—*mfg*	334519	3829
Surgical and Medical Instrument—*mfg*	339112	3829
Shade cloth, coated or impregnated: Fabric Coating Mills—*mfg*	31332	2295
Shade cloth, window–cotton: Broadwoven Fabric Mills—*mfg*	31321	2211
Shade pulls, window: Blind and Shade—*mfg*	33792	2591
Shades, canvas: Canvas and Related Product Mills—*mfg*	314912	2394
Shades, lamp and candle–except glass and metal: Residential Electric Lighting Fixture—*mfg*	335121	3999
Shades, lamp–glass: Pressed and Blown Glass and Glassware, Other—*mfg*	327212	3229
Shades, lamp–metal: Residential Electric Lighting Fixture—*mfg*	335121	3645
Shades, porch–made of wood slats: Blind and Shade—*mfg*	33792	2591
Shades, window–except canvas: Blind and Shade—*mfg*	33792	2591
Shaft sinking for nonmetallic minerals, except fuels–on a contract basis: Geophysical Surveying and Mapping Services—*prof*	54136	1481
Non-Metallic Minerals (except Fuels) Support Activities—*mining*	213115	1481
Shaft sinking, anthracite mining–on a contract basis: Coal Support Activities—*mining*	213113	1241
Shaft sinking, bituminous coal and lignite mining–on a contract basis: Coal Support Activities—*mining*	213113	1241
Shaft sinking, metal mining–on a contract basis: Geophysical Surveying and Mapping Services—*prof*	54136	1081
Metal Support Activities—*mining*	213114	1081
Shafts, flexible: Mechanical Power Transmission Equipment—*mfg*	333613	3568
Shafts, golf club: Sporting and Athletic Goods—*mfg*	33992	3949
Shakes (hand split shingles): Cut Stock, Resawing Lumber, and Planing—*mfg*	321912	2429
Sawmills—*mfg*	321113	2429
Wood Product, All Other Miscellaneous—*mfg*	321999	2429
Shale (common) quarrying-not in conjunction with manufacturing: Clay and Ceramic and Refractory Minerals—*mining*	212325	1459
Shale, expanded: Ground or Treated Mineral and Earth—*mfg*	327992	3295
Shampoos, hair: Soap and Other Detergent—*mfg*	325611	2844
Toilet Preparation—*mfg*	32562	2844
Shanks, shoe: Fastener, Button, Needle and Pin—*mfg*	339993	3131
Leather Good, All Other—*mfg*	316999	3131
Wood Product, All Other Miscellaneous—*mfg*	321999	3131
Shantungs, manmade fiber and silk: Broadwoven Fabric Mills—*mfg*	31321	2221
Shapers and slotters, metal cutting: Machine Tool (Metal Cutting Types)—*mfg*	333512	3541
Shapers, woodworking machinery: Sawmill and Woodworking Machinery—*mfg*	33321	3553
Shaping tools (machine tool accessories): Cutting Tool and Machine Tool Accessory—*mfg*	333515	3545
Hand and Edge Tool—*mfg*	332212	3545
Sharks, catching of: Finfish Fishing—*ag*	114111	912
Sharpening stone quarrying: Crushed and Broken Stone and Quarrying, Other—*mining*	212319	1499
Non-Metallic Mineral, All Other—*mining*	212399	1499
Shaving brushes: Broom, Brush and Mop—*mfg*	339994	3991
Shaving machines (metalworking): Machine Tool (Metal Cutting Types)—*mfg*	333512	3541
Shaving preparations–e.g., cakes, creams, lotions, powders, tablets: Soap and Other Detergent—*mfg*	325611	2844
Toilet Preparation—*mfg*	32562	2844
Shawls: Outerwear Knitting Mills—*mfg*	315191	2253
Shear knives: Cutting Tool and Machine Tool Accessory—*mfg*	333515	3545
Hand and Edge Tool—*mfg*	332212	3545
Shearing machines, power: Machine Tool (Metal Forming Types)—*mfg*	333513	3542
Shearling (prepared sheepskin): Leather and Hide Tanning and Finishing—*mfg*	31611	3111
Shears, hand: Cutlery and Flatware (except Precious)—*mfg*	332211	3421

Shell slugs, steel–made in steel works or rolling mills: Iron and Steel Mills—*mfg*	331111	3312
Petroleum and Coal Productsa, All Other—*mfg*	324199	3312
Shellac: Paint and Wallpaper Stores—*retail*	44412	5198
Paint, Varnish and Supplies—*whlse*	42295	5198
Shellac, protective coating: Paint and Coating—*mfg*	32551	2851
Shellers, nut (agricultural machinery): Farm Machinery and Equipment—*mfg*	333111	3523
Shellfish Farming	**112512**	**921**
Shellfish Fishing	**114112**	**913**
Shellfish, canned and cured: Seafood Canning—*mfg*	311711	2091
Shellfish, catching of: Shellfish Fishing—*ag*	114112	913
Shellfish, fresh and frozen: Fresh and Frozen Seafood Processing—*mfg*	311712	2092
Shellfish, fresh–shucked, picked, or packed: Fresh and Frozen Seafood Processing—*mfg*	311712	2092
Shells, artillery–more than 30 mm (or more than 1.18 inch): Ammunition (except Small Arms)—*mfg*	332993	3483
Shells, small arms–30 mm. (or 1.18 inch)or less: Small Arms Ammunition—*mfg*	332992	3482
Sheltered workshops: Vocational Rehabilitation Services—*hlth*	62431	8331
Shelving: Equipment, Other Commercial—*whlse*	42144	5046
Shelving angles and slotted bars, exceptwood: Showcase, Partition, Shelving, and Locker—*mfg*	337215	2542
Shelving without rigid framework, madefrom purchased wire: Fabricated Wire Product, Other—*mfg*	332618	3496
Shelving, office and store–except wood: Showcase, Partition, Shelving, and Locker—*mfg*	337215	2542
Shelving, office and store–wood: Architectural Woodwork and Millwork, Custom—*mfg*	337212	2541
Showcase, Partition, Shelving, and Locker—*mfg*	337215	2541
Wood Kitchen Cabinet and Counter Top—*mfg*	33711	2541
Sherardizing of metals and metal products, for the trade: Costume Jewelry and Novelty—*mfg*	339914	3479
Jewelry (except Costume)—*mfg*	339911	3479
Metal Coating, Engraving (except Jewelry and Silverware), and Allied Services to Manufacturers—*mfg*	332812	3479
Silverware and Plated Ware—*mfg*	339912	3479
Sherardizing ovens: Industrial Process Furnace and Oven—*mfg*	333994	3567
Sherbets and ices: Ice Cream and Frozen Dessert—*mfg*	31152	2024
Sheriffs' offices: Police Protection—*pub*	92212	9221
Shifting of floating equipment within harbors: Coastal and Great Lakes Freight—*trans*	483113	4492
Inland Water Freight—*trans*	483211	4492
Navigational Services to Shipping—*trans*	48833	4492
Shims, metal: Fabricated Metal Product, All Other Miscellaneous—*mfg*	332999	3499
Shingle bolts, wood–hewn: Logging—*ag*	11331	2411
Shingle mills, wood: Cut Stock, Resawing Lumber, and Planing—*mfg*	321912	2429
Sawmills—*mfg*	321113	2429
Wood Product, All Other Miscellaneous—*mfg*	321999	2429
Shingles, asbestos cement: Motor Vehicle Brake System—*mfg*	33634	3292
Nonmetallic Mineral Product, All Other Miscellaneous—*mfg*	327999	3292
Shingles, asphalt or tar saturated felt:strip and individual: Asphalt Shingle and Coating Materials—*mfg*	324122	2952
Shingles, except wood: Roofing, Siding and Insulation Material—*whlse*	42133	5033
Shingles, wood: Building Material Dealers, Other—*retail*	44419	5031
Shingles, wood–sawed or hand split: Cut Stock, Resawing Lumber, and Planing—*mfg*	321912	2429
Sawmills—*mfg*	321113	2429
Wood Product, All Other Miscellaneous—*mfg*	321999	2429
Ship and Boat Building	**3366**	
Ship and Boat Building	**33661**	
Ship boiler and tank cleaning and repair–contractors: Water, Other Support Activities for—*trans*	48839	7699
Ship Building and Repairing	**336611**	**3731**
Ship capstans: Construction Machinery—*mfg*	33312	3531
Overhead Traveling Crane, Hoist and Monorail System—*mfg*	333923	3531
Railroad Rolling Stock—*mfg*	33651	3531
Ship cleaning, except hold cleaning: Air, Rail, and Water Equipment Rental and Leasing, Commercial—*real*	532411	4499
Navigational Services to Shipping—*trans*	48833	4499
Port and Harbor Operations—*trans*	48831	4499
Water, Other Support Activities for—*trans*	48839	4499
Ship cranes and derricks: Construction Machinery—*mfg*	33312	3531
Overhead Traveling Crane, Hoist and Monorail System—*mfg*	333923	3531
Railroad Rolling Stock—*mfg*	33651	3531
Ship crew registries: Employment Placement Agencies—*admin*	56131	7361
Human Resources and Executive Search Consulting Services—*prof*	541612	7361
Ship furniture: Institutional Furniture—*mfg*	337127	2599
Ship hold cleaning: Marine Cargo Handling—*trans*	48832	4491
Port and Harbor Operations—*trans*	48831	4491
Ship joinery-contractors: Carpentry Contractors—*const*	23551	1751
Ship models, except toy and hobby models: Fabricated Metal Product, All Other Miscellaneous—*mfg*	332999	3999
Plastics Product, All Other—*mfg*	326199	3999
Wood Product, All Other Miscellaneous—*mfg*	321999	3999
Ship painting–contractors: Painting and Wall Covering Contractors—*const*	23521	1721
Ship propellers–cast brass, bronze, copper and copper base: Copper Foundries—*mfg*	331525	3366
Ship registers–survey and classification of ships and marine equipment: Air, Rail, and Water Equipment Rental and Leasing, Commercial—*real*	532411	4499

ALPHABETICAL INDEX	NAICS	SIC
Navigational Services to Shipping—*trans*	48833	4499
Port and Harbor Operations—*trans*	48831	4499
Water, Other Support Activities for—*trans*	48839	4499
Ship scaling–contractors: Water, Other Support Activities for—*trans*	48839	7699
Ship sections, prefabricated metal: Fabricated Structural Metal—*mfg*	332312	3441
Ship winches: Construction Machinery—*mfg*	33312	3531
Overhead Traveling Crane, Hoist and Monorail System—*mfg*	333923	3531
Railroad Rolling Stock—*mfg*	33651	3531
Shipboard cable, nonferrous: Aluminum Rolling and Drawing, Other—*mfg*	331319	3357
Communication and Energy Wire, Other—*mfg*	335929	3357
Copper Wire (except Mechanical) Drawing—*mfg*	331422	3357
Fiber Optic Cable—*mfg*	335921	3357
Nonferrous Metal (except Copper and Aluminum) Rolling, Drawing and Extruding—*mfg*	331491	3357
Shipbuilding and repairing: Ship Building and Repairing—*mfg*	336611	3731
Shipping and steamship company associations: Business Associations—*serv*	81391	8611
Shipping bags or sacks, including multiwall and heavy duty: Uncoated Paper and Multiwall Bag—*mfg*	322224	2674
Shipping barrels, kegs, and pails–metal-light and heavy types: Metal Container, Other—*mfg*	332439	3412
Shipping cases and drums, wood–wirebound: Wood Container and Pallet—*mfg*	32192	2449
Shipping cases, wood–nailed or lockcorner: Wood Container and Pallet—*mfg*	32192	2441
Shipping documents preparation: Freight Arrangement—*trans*	48851	4731
Management Consulting Services, Other—*prof*	541618	4731
Shipping hampers, vulcanized fiber: Fiber Can, Tube, Drum, and Similar Products—*mfg*	322214	2655
Shipping pads, plastics foam: Polystyrene Foam Product—*mfg*	32614	3086
Urethane and Other Foam Product (except Polystyrene)—*mfg*	32615	3086
Shipping sack paper: Newsprint Mills—*mfg*	322122	2621
Paper (except Newsprint) Mills—*mfg*	322121	2621
Shipping sacks, paper: Uncoated Paper and Multiwall Bag—*mfg*	322224	2674
Shipping supplies, paper and disposable plastics (e.g., cartons, gummed tapes): Industrial and Personal Service Paper—*whlse*	42213	5113
Ships: Transportation Equipment and Supplies (except Motor Vehicle)—*whlse*	42186	5088
Shirt (except Work Shirt) Manufacturing, Men's and Boys' Cut and Sew	**315223**	**2361**
Shirt and slack suits, nontailored: Cut and Sew Apparel, All Other—*mfg*	315299	2329
Men's and Boys' Cut and Sew Apparel Contractors—*mfg*	315211	2329
Men's and Boys' Cut and Sew Other Outerwear—*mfg*	315228	2329
Shirt linings: Apparel Accessories and Apparel, Other—*mfg*	315999	2396

ALPHABETICAL INDEX	NAICS	SIC
Textile Product Mills, All Other Miscellaneous—*mfg*	314999	2396
Shirt studs, except precious metal and precious or semiprecious stones: Fastener, Button, Needle and Pin—*mfg*	339993	3965
Shirt studs, precious metal and precious or semiprecious stones: Jewelry (except Costume)—*mfg*	339911	3911
Shirt supply service: Linen Supply—*serv*	812331	7213
Shirting fabrics, cotton: Broadwoven Fabric Mills—*mfg*	31321	2211
Shirting fabrics, manmade fiber and silk: Broadwoven Fabric Mills—*mfg*	31321	2221
Shirts, custom made: Clothing Accessories Stores—*retail*	44815	5699
Clothing Stores, Other—*retail*	44819	5699
Shirts, men's and boys': Men's and Boys' Clothing and Furnishings—*whlse*	42232	5136
Shirts, outerwear: Infants' Cut and Sew Apparel—*mfg*	315291	2361
Men's and Boys' Cut and Sew Apparel Contractors—*mfg*	315211	2361
Men's and Boys' Cut and Sew Shirt (except Work Shirt)—*mfg*	315223	2361
Outerwear Knitting Mills—*mfg*	315191	2253
Women's and Girls' Cut and Sew Apparel Contractors—*mfg*	315212	2361
Women's and Girls' Cut and Sew Apparel Contractors—*mfg*	315212	2331
Women's and Girls' Cut and Sew Blouse and Shirt—*mfg*	315232	2361
Women's and Girls' Cut and Sew Blouse and Shirt—*mfg*	315232	2331
Women's and Girls' Cut and Sew Dress—*mfg*	315233	2361
Men's and Boys' Cut and Sew Apparel Contractors—*mfg*	315211	2321
Men's and Boys' Cut and Sew Shirt (except Work Shirt)—*mfg*	315223	2321
Shirts, underwear: Men's and Boys' Cut and Sew Apparel Contractors—*mfg*	315211	2322
Men's and Boys' Cut and Sew Underwear and Nightwear—*mfg*	315221	2322
Underwear and Nightwear Knitting Mills—*mfg*	315192	2254
Shirts, work: Men's and Boys' Cut and Sew Apparel Contractors—*mfg*	315211	2326
Men's and Boys' Cut and Sew Work Clothing—*mfg*	315225	2326
Shock absorbers, motor vehicle: Motor Vehicle Parts, All Other—*mfg*	336399	3714
Motor Vehicle Steering and Suspension Components (except Spring)—*mfg*	33633	3714
Shock wave metal forming machines: Machine Tool (Metal Forming Types)—*mfg*	333513	3542
Shoe accessories: Footwear—*whlse*	42234	5139
Shoe bags: Household Textile Product Mills, Other—*mfg*	314129	2392
Textile Bag Mills—*mfg*	314911	2392
Shoe board: Paperboard Mills—*mfg*	32213	2631
Shoe cleaners and polishes: Polish and Other Sanitation Good—*mfg*	325612	2842
Shoe cut stock: Fastener, Button, Needle and Pin—*mfg*	339993	3131
Leather Good, All Other—*mfg*	316999	3131
Wood Product, All Other Miscellaneous—*mfg*	321999	3131
Shoe cut stock and findings: Fastener, Button, Needle and Pin—*mfg*	339993	3131
Leather Good, All Other—*mfg*	316999	3131

Description	NAICS	SIC
Wood Product, All Other Miscellaneous—*mfg*	321999	3131
Shoe designers: Industrial Design Services—*prof*	54142	7389
Shoe display forms-regardless of material: Manufacturing, All Other Miscellaneous—*mfg*	339999	2499
Wood Container and Pallet—*mfg*	32192	2499
Wood Product, All Other Miscellaneous—*mfg*	321999	2499
Shoe dyeing for the trade: Footwear, Other—*mfg*	316219	3149
Shoe dyeing shops: Footwear and Leather Goods Repair—*serv*	81143	7251
Shoe fabrics: Broadwoven Fabric Mills—*mfg*	31321	2211
Shoe heels: Cosmetics, Beauty Supplies and Perfume Stores—*retail*	44612	5087
Service Establishment Equipment and Supplies—*whlse*	42185	5087
Shoe heels, finished wood or leather: Fastener, Button, Needle and Pin—*mfg*	339993	3131
Leather Good, All Other—*mfg*	316999	3131
Wood Product, All Other Miscellaneous—*mfg*	321999	3131
Shoe heels, plastics: Plastics Pipe and Pipe Fitting—*mfg*	326122	3089
Plastics Product, All Other—*mfg*	326199	3089
Unsupported Plastics Profile Shape—*mfg*	326121	3089
Shoe heels–rubber, composition, and fiber: Fabric Coating Mills—*mfg*	31332	3069
Rubber Product, All Other—*mfg*	326299	3069
Shoe kits, regardless of material: Luggage—*mfg*	316991	3161
Shoe laces, except leather: Narrow Fabric Mills—*mfg*	313221	2241
Shoe laces, leather: Fastener, Button, Needle and Pin—*mfg*	339993	3131
Leather Good, All Other—*mfg*	316999	3131
Wood Product, All Other Miscellaneous—*mfg*	321999	3131
Shoe linings: Knit Fabric and Lace Mills, Other—*mfg*	313249	2259
Weft Knit Fabric Mills—*mfg*	313241	2259
Shoe linings, leather: Fastener, Button, Needle and Pin—*mfg*	339993	3131
Leather Good, All Other—*mfg*	316999	3131
Wood Product, All Other Miscellaneous—*mfg*	321999	3131
Shoe making and repalring machinery: Industrial Machinery, All Other—*mfg*	333298	3559
Machinery, Other Commercial and Service Industry—*mfg*	333319	3559
Shoe manufacturing and repairing machinery: Industrial Machinery and Equipment—*whlse*	42183	5084
Shoe patterns: Cosmetics, Beauty Supplies and Perfume Stores—*retail*	44612	5087
Service Establishment Equipment and Supplies—*whlse*	42185	5087
Shoe pegs: Fastener, Button, Needle and Pin—*mfg*	339993	3131
Leather Good, All Other—*mfg*	316999	3131
Wood Product, All Other Miscellaneous—*mfg*	321999	3131
Shoe polishers, electric: Electric Housewares and Household Fan—*mfg*	335211	3634
Heating Equipment (except Electric and Warm Air Furnaces)—*mfg*	333414	3634
Shoe repair materials: Cosmetics, Beauty Supplies and Perfume Stores—*retail*	44612	5087
Service Establishment Equipment and Supplies—*whlse*	42185	5087
Shoe repair shops: Footwear and Leather Goods Repair—*serv*	81143	7251
Shoe soles and soling strips–rubber, composition, and fiber: Fabric Coating Mills—*mfg*	31332	3069
Rubber Product, All Other—*mfg*	326299	3069
Shoe soles and soling strips-plastics: Plastics Pipe and Pipe Fitting—*mfg*	326122	3089
Plastics Product, All Other—*mfg*	326199	3089
Unsupported Plastics Profile Shape—*mfg*	326121	3089
Shoe soles–except rubber, composition, plastics, and fiber: Fastener, Button, Needle and Pin—*mfg*	339993	3131
Leather Good, All Other—*mfg*	316999	3131
Wood Product, All Other Miscellaneous—*mfg*	321999	3131
Shoe stamps, steel: Marking Device—*mfg*	339943	3953
Shoe Stores	**44821**	**5661**
Shoe Stores	**4482**	
Shoe stores, secondhand: Non-Depository Credit Intermediation, All Other—*fin*	522298	5932
Used Merchandise Stores—*retail*	45331	5932
Shoe stretchers, regardless of material: Manufacturing, All Other Miscellaneous—*mfg*	339999	2499
Wood Container and Pallet—*mfg*	32192	2499
Wood Product, All Other Miscellaneous—*mfg*	321999	2499
Shoe trees, regardless of material: Manufacturing, All Other Miscellaneous—*mfg*	339999	2499
Wood Container and Pallet—*mfg*	32192	2499
Wood Product, All Other Miscellaneous—*mfg*	321999	2499
Shoes: Footwear—*whlse*	42234	5139
Shoes, children's and infants'–excepthouse slippers and rubber footwear: Footwear, Other—*mfg*	316219	3149
Shoes, doll: Doll and Stuffed Toy—*mfg*	339931	3942
Shoes, extension–orthopedic: Surgical Appliance and Supplies—*mfg*	339113	3842
Shoes, men's–except house slippers, athletic, rubber, and extension shoes: Men's Footwear (except Athletic)—*mfg*	316213	3143
Shoes, plastics soles molded to fabric uppers: Rubber and Plastics Footwear—*mfg*	316211	3021
Shoes, rubber or rubber soled fabric uppers: Rubber and Plastics Footwear—*mfg*	316211	3021
Shoes, women's–except house slippers, athletic, and rubber footwear: Women's Footwear (except Athletic)—*mfg*	316214	3144
Shoeshine parlors: Footwear and Leather Goods Repair—*serv*	81143	7251
Shook, box-rnfg: Wood Container and Pallet—*mfg*	32192	2441
Shooting clubs, membership: Fitness and Recreational Sports Centers—*arts*	71394	7997
Shooting galleries: Fitness and Recreational Sports Centers—*arts*	71394	7999
Shooting ranges, operation of: Fitness and Recreational Sports Centers—*arts*	71394	7999
Shooting wells on a contract basis: Oil and Gas Operations Support Activities—*mining*	213112	1389

ALPHABETICAL INDEX	NAICS	SIC
Shopping bags, uncoated paper: Uncoated Paper and Multiwall Bag—*mfg*	322224	2674
Shopping center construction–general contractors: Building, Commercial and Institutional—*const*	23332	1542
Shopping centers, property operation only: Lessors of Nonresidential Buildings (except Miniwarehouses)—*real*	53112	6512
Promoters of Performing Arts, Sports and Similar Events with Facilities—*arts*	71131	6512
Shopping news advertising and distributing service: Advertising Material Distribution Services—*prof*	54187	7319
Advertising, Other Services Related to—*prof*	54189	7319
Display Advertising—*prof*	54185	7319
Media Buying Agencies—*prof*	54183	7319
Nonscheduled Air, Other—*trans*	481219	7319
Shopping news–publishing and printing, or publishing only: Database and Directory Publishers—*info*	51114	2741
Music Publishers—*info*	51223	2741
Publishers, All Other—*info*	511199	2741
Shopping service for individuals: Personal Services, All Other—*serv*	81299	7299
Shoring and underpinning work–contractors: Trade Contractors, All Other Special—*const*	23599	1799
Short Line Railroads	**482112**	**4013**
Shortening, vegetable: Grocery and Related Products, Other—*whlse*	42249	5149
Shortenings, compound and vegetable: Fats and Oils Refining and Blending—*mfg*	311225	2079
Oilseed Processing, Other—*mfg*	311223	2079
Soybean Processing—*mfg*	311222	2079
Shorthand machines: Lead Pencil and Art Good—*mfg*	339942	3579
Office Machinery—*mfg*	333313	3579
Watch, Clock, and Part—*mfg*	334518	3579
Shorts: Underwear and Nightwear Knitting Mills—*mfg*	315192	2254
Shorts, outerwear: Apparel Accessories and Apparel, Other—*mfg*	315999	2339
Cut and Sew Apparel, All Other—*mfg*	315299	2329
Cut and Sew Apparel, All Other—*mfg*	315299	2339
Men's and Boys' Cut and Sew Apparel Contractors—*mfg*	315211	2329
Men's and Boys' Cut and Sew Other Outerwear—*mfg*	315228	2329
Women's and Girls' Cut and Sew Apparel Contractors—*mfg*	315212	2339
Women's and Girls' Cut and Sew Other Outerwear—*mfg*	315238	2339
Shorts, underwear: Men's and Boys' Cut and Sew Apparel Contractors—*mfg*	315211	2322
Men's and Boys' Cut and Sew Underwear and Nightwear—*mfg*	315221	2322
Underwear and Nightwear Knitting Mills—*mfg*	315192	2254
Shot peening-treating steel to reduce fatigue: Metal Heat Treating—*mfg*	332811	3398
Shot, BB: Small Arms Ammunition—*mfg*	332992	3482
Shot, lead: Small Arms Ammunition—*mfg*	332992	3482
Shot, pellet: Small Arms Ammunition—*mfg*	332992	3482

ALPHABETICAL INDEX	NAICS	SIC
Shot, steel ammunition: Small Arms Ammunition—*mfg*	332992	3482
Shot-hole drilling service, oil and gas field–on a contract basis: Oil and Gas Operations Support Activities—*mining*	213112	1389
Shotgun ammunition: Small Arms Ammunition—*mfg*	332992	3482
Shotguns and parts: Small Arms—*mfg*	332994	3484
Shoulder pads: Broadwoven Fabric Finishing Mills—*mfg*	313311	5131
Piece Goods, Notions and Other Dry Goods—*whlse*	42231	5131
Textile and Fabric Finishing (except Broadwoven Fabric) Mills—*mfg*	313312	5131
Shoulder pads–for coats, suits, etc.: Apparel Accessories and Apparel, Other—*mfg*	315999	2396
Textile Product Mills, All Other Miscellaneous—*mfg*	314999	2396
Shoulder straps, for women's underwear: Apparel Accessories and Apparel, Other—*mfg*	315999	2396
Textile Product Mills, All Other Miscellaneous—*mfg*	314999	2396
Shoulderettes: Outerwear Knitting Mills—*mfg*	315191	2253
Shovel loaders: Construction Machinery—*mfg*	33312	3531
Overhead Traveling Crane, Hoist and Monorail System—*mfg*	333923	3531
Railroad Rolling Stock—*mfg*	33651	3531
Shovels, hand: Hand and Edge Tool—*mfg*	332212	3423
Shovels, power: Construction and (except Petroleum) Machinery and Equipment—*whlse*	42181	5082
Construction Machinery—*mfg*	33312	3531
Overhead Traveling Crane, Hoist and Monorail System—*mfg*	333923	3531
Railroad Rolling Stock—*mfg*	33651	3531
Show cases, refrigerated: Refrigeration Equipment and Supplies—*whlse*	42174	5078
Showcase, Partition, Shelving, and Locker Manufacturing	**337215**	**2426**
Showcases, not refrigerated–except wood: Showcase, Partition, Shelving, and Locker—*mfg*	337215	2542
Showcases, not refrigerated–wood: Architectural Woodwork and Millwork, Custom—*mfg*	337212	2541
Showcase, Partition, Shelving, and Locker—*mfg*	337215	2541
Wood Kitchen Cabinet and Counter Top—*mfg*	33711	2541
Showcases, refrigerated: Air-Conditioning and Warm Air Heating Equipment and Commercial and Industrial Refrigeration Equipment—*mfg*	333415	3585
Motor Vehicle Air-Conditioning—*mfg*	336391	3585
Shower curtains: Household Textile Product Mills, Other—*mfg*	314129	2392
Shower doors–made from purchased glass: Glass Product Made of Purchased Glass—*mfg*	327215	3231
Shower receptors, concrete: Concrete Pipe—*mfg*	327332	3272
Concrete Product, Other—*mfg*	32739	3272
Nonmetallic Mineral Product, All Other Miscellaneous—*mfg*	327999	3272
Shower receptors, metal: Enameled Iron and Metal Sanitary Ware—*mfg*	332998	3431

Description	NAICS	SIC
Shower rods: Fabricated Metal Product, All Other Miscellaneous—*mfg*	332999	3432
Plumbing Fixture Fitting and Trim—*mfg*	332913	3432
Shower sandals or slippers, rubber: Rubber and Plastics Footwear—*mfg*	316211	3021
Shower stalls, metal: Enameled Iron and Metal Sanitary Ware—*mfg*	332998	3431
Shower stalls, plastics: Plastics Plumbing Fixture—*mfg*	326191	3088
Showing of cattle, hogs, sheep, goats, andpoultry: Animal Production Support Activities—*ag*	11521	751
Showing of pets and other animal specialties: Animal Production Support Activities—*ag*	11521	752
Pet Care (except Veterinary) Services—*serv*	81291	752
Shredders (agricultural machinery): Farm Machinery and Equipment—*mfg*	333111	3523
Shredding peat: Crushed and Broken Stone and Quarrying, Other—*mining*	212319	1499
Non-Metallic Mineral, All Other—*mining*	212399	1499
Shrimp, canned and cured: Seafood Canning—*mfg*	311711	2091
Shrimp, catching of: Shellfish Fishing—*ag*	114112	913
Shrimp, fresh and frozen: Fresh and Frozen Seafood Processing—*mfg*	311712	2092
Shrines, religious: Religious Organizations—*serv*	81311	8661
Shrink-mixed concrete: Ready-Mix Concrete—*mfg*	32732	3273
Shrinking cloth of wool, mohair, and similar animal fibers–for the trade: Broadwoven Fabric Finishing Mills—*mfg*	313311	2231
Broadwoven Fabric Mills—*mfg*	31321	2231
Textile and Fabric Finishing (except Broadwoven Fabric) Mills—*mfg*	313312	2231
Shrinking cotton broadwoven fabrics for the trade: Broadwoven Fabric Finishing Mills—*mfg*	313311	2261
Shrinking manmade fiber and silk broad-woven fabrics for the trade: Broadwoven Fabric Finishing Mills—*mfg*	313311	2262
Shrubberies, except forest shrubbery–growing of: Floriculture Production—*ag*	111422	181
Nursery and Tree Production—*ag*	111421	181
Shunts, instrument: Electronic Coil, Transformer, and Other Inductor—*mfg*	334416	3825
Instrument for Measuring and Testing Electricity and Electrical Signals—*mfg*	334515	3825
Shutters, camera: Photographic and Photocopying Equipment—*mfg*	333315	3861
Photographic Film, Paper, Plate and Chemical—*mfg*	325992	3861
Shutters, door and window–metal: Metal Window and Door—*mfg*	332321	3442
Shutters, door and window–wood and covered wood: Millwork (including Flooring), Other—*mfg*	321918	2431
Wood Window and Door—*mfg*	321911	2431
Shutters, plastics: Plastics Pipe and Pipe Fitting—*mfg*	326122	3089
Plastics Product, All Other—*mfg*	326199	3089
Unsupported Plastics Profile Shape—*mfg*	326121	3089
Shuttle blocks–hardwood: Cut Stock, Resawing Lumber, and Planing—*mfg*	321912	2426
Millwork (including Flooring), Other—*mfg*	321918	2426
Showcase, Partition, Shelving, and Locker—*mfg*	337215	2426
Wood Product, All Other Miscellaneous—*mfg*	321999	2426
Shuttle cars, underground: Mining Machinery and Equipment—*mfg*	333131	3532
Shuttles for textile weaving: Textile Machinery—*mfg*	333292	3552
Sick benefit associations, mutual: Direct Health and Medical Insurance Carriers—*fin*	524114	6321
Insurance Funds, Other—*fin*	52519	6321
Reinsurance Carriers—*fin*	52413	6321
Sickles, hand: Hand and Edge Tool—*mfg*	332212	3423
Siderite mining: Iron Ore—*mining*	21221	1011
Sidewalk construction, except public–contractors: Concrete Contractors—*const*	23571	1771
Drywall, Plastering, Acoustical and Insulation Contractors—*const*	23542	1771
Sidewalk construction, public–contractors: Highway and Street—*const*	23411	1611
Siding, asbestos cement: Motor Vehicle Brake System—*mfg*	33634	3292
Nonmetallic Mineral Product, All Other Miscellaneous—*mfg*	327999	3292
Siding, asphalt brick: Asphalt Shingle and Coating Materials—*mfg*	324122	2952
Siding, dressed lumber: Cut Stock, Resawing Lumber, and Planing—*mfg*	321912	2421
Millwork (including Flooring), Other—*mfg*	321918	2421
Sawmills—*mfg*	321113	2421
Wood Product, All Other Miscellaneous—*mfg*	321999	2421
Siding, except wood: Roofing, Siding and Insulation Material—*whlse*	42133	5033
Siding, insulating–impregnated: Asphalt Shingle and Coating Materials—*mfg*	324122	2952
Siding, insulating–paper, impregnated or not: Newsprint Mills—*mfg*	322122	2621
Paper (except Newsprint) Mills—*mfg*	322121	2621
Siding, plastics: Plastics Pipe and Pipe Fitting—*mfg*	326122	3089
Plastics Product, All Other—*mfg*	326199	3089
Unsupported Plastics Profile Shape—*mfg*	326121	3089
Siding, precast stone: Concrete Pipe—*mfg*	327332	3272
Concrete Product, Other—*mfg*	32739	3272
Nonmetallic Mineral Product, All Other Miscellaneous—*mfg*	327999	3272
Siding, sheet metal: Metal Container, Other—*mfg*	332439	3444
Sheet Metal Work—*mfg*	332322	3444
Siding–contractors: Roofing, Siding and Sheet Metal Contractors—*const*	23561	1761
Sienna mining: Chemical and Fertilizer Mineral, Other—*mining*	212393	1479
Siennas: Carbon Black—*mfg*	325182	2816
Inorganic Dye and Pigment—*mfg*	325131	2816
Sieves, made from purchased wire: Fabricated Wire Product, Other—*mfg*	332618	3496
Sifting and screening machines for general industrial use: General Purpose Machinery , All Other—*mfg*	333999	3569

ALPHABETICAL INDEX	NAICS	SIC
Sifting machines, food: Food Product Machinery—*mfg*	333294	3556
Sighting and fire control equipment, optical: Optical Instrument and Lens—*mfg*	333314	3827
Sights, gun–except optical 30 mm. (or 1.18inch) or less: Small Arms—*mfg*	332994	3484
Sights, gun–except optical-more than 30mm. (or more than 1.18 inch): Ordnance and Accessories, Other—*mfg*	332995	3489
Sights, telescopic: Optical Instrument and Lens—*mfg*	333314	3827
Sightseeing airplane services: Ambulance Services—*hlth*	62191	4522
Nonscheduled Chartered Freight Air—*trans*	481212	4522
Nonscheduled Chartered Passenger Air—*trans*	481211	4522
Scenic and Sightseeing, Other—*trans*	48799	4522
Sightseeing boats: Inland Water Passenger—*trans*	483212	4489
Scenic and Sightseeing, Water—*trans*	48721	4489
Sightseeing buses: Scenic and Sightseeing, Land—*trans*	48711	4119
Sign Manufacturing	**33995**	**3993**
Sign painting and lettering shops: Design Services, Other Specialized—*prof*	54149	7389
Signal and control cable, nonferrous: Aluminum Rolling and Drawing, Other—*mfg*	331319	3357
Communication and Energy Wire, Other—*mfg*	335929	3357
Copper Wire (except Mechanical) Drawing—*mfg*	331422	3357
Fiber Optic Cable—*mfg*	335921	3357
Nonferrous Metal (except Copper and Aluminum) Rolling, Drawing and Extruding—*mfg*	331491	3357
Signal flares, marine: Basic Organic Chemical. All Other—*mfg*	325199	2899
Chemical Product, All Other Miscellaneous—*mfg*	325998	2899
Signal generators and averages: Electronic Coil. Transformer, and Other Inductor—*mfg*	334416	3825
Instrument for Measuring and Testing Electricity and Electrical Signals—*mfg*	334515	3825
Signaling apparatus, electric: Communications Equipment, Other—*mfg*	33429	3669
Signaling equipment, electrical: Building Material Dealers, Other—*retail*	44419	5063
Electrical Apparatus and Equipment. Wiring Supplies and Material—*whlse*	42161	5063
Signaling transformers, electric: Power, Distribution and Specialty Transformer—*mfg*	335311	3612
Signals, directional–motor vehicle: Motor Vehicle Body—*mfg*	336211	3714
Motor Vehicle Electrical and Electronic Equipment, Other—*mfg*	336322	3714
Motor Vehicle Parts, All Other—*mfg*	336399	3714
Signals–railway, highway, and traffic-electric: Communications Equipment, Other—*mfg*	33429	3669
Signboards, wood: Manufacturing, All Other Miscellaneous—*mfg*	339999	2499
Wood Container and Pallet—*mfg*	32192	2499
Wood Product, All Other Miscellaneous—*mfg*	321999	2499

ALPHABETICAL INDEX	NAICS	SIC
Signs, electrical: Equipment, Other Commercial—*whlse*	42144	5046
Signs, except electric: Durable Goods, Other Miscellaneous—*whlse*	42199	5099
Signs, not made in custom sign painting shops: Sign—*mfg*	33995	3993
Silesia, cotton: Broadwoven Fabric Mills—*mfg*	31321	2211
Silica gel: Basic Inorganic Chemical, All Other—*mfg*	325188	2819
Chemical Product, All Other Miscellaneous—*mfg*	325998	2819
Silica mining: Industrial Sand—*mining*	212322	1446
Silica sand mining: Industrial Sand—*mining*	212322	1446
Silica, amorphous: Basic Inorganic Chemical, All Other—*mfg*	325188	2819
Chemical Product, All Other Miscellaneous—*mfg*	325998	2819
Silicofluorides: Basic Inorganic Chemical. All Other—*mfg*	325188	2819
Chemical Product, All Other Miscellaneous—*mfg*	325998	2819
Silicon carbide abrasives: Abrasive Product—*mfg*	32791	3291
Fabricated Metal Product, All Other Miscellaneous—*mfg*	332999	3291
Silicon refining, primary (over 99 percent pure): Primary Smelting and Refining of Nonferrous Metal (except Copper and Aluminum)—*mfg*	331419	3339
Silicon wafers, chemically doped: Semiconductor and Related Device—*mfg*	334413	3674
Silicon, epitaxial (silicon alloy): Primary Smelting and Refining of Nonferrous Metal (except Copper and Aluminum)—*mfg*	331419	3339
Silicon, pure: Primary Smelting and Refining of Nonferrous Metai (except Copper and Aluminum)—*mfg*	331419	3339
Silicon, ultra high purity–treated purchased materials: Ground or Treated Mineral and Earth—*mfg*	327992	3295
Silicone fluid solution (fluid for sonar transducers): Plastics Material and Resin—*mfg*	325211	2821
Silicone resins: Plastics Material and Resin—*mfg*	325211	2821
Silicone rubbers: Synthetic Rubber—*mfg*	325212	2822
Silicones: Basic Organic Chemical, All Other—*mfg*	325199	2869
Silk (raw) production and silkworm farms: Animal Production. All Other—*ag*	11299	279
Apiculture—*ag*	11291	279
Silk broadwoven fabric finishing: Broadwoven Fabric Finishing Mills—*mfg*	313311	2262
Silk broadwoven fabrics: Broadwoven Fabric Mills—*mfg*	31321	2221
Silk narrow fabrics: Narrow Fabric Mills—*mfg*	313221	2241
Silk piece goods: Broadwoven Fabric Finishing Mills—*mfg*	313311	5131
Piece Goods, Notions and Other Dry Goods—*whlse*	42231	5131
Textile and Fabric Finishing (except Broadwoven Fabric) Mills—*mfg*	313312	5131
Silk screen design: Graphic Design Services—*prof*	54143	7336
Silk screening on fabric articles: Apparel Accessories and Apparel. Other—*mfg*	315999	2396
Screen Printing, Commercial—*mfg*	323113	2396
Silk screens for the textile industry: Textile Machinery—*mfg*	333292	3552

Silk thread: Textile and Fabric Finishing (except Broadwoven Fabric) Mills—*mfg*	313312	2284
Thread Mills—*mfg*	313113	2284
Silk throwing, twisting, winding, or spooling: Textile and Fabric Finishing (except Broadwoven Fabric) Mills—*mfg*	313312	2282
Yarn Texturing, Throwing and Twisting Mills—*mfg*	313112	2282
Silk yarn, spinning: Yarn Spinning Mills—*mfg*	313111	2281
Silk yarns: Nondurable Goods, Other Miscellaneous—*whlse*	42299	5199
Silk, raw: Farm Product Raw Material, Other—*whlse*	42259	5159
Sillimanite mining: Clay and Ceramic and Refractory Minerals—*mining*	212325	1459
Sills, concrete: Concrete Pipe—*mfg*	327332	3272
Concrete Product, Other—*mfg*	32739	3272
Nonmetallic Mineral Product, All Other Miscellaneous—*mfg*	327999	3272
Silo construction, agricultural–general contractors: Building, Commercial and Institutional—*const*	23332	1542
Silo fillers (agricultural machinery): Farm Machinery and Equipment—*mfg*	333111	3523
Silo staves, cast stone: Concrete Pipe—*mfg*	327332	3272
Concrete Product, Other—*mfg*	32739	3272
Nonmetallic Mineral Product, All Other Miscellaneous—*mfg*	327999	3272
Silo staves, wood: Millwork (including Flooring), Other—*mfg*	321918	2431
Wood Window and Door—*mfg*	321911	2431
Silo stock, wood–sawed: Cut Stock, Resawing Lumber, and Planing—*mfg*	321912	2421
Millwork (including Flooring), Other—*mfg*	321918	2421
Sawmills—*mfg*	321113	2421
Wood Product, All Other Miscellaneous—*mfg*	321999	2421
Silo tile: Brick and Structural Clay Tile—*mfg*	327121	3251
Silo unloaders: Farm Machinery and Equipment—*mfg*	333111	3523
Silos, cement Cbatch plant): Construction Machinery—*mfg*	33312	3531
Overhead Traveling Crane, Hoist and Monorail System—*mfg*	333923	3531
Railroad Rolling Stock—*mfg*	33651	3531
Silos, metal: Prefabricated Metal Building and Component—*mfg*	332311	3448
Silos, prefabricated concrete: Concrete Pipe—*mfg*	327332	3272
Concrete Product, Other—*mfg*	32739	3272
Nonmetallic Mineral Product, All Other Miscellaneous—*mfg*	327999	3272
Silver and silver alloy bars, rods, sheets, strip, and tubing: Nonferrous Metal (except Copper and Aluminum) Rolling, Drawing and Extruding—*mfg*	331491	3356
Silver bromide, chioride, and nitrate: Basic Inorganic Chemical, All Other—*mfg*	325188	2819
Chemical Product, All Other Miscellaneous—*mfg*	325998	2819
Silver compounds, inorganic: Basic Inorganic Chemical, All Other—*mfg*	325188	2819
Chemical Product, All Other Miscellaneous—*mfg*	325998	2819
Silver foil and leaf: Fabricated Metal Product, All Other Miscellaneous—*mfg*	332999	3497
Laminated Aluminum Foil for Flexible Packaging Uses—*mfg*	322225	3497
Silver ore: Coal and Other Mineral and Ore—*whlse*	42152	5052
Silver Ore Mining	**212222**	**1044**
Silver powder, except artists' materials: Electroplating, Plating, Polishing, Anodizing and Coloring—*mfg*	332813	3399
Iron and Steel Mills—*mfg*	331111	3399
Secondary Smelting, Refining, and Alloying of Copper—*mfg*	331423	3399
Secondary Smelting, Refining, and Alloying of Nonferrous Metal (except Copper and Aluminum)—*mfg*	331492	3399
Silver recovery equipment, electrolytic: Industrial Machinery, All Other—*mfg*	333298	3559
Machinery, Other Commercial and Service Industry—*mfg*	333319	3559
Silver refining, primary: Primary Smelting and Refining of Nonferrous Metal (except Copper and Aluminum)—*mfg*	331419	3339
Silver rolling and drawing: Nonferrous Metal (except Copper and Aluminum) Rolling, Drawing and Extruding—*mfg*	331491	3356
Silver smelting and refining, secondary: Secondary Smelting and Alloying of Aluminum—*mfg*	331314	3341
Secondary Smelting, Refining, and Alloying of Nonferrous Metal (except Copper and Aluminum)—*mfg*	331492	3341
Silver, recovery of–from used photographic film: Secondary Smelting and Alloying of Aluminum—*mfg*	331314	3341
Secondary Smelting, Refining, and Alloying of Nonferrous Metal (except Copper and Aluminum)—*mfg*	331492	3341
Silvered glass, made from purchased glass: Glass Product Made of Purchased Glass—*mfg*	327215	3231
Silversmithing: Cutlery and Flatware (except Precious)—*mfg*	332211	3914
Silverware and Plated Ware—*mfg*	339912	3914
Silverware: Jewelry Stores—*retail*	44831	5944
Silverware and plated ware: Jewelry, Watch, Precious Stone and Precious Metal—*whlse*	42194	5094
Silverware and Plated Ware Manufacturing	**339912**	**3914**
Silverware chests, wood (floor standing): Nonupholstered Wood Household Furniture—*mfg*	337122	2511
Silverware–nickel silver, silver plated, solid silver, and sterling: Cutlery and Flatware (except Precious)—*mfg*	332211	3914
Silverware and Plated Ware—*mfg*	339912	3914
Singing societies: Child and Youth Services—*hlth*	62411	8641
Civic and Social Organizations—*serv*	81341	8641
Single Family Housing Construction	**23321**	**1531**
Single-family home improvements–general contractors: Single Family Housing—*const*	23321	1521
Sink tops, plastics laminated: Architectural Woodwork and Millwork, Custom—*mfg*	337212	2541
Showcase, Partition, Shelving, and Locker—*mfg*	337215	2541
Wood Kitchen Cabinet and Counter Top—*mfg*	33711	2541
Sinkers (fishing tackle): Sporting and Athletic Goods—*mfg*	33992	3949
Sinking shafts for bituminous coal, anthracite, and lignite on a contract basis: Coal Support Activities—*mining*	213113	1241

ALPHABETICAL INDEX	NAICS	SIC
Sinking shafts for metal mining–on a contract basis: Geophysical Surveying and Mapping Services—*prof*	54136	1081
Metal Support Activities—*mining*	213114	1081
Sinks, plastics: Plastics Plumbing Fixture—*mfg*	326191	3088
Sinks, vitreous china: Vitreous China Plumbing Fixture and China and Earthenware Fittings and Bathroom Accessories—*mfg*	327111	3261
Sinks–enameled iron, cast iron, and pressed metal: Enameled Iron and Metal Sanitary Ware—*mfg*	332998	3431
Sinkware, plastics: Plastics Pipe and Pipe Fitting—*mfg*	326122	3089
Plastics Product, All Other—*mfg*	326199	3089
Unsupported Plastics Profile Shape—*mfg*	326121	3089
Sintering of iron ore at the mine: Iron Ore—*mining*	21221	1011
Siphons, soda water: Air-Conditioning and Warm Air Heating Equipment and Commercial and Industrial Refrigeration Equipment—*mfg*	333415	3585
Motor Vehicle Air-Conditioning—*mfg*	336391	3585
Sirens, electric–vehicle, marine, industrial, and air raid: Communications Equipment, Other—*mfg*	33429	3669
Site location consultants: Administrative Management and General Management Consulting Services—*prof*	541611	8742
Human Resources and Executive Search Consulting Services—*prof*	541612	8742
Marketing Consulting Services—*prof*	541613	8742
Process, Physical, Distribution and Logistics Consulting Services—*prof*	541614	8742
Size, glue: Basic Organic Chemical, All Other—*mfg*	325199	2899
Chemical Product, All Other Miscellaneous—*mfg*	325998	2899
Sizes, artists'–gold and bronze: Chemical Product, All Other Miscellaneous—*mfg*	325998	3952
Institutional Furniture—*mfg*	337127	3952
Lead Pencil and Art Good—*mfg*	339942	3952
Sizes–animal, vegetable, and synthetic plastics materials: Basic Organic Chemical, All Other—*mfg*	325199	2899
Chemical Product, All Other Miscellaneous—*mfg*	325998	2899
Skateboards: Sporting and Athletic Goods—*mfg*	33992	3949
Skates and parts, ice and roller: Sporting and Athletic Goods—*mfg*	33992	3949
Skating instruction, ice or roller: Fitness and Recreational Sports Centers—*arts*	71394	7999
Sports and Recreation Instruction—*educ*	61162	7999
Skeet shooting facilities, except membership clubs: Fitness and Recreational Sports Centers—*arts*	71394	7999
Skelp, iron and steel: Iron and Steel Mills—*mfg*	331111	3312
Petroleum and Coal Productsa, All Other—*mfg*	324199	3312
Sketching boxes, artists': Chemical Product, All Other Miscellaneous—*mfg*	325998	3952
Institutional Furniture—*mfg*	337127	3952
Lead Pencil and Art Good—*mfg*	339942	3952
Skewers, wood: Manufacturing, All Other Miscellaneous—*mfg*	339999	2499
Wood Container and Pallet—*mfg*	32192	2499
Wood Product, All Other Miscellaneous—*mfg*	321999	2499
Ski instruction: Sports and Recreation Instruction—*educ*	61162	7999
Ski jackets, vests, and pants: Apparel Accessories and Apparel, Other—*mfg*	315999	2339
Cut and Sew Apparel, All Other—*mfg*	315299	2339
Women's and Girls' Cut and Sew Apparel Contractors—*mfg*	315212	2339
Women's and Girls' Cut and Sew Other Outerwear—*mfg*	315238	2339
Ski lifts, cable lifts, and ski tows operated separately from lodges: Skiing Facilities—*arts*	71392	7999
Ski lodges and resorts: Bed and Breakfast Inns—*accom*	721191	7011
Casino Hotels—*accom*	72112	7011
Hotels (except Casino Hotels) and Motels—*accom*	72111	7011
Traveler Accommodation, All Other—*accom*	721199	7011
Ski pants: Cut and Sew Apparel, All Other—*mfg*	315299	2329
Ski rental concessions: Skiing Facilities—*arts*	71392	7999
Ski suits: Apparel Accessories and Apparel, Other—*mfg*	315999	2339
Cut and Sew Apparel, All Other—*mfg*	315299	2329
Cut and Sew Apparel, All Other—*mfg*	315299	2339
Outerwear Knitting Mills—*mfg*	315191	2253
Women's and Girls' Cut and Sew Apparel Contractors—*mfg*	315212	2339
Women's and Girls' Cut and Sew Other Outerwear—*mfg*	315238	2339
Ski tow erection–general contractors: Heavy, All Other—*const*	23499	1629
Industrial Nonbuilding Structure—*const*	23493	1629
Skid boxes, metsl: Fabricated Metal Product, All Other Miscellaneous—*mfg*	332999	3537
Industrial Truck, Tractor, Trailer and Stacker Machinery—*mfg*	333924	3537
Metal Container, Other—*mfg*	332439	3537
Skid chains, made from purchased wire: Fabricated Wire Product, Other—*mfg*	332618	3496
Skid tanks, metal plate: Air-Conditioning and Warm Air Heating Equipment and Commercial and Industrial Refrigeration Equipment—*mfg*	333415	3443
Metal Tank (Heavy Gauge)—*mfg*	33242	3443
Plate Work—*mfg*	332313	3443
Power Boiler and Heat Exchanger—*mfg*	33241	3443
Skidding logs: Logging—*ag*	11331	2411
Skids and pallets, wood or wood and metal combination: Wood Container and Pallet—*mfg*	32192	2448
Skids, metsl: Fabricated Metal Product, All Other Miscellaneous—*mfg*	332999	3537
Industrial Truck, Tractor, Trailer and Stacker Machinery—*mfg*	333924	3537
Metal Container, Other—*mfg*	332439	3537
Skiffs, building and repairing: Boat Building—*mfg*	336612	3732
Personal and Household Goods Repair and Maintenance, Other—*serv*	81149	3732

Entry	NAICS	SIC
Skiing equipment: Sporting and Recreational Goods and Supplies—*whlse*	42191	5091
Sporting Goods Stores—*retail*	45111	5941
Skiing Facilities	**71392**	**7999**
Skill training centers: Vocational Rehabilitation Services—*hlth*	62431	8331
Skim milk–concentrated, dried, and powdered: Dry, Condensed, and Evaporated Dairy Product—*mfg*	311514	2023
Skin diving and scuba equipment: Sporting Goods Stores—*retail*	45111	5941
Skin diving equipment, except clothing: Sporting and Athletic Goods—*mfg*	33992	3949
Skin grafting equipment: Surgical and Medical Instrument—*mfg*	339112	3841
Skins, raw: Farm Product Raw Material, Other—*whlse*	42259	5159
Skins–tanning, currying and finishing: Leather and Hide Tanning and Finishing—*mfg*	31611	3111
Skirt linings: Apparel Accessories and Apparel, Other—*mfg*	315999	2396
Textile Product Mills, All Other Miscellaneous—*mfg*	314999	2396
Skirting leather: Leather and Hide Tanning and Finishing—*mfg*	31611	3111
Skirtings: Broadwoven Fabric Finishing Mills—*mfg*	313311	2231
Broadwoven Fabric Mills—*mfg*	31321	2231
Textile and Fabric Finishing (except Broadwoven Fabric) Mills—*mfg*	313312	2231
Skirts: Outerwear Knitting Mills—*mfg*	315191	2253
Women's, Children's, and Infants' and Accessories—*whlse*	42233	5137
Skirts, except tennis skirts: Women's and Girls' Cut and Sew Apparel Contractors—*mfg*	315212	2337
Women's and Girls' Cut and Sew Suit, Coat, Tailored Jacket and Skirt—*mfg*	315234	2337
Skirts, plastics (siding): Plastics Pipe and Pipe Fitting—*mfg*	326122	3089
Plastics Product, All Other—*mfg*	326199	3089
Unsupported Plastics Profile Shape—*mfg*	326121	3089
Skirts, tennis: Apparel Accessories and Apparel, Other—*mfg*	315999	2339
Cut and Sew Apparel, All Other—*mfg*	315299	2339
Women's and Girls' Cut and Sew Apparel Contractors—*mfg*	315212	2339
Women's and Girls' Cut and Sew Other Outerwear—*mfg*	315238	2339
Skis and skiing equipment, except apparel: Sporting and Athletic Goods—*mfg*	33992	3949
Skivers, leather: Leather and Hide Tanning and Finishing—*mfg*	31611	3111
Sky writing: Advertising Material Distribution Services—*prof*	54187	7319
Advertising, Other Services Related to—*prof*	54189	7319
Display Advertising—*prof*	54185	7319
Media Buying Agencies—*prof*	54183	7319
Nonscheduled Air, Other—*trans*	481219	7319
Skylight glass: Flat Glass—*mfg*	327211	3211
Skylight installation-contractors: Roofing, Siding and Sheet Metal Contractors—*const*	23561	1761
Skylights, sheet metal: Metal Container, Other—*mfg*	332439	3444
Sheet Metal Work—*mfg*	332322	3444
Slabs, aluminum–primary: Primary Aluminum Production—*mfg*	331312	3334
Slabs, copper–primary: Primary Smelting and Refining of Copper—*mfg*	331411	3331
Slabs, crossing–concrete: Concrete Pipe—*mfg*	327332	3272
Concrete Product, Other—*mfg*	32739	3272
Nonmetallic Mineral Product, All Other Miscellaneous—*mfg*	327999	3272
Slabs, primary–nonferrous metals, except copper and aluminum: Primary Smelting and Refining of Nonferrous Metal (except Copper and Aluminum)—*mfg*	331419	3339
Slabs, steel: Iron and Steel Mills—*mfg*	331111	3312
Petroleum and Coal Productsa, All Other—*mfg*	324199	3312
Slacks: Apparel Accessories and Apparel, Other—*mfg*	315999	2339
Cut and Sew Apparel, All Other—*mfg*	315299	2339
Outerwear Knitting Mills—*mfg*	315191	2253
Women's and Girls' Cut and Sew Apparel Contractors—*mfg*	315212	2339
Women's and Girls' Cut and Sew Other Outerwear—*mfg*	315238	2339
Slacks (separate): Men's and Boys' Cut and Sew Apparel Contractors—*mfg*	315211	2325
Men's and Boys' Cut and Sew Trouser, Slack and Jean—*mfg*	315224	2325
Slacks, jean-cut casual: Men's and Boys' Cut and Sew Apparel Contractors—*mfg*	315211	2325
Men's and Boys' Cut and Sew Trouser, Slack and Jean—*mfg*	315224	2325
Slag mixers: Construction Machinery—*mfg*	33312	3531
Overhead Traveling Crane, Hoist and Monorail System—*mfg*	333923	3531
Railroad Rolling Stock—*mfg*	33651	3531
Slag, crushed or ground: Ground or Treated Mineral and Earth—*mfg*	327992	3295
Slashing machines (textile machinery): Textile Machinery—*mfg*	333292	3552
Slate and slate products: Cut Stone and Stone Product—*mfg*	327991	3281
Slate, crushed and broken: Crushed and Broken Stone and Quarrying, Other—*mining*	212319	1429
Slate, dimension: Dimension Stone and Quarrying—*mining*	212311	1411
Slats, trunk–wood: Wood Container and Pallet—*mfg*	32192	2441
Slaughtering of animals, except for human consumption: Animal (except Poultry) Slaughtering—*mfg*	311611	2048
Animal Food, Other—*mfg*	311119	2048
Slaughtering plants–except animals not for human consumption: Animal (except Poultry) Slaughtering—*mfg*	311611	2011
Slaughtering, custom–for individuals: Animal Production Support Activities—*ag*	11521	751
Slaw, cole–in bulk: Food, All Other Miscellaneous—*mfg*	311999	2099
Sledges (handtools): Hand and Edge Tool—*mfg*	332212	3423
Sleds, children's: Game, Toy, and Children's Vehicle—*mfg*	339932	3944
Sleeper mechanisms, for convertible beds: Hardware—*mfg*	33251	3429
Sleeping bags: Textile Product Mills, All Other Miscellaneous—*mfg*	314999	2399
Sleeping car and other passenger car operations, not performed by railroads: Rail Support Activities—*trans*	48821	4789
Scenic and Sightseeing, Land—*trans*	48711	4789
Transportation, All Other Support Activities—*trans*	488999	4789
Sleeping cars, railroad: Pump and Pumping Equipment—*mfg*	333911	3743
Railroad Rolling Stock—*mfg*	33651	3743

ALPHABETICAL INDEX	NAICS	SIC
Sleeves, pump–rubber: Fabric Coating Mills—*mfg*	31332	3069
Rubber Product, All Other—*mfg*	326299	3069
Sleeves, welders'–leather: Leather Good, All Other—*mfg*	316999	3199
Sleeving, textile–saturated: Fabric Coating Mills—*mfg*	31332	2295
Slenderizing salons: Fitness and Recreational Sports Centers—*arts*	71394	7991
Slicing machines, fruit and vegetable–commercial types: Food Product Machinery—*mfg*	333294	3556
Slide fastener tapes: Narrow Fabric Mills—*mfg*	313221	2241
Slide fasteners (zippers): Fastener, Button, Needle and Pin—*mfg*	339993	3965
Slide film producers: Graphic Design Services—*prof*	54143	7336
Slings, lifting–made from purchased wire: Fabricated Wire Product, Other—*mfg*	332618	3496
Slings, rope: Rope, Cordage and Twine Mills—*mfg*	314991	2298
Slip clay mining: Kaolin and Ball Clay—*mining*	212324	1455
Slipcover fabrics, cotton: Broadwoven Fabric Mills—*mfg*	31321	2211
Slipcover fabrics, manmade fiber and silk: Broadwoven Fabric Mills—*mfg*	31321	2221
Slipcover stores: Curtain and Drapery Mills—*mfg*	314121	5714
Sewing, Needlework and Piece Goods Stores—*retail*	45113	5714
Window Treatment Stores—*retail*	442291	5714
Slipeovers, furniture: Home Furnishing—*whlse*	42122	5023
Slipeovers–made of fabrics, plastics, and other material except paper: Household Textile Product Mills, Other—*mfg*	314129	2392
Slipper socks: Hosiery and Sock Mills, Other—*mfg*	315119	2252
Sheer Hosiery Mills—*mfg*	315111	2252
Slipper socks, made from purchased socks: House Slipper—*mfg*	316212	3142
Slippers, ballet: Footwear, Other—*mfg*	316219	3149
Slippers, house: House Slipper—*mfg*	316212	3142
Sliprings for motors and generators: Motor and Generator—*mfg*	335312	3621
Slips: Infants' Cut and Sew Apparel—*mfg*	315291	2341
Underwear and Nightwear Knitting Mills—*mfg*	315192	2254
Women's and Girls' Cut and Sew Apparel Contractors—*mfg*	315212	2341
Women's and Girls' Cut and Sew Lingerie, Loungewear and Nightwear—*mfg*	315231	2341
Slipsheeting machines: Lead Pencil and Art Good—*mfg*	339942	3579
Office Machinery—*mfg*	333313	3579
Watch, Clock, and Part—*mfg*	334518	3579
Slit lamps (ophthalmic goods): Surgical and Medical Instrument—*mfg*	339112	3841
Slitters, rotary (metalworking machines): Other Metalworking Machinery, Other—*mfg*	333518	3549
Slot machines, operation of: Amusement and Recreation Industries, All Other—*arts*	71399	7993
Amusement Arcades—*arts*	71312	7993
Gambling Industries, Other—*arts*	71329	7993
Slotcar racetracks: Amusement and Recreation Industries, All Other—*arts*	71399	7999

ALPHABETICAL INDEX	NAICS	SIC
Slotting machines (machine tools): Machine Tool (Metal Cutting Types)—*mfg*	333512	3541
Slubs and nubs (cutting up fibers for use in tweeds): Broadwoven Fabric Mills—*mfg*	31321	2299
Narrow Fabric Mills—*mfg*	313221	2299
Nonwoven Fabric Mills—*mfg*	31323	2299
Textile and Fabric Finishing (except Broadwoven Fabric) Mills—*mfg*	313312	2299
Textile Product Mills, All Other Miscellaneous—*mfg*	314999	2299
Thread Mills—*mfg*	313113	2299
Yarn Spinning Mills—*mfg*	313111	2299
Sludge disposal sites: Hazardous Waste Collection—*admin*	562112	4953
Hazardous Waste Treatment and Disposal—*admin*	562211	4953
Materials Recovery Facilities—*admin*	56292	4953
Nonhazardous Waste Treatment and Disposal, Other—*admin*	562219	4953
Solid Waste Collection—*admin*	562111	4953
Solid Waste Combustors and Incinerators—*admin*	562213	4953
Solid Waste Landfill—*admin*	562212	4953
Waste Collection, Other—*admin*	562119	4953
Sludge processing equipment: Machinery, Other Commercial and Service Industry—*mfg*	333319	3589
Sludge tables: Fabricated Metal Product, All Other Miscellaneous—*mfg*	332999	3599
General Purpose Machinery , All Other—*mfg*	333999	3599
Machine Shops—*mfg*	33271	3599
Machinery, Other Commercial and Service Industry—*mfg*	333319	3599
Slugs, aluminum: Aluminum Rolling and Drawing, Other—*mfg*	331319	3355
Slugs, copper and copper alloy: Copper Rolling, Drawing and Extruding—*mfg*	331421	3351
Slugs, printers': Printing Machinery and Equipment—*mfg*	333293	3555
Slumped brick: Brick and Structural Clay Tile—*mfg*	327121	3251
Slurry pipeline operation: Pipeline, All Other—*trans*	48699	4619
Slush pits and cellars, excavation of–on a contract basis: Oil and Gas Operations Support Activities—*mining*	213112	1389
Slushing compounds, gun: Basic Organic Chemical, All Other—*mfg*	325199	2899
Chemical Product, All Other Miscellaneous—*mfg*	325998	2899
Small Arms Ammunition Manufacturing	**332992**	**3482**
Small arms ammunition, 80 mm. (or 1.18 inch) or less: Small Arms Ammunition—*mfg*	332992	3482
Small Arms Manufacturing	**332994**	**3484**
Small Electrical Appliance Manufacturing	**33521**	
Small game dressing: Food, All Other Miscellaneous—*mfg*	311999	2015
Poultry Processing—*mfg*	311615	2015
Smelting and refining machinery and equipment, except ovens: Industrial Machinery, All Other—*mfg*	333298	3559
Machinery, Other Commercial and Service Industry—*mfg*	333319	3559

Smelting and refining of lead, primary: Primary Smelting and Refining of Nonferrous Metal (except Copper and Aluminum)—*mfg*	331419	3339
Smelting and refining of nonferrous metals, secondary: Secondary Smelting and Alloying of Aluminum—*mfg*	331314	3341
Secondary Smelting, Refining, and Alloying of Copper—*mfg*	331423	3341
Secondary Smelting, Refining, and Alloying of Nonferrous Metal (except Copper and Aluminum)—*mfg*	331492	3341
Smelting and refining of zinc, primary: Primary Smelting and Refining of Nonferrous Metal (except Copper and Aluminum)—*mfg*	331419	3339
Smelting machinery and equipment: Industrial Machinery and Equipment—*whlse*	42183	5084
Smelting of nonferrous metal, primary–except copper and aluminum: Primary Smelting and Refining of Nonferrous Metal (except Copper and Aluminum)—*mfg*	331419	3339
Smelting ovens: Industrial Process Furnace and Oven—*mfg*	333994	3567
Smelting pots and retorts: Air-Conditioning and Warm Air Heating Equipment and Commercial and Industrial Refrigeration Equipment—*mfg*	333415	3443
Metal Tank (Heavy Gauge)—*mfg*	33242	3443
Plate Work—*mfg*	332313	3443
Power Boiler and Heat Exchanger—*mfg*	33241	3443
Smithsonite mining: Lead Ore and Zinc Ore—*mining*	212231	1031
Smocks: Apparel Accessories and Apparel, Other—*mfg*	315999	2339
Cut and Sew Apparel, All Other—*mfg*	315299	2339
Women's and Girls' Cut and Sew Apparel Contractors—*mfg*	315212	2339
Women's and Girls' Cut and Sew Other Outerwear—*mfg*	315238	2339
Smoke detectors: Communications Equipment, Other—*mfg*	33429	3669
Smoke generators (ordnance): Ordnance and Accessories, Other—*mfg*	332995	3489
Smoked meats: Meat Processed from Carcasses—*mfg*	311612	2013
Smokeless powder: Explosives—*mfg*	32592	2892
Smokers' articles, pottery: Vitreous China, Fine Earthenware and Other Pottery Product—*mfg*	327112	3269
Smokers' glassware–ashtrays, tobacco jars, etc.: Pressed and Blown Glass and Glassware, Other—*mfg*	327212	3229
Smokers' supplies: Nondurable Goods, Other Miscellaneous—*whlse*	42299	5199
Smokestacks, boiler plate: Air-Conditioning and Warm Air Heating Equipment and Commercial and Industrial Refrigeration Equipment—*mfg*	333415	3443
Metal Tank (Heavy Gauge)—*mfg*	33242	3443
Plate Work—*mfg*	332313	3443
Power Boiler and Heat Exchanger—*mfg*	33241	3443
Smoking stands, metal: Metal Household Furniture—*mfg*	337124	2514
Smoking stands, wood: Nonupholstered Wood Household Furniture—*mfg*	337122	2511
Smoking tobacco: Tobacco and Tobacco Product—*whlse*	42294	5194
Tobacco Product, Other—*mfg*	312229	2131
Smyrna carpets and rugs, machine woven: Carpet and Rug Mills—*mfg*	31411	2273
Snack and Nonalcoholic Beverage Bars	**722213**	**5461**
Snack bars: Cafeterias—*accom*	722212	5812
Caterers—*accom*	72232	5812
Foodservice Contractors—*accom*	72231	5812
Full-Service Restaurants—*accom*	72211	5812
Limited-Service Restaurants—*accom*	722211	5812
Snack and Nonalcoholic Beverage Bars—*accom*	722213	5812
Theater Companies and Dinner Theaters—*arts*	71111	5812
Snack Food Manufacturing	**31191**	
Snack Food Manufacturing, Other	**311919**	**2096**
Snack shops: Cafeterias—*accom*	722212	5812
Caterers—*accom*	72232	5812
Foodservice Contractors—*accom*	72231	5812
Full-Service Restaurants—*accom*	72211	5812
Limited-Service Restaurants—*accom*	722211	5812
Snack and Nonalcoholic Beverage Bars—*accom*	722213	5812
Theater Companies and Dinner Theaters—*arts*	71111	5812
Snagging grinders: Power-Driven Hand Tool—*mfg*	333991	3546
Snap bean farms (bush and pole): Vegetable (except Potato) and Melon Farming, Other—*ag*	111219	161
Snap switches, (electric wiring devices): Current-Carrying Wiring Device—*mfg*	335931	3643
Snips, tinners': Cutlery and Flatware (except Precious)—*mfg*	332211	3421
Snow fence lath: Cut Stock, Resawing Lumber, and Planing—*mfg*	321912	2421
Millwork (including Flooring), Other—*mfg*	321918	2421
Sawmills—*mfg*	321113	2421
Wood Product, All Other Miscellaneous—*mfg*	321999	2421
Snow fenoe: Manufacturing, All Other Miscellaneous—*mfg*	339999	2499
Wood Container and Pallet—*mfg*	32192	2499
Wood Product, All Other Miscellaneous—*mfg*	321999	2499
Snow making machinery: Air-Conditioning and Warm Air Heating Equipment and Commercial and Industrial Refrigeration Equipment—*mfg*	333415	3585
Motor Vehicle Air-Conditioning—*mfg*	336391	3585
Snowblowers and throwers, residential: Hand and Edge Tool—*mfg*	332212	3524
Lawn and Garden Tractor and Home Lawn and Garden Equipment—*mfg*	333112	3524
Snowmobiles: Automobile and Other Motor Vehicle—*whlse*	42111	5012
Motor Vehicle Dealers, All Other—*retail*	441229	5599
Transportation Equipment, All Other—*mfg*	336999	3799
Snowplow attschments: Construction Machinery—*mfg*	33312	3531
Overhead Traveling Crane, Hoist and Monorail System—*mfg*	333923	3531
Railroad Rolling Stock—*mfg*	33651	3531
Snowplowing: Airport Operations, Other—*trans*	488119	4959
Exterminating and Pest Control Services—*admin*	56171	4959
Remediation Services—*admin*	56291	4959
Waste Management Services, All Other Miscellaneous—*admin*	562998	4959

ALPHABETICAL INDEX	NAICS	SIC
Snowplows (motor vehicles): Automobile—*mfg*	336111	3711
Heavy Duty Truck—*mfg*	33612	3711
Light Truck and Utility Vehicle—*mfg*	336112	3711
Military Armored Vehicle, Tank and Tank Component—*mfg*	336992	3711
Motor Vehicle Body—*mfg*	336211	3711
Snowshoes: Sporting and Athletic Goods—*mfg*	33992	3949
Snowsuits: Apparel Accessories and Apparel, Other—*mfg*	315999	2339
Cut and Sew Apparel, All Other—*mfg*	315299	2339
Cut and Sew Apparel, All Other—*mfg*	315299	2329
Women's and Girls' Cut and Sew Apparel Contractors—*mfg*	315212	2339
Women's and Girls' Cut and Sew Other Outerwear—*mfg*	315238	2339
Snubbers for CATV systems: Noncurrent-Carrying Wiring Device—*mfg*	335932	3644
Snuff: Tobacco and Tobacco Product—*whlse*	42294	5194
Tobacco Product, Other—*mfg*	312229	2131
Soap and Cleaning Compound Manufacturing	**32561**	
Soap and Other Detergent Manufacturing	**325611**	**2844**
Soap dishes, vitreous china and earthenware: Vitreous China Plumbing Fixture and China and Earthenware Fittings and Bathroom Accessories—*mfg*	327111	3261
Soap dispensers: Plastics Product, All Other—*mfg*	326199	3999
Soap impregnated papers and paper washcloths: Soap and Other Detergent—*mfg*	325611	2844
Toilet Preparation—*mfg*	32562	2844
Soap, chips, and powder–laundry: Chemical and Allied Products, Other—*whlse*	42269	5169
Soap, Cleaning Compound and Toilet Preparation Manufacturing	**3256**	
Soap, saddle: Polish and Other Sanitation Good—*mfg*	325612	2842
Soap, tailet: Drug, Drug Proprietaries and Druggists' Sundries—*whlse*	42221	5122
Soap–granulated, liquid, cake, flaked, and chip: Soap and Other Detergent—*mfg*	325611	2841
Soaps, naphthenic acid: Basic Organic Chemical, All Other—*mfg*	325199	2869
Soapstone quarrying: Crushed and Broken Stone and Quarrying, Other—*mining*	212319	1499
Non-Metallic Mineral, All Other—*mining*	212399	1499
Soccer clubs, except professional and semiprofessional: Fitness and Recreational Sports Centers—*arts*	71394	7997
Soccer clubs, professional or semiprofessional: Agents and Managers for Artists, Athletes, Entertainers and Other Public Figures—*arts*	71141	7941
Promoters of Performing Arts, Sports and Similar Events with Facilities—*arts*	71131	7941
Promoters of Performing Arts, Sports and Similar Events without Facilities—*arts*	71132	7941
Spectator Sports, Other—*arts*	711219	7941

ALPHABETICAL INDEX	NAICS	SIC
Sports Teams and Clubs—*arts*	711211	7941
Soccer equipment, except apparel: Sporting and Athletic Goods—*mfg*	33992	3949
Social Advocacy Organizations	**81331**	
Social Advocacy Organizations	**8133**	
Social Advocacy Organizations, Other	**813319**	**8399**
Social Assistance	**624**	
Social change associations: Grantmaking and Giving Services, Other—*serv*	813219	8399
Social Advocacy Organizations, Other—*serv*	813319	8399
Voluntary Health Organizations—*serv*	813212	8399
Social clubs, membership: Child and Youth Services—*hlth*	62411	8641
Civic and Social Organizations—*serv*	81341	8641
Social escort service: Personal Services, All Other—*serv*	81299	7299
Social service centers: Child and Youth Services—*hlth*	62411	8322
Community Food Services—*hlth*	62421	8322
Community Housing Services, Other—*hlth*	624229	8322
Emergency and Other Relief Services—*hlth*	62423	8322
Individual and Family Services, Other—*hlth*	62419	8322
Parole Offices and Probation Offices—*pub*	92215	8322
Services for the Elderly and Persons with Disabilities—*hlth*	62412	8322
Temporary Shelters—*hlth*	624221	8322
Social service information exchanges–e.g., alcoholism, drug addiction: Grantmaking and Giving Services, Other—*serv*	813219	8399
Social Advocacy Organizations, Other—*serv*	813319	8399
Voluntary Health Organizations—*serv*	813212	8399
Social, Human Resource and Income Maintenance Programs, Administration of	**92313**	**9441**
Sociological research, commercial: Marketing Research and Public Opinion Polling—*prof*	54191	8732
Research and Development in the Social Sciences and Humanities—*prof*	54173	8732
Sociological research, noncommercial: Research and Development in the Life Sciences—*prof*	54172	8733
Research and Development in the Physical Sciences and Engineering Sciences—*prof*	54171	8733
Research and Development in the Social Sciences and Humanities—*prof*	54173	8733
Sockets (machine tool accessories): Cutting Tool and Machine Tool Accessory—*mfg*	333515	3545
Hand and Edge Tool—*mfg*	332212	3545
Sockets, electric: Current-Carrying Wiring Device—*mfg*	335931	3643
Sockets, electronic tube: Electronic Component, Other—*mfg*	334419	3679
Motor Vehicle Electrical and Electronic Equipment, Other—*mfg*	336322	3679
Printed Circuit/Electronics Assembly—*mfg*	334418	3679
Radio and Television Broadcasting and Wireless Communications Equipment—*mfg*	33422	3679

ALPHABETICAL INDEX	NAICS	SIC
Sodium silicate: Basic Inorganic Chemical, All Other—*mfg*	325188	2819
Chemical Product, All Other Miscellaneous—*mfg*	325998	2819
Sodium silicofluoride: Basic Inorganic Chemical, All Other—*mfg*	325188	2819
Chemical Product, All Other Miscellaneous—*mfg*	325998	2819
Sodium stannate: Basic Inorganic Chemical, All Other—*mfg*	325188	2819
Chemical Product, All Other Miscellaneous—*mfg*	325998	2819
Sodium sulfate-bulk or tablets: Basic Inorganic Chemical, All Other—*mfg*	325188	2819
Chemical Product, All Other Miscellaneous—*mfg*	325998	2819
Sodium sulfoxalate formaldehyde: Basic Organic Chemical, All Other—*mfg*	325199	2869
Sodium tetrahorate, not produced at mines: Basic Inorganic Chemical, All Other—*mfg*	325188	2819
Chemical Product, All Other Miscellaneous—*mfg*	325998	2819
Sodium thiosulfate: Basic Inorganic Chemical, All Other—*mfg*	325188	2819
Chemical Product, All Other Miscellaneous—*mfg*	325998	2819
Sodium tungstate: Basic Inorganic Chemical, All Other—*mfg*	325188	2819
Chemical Product, All Other Miscellaneous—*mfg*	325998	2819
Sodium uranate: Basic Inorganic Chemical, All Other—*mfg*	325188	2819
Chemical Product, All Other Miscellaneous—*mfg*	325998	2819
Sodium, metallic: Basic Inorganic Chemical, All Other—*mfg*	325188	2819
Chemical Product, All Other Miscellaneous—*mfg*	325998	2819
Sofas, convertible: Mattress—*mfg*	33791	2515
Upholstered Household Furniture—*mfg*	337121	2515
Sofas, upholstered on wood frames, except convertible beds: Upholstered Household Furniture—*mfg*	337121	2512
Soffit, plastics (siding): Plastics Pipe and Pipe Fitting—*mfg*	326122	3089
Plastics Product, All Other—*mfg*	326199	3089
Unsupported Plastics Profile Shape—*mfg*	326121	3089
Soft Drink and Ice Manufacturing	**31211**	
Soft Drink Manufacturing	**312111**	**2086**
Soft drink stands: Cafeterias—*accom*	722212	5812
Caterers—*accom*	72232	5812
Foodservice Contractors—*accom*	72231	5812
Full-Service Restaurants—*accom*	72211	5812
Limited-Service Restaurants—*accom*	722211	5812
Snack and Nonalcoholic Beverage Bars—*accom*	722213	5812
Theater Companies and Dinner Theaters—*arts*	71111	5812
Soft drinks: Grocery and Related Products, Other—*whlse*	42249	5149
Soft drinks, bottled or canned: Bottled Water—*mfg*	312112	2086
Soft Drink—*mfg*	312111	2086
Soft fiber cordage and twine: Rope, Cordage and Twine Mills—*mfg*	314991	2298
Softeners (textile assistants): Surface Active Agent—*mfg*	325613	2843
Software programming, custom: Custom Computer Programming Services, Custom—*prof*	541511	7371
Software Publishers	**5112**	
Software Reproducing	**334611**	**7372**

ALPHABETICAL INDEX	NAICS	SIC
Software systems analysis and design, custom: Custom Computer Programming Services, Custom—*prof*	541511	7371
Software, computer: Computer and Computer Peripheral Equipment and Software—*whlse*	42143	5045
Computer and Software Stores—*retail*	44312	5045
Software, computer–prepackaged: Publishers—*info*	51121	7372
Software Reproducing—*mfg*	334611	7372
Softwood distillates: Gum and Wood Chemical—*mfg*	325191	2861
Softwood plywood composites: Softwood Veneer and Plywood—*mfg*	321212	2436
Softwood Veneer and Plywood Manufacturing	**321212**	**2436**
Softwood veneer or plywood: Softwood Veneer and Plywood—*mfg*	321212	2436
Soil compacting service–contractors: Heavy, All Other—*const*	23499	1629
Industrial Nonbuilding Structure—*const*	23493	1629
Soil compactors–vibratory: Construction Machinery—*mfg*	33312	3531
Overhead Traveling Crane, Hoist and Monorail System—*mfg*	333923	3531
Railroad Rolling Stock—*mfg*	33651	3531
Soil conditioners: Pesticide and Other Agricultural Chemical—*mfg*	32532	2879
Soil conservation services: Land, Mineral, Wildlife, and Forest Conservation—*pub*	92412	9512
Soil pipe, cast iron: Iron Foundries—*mfg*	331511	3321
Soil Preparation, Planting, and Cultivating	**115112**	**721**
Soil pulverizers and packers (agricultural machinery): Farm Machinery and Equipment—*mfg*	333111	3523
Soil testing kits: Basic Organic Chemical, All Other—*mfg*	325199	2899
Chemical Product, All Other Miscellaneous—*mfg*	325998	2899
Soil, top: Nursery and Garden Centers—*retail*	44422	5261
Outdoor Power Equipment Stores—*retail*	44421	5261
Stores (except Tobacco Stores), All Other Miscellaneous—*retail*	453998	5261
Solar cells: Semiconductor and Related Device—*mfg*	334413	3674
Solar energy collectors, liquid or gas: Heating Equipment (except Electric and Warm Air Furnaces)—*mfg*	333414	3433
Solar heaters: Heating Equipment (except Electric and Warm Air Furnaces)—*mfg*	333414	3433
Solar heating apparatus-contractors: Plumbing, Heating and Air-Conditioning Contractors—*const*	23511	1711
Solar heating panels and equipment: Building Material Dealers, Other—*retail*	44419	5074
Plumbing and Heating Equipment and Supplies (Hydronics)—*whlse*	42172	5074
Solar powered turbinegenerator sets: Turbine and Turbine Generator Set Unit—*mfg*	333611	3511
Solar reflecting insulation film-contractors: Drywall, Plastering, Acoustical and Insulation Contractors—*const*	23542	1742
Solarimeters: Measuring and Controlling Device, Other—*mfg*	334519	3829
Surgical and Medical Instrument—*mfg*	339112	3829
Solder (base metal), pig and ingot–secondary: Secondary Smelting and Alloying of Aluminum—*mfg*	331314	3341

Description	NAICS	SIC
Secondary Smelting, Refining, and Alloying of Copper—*mfg*	331423	3341
Secondary Smelting, Refining, and Alloying of Nonferrous Metal (except Copper and Aluminum)—*mfg*	331492	3341
Solder wire, bar–acid core and rosin core: Nonferrous Metal (except Copper and Aluminum) Rolling, Drawing and Extruding—*mfg*	331491	3356
Soldering equipment, except soldering irons: Power, Distribution and Specialty Transformer—*mfg*	335311	3548
Welding and Soldering Equipment—*mfg*	333992	3548
Soldering fluxes: Basic Organic Chemical, All Other—*mfg*	325199	2899
Chemical Product, All Other Miscellaneous—*mfg*	325998	2899
Soldering for the jewelry trade: Jewelers' Material and Lapidary Work—*mfg*	339913	3915
Soldering guns and tools, hand–electric: Hand and Edge Tool—*mfg*	332212	3423
Soldering iron tips and tiplets: Hand and Edge Tool—*mfg*	332212	3423
Soldering irons and coppers: Hand and Edge Tool—*mfg*	332212	3423
Solderless connectors (electric wiring devices): Current-Carrying Wiring Device—*mfg*	335931	3643
Sole leather: Leather and Hide Tanning and Finishing—*mfg*	31611	3111
Solenoid switches, industrial: Relay and Industrial Control—*mfg*	335314	3625
Solenoid valves, fluid power–metal: Fluid Power Valve and Hose Fitting—*mfg*	332912	3492
Solenoids for electronic applications: Electronic Component, Other—*mfg*	334419	3679
Motor Vehicle Electrical and Electronic Equipment, Other—*mfg*	336322	3679
Printed Circuit/Electronics Assembly—*mfg*	334418	3679
Radio and Television Broadcasting and Wireless Communications Equipment—*mfg*	33422	3679
Soles, boot and shoe–except rubber, composition, plastics, and fiber: Fastener, Button, Needle and Pin—*mfg*	339993	3131
Leather Good, All Other—*mfg*	316999	3131
Wood Product, All Other Miscellaneous—*mfg*	321999	3131
Soles, boot and shoe–plastics: Plastics Pipe and Pipe Fitting—*mfg*	326122	3089
Plastics Product, All Other—*mfg*	326199	3089
Unsupported Plastics Profile Shape—*mfg*	326121	3089
Soles, boot and shoe–rubber, composition, and fiber: Fabric Coating Mills—*mfg*	31332	3069
Rubber Product, All Other—*mfg*	326299	3069
Soles, shoe: Cosmetics, Beauty Supplies and Perfume Stores—*retail*	44612	5087
Service Establishment Equipment and Supplies—*whlse*	42185	5087
Solid fuel propellants, inorganic: Basic Inorganic Chemical, All Other—*mfg*	325188	2819
Chemical Product, All Other Miscellaneous—*mfg*	325998	2819
Solid fuel propellants, organic: Basic Organic Chemical, All Other—*mfg*	325199	2869
Solid Waste Collection	**562111**	**4953**
Solid Waste Combustors and Incinerators	**562213**	**4953**
Solid Waste Landfill	**562212**	**4953**
Solid-state electronic devices: Semiconductor and Related Device—*mfg*	334413	3674
Soling strips, boot and shoe–plastics: Plastics Pipe and Pipe Fitting—*mfg*	326122	3089
Plastics Product, All Other—*mfg*	326199	3089
Unsupported Plastics Profile Shape—*mfg*	326121	3089
Soling strips, boot and shoe–rubber, composition, and fiber: Fabric Coating Mills—*mfg*	31332	3069
Rubber Product, All Other—*mfg*	326299	3069
Solite, ground or otherwise treated: Ground or Treated Mineral and Earth—*mfg*	327992	3295
Soluble oils and greases: Surface Active Agent—*mfg*	325613	2843
Solutions, pharmaceutical: Pharmaceutical Preparation—*mfg*	325412	2834
Solvent naphtha, made in chemical plants: Cyclic Crude and Intermediate—*mfg*	325192	2865
Petrochemical—*mfg*	32511	2865
Solvents, carbon: Basic Organic Chemical, All Other—*mfg*	325199	2899
Chemical Product, All Other Miscellaneous—*mfg*	325998	2899
Solvents, degreasing: Polish and Other Sanitation Good—*mfg*	325612	2842
Solvents, drain pipe: Polish and Other Sanitation Good—*mfg*	325612	2842
Solvents, organic: Basic Organic Chemical, All Other—*mfg*	325199	2869
Ethyl Alcohol—*mfg*	325193	2869
Solvents, produced in petroleum refineries: Petroleum Refineries—*mfg*	32411	2911
Sonabuoys: Search, Detection, Navigation, Guidance, Aeronautical, and Nautical System and Instrument—*mfg*	334511	3812
Sonar fish finders: Search, Detection, Navigation, Guidance, Aeronautical, and Nautical System and Instrument—*mfg*	334511	3812
Sonar Systems and equipment: Search, Detection, Navigation, Guidance, Aeronautical, and Nautical System and Instrument—*mfg*	334511	3812
Song writers: Independent Artists, Writers, and Performers—*arts*	71151	8999
Music Publishers—*info*	51223	8999
Record Production—*info*	51221	8999
Sorbitol: Basic Organic Chemical, All Other—*mfg*	325199	2869
Sorghum farms, except for syrup: Grain Farming, All Other—*ag*	111199	119
Sorghum grain flour: Flour Milling—*mfg*	311211	2041
Sorghum, including custom refining: Food, All Other Miscellaneous—*mfg*	311999	2099
Sororities, except residential: Child and Youth Services—*hlth*	62411	8641
Sorority residential houses: Hotels (except Casino Hotels) and Motels—*accom*	72111	7041
Rooming and Boarding Houses—*accom*	72131	7041
Sorters, filing–office: Lead Pencil and Art Good—*mfg*	339942	3579
Office Machinery—*mfg*	333313	3579
Watch, Clock, and Part—*mfg*	334518	3579
Sorters, punch card: Computer Peripheral Equipment, Other—*mfg*	334119	3577
Sorting machines for agricultural products: Farm Machinery and Equipment—*mfg*	333111	3523

ALPHABETICAL INDEX	NAICS	SIC
Sorting machines, card: Computer Peripheral Equipment, Other—*mfg*	334119	3577
Sorting racks, mail–except wood: Showcase, Partition, Shelving, and Locker—*mfg*	337215	2542
Sorting, grading, and packing of fruits and vegetables: Postharvest Crop Activities (except Cotton Ginning)—*ag*	115114	723
Sound equipment installation-contractors: Electrical Contractors—*const*	23531	1731
Security Systems Services (except Locksmiths)—*admin*	561621	1731
Sound recording and reproducing equipment, motion picture: Photographic and Photocopying Equipment—*mfg*	333315	3861
Photographic Film, Paper, Plate and Chemical—*mfg*	325992	3861
Sound Recording Industries	**5122**	
Sound Recording Industries, Other	**51229**	**7922**
Sound Recording Studios	**51224**	**7389**
Soup mixes: Dried and Dehydrated Food—*mfg*	311423	2034
Flour Milling—*mfg*	311211	2034
Soup powders: Dried and Dehydrated Food—*mfg*	311423	2034
Flour Milling—*mfg*	311211	2034
Soup, frozen: Packaged Frozen Food—*whlse*	42242	5142
Soups, dehydrated: Dried and Dehydrated Food—*mfg*	311423	2034
Flour Milling—*mfg*	311211	2034
Soups, except frozen: Grocery and Related Products, Other—*whlse*	42249	5149
Soups, except seafood–canned: Canning, Specialty—*mfg*	311422	2032
Food, All Other Miscellaneous—*mfg*	311999	2032
Soups, fish and seafood–canned: Seafood Canning—*mfg*	311711	2091
Soups, fish and seafood–frozen: Fresh and Frozen Seafood Processing—*mfg*	311712	2092
Soups, frozen–except seafood: Frozen Specialty Food—*mfg*	311412	2038
Sour cream: Fluid Milk—*mfg*	311511	2026
Souvenir cards, lithographed: Lithographic Printing, Commercial—*mfg*	323110	2752
Quick Printing—*mfg*	323114	2752
Souvenir cards–except lithographed or gravure: Digital Printing—*mfg*	323115	2759
Flexographic Printing, Commercial—*mfg*	323112	2759
Printing, Other Commercial—*mfg*	323119	2759
Quick Printing—*mfg*	323114	2759
Souvenir cards–gravure printing: Gravure Printing, Commercial—*mfg*	323111	2754
Souvenir shops: Gift, Novelty and Souvenir Stores—*retail*	45322	5947
Soy sauce: Fruit and Vegetable Canning—*mfg*	311421	2035
Mayonnaise, Dressing and Other Prepared Sauce—*mfg*	311941	2035
Soyate driers: Paint and Coating—*mfg*	32551	2851
Soybean cooking and salad oil: Fats and Oils Refining and Blending—*mfg*	311225	2079
Oilseed Processing, Other—*mfg*	311223	2079
Soybean Processing—*mfg*	311222	2079
Soybean Farming	**11111**	**116**
Soybean farms: Soybean Farming—*ag*	11111	116
Soybean fibers (manmade textile materials): Noncellulosic Organic Fiber—*mfg*	325222	2824
Soybean flour and grits: Fats and Oils Refining and Blending—*mfg*	311225	2075
Soybean Processing—*mfg*	311222	2075
Soybean oil, cake, and meal: Fats and Oils Refining and Blending—*mfg*	311225	2075
Soybean Processing—*mfg*	311222	2075
Soybean oil, deodorized: Fats and Oils Refining and Blending—*mfg*	311225	2075
Soybean Processing—*mfg*	311222	2075
Soybean plastics: Plastics Material and Resin—*mfg*	325211	2821
Soybean Processing	**311222**	**2075**
Soybean protein concentrates: Fats and Oils Refining and Blending—*mfg*	311225	2075
Soybean Processing—*mfg*	311222	2075
Soybean protein isolates: Fats and Oils Refining and Blending—*mfg*	311225	2075
Soybean Processing—*mfg*	311222	2075
Soybeans: Grain and Field Bean—*whlse*	42251	5153
Space capsules: Guided Missile and Space Vehicle Parts and Auxiliary Equipment, Other—*mfg*	336419	3769
Space flight operations: Space Research and Technology—*pub*	92711	9661
Space flight operations, except: Rail Support Activities—*trans*	48821	4789
Scenic and Sightseeing, Land—*trans*	48711	4789
Transportation, All Other Support Activities—*trans*	488999	4789
Space heaters, except electric: Heating Equipment (except Electric and Warm Air Furnaces)—*mfg*	333414	3433
Space propulsion units and parts: Transportation Equipment and Supplies (except Motor Vehicle)—*whlse*	42186	5088
Space research and development: Space Research and Technology—*pub*	92711	9661
Space Research and Technology	**9271**	
Space Research and Technology	**927**	
Space Research and Technology	**92711**	**9661**
Space satellite communications equipment: Radio and Television Broadcasting and Wireless Communications Equipment—*mfg*	33422	3663
Space simulation chambers, metal plate: Air-Conditioning and Warm Air Heating Equipment and Commercial and Industrial Refrigeration Equipment—*mfg*	333415	3443
Metal Tank (Heavy Gauge)—*mfg*	33242	3443
Plate Work—*mfg*	332313	3443
Power Boiler and Heat Exchanger—*mfg*	33241	3443
Space vehicle guidance systems and equipment: Search, Detection, Navigation, Guidance, Aeronautical, and Nautical System and Instrument—*mfg*	334511	3812

Entry	NAICS	SIC
Space vehicles, complete: Guided Missile and Space Vehicle—*mfg*	336414	3761
Spades, hand: Hand and Edge Tool—*mfg*	332212	3423
Spaghetti: Grocery and Related Products, Other—*whlse*	42249	5149
Spaghetti and meatballs, frozen: Frozen Specialty Food—*mfg*	311412	2038
Spaghetti sauce: Fruit and Vegetable Canning—*mfg*	311421	2033
Spaghetti, cannod: Canning, Specialty—*mfg*	311422	2032
Food, All Other Miscellaneous—*mfg*	311999	2032
Spaghetti, dry: Pasta—*mfg*	311823	2098
Spandex broadwoven fabrics: Broadwoven Fabric Mills—*mfg*	31321	2221
Spanish floor tile, concrete: Concrete Pipe—*mfg*	327332	3272
Concrete Product, Other—*mfg*	32739	3272
Nonmetallic Mineral Product, All Other Miscellaneous—*mfg*	327999	3272
Spanish foods, canned: Canning, Specialty—*mfg*	311422	2032
Food, All Other Miscellaneous—*mfg*	311999	2032
Spanish moss, gathering of: Crop Farming, All Other Miscellaneous—*ag*	111998	831
Forest Nurseries and Gathering of Forest Products—*ag*	11321	831
Spaoe suits: Surgical Appliance and Supplies—*mfg*	339113	3842
Spar, ground or otherwise treated: Ground or Treated Mineral and Earth—*mfg*	327992	3295
Spark plug testing instruments, electric: Electronic Coil, Transformer, and Other Inductor—*mfg*	334416	3825
Instrument for Measuring and Testing Electricity and Electrical Signals—*mfg*	334515	3825
Spark plugs for internal combustion engines: Motor Vehicle Electrical and Electronic Equipment, Other—*mfg*	336322	3694
Spark plugs, porcelain: Porcelain Electrical Supply—*mfg*	327113	3264
Spars, wood: Manufacturing, All Other Miscellaneous—*mfg*	339999	2499
Wood Container and Pallet—*mfg*	32192	2499
Wood Product, All Other Miscellaneous—*mfg*	321999	2499
Spas, health fitness–except resort lodges: Fitness and Recreational Sports Centers—*arts*	71394	7991
Spats: Leather Good, All Other—*mfg*	316999	3199
Spatulas, rubber: Fabric Coating Mills—*mfg*	31332	3069
Rubber Product, All Other—*mfg*	326299	3069
Speaker systems: Audio and Video Equipment—*mfg*	33431	3651
Spearguns: Sporting and Athletic Goods—*mfg*	33992	3949
Spearmint oil: Spice and Extract—*mfg*	311942	2899
Spears, fishing: Sporting and Athletic Goods—*mfg*	33992	3949
Special food board: Paperboard Mills—*mfg*	32213	2631
Specialty leathers: Leather and Hide Tanning and Finishing—*mfg*	31611	3111
Specialty transformers: Power, Distribution and Specialty Transformer—*mfg*	335311	3612
Specific ion measuring instruments, laboratory type: Analytical Laboratory Instrument—*mfg*	334516	3826
Spectacle glass: Flat Glass—*mfg*	327211	3211
Spectacles: Ophthalmic Goods—*mfg*	339115	3851
Spectator seating installation–contractors: Trade Contractors, All Other Special—*const*	23599	1799
Spectator Sports	**7112**	
Spectator Sports	**71121**	
Spectator Sports, Other	**711219**	**7948**
Spectrofluorometers: Analytical Laboratory Instrument—*mfg*	334516	3826
Spectrographs: Analytical Laboratory Instrument—*mfg*	334516	3826
Spectrometers, liquid scintillation and nuclear: Measuring and Controlling Device, Other—*mfg*	334519	3829
Surgical and Medical Instrument—*mfg*	339112	3829
Spectrometers–electron diffraction, mass, nmr, raman, X-ray: Analytical Laboratory Instrument—*mfg*	334516	3826
Spectrophotometers–atomic absorption, atomic emission, flame, fluorescence, infrared, raman, visible, ultraviolet-mf: Analytical Laboratory Instrument—*mfg*	334516	3826
Spectrum analyzers: Electronic Coil, Transformer, and Other Inductor—*mfg*	334416	3825
Instrument for Measuring and Testing Electricity and Electrical Signals—*mfg*	334515	3825
Speculative builders: Building, Commercial and Institutional—*const*	23332	1531
Manufacturing and Industrial Building—*const*	23331	1531
Multifamily Housing—*const*	23322	1531
Single Family Housing—*const*	23321	1531
Speculums: Surgical and Medical Instrument—*mfg*	339112	3841
Speech clinicians, offices of: Health Practitioners, Offices Of Miscellaneous—*hlth*	621399	8049
Mental Health Practitioners (except Physicians), Offices Of—*hlth*	62133	8049
Physical, Occupational and Speech Therapists and Audiologists, Offices Of—*hlth*	62134	8049
Speech pathologists, offices of: Health Practitioners, Offices Of Miscellaneous—*hlth*	621399	8049
Mental Health Practitioners (except Physicians), Offices Of—*hlth*	62133	8049
Physical, Occupational and Speech Therapists and Audiologists, Offices Of—*hlth*	62134	8049
Speed Changer, Industrial High-Speed Drive and Gear Manufacturing	**333612**	**3566**
Speed changers (power transmission equipment): Speed Changer, Industrial High-Speed Drive and Gear—*mfg*	333612	3566
Speed indicators and recorders, vehicle: Totalizing Fluid Meter and Counting Device—*mfg*	334514	3824
Speed reading courses: Language Schools—*educ*	61163	8299
Speed reducers (power transmission equipment): Speed Changer, Industrial High-Speed Drive and Gear—*mfg*	333612	3566
Speed shops: Automotive Parts and Accessories Stores—*retail*	44131	5531
Tire Dealers—*retail*	44132	5531
Speedometers: Totalizing Fluid Meter and Counting Device—*mfg*	334514	3824
Speedway operation: Race Tracks—*arts*	711212	7948
Spectator Sports, Other—*arts*	711219	7948
Spelter (zinc), primary: Primary Smelting and Refining of Nonferrous Metal (except Copper and Aluminum)—*mfg*	331419	3339
Sperm banks: Blood and Organ Banks—*hlth*	621991	8099

ALPHABETICAL INDEX	NAICS	SIC
Sphagnum moss, gathering of: Crop Farming, All Other Miscellaneous—*ag*	111998	831
Forest Nurseries and Gathering of Forest Products—*ag*	11321	831
Sphalerite mining: Lead Ore and Zinc Ore—*mining*	212231	1031
Spheres, for liqrnds or gas–metal plate: Air-Conditioning and Warm Air Heating Equipment and Commercial and Industrial Refrigeration Equipment—*mfg*	333415	3443
Metal Tank (Heavy Gauge)—*mfg*	33242	3443
Plate Work—*mfg*	332313	3443
Power Boiler and Heat Exchanger—*mfg*	33241	3443
Sphygmomanometers: Surgical and Medical Instrument—*mfg*	339112	3841
Spice and Extract Manufacturing	**311942**	**2095**
Spice and herb stores: Food (Health) Supplement Stores—*retail*	446191	5499
Food Stores, All Other Specialty—*retail*	445299	5499
Limited-Service Restaurants—*accom*	722211	5499
Meat Markets—*retail*	44521	5499
Spices: Grocery and Related Products, Other—*whlse*	42249	5149
Spices, including grinding: Spice and Extract—*mfg*	311942	2099
Spiegeleisen: Electrometallurgical Ferroalloy Product—*mfg*	331112	3313
Secondary Smelting, Refining, and Alloying of Nonferrous Metal (except Copper and Aluminum)—*mfg*	331492	3313
Spigots, metal and plastics: Fabricated Metal Product, All Other Miscellaneous—*mfg*	332999	3432
Plumbing Fixture Fitting and Trim—*mfg*	332913	3432
Spigots, wood: Manufacturing, All Other Miscellaneous—*mfg*	339999	2499
Wood Container and Pallet—*mfg*	32192	2499
Wood Product, All Other Miscellaneous—*mfg*	321999	2499
Spike rods, made in steel works or rolling mills: Iron and Steel Mills—*mfg*	331111	3312
Petroleum and Coal Productsa, All Other—*mfg*	324199	3312
Spikes, nonferrous metal (including wire): Iron and Steel Mills—*mfg*	331111	3399
Secondary Smelting and Alloying of Aluminum—*mfg*	331314	3399
Secondary Smelting, Refining, and Alloying of Copper—*mfg*	331423	3399
Secondary Smelting, Refining, and Alloying of Nonferrous Metal (except Copper and Aluminum)—*mfg*	331492	3399
Spikes, steel–wire or cut: Fabricated Wire Product, Other—*mfg*	332618	3315
Steel Wire Drawing—*mfg*	331222	3315
Spindle banding: Narrow Fabric Mills—*mfg*	313221	2241
Spindles, textile: Textile Machinery—*mfg*	333292	3552
Spinners, aircraft propeller: Aircraft Part and Auxiliary Equipment, Other—*mfg*	336413	3728
Fluid Power Valve and Hose Fitting—*mfg*	332912	3728
Spinning lathes: Machine Tool (Metal Forming Types)—*mfg*	333513	3542
Spinning machines, metal: Machine Tool (Metal Forming Types)—*mfg*	333513	3542
Spinning machines, textile: Textile Machinery—*mfg*	333292	3552
Spinning metal, for the trade: Metal Stamping—*mfg*	332116	3469
Spinning thread–cotton, silk, manmade fibers, and wool: Textile and Fabric Finishing (except Broadwoven Fabric) Mills—*mfg*	313312	2284
Thread Mills—*mfg*	313113	2284
Spinning wool carpet and rug yarn–wool, mohair, or animal fiber: Yarn Spinning Mills—*mfg*	313111	2281
Spinning yarn–cotton, silk, wool, and manmade staple: Yarn Spinning Mills—*mfg*	313111	2281
Spiral cloth, made from purchased wire: Fabricated Wire Product, Other—*mfg*	332618	3496
Spirit duplicating fluid: Basic Organic Chemical, All Other—*mfg*	325199	2899
Chemical Product, All Other Miscellaneous—*mfg*	325998	2899
Spirits: Wine and Distilled Alcoholic Beverage—*whlse*	42282	5182
Spirits, neutral, except fruit-for beverage purposes: Distilleries—*mfg*	31214	2085
Spirits, pharmaceutical: Pharmaceutical Preparation—*mfg*	325412	2834
Splicers, motion picture film: Photographic and Photocopying Equipment—*mfg*	333315	3861
Photographic Film, Paper, Plate and Chemical—*mfg*	325992	3861
Spline rolling machines: Machine Tool (Metal Forming Types)—*mfg*	333513	3542
Splint baskets, for fruits and vegetables: Wood Container and Pallet—*mfg*	32192	2449
Splints, pneumatic and wood: Surgical Appliance and Supplies—*mfg*	339113	3842
Splits, leather: Leather and Hide Tanning and Finishing—*mfg*	31611	3111
Spodumene mining: Chemical and Fertilizer Mineral, Other—*mining*	212393	1479
Spokes, wood: Manufacturing, All Other Miscellaneous—*mfg*	339999	2499
Wood Container and Pallet—*mfg*	32192	2499
Wood Product, All Other Miscellaneous—*mfg*	321999	2499
Sponge goods, bakery, except frozen: Bakeries, Commercial—*mfg*	311812	2051
Sponge iron: Iron and Steel Mills—*mfg*	331111	3312
Petroleum and Coal Productsa, All Other—*mfg*	324199	3312
Sponge rubber and sponge rubber products: Fabric Coating Mills—*mfg*	31332	3069
Rubber Product, All Other—*mfg*	326299	3069
Sponges: Nondurable Goods, Other Miscellaneous—*whlse*	42299	5199
Sponges, gathering of: Crop Farming, All Other Miscellaneous—*ag*	111998	919
Marine Fishing, Other—*ag*	114119	919
Sponges, plastics: Plastics Pipe and Pipe Fitting—*mfg*	326122	3089
Plastics Product, All Other—*mfg*	326199	3089
Unsupported Plastics Profile Shape—*mfg*	326121	3089
Sponges, rubber: Fabric Coating Mills—*mfg*	31332	3069
Rubber Product, All Other—*mfg*	326299	3069
Sponges, scouring–metallic: Abrasive Product—*mfg*	32791	3291
Fabricated Metal Product, All Other Miscellaneous—*mfg*	332999	3291
Sponges, surgical: Surgical Appliance and Supplies—*mfg*	339113	3842
Sponging and refinishing cloth–wool and similar animal fiber for the trade: Broadwoven Fabric Finishing Mills—*mfg*	313311	2231
Broadwoven Fabric Mills—*mfg*	31321	2231

Description	NAICS	SIC
Textile and Fabric Finishing (except Broadwoven Fabric) Mills—*mfg*	313312	2231
Spool blocks and blanks, wood: Cut Stock, Resawing Lumber, and Planing—*mfg*	321912	2426
Millwork (including Flooring), Other—*mfg*	321918	2426
Showcase, Partition, Shelving, and Locker—*mfg*	337215	2426
Wood Product, All Other Miscellaneous—*mfg*	321999	2426
Spooling yarn–cotton, silk, and manmade fiber continuous filament: Textile and Fabric Finishing (except Broadwoven Fabric) Mills—*mfg*	313312	2282
Yarn Texturing, Throwing and Twisting Mills—*mfg*	313112	2282
Spooling yarn–wool, mohair, or similar animal fibers: Textile and Fabric Finishing (except Broadwoven Fabric) Mills—*mfg*	313312	2282
Yarn Texturing, Throwing and Twisting Mills—*mfg*	313112	2282
Spools, except for textile machinery:wood: Manufacturing, All Other Miscellaneous—*mfg*	339999	2499
Wood Container and Pallet—*mfg*	32192	2499
Wood Product, All Other Miscellaneous—*mfg*	321999	2499
Spools, fiber (metal-end or all-fiber): Fiber Can, Tube, Drum, and Similar Products—*mfg*	322214	2655
Spools, textile machinery–wood: Textile Machinery—*mfg*	333292	3552
Spoons, paper–except those made from pressed or molded pulp: Non-Folding Sanitary Food Container—*mfg*	322215	2656
Spoons, pressed and molded pulp: Coated and Laminated Paper—*mfg*	322222	2679
Converted Paper Product, All Other—*mfg*	322298	2679
Die-Cut Paper and Paperboard Office Supplies—*mfg*	322231	2679
Non-Folding Sanitary Food Container—*mfg*	322215	2679
Spoons–silver, nickel silver, pewter, stainless steel, and plated: Cutlery and Flatware (except Precious)—*mfg*	332211	3914
Silverware and Plated Ware—*mfg*	339912	3914
Sport shirts: Men's and Boys' Cut and Sew Apparel Contractors—*mfg*	315211	2321
Men's and Boys' Cut and Sew Shirt (except Work Shirt)—*mfg*	315223	2321
Sporting and Athletic Goods Manufacturing	**33992**	**3949**
Sporting and Recreational Goods and Supplies Wholesalers	**42191**	**5091**
Sporting camps: Recreational and Vacation Camps—*accom*	721214	7032
Sporting goods rental: Recreational Goods Rental—*real*	532292	7999
Sporting Goods Stores	**45111**	**5941**
Sporting Goods, Hobby and Musical Instrument Stores	**4511**	
Sporting Goods, Hobby, Book and Music Stores	**451**	
Sporting goods, including firearms, ammunition, and bicycles: Sporting and Recreational Goods and Supplies—*whlse*	42191	5091
Sporting goods–except clothing, footwear, small arms, and ammunition: Sporting and Athletic Goods—*mfg*	33992	3949
Sporting powder (explosive): Explosives—*mfg*	32592	2892
Sports and recreation clubs, membership–except physical fitness: Fitness and Recreational Sports Centers—*arts*	71394	7997
Sports and Recreation Instruction	**61162**	**7999**
Sports apparel stores: Clothing Accessories Stores—*retail*	44815	5699
Clothing Stores, Other—*retail*	44819	5699
Sports clothing, nontailored: Cut and Sew Apparel, All Other—*mfg*	315299	2329
Sports field operation (sports promotion): Agents and Managers for Artists, Athletes, Entertainers and Other Public Figures—*arts*	71141	7941
Promoters of Performing Arts, Sports and Similar Events with Facilities—*arts*	71131	7941
Promoters of Performing Arts, Sports and Similar Events without Facilities—*arts*	71132	7941
Spectator Sports, Other—*arts*	711219	7941
Sports Teams and Clubs—*arts*	711211	7941
Sports promotion–baseball, football, boxing, etc.: Agents and Managers for Artists, Athletes, Entertainers and Other Public Figures—*arts*	71141	7941
Promoters of Performing Arts, Sports and Similar Events with Facilities—*arts*	71131	7941
Promoters of Performing Arts, Sports and Similar Events without Facilities—*arts*	71132	7941
Spectator Sports, Other—*arts*	711219	7941
Sports Teams and Clubs—*arts*	711211	7941
Sports shirts: Outerwear Knitting Mills—*mfg*	315191	2253
Sports Teams and Clubs	**711211**	**7941**
Sportswear, men's and boys': Men's and Boys' Clothing and Furnishings—*whlse*	42232	5136
Sportswear–women's and children's: Women's, Children's, and Infants' and Accessories—*whlse*	42233	5137
Spot welding apparatus, gas and electric: Power, Distribution and Specialty Transformer—*mfg*	335311	3548
Welding and Soldering Equipment—*mfg*	333992	3548
Spotlights, except vehicular: Lighting Equipment, Other—*mfg*	335129	3648
Spotlights, motor vehicle: Vehicular Lighting Equipment—*mfg*	336321	3647
Spotting boards (sighting and fire control equipment): Optical Instrument and Lens—*mfg*	333314	3827
Spouting, plastics–glass fiber reinforced: Plastics Pipe and Pipe Fitting—*mfg*	326122	3089
Plastics Product, All Other—*mfg*	326199	3089
Unsupported Plastics Profile Shape—*mfg*	326121	3089
Spouts, sheet metal: Metal Container, Other—*mfg*	332439	3444
Sheet Metal Work—*mfg*	332322	3444
Spray nozzles, aerosol: Other Metal Valve and Pipe Fitting, Other—*mfg*	332919	3499
Sprayers, hand–agricultural: Farm Machinery and Equipment—*mfg*	333111	3523
Hand and Edge Tool—*mfg*	332212	3523
Sprayers, hand–except agricultural: Air and Gas Compressor—*mfg*	333912	3563
Spraying crops, with or without fertilizing: Nonscheduled Air, Other—*trans*	481219	721
Soil Preparation, Planting, and Cultivating—*ag*	115112	721
Spraying machines (agricultural machinery): Farm Machinery and Equipment—*mfg*	333111	3523

ALPHABETICAL INDEX	NAICS	SIC
Spraying outfits for metals, paints, and chemicals (compressor units): Air and Gas Compressor—*mfg*	333912	3563
Spreaders and finishers, construction: Construction Machinery—*mfg*	33312	3531
Overhead Traveling Crane, Hoist and Monorail System—*mfg*	333923	3531
Railroad Rolling Stock—*mfg*	33651	3531
Spreaders, fertilizer: Farm Machinery and Equipment—*mfg*	333111	3523
Spreading lime for crops: Soil Preparation, Planting, and Cultivating—*ag*	115112	711
Spreads, sandwich–cheese: Cheese—*mfg*	311513	2022
Spreads, sandwich–meat: Meat Processed from Carcasses—*mfg*	311612	2013
Spreads, sandwich–salad dressing based: Fruit and Vegetable Canning—*mfg*	311421	2035
Mayonnaise, Dressing and Other Prepared Sauce—*mfg*	311941	2035
Spring and Wire Product Manufacturing	**33261**	
Spring and Wire Product Manufacturing	**3326**	
Spring cushions: Mattress—*mfg*	33791	2515
Upholstered Household Furniture—*mfg*	337121	2515
Spring pins, metal: Bolt, Nut, Screw, Rivet and Washer—*mfg*	332722	3452
Spring pins, plastics: Plastics Pipe and Pipe Fitting—*mfg*	326122	3089
Plastics Product, All Other—*mfg*	326199	3089
Unsupported Plastics Profile Shape—*mfg*	326121	3089
Spring units for seats, made from purchased wire: Watch, Clock, and Part—*mfg*	334518	3495
Wire Spring—*mfg*	332612	3495
Spring washers, metal: Bolt, Nut, Screw, Rivet and Washer—*mfg*	332722	3452
Spring washers, plastics: Plastics Pipe and Pipe Fitting—*mfg*	326122	3089
Plastics Product, All Other—*mfg*	326199	3089
Unsupported Plastics Profile Shape—*mfg*	326121	3089
Spring winding and forming machines: Machine Tool (Metal Forming Types)—*mfg*	333513	3542
Springs, assembled–bed and box: Mattress—*mfg*	33791	2515
Upholstered Household Furniture—*mfg*	337121	2515
Springs, except complete bedsprings–made from purchased wire: Watch, Clock, and Part—*mfg*	334518	3495
Wire Spring—*mfg*	332612	3495
Springs, precision–clock, gun, instrument, and mechanical: Watch, Clock, and Part—*mfg*	334518	3495
Wire Spring—*mfg*	332612	3495
Springs, steel–except wire: Steel Spring (except Wire)—*mfg*	332611	3493
Sprinkler system installation-contractors: Plumbing, Heating and Air-Conditioning Contractors—*const*	23511	1711
Sprinkler systems, except agricultural: Cosmetics, Beauty Supplies and Perfume Stores—*retail*	44612	5087
Service Establishment Equipment and Supplies—*whlse*	42185	5087
Sprinkler systems, fire–automatic: General Purpose Machinery , All Other—*mfg*	333999	3569
Sprinklers, lawn: Fabricated Metal Product, All Other Miscellaneous—*mfg*	332999	3432
Plumbing Fixture Fitting and Trim—*mfg*	332913	3432
Sprockets: Industrial Machinery and Equipment—*whlse*	42183	5085
Industrial Supplies—*whlse*	42184	5085
Sprockets (power transmission equipment): Mechanical Power Transmission Equipment—*mfg*	333613	3568
Sprouts, made in malthouses: Malt—*mfg*	311213	2083
Spruce gum, gathering of: Crop Farming, All Other Miscellaneous—*ag*	111998	831
Forest Nurseries and Gathering of Forest Products—*ag*	11321	831
Spudding in oil and gas wells on a contract basis: Drilling Oil and Gas Wells—*mining*	213111	1381
Spumoni: Ice Cream and Frozen Dessert—*mfg*	31152	2024
Spun metal products: Metal Stamping—*mfg*	332116	3469
Spun yarn–cotton, silk, manmade fiber, wool, and animal fiber: Yarn Spinning Mills—*mfg*	313111	2281
Spunbonded fabrics: Nonwoven Fabric Mills—*mfg*	31323	2297
Spyglasses: Optical Instrument and Lens—*mfg*	333314	3827
Squab farms: Poultry Production, Other—*ag*	11239	259
Squares for walls and ceilings, concrete: Concrete Pipe—*mfg*	327332	3272
Concrete Product, Other—*mfg*	32739	3272
Nonmetallic Mineral Product, All Other Miscellaneous—*mfg*	327999	3272
Squares, carpenter: Hand and Edge Tool—*mfg*	332212	3423
Squash equipment, except apparel: Sporting and Athletic Goods—*mfg*	33992	3949
Squash farms: Vegetable (except Potato) and Melon Farming, Other—*ag*	111219	161
Squibbs, electric: Explosives—*mfg*	32592	2892
Squid, catching of: Shellfish Fishing—*ag*	114112	913
Stabilizers, aircraft: Aircraft Part and Auxiliary Equipment, Other—*mfg*	336413	3728
Fluid Power Valve and Hose Fitting—*mfg*	332912	3728
Stabilizing bars (cargo), metal: Fabricated Metal Product, All Other Miscellaneous—*mfg*	332999	3499
Stables, racing: Race Tracks—*arts*	711212	7948
Spectator Sports, Other—*arts*	711219	7948
Stackers, hay and grain: Conveyor and Conveying Equipment—*mfg*	333922	3523
Farm Machinery and Equipment—*mfg*	333111	3523
Stackers, industrial: Industrial Machinery and Equipment—*whlse*	42183	5084
Stackers, power (industrial truck stackers): Fabricated Metal Product, All Other Miscellaneous—*mfg*	332999	3537
Industrial Truck, Tractor, Trailer and Stacker Machinery—*mfg*	333924	3537
Metal Container, Other—*mfg*	332439	3537
Stacking carts: Fabricated Metal Product, All Other Miscellaneous—*mfg*	332999	3537
Industrial Truck, Tractor, Trailer and Stacker Machinery—*mfg*	333924	3537

Description	NAICS	SIC
Metal Container, Other—*mfg*	332439	3537
Stacking machines, automatic: Fabricated Metal Product, All Other Miscellaneous—*mfg*	332999	3537
Industrial Truck, Tractor, Trailer and Stacker Machinery—*mfg*	333924	3537
Metal Container, Other—*mfg*	332439	3537
Stadium construction–general contractors: Building, Commercial and Institutional—*const*	23332	1542
Stadium seating: Institutional Furniture—*mfg*	337127	2531
Stadiums (sports promotion): Agents and Managers for Artists, Athletes, Entertainers and Other Public Figures—*arts*	71141	7941
Promoters of Performing Arts, Sports and Similar Events with Facilities—*arts*	71131	7941
Promoters of Performing Arts, Sports and Similar Events without Facilities—*arts*	71132	7941
Spectator Sports, Other—*arts*	711219	7941
Sports Teams and Clubs—*arts*	711211	7941
Stage lighting equipment: Lighting Equipment, Other—*mfg*	335129	3648
Stain removers: Polish and Other Sanitation Good—*mfg*	325612	2842
Stained glass, made from purchased glass: Glass Product Made of Purchased Glass—*mfg*	327215	3231
Stainless steel: Iron and Steel Mills—*mfg*	331111	3312
Petroleum and Coal Productsa, All Other—*mfg*	324199	3312
Stainless steel, brazing (hardening) for the trade: Metal Heat Treating—*mfg*	332811	3398
Stains, biological: Organic Dye and Pigment—*mfg*	325132	2865
Petrochemical—*mfg*	32511	2865
Stains–varnish, oil, and wax: Paint and Coating—*mfg*	32551	2851
Stair elevators–motor powered: Elevator and Moving Stairway—*mfg*	333921	3534
Stair railings, metal: Ornamental and Architectural Metal Work—*mfg*	332323	3446
Stair railings, wood: Millwork (including Flooring), Other—*mfg*	321918	2431
Wood Window and Door—*mfg*	321911	2431
Stair treads, fabricated metal: Ornamental and Architectural Metal Work—*mfg*	332323	3446
Stair treads, rubber: Fabric Coating Mills—*mfg*	31332	3069
Rubber Product, All Other—*mfg*	326299	3069
Staircases and stairs, wood: Millwork (including Flooring), Other—*mfg*	321918	2431
Wood Window and Door—*mfg*	321911	2431
Staircases, prefabricated metal: Ornamental and Architectural Metal Work—*mfg*	332323	3446
Stairs, prefabricated metal: Ornamental and Architectural Metal Work—*mfg*	332323	3446
Stairways, moving: Elevator and Moving Stairway—*mfg*	333921	3534
Stakes, surveyors'–wood: Manufacturing, All Other Miscellaneous—*mfg*	339999	2499
Wood Container and Pallet—*mfg*	32192	2499
Wood Product, All Other Miscellaneous—*mfg*	321999	2499
Stalk choppers, shredders: Farm Machinery and Equipment—*mfg*	333111	3523
Stall urinals, vitreous china: Vitreous China Plumbing Fixture and China and Earthenware Fittings and Bathroom Accessories—*mfg*	327111	3261
Stamp and cash boxes, stamped metal: Metal Stamping—*mfg*	332116	3469
Stamp pad ink: Basic Organic Chemical, All Other—*mfg*	325199	2899
Chemical Product, All Other Miscellaneous—*mfg*	325998	2899
Stamp pads: Marking Device—*mfg*	339943	3953
Stamping devices, hand: Marking Device—*mfg*	339943	3953
Stamping fabrics for embroidering: Apparel Accessories and Apparel, Other—*mfg*	315999	2396
Screen Printing, Commercial—*mfg*	323113	2396
Textile Product Mills, All Other Miscellaneous—*mfg*	314999	2396
Stamping ink: Basic Organic Chemical, All Other—*mfg*	325199	2899
Chemical Product, All Other Miscellaneous—*mfg*	325998	2899
Stamping metal, for the trade: Metal Stamping—*mfg*	332116	3469
Stamping mill mining machinery: Mining Machinery and Equipment—*mfg*	333131	3532
Stamping on finished fabric articles: Apparel Accessories and Apparel, Other—*mfg*	315999	2396
Screen Printing, Commercial—*mfg*	323113	2396
Textile Product Mills, All Other Miscellaneous—*mfg*	314999	2396
Stamps, hand–time, date, postmark, cancelling, shoe, and textile marking: Marking Device—*mfg*	339943	3953
Stamps, mail-order: Electronic Shopping and Mail-Order Houses—*retail*	45411	5961
Stamps, philatelist: Toy and Hobby Goods and Supplies—*whlse*	42192	5092
Stamps, philatelist-retail–except mail-order: Stores (except Tobacco Stores), All Other Miscellaneous—*retail*	453998	5999
Stanchions and standards, barn: Farm Machinery and Equipment—*mfg*	333111	3523
Stand boards: Sporting and Athletic Goods—*mfg*	33992	3949
Standard cells: Electronic Coil, Transformer, and Other Inductor—*mfg*	334416	3825
Instrument for Measuring and Testing Electricity and Electrical Signals—*mfg*	334515	3825
Standardizing of metals and metal products, for the trade: Costume Jewelry and Novelty—*mfg*	339914	3479
Jewelry (except Costume)—*mfg*	339911	3479
Metal Coating, Engraving (except Jewelry and Silverware), and Allied Services to Manufacturers—*mfg*	332812	3479
Silverware and Plated Ware—*mfg*	339912	3479
Standards and calibration equipment for electrical measuring, except laboratory: Electronic Coil, Transformer, and Other Inductor—*mfg*	334416	3825
Instrument for Measuring and Testing Electricity and Electrical Signals—*mfg*	334515	3825
Standing wave ratio measuring equipment: Electronic Coil, Transformer, and Other Inductor—*mfg*	334416	3825

ALPHABETICAL INDEX	NAICS	SIC
Instrument for Measuring and Testing Electricity and Electrical Signals—*mfg*	334515	3825
Standpipes: Air-Conditioning and Warm Air Heating Equipment and Commercial and Industrial Refrigeration Equipment—*mfg*	333415	3443
Metal Tank (Heavy Gauge)—*mfg*	33242	3443
Plate Work—*mfg*	332313	3443
Power Boiler and Heat Exchanger—*mfg*	33241	3443
Stands, camera and projector: Photographic and Photocopying Equipment—*mfg*	333315	3861
Photographic Film, Paper, Plate and Chemical—*mfg*	325992	3861
Stands, ground servicing aircraft: Fabricated Metal Product, All Other Miscellaneous—*mfg*	332999	3537
Industrial Truck, Tractor, Trailer and Stacker Machinery—*mfg*	333924	3537
Metal Container, Other—*mfg*	332439	3537
Stands, merchandise display–except wood: Showcase, Partition, Shelving, and Locker—*mfg*	337215	2542
Stands, merchandise display–wood: Architectural Woodwork and Millwork, Custom—*mfg*	337212	2541
Showcase, Partition, Shelving, and Locker—*mfg*	337215	2541
Wood Kitchen Cabinet and Counter Top—*mfg*	33711	2541
Stands, music: Musical Instrument—*mfg*	339992	3931
Stands–telephone, bedside, and smoking-wood: Nonupholstered Wood Household Furniture—*mfg*	337122	2511
Stannic and stannous chloride: Basic Inorganic Chemical, All Other—*mfg*	325188	2819
Chemical Product, All Other Miscellaneous—*mfg*	325998	2819
Staple removers: Lead Pencil and Art Good—*mfg*	339942	3579
Office Machinery—*mfg*	333313	3579
Watch, Clock, and Part—*mfg*	334518	3579
Staples: Hardware—*whlse*	42171	5072
Staples, nonferrous metal (including wire): Iron and Steel Mills—*mfg*	331111	3399
Secondary Smelting and Alloying of Aluminum—*mfg*	331314	3399
Secondary Smelting, Refining, and Alloying of Copper—*mfg*	331423	3399
Secondary Smelting, Refining, and Alloying of Nonferrous Metal (except Copper and Aluminum)—*mfg*	331492	3399
Staples, steel–wire or cut: Fabricated Wire Product, Other—*mfg*	332618	3315
Steel Wire Drawing—*mfg*	331222	3315
Staples, wire–made from purchased wire: Fabricated Wire Product, Other—*mfg*	332618	3496
Stapling machines, office: Lead Pencil and Art Good—*mfg*	339942	3579
Office Machinery—*mfg*	333313	3579
Watch, Clock, and Part—*mfg*	334518	3579
Star routes, local: Freight (except Used Goods) Trucking, Local Specialized—*trans*	48422	4212
General Freight Trucking, Local—*trans*	48411	4212
Starch and Vegetable Fats and Oils Manufacturing	**31122**	
Starch preparations, laundry: Polish and Other Sanitation Good—*mfg*	325612	2842
Starch, instant: Wet Corn Milling—*mfg*	311221	2046
Starch, liquid: Wet Corn Milling—*mfg*	311221	2046
Starches: Grocery and Related Products, Other—*whlse*	42249	5149
Starches, edible and industrial: Wet Corn Milling—*mfg*	311221	2046
Starches, plastics: Polish and Other Sanitation Good—*mfg*	325612	2842
Started pullet farms: Chicken Egg Production—*ag*	11231	252
Starter and generator repair, automotive: Automotive Mechanical and Electrical Repair and Maintenance, Other—*serv*	811118	7539
Starter and starter parts, internal combustion engine: Motor Vehicle Electrical and Electronic Equipment, Other—*mfg*	336322	3694
Starters, aircraft–nonelectric: Aircraft Engine and Engine Parts—*mfg*	336412	3724
Starters, electric motor: Relay and Industrial Control—*mfg*	335314	3625
Starters, fluorescent: Current-Carrying Wiring Device—*mfg*	335931	3643
Starting equipment, for streetcars: Motor and Generator—*mfg*	335312	3621
Starting switches, fluorescent lamp: Current-Carrying Wiring Device—*mfg*	335931	3643
State banks, commercial: Banking, Commercial—*fin*	52211	6022
Credit Card Issuing—*fin*	52221	6022
Depository Credit Intermediation, Other—*fin*	52219	6022
Trust, Fiduciary and Custody Activities—*fin*	523991	6022
State credit unions, not federally chartered: Credit Unions—*fin*	52213	6062
State education departments: Education Programs, Administration of—*pub*	92311	9411
State police: Police Protection—*pub*	92212	9221
State tax commissions: Public Finance—*pub*	92113	9311
Static power supply converters for electronic applications: Electronic Component, Other—*mfg*	334419	3679
Motor Vehicle Electrical and Electronic Equipment, Other—*mfg*	336322	3679
Printed Circuit/Electronics Assembly—*mfg*	334418	3679
Radio and Television Broadcasting and Wireless Communications Equipment—*mfg*	33422	3679
Static pressure regulators: Automatic Environmental Control for Residential, Commercial and Appliance Use—*mfg*	334512	3822
Station wagons (motor vehicles): Automobile—*mfg*	336111	3711
Heavy Duty Truck—*mfg*	33612	3711
Light Truck and Utility Vehicle—*mfg*	336112	3711
Military Armored Vehicle, Tank and Tank Component—*mfg*	336992	3711
Motor Vehicle Body—*mfg*	336211	3711
Stationary and Office Supplies Wholesalers	**42212**	**5112**
Stationers' glassware–inkwell, clip cups, etc.: Pressed and Blown Glass and Glassware, Other—*mfg*	327212	3229
Stationers' sundries, rubber: Fabric Coating Mills—*mfg*	31332	3069
Rubber Product, All Other—*mfg*	326299	3069
Stationery: Stationery, Tablet, and Related Product—*mfg*	322233	2678
Stationery and stationery supplies: Office Supplies and Stationery Stores—*retail*	45321	5112
Stationary and Office Supplies—*whlse*	42212	5112

Description	NAICS	SIC
Stationery articles, pottery: Vitreous China, Fine Earthenware and Other Pottery Product—*mfg*	327112	3269
Stationery Product Manufacturing	**32223**	
Stationery stores: Office Supplies and Stationery Stores—*retail*	45321	5943
Stationery, Tablet, and Related Product Manufacturing	**322233**	**2678**
Stationery–except lithographed or gravure: Digital Printing—*mfg*	323115	2759
Flexographic Printing, Commercial—*mfg*	323112	2759
Printing, Other Commercial—*mfg*	323119	2759
Quick Printing—*mfg*	323114	2759
Stationery–gravure printing: Gravure Printing, Commercial—*mfg*	323111	2754
Stations operated by railway terminal companies: Rail Support Activities—*trans*	48821	4013
Short Line Railroads—*trans*	482112	4013
Stations, cream: Dairy Product (except Dried or Canned)—*whlse*	42243	5143
Statistical reports (periodicals), publishing and printing, or publishing only: Periodical Publishers—*info*	51112	2721
Stators for motors: Motor and Generator—*mfg*	335312	3621
Statuary: Nondurable Goods, Other Miscellaneous—*whlse*	42299	5199
Statuary, marble: Cut Stone and Stone Product—*mfg*	327991	3281
Statuary–gypsum, clay, papier-mache, scagliola, and metal-factory productiononly: Gypsum and Gypsum Product—*mfg*	32742	3299
Nonmetallic Mineral Product, All Other Miscellaneous—*mfg*	327999	3299
Stave bolts, wood–hewn: Logging—*ag*	11331	2411
Staves, barrel–sawed or split: Cut Stock, Resawing Lumber, and Planing—*mfg*	321912	2429
Sawmills—*mfg*	321113	2429
Wood Product, All Other Miscellaneous—*mfg*	321999	2429
Staves, silo–concrete: Concrete Pipe—*mfg*	327332	3272
Concrete Product, Other—*mfg*	32739	3272
Nonmetallic Mineral Product, All Other Miscellaneous—*mfg*	327999	3272
Stays, shoe: Fastener, Button, Needle and Pin—*mfg*	339993	3131
Leather Good, All Other—*mfg*	316999	3131
Wood Product, All Other Miscellaneous—*mfg*	321999	3131
Steam and Air-Conditioning Supply	**22133**	**4961**
Steam and other packing: Gasket, Packing, and Sealing Device—*mfg*	339991	3053
Steam baths: Personal Care Services, Other—*serv*	812199	7299
Steam cleaning of building exteriors–contractors: Trade Contractors, All Other Special—*const*	23599	1799
Steam condensers: Air-Conditioning and Warm Air Heating Equipment and Commercial and Industrial Refrigeration Equipment—*mfg*	333415	3443
Metal Tank (Heavy Gauge)—*mfg*	33242	3443
Plate Work—*mfg*	332313	3443
Power Boiler and Heat Exchanger—*mfg*	33241	3443
Steam cookers, restaurant type: Machinery, Other Commercial and Service Industry—*mfg*	333319	3589
Steam engines, except locomotives: Turbine and Turbine Generator Set Unit—*mfg*	333611	3511
Steam fitting–contractors: Plumbing, Heating and Air-Conditioning Contractors—*const*	23511	1711
Steam fittings: Building Material Dealers, Other–-*retail*	44419	5074
Plumbing and Heating Equipment and Supplies (Hydronics)—*whlse*	42172	5074
Steam fittings and specialties, except plumbers' brass goods and fittings, metal: Fabricated Metal Product, All Other Miscellaneous—*mfg*	332999	3494
Other Metal Valve and Pipe Fitting, Other—*mfg*	332919	3494
Steam governors: Turbine and Turbine Generator Set Unit—*mfg*	333611	3511
Steam heating apparatus, domestic: Heating Equipment (except Electric and Warm Air Furnaces)—*mfg*	333414	3433
Steam heating systems (suppliers of heat): Steam and Air-Conditioning Supply—*util*	22133	4961
Steam jet aftercoolers: Air-Conditioning and Warm Air Heating Equipment and Commercial and Industrial Refrigeration Equipment—*mfg*	333415	3443
Metal Tank (Heavy Gauge)—*mfg*	33242	3443
Plate Work—*mfg*	332313	3443
Power Boiler and Heat Exchanger—*mfg*	33241	3443
Steam jet inter condensers: Air-Conditioning and Warm Air Heating Equipment and Commercial and Industrial Refrigeration Equipment—*mfg*	333415	3443
Metal Tank (Heavy Gauge)—*mfg*	33242	3443
Plate Work—*mfg*	332313	3443
Power Boiler and Heat Exchanger—*mfg*	33241	3443
Steam pressure controls, residential and commercial type: Automatic Environmental Control for Residential, Commercial and Appliance Use—*mfg*	334512	3822
Steam separators (machinery): General Purpose Machinery , All Other—*mfg*	333999	3569
Steam supply systems, including geothermal: Steam and Air-Conditioning Supply—*util*	22133	4961
Steam tables: Machinery, Other Commercial and Service Industry—*mfg*	333319	3589
Steam traps, over 15 lbs. w.s.p.: Industrial Valve—*mfg*	332911	3491
Steam turbine generator set units, complete: Turbine and Turbine Generator Set Unit—*mfg*	333611	3511
Steam turbines: Turbine and Turbine Generator Set Unit—*mfg*	333611	3511
Steamship leasing: Air, Rail, and Water Equipment Rental and Leasing, Commercial—*real*	532411	4499
Navigational Services to Shipping—*trans*	48833	4499
Port and Harbor Operations—*trans*	48831	4499
Water, Other Support Activities for—*trans*	48839	4499
Steamship ticket offices, not operated by transportation companies: Transportation, All Other Support Activities—*trans*	488999	4729
Travel Arrangement and Reservation Services, All Other—*admin*	561599	4729
Stearic acid: Basic Organic Chemical, All Other—*mfg*	325199	2899
Chemical Product, All Other Miscellaneous—*mfg*	325998	2899

ALPHABETICAL INDEX	NAICS	SIC
Stearic acid esters: Basic Organic Chemical, All Other—*mfg*	325199	2869
Stearic acid salts: Basic Organic Chemical, All Other—*mfg*	325199	2869
Stearin, animal–inedible: Fats and Oils Refining and Blending—*mfg*	311225	2077
Fresh and Frozen Seafood Processing—*mfg*	311712	2077
Rendering and Meat By-product Processing—*mfg*	311613	2077
Seafood Canning—*mfg*	311711	2077
Steatite mining: Crushed and Broken Stone and Quarrying, Other—*mining*	212319	1499
Non-Metallic Mineral, All Other—*mining*	212399	1499
Steatite porcelain insulators: Porcelain Electrical Supply—*mfg*	327113	3264
Steatite, ground or otherwise treated: Ground or Treated Mineral and Earth—*mfg*	327992	3295
Steel: Metal Service Centers and Offices—*whlse*	42151	5051
Steel balls: Iron and Steel Mills—*mfg*	331111	3399
Secondary Smelting, Refining, and Alloying of Copper—*mfg*	331423	3399
Secondary Smelting, Refining, and Alloying of Nonferrous Metal (except Copper and Aluminum)—*mfg*	331492	3399
Steel bars, sheets, and strip–cold-rolled-not made in hot-rolling mills: Cold-Rolled Steel Shape—*mfg*	331221	3316
Steel castings, except investment: Steel Foundries, (except Investment)—*mfg*	331513	3325
Steel Foundries, (except Investment)	**331513**	**3325**
Steel foundries, except investment: Steel Foundries, (except Investment)—*mfg*	331513	3325
Steel Investment Foundries	**331512**	**3324**
Steel joists, open web–long-span series: Fabricated Structural Metal—*mfg*	332312	3441
Steel line engraving, for the printing trade: Digital Printing—*mfg*	323115	2759
Flexographic Printing, Commercial—*mfg*	323112	2759
Printing, Other Commercial—*mfg*	323119	2759
Quick Printing—*mfg*	323114	2759
Steel railroad car racks (for transporting motor vehicles fabricated): Fabricated Structural Metal—*mfg*	332312	3441
Steel rolling machinery: Rolling Mill Machinery and Equipment—*mfg*	333516	3547
Steel shot abrasives: Abrasive Product—*mfg*	32791	3291
Fabricated Metal Product, All Other Miscellaneous—*mfg*	332999	3291
Steel Spring (except Wire) Manufacturing	**332611**	**3493**
Steel springs, except wire: Steel Spring (except Wire)—*mfg*	332611	3493
Steel tire cord and tire cord fabrics: Tire Cord and Tire Fabric Mills—*mfg*	314992	2296
Steel wire cages, made in wire-drawing plants: Fabricated Wire Product, Other—*mfg*	332618	3315
Steel Wire Drawing—*mfg*	331222	3315
Steel Wire Drawing	**331222**	**3315**
Steel wool: Abrasive Product—*mfg*	32791	3291
Fabricated Metal Product, All Other Miscellaneous—*mfg*	332999	3291

ALPHABETICAL INDEX	NAICS	SIC
Steel work, structural–contractors: Structural Steel Erection Contractors—*const*	23591	1791
Steel works producing bars, rods, plates, sheets, structural shapes, etc.: Iron and Steel Mills—*mfg*	331111	3312
Petroleum and Coal Productsa, All Other—*mfg*	324199	3312
Steelwork, ornamental–contractors: Trade Contractors, All Other Special—*const*	23599	1799
Steeplejacks: Trade Contractors, All Other Special—*const*	23599	1799
Steepwater concentrate: Wet Corn Milling—*mfg*	311221	2046
Steering mechanisms, motor vehicle: Motor Vehicle Parts, All Other—*mfg*	336399	3714
Motor Vehicle Steering and Suspension Components (except Spring)—*mfg*	33633	3714
Stemming and redrying of tobacco: Tobacco Product, Other—*mfg*	312229	2141
Tobacco Stemming and Redrying—*mfg*	31221	2141
Stemware, glass: Pressed and Blown Glass and Glassware, Other—*mfg*	327212	3229
Stencil board: Converted Paper Product, All Other—*mfg*	322298	2675
Die-Cut Paper and Paperboard Office Supplies—*mfg*	322231	2675
Paperboard Mills—*mfg*	32213	2631
Surface-Coated Paperboard—*mfg*	322292	2675
Stencil cards for addressing machines: Converted Paper Product, All Other—*mfg*	322298	2675
Die-Cut Paper and Paperboard Office Supplies—*mfg*	322231	2675
Surface-Coated Paperboard—*mfg*	322292	2675
Stencil correction compounds: Basic Organic Chemical, All Other—*mfg*	325199	2899
Chemical Product, All Other Miscellaneous—*mfg*	325998	2899
Stencil paper for typewriters: Carbon Paper and Inked Ribbon—*mfg*	339944	3955
Stencil paper, gelatin or spirit process: Carbon Paper and Inked Ribbon—*mfg*	339944	3955
Stencils for use in painting and marking:e.g., metal, cardboard: Marking Device—*mfg*	339943	3953
Stenographers, public: Court Reporting and Stenotype Services—*admin*	561492	7338
Document Preparation Services—*admin*	56141	7338
Stenographic service: Court Reporting and Stenotype Services—*admin*	561492	7338
Document Preparation Services—*admin*	56141	7338
Step positioners for transmitting equipment: Electronic Component, Other—*mfg*	334419	3679
Motor Vehicle Electrical and Electronic Equipment, Other—*mfg*	336322	3679
Printed Circuit/Electronics Assembly—*mfg*	334418	3679
Radio and Television Broadcasting and Wireless Communications Equipment—*mfg*	33422	3679
Step-ins: Underwear and Nightwear Knitting Mills—*mfg*	315192	2254

Stepladders, metal: Fabricated Metal Product, All Other Miscellaneous—*mfg*	332999	3499
Stepladders, wood: Manufacturing, All Other Miscellaneous—*mfg*	339999	2499
Wood Container and Pallet—*mfg*	32192	2499
Wood Product, All Other Miscellaneous—*mfg*	321999	2499
Steps, prefabricated concrete: Concrete Pipe—*mfg*	327332	3272
Concrete Product, Other—*mfg*	32739	3272
Nonmetallic Mineral Product, All Other Miscellaneous—*mfg*	327999	3272
Stereo cabinets, woocl: Wood Television, Radio, and Sewing Machine Cabinet—*mfg*	337129	2517
Stereo equipment: Electrical Appliance, Television and Radio Set—*whlse*	42162	5064
Stereo regular elastomers: Synthetic Rubber—*mfg*	325212	2822
Stereophonic equipment repair: Communication Equipment Repair and Maintenance—*serv*	811213	7622
Consumer Electronics Repair and Maintenance—*serv*	811211	7622
Radio, Television and Other Electronics Stores—*retail*	443112	7622
Stereopticons: Photographic and Photocopying Equipment—*mfg*	333315	3861
Photographic Film, Paper, Plate and Chemical—*mfg*	325992	3861
Stereotopographs: Measuring and Controlling Device, Other—*mfg*	334519	3829
Surgical and Medical Instrument—*mfg*	339112	3829
Stereotype plates: Prepress Services—*mfg*	323122	2796
Stereotyping for the trade: Prepress Services—*mfg*	323122	2796
Stereotyping machines: Printing Machinery and Equipment—*mfg*	333293	3555
Sterilizers, dental: Dental Equipment and Supplies—*mfg*	339114	3843
Sterilizers, hospital and surgical: Electromedical and Electrotherapeutic Apparatus—*mfg*	334510	3842
Surgical Appliance and Supplies—*mfg*	339113	3842
Sterilizing chambers, metal plate: Air-Conditioning and Warm Air Heating Equipment and Commercial and Industrial Refrigeration Equipment—*mfg*	333415	3443
Metal Tank (Heavy Gauge)—*mfg*	33242	3443
Plate Work—*mfg*	332313	3443
Power Boiler and Heat Exchanger—*mfg*	33241	3443
Stethoscopes and stethographs: Surgical and Medical Instrument—*mfg*	339112	3841
Stevedoring: Marine Cargo Handling—*trans*	48832	4491
Port and Harbor Operations—*trans*	48831	4491
Stew, beef and lamb: Meat Processed from Carcasses—*mfg*	311612	2013
Stews, fish and seafood–canned: Seafood Canning—*mfg*	311711	2091
Stews, fish and seafood–frozen: Fresh and Frozen Seafood Processing—*mfg*	311712	2092
Sticks, abrasive: Abrasive Product—*mfg*	32791	3291
Fabricated Metal Product, All Other Miscellaneous—*mfg*	332999	3291
Sticks, printers': Printing Machinery and Equipment—*mfg*	333293	3555
Sticks, sports–e.g., hockey, lacrosse: Sporting and Athletic Goods—*mfg*	33992	3949
Stilbene dyes: Organic Dye and Pigment—*mfg*	325132	2865
Petrochemical—*mfg*	32511	2865
Still film producers: Graphic Design Services—*prof*	54143	7336
Stills, pressure–metal plate: Air-Conditioning and Warm Air Heating Equipment and Commercial and Industrial Refrigeration Equipment—*mfg*	333415	3443
Metal Tank (Heavy Gauge)—*mfg*	33242	3443
Plate Work—*mfg*	332313	3443
Power Boiler and Heat Exchanger—*mfg*	33241	3443
Stirrups, wood and metal: Leather Good, All Other—*mfg*	316999	3199
Stitching, decorative and novelty–for the trade: Men's and Boys' Cut and Sew Apparel Contractors—*mfg*	315211	2395
Textile Product Mills, All Other Miscellaneous—*mfg*	314999	2395
Women's and Girls' Cut and Sew Apparel Contractors—*mfg*	315212	2395
Stock accident and health insurance: Direct Health and Medical Insurance Carriers—*fin*	524114	6321
Insurance Funds, Other—*fin*	52519	6321
Reinsurance Carriers—*fin*	52413	6321
Stock brokers and dealers: Financial Investment Activities, Miscellaneous—*fin*	523999	6211
Intermediation, Miscellaneous—*fin*	52391	6211
Investment Banking and Securities Dealing—*fin*	52311	6211
Securities Brokerage—*fin*	52312	6211
Stock car racing: Race Tracks—*arts*	711212	7948
Spectator Sports, Other—*arts*	711219	7948
Stock certificates, engraved: Digital Printing—*mfg*	323115	2759
Flexographic Printing, Commercial—*mfg*	323112	2759
Printing, Other Commercial—*mfg*	323119	2759
Quick Printing—*mfg*	323114	2759
Stock companies, theatrical: Theater Companies and Dinner Theaters—*arts*	71111	7922
Stock exchanges: Securities and Commodity Exchanges—*fin*	52321	6231
Stock feeds, dry: Animal Food, Other—*mfg*	311119	2048
Stock fire, marine, and casualty insurance: Direct Property and Casualty Insurance Carriers—*fin*	524126	6331
Insurance Funds, Other—*fin*	52519	6331
Reinsurance Carriers—*fin*	52413	6331
Stock life insurance: Direct Life Insurance Carriers—*fin*	524113	6311
Reinsurance Carriers—*fin*	52413	6311
Stock transfer agents: Financial Investment Activities, Miscellaneous—*fin*	523999	6289
Trust, Fiduciary and Custody Activities—*fin*	523991	6289
Stock, chair–hardwood-turned, shaped, or carved: Cut Stock, Resawing Lumber, and Planing—*mfg*	321912	2426
Millwork (including Flooring), Other—*mfg*	321918	2426
Showcase, Partition, Shelving, and Locker—*mfg*	337215	2426
Wood Product, All Other Miscellaneous—*mfg*	321999	2426
Stockinette, surgical: Surgical Appliance and Supplies—*mfg*	339113	3842
Stockinettes: Underwear and Nightwear Knitting Mills—*mfg*	315192	2259
Stockings, except women's and misses' full-length and knee-length: Hosiery and Sock Mills, Other—*mfg*	315119	2252

ALPHABETICAL INDEX	NAICS	SIC
Sheer Hosiery Mills—*mfg*	315111	2252
Stockings, women's full-length and knee-length, except socks: Sheer Hosiery Mills--*mfg*	315111	2251
Stockyards, exclusively for fattening cattle: Cattle Feedlots—*ag*	112112	211
Stockyards, not primarily for fattening or selling livestock: Rail Support Activities—*trans*	48821	4789
Scenic and Sightseeing, Land—*trans*	48711	4789
Transportation, All Other Support Activities—*trans*	488999	4789
Stogies: Tobacco Product, Other—*mfg*	312229	2121
Stokers, mechanical–domestic and industrial: Heating Equipment (except Electric and Warm Air Furnaces)—*mfg*	333414	3433
Stone forks (handtools): Hand and Edge Tool—*mfg*	332212	3423
Stone Mining and Quarrying	**21231**	
Stone pulverizers, stationary: Mining Machinery and Equipment—*mfg*	333131	3532
Stone setting-contractors: Masonry and Stone Contractors—*const*	23541	1741
Stone tumblers: Industrial Machinery, All Other—*mfg*	333298	3559
Machinery, Other Commercial and Service Industry—*mfg*	333319	3559
Stone working machinery: Industrial Machinery, All Other—*mfg*	333298	3559
Machinery, Other Commercial and Service Industry—*mfg*	333319	3559
Stone, building: Brick, Stone and Related Material—*whlse*	42132	5032
Building Material Dealers, Other—*retail*	44419	5032
Stone, cast concrete: Concrete Pipe—*mfg*	327332	3272
Concrete Product, Other—*mfg*	32739	3272
Nonmetallic Mineral Product, All Other Miscellaneous—*mfg*	327999	3272
Stone, crushed or broken: Brick, Stone and Related Material—*whlse*	42132	5032
Building Material Dealers, Other—*retail*	44419	5032
Stone, cut and shaped: Cut Stone and Stone Product—*mfg*	327991	3281
Stone, quarrying and processing of own stone products: Cut Stone and Stone Product—*mfg*	327991	3281
Stonecutters' handtools: Hand and Edge Tool—*mfg*	332212	3423
Stones, abrasive: Abrasive Product—*mfg*	32791	3291
Fabricated Metal Product, All Other Miscellaneous—*mfg*	332999	3291
Stones, crystalline–rough: Jewelry Stores—*retail*	44831	5999
Stores (except Tobacco Stores), All Other Miscellaneous—*retail*	453998	5999
Stones, synthetic–for gem stones and industrial use: Gypsum and Gypsum Product—*mfg*	32742	3299
Nonmetallic Mineral Product, All Other Miscellaneous—*mfg*	327999	3299
Stones–preparation of real and imitation gems for settings: Jewelers' Material and Lapidary Work—*mfg*	339913	3915
Stoneware clay mining: Clay and Ceramic and Refractory Minerals—*mining*	212325	1459
Stoneware, chemical (pottery products): Vitreous China, Fine Earthenware and Other Pottery Product—*mfg*	327112	3269
Stonework erection–contractors: Masonry and Stone Contractors—*const*	23541	1741
Stools, factory: Institutional Furniture—*mfg*	337127	2599

ALPHABETICAL INDEX	NAICS	SIC
Stools, household–metal: Metal Household Furniture—*mfg*	337124	2514
Stools, household–wood: Nonupholstered Wood Household Furniture—*mfg*	337122	2511
Stools, metal–with casters–not household or office: Institutional Furniture—*mfg*	337127	2599
Stools, office–rotating-except wood: Nonwood Office Furniture—*mfg*	337214	2522
Stools, office–wood: Wood Office Furniture—*mfg*	337211	2521
Stools, precast terrazzo: Concrete Pipe—*mfg*	327332	3272
Concrete Product, Other—*mfg*	32739	3272
Nonmetallic Mineral Product, All Other Miscellaneous—*mfg*	327999	3272
Stop cocks, except drain–metal: Fabricated Metal Product, All Other Miscellaneous—*mfg*	332999	3494
Other Metal Valve and Pipe Fitting, Other—*mfg*	332919	3494
Stopcocks (plumbers' supplies): Fabricated Metal Product, All Other Miscellaneous—*mfg*	332999	3432
Plumbing Fixture Fitting and Trim—*mfg*	332913	3432
Stoppers, cork: Manufacturing, All Other Miscellaneous—*mfg*	339999	2499
Wood Container and Pallet—*mfg*	32192	2499
Wood Product, All Other Miscellaneous—*mfg*	321999	2499
Stoppers, ear: Surgical Appliance and Supplies—*mfg*	339113	3842
Stoppers, glasshouse–clay: Clay Refractory—*mfg*	327124	3255
Stoppers, rubber: Fabric Coating Mills—*mfg*	31332	3069
Rubber Product, All Other—*mfg*	326299	3069
Storage and repair of fur and other garments for individuals: Personal and Household Goods Repair and Maintenance, Other—*serv*	81149	7219
Storage batteries: Storage Battery—*mfg*	335911	3691
Storage batteries, industrial: Building Material Dealers, Other—*retail*	44419	5063
Electrical Apparatus and Equipment, Wiring Supplies and Material—*whlse*	42161	5063
Storage battery chargers, engine generatortype: Motor and Generator—*mfg*	335312	3621
Storage Battery Manufacturing	**335911**	**3691**
Storage chests, household–wood: Nonupholstered Wood Household Furniture—*mfg*	337122	2511
Storage devices, computer: Computer Storage Device—*mfg*	334112	3572
Storage fixtures, except wood: Showcase, Partition, Shelving, and Locker—*mfg*	337215	2542
Storage fixtures, wood: Architectural Woodwork and Millwork, Custom—*mfg*	337212	2541
Showcase, Partition, Shelving, and Locker—*mfg*	337215	2541
Wood Kitchen Cabinet and Counter Top—*mfg*	33711	2541
Storage of goods at foreign trade zones: General Warehousing and Storage Facilities—*trans*	49311	4226
Refrigerated Warehousing and Storage Facilities—*trans*	49312	4226
Warehousing and Storage Facilities, Other—*trans*	49319	4226

Entry	NAICS	SIC
Storage of household goods–combined withlocal trucking: Freight (except Used Goods) Trucking, Local Specialized—*trans*	48422	4214
General Freight Trucking, Local—*trans*	48411	4214
Used Household and Office Goods Moving—*trans*	48421	4214
Storage of household goods–without localtrucking: General Warehousing and Storage Facilities—*trans*	49311	4226
Refrigerated Warehousing and Storage Facilities—*trans*	49312	4226
Warehousing and Storage Facilities, Other—*trans*	49319	4226
Storage of natural gas: Pipeline of Natural Gas—*trans*	48621	4922
Storage other than cold storage, farm product: Farm Product Warehousing and Storage Facilities—*trans*	49313	4221
Storage tanks, concrete: Concrete Pipe—*mfg*	327332	3272
Concrete Product, Other—*mfg*	32739	3272
Nonmetallic Mineral Product, All Other Miscellaneous—*mfg*	327999	3272
Storage tanks, metal plate: Air-Conditioning and Warm Air Heating Equipment and Commercial and Industrial Refrigeration Equipment—*mfg*	333415	3443
Metal Tank (Heavy Gauge)—*mfg*	33242	3443
Plate Work—*mfg*	332313	3443
Power Boiler and Heat Exchanger—*mfg*	33241	3443
Storage tanks, metal–erection–contractors: Structural Steel Erection Contractors—*const*	23591	1791
Storage, frozen or refrigerated goods: Refrigerated Warehousing and Storage Facilities—*trans*	49312	4222
Storage, furniture–without local trucking: General Warehousing and Storage Facilities—*trans*	49311	4226
Refrigerated Warehousing and Storage Facilities—*trans*	49312	4226
Warehousing and Storage Facilities, Other—*trans*	49319	4226
Storage, general: General Warehousing and Storage Facilities—*trans*	49311	4225
Lessors of Miniwarehouses and Self Storage Units—*real*	53113	4225
Storage, special–except farm products and cold storage: General Warehousing and Storage Facilities—*trans*	49311	4226
Refrigerated Warehousing and Storage Facilities—*trans*	49312	4226
Warehousing and Storage Facilities, Other—*trans*	49319	4226
Store construction–general contractors: Building, Commercial and Institutional—*const*	23332	1542
Store fixture installation–contractors: Carpentry Contractors—*const*	23551	1751
Store front installation, metal–contractors: Structural Steel Erection Contractors—*const*	23591	1791
Store fronts, porcelain enameled: Metal Stamping—*mfg*	332116	3469
Store fronts, prefabricated–metal, except porcelain enameled: Metal Window and Door—*mfg*	332321	3442
Store fronts, prefabricated–wood: Architectural Woodwork and Millwork, Custom—*mfg*	337212	2541
Showcase, Partition, Shelving, and Locker—*mfg*	337215	2541
Wood Kitchen Cabinet and Counter Top—*mfg*	33711	2541
Store Retailers (except Tobacco Stores), All Other Miscellaneous	**453998**	**5261**
Store Retailers, All Other Miscellaneous	**45399**	
Store Retailers, Miscellaneous	**453**	
Store Retailers, Other Miscellaneous	**4539**	
Storm doors and windows, metal: Metal Window and Door—*mfg*	332321	3442
Storm windows and sash, wood or metal: Building Material Dealers, Other—*retail*	44419	5211
Home Centers—*retail*	44411	5211
Storm windows, wood: Millwork (including Flooring), Other—*mfg*	321918	2431
Wood Window and Door—*mfg*	321911	2431
Stout (alcoholic beverage)-m/g: Breweries—*mfg*	31212	2082
Stove boards, sheet metal: Metal Container, Other—*mfg*	332439	3444
Sheet Metal Work—*mfg*	332322	3444
Stove lining, clay: Structural Clay Product, Other—*mfg*	327123	3259
Stove pipe and flues, sheet metal: Metal Container, Other—*mfg*	332439	3444
Sheet Metal Work—*mfg*	332322	3444
Stove polish: Polish and Other Sanitation Good—*mfg*	325612	2842
Stove repair shops: Appliance Repair and Maintenance—*serv*	811412	7699
Personal and Household Goods Repair and Maintenance, Other—*serv*	81149	7699
Stoves and related electric and gas appliances: Household Appliance Stores—*retail*	443111	5722
Stoves, commercial: Machinery, Other Commercial and Service Industry—*mfg*	333319	3589
Stoves, cooking or heating, household–electric: Electrical Appliance, Television and Radio Set—*whlse*	42162	5064
Stoves, cooking–except electric: Building Material Dealers, Other—*retail*	44419	5074
Plumbing and Heating Equipment and Supplies (Hydronics)—*whlse*	42172	5074
Stoves, disk: Household Cooking Appliance—*mfg*	335221	3631
Stoves, household–cooking: Household Cooking Appliance—*mfg*	335221	3631
Stoves. household–heating-except electric: Heating Equipment (except Electric and Warm Air Furnaces)—*mfg*	333414	3433
Stoves, wood and coal burning: Heating Equipment (except Electric and Warm Air Furnaces)—*mfg*	333414	3433
Stoves. wood burning: Building Material Dealers, Other—*retail*	44419	5074
Plumbing and Heating Equipment and Supplies (Hydronics)—*whlse*	42172	5074
Straddle carriers, mobile: Fabricated Metal Product, All Other Miscellaneous—*mfg*	332999	3537
Industrial Truck, Tractor, Trailer and Stacker Machinery—*mfg*	333924	3537
Metal Container, Other—*mfg*	332439	3537
Straight razors: Cutlery and Flatware (except Precious)—*mfg*	332211	3421
Straightening machinery (rolling mill equipment): Rolling Mill Machinery and Equipment—*mfg*	333516	3547
Strain gages, solid-state: Semiconductor and Related Device—*mfg*	334413	3674
Strainers. line–for use in piping systems-metal: Fabricated Metal Product, All Other Miscellaneous—*mfg*	332999	3494
Other Metal Valve and Pipe Fitting, Other—*mfg*	332919	3494
Strainers, oil–motor vehicle: Gasoline Engine and Engine Parts—*mfg*	336312	3714

Entry	NAICS	SIC
Strip, copper and copper alloy: Copper Rolling, Drawing and Extruding—*mfg*	331421	3351
Strip, metal: Metal Service Centers and Offices—*whlse*	42151	5051
Strip–lead, magnesium, nickel, tin, titanium, zinc, and their alloys: Nonferrous Metal (except Copper and Aluminum) Rolling, Drawing and Extruding—*mfg*	331491	3356
Stripping services–bituminous coal, anthracite, and lignite on a contract basis: Coal Support Activities—*mining*	213113	1241
Strips, galvanized iron and steel–made in steel works or rolling mills: Iron and Steel Mills—*mfg*	331111	3312
Petroleum and Coal Productsa, All Other—*mfg*	324199	3312
Strips, iron and steel–made in steel worksor hot-rolling mills: Iron and Steel Mills—*mfg*	331111	3312
Petroleum and Coal Productsa, All Other—*mfg*	324199	3312
Strips, liner–rubber: Fabric Coating Mills—*mfg*	31332	3069
Rubber Product, All Other—*mfg*	326299	3069
Strips, rayon: Cellulosic Organic Fiber—*mfg*	325221	2823
Strips, viscose: Cellulosic Organic Fiber—*mfg*	325221	2823
Stroboscopes: Electronic Coil, Transformer, and Other Inductor—*mfg*	334416	3825
Instrument for Measuring and Testing Electricity and Electrical Signals—*mfg*	334515	3825
Strobotrons: Electric Lamp Bulb and Part—*mfg*	33511	3641
Strollers, baby (vehicles): Game, Toy, and Children's Vehicle—*mfg*	339932	3944
Strontianite mining: Chemical and Fertilizer Mineral, Other—*mining*	212393	1479
Strontium carbonate, precipitated, and oxide: Basic Inorganic Chemical, All Other—*mfg*	325188	2819
Chemical Product, All Other Miscellaneous—*mfg*	325998	2819
Strontium mineral mining: Chemical and Fertilizer Mineral, Other—*mining*	212393	1479
Strontium nitrate: Basic Inorganic Chemical, All Other—*mfg*	325188	2819
Chemical Product, All Other Miscellaneous—*mfg*	325998	2819
Strops, razor: Leather Good, All Other—*mfg*	316999	3199
Structural assemblies, prefabricated–non-wood: Building Material Dealers, Other—*retail*	44419	5039
Construction Material, Other—*whlse*	42139	5039
Structural assemblies, prefabricated–wood: Building Material Dealers, Other—*retail*	44419	5031
Structural Clay Product Manufacturing, Other	**327123**	**3259**
Structural clay products: Building Material Dealers, Other—*retail*	44419	5211
Home Centers—*retail*	44411	5211
Structural glass, flat: Flat Glass—*mfg*	327211	3211
Structural lumber and timber, treated: Wood Preservation—*mfg*	321114	2491
Structural members, laminated wood–arches, trusses, timbers, and parallelchord ceilings: Cut Stock, Resawing Lumber, and Planing—*mfg*	321912	2439
Engineered Wood Member (except Truss)—*mfg*	321213	2439
Truss—*mfg*	321214	2439
Structural mills (rolling mill machinery): Rolling Mill Machinery and Equipment—*mfg*	333516	3547
Structural shapes, iron and steel: Iron and Steel Mills—*mfg*	331111	3312
Metal Service Centers and Offices—*whlse*	42151	5051
Petroleum and Coal Productsa, All Other—*mfg*	324199	3312
Structural shapes, rolled aluminum: Aluminum Rolling and Drawing, Other—*mfg*	331319	3355
Structural Steel Erection Contractors	**23591**	**1791**
Structural steel erection-contractors: Structural Steel Erection Contractors—*const*	23591	1791
Structural steel, fabricated: Fabricated Structural Metal—*mfg*	332312	3441
Structural tile, clay: Brick and Structural Clay Tile—*mfg*	327121	3251
Structural toy sets: Game, Toy, and Children's Vehicle—*mfg*	339932	3944
Strychnine and derivatives: Medicinal and Botanical—*mfg*	325411	2833
Stucco: Brick, Stone and Related Material—*whlse*	42132	5032
Building Material Dealers, Other—*retail*	44419	5032
Gypsum and Gypsum Product—*mfg*	32742	3299
Nonmetallic Mineral Product, All Other Miscellaneous—*mfg*	327999	3299
Stucco construction-contractors: Concrete Contractors—*const*	23571	1771
Drywall, Plastering, Acoustical and Insulation Contractors—*const*	23542	1771
Stud bases or mounts for semiconductor devices: Semiconductor and Related Device—*mfg*	334413	3674
Stud mills: Cut Stock, Resawing Lumber, and Planing—*mfg*	321912	2421
Millwork (including Flooring), Other—*mfg*	321918	2421
Sawmills—*mfg*	321113	2421
Wood Product, All Other Miscellaneous—*mfg*	321999	2421
Student exchange programs: Educational Support Services—*educ*	61171	8299
Schools and Instruction, All Other Miscellaneous—*educ*	611699	8299
Student Loan Marketing Association: International Trade Financing—*fin*	522293	6111
Non-Depository Credit Intermediation, All Other—*fin*	522298	6111
Secondary Market Financing—*fin*	522294	6111
Studio equipment, radio and television broadcasting: Radio and Television Broadcasting and Wireless Communications Equipment—*mfg*	33422	3663
Studio property rental for motion picture film production: Independent Artists, Writers, and Performers—*arts*	71151	7819
Machinery and Equipment Rental and Leasing, Other Commercial and Industrial—*real*	53249	7819
Motion Picture and Video Industries, Other—*info*	512199	7819
Studios, dance: Amusement and Recreation Industries, All Other—*arts*	71399	7911
Fine Arts Schools—*educ*	61161	7911
Studios, portrait photography: Photography Studios, Portrait—*prof*	541921	7221
Studs, sheet metal: Metal Container, Other—*mfg*	332439	3444
Sheet Metal Work—*mfg*	332322	3444
Studs, shirt–except precious metal and precious or semiprecious stones: Fastener, Button, Needle and Pin—*mfg*	339993	3965
Study commissioas, legislative: Legislative Bodies—*pub*	92112	9121

ALPHABETICAL INDEX	NAICS	SIC
Stuffed toys (including animals): Doll and Stuffed Toy—*mfg*	339931	3942
Stuffers, sausage: Food Product Machinery—*mfg*	333294	3556
Stumping for turpentine or powder manufacturing: Logging—*ag*	11331	2411
Stumps: Logging—*ag*	11331	2411
Styli, phonograph record cutting: Electronic Component, Other—*mfg*	334419	3679
Printed Circuit/Electronics Assembly—*mfg*	334418	3679
Radio and Television Broadcasting and Wireless Communications Equipment—*mfg*	33422	3679
Styling of fashions, apparel, furniture, andtextiles: Design Services, Other Specialized—*prof*	54149	7389
Styling wigs for the trade: Design Services, Other Specialized—*prof*	54149	7389
Stylographic pens: Pen and Mechanical Pencil—*mfg*	339941	3951
Styphnic acid: Explosives—*mfg*	32592	2892
Styrene: Cyclic Crude and Intermediate—*mfg*	325192	2865
Petrochemical—*mfg*	32511	2865
Styrene monomer: Cyclic Crude and Intermediate—*mfg*	325192	2865
Petrochemical—*mfg*	32511	2865
Styrene resins: Plastics Material and Resin—*mfg*	325211	2821
Styrene-acrylonitrile resins: Plastics Material and Resin—*mfg*	325211	2821
Styrene-butadiene rubbers (50 percent or less styrene content): Synthetic Rubber—*mfg*	325212	2822
Styrene-chloroprene rubbers: Synthetic Rubber—*mfg*	325212	2822
Styrene-isoprene rubbers: Synthetic Rubber—*mfg*	325212	2822
Subbituminous coal surface mining: Bituminous Coal and Lignite Surface—*mining*	212111	1221
Subbituminous coal underground mining: Bituminous Coal Underground—*mining*	212112	1222
Subgraders, construction equipment: Construction Machinery—*mfg*	33312	3531
Overhead Traveling Crane, Hoist and Monorail System—*mfg*	333923	3531
Railroad Rolling Stock—*mfg*	33651	3531
Sublimate, corrosive: Basic Inorganic Chemical, All Other—*mfg*	325188	2819
Chemical Product, All Other Miscellaneous—*mfg*	325998	2819
Submachine guns and parts: Small Arms—*mfg*	332994	3484
Submarine rock removal-general contractom: Heavy, All Other—*const*	23499	1629
Industrial Nonbuilding Structure—*const*	23493	1629
Submarine sandwich shops: Cafeterias—*accom*	722212	5812
Caterers—*accom*	72232	5812
Foodservice Contractors—*accom*	72231	5812
Full-Service Restaurants—*accom*	72211	5812
Limited-Service Restaurants—*accom*	722211	5812
Snack and Nonalcoholic Beverage Bars—*accom*	722213	5812
Theater Companies and Dinner Theaters—*arts*	71111	5812
Submarine tenders, building and repairing: Ship Building and Repairing—*mfg*	336611	3731
Subpresses, metalworking: Die and Tool, Die Set, Jig and Fixture, Special—*mfg*	333514	3544

ALPHABETICAL INDEX	NAICS	SIC
Industrial Mold—*mfg*	333511	3544
Subscription television services: Cable and Other Program Distribution—*info*	51322	4841
Cable Networks—*info*	51321	4841
Subsoiler attachments, tractor-mounted: Construction Machinery—*mfg*	33312	3531
Overhead Traveling Crane, Hoist and Monorail System—*mfg*	333923	3531
Railroad Rolling Stock—*mfg*	33651	3531
Suburban and urban railway operation: Bus and Motor Vehicle Transit Systems—*trans*	485113	4111
Commuter Rail Systems—*trans*	485112	4111
Mixed Mode Transit Systems—*trans*	485111	4111
Transit and Ground Passenger, All Other—*trans*	485999	4111
Urban Transit Systems, Other—*trans*	485119	4111
Subway construction–general contractors: Heavy, All Other—*const*	23499	1629
Industrial Nonbuilding Structure—*const*	23493	1629
Subway operation: Bus and Motor Vehicle Transit Systems—*trans*	485113	4111
Commuter Rail Systems—*trans*	485112	4111
Mixed Mode Transit Systems—*trans*	485111	4111
Transit and Ground Passenger, All Other—*trans*	485999	4111
Urban Transit Systems, Other—*trans*	485119	4111
Suction therapy apparatus: Surgical and Medical Instrument—*mfg*	339112	3841
Sueding cotton broadwoven goods: Broadwoven Fabric Finishing Mills—*mfg*	313311	2261
Sueding manmade fiber and silk broadwoven fabrics: Broadwoven Fabric Finishing Mills—*mfg*	313311	2262
Sugar and Confectionery Product Manufacturing	**3113**	
Sugar Beet Farming	**111991**	**133**
Sugar beets, machine harvesting of: Crop Harvesting, Primarily by Machine—*ag*	115113	722
Sugar grinding: Food, All Other Miscellaneous—*mfg*	311999	2099
Sugar Manufacturing	**31131**	
Sugar of milk: Dry, Condensed, and Evaporated Dairy Product—*mfg*	311514	2023
Sugar plant machinery: Food Product Machinery—*mfg*	333294	3556
Sugar, burnt (food color): Flavoring Syrup and Concentrate—*mfg*	31193	2087
Food, All Other Miscellaneous—*mfg*	311999	2087
Spice and Extract—*mfg*	311942	2087
Sugar, corn: Wet Corn Milling—*mfg*	311221	2046
Sugar, granulated–made from purchased raw cane sugar or sugar syrup: Cane Sugar Refining—*mfg*	311312	2062
Sugar, granulated–made from sugarbeets: Beet Sugar—*mfg*	311313	2063
Sugar, granulated–made from sugarcane: Sugarcane Mills—*mfg*	311311	2061
Sugar, industrial maple–made in plants producing maple syrup: Food, All Other Miscellaneous—*mfg*	311999	2099
Sugar, invert–made from purchased raw cane sugar or sugar syrup: Cane Sugar Refining—*mfg*	311312	2062
Sugar, invert–made from sugar beets: Beet Sugar—*mfg*	311313	2063

Description	NAICS	SIC
Sugar, invert–made from sugarcane: Sugarcane Mills—*mfg*	311311	2061
Sugar, liquid–made from sugar beets: Beet Sugar—*mfg*	311313	2063
Sugar, powdered: Food, All Other Miscellaneous—*mfg*	311999	2099
Sugar, powdered–made from purchased raw cane sugar or sugar syrup: Cane Sugar Refining—*mfg*	311312	2062
Sugar, powdered–made from sugar beets: Beet Sugar—*mfg*	311313	2063
Sugar, powdered–made from sugarcane: Sugarcane Mills—*mfg*	311311	2061
Sugar, raw: Farm Product Raw Material, Other—*whlse*	42259	5159
Sugar, raw–made from sugarcane: Sugarcane Mills—*mfg*	311311	2061
Sugar, refined: Grocery and Related Products, Other—*whlse*	42249	5149
Sugar, refined–made from purchased raw cane sugar or sugar syrup: Cane Sugar Refining—*mfg*	311312	2062
Sugar–clarified, granulated, and raw-made from sugarcane: Sugarcane Mills—*mfg*	311311	2061
Sugarbeet farms: Sugar Beet Farming—*ag*	111991	133
Sugarcane Farming—*ag*	11193	133
Sugarcane Farming	**11193**	**133**
Sugarcane farms: Sugar Beet Farming—*ag*	111991	133
Sugarcane Farming—*ag*	11193	133
Sugarcane Mills	**311311**	**2061**
Sugarcane, machine harvesting of: Crop Harvesting, Primarily by Machine—*ag*	115113	722
Suit and coat findings–coat fronts and linings: Apparel Accessories and Apparel, Other—*mfg*	315999	2396
Suit trimmings, fabric: Apparel Accessories and Apparel, Other—*mfg*	315999	2396
Suit, Coat and Overcoat Manufacturing, Men's and Boys' Cut and Sew	**315222**	**2369**
Suit, Coat, Tailored Jacket and Skirt Manufacturing, Women's and Girls' Cut and Sew	**315234**	**2369**
Suitcase hardware, including locks: Hardware—*mfg*	33251	3429
Suitcase shells, plastics: Plastics Pipe and Pipe Fitting—*mfg*	326122	3089
Plastics Product, All Other—*mfg*	326199	3089
Unsupported Plastics Profile Shape—*mfg*	326121	3089
Suitcases, regardless of material: Luggage—*mfg*	316991	3161
Suiting fabrics, cotton: Broadwoven Fabric Mills—*mfg*	31321	2211
Suiting fabrics, manmade fiber and silk: Broadwoven Fabric Mills—*mfg*	31321	2221
Suitings–wool, mohair, and similar animal fibers: Broadwoven Fabric Finishing Mills—*mfg*	313311	2231
Broadwoven Fabric Mills—*mfg*	31321	2231
Textile and Fabric Finishing (except Broadwoven Fabric) Mills—*mfg*	313312	2231
Suits: Outerwear Knitting Mills—*mfg*	315191	2253
Suits, except playsuits and athletic: Women's and Girls' Cut and Sew Apparel Contractors—*mfg*	315212	2337
Women's and Girls' Cut and Sew Suit, Coat, Tailored Jacket and Skirt—*mfg*	315234	2337
Suits, firefighting–asbestos: Surgical Appliance and Supplies—*mfg*	339113	3842
Suits, men's and boys': Men's and Boys' Clothing and Furnishings—*whlse*	42232	5136
Suits, tailored: Men's and Boys' Cut and Sew Apparel Contractors—*mfg*	315211	2311
Men's and Boys' Cut and Sew Suit, Coat and Overcoat—*mfg*	315222	2311
Suits, work: Men's and Boys' Cut and Sew Apparel Contractors—*mfg*	315211	2326
Men's and Boys' Cut and Sew Work Clothing—*mfg*	315225	2326
Suits–warmup, jogging, snow, and ski: Apparel Accessories and Apparel, Other—*mfg*	315999	2339
Cut and Sew Apparel, All Other—*mfg*	315299	2339
Cut and Sew Apparel, All Other—*mfg*	315299	2329
Women's and Girls' Cut and Sew Apparel Contractors—*mfg*	315212	2339
Women's and Girls' Cut and Sew Other Outerwear—*mfg*	315238	2339
Suits–women's, children's, and infants': Women's, Children's, and Infants' and Accessories—*whlse*	42233	5137
Sulfa drugs–bulk, uncompounded: Medicinal and Botanical—*mfg*	325411	2833
Sulfate of potash and potash magnesia, not produced at mines: Basic Inorganic Chemical, All Other—*mfg*	325188	2819
Chemical Product, All Other Miscellaneous—*mfg*	325998	2819
Sulfides and sulfites: Basic Inorganic Chemical, All Other—*mfg*	325188	2819
Chemical Product, All Other Miscellaneous—*mfg*	325998	2819
Sulfocyanides: Basic Inorganic Chemical, All Other—*mfg*	325188	2819
Chemical Product, All Other Miscellaneous—*mfg*	325998	2819
Sulfonamides: Medicinal and Botanical—*mfg*	325411	2833
Sulfonated naphthalene: Basic Organic Chemical, All Other—*mfg*	325199	2869
Sulfonated oils, fats, and greases: Surface Active Agent—*mfg*	325613	2843
Sulfur chloride: Basic Inorganic Chemical, All Other—*mfg*	325188	2819
Chemical Product, All Other Miscellaneous—*mfg*	325998	2819
Sulfur dioxide: Basic Inorganic Chemical, All Other—*mfg*	325188	2819
Chemical Product, All Other Miscellaneous—*mfg*	325998	2819
Sulfur dust (insecticide): Pesticide and Other Agricultural Chemical—*mfg*	32532	2879
Sulfur hexafluoride gas: Basic Inorganic Chemical, All Other—*mfg*	325188	2819
Chemical Product, All Other Miscellaneous—*mfg*	325998	2819
Sulfur mining, native: Chemical and Fertilizer Mineral, Other—*mining*	212393	1479
Sulfur, ground or otherwise treated: Chemical and Fertilizer Mineral, Other—*mining*	212393	1479
Sulfur, recovered or refined, including from sour natural gas: Basic Inorganic Chemical, All Other—*mfg*	325188	2819
Chemical Product, All Other Miscellaneous—*mfg*	325998	2819
Sulfuric acid: Basic Inorganic Chemical, All Other—*mfg*	325188	2819
Chemical Product, All Other Miscellaneous—*mfg*	325998	2819
Sulkies, baby (vehicles): Game, Toy, and Children's Vehicle—*mfg*	339932	3944
Sumac extract: Gum and Wood Chemical—*mfg*	325191	2861
Summer camps, except day and sports instructional: Recreational and Vacation Camps—*accom*	721214	7032
Sump pump installation and servicing–contractors: Plumbing, Heating and Air-Conditioning Contractors—*const*	23511	1711

ALPHABETICAL INDEX	NAICS	SIC
Sunflower farms: Oilseed (except Soybean) Farming—*ag*	11112	119
Sunflower seed oil: Fats and Oils Refining and Blending—*mfg*	311225	2076
Oilseed Processing, Other—*mfg*	311223	2076
Sunglasses and goggles: Ophthalmic Goods—*mfg*	339115	3851
Suntan lotions and oils: Soap and Other Detergent—*mfg*	325611	2844
Toilet Preparation—*mfg*	32562	2844
Supermarkets and Other Grocery (except Convenience) Stores	**44511**	**5411**
Supermarkets, grocery: Convenience Stores—*retail*	44512	5411
Gasoline Stations with Convenience Stores—*retail*	44711	5411
Supermarkets and Other Grocery (except Convenience) Stores—*retail*	44511	5411
Warehouse Clubs and Superstores—*retail*	45291	5411
Superphosphates, ammoniated and not ammoniated: Phosphatic Fertilizer—*mfg*	325312	2874
Supply agencies: General Government, All Other—*pub*	92119	9199
Support Services, All Other	**56199**	**7389**
Support Services, Other	**5619**	
Supports–abdominal, ankle, arch, and kneecap: Surgical Appliance and Supplies—*mfg*	339113	3842
Suppositories: Pharmaceutical Preparation—*mfg*	325412	2834
Surety insurance: Direct Property and Casualty Insurance Carriers—*fin*	524126	6351
Reinsurance Carriers—*fin*	52413	6351
Surface Active Agent Manufacturing	**325613**	**2843**
Surface active agents: Chemical and Allied Products, Other—*whlse*	42269	5169
Surface Active Agent—*mfg*	325613	2843
Surface area analyzers: Analytical Laboratory Instrument—*mfg*	334516	3826
Surface burner controls, temperature: Automatic Environmental Control for Residential, Commercial and Appliance Use—*mfg*	334512	3822
Surface-Coated Paperboard Manufacturing	**322292**	**2675**
Surfacers (woodworking machines): Sawmill and Woodworking Machinery—*mfg*	33321	3553
Surfacers, concrete grinding: Construction Machinery—*mfg*	33312	3531
Overhead Traveling Crane, Hoist and Monorail System—*mfg*	333923	3531
Railroad Rolling Stock—*mfg*	33651	3531
Surfboards: Sporting and Athletic Goods—*mfg*	33992	3949
Surge tanks, metal plate: Air-Conditioning and Warm Air Heating Equipment and Commercial and Industrial Refrigeration Equipment—*mfg*	333415	3443
Metal Tank (Heavy Gauge)—*mfg*	33242	3443
Plate Work—*mfg*	332313	3443
Power Boiler and Heat Exchanger—*mfg*	33241	3443
Surgeons (M.D.), offices of: Freestanding Ambulatory Surgical and Emergency Centers—*hlth*	621493	8011
HMO Medical Centers—*hlth*	621491	8011
Physicians (except Mental Health Specialists), Offices Of—*hlth*	621111	8011
Physicians, Mental Health Specialists, Offices Of—*hlth*	621112	8011
Surgeons' gloves, rubber: Fabric Coating Mills—*mfg*	31332	3069
Rubber Product, All Other—*mfg*	326299	3069
Surgery on orchard trees and vines: Nonscheduled Air, Other—*trans*	481219	721
Soil Preparation, Planting, and Cultivating—*ag*	115112	721
Surgical and Medical Instrument Manufacturing	**339112**	**3829**
Surgical and medical instruments: Health and Personal Care Stores, All Other—*retail*	446199	5047
Medical, Dental and Hospital Equipment and Supplies—*whlse*	42145	5047
Surgical and medical tubing–extruded and lathe-cut: Rubber Product for Mechanical Use—*mfg*	326291	3061
Surgical Appliance and Supplies Manufacturing	**339113**	**3842**
Surgical appliances and supplies, except medical instruments: Electromedical and Electrotherapeutic Apparatus—*mfg*	334510	3842
Surgical Appliance and Supplies—*mfg*	339113	3842
Surgical equipment: Health and Personal Care Stores, All Other—*retail*	446199	5047
Medical, Dental and Hospital Equipment and Supplies—*whlse*	42145	5047
Surgical fabrics, cotton: Broadwoven Fabric Mills—*mfg*	31321	2211
Surgical instrument repair: Electronic and Precision Equipment Repair and Maintenance, Other—*serv*	811219	7699
Surgical instruments and apparatus, except electromedical: Surgical and Medical Instrument—*mfg*	339112	3841
Surgical knife blades and handles: Surgical and Medical Instrument—*mfg*	339112	3841
Surgical stapling devices: Surgical and Medical Instrument—*mfg*	339112	3841
Surgical support systems–heart-lung machines, except iron lungs and blood flowsystems: Electromedical and Electrotherapeutic Apparatus—*mfg*	334510	3845
Irradiation Apparatus—*mfg*	334517	3845
Surveillance ovens, for aging and testing powder: General Purpose Machinery , All Other—*mfg*	333999	3569
Surveying and Mapping (except Geophysical) Services	**54137**	**8713**
Surveying instrument repair: Electronic and Precision Equipment Repair and Maintenance, Other—*serv*	811219	7699
Surveying instruments: Measuring and Controlling Device, Other—*mfg*	334519	3829
Surgical and Medical Instrument—*mfg*	339112	3829
Surveying wells on a contract basis, except seismographic: Oil and Gas Operations Support Activities—*mining*	213112	1389
Surveying–land, water, and aerial: Geophysical Surveying and Mapping Services—*prof*	54136	8713
Surveying and Mapping (except Geophysical) Services—*prof*	54137	8713
Surveyors' stakes, wood: Manufacturing, All Other Miscellaneous—*mfg*	339999	2499
Wood Container and Pallet—*mfg*	32192	2499
Wood Product, All Other Miscellaneous—*mfg*	321999	2499

Surveyors, marine cargo: Road, Other Support Activities for—*trans*	48849	4785
Water, Other Support Activities for—*trans*	48839	4785
Survival schools: Schools and Instruction, All Other Miscellaneous—*educ*	611699	8299
Suspenders: Apparel Accessories and Apparel, Other—*mfg*	315999	2389
Suspensories: Surgical Appliance and Supplies—*mfg*	339113	3842
Sutures: Surgical Appliance and Supplies—*mfg*	339113	3842
Swabbing wells–on a contract basis: Oil and Gas Operations Support Activities—*mining*	213112	1389
Swabs, sanitary cotton: Surgical Appliance and Supplies—*mfg*	339113	3842
Swage blocks: Fabricated Metal Product, All Other Miscellaneous—*mfg*	332999	3599
General Purpose Machinery , All Other—*mfg*	333999	3599
Machine Shops—*mfg*	33271	3599
Machinery, Other Commercial and Service Industry—*mfg*	333319	3599
Swaging machines: Machine Tool (Metal Forming Types)—*mfg*	333513	3542
Swatches and samples, mounting for the trade: Tradebinding and Related Work—*mfg*	323121	2789
Swatters, fly: Fabricated Metal Product, All Other Miscellaneous—*mfg*	332999	3999
Plastics Product, All Other—*mfg*	326199	3999
Sweat bands: Outerwear Knitting Mills—*mfg*	315191	2253
Sweat pants: Apparel Accessories and Apparel, Other—*mfg*	315999	2339
Cut and Sew Apparel, All Other—*mfg*	315299	2339
Cut and Sew Apparel, All Other—*mfg*	315299	2329
Outerwear Knitting Mills—*mfg*	315191	2253
Women's and Girls' Cut and Sew Apparel Contractors—*mfg*	315212	2339
Women's and Girls' Cut and Sew Other Outerwear—*mfg*	315238	2339
Sweat shirts: Infants' Cut and Sew Apparel—*mfg*	315291	2361
Men's and Boys' Cut and Sew Apparel Contractors—*mfg*	315211	2361
Men's and Boys' Cut and Sew Shirt (except Work Shirt)—*mfg*	315223	2361
Outerwear Knitting Mills—*mfg*	315191	2253
Women's and Girls' Cut and Sew Apparel Contractors—*mfg*	315212	2361
Women's and Girls' Cut and Sew Blouse and Shirt—*mfg*	315232	2361
Women's and Girls' Cut and Sew Dress—*mfg*	315233	2361
Sweatband leather: Leather and Hide Tanning and Finishing—*mfg*	31611	3111
Sweatbands, hat and cap: Apparel Accessories and Apparel, Other—*mfg*	315999	2396
Sweater jackets: Cut and Sew Apparel, All Other—*mfg*	315299	2329
Men's and Boys' Cut and Sew Apparel Contractors—*mfg*	315211	2329
Men's and Boys' Cut and Sew Other Outerwear—*mfg*	315228	2329
Sweater vests: Cut and Sew Apparel, All Other—*mfg*	315299	2329
Men's and Boys' Cut and Sew Apparel Contractors—*mfg*	315211	2329
Men's and Boys' Cut and Sew Other Outerwear—*mfg*	315228	2329
Sweaters: Cut and Sew Apparel, All Other—*mfg*	315299	2329
Men's and Boys' Cut and Sew Apparel Contractors—*mfg*	315211	2329
Men's and Boys' Cut and Sew Other Outerwear—*mfg*	315228	2329
Sweaters and sweater coats: Outerwear Knitting Mills—*mfg*	315191	2253
Sweatshirts: Men's and Boys' Cut and Sew Apparel Contractors—*mfg*	315211	2321
Men's and Boys' Cut and Sew Shirt (except Work Shirt)—*mfg*	315223	2321
Women's and Girls' Cut and Sew Apparel Contractors—*mfg*	315212	2331
Women's and Girls' Cut and Sew Blouse and Shirt—*mfg*	315232	2331
Sweep generators: Electronic Coil, Transformer, and Other Inductor—*mfg*	334416	3825
Instrument for Measuring and Testing Electricity and Electrical Signals—*mfg*	334515	3825
Sweep oscillators: Electronic Coil, Transformer, and Other Inductor—*mfg*	334416	3825
Instrument for Measuring and Testing Electricity and Electrical Signals—*mfg*	334515	3825
Sweepers, carpet–except household electric vacuum sweepers: Machinery, Other Commercial and Service Industry—*mfg*	333319	3589
Sweepers, electric–vacuum-household: Household Vacuum Cleaner—*mfg*	335212	3635
Sweepers, electric–vacuum-industrial: Machinery, Other Commercial and Service Industry—*mfg*	333319	3589
Sweepers, street (motor vehicles): Automobile—*mfg*	336111	3711
Heavy Duty Truck—*mfg*	33612	3711
Light Truck and Utility Vehicle—*mfg*	336112	3711
Military Armored Vehicle, Tank and Tank Component—*mfg*	336992	3711
Motor Vehicle Body—*mfg*	336211	3711
Sweeping compounds, oil and water absorbent, clay or sawdust: Polish and Other Sanitation Good—*mfg*	325612	2842
Sweeping service–road, airport, parking lot, etc.: Airport Operations, Other—*trans*	488119	4959
Exterminating and Pest Control Services—*admin*	56171	4959
Remediation Services—*admin*	56291	4959
Waste Management Services, All Other Miscellaneous—*admin*	562998	4959
Sweet corn farms: Vegetable (except Potato) and Melon Farming, Other—*ag*	111219	161
Sweet pepper farms: Vegetable (except Potato) and Melon Farming, Other—*ag*	111219	161
Sweet potato curing: Postharvest Crop Activities (except Cotton Ginning)—*ag*	115114	723
Sweet potato farms: Crop Farming, All Other Miscellaneous—*ag*	111998	139
Hay Farming—*ag*	11194	139
Peanut Farming—*ag*	111992	139
Vegetable (except Potato) and Melon Farming, Other—*ag*	111219	139
Sweet yeast goods, except frozen: Bakeries, Commercial—*mfg*	311812	2051
Sweet yeast goods, frozen: Frozen Bakery Product—*mfg*	311813	2053
Sweetners, synthetic: Basic Organic Chemical, All Other—*mfg*	325199	2869
Swimming clubs, membership: Fitness and Recreational Sports Centers—*arts*	71394	7997
Swimming pool cleaning and maintenance: Personal Services, All Other—*serv*	81299	7389
Swimming pool construction–contractors: Trade Contractors, All Other Special—*const*	23599	1799

ALPHABETICAL INDEX	NAICS	SIC
Swimming pool covers and blankets, fabric: Canvas and Related Product Mills—*mfg*	314912	2394
Swimming pool covers and blankets–plastics: Plastics Pipe and Pipe Fitting—*mfg*	326122	3089
Plastics Product, All Other—*mfg*	326199	3089
Unsupported Plastics Profile Shape—*mfg*	326121	3089
Swimming pool filter systems (homepools): Machinery, Other Commercial and Service Industry—*mfg*	333319	3589
Swimming pool lighting fixtures: Lighting Equipment, Other—*mfg*	335129	3648
Swimming pools and equipment: Sporting and Recreational Goods and Supplies—*whlse*	42191	5091
Swimming pools, except membership: Fitness and Recreational Sports Centers—*arts*	71394	7999
Swimming pools, home–not installed: Stores (except Tobacco Stores), All Other Miscellaneous—*retail*	453998	5999
Swimming pools, plastics: Sporting and Athletic Goods—*mfg*	33992	3949
Swimsuits: Apparel Accessories and Apparel, Other—*mfg*	315999	2339
Cut and Sew Apparel, All Other—*mfg*	315299	2339
Cut and Sew Apparel, All Other—*mfg*	315299	2329
Outerwear Knitting Mills—*mfg*	315191	2253
Women's and Girls' Cut and Sew Apparel Contractors—*mfg*	315212	2339
Women's and Girls' Cut and Sew Other Outerwear—*mfg*	315238	2339
Swimwear: Cut and Sew Apparel, All Other—*mfg*	315299	2329
Swings, porch–metal: Metal Household Furniture—*mfg*	337124	2514
Swings, porch–wood: Nonupholstered Wood Household Furniture—*mfg*	337122	2511
Swiss loom embroideries: Men's and Boys' Cut and Sew Apparel Contractors—*mfg*	315211	2395
Textile Product Mills, All Other Miscellaneous—*mfg*	314999	2395
Women's and Girls' Cut and Sew Apparel Contractors—*mfg*	315212	2395
Switch boxes, electric: Noncurrent-Carrying Wiring Device—*mfg*	335932	3644
Switch cutouts: Current-Carrying Wiring Device—*mfg*	335931	3643
Switchboard panels, slate: Cut Stone and Stone Product—*mfg*	327991	3281
Switchboards and parts, power: Switchgear and Switchboard Apparatus—*mfg*	335313	3613
Switchboards, electrical distribution: Building Material Dealers, Other—*retail*	44419	5063
Electrical Apparatus and Equipment, Wiring Supplies and Material—*whlse*	42161	5063
Switchboards, telephone and telegraph: Electronic Coil, Transformer, and Other Inductor—*mfg*	334416	3661
Printed Circuit/Electronics Assembly—*mfg*	334418	3661
Telephone Apparatus—*mfg*	33421	3661
Switches for electric wiring–e.g., snap, tumbler, pressure, push button: Current-Carrying Wiring Device—*mfg*	335931	3643
Switches, electric power–except snap, push button, tumbler, and solenoid: Switchgear and Switchboard Apparatus—*mfg*	335313	3613

ALPHABETICAL INDEX	NAICS	SIC
Switches, electronic: Electronic Component, Other—*mfg*	334419	3679
Motor Vehicle Electrical and Electronic Equipment, Other—*mfg*	336322	3679
Printed Circuit/Electronics Assembly—*mfg*	334418	3679
Radio and Television Broadcasting and Wireless Communications Equipment—*mfg*	33422	3679
Switches, except electronic: Building Material Dealers, Other—*retail*	44419	5063
Electrical Apparatus and Equipment, Wiring Supplies and Material—*whlse*	42161	5063
Switches, flow activated electrical: Relay and Industrial Control—*mfg*	335314	3625
Switches, pneumatic positioning remote: Automatic Environmental Control for Residential, Commercial and Appliance Use—*mfg*	334512	3822
Switches, railroad–forged-not made in rolling mills: Iron and Steel Forging—*mfg*	332111	3462
Switches, silicon control: Semiconductor and Related Device—*mfg*	334413	3674
Switches, stepping: Electronic Component, Other—*mfg*	334419	3679
Motor Vehicle Electrical and Electronic Equipment, Other—*mfg*	336322	3679
Printed Circuit/Electronics Assembly—*mfg*	334418	3679
Radio and Television Broadcasting and Wireless Communications Equipment—*mfg*	33422	3679
Switches, thermostatic: Automatic Environmental Control for Residential, Commercial and Appliance Use—*mfg*	334512	3822
Switchgear: Building Material Dealers, Other—*retail*	44419	5063
Electrical Apparatus and Equipment, Wiring Supplies and Material—*whlse*	42161	5063
Switchgear and Switchboard Apparatus Manufacturing	**335313**	**3613**
Switchgear and switchgear accessories: Switchgear and Switchboard Apparatus—*mfg*	335313	3613
Switching equipment power: Switchgear and Switchboard Apparatus—*mfg*	335313	3613
Switching equipment, telephone: Electronic Coil, Transformer, and Other Inductor—*mfg*	334416	3661
Printed Circuit/Electronics Assembly—*mfg*	334418	3661
Telephone Apparatus—*mfg*	33421	3661
Switching locomotives and parts, electric and nonelectric: Pump and Pumping Equipment—*mfg*	333911	3743
Railroad Rolling Stock—*mfg*	33651	3743
Swivels (fishing equipment): Sporting and Athletic Goods—*mfg*	33992	3949
Swords: Cutlery and Flatware (except Precious)—*mfg*	332211	3421
Syenite (except nepheline), dimension: Dimension Stone and Quarrying—*mining*	212311	1411
Syenite, except nepheline–crushed and broken: Crushed and Broken Granite and Quarrying—*mining*	212313	1423
Syenite, nepheline: Clay and Ceramic and Refractory Minerals—*mining*	212325	1459
Sylvanite mining: Gold Ore—*mining*	212221	1041

Description	NAICS	SIC
Symphony orchestras: Independent Artists, Writers, and Performers—*arts*	71151	7929
Musical Groups and Artists—*arts*	71113	7929
Performing Arts Companies, Other—*arts*	71119	7929
Synchronizers, aircraft engine: Measuring and Controlling Device, Other—*mfg*	334519	3829
Surgical and Medical Instrument—*mfg*	339112	3829
Synchronous condensers and timing motors, electric: Motor and Generator—*mfg*	335312	3621
Synchros: Motor and Generator—*mfg*	335312	3621
Synchroscopes: Electronic Coil, Transformer, and Other Inductor—*mfg*	334416	3825
Instrument for Measuring and Testing Electricity and Electrical Signals—*mfg*	334515	3825
Synthesizers, music: Musical Instrument—*mfg*	339992	3931
Synthetic filament extruding machines: Industrial Machinery, All Other—*mfg*	333298	3559
Machinery, Other Commercial and Service Industry—*mfg*	333319	3559
Rubber and Plastics Industry Machinery—*mfg*	33322	3559
Synthetic Fuels Corporation: International Trade Financing—*fin*	522293	6111
Non-Depository Credit Intermediation, All Other—*fin*	522298	6111
Secondary Market Financing—*fin*	522294	6111
Synthetic natural gas from naphtha, production and distribution: Natural Gas Distribution—*util*	22121	4925
Synthetic rubber: Chemical and Allied Products, Other—*whlse*	42269	5169
Synthetic Rubber Manufacturing	**325212**	**2822**
Synthetic stones, for gem stones and industrial use: Gypsum and Gypsum Product—*mfg*	32742	3299
Nonmetallic Mineral Product, All Other Miscellaneous—*mfg*	327999	3299
Syringes, fountain–rubber: Fabric Coating Mills—*mfg*	31332	3069
Rubber Product, All Other—*mfg*	326299	3069
Syringes, hypodermic: Surgical and Medical Instrument—*mfg*	339112	3841
Syrup, cane–made from sugarcane: Sugarcane Mills—*mfg*	311311	2061
Syrup, corn–unmixed: Wet Corn Milling—*mfg*	311221	2046
Syrup, made from purchased raw cane sugar or sugar syrup: Cane Sugar Refining—*mfg*	311312	2062
Syrup, made from sugar beets: Beet Sugar—*mfg*	311313	2063
Syrups, beverage: Flavoring Syrup and Concentrate—*mfg*	31193	2087
Food, All Other Miscellaneous—*mfg*	311999	2087
Spice and Extract—*mfg*	311942	2087
Syrups, chocolate: Chocolate and Confectionery from Cacao Beans—*mfg*	31132	2066
Syrups, except for fountain use: Grocery and Related Products, Other—*whlse*	42249	5149
Syrups, flavoring: Flavoring Syrup and Concentrate—*mfg*	31193	2087
Food, All Other Miscellaneous—*mfg*	311999	2087
Spice and Extract—*mfg*	311942	2087
Syrups, fountain: Confectionery—*whlse*	42245	5145
Syrups, malt: Breweries—*mfg*	31212	2082
Syrups, pharmaceutical: Pharmaceutical Preparation—*mfg*	325412	2834
Syrups, refiners': Cane Sugar Refining—*mfg*	311312	2062
Syrups, sweetening–honey, maple syrup, sorghum: Food, All Other Miscellaneous—*mfg*	311999	2099
Systems analysis and design, computer software: Custom Computer Programming Services, Custom—*prof*	541511	7371
Systems engineering consulting, except professional engineering or computer related: Educational Support Services—*educ*	61171	8748
Management Consulting Services, Other—*prof*	541618	8748
Scientific and Technical Consulting Services, Other—*prof*	54169	8748
Systems integration, computer: Computer Systems Design Services—*prof*	541512	7373
T-hirts, outerwear: Outerwear Knitting Mills—*mfg*	315191	2253
T-hirts, underwear: Men's and Boys' Cut and Sew Apparel Contractors—*mfg*	315211	2322
Men's and Boys' Cut and Sew Underwear and Nightwear—*mfg*	315221	2322
T-shirts: Outerwear Knitting Mills—*mfg*	315191	2253
T-shirts, outerwear: Infants' Cut and Sew Apparel—*mfg*	315291	2361
Men's and Boys' Cut and Sew Apparel Contractors—*mfg*	315211	2361
Men's and Boys' Cut and Sew Apparel Contractors—*mfg*	315211	2321
Men's and Boys' Cut and Sew Shirt (except Work Shirt)—*mfg*	315223	2361
Men's and Boys' Cut and Sew Shirt (except Work Shirt)—*mfg*	315223	2321
Women's and Girls' Cut and Sew Apparel Contractors—*mfg*	315212	2361
Women's and Girls' Cut and Sew Apparel Contractors—*mfg*	315212	2331
Women's and Girls' Cut and Sew Blouse and Shirt—*mfg*	315232	2331
Women's and Girls' Cut and Sew Blouse and Shirt—*mfg*	315232	2361
Women's and Girls' Cut and Sew Dress—*mfg*	315233	2361
T-shirts, underwear: Infants' Cut and Sew Apparel—*mfg*	315291	2341
Underwear and Nightwear Knitting Mills—*mfg*	315192	2254
Women's and Girls' Cut and Sew Apparel Contractors—*mfg*	315212	2341
Women's and Girls' Cut and Sew Lingerie, Loungewear and Nightwear—*mfg*	315231	2341
T-squares (drafting): Measuring and Controlling Device, Other—*mfg*	334519	3829
Surgical and Medical Instrument—*mfg*	339112	3829
Table and kitchen cutlery, all metal: Cutlery and Flatware (except Precious)—*mfg*	332211	3914
Silverware and Plated Ware—*mfg*	339912	3914
Table articles, coarse earthenware: Vitreous China, Fine Earthenware and Other Pottery Product—*mfg*	327112	3269
Table articles, fine earthenware (whiteware): Vitreous China, Fine Earthenware and Other Pottery Product—*mfg*	327112	3263
Table articles, vitreous china: Vitreous China, Fine Earthenware and Other Pottery Product—*mfg*	327112	3262
Table cover fabrics, cotton: Broadwoven Fabric Mills—*mfg*	31321	2211
Table cover supply service: Linen Supply—*serv*	812331	7213
Table covers, lace: Knit Fabric and Lace Mills, Other—*mfg*	313249	2258
Textile and Fabric Finishing (except Broadwoven Fabric) Mills—*mfg*	313312	2258
Table cutlery, all metal: Cutlery and Flatware (except Precious)—*mfg*	332211	3914

ALPHABETICAL INDEX	NAICS	SIC
Silverware and Plated Ware—*mfg*	339912	3914
Table cutlery, except table cutlery with handles of metal: Cutlery and Flatware (except Precious)—*mfg*	332211	3421
Table damask, cotton: Broadwoven Fabric Mills—*mfg*	31321	2211
Table lamps: Residential Electric Lighting Fixture—*mfg*	335121	3645
Table linens: Home Furnishing—*whlse*	42122	5023
Table mats, plastics and textiles: Household Textile Product Mills, Other—*mfg*	314129	2392
Table oils: Fats and Oils Refining and Blending—*mfg*	311225	2079
Oilseed Processing, Other—*mfg*	311223	2079
Soybean Processing—*mfg*	311222	2079
Table or counter tops, plastics laminated: Architectural Woodwork and Millwork, Custom—*mfg*	337212	2541
Showcase, Partition, Shelving, and Locker—*mfg*	337215	2541
Wood Kitchen Cabinet and Counter Top—*mfg*	33711	2541
Table pads and padding, asbestos: Motor Vehicle Brake System—*mfg*	33634	3292
Nonmetallic Mineral Product, All Other Miscellaneous—*mfg*	327999	3292
Table pads and padding, felt–except woven: Broadwoven Fabric Mills—*mfg*	31321	2299
Narrow Fabric Mills—*mfg*	313221	2299
Nonwoven Fabric Mills—*mfg*	31323	2299
Textile and Fabric Finishing (except Broadwoven Fabric) Mills—*mfg*	313312	2299
Textile Product Mills, All Other Miscellaneous—*mfg*	314999	2299
Thread Mills—*mfg*	313113	2299
Yarn Spinning Mills—*mfg*	313111	2299
Table scarves: Household Textile Product Mills, Other—*mfg*	314129	2392
Table slides, for extension tables–wood: Cut Stock, Resawing Lumber, and Planing—*mfg*	321912	2426
Millwork (including Flooring), Other—*mfg*	321918	2426
Showcase, Partition, Shelving, and Locker—*mfg*	337215	2426
Wood Product, All Other Miscellaneous—*mfg*	321999	2426
Table tops, made from purchased glass: Glass Product Made of Purchased Glass—*mfg*	327215	3231
Table tops, marble: Cut Stone and Stone Product—*mfg*	327991	3281
Table tops, porcelain enameled: Metal Stamping—*mfg*	332116	3469
Tablecloths: Household Textile Product Mills, Other—*mfg*	314129	2392
Tablecloths, plastics: Household Textile Product Mills, Other—*mfg*	314129	2392
Tables, household–metal: Metal Household Furniture—*mfg*	337124	2514
Tables, household–wood: Nonupholstered Wood Household Furniture—*mfg*	337122	2511
Tables, lift–hydraulic: Fabricated Metal Product, All Other Miscellaneous—*mfg*	332999	3537
Industrial Truck, Tractor, Trailer and Stacker Machinery—*mfg*	333924	3537
Metal Container, Other—*mfg*	332439	3537
Tables, office–except wood: Nonwood Office Furniture—*mfg*	337214	2522

ALPHABETICAL INDEX	NAICS	SIC
Tables, office–wood: Wood Office Furniture—*mfg*	337211	2521
Tables, onerating: Surgical and Medical Instrument—*mfg*	339112	3841
Tables, rotary–indexing: Cutting Tool and Machine Tool Accessory—*mfg*	333515	3545
Hand and Edge Tool—*mfg*	332212	3545
Tables, sludge: Fabricated Metal Product, All Other Miscellaneous—*mfg*	332999	3599
General Purpose Machinery , All Other—*mfg*	333999	3599
Machine Shops—*mfg*	33271	3599
Machinery, Other Commercial and Service Industry—*mfg*	333319	3599
Tables–billiard, pool, bagatelle, and pingpong: Sporting and Athletic Goods—*mfg*	33992	3949
Tablets and pads, book and writing: Stationery, Tablet, anJ Related Product—*mfg*	322233	2678
Tablets, metal: Fabricated Metal Product, All Other Miscellaneous—*mfg*	332999	3499
Tablets, pharmaceutical: Pharmaceutical Preparation—*mfg*	325412	2834
Tableware, commercial–vitreous china: Vitreous China, Fine Earthenware and Other Pottery Product—*mfg*	327112	3262
Tableware, glass and glass ceramic: Pressed and Blown Glass and Glassware, Other—*mfg*	327212	3229
Tableware, plastics–except foam: Plastics Pipe and Pipe Fitting—*mfg*	326122	3089
Plastics Product, All Other—*mfg*	326199	3089
Unsupported Plastics Profile Shape—*mfg*	326121	3089
Tableware–commercial and household-semivitreous: Vitreous China, Fine Earthenware and Other Pottery Product—*mfg*	327112	3263
Tabulating card set forms (business forms): Manifold Business Form Printing—*mfg*	323116	2761
Tabulating cards, printed or unprinted–die-cut from purchased paperboard: Converted Paper Product, All Other—*mfg*	322298	2675
Die-Cut Paper and Paperboard Office Supplies—*mfg*	322231	2675
Surface-Coated Paperboard—*mfg*	322292	2675
Tabulating servioe, computer: Data Processing Services—*info*	51421	7374
Tabulation cards: Office Supplies and Stationery Stores—*retail*	45321	5112
Stationary and Office Supplies—*whlse*	42212	5112
Tachometer generators: Electronic Coil, Transformer, and Other Inductor—*mfg*	334416	3825
Instrument for Measuring and Testing Electricity and Electrical Signals—*mfg*	334515	3825
Tachometer, centrifugal: Totalizing Fluid Meter and Counting Device—*mfg*	334514	3824
Tackifiers, organic: Basic Organic Chemical, All Other—*mfg*	325199	2869
Tackle blocks, metal: Hardware—*mfg*	33251	3429
Tackle blocks, wood: Manufacturing, All Other Miscellaneous—*mfg*	339999	2499
Wood Container and Pallet—*mfg*	32192	2499
Wood Product, All Other Miscellaneous—*mfg*	321999	2499

Entry	NAICS	SIC
Tackle, fishing–except nets, seines, and line: Sporting and Athletic Goods—*mfg*	33992	3949
Tacks: Hardware—*whlse*	42171	5072
Tacks, nonferrous metal (including wire): Iron and Steel Mills—*mfg*	331111	3399
Secondary Smelting and Alloying of Aluminum—*mfg*	331314	3399
Secondary Smelting, Refining, and Alloying of Copper—*mfg*	331423	3399
Secondary Smelting, Refining, and Alloying of Nonferrous Metal (except Copper and Aluminum)—*mfg*	331492	3399
Tacks, steel–wire or cut: Fabricated Wire Product, Other—*mfg*	332618	3315
Steel Wire Drawing—*mfg*	331222	3315
Taconite mining: Iron Ore—*mining*	21221	1011
Taffetas: Broadwoven Fabric Mills—*mfg*	31321	2221
Tagboard: Paperboard Mills—*mfg*	32213	2631
Taghoard, made in paper: Newsprint Mills—*mfg*	322122	2621
Paper (except Newsprint) Mills—*mfg*	322121	2621
Tags, lithographed: Lithographic Printing, Commercial—*mfg*	323110	2752
Quick Printing—*mfg*	323114	2752
Tags, paper–unprinted: Coated and Laminated Paper—*mfg*	322222	2679
Converted Paper Product, All Other—*mfg*	322298	2679
Die-Cut Paper and Paperboard Office Supplies—*mfg*	322231	2679
Non-Folding Sanitary Food Container—*mfg*	322215	2679
Tags, printed–except lithographed or gravure: Digital Printing—*mfg*	323115	2759
Flexographic Printing, Commercial—*mfg*	323112	2759
Printing, Other Commercial—*mfg*	323119	2759
Quick Printing—*mfg*	323114	2759
Tail lights, motor vehicle: Vehicular Lighting Equipment—*mfg*	336321	3647
Tailor shops, except custom or merchant tailors: Personal and Household Goods Repair and Maintenance, Other—*serv*	81149	7219
Tailored dress and sport coats: Men's and Boys' Cut and Sew Apparel Contractors—*mfg*	315211	2311
Men's and Boys' Cut and Sew Suit, Coat and Overcoat—*mfg*	315222	2311
Tailors' chalk: Chemical Product, All Other Miscellaneous—*mfg*	325998	3952
Institutional Furniture—*mfg*	337127	3952
Lead Pencil and Art Good—*mfg*	339942	3952
Tailors' pressing blocks, wood: Manufacturing, All Other Miscellaneous—*mfg*	339999	2499
Wood Container and Pallet—*mfg*	32192	2499
Wood Product, All Other Miscellaneous—*mfg*	321999	2499
Tailors' scissors: Cutlery and Flatware (except Precious)—*mfg*	332211	3421
Tailors' shears, hand: Cutlery and Flatware (except Precious)—*mfg*	332211	3421
Tailors' supplies: Cosmetics, Beauty Supplies and Perfume Stores—*retail*	44612	5087
Service Establishment Equipment and Supplies—*whlse*	42185	5087
Tailors, custom: Clothing Accessories Stores—*retail*	44815	5699
Clothing Stores, Other—*retail*	44819	5699
Talc mining: Crushed and Broken Stone and Quarrying, Other—*mining*	212319	1499
Non-Metallic Mineral, All Other—*mining*	212399	1499
Talc, ground or otherwise treated: Ground or Treated Mineral and Earth—*mfg*	327992	3295
Talcum powders: Soap and Other Detergent—*mfg*	325611	2844
Toilet Preparation—*mfg*	32562	2844
Talfrail logs: Search, Detection, Navigation, Guidance, Aeronautical, and Nautical System and Instrument—*mfg*	334511	3812
Tall oil, except skimmings: Gum and Wood Chemical—*mfg*	325191	2861
Tallate driers: Paint and Coating—*mfg*	32551	2851
Tallow rendering, inedible: Fats and Oils Refining and Blending—*mfg*	311225	2077
Fresh and Frozen Seafood Processing—*mfg*	311712	2077
Rendering and Meat By-product Processing—*mfg*	311613	2077
Seafood Canning—*mfg*	311711	2077
Tallow, vegetable: Fats and Oils Refining and Blending—*mfg*	311225	2076
Oilseed Processing, Other—*mfg*	311223	2076
Tally counters: Totalizing Fluid Meter and Counting Device—*mfg*	334514	3824
Tallying meters–except electrical instruments, watches, and clocks: Totalizing Fluid Meter and Counting Device—*mfg*	334514	3824
Tamales, canned: Canning, Specialty—*mfg*	311422	2032
Food, All Other Miscellaneous—*mfg*	311999	2032
Tampers, powered: Construction Machinery—*mfg*	33312	3531
Overhead Traveling Crane, Hoist and Monorail System—*mfg*	333923	3531
Railroad Rolling Stock—*mfg*	33651	3531
Tamping equipment, rail: Construction Machinery—*mfg*	33312	3531
Overhead Traveling Crane, Hoist and Monorail System—*mfg*	333923	3531
Railroad Rolling Stock—*mfg*	33651	3531
Tampions for guns more than 30 mm. (or more than 1.18 inch): Ordnance and Accessories, Other—*mfg*	332995	3489
Tampons: Sanitary Paper Product—*mfg*	322291	2676
Tangerine groves and farms: Citrus (except Orange) Groves—*ag*	11132	174
Orange Groves—*ag*	11131	174
Tank artillery: Ordnance and Accessories, Other—*mfg*	332995	3489
Tank blocks, glasshouse–clay: Clay Refractory—*mfg*	327124	3255
Tank cleaning, ship: Water, Other Support Activities for—*trans*	48839	7699
Tank components, specialized–military: Military Armored Vehicle, Tank and Tank Component—*mfg*	336992	3795
Tank engines and engine parts, internal combustion–military: Engine Equipment, Other—*mfg*	333618	3519
Motor Vehicle Parts, All Other—*mfg*	336399	3519
Tank freight cars and car equipment: Pump and Pumping Equipment—*mfg*	333911	3743
Railroad Rolling Stock—*mfg*	33651	3743
Tank liner brick, vitrified clay: Structural Clay Product, Other—*mfg*	327123	3259
Tank recovery vehicles: Military Armored Vehicle, Tank and Tank Component—*mfg*	336992	3795
Tank tops: Infants' Cut and Sew Apparel—*mfg*	315291	2361
Men's and Boys' Cut and Sew Apparel Contractors—*mfg*	315211	2321
Men's and Boys' Cut and Sew Apparel Contractors—*mfg*	315211	2361
Men's and Boys' Cut and Sew Shirt (except Work Shirt)—*mfg*	315223	2361

ALPHABETICAL INDEX	NAICS	SIC
Men's and Boys' Cut and Sew Shirt (except Work Shirt)—*mfg*	315223	2321
Outerwear Knitting Mills—*mfg*	315191	2253
Women's and Girls' Cut and Sew Apparel Contractors—*mfg*	315212	2361
Women's and Girls' Cut and Sew Blouse and Shirt—*mfg*	315232	2361
Women's and Girls' Cut and Sew Dress—*mfg*	315233	2361
Tank tops, outerwear: Women's and Girls' Cut and Sew Apparel Contractors—*mfg*	315212	2331
Women's and Girls' Cut and Sew Blouse and Shirt—*mfg*	315232	2331
Tank towers, metal plate: Air-Conditioning and Warm Air Heating Equipment and Commercial and Industrial Refrigeration Equipment—*mfg*	333415	3443
Metal Tank (Heavy Gauge)—*mfg*	33242	3443
Plate Work—*mfg*	332313	3443
Power Boiler and Heat Exchanger—*mfg*	33241	3443
Tank truck meters: Totalizing Fluid Meter and Counting Device—*mfg*	334514	3824
Tank turbines: Turbine and Turbine Generator Set Unit—*mfg*	333611	3511
Tankers (ships), building and repairing: Ship Building and Repairing—*mfg*	336611	3731
Tanks and tank components: Transportation Equipment and Supplies (except Motor Vehicle)—*whlse*	42186	5088
Tanks for tank trucks, metal plate: Air-Conditioning and Warm Air Heating Equipment and Commercial and Industrial Refrigeration Equipment—*mfg*	333415	3443
Metal Tank (Heavy Gauge)—*mfg*	33242	3443
Plate Work—*mfg*	332313	3443
Power Boiler and Heat Exchanger—*mfg*	33241	3443
Tanks, concrete: Concrete Pipe—*mfg*	327332	3272
Concrete Product, Other—*mfg*	32739	3272
Nonmetallic Mineral Product, All Other Miscellaneous—*mfg*	327999	3272
Tanks, flush–vitreous china: Vitreous China Plumbing Fixture and China and Earthenware Fittings and Bathroom Accessories—*mfg*	327111	3261
Tanks, fuel–aircraft: Aircraft Part and Auxiliary Equipment, Other—*mfg*	336413	3728
Fluid Power Valve and Hose Fitting—*mfg*	332912	3728
Tanks, gas–motor vehicle: Gasoline Engine and Engine Parts—*mfg*	336312	3714
Motor Vehicle Parts, All Other—*mfg*	336399	3714
Tanks, metal plate–lined: Air-Conditioning and Warm Air Heating Equipment and Commercial and Industrial Refrigeration Equipment—*mfg*	333415	3443
Metal Tank (Heavy Gauge)—*mfg*	33242	3443
Plate Work—*mfg*	332313	3443
Power Boiler and Heat Exchanger—*mfg*	33241	3443
Tanks, military–including factory rebuilding: Military Armored Vehicle, Tank and Tank Component—*mfg*	336992	3795
Tanks, soda water: Air-Conditioning and Warm Air Heating Equipment and Commercial and Industrial Refrigeration Equipment—*mfg*	333415	3585
Motor Vehicle Air-Conditioning—*mfg*	336391	3585
Tanks, standard and custom fabricated–metal plate-made in boiler shops: Air-Conditioning and Warm Air Heating Equipment and Commercial and Industrial Refrigeration Equipment—*mfg*	333415	3443
Metal Tank (Heavy Gauge)—*mfg*	33242	3443
Plate Work—*mfg*	332313	3443
Power Boiler and Heat Exchanger—*mfg*	33241	3443
Tanks, wood–coopered: Wood Container and Pallet—*mfg*	32192	2449
Tanks–photographic developing, fixing, and washing: Photographic and Photocopying Equipment—*mfg*	333315	3861
Photographic Film, Paper, Plate and Chemical—*mfg*	325992	3861
Tanneries, leather: Leather and Hide Tanning and Finishing—*mfg*	31611	3111
Tannery machines: Industrial Machinery, All Other—*mfg*	333298	3559
Machinery, Other Commercial and Service Industry—*mfg*	333319	3559
Tannic acid: Basic Organic Chemical, All Other—*mfg*	325199	2869
Tanning agents, syntbetic organic: Basic Organic Chemical, All Other—*mfg*	325199	2869
Tanning agents, synthetic inorganic: Basic Inorganic Chemical, All Other—*mfg*	325188	2819
Chemical Product, All Other Miscellaneous—*mfg*	325998	2819
Tanning and currying furs: Leather and Hide Tanning and Finishing—*mfg*	31611	3999
Tanning extracts and materials, natural: Gum and Wood Chemical—*mfg*	325191	2861
Tanning salons: Personal Care Services, Other—*serv*	812199	7299
Tantalite mining: Copper Ore and Nickel Ore—*mining*	212234	1061
Metal Ore, All Other—*mining*	212299	1061
Tantalum ore mining: Copper Ore and Nickel Ore—*mining*	212234	1061
Metal Ore, All Other—*mining*	212299	1061
Tantalum refining: Primary Smelting and Refining of Nonferrous Metal (except Copper and Aluminum)—*mfg*	331419	3339
Tap rooms (drinking places): Drinking Places (Alcoholic Beverages)—*accom*	72241	5813
Tape cleaners, magnetic–computer peripheral equipment: Computer Peripheral Equipment, Other—*mfg*	334119	3577
Tape distribution for television: Durable Goods, Other Miscellaneous—*whlse*	42199	7822
Motion Picture and Video Distribution—*info*	51212	7822
Tape players and recorders, household: Electrical Appliance, Television and Radio Set—*whlse*	42162	5064
Tape players, household: Audio and Video Equipment—*mfg*	33431	3651
Tape print units, computer peripheral equipment: Computer Peripheral Equipment, Other—*mfg*	334119	3577

Description	NAICS	SIC
Tape production, video or motion picture: Motion Picture and Video Production—*info*	51211	7812
Tape recertification service: Computer Related Services, Other—*prof*	541519	7379
Computer Systems Design Services—*prof*	541512	7379
Tape recorder repair: Communication Equipment Repair and Maintenance—*serv*	811213	7622
Consumer Electronics Repair and Maintenance—*serv*	811211	7622
Radio, Television and Other Electronics Stores—*retail*	443112	7622
Tape recorders and players: Automotive Parts and Accessories Stores—*retail*	44131	5731
Radio, Television and Other Electronics Stores—*retail*	443112	5731
Tape recorders for data computers: Computer Storage Device—*mfg*	334112	3572
Tape recorders, household: Audio and Video Equipment—*mfg*	33431	3651
Tape storage units, computer: Computer Storage Device—*mfg*	334112	3572
Tape stores, audio and video: Prerecorded Tape, Compact Disc and Record Stores—*retail*	45122	5735
Tape transports, magnetic: Computer Storage Device—*mfg*	334112	3572
Tape, adhesive–medicated or nonmedicated: Surgical Appliance and Supplies—*mfg*	339113	3842
Tape, asbestos: Motor Vehicle Brake System—*mfg*	33634	3292
Nonmetallic Mineral Product, All Other Miscellaneous—*mfg*	327999	3292
Tape, audio magnetic–prerecorded: Integrated Record Production/Distribution—*info*	51222	3652
Prerecorded Compact Disc (except Software), Tape, and Record Reproducing—*mfg*	334612	3652
Tape, cellophane adhesive-rnfpm: Coated and Laminated Paper—*mfg*	322222	2672
Tape, friction–rubber: Fabric Coating Mills—*mfg*	31332	3069
Rubber Product, All Other—*mfg*	326299	3069
Tape, gummed–cloth and paper base: Coated and Laminated Paper—*mfg*	322222	2672
Tape, hook-and-eye and snap fastener: Fastener, Button, Needle and Pin—*mfg*	339993	3965
Tape, magnetic recording–blank: Magnetic and Optical Recording Media—*mfg*	334613	3695
Tape, masking-rnfg: Coated and Laminated Paper—*mfg*	322222	2672
Tape, pressure sensitive (including friction), rubber: Fabric Coating Mills—*mfg*	31332	3069
Rubber Product, All Other—*mfg*	326299	3069
Tape, pressure sensitive–except rubber backed: Coated and Laminated Paper—*mfg*	322222	2672
Tape, telegraph–paper: Coated and Laminated Paper—*mfg*	322222	2679
Converted Paper Product, All Other—*mfg*	322298	2679
Die-Cut Paper and Paperboard Office Supplies—*mfg*	322231	2679
Non-Folding Sanitary Food Container—*mfg*	322215	2679
Tape, textile: Broadwoven Fabric Finishing Mills—*mfg*	313311	5131
Piece Goods, Notions and Other Dry Goods—*whlse*	42231	5131
Textile and Fabric Finishing (except Broadwoven Fabric) Mills—*mfg*	313312	5131
Tape, varnished–plastics and other coated–except magnetic: Fabric Coating Mills—*mfg*	31332	2295
Tapes, audio and video recording: Electronic Parts and Equipment, Other—*whlse*	42169	5065
Tapes, audio prerecorded: Durable Goods, Other Miscellaneous—*whlse*	42199	5099
Tapes, fabric: Narrow Fabric Mills—*mfg*	313221	2241
Tapes, surveyors': Measuring and Controlling Device, Other—*mfg*	334519	3829
Surgical and Medical Instrument—*mfg*	339112	3829
Tapes, video, recorded: Durable Goods, Other Miscellaneous—*whlse*	42199	7822
Motion Picture and Video Distribution—*info*	51212	7822
Tapestry fabrics, cotton: Broadwoven Fabric Mills—*mfg*	31321	2211
Tapestry fabrics, manmade fiber and silk: Broadwoven Fabric Mills—*mfg*	31321	2221
Taping and finishing drywall–contractors: Drywall, Plastering, Acoustical and Insulation Contractors—*const*	23542	1742
Tapioca: Wet Corn Milling—*mfg*	311221	2046
Tapping attachments: Industrial Machinery and Equipment—*whlse*	42183	5084
Tapping machines: Machine Tool (Metal Cutting Types)—*mfg*	333512	3541
Taps, current–attachment plug and screw shell types: Current-Carrying Wiring Device—*mfg*	335931	3643
Taps, machine tool: Cutting Tool and Machine Tool Accessory—*mfg*	333515	3545
Hand and Edge Tool—*mfg*	332212	3545
Taps, shoe–regardless of material: Fastener, Button, Needle and Pin—*mfg*	339993	3131
Leather Good, All Other—*mfg*	316999	3131
Wood Product, All Other Miscellaneous—*mfg*	321999	3131
Tar acid resins: Plastics Material and Resin—*mfg*	325211	2821
Tar and asphalt mixtures for paving, not made in petroleum refineries: Asphalt Paving Mixture and Block—*mfg*	324121	2951
Tar and tar oils, products of wood distillation: Gum and Wood Chemical—*mfg*	325191	2861
Tar or residuum, produced in petroleum refineries: Petroleum Refineries—*mfg*	32411	2911
Tar paper, building and roofing: Newsprint Mills—*mfg*	322122	2621
Paper (except Newsprint) Mills—*mfg*	322121	2621
Tar paper, roofing: Asphalt Shingle and Coating Materials—*mfg*	324122	2952
Tar paper–except building or roofing and packaging: Coated and Laminated Paper—*mfg*	322222	2672
Tar sands mining: Crude Petroleum and Natural Gas Extraction—*mining*	211111	1311
Tar, derived from chemical recovery coke ovens: Iron and Steel Mills—*mfg*	331111	3312
Petroleum and Coal Productsa, All Other—*mfg*	324199	3312
Tar, product of coal tar distillation: Cyclic Crude and Intermediate—*mfg*	325192	2865
Petrochemical—*mfg*	32511	2865
Target drones for use by ships, metal: Fabricated Metal Product, All Other Miscellaneous—*mfg*	332999	3499

ALPHABETICAL INDEX	NAICS	SIC
Target drones, aircraft: Aircraft Part and Auxiliary Equipment, Other—*mfg*	336413	3728
Fluid Power Valve and Hose Fitting—*mfg*	332912	3728
Target shooting equipment, except small arms and ammunition: Sporting and Athletic Goods—*mfg*	33992	3949
Targets, archery and rifle shooting: Sporting and Athletic Goods—*mfg*	33992	3949
Targets, clay: Sporting and Athletic Goods—*mfg*	33992	3949
Targets, trailer type–aircraft: Aircraft Part and Auxiliary Equipment, Other—*mfg*	336413	3728
Fluid Power Valve and Hose Fitting—*mfg*	332912	3728
Tariff consultant: Freight Arrangement—*trans*	48851	4731
Management Consulting Services, Other—*prof*	541618	4731
Tariff rate information service: Freight Arrangement—*trans*	48851	4731
Management Consulting Services, Other—*prof*	541618	4731
Tarlatan, cotton: Broadwoven Fabric Mills—*mfg*	31321	2211
Tarpaulins, fabric: Canvas and Related Product Mills—*mfg*	314912	2394
Tartaric acid and metallic salts: Basic Organic Chemical, All Other—*mfg*	325199	2869
Tartrates: Basic Organic Chemical, All Other—*mfg*	325199	2869
Tatting thread–cotton, silk, manmade fibers, and wool: Textile and Fabric Finishing (except Broadwoven Fabric) Mills—*mfg*	313312	2284
Thread Mills—*mfg*	313113	2284
Tattoo parlors: Personal Services, All Other—*serv*	81299	7299
Taverns (drinking places): Drinking Places (Alcoholic Beverages)—*accom*	72241	5813
Tax certificate dealers: Financial Investment Activities, Miscellaneous—*fin*	523999	6211
Intermediation, Miscellaneous—*fin*	52391	6211
Investment Banking and Securities Dealing—*fin*	52311	6211
Securities Brokerage—*fin*	52312	6211
Tax certIficate sale and redemption agencies: Commodity Contracts Dealing—*fin*	52313	6099
Credit Intermediation, Other Activities Related to—*fin*	52239	6099
Financial Investment Activities, Miscellaneous—*fin*	523999	6099
Financial Transactions Processing, Reserve, and Clearing House Activities—*fin*	52232	6099
Trust, Fiduciary and Custody Activities—*fin*	523991	6099
Tax collection agencies–collecting for acity, county, or State: Financial Transactions Processing, Reserve, and Clearing House Activities—*fin*	52232	7389
Tax liens–holding, buying, and selling: Commodity Contracts Dealing—*fin*	52313	6799
Financial Investment Activities, Miscellaneous—*fin*	523999	6799
Intermediation, Miscellaneous—*fin*	52391	6799
Portfolio Management—*fin*	52392	6799
Tax Preparation Services	**541213**	**7291**

ALPHABETICAL INDEX	NAICS	SIC
Tax return preparation services without accounting, auditing, or bookkeepingservices: Tax Preparation Services—*prof*	541213	7291
Tax title dealers–agencies for city, county, or State: Legal Services, All Other—*prof*	541199	7389
Taxation departments: Public Finance—*pub*	92113	9311
Taxi and Limousine Service	**4853**	
Taxi Service	**48531**	**4121**
Taxicab card advertising: Advertising Material Distribution Services—*prof*	54187	7319
Advertising, Other Services Related to—*prof*	54189	7319
Display Advertising—*prof*	54185	7319
Media Buying Agencies—*prof*	54183	7319
Nonscheduled Air, Other—*trans*	481219	7319
Taxicab operation: Taxi Service—*trans*	48531	4121
Taxicabs: Automobile—*mfg*	336111	3711
Automobile and Other Motor Vehicle—*whlse*	42111	5012
Heavy Duty Truck—*mfg*	33612	3711
Light Truck and Utility Vehicle—*mfg*	336112	3711
Military Armored Vehicle, Tank and Tank Component—*mfg*	336992	3711
Motor Vehicle Body—*mfg*	336211	3711
Taximeters: Totalizing Fluid Meter and Counting Device—*mfg*	334514	3824
Taxpayers' associations: Civic and Social Organizations—*serv*	81341	8641
Tea: Grocery and Related Products, Other—*whlse*	42249	5149
Tea bags, fabric: Textile Bag Mills—*mfg*	314911	2393
Tea blending: Coffee and Tea—*mfg*	31192	2099
Tea kettles, electric: Electric Housewares and Household Fan—*mfg*	335211	3634
Heating Equipment (except Electric and Warm Air Furnaces)—*mfg*	333414	3634
Tea kettles, glass and glass ceramic: Pressed and Blown Glass and Glassware, Other—*mfg*	327212	3229
Tea rooms: Cafeterias—*accom*	722212	5812
Caterers—*accom*	72232	5812
Foodservice Contractors—*accom*	72231	5812
Full-Service Restaurants—*accom*	72211	5812
Limited-Service Restaurants—*accom*	722211	5812
Snack and Nonalcoholic Beverage Bars—*accom*	722213	5812
Theater Companies and Dinner Theaters—*arts*	71111	5812
Tea stores: Food (Health) Supplement Stores—*retail*	446191	5499
Food Stores, All Other Specialty—*retail*	445299	5499
Limited-Service Restaurants—*accom*	722211	5499
Meat Markets—*retail*	44521	5499
Tea wagons, metal: Metal Household Furniture—*mfg*	337124	2514
Tea wagons, wood: Nonupholstered Wood Household Furniture—*mfg*	337122	2511
Tea, iced–bottled or canned: Bottled Water—*mfg*	312112	2086
Soft Drink—*mfg*	312111	2086

Entry	NAICS	SIC
Teaberries, gathering of: Crop Farming, All Other Miscellaneous—*ag*	111998	831
Forest Nurseries and Gathering of Forest Products—*ag*	11321	831
Teacher certification bureaus: Education Programs, Administration of—*pub*	92311	9411
Teachers' registries: Employment Placement Agencies—*admin*	56131	7361
Human Resources and Executive Search Consulting Services—*prof*	541612	7361
Teaching machines and aids, electronic: Electrical Equipment and Component, All Other Miscellaneous—*mfg*	335999	3699
Machinery, Other Commercial and Service Industry—*mfg*	333319	3699
Teakettles, except electric–stamped metal: Kitchen Utensil, Pot and Pan—*mfg*	332214	3469
Tear gas: Basic Organic Chemical, All Other—*mfg*	325199	2869
Teaseling cotton broadwoven goods: Broadwoven Fabric Finishing Mills—*mfg*	313311	2261
Teaseling manmade fiber and silk broad-woven fabrics: Broadwoven Fabric Finishing Mills—*mfg*	313311	2262
Technetium products: In-Vitro Diagnostic Substance—*mfg*	325413	2835
Pharmaceutical Preparation—*mfg*	325412	2835
Technical and Trade Schools	**61151**	
Technical and Trade Schools	**6115**	
Technical and Trade Schools, Other	**611519**	**8243**
Technical glassware and glass products, pressed or blown: Pressed and Blown Glass and Glassware, Other—*mfg*	327212	3229
Technical glassware, made from purchased glass: Glass Product Made of Purchased Glass—*mfg*	327215	3231
Technical institutes: Junior Colleges—*educ*	61121	8222
Technical manuals and papers–publishing and printing, or publishing only: Database and Directory Publishers—*info*	51114	2741
Music Publishers—*info*	51223	2741
Publishers, All Other—*info*	511199	2741
Teddies: Infants' Cut and Sew Apparel—*mfg*	315291	2341
Women's and Girls' Cut and Sew Apparel Contractors—*mfg*	315212	2341
Women's and Girls' Cut and Sew Lingerie, Loungewear and Nightwear—*mfg*	315231	2341
Tee shirts, custom printed: Clothing Accessories Stores—*retail*	44815	5699
Clothing Stores, Other—*retail*	44819	5699
Teeth, artificial–made in dental laboratories to order for the profession: Dental Laboratories—*mfg*	339116	8072
Teeth, artificial–not made in dental laboratories: Dental Equipment and Supplies—*mfg*	339114	3843
Teeth, bucket and scarifier: Construction Machinery—*mfg*	33312	3531
Overhead Traveling Crane, Hoist and Monorail System—*mfg*	333923	3531
Railroad Rolling Stock—*mfg*	33651	3531
Teething rings, rubber: Fabric Coating Mills—*mfg*	31332	3069
Rubber Product, All Other—*mfg*	326299	3069
Telecommunications	**5133**	
Telecommunications equipment installation-contractors: Electrical Contractors—*const*	23531	1731
Security Systems Services (except Locksmiths)—*admin*	561621	1731
Telecommunications Resellers	**51333**	**4813**
Telecommunications, Other	**51339**	**4899**
Telegram services: Wired Telecommunications Carriers—*info*	51331	4822
Telegraph and telephone carrier and i peater equipment: Electronic Coil, Transformer, and Other Inductor—*mfg*	334416	3661
Printed Circuit/Electronics Assembly—*mfg*	334418	3661
Telephone Apparatus—*mfg*	33421	3661
Telegraph cable services: Wired Telecommunications Carriers—*info*	51331	4822
Telegraph equipment: Electronic Parts and Equipment, Other—*whlse*	42169	5065
Telegraph line construction–general contractors: Power and Communication Transmission Line—*const*	23492	1623
Water, Sewer, and Pipeline—*const*	23491	1623
Telegraph office switching equipment: Electronic Coil, Transformer, and Other Inductor—*mfg*	334416	3661
Printed Circuit/Electronics Assembly—*mfg*	334418	3661
Telephone Apparatus—*mfg*	33421	3661
Telegraph services: Wired Telecommunications Carriers—*info*	51331	4822
Telegraph station equipment and parts, wire: Electronic Coil, Transformer, and Other Inductor—*mfg*	334416	3661
Printed Circuit/Electronics Assembly—*mfg*	334418	3661
Telephone Apparatus—*mfg*	33421	3661
Telegraph tape, paper: Coated and Laminated Paper—*mfg*	322222	2679
Converted Paper Product, All Other—*mfg*	322298	2679
Die-Cut Paper and Paperboard Office Supplies—*mfg*	322231	2679
Non-Folding Sanitary Food Container—*mfg*	322215	2679
Telemarketing (telephone marketing) service on a contract or fee basis: Telemarketing Bureaus—*admin*	561422	7389
Telemarketing Bureaus	**561422**	**7389**
Telemetering equipment, electronic: Radio and Television Broadcasting and Wireless Communications Equipment—*mfg*	33422	3663
Telemetering instruments, industrial process type: Instruments and Related Products for Measuring, Displaying, and Controlling Industrial Process Variables—*mfg*	334513	3823
Telephone and telephone equipment installation-contractors: Electrical Contractors—*const*	23531	1731
Security Systems Services (except Locksmiths)—*admin*	561621	1731
Telephone answering machines: Electronic Coil, Transformer, and Other Inductor—*mfg*	334416	3661
Printed Circuit/Electronics Assembly—*mfg*	334418	3661
Telephone Apparatus—*mfg*	33421	3661
Telephone Answering Services	**561421**	**7389**
Telephone Apparatus Manufacturing	**33421**	**3661**
Telephone booths, cleaning and maintenance of: Janitorial Services—*admin*	56172	7349

ALPHABETICAL INDEX	NAICS	SIC
Telephone booths, except wood: Showcase, Partition, Shelving, and Locker—*mfg*	337215	2542
Telephone booths, wood: Architectural Woodwork and Millwork, Custom—*mfg*	337212	2541
Showcase, Partition, Shelving, and Locker—*mfg*	337215	2541
Wood Kitchen Cabinet and Counter Top—*mfg*	33711	2541
Telephone Call Centers	**56142**	
Telephone central office equipment, dial and manual: Electronic Coil, Transformer, and Other Inductor—*mfg*	334416	3661
Printed Circuit/Electronics Assembly—*mfg*	334418	3661
Telephone Apparatus—*mfg*	33421	3661
Telephone counseling service: Child and Youth Services—*hlth*	62411	8322
Community Food Services—*hlth*	62421	8322
Community Housing Services, Other—*hlth*	624229	8322
Emergency and Other Relief Services—*hlth*	62423	8322
Individual and Family Services, Other—*hlth*	62419	8322
Parole Offices and Probation Offices—*pub*	92215	8322
Services for the Elderly and Persons with Disabilities—*hlth*	62412	8322
Temporary Shelters—*hlth*	624221	8322
Telephone dialing devices, automatic: Electronic Coil, Transformer, and Other Inductor—*mfg*	334416	3661
Printed Circuit/Electronics Assembly—*mfg*	334418	3661
Telephone Apparatus—*mfg*	33421	3661
Telephone directories, except lithographed or gravure (not publishing): Digital Printing—*mfg*	323115	2759
Flexographic Printing, Commercial—*mfg*	323112	2759
Printing, Other Commercial—*mfg*	323119	2759
Quick Printing—*mfg*	323114	2759
Telephone directories, gravure printing–not publishing: Gravure Printing, Commercial—*mfg*	323111	2754
Telephone directories–publishing and printing, or publishing only: Database and Directory Publishers—*info*	51114	2741
Music Publishers—*info*	51223	2741
Publishers, All Other—*info*	511199	2741
Telephone equipment: Electronic Parts and Equipment, Other—*whlse*	42169	5065
Telephone line construction–general contractors: Power and Communication Transmission Line—*const*	23492	1623
Water, Sewer, and Pipeline—*const*	23491	1623
Telephone set repair: Communication Equipment Repair and Maintenance—*serv*	811213	7629
Consumer Electronics Repair and Maintenance—*serv*	811211	7629
Telephone sets, except cellular radio telephone: Electronic Coil, Transformer, and Other Inductor—*mfg*	334416	3661
Printed Circuit/Electronics Assembly—*mfg*	334418	3661
Telephone Apparatus—*mfg*	33421	3661

ALPHABETICAL INDEX	NAICS	SIC
Telephone solicitation service on a contract or fee basis: Telemarketing Bureaus—*admin*	561422	7389
Telephone stands, wood: Nonupholstered Wood Household Furniture—*mfg*	337122	2511
Telephone station equipment and parts, wire: Electronic Coil, Transformer, and Other Inductor—*mfg*	334416	3661
Printed Circuit/Electronics Assembly—*mfg*	334418	3661
Telephone Apparatus—*mfg*	33421	3661
Telephone stores: Stores (except Tobacco Stores), All Other Miscellaneous—*retail*	453998	5999
Telephones, cellular radio: Radio and Television Broadcasting and Wireless Communications Equipment—*mfg*	33422	3663
Telephones, sound powered (no battery): Electronic Coil, Transformer, and Other Inductor—*mfg*	334416	3661
Printed Circuit/Electronics Assembly—*mfg*	334418	3661
Telephone Apparatus—*mfg*	33421	3661
Telephones, underwater: Electronic Coil, Transformer, and Other Inductor—*mfg*	334416	3661
Printed Circuit/Electronics Assembly—*mfg*	334418	3661
Telephone Apparatus—*mfg*	33421	3661
Teleprinters (computer terminals): Computer Terminal—*mfg*	334113	3575
Teleproduction and Other Post-Production Services	**512191**	**7819**
Telescopes: Optical Instrument and Lens—*mfg*	333314	3827
Stores (except Tobacco Stores), All Other Miscellaneous—*retail*	453998	5999
Telescopic sights: Optical Instrument and Lens—*mfg*	333314	3827
Teletypewriter paper, rolls with carbon: Coated and Laminated Paper—*mfg*	322222	2679
Converted Paper Product, All Other—*mfg*	322298	2679
Die-Cut Paper and Paperboard Office Supplies—*mfg*	322231	2679
Non-Folding Sanitary Food Container—*mfg*	322215	2679
Teletypewriter services: Wired Telecommunications Carriers—*info*	51331	4822
Television and radio chassis–stamped metal: Metal Stamping—*mfg*	332116	3469
Television and radio stations, service and repair of-contractors: Trade Contractors, All Other Special—*const*	23599	1799
Television and radio time, sale of–not auxiliary to television or radio broadcasting: Media Representatives—*prof*	54184	7313
Television Broadcasting	**51312**	**4833**
Television broadcasting stations: Television Broadcasting—*info*	51312	4833
Television cabinets, plastics: Household Furniture (except Wood and Metal)—*mfg*	337125	2519
Television cabinets, wood: Wood Television, Radio, and Sewing Machine Cabinet—*mfg*	337129	2517
Television closed-circuit equipment: Radio and Television Broadcasting and Wireless Communications Equipment—*mfg*	33422	3663
Television employment agencies: Employment Placement Agencies—*admin*	56131	7922

Entry	NAICS	SIC
Television film production: Motion Picture and Video Production—*info*	51211	7812
Television monitors: Radio and Television Broadcasting and Wireless Communications Equipment—*mfg*	33422	3663
Television receiving and transmitting tubes: Electronic Parts and Equipment, Other—*whlse*	42169	5065
Television receiving sets: Audio and Video Equipment—*mfg*	33431	3651
Television rental and leasing: Consumer Electronics and Appliances Rental—*real*	53221	7359
Television repair shops: Communication Equipment Repair and Maintenance—*serv*	811213	7622
Consumer Electronics Repair and Maintenance—*serv*	811211	7622
Radio, Television and Other Electronics Stores—*retail*	443112	7622
Television schedules–publishing and printing, or publishing only: Periodical Publishers—*info*	51112	2721
Television set stores: Automotive Parts and Accessories Stores—*retail*	44131	5731
Radio, Television and Other Electronics Stores—*retail*	443112	5731
Television sets: Electrical Appliance, Television and Radio Set—*whlse*	42162	5064
Television tape services (e.g., editing and transfers): Independent Artists, Writers, and Performers—*arts*	71151	7819
Motion Picture and Video Industries, Other—*info*	512199	7819
Prerecorded Compact Disc (except Software), Tape, and Record Reproducing—*mfg*	334612	7819
Teleproduction and Other Post-Production Services—*info*	512191	7819
Television tower sections, prefabricated metal: Fabricated Structural Metal—*mfg*	332312	3441
Television transmitting antennas and ground equipment: Radio and Television Broadcasting and Wireless Communications Equipment—*mfg*	33422	3663
Television transmitting tower construction–general contractors: Power and Communication Transmission Line—*const*	23492	1623
Water, Sewer, and Pipeline—*const*	23491	1623
Television tube blanks, glass: Pressed and Blown Glass and Glassware, Other—*mfg*	327212	3229
Television tubes: Electron Tube—*mfg*	334411	3671
Television, mail-order home shopping: Electronic Shopping and Mail-Order Houses—*retail*	45411	5961
Television, subscription or closed circuit: Cable and Other Program Distribution—*info*	51322	4841
Cable Networks—*info*	51321	4841
Telex services: Wired Telecommunications Carriers—*info*	51331	4822
Telluride (gold) mining: Gold Ore—*mining*	212221	1041
Tellurium refining, primary: Primary Smelting and Refining of Nonferrous Metal (except Copper and Aluminum)—*mfg*	331419	3339
Temperature controls, automatic–residential and commercial types: Automatic Environmental Control for Residential, Commercial and Appliance Use—*mfg*	334512	3822
Temperature instruments–industrial process type, except glass and bimetal: Instruments and Related Products for Measuring, Displaying, and Controlling Industrial Process Variables—*mfg*	334513	3823
Temperature sensors for motor windings: Automatic Environmental Control for Residential, Commercial and Appliance Use—*mfg*	334512	3822
Temperature testing chambers: General Purpose Machinery , All Other—*mfg*	333999	3569
Tempered glass: Flat Glass—*mfg*	327211	3211
Tempered glass, made from purchased glass: Glass Product Made of Purchased Glass—*mfg*	327215	3231
Tempering of metal for the trade: Metal Heat Treating—*mfg*	332811	3398
Templates, drafting: Measuring and Controlling Device, Other—*mfg*	334519	3829
Surgical and Medical Instrument—*mfg*	339112	3829
Temples: Religious Organizations—*serv*	81311	8661
Temples and fronts, ophthalmic: Ophthalmic Goods—*mfg*	339115	3851
Temporary help service: Employee Leasing Services—*admin*	56133	7363
Temporary Help Services—*admin*	56132	7363
Temporary Help Services	**56132**	**7363**
Temporary Shelters	**624221**	**8322**
Ten pin centers: Bowling Centers—*arts*	71395	7933
Tenant associations, except property management: Civic and Social Organizations—*serv*	81341	8641
Tenders (ships), building and repairing: Ship Building and Repairing—*mfg*	336611	3731
Tenders, baby (vehicles): Game, Toy, and Children's Vehicle—*mfg*	339932	3944
Tenders, locomotive: Pump and Pumping Equipment—*mfg*	333911	3743
Railroad Rolling Stock—*mfg*	33651	3743
Tennis clubs, membership: Fitness and Recreational Sports Centers—*arts*	71394	7997
Tennis clubs, nonmembership: Fitness and Recreational Sports Centers—*arts*	71394	7999
Tennis court construction, outdoor–general contractors: Heavy, All Other—*const*	23499	1629
Industrial Nonbuilding Structure—*const*	23493	1629
Tennis courts, outdoor and indoor–operation of, nonmembership: Fitness and Recreational Sports Centers—*arts*	71394	7999
Tennis goods and equipment: Sporting Goods Stores—*retail*	45111	5941
Tennis goods–e.g., balls, frames, rackets: Sporting and Athletic Goods—*mfg*	33992	3949
Tennis shirts: Outerwear Knitting Mills—*mfg*	315191	2253
Tenoners (woodworking machines): Sawmill and Woodworking Machinery—*mfg*	33321	3553
Tensile strength testing equipment: Measuring and Controlling Device, Other—*mfg*	334519	3829
Surgical and Medical Instrument—*mfg*	339112	3829
Tent poles, wood: Manufacturing, All Other Miscellaneous—*mfg*	339999	2499
Wood Container and Pallet—*mfg*	32192	2499

ALPHABETICAL INDEX	NAICS	SIC
Wood Product, All Other Miscellaneous—*mfg*	321999	2499
Tent shops: Stores (except Tobacco Stores), All Other Miscellaneous—*retail*	453998	5999
Tent-type camping trailers: Travel Trailer and Camper—*mfg*	336214	3792
Tentage: Broadwoven Fabric Mills—*mfg*	31321	2211
Tents: Canvas and Related Product Mills—*mfg*	314912	2394
Terminal and switching companies, railroad: Rail Support Activities—*trans*	48821	4013
Short Line Railroads—*trans*	482112	4013
Terminal operation, waterfront: Marine Cargo Handling—*trans*	48832	4491
Port and Harbor Operations—*trans*	48831	4491
Terminal services, coordinated–at airports: Airport Operations, Other—*trans*	488119	4581
Terminals and connectors for electrical devices: Current-Carrying Wiring Device—*mfg*	335931	3643
Terminals, computer: Computer Terminal—*mfg*	334113	3575
Terminals, freight trucking–with or without maintenance facilities: Road, Other Support Activities for—*trans*	48849	4231
Termite control: Exterminating and Pest Control Services—*admin*	56171	7342
Janitorial Services—*admin*	56172	7342
Terneplate: Iron and Steel Mills—*mfg*	331111	3312
Metal Service Centers and Offices—*whlse*	42151	5051
Petroleum and Coal Productsa, All Other—*mfg*	324199	3312
Ternes, iron and steel–long or short: Iron and Steel Mills—*mfg*	331111	3312
Petroleum and Coal Productsa, All Other—*mfg*	324199	3312
Terpineol: Basic Organic Chemical, All Other—*mfg*	325199	2869
Terra cotta: Brick, Stone and Related Material—*whlse*	42132	5032
Building Material Dealers, Other—*retail*	44419	5032
Terra cotta, architectural–clay: Structural Clay Product, Other—*mfg*	327123	3259
Terrapins, catching of: Crop Farming, All Other Miscellaneous—*ag*	111998	919
Marine Fishing, Other—*ag*	114119	919
Terrazzo products, precast: Concrete Pipe—*mfg*	327332	3272
Concrete Product, Other—*mfg*	32739	3272
Nonmetallic Mineral Product, All Other Miscellaneous—*mfg*	327999	3272
Terrazzo work–contractors: Drywall, Plastering, Acoustical and Insulation Contractors—*const*	23542	1743
Tile, Marble, Terrazzo and Mosaic Contractors—*const*	23543	1743
Terry woven fabrics, cotton: Broadwoven Fabric Mills—*mfg*	31321	2211
Tert-butylated bis (p-phenoxyphenyl) ether fluid: Basic Organic Chemical, All Other—*mfg*	325199	2869
Test boring for construction-contractors: Trade Contractors, All Other Special—*const*	23599	1799
Test development and evaluation service, educational or personnel: Educational Support Services—*educ*	61171	8748
Management Consulting Services, Other—*prof*	541618	8748
Scientific and Technical Consulting Services, Other—*prof*	54169	8748

ALPHABETICAL INDEX	NAICS	SIC
Test drilling for metal mining–on a contract basis: Geophysical Surveying and Mapping Services—*prof*	54136	1081
Metal Support Activities—*mining*	213114	1081
Test drilling for nonmetallic minerals except fuel–on a contract basis: Geophysical Surveying and Mapping Services—*prof*	54136	1481
Non-Metallic Minerals (except Fuels) Support Activities—*mining*	213115	1481
Test equipment for electronic and electrical circuits and equipment: Electronic Coil, Transformer, and Other Inductor—*mfg*	334416	3825
Instrument for Measuring and Testing Electricity and Electrical Signals—*mfg*	334515	3825
Test plugs–plumbers' handtools: Hand and Edge Tool—*mfg*	332212	3423
Test sets, ignition harness: Electronic Coil, Transformer, and Other Inductor—*mfg*	334416	3825
Instrument for Measuring and Testing Electricity and Electrical Signals—*mfg*	334515	3825
Test tubes, made from purchased glass: Glass Product Made of Purchased Glass—*mfg*	327215	3231
Testers for checking hydraulic controls on aircraft: Measuring and Controlling Device, Other—*mfg*	334519	3829
Surgical and Medical Instrument—*mfg*	339112	3829
Testing and measuring equipment, electrical–except automotive: Industrial Machinery and Equipment—*whlse*	42183	5084
Testing chambers for altitude, temperature, ordnance, and power: General Purpose Machinery , All Other—*mfg*	333999	3569
Testing equipment, electrical–automotive: Automotive Parts and Accessories Stores—*retail*	44131	5013
Motor Vehicle Supplies and New Part—*whlse*	42112	5013
Testing equipment–abrasion, shearing strength, tensile strength, and torsion: Measuring and Controlling Device, Other—*mfg*	334519	3829
Surgical and Medical Instrument—*mfg*	339112	3829
Testing Laboratories	**54138**	**8734**
Testing laboratories, except clinical: Testing Laboratories—*prof*	54138	8734
Veterinary Services—*prof*	54194	8734
Testing laboratories, medical–analytic or diagnostic: Diagnostic Imaging Centers—*hlth*	621512	8071
Medical Laboratories—*hlth*	621511	8071
Testing services, educational or personnel: Educational Support Services—*educ*	61171	8748
Management Consulting Services, Other—*prof*	541618	8748
Scientific and Technical Consulting Services, Other—*prof*	54169	8748
Tetrachloroethylene: Basic Organic Chemical, All Other—*mfg*	325199	2869
Tetraethyl lead: Basic Organic Chemical, All Other—*mfg*	325199	2869
Tetryl (explosives): Explosives—*mfg*	32592	2892
Text paper: Newsprint Mills—*mfg*	322122	2621
Paper (except Newsprint) Mills—*mfg*	322121	2621
Textbooks–printing or printing and binding, not publishing: Book Printing—*mfg*	323117	2732

Description	NAICS	SIC
Textbooks–publishing and printing, or publishing only: Book Publishers—*info*	51113	2731
Music Publishers—*info*	51223	2731
Textile and Fabric Finishing (except Broadwoven Fabric) Mills	**313312**	**2257**
Textile and Fabric Finishing and Fabric Coating Mills	**3133**	
Textile and Fabric Finishing Mills	**31331**	
Textile Bag and Canvas Mills	**31491**	
Textile Bag Mills	**314911**	**2393**
Textile converters except knit goods: Broadwoven Fabric Finishing Mills—*mfg*	313311	5131
Piece Goods, Notions and Other Dry Goods—*whlse*	42231	5131
Textile and Fabric Finishing (except Broadwoven Fabric) Mills—*mfg*	313312	5131
Textile designers: Industrial Design Services—*prof*	54142	7389
Textile finishing agents: Surface Active Agent—*mfg*	325613	2843
Textile finishing machinery–bleaching, dyeing, mercerizing, and printing: Textile Machinery—*mfg*	333292	3552
Textile Furnishings Mills	**3141**	
Textile glass fibers: Pressed and Blown Glass and Glassware, Other—*mfg*	327212	3229
Textile guides, porcelain: Vitreous China, Fine Earthenware and Other Pottery Product—*mfg*	327112	3269
Textile leathers–apron picker leather, and mill strapping: Leather Good, All Other—*mfg*	316999	3199
Textile machinery and equipment: Industrial Machinery and Equipment—*whlse*	42183	5084
Textile Machinery Manufacturing	**333292**	**3552**
Textile machinery parts: Textile Machinery—*mfg*	333292	3552
Textile machinery, except sewing machines: Textile Machinery—*mfg*	333292	3552
Textile marking stamps, hand: Marking Device—*mfg*	339943	3953
Textile Mills	**313**	
Textile mills, broadwoven cotton: Broadwoven Fabric Mills—*mfg*	31321	2211
Textile mills, broadwoven–silk, and manmade fiber including glass: Broadwoven Fabric Mills—*mfg*	31321	2221
Textile mills, narrow woven fabric–cotton, wool, silk, and manmade fibers-including glass: Narrow Fabric Mills—*mfg*	313221	2241
Textile mills–linen, jute, hemp, and ramie yarn, thread, and fabrics: Broadwoven Fabric Mills—*mfg*	31321	2299
Narrow Fabric Mills—*mfg*	313221	2299
Nonwoven Fabric Mills—*mfg*	31323	2299
Textile and Fabric Finishing (except Broadwoven Fabric) Mills—*mfg*	313312	2299
Textile Product Mills, All Other Miscellaneous—*mfg*	314999	2299
Thread Mills—*mfg*	313113	2299
Yarn Spinning Mills—*mfg*	313111	2299
Textile printers' supplies: Industrial Machinery and Equipment—*whlse*	42183	5085
Industrial Supplies—*whlse*	42184	5085
Textile printing machines: Textile Machinery—*mfg*	333292	3552
Textile processing assistants: Surface Active Agent—*mfg*	325613	2843
Textile Product Mills, All Other	**31499**	
Textile Product Mills	**314**	
Textile Product Mills, All Other Miscellaneous	**314999**	**2395**
Textile Product Mills, Other	**3149**	
Textile reels, fiber: Fiber Can, Tube, Drum, and Similar Products—*mfg*	322214	2655
Textile scouring compounds and wetting agents: Surface Active Agent—*mfg*	325613	2843
Textile soap: Soap and Other Detergent—*mfg*	325611	2841
Textile spinning bobbins, fiber (metal-end or all-fiber): Fiber Can, Tube, Drum, and Similar Products—*mfg*	322214	2655
Textile turnings and shapes, wood: Textile Machinery—*mfg*	333292	3552
Textile warehousing: General Warehousing and Storage Facilities—*trans*	49311	4226
Refrigerated Warehousing and Storage Facilities—*trans*	49312	4226
Warehousing and Storage Facilities, Other—*trans*	49319	4226
Textile warping, on a contract basis: Broadwoven Fabric Mills—*mfg*	31321	2221
Textile waste: Recyclable Material—*whlse*	42193	5093
Textiles: Broadwoven Fabric Finishing Mills—*mfg*	313311	5131
Piece Goods, Notions and Other Dry Goods—*whlse*	42231	5131
Textile and Fabric Finishing (except Broadwoven Fabric) Mills—*mfg*	313312	5131
Textiles, asbestos–except packing: Motor Vehicle Brake System—*mfg*	33634	3292
Nonmetallic Mineral Product, All Other Miscellaneous—*mfg*	327999	3292
Textiles, bonded fiber–except felt: Nonwoven Fabric Mills—*mfg*	31323	2297
Textured fibers and yarns, noncellulosic:made in chemical plants: Noncellulosic Organic Fiber—*mfg*	325222	2824
Textured yarns: Textile and Fabric Finishing (except Broadwoven Fabric) Mills—*mfg*	313312	2282
Yarn Texturing, Throwing and Twisting Mills—*mfg*	313112	2282
Textured yarns and fibers, cellulosic–made in chemical plants: Cellulosic Organic Fiber—*mfg*	325221	2823
Thacetate fibers: Cellulosic Organic Fiber—*mfg*	325221	2823
Theater buildings (ownership and operation): Lessors of Nonresidential Buildings (except Miniwarehouses)—*real*	53112	6512
Promoters of Performing Arts, Sports and Similar Events with Facilities—*arts*	71131	6512
Theater Companies and Dinner Theaters	**71111**	**7922**
Theater seats: Furniture—*whlse*	42121	5021
Furniture Stores—*retail*	44211	5021
Theaters, dinner: Cafeterias—*accom*	722212	5812
Caterers—*accom*	72232	5812
Foodservice Contractors—*accom*	72231	5812
Full-Service Restaurants—*accom*	72211	5812
Limited-Service Restaurants—*accom*	722211	5812
Snack and Nonalcoholic Beverage Bars—*accom*	722213	5812
Theater Companies and Dinner Theaters—*arts*	71111	5812

ALPHABETICAL INDEX	NAICS	SIC
Theaters, motion picture–drive-in: Drive-In Motion Picture Theaters—*info*	512132	7833
Theaters, motion picture–except drive-in: Motion Picture Theaters, Except Drive-Ins.—*info*	512131	7832
Theatrical booking agencies, except motion picture: Promoters of Performing Arts, Sports and Similar Events without Facilities—*arts*	71132	7922
Theatrical booking agencies, motion picture: Motion Picture and Video Distribution—*info*	51212	7829
Motion Picture and Video Industries, Other—*info*	512199	7829
Theatrical companies: Theater Companies and Dinner Theaters—*arts*	71111	7922
Theatrical costumes: Cut and Sew Apparel, All Other—*mfg*	315299	2389
Theatrical employment agencies: Employment Placement Agencies—*admin*	56131	7922
Theatrical equipment rental: Machinery and Equipment Rental and Leasing, Other Commercial and Industrial—*real*	53249	7922
Theatrical furniture: Institutional Furniture—*mfg*	337127	2531
Theatrical production, except motion picture: Promoters of Performing Arts, Sports and Similar Events without Facilities—*arts*	71132	7922
Theatrical scenery: Wood Product, All Other Miscellaneous—*mfg*	321999	3999
Theatrical ticket agencies: Promoters of Performing Arts, Sports and Similar Events without Facilities—*arts*	71132	7922
Theme parks, amusement: Amusement and Theme Parks—*arts*	71311	7996
Theobromine: Medicinal and Botanical—*mfg*	325411	2833
Theodolites, surveying: Measuring and Controlling Device, Other—*mfg*	334519	3829
Surgical and Medical Instrument—*mfg*	339112	3829
Theological seminaries: Colleges, Universities and Professional Schools—*educ*	61131	8221
Therapeutic X-ray apparatus and tubes–medical, industrial, and research: Irradiation Apparatus—*mfg*	334517	3844
Therapy equipment: Health and Personal Care Stores, All Other—*retail*	446199	5047
Medical, Dental and Hospital Equipment and Supplies—*whlse*	42145	5047
Thermal analysis instruments, laboratory type: Analytical Laboratory Instrument—*mfg*	334516	3826
Thermal conductivity instruments and sensors: Analytical Laboratory Instrument—*mfg*	334516	3826
Thermal conductivity instruments, industrial process type: Instruments and Related Products for Measuring, Displaying, and Controlling Industrial Process Variables—*mfg*	334513	3823
Thermionic devices, solid-state: Semiconductor and Related Device—*mfg*	334413	3674
Thermistors, except temperature sensors: Electronic Resistor—*mfg*	334415	3676

ALPHABETICAL INDEX	NAICS	SIC
Thermistors, industrial process type: Instruments and Related Products for Measuring, Displaying, and Controlling Industrial Process Variables—*mfg*	334513	3823
Thermocouples, except industrial process, aircraft type, and glass vacuum: Measuring and Controlling Device, Other—*mfg*	334519	3829
Surgical and Medical Instrument—*mfg*	339112	3829
Thermocouples, industrial process type: Instruments and Related Products for Measuring, Displaying, and Controlling Industrial Process Variables—*mfg*	334513	3823
Thermocouples, vacuum–glass: Automatic Environmental Control for Residential, Commercial and Appliance Use—*mfg*	334512	3822
Thermoelectric devices, solid-state: Semiconductor and Related Device—*mfg*	334413	3674
Thermoelectric generators: Electrical Equipment and Component, All Other Miscellaneous—*mfg*	335999	3629
Thermogravimetric analyzers: Analytical Laboratory Instrument—*mfg*	334516	3826
Thermohydrometers: Measuring and Controlling Device, Other—*mfg*	334519	3829
Surgical and Medical Instrument—*mfg*	339112	3829
Thermometer cases, rubber: Fabric Coating Mills—*mfg*	31332	3069
Rubber Product, All Other—*mfg*	326299	3069
Thermometers, filled system–industrial process type: Instruments and Related Products for Measuring, Displaying, and Controlling Industrial Process Variables—*mfg*	334513	3823
Thermometers, liquid-in-glass and bimetaltypes: Measuring and Controlling Device, Other—*mfg*	334519	3829
Surgical and Medical Instrument—*mfg*	339112	3829
Thermoplastics coated paper for packaging: Coated and Laminated Packaging Paper and Plastics Film—*mfg*	322221	2671
Unsupported Plastics Packaging Film and Sheet—*mfg*	326112	2671
Thermoplastics coated paper, except forpackaging: Coated and Laminated Paper—*mfg*	322222	2672
Thermoplastics laminates–rods, tubes, plates, and sheet, except flexible packaging: Laminated Plastics Plate, Sheet and Shape—*mfg*	32613	3083
Thermosetting laminates–rods, tubes, plates, and sheet, except flexible packaging: Laminated Plastics Plate, Sheet and Shape—*mfg*	32613	3083
Thermostat repair: Electronic and Precision Equipment Repair and Maintenance, Other—*serv*	811219	7699
Thermostatic traps, heating–metal: Industrial Valve—*mfg*	332911	3491
Thermostats, motor vehicle: Gasoline Engine and Engine Parts—*mfg*	336312	3714
Motor Vehicle Parts, All Other—*mfg*	336399	3714
Thermostats–air-conditioning, refrigeration, comfort heating, appliance: Automatic Environmental Control for Residential, Commercial and Appliance Use—*mfg*	334512	3822

Description	NAICS	SIC
Thickness gauging instruments, ultrasonic: Measuring and Controlling Device, Other—*mfg*	334519	3829
Surgical and Medical Instrument—*mfg*	339112	3829
Thimbles, chimney–clay: Structural Clay Product, Other—*mfg*	327123	3259
Thimbles, wire rope: Hardware—*mfg*	33251	3429
Thin film circuits: Semiconductor and Related Device—*mfg*	334413	3674
Thin paper: Newsprint Mills—*mfg*	322122	2621
Paper (except Newsprint) Mills—*mfg*	322121	2621
Thin water (admixture): Surface Active Agent—*mfg*	325613	2843
Thinner, lacquer: Paint and Coating—*mfg*	32551	2851
Thinners, paint–prepared: Paint and Coating—*mfg*	32551	2851
Thinning of crops, mechanical and chemical: Nonscheduled Air, Other—*trans*	481219	721
Soil Preparation, Planting, and Cultivating—*ag*	115112	721
Thiocyanates, inorganic: Basic Inorganic Chemical, All Other—*mfg*	325188	2819
Chemical Product, All Other Miscellaneous—*mfg*	325998	2819
Thiocyanates, organic (formulated): Pesticide and Other Agricultural Chemical—*mfg*	32532	2879
Thioglycolic acid, for permanent wave locations: Basic Organic Chemical, All Other—*mfg*	325199	2869
Thiol rubbers: Synthetic Rubber—*mfg*	325212	2822
Third axle attachments or six wheel units for motor vehicles: Motor Vehicle Parts, All Other—*mfg*	336399	3714
Motor Vehicle Steering and Suspension Components (except Spring)—*mfg*	33633	3714
Third Party Administration for Insurance and Pension Funds	**524292**	**6411**
Thorium ore mining: Metal Ore, All Other—*mining*	212299	1099
Thousand Island dressing: Fruit and Vegetable Canning—*mfg*	311421	2035
Mayonnaise, Dressing and Other Prepared Sauce—*mfg*	311941	2035
Thpe: Meat Processed from Carcasses—*mfg*	311612	2013
Thread cutting dies: Cutting Tool and Machine Tool Accessory—*mfg*	333515	3545
Hand and Edge Tool—*mfg*	332212	3545
Thread gauges (machinists' precision tools): Cutting Tool and Machine Tool Accessory—*mfg*	333515	3545
Hand and Edge Tool—*mfg*	332212	3545
Thread making machines (spinning machinery), textile: Textile Machinery—*mfg*	333292	3552
Thread Mills	**313113**	**2299**
Thread rolling machines: Machine Tool (Metal Forming Types)—*mfg*	333513	3542
Thread, asbestos: Motor Vehicle Brake System—*mfg*	33634	3292
Nonmetallic Mineral Product, All Other Miscellaneous—*mfg*	327999	3292
Thread, elastic–fabric covered: Narrow Fabric Mills—*mfg*	313221	2241
Thread, except industrial: Broadwoven Fabric Finishing Mills—*mfg*	313311	5131
Piece Goods, Notions and Other Dry Goods—*whlse*	42231	5131
Textile and Fabric Finishing (except Broadwoven Fabric) Mills—*mfg*	313312	5131
Thread, fabric covered rubber: Narrow Fabric Mills—*mfg*	313221	2241
Thread, rubber–except fabric covered: Fabric Coating Mills—*mfg*	31332	3069
Rubber Product, All Other—*mfg*	326299	3069
Thread, sewing, except industrial: Broadwoven Fabric Finishing Mills—*mfg*	313311	5131
Piece Goods, Notions and Other Dry Goods—*whlse*	42231	5131
Textile and Fabric Finishing (except Broadwoven Fabric) Mills—*mfg*	313312	5131
Thread–except flax, hemp, and ramie: Textile and Fabric Finishing (except Broadwoven Fabric) Mills—*mfg*	313312	2284
Thread Mills—*mfg*	313113	2284
Thread–linen, hemp, and ramie: Broadwoven Fabric Mills—*mfg*	31321	2299
Narrow Fabric Mills—*mfg*	313221	2299
Nonwoven Fabric Mills—*mfg*	31323	2299
Textile and Fabric Finishing (except Broadwoven Fabric) Mills—*mfg*	313312	2299
Textile Product Mills, All Other Miscellaneous—*mfg*	314999	2299
Thread Mills—*mfg*	313113	2299
Yarn Spinning Mills—*mfg*	313111	2299
Threading machines (machine tools): Machine Tool (Metal Cutting Types)—*mfg*	333512	3541
Threading toolholders: Cutting Tool and Machine Tool Accessory—*mfg*	333515	3545
Hand and Edge Tool—*mfg*	332212	3545
Threading tools: Industrial Machinery and Equipment—*whlse*	42183	5084
Threading tools (machine tool accessories): Cutting Tool and Machine Tool Accessory—*mfg*	333515	3545
Hand and Edge Tool—*mfg*	332212	3545
Threshing service: Crop Harvesting, Primarily by Machine—*ag*	115113	722
Thresholds, precast terrazzo: Concrete Pipe—*mfg*	327332	3272
Concrete Product, Other—*mfg*	32739	3272
Nonmetallic Mineral Product, All Other Miscellaneous—*mfg*	327999	3272
Throwing, winding, or spooling of yarn–silk, wool and manmade fiber continuous filament: Textile and Fabric Finishing (except Broadwoven Fabric) Mills—*mfg*	313312	2282
Yarn Texturing, Throwing and Twisting Mills—*mfg*	313112	2282
Thrust power indicators, aircraft engine: Measuring and Controlling Device, Other—*mfg*	334519	3829
Surgical and Medical Instrument—*mfg*	339112	3829
Thyristors: Semiconductor and Related Device—*mfg*	334413	3674
Thyroid preparations: Pharmaceutical Preparation—*mfg*	325412	2834
Ticket agencies, theatrical: Promoters of Performing Arts, Sports and Similar Events without Facilities—*arts*	71132	7922
Ticket counting machines: Lead Pencil and Art Good—*mfg*	339942	3579
Office Machinery—*mfg*	333313	3579
Watch, Clock, and Part—*mfg*	334518	3579
Ticket offices, transportation–not operated by transportation companies: Transportation, All Other Support Activities—*trans*	488999	4729
Travel Arrangement and Reservation Services, All Other—*admin*	561599	4729
Tickets, lithographed: Lithographic Printing, Commercial—*mfg*	323110	2752

ALPHABETICAL INDEX	NAICS	SIC
Quick Printing—*mfg*	323114	2752
Tickets, pin–paper: Coated and Laminated Paper—*mfg*	322222	2679
Converted Paper Product, All Other—*mfg*	322298	2679
Die-Cut Paper and Paperboard Office Supplies—*mfg*	322231	2679
Non-Folding Sanitary Food Container—*mfg*	322215	2679
Tickets, printed–except lithographed or gravure: Digital Printing—*mfg*	323115	2759
Flexographic Printing, Commercial—*mfg*	323112	2759
Printing, Other Commercial—*mfg*	323119	2759
Quick Printing—*mfg*	323114	2759
Tickets–gravure printing: Gravure Printing, Commercial—*mfg*	323111	2754
Tickings: Broadwoven Fabric Mills—*mfg*	31321	2211
Tie plates, iron and steel: Iron and Steel Mills—*mfg*	331111	3312
Petroleum and Coal Productsa, All Other—*mfg*	324199	3312
Tie rods, motor vehicle: Gasoline Engine and Engine Parts—*mfg*	336312	3714
Motor Vehicle Parts, All Other—*mfg*	336399	3714
Tie shops: Clothing Accessories Stores—*retail*	44815	5611
Men's Clothing Stores—*retail*	44811	5611
Tie tapes, woven or braided: Narrow Fabric Mills—*mfg*	313221	2241
Tie wires, made in wire-drawing plants: Fabricated Wire Product, Other—*mfg*	332618	3315
Steel Wire Drawing—*mfg*	331222	3315
Tierces (cooperage): Wood Container and Pallet—*mfg*	32192	2449
Ties: Apparel Accessories and Apparel, Other—*mfg*	315999	2339
Cut and Sew Apparel, All Other—*mfg*	315299	2339
Outerwear Knitting Mills—*mfg*	315191	2253
Women's and Girls' Cut and Sew Apparel Contractors—*mfg*	315212	2339
Women's and Girls' Cut and Sew Other Outerwear—*mfg*	315238	2339
Ties, bale–made from purchased wire: Fabricated Wire Product, Other—*mfg*	332618	3496
Ties, form–metal: Fabricated Metal Product, All Other Miscellaneous—*mfg*	332999	3599
General Purpose Machinery , All Other—*mfg*	333999	3599
Machine Shops—*mfg*	33271	3599
Machinery, Other Commercial and Service Industry—*mfg*	333319	3599
Ties, handsewn: Men's and Boys' Neckwear—*mfg*	315993	2323
Ties, men's and boys': Men's and Boys' Clothing and Furnishings—*whlse*	42232	5136
Ties, railroad cross bridge and switch–treated: Wood Preservation—*mfg*	321114	2491
Ties, railroad–concrete: Concrete Pipe—*mfg*	327332	3272
Concrete Product, Other—*mfg*	32739	3272
Nonmetallic Mineral Product, All Other Miscellaneous—*mfg*	327999	3272
Ties, railroad–sawed: Cut Stock, Resawing Lumber, and Planing—*mfg*	321912	2421
Millwork (including Flooring), Other—*mfg*	321918	2421
Sawmills—*mfg*	321113	2421

ALPHABETICAL INDEX	NAICS	SIC
Wood Product, All Other Miscellaneous—*mfg*	321999	2421
Tights, except women's: Hosiery and Sock Mills, Other—*mfg*	315119	2252
Sheer Hosiery Mills—*mfg*	315111	2252
Tights, women's: Sheer Hosiery Mills—*mfg*	315111	2251
Tile and brick dealers: Building Material Dealers, Other—*retail*	44419	5211
Home Centers—*retail*	44411	5211
Tile installation, asphalt-contractors: Floor Laying and Other Floor Contractors—*const*	23552	1752
Tile installation, ceramic-contractors: Drywall, Plastering, Acoustical and Insulation Contractors—*const*	23542	1743
Tile, Marble, Terrazzo and Mosaic Contractors—*const*	23543	1743
Tile installation, wall–plastics–contractors: Trade Contractor., All Other Special—*const*	23599	1799
Tile making machines: Industrial Machinery, All Other—*mfg*	333298	3559
Machinery, Other Commercial and Service Industry—*mfg*	333319	3559
Rubber and Plastics Industry Machinery—*mfg*	33322	3559
Tile setting, ceramic–contractors: Drywall, Plastering, Acoustical and Insulation Contractors—*const*	23542	1743
Tile, Marble, Terrazzo and Mosaic Contractors—*const*	23543	1743
Tile, acoustical–mineral wool: Mineral Wool—*mfg*	327993	3296
Tile, ceramic wall and floor: Ceramic Wall and Floor Tile—*mfg*	327122	3253
Tile, clay floor and wall–enameled: Ceramic Wall and Floor Tile—*mfg*	327122	3253
Tile, clay or other ceramic–except refractory: Brick, Stone and Related Material—*whlse*	42132	5032
Building Material Dealers, Other—*retail*	44419	5032
Tile, clay refractory: Clay Refractory—*mfg*	327124	3255
Tile, clay–structural: Brick and Structural Clay Tile—*mfg*	327121	3251
Tile, cork: Manufacturing, All Other Miscellaneous—*mfg*	339999	2499
Wood Container and Pallet—*mfg*	32192	2499
Wood Product, All Other Miscellaneous—*mfg*	321999	2499
Tile, filter under-drain–clay: Structural Clay Product, Other—*mfg*	327123	3259
Tile, floor and wall–stamped metal: Metal Stamping—*mfg*	332116	3469
Tile, floor–asphalt: Motor Vehicle Brake System—*mfg*	33634	3292
Nonmetallic Mineral Product, All Other Miscellaneous—*mfg*	327999	3292
Tile, floor–supported plastics: Resilient Floor Covering—*mfg*	326192	3996
Tile, gypsum: Gypsum and Gypsum Product—*mfg*	32742	3275
Tile, Marble, Terrazzo and Mosaic Contractors	**23543**	**1743**
Tile, precast terrazzo or concrete: Concrete Pipe—*mfg*	327332	3272
Concrete Product, Other—*mfg*	32739	3272
Nonmetallic Mineral Product, All Other Miscellaneous—*mfg*	327999	3272
Tile, roofing and drain–clay: Structural Clay Product, Other—*mfg*	327123	3259
Tile, rubber: Fabric Coating Mills—*mfg*	31332	3069
Rubber Product, All Other—*mfg*	326299	3069
Tile, sand lime: Gypsum and Gypsum Product—*mfg*	32742	3299
Nonmetallic Mineral Product, All Other Miscellaneous—*mfg*	327999	3299
Tile, sewer–clay: Structural Clay Product, Other—*mfg*	327123	3259

Entry	NAICS	SIC
Tile, structural clay: Brick, Stone and Related Material—*whlse*	42132	5032
Building Material Dealers, Other—*retail*	44419	5032
Tile, vinyl asbestos: Motor Vehicle Brake System—*mfg*	33634	3292
Nonmetallic Mineral Product, All Other Miscellaneous—*mfg*	327999	3292
Tile, wall–fiberboard: Reconstituted Wood Product—*mfg*	321219	2493
Till baskets, veneer and splint: Wood Container and Pallet—*mfg*	32192	2449
Timber (product of logging camps): Logging—*ag*	11331	2411
Timber products, rough: Durable Goods, Other Miscellaneous—*whlse*	42199	5099
Timber removal, underwater–contractors: Heavy, All Other—*const*	23499	1629
Industrial Nonbuilding Structure—*const*	23493	1629
Timber Tract Operations	**1131**	
Timber Tract Operations	**11311**	**811**
Timber tracts: Nursery and Tree Production—*ag*	111421	811
Timber Tract Operations—*ag*	11311	811
Timber valuation: Forestry Support Activities—*ag*	11531	851
Timber, structural–treated: Wood Preservation—*mfg*	321114	2491
Timbers, mine–hewn: Logging—*ag*	11331	2411
Timbers, structural–laminated lumber: Cut Stock, Resawing Lumber, and Planing—*mfg*	321912	2439
Engineered Wood Member (except Truss)—*mfg*	321213	2439
Truss—*mfg*	321214	2439
Time code generators: Electronic Coil, Transformer, and Other Inductor—*mfg*	334416	3825
Instrument for Measuring and Testing Electricity and Electrical Signals—*mfg*	334515	3825
Time cycle and program controllers, industrial process type: Instruments and Related Products for Measuring, Displaying, and Controlling Industrial Process Variables—*mfg*	334513	3823
Time locks: Hardware—*mfg*	33251	3429
Time program controls, air-conditioning systems: Automatic Environmental Control for Residential, Commercial and Appliance Use—*mfg*	334512	3822
Time recording cards, die-cut from purchased paperboard: Converted Paper Product, All Other—*mfg*	322298	2675
Die-Cut Paper and Paperboard Office Supplies—*mfg*	322231	2675
Surface-Coated Paperboard—*mfg*	322292	2675
Time sharing, computer: Data Processing Services—*info*	51421	7374
Time switches: Building Material Dealers, Other—*retail*	44419	5063
Electrical Apparatus and Equipment, Wiring Supplies and Material—*whlse*	42161	5063
Time switches, electrical switchgear apparatus: Switchgear and Switchboard Apparatus—*mfg*	335313	3613
Time-share condominium exchanges: Personal Services, All Other—*serv*	81299	7389
Time-sharing real estate–sales, leasing, and rentals: Real Estate, Other Activities Related to—*real*	53139	6531
Time-stamps containing clock mechanisms: Lead Pencil and Art Good—*mfg*	339942	3579
Office Machinery—*mfg*	333313	3579
Watch, Clock, and Part—*mfg*	334518	3579
Timeclocks and time recording devices: Lead Pencil and Art Good—*mfg*	339942	3579
Office Machinery—*mfg*	333313	3579
Watch, Clock, and Part—*mfg*	334518	3579
Timers for industrial use, clockwork mechanism only: Watch, Clock, and Part—*mfg*	334518	3873
Timing devices, mechanical and solid-state, except clockwork: Relay and Industrial Control—*mfg*	335314	3625
Timing motors, synchronous–electric: Motor and Generator—*mfg*	335312	3621
Timothy farms: Crop Farming, All Other Miscellaneous—*ag*	111998	139
Hay Farming—*ag*	11194	139
Peanut Farming—*ag*	111992	139
Vegetable (except Potato) and Melon Farming, Other—*ag*	111219	139
Tin and tin alloy bars, pipe, rods, sheets, strip, and tubing: Nonferrous Metal (except Copper and Aluminum) Rolling, Drawing and Extruding—*mfg*	331491	3356
Tin and tin base metals, shapes, forms, etc.: Metal Service Centers and Offices—*whlse*	42151	5051
Tin base alloys, primary: Primary Smelting and Refining of Nonferrous Metal (except Copper and Aluminum)—*mfg*	331419	3339
Tin cans: Metal Can—*mfg*	332431	3411
Tin chloride: Basic Inorganic Chemical, All Other—*mfg*	325188	2819
Chemical Product, All Other Miscellaneous—*mfg*	325998	2819
Tin compounds, inorganic: Basic Inorganic Chemical, All Other—*mfg*	325188	2819
Chemical Product, All Other Miscellaneous—*mfg*	325998	2819
Tin foil, not made in rolling mills: Fabricated Metal Product, All Other Miscellaneous—*mfg*	332999	3497
Laminated Aluminum Foil for Flexible Packaging Uses—*mfg*	322225	3497
Tin ore mining: Metal Ore, All Other—*mining*	212299	1099
Tin oxide: Basic Inorganic Chemical, All Other—*mfg*	325188	2819
Chemical Product, All Other Miscellaneous—*mfg*	325998	2819
Tin plate: Metal Service Centers and Offices—*whlse*	42151	5051
Tin plate bars: Metal Service Centers and Offices—*whlse*	42151	5051
Tin refining, primary: Primary Smelting and Refining of Nonferrous Metal (except Copper and Aluminum)—*mfg*	331419	3339
Tin rolling and drawing: Nonferrous Metal (except Copper and Aluminum) Rolling, Drawing and Extruding—*mfg*	331491	3356
Tin salts: Basic Inorganic Chemical, All Other—*mfg*	325188	2819
Chemical Product, All Other Miscellaneous—*mfg*	325998	2819
Tin smelting and refining, secondary: Secondary Smelting and Alloying of Aluminum—*mfg*	331314	3341
Secondary Smelting, Refining, and Alloying of Nonferrous Metal (except Copper and Aluminum)—*mfg*	331492	3341
Tin-free steel: Iron and Steel Mills—*mfg*	331111	3312
Petroleum and Coal Productsa, All Other—*mfg*	324199	3312
Tinctures, pharmaceutical: Pharmaceutical Preparation—*mfg*	325412	2834

ALPHABETICAL INDEX	NAICS	SIC
Tinners' handtools, except snips: Hand and Edge Tool—*mfg*	332212	3423
Tinners' snips: Cutlery and Flatware (except Precious)—*mfg*	332211	3421
Tinplate: Iron and Steel Mills—*mfg*	331111	3312
Petroleum and Coal Productsa, All Other—*mfg*	324199	3312
Tinsmithing repair, except construction: Machinery and Equipment (except Automotive and Electronic) Repair and Maintenance, Commercial and Industrial—*serv*	81131	7699
Tinsmithing, in connection with construction work-contractors: Roofing, Siding and Sheet Metal Contractors—*const*	23561	1761
Tinting glass–contractors: Glass and Glazing Contractors—*const*	23592	1799
Tints and dyes, household: Basic Organic Chemical, All Other—*mfg*	325199	2899
Chemical Product, All Other Miscellaneous—*mfg*	325998	2899
Tinware stores: Home Furnishings Stores, All Other—*retail*	442299	5719
Window Treatment Stores—*retail*	442291	5719
Tip printing and stamping on fabric articles: Apparel Accessories and Apparel, Other—*mfg*	315999	2396
Screen Printing, Commercial—*mfg*	323113	2396
Tipple construction–general contractors: Heavy, All Other—*const*	23499	1629
Industrial Nonbuilding Structure—*const*	23493	1629
Tips, cutting tool: Cutting Tool and Machine Tool Accessory—*mfg*	333515	3545
Hand and Edge Tool—*mfg*	332212	3545
Tips, shoe–regardless of material: Fastener, Button, Needle and Pin—*mfg*	339993	3131
Leather Good, All Other—*mfg*	316999	3131
Wood Product, All Other Miscellaneous—*mfg*	321999	3131
Tire (automobile) dealers: Automotive Parts and Accessories Stores—*retail*	44131	5531
Tire Dealers—*retail*	44132	5531
Tire and tube repair materials: Tire and Tube—*whlse*	42113	5014
Tire Dealers—*retail*	44132	5014
Tire and Tube Wholesalers	**42113**	**5014**
Tire chains, made from purchased wire: Fabricated Wire Product, Other—*mfg*	332618	3496
Tire cord: Tire Cord and Tire Fabric Mills—*mfg*	314992	2296
Tire Cord and Tire Fabric Mills	**314992**	**2296**
Tire covers: Motor Vehicle Fabric Accessories and Seat—*mfg*	33636	2399
Tire Dealers	**44132**	**5531**
Tire dealers, automotive: Automotive Parts and Accessories Stores—*retail*	44131	5531
Tire Dealers—*retail*	44132	5531
Tire fabric: Tire Cord and Tire Fabric Mills—*mfg*	314992	2296
Tire grooving machines: Industrial Machinery, All Other—*mfg*	333298	3559
Machinery, Other Commercial and Service Industry—*mfg*	333319	3559
Rubber and Plastics Industry Machinery—*mfg*	33322	3559
Tire inflators, hand or compressor operated: Air and Gas Compressor—*mfg*	333912	3563
Tire Manufacturing	**32621**	
Tire Manufacturing (except Retreading)	**326211**	**3011**
Tire recapping: Automotive Repair and Maintenance, All Other—*serv*	811198	7534
Tire Retreading—*mfg*	326212	7534
Tire repair shops: Automotive Repair and Maintenance, All Other—*serv*	811198	7534
Tire Retreading—*mfg*	326212	7534
Tire Retreading	**326212**	**7534**
Tire retreading machinery and equipment: Industrial Machinery, All Other—*mfg*	333298	3559
Machinery, Other Commercial and Service Industry—*mfg*	333319	3559
Rubber and Plastics Industry Machinery—*mfg*	33322	3559
Tire shredding machinery: Industrial Machinery, All Other—*mfg*	333298	3559
Machinery, Other Commercial and Service Industry—*mfg*	333319	3559
Rubber and Plastics Industry Machinery—*mfg*	33322	3559
Tire studding and restudding: Automotive Repair and Maintenance, All Other—*serv*	811198	7534
Tire Retreading—*mfg*	326212	7534
Tire sundries and tire repair materials, rubber: Tire (except Retreading)—*mfg*	326211	3011
Tire valve cores: Motor Vehicle Parts, All Other—*mfg*	336399	3714
Tire, battery, and accessory dealers: Automotive Parts and Accessories Stores—*retail*	44131	5531
Tire Dealers—*retail*	44132	5531
Tires and tubes, new: Tire and Tube—*whlse*	42113	5014
Tire Dealers—*retail*	44132	5014
Tires, cushion or solid rubber: Tire (except Retreading)—*mfg*	326211	3011
Tires, plastics: Plastics Pipe and Pipe Fitting—*mfg*	326122	3089
Plastics Product, All Other—*mfg*	326199	3089
Unsupported Plastics Profile Shape—*mfg*	326121	3089
Tires, used: Tire and Tube—*whlse*	42113	5014
Tire Dealers—*retail*	44132	5014
Tiring, continuous lengths–rubber, with or without metal core: Tire (except Retreading)—*mfg*	326211	3011
Tissue dispensers, plastics: Plastics Pipe and Pipe Fitting—*mfg*	326122	3089
Plastics Product, All Other—*mfg*	326199	3089
Unsupported Plastics Profile Shape—*mfg*	326121	3089
Tissue paper: Newsprint Mills—*mfg*	322122	2621
Paper (except Newsprint) Mills—*mfg*	322121	2621
Tissues, cleansing: Sanitary Paper Product—*mfg*	322291	2676
Titania porcelain insulators: Porcelain Electrical Supply—*mfg*	327113	3264
Titaniferous-magnetite mining, valued chiefly for titanium content: Metal Ore, All Other—*mining*	212299	1099
Titanium and titanium alloy bars, rods, billets, sheets, strip, and tubing: Nonferrous Metal (except Copper and Aluminum) Rolling, Drawing and Extruding—*mfg*	331491	3356

Entry	NAICS	SIC
Titanium castings, except die-castings: Nonferrous Foundries, Other—*mfg*	331528	3369
Titanium die-castings: Nonferrous (except Aluminum) Die-Castings—*mfg*	331522	3364
Titanium forgings, not made in hot-rolling mills: Nonferrous Forging—*mfg*	332112	3463
Titanium from sponge: Nonferrous Metal (except Copper and Aluminum) Rolling, Drawing and Extruding—*mfg*	331491	3356
Titanium metal sponge and granules: Primary Smelting and Refining of Nonferrous Metal (except Copper and Aluminum)—*mfg*	331419	3339
Titanium ore mining: Metal Ore, All Other—*mining*	212299	1099
Titanium pigments: Carbon Black—*mfg*	325182	2816
Inorganic Dye and Pigment—*mfg*	325131	2816
Title Abstract and Settlement Offices	**541191**	**6541**
Title abstract companies: Title Abstract and Settlement Offices—*prof*	541191	6541
Title and trust companies: Title Abstract and Settlement Offices—*prof*	541191	6541
Title insurance: Direct Title Insurance Carriers—*fin*	524127	6361
Reinsurance Carriers—*fin*	52413	6361
Title reconveyance companies: Title Abstract and Settlement Offices—*prof*	541191	6541
Title search companies: Title Abstract and Settlement Offices—*prof*	541191	6541
Titlers, motion picture film: Photographic and Photocopying Equipment—*mfg*	333315	3861
Photographic Film, Paper, Plate and Chemical—*mfg*	325992	3861
Titling of motion picture film: Independent Artists, Writers, and Performers—*arts*	71151	7819
Motion Picture and Video Industries, Other—*info*	512199	7819
Prerecorded Compact Disc (except Software), Tape, and Record Reproducing—*mfg*	334612	7819
Titrimeters: Analytical Laboratory Instrument—*mfg*	334516	3826
TNT (trinitrotoluene): Explosives—*mfg*	32592	2892
Toasters, electric: Electrical Appliance, Television and Radio Set—*whlse*	42162	5064
Toasters, household–electric: Electric Housewares and Household Fan—*mfg*	335211	3634
Heating Equipment (except Electric and Warm Air Furnaces)—*mfg*	333414	3634
Tobacco and Tobacco Product Wholesalers	**42294**	**5194**
Tobacco auctioning and warehousing: Farm Product Raw Material, Other—*whlse*	42259	5159
Tobacco cloths: Broadwoven Fabric Mills—*mfg*	31321	2211
Tobacco curers: Farm Machinery and Equipment—*mfg*	333111	3523
Tobacco Farming	**11191**	**132**
Tobacco farms: Tobacco Farming—*ag*	11191	132
Tobacco grading: Postharvest Crop Activities (except Cotton Ginning)—*ag*	115114	723
Tobacco harvesters: Farm Machinery and Equipment—*mfg*	333111	3523
Tobacco hogshead stock: Cut Stock, Resawing Lumber, and Planing—*mfg*	321912	2421
Millwork (including Flooring), Other—*mfg*	321918	2421
Sawmills—*mfg*	321113	2421
Wood Product, All Other Miscellaneous—*mfg*	321999	2421
Tobacco hogsheads: Wood Container and Pallet—*mfg*	32192	2449
Tobacco jars, glass: Pressed and Blown Glass and Glassware, Other—*mfg*	327212	3229
Tobacco Manufacturing	**3122**	
Tobacco pipe mouthpieces, hard rubber: Fabric Coating Mills—*mfg*	31332	3069
Rubber Product, All Other—*mfg*	326299	3069
Tobacco pouches, regardless of material: Personal Leather Good (except Women's Handbag and Purse)—*mfg*	316993	3172
Tobacco Product Manufacturing	**31222**	
Tobacco Product Manufacturing, Other	**312229**	**2131**
Tobacco products machinery: Industrial Machinery, All Other—*mfg*	333298	3559
Machinery, Other Commercial and Service Industry—*mfg*	333319	3559
Rubber and Plastics Industry Machinery—*mfg*	33322	3559
Tobacco products, manufactured: Tobacco and Tobacco Product—*whlse*	42294	5194
Tobacco Stemming and Redrying	**31221**	**2141**
Tobacco Stores	**453991**	**5993**
Tobacco thrashing (mechanical stemming): Tobacco Product, Other—*mfg*	312229	2141
Tobacco Stemming and Redrying—*mfg*	31221	2141
Tobacco warehousing and storage: Farm Product Warehousing and Storage Facilities—*trans*	49313	4221
Tobacco, except leaf: Tobacco and Tobacco Product—*whlse*	42294	5194
Tobacco, leaf (including exporters): Farm Product Raw Material, Other—*whlse*	42259	5159
Tobacco, stemming and redrying of: Tobacco Product, Other—*mfg*	312229	2141
Tobacco Stemming and Redrying—*mfg*	31221	2141
Tobacco–chewing, smoking, and snuff: Tobacco Product, Other—*mfg*	312229	2131
Tobacconists: Tobacco Stores—*retail*	453991	5993
Toboggans: Sporting and Athletic Goods—*mfg*	33992	3949
Toe caps, leather or metal: Fastener, Button, Needle and Pin—*mfg*	339993	3131
Leather Good, All Other—*mfg*	316999	3131
Wood Product, All Other Miscellaneous—*mfg*	321999	3131
Tofu frozen desserts: Ice Cream and Frozen Dessert—*mfg*	31152	2024
Tofu, except frozen desserts: Food, All Other Miscellaneous—*mfg*	311999	2099
Perishable Prepared Food—*mfg*	311991	2099
Toggle bolts, metal: Bolt, Nut, Screw, Rivet and Washer—*mfg*	332722	3452
Toggle bolts, plastics: Plastics Pipe and Pipe Fitting—*mfg*	326122	3089
Plastics Product, All Other—*mfg*	326199	3089
Unsupported Plastics Profile Shape—*mfg*	326121	3089
Toilet articles: Drug, Drug Proprietaries and Druggists' Sundries—*whlse*	42221	5122
Toilet brushes: Broom, Brush and Mop—*mfg*	339994	3991

ALPHABETICAL INDEX	NAICS	SIC
Toilet creams, powders, and waters: Soap and Other Detergent—*mfg*	325611	2844
Toilet Preparation—*mfg*	32562	2844
Toilet fixtures, plastics: Plastics Plumbing Fixture—*mfg*	326191	3088
Toilet fixtures, vitreous china: Vitreous China Plumbing Fixture and China and Earthenware Fittings and Bathroom Accessories—*mfg*	327111	3261
Toilet fixtures–enameled iron, cast iron, and pressed metal: Enameled Iron and Metal Sanitary Ware—*mfg*	332998	3431
Toilet kits and cases, regardless of material: Personal Leather Good (except Women's Handbag and Purse)—*mfg*	316993	3172
Toilet paper: Sanitary Paper Product—*mfg*	322291	2676
Toilet Preparation Manufacturing	**32562**	**2844**
Toilet preparations: Drug, Drug Proprietaries and Druggists' Sundries—*whlse*	42221	5122
Soap and Other Detergent—*mfg*	325611	2844
Toilet Preparation—*mfg*	32562	2844
Toilet seats, wood: Manufacturing, All Other Miscellaneous—*mfg*	339999	2499
Wood Container and Pallet—*mfg*	32192	2499
Wood Product, All Other Miscellaneous—*mfg*	321999	2499
Toilet soap: Drug, Drug Proprietaries and Druggists' Sundries—*whlse*	42221	5122
Toilet tissue stock: Newsprint Mills—*mfg*	322122	2621
Paper (except Newsprint) Mills—*mfg*	322121	2621
Toilet ware, metal–except silver, nickel silver, pewter, and plated: Fabricated Metal Product, All Other Miscellaneous—*mfg*	332999	3499
Toilet ware–silver, nickel silver, pewter, and plated: Cutlery and Flatware (except Precious)—*mfg*	332211	3914
Silverware and Plated Ware—*mfg*	339912	3914
Toiletries: Drug, Drug Proprietaries and Druggists' Sundries—*whlse*	42221	5122
Toll booths, automatic: Measuring and Controlling Device, Other—*mfg*	334519	3829
Surgical and Medical Instrument—*mfg*	339112	3829
Toll bridge operation: Road, Other Support Activities for—*trans*	48849	4785
Water, Other Support Activities for—*trans*	48839	4785
Toll roads, operation of: Road, Other Support Activities for—*trans*	48849	4785
Water, Other Support Activities for—*trans*	48839	4785
Toll switching equipment, telephone: Electronic Coil, Transformer, and Other Inductor—*mfg*	334416	3661
Printed Circuit/Electronics Assembly—*mfg*	334418	3661
Telephone Apparatus—*mfg*	33421	3661
Toluene, made in chemical plants: Cyclic Crude and Intermediate—*mfg*	325192	2865
Petrochemical—*mfg*	32511	2865
Toluidines: Cyclic Crude and Intermediate—*mfg*	325192	2865
Petrochemical—*mfg*	32511	2865
Tomato farms: Vegetable (except Potato) and Melon Farming, Other—*ag*	111219	161

ALPHABETICAL INDEX	NAICS	SIC
Tomato harvesters: Farm Machinery and Equipment—*mfg*	333111	3523
Tomato juice and cocktails, canned: Fruit and Vegetable Canning—*mfg*	311421	2033
Tomato paste: Fruit and Vegetable Canning—*mfg*	311421	2033
Tomato puree: Fruit and Vegetable Canning—*mfg*	311421	2033
Tomato sauce: Fruit and Vegetable Canning—*mfg*	311421	2033
Tomatoes grown under cover: Food Crops Grown Under Cover, Other—*ag*	111419	182
Mushroom Production—*ag*	111411	182
Tombstones: Stores (except Tobacco Stores), All Other Miscellaneous—*retail*	453998	5999
Tombstones, cut stone–not including only finishing or lettering to order: Cut Stone and Stone Product—*mfg*	327991	3281
Tombstones, precast terrazzo or concrete: Concrete Pipe—*mfg*	327332	3272
Concrete Product, Other—*mfg*	32739	3272
Nonmetallic Mineral Product, All Other Miscellaneous—*mfg*	327999	3272
Toners (reduced or full strength organic colors): Organic Dye and Pigment—*mfg*	325132	2865
Petrochemical—*mfg*	32511	2865
Toners, prepared photographic, pack-aged: Photographic and Photocopying Equipment—*mfg*	333315	3861
Photographic Film, Paper, Plate and Chemical—*mfg*	325992	3861
Tongs, oyster: Hand and Edge Tool—*mfg*	332212	3423
Tongue depressors: Surgical Appliance and Supplies—*mfg*	339113	3842
Tongues, boot and shoe–leather: Fastener, Button, Needle and Pin—*mfg*	339993	3131
Leather Good, All Other—*mfg*	316999	3131
Wood Product, All Other Miscellaneous—*mfg*	321999	3131
Tonics, hair: Soap and Other Detergent—*mfg*	325611	2844
Toilet Preparation—*mfg*	32562	2844
Tonometers, medical: Surgical and Medical Instrument—*mfg*	339112	3841
Tool boxes, stamped metal: Metal Stamping—*mfg*	332116	3469
Tool chests, wood: Wood Container and Pallet—*mfg*	32192	2441
Tool designers: Industrial Design Services—*prof*	54142	7389
Tool handles, plastics: Plastics Pipe and Pipe Fitting—*mfg*	326122	3089
Plastics Product, All Other—*mfg*	326199	3089
Unsupported Plastics Profile Shape—*mfg*	326121	3089
Tool handles, wood–turned and shaped: Manufacturing, All Other Miscellaneous—*mfg*	339999	2499
Wood Container and Pallet—*mfg*	32192	2499
Wood Product, All Other Miscellaneous—*mfg*	321999	2499
Tool rental and leasing: Consumer Goods Rental, All Other—*real*	532299	7359
Tool sharpening and repair shops: Machinery and Equipment (except Automotive and Electronic) Repair and Maintenance, Commercial and Industrial—*serv*	81131	7699
Tool stands, factory: Institutional Furniture—*mfg*	337127	2599
Tool steel: Iron and Steel Mills—*mfg*	331111	3312

Entry	NAICS	SIC
Petroleum and Coal Productsa, All Other—*mfg*	324199	3312
Toolholders: Cutting Tool and Machine Tool Accessory—*mfg*	333515	3545
Hand and Edge Tool—*mfg*	332212	3545
Toolholders (e.g., chucks, turrets): Industrial Machinery and Equipment—*whlse*	42183	5084
Tools and accessories for machine tools: Cutting Tool and Machine Tool Accessory—*mfg*	333515	3545
Hand and Edge Tool—*mfg*	332212	3545
Tools and equipment for use with sporting arms: Hand and Edge Tool—*mfg*	332212	3423
Tools and equipment, automotive: Automotive Parts and Accessories Stores—*retail*	44131	5013
Motor Vehicle Supplies and New Part—*whlse*	42112	5013
Tools, dentists': Dental Equipment and Supplies—*mfg*	339114	3843
Tools, edge–woodworking-augers, bits, gimlets, countersinks, etc.: Hand and Edge Tool—*mfg*	332212	3423
Tools, hand–except power-driven tools and saws: Hand and Edge Tool—*mfg*	332212	3423
Tools, hand–power-driven, wood-working or metal-working: Power-Driven Hand Tool—*mfg*	333991	3546
Tools, machine–metal cutting types: Machine Tool (Metal Cutting Types)—*mfg*	333512	3541
Tools, machinists' precision: Industrial Machinery and Equipment—*whlse*	42183	5084
Tools, power and hand: Hardware Stores—*retail*	44413	5251
Tools–drilling, etc.-for artesian, gas, and oil wells: Oil and Gas Field Machinery and Equipment—*mfg*	333132	3533
Toothbrushes, electric: Electric Housewares and Household Fan—*mfg*	335211	3634
Electrical Appliance, Television and Radio Set—*whlse*	42162	5064
Heating Equipment (except Electric and Warm Air Furnaces)—*mfg*	333414	3634
Toothbrushes, except electric: Broom, Brush and Mop—*mfg*	339994	3991
Drug, Drug Proprietaries and Druggists' Sundries—*whlse*	42221	5122
Toothpastes and powders: Soap and Other Detergent—*mfg*	325611	2844
Toilet Preparation—*mfg*	32562	2844
Toothpicks, wood: Manufacturing, All Other Miscellaneous—*mfg*	339999	2499
Wood Container and Pallet—*mfg*	32192	2499
Wood Product, All Other Miscellaneous—*mfg*	321999	2499
Top lift sheets, rubber: Fabric Coating Mills—*mfg*	31332	3069
Rubber Product, All Other—*mfg*	326299	3069
Top lifts, boot and shoe: Fastener, Button, Needle and Pin—*mfg*	339993	3131
Leather Good, All Other—*mfg*	316999	3131
Wood Product, All Other Miscellaneous—*mfg*	321999	3131
Top repair, automotive: Automotive Body, Paint and Interior Repair and Maintenance—*serv*	811121	7532
Top roll covering, for textile mill machinery–rubber: Fabric Coating Mills—*mfg*	31332	3069
Rubber Product, All Other—*mfg*	326299	3069
Topaz (nongem) mining: Clay and Ceramic and Refractory Minerals—*mining*	212325	1459
Topcoats: Men's and Boys' Cut and Sew Apparel Contractors—*mfg*	315211	2311
Men's and Boys' Cut and Sew Suit, Coat and Overcoat—*mfg*	315222	2311
Toppings, soda fountain: Confectionery—*whlse*	42245	5145
Tops, automobile–stamped metal: Motor Vehicle Metal Stamping—*mfg*	33637	3465
Tops, bottle; die-cut from purchased paper or paperboard: Converted Paper Product, All Other—*mfg*	322298	2675
Die-Cut Paper and Paperboard Office Supplies—*mfg*	322231	2675
Surface-Coated Paperboard—*mfg*	322292	2675
Tops, chimney–clay: Structural Clay Product, Other—*mfg*	327123	3259
Tops, combing and converting: Broadwoven Fabric Mills—*mfg*	31321	2299
Narrow Fabric Mills—*mfg*	313221	2299
Nonwoven Fabric Mills—*mfg*	31323	2299
Textile and Fabric Finishing (except Broadwoven Fabric) Mills—*mfg*	313312	2299
Textile Product Mills, All Other Miscellaneous—*mfg*	314999	2299
Thread Mills—*mfg*	313113	2299
Yarn Spinning Mills—*mfg*	313111	2299
Tops, jar–stamped metal: Crown and Closure—*mfg*	332115	3466
Tops, manmade fiber: Broadwoven Fabric Mills—*mfg*	31321	2299
Narrow Fabric Mills—*mfg*	313221	2299
Nonwoven Fabric Mills—*mfg*	31323	2299
Textile and Fabric Finishing (except Broadwoven Fabric) Mills—*mfg*	313312	2299
Textile Product Mills, All Other Miscellaneous—*mfg*	314999	2299
Thread Mills—*mfg*	313113	2299
Yarn Spinning Mills—*mfg*	313111	2299
Tops, motor vehicle–except stamped metal: Motor Vehicle Body—*mfg*	336211	3714
Motor Vehicle Parts, All Other—*mfg*	336399	3714
Tops, plastics (e.g., dispenser, shaker): Plastics Pipe and Pipe Fitting—*mfg*	326122	3089
Plastics Product, All Other—*mfg*	326199	3089
Unsupported Plastics Profile Shape—*mfg*	326121	3089
Tops, truck: Motor Vehicle Body—*mfg*	336211	3713
Tops, wool: Farm Product Raw Material, Other—*whlse*	42259	5159
Torches (fireworks): Basic Organic Chemical, All Other—*mfg*	325199	2899
Chemical Product, All Other Miscellaneous—*mfg*	325998	2899
Torpedo tubes (ordnance): Ordnance and Accessories, Other—*mfg*	332995	3489
Torpedoes and parts (ordnance): Ammunition (except Small Arms)—*mfg*	332993	3483
Torpedoes, railroad: Basic Organic Chemical, All Other—*mfg*	325199	2899
Chemical Product, All Other Miscellaneous—*mfg*	325998	2899
Torpedoes, well shooting (explosives): Explosives—*mfg*	32592	2892
Torque converters, except motor vehicle: Speed Changer, Industrial High-Speed Drive and Gear—*mfg*	333612	3566
Torque motors, electric: Motor and Generator—*mfg*	335312	3621

ALPHABETICAL INDEX	NAICS	SIC
Torsion bar springs: Steel Spring (except Wire)—*mfg*	332611	3493
Torsion testing equipment: Measuring and Controlling Device, Other—*mfg*	334519	3829
Surgical and Medical Instrument—*mfg*	339112	3829
Tortilla Manufacturing	**31183**	**2099**
Tortillas, canned: Canning, Specialty—*mfg*	311422	2032
Food, All Other Miscellaneous—*mfg*	311999	2032
Tortillas, fresh or refrigerated: Tortilla—*mfg*	31183	2099
Totalizing Fluid Meter and Counting Device Manufacturing	**334514**	**3824**
Totalizing meters, consumption registering, except aircraft: Totalizing Fluid Meter and Counting Device—*mfg*	334514	3824
Tour operation (travel): Tour Operators—*admin*	56152	4725
Tour Operators	**56152**	**4725**
Tourist agencies for the arrangement of transportation, lodging, and car rental: Travel Agencies—*admin*	56151	4724
Tourist attractions, natural wonder–commercial: Nature Parks and Other Similar Institutions—*arts*	71219	7999
Scenic and Sightseeing, Land—*trans*	48711	7999
Travel Arrangement and Reservation Services, All Other—*admin*	561599	7999
Tourist cabins: Bed and Breakfast Inns—*accom*	721191	7011
Casino Hotels—*accom*	72112	7011
Hotels (except Casino Hotels) and Motels—*accom*	72111	7011
Traveler Accommodation, All Other—*accom*	721199	7011
Tourist camps: Bed and Breakfast Inns—*accom*	721191	7011
Casino Hotels—*accom*	72112	7011
Hotels (except Casino Hotels) and Motels—*accom*	72111	7011
Traveler Accommodation, All Other—*accom*	721199	7011
Tourist courts: Bed and Breakfast Inns—*accom*	721191	7011
Casino Hotels—*accom*	72112	7011
Hotels (except Casino Hotels) and Motels—*accom*	72111	7011
Traveler Accommodation, All Other—*accom*	721199	7011
Tourist guides: Nature Parks and Other Similar Institutions—*arts*	71219	7999
Travel Arrangement and Reservation Services, All Other—*admin*	561599	7999
Tourist information bureaus: Convention and Visitors Bureaus—*admin*	561591	7389
Travel Arrangement and Reservation Services, All Other—*admin*	561599	7389
Tours, except sightseeing buses, boats, and airplanes: Tour Operators—*admin*	56152	4725
Tow targets, aircraft: Aircraft Part and Auxiliary Equipment, Other—*mfg*	336413	3728
Fluid Power Valve and Hose Fitting—*mfg*	332912	3728
Tow to top mills: Broadwoven Fabric Mills—*mfg*	31321	2299
Narrow Fabric Mills—*mfg*	313221	2299
Nonwoven Fabric Mills—*mfg*	31323	2299
Textile and Fabric Finishing (except Broadwoven Fabric) Mills—*mfg*	313312	2299
Textile Product Mills, All Other Miscellaneous—*mfg*	314999	2299

ALPHABETICAL INDEX	NAICS	SIC
Thread Mills—*mfg*	313113	2299
Yarn Spinning Mills—*mfg*	313111	2299
Tow-in parking lots: Parking Lots and Garages—*serv*	81293	7521
Towboats, building and repairing: Ship Building and Repairing—*mfg*	336611	3731
Towel bar holders, vitreous china and earthenware: Vitreous China Plumbing Fixture and China and Earthenware Fittings and Bathroom Accessories—*mfg*	327111	3261
Towel supply service, except wiping: Linen Supply—*serv*	812331	7213
Towel supply service, wiping: Industrial Launderers—*serv*	812332	7218
Towelettes, premoistened: Soap and Other Detergent—*mfg*	325611	2844
Toilet Preparation—*mfg*	32562	2844
Toweling paper: Newsprint Mills—*mfg*	322122	2621
Paper (except Newsprint) Mills—*mfg*	322121	2621
Towels: Knit Fabric and Lace Mills, Other—*mfg*	313249	2259
Weft Knit Fabric Mills—*mfg*	313241	2259
Towels and toweling, cotton–made in weaving mills: Broadwoven Fabric Mills—*mfg*	31321	2211
Towels and towelings, linen and linen-and-cotton mixtures: Broadwoven Fabric Mills—*mfg*	31321	2299
Narrow Fabric Mills—*mfg*	313221	2299
Nonwoven Fabric Mills—*mfg*	31323	2299
Textile and Fabric Finishing (except Broadwoven Fabric) Mills—*mfg*	313312	2299
Textile Product Mills, All Other Miscellaneous—*mfg*	314999	2299
Thread Mills—*mfg*	313113	2299
Yarn Spinning Mills—*mfg*	313111	2299
Towels, fabric and nonwoven textiles: Household Textile Product Mills, Other—*mfg*	314129	2392
Towels, paper: Industrial and Personal Service Paper—*whlse*	42213	5113
Sanitary Paper Product—*mfg*	322291	2676
Tower sections, transmission–prefabricated metal: Fabricated Structural Metal—*mfg*	332312	3441
Towers, cooling–wood or wood and sheet-metal combination: Manufacturing, All Other Miscellaneous—*mfg*	339999	2499
Wood Container and Pallet—*mfg*	32192	2499
Wood Product, All Other Miscellaneous—*mfg*	321999	2499
Towers, tank–metal plate: Air-Conditioning and Warm Air Heating Equipment and Commercial and Industrial Refrigeration Equipment—*mfg*	333415	3443
Metal Tank (Heavy Gauge)—*mfg*	33242	3443
Plate Work—*mfg*	332313	3443
Power Boiler and Heat Exchanger—*mfg*	33241	3443
Towers–bubble, cooling, fractionating-metal plate: Air-Conditioning and Warm Air Heating Equipment and Commercial and Industrial Refrigeration Equipment—*mfg*	333415	3443
Metal Tank (Heavy Gauge)—*mfg*	33242	3443
Plate Work—*mfg*	332313	3443

Power Boiler and Heat Exchanger—*mfg*	33241	3443
Towing bars and systems: Transportation Equipment, All Other—*mfg*	336999	3799
Towing service, automotive: Automotive Oil Change and Lubrication Shops—*serv*	811191	7549
Automotive Repair and Maintenance, All Other—*serv*	811198	7549
Motor Vehicle Towing—*trans*	48841	7549
Towing services, marine: Coastal and Great Lakes Freight—*trans*	483113	4492
Inland Water Freight—*trans*	483211	4492
Navigational Services to Shipping—*trans*	48833	4492
Townhouse construction–general contractors: Single Family Housing—*const*	23321	1521
Toxins: Biological Product (except Diagnostic)—*mfg*	325414	2836
Toxoids, except in vitro and in vivo: Biological Product (except Diagnostic)—*mfg*	325414	2836
Toy and game stores: Hobby, Toy and Game Stores—*retail*	45112	5945
Toy and Hobby Goods and Supplies Wholesalers	**42192**	**5092**
Toy transformers: Power, Distribution and Specialty Transformer—*mfg*	335311	3612
Toys (including electronic): Toy and Hobby Goods and Supplies—*whlse*	42192	5092
Toys, doll: Doll and Stuffed Toy—*mfg*	339931	3942
Toys, rubber–except dolls: Fabric Coating Mills—*mfg*	31332	3069
Rubber Product, All Other—*mfg*	326299	3069
Toys, stuffed: Doll and Stuffed Toy—*mfg*	339931	3942
Toys–except dolls, bicycles, rubber toys, and stuffed toys: Game, Toy, and Children's Vehicle—*mfg*	339932	3944
Trace elements (agricultural chemicals): Pesticide and Other Agricultural Chemical—*mfg*	32532	2879
Tracer igniters for ammunition more than 30 mm. (or more than 1.18 inch): Ammunition (except Small Arms)—*mfg*	332993	3483
Tracing cloth (drafting material): Chemical Product, All Other Miscellaneous—*mfg*	325998	3952
Institutional Furniture—*mfg*	337127	3952
Lead Pencil and Art Good—*mfg*	339942	3952
Tracing cloth, cotton: Broadwoven Fabric Mills—*mfg*	31321	2211
Track and field athletic equipment, except apparel and footwear: Sporting and Athletic Goods—*mfg*	33992	3949
Track spikes: Metal Service Centers and Offices—*whlse*	42151	5051
Track-laying equipment: Construction and (except Petroleum) Machinery and Equipment—*whlse*	42181	5082
Tracking missiles by telemetry and photography on a contract basis: Cellular and Other Wireless Telecommunications—*info*	513322	4899
Satellite Telecommunications—*info*	51334	4899
Telecommunications, Other—*info*	51339	4899
Trackless trolley buses: Pump and Pumping Equipment—*mfg*	333911	3743
Railroad Rolling Stock—*mfg*	33651	3743
Traction apparatus: Surgical Appliance and Supplies—*mfg*	339113	3842
Tractor repair: Home and Garden Equipment Repair and Maintenance—*serv*	811411	7699

Machinery and Equipment (except Automotive and Electronic) Repair and Maintenance, Commercial and Industrial—*serv*	81131	7699
Tractor-mounting equipment: Construction and (except Petroleum) Machinery and Equipment—*whlse*	42181	5082
Tractors, agricultural: Farm and Garden Machinery and Equipment—*whlse*	42182	5083
Outdoor Power Equipment Stores—*retail*	44421	5083
Tractors, construction: Construction and (except Petroleum) Machinery and Equipment—*whlse*	42181	5082
Construction Machinery—*mfg*	33312	3531
Overhead Traveling Crane, Hoist and Monorail System—*mfg*	333923	3531
Railroad Rolling Stock—*mfg*	33651	3531
Tractors, crawler: Construction Machinery—*mfg*	33312	3531
Overhead Traveling Crane, Hoist and Monorail System—*mfg*	333923	3531
Railroad Rolling Stock—*mfg*	33651	3531
Tractors, industrial: Industrial Machinery and Equipment—*whlse*	42183	5084
Tractors, industrial–for use in plants, depots, docks, and terminals: Fabricated Metal Product, All Other Miscellaneous—*mfg*	332999	3537
Industrial Truck, Tractor, Trailer and Stacker Machinery—*mfg*	333924	3537
Metal Container, Other—*mfg*	332439	3537
Tractors, lawn and garden: Hand and Edge Tool—*mfg*	332212	3524
Lawn and Garden Tractor and Home Lawn and Garden Equipment—*mfg*	333112	3524
Tractors, track-laying: Construction Machinery—*mfg*	33312	3531
Overhead Traveling Crane, Hoist and Monorail System—*mfg*	333923	3531
Railroad Rolling Stock—*mfg*	33651	3531
Tractors, truck: Automobile and Other Motor Vehicle—*whlse*	42111	5012
Tractors, truck–for highway use: Automobile—*mfg*	336111	3711
Heavy Duty Truck—*mfg*	33612	3711
Light Truck and Utility Vehicle—*mfg*	336112	3711
Military Armored Vehicle, Tank and Tank Component—*mfg*	336992	3711
Motor Vehicle Body—*mfg*	336211	3711
Tractors, wheel–farm type: Farm Machinery and Equipment—*mfg*	333111	3523
Trade associations: Business Associations—*serv*	81391	8611
Trade binding services: Tradebinding and Related Work—*mfg*	323121	2789
Trade commissions: General Economic Programs, Administration of—*pub*	92611	9611
Trade Contractors, All Other Special	**23599**	**1799**
Trade Contractors, Other Special	**2359**	
Trade Contractors, Special	**235**	
Trade journals, publishing and printing, or publishing only: Periodical Publishers—*info*	51112	2721
Trade schools: Apprenticeship Training—*educ*	611513	8249
Technical and Trade Schools, Other—*educ*	611519	8249
Trade show arrangement: Convention and Trade Show Organizers—*admin*	56192	7389
Convention and Visitors Bureaus—*admin*	561591	7389
Trade unions, local or national: Labor Unions and Similar Labor Organizations—*serv*	81393	8631

ALPHABETICAL INDEX	NAICS	SIC
Tradebinding and Related Work	**323121**	**2789**
Traders, commodity contract: Commodity Brokerage—*fin*	52314	6221
Commodity Contracts Dealing—*fin*	52313	6221
Traders. security: Financial Investment Activities, Miscellaneous—*fin*	523999	6211
Intermediation, Miscellaneous—*fin*	52391	6211
Investment Banking and Securities Dealing—*fin*	52311	6211
Securities Brokerage—*fin*	52312	6211
Trading companies, commodity contract: Commodity Contracts Dealing—*fin*	52313	6799
Financial Investment Activities, Miscellaneous—*fin*	523999	6799
Intermediation, Miscellaneous—*fin*	52391	6799
Portfolio Management—*fin*	52392	6799
Trading stamps, lithographed: Lithographic Printing, Commercial—*mfg*	323110	2752
Quick Printing—*mfg*	323114	2752
Trading stamps, printed–except lithographed or gravure: Digital Printing—*mfg*	323115	2759
Flexographic Printing, Commercial—*mfg*	323112	2759
Printing, Other Commercial—*mfg*	323119	2759
Quick Printing—*mfg*	323114	2759
Trading stamps–gravure printing: Gravure Printing, Commercial—*mfg*	323111	2754
Traffic consultants: Educational Support Services—*educ*	61171	8748
Management Consulting Services, Other—*prof*	541618	8748
Scientific and Technical Consulting Services, Other—*prof*	54169	8748
Traffic lane painting–contractors: Painting and Wall Covering Contractors—*const*	23521	1721
Traffic signals, electric: Communications Equipment, Other—*mfg*	33429	3669
Trail building–general contractors: Heavy, All Other—*const*	23499	1629
Industrial Nonbuilding Structure—*const*	23493	1629
Trailer camp construction–general contractors: Heavy, All Other—*const*	23499	1629
Industrial Nonbuilding Structure—*const*	23493	1629
Trailer hitches: Transportation Equipment, All Other—*mfg*	336999	3799
Trailer parks for transients: RV (Recreational Vehicle) Parks and Campgrounds—*accom*	721211	7033
Trailer rental: Truck, Utility Trailer, and RV (Recreational Vehicle) Rental and Leasing—*real*	53212	7519
Trailers and wagons, farm: Farm Machinery and Equipment—*mfg*	333111	3523
Trailers for automobiles, except travel and mobile home: Transportation Equipment, All Other—*mfg*	336999	3799
Trailers for passenger automobiles: Automobile and Other Motor Vehicle—*whlse*	42111	5012
Trailers for transporting horses, except fifth-wheel type: Transportation Equipment, All Other—*mfg*	336999	3799

ALPHABETICAL INDEX	NAICS	SIC
Trailers for trucks, new and used: Automobile and Other Motor Vehicle—*whlse*	42111	5012
Trailers, boat: Transportation Equipment, All Other—*mfg*	336999	3799
Trailers, camping: Travel Trailer and Camper—*mfg*	336214	3792
Trailers, fifth-wheel type–for transporting horses: Truck Trailer—*mfg*	336212	3715
Trailers, house–except as permanent dwellings: Travel Trailer and Camper—*mfg*	336214	3792
Trailers, industrial: Industrial Machinery and Equipment—*whlse*	42183	5084
Trailers, motor truck: Truck Trailer—*mfg*	336212	3715
Trailers, truck–for use in plants, depots, docks, and terminals: Fabricated Metal Product, All Other Miscellaneous—*mfg*	332999	3537
Industrial Truck, Tractor, Trailer and Stacker Machinery—*mfg*	333924	3537
Metal Container, Other—*mfg*	332439	3537
Trailers, utility: Motor Vehicle Dealers, All Other—*retail*	441229	5599
Train cars and equipment, freight or passenger: Pump and Pumping Equipment—*mfg*	333911	3743
Railroad Rolling Stock—*mfg*	33651	3743
Training aids, aircraft–except electronic: Aircraft Part and Auxiliary Equipment, Other—*mfg*	336413	3728
Fluid Power Valve and Hose Fitting—*mfg*	332912	3728
Training horses, except racing: Animal Production Support Activities—*ag*	11521	752
Pet Care (except Veterinary) Services—*serv*	81291	752
Training motion picture production: Motion Picture and Video Production—*info*	51211	7812
Training of pets and other animal special-ties: Animal Production Support Activities—*ag*	11521	752
Pet Care (except Veterinary) Services—*serv*	81291	752
Training pants (underwear) except rubber or rubberized fabric: Infants' Cut and Sew Apparel—*mfg*	315291	2341
Women's and Girls' Cut and Sew Apparel Contractors—*mfg*	315212	2341
Women's and Girls' Cut and Sew Lingerie, Loungewear and Nightwear—*mfg*	315231	2341
Training racehorses: Race Tracks—*arts*	711212	7948
Spectator Sports, Other—*arts*	711219	7948
Training schools for delinquents: Homes for the Elderly—*hlth*	623312	8361
Residential Care Facilities, Other—*hlth*	62399	8361
Residential Mental Health and Substance Abuse Facilities—*hlth*	62322	8361
Trains and equipment, toy–electric and mechanical: Game, Toy, and Children's Vehicle—*mfg*	339932	3944
Trampoline operation: Fitness and Recreational Sports Centers—*arts*	71394	7999
Tramways, aerial–except amusement and scenic: Transit and Ground Passenger, All Other—*trans*	485999	4119
Transportation, Special Needs—*trans*	485991	4119
Tranquilizers and mental drug preparations: Pharmaceutical Preparation—*mfg*	325412	2834

Entry	NAICS	SIC
Transceivers: Radio and Television Broadcasting and Wireless Communications Equipment—*mfg*	33422	3663
Transcutaneous electrical nerve stimulators (TENS): Electromedical and Electrotherapeutic Apparatus—*mfg*	334510	3845
Irradiation Apparatus—*mfg*	334517	3845
Transducers for use in measuring and testing instruments and equipments: Electronic Component, Other—*mfg*	334419	3679
Motor Vehicle Electrical and Electronic Equipment, Other—*mfg*	336322	3679
Printed Circuit/Electronics Assembly—*mfg*	334418	3679
Radio and Television Broadcasting and Wireless Communications Equipment—*mfg*	33422	3679
Transducers, pressure: Measuring and Controlling Device, Other—*mfg*	334519	3829
Surgical and Medical Instrument—*mfg*	339112	3829
Transfer agents, securities: Financial Investment Activities, Miscellaneous—*fin*	523999	6289
Trust, Fiduciary and Custody Activities—*fin*	523991	6289
Transfer paper, gold and silver: Coated and Laminated Paper—*mfg*	322222	2672
Transferring designs (lithographing): Lithographic Printing, Commercial—*mfg*	323110	2752
Quick Printing—*mfg*	323114	2752
Transfers, decalcomania and dry–lithographed: Lithographic Printing, Commercial—*mfg*	323110	2752
Quick Printing—*mfg*	323114	2752
Transformers (separate) for arc-welders: Power, Distribution and Specialty Transformer—*mfg*	335311	3548
Welding and Soldering Equipment—*mfg*	333992	3548
Transformers, electric power: Power, Distribution and Specialty Transformer—*mfg*	335311	3612
Transformers, electric–except electronic: Building Material Dealers, Other—*retail*	44419	5063
Electrical Apparatus and Equipment, Wiring Supplies and Material—*whlse*	42161	5063
Transformers, electronic: Electronic Parts and Equipment, Other—*whlse*	42169	5065
Transformers, electronic types: Electronic Coil, Transformer, and Other Inductor—*mfg*	334416	3677
Transformers, for electronic meters: Power, Distribution and Specialty Transformer—*mfg*	335311	3612
Transformers, ignition–for use on domestic fuel burners: Power, Distribution and Specialty Transformer—*mfg*	335311	3612
Transformers, instrument–except portable: Power, Distribution and Specialty Transformer—*mfg*	335311	3612
Transformers, instrument–portable: Electronic Coil, Transformer, and Other Inductor—*mfg*	334416	3825
Instrument for Measuring and Testing Electricity and Electrical Signals—*mfg*	334515	3825
Transformers, reactor: Power, Distribution and Specialty Transformer—*mfg*	335311	3612

Entry	NAICS	SIC
Transformers–power supply electronictype: Electronic Coil, Transformer, and Other Inductor—*mfg*	334416	3677
Transient photographers: Photography Studios, Portrait—*prof*	541921	7221
Transistors: Electronic Parts and Equipment, Other—*whlse*	42169	5065
Semiconductor and Related Device—*mfg*	334413	3674
Transit advertising: Advertising Material Distribution Services—*prof*	54187	7319
Advertising, Other Services Related to—*prof*	54189	7319
Display Advertising—*prof*	54185	7319
Media Buying Agencies—*prof*	54183	7319
Nonscheduled Air, Other—*trans*	481219	7319
Transit and Ground Passenger Transportation	**485**	
Transit and Ground Passenger Transportation, All Other	**485999**	**4119**
Transit and Ground Passenger Transportation, Other	**4859**	
Transit and Ground Passenger Transportation, Other	**48599**	
Transit systems and authorities-nonoperating: Air Traffic Control—*trans*	488111	9621
Transportation Programs, Regulation and Administration of—*pub*	92612	9621
Transits, surveying: Measuring and Controlling Device, Other—*mfg*	334519	3829
Surgical and Medical Instrument—*mfg*	339112	3829
Translation and Interpretation Services	**54193**	**7389**
Transmission and distribution of naturalgas: Natural Gas Distribution—*util*	22121	4923
Pipeline of Natural Gas—*trans*	48621	4923
Transmission and distribution voltage regulators: Power, Distribution and Specialty Transformer—*mfg*	335311	3612
Transmission belting, leather: Leather Good, All Other—*mfg*	316999	3199
Transmission equipment, electrical: Building Material Dealers, Other—*retail*	44419	5063
Electrical Apparatus and Equipment, Wiring Supplies and Material—*whlse*	42161	5063
Transmission fluid: Petroleum Lubricating Oil and Grease—*mfg*	324191	2992
Transmission housings and parts, motorvehicle: Motor Vehicle Parts, All Other—*mfg*	336399	3714
Motor Vehicle Steering and Suspension Components (except Spring)—*mfg*	33633	3714
Motor Vehicle Transmission and Power Train Parts—*mfg*	33635	3714
Transmission line construction–general contractors: Power and Communication Transmission Line—*const*	23492	1623
Water, Sewer, and Pipeline—*const*	23491	1623
Transmission of electric power: Electric Bulk Power Transmission and Control—*util*	221121	4911
Electric Power Distribution—*util*	221122	4911
Electric Power Generation, Other—*util*	221119	4911
Fossil Fuel Electric Power Generation—*util*	221112	4911
Hydroelectric Power Generation—*util*	221111	4911
Nuclear Electric Power Generation—*util*	221113	4911
Transmission of natural gas: Pipeline of Natural Gas—*trans*	48621	4922
Transmission repair, automotive: Automotive Transmission Repair—*serv*	811113	7537

ALPHABETICAL INDEX	NAICS	SIC
Transmission towers: Fabricated Structural Metal—*mfg*	332312	3441
Transmissions, aircraft: Aircraft Part and Auxiliary Equipment, Other—*mfg*	336413	3728
Fluid Power Valve and Hose Fitting—*mfg*	332912	3728
Transmissions, automotive–installation, repair, or sale and installation: Automotive Transmission Repair—*serv*	811113	7537
Transmissions, hydrostatic drives: Fluid Power Pump and Motor—*mfg*	333996	3594
Transmissions, motor vehicle: Motor Vehicle Parts, All Other—*mfg*	336399	3714
Motor Vehicle Steering and Suspension Components (except Spring)—*mfg*	33633	3714
Motor Vehicle Transmission and Power Train Parts—*mfg*	33635	3714
Transmitter-receivers, radio: Radio and Television Broadcasting and Wireless Communications Equipment—*mfg*	33422	3663
Transmitters: Electronic Parts and Equipment, Other—*whlse*	42169	5065
Transmitters of process variables, standard signal conversion: Instruments and Related Products for Measuring, Displaying, and Controlling Industrial Process Variables—*mfg*	334513	3823
Transmitting apparatus, radio and television: Radio and Television Broadcasting and Wireless Communications Equipment—*mfg*	33422	3663
Transmitting electron tubes: Electron Tube—*mfg*	334411	3671
Transplanters: Farm Machinery and Equipment—*mfg*	333111	3523
Transport clearinghouse: Freight Arrangement—*trans*	48851	4731
Management Consulting Services, Other—*prof*	541618	4731
Transport vessels, passenger and troop–building and repairing: Ship Building and Repairing—*mfg*	336611	3731
Transportation	**48-49**	
Transportation brokerage: Freight Arrangement—*trans*	48851	4731
Management Consulting Services, Other—*prof*	541618	4731
Transportation departments: Air Traffic Control—*trans*	488111	9621
Transportation Programs, Regulation and Administration of—*pub*	92612	9621
Transportation Equipment and Supplies (except Motor Vehicle) Wholesalers	**42186**	**5088**
Transportation equipment and supplies, except motor vehicles: Transportation Equipment and Supplies (except Motor Vehicle)—*whlse*	42186	5088
Transportation Equipment Manufacturing	**336**	
Transportation Equipment Manufacturing, All Other	**336999**	**3799**
Transportation Equipment Manufacturing, Other	**33699**	
Transportation Equipment Manufacturing, Other	**3369**	
Transportation of freight on bays andsounds of the oceans: Inland Water Freight—*trans*	483211	4449
Transportation Programs, Regulation and Administration of	**92612**	**9621**
Transportation rate services: Freight Arrangement—*trans*	48851	4731
Management Consulting Services, Other—*prof*	541618	4731
Transportation regulatory agencies: Air Traffic Control—*trans*	488111	9621
Transportation Programs, Regulation and Administration of—*pub*	92612	9621
Transportation schedules, gravure printing: Gravure Printing, Commercial—*mfg*	323111	2754
Transportation schedules, lithographed: Lithographic Printing, Commercial—*mfg*	323110	2752
Quick Printing—*mfg*	323114	2752
Transportation schedules, printing–except lithographed or gravure: Digital Printing—*mfg*	323115	2759
Flexographic Printing, Commercial—*mfg*	323112	2759
Printing, Other Commercial—*mfg*	323119	2759
Quick Printing—*mfg*	323114	2759
Transportation Support Activities	**488**	
Transportation, All Other Support Activities	**488999**	**4789**
Transportation, Other Support Activities for	**48899**	
Transportation, Other Support Activities for	**4889**	
Transportation, railroad–line-haul: Line-Haul Railroads—*trans*	482111	4011
Transportation, Special Needs	**485991**	**4119**
Trap racks (clay targets): Sporting and Athletic Goods—*mfg*	33992	3949
Trap rock, crushed and broken: Crushed and Broken Stone and Quarrying, Other—*mining*	212319	1429
Trap rock, dimension: Dimension Stone and Quarrying—*mining*	212311	1411
Trapping carried on as a business enterprise: Hunting and Trapping—*ag*	11421	971
Traps, animal and fish–made from purchased wire: Fabricated Wire Product, Other—*mfg*	332618	3496
Traps, drummers': Musical Instrument—*mfg*	339992	3931
Traps, water: Fabricated Metal Product, All Other Miscellaneous—*mfg*	332999	3432
Plumbing Fixture Fitting and Trim—*mfg*	332913	3432
Trapshooting facilities, except membership clubs: Fitness and Recreational Sports Centers—*arts*	71394	7999
Trash bags, plastics film, foil, and coated paper: Plastics, Foil, and Coated Paper Bag—*mfg*	322223	2673
Unsupported Plastics Bag—*mfg*	326111	2673
Trash compactors, household: Major Household Appliance, Other—*mfg*	335228	3639
Trash containers, plastics: Plastics Pipe and Pipe Fitting—*mfg*	326122	3089
Plastics Product, All Other—*mfg*	326199	3089
Unsupported Plastics Profile Shape—*mfg*	326121	3089
Trash racks, metal plate: Air-Conditioning and Warm Air Heating Equipment and Commercial and Industrial Refrigeration Equipment—*mfg*	333415	3443
Metal Tank (Heavy Gauge)—*mfg*	33242	3443
Plate Work—*mfg*	332313	3443
Power Boiler and Heat Exchanger—*mfg*	33241	3443
Travel Agencies	**56151**	**4724**
Travel Arrangement and Reservation Services	**5615**	

Entry	NAICS	SIC
Travel Arrangement and Reservation Services, All Other	**561599**	**7389**
Travel Arrangement and Reservation Services, Other	**56159**	
Travel bureaus: Travel Agencies—*admin*	56151	4724
Travel Trailer and Camper Manufacturing	**336214**	**3799**
Travel trailer chassis: Travel Trailer and Camper—*mfg*	336214	3792
Travel trailers, automobile–new and used: Recreational Vehicle Dealers—*retail*	44121	5561
Traveler Accommodation	**7211**	
Traveler Accommodation, All Other	**721199**	**7011**
Traveler Accommodation, Other	**72119**	
Traveler's aid centers: Child and Youth Services—*hlth*	62411	8322
Community Food Services—*hlth*	62421	8322
Community Housing Services, Other—*hlth*	624229	8322
Emergency and Other Relief Services—*hlth*	62423	8322
Individual and Family Services, Other—*hlth*	62419	8322
Parole Offices and Probation Offices—*pub*	92215	8322
Services for the Elderly and Persons with Disabilities—*hlth*	62412	8322
Temporary Shelters—*hlth*	624221	8322
Traveling bags, regardless of material: Luggage—*mfg*	316991	3161
Traveling wave tubes: Electron Tube—*mfg*	334411	3671
Travertine, crushed and broken: Crushed and Broken Limestone and Quarrying—*mining*	212312	1422
Travertine, dimension: Dimension Stone and Quarrying—*mining*	212311	1411
Trawl twin: Rope, Cordage and Twine Mills—*mfg*	314991	2298
Trawlers, building and repalring: Ship Building and Repairing—*mfg*	336611	3731
Tray trucks, restaurant: Institutional Furniture—*mfg*	337127	2599
Trays, carrier–wood: Wood Container and Pallet—*mfg*	32192	2441
Trays, glass: Pressed and Blown Glass and Glassware, Other—*mfg*	327212	3229
Trays, laundry–concrete: Concrete Pipe—*mfg*	327332	3272
Concrete Product, Other—*mfg*	32739	3272
Nonmetallic Mineral Product, All Other Miscellaneous—*mfg*	327999	3272
Trays, made from purchased wire: Fabricated Wire Product, Other—*mfg*	332618	3496
Trays, photographic printing and processing: Photographic and Photocopying Equipment—*mfg*	333315	3861
Photographic Film, Paper, Plate and Chemical—*mfg*	325992	3861
Trays, plastics–except foam: Plastics Pipe and Pipe Fitting—*mfg*	326122	3089
Plastics Product, All Other—*mfg*	326199	3089
Unsupported Plastics Profile Shape—*mfg*	326121	3089
Trays, rubber: Fabric Coating Mills—*mfg*	31332	3069
Rubber Product, All Other—*mfg*	326299	3069
Trays, warming–electric: Electric Housewares and Household Fan—*mfg*	335211	3634
Heating Equipment (except Electric and Warm Air Furnaces)—*mfg*	333414	3634
Trays–silver, nickel silver, pewter, stainless steel, and plated: Cutlery and Flatware (except Precious)—*mfg*	332211	3914
Silverware and Plated Ware—*mfg*	339912	3914

Entry	NAICS	SIC
Trays–wood, wicker, and bagasse: Manufacturing, All Other Miscellaneous—*mfg*	339999	2499
Wood Container and Pallet—*mfg*	32192	2499
Wood Product, All Other Miscellaneous—*mfg*	321999	2499
Tread rubber (camelback): Tire (except Retreading)—*mfg*	326211	3011
Treadmills: Sporting and Athletic Goods—*mfg*	33992	3949
Treads, stair–fabricated metal: Ornamental and Architectural Metal Work—*mfg*	332323	3446
Treads, stair–rubber: Fabric Coating Mills—*mfg*	31332	3069
Rubber Product, All Other—*mfg*	326299	3069
Treasurers' offices: Public Finance—*pub*	92113	9311
Treated mats, rugs, mops, dust tool covers, and cloth supply service: Industrial Launderers—*serv*	812332	7218
Treating wood products with creosote or other Preservatives: Wood Preservation—*mfg*	321114	2491
Tree farms: Nursery and Tree Production—*ag*	111421	811
Timber Tract Operations—*ag*	11311	811
Tree Nut Farming	**111335**	**173**
Tree nut groves and farms: Tree Nut Farming—*ag*	111335	173
Tree seed gathering, extracting, and selling: Crop Farming, All Other Miscellaneous—*ag*	111998	831
Forest Nurseries and Gathering of Forest Products—*ag*	11321	831
Tree shakers (nuts, 80ft fruits, and citrus): Farm Machinery and Equipment—*mfg*	333111	3523
Hand and Edge Tool—*mfg*	332212	3523
Tree trimming for public utility lines: Landscaping Services—*admin*	56173	783
Trees, Christmas, artificial: Fabricated Metal Product, All Other Miscellaneous—*mfg*	332999	3999
Trees, orchard–cultivation of: Nonscheduled Air, Other—*trans*	481219	721
Soil Preparation, Planting, and Cultivating—*ag*	115112	721
Trees, orchard–planting, pruning, bracing, spraying, removal, and surgery: Nonscheduled Air. Other—*trans*	481219	721
Soil Preparation, Planting, and Cultivating—*ag*	115112	721
Trees, ornamental–planting, pruning, bracing, spraying, removal, and surgery: Landscaping Services—*admin*	56173	783
Trellises, wood: Millwork (including Flooring), Other—*mfg*	321918	2431
Wood Window and Door—*mfg*	321911	2431
Trenching machines: Construction Machinery—*mfg*	33312	3531
Overhead Traveling Crane. Hoist and Monorail System—*mfg*	333923	3531
Railroad Rolling Stock—*mfg*	33651	3531
Trenching-contractors: Heavy, All Other—*const*	23499	1629
Industrial Nonbuilding Structure—*const*	23493	1629
Trestle construction–general contractors: Bridge and Tunnel—*const*	23412	1622
Trestles, wood–treated: Wood Preservation—*mfg*	321114	2491
Trichloroethylene: Basic Organic Chemical, All Other—*mfg*	325199	2869
Trichlorophenoxyacetic acid: Basic Organic Chemical, All Other—*mfg*	325199	2869
Trichlorotrifluoroethane tetrachlorodifluorcethane isopropyl alcohol: Basic Organic Chemical. All Other—*mfg*	325199	2869

ALPHABETICAL INDEX	NAICS	SIC
Ethyl Alcohol—*mfg*	325193	2869
Tricot fabrics: Knit Fabric and Lace Mills, Other—*mfg*	313249	2258
Textile and Fabric Finishing (except Broadwoven Fabric) Mills—*mfg*	313312	2258
Tricresyl phosphate: Basic Organic Chemical, All Other—*mfg*	325199	2869
Tricycles, children's: Game, Toy, and Children's Vehicle—*mfg*	339932	3944
Tridecyl alcohol: Basic Organic Chemical, All Other—*mfg*	325199	2869
Ethyl Alcohol—*mfg*	325193	2869
Trim and body parts, automobile–stamped metal: Motor Vehicle Metal Stamping—*mfg*	33637	3465
Trim and finish–contractors: Carpentry Contractors—*const*	23551	1751
Trim and molding, except automobile–metal: Metal Window and Door—*mfg*	332321	3442
Trim, sheet metal: Building Material Dealers, Other—*retail*	44419	5031
Trim, wood and covered wood: Millwork (including Flooring), Other—*mfg*	321918	2431
Wood Window and Door—*mfg*	321911	2431
Trimethyltrithiophosphite (rocket propellants): Basic Organic Chemical, All Other—*mfg*	325199	2869
Trimmers, hedge–except power: Cutlery and Flatware (except Precious)—*mfg*	332211	3421
Trimmers, hedge–power: Hand and Edge Tool—*mfg*	332212	3524
Lawn and Garden Tractor and Home Lawn and Garden Equipment—*mfg*	333112	3524
Trimming felts, except woven: Broadwoven Fabric Mills—*mfg*	31321	2299
Narrow Fabric Mills—*mfg*	313221	2299
Nonwoven Fabric Mills—*mfg*	31323	2299
Textile and Fabric Finishing (except Broadwoven Fabric) Mills—*mfg*	313312	2299
Textile Product Mills, All Other Miscellaneous—*mfg*	314999	2299
Thread Mills—*mfg*	313113	2299
Yarn Spinning Mills—*mfg*	313111	2299
Trimmings, apparel: Broadwoven Fabric Finishing Mills—*mfg*	313311	5131
Piece Goods, Notions and Other Dry Goods—*whlse*	42231	5131
Textile and Fabric Finishing (except Broadwoven Fabric) Mills—*mfg*	313312	5131
Trimmings, fabric–auto, furniture, millinery, dress, coat, and suit: Apparel Accessories and Apparel, Other—*mfg*	315999	2396
Motor Vehicle Fabric Accessories and Seat—*mfg*	33636	2396
Trimmings, fur: Fur and Leather Apparel—*mfg*	315292	2371
Trimmings, hat: Apparel Accessories and Apparel, Other—*mfg*	315999	2396
Trimmings, precious metal–e.g., for canes, umbrellas: Jewelry (except Costume)—*mfg*	339911	3911
Trimmings, shoe–leather: Fastener, Button, Needle and Pin—*mfg*	339993	3131
Leather Good, All Other—*mfg*	316999	3131
Wood Product, All Other Miscellaneous—*mfg*	321999	3131
Trimmings, textile: Narrow Fabric Mills—*mfg*	313221	2241

ALPHABETICAL INDEX	NAICS	SIC
Trimmings, trunk–metal: Hardware—*mfg*	33251	3429
Trinitrotoluene (TNT): Explosives—*mfg*	32592	2892
Triphenyl phosphate: Basic Organic Chemical, All Other—*mfg*	325199	2869
Triplet magnifying instruments, optical: Optical Instrument and Lens—*mfg*	333314	3827
Tripods, camera and projector: Photographic and Photocopying Equipment—*mfg*	333315	3861
Photographic Film, Paper, Plate and Chemical—*mfg*	325992	3861
Tripoli: Abrasive Product—*mfg*	32791	3291
Fabricated Metal Product, All Other Miscellaneous—*mfg*	332999	3291
Tripoli mining: Crushed and Broken Stone and Quarrying, Other—*mining*	212319	1499
Non-Metallic Mineral, All Other—*mining*	212399	1499
Tripping transformers: Power, Distribution and Specialty Transformer—*mfg*	335311	3612
Trocars: Surgical and Medical Instrument—*mfg*	339112	3841
Trolley buses, trackless: Pump and Pumping Equipment—*mfg*	333911	3743
Railroad Rolling Stock—*mfg*	33651	3743
Trolley line material, overhead: Current-Carrying Wiring Device—*mfg*	335931	3643
Trolley operation, except amusement andscenic: Bus and Motor Vehicle Transit Systems—*trans*	485113	4111
Commuter Rail Systems—*trans*	485112	4111
Mixed Mode Transit Systems—*trans*	485111	4111
Transit and Ground Passenger, All Other—*trans*	485999	4111
Urban Transit Systems, Other—*trans*	485119	4111
Trombones and parts: Musical Instrument—*mfg*	339992	3931
Trona mining: Potash, Soda, and Borate Mineral—*mining*	212391	1474
Trophies: Jewelry, Watch, Precious Stone and Precious Metal—*whlse*	42194	5094
Trophies, metal–except silver, nickelsilver, pewter, and plated: Fabricated Metal Product, All Other Miscellaneous—*mfg*	332999	3499
Trophies–silver, nickel silver, pewter, and plated: Cutlery and Flatware (except Precious)—*mfg*	332211	3914
Silverware and Plated Ware—*mfg*	339912	3914
Trophy bases, woed: Manufacturing, All Other Miscellaneous—*mfg*	339999	2499
Wood Container and Pallet—*mfg*	32192	2499
Wood Product, All Other Miscellaneous—*mfg*	321999	2499
Trophy shops: Stores (except Tobacco Stores), All Other Miscellaneous—*retail*	453998	5999
Tropical aquarium fish farms: Animal Aquaculture, Other—*ag*	112519	273
Finfish Farming and Fish Hatcheries—*ag*	112511	273
Shellfish Farming—*ag*	112512	273
Tropical fruit farms: Fruit and Tree Nut Combination Farming—*ag*	111336	179
Noncitrus Fruit Farming, Other—*ag*	111339	179
Trouble lights: Lighting Equipment, Other—*mfg*	335129	3699
Troughs, elevator–sheet metal: Metal Container, Other—*mfg*	332439	3444

Entry	NAICS	SIC
Sheet Metal Work—*mfg*	332322	3444
Troughs, industrial–metal plate: Air-Conditioning and Warm Air Heating Equipment and Commercial and Industrial Refrigeration Equipment—*mfg*	333415	3443
Metal Tank (Heavy Gauge)—*mfg*	33242	3443
Plate Work—*mfg*	332313	3443
Power Boiler and Heat Exchanger—*mfg*	33241	3443
Troughs, water: Farm Machinery and Equipment—*mfg*	333111	3523
Trouser pressers, electric: Electric Housewares and Household Fan—*mfg*	335211	3634
Heating Equipment (except Electric and Warm Air Furnaces)—*mfg*	333414	3634
Trouser, Slack and Jean Manufacturing, Men's and Boys' Cut and Sew	**315224**	**2369**
Trouserings, cotton: Broadwoven Fabric Mills—*mfg*	31321	2211
Trouserings–wool, mohair, and similaranimal fibers: Broadwoven Fabric Finishing Mills—*mfg*	313311	2231
Broadwoven Fabric Mills—*mfg*	31321	2231
Textile and Fabric Finishing (except Broadwoven Fabric) Mills—*mfg*	313312	2231
Trousers: Outerwear Knitting Mills—*mfg*	315191	2253
Trousers (separate): Men's and Boys' Cut and Sew Apparel Contractors—*mfg*	315211	2325
Men's and Boys' Cut and Sew Trouser, Slack and Jean—*mfg*	315224	2325
Trousers, men's and boys': Men's and Boys' Clothing and Furnishings—*whlse*	42232	5136
Trout farms: Animal Aquaculture, Other—*ag*	112519	273
Finfish Farming and Fish Hatcheries—*ag*	112511	273
Shellfish Farming—*ag*	112512	273
Trowels: Hand and Edge Tool—*mfg*	332212	3423
Truck and automobile assembly plant construction–general contractors: Building, Commercial and Institutional—*const*	23332	1541
Manufacturing and Industrial Building—*const*	23331	1541
Truck bodies, motor vehicle: Motor Vehicle Body—*mfg*	336211	3713
Truck cabs for motor vehicles: Motor Vehicle Body—*mfg*	336211	3713
Truck campers (slide-in campers): Travel Trailer and Camper—*mfg*	336214	3792
Truck controls, industrial battery: Relay and Industrial Control—*mfg*	335314	3625
Truck driving schools: Apprenticeship Training—*educ*	611513	8249
Technical and Trade Schools, Other—*educ*	611519	8249
Truck engine repair, except industrial: General Automotive Repair—*serv*	811111	7538
Truck farms: Vegetable (except Potato) and Melon Farming, Other—*ag*	111219	161
Truck finance leasing: International Trade Financing—*fin*	522293	6159
Non-Depository Credit Intermediation, All Other—*fin*	522298	6159
Sales Financing—*fin*	52222	6159
Truck leasing, except industrial trucks and finance leasing–without drivers: Truck, Utility Trailer, and RV (Recreational Vehicle) Rental and Leasing—*real*	53212	7513
Truck leasing, without drivers–except finance (equity) leasing: Truck, Utility Trailer, and RV (Recreational Vehicle) Rental and Leasing—*real*	53212	7513
Truck rental and leasing, industrial: Construction, and Forestry Machinery and Equipment Rental and Leasing—*real*	532412	7359
Machinery and Equipment Rental and Leasing, Other Commercial and Industrial—*real*	53249	7359
Truck rental for local use, with drivers: Freight (except Used Goods) Trucking, Local Specialized—*trans*	48422	4212
General Freight Trucking, Local—*trans*	48411	4212
Used Household and Office Goods Moving—*trans*	48421	4212
Truck rental, except industrial–withoutdrivers: Truck, Utility Trailer, and RV (Recreational Vehicle) Rental and Leasing—*real*	53212	7513
Truck route laundry and drycleaning, notoperated by laundries or cleaners: Garment Pressing, and Agents for Laundries—*serv*	812391	7212
Truck stops: Gasoline Stations with Convenience Stores—*retail*	44711	5541
Gasoline Stations, Other—*retail*	44719	5541
Truck tires and tubes: Tire and Tube—*whlse*	42113	5014
Tire Dealers—*retail*	44132	5014
Truck tractors: Automobile and Other Motor Vehicle—*whlse*	42111	5012
Truck tractors for highway use: Automobile—*mfg*	336111	3711
Heavy Duty Truck—*mfg*	33612	3711
Light Truck and Utility Vehicle—*mfg*	336112	3711
Military Armored Vehicle, Tank and Tank Component—*mfg*	336992	3711
Motor Vehicle Body—*mfg*	336211	3711
Truck Trailer Manufacturing	**336212**	**3715**
Truck trailers: Automobile and Other Motor Vehicle—*whlse*	42111	5012
Truck Trailer—*mfg*	336212	3715
Truck trailers for use in plants, depots, docks, and terminals: Fabricated Metal Product, All Other Miscellaneous—*mfg*	332999	3537
Industrial Truck, Tractor, Trailer and Stacker Machinery—*mfg*	333924	3537
Metal Container, Other—*mfg*	332439	3537
Truck Transportation	**484**	
Truck transportation brokers: Freight Arrangement—*trans*	48851	4731
Management Consulting Services, Other—*prof*	541618	4731
Truck, Utility Trailer, and RV (Recreational Vehicle) Rental and Leasing	**53212**	**7519**
Truck-mixed concrete: Ready-Mix Concrete—*mfg*	32732	3273
Truckheds: Motor Vehicle Body—*mfg*	336211	3713
Trucking logs: Freight (except Used Goods) Trucking, Local Specialized—*trans*	48422	4212
General Freight Trucking, Local—*trans*	48411	4212
Trucking rental with drivers, except forlocal use: Freight (except Used Goods) Trucking, Long-Distance, Specialized—*trans*	48423	4213
General Freight Trucking, Long-Distance, Less Than Truckload—*trans*	484122	4213
General Freight Trucking, Long-Distance, Truckload—*trans*	484121	4213
Used Household and Office Goods Moving—*trans*	48421	4213

ALPHABETICAL INDEX	NAICS	SIC
Trucking terminals, freight–with or with-out maintenance facilities: Road, Other Support Activities for—*trans*	48849	4231
Trucking timber: Freight (except Used Goods) Trucking, Local Specialized—*trans*	48422	4212
General Freight Trucking, Local—*trans*	48411	4212
Trucking, except local: Freight (except Used Goods) Trucking, Long-Distance, Specialized—*trans*	48423	4213
General Freight Trucking, Long-Distance, Less Than Truckload—*trans*	484122	4213
General Freight Trucking, Long-Distance, Truckload—*trans*	484121	4213
Used Household and Office Goods Moving—*trans*	48421	4213
Trucking, local–combined with storage: Freight (except Used Goods) Trucking, Local Specialized—*trans*	48422	4214
General Freight Trucking, Local—*trans*	48411	4214
Used Household and Office Goods Moving—*trans*	48421	4214
Trucking, local–without storage: Freight (except Used Goods) Trucking, Local Specialized—*trans*	48422	4212
General Freight Trucking, Local—*trans*	48411	4212
Trucks: Automobile and Other Motor Vehicle—*whlse*	42111	5012
Trucks, industrial: Industrial Machinery and Equipment—*whlse*	42183	5084
Trucks, industrial (except mining)–for freight, baggage, etc.: Fabricated Metal Product, All Other Miscellaneous—*mfg*	332999	3537
Industrial Truck, Tractor, Trailer and Stacker Machinery—*mfg*	333924	3537
Metal Container, Other—*mfg*	332439	3537
Trucks, motor–except off-highway: Automobile—*mfg*	336111	3711
Heavy Duty Truck—*mfg*	33612	3711
Light Truck and Utility Vehicle—*mfg*	336112	3711
Military Armored Vehicle, Tank and Tank Component—*mfg*	336992	3711
Motor Vehicle Body—*mfg*	336211	3711
Trucks, off-highway: Construction Machinery—*mfg*	33312	3531
Overhead Traveling Crane, Hoist and Monorail System—*mfg*	333923	3531
Railroad Rolling Stock—*mfg*	33651	3531
Trucktops: Motor Vehicle Body—*mfg*	336211	3713
Truckwashing: Car Washes—*serv*	811192	7542
Truffles grown under cover: Food Crops Grown Under Cover, Other—*ag*	111419	182
Mushroom Production—*ag*	111411	182
Trumpets and parts: Musical Instrument—*mfg*	339992	3931
Trunk hardware, including locks: Hardware—*mfg*	33251	3429
Trunk slats, wood: Wood Container and Pallet—*mfg*	32192	2441
Trunks, luggage: Luggage and Leather Goods Stores—*retail*	44832	5948
Trunks, regardless of material: Luggage—*mfg*	316991	3161
Truss Manufacturing	**321214**	**2439**
Truss plates, metal: Air-Conditioning and Warm Air Heating Equipment and Commercial and Industrial Refrigeration Equipment—*mfg*	333415	3443
Metal Tank (Heavy Gauge)—*mfg*	33242	3443

ALPHABETICAL INDEX	NAICS	SIC
Plate Work—*mfg*	332313	3443
Power Boiler and Heat Exchanger—*mfg*	33241	3443
Trusses, laminated lumber: Cut Stock, Resawing Lumber, and Planing—*mfg*	321912	2439
Engineered Wood Member (except Truss)—*mfg*	321213	2439
Truss—*mfg*	321214	2439
Trusses, wood: Cut Stock, Resawing Lumber, and Planing—*mfg*	321912	2439
Engineered Wood Member (except Truss)—*mfg*	321213	2439
Truss—*mfg*	321214	2439
Trusses–orthopedic and surgical: Surgical Appliance and Supplies—*mfg*	339113	3842
Trust companies (accepting deposits), commercial–State: Banking, Commercial—*fin*	52211	6022
Credit Card Issuing—*fin*	52221	6022
Depository Credit Intermediation, Other—*fin*	52219	6022
Trust, Fiduciary and Custody Activities—*fin*	523991	6022
Trust companies with deposits, commercial–national: Banking, Commercial—*fin*	52211	6021
Credit Card Issuing—*fin*	52221	6021
Trust, Fiduciary and Custody Activities—*fin*	523991	6021
Trust companies, nondeposit: Trust, Fiduciary and Custody Activities—*fin*	523991	6091
Trust deeds, purchase and sale of: Financial Transactions Processing, Reserve, and Clearing House Activities—*fin*	52232	6153
Non-Depository Credit Intermediation, All Other—*fin*	522298	6153
Sales Financing—*fin*	52222	6153
Trust, Fiduciary and Custody Activities	**523991**	**6022**
Trustees–except for educational, religious, or charitable trusts: Insurance Funds, Other—*fin*	52519	6733
Portfolio Management—*fin*	52392	6733
Trust, Fiduciary and Custody Activities—*fin*	523991	6733
Trusts, Estates, and Agency Accounts—*fin*	52592	6733
Trusts except educational, religious, andcharitable–management of: Insurance Funds, Other—*fin*	52519	6733
Portfolio Management—*fin*	52392	6733
Trust, Fiduciary and Custody Activities—*fin*	523991	6733
Trusts, Estates, and Agency Accounts—*fin*	52592	6733
Trusts, charitable–management of: Grantmaking Foundations—*serv*	813211	6732
Trusts, educational–management of: Grantmaking Foundations—*serv*	813211	6732
Trusts, Estates, and Agency Accounts	**52592**	**6733**
Trusts, personal investment–managementof: Insurance Funds, Other—*fin*	52519	6733
Portfolio Management—*fin*	52392	6733
Trust, Fiduciary and Custody Activities—*fin*	523991	6733
Trusts, Estates, and Agency Accounts—*fin*	52592	6733
Trusts, religious–management of: Grantmaking Foundations—*serv*	813211	6732

Description	NAICS	SIC
Tube and hose fittings and assemblies, fluid power–metal: Fluid Power Valve and Hose Fitting—*mfg*	332912	3492
Tube blooms, aluminum–extruded: Aluminum Extruded Product—*mfg*	331316	3354
Tube fabricating (contract bending and shaping); metal: Fabricated Pipe and Pipe Fitting—*mfg*	332996	3498
Tube fins, stamped metal: Metal Stamping—*mfg*	332116	3469
Tube fittings and assemblies, fluid power–metal: Fluid Power Valve and Hose Fitting—*mfg*	332912	3492
Tube mill machinery: Rolling Mill Machinery and Equipment—*mfg*	333516	3547
Tube retainers, electronic: Electronic Component, Other—*mfg*	334419	3679
Motor Vehicle Electrical and Electronic Equipment, Other—*mfg*	336322	3679
Printed Circuit/Electronics Assembly—*mfg*	334418	3679
Radio and Television Broadcasting and Wireless Communications Equipment—*mfg*	33422	3679
Tube rounds: Iron and Steel Mills—*mfg*	331111	3312
Petroleum and Coal Productsa, All Other—*mfg*	324199	3312
Tube spacers, mica: Electronic Component, Other—*mfg*	334419	3679
Motor Vehicle Electrical and Electronic Equipment, Other—*mfg*	336322	3679
Printed Circuit/Electronics Assembly—*mfg*	334418	3679
Radio and Television Broadcasting and Wireless Communications Equipment—*mfg*	33422	3679
Tube testers: Electronic Coil, Transformer, and Other Inductor—*mfg*	334416	3825
Instrument for Measuring and Testing Electricity and Electrical Signals—*mfg*	334515	3825
Tube transformer assemblies used in firing electronic tubes: Electronic Component, Other—*mfg*	334419	3679
Motor Vehicle Electrical and Electronic Equipment, Other—*mfg*	336322	3679
Printed Circuit/Electronics Assembly—*mfg*	334418	3679
Radio and Television Broadcasting and Wireless Communications Equipment—*mfg*	33422	3679
Tube, aluminum–extruded or drawn: Aluminum Extruded Product—*mfg*	331316	3354
Tuberculins: Biological Product (except Diagnostic)—*mfg*	325414	2836
Tuberculosis and other respiratory illness hospitals: General Medical and Surgical Hospitals—*hlth*	62211	8069
Hospitals (except Psychiatric and Substance Abuse), Specialty—*hlth*	62231	8069
Psychiatric and Substance Abuse Hospitals—*hlth*	62221	8069
Tubes for operating above the X-ray spectrum (with shorter wavelength): Electron Tube—*mfg*	334411	3671
Tubes, cathode ray: Electron Tube—*mfg*	334411	3671
Tubes, collapsible–for viscous products-tin, lead, and aluminum: Fabricated Metal Product, All Other Miscellaneous—*mfg*	332999	3499
Tubes, electron: Electron Tube—*mfg*	334411	3671
Tubes, electronic–receiving and transmitting, and industrial: Electronic Parts and Equipment, Other—*whlse*	42169	5065
Tubes, fiber or paper (with or without metal ends): Fiber Can, Tube, Drum, and Similar Products—*mfg*	322214	2655
Tubes, for chemical and electrical uses–impregnated paper or fiber: Fiber Can, Tube, Drum, and Similar Products—*mfg*	322214	2655
Tubes, hard rubber: Fabric Coating Mills—*mfg*	31332	3069
Rubber Product, All Other—*mfg*	326299	3069
Tubes, inner–airplane, automobile, bicycle, motorcycle, and tractor: Tire (except Retreading)—*mfg*	326211	3011
Tubes, iron and steel–made in steel works or rolling mills: Iron and Steel Mills—*mfg*	331111	3312
Petroleum and Coal Productsa, All Other—*mfg*	324199	3312
Tubes, klystron: Electron Tube—*mfg*	334411	3671
Tubes, laminated plastics: Laminated Plastics Plate, Sheet and Shape—*mfg*	32613	3083
Tubes, porcelain: Porcelain Electrical Supply—*mfg*	327113	3264
Tubes, seamless steel: Iron and Steel Pipes and Tubes from Purchased Steel—*mfg*	33121	3317
Tubes, television receiving type–cathode ray: Electron Tube—*mfg*	334411	3671
Tubes, unsupported plastics: Unsupported Plastics Profile Shape—*mfg*	326121	3082
Tubes, welded–aluminum: Aluminum Sheet, Plate and Foil—*mfg*	331315	3353
Tubes, wrought–welded, lock joint, and heavy riveted: Iron and Steel Pipes and Tubes from Purchased Steel—*mfg*	33121	3317
Tubes, X-ray: Irradiation Apparatus—*mfg*	334517	3844
Tubing for electrical purposes, quartz: Gypsum and Gypsum Product—*mfg*	32742	3299
Nonmetallic Mineral Product, All Other Miscellaneous—*mfg*	327999	3299
Tubing, asbestos: Motor Vehicle Brake System—*mfg*	33634	3292
Nonmetallic Mineral Product, All Other Miscellaneous—*mfg*	327999	3292
Tubing, copper and copper alloy: Copper Rolling, Drawing and Extruding—*mfg*	331421	3351
Tubing, flexible metallic: Fabricated Metal Product, All Other Miscellaneous—*mfg*	332999	3599
General Purpose Machinery , All Other—*mfg*	333999	3599
Machine Shops—*mfg*	33271	3599
Machinery, Other Commercial and Service Industry—*mfg*	333319	3599
Tubing, glass: Pressed and Blown Glass and Glassware, Other—*mfg*	327212	3229
Tubing, mechanical and hypodermic sizes–cold-drawn stainless steel: Iron and Steel Pipes and Tubes from Purchased Steel—*mfg*	33121	3317
Tubing, metal: Metal Service Centers and Offices—*whlse*	42151	5051
Tubing, pillow: Broadwoven Fabric Mills—*mfg*	31321	2211
Tubing, rubber–except extruded and lathe-cut: Fabric Coating Mills—*mfg*	31332	3069
Rubber Product, All Other—*mfg*	326299	3069
Tubing, seamless–cotton: Broadwoven Fabric Mills—*mfg*	31321	2211
Tubing, seamless–steel: Iron and Steel Mills—*mfg*	331111	3312
Petroleum and Coal Productsa, All Other—*mfg*	324199	3312
Tubing, textile–varnished: Fabric Coating Mills—*mfg*	31332	2295
Tubing, wrought–made in steel works or rolling mills: Iron and Steel Mills—*mfg*	331111	3312
Petroleum and Coal Productsa, All Other—*mfg*	324199	3312

ALPHABETICAL INDEX	NAICS	SIC
Tubing–lead magnesium, nickel, titanium, zinc, and their ailoys: Nonferrous Metal (except Copper and Aluminum) Rolling, Drawing and Extruding—*mfg*	331491	3356
Tubs, laundry and bath–enameled iron, cast iron, and pressed metal: Enameled Iron and Metal Sanitary Ware—*mfg*	332998	3431
Tubs, plastics (containers): Plastics Pipe and Pipe Fitting—*mfg*	326122	3089
Plastics Product, All Other—*mfg*	326199	3089
Unsupported Plastics Profile Shape—*mfg*	326121	3089
Tubs, plastics–bath, shower, and laundry: Plastics Plumbing Fixture—*mfg*	326191	3088
Tubs, wood–coopered: Wood Container and Pallet—*mfg*	32192	2449
Tuck pointing-contractors: Masonry and Stone Contractors—*const*	23541	1741
Tucking, for the trade: Men's and Boys' Cut and Sew Apparel Contractors—*mfg*	315211	2395
Textile Product Mills, All Other Miscellaneous—*mfg*	314999	2395
Women's and Girls' Cut and Sew Apparel Contractors—*mfg*	315212	2395
Tufting machines: Textile Machinery—*mfg*	333292	3552
Tugboat service: Coastal and Great Lakes Freight—*trans*	483113	4492
Inland Water Freight—*trans*	483211	4492
Navigational Services to Shipping—*trans*	48833	4492
Tugboats, building and repairing: Ship Building and Repairing—*mfg*	336611	3731
Tumblers, glass: Pressed and Blown Glass and Glassware, Other—*mfg*	327212	3229
Tumblers, plastics–except foam: Plastics Pipe and Pipe Fitting—*mfg*	326122	3089
Plastics Product, All Other—*mfg*	326199	3089
Unsupported Plastics Profile Shape—*mfg*	326121	3089
Tumbling (cleaning and polishing) of machine parts, for the trade: Electroplating, Plating, Polishing, Anodizing and Coloring—*mfg*	332813	3471
Tuna fish, canned: Seafood Canning—*mfg*	311711	2091
Tuna, catching of: Finfish Fishing—*ag*	114111	912
Tuners, FM and AM: Audio and Video Equipment—*mfg*	33431	3651
Tung oil: Fats and Oils Refining and Blending—*mfg*	311225	2076
Oilseed Processing, Other—*mfg*	311223	2076
Tungsten basic shapes: Nonferrous Metal (except Copper and Aluminum) Rolling, Drawing and Extruding—*mfg*	331491	3356
Tungsten carbide abrasives: Abrasive Product—*mfg*	32791	3291
Fabricated Metal Product, All Other Miscellaneous—*mfg*	332999	3291
Tungsten carbide powder by metallurgical process: Electrometallurgical Ferroalloy Product—*mfg*	331112	3313
Secondary Smelting, Refining, and Alloying of Nonferrous Metal (except Copper and Aluminum)—*mfg*	331492	3313
Tungsten carbide powder, except abrasivesor by metallurgical process: Basic Inorganic Chemical, All Other—*mfg*	325188	2819
Chemical Product, All Other Miscellaneous—*mfg*	325998	2819
Tungsten ore mining: Copper Ore and Nickel Ore—*mining*	212234	1061
Metal Ore, All Other—*mining*	212299	1061

ALPHABETICAL INDEX	NAICS	SIC
Tuning of pianos and organs: Electronic and Precision Equipment Repair and Maintenance, Other—*serv*	811219	7699
Personal and Household Goods Repair and Maintenance, Other—*serv*	81149	7699
Tunnel construction–general contractors: Bridge and Tunnel—*const*	23412	1622
Tunnel diodes: Semiconductor and Related Device—*mfg*	334413	3674
Tunnel kiln cars: Fabricated Metal Product, All Other Miscellaneous—*mfg*	332999	3537
Industrial Truck, Tractor, Trailer and Stacker Machinery—*mfg*	333924	3537
Metal Container, Other—*mfg*	332439	3537
Tunnel lining, metal plate: Air-Conditioning and Warm Air Heating Equipment and Commercial and Industrial Refrigeration Equipment—*mfg*	333415	3443
Metal Tank (Heavy Gauge)—*mfg*	33242	3443
Plate Work—*mfg*	332313	3443
Power Boiler and Heat Exchanger—*mfg*	33241	3443
Tunnel operation, vehicular: Road, Other Support Activities for—*trans*	48849	4785
Water, Other Support Activities for—*trans*	48839	4785
Tunneling, anthracite mine–on a contract basis: Coal Support Activities—*mining*	213113	1241
Tunneling–bituminous coal, anthracite, and lignite on a contract basis: Coal Support Activities—*mining*	213113	1241
Tunnels, vacuum–metal plate: Air-Conditioning and Warm Air Heating Equipment and Commercial and Industrial Refrigeration Equipment—*mfg*	333415	3443
Metal Tank (Heavy Gauge)—*mfg*	33242	3443
Plate Work—*mfg*	332313	3443
Power Boiler and Heat Exchanger—*mfg*	33241	3443
Tunnels, wind: Air-Conditioning and Warm Air Heating Equipment and Commercial and Industrial Refrigeration Equipment—*mfg*	333415	3443
Metal Tank (Heavy Gauge)—*mfg*	33242	3443
Plate Work—*mfg*	332313	3443
Power Boiler and Heat Exchanger—*mfg*	33241	3443
Turbidity instruments, industrial process type: Instruments and Related Products for Measuring, Displaying, and Controlling Industrial Process Variables—*mfg*	334513	3823
Turbidometers: Analytical Laboratory Instrument—*mfg*	334516	3826
Turbine and Turbine Generator Set Unit Manufacturing	**333611**	**3511**
Turbine engine forgings, ferrous–not made in rolling mills: Iron and Steel Forging—*mfg*	332111	3462
Turbine flow meters, industrial process type: Instruments and Related Products for Measuring, Displaying, and Controlling Industrial Process Variables—*mfg*	334513	3823
Turbine generator set units, complete–steam, gas, and hydraulic: Turbine and Turbine Generator Set Unit—*mfg*	333611	3511

Entry	NAICS	SIC
Turbine meters, consumption registering: Totalizing Fluid Meter and Counting Device—*mfg*	334514	3824
Turbines, aircraft type: Aircraft Engine and Engine Parts—*mfg*	336412	3724
Turbines–steam, hydraulic, and gas-except aircraft type: Turbine and Turbine Generator Set Unit—*mfg*	333611	3511
Turbogenerators: Turbine and Turbine Generator Set Unit—*mfg*	333611	3511
Turbosuperchargem, aircraft: Aircraft Engine and Engine Parts—*mfg*	336412	3724
Turf equipment, commercial: Farm Machinery and Equipment—*mfg*	333111	3523
Turf installation, except artificial: Landscaping Services—*admin*	56173	782
Turhoblowers, industrial: Air Purification Equipment—*mfg*	333411	3564
Industrial and Commercial Fan and Blower—*mfg*	333412	3564
Turkey egg farms and ranches: Turkey Production—*ag*	11233	253
Turkey farms and ranches: Turkey Production—*ag*	11233	253
Turkey Production	**11233**	**253**
Turkey red oil: Surface Active Agent—*mfg*	325613	2843
Turkeys, processed–fresh, frozen, canned, or cooked: Food, All Other Miscellaneous—*mfg*	311999	2015
Poultry Processing—*mfg*	311615	2015
Turkeys–slaughtering and dressing: Food, All Other Miscellaneous—*mfg*	311999	2015
Poultry Processing—*mfg*	311615	2015
Turkish baths: Personal Care Services, Other—*serv*	812199	7299
Turnbuckles: Hardware—*mfg*	33251	3429
Turned and carved wood (except furniture): Manufacturing, All Other Miscellaneous—*mfg*	339999	2499
Wood Container and Pallet—*mfg*	32192	2499
Wood Product, All Other Miscellaneous—*mfg*	321999	2499
Turned Product and Screw, Nut and Bolt Manufacturing	**33272**	
Turning machines (lathes): Machine Tool (Metal Cutting Types)—*mfg*	333512	3541
Turnings, furniture–wood: Cut Stock, Resawing Lumber, and Planing—*mfg*	321912	2426
Millwork (including Flooring), Other—*mfg*	321918	2426
Showcase, Partition, Shelving, and Locker—*mfg*	337215	2426
Wood Product, All Other Miscellaneous—*mfg*	321999	2426
Turnkey vendors, computer systems: Computer Systems Design Services—*prof*	541512	7373
Turnstiles, equipped with counting mechanisms: Measuring and Controlling Device, Other—*mfg*	334519	3829
Surgical and Medical Instrument—*mfg*	339112	3829
Turntables, for phonographs: Audio and Video Equipment—*mfg*	33431	3651
Turpentine: Chemical and Allied Products, Other—*whlse*	42269	5169
Turpentine, produced by distillation of pine gum or pine wood: Gum and Wood Chemical—*mfg*	325191	2861
Turquoise mining: Crushed and Broken Stone and Quarrying, Other—*mining*	212319	1499
Non-Metallic Mineral, All Other—*mining*	212399	1499
Turret lathes, metal cutting: Machine Tool (Metal Cutting Types)—*mfg*	333512	3541
Turret test fixtures, aircraft: Aircraft Part and Auxiliary Equipment, Other—*mfg*	336413	3728
Fluid Power Valve and Hose Fitting—*mfg*	332912	3728
Turrets and turret drives, aircraft: Aircraft Part and Auxiliary Equipment, Other—*mfg*	336413	3728
Fluid Power Valve and Hose Fitting—*mfg*	332912	3728
Turrets, gun–for artillery more than 30 mm. (or more than 1.18 inch): Ordnance and Accessories, Other—*mfg*	332995	3489
Turtles, catching of: Crop Farming, All Other Miscellaneous—*ag*	111998	919
Marine Fishing, Other—*ag*	114119	919
Tutoring: Exam Preparation and Tutoring—*educ*	611691	8299
Tuxedo rental: Formal Wear and Costume Rental—*real*	53222	7299
Tuxedos: Men's and Boys' Cut and Sew Apparel Contractors—*mfg*	315211	2311
Men's and Boys' Cut and Sew Suit, Coat and Overcoat—*mfg*	315222	2311
Twills, cotton: Broadwoven Fabric Mills—*mfg*	31321	2211
Twills, manmade fiber: Broadwoven Fabric Mills—*mfg*	31321	2221
Twine: Industrial Machinery and Equipment—*whlse*	42183	5085
Industrial Supplies—*whlse*	42184	5085
Rope, Cordage and Twine Mills—*mfg*	314991	2298
Twist drills: Industrial Machinery and Equipment—*whlse*	42183	5084
Twisting yarn–silk, wool, and manmade fiber continuous filament: Textile and Fabric Finishing (except Broadwoven Fabric) Mills—*mfg*	313312	2282
Yarn Texturing, Throwing and Twisting Mills—*mfg*	313112	2282
Type, rubber: Fabric Coating Mills—*mfg*	31332	3069
Rubber Product, All Other—*mfg*	326299	3069
Type–lead, steel, brass, copper faced, etc.: Printing Machinery and Equipment—*mfg*	333293	3555
Typecases, printers': Printing Machinery and Equipment—*mfg*	333293	3555
Typecasting, founding, and melting machines: Printing Machinery and Equipment—*mfg*	333293	3555
Typecetting for the printing trade: Prepress Services—*mfg*	323122	2791
Typesetting machines–intertypes, linotypes, monotypes, etc.: Printing Machinery and Equipment—*mfg*	333293	3555
Typesetting, computer controlled: Prepress Services—*mfg*	323122	2791
Typewriter repair, including electric: Electronic and Precision Equipment Repair and Maintenance, Other—*serv*	811219	7699
Personal and Household Goods Repair and Maintenance, Other—*serv*	81149	7699
Typewriter ribbon cloth, cotton: Broadwoven Fabric Mills—*mfg*	31321	2211
Typewriter ribbon cloth, manmade fiber: Broadwoven Fabric Mills—*mfg*	31321	2221
Typewriter ribbons, cloth or paper: Carbon Paper and Inked Ribbon—*mfg*	339944	3955
Typewriter stores: Stores (except Tobacco Stores), All Other Miscellaneous—*retail*	453998	5999
Typewriters: Lead Pencil and Art Good—*mfg*	339942	3579
Office Equipment—*whlse*	42142	5044
Office Machinery—*mfg*	333313	3579

ALPHABETICAL INDEX	NAICS	SIC
Watch, Clock, and Part—*mfg*	334518	3579
Typing service: Court Reporting and Stenotype Services—*admin*	561492	7338
Document Preparation Services—*admin*	56141	7338
Typographic composition: Prepress Services—*mfg*	323122	2791
Typographic numbering machines: Printing Machinery and Equipment—*mfg*	333293	3555
Tyuyamunite mining: Uranium-Radium-Vanadium Ore—*mining*	212291	1094
U.S. attorneys' offices: Legal Counsel and Prosecution—*pub*	92213	9222
Ukuleles and parts: Musical Instrument—*mfg*	339992	3931
Ulexite mining: Potash, Soda, and Borate Mineral—*mining*	212391	1474
Ultramarine pigments: Carbon Black—*mfg*	325182	2816
Inorganic Dye and Pigment—*mfg*	325131	2816
Ultrasonic assisted grinding machines (metalworking): Machine Tool (Metal Cutting Types)—*mfg*	333512	3541
Ultrasonic cleaning equipment, except medical and dental: Electrical Equipment and Component, All Other Miscellaneous—*mfg*	335999	3699
Machinery, Other Commercial and Service Industry—*mfg*	333319	3699
Ultrasonic dental equipment: Dental Equipment and Supplies—*mfg*	339114	3843
Ultrasonic generators sold separately for inclusion in tools and equipment: Electrical Equipment and Component, All Other Miscellaneous—*mfg*	335999	3699
Machinery, Other Commercial and Service Industry—*mfg*	333319	3699
Ultrasonic medical cleaning equipment: Surgical and Medical Instrument—*mfg*	339112	3841
Ultrasonic medical equipment, except cleaning: Electromedical and Electrotherapeutic Apparatus—*mfg*	334510	3845
Irradiation Apparatus—*mfg*	334517	3845
Ultrasonic metal cutting machine tools: Machine Tool (Metal Cutting Types)—*mfg*	333512	3541
Ultrasonic scanning devices, medical: Electromedical and Electrotherapeutic Apparatus—*mfg*	334510	3845
Irradiation Apparatus—*mfg*	334517	3845
Ultrasonic testing equipment: Measuring and Controlling Device, Other—*mfg*	334519	3829
Surgical and Medical Instrument—*mfg*	339112	3829
Ultrasonic welding machines and equipment: Electrical Equipment and Component, All Other Miscellaneous—*mfg*	335999	3699
Machinery, Other Commercial and Service Industry—*mfg*	333319	3699
Ultrasonically assisted metal forming machines: Machine Tool (Metal Forming Types)—*mfg*	333513	3542
Ultraviolet lamp fixtures: Lighting Equipment, Other—*mfg*	335129	3648
Ultraviolet lamps: Electric Lamp Bulb and Part—*mfg*	33511	3641
Ultraviolet sensors, solid-state: Semiconductor and Related Device—*mfg*	334413	3674
Ultraviolet-type analytical instruments: Analytical Laboratory Instrument—*mfg*	334516	3826
Umber mining: Chemical and Fertilizer Mineral, Other—*mining*	212393	1479

ALPHABETICAL INDEX	NAICS	SIC
Umbers: Carbon Black—*mfg*	325182	2816
Inorganic Dye and Pigment—*mfg*	325131	2816
Umbrella cloth, cotton: Broadwoven Fabric Mills—*mfg*	31321	2211
Umbrella handles and trimmings, precious metal: Jewelry (except Costume)—*mfg*	339911	3911
Umbrella stores: Clothing Accessories Stores—*retail*	44815	5699
Clothing Stores, Other—*retail*	44819	5699
Umbrellas and parts, except precious metal: Fabricated Metal Product, All Other Miscellaneous—*mfg*	332999	3999
Umbrellas, men's and boys': Men's and Boys' Clothing and Furnishings—*whlse*	42232	5136
Umbrellas–beach, garden, and wagon: Fabricated Metal Product, All Other Miscellaneous—*mfg*	332999	3999
Unclassified Establishments	**9999**	
Unclassified Establishments	**99999**	**9999**
Unclassified Establishments	**999**	
Unclassified Establishments	**99**	
Uncoated Paper and Multiwall Bag Manufacturing	**322224**	**2674**
Undercoating service, automotive: Automotive Oil Change and Lubrication Shops—*serv*	811191	7549
Automotive Repair and Maintenance, All Other—*serv*	811198	7549
Motor Vehicle Towing—*trans*	48841	7549
Undercoatings, paint: Paint and Coating—*mfg*	32551	2851
Underpass construction–general contractors: Bridge and Tunnel—*const*	23412	1622
Underpinning work-contractors: Trade Contractors, All Other Special—*const*	23599	1799
Undertakers: Cemeteries and Crematories—*serv*	81222	7261
Funeral Homes—*serv*	81221	7261
Undertakers' equipment and supplies: Cosmetics, Beauty Supplies and Perfume Stores—*retail*	44612	5087
Service Establishment Equipment and Supplies—*whlse*	42185	5087
Underwater lighting fLxtures: Lighting Equipment, Other—*mfg*	335129	3648
Underwater sports equipment: Sporting and Recreational Goods and Supplies—*whlse*	42191	5091
Underwear: Infants' Cut and Sew Apparel—*mfg*	315291	2341
Men's and Boys' Cut and Sew Apparel Contractors—*mfg*	315211	2322
Men's and Boys' Cut and Sew Underwear and Nightwear—*mfg*	315221	2322
Underwear and Nightwear Knitting Mills—*mfg*	315192	2254
Women's and Girls' Cut and Sew Apparel Contractors—*mfg*	315212	2341
Women's and Girls' Cut and Sew Lingerie, Loungewear and Nightwear—*mfg*	315231	2341
Underwear and Nightwear Knitting Mills	**315192**	**2259**
Underwear and Nightwear Manufacturing, Men's and Boys' Cut and Sew	**315221**	**2341**
Underwear fabrics, except knit–manmade fiber and silk: Broadwoven Fabric Mills—*mfg*	31321	2221

Entry	NAICS	SIC
Underwear fabrics, woven–cotton: Broadwoven Fabric Mills—*mfg*	31321	2211
Underwear, men's and boys': Men's and Boys' Clothing and Furnishings—*whlse*	42232	5136
Underwear–women's, children's, and infants': Women's, Children's, and Infants' and Accessories—*whlse*	42233	5137
Underwriters, security: Financial Investment Activities, Miscellaneous—*fin*	523999	6211
Intermediation, Miscellaneous—*fin*	52391	6211
Investment Banking and Securities Dealing—*fin*	52311	6211
Securities Brokerage—*fin*	52312	6211
Undocking of ocean vessels: Coastal and Great Lakes Freight—*trans*	483113	4492
Inland Water Freight—*trans*	483211	4492
Navigational Services to Shipping—*trans*	48833	4492
Unemployment insurance offices: Social, Human Resource and Income Maintenance Programs, Administration of—*pub*	92313	9441
Uniform hats and caps, except protective head gear: Hat, Cap and Millinery—*mfg*	315991	2353
Uniform shirts, except athletic or work: Men's and Boys' Cut and Sew Apparel Contractors—*mfg*	315211	2321
Men's and Boys' Cut and Sew Shirt (except Work Shirt)—*mfg*	315223	2321
Uniform supply service, except industrial: Linen Supply—*serv*	812331	7213
Uniforms: Clothing Accessories Stores—*retail*	44815	5699
Clothing Stores, Other—*retail*	44819	5699
Uniforms, athletic: Apparel Accessories and Apparel, Other—*mfg*	315999	2339
Cut and Sew Apparel, All Other—*mfg*	315299	2329
Cut and Sew Apparel, All Other—*mfg*	315299	2339
Women's and Girls' Cut and Sew Apparel Contractors—*mfg*	315212	2339
Women's and Girls' Cut and Sew Other Outerwear—*mfg*	315238	2339
Uniforms, band: Cut and Sew Apparel, All Other—*mfg*	315299	2389
Uniforms, except athletic and service apparel: Women's and Girls' Cut and Sew Apparel Contractors—*mfg*	315212	2337
Women's and Girls' Cut and Sew Suit, Coat, Tailored Jacket and Skirt—*mfg*	315234	2337
Uniforms, men's and boys': Men's and Boys' Clothing and Furnishings—*whlse*	42232	5136
Uniforms, nontailored work type: Men's and Boys' Cut and Sew Apparel Contractors—*mfg*	315211	2326
Men's and Boys' Cut and Sew Work Clothing—*mfg*	315225	2326
Uniforms, tailored: Men's and Boys' Cut and Sew Apparel Contractors—*mfg*	315211	2311
Men's and Boys' Cut and Sew Suit, Coat and Overcoat—*mfg*	315222	2311
Uniforms, washable service apparel (nurses', maid, waitresses', laboratory): Apparel Accessories and Apparel, Other—*mfg*	315999	2339
Cut and Sew Apparel, All Other—*mfg*	315299	2339
Women's and Girls' Cut and Sew Apparel Contractors—*mfg*	315212	2339
Women's and Girls' Cut and Sew Other Outerwear—*mfg*	315238	2339
Uniforms, work: Men's and Boys' Cut and Sew Apparel Contractors—*mfg*	315211	2326
Men's and Boys' Cut and Sew Work Clothing—*mfg*	315225	2326
Uniforms–women's and children's: Women's, Children's, and Infants' and Accessories—*whlse*	42233	5137
Union suits: Underwear and Nightwear Knitting Mills—*mfg*	315192	2254
Union trust funds: Health and Welfare Funds—*fin*	52512	6371
Pension Funds—*fin*	52511	6371
Portfolio Management—*fin*	52392	6371
Third Party Administration for Insurance and Pension Funds—*fin*	524292	6371
Union welfare, benefit, and health funds: Health and Welfare Funds—*fin*	52512	6371
Pension Funds—*fin*	52511	6371
Portfolio Management—*fin*	52392	6371
Third Party Administration for Insurance and Pension Funds—*fin*	524292	6371
Unions, pipe–metal: Fabricated Metal Product, All Other Miscellaneous—*mfg*	332999	3494
Other Metal Valve and Pipe Fitting, Other—*mfg*	332919	3494
Unions, plastics: Plastics Pipe and Pipe Fitting—*mfg*	326122	3089
Plastics Product, All Other—*mfg*	326199	3089
Unsupported Plastics Profile Shape—*mfg*	326121	3089
Unisex clothing stores: Family Clothing Stores—*retail*	44814	5651
Unisex clothing–women's and children's: Women's, Children's, and Infants' and Accessories—*whlse*	42233	5137
Unisex hairdressers: Beauty Salons—*serv*	812112	7231
Cosmetology and Barber Schools—*educ*	611511	7231
Nail Salons—*serv*	812113	7231
Unit heaters, domestic–except electric: Heating Equipment (except Electric and Warm Air Furnaces)—*mfg*	333414	3433
Unit heaters, household–electric: Electric Housewares and Household Fan—*mfg*	335211	3634
Heating Equipment (except Electric and Warm Air Furnaces)—*mfg*	333414	3634
Unit investment trusts: Financial Vehicles, Other—*fin*	52599	6726
Unit sets (manifold business forms): Manifold Business Form Printing—*mfg*	323116	2761
Unit substations: Building Material Dealers, Other—*retail*	44419	5063
Electrical Apparatus and Equipment, Wiring Supplies and Material—*whlse*	42161	5063
United fund councils: Grantmaking and Giving Services, Other—*serv*	813219	8399
Social Advocacy Organizations, Other—*serv*	813319	8399
Voluntary Health Organizations—*serv*	813212	8399
United Nations: International Affairs—*pub*	92812	9721
United States Postal Service: Postal Service—*trans*	49111	4311
Universal carriers, military: Automobile—*mfg*	336111	3711
Heavy Duty Truck—*mfg*	33612	3711
Light Truck and Utility Vehicle—*mfg*	336112	3711
Military Armored Vehicle, Tank and Tank Component—*mfg*	336992	3711
Motor Vehicle Body—*mfg*	336211	3711
Universal joints, except motor vehicle: Mechanical Power Transmission Equipment—*mfg*	333613	3568
Universal joints, motor vehicle: Motor Vehicle Parts, All Other—*mfg*	336399	3714

ALPHABETICAL INDEX	NAICS	SIC
Motor Vehicle Steering and Suspension Components (except Spring)—*mfg*	33633	3714
Motor Vehicle Transmission and Power Train Parts—*mfg*	33635	3714
Universities: Colleges, Universities and Professional Schools—*educ*	61131	8221
University clubs: Child and Youth Services—*hlth*	62411	8641
Unloading vessels: Marine Cargo Handling—*trans*	48832	4491
Port and Harbor Operations—*trans*	48831	4491
Unsupported Plastics Bag Manufacturing	**326111**	**2673**
Unsupported Plastics Film and Sheet (except Packaging) Manufacturing	**326113**	**3081**
Unsupported Plastics Film, Sheet and Bag Manufacturing	**32611**	
Unsupported Plastics Packaging Film and Sheet Manufacturing	**326112**	**2671**
Unsupported Plastics Profile Shape Manufacturing	**326121**	**3089**
Upholstered furniture, household–on wood frames, except dual-purpose sleep furniture: Upholstered Household Furniture—*mfg*	337121	2512
Upholstered Household Furniture Manufacturing	**337121**	**2515**
Upholsterers' equipment and supplies, except fabrics: Cosmetics, Beauty Supplies and Perfume Stores—*retail*	44612	5087
Service Establishment Equipment and Supplies—*whlse*	42185	5087
Upholstery cleaning on customers' premises: Carpet and Upholstery Cleaning Services—*admin*	56174	7217
Upholstery fabrics, cotton: Broadwoven Fabric Mills—*mfg*	31321	2211
Upholstery fabrics, manmade fiber and silk: Broadwoven Fabric Mills—*mfg*	31321	2221
Upholstery fabrics, wool: Broadwoven Fabric Finishing Mills—*mfg*	313311	2231
Broadwoven Fabric Mills—*mfg*	31321	2231
Textile and Fabric Finishing (except Broadwoven Fabric) Mills—*mfg*	313312	2231
Upholstery filling and padding: Cosmetics, Beauty Supplies and Perfume Stores—*retail*	44612	5087
Service Establishment Equipment and Supplies—*whlse*	42185	5087
Upholstery filling, textile: Broadwoven Fabric Mills—*mfg*	31321	2299
Narrow Fabric Mills—*mfg*	313221	2299
Nonwoven Fabric Mills—*mfg*	31323	2299
Textile and Fabric Finishing (except Broadwoven Fabric) Mills—*mfg*	313312	2299
Textile Product Mills, All Other Miscellaneous—*mfg*	314999	2299
Thread Mills—*mfg*	313113	2299
Yarn Spinning Mills—*mfg*	313111	2299
Upholstery leather: Leather and Hide Tanning and Finishing—*mfg*	31611	3111
Upholstery materials stores: Curtain and Drapery Mills—*mfg*	314121	5714
Sewing, Needlework and Piece Goods Stores—*retail*	45113	5714
Window Treatment Stores—*retail*	442291	5714
Upholstery repair, automotive: Automotive Body, Paint and Interior Repair and Maintenance—*serv*	811121	7532
Upholstery springs, unassembled–made from purchased wire: Watch, Clock, and Part—*mfg*	334518	3495
Wire Spring—*mfg*	332612	3495
Upper leather: Leather and Hide Tanning and Finishing—*mfg*	31611	3111
Uppers (shoe cut stock): Fastener, Button, Needle and Pin—*mfg*	339993	3131
Leather Good, All Other—*mfg*	316999	3131
Wood Product, All Other Miscellaneous—*mfg*	321999	3131
Upset forgings, iron and steel–not made in rolling mills: Iron and Steel Forging—*mfg*	332111	3462
Upsetters (forging machines): Machine Tool (Metal Forming Types)—*mfg*	333513	3542
Uraninite (pitchblende) mining: Uranium-Radium-Vanadium Ore—*mining*	212291	1094
Uranium ore mining: Uranium-Radium-Vanadium Ore—*mining*	212291	1094
Uranium slug, radioactive: Basic Inorganic Chemical, All Other—*mfg*	325188	2819
Chemical Product, All Other Miscellaneous—*mfg*	325998	2819
Uranium-Radium-Vanadium Ore Mining	**212291**	**1094**
Urban and suburban railway operation: Bus and Motor Vehicle Transit Systems—*trans*	485113	4111
Commuter Rail Systems—*trans*	485112	4111
Mixed Mode Transit Systems—*trans*	485111	4111
Transit and Ground Passenger, All Other—*trans*	485999	4111
Urban Transit Systems, Other—*trans*	485119	4111
Urban mortgage companies: Credit Intermediation, Other Activities Related to—*fin*	52239	6162
Real Estate Credit—*fin*	522292	6162
Urban Planning and Community and Rural Development, Administration of	**92512**	**9532**
Urban planning commissions: Urban Planning and Community and Rural Development, Administration of—*pub*	92512	9532
Urban renewal agencies: Urban Planning and Community and Rural Development, Administration of—*pub*	92512	9532
Urban Transit Systems	**48511**	
Urban Transit Systems	**4851**	
Urban Transit Systems, Other	**485119**	**4111**
Urea: Nitrogenous Fertilizer—*mfg*	325311	2873
Urea resins: Plastics Material and Resin—*mfg*	325211	2821
Urethane and Other Foam Product (except Polystyrene) Manufacturing	**32615**	**3086**
Urethane rubbers: Synthetic Rubber—*mfg*	325212	2822
Urinals, plastics: Plastics Plumbing Fixture—*mfg*	326191	3088
Urinals, rubber: Fabric Coating Mills—*mfg*	31332	3069
Rubber Product, All Other—*mfg*	326299	3069
Urinals, vitreous china: Vitreous China Plumbing Fixture and China and Earthenware Fittings and Bathroom Accessories—*mfg*	327111	3261

Entry	NAICS	SIC
Urinals–enameled iron, cast iron, and pressed metal: Enameled Iron and Metal Sanitary Ware—*mfg*	332998	3431
Urinalysis lahoratories: Diagnostic Imaging Centers—*hlth*	621512	8071
Medical Laboratories—*hlth*	621511	8071
Urns, cut stone: Cut Stone and Stone Product—*mfg*	327991	3281
Urns, electric–household: Electric Housewares and Household Fan—*mfg*	335211	3634
Heating Equipment (except Electric and Warm Air Furnaces)—*mfg*	333414	3634
Urns, gypsum or papier-mache–factory production only: Gypsum and Gypsum Product—*mfg*	32742	3299
Nonmetallic Mineral Product, All Other Miscellaneous—*mfg*	327999	3299
Urologists, offices of: Freestanding Ambulatory Surgical and Emergency Centers—*hlth*	621493	8011
HMO Medical Centers—*hlth*	621491	8011
Physicians (except Mental Health Specialists), Offices Of—*hlth*	621111	8011
Physicians, Mental Health Specialists, Offices Of—*hlth*	621112	8011
Used Car Dealers	**44112**	**5521**
Used Household and Office Goods Moving	**48421**	**4213**
Used Merchandise Stores	**4533**	
Used Merchandise Stores	**45331**	**5932**
Usher service: Employee Leasing Services—*admin*	56133	7363
Temporary Help Services—*admin*	56132	7363
Utensils, cast aluminum: Aluminum Foundries—*mfg*	331524	3365
Utensils, metal, except cast–household, commercial, and hospital: Kitchen Utensil, Pot and Pan—*mfg*	332214	3469
Utensils, paper–except those made from pressed or molded pulp: Non-Folding Sanitary Food Container—*mfg*	322215	2656
Utensils, porcelain enameled–household, commercial, and hospital: Kitchen Utensil, Pot and Pan—*mfg*	332214	3469
Utensils, pressed and molded pulp: Coated and Laminated Paper—*mfg*	322222	2679
Converted Paper Product, All Other—*mfg*	322298	2679
Die-Cut Paper and Paperboard Office Supplies—*mfg*	322231	2679
Non-Folding Sanitary Food Container—*mfg*	322215	2679
Utensils, retinning of–not done in rolling mills: Costume Jewelry and Novelty—*mfg*	339914	3479
Jewelry (except Costume)—*mfg*	339911	3479
Metal Coating, Engraving (except Jewelry and Silverware), and Allied Services to Manufacturers—*mfg*	332812	3479
Silverware and Plated Ware—*mfg*	339912	3479
Utilities	**22**	
Utilities	**221**	
Utilities, combination of: Electric Bulk Power Transmission and Control—*util*	221121	4939
Electric Power Distribution—*util*	221122	4939
Electric Power Generation, Other—*util*	221119	4939
Fossil Fuel Electric Power Generation—*util*	221112	4939
Hydroelectric Power Generation—*util*	221111	4939
Natural Gas Distribution—*util*	22121	4939
Nuclear Electric Power Generation—*util*	221113	4939
Utility buildings, prefabricated–metal: Prefabricated Metal Building and Component—*mfg*	332311	3448
Utility carriers, car top: Metal Container, Other—*mfg*	332439	3429
Utility containers, plastics: Plastics Pipe and Pipe Fitting—*mfg*	326122	3089
Plastics Product, All Other—*mfg*	326199	3089
Unsupported Plastics Profile Shape—*mfg*	326121	3089
Utility line tree trimming services: Landscaping Services—*admin*	56173	783
Utility software, computer–prepackaged: Publishers—*info*	51121	7372
Software Reproducing—*mfg*	334611	7372
Utility trailer rental: Truck, Utility Trailer, and RV (Recreational Vehicle) Rental and Leasing—*real*	53212	7519
Utility trailers-retall: Motor Vehicle Dealers, All Other—*retail*	441229	5599
V-belts, rubber or plastics: Rubber and Plastics Hoses and Belting—*mfg*	32622	3052
Vacation funds for employees: Insurance Funds, Other—*fin*	52519	6733
Portfolio Management—*fin*	52392	6733
Trust, Fiduciary and Custody Activities—*fin*	523991	6733
Trusts, Estates, and Agency Accounts—*fin*	52592	6733
Vaccinating livestock, except by veterinarians: Animal Production Support Activities—*ag*	11521	751
Vaccinating pets and other animal specialties, except by veterinarians: Animal Production Support Activities—*ag*	11521	752
Pet Care (except Veterinary) Services—*serv*	81291	752
Vaccines: Biological Product (except Diagnostic)—*mfg*	325414	2836
Vacuum 'cleaners, household: Electrical Appliance, Television and Radio Set—*whlse*	42162	5064
Vacuum bottles and jugs: Metal Container, Other—*mfg*	332439	3429
Vacuum brakes, motor vehicle: Motor Vehicle Brake System—*mfg*	33634	3714
Motor Vehicle Parts, All Other—*mfg*	336399	3714
Vacuum brakes, railway: Pump and Pumping Equipment—*mfg*	333911	3743
Railroad Rolling Stock—*mfg*	33651	3743
Vacuum cleaner hose, plastics or rubber: Rubber and Plastics Hoses and Belting—*mfg*	32622	3052
Vacuum cleaner stores: Household Appliance Stores—*retail*	443111	5722
Vacuum cleaners and sweepers, electric–household: Household Vacuum Cleaner—*mfg*	335212	3635
Vacuum cleaners and sweepers, electric–industrial and commercial: Machinery, Other Commercial and Service Industry—*mfg*	333319	3589
Vacuum cleaning systems: Cosmetics, Beauty Supplies and Perfume Stores—*retail*	44612	5087
Service Establishment Equipment and Supplies—*whlse*	42185	5087
Vacuum cleaning systems, built-in-contractors: Building Equipment and Other Machinery Installation Contractors—*const*	23595	1796
Vacuum furnaces and ovens: Industrial Process Furnace and Oven—*mfg*	333994	3567
Vacuum pumps, except laboratory: Air and Gas Compressor—*mfg*	333912	3563
Vacuum relays: Relay and Industrial Control—*mfg*	335314	3625

ALPHABETICAL INDEX	NAICS	SIC
Vacuum tanks, metal plate: Air-Conditioning and Warm Air Heating Equipment and Commercial and Industrial Refrigeration Equipment—*mfg*	333415	3443
Metal Tank (Heavy Gauge)—*mfg*	33242	3443
Plate Work—*mfg*	332313	3443
Power Boiler and Heat Exchanger—*mfg*	33241	3443
Vacuum tube bridges (electrical measuring instruments): Electronic Coil, Transformer, and Other Inductor—*mfg*	334416	3825
Instrument for Measuring and Testing Electricity and Electrical Signals—*mfg*	334515	3825
Vacuum tubes: Electron Tube—*mfg*	334411	3671
Vacuum tunnels, metal plate: Air-Conditioning and Warm Air Heating Equipment and Commercial and Industrial Refrigeration Equipment—*mfg*	333415	3443
Metal Tank (Heavy Gauge)—*mfg*	33242	3443
Plate Work—*mfg*	332313	3443
Power Boiler and Heat Exchanger—*mfg*	33241	3443
Vacuuming of airport runways: Airport Operations, Other—*trans*	488119	4959
Exterminating and Pest Control Services—*admin*	56171	4959
Remediation Services—*admin*	56291	4959
Waste Management Services, All Other Miscellaneous—*admin*	562998	4959
Vacuums, residential lawn: Hand and Edge Tool—*mfg*	332212	3524
Lawn and Garden Tractor and Home Lawn and Garden Equipment—*mfg*	333112	3524
Valentine cards, except hand painted: Flexographic Printing, Commercial—*mfg*	323112	2771
Gravure Printing, Commercial—*mfg*	323111	2771
Greeting Card Publishers—*info*	511191	2771
Lithographic Printing, Commercial—*mfg*	323110	2771
Printing, Other Commercial—*mfg*	323119	2771
Screen Printing, Commercial—*mfg*	323113	2771
Valet apparel service: Garment Pressing, and Agents for Laundries—*serv*	812391	7212
Valet parking: Personal Services, All Other—*serv*	81299	7299
Valises, regardless of material: Luggage—*mfg*	316991	3161
Valonia extract: Gum and Wood Chemical—*mfg*	325191	2861
Value-added resellers, computer systems: Computer Systems Design Services—*prof*	541512	7373
Valve cores, tire: Motor Vehicle Parts, All Other—*mfg*	336399	3714
Motor Vehicle Steering and Suspension Components (except Spring)—*mfg*	33633	3714
Valve grinding machines: Machine Tool (Metal Cutting Types)—*mfg*	333512	3541
Valves and fittings, except plumbers': Industrial Machinery and Equipment—*whlse*	42183	5085
Industrial Supplies—*whlse*	42184	5085
Valves, air ventilating: Industrial Valve—*mfg*	332911	3491

ALPHABETICAL INDEX	NAICS	SIC
Valves, automatic control–fluid power–metal: Fluid Power Valve and Hose Fitting—*mfg*	332912	3492
Valves, automatic control–industrial, except fluid power: Industrial Valve—*mfg*	332911	3491
Valves, engine–intake and exhaust: Carburetor, Piston, Piston Ring and Valve—*mfg*	336311	3592
Valves, hard rubber: Fabric Coating Mills—*mfg*	31332	3069
Rubber Product, All Other—*mfg*	326299	3069
Valves, hydraulic and pneumatic control–fluid power-metal: Fluid Power Valve and Hose Fitting—*mfg*	332912	3492
Valves, industrial–gate, globe, check, pop safety, and relief: Industrial Valve—*mfg*	332911	3491
Valves, nuclear: Industrial Valve—*mfg*	332911	3491
Valves, PCV: Gasoline Engine and Engine Parts—*mfg*	336312	3714
Motor Vehicle Parts, All Other—*mfg*	336399	3714
Valves, plumbing and heating: Building Material Dealers, Other—*retail*	44419	5074
Plumbing and Heating Equipment and Supplies (Hydronics)—*whlse*	42172	5074
Valves, plumbing and heating–metal: Fabricated Metal Product, All Other Miscellaneous—*mfg*	332999	3494
Other Metal Valve and Pipe Fitting, Other—*mfg*	332919	3494
Valves, power transfer–except fluid power: Industrial Valve—*mfg*	332911	3491
Valves, relief–over 15 lbs. w.s.p.: Industrial Valve—*mfg*	332911	3491
Valves, solenoid–except fluid power: Industrial Valve—*mfg*	332911	3491
Vamps, leather: Fastener, Button, Needle and Pin—*mfg*	339993	3131
Leather Good, All Other—*mfg*	316999	3131
Wood Product, All Other Miscellaneous—*mfg*	321999	3131
Van conversions, except on a factory basis: Automotive Body, Paint and Interior Repair and Maintenance—*serv*	811121	7532
Van-type bodies, all purpose: Motor Vehicle Body—*mfg*	336211	3713
Vanadium ore mining: Uranium-Radium-Vanadium Ore—*mining*	212291	1094
Vanes, weather: Fabricated Metal Product, All Other Miscellaneous—*mfg*	332999	3599
General Purpose Machinery , All Other—*mfg*	333999	3599
Machine Shops—*mfg*	33271	3599
Machinery, Other Commercial and Service Industry—*mfg*	333319	3599
Vanillin, synthetic: Basic Organic Chemical, All Other—*mfg*	325199	2869
Vanities, bathroom, wood–to be installed: Wood Kitchen Cabinet and Counter Top—*mfg*	33711	2434
Vanities, household–metal: Metal Household Furniture—*mfg*	337124	2514
Vanity cases, except precious metal and leather: Costume Jewelry and Novelty—*mfg*	339914	3961
Vanity cases, leather: Personal Leather Good (except Women's Handbag and Purse)—*mfg*	316993	3172
Vanity cases, precious metal: Jewelry (except Costume)—*mfg*	339911	3911
Vanity dressers: Nonupholstered Wood Household Furniture—*mfg*	337122	2511

Entry	NAICS	SIC
Vanpool operation: School and Employee Bus—*trans*	48541	4119
Transit and Ground Passenger, All Other—*trans*	485999	4119
Transportation, Special Needs—*trans*	485991	4119
Vans: Automobile and Other Motor Vehicle—*whlse*	42111	5012
Vans, self-propelled–conversion on a factory basis for recreational use: Motor Home—*mfg*	336213	3716
Vapor heating controls: Automatic Environmental Control for Residential, Commercial and Appliance Use—*mfg*	334512	3822
Vapor lamps, electric: Electric Lamp Bulb and Part—*mfg*	33511	3641
Vapor separators (machinery): General Purpose Machinery , All Other—*mfg*	333999	3569
Vaporizers, electric–household: Electric Housewares and Household Fan—*mfg*	335211	3634
Heating Equipment (except Electric and Warm Air Furnaces)—*mfg*	333414	3634
Variable capacitance diodes: Semiconductor and Related Device—*mfg*	334413	3674
Variety bags, uncoated paper: Uncoated Paper and Multiwall Bag—*mfg*	322224	2674
Variety meats edible organs: Animal (except Poultry) Slaughtering—*mfg*	311611	2011
Variety stores, limited price: General Merchandise Stores, All Other—*retail*	45299	5331
Varistors: Electronic Resistor—*mfg*	334415	3676
Varnish brushes: Broom, Brush and Mop—*mfg*	339994	3991
Varnish removers: Paint and Coating—*mfg*	32551	2851
Varnish stains: Paint and Coating—*mfg*	32551	2851
Varnishes: Paint and Coating—*mfg*	32551	2851
Paint and Wallpaper Stores—*retail*	44412	5198
Paint, Varnish and Supplies—*whlse*	42295	5198
Varnishing of metal products, for the trade: Costume Jewelry and Novelty—*mfg*	339914	3479
Jewelry (except Costume)—*mfg*	339911	3479
Metal Coating, Engraving (except Jewelry and Silverware), and Allied Services to Manufacturers—*mfg*	332812	3479
Silverware and Plated Ware—*mfg*	339912	3479
Varnishing of textiles: Fabric Coating Mills—*mfg*	31332	2295
Vases, cut stone: Cut Stone and Stone Product—*mfg*	327991	3281
Vases, glass: Pressed and Blown Glass and Glassware, Other—*mfg*	327212	3229
Vases, gypsum or papier-mache–factory production only: Gypsum and Gypsum Product—*mfg*	32742	3299
Nonmetallic Mineral Product, All Other Miscellaneous—*mfg*	327999	3299
Vases, pottery (china, earthenware, and stoneware): Vitreous China, Fine Earthenware and Other Pottery Product—*mfg*	327112	3269
Vat dyeing of manmade fiber and silk broadwoven fabrics: Broadwoven Fabric Finishing Mills—*mfg*	313311	2262
Vat dyes, synthetic: Organic Dye and Pigment—*mfg*	325132	2865
Petrochemical—*mfg*	32511	2865
Vats, metal plate: Air-Conditioning and Warm Air Heating Equipment and Commercial and Industrial Refrigeration Equipment—*mfg*	333415	3443
Metal Tank (Heavy Gauge)—*mfg*	33242	3443
Plate Work—*mfg*	332313	3443
Power Boiler and Heat Exchanger—*mfg*	33241	3443
Vats, sheet metal: Metal Container, Other—*mfg*	332439	3444
Sheet Metal Work—*mfg*	332322	3444
Vats, wood–coopered: Wood Container and Pallet—*mfg*	32192	2449
Vats, wood–except coopered: Manufacturing, All Other Miscellaneous—*mfg*	339999	2499
Wood Container and Pallet—*mfg*	32192	2499
Wood Product, All Other Miscellaneous—*mfg*	321999	2499
Vaudeville companies: Theater Companies and Dinner Theaters—*arts*	71111	7922
Vault doors and linings, metal: Metal Container, Other—*mfg*	332439	3499
Vaults and safes: Office Equipment—*whlse*	42142	5044
Vaults, except burial vaults–metal: Metal Container, Other—*mfg*	332439	3499
Vaults, grave–concrete and precast terrazzo: Concrete Pipe—*mfg*	327332	3272
Concrete Product, Other—*mfg*	32739	3272
Nonmetallic Mineral Product, All Other Miscellaneous—*mfg*	327999	3272
Vaults, grave–metal: Burial Casket—*mfg*	339995	3995
Veal: Animal (except Poultry) Slaughtering—*mfg*	311611	2011
Vegetable (except Potato) and Melon Farming, Other	**111219**	**139**
Vegetable and fruit stands: Fruit and Vegetable Markets—*retail*	44523	5431
Vegetable and Melon Farming	**11121**	
Vegetable and Melon Farming	**1112**	
Vegetable baskets, veneer and splint: Wood Container and Pallet—*mfg*	32192	2449
Vegetable bedding plants, growing of: Floriculture Production—*ag*	111422	181
Nursery and Tree Production—*ag*	111421	181
Vegetable cake and meal: Nondurable Goods, Other Miscellaneous—*whlse*	42299	5199
Vegetable cooking and salad oils, except corn oil–refined: Fats and Oils Refining and Blending—*mfg*	311225	2079
Oilseed Processing, Other—*mfg*	311223	2079
Soybean Processing—*mfg*	311222	2079
Vegetable cooking oil: Grocery and Related Products, Other—*whlse*	42249	5149
Vegetable crates, wood–wirebound: Wood Container and Pallet—*mfg*	32192	2449
Vegetable drying: Postharvest Crop Activities (except Cotton Ginning)—*ag*	115114	723
Vegetable farms: Vegetable (except Potato) and Melon Farming, Other—*ag*	111219	161
Vegetable flour, meal, and powders: Dried and Dehydrated Food—*mfg*	311423	2034
Flour Milling—*mfg*	311211	2034
Vegetable gelatin (agar-agar): Medicinal and Botanical—*mfg*	325411	2833

ALPHABETICAL INDEX	NAICS	SIC
Vegetable grading, cleaning and sorting machines–farm: Farm Machinery and Equipment—*mfg*	333111	3523
Vegetable juices–canned, bottled and bulk: Fruit and Vegetable Canning—*mfg*	311421	2033
Vegetable markets and stands: Fruit and Vegetable Markets—*retail*	44523	5431
Vegetable oil processing machinery: Food Product Machinery—*mfg*	333294	3556
Vegetable oils, medicinal grade–refined and ooncentrated: Medicinal and Botanical—*mfg*	325411	2833
Vegetable pie mixes: Fruit and Vegetable Canning—*mfg*	311421	2033
Vegetable precooling, not in connection with transportation: Postharvest Crop Activities (except Cotton Ginning)—*ag*	115114	723
Vegetable purees: Fruit and Vegetable Canning—*mfg*	311421	2033
Vegetable sauces, except tomato: Fruit and Vegetable Canning—*mfg*	311421	2035
Mayonnaise, Dressing and Other Prepared Sauce—*mfg*	311941	2035
Vegetable sorting, grading, and packing: Postharvest Crop Activities (except Cotton Ginning)—*ag*	115114	723
Vegetable tallow: Fats and Oils Refining and Blending—*mfg*	311225	2076
Oilseed Processing, Other—*mfg*	311223	2076
Vegetable vacuum cooling: Postharvest Crop Activities (except Cotton Ginning)—*ag*	115114	723
Vegetables grown under cover: Food Crops Grown Under Cover, Other—*ag*	111419	182
Mushroom Production—*ag*	111411	182
Vegetables peeled for the trade: Perishable Prepared Food—*mfg*	311991	2099
Vegetables, canned: Fruit and Vegetable Canning—*mfg*	311421	2033
Vegetables, dried or dehydrated: Dried and Dehydrated Food—*mfg*	311423	2034
Flour Milling—*mfg*	311211	2034
Vegetables, fresh: Fresh Fruit and Vegetable—*whlse*	42248	5148
Vegetables, machine harvesting of: Crop Harvesting, Primarily by Machine—*ag*	115113	722
Vegetables, pickled and brined: Fruit and Vegetable Canning—*mfg*	311421	2035
Mayonnaise, Dressing and Other Prepared Sauce—*mfg*	311941	2035
Vegetables, quick frozen and coldpack (frozen): Frozen Fruit, Juice and Vegetable—*mfg*	311411	2037
Vegetables, sulphured: Dried and Dehydrated Food—*mfg*	311423	2034
Flour Milling—*mfg*	311211	2034
Vehicle lumber, treated: Wood Preservation—*mfg*	321114	2491
Vehicle stock, hardwood: Cut Stock, Resawing Lumber, and Planing—*mfg*	321912	2426
Millwork (including Flooring), Other—*mfg*	321918	2426
Showcase, Partition, Shelving, and Locker—*mfg*	337215	2426
Wood Product, All Other Miscellaneous—*mfg*	321999	2426
Vehicle tank meters: Totalizing Fluid Meter and Counting Device—*mfg*	334514	3824
Vehicles except bicycles, children's: Game, Toy, and Children's Vehicle—*mfg*	339932	3944
Vehicles, children's: Toy and Hobby Goods and Supplies—*whlse*	42192	5092

ALPHABETICAL INDEX	NAICS	SIC
Vehicles, motor–including amphibian: Automobile—*mfg*	336111	3711
Heavy Duty Truck—*mfg*	33612	3711
Light Truck and Utility Vehicle—*mfg*	336112	3711
Military Armored Vehicle, Tank and Tank Component—*mfg*	336992	3711
Motor Vehicle Body—*mfg*	336211	3711
Vehicular Lighting Equipment Manufacturing	**336321**	**3647**
Veils and veiling, hat: Apparel Accessories and Apparel, Other—*mfg*	315999	2396
Vellum leather: Leather and Hide Tanning and Finishing—*mfg*	31611	3111
Velours: Broadwoven Fabric Mills—*mfg*	31321	2211
Velveteens: Broadwoven Fabric Mills—*mfg*	31321	2211
Velvets, manmade fiber and silk: Broadwoven Fabric Mills—*mfg*	31321	2221
Vending Machine Operators	**45421**	**5962**
Vending Machine Operators	**4542**	
Vending machine sale of products: Vending Machine Operators—*retail*	45421	5962
Vending machines: Equipment, Other Commercial—*whlse*	42144	5046
Vending machines for merchandise–coin-operated: Automatic Vending Machine—*mfg*	333311	3581
Vending machines, rental only: Machinery and Equipment Rental and Leasing, Other Commercial and Industrial—*real*	53249	7359
Veneer: Building Material Dealers, Other—*retail*	44419	5031
Veneer baskets, for fruits and vegetables: Wood Container and Pallet—*mfg*	32192	2449
Veneer logs: Logging—*ag*	11331	2411
Veneer mill machines: Sawmill and Woodworking Machinery—*mfg*	33321	3553
Veneer mills, hardwood: Hardwood Veneer and Plywood—*mfg*	321211	2435
Veneer mills, softwood: Softwood Veneer and Plywood—*mfg*	321212	2436
Veneer work, inlaid: Manufacturing, All Other Miscellaneous—*mfg*	339999	2499
Wood Container and Pallet—*mfg*	32192	2499
Wood Product, All Other Miscellaneous—*mfg*	321999	2499
Veneer, Plywood and Engineered Wood Product Manufacturing	**3212**	
Veneer, Plywood, and Engineered Wood Product Manufacturing	**32121**	
Venetian blind cleaning, including work done on owners' premises: Janitorial Services—*admin*	56172	7349
Venetian blind machines (woodworking machinery): Sawmill and Woodworking Machinery—*mfg*	33321	3553
Venetian blind repair shops: Buildings and Dwellings, Other Services to—*admin*	56179	7699
Personal and Household Goods Repair and Maintenance, Other—*serv*	81149	7699
Venetian blind shops: Home Furnishings Stores, All Other—*retail*	442299	5719
Window Treatment Stores—*retail*	442291	5719
Venetian blind slats, wood: Millwork (including Flooring), Other—*mfg*	321918	2431
Wood Window and Door—*mfg*	321911	2431
Venetian blind tapes: Narrow Fabric Mills—*mfg*	313221	2241
Venetian blinds: Blind and Shade—*mfg*	33792	2591

ALPHABETICAL INDEX	NAICS	SIC
Vibration meters, analyzers, and calibrators: Measuring and Controlling Device, Other—*mfg*	334519	3829
Surgical and Medical Instrument—*mfg*	339112	3829
Vibrators for concrete construction: Construction Machinery—*mfg*	33312	3531
Overhead Traveling Crane, Hoist and Monorail System—*mfg*	333923	3531
Railroad Rolling Stock—*mfg*	33651	3531
Vibrators, electric–designed for beauty and barber shops: Hand and Edge Tool—*mfg*	332212	3999
Vibrators, interrupter: Power, Distribution and Specialty Transformer—*mfg*	335311	3612
Video camera stores: Automotive Parts and Accessories Stores—*retail*	44131	5731
Radio, Television and Other Electronics Stores—*retail*	443112	5731
Video camera-audio recorders, household: Audio and Video Equipment—*mfg*	33431	3651
Video cassette recorders/players: Audio and Video Equipment—*mfg*	33431	3651
Video disc players: Electrical Appliance, Television and Radio Set—*whlse*	42162	5064
Video disk rental to the general public: Video Tape and Disc Rental—*real*	53223	7841
Video game arcades: Amusement and Recreation Industries, All Other—*arts*	71399	7993
Amusement Arcades—*arts*	71312	7993
Gambling Industries, Other—*arts*	71329	7993
Video game machines, except coin-operated: Game, Toy, and Children's Vehicle—*mfg*	339932	3944
Video photography, portrait: Photography Studios, Portrait—*prof*	541921	7221
Video recorder and player rental and lease: Automotive Mechanical and Electrical Repair and Maintenance, Other—*serv*	811118	7539
Video recorder or player repair: Communication Equipment Repair and Maintenance—*serv*	811213	7622
Consumer Electronics Repair and Maintenance—*serv*	811211	7622
Radio, Television and Other Electronics Stores—*retail*	443112	7622
Video recording tape, blank: Magnetic and Optical Recording Media—*mfg*	334613	3695
Video Tape and Disc Rental	**53223**	**7841**
Video tape or disk reproduction: Independent Artists, Writers, and Performers—*arts*	71151	7819
Motion Picture and Video Industries, Other—*info*	512199	7819
Prerecorded Compact Disc (except Software), Tape, and Record Reproducing—*mfg*	334612	7819
Teleproduction and Other Post-Production Services—*info*	512191	7819
Video tape production: Motion Picture and Video Production—*info*	51211	7812
Video tape recorder stores: Automotive Parts and Accessories Stores—*retail*	44131	5731
Radio, Television and Other Electronics Stores—*retail*	443112	5731
Video tape rental to the general public: Video Tape and Disc Rental—*real*	53223	7841
Video tape stores: Prerecorded Tape, Compact Disc and Record Stores—*retail*	45122	5735
Video tapes, recorded: Durable Goods, Other Miscellaneous—*whlse*	42199	7822
Motion Picture and Video Distribution—*info*	51212	7822
Video triggers (remote control television devices): Audio and Video Equipment—*mfg*	33431	3651
Video triggers, except remote control television devices: Electronic Component, Other—*mfg*	334419	3679
Motor Vehicle Electrical and Electronic Equipment, Other—*mfg*	336322	3679
Printed Circuit/Electronics Assembly—*mfg*	334418	3679
Radio and Television Broadcasting and Wireless Communications Equipment—*mfg*	33422	3679
Vienna sausage: Meat Processed from Carcasses—*mfg*	311612	2013
Vinal broadwoven fabrics: Broadwoven Fabric Mills—*mfg*	31321	2221
Vine pullers: Farm Machinery and Equipment—*mfg*	333111	3523
Hand and Edge Tool—*mfg*	332212	3523
Vinegar: Food, All Other Miscellaneous—*mfg*	311999	2099
Vinegar pickles and relishes: Fruit and Vegetable Canning—*mfg*	311421	2035
Mayonnaise, Dressing and Other Prepared Sauce—*mfg*	311941	2035
Vineyard cultivation services: Nonscheduled Air, Other—*trans*	481219	721
Soil Preparation, Planting, and Cultivating—*ag*	115112	721
Vineyard management and maintenance, with or without crop services: Farm Management Services—*ag*	115116	762
Vineyards: Grape Vineyards—*ag*	111332	172
Vinyl acetate: Basic Organic Chemical, All Other—*mfg*	325199	2869
Vinyl and vinyl copolymer film and sheet, unsupported: Unsupported Plastics Film and Sheet (except Packaging)—*mfg*	326113	3081
Vinyl asbestos tile: Motor Vehicle Brake System—*mfg*	33634	3292
Nonmetallic Mineral Product, All Other Miscellaneous—*mfg*	327999	3292
Vinyl coated fabrics: Fabric Coating Mills—*mfg*	31332	2295
Vinyl coatings, strippable: Paint and Coating—*mfg*	32551	2851
Vinyl fibers: Noncellulosic Organic Fiber—*mfg*	325222	2824
Vinyl floor tile and sheet installation–contractors: Floor Laying and Other Floor Contractors—*const*	23552	1752
Vinyl plastisol: Paint and Coating—*mfg*	32551	2851
Vinyl resins: Plastics Material and Resin—*mfg*	325211	2821
Vinylidene chloride fibers: Noncellulosic Organic Fiber—*mfg*	325222	2824
Vinyon broadwoven fabrics: Broadwoven Fabric Mills—*mfg*	31321	2221
Violas and parts: Musical Instrument—*mfg*	339992	3931
Violins and parts: Musical Instrument—*mfg*	339992	3931
Viral test diagnostic reagents: In-Vitro Diagnostic Substance—*mfg*	325413	2835
Pharmaceutical Preparation—*mfg*	325412	2835
Viruses: Biological Product (except Diagnostic)—*mfg*	325414	2836
Viscosimeters, except industrial press type: Measuring and Controlling Device, Other—*mfg*	334519	3829

Surgical and Medical Instrument—*mfg*	339112	3829
Viscosimeters, industrial process type: Instruments and Related Products for Measuring, Displaying, and Controlling Industrial Process Variables—*mfg*	334513	3823
Vises, carpenters': Hand and Edge Tool—*mfg*	332212	3423
Vises, except machine: Hand and Edge Tool—*mfg*	332212	3423
Vises, machine (machine tool accessories): Cutting Tool and Machine Tool Accessory—*mfg*	333515	3545
Hand and Edge Tool—*mfg*	332212	3545
Visiting cards, lithographed: Lithographic Printing, Commercial—*mfg*	323110	2752
Quick Printing—*mfg*	323114	2752
Visiting cards, printed–except lithographed or gravure: Digital Printing—*mfg*	323115	2759
Flexographic Printing, Commercial—*mfg*	323112	2759
Printing, Other Commercial—*mfg*	323119	2759
Quick Printing—*mfg*	323114	2759
Visiting cards–gravure printing: Gravure Printing, Commercial—*mfg*	323111	2754
Visiting nurse associations: Home Health Care Services—*hlth*	62161	8082
Visors, cap: Apparel Accessories and Apparel, Other—*mfg*	315999	2396
Visose fibers, bands, strips, and yarn: Cellulosic Organic Fiber—*mfg*	325221	2823
Vitamin and mineral enriched rice: Rice Milling—*mfg*	311212	2044
Vitamin food stores: Food (Health) Supplement Stores—*retail*	446191	5499
Food Stores, All Other Specialty—*retail*	445299	5499
Limited-Service Restaurants—*accom*	722211	5499
Meat Markets—*retail*	44521	5499
Vitamin preparations: Pharmaceutical Preparation—*mfg*	325412	2834
Vitamins: Drug, Drug Proprietaries and Druggists' Sundries—*whlse*	42221	5122
Vitamins, natural and synthetic–bulk, uncompounded: Medicinal and Botanical—*mfg*	325411	2833
Vitreous China Plumbing Fixture and China and Earthenware Fittings and Bathroom Accessories Manufacturing	**327111**	**3261**
Vitreous China, Fine Earthenware and Other Pottery Product Manufacturing	**327112**	**3263**
Vocational apprenticeship training: Apprenticeship Training—*educ*	611513	8249
Technical and Trade Schools, Other—*educ*	611519	8249
Vocational counseling except rehabilitation counseling: Educational Support Services—*educ*	61171	8299
Schools and Instruction, All Other Miscellaneous—*educ*	611699	8299
Vocational high schools: Elementary and Secondary Schools—*educ*	61111	8211
Vocational rehabilitation agencies: Vocational Rehabilitation Services—*hlth*	62431	8331
Vocational rehabilitation counseling: Vocational Rehabilitation Services—*hlth*	62431	8331
Vocational Rehabilitation Services	**6243**	
Vocational Rehabilitation Services	**62431**	**8331**
Vocational schools–except high schools, data processing, or business: Apprenticeship Training—*educ*	611513	8249
Technical and Trade Schools, Other—*educ*	611519	8249
Vocational training agencies, except schools: Vocational Rehabilitation Services—*hlth*	62431	8331
Vodka: Distilleries—*mfg*	31214	2085
Voice controls: Electronic Component, Other—*mfg*	334419	3679
Motor Vehicle Electrical and Electronic Equipment, Other—*mfg*	336322	3679
Printed Circuit/Electronics Assembly—*mfg*	334418	3679
Radio and Television Broadcasting and Wireless Communications Equipment—*mfg*	33422	3679
Voice telephone communications, except radio telephone: Telecommunications Resellers—*info*	51333	4813
Wired Telecommunications Carriers—*info*	51331	4813
Voids and pans, fiber and cardboard: Fiber Can, Tube, Drum, and Similar Products—*mfg*	322214	2655
Voiles, cotton: Broadwoven Fabric Mills—*mfg*	31321	2211
Voiles, manmade fiber and silk: Broadwoven Fabric Mills—*mfg*	31321	2221
Volcanic ash mining: Crushed and Broken Stone and Quarrying, Other—*mining*	212319	1499
Non-Metallic Mineral, All Other—*mining*	212399	1499
Volcanic rock, crushed and broken: Crushed and Broken Stone and Quarrying, Other—*mining*	212319	1429
Volcanic rock, dimension: Dimension Stone and Quarrying—*mining*	212311	1411
Volt-ohm milliammeters: Electronic Coil, Transformer, and Other Inductor—*mfg*	334416	3825
Instrument for Measuring and Testing Electricity and Electrical Signals—*mfg*	334515	3825
Voltage regulating transformers, electric power: Power, Distribution and Specialty Transformer—*mfg*	335311	3612
Voltage regulators, motor vehicle: Motor Vehicle Electrical and Electronic Equipment, Other—*mfg*	336322	3694
Voltage regulators, transmission and distribution: Power, Distribution and Specialty Transformer—*mfg*	335311	3612
Voltmeters: Electronic Coil, Transformer, and Other Inductor—*mfg*	334416	3825
Instrument for Measuring and Testing Electricity and Electrical Signals—*mfg*	334515	3825
Volume guns (irrigation equipment): Farm Machinery and Equipment—*mfg*	333111	3523
Voluntary Health Organizations	**813212**	**8399**
Voting machines: Cosmetics, Beauty Supplies and Perfume Stores—*retail*	44612	5087
Lead Pencil and Art Good—*mfg*	339942	3579
Office Machinery—*mfg*	333313	3579
Service Establishment Equipment and Supplies—*whlse*	42185	5087
Watch, Clock, and Part—*mfg*	334518	3579
Vulcanized fiber boxes: Fiber Can, Tube, Drum, and Similar Products—*mfg*	322214	2655
Vulcanized fiber plate, sheet, rods and tubes: Plastics Pipe and Pipe Fitting—*mfg*	326122	3089
Plastics Product, All Other—*mfg*	326199	3089
Unsupported Plastics Profile Shape—*mfg*	326121	3089

ALPHABETICAL INDEX	NAICS	SIC
Vulcanized oils: Synthetic Rubber—*mfg*	325212	2822
Vulcanizing tires and tubes: Automotive Repair and Maintenance, All Other—*serv*	811198	7534
Tire Retreading—*mfg*	326212	7534
Wading pools, plastics coated fabric: Sporting and Athletic Goods—*mfg*	33992	3949
Wads and wadding, textile: Broadwoven Fabric Mills—*mfg*	31321	2299
Narrow Fabric Mills—*mfg*	313221	2299
Nonwoven Fabric Mills—*mfg*	31323	2299
Textile and Fabric Finishing (except Broadwoven Fabric) Mills—*mfg*	313312	2299
Textile Product Mills, All Other Miscellaneous—*mfg*	314999	2299
Thread Mills—*mfg*	313113	2299
Yarn Spinning Mills—*mfg*	313111	2299
Wads, ammunition–30 mm. (or 1.18 inch) or less: Small Arms Ammunition—*mfg*	332992	3482
Waferboard: Reconstituted Wood Product—*mfg*	321219	2493
Wafers (semiconductor devices): Semiconductor and Related Device—*mfg*	334413	3674
Wafers, sugar: Bakeries, Commercial—*mfg*	311812	2052
Cookie and Cracker—*mfg*	311821	2052
Snack Food, Other—*mfg*	311919	2052
Waffare countermeasures equipment: Search, Detection, Navigation, Guidance, Aeronautical, and Nautical System and Instrument—*mfg*	334511	3812
Waffle cloth, cotton: Broadwoven Fabric Mills—*mfg*	31321	2211
Waffle irons, electric: Electric Housewares and Household Fan—*mfg*	335211	3634
Electrical Appliance, Television and Radio Set—*whlse*	42162	5064
Heating Equipment (except Electric and Warm Air Furnaces)—*mfg*	333414	3634
Waffles, frozen: Frozen Specialty Food—*mfg*	311412	2038
Wage control agencies: Regulation, Licensing, and Inspection of Miscellaneous Commercial Sectors—*pub*	92615	9651
Wagons and trailers, farm: Farm Machinery and Equipment—*mfg*	333111	3523
Wagons for residential lawn and garden use: Hand and Edge Tool—*mfg*	332212	3524
Lawn and Garden Tractor and Home Lawn and Garden Equipment—*mfg*	333112	3524
Wagons, children's–coaster, express, and play: Game, Toy, and Children's Vehicle—*mfg*	339932	3944
Wagons, ice cream: Direct Selling Establishments, Other—*retail*	45439	5963
Mobile Foodservices—*accom*	72233	5963
Wailcovering stores: Building Material Dealers, Other—*retail*	44419	5231
Paint and Wallpaper Stores—*retail*	44412	5231
Paint, Varnish and Supplies—*whlse*	42295	5231
Wainscoting, rubber: Fabric Coating Mills—*mfg*	31332	3069
Rubber Product, All Other—*mfg*	326299	3069

ALPHABETICAL INDEX	NAICS	SIC
Wainscots, wood: Millwork (including Flooring), Other—*mfg*	321918	2431
Wood Window and Door—*mfg*	321911	2431
Waistbands, trouser: Apparel Accessories and Apparel, Other—*mfg*	315999	2396
Walkers: Surgical Appliance and Supplies—*mfg*	339113	3842
Walkers, baby (vehicles): Game, Toy, and Children's Vehicle—*mfg*	339932	3944
Walkways, moving: Elevator and Moving Stairway—*mfg*	333921	3534
Wall base, precast terrazzo: Concrete Pipe—*mfg*	327332	3272
Concrete Product, Other—*mfg*	32739	3272
Nonmetallic Mineral Product, All Other Miscellaneous—*mfg*	327999	3272
Wall cases, oflice–except wood: Nonwood Office Furniture—*mfg*	337214	2522
Wall coping, clay: Structural Clay Product, Other—*mfg*	327123	3259
Wall coverings, plastics: Plastics Pipe and Pipe Fitting—*mfg*	326122	3089
Plastics Product, All Other—*mfg*	326199	3089
Unsupported Plastics Profile Shape—*mfg*	326121	3089
Wall heaters, except electric: Heating Equipment (except Electric and Warm Air Furnaces)—*mfg*	333414	3433
Wall heaters, household–electric: Electric Housewares and Household Fan—*mfg*	335211	3634
Heating Equipment (except Electric and Warm Air Furnaces)—*mfg*	333414	3634
Wall lamps: Residential Electric Lighting Fixture—*mfg*	335121	3645
Wall squares, concrete: Concrete Pipe—*mfg*	327332	3272
Concrete Product, Other—*mfg*	32739	3272
Nonmetallic Mineral Product, All Other Miscellaneous—*mfg*	327999	3272
Wall tile, ceramic: Ceramic Wall and Floor Tile—*mfg*	327122	3253
Wall tile, fiberboard: Reconstituted Wood Product—*mfg*	321219	2493
Wallboard: Building Material Dealers, Other—*retail*	44419	5031
Wallboard (composition) dealers: Building Material Dealers, Other—*retail*	44419	5211
Home Centers—*retail*	44411	5211
Wallboard, gypsum: Gypsum and Gypsum Product—*mfg*	32742	3275
Wallboard, wood fiber–cellular fiber or hard pressed: Reconstituted Wood Product—*mfg*	321219	2493
Wallcoverings, rubber: Fabric Coating Mills—*mfg*	31332	3069
Rubber Product, All Other—*mfg*	326299	3069
Wallcoverings–paper: Coated and Laminated Paper—*mfg*	322222	2679
Converted Paper Product, All Other—*mfg*	322298	2679
Die-Cut Paper and Paperboard Office Supplies—*mfg*	322231	2679
Non-Folding Sanitary Food Container—*mfg*	322215	2679
Wallets, regardless of material: Personal Leather Good (except Women's Handbag and Purse)—*mfg*	316993	3172
Wallpaper: Coated and Laminated Paper—*mfg*	322222	2679
Converted Paper Product, All Other—*mfg*	322298	2679
Die-Cut Paper and Paperboard Office Supplies—*mfg*	322231	2679
Non-Folding Sanitary Food Container—*mfg*	322215	2679
Paint and Wallpaper Stores—*retail*	44412	5198
Paint, Varnish and Supplies—*whlse*	42295	5198

Description	NAICS	SIC
Wallpaper cleaners: Polish and Other Sanitation Good—*mfg*	325612	2842
Wallpaper removal-contractors: Painting and Wall Covering Contractors—*const*	23521	1799
Wallpaper stock hanging paper: Newsprint Mills—*mfg*	322122	2621
Paper (except Newsprint) Mills—*mfg*	322121	2621
Wallpaper stores: Building Material Dealers, Other—*retail*	44419	5231
Paint and Wallpaper Stores—*retail*	44412	5231
Paint, Varnish and Supplies—*whlse*	42295	5231
Wallpaper, embossed plastics–made on textile backing: Coated and Laminated Paper—*mfg*	322222	2679
Converted Paper Product, All Other—*mfg*	322298	2679
Die-Cut Paper and Paperboard Office Supplies—*mfg*	322231	2679
Non-Folding Sanitary Food Container—*mfg*	322215	2679
Walls, retaining–block, stone, or brick–contractors: Masonry and Stone Contractors—*const*	23541	1741
Walnut groves and farms: Tree Nut Farming—*ag*	111335	173
Walnut hulling and shelling: Postharvest Crop Activities (except Cotton Ginning)—*ag*	115114	723
Walnut oil: Fats and Oils Refining and Blending—*mfg*	311225	2076
Oilseed Processing, Other—*mfg*	311223	2076
Walnut oil, artists': Chemical Product, All Other Miscellaneous—*mfg*	325998	3952
Institutional Furniture—*mfg*	337127	3952
Lead Pencil and Art Good—*mfg*	339942	3952
Wardrobe bags: Household Textile Product Mills, Other—*mfg*	314129	2392
Wardrobe bags (closet accessories), plastics film or coated paper: Plastics, Foil, and Coated Paper Bag—*mfg*	322223	2673
Unsupported Plastics Bag—*mfg*	326111	2673
Wardrobe bags (luggage): Luggage—*mfg*	316991	3161
Wardrobe rental for motion picture film production: Formal Wear and Costume Rental—*real*	53222	7819
Independent Artists, Writers, and Performers—*arts*	71151	7819
Motion Picture and Video Industries, Other—*info*	512199	7819
Wardrobe service, except theatrical: Formal Wear and Costume Rental—*real*	53222	7299
Wardrobes, household–wood: Nonupholstered Wood Household Furniture—*mfg*	337122	2511
Warehouse Clubs and Superstores	**45291**	**5411**
Warehouse construction–general contractors: Building, Commercial and Institutional—*const*	23332	1541
Manufacturing and Industrial Building—*const*	23331	1541
Warehousing and Storage Facilities	**4931**	
Warehousing and Storage Facilities	**493**	
Warehousing and Storage Facilities, Other	**49319**	**4226**
Warehousing and storage, farm product–other than refrigerated: Farm Product Warehousing and Storage Facilities—*trans*	49313	4221
Warehousing of goods at foreign tradezones: General Warehousing and Storage Facilities—*trans*	49311	4226
Refrigerated Warehousing and Storage Facilities—*trans*	49312	4226
Warehousing and Storage Facilities, Other—*trans*	49319	4226
Warehousing of household goods, without local trucking: General Warehousing and Storage Facilities—*trans*	49311	4226
Refrigerated Warehousing and Storage Facilities—*trans*	49312	4226
Warehousing and Storage Facilities, Other—*trans*	49319	4226
Warehousing, cold storage or refrigerated: Refrigerated Warehousing and Storage Facilities—*trans*	49312	4222
Warehousing, general: General Warehousing and Storage Facilities—*trans*	49311	4225
Lessors of Miniwarehouses and Self Storage Units—*real*	53113	4225
Warehousing, self-storage: General Warehousing and Storage Facilities—*trans*	49311	4225
Lessors of Miniwarehouses and Self Storage Units—*real*	53113	4225
Warehousing, special–except farm products and cold storage: General Warehousing and Storage Facilities—*trans*	49311	4226
Refrigerated Warehousing and Storage Facilities—*trans*	49312	4226
Warehousing and Storage Facilities, Other—*trans*	49319	4226
Warm Air Heating and Air-Conditioning Equipment and Supplies Wholesalers	**42173**	**5075**
Warm air heating and cooling equipment: Warm Air Heating and Air-Conditioning Equipment and Supplies—*whlse*	42173	5075
Warmers, bottle–plastics, except foam: Plastics Pipe and Pipe Fitting—*mfg*	326122	3089
Plastics Product, All Other—*mfg*	326199	3089
Unsupported Plastics Profile Shape—*mfg*	326121	3089
Warmup and jogging suits: Outerwear Knitting Mills—*mfg*	315191	2253
Warmup suits: Apparel Accessories and Apparel, Other—*mfg*	315999	2339
Cut and Sew Apparel, All Other—*mfg*	315299	2329
Cut and Sew Apparel, All Other—*mfg*	315299	2339
Women's and Girls' Cut and Sew Apparel Contractors—*mfg*	315212	2339
Women's and Girls' Cut and Sew Other Outerwear—*mfg*	315238	2339
Warp (flat) knit fabrics: Knit Fabric and Lace Mills, Other—*mfg*	313249	2258
Textile and Fabric Finishing (except Broadwoven Fabric) Mills—*mfg*	313312	2258
Warp and knot tying machines (textile machinery): Textile Machinery—*mfg*	333292	3552
Warp knit fabrics: Broadwoven Fabric Finishing Mills—*mfg*	313311	5131
Piece Goods, Notions and Other Dry Goods—*whlse*	42231	5131
Textile and Fabric Finishing (except Broadwoven Fabric) Mills—*mfg*	313312	5131
Warping machines (textile machinery): Textile Machinery—*mfg*	333292	3552
Warranty insurance, automobile: Direct Insurance (except Life, Health and Medical) Carriers, Other—*fin*	524128	6399
Warranty insurance, home: Direct Property and Casualty Insurance Carriers—*fin*	524126	6351
Reinsurance Carriers—*fin*	52413	6351
Wash foundations, precast terrazzo: Concrete Pipe—*mfg*	327332	3272
Concrete Product, Other—*mfg*	32739	3272
Nonmetallic Mineral Product, All Other Miscellaneous—*mfg*	327999	3272

ALPHABETICAL INDEX	NAICS	SIC
Washable service apparel–hospital, professional, barbers', etc.: Men's and Boys' Cut and Sew Apparel Contractors—*mfg*	315211	2326
Men's and Boys' Cut and Sew Work Clothing—*mfg*	315225	2326
Washboards, wood and part wood: Manufacturing, All Other Miscellaneous—*mfg*	339999	2499
Wood Container and Pallet—*mfg*	32192	2499
Wood Product, All Other Miscellaneous—*mfg*	321999	2499
Washcloths: Household Textile Product Mills, Other—*mfg*	314129	2392
Knit Fabric and Lace Mills, Other—*mfg*	313249	2259
Weft Knit Fabric Mills—*mfg*	313241	2259
Washcloths, woven–made in weaving mills: Broadwoven Fabric Mills—*mfg*	31321	2211
Washeries construction, mining–general contractors: Heavy, All Other—*const*	23499	1629
Industrial Nonbuilding Structure—*const*	23493	1629
Washeries, anthracite: Anthracite—*mining*	212113	1231
Washeries, bituminous coal or lignite: Bituminous Coal and Lignite Surface—*mining*	212111	1221
Washers, aggregate and sand–stationary type: Mining Machinery and Equipment—*mfg*	333131	3532
Washers, bottle–for food products: Packaging Machinery—*mfg*	333993	3565
Washers, hardware: Hardware—*whlse*	42171	5072
Washers, leather: Gasket, Packing, and Sealing Device—*mfg*	339991	3053
Washers, metal: Bolt, Nut, Screw, Rivet and Washer—*mfg*	332722	3452
Washers, photographic print and film: Photographic and Photocopying Equipment—*mfg*	333315	3861
Photographic Film, Paper, Plate and Chemical—*mfg*	325992	3861
Washers, plastics: Plastics Pipe and Pipe Fitting—*mfg*	326122	3089
Plastics Product, All Other—*mfg*	326199	3089
Unsupported Plastics Profile Shape—*mfg*	326121	3089
Washes, cosmetic: Soap and Other Detergent—*mfg*	325611	2844
Toilet Preparation—*mfg*	32562	2844
Washing and polishing, automotive: Car Washes—*serv*	811192	7542
Washing compounds: Soap and Other Detergent—*mfg*	325611	2841
Washing machine parts, porcelain enameled: Kitchen Utensil, Pot and Pan—*mfg*	332214	3469
Washing machine repair: Appliance Repair and Maintenance—*serv*	811412	7629
Household Appliance Stores—*retail*	443111	7629
Washing machines, household–electric: Electrical Appliance, Television and Radio Set—*whlse*	42162	5064
Washing machines, household–including coin-operated: Household Laundry Equipment—*mfg*	335224	3633
Washing machines, laundry–commercial, including coin-operated: Laundry, Drycleaning and Pressing Machine, Commercial—*mfg*	333312	3582
Washing soda (sal soda): Alkalies and Chlorine—*mfg*	325181	2812

ALPHABETICAL INDEX	NAICS	SIC
Washroom sanitation service: Exterminating and Pest Control Services—*admin*	56171	7342
Janitorial Services—*admin*	56172	7342
Waste bags, plastics film and laminated: Plastics, Foil, and Coated Paper Bag—*mfg*	322223	2673
Unsupported Plastics Bag—*mfg*	326111	2673
Waste bottles and boxes: Recyclable Material—*whlse*	42193	5093
Waste Collection	**56211**	
Waste Collection	**5621**	
Waste Collection, Other	**562119**	**4953**
Waste disposal plant construction–general contractors: Heavy, All Other—*const*	23499	1629
Industrial Nonbuilding Structure—*const*	23493	1629
Waste Management and Remediation Services	**562**	
Waste Management and Remediation, Administrative and Support Services	**56**	
Waste management program administration: Air and Water Resource and Solid Waste Management—*pub*	92411	9511
Waste Management Services, All Other	**56299**	
Waste Management Services, All Other Miscellaneous	**562998**	**4959**
Waste materials disposal at sea: Hazardous Waste Collection—*admin*	562112	4953
Hazardous Waste Treatment and Disposal—*admin*	562211	4953
Materials Recovery Facilities—*admin*	56292	4953
Nonhazardous Waste Treatment and Disposal, Other—*admin*	562219	4953
Solid Waste Collection—*admin*	562111	4953
Solid Waste Combustors and Incinerators—*admin*	562213	4953
Solid Waste Landfill—*admin*	562212	4953
Waste Collection, Other—*admin*	562119	4953
Waste rags: Recyclable Material—*whlse*	42193	5093
Waste Treatment and Disposal	**56221**	
Waste Treatment and Disposal	**5622**	
Waste, rubber: Recyclable Material—*whlse*	42193	5093
Waste, textile: Recyclable Material—*whlse*	42193	5093
Waste, textile mill–processing of: Broadwoven Fabric Mills—*mfg*	31321	2299
Narrow Fabric Mills—*mfg*	313221	2299
Nonwoven Fabric Mills—*mfg*	31323	2299
Textile and Fabric Finishing (except Broadwoven Fabric) Mills—*mfg*	313312	2299
Textile Product Mills, All Other Miscellaneous—*mfg*	314999	2299
Thread Mills—*mfg*	313113	2299
Yarn Spinning Mills—*mfg*	313111	2299
Wastebaskets, fiber (metal-end or all fiber): Fiber Can, Tube, Drum, and Similar Products—*mfg*	322214	2655
Wastebaskets, stamped metal: Kitchen Utensil, Pot and Pan—*mfg*	332214	3469
Wastepaper, including paper recycling: Recyclable Material—*whlse*	42193	5093
Watch crystals, made from purchased glass: Glass Product Made of Purchased Glass—*mfg*	327215	3231

Description	NAICS	SIC
Watch jewels: Jewelers' Material and Lapidary Work—*mfg*	339913	3915
Watch repair shops: Personal and Household Goods Repair and Maintenance, Other—*serv*	81149	7631
Watch straps, except metal: Personal Leather Good (except Women's Handbag and Purse)—*mfg*	316993	3172
Watch, Clock, and Part Manufacturing	**334518**	**3579**
Watchbands, base metal: Costume Jewelry and Novelty—*mfg*	339914	3961
Watchbands, precious metal: Jewelry (except Costume)—*mfg*	339911	3911
Watchcases: Jewelry, Watch, Precious Stone and Precious Metal—*whlse*	42194	5094
Watch, Clock, and Part—*mfg*	334518	3873
Watches and parts: Jewelry, Watch, Precious Stone and Precious Metal—*whlse*	42194	5094
Watches and parts–except crystals and jewels: Watch, Clock, and Part—*mfg*	334518	3873
Watches, including custom made: Jewelry Stores—*retail*	44831	5944
Water bottles, glass: Glass Container—*mfg*	327213	3221
Water bottles, rubber: Fabric Coating Mills—*mfg*	31332	3069
Rubber Product, All Other—*mfg*	326299	3069
Water closets, plastics: Plastics Plumbing Fixture—*mfg*	326191	3088
Water closets–enameled iron, cast iron, and pressed metal: Enameled Iron and Metal Sanitary Ware—*mfg*	332998	3431
Water colors, artists': Chemical Product, All Other Miscellaneous—*mfg*	325998	3952
Institutional Furniture—*mfg*	337127	3952
Lead Pencil and Art Good—*mfg*	339942	3952
Water conditioners, for swimming pools: Machinery, Other Commercial and Service Industry—*mfg*	333319	3589
Water conditioning equipment: Building Material Dealers, Other—*retail*	44419	5074
Plumbing and Heating Equipment and Supplies (Hydronics)—*whlse*	42172	5074
Water control and quality agencies: Air and Water Resource and Solid Waste Management—*pub*	92411	9511
Water coolers, electric: Air-Conditioning and Warm Air Heating Equipment and Commercial and Industrial Refrigeration Equipment—*mfg*	333415	3585
Motor Vehicle Air-Conditioning—*mfg*	336391	3585
Water decontamination or purification tablets: Pharmaceutical Preparation—*mfg*	325412	2834
Water distribution or supply systems for irrigation: Water Supply and Irrigation Systems—*util*	22131	4971
Water filters and softeners, household type: Machinery, Other Commercial and Service Industry—*mfg*	333319	3589
Water glass: Basic Inorganic Chemical, All Other—*mfg*	325188	2819
Chemical Product, All Other Miscellaneous—*mfg*	325998	2819
Water heater controls: Automatic Environmental Control for Residential, Commercial and Appliance Use—*mfg*	334512	3822
Water heaters, electric: Electrical Appliance, Television and Radio Set—*whlse*	42162	5064
Water heaters, except electric: Building Material Dealers, Other—*retail*	44419	5074
Plumbing and Heating Equipment and Supplies (Hydronics)—*whlse*	42172	5074
Water heaters, household–including nonelectric: Major Household Appliance, Other—*mfg*	335228	3639
Water intake well drilling–on a contract basis: Drilling Oil and Gas Wells—*mining*	213111	1381
Water leak detectors: Fabricated Metal Product, All Other Miscellaneous—*mfg*	332999	3599
General Purpose Machinery , All Other—*mfg*	333999	3599
Machine Shops—*mfg*	33271	3599
Machinery, Other Commercial and Service Industry—*mfg*	333319	3599
Water main line construction–general contractors: Power and Communication Transmission Line—*const*	23492	1623
Water, Sewer, and Pipeline—*const*	23491	1623
Water paints: Paint and Coating—*mfg*	32551	2851
Water pipe, cast iron: Iron Foundries—*mfg*	331511	3321
Water pollution control agencies: Air and Water Resource and Solid Waste Management—*pub*	92411	9511
Water power project construction–general contractors: Heavy, All Other—*const*	23499	1629
Industrial Nonbuilding Structure—*const*	23493	1629
Water pulsating devices, electric: Electric Housewares and Household Fan—*mfg*	335211	3634
Heating Equipment (except Electric and Warm Air Furnaces)—*mfg*	333414	3634
Water pump installation and servicing–contractors: Plumbing, Heating and Air-Conditioning Contractors—*const*	23511	1711
Water pumps, industrial: Industrial Machinery and Equipment—*whlse*	42183	5084
Water purification equipment, household type: Machinery, Other Commercial and Service Industry—*mfg*	333319	3589
Water quality monitoring and control systems: Instruments and Related Products for Measuring, Displaying, and Controlling Industrial Process Variables—*mfg*	334513	3823
Water repellency finishing of cotton broad-woven fabrics: Broadwoven Fabric Finishing Mills—*mfg*	313311	2261
Water softeners: Building Material Dealers, Other—*retail*	44419	5074
Plumbing and Heating Equipment and Supplies (Hydronics)—*whlse*	42172	5074
Water softeners, household type: Machinery, Other Commercial and Service Industry—*mfg*	333319	3589
Water Supply and Irrigation Systems	**22131**	**4971**
Water supply systems, except irrigation: Water Supply and Irrigation Systems—*util*	22131	4941

ALPHABETICAL INDEX	NAICS	SIC
Water system balancing and testing-contractors: Plumbing, Heating and Air-Conditioning Contractors—*const*	23511	1711
Water tanks, metal plate: Air-Conditioning and Warm Air Heating Equipment and Commercial and Industrial Refrigeration Equipment—*mfg*	333415	3443
Metal Tank (Heavy Gauge)—*mfg*	33242	3443
Plate Work—*mfg*	332313	3443
Power Boiler and Heat Exchanger—*mfg*	33241	3443
Water taxis, operation of: Inland Water Passenger—*trans*	483212	4489
Scenic and Sightseeing, Water—*trans*	48721	4489
Water temperature gauges, motor vehicle: Measuring and Controlling Device, Other—*mfg*	334519	3829
Surgical and Medical Instrument—*mfg*	339112	3829
Water Transportation	**483**	
Water transportation of freight to noncontiguous territories: Coastal and Great Lakes Freight—*trans*	483113	4424
Water Transportation Support Activities	**4883**	
Water Transportation, Other Support Activities for	**48839**	**4785**
Water traps: Fabricated Metal Product, All Other Miscellaneous—*mfg*	332999	3432
Plumbing Fixture Fitting and Trim—*mfg*	332913	3432
Water treating compounds: Basic Organic Chemical, All Other—*mfg*	325199	2899
Chemical Product, All Other Miscellaneous—*mfg*	325998	2899
Water treatment equipment, industrial: Machinery, Other Commercial and Service Industry—*mfg*	333319	3589
Water treatment plant construction–general contractors: Heavy, All Other—*const*	23499	1629
Industrial Nonbuilding Structure—*const*	23493	1629
Water troughs: Farm Machinery and Equipment—*mfg*	333111	3523
Water turbines: Turbine and Turbine Generator Set Unit—*mfg*	333611	3511
Water valves, except plumbers' brass goods and fittings, metal: Fabricated Metal Product, All Other Miscellaneous—*mfg*	332999	3494
Other Metal Valve and Pipe Fitting, Other—*mfg*	332919	3494
Water Well Drilling Contractors	**2358**	
Water Well Drilling Contractors	**23581**	**1781**
Water well drilling machinery: Oil and Gas Field Machinery and Equipment—*mfg*	333132	3533
Water well drilling-contractors: Water Well Drilling Contractors—*const*	23581	1781
Water works valves: Industrial Valve—*mfg*	332911	3491
Water, distilled: Basic Organic Chemical, All Other—*mfg*	325199	2899
Chemical Product, All Other Miscellaneous—*mfg*	325998	2899
Water, mineral: Food (Health) Supplement Stores—*retail*	446191	5499
Food Stores, All Other Specialty—*retail*	445299	5499
Limited-Service Restaurants—*accom*	722211	5499
Meat Markets—*retail*	44521	5499
Water, pasteurized–bottled or canned: Bottled Water—*mfg*	312112	2086
Soft Drink—*mfg*	312111	2086
Water, Sewage and Other Systems	**2213**	.
Water, Sewer, and Pipeline Construction	**23491**	**1623**
Water, sterile–for injections: Pharmaceutical Preparation—*mfg*	325412	2834
Waterbeds: Furniture—*whlse*	42121	5021
Furniture Stores—*retail*	44211	5021
Furniture Stores—*retail*	44211	5712
Nonupholstered Wood Household Furniture—*mfg*	337122	5712
Upholstered Household Furniture—*mfg*	337121	5712
Wood Kitchen Cabinet and Counter Top—*mfg*	33711	5712
Waterfront terminal operation: Marine Cargo Handling—*trans*	48832	4491
Port and Harbor Operations—*trans*	48831	4491
Watering pots, plastics: Plastics Pipe and Pipe Fitting—*mfg*	326122	3089
Plastics Product, All Other—*mfg*	326199	3089
Unsupported Plastics Profile Shape—*mfg*	326121	3089
Watermelon farms: Vegetable (except Potato) and Melon Farming, Other—*ag*	111219	161
Watermeters, consumption registering: Totalizing Fluid Meter and Counting Device—*mfg*	334514	3824
Waterproof and water-repellent outerwear, except vulcanized rubber, oiled and wool: Apparel Accessories and Apparel, Other—*mfg*	315999	2385
Infants' Cut and Sew Apparel—*mfg*	315291	2385
Men's and Boys' Cut and Sew Apparel Contractors—*mfg*	315211	2385
Men's and Boys' Cut and Sew Other Outerwear—*mfg*	315228	2385
Men's and Boys' Cut and Sew Suit, Coat and Overcoat—*mfg*	315222	2385
Women's and Girls' Cut and Sew Apparel Contractors—*mfg*	315212	2385
Women's and Girls' Cut and Sew Other Outerwear—*mfg*	315238	2385
Women's and Girls' Cut and Sew Suit, Coat, Tailored Jacket and Skirt—*mfg*	315234	2385
Waterproof cardboard: Converted Paper Product, All Other—*mfg*	322298	2675
Die-Cut Paper and Paperboard Office Supplies—*mfg*	322231	2675
Surface-Coated Paperboard—*mfg*	322292	2675
Waterproof outergarments, men's and boys': Men's and Boys' Clothing and Furnishings—*whlse*	42232	5136
Waterproof outergarments–women's and children's: Women's, Children's, and Infants' and Accessories—*whlse*	42233	5137
Waterproof wrapping paper: Coated and Laminated Packaging Paper and Plastics Film—*mfg*	322221	2671
Unsupported Plastics Packaging Film and Sheet—*mfg*	326112	2671
Waterproofing compounds: Basic Organic Chemical, All Other—*mfg*	325199	2899
Chemical Product, All Other Miscellaneous—*mfg*	325998	2899
Waterproofing-contractors: Trade Contractors, All Other Special—*const*	23599	1799
Waterslides, operation of: Amusement and Recreation Industries, All Other—*arts*	71399	7999
Fitness and Recreational Sports Centers—*arts*	71394	7999

Entry	NAICS	SIC
Waterway construction–general contractors: Heavy, All Other—*const*	23499	1629
Industrial Nonbuilding Structure—*const*	23493	1629
Watt-hour and demand meters, combined: Electronic Coil, Transformer, and Other Inductor—*mfg*	334416	3825
Instrument for Measuring and Testing Electricity and Electrical Signals—*mfg*	334515	3825
Watt-hour and time switch meters, combined: Electronic Coil, Transformer, and Other Inductor—*mfg*	334416	3825
Instrument for Measuring and Testing Electricity and Electrical Signals—*mfg*	334515	3825
Watt-hour meters, electric: Electronic Coil, Transformer, and Other Inductor—*mfg*	334416	3825
Instrument for Measuring and Testing Electricity and Electrical Signals—*mfg*	334515	3825
Wattle extract: Gum and Wood Chemical—*mfg*	325191	2861
Wattmeters: Electronic Coil, Transformer, and Other Inductor—*mfg*	334416	3825
Instrument for Measuring and Testing Electricity and Electrical Signals—*mfg*	334515	3825
Wave pools, operation of: Amusement and Recreation Industries, All Other—*arts*	71399	7999
Waveform measuring and/or analyzing equipment: Electronic Coil, Transformer, and Other Inductor—*mfg*	334416	3825
Instrument for Measuring and Testing Electricity and Electrical Signals—*mfg*	334515	3825
Waveguide pressurization equipment: Electrical Equipment and Component, All Other Miscellaneous—*mfg*	335999	3699
Machinery, Other Commercial and Service Industry—*mfg*	333319	3699
Waveguides and fittings: Electronic Component, Other—*mfg*	334419	3679
Motor Vehicle Electrical and Electronic Equipment, Other—*mfg*	336322	3679
Printed Circuit/Electronics Assembly—*mfg*	334418	3679
Radio and Television Broadcasting and Wireless Communications Equipment—*mfg*	33422	3679
Wax museums, commercial: Historical Sites—*arts*	71212	8412
Museums—*arts*	71211	8412
Wax removers: Polish and Other Sanitation Good—*mfg*	325612	2842
Wax, artists': Chemical Product, All Other Miscellaneous—*mfg*	325998	3952
Institutional Furniture—*mfg*	337127	3952
Lead Pencil and Art Good—*mfg*	339942	3952
Wax, core: Basic Organic Chemical, All Other—*mfg*	325199	2899
Chemical Product, All Other Miscellaneous—*mfg*	325998	2899
Wax, dental: Dental Equipment and Supplies—*mfg*	339114	3843
Wax, paraffin–produced in petroleum refineries: Petroleum Refineries—*mfg*	32411	2911
Wax, sealing: Adhesive—*mfg*	32552	2891
Waxed paper for packaging: Coated and Laminated Packaging Paper and Plastics Film—*mfg*	322221	2671
Unsupported Plastics Packaging Film and Sheet—*mfg*	326112	2671
Waxed paper, except for packaging: Coated and Laminated Paper—*mfg*	322222	2672
Waxes for wood, fabricated leather, andother materials: Polish and Other Sanitation Good—*mfg*	325612	2842
Waxes, except petroleum: Chemical and Allied Products, Other—*whlse*	42269	5169
Waxes, petroleum–not produced in petroleum refineries: Petroleum and Coal Productsa, All Other—*mfg*	324199	2999
Waxing and polishing, automotive: Car Washes—*serv*	811192	7542
Waxing of cloth: Fabric Coating Mills—*mfg*	31332	2295
Weather forecasters: Scientific and Technical Consulting Services, Other—*prof*	54169	8999
Weather modification (rain makers): Scientific and Technical Consulting Services, Other—*prof*	54169	8999
Weather strip, metal: Metal Window and Door—*mfg*	332321	3442
Weather strip, sponge rubber: Fabric Coating Mills—*mfg*	31332	3069
Rubber Product, All Other—*mfg*	326299	3069
Weather strip, wood: Millwork (including Flooring), Other—*mfg*	321918	2431
Wood Window and Door—*mfg*	321911	2431
Weather stripping-contra tors: Trade Contractors, All Other Special—*const*	23599	1799
Weather tracking equipment: Measuring and Controlling Device, Other—*mfg*	334519	3829
Surgical and Medical Instrument—*mfg*	339112	3829
Weather vanes: Fabricated Metal Product, All Other Miscellaneous—*mfg*	332999	3599
General Purpose Machinery , All Other—*mfg*	333999	3599
Machine Shops—*mfg*	33271	3599
Machinery, Other Commercial and Service Industry—*mfg*	333319	3599
Weatherproof wire and cable, nonferrous: Aluminum Rolling and Drawing, Other—*mfg*	331319	3357
Communication and Energy Wire, Other—*mfg*	335929	3357
Copper Wire (except Mechanical) Drawing—*mfg*	331422	3357
Fiber Optic Cable—*mfg*	335921	3357
Nonferrous Metal (except Copper and Aluminum) Rolling, Drawing and Extruding—*mfg*	331491	3357
Weaving mills, broadwoven fabrics–wool, mohair, and similar animal fibers: Broadwoven Fabric Finishing Mills—*mfg*	313311	2231
Broadwoven Fabric Mills—*mfg*	31321	2231
Textile and Fabric Finishing (except Broadwoven Fabric) Mills—*mfg*	313312	2231
Weaving mills, cotton broadwoven fabrics: Broadwoven Fabric Mills—*mfg*	31321	2211
Weaving mills, narrow fabric–cotton, wool, silk, and manmade fibers-including glass: Narrow Fabric Mills—*mfg*	313221	2241
Weaving yarn–cotton, silk, wool, and manmade staple: Yarn Spinning Mills—*mfg*	313111	2281
Webbing, jute: Broadwoven Fabric Mills—*mfg*	31321	2299
Narrow Fabric Mills—*mfg*	313221	2299
Nonwoven Fabric Mills—*mfg*	31323	2299

ALPHABETICAL INDEX	NAICS	SIC
Textile and Fabric Finishing (except Broadwoven Fabric) Mills—*mfg*	313312	2299
Textile Product Mills, All Other Miscellaneous—*mfg*	314999	2299
Thread Mills—*mfg*	313113	2299
Yarn Spinning Mills—*mfg*	313111	2299
Webbing, woven–except jute: Narrow Fabric Mills—*mfg*	313221	2241
Webbing–cane, reed, and rattan: Manufacturing, All Other Miscellaneous—*mfg*	339999	2499
Wood Container and Pallet—*mfg*	32192	2499
Wood Product, All Other Miscellaneous—*mfg*	321999	2499
Webs, strapping: Narrow Fabric Mills—*mfg*	313221	2241
Wedding chapels, privately operated: Personal Services, All Other—*serv*	81299	7299
Wedding dresses: Women's and Girls' Cut and Sew Apparel Contractors—*mfg*	315212	2335
Women's and Girls' Cut and Sew Dress—*mfg*	315233	2335
Weed control, crop–after planting: Nonscheduled Air, Other—*trans*	481219	721
Soil Preparation, Planting, and Cultivating—*ag*	115112	721
Weed control, crop–before planting: Soil Preparation, Planting, and Cultivating—*ag*	115112	711
Weeding machines, farm: Farm Machinery and Equipment—*mfg*	333111	3523
Weft Knit Fabric Mills	**313241**	**2259**
Weft knit fabrics: Broadwoven Fabric Finishing Mills—*mfg*	313311	5131
Piece Goods, Notions and Other Dry Goods—*whlse*	42231	5131
Textile and Fabric Finishing (except Broadwoven Fabric) Mills—*mfg*	313312	2257
Textile and Fabric Finishing (except Broadwoven Fabric) Mills—*mfg*	313312	5131
Weft Knit Fabric Mills—*mfg*	313241	2257
Weighing machines and apparatus, except laboratory: Scale and Balance (except Laboratory)—*mfg*	333997	3596
Weighing services connected with transportation: Road, Other Support Activities for—*trans*	48849	4785
Water, Other Support Activities for—*trans*	48839	4785
Welded steel wire fabric, made in wire-drawing plants: Fabricated Wire Product, Other—*mfg*	332618	3315
Steel Wire Drawing—*mfg*	331222	3315
Welders' aprons, leather: Leather Good, All Other—*mfg*	316999	3199
Welders' gloves: Glove and Mitten—*mfg*	315992	3151
Welders' hoods: Surgical Appliance and Supplies—*mfg*	339113	3842
Welders' jackets, leggings, and sleeves–leather: Leather Good, All Other—*mfg*	316999	3199
Welding accessories, electric and gas: Power, Distribution and Specialty Transformer—*mfg*	335311	3548
Welding and Soldering Equipment—*mfg*	333992	3548
Welding and cutting apparatus, gas or electric: Power, Distribution and Specialty Transformer—*mfg*	335311	3548
Welding and Soldering Equipment—*mfg*	333992	3548
Welding and Soldering Equipment Manufacturing	**333992**	**3548**
Welding contractors, operating at site of construction: Trade Contractors, All Other Special—*const*	23599	1799
Welding fluxes: Basic Organic Chemical, All Other—*mfg*	325199	2899
Chemical Product, All Other Miscellaneous—*mfg*	325998	2899
Welding machinery and equipment: Industrial Machinery and Equipment—*whlse*	42183	5084
Welding positioners (jigs): Die and Tool, Die Set, Jig and Fixture, Special—*mfg*	333514	3544
Industrial Mold—*mfg*	333511	3544
Welding rods: Nonferrous Metal (except Copper and Aluminum) Rolling, Drawing and Extruding—*mfg*	331491	3356
Welding shops, including automotive: Personal and Household Goods Repair and Maintenance, Other—*serv*	81149	7692
Welding wire, bare and coated: Power, Distribution and Specialty Transformer—*mfg*	335311	3548
Welding and Soldering Equipment—*mfg*	333992	3548
Weldments: Air-Conditioning and Warm Air Heating Equipment and Commercial and Industrial Refrigeration Equipment—*mfg*	333415	3443
Metal Tank (Heavy Gauge)—*mfg*	33242	3443
Plate Work—*mfg*	332313	3443
Power Boiler and Heat Exchanger—*mfg*	33241	3443
Welfare pensions: Health and Welfare Funds—*fin*	52512	6371
Pension Funds—*fin*	52511	6371
Portfolio Management—*fin*	52392	6371
Third Party Administration for Insurance and Pension Funds—*fin*	524292	6371
Well adapters, tipless–metal: Fabricated Metal Product, All Other Miscellaneous—*mfg*	332999	3494
Other Metal Valve and Pipe Fitting, Other—*mfg*	332919	3494
Well casing, wrought–welded, lock joint, and heavy riveted: Iron and Steel Pipes and Tubes from Purchased Steel—*mfg*	33121	3317
Well casings, iron and steel–made in steel works or rolling mills: Iron and Steel Mills—*mfg*	331111	3312
Petroleum and Coal Productsa, All Other—*mfg*	324199	3312
Well curbing, concrete: Concrete Pipe—*mfg*	327332	3272
Concrete Product, Other—*mfg*	32739	3272
Nonmetallic Mineral Product, All Other Miscellaneous—*mfg*	327999	3272
Well drilling, water–except oil or gas field water intake–contractors: Water Well Drilling Contractors—*const*	23581	1781
Well drilling–gas, oil, and water intake-on a contract basis: Drilling Oil and Gas Wells—*mining*	213111	1381
Well foundation grading, oil and gas wells–on a contract basis: Oil and Gas Operations Support Activities—*mining*	213112	1389
Well logging equipment: Oil and Gas Field Machinery and Equipment—*mfg*	333132	3533

Description	NAICS	SIC
Well logging–on a contract basis: Oil and Gas Operations Support Activities—*mining*	213112	1389
Well plugging and abandoning, oil and gas wells–on a contract basis: Oil and Gas Operations Support Activities—*mining*	213112	1389
Well points (drilling equipment): Construction and (except Petroleum) Machinery and Equipment—*whlse*	42181	5082
Well pumping, oil and gas–on a contract basis: Oil and Gas Operations Support Activities—*mining*	213112	1389
Well servicing, oil and gas wells–on a contract basis: Oil and Gas Operations Support Activities—*mining*	213112	1389
Well shooting torpedoes (explosives): Explosives—*mfg*	32592	2892
Well surveying machinery: Oil and Gas Field Machinery and Equipment—*mfg*	333132	3533
Wellpoint systems: Construction Machinery—*mfg*	33312	3531
Overhead Traveling Crane, Hoist and Monorail System—*mfg*	333923	3531
Railroad Rolling Stock—*mfg*	33651	3531
Wells, light–sheet metal: Metal Container, Other—*mfg*	332439	3444
Sheet Metal Work—*mfg*	332322	3444
Welting leather: Leather and Hide Tanning and Finishing—*mfg*	31611	3111
Welting, leather (cut stock and findings): Fastener, Button, Needle and Pin—*mfg*	339993	3131
Leather Good, All Other—*mfg*	316999	3131
Wood Product, All Other Miscellaneous—*mfg*	321999	3131
Welts: Textile Product Mills, All Other Miscellaneous—*mfg*	314999	2399
Wet blues: Leather and Hide Tanning and Finishing—*mfg*	31611	3111
Wet Corn Milling	**311221**	**2046**
Wet corn milling products: Grocery and Related Products, Other—*whlse*	42249	5149
Wet machine board: Paperboard Mills—*mfg*	32213	2631
Wet suits, rubber: Fabric Coating Mills—*mfg*	31332	3069
Rubber Product, All Other—*mfg*	326299	3069
Wetting agents: Surface Active Agent—*mfg*	325613	2843
Whale oil, refined: Fats and Oils Refining and Blending—*mfg*	311225	2077
Fresh and Frozen Seafood Processing—*mfg*	311712	2077
Rendering and Meat By-product Processing—*mfg*	311613	2077
Seafood Canning—*mfg*	311711	2077
Wharf construction–general contractors: Heavy, All Other—*const*	23499	1629
Industrial Nonbuilding Structure—*const*	23493	1629
Whatnot shelves, wood: Nonupholstered Wood Household Furniture—*mfg*	337122	2511
Wheat: Grain and Field Bean—*whlse*	42251	5153
Wheat Farming	**11114**	**111**
Wheat farms: Wheat Farming—*ag*	11114	111
Wheat flakes: Breakfast Cereal—*mfg*	31123	2043
Coffee and Tea—*mfg*	31192	2043
Wheat flour: Flour Milling—*mfg*	311211	2041
Wheat germ: Flour Milling—*mfg*	311211	2041
Wheat gluten: Wet Corn Milling—*mfg*	311221	2046
Wheat mill feed: Flour Milling—*mfg*	311211	2041
Wheat starch: Wet Corn Milling—*mfg*	311221	2046
Wheatstone bridges (electrical measuring instruments): Electronic Coil, Transformer, and Other Inductor—*mfg*	334416	3825
Instrument for Measuring and Testing Electricity and Electrical Signals—*mfg*	334515	3825
Wheel alignment, automotive: Automotive Mechanical and Electrical Repair and Maintenance, Other—*serv*	811118	7539
Wheel balancing equipment, automotive: Industrial Machinery, All Other—*mfg*	333298	3559
Machinery, Other Commercial and Service Industry—*mfg*	333319	3559
Wheel chairs: Surgical Appliance and Supplies—*mfg*	339113	3842
Wheel mounting and balancing equipment, automotive: Industrial Machinery, All Other—*mfg*	333298	3559
Machinery, Other Commercial and Service Industry—*mfg*	333319	3559
Wheel position indicators and transmitters, aircraft: Search, Detection, Navigation, Guidance, Aeronautical, and Nautical System and Instrument—*mfg*	334511	3812
Wheel pullers, handtools: Hand and Edge Tool—*mfg*	332212	3423
Wheel turning equipment, diamond point and other (machine tool accessories): Cutting Tool and Machine Tool Accessory—*mfg*	333515	3545
Hand and Edge Tool—*mfg*	332212	3545
Wheelbarrows: Hand and Edge Tool—*mfg*	332212	3799
Wheels, abrasive–dental: Dental Equipment and Supplies—*mfg*	339114	3843
Wheels, abrasive–except dental: Abrasive Product—*mfg*	32791	3291
Fabricated Metal Product, All Other Miscellaneous—*mfg*	332999	3291
Wheels, aircraft: Aircraft Part and Auxiliary Equipment, Other—*mfg*	336413	3728
Fluid Power Valve and Hose Fitting—*mfg*	332912	3728
Wheels, car and locomotive–forged-not made in rolling mills: Iron and Steel Forging—*mfg*	332111	3462
Wheels, car and locomotive–iron and steel: Iron and Steel Mills—*mfg*	331111	3312
Petroleum and Coal Productsa, All Other—*mfg*	324199	3312
Wheels, diamond abrasive: Abrasive Product—*mfg*	32791	3291
Fabricated Metal Product, All Other Miscellaneous—*mfg*	332999	3291
Wheels, grinding–artificial: Abrasive Product—*mfg*	32791	3291
Fabricated Metal Product, All Other Miscellaneous—*mfg*	332999	3291
Wheels, motor vehicle: Motor Vehicle Body—*mfg*	336211	3714
Motor Vehicle Brake System—*mfg*	33634	3714
Motor Vehicle Parts, All Other—*mfg*	336399	3714
Motor Vehicle Steering and Suspension Components (except Spring)—*mfg*	33633	3714
Wheels, motor vehicle–new: Automotive Parts and Accessories Stores—*retail*	44131	5013
Motor Vehicle Supplies and New Part—*whlse*	42112	5013
Wheels, stamped metal, disc type–wheelbarrow, stroller, lawnmower: Fabricated Metal Product, All Other Miscellaneous—*mfg*	332999	3499
Whetstone quarrying: Crushed and Broken Stone and Quarrying, Other—*mining*	212319	1499

ALPHABETICAL INDEX	NAICS	SIC
Non-Metallic Mineral, All Other—*mining*	212399	1499
Whetstones, artificial: Abrasive Product—*mfg*	32791	3291
Fabricated Metal Product, All Other Miscellaneous—*mfg*	332999	3291
Whey butter: Creamery Butter—*mfg*	311512	2021
Whey, raw–liquid: Cheese—*mfg*	311513	2022
Whey–concentrated, condensed, dried, evaporated, and powdered: Dry, Condensed, and Evaporated Dairy Product—*mfg*	311514	2023
Whimseys and miniatures (millinery): Hat, Cap and Millinery—*mfg*	315991	2353
Whipped cream: Fluid Milk—*mfg*	311511	2026
Whipped topping, dry mix: Dry, Condensed, and Evaporated Dairy Product—*mfg*	311514	2023
Whipped topping, except frozen or dry mix: Fluid Milk—*mfg*	311511	2026
Whipped topping, frozen: Frozen Specialty Food—*mfg*	311412	2038
Whippers, household–electric: Electric Housewares and Household Fan—*mfg*	335211	3634
Heating Equipment (except Electric and Warm Air Furnaces)—*mfg*	333414	3634
Whips, horse: Leather Good, All Other—*mfg*	316999	3199
Whipstocks: Leather Good, All Other—*mfg*	316999	3199
Whirlpool baths: Stores (except Tobacco Stores), All Other Miscellaneous—*retail*	453998	5999
Whirlpool baths, hydrotherapy equipment: Electromedical and Electrotherapeutic Apparatus—*mfg*	334510	3842
Whisk brooms: Broom, Brush and Mop—*mfg*	339994	3991
Whiskey warehousing: General Warehousing and Storage Facilities—*trans*	49311	4226
Refrigerated Warehousing and Storage Facilities—*trans*	49312	4226
Warehousing and Storage Facilities, Other—*trans*	49319	4226
Whiskey–hourben, rye, scotch type, and corn: Distilleries—*mfg*	31214	2085
White lead pigments: Carbon Black—*mfg*	325182	2816
Inorganic Dye and Pigment—*mfg*	325131	2816
White metal castings, except die-castings–lead, antimony, and tin: Nonferrous Foundries, Other—*mfg*	331528	3369
Whiteprint (diazo) paper and cloth, sensitized: Photographic and Photocopying Equipment—*mfg*	333315	3861
Photographic Film, Paper, Plate and Chemical—*mfg*	325992	3861
Whiteprint (diazotype) reproduction machines and equipment: Photographic and Photocopying Equipment—*mfg*	333315	3861
Photographic Film, Paper, Plate and Chemical—*mfg*	325992	3861
Whiteprinting equipment: Office Equipment—*whlse*	42142	5044
Whiteware, fine type semivitreous tableware and kitchenware: Vitreous China, Fine Earthenware and Other Pottery Product—*mfg*	327112	3263
Whitewashing-contractors: Painting and Wall Covering Contractors—*const*	23521	1721
Whiting: Carbon Black—*mfg*	325182	2816
Inorganic Dye and Pigment—*mfg*	325131	2816
Whiting mining, crushed and broken: Crushed and Broken Limestone and Quarrying—*mining*	212312	1422
Whiting, catching of: Finfish Fishing—*ag*	114111	912
Whole body counters, nuclear: Measuring and Controlling Device, Other—*mfg*	334519	3829
Surgical and Medical Instrument—*mfg*	339112	3829
Wholesale tour operator: Tour Operators—*admin*	56152	4725
Wholesale Trade	**42**	
Wholesale Trade, Durable Goods	**421**	
Wholesale Trade, Nondurable Goods	**422**	
Wick, ashestos: Motor Vehicle Brake System—*mfg*	33634	3292
Nonmetallic Mineral Product, All Other Miscellaneous—*mfg*	327999	3292
Wicker furniture: Household Furniture (except Wood and Metal)—*mfg*	337125	2519
Wicking: Narrow Fabric Mills—*mfg*	313221	2241
Wig, toupee, and wiglet stores: Clothing Accessories Stores—*retail*	44815	5699
Clothing Stores, Other—*retail*	44819	5699
Wignan, cotton: Broadwoven Fabric Mills—*mfg*	31321	2211
Wigs: Nondurable Goods, Other Miscellaneous—*whlse*	42299	5199
Wildlife conservation agencies: Land, Mineral, Wildlife, and Forest Conservation—*pub*	92412	9512
Wildlife management: Hunting and Trapping—*ag*	11421	971
Willemite mining: Lead Ore and Zinc Ore—*mining*	212231	1031
Willow furniture: Household Furniture (except Wood and Metal)—*mfg*	337125	2519
Willow ware, except furniture: Manufacturing, All Other Miscellaneous—*mfg*	339999	2499
Wood Container and Pallet—*mfg*	32192	2499
Wood Product, All Other Miscellaneous—*mfg*	321999	2499
Wilton carpets: Carpet and Rug Mills—*mfg*	31411	2273
Winches: Industrial Machinery and Equipment—*whlse*	42183	5084
Winches, all types: Construction Machinery—*mfg*	33312	3531
Overhead Traveling Crane, Hoist and Monorail System—*mfg*	333923	3531
Railroad Rolling Stock—*mfg*	33651	3531
Wind and water erosion control agencies: Land, Mineral, Wildlife, and Forest Conservation—*pub*	92412	9512
Wind correctors, military: Optical Instrument and Lens—*mfg*	333314	3827
Wind direction indicators: Measuring and Controlling Device, Other—*mfg*	334519	3829
Surgical and Medical Instrument—*mfg*	339112	3829
Wind machines (frost protection equipment): Farm and Garden Machinery and Equipment—*whlse*	42182	5083
Outdoor Power Equipment Stores—*retail*	44421	5083
Wind powered turbine generator sets: Turbine and Turbine Generator Set Unit—*mfg*	333611	3511

Entry	NAICS	SIC
Wind tunnels: Air-Conditioning and Warm Air Heating Equipment and Commercial and Industrial Refrigeration Equipment—*mfg*	333415	3443
Metal Tank (Heavy Gauge)—*mfg*	33242	3443
Plate Work—*mfg*	332313	3443
Power Boiler and Heat Exchanger—*mfg*	33241	3443
Windbreakers: Apparel Accessories and Apparel, Other—*mfg*	315999	2339
Cut and Sew Apparel, All Other—*mfg*	315299	2329
Cut and Sew Apparel, All Other—*mfg*	315299	2339
Men's and Boys' Cut and Sew Apparel Contractors—*mfg*	315211	2329
Men's and Boys' Cut and Sew Other Outerwear—*mfg*	315228	2329
Women's and Girls' Cut and Sew Apparel Contractors—*mfg*	315212	2339
Women's and Girls' Cut and Sew Other Outerwear—*mfg*	315238	2339
Winders (textile machinery): Textile Machinery—*mfg*	333292	3552
Winding yarn–cotton, silk, wool, and man-made fiber continuous filament: Textile and Fabric Finishing (except Broadwoven Fabric) Mills—*mfg*	313312	2282
Yarn Texturing, Throwing and Twisting Mills—*mfg*	313112	2282
Winding yarn–wool, mohair, or similar animal fibers: Textile and Fabric Finishing (except Broadwoven Fabric) Mills—*mfg*	313312	2282
Yarn Texturing, Throwing and Twisting Mills—*mfg*	313112	2282
Windmill heads and towers: Farm Machinery and Equipment—*mfg*	333111	3523
Windmills for generating power: Turbine and Turbine Generator Set Unit—*mfg*	333611	3511
Windmills for pumping water (agricultural machinery): Farm Machinery and Equipment—*mfg*	333111	3523
Window and door (prefabricated) installation-contractors: Carpentry Contractors—*const*	23551	1751
Window backs, store and lunchroom–prefabricated-wood: Architectural Woodwork and Millwork, Custom—*mfg*	337212	2541
Showcase, Partition, Shelving, and Locker—*mfg*	337215	2541
Wood Kitchen Cabinet and Counter Top—*mfg*	33711	2541
Window cleaning preparations: Polish and Other Sanitation Good—*mfg*	325612	2842
Window cleaning service: Janitorial Services—*admin*	56172	7349
Window cutouts and displays: Sign—*mfg*	33995	3993
Window frames and sash, metal: Metal Window and Door—*mfg*	332321	3442
Window frames and sash, plastics: Plastics Pipe and Pipe Fitting—*mfg*	326122	3089
Plastics Product, All Other—*mfg*	326199	3089
Unsupported Plastics Profile Shape—*mfg*	326121	3089
Window frames and sash, wood and covered wood: Millwork (including Flooring), Other—*mfg*	321918	2431
Wood Window and Door—*mfg*	321911	2431
Window frames, all materials: Building Material Dealers, Other—*retail*	44419	5031
Window frames, plastics: Plastics Pipe and Pipe Fitting—*mfg*	326122	3089
Plastics Product, All Other—*mfg*	326199	3089
Unsupported Plastics Profile Shape—*mfg*	326121	3089
Window glass: Building Material Dealers, Other—*retail*	44419	5039
Construction Material, Other—*whlse*	42139	5039
Window glass, clear and colored: Flat Glass—*mfg*	327211	3211
Window screening, plastics: Plastics Pipe and Pipe Fitting—*mfg*	326122	3089
Plastics Product, All Other—*mfg*	326199	3089
Unsupported Plastics Profile Shape—*mfg*	326121	3089
Window screens, metal frame: Metal Window and Door—*mfg*	332321	3442
Window screens, wood: Millwork (including Flooring), Other—*mfg*	321918	2431
Wood Window and Door—*mfg*	321911	2431
Window shade cloth, cotton: Broadwoven Fabric Mills—*mfg*	31321	2211
Window shade cloth, impregnated or coated: Fabric Coating Mills—*mfg*	31332	2295
Window shade installation–contractors: Trade Contractors, All Other Special—*const*	23599	1799
Window shade repair shops: Buildings and Dwellings, Other Services to—*admin*	56179	7699
Personal and Household Goods Repair and Maintenance, Other—*serv*	81149	7699
Window shade rollers and fittings: Blind and Shade—*mfg*	33792	2591
Window shade shops: Home Furnishings Stores, All Other—*retail*	442299	5719
Window Treatment Stores—*retail*	442291	5719
Window shades, except canvas: Blind and Shade—*mfg*	33792	2591
Window sills, cast stone: Concrete Pipe—*mfg*	327332	3272
Concrete Product, Other—*mfg*	32739	3272
Nonmetallic Mineral Product, All Other Miscellaneous—*mfg*	327999	3272
Window tinting, automotive: Automotive Oil Change and Lubrication Shops—*serv*	811191	7549
Automotive Repair and Maintenance, All Other—*serv*	811198	7549
Motor Vehicle Towing—*trans*	48841	7549
Window Treatment Stores	**442291**	**5719**
Window trim, wood and covered wood: Millwork (including Flooring), Other—*mfg*	321918	2431
Wood Window and Door—*mfg*	321911	2431
Window units, wood and covered wood: Millwork (including Flooring), Other—*mfg*	321918	2431
Wood Window and Door—*mfg*	321911	2431
Windows and doors: Building Material Dealers, Other—*retail*	44419	5031
Windows, louver–all metal or metal frame: Metal Window and Door—*mfg*	332321	3442
Windows, louver–plastics: Plastics Pipe and Pipe Fitting—*mfg*	326122	3089
Plastics Product, All Other—*mfg*	326199	3089
Unsupported Plastics Profile Shape—*mfg*	326121	3089
Windows, louver–wood: Millwork (including Flooring), Other—*mfg*	321918	2431
Wood Window and Door—*mfg*	321911	2431
Windows, stained glass–made from purchased glass: Glass Product Made of Purchased Glass—*mfg*	327215	3231
Windows, storm–plastics: Plastics Pipe and Pipe Fitting—*mfg*	326122	3089
Plastics Product, All Other—*mfg*	326199	3089
Unsupported Plastics Profile Shape—*mfg*	326121	3089

ALPHABETICAL INDEX	NAICS	SIC
Windows, storm–wood or metal: Building Material Dealers, Other—*retail*	44419	5211
Home Centers—*retail*	44411	5211
Windrowers (agricultural machinery): Farm Machinery and Equipment—*mfg*	333111	3523
Windshield frames, motor vehicle-m[g: Motor Vehicle Body—*mfg*	336211	3714
Motor Vehicle Parts, All Other—*mfg*	336399	3714
Windshield wiper systems, all types: Motor Vehicle Body—*mfg*	336211	3714
Motor Vehicle Parts, All Other—*mfg*	336399	3714
Windshields, made from purchased glass: Glass Product Made of Purchased Glass—*mfg*	327215	3231
Windshields, plastics: Plastics Pipe and Pipe Fitting—*mfg*	326122	3089
Plastics Product, All Other—*mfg*	326199	3089
Unsupported Plastics Profile Shape—*mfg*	326121	3089
Windsurfing boards and equipment: Sporting and Athletic Goods—*mfg*	33992	3949
Wine and Distilled Alcoholic Beverage Wholesalers	**42282**	**5182**
Wine cellars, bonded–engaged in blending wines: Wineries—*mfg*	31213	2084
Wine coolers (beverages): Wineries—*mfg*	31213	2084
Wine coolers, alcoholic: Wine and Distilled Alcoholic Beverage—*whlse*	42282	5182
Wine, packaged: Beer, Wine and Liquor Stores—*retail*	44531	5921
Winebars: Drinking Places (Alcoholic Beverages)—*accom*	72241	5813
Wineries	**31213**	**2084**
Wines: Wine and Distilled Alcoholic Beverage—*whlse*	42282	5182
Wineries—*mfg*	31213	2084
Wing assemblies and parts, aircraft: Aircraft Part and Auxiliary Equipment, Other—*mfg*	336413	3728
Fluid Power Valve and Hose Fitting—*mfg*	332912	3728
Winterfronts, motor vehicle: Motor Vehicle Body—*mfg*	336211	3714
Motor Vehicle Parts, All Other—*mfg*	336399	3714
Wintergreen oil: Spice and Extract—*mfg*	311942	2899
Wipers, windshield–motor vehicle: Motor Vehicle Body—*mfg*	336211	3714
Motor Vehicle Parts, All Other—*mfg*	336399	3714
Wiping rags, including washing and reconditioning: Recyclable Material—*whlse*	42193	5093
Wiping towel supply service: Industrial Launderers—*serv*	812332	7218
Wire and cables, interior: Building Material Dealers, Other—*retail*	44419	5063
Electrical Apparatus and Equipment, Wiring Supplies and Material—*whlse*	42161	5063
Wire and wire products–except insulated wire, and nails and spikes: Fabricated Wire Product, Other—*mfg*	332618	3496
Wire carts–household, grocery, and industrial-made in wiredrawing plants: Fabricated Wire Product, Other—*mfg*	332618	3315
Steel Wire Drawing—*mfg*	331222	3315
Wire cloth, nonferrous–made in wiredrawing plants: Aluminum Rolling and Drawing, Other—*mfg*	331319	3357
Communication and Energy Wire, Other—*mfg*	335929	3357
Copper Wire (except Mechanical) Drawing—*mfg*	331422	3357
Fiber Optic Cable—*mfg*	335921	3357
Nonferrous Metal (except Copper and Aluminum) Rolling, Drawing and Extruding—*mfg*	331491	3357
Wire cloth, steel–made in wiredrawing plants: Fabricated Wire Product, Other—*mfg*	332618	3315
Steel Wire Drawing—*mfg*	331222	3315
Wire fence, gates, and accessories: Building Material Dealers, Other—*retail*	44419	5039
Construction Material, Other—*whlse*	42139	5039
Wire garment hangers, steel–made in wiredrawing plants: Fabricated Wire Product, Other—*mfg*	332618	3315
Steel Wire Drawing—*mfg*	331222	3315
Wire or cable telegraph: Wired Telecommunications Carriers—*info*	51331	4822
Wire products, ferrous–made in wiredrawing plants: Fabricated Wire Product, Other—*mfg*	332618	3315
Steel Wire Drawing—*mfg*	331222	3315
Wire products, iron and steel–made in steel works or rolling mills: Iron and Steel Mills—*mfg*	331111	3312
Petroleum and Coal Productsa, All Other—*mfg*	324199	3312
Wire rods: Metal Service Centers and Offices—*whlse*	42151	5051
Wire rope centers: Rope, Cordage and Twine Mills—*mfg*	314991	2298
Wire rope or cable, insulated: Building Material Dealers, Other—*retail*	44419	5063
Electrical Apparatus and Equipment, Wiring Supplies and Material—*whlse*	42161	5063
Wire rope or cable, not insulated: Metal Service Centers and Offices—*whlse*	42151	5051
Wire screening: Metal Service Centers and Offices—*whlse*	42151	5051
Wire screening, nonferrous–made in wiredrawing plants: Aluminum Rolling and Drawing, Other—*mfg*	331319	3357
Communication and Energy Wire, Other—*mfg*	335929	3357
Copper Wire (except Mechanical) Drawing—*mfg*	331422	3357
Fiber Optic Cable—*mfg*	335921	3357
Nonferrous Metal (except Copper and Aluminum) Rolling, Drawing and Extruding—*mfg*	331491	3357
Wire Spring Manufacturing	**332612**	**3495**
Wire telephone: Telecommunications Resellers—*info*	51333	4813
Wired Telecommunications Carriers—*info*	51331	4813
Wire winding of purchased wire: Fabricated Wire Product, Other—*mfg*	332618	3496
Wire, aluminum–made in rolling mills: Aluminum Rolling and Drawing, Other—*mfg*	331319	3355
Wire, concrete reinforcing–made from purchased wire: Fabricated Wire Product, Other—*mfg*	332618	3496

Description	NAICS	SIC
Wire, copper and copper alloy–made in brass mills: Copper Rolling, Drawing and Extruding—*mfg*	331421	3351
Wire, ferrous–made in wiredrawing plants: Fabricated Wire Product, Other—*mfg*	332618	3315
Steel Wire Drawing—*mfg*	331222	3315
Wire, flat–cold-rolled strip-not made in hot-rolling mills: Cold-Rolled Steel Shape—*mfg*	331221	3316
Wire, insulated: Building Material Dealers, Other—*retail*	44419	5063
Electrical Apparatus and Equipment, Wiring Supplies and Material—*whlse*	42161	5063
Wire, nonferrous except copper and aluminum–made in rolling mills: Nonferrous Metal (except Copper and Aluminum) Rolling, Drawing and Extruding—*mfg*	331491	3356
Wire, nonferrous–bare, insulated, or armored: Aluminum Rolling and Drawing, Other—*mfg*	331319	3357
Communication and Energy Wire, Other—*mfg*	335929	3357
Copper Wire (except Mechanical) Drawing—*mfg*	331422	3357
Fiber Optic Cable—*mfg*	335921	3357
Nonferrous Metal (except Copper and Aluminum) Rolling, Drawing and Extruding—*mfg*	331491	3357
Wire, not insulated: Metal Service Centers and Offices—*whlse*	42151	5051
Wire, steel–insulated or armored: Fabricated Wire Product, Other—*mfg*	332618	3315
Steel Wire Drawing—*mfg*	331222	3315
Wired Telecommunications Carriers	**51331**	**4822**
Wiredrawing and fabricating machinery and equipment, except dies: Other Metalworking Machinery, Other—*mfg*	333518	3549
Wiredrawing and straightening dies: Die and Tool, Die Set, Jig and Fixture, Special—*mfg*	333514	3544
Industrial Mold—*mfg*	333511	3544
Wireless Telecommunications Carriers (except Satellite)	**51332**	
Wiring boards: Printed Circuit Board—*mfg*	334412	3672
Wiring Device Manufacturing	**33593**	
Wiring devices: Building Material Dealers, Other—*retail*	44419	5063
Electrical Apparatus and Equipment, Wiring Supplies and Material—*whlse*	42161	5063
Wiring harness sets motor vehicles–except ignition: Motor Vehicle Electrical and Electronic Equipment, Other—*mfg*	336322	3714
Motor Vehicle Parts, All Other—*mfg*	336399	3714
Wiring materials, interior: Building Material Dealers, Other—*retail*	44419	5063
Electrical Apparatus and Equipment, Wiring Supplies and Material—*whlse*	42161	5063
Wiring supplies: Building Material Dealers, Other—*retail*	44419	5063
Electrical Apparatus and Equipment, Wiring Supplies and Material—*whlse*	42161	5063
Wolframite mining: Copper Ore and Nickel Ore—*mining*	212234	1061
Metal Ore, All Other—*mining*	212299	1061
Women's bureaus: Social, Human Resource and Income Maintenance Programs, Administration of—*pub*	92313	9441
Women's Clothing Stores	**44812**	**5621**
Women's Footwear (except Athletic) Manufacturing	**316214**	**3144**
Women's Handbag and Purse Manufacturing	**316992**	**3171**
Women's, Children's, and Infants' and Accessories Wholesalers	**42233**	**5137**
Wood alcohol, natural: Gum and Wood Chemical—*mfg*	325191	2861
Wood carvings: Nondurable Goods, Other Miscellaneous—*whlse*	42299	5199
Wood chips: Durable Goods, Other Miscellaneous—*whlse*	42199	5099
Wood chips produced at mill: Cut Stock, Resawing Lumber, and Planing—*mfg*	321912	2421
Millwork (including Flooring), Other—*mfg*	321918	2421
Sawmills—*mfg*	321113	2421
Wood Product, All Other Miscellaneous—*mfg*	321999	2421
Wood chips, produced in the field: Logging—*ag*	11331	2411
Wood Container and Pallet Manufacturing	**32192**	**2448**
Wood creosote: Gum and Wood Chemical—*mfg*	325191	2861
Wood dealers, fuel: Fuel Dealers, Other—*retail*	454319	5989
Wood distillates: Gum and Wood Chemical—*mfg*	325191	2861
Wood drying kilns: Industrial Machinery, All Other—*mfg*	333298	3559
Machinery, Other Commercial and Service Industry—*mfg*	333319	3559
Wood fence–pickets, poling, rails-treated: Wood Preservation—*mfg*	321114	2491
Wood fillers and sealers: Paint and Coating—*mfg*	32551	2851
Wood flooring–contractors: Floor Laying and Other Floor Contractors—*const*	23552	1752
Wood flour: Manufacturing, All Other Miscellaneous—*mfg*	339999	2499
Wood Container and Pallet—*mfg*	32192	2499
Wood Product, All Other Miscellaneous—*mfg*	321999	2499
Wood heel blocks, for sale as such: Fastener, Button, Needle and Pin—*mfg*	339993	3131
Leather Good, All Other—*mfg*	316999	3131
Wood Product, All Other Miscellaneous—*mfg*	321999	3131
Wood heels, finished (shoe findings): Fastener, Button, Needle and Pin—*mfg*	339993	3131
Leather Good, All Other—*mfg*	316999	3131
Wood Product, All Other Miscellaneous—*mfg*	321999	3131
Wood Kitchen Cabinet and Counter Top Manufacturing	**33711**	**2541**
Wood Office Furniture Manufacturing	**337211**	**2521**
Wood oils, product of hardwood distillation: Gum and Wood Chemical—*mfg*	325191	2861
Wood Preservation	**321114**	**2491**
Wood Product Manufacturing	**321**	
Wood Product Manufacturing, All Other	**32199**	
Wood Product Manufacturing, All Other Miscellaneous	**321999**	**2421**
Wood Product Manufacturing, Other	**3219**	
Wood products, creosoted: Wood Preservation—*mfg*	321114	2491
Wood pulp: Paper (except Newsprint) Mills—*mfg*	322121	2611
Paperboard Mills—*mfg*	32213	2611
Pulp Mills—*mfg*	32211	2611
Wood screws, metal: Bolt, Nut, Screw, Rivet and Washer—*mfg*	332722	3452
Wood siding: Building Material Dealers, Other—*re.ail*	44419	5031

ALPHABETICAL INDEX	NAICS	SIC
Wood stains: Paint and Coating—*mfg*	32551	2851
Wood Television, Radio, and Sewing Machine Cabinet Manufacturing	**337129**	**2517**
Wood Window and Door Manufacturing	**321911**	**2431**
Wood wool (excelsior): Cut Stock, Resawing Lumber, and Planing—*mfg*	321912	2429
Sawmills—*mfg*	321113	2429
Wood Product, All Other Miscellaneous—*mfg*	321999	2429
Wood, except furniture–turned and carved: Manufacturing, All Other Miscellaneous—*mfg*	339999	2499
Wood Container and Pallet—*mfg*	32192	2499
Wood Product, All Other Miscellaneous—*mfg*	321999	2499
Wood, plastic: Basic Organic Chemical, All Other—*mfg*	325199	2899
Chemical Product, All Other Miscellaneous—*mfg*	325998	2899
Woodburning stoves: Home Furnishings Stores, All Other—*retail*	442299	5719
Window Treatment Stores—*retail*	442291	5719
Woodenware, kitchen and household: Manufacturing, All Other Miscellaneous—*mfg*	339999	2499
Wood Container and Pallet—*mfg*	32192	2499
Wood Product, All Other Miscellaneous—*mfg*	321999	2499
Woodwind and brass wind musical instrument: Musical Instrument—*mfg*	339992	3931
Woodwork, interior and ornamental–e.g., windows, doors, sash, and mantels: Millwork (including Flooring), Other—*mfg*	321918	2431
Wood Window and Door—*mfg*	321911	2431
Woodworking machinery: Industrial Machinery and Equipment—*whlse*	42183	5084
Woodworking machines: Sawmill and Woodworking Machinery—*mfg*	33321	3553
Wool and mohair warehousing: Farm Product Warehousing and Storage Facilities—*trans*	49313	4221
Wool and worsted finishing machines: Textile Machinery—*mfg*	333292	3552
Wool broad woven fabrics: Broadwoven Fabric Finishing Mills—*mfg*	313311	2231
Broadwoven Fabric Mills—*mfg*	31321	2231
Textile and Fabric Finishing (except Broadwoven Fabric) Mills—*mfg*	313312	2231
Wool felts, pressed or needle loom: Broadwoven Fabric Mills—*mfg*	31321	2299
Narrow Fabric Mills—*mfg*	313221	2299
Nonwoven Fabric Mills—*mfg*	31323	2299
Textile and Fabric Finishing (except Broadwoven Fabric) Mills—*mfg*	313312	2299
Textile Product Mills, All Other Miscellaneous—*mfg*	314999	2299
Thread Mills—*mfg*	313113	2299
Yarn Spinning Mills—*mfg*	313111	2299
Wool felts, woven: Broadwoven Fabric Finishing Mills—*mfg*	313311	2231
Broadwoven Fabric Mills—*mfg*	31321	2231
Textile and Fabric Finishing (except Broadwoven Fabric) Mills—*mfg*	313312	2231
Wool grease, mohair, and similar fibers: Broadwoven Fabric Mills—*mfg*	31321	2299
Narrow Fabric Mills—*mfg*	313221	2299
Nonwoven Fabric Mills—*mfg*	31323	2299
Textile and Fabric Finishing (except Broadwoven Fabric) Mills—*mfg*	313312	2299
Textile Product Mills, All Other Miscellaneous—*mfg*	314999	2299
Thread Mills—*mfg*	313113	2299
Yarn Spinning Mills—*mfg*	313111	2299
Wool narrow woven goods: Narrow Fabric Mills—*mfg*	313221	2241
Wool production: Goat Farming—*ag*	11242	214
Sheep Farming—*ag*	11241	214
Wool scouring and carbonizing: Broadwoven Fabric Mills—*mfg*	31321	2299
Narrow Fabric Mills—*mfg*	313221	2299
Nonwoven Fabric Mills—*mfg*	31323	2299
Textile and Fabric Finishing (except Broadwoven Fabric) Mills—*mfg*	313312	2299
Textile Product Mills, All Other Miscellaneous—*mfg*	314999	2299
Thread Mills—*mfg*	313113	2299
Yarn Spinning Mills—*mfg*	313111	2299
Wool shoddy: Broadwoven Fabric Mills—*mfg*	31321	2299
Narrow Fabric Mills—*mfg*	313221	2299
Nonwoven Fabric Mills—*mfg*	31323	2299
Textile and Fabric Finishing (except Broadwoven Fabric) Mills—*mfg*	313312	2299
Textile Product Mills, All Other Miscellaneous—*mfg*	314999	2299
Thread Mills—*mfg*	313113	2299
Yarn Spinning Mills—*mfg*	313111	2299
Wool tops and noils: Farm Product Raw Material, Other—*whlse*	42259	5159
Wool tops, combing and converting: Broadwoven Fabric Mills—*mfg*	31321	2299
Narrow Fabric Mills—*mfg*	313221	2299
Nonwoven Fabric Mills—*mfg*	31323	2299
Textile and Fabric Finishing (except Broadwoven Fabric) Mills—*mfg*	313312	2299
Textile Product Mills, All Other Miscellaneous—*mfg*	314999	2299
Thread Mills—*mfg*	313113	2299
Yarn Spinning Mills—*mfg*	313111	2299
Wool waste processing: Broadwoven Fabric Mills—*mfg*	31321	2299
Narrow Fabric Mills—*mfg*	313221	2299
Nonwoven Fabric Mills—*mfg*	31323	2299
Textile and Fabric Finishing (except Broadwoven Fabric) Mills—*mfg*	313312	2299
Textile Product Mills, All Other Miscellaneous—*mfg*	314999	2299
Thread Mills—*mfg*	313113	2299
Yarn Spinning Mills—*mfg*	313111	2299

ALPHABETICAL INDEX	NAICS	SIC
Printing, Other Commercial—*mfg*	323119	2759
Quick Printing—*mfg*	323114	2759
Wrappers–gravure printing: Gravure Printing, Commercial—*mfg*	323111	2754
Wrapping machines: Packaging Machinery—*mfg*	333993	3565
Wrapping paper: Newsprint Mills—*mfg*	322122	2621
Paper (except Newsprint) Mills—*mfg*	322121	2621
Wrapping paper and products: Industrial and Personal Service Paper—*whlse*	42213	5113
Wrapping paper, coated or laminated: Coated and Laminated Packaging Paper and Plastics Film—*mfg*	322221	2671
Unsupported Plastics Packaging Film and Sheet—*mfg*	326112	2671
Wrecker service (towing), automotive: Automotive Oil Change and Lubrication Shops—*serv*	811191	7549
Automotive Repair and Maintenance, All Other—*serv*	811198	7549
Motor Vehicle Towing—*trans*	48841	7549
Wrecking and Demolition Contractors	**23594**	**1795**
Wrecking of buildings or other structures, except marine–contractors: Wrecking and Demolition Contractors—*const*	23594	1795
Wrenches (handtools): Hand and Edge Tool—*mfg*	332212	3423
Wringers, domestic laundry: Household Laundry Equipment—*mfg*	335224	3633
Wringers, mop: Machinery, Other Commercial and Service Industry—*mfg*	333319	3589
Wristlets: Outerwear Knitting Mills—*mfg*	315191	2253
Writers: Independent Artists, Writers, and Performers—*arts*	71151	8999
Writing ink: Office Supplies and Stationery Stores—*retail*	45321	5112
Stationary and Office Supplies—*whlse*	42212	5112
Writing ink and fluids: Basic Organic Chemical, All Other—*mfg*	325199	2899
Chemical Product, All Other Miscellaneous—*mfg*	325998	2899
Writing paper: Newsprint Mills—*mfg*	322122	2621
Paper (except Newsprint) Mills—*mfg*	322121	2621
Writing paper and envelopes, boxed sets: Stationery, Tablet, and Related Product—*mfg*	322233	2678
Writing supplies: Office Supplies and Stationery Stores—*retail*	45321	5943
Writing tablets: Stationery, Tablet, and Related Product—*mfg*	322233	2678
Wrought pipe and tubes–welded, lockjoint, and heavy riveted: Iron and Steel Pipes and Tubes from Purchased Steel—*mfg*	33121	3317
Wrought pipe and tubing, made in steelworks or rolling mills: Iron and Steel Mills—*mfg*	331111	3312
Petroleum and Coal Productsa, All Other—*mfg*	324199	3312
Wulfenite mining: Copper Ore and Nickel Ore—*mining*	212234	1061
Metal Ore, All Other—*mining*	212299	1061
Wurizilite mining: Crushed and Broken Stone and Quarrying, Other—*mining*	212319	1499
Non-Metallic Mineral, All Other—*mining*	212399	1499
X-ray apparatus and tubes–medical, industrial, research, and control: Irradiation Apparatus—*mfg*	334517	3844
X-ray film: Photographic and Photocopying Equipment—*mfg*	333315	3861

ALPHABETICAL INDEX	NAICS	SIC
Photographic Film, Paper, Plate and Chemical—*mfg*	325992	3861
X-ray generators: Irradiation Apparatus—*mfg*	334517	3844
X-ray inspection service, industrial: Testing Laboratories—*prof*	54138	8734
Veterinary Services—*prof*	54194	8734
X-ray laboratories, including dental (not manufacturing): Diagnostic Imaging Centers—*hlth*	621512	8071
Medical Laboratories—*hlth*	621511	8071
X-ray machines and parts, medical: Health and Personal Care Stores, All Other—*retail*	446199	5047
Medical, Dental and Hospital Equipment and Supplies—*whlse*	42145	5047
X-ray plates, sensitized: Photographic and Photocopying Equipment—*mfg*	333315	3861
Photographic Film, Paper, Plate and Chemical—*mfg*	325992	3861
X-Y recorders (plotters), except computer peripheral equipment: Electronic Coil, Transformer, and Other Inductor—*mfg*	334416	3825
Instrument for Measuring and Testing Electricity and Electrical Signals—*mfg*	334515	3825
Xanthone (formulated): Pesticide and Other Agricultural Chemical—*mfg*	32532	2879
Xylene, made in chemical plants: Cyclic Crude and Intermediate—*mfg*	325192	2865
Petrochemical—*mfg*	32511	2865
Xylophones and parts: Musical Instrument—*mfg*	339992	3931
Y bends and branches, pipe–metal: Fabricated Metal Product, All Other Miscellaneous—*mfg*	332999	3494
Other Metal Valve and Pipe Fitting, Other—*mfg*	332919	3494
Yacht basins, operation of: Marinas—*arts*	71393	4493
Yacht clubs, membership: Fitness and Recreational Sports Centers—*arts*	71394	7997
Golf Courses and Country Clubs—*arts*	71391	7997
Yam farms: Crop Farming, All Other Miscellaneous—*ag*	111998	139
Hay Farming—*ag*	11194	139
Peanut Farming—*ag*	111992	139
Vegetable (except Potato) and Melon Farming, Other—*ag*	111219	139
Yard goods: Broadwoven Fabric Finishing Mills—*mfg*	313311	5131
Piece Goods, Notions and Other Dry Goods—*whlse*	42231	5131
Textile and Fabric Finishing (except Broadwoven Fabric) Mills—*mfg*	313312	5131
Yard goods stores: Sewing, Needlework and Piece Goods Stores—*retail*	45113	5949
Yardsticks, metal: Hand and Edge Tool—*mfg*	332212	3423
Yardsticks, wood: Manufacturing, All Other Miscellaneous—*mfg*	339999	2499
Wood Container and Pallet—*mfg*	32192	2499
Wood Product, All Other Miscellaneous—*mfg*	321999	2499
Yarn bleaching, dyeing, and finishing–wool, mohair, and similar animal fibers: Broadwoven Fabric Finishing Mills—*mfg*	313311	2231
Broadwoven Fabric Mills—*mfg*	31321	2231

Description	NAICS	SIC
Textile and Fabric Finishing (except Broadwoven Fabric) Mills—*mfg*	313312	2231
Yarn bleaching, dyeing, and other finishing–except wool: Broadwoven Fabric Finishing Mills—*mfg*	313311	2269
Textile and Fabric Finishing (except Broadwoven Fabric) Mills—*mfg*	313312	2269
Yarn shops (knitting): Sewing, Needlework and Piece Goods Stores—*retail*	45113	5949
Yarn Spinning Mills	**313111**	**2299**
Yarn spinning–cotton, silk, and manmade staple: Yarn Spinning Mills—*mfg*	313111	2281
Yarn Texturing, Throwing and Twisting Mills	**313112**	**2282**
Yarn texturizing machines: Textile Machinery—*mfg*	333292	3552
Yarn, animal fiber–twisting, winding, and spooling: Textile and Fabric Finishing (except Broadwoven Fabric) Mills—*mfg*	313312	2282
Yarn Texturing, Throwing and Twisting Mills—*mfg*	313112	2282
Yarn, asbestos: Motor Vehicle Brake System—*mfg*	33634	3292
Nonmetallic Mineral Product, All Other Miscellaneous—*mfg*	327999	3292
Yarn, carpet and rug–animal fiber-spinning, twisting and spooling: Yarn Spinning Mills—*mfg*	313111	2281
Yarn, cellulosic–made in chemical plants: Cellulosic Organic Fiber—*mfg*	325221	2823
Yarn, dyed fabrics, cotton: Broadwoven Fabric Mills—*mfg*	31321	2211
Yarn, elastic–fabric covered: Narrow Fabric Mills—*mfg*	313221	2241
Yarn, fiberglass–made in glass plants: Pressed and Blown Glass and Glassware, Other—*mfg*	327212	3229
Yarn, specialty and novelty: Broadwoven Fabric Mills—*mfg*	31321	2299
Narrow Fabric Mills—*mfg*	313221	2299
Nonwoven Fabric Mills—*mfg*	31323	2299
Textile and Fabric Finishing (except Broadwoven Fabric) Mills—*mfg*	313312	2299
Textile Product Mills, All Other Miscellaneous—*mfg*	314999	2299
Thread Mills—*mfg*	313113	2299
Yarn Spinning Mills—*mfg*	313111	2299
Yarn, spun–cotton, silk, manmade fiber, wool, and animal fiber: Yarn Spinning Mills—*mfg*	313111	2281
Yarn, viscose: Cellulosic Organic Fiber—*mfg*	325221	2823
Yarn–cotton, silk, wool, and manmade staple: Yarn Spinning Mills—*mfg*	313111	2281
Yarn–flax, jute, hemp, and ramie: Broadwoven Fabric Mills—*mfg*	31321	2299
Narrow Fabric Mills—*mfg*	313221	2299
Nonwoven Fabric Mills—*mfg*	31323	2299
Textile and Fabric Finishing (except Broadwoven Fabric) Mills—*mfg*	313312	2299
Textile Product Mills, All Other Miscellaneous—*mfg*	314999	2299
Thread Mills—*mfg*	313113	2299
Yarn Spinning Mills—*mfg*	313111	2299
Yarn–metallic, ceramic, or paper fibers: Broadwoven Fabric Mills—*mfg*	31321	2299
Narrow Fabric Mills—*mfg*	313221	2299
Nonwoven Fabric Mills—*mfg*	31323	2299
Textile and Fabric Finishing (except Broadwoven Fabric) Mills—*mfg*	313312	2299
Textile Product Mills, All Other Miscellaneous—*mfg*	314999	2299
Thread Mills—*mfg*	313113	2299
Yarn Spinning Mills—*mfg*	313111	2299
Yarns: Nondurable Goods, Other Miscellaneous—*whlse*	42299	5199
Yarns, fabric covered rubber: Narrow Fabric Mills—*mfg*	313221	2241
Yarns, plastics coated–made from purchased yarns: Fabric Coating Mills—*mfg*	31332	2295
Yearbooks–publishing and printing, or publishing only: Database and Directory Publishers—*info*	51114	2741
Music Publishers—*info*	51223	2741
Publishers, All Other—*info*	511199	2741
Yeast: Food, All Other Miscellaneous—*mfg*	311999	2099
Grocery and Related Products, Other—*whlse*	42249	5149
Yogurt: Dairy Product (except Dried or Canned)—*whlse*	42243	5143
Yogurt mix: Dry, Condensed, and Evaporated Dairy Product—*mfg*	311514	2023
Yogurt, except frozen: Fluid Milk—*mfg*	311511	2026
Yogurt, frozen: Ice Cream and Frozen Dessert—*mfg*	31152	2024
Youth associations, except hotel units: Child and Youth Services—*hlth*	62411	8641
Youth centers: Child and Youth Services—*hlth*	62411	8322
Community Food Services—*hlth*	62421	8322
Community Housing Services, Other—*hlth*	624229	8322
Emergency and Other Relief Services—*hlth*	62423	8322
Individual and Family Services, Other—*hlth*	62419	8322
Parole Offices and Probation Offices—*pub*	92215	8322
Services for the Elderly and Persons with Disabilities—*hlth*	62412	8322
Temporary Shelters—*hlth*	624221	8322
Youth self-help organizations: Child and Youth Services—*hlth*	62411	8322
Community Food Services—*hlth*	62421	8322
Community Housing Services, Other—*hlth*	624229	8322
Emergency and Other Relief Services—*hlth*	62423	8322
Individual and Family Services, Other—*hlth*	62419	8322
Parole Offices and Probation Offices—*pub*	92215	8322
Services for the Elderly and Persons with Disabilities—*hlth*	62412	8322
Temporary Shelters—*hlth*	624221	8322
Zein fibers: Noncellulosic Organic Fiber—*mfg*	325222	2824
Zener diodes: Semiconductor and Related Device—*mfg*	334413	3674
Zinc: Metal Service Centers and Offices—*whlse*	42151	5051
Zinc and zinc alloy bars, plates, pipe, rods, sheets, tubing, and wire: Nonferrous Metal (except Copper and Aluminum) Rolling, Drawing and Extruding—*mfg*	331491	3356
Zinc castings, except die-castings: Nonferrous Foundries, Other—*mfg*	331528	3369
Zinc chloride: Basic Inorganic Chemical, All Other—*mfg*	325188	2819
Chemical Product, All Other Miscellaneous—*mfg*	325998	2819

ALPHABETICAL INDEX	NAICS	SIC
Zinc die-castings: Nonferrous (except Aluminum) Die-Castings—*mfg*	331522	3364
Zinc dust, primary: Primary Smelting and Refining of Nonferrous Metal (except Copper and Aluminum)—*mfg*	331419	3339
Zinc dust, reclaimed: Secondary Smelting and Alloying of Aluminum—*mfg*	331314	3341
Secondary Smelting, Refining, and Alloying of Nonferrous Metal (except Copper and Aluminum)—*mfg*	331492	3341
Zinc foil, not made in rolling mills: Fabricated Metal Product, All Other Miscellaneous—*mfg*	332999	3497
Laminated Aluminum Foil for Flexible Packaging Uses—*mfg*	322225	3497
Zinc ointment: Pharmaceutical Preparation—*mfg*	325412	2834
Zinc ore: Coal and Other Mineral and Ore—*whlse*	42152	5052
Zinc ore mining: Lead Ore and Zinc Ore—*mining*	212231	1031
Zinc oxide in oil, paint: Paint and Coating—*mfg*	32551	2851
Zinc oxide pigments: Carbon Black—*mfg*	325182	2816
Inorganic Dye and Pigment—*mfg*	325131	2816
Zinc pigments–zinc yellow and zinc sulfide: Carbon Black—*mfg*	325182	2816
Inorganic Dye and Pigment—*mfg*	325131	2816
Zinc rolling, drawing, and extruding: Nonferrous Metal (except Copper and Aluminum) Rolling, Drawing and Extruding—*mfg*	331491	3356
Zinc slabs, ingots, and refinery shapes–primary: Primary Smelting and Refining of Nonferrous Metal (except Copper and Aluminum)—*mfg*	331419	3339
Zinc smelting and refining, secondary: Secondary Smelting and Alloying of Aluminum—*mfg*	331314	3341
Secondary Smelting, Refining, and Alloying of Nonferrous Metal (except Copper and Aluminum)—*mfg*	331492	3341
Zinc-blende (sphalerite) mining: Lead Ore and Zinc Ore—*mining*	212231	1031
Zincite mining: Lead Ore and Zinc Ore—*mining*	212231	1031
Zipper making machinery: Industrial Machinery, All Other—*mfg*	333298	3559
Machinery, Other Commercial and Service Industry—*mfg*	333319	3559
Rubber and Plastics Industry Machinery—*mfg*	33322	3559
Zipper tape: Narrow Fabric Mills—*mfg*	313221	2241
Zippers: Broadwoven Fabric Finishing Mills—*mfg*	313311	5131
Piece Goods, Notions and Other Dry Goods—*whlse*	42231	5131
Textile and Fabric Finishing (except Broadwoven Fabric) Mills—*mfg*	313312	5131
Zippers (slide fasteners): Fastener, Button, Needle and Pin—*mfg*	339993	3965
Zirconium and zirconium alloy bars, rods, billets, sheets, strip, and tubing: Nonferrous Metal (except Copper and Aluminum) Rolling, Drawing and Extruding—*mfg*	331491	3356
Zirconium metal sponge and granules: Primary Smelting and Refining of Nonferrous Metal (except Copper and Aluminum)—*mfg*	331419	3339
Zirconium ore mining: Metal Ore, All Other—*mining*	212299	1099
Zithers and parts: Musical Instrument—*mfg*	339992	3931
Zoning boards and commissions: Urban Planning and Community and Rural Development, Administration of—*pub*	92512	9532
Zoological gardens: Nature Parks and Other Similar Institutions—*arts*	71219	8422
Zoos and Botanical Gardens—*arts*	71213	8422
Zoos and Botanical Gardens	**71213**	**8422**
Zwieback: Bakeries, Commercial—*mfg*	311812	2052
Cookie and Cracker—*mfg*	311821	2052
Snack Food, Other—*mfg*	311919	2052

NOTES

NOTES

NOTES

Table 4. Alphabetical Listing of 1987 SIC

Appendix C

Glossary of Abbreviations

admin .... administration
& .... and
etc .... et cetera (and so forth)
exc. or ex .... except
Intl .... International
inst .... institutions
mach .... machinery
misc .... miscellaneous
mfg .... manufacturing
mfpm .... made from purchased materials or materials transferred from another establishment
mitse .... made in the same establishment as the basic materials
nec .... not elsewhere classified
trans .... transportation

Alphabetic Index

A

2282 Acrylic and modacrylic filament yarn: throwing, winding, or spooling—*mfg*
2221 Acrylic broadwoven fabrics—*mfg*
2824 Acrylic fibers—*mfg*
2821 Acrylic resins—*mfg*
2822 Acrylic rubbers—*mfg*
2281 Acrylic yarn, made from purchased staple: spun—*mfg*
2869 Acrylonitrile—*mfg*
2824 Acrylonitrile fibers—*mfg*
2821 Acrylonitrile-butadiene-styrene resins—*mfg*
3829 Actinometers, meteorological—*mfg*
2819 Activated carbon and charcoal—*mfg*
8322 Activity centers, elderly or handicapped
7929 Actors
7929 Actresses
8999 Actuaries, consulting
3593 Actuators, fluid power: hydraulic and pneumatic—*mfg*
8049 Acupuncturists, except M.D.: offices of
3728 Adapter assemblies, hydromatic propeller—*mfg*
3537 Adapters for multiweapon rack loading on aircraft—*mfg*
3483 Adapters, bombcluster—*mfg*
2679 Adding machine rolls, paper—mfpm—*mfg*
3578 Adding machines—*mfg*
5044 Adding machines—wholesale
3313 Additive alloys, except copper—*mfg*
3579 Address labeling machines—*mfg*
7331 Address list compilers
3579 Addressing machines, plates and plate embossers—*mfg*
5044 Addressing machines—wholesale
7331 Addressing service
3842 Adhesive tape and plasters, medicated or nonmedicated—*mfg*
2891 Adhesives—*mfg*
2891 Adhesives, plastics—*mfg*
2869 Adipic acid—*mfg*
2869 Adipic acid esters—*mfg*
2869 Adiponitrile—*mfg*
2822 Adiprene—*mfg*
7322 Adjustment bureaus, except insurance adjustment agencies
6411 Adjustment services, insurance
1542 Administration building construction—general contractors
8742 Administrative management consultants
8741 Administrative management services
6733 Administrators of private estates (nonoperating)
**** Administrators of private estates (operating)—code to principal activity
3259 Adobe brick—*mfg*
8322 Adoption services
2833 Adrenal derivatives: bulk, uncompounded—*mfg*
2834 Adrenal pharmaceutical preparations—*mfg*
8322 Adult day care centers
2791 Advertisement typesetting—*mfg*
7311 Advertising agencies
3555 Advertising and newspaper mats—*mfg*
7311 Advertising consultants (agencies)
8999 Advertising copy, writers of
3999 Advertising curtains—*mfg*
3993 Advertising displays, except printed—*mfg*
2752 Advertising posters, lithographed—*mfg*
7312 Advertising service, outdoor
3993 Advertising specialties—mfpm—*mfg*
5199 Advertising specialties—wholesale
7319 Advertising, aerial
7312 Advertising, billboard
7331 Advertising, direct mail
9111 Advisory commissions, executive
9121 Advisory commissions, legislative
8399 Advocacy groups
3423 Adzes—*mfg*
3565 Aerating machines, for beverages—*mfg*
7319 Aerial advertising
3861 Aerial cameras—*mfg*
0721 Aerial dusting and spraying
1382 Aerial geophysical exploration, oil and gas field: on a contract basis
7335 Aerial photographic service, except mapmaking
7999 Aerial tramways, amusement or scenic
4119 Aerial tramways, except amusement and scenic
3531 Aerial work platforms, hydraulic or electric truck or carrier mounted—*mfg*
7991 Aerobic dance and exercise classes
5088 Aeronautical equipment and supplies—wholesale
3499 Aerosol valves, metal—*mfg*
3443 Aftercooler shells—*mfg*
3443 Aftercoolers, steam jet—*mfg*
2836 Agar culture media, except in vitro and in vivo—*mfg*
2833 Agar-agar (ground)—*mfg*
1499 Agate mining
6081 Agencies of foreign banks
7389 Agents and brokers for authors and nonperforming artists
6211 Agents for mutual funds
7922 Agents or managers for entertainers
6163 Agents, farm or business loan
6531 Agents, real estate
7212 Agents, retail: for laundries and drycleaners

7629 Aircraft electrical equipment repair, except radio
3537 Aircraft engine cradles—*mfg*
3724 Aircraft engines and engine parts, internal combustion and jet propulsion—*mfg*
5088 Aircraft engines and engine parts—wholesale
5088 Aircraft equipment and supplies—wholesale
3812 Aircraft flight instruments—*mfg*
2273 Aircraft floor coverings, except rubber or plastics—*mfg*
3462 Aircraft forgings, ferrous: not made in rolling mills—*mfg*
3463 Aircraft forgings, nonferrous: not made in hot-rolling mills—*mfg*
5172 Aircraft fueling services—wholesale
3429 Aircraft hardware—*mfg*
9621 Aircraft inspection—government
3647 Aircraft lighting fixtures—*mfg*
3537 Aircraft loading hoists—*mfg*
**** Aircraft modification centers—classify according to principal activity
3728 Aircraft power transmission equipment—*mfg*
3728 Aircraft propeller parts—*mfg*
3728 Aircraft propellers, variable and fixed pitch—*mfg*
7622 Aircraft radio equipment repair
2531 Aircraft seats—*mfg*
4581 Aircraft servicing and repairing, except on a factory basis
4581 Aircraft storage at airports
4581 Aircraft upholstery repair
3564 Aircurtains (blower)—*mfg*
3724 Airfoils, aircraft engine—*mfg*
3728 Airframe assemblies, except for guided missiles—*mfg*
3769 Airframe assemblies, for guided missiles—*mfg*
3812 Airframe equipment instruments—*mfg*
4581 Airfreight handling at airports
4729 Airline ticket offices, not operated by transportation companies
3443 Airlocks—*mfg*
3728 Airplane brake expanders—*mfg*
2211 Airplane cloth, cotton—*mfg*
3999 Airplane models, except toy and hobby models—*mfg*
3944 Airplane models, toy and hobby—*mfg*
7359 Airplane rental and leasing
3721 Airplanes, fixed or rotary wing—*mfg*
4581 Airplanes, janitorial services on
3944 Airplanes, toy—*mfg*
4581 Airport hangar rental
6519 Airport leasing, if not operating airport
4581 Airport leasing, if operating airport
3612 Airport lighting transformers—*mfg*
4111 Airport limousine scheduled service
1611 Airport runway construction—general contractors
4581 Airport terminal services
4111 Airport transportation service, local: road or rail
4581 Airports
3721 Airships—*mfg*
3812 Airspeed instrumentation (aeronautical instruments)—*mfg*
1499 Alabaster mining
5063 Alarm signal systems—wholesale
2782 Albums—*mfg*
5112 Albums (photo) and scrapbooks—wholesale
2085 Alcohol for medicinal and beverage purposes, ethyl or grain—*mfg*
2821 Alcohol resins, polyvinyl—*mfg*
8093 Alcohol treatment, outpatient clinics
2869 Alcohol, aromatic—*mfg*
2869 Alcohol, fatty: powdered—*mfg*
5169 Alcohol, industrial—wholesale
2861 Alcohol, methyl: natural—*mfg*
2869 Alcohol, methyl: synthetic (methanol)—*mfg*
2861 Alcohol, wood: natural (methanol)—*mfg*
9651 Alcoholic beverage control boards—government
8322 Alcoholism counseling, nonresidential: except medical treatment
8361 Alcoholism rehabilitation centers, residential: with health care incidental
8069 Alcoholism rehabilitation hospitals
2869 Alcohols, industrial: denatured (nonbeverage)—*mfg*
2869 Alcohols, polyhydric—*mfg*
2082 Ale—*mfg*
5181 Ale—wholesale
0139 Alfalfa farms
2048 Alfalfa, cubed—*mfg*
2048 Alfalfa, prepared as feed for animals—*mfg*
5191 Alfalfa—wholesale
2869 Algin products—*mfg*
3829 Alidades, surveying—*mfg*
3728 Alighting assemblies (landing gear), aircraft—*mfg*
2819 Alkali metals—*mfg*
2812 Alkalies, not produced at mines—*mfg*
5169 Alkalies—wholesale
3691 Alkaline cell storage batteries—*mfg*
2833 Alkaloids and salts—*mfg*
2821 Alkyd resins—*mfg*
2865 Alkylated diphenylamines, mixed—*mfg*
2865 Alkylated phenol, mixed—*mfg*

2655 Ammunition cans or tubes, paperboard laminated with metal foil—mfpm—*mfg*
3484 Ammunition carts, machine gun—*mfg*
3483 Ammunition loading and assembling plants—*mfg*
5099 Ammunition, except sporting—wholesale
5091 Ammunition, sporting—wholesale
5941 Ammunition—retail
3825 Ampere-hour meters—*mfg*
3711 Amphibian motor vehicles, except tanks—*mfg*
3795 Amphibian tanks, military—*mfg*
3663 Amplifiers: RF power and IF—*mfg*
3651 Amplifiers: radio, public address, or musical instrument—*mfg*
3699 Amplifiers; magnetic, pulse, and maser—*mfg*
3221 Ampoules, glass—*mfg*
7996 Amusement centers and parks (not fairs, circuses, or carnivals)
7999 Amusement concessions
7993 Amusement device parlors, coin-operated
3999 Amusement machines, coin-operated: except coin-operated phonographs—*mfg*
7993 Amusement machines, coin-operated: operation of
7996 Amusement parks
7999 Amusement rides
3599 Amusement rides for carnivals—*mfg*
2869 Amyl acetate and alcohol—*mfg*
2834 Analgesics—*mfg*
3825 Analog-to-digital converters, electronic instrumentation type—*mfg*
5049 Analytical instruments: photometers, spectrographs, and chromatographic instruments—wholesale
3825 Analyzers for testing electrical characteristics—*mfg*
3823 Analyzers, industrial process type—*mfg*
3829 Anamometers—*mfg*
3462 Anchors, forged: not made in rolling mills—*mfg*
1459 Andalusite mining
3429 Andirons—*mfg*
3841 Anesthesia apparatus—*mfg*
8011 Anesthesiologists, offices of
2833 Anesthetics, in bulk form—*mfg*
2834 Anesthetics, packaged—*mfg*
2835 Angiourographic diagnostic agents—*mfg*
3429 Angle irons, hardware—*mfg*
3545 Angle rings—*mfg*
3812 Angle-of-attack instrumentation—*mfg*
3812 Angle-of-yaw instrumentation—*mfg*
2873 Anhydrous ammonia—*mfg*
2021 Anhydrous butterfat—*mfg*
2824 Anidex fibers—*mfg*
2865 Aniline—*mfg*
2865 Aniline oil—*mfg*
3496 Animal and fish traps, made from purchased wire—*mfg*
2816 Animal black—*mfg*
6553 Animal cemetery operation
3523 Animal clippers, hand and electric—*mfg*
8422 Animal exhibits
5191 Animal feeds, except pet—wholesale
2048 Animal feeds, prepared: except dog and cat—*mfg*
2282 Animal fiber yarn: twisting, winding, or spooling—*mfg*
5159 Animal hair—wholesale
0741 Animal hospitals for livestock
0742 Animal hospitals for pets and other animal specialties
8699 Animal humane societies
2077 Animal oils, except medicinal grade—*mfg*
2833 Animal oils, medicinal grade: refined and concentrated—*mfg*
2834 Animal remedies—*mfg*
0752 Animal shelters
7999 Animal shows in circuses, fairs, and carnivals
0291 Animal specialty and livestock farms, general
0971 Animal trapping, commercial
3429 Animal traps, iron and steel: except wire—*mfg*
2899 Anise oil—*mfg*
3842 Ankle supports, orthopedic—*mfg*
2252 Anklets, hosiery—*mfg*
2861 Annato extract—*mfg*
3443 Annealing boxes, pots, and covers—*mfg*
3398 Annealing of metal for the trade—*mfg*
2759 Announcements, engraved—*mfg*
8999 Announcers, radio and television service
3823 Annunciators, relay and solid-state types: industrial display—*mfg*
5051 Anode metal—wholesale
3559 Anodizing equipment (except rolling mill lines)—*mfg*
3471 Anodizing of metals and formed products, for the trade—*mfg*
5064 Answering machines, telephone—wholesale
2879 Ant poisons—*mfg*
2834 Antacids—*mfg*
1799 Antenna installation, except household type—contractors
5731 Antenna stores, household—retail
7622 Antennas, household: installation and service
3679 Antennas, receiving: automobile, home, and portable—*mfg*

2873 Aqua ammonia, made in ammonia plants—*mfg*
3499 Aquarium accessories, metal—*mfg*
3089 Aquarium accessories, plastics—*mfg*
8422 Aquariums
3231 Aquariums and reflectors, made from purchased glass—*mfg*
1623 Aqueduct construction—general contractors
7389 Arbitration and conciliation services
3542 Arbor presses—*mfg*
8422 Arboreta
0783 Arborist services
3545 Arbors (machine tool accessories)—*mfg*
3845 Arc lamp units, electrotherapeutic: except infrared and ultraviolet—*mfg*
3648 Arc lamps, except electrotherapeutic—*mfg*
3648 Arc lighting fixtures—*mfg*
3548 Arc-welding generators—*mfg*
3548 Arc-welder transformers (separate)—*mfg*
3548 Arc-welders, transformer-rectifier—*mfg*
3548 Arc-welding generators, a.c. and d.c.—*mfg*
7993 Arcades, amusement
3842 Arch supports, orthopedic—*mfg*
8733 Archeological expeditions
3949 Archery equipment—*mfg*
5091 Archery equipment—wholesale
7999 Archery ranges, operation of
2439 Arches, laminated lumber—*mfg*
5049 Architects' equipment and supplies—wholesale
3271 Architectural block, concrete: e.g., fluted, screen, split, slump, ground face—*mfg*
8712 Architectural engineering services
3446 Architectural metal work, ferrous and nonferrous—*mfg*
5039 Architectural metal work—wholesale
3299 Architectural sculptures, plaster of paris: factory production only—*mfg*
3299 Architectural sculptures: gypsum, clay or papier mache—*mfg*
8712 Architectural services
1761 Architectural sheet metal work—contractors
5999 Architectural supplies—retail
3259 Architectural terra cotta—*mfg*
3021 Arctics, rubber or rubber soled fabric—*mfg*
3648 Area and sports luminaries—*mfg*
3272 Areaways, basement window: concrete—*mfg*
7941 Arenas, boxing and wrestling (sports promotion): professional
1411 Argillite, dimension—quarrying
2813 Argon—*mfg*
2389 Arm bands, elastic—mfpm—*mfg*
3625 Armature relays—*mfg*
7694 Armature rewinding
3621 Armatures, industrial—*mfg*
3694 Armatures, motor vehicle—*mfg*
3483 Arming and fusing devices for missiles—*mfg*
3462 Armor plate, forged iron and steel: not made in rolling mills—*mfg*
3312 Armor plate, made in steel works or rolling mills—*mfg*
3357 Armored cable or conductor, nonferrous—mfpm—*mfg*
7381 Armored car service
9711 Army
2911 Aromatic chemicals, made in petroleum refineries—*mfg*
5169 Aromatic chemicals—wholesale
4729 Arrangement of carpools and vanpools
3643 Arrestors and coils, lightning—*mfg*
3949 Arrows, archery—*mfg*
2879 Arsenates: calcium, copper, and lead-formulated—*mfg*
1479 Arsenic mineral mining
2879 Arsenites, formulated—*mfg*
7335 Art and illustration, commercial
3269 Art and ornamental ware, pottery—*mfg*
8699 Art councils
5999 Art dealers—retail
8412 Art galleries, not primarily selling
3231 Art glass, made from purchased glass—*mfg*
3229 Art glassware, made in glassmaking plants—*mfg*
3299 Art goods: plaster of paris, papier-mache, and scagliola—*mfg*
5199 Art goods—wholesale
3272 Art marble, concrete—*mfg*
2395 Art needlework—mfpm—*mfg*
8999 Art restoration
8249 Art schools, commercial
8299 Art schools, except commercial
2273 Art squares, textile fiber—*mfg*
2273 Art squares: twisted paper, grass, reed, coir, sisal, jute, and rag—*mfg*
2033 Artichokes in olive oil, canned—*mfg*
3999 Artificial and preserved flowers, foliage, fruits, and vines: except glass—*mfg*
3999 Artificial flower arrangements—*mfg*
5999 Artificial flowers—retail
5193 Artificial flowers—wholesale
3812 Artificial horizon instrumentation—*mfg*
0752 Artificial insemination services: animal specialties
0751 Artificial insemination services: livestock
5999 Artificial limb stores—retail
8999 Artificial nucleation (cloud seeding)

3161 Attache cases, regardless of material—*mfg*
3546 Attachments for portable drills—*mfg*
3679 Attenuators—*mfg*
3564 Attic fans—*mfg*
8111 Attorneys
9222 Attorneys general's offices
5999 Auction rooms (general merchandise)—retail
**** Auction, specialized—code according to product sold
7389 Auctioneering service on a commission or fee basis
5154 Auctioning livestock—wholesale
2517 Audio cabinets, wood—*mfg*
3695 Audio range tapes, blank—*mfg*
3651 Audio recorders and players: automotive and household—*mfg*
3825 Audiofrequency oscillators—*mfg*
3845 Audiological equipment, electromedical—*mfg*
8049 Audiologists, offices of
3825 Audiometers, except medical—*mfg*
7812 Audiovisual motion picture program production
8721 Auditing service, accounts
1542 Auditorium construction—general contractors
4731 Auditors, freight rate
3532 Auger mining equipment—*mfg*
1241 Auger mining services: bituminous coal, anthracite, and lignite on a contract basis
3423 Augers (edge tools)—*mfg*
8999 Authors
7389 Authors' agents and brokers
7011 Auto courts
7549 Auto emissions testing, without repairs
2241 Auto wind lace—*mfg*
3843 Autoclaves, dental—*mfg*
3842 Autoclaves, hospital and surgical—*mfg*
3443 Autoclaves, industrial—*mfg*
3821 Autoclaves, laboratory—*mfg*
3721 Autogiros—*mfg*
5999 Autograph and philatelist supply stores—retail
2761 Autographic register forms, printed—*mfg*
3845 Automated blood and body fluid analyzers, except laboratory—*mfg*
6099 Automated clearinghouses
3826 Automatic chemical analyzers, laboratory type—*mfg*
3541 Automatic chucking machines—*mfg*
7215 Automatic laundry
3812 Automatic pilots—*mfg*
3541 Automatic screw machines—*mfg*
3578 Automatic teller machines (ATM)—*mfg*
7537 Automatic transmission repair, automotive
5812 Automats (eating places)
5531 Automobile accessory dealers—retail
5511 Automobile agencies (dealers)—retail
5531 Automobile air-conditioning equipment, sale and installation—retail
5012 Automobile auction—wholesale
5531 Automobile battery dealers—retail
3711 Automobile bodies, passenger car—*mfg*
4226 Automobile dead storage
8299 Automobile driving instruction
5013 Automobile engine testing equipment, electrical—wholesale
5015 Automobile engines, used—wholesale or retail
6159 Automobile finance leasing
2273 Automobile floor coverings, except rubber or plastics—*mfg*
5013 Automobile glass—wholesale
3429 Automobile hardware—*mfg*
3052 Automobile hose, plastics or rubber—*mfg*
3792 Automobile house trailer chassis—*mfg*
6331 Automobile insurance
7515 Automobile leasing, except finance leasing: without drivers
3469 Automobile license tags, stamped metal—*mfg*
3534 Automobile lifts (elevators)—*mfg*
6141 Automobile loans (may include automobile insurance)
8699 Automobile owners' associations and clubs
5531 Automobile parts dealers—retail
5015 Automobile parts, used—wholesale or retail
2842 Automobile polishes—*mfg*
8734 Automobile proving and testing grounds
7389 Automobile recovery service
4119 Automobile rental with drivers
7514 Automobile rental, without drivers
7389 Automobile repossession service
2399 Automobile seat covers—*mfg*
3499 Automobile seat frames, metal—*mfg*
2531 Automobile seats—*mfg*
5013 Automobile service station equipment—wholesale
5541 Automobile service stations—retail
7389 Automobile shows, flower shows, and home shows: promoters of
3496 Automobile skid chains, made from purchased wire—*mfg*
3493 Automobile springs—*mfg*
5531 Automobile tire dealers—retail
5014 Automobile tires and tubes—wholesale
3799 Automobile trailer chassis, except travel trailer—*mfg*

B

8811 Babysitting (private households employing babysitters in the home)
7299 Babysitting bureaus
3531 Backfillers, self-propelled—*mfg*
3432 Backflow preventors—*mfg*
3531 Backhoes—*mfg*
5941 Backpacking, hiking, and mountaineering equipment—retail
2514 Backs for metal household furniture—*mfg*
2013 Bacon, slab and sliced—mfpm—*mfg*
2011 Bacon, slab and sliced—mitse—*mfg*
2836 Bacterial vaccines—*mfg*
2836 Bacterins, except in vitro and in vivo—*mfg*
8071 Bacteriological laboratories (not manufacturing)
2836 Bacteriological media, except in vitro and in vivo—*mfg*
3999 Badges for policemen and firemen—metal—*mfg*
2399 Badges, made from fabric—*mfg*
3949 Badminton equipment—*mfg*
3443 Baffles—*mfg*
3554 Bag and envelope making machinery (paper machinery)—*mfg*
3111 Bag leather—*mfg*
3483 Bag loading plants, ammunition—*mfg*
3565 Bag opening, filling and closing machines—*mfg*
2621 Bag paper—mitse—*mfg*
5093 Bag reclaiming—wholesale
3559 Bag sewing and closing machines (industrial sewing machines)—*mfg*
3949 Bagatelle tables—*mfg*
5461 Bagel stores—retail
2051 Bagels—*mfg*
4212 Baggage transfer
5149 Bagging of tea
2299 Bagging, jute: made in jute weaving mills—*mfg*
3161 Bags (luggage), regardless of material—*mfg*
2259 Bags and bagging—mitse—*mfg*
2393 Bags and containers, textile: except sleeping bags—insulated or not—mfpm—*mfg*
2392 Bags, blanket: plastics—*mfg*
3199 Bags, feed: for horses—*mfg*
2392 Bags, garment storage: except paper or plastics film—*mfg*
3949 Bags, golf—*mfg*
2392 Bags, laundry—mfpm—*mfg*
5113 Bags, paper and disposable plastics—wholesale
2674 Bags, paper: uncoated—mfpm—*mfg*
2759 Bags, plastics: printed only, except lithographed or gravure (bags not made in printing plants)—*mfg*
3949 Bags, rosin—*mfg*
3069 Bags, rubber or rubberized fabric—*mfg*
2399 Bags, sleeping—*mfg*
3949 Bags, striking (punching)—*mfg*
2393 Bags, textile: including canvas—except laundry, garment, and sleeping—mfpm—*mfg*
5199 Bags, textile—wholesale
1389 Bailing wells on a contract basis
3443 Bails, ladle—*mfg*
5941 Bait and tackle shops—retail
5091 Bait, artificial—wholesale
3949 Bait, fishing: artificial—*mfg*
2032 Baked beans without meat: canned—*mfg*
5461 Bakeries with baking on the premises—retail
5461 Bakeries without baking on the premises—retail
5461 Bakeries—retail
2026 Bakers' cheese—*mfg*
2087 Bakers' colors, except synthetic—*mfg*
2499 Bakers' equipment, wood—*mfg*
1629 Bakers' oven construction—general contractors
2326 Bakers' service apparel, washable—*mfg*
5963 Bakery goods, purchased: house-to-house—retail
3556 Bakery machinery—*mfg*
5461 Bakery products produced primarily for sale on the premises—retail
2052 Bakery products, dry: e.g., biscuits, crackers, pretzels—*mfg*
2051 Bakery products, fresh: bread, cakes, doughnuts, and pastries—*mfg*
2053 Bakery products, frozen: except bread and bread-type rolls—*mfg*
5142 Bakery products, frozen—wholesale
2051 Bakery products, partially cooked: except frozen—*mfg*
5149 Bakery products—wholesale
2079 Baking and frying fats (shortening)—*mfg*
2066 Baking chocolate—*mfg*
2851 Baking japans—*mfg*
2099 Baking powder—*mfg*
3596 Balances, except laboratory—*mfg*
5046 Balances, except laboratory—wholesale
3821 Balances, laboratory—*mfg*
3559 Balancing equipment, automotive wheel—*mfg*
3446 Balconies, metal—*mfg*
2261 Bale dyeing of cotton broadwoven products—*mfg*
2262 Bale dyeing of manmade fiber and silk broadwoven fabrics—*mfg*
3523 Bale throwers—*mfg*
3496 Bale ties, made from purchased wire—*mfg*

1479 Barium ore mining
2816 Barium sulfate, precipitated (blanc fixe)—*mfg*
3295 Barium, ground or otherwise treated—*mfg*
2211 Bark cloth, cotton—*mfg*
0831 Barks, gathering of
0119 Barley farms
5153 Barley—wholesale
2258 Barmen laces—*mfg*
3523 Barn cleaners—*mfg*
3523 Barn stanchions and standards—*mfg*
3829 Barographs—*mfg*
3829 Barometers, mercury and aneroid types—*mfg*
3443 Barometric condensers—*mfg*
2429 Barrel heading and staves, sawed or split—*mfg*
3484 Barrels, gun: 30 mm. (or 1.18 inch) or less—*mfg*
3489 Barrels, gun: more than 30 mm. (or more than 1.18 inch)—*mfg*
5085 Barrels, new and reconditioned—wholesale
3412 Barrels, shipping: steel and other metal—*mfg*
2449 Barrels, wood: coopered—*mfg*
3499 Barricades, metal—*mfg*
5813 Bars (alcoholic beverage drinking places)
8641 Bars and restaurants owned and operated for members of organizations only
3354 Bars, aluminum: extruded—*mfg*
3355 Bars, aluminum: rolled—*mfg*
2064 Bars, candy: including chocolate covered bars—*mfg*
2066 Bars, candy: solid chocolate—*mfg*
3449 Bars, concrete reinforcing: fabricated steel—*mfg*
5051 Bars, concrete reinforcing—wholesale
3351 Bars, copper and copper alloy—*mfg*
3312 Bars, iron: made in steel works or rolling mills—*mfg*
5051 Bars, metal—wholesale
3423 Bars, prying (handtools)—*mfg*
3331 Bars, refinery: primary copper—*mfg*
3316 Bars, steel: cold-rolled—not made in hot-rolling mills—*mfg*
3312 Bars, steel: made in steel works or hot-rolling mills—*mfg*
3356 Bars: lead, magnesium, nickel, tin, titanium, zinc, and their alloys—*mfg*
7389 Bartering services for businesses
7299 Bartering services for individuals
3229 Barware, glass—*mfg*
2816 Barytes pigments—*mfg*
1429 Basalt, crushed and broken—quarrying
1411 Basalt, dimension—quarrying
8744 Base maintenance (providing personnel on continuing basis)
2353 Baseball caps, except plastics—*mfg*
7997 Baseball clubs, except professional and semiprofessional
7941 Baseball clubs, professional or semiprofessional
3949 Baseball equipment and supplies, except uniforms and footwear—*mfg*
7999 Baseball instruction schools
2329 Baseball uniforms: men's and boys'—*mfg*
2431 Baseboards, floor: wood—*mfg*
3442 Baseboards, metal—*mfg*
3949 Bases, baseball—*mfg*
2844 Bases, perfume: blending and compounding—*mfg*
2211 Basket weave fabrics, cotton—*mfg*
7941 Basketball clubs, professional or semi-professional
7999 Basketball instruction schools
2329 Basketball uniforms: men's and boys'—*mfg*
3949 Basketballs and basketball equipment and supplies, except uniforms and footwear—*mfg*
2499 Baskets, except fruit, vegetable, fish, and bait: (e.g., rattan, reed, straw)—*mfg*
3949 Baskets, fish and bait—*mfg*
2449 Baskets, fruit and vegetable: e.g., till, berry, climax, round stave—*mfg*
3496 Baskets, made from purchased wire—*mfg*
3315 Baskets, steel: made in wiredrawing plants—*mfg*
3944 Baskets, toy—*mfg*
5199 Baskets: reed, rattan, willow, and wood—wholesale
2519 Bassinets, reed and rattan—*mfg*
3931 Bassoons—*mfg*
1099 Bastnasite ore mining
3531 Batching plants, bituminous—*mfg*
3531 Batching plants, for aggregate concrete and bulk cement—*mfg*
7999 Bath houses, independently operated
2392 Bath mitts (washcloths)—*mfg*
2844 Bath salts—*mfg*
3069 Bath sprays, rubber—*mfg*
1799 Bathtub refinishing—contractors
7997 Bathing beaches, membership
7999 Bathing beaches, public
3069 Bathing caps and suits, rubber—mitse—*mfg*
5699 Bathing suit stores—retail
2369 Bathing suits: girls', children's, and infants'—mfpm—*mfg*
2329 Bathing suits: men's and boys'—mfpm—*mfg*

3556 Biscuit cutters (machines)—*mfg*
2041 Biscuit dough, canned—mitse—*mfg*
2045 Biscuit mixes and doughs—mfpm—*mfg*
2051 Biscuits, baked: baking powder and raised—*mfg*
2052 Biscuits, baked: dry, except baking powder and raised—*mfg*
3339 Bismuth refining, primary—*mfg*
3423 Bits (edge tools for woodworking)—*mfg*
3545 Bits for use on lathes, planers, shapers, etc.—*mfg*
3532 Bits, rock: except oil and gas field tools—*mfg*
3533 Bits, rock: oil and gas field tools—*mfg*
2087 Bitters (flavoring concentrates)—*mfg*
1499 Bitumens (native) mining
3531 Bituminous batching plants—*mfg*
1221 Bituminous coal cleaning plants
1221 Bituminous coal crushing
1241 Bituminous coal mining services on a contract basis
1221 Bituminous coal screening plants
1241 Bituminous coal stripping service: on a contract basis
1222 Bituminous coal stripping: except on a contract, fee, or other basis
1221 Bituminous coal washeries
1499 Bituminous limestone quarrying
1241 Bituminous or lignite auger mining service: on a contract basis
2851 Bituminous paints—*mfg*
5082 Bituminous processing equipment—wholesale
1499 Bituminous sandstone quarrying
2816 Black pigments, except carbon black—*mfg*
5051 Black plate, iron and steel—wholesale
0171 Blackberry farms
3281 Blackboards, slate—*mfg*
2531 Blackboards, wood—*mfg*
2842 Blackings—*mfg*
3312 Blackplate—*mfg*
7699 Blacksmith shops
3199 Blacksmiths' aprons, leather—*mfg*
2061 Blackstrap molasses—*mfg*
1771 Blacktop work: private driveways and private parking areas—contractors
3531 Blades for graders, scrapers, dozers, and snowplows—*mfg*
3728 Blades, aircraft propeller: metal or wood—*mfg*
3421 Blades, knife and razor—*mfg*
3425 Blades, saw: for hand or power saws—*mfg*
2816 Blanc fixe (barium sulfate, precipitated)—*mfg*
3482 Blank cartridges, 30 mm. (or 1.18 inch) or less—*mfg*
2782 Blankbook making—*mfg*
5112 Blankbooks—wholesale
2392 Blanket bags, plastic—*mfg*
2221 Blanketings, manmade fiber—*mfg*
2211 Blankets and blanketings, cotton—mitse—*mfg*
2231 Blankets and blanketings, wool and similar animal fibers—mitse—*mfg*
3292 Blankets, asbestos—*mfg*
3634 Blankets, electric—*mfg*
2399 Blankets, horse—mfpm—*mfg*
3292 Blankets, insulating for aircraft: asbestos—*mfg*
2679 Blankets, insulating: paper—mfpm—*mfg*
3069 Blankets, printers': rubber—*mfg*
2392 Blankets—mfpm—*mfg*
5023 Blankets—wholesale
3229 Blanks for electric light bulbs, glass—*mfg*
3965 Blanks, button—*mfg*
3545 Blanks, cutting tool—*mfg*
3545 Blanks, tips and inserts: cutting tools—*mfg*
5084 Blanks, tips and inserts—wholesale
2426 Blanks, wood: for bowling pins, handles, and textile machinery accessories—*mfg*
3569 Blast cleaning equipment, dustless: except metalworking—*mfg*
3312 Blast furnace products—*mfg*
3295 Blast furnace slag—*mfg*
1446 Blast sand mining
2298 Blasting mats, rope—*mfg*
2892 Blasting powder and blasting caps—*mfg*
1629 Blasting, except building demolition—contractors
2819 Bleach (calcium hypochlorite), industrial—*mfg*
2819 Bleach (sodium hypochlorite), industrial—*mfg*
2531 Bleacher seating, portable—*mfg*
2844 Bleaches, hair—*mfg*
2842 Bleaches, household: liquid or dry—*mfg*
2819 Bleaches, industrial—*mfg*
3999 Bleaching and dyeing of sponges—*mfg*
2261 Bleaching cotton broadwoven fabrics—*mfg*
3552 Bleaching machinery, textile—*mfg*
2262 Bleaching manmade fiber and silk broadwoven fabrics—*mfg*
2819 Bleaching powder, industrial—*mfg*
2269 Bleaching raw stock, yarn, and narrow fabrics: except knit and wool—*mfg*
2231 Bleaching yarn and fabrics, wool and similar animal fibers: except knit—*mfg*
2261 Bleaching, kier: continuous machine—*mfg*
3825 Bleed control cabinets (engine testers)—*mfg*
1031 Blende (zinc) mining

3732 Boats, fiberglass: building and repairing—*mfg*
3089 Boats, nonrigid: plastics—*mfg*
7999 Boats, party fishing: operation of
5091 Boats, pleasure: canoes, motorboats, and sailboats—wholesale
3732 Boats, rigid: plastics—*mfg*
3732 Boats: motorboats, sailboats, rowboats, and canoes—building and repairing—*mfg*
2426 Bobbin blocks and blanks, wood—*mfg*
2258 Bobbinet (lace goods)—*mfg*
3552 Bobbins for textile machinery—*mfg*
2655 Bobbins, fiber—mfpm—*mfg*
3949 Bobsleds—*mfg*
7212 Bobtailers, laundry and drycleaning
3728 Bodies, aircraft: not complete aircraft—*mfg*
5012 Bodies, automotive—wholesale
3713 Bodies, dump—*mfg*
3711 Bodies, passenger automobile—*mfg*
3713 Bodies, truck (motor vehicle)—*mfg*
3465 Body parts, automotive: stamped—*mfg*
2844 Body powder—*mfg*
7532 Body repair, automotive
7532 Body shops, automotive
2253 Body stockings—mitse—*mfg*
3489 Bofors guns—*mfg*
1799 Boiler and pipe, insulation of—contractors
3443 Boiler casings: metal plate—*mfg*
7699 Boiler cleaning
2899 Boiler compounds, antiscaling—*mfg*
3823 Boiler controls: industrial, power, and marine type—*mfg*
3494 Boiler couplings and drains, metal—*mfg*
3292 Boiler covering (heat insulating material), except felt—*mfg*
2299 Boiler covering, felt—*mfg*
1711 Boiler erection and installation—contractors
3491 Boiler gauge cocks—*mfg*
6331 Boiler insurance
7699 Boiler repair shops, except manufacturing
3443 Boiler shop products: industrial boilers, smokestacks, and steel tanks—*mfg*
3599 Boiler tube cleaners—*mfg*
3317 Boiler tubes, wrought—mfpm—*mfg*
3433 Boilers, low-pressure heating: steam or hot water—*mfg*
5074 Boilers, power: industrial—wholesale
5074 Boilers, steam and hot water heating—wholesale
3443 Boilers: industrial, power, and marine—*mfg*
0161 Bok choy farms
2013 Bologna—mfpm—*mfg*
3261 Bolt caps, vitreous china and earthenware—*mfg*
3452 Bolts, metal—*mfg*
5072 Bolts, nuts, rivets, and screws—wholesale
3089 Bolts, plastics—*mfg*
2411 Bolts, wood: e.g., handle, heading, shingle, stave—*mfg*
3537 Bomb lifts—*mfg*
3483 Bomb loading and assembling plants—*mfg*
3728 Bomb racks, aircraft—*mfg*
3537 Bomb trucks—*mfg*
2211 Bombazine, cotton—*mfg*
3483 Bombcluster adapters—*mfg*
3483 Bombs and parts—*mfg*
2899 Bombs, flashlight—*mfg*
6162 Bond and mortgage companies
6211 Bond dealers and brokers
2621 Bond paper—mitse—*mfg*
2084 Bonded wine cellars, engaged in blending wines—*mfg*
2297 Bonded-fiber fabrics, except felt—*mfg*
3479 Bonderizing of metal and metal products, for the trade—*mfg*
6289 Bondholders protective committees
6351 Bonding for guaranteeing job completion
6351 Bonding of employees
6351 Bonding, fidelity or surety
7389 Bondspersons
2816 Bone black—*mfg*
3262 Bone china—*mfg*
3841 Bone drills—*mfg*
3999 Bone novelties—*mfg*
3841 Bone plates and screws—*mfg*
3841 Bone rongeurs—*mfg*
2211 Book cloth—mitse—*mfg*
2731 Book club publishing and printing, or publishing only—*mfg*
5961 Book clubs, not publishing
3499 Book ends, metal—*mfg*
2789 Book gilding, bronzing, edging, deckling, embossing, and gold stamping—*mfg*
3999 Book matches—*mfg*
2672 Book paper, coated—mfpm—*mfg*
2621 Book paper—mitse—*mfg*
5942 Book stores selling new books and magazines—retail
5932 Book stores, secondhand—retail
3251 Book tile, clay—*mfg*
3111 Bookbinders' leather—*mfg*
3555 Bookbinders' machines—*mfg*
2789 Bookbinding: edition, job, library, and trade—*mfg*
2514 Bookcases, household: metal—*mfg*
2511 Bookcases, household: wood—*mfg*
2522 Bookcases, office: except wood—*mfg*
2521 Bookcases, office: wood—*mfg*

2341 Briefs: women's, misses', children's, and infants'—mfpm—*mfg*
1479 Brimstone mining
2819 Brine—*mfg*
2035 Brining of fruits and vegetables—*mfg*
2999 Briquettes (fuel bricks): made with petroleum binder—*mfg*
2499 Briquettes, sawdust or bagasse: nonpetroleum binder—*mfg*
3999 Bristles, dressing of—*mfg*
5159 Bristles—wholesale
2631 Bristols, bogus—mitse—*mfg*
2621 Bristols, except bogus—mitse—*mfg*
3356 Britannia metal, rolling and drawing—*mfg*
3545 Broaches (machine tool accessories)—*mfg*
3843 Broaches, dental—*mfg*
5084 Broaches—wholesale
3541 Broaching machines—*mfg*
3663 Broadcast equipment (including studio), radio and television—*mfg*
4832 Broadcasting stations, radio
4833 Broadcasting stations, television
2211 Broadcloth, cotton—*mfg*
2211 Broadwoven fabrics, cotton—*mfg*
2221 Broadwoven fabrics, silk and manmade fiber—*mfg*
2299 Broadwoven fabrics: linen, jute, hemp, and ramie—*mfg*
5131 Broadwoven fabrics—wholesale
2211 Brocade, cotton—*mfg*
2211 Brocatelle, cotton—*mfg*
0161 Broccoli farms
0251 Broiler chickens, raising of
3634 Broilers, electric—*mfg*
6531 Brokers of manufactured homes, on site
7389 Brokers, business (buying and selling business enterprises)
6221 Brokers, commodity contract
4731 Brokers, custom house
6163 Brokers, farm or business loan
6411 Brokers, insurance
6531 Brokers, real estate
6211 Brokers, security
4731 Brokers, shipping
4731 Brokers, transportation
2819 Bromine, elemental—*mfg*
2869 Bromochloromethane—*mfg*
3845 Bronchoscopes, electromedical—*mfg*
3841 Bronchoscopes, except electromedical—*mfg*
3364 Bronze die castings—*mfg*
3366 Bronze foundries—*mfg*
2893 Bronze ink—*mfg*
3351 Bronze rolling and drawing—*mfg*
3341 Bronze smelting and refining, secondary—*mfg*
3952 Bronze, artists': mixtures, powders, paints, etc.—*mfg*
3555 Bronzing and dusting machines for the printing trade—*mfg*
7389 Bronzing baby shoes
2789 Bronzing books, cards, or paper—*mfg*
3523 Brooders—*mfg*
3559 Broom making machinery—*mfg*
5199 Broom, mop, and paint handles—wholesale
0139 Broomcorn farms
5159 Broomcorn—wholesale
3991 Brooms, hand and machine: bamboo, wire, fiber, splint, or other material—*mfg*
3711 Brooms, powered (motor vehicles)—*mfg*
5719 Brooms—retail
2032 Broth, except seafood: canned—*mfg*
2051 Brown bread, Boston and other: canned—*mfg*
1221 Brown coal mining
1011 Brown ore mining
3861 Brownprint paper and cloth, sensitized—*mfg*
3861 Brownprint reproduction machines and equipment—*mfg*
5044 Brownprinting equipment—wholesale
2833 Brucine and derivatives—*mfg*
1459 Brucite mining
3624 Brush blocks, carbon or molded graphite—*mfg*
2426 Brush blocks, wood: turned and shaped—*mfg*
1629 Brush clearing or cutting—contractors
3089 Brush handles, plastics—*mfg*
3624 Brushes and brush stock contacts: carbon and graphite—electric—*mfg*
3991 Brushes for vacuum cleaners, carpet sweepers, and other rotary machines—*mfg*
3952 Brushes, air: artists'—*mfg*
5963 Brushes, house-to-house or party plan selling—retail
3991 Brushes, household and industrial—*mfg*
3069 Brushes, rubber—*mfg*
5719 Brushes—retail
3541 Brushing machines (metalworking machinery)—*mfg*
3089 Bubble formed packaging, plastics—*mfg*
3443 Bubble towers—*mfg*
3432 Bubblers, drinking fountain—*mfg*
3531 Bucket and scarifier teeth—*mfg*
3535 Bucket type conveyor systems for general industrial use—*mfg*

3542 Bulldozers, metalworking—*mfg*
3482 Bullet jackets and cores, 30 mm. (or 1.18 inch) or less—*mfg*
2499 Bulletin boards, wood and cork—*mfg*
3842 Bulletproof vests—*mfg*
1041 Bullion, gold: produced at mine, mill, or dredge site
5094 Bullion, precious metals—wholesale
1044 Bullion, silver: produced at mine or mill site
7532 Bump shops (automotive repair)
3714 Bumpers and bumperettes, motor vehicle—*mfg*
3462 Bumping posts, railroad: forged—not made in rolling mills—*mfg*
2499 Bungs, wood—*mfg*
2051 Buns, bread-type (e.g., hamburger, hot dog), including frozen—*mfg*
2051 Buns, sweet, except frozen—*mfg*
3821 Bunsen burners—*mfg*
2211 Bunting—mitse—*mfg*
2369 Buntings: infants'—mfpm—*mfg*
3823 Buoyancy instruments, industrial process type—*mfg*
3089 Buoys and floats, plastics—*mfg*
2499 Buoys, cork—*mfg*
3443 Buoys, metal—*mfg*
9221 Bureaus of criminal investigations—government
9651 Bureaus of standards—government
3669 Burglar alarm apparatus, electric—*mfg*
1731 Burglar alarm installation—contractors
7382 Burglar alarm monitoring and maintenance
6331 Burglary and theft insurance
3995 Burial cases, metal and wood—*mfg*
2389 Burial garments—mfpm—*mfg*
6311 Burial insurance societies
3272 Burial vaults, concrete and precast terrazzo—*mfg*
3995 Burial vaults, fiberglass—*mfg*
3281 Burial vaults, stone—*mfg*
2299 Burlap, jute—*mfg*
5199 Burlap—wholesale
7922 Burlesque companies
1459 Burley mining
2231 Burling and mending wool cloth for the trade—*mfg*
2411 Burls, wood—*mfg*
5074 Burners, fuel oil and distillate oil—wholesale
3433 Burners, gas: domestic—*mfg*
3433 Burners, oil: domestic and industrial—*mfg*
3398 Burning metal for the trade—*mfg*
3952 Burnishers and cushions, gilders'—*mfg*
3569 Burnishing and washing machines, brake—*mfg*
2842 Burnishing ink—*mfg*
3541 Burnishing machines (machine tools)—*mfg*
3199 Burnt leather goods for the trade—*mfg*
2087 Burnt sugar (food color)—*mfg*
3999 Burnt wood articles—*mfg*
0272 Burro farms
1499 Burrstone quarrying
3843 Burs, dental—*mfg*
3613 Bus bar structures—*mfg*
3643 Bus bars (electrical conductors)—*mfg*
5063 Bus bars and trolley ducts—wholesale
3713 Bus bodies, motor vehicle—*mfg*
7319 Bus card advertising
4142 Bus charter service, except local
4141 Bus charter service, local
4111 Bus line operation, local
4131 Bus lines, intercity
4173 Bus terminal operation
4729 Bus ticket offices, not operated by transportation companies
3715 Bus trailers, tractor type—*mfg*
7542 Bus washing
3462 Bus, truck and trailer forgings, ferrous: not made in rolling mills—*mfg*
3711 Buses, motor: except trackless trolley—*mfg*
4151 Buses, school: operation of
4119 Buses, sightseeing: operation of
3743 Buses, trackless trolley—*mfg*
5012 Buses—wholesale
3423 Bush hooks—*mfg*
3366 Bushings and bearings, except die-castings: brass, bronze, and copper—*mfg*
3325 Bushings, cast steel: except investment—*mfg*
3069 Bushings, rubber—*mfg*
2499 Bushings, wood—*mfg*
8611 Business associations, other than civic and social
7389 Business brokers (buying and selling business enterprises)
8244 Business colleges and schools, not of college grade
6153 Business credit institutions, short-term
8732 Business economists, commercial
2759 Business forms, except manifold, lithographed or gravure printed—*mfg*
2754 Business forms, except manifold: gravure printing—*mfg*
2752 Business forms, except manifold: lithographed—*mfg*
2761 Business forms, manifold—*mfg*
5112 Business forms—wholesale
7629 Business machine repair, electrical

Description	NAICS	SIC
Venoms: Biological Product (except Diagnostic)—*mfg*	325414	2836
Ventilating equipment and supplies: Warm Air Heating and Air-Conditioning Equipment and Supplies—*whlse*	42173	5075
Ventilating fans, electric–household-kitchen: Electric Housewares and Household Fan—*mfg*	335211	3634
Heating Equipment (except Electric and Warm Air Furnaces)—*mfg*	333414	3634
Ventilating work, with or without sheet metalwork-contractors: Plumbing, Heating and Air-Conditioning Contractors—*const*	23511	1711
Ventilating, blowing, and exhaust fans–except household and kitchen: Air Purification Equipment—*mfg*	333411	3564
Industrial and Commercial Fan and Blower—*mfg*	333412	3564
Ventilation of railroad cars: Air, Rail, and Water Equipment Rental and Leasing, Commercial—*real*	532411	4741
Rail Support Activities—*trans*	48821	4741
Ventilation, Heating, Air-Conditioning and Commercial Refrigeration Equipment Manufacturing	**3334**	
Ventilation, Heating, Air-Conditioning and Commercial Refrigeration Equipment Manufacturing	**33341**	
Ventilators, sheet metal: Metal Container, Other—*mfg*	332439	3444
Sheet Metal Work—*mfg*	332322	3444
Venture capital companies: Commodity Contracts Dealing—*fin*	52313	6799
Financial Investment Activities, Miscellaneous—*fin*	523999	6799
Intermediation, Miscellaneous—*fin*	52391	6799
Portfolio Management—*fin*	52392	6799
Verde' antique, crushed and broken: Crushed and Broken Stone and Quarrying, Other—*mining*	212319	1429
Verde' antique, dimension: Dimension Stone and Quarrying—*mining*	212311	1411
Verifiers: Computer Peripheral Equipment, Other—*mfg*	334119	3577
Vermicelli: Pasta—*mfg*	311823	2098
Vermiculite mining: Crushed and Broken Stone and Quarrying, Other—*mining*	212319	1499
Non-Metallic Mineral, All Other—*mining*	212399	1499
Vermiculite, exfoliated: Ground or Treated Mineral and Earth—*mfg*	327992	3295
Vermifuges: Pharmaceutical Preparation—*mfg*	325412	2834
Vermilion pigments: Carbon Black—*mfg*	325182	2816
Inorganic Dye and Pigment—*mfg*	325131	2816
Verniers (machinists' precision tools): Cutting Tool and Machine Tool Accessory—*mfg*	333515	3545
Hand and Edge Tool—*mfg*	332212	3545
Vertical turning and boring machines (metalworking): Machine Tool (Metal Cutting Types)—*mfg*	333512	3541
Vessels, pressure–industrial-metal plate (made in boiler shops): Air-Conditioning and Warm Air Heating Equipment and Commercial and Industrial Refrigeration Equipment—*mfg*	333415	3443
Metal Tank (Heavy Gauge)—*mfg*	33242	3443
Plate Work—*mfg*	332313	3443
Power Boiler and Heat Exchanger—*mfg*	33241	3443
Vessels, process and storage–metal plate (made in boiler shops): Air-Conditioning and Warm Air Heating Equipment and Commercial and Industrial Refrigeration Equipment—*mfg*	333415	3443
Metal Tank (Heavy Gauge)—*mfg*	33242	3443
Plate Work—*mfg*	332313	3443
Power Boiler and Heat Exchanger—*mfg*	33241	3443
Vestments, academic and clerical: Cut and Sew Apparel, All Other—*mfg*	315299	2389
Vests, except tailored: Women's and Girls' Cut and Sew Apparel Contractors—*mfg*	315212	2337
Women's and Girls' Cut and Sew Suit, Coat, Tailored Jacket and Skirt—*mfg*	315234	2337
Vests, leather or sheet-lined: Fur and Leather Apparel—*mfg*	315292	2386
Vests, nontailored including sweater: Cut and Sew Apparel, All Other—*mfg*	315299	2329
Men's and Boys' Cut and Sew Apparel Contractors—*mfg*	315211	2329
Men's and Boys' Cut and Sew Other Outerwear—*mfg*	315228	2329
Vests, not tailored: Apparel Accessories and Apparel, Other—*mfg*	315999	2339
Cut and Sew Apparel, All Other—*mfg*	315299	2339
Women's and Girls' Cut and Sew Apparel Contractors—*mfg*	315212	2339
Women's and Girls' Cut and Sew Other Outerwear—*mfg*	315238	2339
Vests, tailored: Men's and Boys' Cut and Sew Apparel Contractors—*mfg*	315211	2311
Men's and Boys' Cut and Sew Suit, Coat and Overcoat—*mfg*	315222	2311
Veteran's Affairs, Administration of	**92314**	**9451**
Veterans' affairs offices: Veteran's Affairs, Administration of—*pub*	92314	9451
Veterans' organizations: Civic and Social Organizations—*serv*	81341	8641
Veterinarians for livestock: Veterinary Services—*prof*	54194	741
Veterinarians for pets and other animal specialties: Veterinary Services—*prof*	54194	742
Veterinarians' instruments and apparatus: Surgical and Medical Instrument—*mfg*	339112	3841
Veterinary pharmaceutical preparations: Pharmaceutical Preparation—*mfg*	325412	2834
Veterinary Services	**54194**	**742**
Veterinary services for livestock: Veterinary Services—*prof*	54194	741
Veterinary services for pets and other animal specialties: Veterinary Services—*prof*	54194	742
Veterinary testing laboratories: Testing Laboratories—*prof*	54138	8734
Veterinary Services—*prof*	54194	8734
Viaduct construction–general contractors: Bridge and Tunnel—*const*	23412	1622
Vials, glass–made in glassmaking establishments: Glass Container—*mfg*	327213	3221
Vials, made from purchased glass: Glass Product Made of Purchased Glass—*mfg*	327215	3231
Vials, plastics: Plastics Pipe and Pipe Fitting—*mfg*	326122	3089
Plastics Product, All Other—*mfg*	326199	3089
Unsupported Plastics Profile Shape—*mfg*	326121	3089
Vibraphones: Musical Instrument—*mfg*	339992	3931

C

4119 Cable cars, aerial: except amusement and scenic
4111 Cable cars, except aerial, amusement and scenic
5063 Cable conduit—wholesale
1623 Cable laying construction—contractors
7999 Cable lifts, amusement or scenic: operated separately from lodges
4813 Cable service, telephone
1799 Cable splicing service, nonelectrical—contractors
1731 Cable splicing, electrical—contractors
3663 Cable television equipment—*mfg*
1731 Cable television hookup—contractors
1623 Cable television line construction— contractors
4841 Cable television services
3829 Cable testing machines—*mfg*
3443 Cable trays, metal plate—*mfg*
3355 Cable, aluminum: made in rolling mills—*mfg*
2298 Cable, fiber—*mfg*
3357 Cable, nonferrous: bare, insulated, or armored—mfpm—*mfg*
3315 Cable, steel: insulated or armored—*mfg*
3496 Cable, uninsulated wire: made from purchased wire—*mfg*
5051 Cable, wire: not insulated—wholesale
4822 Cablegram services
3537 Cabs for industrial trucks and tractors—*mfg*
3523 Cabs, agricultural machinery—*mfg*
3531 Cabs, construction machinery—*mfg*
4789 Cabs, horse-drawn: for hire
2066 Cacao bean products: chocolate, cocoa butter, and cocoa—*mfg*
2066 Cacao beans: shelling, roasting, and grinding for making chocolate liquor—*mfg*
3799 Caddy cars—*mfg*
3949 Caddy carts—*mfg*
3339 Cadmium refining, primary—*mfg*
5812 Cafes
3589 Cafeteria food warming equipment—*mfg*
2599 Cafeteria furniture—*mfg*
5021 Cafeteria furniture—wholesale
5812 Cafeterias
2833 Caffeine and derivatives—*mfg*
2384 Caftans—mfpm—*mfg*
3532 Cages, mine shaft—*mfg*
3496 Cages, wire: made from purchased wire—*mfg*
1629 Caisson drilling—contractors
3489 Caisson limbers—*mfg*
3443 Caissons, metal plate—*mfg*
5999 Cake decorating supplies—retail
2099 Cake fillings, except fruits, vegetables and meat—*mfg*
2045 Cake flour—mfpm—*mfg*
2041 Cake flour—mitse—*mfg*
2099 Cake frosting mixes, dry—*mfg*
2045 Cake mixes—mfpm—*mfg*
2064 Cake ornaments, confectionery—*mfg*
2046 Cake, corn oil—*mfg*
2051 Cakes, bakery, except frozen—*mfg*
5142 Cakes, frozen: packaged—wholesale
2053 Cakes, frozen: pound, layer, and cheese—*mfg*
1031 Calamine mining
1041 Calaverite mining
1422 Calcareous tufa, crushed and broken—quarrying
1411 Calcareous tufa, dimension—quarrying
2851 Calcimines, dry and paste—*mfg*
5198 Calcimines—wholesale
2999 Calcined petroleum coke—mfpm—*mfg*
3567 Calcining kilns (industrial furnaces)—*mfg*
1499 Calcite mining
2861 Calcium acetate, product of hardwood distillation—*mfg*
2879 Calcium arsenate and arsenite, formulated—*mfg*
2819 Calcium carbide, chloride, and hypochlorite—*mfg*
2819 Calcium compounds, inorganic—*mfg*
2874 Calcium meta-phosphates—*mfg*
2819 Calcium metal—*mfg*
2869 Calcium oxalate—*mfg*
2843 Calcium salts of sulfonated oils, fats, or greases—*mfg*
3578 Calculating machines, operator paced—*mfg*
5044 Calculating machines—wholesale
7374 Calculating service, computer
3999 Calendars, framed—*mfg*
2754 Calendars, gravure printing: not publishing—*mfg*
2752 Calendars, lithographed: not published—*mfg*
2759 Calendars, printed: except lithographed or gravure—*mfg*
2741 Calendars: publishing and printing, or publishing only—*mfg*
2261 Calendering of cotton broadwoven fabrics—*mfg*
2262 Calendering of manmade fiber and silk broadwoven fabrics—*mfg*
2231 Calendering of wool, mohair, and similar animal fiber fabrics: except knit—*mfg*
3523 Calf savers (farm equipment)—*mfg*
2013 Calf's-foot jelly—*mfg*
8734 Calibration and certification (testing)

2221 Canton crepes—*mfg*
2211 Canton flannels, cotton—*mfg*
2421 Cants, resawed (lumber)—*mfg*
3952 Canvas board, artists'—*mfg*
2394 Canvas products, except bags and knapsacks—mfpm—*mfg*
5199 Canvas products—wholesale
3021 Canvas shoes, rubber soled—*mfg*
3952 Canvas, artists': prepared on frames—*mfg*
2211 Canvas—mitse—*mfg*
5963 Canvassers (door-to-door), headquarters for retail sale of merchandise
2396 Cap fronts and visors—*mfg*
3469 Capacitor and condenser cans and cases: stamped metal—*mfg*
2621 Capacitor paper—mitse—*mfg*
3629 Capacitors, a.c.: for motors and fluorescent lamp ballasts—*mfg*
3675 Capacitors, electronic: fixed and variable—*mfg*
5065 Capacitors, electronic—wholesale
3629 Capacitors, except electronic: fixed and variable—*mfg*
5063 Capacitors, except electronic—wholesale
2337 Capes, except fur and vulcanized rubber: women's, misses', and juniors'—mfpm—*mfg*
2371 Capes, fur—*mfg*
3069 Capes, vulcanized rubber and rubberized fabric—mitse—*mfg*
2869 Caprolactam—*mfg*
2389 Caps and gowns, academic—mfpm—*mfg*
5137 Caps and gowns: women's and children's—wholesale
3643 Caps and plugs, attachment: electric—*mfg*
3466 Caps and tops, bottle: stamped metal—*mfg*
2675 Caps and tops, bottle: die cut from purchased paper or paperboard—mfpm—*mfg*
2892 Caps, blasting and detonating—*mfg*
3261 Caps, bolt: vitreous china and earthenware—*mfg*
3483 Caps, bomb—*mfg*
2353 Caps, cloth—mfpm—*mfg*
2899 Caps, for toy pistols—*mfg*
2371 Caps, fur—*mfg*
3131 Caps, heel and toe: leather or metal—*mfg*
2386 Caps, leather—*mfg*
5136 Caps, men's and boys'—wholesale
3089 Caps, plastics—*mfg*
3069 Caps, rubber—mitse—*mfg*
2353 Caps: textiles, straw, fur-felt, and wool-felt—mfpm—*mfg*
5137 Caps: women's and children's—wholesale
2253 Caps—mitse—*mfg*
3531 Capstans, ship—*mfg*
2899 Capsules, gelatin: empty—*mfg*
3711 Car bodies, including fiberglass—*mfg*
3532 Car dumpers, mining—*mfg*
4482 Car lighters (ferries)
4789 Car loading
3429 Car seals, metal—*mfg*
7299 Car title and tag service
3321 Car wheels, railroad: chilled cast iron—*mfg*
3312 Car wheels, rolled—*mfg*
3089 Carafes, plastics—*mfg*
2819 Carbide—*mfg*
3484 Carbines, 30 mm. (or 1.18 inch) or less—*mfg*
2821 Carbohydrate plastics—*mfg*
2892 Carbohydrates, nitrated (explosives)—*mfg*
3845 Carbon arc lamp units, electrotherapeutic: except infrared and ultraviolet—*mfg*
2869 Carbon bisulfide (disulfide)—*mfg*
2895 Carbon black—*mfg*
5169 Carbon black—wholesale
3297 Carbon brick—*mfg*
2813 Carbon dioxide—*mfg*
3955 Carbon paper—*mfg*
5112 Carbon paper—wholesale
2899 Carbon removing solvent—*mfg*
3624 Carbon specialties for electrical use—*mfg*
2869 Carbon tetrachloride—*mfg*
2819 Carbon, activated—*mfg*
2086 Carbonated beverages, nonalcoholic: bottled or canned—*mfg*
2812 Carbonates, potassium and sodium: not produced at mines—*mfg*
2299 Carbonized rags—*mfg*
3552 Carbonizing equipment (wool processing machinery)—*mfg*
2299 Carbonizing of wool, mohair, and similar fibers—*mfg*
3624 Carbons, electric—*mfg*
3624 Carbons, lighting—*mfg*
3221 Carboys, glass—*mfg*
7539 Carburetor repair
3592 Carburetors, all types—*mfg*
7319 Card advertising
3172 Card cases, except precious metal—*mfg*
3552 Card clothing for textile machines—*mfg*
2675 Card cutting—mfpm—*mfg*
3577 Card punching and sorting machines—*mfg*
7999 Card rooms
3577 Card-type conversion equipment, computer peripheral equipment—*mfg*
5113 Cardboard and products—wholesale
2675 Cardboard foundations and cutouts—mfpm—*mfg*
2675 Cardboard panels and cutouts—mfpm—*mfg*

3496 Carts, grocery: made from purchased wire—*mfg*
3484 Carts, machine gun and machine gun ammunition—*mfg*
2599 Carts, restaurant—*mfg*
2499 Carved and turned wood (except furniture)—*mfg*
3553 Carving machine, woodworking—*mfg*
3914 Carving sets, with metal handles and blades—*mfg*
3421 Carving sets: except all metal—*mfg*
2426 Carvings, furniture: wood—*mfg*
5087 Carwash equipment and supplies—wholesale
7542 Carwashes
3589 Carwashing machinery, including coin-operated—*mfg*
3111 Case leather—*mfg*
2824 Casein fibers—*mfg*
2821 Casein plastics—*mfg*
3089 Casein products, molded for the trade—*mfg*
2023 Casein, dry and wet—*mfg*
2211 Casement cloth, cotton—*mfg*
3442 Casements, aluminum—*mfg*
3873 Cases for watches—*mfg*
2522 Cases, filing: except wood—*mfg*
2521 Cases, filing: wood—*mfg*
3949 Cases, gun and rod (sporting equipment)—*mfg*
3172 Cases, jewelry: regardless of material—*mfg*
3161 Cases, luggage—*mfg*
2655 Cases, mailing: paper fiber (metal-end or all-fiber)—mfpm—*mfg*
3161 Cases, musical instrument—*mfg*
2441 Cases, packing: wood—nailed or lock corner—*mfg*
3089 Cases, plastics—*mfg*
2441 Cases, shipping: wood—nailed or lock corner—*mfg*
2449 Cases, shipping: wood—wirebound—*mfg*
3585 Cases, show and display: refrigerated—*mfg*
2517 Cases: radio, phonograph, and sewing machine—wood—*mfg*
3911 Cases: cigar, cigarette, and vanity—precious metal—*mfg*
3469 Cash and stamp boxes, stamped metal—*mfg*
0119 Cash grain farms: except wheat, rice, corn, and soybeans
3578 Cash registers, including adding machines with cash drawers—*mfg*
5044 Cash registers—wholesale
2869 Casing fluids for curing fruits, spices, and tobacco—*mfg*
3443 Casing, boiler: metal plate—*mfg*
1321 Casing-head butane and propane production
3769 Casings for missiles and missile components shipping and storage—*mfg*
3443 Casings, scroll—*mfg*
3444 Casings, sheet metal—*mfg*
7011 Casino hotels
3429 Casket hardware—*mfg*
5087 Caskets, burial—wholesale
3995 Caskets, metal and wood—*mfg*
2449 Casks, wood: coopered—*mfg*
3634 Casseroles, electric—*mfg*
5099 Cassettes, prerecorded: audio—wholesale
5065 Cassettes, recording—wholesale
3321 Cast iron pipe—*mfg*
5051 Cast iron pipe—wholesale
3325 Cast steel railroad car wheels—*mfg*
3272 Cast stone, concrete—*mfg*
3255 Castable refractories, clay—*mfg*
3297 Castable refractories, nonclay—*mfg*
3429 Casters, furniture—*mfg*
3429 Casters, industrial—*mfg*
7922 Casting agencies, theatrical: except motion picture
7819 Casting bureaus, motion picture
7922 Casting bureaus, theatrical: except motion picture
3089 Casting of plastics for the trade, except foam plastics—*mfg*
3365 Castings, aluminum: except die-castings—*mfg*
3321 Castings, compacted graphite iron—*mfg*
3369 Castings, except die-castings and castings of aluminum and copper—*mfg*
3366 Castings, except die-castings: brass, bronze, copper, and copper-base alloy—*mfg*
3321 Castings, gray iron and semisteel—*mfg*
3322 Castings, malleable iron—*mfg*
3369 Castings, precision, except die-castings: industrial and aircraft use—cobalt-chromium—*mfg*
5051 Castings, rough: iron and steel—wholesale
3069 Castings, rubber—*mfg*
3325 Castings, steel: except investment—*mfg*
2076 Castor oil and pomace—*mfg*
3143 Casual shoes, men's: except athletic and rubber footwear—*mfg*
6531 Casualty insurance and reinsurance
0279 Cat farms
2047 Cat food—*mfg*
5961 Catalog (order taking) offices of mail-order houses—retail
2621 Catalog paper—mitse—*mfg*
5399 Catalog showrooms, general merchandise: except catalog mail-order—retail

6019 Central liquidity facility
1629 Central station construction—general contractors
3273 Central-mixed concrete—*mfg*
3569 Centrifugal purifiers—*mfg*
3569 Centrifuges, industrial—*mfg*
3821 Centrifuges, laboratory—*mfg*
3269 Ceramic articles for craft shops—*mfg*
5032 Ceramic construction materials, except refractory—wholesale
3299 Ceramic fiber—*mfg*
3251 Ceramic glazed brick, clay—*mfg*
3567 Ceramic kilns and furnaces—*mfg*
3253 Ceramic tile, floor and wall—*mfg*
5032 Ceramic wall and floor tile—wholesale
8299 Ceramics schools
5945 Ceramics supplies—retail
2043 Cereal preparations and breakfast foods—*mfg*
2041 Cereals, cracked grain—mitse—*mfg*
1099 Cerium ore mining
2819 Cerium salts—*mfg*
1031 Cerrusite mining
2759 Certificates, security: engraved—*mfg*
8721 Certified public accountants (CPAs)
3842 Cervical collars—*mfg*
2819 Cesium metal—*mfg*
7699 Cesspool cleaning
1711 Cesspool construction—contractors
3728 Chaffing dispensers, aircraft—*mfg*
3634 Chafing dishes, electric—*mfg*
3429 Chain fittings—*mfg*
3446 Chain ladders, metal—*mfg*
3315 Chain link fencing, steel: made in wiredrawing plants—*mfg*
3546 Chain saws, portable—*mfg*
3425 Chain type saw blades—*mfg*
3568 Chain, power transmission—*mfg*
5085 Chain, power transmission—wholesale
3496 Chain, welded: made from purchased wire—*mfg*
3496 Chain, wire: made from purchased wire—*mfg*
3462 Chains, forged steel: not made in rolling mills—*mfg*
3829 Chains, surveyors'—*mfg*
5251 Chainsaws—retail
5084 Chainsaws—wholesale
2515 Chair and couch springs, assembled—*mfg*
2515 Chair beds, on frames of any material—*mfg*
2392 Chair covers, cloth—*mfg*
2426 Chair frames for upholstered furniture, wood—*mfg*
3499 Chair frames, metal—*mfg*
3429 Chair glides—*mfg*
2392 Chair pads, except felt—*mfg*
2426 Chair seats, hardwood—*mfg*
2426 Chair stock, hardwood: turned, shaped, or carved—*mfg*
2511 Chairs, bentwood—*mfg*
2519 Chairs, cane—*mfg*
3843 Chairs, dentists'—*mfg*
2511 Chairs, household: except upholstered—wood—*mfg*
2514 Chairs, household: metal—*mfg*
3999 Chairs, hydraulic: barber and beauty shop—*mfg*
5087 Chairs, hydraulic: beauty and barber shop—wholesale
2522 Chairs, office: except wood—*mfg*
2521 Chairs, office: wood—*mfg*
2531 Chairs, portable folding—*mfg*
2531 Chairs, tablet arm—*mfg*
2512 Chairs, upholstered on wood frames, except convertible beds—*mfg*
3842 Chairs, wheel—*mfg*
5021 Chairs: household, office, and public building—wholesale
1021 Chalcocite mining
1021 Chalcopyrite mining
1422 Chalk mining, crushed and broken—quarrying
3949 Chalk, billiard—*mfg*
1422 Chalk, ground or otherwise treated
3952 Chalk: e.g., carpenters', blackboard, marking, artists', tailors'—*mfg*
3281 Chalkboards, slate—*mfg*
2531 Chalkboards, wood—*mfg*
8611 Chambers of Commerce
2211 Chambrays—*mfg*
3541 Chamfering machines—*mfg*
3111 Chamois leather—*mfg*
5199 Chamois leather—wholesale
3646 Chandeliers, commercial—*mfg*
3645 Chandeliers, residential—*mfg*
3578 Change making machines—*mfg*
2895 Channel black—*mfg*
1629 Channel construction—general contractors
1629 Channel cutoff construction—general contractors
3446 Channels, furring—*mfg*
2819 Charcoal, activated—*mfg*
2861 Charcoal, except activated—*mfg*
5199 Charcoal—wholesale
7389 Charge account service (shopping plates)—collection by individual firms
3629 Chargers, battery: rectifying or nonrotating—*mfg*
6732 Charitable trusts, management of

2869 Citrates—*mfg*
2869 Citric acid—*mfg*
2899 Citronella oil—*mfg*
2869 Citronellal—*mfg*
0721 Citrus grove cultivation services
0762 Citrus grove management and maintenance, with or without crop services
0174 Citrus groves and farms
5084 Citrus processing machinery—wholesale
2048 Citrus seed meal—*mfg*
4111 City and suburban bus line operation
9121 City and town councils
9111 City and town managers' offices
8748 City planners, except professional engineering
8641 Civic associations
1542 Civic center construction—general contractors
9199 Civil rights commissions—government
9199 Civil service commissions—government
8299 Civil service schools
9211 Civilian courts
6411 Claim adjusters insurance: not employed by insurance companies
2091 Clam bouillon, broth, chowder, juice: bottled or canned—*mfg*
3423 Clamps, hand—*mfg*
3429 Clamps, hose—*mfg*
3545 Clamps, machine tool—*mfg*
3429 Clamps, metal—*mfg*
3841 Clamps, surgical—*mfg*
0913 Clams, digging of
3532 Clarifying machinery, mineral—*mfg*
3931 Clarinets and parts—*mfg*
3131 Clasps, shoe—*mfg*
7929 Classical music groups or artists
3532 Classifiers, metallurgical and mining—*mfg*
2631 Clay coated board—mitse—*mfg*
5032 Clay construction materials, except refractory—wholesale
3295 Clay for petroleum refining, chemically processed—*mfg*
3255 Clay refractories—*mfg*
3295 Clay, ground or otherwise treated—*mfg*
3952 Clay, modeling—*mfg*
1459 Clays (common) quarrying—not in conjunction with manufacturing
3559 Clayworking and tempering machines—*mfg*
7218 Clean room apparel supply service
1541 Clean room construction—general contractors
3714 Cleaners, air: motor vehicle—*mfg*
3599 Cleaners, boiler tube—*mfg*
2844 Cleaners, denture—*mfg*
3589 Cleaners, electric vacuum: industrial—*mfg*
3635 Cleaners, electric: vacuum—household—*mfg*
7212 Cleaners, not operating own drycleaning plants
2851 Cleaners, paintbrush—*mfg*
3999 Cleaners, pipe and cigarette holder—*mfg*
3471 Cleaning and descaling metal products, for the trade—*mfg*
7216 Cleaning and dyeing plants, except rug cleaning
7212 Cleaning and laundry pickup stations, not owned by laundries or cleaners
7542 Cleaning and polishing (detailing) new autos for dealers on a contract or fee basis
2044 Cleaning and polishing of rice—*mfg*
2842 Cleaning and polishing preparations—*mfg*
7699 Cleaning and reglazing of baking pans
7217 Cleaning and repairing plants, rug and carpet
7699 Cleaning bricks
1799 Cleaning building exteriors—contractors
3699 Cleaning equipment, ultrasonic: except medical and dental—*mfg*
1389 Cleaning lease tanks, oil and gas field: on a contract basis
3547 Cleaning lines, electrolytic (rolling mill equipment)—*mfg*
3532 Cleaning machinery, mineral—*mfg*
3523 Cleaning machines for fruits, grains, and vegetables: farm—*mfg*
1799 Cleaning new buildings after construction—contractors
5149 Cleaning of dry foods and spices—wholesale
4741 Cleaning of railroad cars
1221 Cleaning plants, bituminous coal
0751 Cleaning poultry coops
4789 Cleaning railroad ballasts
1389 Cleaning wells on a contract basis
2621 Cleansing tissue stock—mitse—*mfg*
2676 Cleansing tissues—mfpm—*mfg*
3647 Clearance lamps and reflectors, motor vehicle—*mfg*
1629 Clearing of land—general contractors
6099 Clearinghouse associations: bank or check
6289 Clearinghouses, commodity exchange
6289 Clearinghouses, security exchange
3264 Cleats, porcelain—*mfg*
3421 Cleavers—*mfg*
2389 Clergy's vestments—*mfg*
2449 Climax baskets—*mfg*
2835 Clinical chemistry reagents (including toxicology)—*mfg*
2835 Clinical chemistry standards and controls (including toxicology)—*mfg*

3568 Clutches, except motor vehicle—*mfg*
**** Clutches, vehicle—classify by type of vehicle
2835 Coagulation diagnostic reagents—*mfg*
2836 Coagulation products—*mfg*
3532 Coal breakers, cutters, and pulverizers—*mfg*
3444 Coal chutes, prefabricated sheet metal—*mfg*
5989 Coal dealers—retail
3312 Coal gas, derived from chemical recovery coke ovens—*mfg*
1311 Coal gasification at the mine site
1311 Coal liquefaction at the mine site
1231 Coal mining, anthracite
1221 Coal mining, bituminous: surface
1222 Coal mining, bituminous—underground
1221 Coal mining—brown
4619 Coal pipeline operation
1221 Coal preparation plants, bituminous or lignite
1311 Coal pyrolysis at the mine site
3312 Coal tar crudes, derived from chemical recovery coke ovens—*mfg*
2865 Coal tar crudes, derived from coal tar distillation—*mfg*
2865 Coal tar distillates—*mfg*
2865 Coal tar intermediates—*mfg*
2951 Coal tar paving materials, not made in petroleum refineries—*mfg*
5169 Coal tar products, primary and intermediate—wholesale
2821 Coal tar resins—*mfg*
5052 Coal—wholesale
3751 Coaster brakes, bicycle—*mfg*
4424 Coastwise transportation of freight
2369 Coat and legging sets: girls' and children's—mfpm—*mfg*
3496 Coat hangers, made from purchased wire—*mfg*
2396 Coat linings, fronts, and pads: for men's coats—*mfg*
2371 Coat linings, fur—*mfg*
7213 Coat supply service
2396 Coat trimmings fabric—mfpm—*mfg*
5131 Coated fabrics—wholesale
2671 Coated paper for packaging—mfpm—*mfg*
3479 Coating (hot dipping) of metals and formed products, for the trade—*mfg*
3554 Coating and finishing machinery, paper—*mfg*
2295 Coating and impregnating of fabrics, except rubberizing—*mfg*
3479 Coating and wrapping steel pipe—*mfg*
2952 Coating compounds, tar—mfpm—*mfg*
1799 Coating of concrete structures with plastics—contractors
3479 Coating of metals with plastics and resins, for the trade—*mfg*
3479 Coating of metals with silicon, for the trade—*mfg*
2851 Coating, air curing—*mfg*
3479 Coating, rust preventive—*mfg*
2066 Coatings, chocolate—*mfg*
2337 Coats, except fur and raincoats: women's, misses', and juniors'—mfpm—*mfg*
2329 Coats, except tailored or work: men's and boys'—mfpm—*mfg*
2371 Coats, fur—*mfg*
2386 Coats, leather or sheep-lined—*mfg*
5136 Coats, men's and boys'—wholesale
2329 Coats, oiled fabric and blanket-lined: men's and boys'—mfpm—*mfg*
2339 Coats, service apparel (e.g., medical and lab)—*mfg*
2311 Coats, tailored: men's and boys'—mfpm—*mfg*
2369 Coats: girls', children's, and infants'—mfpm—*mfg*
5137 Coats: women's, children's, and infants'—wholesale
3357 Coaxial cable, nonferrous—*mfg*
5063 Coaxial cable—wholesale
2819 Cobalt 60 (radioactive)—*mfg*
2819 Cobalt chloride—*mfg*
1061 Cobalt ore mining
3339 Cobalt refining, primary—*mfg*
2819 Cobalt sulfate—*mfg*
2833 Cocaine and derivatives—*mfg*
3432 Cocks, drain (including basin)—*mfg*
5813 Cocktail lounges
2087 Cocktail mixes, nonalcoholic—*mfg*
2085 Cocktails, alcoholic—*mfg*
5182 Cocktails, alcoholic: premixed—wholesale
2066 Cocoa butter—*mfg*
2066 Cocoa mix, instant—*mfg*
2066 Cocoa, powdered: mixed with other substances—*mfg*
2076 Coconut oil—*mfg*
2099 Coconut, desiccated and shredded—*mfg*
2843 Cod oil, sulfonated—*mfg*
0912 Cod, catching of
3827 Coddington magnifying instruments—*mfg*
2833 Codeine and derivatives—*mfg*
2091 Codfish: smoked, salted, dried, and pickled—*mfg*
2095 Coffee concentrates (instant coffee)—*mfg*
2095 Coffee extracts—*mfg*
0179 Coffee farms
2087 Coffee flavorings and syrups—*mfg*
3634 Coffee makers, household: electric—*mfg*

2835 Contrast media diagnostic products (e.g., iodine and barium)—*mfg*
3625 Control circuit devices: magnet and solid-state—*mfg*
3625 Control circuit relays, industrial—*mfg*
3621 Control equipment for buses and trucks—*mfg*
3625 Control equipment, electric—*mfg*
3714 Control equipment, motor vehicle: acceleration mechanisms and governors—*mfg*
3613 Control panels, electric power distribution—*mfg*
3559 Control rod drive mechanisms for use on nuclear reactors—*mfg*
3612 Control transformers—*mfg*
3492 Control valves, fluid power: metal—*mfg*
3674 Controlled rectifiers, solid-state—*mfg*
3823 Controllers for process variables: electric, electronic, and pneumatic—*mfg*
9311 Controllers' offices—government
5084 Controlling instruments and accessories, industrial—wholesale
3625 Controls and control accessories, industrial—*mfg*
3625 Controls for adjustable speed drives—*mfg*
3824 Controls, revolution and timing instruments—*mfg*
8059 Convalescent homes for psychiatric patients, with health care
8051 Convalescent homes with continuous nursing care
8059 Convalescent homes with health care
3631 Convection ovens, household: including portable—*mfg*
5074 Convectors—wholesale
5411 Convenience food stores—retail
3643 Convenience outlets, electric—*mfg*
7389 Convention bureaus
7389 Convention decorators
8661 Convents
3621 Converters, phase and rotary: electrical equipment—*mfg*
2515 Convertible sofas—*mfg*
3111 Convertors, leather—*mfg*
3496 Conveyor belts, made from purchased wire—*mfg*
1796 Conveyor system installation—contractors
3535 Conveyor systems for general industrial use—*mfg*
5084 Conveyor systems—wholesale
3523 Conveyors, farm (agricultural machinery)—*mfg*
3469 Cookers, pressure: stamped or drawn—*mfg*
3589 Cookers, steam: restaurant type—*mfg*
5461 Cookie stores—retail
2052 Cookies—*mfg*
5149 Cookies—wholesale
3634 Cooking appliances, household: electric, except convection and microwave ovens—*mfg*
3589 Cooking equipment, commercial—*mfg*
5046 Cooking equipment, commercial—wholesale
2079 Cooking oils, vegetable: except corn oil—refined—*mfg*
5149 Cooking oils—wholesale
8299 Cooking schools
3365 Cooking utensils, cast aluminum: except die-castings—*mfg*
3321 Cooking utensils, cast iron—*mfg*
3229 Cooking utensils, glass and glass ceramic—*mfg*
3262 Cooking ware, china—*mfg*
3263 Cooking ware, fine earthenware—*mfg*
3469 Cooking ware, porcelain enameled—*mfg*
3269 Cooking ware: stoneware, coarse earthenware, and pottery—*mfg*
5719 Cookware—retail
4961 Cooled air suppliers
5078 Coolers, beverage and drinking water: mechanical—wholesale
3585 Coolers, milk and water: electric—*mfg*
3086 Coolers, portable: foamed plastics—*mfg*
4741 Cooling of railroad cars
3724 Cooling systems, aircraft engine—*mfg*
3443 Cooling towers, metal plate—*mfg*
3444 Cooling towers, sheet metal—*mfg*
2499 Cooling towers, wood or wood and sheet metal combination—*mfg*
2449 Cooperage—*mfg*
2429 Cooperage stock mills—*mfg*
2429 Cooperage stock: staves, heading, and hoops—sawed or split—*mfg*
5085 Cooperage stock—wholesale
1531 Cooperative apartment developers on own account
6531 Cooperative apartment manager
6311 Cooperative life insurance organizations
2449 Coopered tubs—*mfg*
5137 Coordinate sets: women's, children's, and infants'—wholesale
3259 Coping, wall: clay—*mfg*
3272 Copings, concrete—*mfg*
2822 Copolymers: butadiene-styrene, butadiene-acrylonitrile, over 50 percent butadiene—*mfg*
3366 Copper and copper-base alloy castings, except die-castings—*mfg*
3366 Copper and copper-base alloy foundries—*mfg*
2879 Copper arsenate, formulated—*mfg*

4783 Crating goods for shipping
0913 Crayfish, catching of
3952 Crayons: chalk, gypsum, charcoal, fusains, pastel, and wax—*mfg*
2869 Cream of tartar—*mfg*
5084 Cream separators, except farm—wholesale
3523 Cream separators, farm—*mfg*
5083 Cream separators, farm—wholesale
3556 Cream separators, industrial—*mfg*
5143 Cream stations—wholesale
2023 Cream substitutes—*mfg*
2026 Cream, aerated—*mfg*
2026 Cream, bottled—*mfg*
2026 Cream, sour—*mfg*
2023 Cream: dried, powdered, and canned—*mfg*
2021 Creamery butter—*mfg*
2844 Creams, cosmetic—*mfg*
2844 Creams, shaving—*mfg*
6351 Credit and other financial responsibility insurance
7323 Credit bureaus and agencies
7389 Credit card service (collection by individual firms)
6153 Credit card service, collection by central agency
7323 Credit clearinghouses
6159 Credit institutions, agricultural
7323 Credit investigation services
6061 Credit unions, Federal
6062 Credit unions, State: not federally chartered
3949 Creels, fish—*mfg*
3552 Creels, textile machinery—*mfg*
3569 Cremating ovens—*mfg*
7261 Crematories
2865 Creosote oil, made in chemical plants—*mfg*
2861 Creosote, wood—*mfg*
2491 Creosoting of wood—*mfg*
2679 Crepe paper—mfpm—*mfg*
2221 Crepe satins—*mfg*
2211 Crepes, cotton—*mfg*
******** Cresines—code according to material from which made
2821 Cresol resins—*mfg*
2821 Cresol-furfural resins—*mfg*
2865 Cresols, made in chemical plants—*mfg*
2865 Cresylic acid, made in chemical plants—*mfg*
2211 Cretonne, cotton—*mfg*
3731 Crew boats, building and repairing—*mfg*
0761 Crew leaders, farm labor: contract
2252 Crew socks—*mfg*
3272 Cribbing, concrete—*mfg*
2514 Cribs, metal—*mfg*
2511 Cribs, wood—*mfg*
3949 Cricket equipment—*mfg*
9229 Criminal justice statistics centers—government
2211 Crinoline—*mfg*
8322 Crisis centers
8322 Crisis intervention centers
2284 Crochet thread: cotton, silk, manmade fibers, and wool—*mfg*
2395 Crochet ware, machine-made—*mfg*
2281 Crochet yarn: cotton, silk, wool, and manmade staple—*mfg*
3634 Crock pots, electric—*mfg*
3269 Crockery—*mfg*
5719 Crockery stores—retail
5023 Crockery—wholesale
2051 Croissants, except frozen—*mfg*
2053 Croissants, frozen—*mfg*
3523 Crop driers, farm—*mfg*
0721 Crop dusting, with/without fertilizing
0191 Crop farms, general
0721 Crop spraying, with/without fertilizing
3199 Crops, riding—*mfg*
3949 Croquet sets—*mfg*
3272 Crossing slabs, concrete—*mfg*
2491 Crossties, treated—*mfg*
8072 Crowns and bridges made in dental laboratories to order for the profession
5085 Crowns and closures, metal—wholesale
3466 Crowns, jar: stamped metal—*mfg*
3255 Crucibles, fire clay—*mfg*
3297 Crucibles: graphite, magnesite, chrome, silica, or other nonclay materials—*mfg*
1311 Crude oil production
5172 Crude oil, except bulk stations and terminals—wholesale
4612 Crude petroleum pipelines
1311 Crude petroleum production
0851 Cruising timber
2051 Crullers, except frozen—*mfg*
3523 Crushers, feed (agricultural machinery)—*mfg*
3569 Crushers, ice: except household—*mfg*
3531 Crushers, mineral: portable—*mfg*
3532 Crushers, mineral: stationary—*mfg*
3821 Crushing and grinding apparatus, laboratory—*mfg*
5084 Crushing machinery and equipment, industrial—wholesale
1221 Crushing plants, bituminous coal
5082 Crushing, pulverizing and screening machinery for construction and mining—wholesale
0273 Crustacean farms
3842 Crutches and walkers—*mfg*
3679 Cryogenic cooling devices (e.g., cryostats) for infrared detectors and masers—*mfg*

1541 Custom builders, industrial and warehouse—general contractors
1542 Custom builders, nonresidential: except industrial and warehouses—general contractors
1522 Custom builders, residential: except single-family—general contractors
1521 Custom builders, single-family houses—general contractors
3087 Custom compounding of purchased resins—*mfg*
3069 Custom compounding of rubber materials—*mfg*
3449 Custom roll formed products, metal—*mfg*
2421 Custom sawmills—*mfg*
5699 Custom tailors—retail
4731 Customhouse brokers
7532 Customizing automobiles, trucks or vans: except on a factory basis
9311 Customs Bureaus
4731 Customs clearance of freight
3231 Cut and engraved glassware, made from purchased glass—*mfg*
5992 Cut flowers—retail
5193 Cut flowers—wholesale
3131 Cut stock for boots and shoes—*mfg*
2421 Cut stock, softwood—*mfg*
3281 Cut stone products—*mfg*
5719 Cutlery stores—retail
3421 Cutlery, except table cutlery with handles of metal—*mfg*
3914 Cutlery, with metal handles and blades—*mfg*
5072 Cutlery—wholesale
3541 Cutoff machines (metalworking machinery)—*mfg*
3993 Cutouts and displays, window and lobby—*mfg*
3613 Cutouts, distribution—*mfg*
2675 Cutouts, paper and paperboard: die-cut from purchased material—*mfg*
3643 Cutouts, switch and fuse—*mfg*
3556 Cutters, biscuit (machines)—*mfg*
3532 Cutters, coal—*mfg*
3523 Cutters, ensilage—*mfg*
3423 Cutters, glass—*mfg*
3545 Cutters, milling—*mfg*
3554 Cutting and folding machines, paper—*mfg*
3544 Cutting dies, for cutting metal—*mfg*
3423 Cutting dies, paper industry—*mfg*
3423 Cutting dies: except metal cutting—*mfg*
3843 Cutting instruments, dental—*mfg*
3541 Cutting machines, pipe (machine tools)—*mfg*
2675 Cutting of cards—mfpm—*mfg*
3111 Cutting of leather—*mfg*
2992 Cutting oils, blending and compounding from purchased material—*mfg*
1629 Cutting right-of-way—general contractors
3545 Cutting tools and bits for use on lathes, planers, shapers, etc.—*mfg*
3549 Cutting up lines—*mfg*
3231 Cutware, made from purchased glass—*mfg*
2819 Cyanides—*mfg*
1459 Cyanite mining
1321 Cycle condensate production (natural gas)
3944 Cycles, sidewalk: children's—*mfg*
5169 Cyclic crudes and intermediates—wholesale
2865 Cyclic crudes, coal tar: product of coal tar distillation—*mfg*
2865 Cyclic intermediates, made in chemical plants—*mfg*
3069 Cyclo rubbers, natural—*mfg*
2822 Cyclo rubbers, synthetic—*mfg*
2865 Cyclohexane—*mfg*
3443 Cyclones, industrial: metal plate—*mfg*
2869 Cyclopropane—*mfg*
2834 Cyclopropane for anesthetic use (U.S.P. par N.F.), packaged—*mfg*
3699 Cyclotrons—*mfg*
3714 Cylinder heads, motor vehicle: gasoline engines—*mfg*
3272 Cylinder pipe, prestressed concrete—*mfg*
3272 Cylinder pipe, pretensioned concrete—*mfg*
3541 Cylinder reboring machines—*mfg*
3496 Cylinder wire cloth, made from purchased wire—*mfg*
3484 Cylinders and clips, gun: 30 mm. (or 1.18 inch) or less—*mfg*
3593 Cylinders, fluid power: hydraulic and pneumatic—*mfg*
3443 Cylinders, pressure: metal plate—*mfg*
3561 Cylinders, pump—*mfg*
3931 Cymbals and parts—*mfg*
3845 Cystoscopes, electromedical—*mfg*
3841 Cystoscopes, except electromedical—*mfg*
2835 Cytology and histology diagnostic products—*mfg*

D

2879 DDT (insecticide), formulated—*mfg*
2869 DDT, technical—*mfg*
5812 Dairy bars
5143 Dairy depots—wholesale
3523 Dairy equipment, farm—*mfg*
5083 Dairy farm machinery and equipment—wholesale
0241 Dairy farms
0241 Dairy heifer replacement farms
0751 Dairy herd improvement associations

3585 Dehumidifiers, except portable: electric—*mfg*
2034 Dehydrated fruits, vegetables, and soups—*mfg*
3556 Dehydrating equipment, food processing—*mfg*
3728 Deicing equipment, aircraft—*mfg*
2899 Deicing fluid—*mfg*
2611 Deinking of newsprint—*mfg*
3679 Delay lines—*mfg*
7319 Delivering advertising, private
3496 Delivery cases, made from purchased wire—*mfg*
3825 Demand meters, electric—*mfg*
2499 Demijohn covers: willow, rattan and reed—*mfg*
1795 Demolition of buildings or other structures, except marine—contractors
7389 Demonstration service, separate from sale
3715 Demountable cargo containers—*mfg*
2869 Denatured alcohol, industrial (nonbeverage)—*mfg*
2211 Denims—*mfg*
3861 Densitometers—*mfg*
3826 Densitometers, analytical—*mfg*
3823 Density and specific gravity instruments, industrial process type—*mfg*
3843 Dental alloys for amalgams—*mfg*
8621 Dental associations
3843 Dental chairs—*mfg*
3843 Dental engines—*mfg*
3843 Dental equipment and supplies—*mfg*
5047 Dental equipment—wholesale
3843 Dental hand instruments, including forceps—*mfg*
8049 Dental hygienists, offices of
7699 Dental instrument repair
6324 Dental insurance (providing services by contracts with health facilities)
8071 Dental laboratories, X-ray
8072 Dental laboratories, except X-ray
3843 Dental laboratory equipment—*mfg*
5047 Dental laboratory equipment—wholesale
3843 Dental metal—*mfg*
8021 Dental surgeons, offices of
2844 Dentifrices—*mfg*
5047 Dentists' professional supplies—wholesale
8021 Dentists, offices and clinics of
2844 Denture cleaners—*mfg*
3843 Denture materials—*mfg*
8072 Dentures made in dental laboratories to order for the profession
7342 Deodorant servicing of rest rooms
2842 Deodorants, nonpersonal—*mfg*
2844 Deodorants, personal—*mfg*
5311 Department stores—retail
2844 Depilatories, cosmetic—*mfg*
7299 Depilatory salons
3471 Depolishing metal, for the trade—*mfg*
6099 Deposit brokers
6399 Deposit or share insurance
3842 Depressors, tongue—*mfg*
3489 Depth charge release pistols and projectors—*mfg*
3483 Depth charges and parts (ordnance)—*mfg*
2834 Dermatological preparations—*mfg*
8011 Dermatologists, offices of
1389 Derrick building, repairing, and dismantling: oil and gas—on a contract basis
3531 Derricks, except oil and gas field—*mfg*
3533 Derricks, oil and gas field—*mfg*
5084 Derricks—wholesale
3559 Desalination equipment—*mfg*
2899 Desalter kits, sea water—*mfg*
3295 Desiccants, activated: clay—*mfg*
2819 Desiccants, activated: silica gel—*mfg*
1521 Designing and erecting combined: single-family houses—general contractors
1542 Designing and erecting, combined: commercial—general contractors
1541 Designing and erecting, combined: industrial—general contractors
1522 Designing and erecting, combined: residential, except single-family—general contractors
8711 Designing: ship, boat, and machine
3634 Desk fans, electric—*mfg*
3646 Desk lamps, commercial—*mfg*
3645 Desk lamps, residential—*mfg*
3999 Desk pads, except paper—*mfg*
2678 Desk pads, paper—mfpm—*mfg*
3281 Desk set bases, onyx—*mfg*
3199 Desk sets, leather—*mfg*
2511 Desks, household: wood—*mfg*
5021 Desks, including school—wholesale
2522 Desks, office: except wood—*mfg*
2521 Desks, office: wood—*mfg*
2024 Dessert pops, frozen: flavored ice, fruit, pudding, and gelatin—*mfg*
2024 Desserts, frozen: except bakery—*mfg*
2099 Desserts, ready-to-mix—*mfg*
3731 Destroyer tenders, building and repairing—*mfg*
7542 Detailing (cleaning and polishing) new autos for dealers on a contract or fee basis
0721 Detasseling of corn
7381 Detective agencies
3829 Detectors, scintillation—*mfg*
9223 Detention centers—government
2841 Detergents, synthetic organic and inorganic alkaline—*mfg*

3519 Diesel and semidiesel engines: for stationary, marine, traction, etc.—*mfg*
3519 Diesel engine parts—*mfg*
7538 Diesel engine repair, automotive
5084 Diesel engines and engine parts, industrial—wholesale
3544 Diesets for metal stamping (presses)—*mfg*
3541 Diesinking machines—*mfg*
7299 Diet workshops
2023 Dietary supplements, dairy and nondairy base—*mfg*
5499 Dietetic food stores—retail
2869 Diethylcyclohexane (mixed isomers)—*mfg*
2869 Diethylene glycol ether—*mfg*
8049 Dieticians, offices of
3823 Differential pressure instruments, industrial process type—*mfg*
3826 Differential thermal analysis instruments—*mfg*
3714 Differentials and parts, motor vehicle—*mfg*
3443 Digesters, process: metal plate—*mfg*
3823 Digital displays of process variables—*mfg*
3663 Digital encoders—*mfg*
3825 Digital panel meters, electricity measuring—*mfg*
3825 Digital test equipment, electronic and electrical circuits and equipment—*mfg*
3825 Digital-to-analog converters, electronic instrumentation type—*mfg*
2834 Digitalis pharmaceutical preparations—*mfg*
2833 Digitoxin—*mfg*
2821 Diisocyanate resins—*mfg*
1629 Dike construction—general contractors
3281 Dimension stone for buildings—*mfg*
2426 Dimension, hardwood—*mfg*
2869 Dimethyl divinyl acetylene (di-isopropenyl acetylene)—*mfg*
2869 Dimethylhydrazine, unsymmetrical—*mfg*
2211 Dimities—*mfg*
5812 Diners (eating places)
2514 Dinette sets, metal—*mfg*
3732 Dinghies, building and repairing—*mfg*
4789 Dining car operations, not performed by line-haul railroad companies
3743 Dining cars and car equipment—*mfg*
2511 Dining room furniture, wood—*mfg*
5812 Dining rooms
5812 Dinner theaters
2038 Dinners, frozen: packaged—*mfg*
5142 Dinners, frozen—wholesale
3089 Dinnerware, plastics: except foam—*mfg*
3825 Diode and transistor testers—*mfg*
3674 Diodes, solid-state (germanium, silicon, etc.)—*mfg*
5065 Diodes—wholesale
1423 Diorite, crushed and broken—quarrying
1411 Diorite, dimension—quarrying
2865 Diphenylamine—*mfg*
2836 Diphtheria toxin—*mfg*
9721 Diplomatic services—government
3469 Dippers, ice cream—*mfg*
3479 Dipping metal in plastics solution as a preservative, for the trade—*mfg*
2879 Dips, cattle and sheep—*mfg*
2022 Dips, cheese-based—*mfg*
2099 Dips, except cheese and sour cream based—*mfg*
2026 Dips, sour cream based—*mfg*
4841 Direct broadcast satellite (DBS) services
7331 Direct mail advertising service
5963 Direct selling organizations (headquarters of door-to-door canvassers)—retail
6153 Direct working capital financing
1381 Directional drilling of oil and gas wells on a contract basis
3714 Directional signals, motor vehicle—*mfg*
2759 Directories, printed: except lithographed or gravure (not publishing)—*mfg*
7389 Directories, telephone: distribution on a contract or fee basis
2754 Directories: gravure printing (not publishing)—*mfg*
2741 Directories: publishing and printing, or publishing only—*mfg*
7819 Directors, motion picture: independent
3721 Dirigibles—*mfg*
1794 Dirt moving—contractors
3589 Dirt sweeping units, industrial—*mfg*
6321 Disability health insurance
9229 Disaster preparedness and management offices—government
8322 Disaster services
3651 Disc players, compact—*mfg*
1629 Discharging station construction, mine—general contractors
5813 Discotheques, alcoholic beverage
7911 Discotheques, except those serving alcoholic beverages
3652 Discs, laser: audio prerecorded—*mfg*
0721 Disease control for crops, with or without fertilizing
2599 Dish carts, restaurant—*mfg*
2392 Dishcloths, nonwoven textile—*mfg*
2211 Dishcloths, woven: made in weaving mills—*mfg*
2259 Dishcloths—mitse—*mfg*
3843 Dishes, abrasive: dental—*mfg*
3263 Dishes, commercial and household: fine earthenware (whiteware)—*mfg*

2851 Driers, paint—*mfg*
3861 Driers, photographic—*mfg*
3523 Driers: grain, hay, and seed (agricultural implements)—*mfg*
3634 Driers: hand, face, and hair—electric—*mfg*
3812 Driftmeters, aeronautical—*mfg*
3545 Drill bits, metalworking—*mfg*
3423 Drill bits, woodworking—*mfg*
3545 Drill bushings (drilling jig)—*mfg*
3541 Drill presses (machine tools)—*mfg*
3533 Drill rigs, all types—*mfg*
3499 Drill stands, metal—*mfg*
3731 Drilling and production platforms, floating, oil and gas—*mfg*
5084 Drilling bits—wholesale
1241 Drilling for bituminous coal, anthracite, and lignite on a contract basis
1081 Drilling for metal mining: on a contract basis
1481 Drilling for nonmetallic minerals, except fuels: on a contract basis
3545 Drilling machine attachments and accessories (machine tool accessories)—*mfg*
3541 Drilling machine tools (metal cutting)—*mfg*
2899 Drilling mud—*mfg*
5169 Drilling mud—wholesale
1381 Drilling of oil and gas wells: on a contract basis
3915 Drilling of pearls—*mfg*
3533 Drilling tools for gas, oil, or water wells—*mfg*
3546 Drilling tools, masonry and concrete: power (portable)—*mfg*
1381 Drilling water intake wells: on a contract basis
1781 Drilling water wells—contractors
1381 Drilling, service well: on a contract basis
3546 Drills (except rock drilling and coring), portable: electric and pneumatic—*mfg*
3545 Drills (machine tool accessories)—*mfg*
3532 Drills and drilling equipment, mining: except oil and gas field—*mfg*
3532 Drills, core—*mfg*
2211 Drills, cotton—*mfg*
3843 Drills, dental—*mfg*
3546 Drills, hand: electric—*mfg*
3423 Drills, hand: except power—*mfg*
3532 Drills, rock: portable—*mfg*
2087 Drink powders and concentrates—*mfg*
2656 Drinking cups, paper: except those made from pressed or molded pulp—mfpm—*mfg*
3431 Drinking fountains, except mechanically refrigerated: metal—*mfg*
3088 Drinking fountains, except mechanically refrigerated: plastics—*mfg*
3585 Drinking fountains, mechanically refrigerated—*mfg*
3261 Drinking fountains, vitreous china—*mfg*
5813 Drinking places, alcoholic beverages
2656 Drinking straws, except glass or plastics—mfpm—*mfg*
3229 Drinking straws, glass—*mfg*
5078 Drinking water coolers, mechanical—wholesale
2086 Drinks, fruit: bottled, canned, or fresh—*mfg*
3568 Drive chains, bicycle and motorcycle—*mfg*
3714 Drive shafts, motor vehicle—*mfg*
7389 Drive-a-way automobile service
5812 Drive-in restaurants
7833 Drive-in theaters
3545 Drivers, drill and cutters (machine tool accessories)—*mfg*
3572 Drives, computer: disk and drum—*mfg*
3566 Drives, high-speed industrial: except hydrostatic—*mfg*
3594 Drives, hydrostatic transmissions—*mfg*
1629 Driving piling—general contractors
2411 Driving timber—*mfg*
2394 Drop cloths, fabric—mfpm—*mfg*
3462 Drop forgings, iron and steel: not made in rolling mills—*mfg*
3542 Drop hammers, for forging and shaping metal—*mfg*
8069 Drug addiction rehabilitation hospitals
2865 Drug dyes, synthetic—*mfg*
2833 Drug grading, grinding, and milling—*mfg*
5122 Drug proprietaries—wholesale
8361 Drug rehabilitation centers, residential: with health care incidental
5912 Drug stores—retail
8093 Drug treatment, outpatient clinics
3069 Druggists' sundries, rubber—*mfg*
5122 Druggists' sundries—wholesale
5122 Drugs—wholesale
7929 Drum and bugle corps (drill teams)
3537 Drum cradles—*mfg*
3572 Drum drives, computer—*mfg*
3931 Drummers' traps—*mfg*
2655 Drums, fiber (metal-end or all-fiber)—mfpm—*mfg*
5085 Drums, new and reconditioned—wholesale
3931 Drums, parts, and accessories (musical instruments)—*mfg*
3089 Drums, plastics (containers)—*mfg*
2449 Drums, plywood—*mfg*
3412 Drums, shipping: metal—*mfg*
2449 Drums, shipping: wood—wirebound—*mfg*
3944 Drums, toy—*mfg*

2253 Dyeing and finishing knit outerwear, except hosiery, gloves, and nightwear—*mfg*
2254 Dyeing and finishing knit underwear—*mfg*
2258 Dyeing and finishing lace goods—*mfg*
2273 Dyeing and finishing of rugs and carpets—*mfg*
2231 Dyeing and finishing of wool and similar animal fibers: except knit—*mfg*
2258 Dyeing and finishing warp knit fabrics—*mfg*
2257 Dyeing and finishing weft knit fabrics—*mfg*
2251 Dyeing and finishing women's full-length and knee-length hosiery, except socks—*mfg*
2261 Dyeing cotton broadwoven fabrics—*mfg*
3999 Dyeing feathers, for the trade—*mfg*
3999 Dyeing furs—*mfg*
2381 Dyeing gloves, woven or knit: for the trade—*mfg*
3552 Dyeing machinery, textile—*mfg*
2262 Dyeing manmade fiber and silk broadwoven fabrics—*mfg*
2269 Dyeing raw stock, yarn, and narrow fabrics: except knit and wool—*mfg*
3999 Dyeing sponges—*mfg*
3999 Dyers' nets—*mfg*
2865 Dyes, food: synthetic—*mfg*
2844 Dyes, hair—*mfg*
2899 Dyes, household—*mfg*
2865 Dyes, synthetic organic—*mfg*
2861 Dyestuffs, natural—*mfg*
5169 Dyestuffs—wholesale
2892 Dynamite—*mfg*
3829 Dynamometer instruments—*mfg*
3621 Dynamos, electric: except automotive—*mfg*
3621 Dynamotors—*mfg*
3699 Dynamotrons—*mfg*
3728 Dynetric balancing stands, aircraft—*mfg*
3429 Dzus fasteners—*mfg*

E

2822 EPDM polymers—*mfg*
3842 Ear stoppers—*mfg*
7353 Earth moving equipment rental and leasing
1629 Earth moving, not connected with building construction—general contractors
1794 Earth moving—contractors
3269 Earthenware table and kitchen articles, coarse—*mfg*
3263 Earthenware: commercial and household—semivitreous—*mfg*
2048 Earthworm food and bedding—*mfg*
0279 Earthworm hatcheries
3952 Easels, artists'—*mfg*
2771 Easter cards, except hand painted—*mfg*
5113 Eating utensils: forks, knives, spoons-disposable plastics—wholesale
3444 Eaves, sheet metal—*mfg*
3281 Ecclesiastical statuary, marble—*mfg*
3299 Ecclesiastical statuary: gypsum, clay, or papier-mache—factory production only—*mfg*
3914 Ecclesiastical ware: silver, nickel silver, pewter, and plated—*mfg*
8748 Economic consulting
9611 Economic development agencies—government
8732 Economic research, commercial
8733 Economic research, noncommercial
3443 Economizers (boilers)—*mfg*
6082 Edge Act Corporations
3423 Edge tools for woodworking: augers, bits, gimlets, countersinks, etc.—*mfg*
2789 Edging books, cards, or paper—*mfg*
2258 Edgings, lace—*mfg*
3861 Editing equipment, motion picture: rewinds, viewers, titlers, and splicers—*mfg*
7819 Editing of motion picture film
7338 Editing service
9411 Education offices, nonoperating
9411 Education statistics centers—government
8748 Educational consulting, except management
7812 Educational motion picture production
8732 Educational research, commercial
8733 Educational research, noncommercial
6732 Educational trusts, management of
0912 Eels, catching of
2834 Effervescent salts—*mfg*
2015 Egg albumen—*mfg*
2675 Egg cartons, die-cut paper and paperboard—mfpm—*mfg*
2679 Egg cartons, molded pulp—mfpm—*mfg*
2679 Egg case filler flats, molded pulp—mfpm—*mfg*
2675 Egg case fillers and flats, die-cut from purchased paper or paperboard—*mfg*
2441 Egg cases, wood—*mfg*
3634 Egg cookers, electric—*mfg*
5499 Egg dealers—retail
0252 Egg farms, chicken
0259 Egg farms, poultry: except chicken and turkey
0253 Egg farms, turkey

3823 Electrodes used in industrial process measurement—*mfg*
3641 Electrodes, cold cathode fluorescent lamp—*mfg*
3548 Electrodes, electric welding—*mfg*
3845 Electroencephalographs—*mfg*
3542 Electroforming machines—*mfg*
3829 Electrogamma ray loggers—*mfg*
3845 Electrogastrograph—*mfg*
3492 Electrohydraulic servo valves, fluid power: metal—*mfg*
3471 Electrolizing steel, for the trade—*mfg*
7299 Electrolysis (hair removal)
2835 Electrolyte diagnostic reagents—*mfg*
3823 Electrolytic conductivity instruments, industrial process type—*mfg*
3826 Electrolytic conductivity instruments, laboratory type—*mfg*
3541 Electrolytic metal cutting machine tools—*mfg*
3625 Electromagnetic brakes and clutches—*mfg*
3824 Electromechanical counters—*mfg*
3845 Electromedical apparatus—*mfg*
5047 Electromedical equipment—wholesale
3845 Electromyographs—*mfg*
3671 Electron beam (beta ray) generator tubes—*mfg*
3699 Electron beam metal cutting, forming, and welding machines—*mfg*
3699 Electron linear accelerators—*mfg*
3826 Electron microprobes—*mfg*
3826 Electron microscopes—*mfg*
3826 Electron paramagnetic spin type apparatus—*mfg*
3559 Electron tube making machinery—*mfg*
3671 Electron tube parts, except glass blanks: bases, getters, and guns—*mfg*
3825 Electron tube test equipment—*mfg*
3671 Electron tubes—*mfg*
3541 Electron-discharge metal cutting machine tools—*mfg*
5065 Electronic coils and transformers—wholesale
3577 Electronic computer subassembly for film reader and phototheodolite—*mfg*
5065 Electronic connectors—wholesale
1731 Electronic control system installation—contractors
3469 Electronic enclosures: stamped or pressed—*mfg*
7359 Electronic equipment rental and leasing, except medical and computer equipment
7629 Electronic equipment repair, except computers and computer peripheral equipment
6099 Electronic funds transfer networks, including switching
3944 Electronic game machines, except coin-operated—*mfg*
3651 Electronic kits for home assembly: radio and television receiving sets, and phonograph equipment—*mfg*
4822 Electronic mail services
3931 Electronic musical instruments—*mfg*
5065 Electronic parts—wholesale
3825 Electronic test equipment for testing electrical characteristics—*mfg*
3824 Electronic totalizing counters—*mfg*
3944 Electronic toys—*mfg*
5065 Electronic tubes: receiving, transmitting, and industrial—wholesale
3826 Electrophoresis instruments—*mfg*
3559 Electroplating machinery and equipment, except rolling mill lines—*mfg*
3471 Electroplating of metals and formed products, for the trade—*mfg*
1721 Electrostatic painting on site (including of lockers and fixtures)—contractors
3699 Electrostatic particle accelerators—*mfg*
3564 Electrostatic precipitators—*mfg*
3641 Electrotherapeutic lamp units for ultraviolet and infrared radiation—*mfg*
3845 Electrotherapy unit—*mfg*
2796 Electrotype plates—*mfg*
2796 Electrotyping for the trade—*mfg*
3555 Electrotyping machines—*mfg*
3826 Elemental analyzers (CHNOS)—*mfg*
8211 Elementary schools
2879 Elements, minor or trace (agricultural chemicals)—*mfg*
1622 Elevated highway construction—general contractors
4111 Elevated railway operation
1791 Elevator front installation, metal—contractors
3534 Elevator fronts—*mfg*
3446 Elevator guide rails, metal—*mfg*
1796 Elevator installation, conversion, and repair—contractors
3534 Elevators and elevator equipment, passenger and freight—*mfg*
3728 Elevators, aircraft—*mfg*
3523 Elevators, farm—*mfg*
4221 Elevators, grain: storage only
3534 Elevators, powered: nonfarm—*mfg*
5084 Elevators—wholesale
9721 Embassies
2395 Emblems, embroidered—*mfg*
2399 Emblems, made from fabrics—*mfg*
3199 Embossed leather goods for the trade—*mfg*

3764 Engines and engine parts, guided missile—*mfg*
3519 Engines and engine parts, internal combustion— military tank—*mfg*
5084 Engines and parts, diesel—wholesale
3714 Engines and parts, except diesel: motor vehicle—*mfg*
3519 Engines, internal combustion: except aircraft and nondiesel automotive—*mfg*
3944 Engines, miniature—*mfg*
3743 Engines, steam (locomotives)—*mfg*
3511 Engines, steam: except locomotives—*mfg*
3519 Engines: diesel and semidiesel and dual fuel—except aircraft—*mfg*
0161 English pea farms
3231 Engraved glassware—*mfg*
3423 Engravers' tools, hand—*mfg*
3479 Engraving jewelry, silverware, and metal for the trade: except printing—*mfg*
3555 Engraving machinery and equipment (printing trades machinery)—*mfg*
2759 Engraving of cards, except greeting cards—*mfg*
3089 Engraving of plastics—*mfg*
2796 Engraving on copper, steel, wood, or rubber plates for printing purposes—*mfg*
2796 Engraving on textile printing plates and cylinders—*mfg*
2796 Engraving, steel line: for printing purposes—*mfg*
7389 Engrossing, e.g., diplomas and resolutions
3861 Enlargers, photographic—*mfg*
2335 Ensemble dresses: women's, misses', and juniors'—mfpm—*mfg*
3523 Ensilage blowers and cutters—*mfg*
7929 Entertainers
7929 Entertainment groups
0721 Entomological service, agricultural
8999 Entomologists, consulting: not with business service laboratories
3555 Envelope printing presses—*mfg*
3579 Envelope stuffing, sealing, and addressing machines—*mfg*
2677 Envelopes, printed or unprinted: paper, glassine, cellophane, and pliofilm—mfpm—*mfg*
2759 Envelopes, printed: except lithographed or gravure—*mfg*
2754 Envelopes: gravure printing—*mfg*
5112 Envelopes—wholesale
9431 Environmental health programs—government
9511 Environmental protection agencies—government
9511 Environmental quality and control agencies—government
2835 Enzyme and isoenzyme diagnostic reagents—*mfg*
2869 Enzymes, except diagnostic substances—*mfg*
2865 Eosine toners—*mfg*
2833 Ephedrine and derivatives—*mfg*
2821 Epichlorohydrin bisphenol—*mfg*
2821 Epichlorohydrin diphenol—*mfg*
2822 Epichlorohydrin elastomers—*mfg*
2891 Epoxy adhesives—*mfg*
1799 Epoxy application—contractors
2851 Epoxy coatings, made from purchased resin—*mfg*
2821 Epoxy resins—*mfg*
9441 Equal employment opportunity offices—government
3952 Eraser guides and shields—*mfg*
3069 Erasers: rubber, or rubber and abrasive combined—*mfg*
1389 Erecting lease tanks, oil and gas field: on a contract basis
1799 Erection and dismantling of forms for poured concrete—contractors
3944 Erector sets, toy—*mfg*
2833 Ergot alkaloids—*mfg*
3534 Escalators, passenger and freight—*mfg*
7299 Escort service
6531 Escrow agents, real estate
6099 Escrow institutions other than real estate
2899 Essential oils—*mfg*
5169 Essential oils—wholesale
2822 Estane—*mfg*
8811 Estates, private
2821 Ester gum—*mfg*
2869 Esters of phosphoric, adipic, lauric, oleic, sebacic, and stearic acids—*mfg*
2869 Esters of phthalic anhydride—*mfg*
2869 Esters of polyhydric alcohols—*mfg*
0851 Estimating timber
3555 Etching machines (printing trades machinery)—*mfg*
2796 Etching on copper, steel, wood, or rubber plates for printing purposes—*mfg*
3479 Etching on metals for purposes other than printing—*mfg*
3479 Etching: photochemical, for the trade—*mfg*
1321 Ethane (natural) production
2869 Ethanol, industrial—*mfg*
2869 Ether—*mfg*
2861 Ethyl acetate, natural—*mfg*
2869 Ethyl acetate, synthetic—*mfg*
2085 Ethyl alcohol for medicinal and beverage purposes—*mfg*

3356 Extruded shapes, nonferrous metals and alloys, except copper and aluminum—*mfg*
3542 Extruding machines (machine tools), metal—*mfg*
3544 Extrusion dies—*mfg*
3355 Extrusion ingot, aluminum: made in rolling mills—*mfg*
3334 Extrusion ingot, aluminum: primary—*mfg*
3841 Eye examining instruments and apparatus—*mfg*
8069 Eye, ear, nose, and throat hospitals: in-patient
3172 Eyeglass cases, regardless of material—*mfg*
3851 Eyeglasses, lenses, and frames—*mfg*
2395 Eyelet making, for the trade—*mfg*
3965 Eyelets, metal: for clothing, fabrics, boots and shoes, and paper—*mfg*
3851 Eyes, glass and plastics—*mfg*

F

3651 FM and AM tuners—*mfg*
2231 Fabric finishing of wool, mohair, and similar animal fibers: except knit—*mfg*
2261 Fabric finishing, cotton broadwoven fabrics—*mfg*
2262 Fabric finishing, manmade fiber and silk broadwoven—*mfg*
2258 Fabric finishing, warp knit—*mfg*
5949 Fabric shops—retail
2842 Fabric softeners—*mfg*
3498 Fabricated pipe and fittings: threading, bending, etc.—of purchased pipe—*mfg*
3441 Fabricated structural steel—*mfg*
2296 Fabrics for reinforcing rubber tires, industrial belting, and fuel cells—*mfg*
2231 Fabrics, animal fiber: broadwoven wool, mohair, and similar animal fibers—*mfg*
2241 Fabrics, animal fiber: narrow woven—*mfg*
2297 Fabrics, bonded fiber: except felt—*mfg*
2211 Fabrics, broadwoven: cotton—*mfg*
2221 Fabrics, broadwoven: manmade fiber and silk—*mfg*
2231 Fabrics, broadwoven: wool, mohair, and similar animal fibers—*mfg*
2257 Fabrics, circular knit—*mfg*
2295 Fabrics, coated and impregnated: except rubberized—*mfg*
2297 Fabrics, nonwoven: except felts—*mfg*
2952 Fabrics, roofing: asphalt or tar saturated—mfpm—*mfg*
3069 Fabrics, rubberized—*mfg*
2258 Fabrics, warp knit—mitse—*mfg*
2257 Fabrics, weft knit—*mfg*
3496 Fabrics, woven wire: made from purchased wire—*mfg*
2299 Fabrics: linen, jute, hemp, ramie—*mfg*
2844 Face creams and lotions—*mfg*
3644 Face plates (wiring devices)—*mfg*
2844 Face powders—*mfg*
6726 Face-amount certificate issuing
7231 Facial salons
2621 Facial tissue stock—mitse—*mfg*
2676 Facial tissues—mfpm—*mfg*
7376 Facilities management services, computer
8744 Facilities management, except computer
8744 Facilities support services, except computer
3541 Facing machines—*mfg*
3251 Facing tile, clay—*mfg*
2899 Facings (chemical foundry supplies)—*mfg*
3661 Facsimile equipment—*mfg*
2754 Facsimile letters: gravure printing—*mfg*
4822 Facsimile transmission services
6153 Factors of commercial paper
1541 Factory construction—general contractors
2599 Factory furniture: stools, work benches, tool stands, and cabinets—*mfg*
3253 Faience tile—*mfg*
2221 Failles—*mfg*
7999 Fairs, agricultural: operation of
2679 False faces, papier-mache—mfpm—*mfg*
5651 Family clothing stores—retail
8322 Family counseling services
8322 Family location services
8322 Family service agencies
3822 Fan control, temperature responsive—*mfg*
3599 Fan forges—*mfg*
3111 Fancy leathers—*mfg*
2672 Fancy paper, coated and glazed: except for packaging—mfpm—*mfg*
2761 Fanfold forms—*mfg*
3564 Fans, except household—*mfg*
3634 Fans, household: kitchen—except attic—*mfg*
3634 Fans, household: electric, except attic fans—*mfg*
5084 Fans, industrial—wholesale
3829 Fare registers: e.g., for streetcars and buses—*mfg*
2043 Farina, cereal breakfast food—*mfg*
2041 Farina, except breakfast food—mitse—*mfg*
1542 Farm building construction, except residential—general contractors
2452 Farm buildings, prefabricated or portable: wood—*mfg*
3448 Farm buildings, prefabricated: metal—*mfg*
8699 Farm bureaus
3523 Farm elevators—*mfg*
8699 Farm granges

9224 Fire departments, including volunteer—government
3669 Fire detection systems, electric—*mfg*
3829 Fire detector systems, nonelectric—*mfg*
3442 Fire doors, metal—*mfg*
1799 Fire escape installation—contractors
3446 Fire escapes, metal—*mfg*
2899 Fire extinguisher charges—*mfg*
3999 Fire extinguishers, portable—*mfg*
7389 Fire extinguishers, service of
5099 Fire extinguishers—wholesale
3491 Fire hydrant valves—*mfg*
6411 Fire loss appraisal
9224 Fire marshals' offices—government
9224 Fire prevention offices—government
0851 Fire prevention, forest
2261 Fire resistance finishing of cotton broadwoven fabrics—*mfg*
2262 Fire resistance finishing of manmade fiber and silk broadwoven fabrics—*mfg*
2899 Fire retardant chemical preparations—*mfg*
1542 Fire station construction—general contractors
3484 Firearms, 30 mm. (or 1.18 inch) or less—*mfg*
5099 Firearms, except sporting—wholesale
5091 Firearms, sporting—wholesale
5941 Firearms—retail
3731 Fireboats, building and repairing—*mfg*
3255 Firebrick, clay—*mfg*
2311 Firefighters' dress uniforms, men's—*mfg*
3569 Firefighting apparatus, except automotive and chemical—*mfg*
5087 Firefighting equipment—wholesale
7389 Firefighting service, other than forestry or public
0851 Firefighting, forest
3569 Firehose, except rubber—*mfg*
3052 Firehose, rubber—*mfg*
3429 Fireplace equipment (hardware)—*mfg*
3433 Fireplace inserts—*mfg*
2999 Fireplace logs, made from coal—*mfg*
5719 Fireplace screens and accessories—retail
5719 Fireplace stores—retail
3272 Fireplaces, concrete—*mfg*
5074 Fireplaces, prefabricated—wholesale
1752 Fireproof flooring construction—contractors
1799 Fireproofing buildings—contractors
3251 Fireproofing tile, clay—*mfg*
2499 Firewood and fuel wood containing fuel binder—*mfg*
5099 Firewood—wholesale
2899 Fireworks—*mfg*
7999 Fireworks display service
5999 Fireworks—retail
5092 Fireworks—wholesale
7699 Firing china to individual order
3269 Firing china, for the trade—*mfg*
2449 Firkins and kits, wood: coopered—*mfg*
3842 First aid, snake bite, and burn kits—*mfg*
2092 Fish and seafood cakes, frozen—*mfg*
2091 Fish and seafood cakes: canned—*mfg*
3556 Fish and shellfish processing machinery—*mfg*
9512 Fish and wildlife conservation—government
2091 Fish egg bait, canned—*mfg*
0273 Fish farms, except hatcheries
2092 Fish fillets—*mfg*
2048 Fish food—*mfg*
0921 Fish hatcheries
2077 Fish liver oils, crude—*mfg*
2833 Fish liver oils, refined and concentrated for medicinal use—*mfg*
5421 Fish markets—retail
2077 Fish meal—*mfg*
2298 Fish nets and seines, made in cordage or twine mills—*mfg*
2077 Fish oil and fish oil meal—*mfg*
2092 Fish sticks—*mfg*
3644 Fish wire (electrical wiring tool)—*mfg*
2091 Fish, canned and cured—*mfg*
5146 Fish, cured—wholesale
5146 Fish, fresh—wholesale
5146 Fish, frozen: except packaged—wholesale
5142 Fish, frozen: packaged—wholesale
5199 Fish, tropical—wholesale
2091 Fish: cured, dried, pickled, salted, and smoked—*mfg*
2092 Fish: fresh and frozen, prepared—*mfg*
0912 Fisheries, finfish
0913 Fisheries, shellfish
7999 Fishing boats, party: operation of
3732 Fishing boats, small—*mfg*
7032 Fishing camps
5941 Fishing equipment—retail
1389 Fishing for tools, oil and gas field: on a contract basis
3421 Fishing knives—*mfg*
2298 Fishing lines, nets, seines: made in cordage or twine mills—*mfg*
2399 Fishing nets—mfpm—*mfg*
7999 Fishing piers and lakes, operation of
0921 Fishing preserves
3949 Fishing tackle (except lines, nets, and seines)—*mfg*
3731 Fishing vessels, large: seiners and trawlers—building and repairing—*mfg*
2819 Fissionable material production—*mfg*
7991 Fitness salons

3999 Flocking metal products for the trade—*mfg*
2261 Flocking of cotton broadwoven fabrics—*mfg*
2262 Flocking of manmade fiber and silk broadwoven fabrics—*mfg*
1629 Flood control project construction—general contractors
3648 Floodlights—*mfg*
3251 Floor arch tile, clay—*mfg*
2431 Floor baseboards, wood—*mfg*
3299 Floor composition, magnesite—*mfg*
2951 Floor composition, mastic: hot and cold—*mfg*
5713 Floor covering stores—retail
3996 Floor coverings, asphalted-felt-base (linoleum)—*mfg*
3089 Floor coverings, plastics—*mfg*
2273 Floor coverings, textile fiber—*mfg*
2273 Floor coverings, tufted—*mfg*
2273 Floor coverings: twisted paper, grass, reed, coir, sisal, jute, and rag—*mfg*
5023 Floor coverings—wholesale
3634 Floor fans, electric—*mfg*
3272 Floor filler tiles, concrete—*mfg*
3441 Floor jacks, metal—*mfg*
3645 Floor lamps—*mfg*
1752 Floor laying, scraping, finishing, and refinishing—contractors
2392 Floor mops—*mfg*
3441 Floor posts, adjustable: metal—*mfg*
3589 Floor sanding, washing, and polishing machines: commercial type—*mfg*
3272 Floor slabs, precast concrete—*mfg*
5713 Floor tile stores—retail
3292 Floor tile, asphalt—*mfg*
3253 Floor tile, ceramic—*mfg*
3272 Floor tile, precast terrazzo—*mfg*
3469 Floor tile, stamped metal—*mfg*
6221 Floor traders, commodity contract
6211 Floor traders, security
2842 Floor wax emulsion—*mfg*
3639 Floor waxers and polishers, household: electric—*mfg*
2842 Floor waxes—*mfg*
7349 Floor waxing service
2421 Flooring (dressed lumber), softwood—*mfg*
3251 Flooring brick, clay—*mfg*
3444 Flooring, cellular steel—*mfg*
2426 Flooring, hardwood—*mfg*
3446 Flooring, open steel (grating)—*mfg*
3069 Flooring, rubber: tile or sheet—*mfg*
2491 Flooring, wood block: treated—*mfg*
1752 Flooring, wood—contractors
5211 Flooring, wood—retail
2452 Floors, prefabricated: wood—*mfg*
3269 Florists' articles, red earthenware—*mfg*
3496 Florists' designs, made from purchased wire—*mfg*
0181 Florists' greens, cultivated: growing of
7389 Florists' telegraph service
5992 Florists—retail
5193 Florists—wholesale
6211 Flotation companies, security
3532 Flotation machinery (mining machinery)—*mfg*
2258 Flouncings, lace—*mfg*
2673 Flour bags, except fabric—mfpm—*mfg*
2393 Flour bags, fabric—mfpm—*mfg*
3556 Flour mill machinery—*mfg*
2041 Flour mills, cereals: except rice—*mfg*
2041 Flour mixes—mitse—*mfg*
2044 Flour, rice—*mfg*
2499 Flour, wood—*mfg*
2045 Flour: blended or self-rising—mfpm—*mfg*
2041 Flour: blended, prepared, or self-rising—mitse—*mfg*
2041 Flour: buckwheat, corn, graham, rye, and wheat—*mfg*
5149 Flour—wholesale
3625 Flow actuated electrical switches—*mfg*
3823 Flow instruments, industrial process type—*mfg*
5191 Flower and field bulbs—wholesale
3299 Flower boxes, plaster of paris: factory production only—*mfg*
5261 Flower bulbs—retail
3089 Flower pots, plastics—*mfg*
3269 Flower pots, red earthenware—*mfg*
5193 Flowers and florists' supplies—wholesale
3999 Flowers, artificial, except glass—*mfg*
5999 Flowers, artificial—retail
5193 Flowers, artificial—wholesale
3231 Flowers, foliage, fruits and vines: artificial glass—made from purchased glass—*mfg*
5992 Flowers, fresh—retail
5193 Flowers, fresh—wholesale
0181 Flowers, growing of
3231 Flowers, made from purchased glass—*mfg*
3999 Flowers, preserved—*mfg*
3259 Flue lining, clay—*mfg*
3444 Flues, stove and furnace: sheet metal—*mfg*
3412 Fluid milk shipping containers, metal—*mfg*
3593 Fluid power actuators, hydraulic and pneumatic—*mfg*
3593 Fluid power cylinders, hydraulic and pneumatic—*mfg*
3593 Fluid power motors—*mfg*
3594 Fluid power pumps and motors—*mfg*
3492 Fluid power valves and fittings—*mfg*

3589 Food warming equipment, commercial—*mfg*
5046 Food warming equipment, commercial—wholesale
3639 Food waste disposal units, household—*mfg*
5961 Food, mail-order—retail
3842 Foot appliances, orthopedic—*mfg*
7997 Football clubs, except professional and semiprofessional
7941 Football clubs, professional or semiprofessional
3949 Footballs and football equipment and supplies, except uniforms and footwear—*mfg*
3021 Footholds, rubber—*mfg*
2389 Footlets—mfpm—*mfg*
5661 Footwear stores—retail
3149 Footwear, children's: house slippers and vulcanized rubber footwear—*mfg*
3149 Footwear, children's: leather or vinyl with molded or vulcanized shoes—*mfg*
3143 Footwear, men's: except house slippers, athletic, and vulcanized rubber footwear—*mfg*
3143 Footwear, men's: leather or vinyl with molded or vulcanized soles—*mfg*
3021 Footwear, rubber or rubber soled fabric—*mfg*
3144 Footwear, women's: except house slippers, athletic, and vulcanized rubber footwear—*mfg*
3144 Footwear, women's: leather or vinyl with molded or vulcanized soles—*mfg*
5139 Footwear—wholesale
3523 Forage blowers—*mfg*
3523 Forage harvesters—*mfg*
**** Force account construction—code according to the use for which constructed
3843 Forceps, dental—*mfg*
3841 Forceps, surgical—*mfg*
6099 Foreign currency exchanges
4731 Foreign forwarding
9721 Foreign missions
4226 Foreign trade zone warehousing, and storage
8734 Forensic laboratories
0851 Forest management plans, preparation of
0831 Forest nurseries
6519 Forest properties, lessors of
5082 Forestry equipment—wholesale
0851 Forestry services
3599 Forges, fan—*mfg*
3542 Forging machinery and hammers—*mfg*
5051 Forgings, ferrous—wholesale
3312 Forgings, iron and steel: made in steel works or rolling mills—*mfg*
3462 Forgings, iron and steel: not made in rolling mills—*mfg*
3463 Forgings, nonferrous metal: not made in hot rolling mills—*mfg*
3483 Forgings, projectile: machined—for ammunition more than 30 mm. (or more than 1.18 inch)—*mfg*
3537 Forklift trucks—*mfg*
3914 Forks, table: all metal—*mfg*
3421 Forks, table: except all metal—*mfg*
3423 Forks: garden, hay and manure, stone and ballast—*mfg*
3315 Form ties, made in wiredrawing plants—*mfg*
2311 Formal jackets, men's and boys'—*mfg*
2869 Formaldehyde (formalin)—*mfg*
2869 Formalin—*mfg*
2869 Formic acid and metallic salts—*mfg*
3444 Forming machine work for the trade, except stampings: sheet metal—*mfg*
3542 Forming machines—*mfg*
2782 Forms and fillers, looseleaf: pen ruled or printed only—*mfg*
3444 Forms for concrete, sheet metal—*mfg*
3269 Forms for dipped rubber products, pottery—*mfg*
1799 Forms for poured concrete, erection and dismantling—contractors
3579 Forms handling equipment for store and office use—*mfg*
2761 Forms, business: manifold or continuous—*mfg*
3443 Forms, collapsible: for tunnels—*mfg*
5051 Forms, concrete construction: steel—wholesale
2499 Forms, display: for boots and shoes—regardless of material—*mfg*
3544 Forms, metal (molds): for foundry and plastics working machinery—*mfg*
3999 Forms: display, dress, and show—except shoe display forms—*mfg*
7999 Fortune tellers
4731 Forwarding, domestic
4731 Forwarding, foreign
8361 Foster homes, group
1794 Foundation digging (excavation)—contractors
2342 Foundation garments, women's—mfpm—*mfg*
5632 Foundation garments—retail
2515 Foundations, bed: spring, foam, and platform—*mfg*
1741 Foundations, building of: block, stone, or brick—contractors
1771 Foundations, building of: poured concrete—contractors

4783 Freight packing and crating
4731 Freight rate auditors
4731 Freight rate information service
4231 Freight trucking terminals, with or without maintenance facilities
2221 French crepes—*mfg*
2035 French dressing—*mfg*
2038 French toast, frozen—*mfg*
3621 Frequency converters (electric generators)—*mfg*
3825 Frequency meters: electrical, mechanical, and electronic—*mfg*
3825 Frequency synthesizers—*mfg*
1743 Fresco work—contractors
3931 Fretted instruments and parts—*mfg*
3499 Friction material, made from powdered metal—*mfg*
3292 Friction materials, asbestos: woven—*mfg*
3069 Friction tape, rubber—*mfg*
2241 Fringes, weaving—*mfg*
3952 Frisket paper (artists' material)—*mfg*
2899 Frit—*mfg*
0279 Frog farms
0919 Frogs, catching of
3312 Frogs, iron and steel: made in steel works or rolling mills—*mfg*
3462 Frogs, railroad: forgings not made in rolling mills—*mfg*
7539 Front end repair, automotive
5082 Front-end loaders—wholesale
3851 Fronts and temples, ophthalmic—*mfg*
2541 Fronts, store: prefabricated—wood—*mfg*
2099 Frosting, prepared—*mfg*
2051 Frozen bread and bread-type rolls—*mfg*
2024 Frozen custard—*mfg*
5812 Frozen custard stands
5143 Frozen dairy desserts—wholesale
2024 Frozen desserts, except bakery—*mfg*
2038 Frozen dinners, packaged—*mfg*
2045 Frozen doughs—mfpm—*mfg*
2041 Frozen doughs—mitse—*mfg*
2092 Frozen fish, packaged—*mfg*
5411 Frozen food and freezer plans, except meat—retail
5421 Frozen food and freezer plans, meat—retail
2673 Frozen food bags—mfpm—*mfg*
2657 Frozen food containers, folding paperboard—mfpm—*mfg*
2656 Frozen food containers, nonfolding paperboard—mfpm—*mfg*
4222 Frozen food locker rental
5142 Frozen foods, packaged—wholesale
2037 Frozen fruits, fruit juices, and vegetables—*mfg*
2092 Frozen prepared fish—*mfg*
2038 Frozen soups, except seafood—*mfg*
5142 Frozen vegetables—wholesale
2046 Fructose—*mfg*
2086 Fruit (fresh) drinks, bottled or canned—*mfg*
2449 Fruit baskets, veneer and splint—*mfg*
2033 Fruit butters—*mfg*
2449 Fruit crates, wood: wirebound—*mfg*
0723 Fruit drying
2034 Fruit flour, meal, and powders—*mfg*
3523 Fruit grading, cleaning, and sorting machines—*mfg*
3221 Fruit jars, glass—*mfg*
2037 Fruit juice concentrates, frozen—*mfg*
2087 Fruit juices, concentrated: for fountain use—*mfg*
2037 Fruit juices, frozen—*mfg*
5142 Fruit juices, frozen—wholesale
2033 Fruit juices: canned—*mfg*
5431 Fruit markets and stands—retail
2064 Fruit peel products: candied, glazed, glace, and crystallized—*mfg*
5149 Fruit peel—wholesale
2033 Fruit pie mixes—*mfg*
2024 Fruit pops, frozen—*mfg*
4741 Fruit precooling, in connection with railroad transportation
0723 Fruit precooling, not in connection with transportation
2033 Fruit purees—*mfg*
0723 Fruit sorting, grading, and packing
0181 Fruit stocks, growing of
5431 Fruit stores—retail
0723 Fruit vacuum cooling
3231 Fruit, artificial: made from purchased glass—*mfg*
5961 Fruit, mail-order—retail
3523 Fruit, vegetable, berry, and grape harvesting machines—*mfg*
0182 Fruits grown under cover
3999 Fruits, artificial and preserved: except glass—*mfg*
3999 Fruits, artificial, except glass—*mfg*
2033 Fruits, canned—*mfg*
2087 Fruits, crushed: for soda fountain use—*mfg*
2034 Fruits, dried or dehydrated—*mfg*
5149 Fruits, dried—wholesale
5145 Fruits, fountain—wholesale
5431 Fruits, fresh—retail
5148 Fruits, fresh—wholesale
5142 Fruits, frozen—wholesale
0722 Fruits, machine harvesting of
2035 Fruits, pickled and brined—*mfg*
2037 Fruits, quick frozen and coldpack (frozen)—*mfg*

5136 Furnishings, except shoes: men's and boys'—wholesale
7217 Furniture cleaning on customers' premises
3469 Furniture components, porcelain enameled—*mfg*
2211 Furniture denim—*mfg*
2426 Furniture dimension stock, hardwood—*mfg*
2421 Furniture dimension stock, softwood—*mfg*
2426 Furniture frames for upholstering, wood—*mfg*
3429 Furniture hardware, including casters—*mfg*
2499 Furniture inlays (veneers)—*mfg*
5712 Furniture made on a custom basis to individual order—retail
3553 Furniture makers' machinery (woodworking)—*mfg*
4214 Furniture moving, local: combined with storage
4212 Furniture moving, local: without storage
3499 Furniture parts, metal—*mfg*
2842 Furniture polish and wax—*mfg*
7641 Furniture refinishing
7359 Furniture rental and leasing
7641 Furniture repairing, redecorating, and remodeling shops
7641 Furniture restoration, antique
3495 Furniture springs, unassembled: made from purchased wire—*mfg*
2426 Furniture squares, hardwood—*mfg*
4226 Furniture storage, without local trucking
5712 Furniture stores, household—retail
5932 Furniture stores, secondhand—retail
3231 Furniture tops, glass: cut, beveled, and polished—*mfg*
2396 Furniture trimmings, fabric—mfpm—*mfg*
2426 Furniture turnings and carvings, wood—*mfg*
5932 Furniture, antique—retail
3999 Furniture, beauty shop and barber shop—*mfg*
2514 Furniture, clubroom: metal—*mfg*
5712 Furniture, custom made—retail
3281 Furniture, cut stone—*mfg*
2599 Furniture, factory: stools, work benches, tool stands, and cabinets—*mfg*
3272 Furniture, garden: concrete—*mfg*
5712 Furniture, household, with or without furnishings and appliances—retail
2511 Furniture, household, wood: porch, lawn, garden, and beach—*mfg*
2511 Furniture, household, wood: unassembled or knock-down—*mfg*
2511 Furniture, household, wood: unfinished—*mfg*
2519 Furniture, household: glass and plastics (including fiberglass)—*mfg*
2514 Furniture, household: metal—*mfg*
2519 Furniture, household: rattan, reed, malacca, fiber, willow, and wicker—*mfg*
2514 Furniture, household: upholstered on metal frames, except dual-purpose sleep furniture—*mfg*
2512 Furniture, household: upholstered on wood frames, except convertible beds—*mfg*
5021 Furniture, juvenile—wholesale
3821 Furniture, laboratory—*mfg*
2522 Furniture, office: except wood—*mfg*
2521 Furniture, office: wood—*mfg*
2599 Furniture, restaurant—*mfg*
5021 Furniture, unfinished—wholesale
2531 Furniture: church, library, school, theater, and other public buildings—*mfg*
2511 Furniture: household, clubroom, novelty—wood, except upholstered—*mfg*
5021 Furniture: household, office, restaurant, and public building—wholesale
5632 Furriers—retail
3446 Furring channels—*mfg*
3251 Furring tile, clay—*mfg*
3999 Furs, dressed: bleached, curried, scraped, tanned, and dyed—*mfg*
5199 Furs, dressed—wholesale
5159 Furs, raw—wholesale
3613 Fuse clips and blocks, electric—*mfg*
3643 Fuse cutouts—*mfg*
3613 Fuse devices, power: 600 volts and over—*mfg*
3613 Fuse mountings, electric power—*mfg*
2892 Fuse powder—*mfg*
3827 Fuse setters (fire control equipment)—*mfg*
2899 Fusees: highway, marine, and railroad—*mfg*
3728 Fuselage assemblies, aircraft—*mfg*
5063 Fuses and accessories—wholesale
3483 Fuses for ammunition more than 30 mm. (or more than 1.18 inch)—*mfg*
3613 Fuses, electric—*mfg*
2892 Fuses, safety—*mfg*
3483 Fuses: mine, torpedo, bomb, depth charge, and chemical warfare projectile—*mfg*
2861 Fustic wood extract—*mfg*
6282 Futures advisory service
6221 Futures brokers, commodity
6221 Futures dealers, commodity
6231 Futures exchanges, contract

G

2211 Gabardine, cotton—*mfg*
1429 Gabbro, crushed and broken—quarrying

2389 Garter belts—mfpm—*mfg*
2389 Garters—mfpm—*mfg*
1623 Gas (natural) compressing station construction—general contractors
1311 Gas (natural) production
3443 Gas absorbers—*mfg*
3826 Gas analyzers, laboratory type—*mfg*
3519 Gas and diesel engine rebuilding, on a factory basis—*mfg*
3823 Gas and liquid analysis instruments, industrial process type—*mfg*
4932 Gas and other services combined (gas less than 95 percent of total)
3671 Gas and vapor tubes—*mfg*
7699 Gas appliance repair service
3822 Gas burner automatic controls, except valves—*mfg*
3433 Gas burners, domestic—*mfg*
3842 Gas capes (cold climate individual protective covers)—*mfg*
3826 Gas chromatographic instruments, laboratory type—*mfg*
1389 Gas compressing, natural gas at the field on a contract basis
1382 Gas field exploration: on a contract basis
3823 Gas flow computers, industrial process type—*mfg*
3433 Gas heaters, room—*mfg*
3443 Gas holders, metal plate—*mfg*
5722 Gas household appliance stores—retail
3433 Gas infrared heating units—*mfg*
1799 Gas leakage detection—contractors
3648 Gas lighting fixtures—*mfg*
5099 Gas lighting fixtures—wholesale
1623 Gas main construction—general contractors
3842 Gas masks—*mfg*
3321 Gas pipe, cast iron—*mfg*
3569 Gas producers (machinery)—*mfg*
3631 Gas ranges, domestic—*mfg*
3569 Gas separators (machinery)—*mfg*
7389 Gas systems, contract conversion from manufactured to natural gas
3443 Gas tanks, metal plate—*mfg*
3714 Gas tanks, motor vehicle—*mfg*
3511 Gas turbine generator set units, complete—*mfg*
3511 Gas turbines and parts, except aircraft type—*mfg*
3511 Gas turbines, mechanical drive—*mfg*
3491 Gas valves and parts, industrial—*mfg*
3548 Gas welding equipment—*mfg*
3496 Gas welding rods, made from purchased wire—*mfg*
1381 Gas well drilling: on a contract basis
3533 Gas well machinery and equipment—*mfg*
1389 Gas well rig building, repairing, and dismantling on a contract basis
3312 Gas, coal: derived from chemical recovery coke ovens—*mfg*
5984 Gas, liquefied petroleum: bottled—retail
4925 Gas, liquefied petroleum: distribution through mains
4925 Gas, manufactured: production and distribution
4925 Gas, mixed natural and manufactured: production and distribution
4924 Gas, natural: distribution
4922 Gas, natural: transmission
4923 Gas, natural: transmission and distribution
2911 Gas, refinery or still oil: produced in petroleum refineries—*mfg*
3433 Gas-oil burners, combination—*mfg*
2869 Gases, chemical warfare—*mfg*
5169 Gases, compressed and liquefied: except liquefied petroleum gas—wholesale
2869 Gases, fluorinated hydrocarbon—*mfg*
2813 Gases, industrial: compressed, liquefied, or solid—*mfg*
5172 Gases, liquefied petroleum: except bulk stations and terminals—wholesale
2911 Gases, liquefied petroleum: produced in petroleum refineries—*mfg*
3053 Gaskets, regardless of material—*mfg*
5085 Gaskets—wholesale
1711 Gasline hookup—contractors
3824 Gasmeters: domestic, large capacity, and industrial—*mfg*
1321 Gasoline (natural) production
5541 Gasoline and oil—retail
2911 Gasoline blending plants—*mfg*
3824 Gasoline dispensing meters (except pumps)—*mfg*
5541 Gasoline filling stations—retail
3599 Gasoline filters, internal combustion engine: except motor vehicle—*mfg*
3586 Gasoline measuring and dispensing pumps—*mfg*
4613 Gasoline pipelines, common carriers
1799 Gasoline pump installation—contractors
5172 Gasoline, except bulk stations and terminals—wholesale
2911 Gasoline, except natural gasoline—*mfg*
5172 Gasoline: buying in bulk and selling to farmers—wholesale
2269 Gassing yarn—*mfg*
3845 Gastroscopes, electromedical—*mfg*
3841 Gastroscopes, except electromedical—*mfg*
3569 Gate and bridge machinery, hydraulic—*mfg*
3452 Gate hooks—*mfg*

1382 Geophysical exploration, oil and gas field: on a contract basis
2221 Georgettes—*mfg*
1781 Geothermal drilling—contractors
4961 Geothermal steam production
2869 Geraniol, synthetic—*mfg*
3339 Germanium refining, primary—*mfg*
3341 Germanium refining, secondary—*mfg*
8999 Ghost writing
5947 Gift shops—retail
2679 Gift wrap paper—mfpm—*mfg*
5199 Gifts and novelties—wholesale
2789 Gilding books, cards, or paper—*mfg*
1499 Gilsonite mining
3423 Gimlets (edge tools)—*mfg*
2241 Gimps—mitse—*mfg*
2085 Gin (alcoholic beverage)—*mfg*
2086 Ginger ale, bottled or canned—*mfg*
2045 Gingerbread mixes—mfpm—*mfg*
2211 Ginghams—*mfg*
0724 Ginning cotton
3559 Ginning machines, cotton—*mfg*
0723 Ginning moss
0724 Gins, cotton: operation of
0831 Ginseng, gathering of
2259 Girdle blanks, elastic—mitse—*mfg*
2259 Girdles (elastic) and other foundation garments—mitse—*mfg*
2342 Girdles, women's and misses'—mfpm—*mfg*
7032 Girls' camps
2252 Girls' hosiery—*mfg*
2064 Glace fruits and nuts—*mfg*
2833 Gland derivatives: bulk, uncompounded—*mfg*
3229 Glass and glassware made in glassmaking establishments: for industrial, scientific, and technical use—*mfg*
3229 Glass blanks for electric light bulbs—*mfg*
5085 Glass bottles—wholesale
3229 Glass brick—*mfg*
2221 Glass broadwoven fabrics—*mfg*
3851 Glass eyes—*mfg*
1793 Glass installation, except automotive—contractors
3559 Glass making machinery: blowing, molding, forming, grinding, etc.—*mfg*
2241 Glass narrow fabrics—*mfg*
7536 Glass replacement and repair, automotive
1446 Glass sand mining
5231 Glass stores—retail
2296 Glass tire cord and tire cord fabrics—*mfg*
2211 Glass toweling, cotton—*mfg*
2842 Glass window cleaning preparations—*mfg*
3296 Glass wool—*mfg*
1793 Glass work, except automotive—contractors
3211 Glass, colored: cathedral and antique—*mfg*
3211 Glass, flat—*mfg*
5039 Glass, flat: except automotive—wholesale
5122 Glass, medical—wholesale
3231 Glass, scientific apparatus: for druggists', hospitals, laboratories—made from purchased glass—*mfg*
3231 Glass, sheet: bent—made from purchased glass—*mfg*
3231 Glass: cut, ground, leaded, laminated, ornamented, and tinted—mfpm—*mfg*
3827 Glasses, field or opera—*mfg*
3851 Glasses, sun or glare—*mfg*
3255 Glasshouse refractories—*mfg*
2674 Glassine bags, uncoated paper—mfpm—*mfg*
2621 Glassine wrapping paper—mitse—*mfg*
3221 Glassware for packing, bottling and home canning—*mfg*
5719 Glassware stores—retail
5932 Glassware, antique—retail
3231 Glassware, cut and engraved—made from purchased glass—*mfg*
3231 Glassware, cutting and engraving—*mfg*
3231 Glassware, decorated: e.g., chipped, engraved, sandblasted, etched—made from purchased glass—*mfg*
3229 Glassware, except glass containers for packing, bottling, and canning—*mfg*
5023 Glassware, household—wholesale
5199 Glassware, novelty—wholesale
3229 Glassware: art, decorative, and novelty—*mfg*
2819 Glauber's salt—*mfg*
1474 Glauber's salt mining
7699 Glazing and cleaning baking pans
2371 Glazing furs—*mfg*
1799 Glazing of concrete surfaces—contractors
3089 Glazing panels, plastics—*mfg*
1793 Glazing work—contractors
3812 Glide slope instrumentation—*mfg*
3721 Gliders (aircraft)—*mfg*
2514 Gliders (furniture), metal—*mfg*
2741 Globe covers (maps): publishing and printing, or publishing only—*mfg*
3999 Globes, geographical—*mfg*
2211 Glove fabrics, cotton—mitse—*mfg*
3111 Glove leather—*mfg*
2241 Glove lining fabrics—*mfg*
2381 Glove linings, except fur—*mfg*
2371 Glove linings, fur—*mfg*
2399 Glove mending on factory basis—*mfg*
5136 Gloves (all materials), men's and boys'—wholesale
3089 Gloves and mittens, plastics—*mfg*

1389 Grading oil and gas well foundations on a contract basis
3523 Grading, cleaning, and sorting machines: fruit, grain, and vegetable—*mfg*
1794 Grading: except for highways, streets, and airport runways—contractors
3822 Gradual switches, pneumatic—*mfg*
3842 Grafts, artificial: for surgery—made of braided or mesh artificial fibers—*mfg*
2041 Graham flour—*mfg*
1499 Grahamite mining
2085 Grain alcohol for medicinal and beverage purposes—*mfg*
2869 Grain alcohol, industrial (nonbeverage)—*mfg*
2041 Grain cereals, cracked—mitse—*mfg*
0723 Grain cleaning
3523 Grain drills, including legume planters (agricultural machinery)—*mfg*
1541 Grain elevator construction—general contractors
5153 Grain elevators, except storage only—wholesale
4221 Grain elevators, storage only
0119 Grain farms: except wheat, rice, corn, and soybeans
0723 Grain fumigation
3523 Grain grading, cleaning, and sorting machines—*mfg*
0723 Grain grinding, custom
4741 Grain leveling in railroad cars
2499 Grain measures, wood: turned and shaped—*mfg*
3556 Grain mill machinery—*mfg*
3523 Grain stackers—*mfg*
5039 Grain storage bins—wholesale
4741 Grain trimming service for railroad shipment
2082 Grain, brewers'—*mfg*
0722 Grain, machine harvesting of
5153 Grain—wholesale
3291 Grains, abrasive: natural and artificial—*mfg*
5032 Granite building stone—wholesale
1423 Granite, crushed and broken—quarrying
3281 Granite, cut and shaped—*mfg*
1411 Granite, dimension—quarrying
2064 Granola bars and clusters—*mfg*
2043 Granola, except bars and clusters—*mfg*
2041 Granular wheat flour—*mfg*
2063 Granulated beet sugar—*mfg*
3821 Granulators, laboratory—*mfg*
0172 Grape farms
0174 Grapefruit groves and farms
2899 Grapefruit oil—*mfg*
2782 Graph paper, ruled—*mfg*
7336 Graphic arts and related design
3861 Graphic arts plates, sensitized—*mfg*
3577 Graphic displays, except graphic terminals: computer peripheral equipment—*mfg*
3825 Graphic recording meters—electric—*mfg*
3624 Graphite electrodes and contacts, electric—*mfg*
1499 Graphite mining
3295 Graphite, natural: ground, pulverized, refined, or blended—*mfg*
3531 Grapples: rock, wood, etc.—*mfg*
3524 Grass catchers, lawnmower—*mfg*
3423 Grass hooks—*mfg*
0139 Grass seed farms
3999 Grasses, artificial and preserved: except glass—*mfg*
3231 Grasses, artificial: made from purchased glass—*mfg*
3446 Gratings (open steel flooring)—*mfg*
3827 Gratings, diffraction—*mfg*
3446 Gratings, tread: fabricated metal—*mfg*
1799 Grave excavation—contractors
3272 Grave markers, concrete—*mfg*
3272 Grave vaults, concrete—*mfg*
3995 Grave vaults, metal—*mfg*
1442 Gravel mining
3299 Gravel painting—*mfg*
5032 Gravel—wholesale
5999 Gravestones, finished—retail
2893 Gravure ink—*mfg*
2796 Gravure plates and cylinders, preparation of—*mfg*
3555 Gravure presses—*mfg*
2754 Gravure printing—*mfg*
2099 Gravy mixes, dry—*mfg*
3321 Gray iron castings—*mfg*
3321 Gray iron foundries—*mfg*
3599 Grease cups, metal—*mfg*
3586 Grease guns (lubricators)—*mfg*
2077 Grease rendering, inedible—*mfg*
3053 Grease retainers, leather—*mfg*
3053 Grease seals, asbestos—*mfg*
3272 Grease traps, concrete—*mfg*
2299 Grease, wool—*mfg*
2621 Greaseproof wrapping paper—mitse—*mfg*
5199 Greases, animal and vegetable—wholesale
2911 Greases, lubricating: produced in petroleum refineries—*mfg*
2992 Greases, lubricating—mfpm—*mfg*
2843 Greases, sulfonated—*mfg*
4432 Great Lakes and St. Lawrence Seaway freight transportation
0161 Green lima bean farms
0161 Green pea farms
0181 Greenhouses for floral products

3484 Gun magazines, 30 mm. (or 1.18 inch) or less—*mfg*
7699 Gun parts made to individual order
3484 Gun sights, except optical: 30 mm. (or 1.18 inch) or less—*mfg*
3827 Gun sights, optical—*mfg*
2899 Gun slushing compounds—*mfg*
3495 Gun springs, precision: made from purchased wire—*mfg*
2426 Gun stocks, wood—*mfg*
3429 Gun trigger locks—*mfg*
3489 Gun turrets and parts for artillery more than 30 mm. (or more than 1.18 inch)—*mfg*
1771 Gunite work—contractors
3674 Gunn effect devices—*mfg*
3297 Gunning mixes, nonclay—*mfg*
2892 Gunpowder—*mfg*
3484 Guns, 30 mm. (or 1.18 inch) or less—*mfg*
3489 Guns, catapult—*mfg*
3423 Guns, caulking—*mfg*
3484 Guns, dart: except toy—*mfg*
3586 Guns, grease (lubricators)—*mfg*
3489 Guns, more than 30 mm. (or more than 1.18 inch)—*mfg*
3546 Guns, pneumatic: chip removal—*mfg*
3944 Guns, toy—*mfg*
3484 Guns: BB and pellet—*mfg*
7699 Gunsmith shops
3842 Gut sutures, surgical—*mfg*
3069 Gutta percha compounds—*mfg*
1761 Gutter installation, metal—contractors
3089 Gutters, plastics: glass fiber reinforced—*mfg*
3444 Gutters, sheet metal—*mfg*
3949 Gymnasium and playground equipment—*mfg*
2329 Gymnasium clothing: men's and boys'—mfpm—*mfg*
5941 Gymnasium equipment—retail
7991 Gymnasiums
7999 Gymnastics instruction
3842 Gynecological supplies and appliances—*mfg*
8011 Gynecologists, offices of
1499 Gypsite mining
1499 Gypsum mining
3275 Gypsum products: e.g., block, board, plaster, lath, rock, tile—*mfg*
3812 Gyrocompasses—*mfg*
3812 Gyrogimbals—*mfg*
3812 Gyropilots—*mfg*
3812 Gyroscopes—*mfg*

H

5611 Haberdashery stores—retail
0912 Haddock, catching of
5131 Hair accessories—wholesale
3523 Hair clippers for animal use, hand and electric—*mfg*
3999 Hair clippers for human use, hand and electric—*mfg*
2844 Hair coloring preparations—*mfg*
3999 Hair curlers, designed for beauty parlors—*mfg*
3634 Hair curlers, electric—*mfg*
3965 Hair curlers, except equipment designed for beauty parlor use—*mfg*
3069 Hair curlers, rubber—*mfg*
3634 Hair dryers, electric: except equipment designed for beauty parlor use—*mfg*
3999 Hair dryers, designed for beauty parlors—*mfg*
3999 Hair goods: braids, nets, switches, toupees, and wigs—*mfg*
3999 Hair nets—*mfg*
3991 Hair pencils (artists' brushes)—*mfg*
2844 Hair preparations: dressings, rinses, tonics, and scalp conditioners—*mfg*
5122 Hair preparations—wholesale
7299 Hair removal (electrolysis)
7241 Hair stylists, men's
7299 Hair weaving or replacement service
5159 Hair, animal—wholesale
2299 Hair, curled: for upholstery, pillow, and quilt filling—*mfg*
3999 Hair, dressing of, for the trade—*mfg*
5199 Hairbrushes—wholesale
2231 Haircloth: wool, mohair, and similar animal fibers—*mfg*
7231 Hairdressers
2844 Hairdressings, dyes, bleaches, tonics, and removers—*mfg*
3999 Hairpin mountings—*mfg*
3965 Hairpins, except rubber—*mfg*
3069 Hairpins, rubber—*mfg*
3495 Hairsprings, made from purchased wire—*mfg*
2026 Half and half—*mfg*
2759 Halftones, engraved—*mfg*
8361 Halfway group homes for persons with social or personal problems
8361 Halfway homes for delinquents and offenders
3674 Hall effect devices—*mfg*
2679 Halloween lanterns, papier-mache—mfpm—*mfg*
3199 Halters (harness)—*mfg*
2064 Halvah (candy)—*mfg*

2046 High fructose syrup—*mfg*

3313 High percentage ferroalloys—*mfg*

3313 High percentage nonferrous additive alloys, except copper—*mfg*

2819 High purity grade chemicals, inorganic: refined from technical grades—*mfg*

2869 High purity grade chemicals, organic: refined from technical grades—*mfg*

8211 High schools

3297 High temperature mortar, nonclay—*mfg*

3443 High vacuum coaters, metal plate—*mfg*

3441 Highway bridge sections, prefabricated metal—*mfg*

4785 Highway bridges, operation of

1622 Highway construction, elevated—general contractors

1611 Highway construction, except elevated—general contractors

2899 Highway fusees—*mfg*

3444 Highway guardrails, sheet metal—*mfg*

1731 Highway lighting and electrical signal construction—contractors

9221 Highway patrols

3669 Highway signals, electric—*mfg*

1611 Highway signs, installation of—contractors

3429 Hinge tubes—*mfg*

3429 Hinges—*mfg*

8699 Historical clubs, other than professional

3799 Hitches, trailer—*mfg*

5092 Hobby kits—wholesale

5945 Hobby shops—retail

3944 Hobbyhorses—*mfg*

3545 Hobs—*mfg*

5084 Hobs—wholesale

7997 Hockey clubs, except professional and semiprofessional

3949 Hockey equipment, except uniforms and footwear—*mfg*

0721 Hoeing

3423 Hoes, garden and masons'—*mfg*

0213 Hog farms

3523 Hog feeding, handling, and watering equipment—*mfg*

3496 Hog rings, made from purchased wire—*mfg*

2011 Hog slaughtering plants—*mfg*

5154 Hogs—wholesale

2449 Hogsheads, wood: coopered—*mfg*

3537 Hoists, aircraft loading—*mfg*

3536 Hoists, except aircraft loading and automobile wrecker hoists—*mfg*

3536 Hoists, hand—*mfg*

3536 Hoists, overhead—*mfg*

5084 Hoists—wholesale

3999 Holders, cigar and cigarette—*mfg*

3952 Holders, pencil—*mfg*

3089 Holders, plastics: papertowel, grocery bag, dust mop and broom—*mfg*

3841 Holders, surgical needle—*mfg*

3861 Holders: photographic film, plate, and paper—*mfg*

6719 Holding companies, except bank

3914 Hollowware, silver, nickel silver, pewter, stainless steel, and plated—*mfg*

3199 Holsters, leather—*mfg*

8082 Home health care services

1522 Home improvements, residential: except single-family—general contractors

1521 Home improvements, single-family—general contractors

2844 Home permanent kits—*mfg*

7221 Home photographers

3651 Home tape recorders: cassette, cartridge, and reel—*mfg*

3541 Home workshop machine tools, metalworking—*mfg*

5932 Homefurnishing stores, secondhand—retail

**** Homefurnishing, except antique—retail—see kind of furnishing

5932 Homefurnishings, antique—retail

5023 Homefurnishings—wholesale

8322 Homemaker's service, primarily nonmedical

8641 Homeowner associations, except property management

8361 Homes for children, with health care incidental

8361 Homes for destitute men and women

8361 Homes for the aged, with health care incidental

8361 Homes for the deaf or blind, with health care incidental

8361 Homes for the emotionally disturbed, with health care incidental

8361 Homes for the mentally handicapped, with health care incidental

8059 Homes for the mentally retarded with health care, except skilled and intermediate care facilities

8361 Homes for the physically handicapped, with health care incidental

2043 Hominy grits prepared as cereal breakfast food—*mfg*

2041 Hominy grits, except breakfast food—*mfg*

2033 Hominy, canned—*mfg*

3556 Homogenizing machinery: dairy, fruit, vegetable, and other foods—*mfg*

3291 Hones—*mfg*

0279 Honey production

0752 Honey straining on the farm

1389 Hot oil treating of oil field tanks: on a contract basis
1389 Hot shot service: on a contract basis
3547 Hot strip mill machinery—*mfg*
3255 Hot top refractories, clay—*mfg*
3297 Hot top refractories, nonclay—*mfg*
2449 Hot tubs, coopered—*mfg*
3088 Hot tubs, plastics or fiberglass—*mfg*
5999 Hot tubs—retail
5091 Hot tubs—wholesale
3639 Hot water heaters, household: including nonelectric—*mfg*
3493 Hot wound springs, except wire springs—*mfg*
3312 Hot-rolled iron and steel products—*mfg*
1522 Hotel construction—general contractors
7389 Hotel reservation service
3262 Hotel tableware and kitchen articles, vitreous china—*mfg*
7041 Hotels operated by organizations for members only
7011 Hotels, except residential
6513 Hotels, residential: operators
7011 Hotels, seasonal
8322 Hotlines
3634 Hotplates, electric—*mfg*
3821 Hotplates, laboratory—*mfg*
1521 House construction, single-family—general contractors
5963 House delivery of purchased milk—retail
8712 House designers
1799 House moving—contractors
1721 House painting—contractors
3142 House slippers—*mfg*
7519 House trailer rental
5963 House-to-house selling of coffee, soda, beer, bottled water, or other products—retail
1521 House: shell erection, single-family—general contractors
7999 Houseboat rentals
3732 Houseboats, building and repairing—*mfg*
2384 Housecoats, except children's and infants'—mfpm—*mfg*
2369 Housecoats: girls', children's, and infants'—mfpm—*mfg*
2253 Housecoats—mitse—*mfg*
2335 Housedresses: women's, misses', and juniors'—mfpm—*mfg*
2392 Housefurnishings, except curtains and draperies—*mfg*
5722 Household appliance stores, electric or gas—retail
2842 Household bleaches, dry or liquid—*mfg*
3991 Household brooms and brushes—*mfg*
3263 Household earthenware, semivitreous—*mfg*
2512 Household furniture upholstered on wood frames, except dual-purpose sleep furniture—*mfg*
2519 Household furniture, glass and plastics—*mfg*
2511 Household furniture, wood: except upholstered—*mfg*
2519 Household furniture: rattan, reed, malacca, fiber, willow, and wicker—*mfg*
5712 Household furniture—retail
5021 Household furniture—wholesale
3069 Household gloves, rubber—*mfg*
4214 Household goods moving, local: combined with storage
4226 Household goods warehousing and storage, without local trucking
2879 Household insecticides—*mfg*
3262 Household tableware and kitchen articles, vitreous china—*mfg*
2899 Household tints and dyes—*mfg*
3365 Household utensils, cast aluminum: except die-castings—*mfg*
3469 Household utensils, porcelain enameled—*mfg*
3469 Household utensils, stamped and pressed metal—*mfg*
2499 Household woodenware—*mfg*
8811 Households, private: employing cooks, maids, chauffeurs, gardeners, etc.
7349 Housekeeping (cleaning service) on a contract or fee basis
9223 Houses of correction—government
2452 Houses, portable: prefabricated wood—except mobile homes—*mfg*
3448 Houses, prefabricated: metal—*mfg*
3792 Housetrailers, except as permanent dwellings—*mfg*
5719 Housewares stores—retail
5963 Housewares: house-to-house, telephone or party plan selling—retail
9531 Housing agencies, nonoperating—government
9531 Housing authorities, nonoperating—government
6531 Housing authorities, operating
3443 Housing cabinets for radium, metal plate—*mfg*
3272 Housing components, prefabricated: concrete—*mfg*
3444 Housings for business machines, sheet metal: except stamped—*mfg*
3469 Housings for business machines, stamped metal—*mfg*
3443 Housings, pressure—*mfg*
3489 Howitzers, more than 30 mm. (or more than 1.18 inch)—*mfg*

I

3429 Ice chests or coolers, portable, except insulated foam plastics—*mfg*
3089 Ice chests or coolers, portable, plastics: except insulated or foam plastics—*mfg*
3086 Ice chests or coolers, portable: foamed plastics—*mfg*
5451 Ice cream (packaged) stores—retail
5143 Ice cream and ices—wholesale
5078 Ice cream cabinets—wholesale
3411 Ice cream cans, metal—*mfg*
2052 Ice cream cones and wafers—*mfg*
2657 Ice cream containers, folding paperboard—mfpm—*mfg*
2656 Ice cream containers, nonfolding paperboard—mfpm—*mfg*
3469 Ice cream dippers—*mfg*
3499 Ice cream freezers, household, nonelectric: metal—*mfg*
3556 Ice cream manufacturing machinery—*mfg*
2023 Ice cream mix, unfrozen: liquid or dry—*mfg*
5812 Ice cream stands
5963 Ice cream wagons—retail
2024 Ice cream: e.g., bulk, packaged, molded, on sticks—*mfg*
3634 Ice crushers, electric—*mfg*
3569 Ice crushers, except household—*mfg*
2097 Ice cubes—*mfg*
5999 Ice dealers—retail
7941 Ice hockey clubs, professional or semiprofessional
3822 Ice maker controls—*mfg*
3585 Ice making machinery—*mfg*
5078 Ice making machines—wholesale
2023 Ice milk mix, unfrozen: liquid or dry—*mfg*
2024 Ice milk: e.g., bulk, packaged, molded, on sticks—*mfg*
2097 Ice plants, operated by public utilities—*mfg*
3949 Ice skates—*mfg*
7999 Ice skating rink operation
2097 Ice, manufactured or artificial: except dry ice—*mfg*
5199 Ice, manufactured or natural—wholesale
2086 Iced tea, bottled or canned—*mfg*
1499 Iceland spar mining (optical grade calcite)
2024 Ices and sherbets—*mfg*
4741 Icing of railroad cars
7389 Identification engraving service
3999 Identification plates—*mfg*
3999 Identification tags, except paper—*mfg*
5043 Identity recorders for photographing checks and fingerprints—wholesale
2899 Igniter grains, boron potassium nitrate—*mfg*
3483 Igniters, tracer: for ammunition more than 30 mm. (or more than 1.18 inch)—*mfg*
3694 Ignition apparatus for internal combustion engines—*mfg*
3694 Ignition cable sets or wire assemblies for internal combustion engines—*mfg*
3822 Ignition controls for gas appliances and furnaces, automatic—*mfg*
7539 Ignition service, automotive
3694 Ignition systems, high frequency—*mfg*
3825 Ignition testing instruments—*mfg*
3612 Ignition transformers—*mfg*
3229 Illuminating glass: light shades, reflectors, lamp chimneys, and globes—*mfg*
2911 Illuminating oil, produced in petroleum refineries—*mfg*
1099 Ilmenite mining
3299 Images, small: gypsum, clay, or papier-mache—factory production only—*mfg*
3634 Immersion heaters, household: electric—*mfg*
9721 Immigration services—government
9431 Immunization program administration—government
3679 Impedance conversion units, high frequency—*mfg*
3825 Impedance measuring equipment—*mfg*
3824 Impeller and counter driven flow meters—*mfg*
3842 Implants, surgical—*mfg*
1389 Impounding and storing salt water in connection with petroleum production
4971 Impounding reservoirs, irrigation
2295 Impregnating and coating of fabrics, except rubberizing—*mfg*
3843 Impression material, dental—*mfg*
2759 Imprinting, except lithographed or gravure—*mfg*
2754 Imprinting: gravure—*mfg*
2835 In vitro diagnostics—*mfg*
2835 In vivo diagnostics—*mfg*
2835 In vivo radioactive reagents—*mfg*
3822 In-built thermostats, filled system and bimetal types—*mfg*
3641 Incandescent filament lamp bulbs, complete—*mfg*
3559 Incandescent lamp making machinery—*mfg*
2899 Incense—*mfg*
3822 Incinerator control systems, residential and commercial types—*mfg*
1796 Incinerator installation, small—contractors
4953 Incinerator operation
3272 Incinerators, concrete—*mfg*

3339 Ingots, primary: nonferrous metals, except copper and aluminum—*mfg*
3312 Ingots, steel—*mfg*
5051 Ingots—wholesale
8049 Inhalation therapists, registered
3841 Inhalation therapy equipment—*mfg*
3841 Inhalators, surgical and medical—*mfg*
2899 Ink and writing fluids, except printing and drawing—*mfg*
2842 Ink eradicators—*mfg*
2842 Ink, burnishing—*mfg*
3952 Ink, drawing: black and colored—*mfg*
2893 Ink, duplicating—*mfg*
2899 Ink, indelible—*mfg*
5085 Ink, printers'—wholesale
2893 Ink, printing: base or finished—*mfg*
2899 Ink, stamp pad—*mfg*
5112 Ink, writing—wholesale
5112 Inked ribbons—wholesale
3229 Inkwells, glass—*mfg*
2499 Inlays for furniture (veneers)—*mfg*
3131 Inner soles, leather—*mfg*
3011 Inner tubes: airplane, automobile, bicycle, motorcycle, and tractor—*mfg*
7011 Inns, furnishing food and lodging
2819 Inorganic acids, except nitric or phosphoric—*mfg*
2833 Inorganic medicinal chemicals: bulk, uncompounded—*mfg*
2816 Inorganic pigments—*mfg*
3577 Input/output equipment, computer: except terminals—*mfg*
0721 Insect control for crops, with or without fertilizing
2879 Insect powder, household—*mfg*
3496 Insect screening, woven wire: made from purchased wire—*mfg*
2879 Insecticides, agricultural—*mfg*
2879 Insecticides, household—*mfg*
5191 Insecticides—wholesale
3545 Inserts, cutting tool—*mfg*
3999 Insignia, military: except textile—*mfg*
2399 Insignia, military: textile—*mfg*
9651 Inspection for labor standards—government
7389 Inspection of commodities, not connected with transportation
2899 Inspection oil, fluorescent—*mfg*
7549 Inspection service, automotive
4785 Inspection services connected with transportation
1796 Installation of machinery and other industrial equipment—contractors
6153 Installment notes, buying of
6153 Installment paper dealer
6141 Installment sales finance, other than banks
2095 Instant coffee—*mfg*
2752 Instant printing, except photocopy service—*mfg*
1542 Institutional building construction, nonresidential—general contractors
3646 Institutional lighting fixtures—*mfg*
3714 Instrument board assemblies, motor vehicle—*mfg*
3812 Instrument landing system instrumentation, airborne or airport—*mfg*
3827 Instrument lenses—*mfg*
3728 Instrument panel mockups: aircraft training units—*mfg*
3825 Instrument relays, all types—*mfg*
3825 Instrument shunts—*mfg*
3495 Instrument springs, precision: made from purchased wire—*mfg*
3612 Instrument transformers, except portable—*mfg*
3829 Instrumentation for reactor controls, auxiliary—*mfg*
3695 Instrumentation type tape, blank—*mfg*
3841 Instruments and apparatus, except electromedical: medical, surgical, ophthalmic, and veterinary—*mfg*
3823 Instruments for industrial process control—*mfg*
3825 Instruments for measuring electrical quantities—*mfg*
3825 Instruments, electric: for testing electrical characteristics—*mfg*
3952 Instruments, lettering: artists'—*mfg*
3841 Instruments, microsurgical: except electromedical—*mfg*
3931 Instruments, musical—*mfg*
3861 Instruments, photographic—*mfg*
3357 Insulated wire and cable, nonferrous—*mfg*
2679 Insulating batts, fills, and blankets: paper—mfpm—*mfg*
2899 Insulating compounds—*mfg*
3255 Insulating firebrick and shapes, clay—*mfg*
3211 Insulating glass, sealed units—mitse—*mfg*
3292 Insulating materials for covering boilers and pipes—*mfg*
2499 Insulating materials, cork—*mfg*
3275 Insulating plaster, gypsum—*mfg*
2493 Insulating siding, board—mitse—*mfg*
2952 Insulating siding, impregnated—mfpm—*mfg*
2241 Insulating tapes and braids, electric, except plastics—*mfg*
3086 Insulation and cushioning: foamed plastics—*mfg*

J

K

L

7819 Laboratories, motion picture
8734 Laboratories, product testing: not manufacturing auxiliaries
8731 Laboratories, research: commercial
8071 Laboratories: biological, medical, and X-ray (picture and treatment)
8731 Laboratory (physical) research and development
0279 Laboratory animal farms (e.g., rats, mice, guinea pigs)
2819 Laboratory chemicals, inorganic—*mfg*
2869 Laboratory chemicals, organic—*mfg*
2326 Laboratory coats: men's—mfpm—*mfg*
5047 Laboratory equipment, dental and medical—wholesale
5049 Laboratory equipment, except medical or dental—wholesale
3821 Laboratory equipment: fume hoods, distillation racks, benches, and cabinets—*mfg*
3231 Laboratory glassware, made from purchased glass—*mfg*
7699 Laboratory instrument repair, except electric
3825 Laboratory standards, electric: resistance, inductance, and capacitance—*mfg*
3069 Laboratory sundries: e.g., cases, covers, funnels, cups, bottles—rubber—*mfg*
3089 Laboratoryware, plastics—*mfg*
0831 Lac production
3552 Lace and net machines—*mfg*
5131 Lace fabrics—wholesale
2258 Lace goods: curtains, bedspreads, table covers, flouncings, and insertions—*mfg*
3111 Lace leather—*mfg*
3552 Lace machine bobbins, wood or metal—*mfg*
2241 Lace, auto wind—*mfg*
2395 Lace, burnt-out—*mfg*
2258 Lace, knit—*mfg*
2675 Lace, paper: die-cut from purchased materials—*mfg*
3131 Laces, boot and shoe: leather—*mfg*
2241 Laces, corset and shoe: textile—*mfg*
2258 Laces: Barmen, bobbinet, levers, and Nottingham—*mfg*
2241 Lacings—mitse—*mfg*
2851 Lacquer bases and dopes—*mfg*
2851 Lacquer thinner—*mfg*
2851 Lacquer, clear and pigmented—*mfg*
3479 Lacquering of metal products, for the trade—*mfg*
3567 Lacquering ovens—*mfg*
2851 Lacquers, plastics—*mfg*
5198 Lacquers—wholesale
3949 Lacrosse equipment—*mfg*
2023 Lactose, edible—*mfg*
3499 Ladder assemblies, combination workstand: metal—*mfg*
3531 Ladder ditchers, vertical boom or wheel—*mfg*
3429 Ladder jacks, metal—*mfg*
2499 Ladder jacks, wood—*mfg*
2426 Ladder round—*mfg*
2426 Ladder rounds or rungs, hardwood—*mfg*
3446 Ladders, chain: metal—*mfg*
3446 Ladders, for permanent installation: metal—*mfg*
3499 Ladders, metal: portable—*mfg*
3089 Ladders, plastics—*mfg*
2499 Ladders, wood—*mfg*
5084 Ladders—wholesale
5137 Ladies' handkerchiefs—wholesale
5137 Ladies' purses—wholesale
3443 Ladle bails—*mfg*
3255 Ladle brick, clay—*mfg*
3443 Ladles, metal plate—*mfg*
4449 Lake freight transportation, except on the Great Lakes
2865 Lake red C toners—*mfg*
2865 Lakes, color—*mfg*
2013 Lamb stew, mfpm—*mfg*
2011 Lamb—mitse—*mfg*
2679 Laminated building paper—mfpm—*mfg*
2675 Laminated cardboard—mfpm—*mfg*
3211 Laminated glass, made from glass produced in the same establishment—*mfg*
3231 Laminated glass, made from purchased glass—*mfg*
3083 Laminated plastics plate, rods, and tubes and sheet, except flexible packaging—*mfg*
2891 Laminating compounds—*mfg*
2295 Laminating of fabrics—*mfg*
7389 Laminating of photographs (coating photographs with plastics)
3399 Laminating steel for the trade—*mfg*
3641 Lamp (bulb) parts, electric—*mfg*
5719 Lamp and shade shops—retail
3281 Lamp bases, onyx—*mfg*
3089 Lamp bases, plastics—*mfg*
3269 Lamp bases, pottery—*mfg*
2816 Lamp black—*mfg*
5063 Lamp bulbs —wholesale
3641 Lamp bulbs and tubes, electric: incandescent filament, fluorescent, and vapor—*mfg*
3641 Lamp bulbs and tubes, health: infrared and ultraviolet radiation—*mfg*
3648 Lamp fixtures, infrared—*mfg*
3496 Lamp frames, wire: made from purchased wire—*mfg*

2869 Lauric acid esters—*mfg*
3431 Lavatories, enameled iron and other metal—*mfg*
3088 Lavatories, plastics—*mfg*
3261 Lavatories, vitreous china—*mfg*
9229 Law enforcement statistics centers—government
8111 Law offices
0782 Lawn care
3524 Lawn edgers, power—*mfg*
0782 Lawn fertilizing services
2514 Lawn furniture, metal—*mfg*
2519 Lawn furniture: except wood, metal, stone, and concrete—*mfg*
5021 Lawn furniture—wholesale
5083 Lawn machinery and equipment—wholesale
0782 Lawn mowing services
0782 Lawn mulching services
3524 Lawn rollers, residential—*mfg*
0782 Lawn seeding services
0782 Lawn spraying services
0782 Lawn sprigging services
1711 Lawn sprinkler system installation—contractors
7699 Lawnmower repair shops
3524 Lawnmowers, hand and power: residential—*mfg*
5261 Lawnmowers—retail
2211 Lawns, cotton—*mfg*
8111 Lawyers
2834 Laxatives—*mfg*
1094 Leaching of uranium, radium or vanadium ores at mine site
3691 Lead acid batteries (storage batteries)—*mfg*
3356 Lead and lead alloy bars, pipe, plates, rods, sheets, strip, and tubing—*mfg*
2879 Lead arsenate, formulated—*mfg*
2892 Lead azide (explosives)—*mfg*
1799 Lead burning—contractors
3364 Lead die-castings—*mfg*
3497 Lead foil, not made in rolling mills—*mfg*
1031 Lead ore mining
5052 Lead ore—wholesale
2816 Lead oxide pigments—*mfg*
2819 Lead oxides, other than pigments—*mfg*
2816 Lead pigments—*mfg*
3339 Lead pigs, blocks, ingots, and refinery shapes: primary—*mfg*
3356 Lead rolling, drawing, and extruding—*mfg*
2819 Lead silicate—*mfg*
3339 Lead smelting and refining, primary—*mfg*
3341 Lead smelting and refining, secondary—*mfg*
3295 Lead, black (natural graphite): ground, refined, or blended—*mfg*
3641 Lead-in wires, electric lamp: made from purchased wire—*mfg*
2851 Lead-in-oil paints—*mfg*
1031 Lead-zinc ore mining
5051 Lead—wholesale
3231 Leaded glass, made from purchased glass—*mfg*
3555 Leads, printers'—*mfg*
3423 Leaf skimmers and swimming pool rakes—*mfg*
3493 Leaf springs: automobile, locomotive, and other vehicle—*mfg*
3497 Leaf, metal—*mfg*
3599 Leak detectors, water—*mfg*
1389 Lease tanks, oil and gas field: erecting, cleaning, and repairing—on a contract basis
7374 Leasing of computer time
7377 Leasing of computers, except finance leasing or by the manufacturer
5199 Leather and cut stock—wholesale
5136 Leather and sheep-lined clothing, men's and boys'—wholesale
5137 Leather and sheep-lined clothing: women's and children's—wholesale
3199 Leather belting for machinery: flat, solid, twisted, and built-up—*mfg*
5085 Leather belting, packing—wholesale
3111 Leather coloring, cutting, embossing, japanning, and welting—*mfg*
3111 Leather converters—*mfg*
2842 Leather dressings and finishes—*mfg*
2865 Leather dyes and stains, synthetic—*mfg*
2843 Leather finishing agents—*mfg*
3151 Leather gloves or mittens—*mfg*
7699 Leather goods repair shops
5199 Leather goods, except footwear, gloves, luggage, and belting—wholesale
5948 Leather goods, including goods made to individual order—retail
3172 Leather goods, small: personal—*mfg*
3131 Leather welting—*mfg*
3559 Leather working machinery—*mfg*
2295 Leather, artificial or imitation—*mfg*
3111 Leather: tanning, currying, and finishing—*mfg*
2631 Leatherboard—mitse—*mfg*
2099 Leavening compounds, prepared—*mfg*
2074 Lecithin, cottonseed—*mfg*
2075 Lecithin, soybean—*mfg*
7389 Lecture bureaus
8999 Lecturers
2782 Ledgers and ledger sheets—*mfg*
2252 Leg warmers—*mfg*

3131 Lifts, heel: leather—*mfg*
3842 Ligatures, medical—*mfg*
1629 Light and power plant construction—general contractors
3641 Light bulbs, electric: complete—*mfg*
5063 Light bulbs, electric—wholesale
3663 Light communications equipment—*mfg*
3674 Light emitting diodes—*mfg*
3861 Light meters, photographic—*mfg*
3812 Light reconnaissance and surveillance systems and equipment—*mfg*
3671 Light sensing and emitting tubes—*mfg*
3674 Light sensitive devices, solid-state—*mfg*
3229 Light shades, glass: pressed or blown—*mfg*
3645 Light shades, metal—*mfg*
3827 Light sources, standard—*mfg*
2899 Lighter fluid—*mfg*
4499 Lighterage
3999 Lighters, cigar and cigarette: except precious metal and electric—*mfg*
5199 Lighters, cigar and cigarette—wholesale
3731 Lighters, marine: building and repairing—*mfg*
3731 Lighthouse tenders, building and repairing—*mfg*
3624 Lighting carbons—*mfg*
3648 Lighting fixtures, airport: runway, approach, taxi, and ramp—*mfg*
3646 Lighting fixtures, commercial—*mfg*
3647 Lighting fixtures, motor vehicle—*mfg*
3645 Lighting fixtures, residential, electric: e.g., garden, patio, walkway, yard—*mfg*
3648 Lighting fixtures, residential, except electric—*mfg*
3645 Lighting fixtures, residential: electric—*mfg*
3647 Lighting fixtures, vehicular—*mfg*
5063 Lighting fixtures: residential, commercial, and industrial—wholesale
3229 Lighting glassware, pressed or blown—*mfg*
7349 Lighting maintenance service (bulb replacement and cleaning)
3612 Lighting transformers, fluorescent—*mfg*
3612 Lighting transformers, street and airport—*mfg*
3643 Lightning arrestors and coils—*mfg*
1799 Lightning conductor erection—contractors
3643 Lightning protection equipment—*mfg*
3645 Lights, yard: electric—*mfg*
2821 Lignin plastics—*mfg*
1221 Lignite mining
1241 Lignite mining services on a contract basis
3489 Limbers, gun and caisson—*mfg*
3842 Limbs, artificial—*mfg*
5211 Lime and plaster dealers—retail
2819 Lime bleaching compounds—*mfg*
2869 Lime citrate—*mfg*
0174 Lime groves and farms
3274 Lime plaster—*mfg*
1422 Lime rock, ground
0711 Lime spreading for crops
5191 Lime, agricultural—wholesale
5032 Lime, except agricultural—wholesale
2879 Lime-sulfur, dry and solution—*mfg*
3281 Limestone, cut and shaped—*mfg*
1411 Limestone, dimension—quarrying
1422 Limestone, except bituminous: crushed and broken—quarrying
5032 Limestone—wholesale
3822 Limit controls, residential and commercial heating types—*mfg*
5331 Limited price variety stores—retail
1011 Limonite mining
4119 Limousine rental with drivers
7514 Limousine rental, without drivers
2879 Lindane, formulated—*mfg*
3531 Line markers, self-propelled—*mfg*
3822 Line or limit control for electric heat—*mfg*
3494 Line strainers, for use in piping systems—metal—*mfg*
3612 Line voltage regulators—*mfg*
3699 Linear accelerators—*mfg*
3824 Linear counters—*mfg*
2824 Linear esters fibers—*mfg*
2796 Linecuts—*mfg*
3842 Linemen's safety belts—*mfg*
2269 Linen fabrics: dyeing, finishing, and printing—*mfg*
5131 Linen piece goods—wholesale
5719 Linen shops—retail
7213 Linen supply service
5023 Linens—wholesale
2631 Liner board, kraft and jute—mitse—*mfg*
3259 Liner brick and plates, for lining sewers, tanks, etc.: vitrified clay—*mfg*
3069 Liner strips, rubber—*mfg*
2394 Liners and covers, fabric: pond, pit, and landfill—mfpm—*mfg*
2675 Liners for freight car doors: reinforced with metal strip—mfpm—*mfg*
3443 Liners, industrial: metal plate—*mfg*
5632 Lingerie stores—retail
5137 Lingerie—wholesale
2834 Liniments—*mfg*
2221 Lining fabrics, manmade fiber and silk: except glove lining fabrics—*mfg*
3111 Lining leather—*mfg*
2621 Lining paper—mitse—*mfg*
3259 Lining, stove and flue: clay—*mfg*
3131 Linings, boot and shoe: leather—*mfg*
2299 Linings, carpet: felt except woven—*mfg*
2392 Linings, carpet: textile, except felt—*mfg*

3452 Lock washers—*mfg*
3089 Lock washers, plastics—*mfg*
7299 Locker rental, except cold storage
2542 Lockers, not refrigerated: except wood—*mfg*
2541 Lockers, not refrigerated: wood—*mfg*
5046 Lockers, not refrigerated—wholesale
3585 Lockers, refrigerated—*mfg*
3429 Locks and lock sets: except safe, vault, and coin-operated—*mfg*
5072 Locks and related materials—wholesale
3581 Locks, coin-operated—*mfg*
3499 Locks, safe and vault: metal—*mfg*
3429 Locks, trigger, for guns—*mfg*
7699 Locksmith shops
3647 Locomotive and railroad car lights—*mfg*
3531 Locomotive cranes—*mfg*
3462 Locomotive wheels, forged: not made in rolling mills—*mfg*
3743 Locomotives, locomotive frames, and parts—*mfg*
1041 Lode gold mining
7041 Lodging houses operated by organizations for members only
7021 Lodging houses, except organization
2452 Log cabins, prefabricated: wood—*mfg*
4449 Log rafting and towing
3531 Log splitters—*mfg*
4212 Log trucking
0171 Loganberry farms
2411 Logging contractors—*mfg*
3531 Logging equipment—*mfg*
5082 Logging equipment—wholesale
4013 Logging railroads
1389 Logging wells on a contract basis
3825 Logic circuit testers—*mfg*
2411 Logs—*mfg*
3699 Logs, fireplace: electric—*mfg*
3433 Logs, fireplace: gas—*mfg*
5099 Logs, hewn ties, posts, and poles—wholesale
2861 Logwood extract—*mfg*
2211 Long cloth, cotton—*mfg*
4813 Long distance telephone communications
4213 Long-distance trucking
3552 Loom bobbins, wood or metal—*mfg*
3552 Looms (textile machinery)—*mfg*
3552 Loopers (textile machinery)—*mfg*
2395 Looping, for the trade—*mfg*
5112 Looseleaf binders—wholesale
2782 Looseleaf devices and binders—*mfg*
2678 Looseleaf fillers and ream paper in filler sizes, except printed—mfpm—*mfg*
2782 Looseleaf forms and fillers, pen ruled or printed only—*mfg*
3851 Lorgnettes—*mfg*
7999 Lotteries, operation of
7999 Lottery clubs and ticket sales to individuals
9311 Lottery control boards—government
3651 Loudspeakers, electrodynamic and magnetic—*mfg*
5813 Lounges, cocktail
2384 Lounging robes and dressing gowns, men's, boys', and women's—mfpm—*mfg*
2369 Lounging robes: girls', children's, and infants'—mfpm—*mfg*
2253 Lounging robes—mitse—*mfg*
2431 Louver windows and doors, glass with wood frame—*mfg*
3442 Louver windows, all metal or metal frame—*mfg*
3444 Louvers, sheet metal—*mfg*
3914 Loving cups, silver, nickel silver, pewter, and plated—*mfg*
2064 Lozenges, candy: nonmedicated—*mfg*
2834 Lozenges, pharmaceutical—*mfg*
2992 Lubricating greases and oils—mfpm—*mfg*
5172 Lubricating oils and greases—wholesale
2992 Lubricating oils, re-refining—mfpm—*mfg*
7549 Lubricating service, automotive
3724 Lubricating systems, aircraft—*mfg*
3569 Lubricating systems, centralized—*mfg*
3569 Lubrication equipment, industrial—*mfg*
3569 Lubrication machinery, automatic—*mfg*
3714 Lubrication systems and parts, motor vehicle—*mfg*
3743 Lubrication systems, locomotive—*mfg*
5948 Luggage and leather goods stores—retail
2211 Luggage fabrics, cotton—*mfg*
3429 Luggage hardware—*mfg*
2396 Luggage linings—*mfg*
3429 Luggage racks, car top—*mfg*
7699 Luggage repair shops
3161 Luggage, regardless of material—*mfg*
5099 Luggage—wholesale
5063 Lugs and connectors, electrical—wholesale
5211 Lumber and building materials dealers—retail
5211 Lumber and planing mill product dealers—retail
2421 Lumber stacking or sticking—*mfg*
4226 Lumber terminals, storage for hire
2426 Lumber, hardwood dimension—*mfg*
2421 Lumber, kiln drying of—*mfg*
5031 Lumber: rough, dressed, and finished—wholesale
2421 Lumber: rough, sawed, or planed—*mfg*
2329 Lumberjackets: men's and boys'—mfpm—*mfg*
2819 Luminous compounds, radium—*mfg*
3646 Luminous panel ceilings—*mfg*

3369 Magnesium castings, except die-castings—*mfg*
2819 Magnesium chloride—*mfg*
2819 Magnesium compounds, inorganic—*mfg*
3364 Magnesium die-castings—*mfg*
3339 Magnesium refining, primary—*mfg*
3356 Magnesium rolling, drawing, and extruding—*mfg*
3341 Magnesium smelting and refining, secondary—*mfg*
3357 Magnet wire, insulated—*mfg*
3674 Magnetic bubble memory device—*mfg*
3824 Magnetic counters—*mfg*
3823 Magnetic flow meters, industrial process type—*mfg*
3542 Magnetic forming machines—*mfg*
3577 Magnetic ink recognition devices, computer peripheral equipment—*mfg*
2899 Magnetic inspection oil and powder—*mfg*
3695 Magnetic recording tape, blank: reels, cassettes, and disks—*mfg*
5065 Magnetic recording tape—wholesale
3845 Magnetic resonance imaging device (diagnostic), nuclear—*mfg*
3826 Magnetic resonance imaging type apparatus, except diagnostic—*mfg*
3572 Magnetic storage devices for computers—*mfg*
3652 Magnetic tape, audio: prerecorded—*mfg*
1011 Magnetite mining
3674 Magnetohydrodynamic (MHD) devices—*mfg*
3829 Magnetometers—*mfg*
3671 Magnetron tubes—*mfg*
3264 Magnets, permanent: ceramic or ferrite—*mfg*
3499 Magnets, permanent: metallic—*mfg*
3851 Magnifiers (readers and simple magnifiers)—*mfg*
3827 Magnifying instruments, optical—*mfg*
7361 Maid registries
7349 Maid service on a contract or fee basis
7331 Mail advertising service
3469 Mail boxes, except collection boxes—*mfg*
4212 Mail carriers, bulk, contract: local
3444 Mail chutes, sheet metal—*mfg*
3444 Mail collection or storage boxes, sheet metal—*mfg*
4215 Mail delivery, private: except air
2542 Mail pouch racks, except wood—*mfg*
3579 Mail tying (bundling) machines—*mfg*
5961 Mail-order houses—retail (not including retail outlets)
4822 Mailgram services
2655 Mailing cases and tubes, paper fiber (metal-end or all-fiber)—mfpm—*mfg*
7331 Mailing list compilers
3579 Mailing machines—*mfg*
5044 Mailing machines—wholesale
2542 Mailing racks, postal service: except wood—*mfg*
7331 Mailing service
3571 Mainframe computers—*mfg*
4173 Maintenance facilities for motor vehicle passenger transportation
7349 Maintenance, building: except repairs
2519 Malacca furniture—*mfg*
4959 Malaria control
2865 Maleic anhydride—*mfg*
3423 Mallets, printers'—*mfg*
3069 Mallets, rubber—*mfg*
3949 Mallets, sports: e.g., polo, croquet—*mfg*
2499 Mallets, wood—*mfg*
2869 Malononitrile, technical grade—*mfg*
2083 Malt byproducts—*mfg*
2082 Malt extract, liquors, and syrups—*mfg*
5149 Malt extract—wholesale
3556 Malt mills—*mfg*
2083 Malt: barley, rye, wheat, and corn—*mfg*
5149 Malt—wholesale
2023 Malted milk—*mfg*
2083 Malthouses—*mfg*
8742 Management engineering consultants
8742 Management information systems consultants
6726 Management investment funds, closed-end
6722 Management investment funds, open-end
0762 Management services, farm
6282 Manager of mutual funds, contract or fee basis
7941 Managers of individual professional athletes
6211 Managers or agents for mutual funds
6531 Managers, real estate
3931 Mandolins and parts—*mfg*
3545 Mandrels—*mfg*
2819 Manganese dioxide powder, synthetic—*mfg*
3313 Manganese metal—*mfg*
1061 Manganese ore mining
1011 Manganiferous ore mining, valued chiefly for iron content
1061 Manganite mining
2861 Mangrove extract—*mfg*
1623 Manhole construction—contractors
3272 Manhole covers and frames, concrete—*mfg*
3321 Manhole covers, metal—*mfg*
7231 Manicure and pedicure salons
2844 Manicure preparations—*mfg*
5112 Manifold business forms—wholesale
3714 Manifolds, motor vehicle: gasoline engine—*mfg*

3498 Manifolds, pipe: fabricated from purchased metal pipe—*mfg*
2675 Manila folders—mfpm—*mfg*
2631 Manila lined board—mitse—*mfg*
2621 Manila wrapping paper—mitse—*mfg*
2284 Manmade fiber thread—*mfg*
5169 Manmade fibers—wholesale
2281 Manmade staple fiber yarn, spun—*mfg*
7389 Mannequin decorating service
5046 Mannequins—wholesale
3999 Mannikins and display forms—*mfg*
3823 Manometers, industrial process type—*mfg*
7363 Manpower pools
8331 Manpower training
1743 Mantel work—contractors
3272 Mantels, concrete—*mfg*
4925 Manufactured gas production and distribution
8611 Manufacturers' institutes
8742 Manufacturing management consultants
5932 Manuscripts, rare—retail
7389 Map drafting service
3829 Map plotting instruments—*mfg*
0831 Maple sap, gathering of
7389 Mapmaking, including aerial
2759 Maps, engraved—*mfg*
2752 Maps, lithographed—*mfg*
2759 Maps, printed: except lithographed or gravure (not publishing)—*mfg*
2754 Maps: gravure printing (not publishing)—*mfg*
2741 Maps: publishing and printing, or publishing only—*mfg*
5032 Marble building stone—wholesale
1743 Marble installation, interior: including finishing—contractors
1741 Marble work, exterior construction—contractors
3281 Marble, building: cut and shaped—*mfg*
1429 Marble, crushed and broken—quarrying
1411 Marble, dimension—quarrying
1479 Marcasite mining
2899 Margaric acid—*mfg*
2079 Margarine oil, except corn—*mfg*
2079 Margarine, including imitation—*mfg*
2079 Margarine-butter blend—*mfg*
5149 Margarine—wholesale
3931 Marimbas—*mfg*
4493 Marinas
2452 Marinas, prefabricated: wood—*mfg*
9711 Marine Corps
3625 Marine and navy auxiliary controls—*mfg*
4493 Marine basins, operation of
4491 Marine cargo handling
1629 Marine construction—general contractors
8711 Marine engineering services
3519 Marine engines: diesel, semidiesel, and other internal combustion—*mfg*
3429 Marine hardware—*mfg*
3499 Marine horns, compressed air or steam: metal—*mfg*
3669 Marine horns, electric—*mfg*
2851 Marine paints—*mfg*
5088 Marine propulsion machinery and equipment—wholesale
3663 Marine radio communications equipment—*mfg*
4499 Marine railways for drydocking, operation of
3731 Marine rigging—*mfg*
4499 Marine salvaging
5541 Marine service stations—retail
5088 Marine supplies (dunnage)—wholesale
5551 Marine supply dealers—retail
4499 Marine surveyors, except cargo
4492 Marine towing
4499 Marine wrecking: ships for scrap
3999 Marionettes (puppets)—*mfg*
3647 Marker lamps, motor vehicle—*mfg*
3951 Markers, soft tip: e.g., felt, fabric, plastics—*mfg*
2499 Market baskets, except fruit and vegetable: veneer and splint—*mfg*
2449 Market baskets, fruit and vegetable: veneer and splint—*mfg*
0161 Market gardens
8732 Market research, commercial
9641 Marketing and consumer services—government
8742 Marketing consultants
5112 Marking devices—wholesale
3549 Marking machines, metalworking—*mfg*
1422 Marl, crushed and broken—quarrying
2033 Marmalade—*mfg*
2499 Marquetry, wood—*mfg*
2211 Marquisettes, cotton—*mfg*
2221 Marquisettes, manmade fiber—*mfg*
7299 Marriage bureaus
8322 Marriage counseling services
9221 Marshals' offices, police
2099 Marshmallow creme—*mfg*
2064 Marshmallows—*mfg*
2064 Marzipan (candy)—*mfg*
3699 Maser amplifiers—*mfg*
2499 Mashers, potato: wood—*mfg*
2672 Masking tape—mfpm—*mfg*
2679 Masks, papier-mache—mfpm—*mfg*
3949 Masks, sports: e.g., baseball, fencing, hockey—*mfg*
3546 Masonry and concrete drilling tools, power: portable—*mfg*
1741 Masonry—contractors

3423 Masons' handtools—*mfg*
3274 Masons' lime—*mfg*
5032 Masons' materials—wholesale
3826 Mass spectrometers—*mfg*
3826 Mass spectroscopy instrumentation—*mfg*
3999 Massage machines, electric: designed for beauty and barber shops—*mfg*
3634 Massage machines, electric: except designed for beauty and barber shop—*mfg*
7299 Massage parlors
2951 Mastic floor composition, hot and cold—*mfg*
2952 Mastic roofing composition—mfpm—*mfg*
2499 Masts, wood—*mfg*
3999 Matches and match books—*mfg*
5199 Matches—wholesale
2211 Matelasse, cotton—*mfg*
5084 Materials handling equipment—wholesale
9431 Maternity and child health program administration—government
2342 Maternity bras and corsets—mfpm—*mfg*
8069 Maternity hospitals
5621 Maternity shops—retail
2631 Matrix board—mitse—*mfg*
2621 Matrix paper—mitse—*mfg*
3496 Mats and matting, made from purchased wire—*mfg*
2273 Mats and matting, textile—*mfg*
3069 Mats and matting: e.g., bath, door—rubber—*mfg*
2273 Mats and matting: twisted paper, grass, reed, coir, sisal, jute, and rag—*mfg*
3555 Mats, advertising and newspaper (matrices)—*mfg*
2299 Mats, felt: except woven—*mfg*
0181 Mats, preseeded: soil erosion—growing of
2295 Mats, varnished glass—*mfg*
3423 Mattocks (handtools)—*mfg*
2392 Mattress pads—*mfg*
2392 Mattress protectors, except rubber—*mfg*
3069 Mattress protectors, rubber—*mfg*
7699 Mattress renovating and repair shops
5712 Mattress stores, including custom made—retail
3272 Mattresses for river revetment, concrete articulated—*mfg*
3292 Mattresses, asbestos—*mfg*
2515 Mattresses, containing felt, foam rubber, urethane, etc.—*mfg*
3069 Mattresses, pneumatic: fabric coated with rubber—*mfg*
2515 Mattresses: innerspring, box spring, and noninnerspring—*mfg*
5021 Mattresses—wholesale
2052 Matzoths—*mfg*
3423 Mauls, metal (handtools)—*mfg*
2499 Mauls, wood—*mfg*
3952 Maulsticks, artists'—*mfg*
1542 Mausoleum construction—general contractors
6553 Mausoleum operation
2035 Mayonnaise—*mfg*
9111 Mayors' offices
8322 Meal delivery programs
2077 Meal, blood—*mfg*
2048 Meal, bone: prepared as feed for animals and fowls—*mfg*
2041 Meal, corn—*mfg*
2046 Meal, gluten—*mfg*
2077 Meal, meat and bone: not prepared as feed—*mfg*
2038 Meals, frozen—*mfg*
7699 Measuring and controlling instrument repair, mechanical
5084 Measuring and testing equipment, electrical, except automotive—wholesale
3825 Measuring equipment for electronic and electrical circuits and equipment—*mfg*
3825 Measuring instruments and meters, electric—*mfg*
3545 Measuring tools and machines, machinists' metalworking type—*mfg*
3824 Measuring wheels—*mfg*
2077 Meat and bone meal and tankage—*mfg*
3556 Meat and poultry processing machinery—*mfg*
2259 Meat bagging—mitse—*mfg*
2013 Meat extracts—mfpm—*mfg*
2011 Meat extracts—mitse—*mfg*
3556 Meat grinders—*mfg*
5421 Meat markets—retail
2011 Meat packing plants—*mfg*
5142 Meat pies, frozen—wholesale
2013 Meat products: cooked, cured, frozen, smoked, and spiced—mfpm—*mfg*
2099 Meat seasonings, except sauces—*mfg*
5142 Meat, frozen: packaged—wholesale
2011 Meat—mitse—*mfg*
5147 Meats, cured or smoked—wholesale
5147 Meats, fresh—wholesale
1711 Mechanical contractors
7993 Mechanical games, coin-operated: operation of
3111 Mechanical leather—*mfg*
3462 Mechanical power transmission forgings, ferrous: not made in rolling mills—*mfg*
3463 Mechanical power transmission forgings, nonferrous: not made in hot-rolling mills—*mfg*
3061 Mechanical rubber goods: molded, extruded, and lathe-cut—*mfg*

3495 Mechanical springs, precision: made from purchased wire—*mfg*
3542 Mechanical-pneumatic or hydraulic metal forming machines—*mfg*
3423 Mechanics' handtools—*mfg*
2841 Mechanics' paste—*mfg*
3873 Mechanisms for clockwork operated devices—*mfg*
3581 Mechanisms for coin-operated machines—*mfg*
5094 Medallions—wholesale
3911 Medals of precious or semiprecious metals—*mfg*
7319 Media buying service
3577 Media-to-media data conversion equipment, computer peripheral equipment—*mfg*
9441 Medical assistance program administration—government
8621 Medical associations
7352 Medical equipment rental and leasing
7629 Medical equipment repair, electrical
7699 Medical equipment repair, except electric
5047 Medical equipment—wholesale
5047 Medical glass—wholesale
6411 Medical insurance claims, processing of: contract or fee basis
8071 Medical laboratories, clinical
8099 Medical photography and art
8733 Medical research, noncommercial
5122 Medical rubber goods—wholesale
6324 Medical service plans
3069 Medical sundries, rubber—*mfg*
2326 Medical uniforms, men's—mfpm—*mfg*
5122 Medicinals and botanicals—wholesale
3221 Medicine bottles, glass—*mfg*
5122 Medicine cabinet sundries—wholesale
3231 Medicine droppers, made from purchased glass—*mfg*
2834 Medicines, capsuled or ampuled—*mfg*
2493 Medium density fiberboard (MDF)—*mfg*
5031 Medium density fiberboard—wholesale
1499 Meerschaum mining or quarrying
2821 Melamine resins—*mfg*
2024 Mellorine—*mfg*
0161 Melon farms
3821 Melting point apparatus, laboratory—*mfg*
3443 Melting pots, for metal—*mfg*
3255 Melting pots, glasshouse: clay—*mfg*
2329 Melton jackets: men's and boys'—mfpm—*mfg*
2678 Memorandum books, except printed—mfpm—*mfg*
2782 Memorandum books, printed—*mfg*
3674 Memories, solid-state—*mfg*
2252 Men's hosiery—*mfg*
5611 Men's wearing apparel—retail
0912 Menhaden, catching of
9431 Mental health agencies—government
8063 Mental hospitals, except for the mentally retarded
8051 Mental retardation hospitals
2759 Menus, except lithographed or gravure printed—*mfg*
2752 Menus, lithographed—*mfg*
2754 Menus: gravure printing—*mfg*
7323 Mercantile credit reporting bureaus
6153 Mercantile financing
2261 Mercerizing cotton broadwoven fabrics—*mfg*
3552 Mercerizing machinery—*mfg*
2269 Mercerizing yarn, braided goods, and narrow fabrics: except knit and wool—*mfg*
2673 Merchandise bags, plastics—mfpm—*mfg*
2674 Merchandise bags, uncoated paper—mfpm—*mfg*
3581 Merchandising machines, automatic—*mfg*
5046 Merchandising machines, automatic—wholesale
5962 Merchandising, automatic (sale of products through vending machines)
5699 Merchant tailors—retail
5159 Merchants of raw farm products, except grain, field beans, and livestock—wholesale
8611 Merchants' associations, not engaged in credit investigations
3629 Mercury arc rectifiers (electrical apparatus)—*mfg*
2892 Mercury azide (explosives)—*mfg*
2819 Mercury chlorides (calomel, corrosive sublimate), except U.S.P.—*mfg*
2833 Mercury chlorides, U.S.P.—*mfg*
2819 Mercury compounds, inorganic—*mfg*
2833 Mercury compounds, medicinal: organic and inorganic—*mfg*
1099 Mercury ore mining
2819 Mercury oxides—*mfg*
2819 Mercury, redistilled—*mfg*
5051 Mercury—wholesale
3496 Mesh, made from purchased wire—*mfg*
3661 Message concentrators—*mfg*
7389 Message service, telephone answering: except beeper service
3841 Metabolism apparatus—*mfg*
2835 Metabolite diagnostic reagents—*mfg*
5039 Metal buildings—wholesale
5169 Metal cyanides—wholesale
3542 Metal deposit forming machines—*mfg*
5031 Metal doors, sash and trim—wholesale
2899 Metal drawing compound lubricants—*mfg*

3429 Metal fasteners, spring and cold-rolled steel, not made in rolling mills—*mfg*
3559 Metal finishing equipment for plating, except rolling mill lines—*mfg*
1791 Metal furring—contractors
3567 Metal melting furnaces, industrial—*mfg*
3674 Metal oxide silicon (MOS) devices—*mfg*
3559 Metal pickling equipment, except rolling mill lines—*mfg*
5169 Metal polishes—wholesale
3541 Metal polishing lathes—*mfg*
5084 Metal refining machinery and equipment—wholesale
5169 Metal salts—wholesale
5074 Metal sanitary ware—wholesale
7389 Metal slitting and shearing on a contract or fee basis
3559 Metal smelting and refining machinery, except furnaces and ovens—*mfg*
2899 Metal treating compounds—*mfg*
5093 Metal waste and scrap—wholesale
3291 Metallic abrasives—*mfg*
5052 Metallic concentrates—wholesale
2671 Metallic covered paper for packaging—mfpm—*mfg*
2672 Metallic covered paper, except for packaging—mfpm—*mfg*
3861 Metallic emulsion sensitized paper and cloth, photographic—*mfg*
5052 Metallic ores—wholesale
2816 Metallic pigments, inorganic—*mfg*
2869 Metallic salts of acyclic organic chemicals—*mfg*
2869 Metallic stearate—*mfg*
2295 Metallizing of fabrics—*mfg*
3827 Metallographs—*mfg*
8734 Metallurgical testing laboratories
5051 Metals, except precious—wholesale
2819 Metals, liquid—*mfg*
5094 Metals, precious—wholesale
5719 Metalware stores—retail
5084 Metalworking machinery—wholesale
5084 Metalworking tools: drills, taps, dies, grinding wheels, and files—wholesale
3829 Meteorogic tracking systems—*mfg*
7699 Meteorological instrument repair
3829 Meteorological instruments—*mfg*
3272 Meter boxes, concrete—*mfg*
3951 Meter pens—*mfg*
7389 Meter readers, remote
3613 Metering panels, electric—*mfg*
3825 Meters, electric: pocket, portable, panelboard, and graphic recording—*mfg*
3825 Meters, power factor and phase angle—*mfg*
3824 Meters: gas, liquid, tallying, and mechanical measuring—except electrical—*mfg*
2861 Methanol, natural (wood alcohol)—*mfg*
2869 Methanol, synthetic (methyl alcohol)—*mfg*
2861 Methyl acetone—*mfg*
2821 Methyl acrylate resins—*mfg*
2861 Methyl alcohol, natural (wood alcohol)—*mfg*
2821 Methyl cellulose plastics—*mfg*
2869 Methyl chloride—*mfg*
2821 Methyl methacrylate resins—*mfg*
2869 Methyl perhydrofluorine—*mfg*
2869 Methyl salicylate—*mfg*
2865 Methyl violet toners—*mfg*
2869 Methylamine—*mfg*
2869 Methylene chloride—*mfg*
2032 Mexican foods, canned—*mfg*
1499 Mica mining
3299 Mica products, built-up and sheet, except radio parts—*mfg*
1429 Mica schist, crushed and broken—quarrying
1411 Mica schist, dimension—quarrying
3299 Mica splitting—*mfg*
3295 Mica, ground or otherwise treated—*mfg*
3299 Mica, laminated—*mfg*
2835 Microbiology, virology, and serology diagnostic products—*mfg*
3674 Microcircuits, integrated (semiconductor)—*mfg*
3571 Microcomputers—*mfg*
3861 Microfiche cameras—*mfg*
3861 Microfiche readers and reader printers—*mfg*
3861 Microfilm equipment: cameras, projectors, and readers—*mfg*
7389 Microfilm recording and developing service
5044 Microfilming equipment—wholesale
1099 Microlite mining
3545 Micrometers—*mfg*
3651 Microphones—*mfg*
3826 Microprobes: electron, ion, laser, X-ray—*mfg*
3674 Microprocessors—*mfg*
3827 Microprojectors—*mfg*
2741 Micropublishing—*mfg*
7699 Microscope repair
3826 Microscopes, electron and proton—*mfg*
3827 Microscopes, except electron, proton, and corneal—*mfg*
3821 Microtomes—*mfg*
3663 Microwave communications equipment—*mfg*
3679 Microwave components—*mfg*

3631 Microwave ovens, household: including portable—*mfg*
5064 Microwave ovens, household—wholesale
3825 Microwave test equipment—*mfg*
3089 Microwaveware, plastics—*mfg*
2361 Middies: girls', children's, and infants'—mfpm—*mfg*
8049 Midwives, offices of
2261 Mildew proofing cotton broadwoven fabrics—*mfg*
2262 Mildew proofing manmade fiber and silk broadwoven fabrics—*mfg*
8211 Military academies, elementary and secondary level
3999 Military insignia, except textile—*mfg*
2899 Military pyrotechnics—*mfg*
9711 Military training schools
2311 Military uniforms, tailored: men's and boys'—*mfg*
3412 Milk (fluid) shipping containers, metal—*mfg*
5143 Milk and cream, fluid—wholesale
5451 Milk and other dairy products stores—retail
3221 Milk bottles, glass—*mfg*
3411 Milk cans, metal—*mfg*
2631 Milk carton board—mitse—*mfg*
2656 Milk cartons, paperboard—mfpm—*mfg*
5143 Milk cooling stations, operated by farm assemblers
5963 Milk delivery and sale of purchased milk, without processing—retail
5143 Milk depots—wholesale
2675 Milk filter disks, die-cut from purchased paper—*mfg*
2621 Milk filter disks—mitse—*mfg*
2026 Milk processing (pasteurizing, homogenizing, vitaminizing, bottling)—*mfg*
3556 Milk processing machinery—*mfg*
0241 Milk production, dairy cattle farm
2026 Milk production, except farm—*mfg*
0214 Milk production, goat farm
5084 Milk products manufacturing machinery and equipment—wholesale
0751 Milk testing for butterfat
2026 Milk, acidophilus—*mfg*
2026 Milk, bottled—*mfg*
5149 Milk, canned or dried—wholesale
2026 Milk, flavored—*mfg*
2026 Milk, reconstituted—*mfg*
2026 Milk, ultra-high temperature—*mfg*
2023 Milk, whole: canned—*mfg*
2023 Milk: concentrated, condensed, dried, evaporated, and powdered—*mfg*
5083 Milking machinery and equipment—wholesale
3523 Milking machines—*mfg*
2023 Milkshake mix—*mfg*
5949 Mill end stores—retail
2269 Mill enders, contract: cotton, silk, and manmade fiber—*mfg*
2231 Mill menders, contract: wool, mohair, and similar animal fibers—*mfg*
3199 Mill strapping for textile mills, leather—*mfg*
5085 Mill supplies—wholesale
3547 Mill tables (rolling mill equipment)—*mfg*
3292 Millboard, asbestos—*mfg*
2353 Millinery—*mfg*
5632 Millinery stores—retail
5131 Millinery supplies—wholesale
2396 Millinery trimmings—mfpm—*mfg*
5137 Millinery—wholesale
3545 Milling machine attachments (machine tool accessories)—*mfg*
3541 Milling machines (machine tools)—*mfg*
2041 Milling of grains, dry, except rice—*mfg*
2044 Milling of rice—*mfg*
3556 Mills and presses: beet, cider, and sugarcane—*mfg*
1499 Millstone quarrying
5211 Millwork and lumber dealers—retail
2431 Millwork products—*mfg*
2491 Millwork, treated—*mfg*
5031 Millwork—wholesale
1796 Millwrights
0119 Milo farms
5044 Mimeograph equipment—wholesale
5112 Mimeograph paper—wholesale
7334 Mimeographing service
2032 Mincemeat, canned—*mfg*
3535 Mine conveyors—*mfg*
1081 Mine development for metal mining: on a contract basis
1481 Mine development for nonmetallic minerals, except fuels: on a contract basis
1629 Mine loading and discharging station construction—general contractors
2491 Mine props, treated—*mfg*
2491 Mine ties, wood: treated—*mfg*
2411 Mine timbers, hewn—*mfg*
5082 Mineral beneficiation machinery—wholesale
2816 Mineral colors and pigments—*mfg*
2048 Mineral feed supplements—*mfg*
2911 Mineral jelly, produced in petroleum refineries—*mfg*
6211 Mineral leases, dealers in
2911 Mineral oils, natural: produced in petroleum refineries—*mfg*
1479 Mineral pigment mining
6211 Mineral royalties, dealers in

5191 Mineral supplements, animal—wholesale
2086 Mineral water, carbonated: bottled or canned—*mfg*
2911 Mineral waxes, natural: produced in petroleum refineries—*mfg*
5033 Mineral wool insulation materials—wholesale
3296 Mineral wool roofing mats—*mfg*
3648 Miners' lamps—*mfg*
3483 Mines and parts (ordnance)—*mfg*
3571 Minicomputers—*mfg*
9651 Minimum wage program administration—government
1629 Mining appurtenance construction—general contractors
3532 Mining cars and trucks (dollies)—*mfg*
3532 Mining equipment, except oil and gas field: rebuilding on a factory basis—*mfg*
3743 Mining locomotives and parts—*mfg*
3532 Mining machinery and equipment, except oil and gas field—*mfg*
5082 Mining machinery and equipment, except petroleum—wholesale
2816 Minium (pigments)—*mfg*
4225 Miniwarehouse warehousing
0271 Mink farms
0273 Minnow farms
0139 Mint farms
7699 Mirror repair shops
5719 Mirrors —retail
3231 Mirrors, framed or unframed: made from purchased glass—*mfg*
3827 Mirrors, optical—*mfg*
3231 Mirrors, transportation equipment: made from purchased glass—*mfg*
1629 Missile facilities construction—general contractors
3462 Missile forgings, ferrous: not made in rolling mills—*mfg*
3463 Missile forgings, nonferrous: not made in hot-rolling mills—*mfg*
3812 Missile guidance systems and equipment—*mfg*
3443 Missile silos and components, metal plate—*mfg*
3483 Missile warheads—*mfg*
3423 Mitre boxes, metal—*mfg*
2211 Mitten flannel, cotton—*mfg*
3151 Mittens, leather—*mfg*
5136 Mittens, men's and boys'—wholesale
3069 Mittens, rubber—*mfg*
5137 Mittens: women's, children's, and infants'—wholesale
2259 Mittens—mitse—*mfg*
2819 Mixed acid—*mfg*
3556 Mixers and whippers, electric: for food manufacturing industries—*mfg*
3443 Mixers for hot metal—*mfg*
5082 Mixers, construction and mining—wholesale
3556 Mixers, feed: except agricultural machinery—*mfg*
3556 Mixers, food: commercial types—*mfg*
3531 Mixers: e.g., concrete, ore, sand, slag, plaster, mortar, bituminous—*mfg*
2045 Mixes, flour: e.g., pancake, cake, biscuit, doughnut—mfpm—*mfg*
2041 Mixes, flour: e.g., pancake, cake, biscuit, doughnut—mitse—*mfg*
2451 Mobile buildings for commercial use (e.g., offices, banks)—*mfg*
2451 Mobile classrooms—*mfg*
3663 Mobile communications equipment—*mfg*
2451 Mobile dwellings—*mfg*
5271 Mobile home equipment—retail
5271 Mobile home parts and accessories—retail
7519 Mobile home rental, except on site
1521 Mobile home repair, on site—general contractors
1799 Mobile home site setup and tie down—contractors
2451 Mobile homes, except recreational—*mfg*
5271 Mobile homes, new and used—retail
5039 Mobile homes—wholesale
3711 Mobile lounges (motor vehicle)—*mfg*
3537 Mobile straddle carriers—*mfg*
3149 Moccasins—*mfg*
2221 Modacrylic broadwoven fabrics—*mfg*
2824 Modacrylic fibers—*mfg*
2281 Modacrylic yarn, made from purchased staple: spun—*mfg*
5092 Model kits—wholesale
7361 Model registries
3952 Modeling clay—*mfg*
8299 Modeling schools, clothes
7363 Modeling service
3842 Models, anatomical—*mfg*
3999 Models, except toy and hobby—*mfg*
3944 Models, toy and hobby: e.g., airplane, boat, ship, railroad equipment—*mfg*
3661 Modems—*mfg*
5065 Modems—wholesale
2521 Modular furniture systems, office, wood—*mfg*
2522 Modular furniture systems, office: except wood—*mfg*
1521 Modular housing, single-family (assembled on site)—general contractors
3674 Modules, solid-state—*mfg*
0214 Mohair production

5043 Motion picture cameras, equipment, and supplies—wholesale

7819 Motion picture consultants

7822 Motion picture distribution, exclusive of production

7832 Motion picture exhibitors for airlines

7832 Motion picture exhibitors, itinerant

3861 Motion picture film—*mfg*

7841 Motion picture film or tape rental to the general public

7812 Motion picture production and distribution

7819 Motion picture reproduction

5043 Motion picture studio and theater equipment—wholesale

7833 Motion picture theaters, drive-in

3711 Motor buses, except trackless trolley—*mfg*

9621 Motor carrier licensing and inspection offices—government

3625 Motor control accessories, including overload relays—*mfg*

3625 Motor control centers—*mfg*

3625 Motor controls, electric—*mfg*

5063 Motor controls, electric—wholesale

3621 Motor generator sets, except automotive and turbogenerators—*mfg*

5561 Motor home dealers—retail

7519 Motor home rental

3716 Motor homes, self-contained: made on purchased chassis—*mfg*

3711 Motor homes, self-contained—mitse—*mfg*

5012 Motor homes—wholesale

3621 Motor housings—*mfg*

7538 Motor repair, automotive

3751 Motor scooters and parts—*mfg*

5571 Motor scooters—retail

5012 Motor scooters—wholesale

3625 Motor starters, contactors, and controllers, industrial—*mfg*

3596 Motor truck scales—*mfg*

3715 Motor truck trailers—*mfg*

3711 Motor trucks, except off-highway—*mfg*

5511 Motor vehicle dealers, new and used cars—retail

5521 Motor vehicle dealers, used cars only—retail

3714 Motor vehicle gasoline engine rebuilding on a factory basis—*mfg*

3429 Motor vehicle hardware—*mfg*

9621 Motor vehicle licensing and inspection offices—government

3714 Motor vehicle parts and accessories, except motor vehicle stampings—*mfg*

5015 Motor vehicle parts, used—wholesale or retail

5064 Motor vehicle radios—wholesale

5014 Motor vehicle tires and tubes—wholesale

5012 Motor vehicles, commercial—wholesale

3711 Motor vehicles, including amphibian—*mfg*

3751 Motorbikes and parts—*mfg*

5551 Motorboat dealers—retail

3732 Motorboats, inboard and outboard: building and repairing—*mfg*

5571 Motorcycle dealers—retail

3647 Motorcycle lamps—*mfg*

5571 Motorcycle parts—retail

5013 Motorcycle parts—wholesale

7948 Motorcycle racing

7999 Motorcycle rental

7699 Motorcycle repair service

3751 Motorcycles and parts—*mfg*

5012 Motorcycles—wholesale

3594 Motors, air or hydraulic (fluid power)—*mfg*

3594 Motors, air or hydraulic fluid power—*mfg*

3621 Motors, electric: except engine starting motors and gear motors—*mfg*

5063 Motors, electric—wholesale

3566 Motors, gear—*mfg*

3594 Motors, pneumatic—*mfg*

3694 Motors, starting: motor vehicle and aircraft—*mfg*

2371 Mounting heads on fur neckpieces—*mfg*

7389 Mounting merchandise on cards on a contract or fee basis

2789 Mounting of maps and samples, for the trade—*mfg*

3999 Mountings, comb and hairpin: except precious metal—*mfg*

3851 Mountings, eyeglass and spectacle—*mfg*

3911 Mountings, gold and silver: for pens, leather goods, and umbrellas—*mfg*

3484 Mounts for guns, 30 mm. (or 1.18 inch) or less—*mfg*

3931 Mouthpieces for musical instruments—*mfg*

3069 Mouthpieces for pipes and cigarette holders, rubber—*mfg*

2844 Mouthwashes—*mfg*

3873 Movements, watch or clock—*mfg*

3523 Mowers and mower-conditioners, hay—*mfg*

5083 Mowers, power—wholesale

0782 Mowing highway center strips and edges

2891 Mucilage—*mfg*

3531 Mud jacks—*mfg*

1389 Mud service, oil field drilling: on a contract basis

7533 Mufflers, automotive: installation, repair, or sales and installation

3714 Mufflers, exhaust: motor vehicle—*mfg*

5136 Mufflers, men's and boys'—wholesale

2323 Mufflers: men's and boys'—mfpm—*mfg*

N

2865 Naphthalene, made in chemical plants—*mfg*
2851 Naphthanate driers—*mfg*
2869 Naphthenic acid soaps—*mfg*
2911 Naphthenic acids, produced in petroleum refineries—*mfg*
2865 Naphthol, alpha and beta—*mfg*
2865 Naphtholsulfonic acids—*mfg*
2621 Napkin stock, paper—mitse—*mfg*
2392 Napkins, fabric and nonwoven textiles—mfpm—*mfg*
2676 Napkins, paper—mfpm—*mfg*
5113 Napkins, paper—wholesale
2676 Napkins, sanitary—mfpm—*mfg*
3552 Napping machines (textile machinery)—*mfg*
2261 Napping of cotton broadwoven fabrics—*mfg*
2262 Napping of manmade fiber and silk broadwoven fabrics—*mfg*
2231 Napping of wool, mohair, and similar animal fiber fabrics—*mfg*
2231 Narrow fabrics, dyeing and finishing: wool, mohair, and similar animal fibers—*mfg*
2241 Narrow fabrics, elastic: woven or braided—*mfg*
2269 Narrow fabrics, except knit and wool: bleaching, dyeing, and finishing—*mfg*
5131 Narrow fabrics—wholesale
2241 Narrow woven fabrics: cotton, rayon, wool, silk, glass, and manmade fiber—*mfg*
2299 Narrow woven fabrics: linen, jute, hemp, and ramie—*mfg*
6111 National Consumer Cooperative Bank
6019 National Credit Union Administration (NCUA)
9711 National Guard
6021 National banks, commercial
2032 Nationality specialty foods, canned—*mfg*
2032 Native foods, canned—*mfg*
2038 Native foods, frozen—*mfg*
1499 Natural abrasives mining (except sand)
1623 Natural gas compressing station construction—general contractors
4924 Natural gas distribution
1321 Natural gas liquids production
1311 Natural gas production
4922 Natural gas storage
4922 Natural gas transmission
4923 Natural gas transmission and distribution
1321 Natural gasoline production
7999 Natural wonders, tourist attraction: commercial
8049 Naturopaths, offices of
7699 Nautical and navigational instrument repair, except electric
3812 Nautical instruments—*mfg*
3489 Naval artillery—*mfg*
3731 Naval ships, building and repairing—*mfg*
2861 Naval stores, gum: processing but not gathering or warehousing—*mfg*
2861 Naval stores, wood—*mfg*
5169 Naval stores—wholesale
3812 Navigational instruments—*mfg*
9711 Navy
2082 Near beer—*mfg*
2371 Neckpieces, fur—*mfg*
2221 Necktie fabrics, manmade fiber and silk: broadwoven—*mfg*
2396 Necktie linings, cutting of—*mfg*
2323 Neckties: men's and boys'—mfpm—*mfg*
2253 Neckties—mitse—*mfg*
5136 Neckwear, men's and boys'—wholesale
2323 Neckwear: men's and boys'—mfpm—*mfg*
2339 Neckwear: women's, misses' and juniors'—mfpm—*mfg*
0175 Nectarine orchards and farms
2033 Nectars, fruit—*mfg*
3841 Needle holders, surgical—*mfg*
3965 Needles, hand and machine—*mfg*
3841 Needles, hypodermic—*mfg*
3841 Needles, suture—*mfg*
5949 Needlework stores—retail
2395 Needlework, art—mfpm—*mfg*
2341 Negligees: women's, misses', children's, and infants'—mfpm—*mfg*
2254 Negligees—mitse—*mfg*
8322 Neighborhood centers
2813 Neon—*mfg*
3993 Neon signs—*mfg*
5046 Neon signs—wholesale
2822 Neoprene—*mfg*
1459 Nepheline syenite quarrying
3826 Nephelometers, except meteorological—*mfg*
3829 Nephoscopes—*mfg*
3552 Net and lace machines—*mfg*
5131 Net goods—wholesale
2211 Nets and nettings—mitse—*mfg*
2399 Nets, fishing—mfpm—*mfg*
3999 Nets, hair—*mfg*
2399 Nets, launderers' and dyers'—*mfg*
2298 Nets, rope—*mfg*
3949 Nets: e.g., badminton, basketball, tennis—not made in weaving mills—*mfg*
2258 Netting made on a lace or net machine—*mfg*
2258 Netting, knit—mitse—*mfg*

3366 Nonferrous foundries: brass, bronze, copper, and copper base alloy—*mfg*

3369 Nonferrous foundries: except aluminum, copper, and copper alloys—*mfg*

3369 Nonferrous metal foundries, except aluminum, copper, and die-castings—*mfg*

3369 Nonferrous metal machinery castings: except aluminum, copper, and die-castings—*mfg*

3341 Nonferrous metal smelting and refining, secondary—*mfg*

5051 Nonferrous metal, except precious: e.g., sheets, bars, rods—wholesale

5093 Nonferrous metals scrap—wholesale

3339 Nonferrous refining, primary: except copper and aluminum—*mfg*

3356 Nonferrous rolling, drawing, and extruding: except copper and aluminum—*mfg*

3339 Nonferrous smelting, primary: except copper and aluminum—*mfg*

5052 Nonmetallic minerals and concentrates, crude: except petroleum—wholesale

6512 Nonresidential buildings, operators of

7812 Nontheatrical motion picture production

2297 Nonwoven fabrics, except felt—*mfg*

2099 Noodles, fried (e.g., Chinese)—*mfg*

2099 Noodles, uncooked: packaged with other ingredients—*mfg*

2098 Noodles: egg, plain, and water—*mfg*

2869 Normal hexyl decalin—*mfg*

3769 Nose cones, guided missile—*mfg*

3842 Nose plugs—*mfg*

7389 Notaries public

6211 Note brokers

2678 Notebooks, including mechanically bound by wire, plastics, etc.—mfpm—*mfg*

5949 Notion stores—retail

5131 Notions—wholesale

2258 Nottingham lace—*mfg*

3499 Novelties and specialties, metal: except advertising novelties—*mfg*

3993 Novelties, advertising—*mfg*

3961 Novelties, costume: except precious metal and gems—*mfg*

3231 Novelties, glass: e.g., fruit, foliage, flowers, animals, made from purchased glass—*mfg*

3199 Novelties, leather—*mfg*

2679 Novelties, paper—mfpm—*mfg*

5199 Novelties, paper—wholesale

2499 Novelties, wood fiber—*mfg*

3999 Novelties: bone, beaded, and shell—*mfg*

2514 Novelty furniture, metal—*mfg*

3229 Novelty glassware: made in glassmaking plants—*mfg*

5961 Novelty merchandise, mail-order—retail

5947 Novelty shops—retail

2395 Novelty stitching, for the trade—*mfg*

3429 Nozzles, fire fighting—*mfg*

3432 Nozzles, lawn hose—*mfg*

3432 Nozzles, plumbers'—*mfg*

3499 Nozzles, spray: aerosol paint, and insecticides—*mfg*

3443 Nuclear core structurals, metal plate—*mfg*

2819 Nuclear cores, inorganic—*mfg*

9631 Nuclear energy inspection and regulation offices

2819 Nuclear fuel reactor cores, inorganic—*mfg*

2819 Nuclear fuel scrap reprocessing—*mfg*

2869 Nuclear fuels, organic—*mfg*

3829 Nuclear instrument modules—*mfg*

3844 Nuclear irradiation equipment—*mfg*

3462 Nuclear power plant forgings, ferrous: not made in rolling mills—*mfg*

3829 Nuclear radiation detection and monitoring instruments—*mfg*

1629 Nuclear reactor containment structure construction—general contractors

3559 Nuclear reactor control rod drive mechanisms—*mfg*

3823 Nuclear reactor controls—*mfg*

3443 Nuclear reactors, military and industrial—*mfg*

3443 Nuclear shielding, metal plate—*mfg*

7032 Nudist camps

3579 Numbering machines, office and store: mechanical—*mfg*

3953 Numbering stamps, with rubber type: hand—*mfg*

3625 Numerical controls—*mfg*

3541 Numerically controlled metal cutting machine tools—*mfg*

5999 Numismatist shops—retail

0831 Nurseries, forest

2514 Nursery furniture, metal—*mfg*

2511 Nursery furniture, wood—*mfg*

8351 Nursery schools

0181 Nursery stock, growing of

5261 Nursery stock, seeds and bulbs—retail

5193 Nursery stock—wholesale

7361 Nurses' registries

8049 Nurses, registered and practical: offices of, except home health care services

8059 Nursing homes except skilled and intermediate care facilities

8052 Nursing homes, intermediate care

8051 Nursing homes, skilled

8249 Nursing schools, practical

0173 Nut (tree) groves and farms

3429 Nut crackers and pickers, metal—*mfg*

0723 Nut hulling and shelling

2079 Nut margarine—*mfg*

O

5159 Oil nuts—wholesale
2851 Oil paints—*mfg*
3829 Oil pressure gauges, motor vehicle—*mfg*
6519 Oil properties, lessors of
1629 Oil refinery construction—general contractors
5084 Oil refining machinery, equipment, and supplies—wholesale
6211 Oil royalties, dealers in
6792 Oil royalty companies
1389 Oil sampling service for oil companies on a contract basis
1311 Oil sand mining
3053 Oil seals, asbestos—*mfg*
3053 Oil seals, leather—*mfg*
3053 Oil seals, rubber—*mfg*
1311 Oil shale mining
4959 Oil spill cleanup
2851 Oil stains—*mfg*
2911 Oil still gas, produced in petroleum refineries—*mfg*
3443 Oil storage tanks, metal plate—*mfg*
2899 Oil treating compounds—*mfg*
7359 Oil well drilling equipment rental and leasing
1381 Oil well drilling: on a contract basis
1389 Oil well logging on a contract basis
5084 Oil well machinery, equipment, and supplies—wholesale
1389 Oil well rig building, repairing, and dismantling: on a contract basis
5084 Oil well supply houses—wholesale
2911 Oil, acid: produced in petroleum refineries—*mfg*
2865 Oil, aniline—*mfg*
2046 Oil, corn: crude and refined—*mfg*
2074 Oil, cottonseed—*mfg*
2865 Oil, creosote: product of coal tar distillation—*mfg*
2079 Oil, hydrogenated: edible—*mfg*
2079 Oil, olive—*mfg*
2079 Oil, partially hydrogenated: edible—*mfg*
2861 Oil, pine: produced by distillation of pine gum or pine wood—*mfg*
2899 Oil, red (oleic acid)—*mfg*
2075 Oil, soybean—*mfg*
2843 Oil, turkey red—*mfg*
2079 Oil, vegetable winter stearin—*mfg*
5093 Oil, waste—wholesale
2295 Oilcloth—*mfg*
2672 Oiled paper—mfpm—*mfg*
2077 Oils, animal—*mfg*
2844 Oils, cosmetic—*mfg*
2899 Oils, essential—*mfg*
5199 Oils, except cooking: animal and vegetable—wholesale
2077 Oils, fish and marine animal: e.g., herring, menhaden, whale (refined), sardine—*mfg*
2077 Oils, fish and marine animal: herring, menhaden, whale (refined), sardine—*mfg*
2992 Oils, lubricating: re-fining—*mfg*
2992 Oils, lubricating—mfpm—*mfg*
2911 Oils, partly refined: sold for rerunning—produced in petroleum refineries—*mfg*
2843 Oils, soluble (textile assistants)—*mfg*
2843 Oils, sulfonated—*mfg*
2079 Oils, vegetable (except corn oil) refined: cooking and salad—*mfg*
2833 Oils, vegetable and animal: medicinal grade—refined and concentrated—*mfg*
2076 Oils, vegetable: except corn, cottonseed, and soybean—*mfg*
2861 Oils, wood: product of hardwood distillation—*mfg*
2911 Oils: fuel, lubricating, and illuminating—produced in petroleum refineries—*mfg*
2865 Oils: light, medium, and heavy: made in chemical plants—*mfg*
5199 Oilseed cake and meal—wholesale
3556 Oilseed crushing and extracting machinery—*mfg*
5159 Oilseeds—wholesale
1499 Oilstone quarrying
3291 Oilstones, artificial—*mfg*
2834 Ointments—*mfg*
2076 Oiticica oil—*mfg*
8322 Old age assistance
8361 Old soldiers' homes
2851 Oleate driers—*mfg*
2824 Olefin fibers—*mfg*
2899 Oleic acid (red oil)—*mfg*
2869 Oleic acid esters—*mfg*
3728 Oleo struts, aircraft—*mfg*
2819 Oleum (fuming sulfuric acid)—*mfg*
0179 Olive groves and farms
2079 Olive oil—*mfg*
2035 Olives, brined: bulk—*mfg*
2034 Olives, dried—*mfg*
2033 Olives, including stuffed: canned—*mfg*
1459 Olivine (nongem) mining
3812 Omnibearing instrumentation—*mfg*
7375 On-line data base information retrieval services
1521 One-family house construction—general contractors
0161 Onion farms
2035 Onions, pickled—*mfg*
1429 Onyx marble, crushed and broken—quarrying
1411 Onyx marble, dimension--quarrying

0783 Ornamental tree planting, pruning, bracing, spraying, removal, and surgery
2431 Ornamental woodwork: e.g., cornices and mantels—*mfg*
3231 Ornamented glass, made from purchased glass—*mfg*
3999 Ornaments, Christmas tree: except glass and electric—*mfg*
3229 Ornaments, Christmas tree: glass—mitse—*mfg*
3231 Ornaments, Christmas tree: made from purchased glass—*mfg*
3699 Ornaments, Christmas tree: electric—*mfg*
3961 Ornaments, costume: except precious metal and gems—*mfg*
3131 Ornaments, shoe—*mfg*
8361 Orphanages
2899 Orris oil—*mfg*
2865 Orthodichlorobenzene—*mfg*
3843 Orthodontic appliances—*mfg*
8072 Orthodontic appliances made in dental laboratories to order for the profession
8021 Orthodontists, offices of
5999 Orthopedic and artificial limb stores—retail
3842 Orthopedic devices and materials—*mfg*
5047 Orthopedic equipment—wholesale
3842 Orthopedic hosiery, elastic—*mfg*
8069 Orthopedic hospitals
8011 Orthopedic physicians, offices of
3275 Orthopedic plaster, gypsum—*mfg*
3149 Orthopedic shoes, children's: except extension shoes—*mfg*
3842 Orthopedic shoes, extension—*mfg*
3143 Orthopedic shoes, men's: except extension shoes—*mfg*
3144 Orthopedic shoes, women's: except extension shoes—*mfg*
3069 Orthopedic sundries, molded rubber—*mfg*
3825 Oscillators, audiofrequency and radiofrequency (instrument types)—*mfg*
3679 Oscillators, except laboratory type—*mfg*
3825 Oscillographs and oscilloscopes—*mfg*
1099 Osmium ore mining
3826 Osmometers—*mfg*
2211 Osnaburgs—*mfg*
2899 Ossein—*mfg*
8031 Osteopathic physicians, offices and clinics of
8099 Osteoperosis centers
3999 Ostrich feathers: curling, dyeing, and renovating for the trade—*mfg*
3845 Otoscopes, electromedical—*mfg*
3841 Otoscopes, except electromedical—*mfg*
5551 Outboard motor dealers—retail
3699 Outboard motors, electric—*mfg*
3519 Outboard motors, except electric—*mfg*
5091 Outboard motors—wholesale
7312 Outdoor advertising service
5712 Outdoor furniture—retail
2253 Outerwear handknitted: for the trade—*mfg*
5136 Outerwear, men's and boys'—wholesale
5137 Outerwear: women's, children's, and infants'—wholesale
2211 Outing flannel, cotton—*mfg*
3644 Outlet boxes (electric wiring devices)—*mfg*
3643 Outlets, convenience: electric—*mfg*
8093 Outpatient detoxification centers
8093 Outpatient mental health clinics
8093 Outpatient treatment clinics for alcoholism and drug addiction
8322 Outreach programs
1629 Oven construction for industrial plants—general contractors
1629 Oven construction, bakers'—general contractors
3822 Oven temperature controls, nonindustrial—*mfg*
3556 Ovens, bakery—*mfg*
3589 Ovens, cafeteria food warming: portable—*mfg*
3631 Ovens, household: excluding portable appliances other than microwave and convection—*mfg*
3634 Ovens, household: portable: except microwave and convection ovens—*mfg*
3567 Ovens, industrial process: except bakery—*mfg*
3821 Ovens, laboratory—*mfg*
3589 Ovens, microwave (cooking equipment): commercial—*mfg*
5046 Ovens, microwave: commercial—wholesale
5064 Ovens, microwave: household—wholesale
3567 Ovens, sherardizing—*mfg*
3569 Ovens, surveillance: for aging and testing powder—*mfg*
3229 Ovenware, glass—*mfg*
3089 Ovenware, plastics—*mfg*
4213 Over-the-road trucking
2326 Overall jackets: men's and boys'—mfpm—*mfg*
2326 Overalls, work: men's and boys'—mfpm—*mfg*
1241 Overburden removal for bituminous coal, anthracite, and lignite on a contract basis
1081 Overburden removal for metal mining: on a contract basis
1481 Overburden removal for nonmetallic minerals, except fuels: on a contract basis

3567 Paint baking and drying ovens—*mfg*
5198 Paint brushes, rollers, and sprayers—wholesale
2851 Paint driers—*mfg*
3559 Paint making machinery—*mfg*
2816 Paint pigments, inorganic—*mfg*
2865 Paint pigments, organic—*mfg*
2851 Paint primers—*mfg*
2851 Paint removers—*mfg*
3991 Paint rollers—*mfg*
3944 Paint sets, children's—*mfg*
7532 Paint shops, automotive
5084 Paint spray equipment, industrial—wholesale
3563 Paint sprayers—*mfg*
2499 Paint sticks, wood—*mfg*
5231 Paint stores—retail
3952 Paint, gold or bronze—*mfg*
2851 Paintbrush cleaners—*mfg*
3991 Paintbrushes—*mfg*
3479 Painting (enameling and varnishing) of metal products, for the trade—*mfg*
3999 Painting instrument dials, for the trade—*mfg*
1721 Painting of buildings and other structures, except roofs—contractors
1721 Painting ships—contractors
1721 Painting traffic lanes—contractors
3952 Paints for burnt wood or leather work, platinum—*mfg*
3952 Paints for china painting—*mfg*
3952 Paints, artists'—*mfg*
2851 Paints, asphalt and bituminous—*mfg*
2851 Paints, plastics texture: paste and dry—*mfg*
2851 Paints, waterproof—*mfg*
2851 Paints: oil and alkyd vehicle, and water thinned—*mfg*
5198 Paints—wholesale
2211 Pajama checks, textile—*mfg*
2322 Pajamas: men's and boys'— mfpm—*mfg*
2341 Pajamas: women's, misses', children's, and infants'—mfpm—*mfg*
2254 Pajamas—mitse—*mfg*
3952 Palettes, artists'—*mfg*
1099 Palladium ore mining
3537 Pallet assemblies for landing mats—*mfg*
2448 Pallet containers, wood or wood and metal combination—*mfg*
3537 Pallet loaders and unloaders—*mfg*
2542 Pallet racks, except wood—*mfg*
2679 Pallet spacers, fiber—mfpm—*mfg*
3537 Palletizers and depalletizers—*mfg*
2653 Pallets, corrugated and solid fiberboard—mfpm—*mfg*
3537 Pallets, metal—*mfg*
2448 Pallets, wood or wood and metal combination—*mfg*
2076 Palm kernel oil—*mfg*
2789 Pamphlets, binding only—*mfg*
2732 Pamphlets: printing or printing and binding, not publishing—*mfg*
2731 Pamphlets: publishing and printing, or publishing only—*mfg*
3479 Pan glazing, for the trade—*mfg*
2353 Panama hats—*mfg*
2045 Pancake batter, refrigerated or frozen—mfpm—*mfg*
2041 Pancake batter, refrigerated or frozen—mitse—*mfg*
2045 Pancake mixes—mfpm—*mfg*
2099 Pancake syrup, blended and mixed—*mfg*
3728 Panel assemblies (hydromatic propeller test stands), aircraft—*mfg*
2521 Panel furniture systems, office, wood—*mfg*
2522 Panel furniture systems, office: except wood—*mfg*
2431 Panel work, wood—*mfg*
3823 Panelboard indicators, recorders and controllers: receiver type—*mfg*
3613 Panelboards and distribution boards, electric—*mfg*
5063 Panelboards—wholesale
5031 Paneling, wood—wholesale
5211 Paneling—retail
3272 Panels and sections, prefabricated: concrete—*mfg*
3448 Panels for prefabricated metal buildings—*mfg*
2452 Panels for prefabricated wood buildings—*mfg*
2675 Panels, cardboard: mfpm—*mfg*
3613 Panels, electric control and metering—*mfg*
2435 Panels, hardwood plywood—*mfg*
3299 Panels, papier-mache or plaster of paris—*mfg*
3275 Panels, plaster: gypsum—*mfg*
2436 Panels, softwood plywood—*mfg*
3827 Panoramic telescopes—*mfg*
2655 Pans and voids, fiber or cardboard—mfpm—*mfg*
3469 Pans, stamped and pressed metal: except tinned—*mfg*
3411 Pans, tinned—*mfg*
2341 Panties: women's, misses', children's, and infants'—mfpm—*mfg*
2254 Panties—mitse—*mfg*
2231 Pantings: wool, mohair, and similar animal fibers—*mfg*
3952 Pantographs for drafting—*mfg*
2339 Pants outfits, except pantsuits: women's, misses', and juniors'—mfpm—*mfg*

8049 Paramedics, offices of
3679 Parametric amplifiers—*mfg*
3674 Parametric diodes—*mfg*
3999 Parasols and frames: handles, parts, and trimmings—except precious metal—*mfg*
4513 Parcel delivery, private: air
4215 Parcel delivery, private: except air
7389 Parcel packing service (packaging)
3111 Parchment leather—*mfg*
2621 Parchment paper—mitse—*mfg*
8641 Parent-teacher associations
2834 Parenteral solutions—*mfg*
2024 Parfait—*mfg*
6159 Pari-mutuel totalizator equipment finance leasing and maintenance
2879 Paris green (insecticide)—*mfg*
3479 Parkerizing, for the trade—*mfg*
3647 Parking lights, automotive—*mfg*
1771 Parking lot construction—contractors
7521 Parking lots
3824 Parking meters—*mfg*
7521 Parking structures
7299 Parking, valet
1611 Parkway construction—general contractors
4789 Parlor car operations, not performed by line-haul railroad companies
8211 Parochial schools, elementary and secondary
8322 Parole offices
2426 Parquet flooring, hardwood—*mfg*
1752 Parquet flooring—contractors
3699 Particle accelerators, high voltage—*mfg*
3826 Particle size analyzers—*mfg*
3821 Particle size reduction apparatus, laboratory—*mfg*
2493 Particleboard—*mfg*
5031 Particleboard—wholesale
2899 Parting compounds (chemical foundry supplies)—*mfg*
3251 Partition tile, clay—*mfg*
3496 Partitions and grillework, made from purchased wire—*mfg*
3446 Partitions and grillework, ornamental metal—*mfg*
2653 Partitions, corrugated and solid fiberboard—mfpm—*mfg*
2522 Partitions, office: not for floor attachment—except wood—*mfg*
2521 Partitions, office: not for floor attachment—wood—*mfg*
2542 Partitions, prefabricated: except wood and free-standing—*mfg*
2541 Partitions, prefabricated: wood—for floor attachment—*mfg*
5046 Partitions—wholesale
7359 Party supplies rental and leasing
5963 Party-plan merchandising—retail
2782 Passbooks—*mfg*
2396 Passementeries—mfpm—*mfg*
1542 Passenger and freight terminal building construction—general contractors
3711 Passenger automobile bodies—*mfg*
3535 Passenger baggage belt loaders—*mfg*
7515 Passenger car leasing, except finance leasing: without drivers
7514 Passenger car rental, without drivers
4111 Passenger transportation, regular route, road or rail: between airports and terminals
4489 Passenger water transportation on rivers and canals
3731 Passenger-cargo vessels, building and repairing—*mfg*
3679 Passive repeaters—*mfg*
7221 Passport photographers
2032 Pasta, canned—*mfg*
2099 Pasta, uncooked: packaged with other ingredients—*mfg*
2891 Paste, adhesive—*mfg*
3399 Paste, metal—*mfg*
3952 Pastels, artists'—*mfg*
2099 Pastes, almond—*mfg*
2033 Pastes, fruit and vegetable—*mfg*
3556 Pasteurizing equipment, dairy and other food—*mfg*
2013 Pastrami—mfpm—*mfg*
2051 Pastries, except frozen: e.g., Danish, French—*mfg*
2499 Pastry boards, wood—*mfg*
2899 Patching plaster, household—*mfg*
7389 Patent brokers
6794 Patent buying and licensing
2631 Patent coated paperboard—mitse—*mfg*
6794 Patent leasing
3111 Patent leather—*mfg*
5122 Patent medicines—wholesale
8111 Patent solicitors' offices
8071 Pathological laboratories
8011 Pathologists (M.D.), offices of
8021 Pathologists, oral: offices of
3845 Patient monitoring equipment: intensive care/coronary care unit—*mfg*
5047 Patient monitoring equipment—wholesale
1771 Patio construction, concrete—contractors
3731 Patrol boats, building and repairing—*mfg*
7389 Patrol of electric transmission or gas lines
3711 Patrol wagons (motor vehicles)—*mfg*
3553 Pattern makers' machinery (woodworking)—*mfg*
3469 Patterns on metal—*mfg*
3543 Patterns, industrial—*mfg*

3827 Percentage correctors—*mfg*
2819 Perchloric acid—*mfg*
2869 Perchloroethylene—*mfg*
3634 Percolators, electric—*mfg*
5064 Percolators, electric—wholesale
3482 Percussion caps, for ammunition of 30 mm. (or 1.18 inch) or less—*mfg*
3931 Percussion musical instruments—*mfg*
3469 Perforated metal, stamped—*mfg*
3443 Perforating on heavy metal—*mfg*
3469 Perforating on light metal—*mfg*
1389 Perforating well casings on a contract basis
3579 Perforators (office machines)—*mfg*
6794 Performance rights, publishing and licensing of
7929 Performing artists
7922 Performing arts center productions
2844 Perfume bases, blending and compounding—*mfg*
2869 Perfume materials, synthetic—*mfg*
2844 Perfumes, natural and synthetic—*mfg*
5122 Perfumes—wholesale
2752 Periodicals, lithographed: not published—*mfg*
2759 Periodicals, printed: except lithographed or gravure (not publishing)—*mfg*
2754 Periodicals: gravure printing (not publishing)—*mfg*
2721 Periodicals: publishing and printing, or publishing only—*mfg*
5192 Periodicals—wholesale
8021 Periodontists, offices of
5734 Peripheral equipment, computer stores—retail
5045 Peripheral equipment, computer—wholesale
3827 Periscopes—*mfg*
3295 Perlite aggregate—*mfg*
1499 Perlite mining
3295 Perlite, expanded—*mfg*
2395 Permanent pleating and pressing, for the trade—*mfg*
3999 Permanent wave equipment and machines—*mfg*
2892 Permissible explosives—*mfg*
2819 Peroxides, inorganic—*mfg*
2865 Persian orange lake—*mfg*
0175 Persimmon orchards and farms
8811 Personal affairs management
8059 Personal care facilities with health care
8059 Personal care homes with health care
3571 Personal computers—*mfg*
8299 Personal development schools
6141 Personal finance companies, small loan: licensed
6719 Personal holding companies, except bank
6733 Personal investment trusts, management of
3172 Personal leather goods, small—*mfg*
3842 Personal safety appliances and equipment—*mfg*
7299 Personal shopping service
9199 Personnel agencies—government
3711 Personnel carriers, for highway use—*mfg*
3829 Personnel dosimetry devices—*mfg*
8742 Personnel management consultants, except employment service
7342 Pest control in structures
0851 Pest control, forest
2879 Pesticides, agricultural—*mfg*
2879 Pesticides, household—*mfg*
5191 Pesticides—wholesale
5999 Pet food stores—retail
2048 Pet food, except dog and cat: canned, frozen, and dry—*mfg*
5149 Pet food—wholesale
0742 Pet hospitals
5999 Pet shops—retail
5199 Pet supplies, except pet food—wholesale
1629 Petrochemical plant construction—general contractors
2911 Petrolatums, produced in petroleum refineries—*mfg*
4226 Petroleum and chemical bulk stations and terminals for hire
5172 Petroleum and its products, except bulk stations and terminals—wholesale
5172 Petroleum brokers—wholesale
5171 Petroleum bulk stations and terminals—wholesale
2911 Petroleum coke, produced in petroleum refineries—*mfg*
8711 Petroleum engineering services
4612 Petroleum pipelines, crude
4613 Petroleum pipelines, refined
2821 Petroleum polymer resins—*mfg*
1311 Petroleum production—crude
1629 Petroleum refinery construction—general contractors
3559 Petroleum refinery equipment—*mfg*
2911 Petroleum refining—*mfg*
2531 Pews, church—*mfg*
3914 Pewter ware—*mfg*
3559 Pharmaceutical machinery—*mfg*
1541 Pharmaceutical manufacturing plant construction—general contractors
2834 Pharmaceuticals—*mfg*
5122 Pharmaceuticals—wholesale
5912 Pharmacies—retail
3825 Phase angle meters—*mfg*

3827 Phototheodolites—*mfg*
3663 Phototransmission equipment—*mfg*
2791 Phototypesetting—*mfg*
3674 Photovoltaic devices, solid-state—*mfg*
7999 Phrenologists
2869 Phthalates—*mfg*
2821 Phthalic alkyd resins—*mfg*
2865 Phthalic anhydride—*mfg*
2821 Phthalic anhydride resins—*mfg*
2865 Phthalocyanine toners—*mfg*
8742 Physical distribution consultants
8099 Physical examination service, except by physicians
7991 Physical fitness centers
3829 Physical properties testing and inspection equipment—*mfg*
8731 Physical research, commercial
8733 Physical research, noncommercial
8049 Physical therapists, offices of
8011 Physicians (M.D.), including specialists: offices and clinics of
8049 Physicians' assistants, offices of
5047 Physicians' equipment—wholesale
5047 Physicians' supplies—wholesale
8031 Physicians, osteopathic: offices and clinics of
8999 Physicists, consulting: not connected with business service laboratories
3841 Physiotherapy equipment, electrical—*mfg*
2833 Physostigmine and derivatives—*mfg*
2879 Phytoactin—*mfg*
3429 Piano hardware—*mfg*
3931 Piano parts and materials, except piano hardware—*mfg*
7359 Piano rental and leasing
5736 Piano stores—retail
7699 Piano tuning and repair
3931 Pianos, all types: e.g., vertical, grand, spinet, player, coin-operated—*mfg*
3931 Piccolos and parts—*mfg*
3552 Picker machines (textile machinery)—*mfg*
2426 Picker stick blanks—*mfg*
3552 Picker sticks for looms—*mfg*
2411 Pickets and paling: round or split—*mfg*
2092 Picking of crab meat—*mfg*
3547 Picklers and pickling lines, sheet and strip (rolling mill equipment)—*mfg*
2035 Pickles and pickle salting—*mfg*
5149 Pickles, preserves, jellies, jams, and sauces—wholesale
3423 Picks (handtools)—*mfg*
7212 Pickup and delivery station laundry not operated by laundries
3792 Pickup coaches (campers), for mounting on pickup trucks—*mfg*
3792 Pickup covers, canopies or caps—*mfg*
3651 Pickup heads, phonograph—*mfg*
5511 Pickups and vans, new and used—retail
5521 Pickups and vans, used only—retail
7999 Picnic grounds operation
3089 Picnic jugs, plastics—*mfg*
2892 Picric acid (explosives)—*mfg*
3812 Pictorial situation instrumentation—*mfg*
2499 Picture frame moldings, finished—*mfg*
5999 Picture frames, ready-made—retail
2499 Picture frames, wood or metal—*mfg*
7699 Picture framing to individual order, not connected with retail art stores
7699 Picture framing, custom
3211 Picture glass—*mfg*
3999 Picture plaques, laminated—*mfg*
2759 Picture post cards: except lithographed or gravure—*mfg*
2752 Picture postcards, lithographed—*mfg*
3671 Picture tube reprocessing—*mfg*
2099 Pie fillings, except fruits, vegetables and meat—*mfg*
5949 Piece goods—retail
5131 Piece goods—wholesale
1629 Pier construction—general contractors
3272 Pier footings, prefabricated concrete—*mfg*
**** Piers and docks, operated by oil firms—code as auxiliary to tanker fleets
7996 Piers, amusement
4491 Piers, including buildings and facilities: operation and maintenance
2051 Pies, bakery, except frozen—*mfg*
2053 Pies, bakery, frozen—*mfg*
5142 Pies, fruit: frozen—wholesale
2032 Pies, meat: canned—*mfg*
3679 Piezoelectric crystals—*mfg*
3312 Pig iron—*mfg*
5051 Pig iron—wholesale
0259 Pigeon farms
3949 Pigeons, clay (targets)—*mfg*
2865 Pigment scarlet lake—*mfg*
5198 Pigments and colors—wholesale
2816 Pigments, inorganic—*mfg*
2865 Pigments, organic: except animal black and bone black—*mfg*
2013 Pigs' feet, cooked and pickled—mfpm—*mfg*
3334 Pigs, aluminum—*mfg*
3331 Pigs, copper—*mfg*
3339 Pigs, lead—*mfg*
3339 Pigs, primary: nonferrous metals, except copper and aluminum—*mfg*
0912 Pilchard, catching of
1629 Pile driving—contractors
2257 Pile fabrics, circular knit—*mfg*
2211 Pile fabrics, cotton—*mfg*
2221 Pile fabrics, manmade fiber and silk—*mfg*

0711 Plowing
3524 Plows (garden tractor equipment)—*mfg*
3523 Plows, agricultural: disc, moldboard, chisel, etc.—*mfg*
3532 Plows, coal—*mfg*
3531 Plows, construction: excavating and grading—*mfg*
3711 Plows, snow (motor vehicles)—*mfg*
1389 Plugging and abandoning wells on a contract basis
3499 Plugs, drain: magnetic—metal—*mfg*
3842 Plugs, ear and nose—*mfg*
3643 Plugs, electric—*mfg*
2499 Plugs, wood—*mfg*
0175 Plum orchards and farms
2032 Plum pudding—*mfg*
3295 Plumbago: ground, refined, or blended—*mfg*
3432 Plumbers' brass goods—*mfg*
5074 Plumbers' brass goods, fittings, and valves—wholesale
3423 Plumbers' handtools—*mfg*
3069 Plumbers' rubber goods—*mfg*
3494 Plumbing and heating valves, metal—*mfg*
5074 Plumbing and heating valves—wholesale
1711 Plumbing and heating—contractors
3432 Plumbing fixture fittings and trim—*mfg*
3463 Plumbing fixture forgings, nonferrous: not made in hot-rolling mills—*mfg*
5074 Plumbing fixtures, equipment, and supplies—wholesale
3088 Plumbing fixtures, plastics—*mfg*
3261 Plumbing fixtures, vitreous china—*mfg*
3431 Plumbing fixtures: enameled iron, cast iron, and pressed metal—*mfg*
1711 Plumbing repair—contractors
1711 Plumbing, with or without sheet metalwork—contractors
3999 Plumes, feather—*mfg*
2211 Plushes, cotton—*mfg*
2221 Plushes, manmade fiber and silk—*mfg*
2435 Plywood, hardwood or hardwood faced—*mfg*
2436 Plywood, softwood—*mfg*
5031 Plywood—wholesale
3011 Pneumatic casings (rubber tires)—*mfg*
3823 Pneumatic controllers, industrial process type—*mfg*
3593 Pneumatic cylinders, fluid power—*mfg*
3492 Pneumatic hose assemblies—*mfg*
3052 Pneumatic hose, rubber or rubberized fabric: e.g., air brake and air line—*mfg*
2394 Pneumatic mattresses—mfpm—*mfg*
3822 Pneumatic relays, air-conditioning type—*mfg*
3535 Pneumatic tube conveyor systems for general industrial use—*mfg*
1796 Pneumatic tube system installation—contractors
3492 Pneumatic valves, including aircraft: fluid power—metal—*mfg*
3421 Pocket knives—*mfg*
3999 Pocketbook frames—*mfg*
2396 Pocketbook linings—*mfg*
7699 Pocketbook repair shops
3172 Pocketbooks, men's: regardless of material—*mfg*
3171 Pocketbooks, women's: of all materials, except precious metal—*mfg*
2211 Pocketing twill, cotton—*mfg*
2396 Pockets for men's and boys' suits and coats—*mfg*
8043 Podiatrists, offices and clinics of
8699 Poetry associations
3578 Point-of-sale devices—*mfg*
2371 Pointing furs—*mfg*
3541 Pointing, chamfering, and burring machines—*mfg*
3843 Points, abrasive: dental—*mfg*
2879 Poison: ant, rat, roach, and rodent—household—*mfg*
3944 Poker chips—*mfg*
3826 Polariscopes—*mfg*
3826 Polarizers—*mfg*
3826 Polarographic equipment—*mfg*
2411 Pole cutting contractors—*mfg*
1623 Pole line construction—general contractors
3644 Pole line hardware—*mfg*
3462 Pole line hardware forgings, ferrous: not made in rolling mills—*mfg*
3463 Pole line hardware forgings, nonferrous: not made in hot-rolling mills—*mfg*
5063 Pole line hardware—wholesale
2491 Poles and pole crossarms, treated—*mfg*
3272 Poles, concrete—*mfg*
2591 Poles, curtain and drapery—*mfg*
2491 Poles, cutting and preserving—*mfg*
2499 Poles, wood: e.g., clothesline, tent, flag—*mfg*
2411 Poles, wood: untreated—*mfg*
9221 Police departments
2353 Police hats and caps, except protective head gear—*mfg*
2499 Police officer's clubs, wood—*mfg*
5999 Police supply stores—retail
2311 Police uniforms, men's—*mfg*
6411 Policyholders' consulting service
2842 Polishes: furniture, automobile, metal, shoe, and stove—*mfg*

1522 Prefabricated building erection, residential: except single-family—general contractors
3448 Prefabricated buildings, metal—*mfg*
2452 Prefabricated buildings, wood—*mfg*
5211 Prefabricated buildings—retail
5039 Prefabricated buildings—wholesale
1521 Prefabricated single-family houses erection—general contractors
2435 Prefinished hardwood plywood—*mfg*
2835 Pregnancy test kits—*mfg*
1521 Premanufactured housing, single-family (assembled on site)—general contractors
3999 Preparation of slides and exhibits, for classroom use—*mfg*
1231 Preparation plants, anthracite
1221 Preparation plants, bituminous coal or lignite
8211 Preparatory schools
2299 Preparing textile fibers for spinning (scouring and combing)—*mfg*
3652 Prerecorded audio magnetic tape—*mfg*
8351 Preschool centers
2033 Preserves, including imitation—*mfg*
2491 Preserving of wood (creosoting)—*mfg*
2261 Preshrinking cotton broadwoven fabrics for the trade—*mfg*
2262 Preshrinking manmade fiber and silk broadwoven fabrics for the trade—*mfg*
2231 Preshrinking wool broad woven fabrics for the trade—*mfg*
9111 President's office
2841 Presoaks—*mfg*
7389 Presorting mail service
3542 Press brakes—*mfg*
7389 Press clipping service
2211 Press cloth—*mfg*
3462 Press forgings, iron and steel: not made in rolling mills—*mfg*
7383 Press services (news syndicates)
7212 Press shops for garments
2631 Pressboard—mitse—*mfg*
5113 Pressed and molded pulp goods—wholesale
2299 Pressed felts—*mfg*
2499 Pressed logs of sawdust and other wood particles, nonpetroleum binder—*mfg*
3469 Pressed metal products (stampings)—*mfg*
2679 Pressed products from wood pulp—mfpm—*mfg*
3523 Presses and balers, farm: hay, cotton, etc.—*mfg*
3542 Presses, arbor—*mfg*
3582 Presses, finishing: commercial laundry and drycleaning—*mfg*
3569 Presses, metal baling—*mfg*
3555 Presses, printing—*mfg*
3553 Presses, woodworking: particleboard, hardboard, medium density fiberboard (MDF), and plywood—*mfg*
3556 Presses: cheese, beet, cider, and sugarcane—*mfg*
3542 Presses: forming, stamping, punching, and shearing (machine tools)—*mfg*
3542 Presses: hydraulic and pneumatic, mechanical and manual—*mfg*
2499 Pressing blocks, tailors': wood—*mfg*
3582 Pressing machines, commercial laundry and drycleaning—*mfg*
3829 Pressure and vacuum indicators, aircraft engine—*mfg*
3492 Pressure control valves, fluid power: metal—*mfg*
3822 Pressure controllers, air-conditioning system type—*mfg*
3365 Pressure cookers, domestic: cast aluminum, except die-castings—*mfg*
3469 Pressure cookers, stamped or drawn—*mfg*
3589 Pressure cookers, steam: commercial—*mfg*
3823 Pressure gauges, dial and digital—*mfg*
3823 Pressure instruments, industrial process type—*mfg*
3321 Pressure pipe, cast iron—*mfg*
3272 Pressure pipe, reinforced concrete—*mfg*
2672 Pressure sensitive paper and tape, except rubber backed—mfpm—*mfg*
5113 Pressure sensitive tape—wholesale
3829 Pressure transducers—*mfg*
3491 Pressure valves, industrial: except power transfer—*mfg*
3443 Pressure vessels, industrial: metal plate—made in boiler shops—*mfg*
3443 Pressurizers and auxiliary equipment, nuclear: metal plate—*mfg*
3272 Prestressed concrete products—*mfg*
5461 Pretzel stores and stands—retail
2052 Pretzels—*mfg*
5149 Pretzels—wholesale
9651 Price control agencies—government
3692 Primary batteries, dry and wet—*mfg*
8011 Primary care medical (M.D.) clinics
3823 Primary elements for process flow measurement: orifice plates—*mfg*
3822 Primary oil burner controls, including stack controls and cadmium cells—*mfg*
3334 Primary production of aluminum—*mfg*
3339 Primary refining of nonferrous metal: except copper and aluminum—*mfg*
3331 Primary smelting and refining of copper—*mfg*
3339 Primary smelting of nonferrous metal: except copper and aluminum—*mfg*

3483 Projectiles, chemical warfare—*mfg*
3483 Projectiles, jet propulsion: complete—*mfg*
5043 Projection apparatus, motion picture and slide: photographic—wholesale
3827 Projection lenses—*mfg*
3861 Projectors, microfilm—*mfg*
3861 Projectors, still and motion picture: silent and sound—*mfg*
3489 Projectors: antisub, depth charge release, grenade, livens, and rocket—*mfg*
3253 Promenade tile, clay—*mfg*
7389 Promoters of home shows and flower shows
7941 Promoters, sports events
7338 Proofreading service
1321 Propane (natural) production
5984 Propane gas, bottled—retail
2819 Propellants for missiles, solid: inorganic—*mfg*
2869 Propellants for missiles, solid: organic—*mfg*
3728 Propeller adapter assemblies, hydromatic—*mfg*
3728 Propeller alining tables—*mfg*
3634 Propeller fans, window-type (household)—*mfg*
3549 Propeller straightening presses—*mfg*
3824 Propeller type meters with registers—*mfg*
3599 Propellers, ship and boat: machined—*mfg*
3366 Propellers, ship and screw: cast brass, bronze, copper, and copper-base—except die-castings—*mfg*
3728 Propellers, variable and fixed pitch and parts—aircraft—*mfg*
6331 Property damage insurance
9311 Property tax assessors' offices
3069 Prophylactics, rubber—*mfg*
5912 Proprietary (nonprescription medicines) stores—retail
5122 Proprietary (patent) medicines—wholesale
2834 Proprietary drug products—*mfg*
3764 Propulsion units for guided missiles and space vehicles—*mfg*
2869 Propylene glycol—*mfg*
2869 Propylene, made in chemical plants—*mfg*
2911 Propylene, produced in petroleum refineries—*mfg*
1081 Prospect drilling for metal mining: on a contract basis
1481 Prospect drilling for nonmetallic minerals except fuels: on a contract basis
3842 Prosthetic appliances and supplies—*mfg*
8021 Prosthodontists, offices of
6289 Protective committees, security holders
7381 Protective service, guard
3579 Protectors, check (machine)—*mfg*
3851 Protectors, eye—*mfg*
3949 Protectors, sports: e.g., baseball, basketball, hockey—*mfg*
3826 Protein analyzers, laboratory type—*mfg*
2824 Protein fibers—*mfg*
2821 Protein plastics—*mfg*
0175 Prune orchards and farms
2034 Prunes, dried—*mfg*
0721 Pruning of orchard trees and vines
3423 Pruning tools—*mfg*
2816 Prussian blue pigments—*mfg*
3423 Prying bars (handtools)—*mfg*
1061 Psilomelane mining
8063 Psychiatric hospitals
8059 Psychiatric patient's convalescent homes
8049 Psychiatric social workers, offices of
8011 Psychiatrists, offices of
8011 Psychoanalysts, offices of
8049 Psychologists, clinical: offices of
8999 Psychologists, industrial
8049 Psychotherapists, except M.D.: offices of
8721 Public accountants, certified
5065 Public address equipment—wholesale
7622 Public address system repair
3651 Public address systems—*mfg*
2531 Public building fixtures—*mfg*
5021 Public building furniture—wholesale
9222 Public defenders' offices
9431 Public health agencies—nonoperating
8732 Public opinion research
9222 Public prosecutors' offices
8743 Public relations services
9229 Public safety bureaus—government
9229 Public safety statistics centers—government
9631 Public service commissions, except transportation
8299 Public speaking schools
8611 Public utility associations
9631 Public utility commissions
6719 Public utility holding companies
6519 Public utility property, lessors of
9441 Public welfare administration, nonoperating
8322 Public welfare centers, offices of
2621 Publication paper—mitse—*mfg*
7313 Publishers' representatives, advertising
2741 Publishing and printing maps, guides, directories, atlases, and sheet music—*mfg*
2731 Publishing and printing, books and pamphlets—*mfg*
2711 Publishing and printing, or publishing only: newspapers—*mfg*
2721 Publishing and printing, or publishing only: periodicals—*mfg*

5137 Purses: women's and children's—wholesale
3991 Push brooms—*mfg*
3799 Pushcarts—*mfg*
3545 Pushers—*mfg*
3199 Puttees, canvas and leather—*mfg*
2851 Putty—*mfg*
3423 Putty knives—*mfg*
2879 Pyrethrin bearing preparations—*mfg*
2879 Pyrethrin concentrates—*mfg*
3829 Pyrheliometers—*mfg*
2822 Pyridine-butadiene copolymers—*mfg*
2822 Pyridine-butadiene rubbers—*mfg*
1479 Pyrites mining
3952 Pyrography materials—*mfg*
2861 Pyroligneous acid—*mfg*
1061 Pyrolusite mining
3297 Pyrolytic graphite—*mfg*
3269 Pyrometer tubes—*mfg*
3823 Pyrometers, industrial process type—*mfg*
3269 Pyrometric cones: earthenware—*mfg*
1499 Pyrophyllite mining
3295 Pyrophyllite, ground or otherwise treated—*mfg*
2899 Pyrotechnic ammunition: flares, signals, flashlight bombs, and rockets—*mfg*
3484 Pyrotechnic pistols and projectors—*mfg*
2821 Pyroxylin—*mfg*
2295 Pyroxylin coated fabrics—*mfg*
1479 Pyrrhotite mining

Q

0259 Quail farms
3253 Quarry tile, clay—*mfg*
5082 Quarrying machinery and equipment—wholesale
3131 Quarters (shoe cut stock)—*mfg*
1499 Quartz crystal mining (pure)
3679 Quartz crystals for electronic application—*mfg*
1429 Quartzite, crushed and broken—quarrying
1411 Quartzite, dimension—quarrying
2861 Quebracho extract—*mfg*
2861 Quercitron extract—*mfg*
2752 Quick printing, except photocopy service—*mfg*
3274 Quicklime—*mfg*
1099 Quicksilver (mercury) ore mining
2299 Quilt filling: curled hair (e.g., cotton waste, moss, hemp tow, kapok)—*mfg*
2395 Quilted fabrics or cloth—*mfg*
7299 Quilting for individuals
5949 Quilting materials and supplies—retail
2395 Quilting, for the trade—*mfg*
2221 Quilts, manmade fiber and silk—mitse—*mfg*
2392 Quilts—mfpm—*mfg*
0175 Quince orchards and farms
2833 Quinine and derivatives—*mfg*
2865 Quinoline dyes—*mfg*
2869 Quinuclidinol ester of benzylic acid—*mfg*
6289 Quotation service, stock

R

2892 RDX (explosives)—*mfg*
3663 RF power amplifiers, and IF amplifiers: sold separately—*mfg*
0271 Rabbit farms
2015 Rabbits, processed: fresh, frozen, canned, or cooked—*mfg*
2015 Rabbits, slaughtering and dressing—*mfg*
7948 Race car drivers and owners
2741 Race track programs: publishing and printing, or publishing only—*mfg*
3562 Races, ball and roller bearing—*mfg*
7389 Racetrack cleaning, except buildings
7948 Racetrack operation: e.g., horse, dog, auto
3644 Raceways—*mfg*
2741 Racing forms: publishing and printing, or publishing only—*mfg*
7948 Racing stables, operation of
3949 Rackets and frames, sports: e.g., tennis, badminton, squash, racketball, lacrosse—*mfg*
3496 Racks without rigid framework, made from purchased wire—*mfg*
2511 Racks, book and magazine: wood—*mfg*
2499 Racks, for drying clothes: wood—*mfg*
2542 Racks, merchandise display and storage: except wood—*mfg*
2541 Racks, merchandise display: wood—*mfg*
3443 Racks, trash: metal plate—*mfg*
2542 Racks: mail pouch, mailing, mail sorting, etc., except wood—*mfg*
7997 Racquetball clubs, membership
7999 Racquetball courts, except membership clubs
4899 Radar station operation
3812 Radar systems and equipment—*mfg*
3825 Radar testing instruments, electric—*mfg*
3731 Radar towers, floating—*mfg*
3829 Radiac equipment (radiation measuring and detecting)—*mfg*
3567 Radiant heating systems, industrial process: e.g., dryers, cookers'—*mfg*
8734 Radiation dosimetry laboratories
3829 Radiation measuring and detecting (radiac) equipment—*mfg*

3493 Railroad equipment springs—*mfg*
4482 Railroad ferries
4731 Railroad freight agencies, not operated by railroad companies
2899 Railroad fusees—*mfg*
3429 Railroad hardware—*mfg*
3743 Railroad locomotives and parts—*mfg*
3999 Railroad models, except toy and hobby models—*mfg*
3944 Railroad models: toy and hobby—*mfg*
6517 Railroad property, lessors of
2531 Railroad seats—*mfg*
3669 Railroad signaling devices, electric—*mfg*
4013 Railroad switching
4013 Railroad terminals
4729 Railroad ticket offices, not operated by transportation companies
2421 Railroad ties, sawed—*mfg*
2899 Railroad torpedoes—*mfg*
3596 Railroad track scales—*mfg*
3462 Railroad wheels, axles, frogs, and related equipment: forged—mfpm—*mfg*
4013 Railroads, belt line
4011 Railroads, electric: line-haul
4011 Railroads, line-haul operating
4013 Railroads, logging
5051 Rails and accessories—wholesale
3355 Rails, aluminum: rolled and drawn—*mfg*
2411 Rails, fence: round or split—*mfg*
3312 Rails, iron and steel—*mfg*
3312 Rails, rerolled or renewed—*mfg*
3351 Rails, rolled and drawn: brass, bronze, and copper—*mfg*
3441 Railway bridge sections, prefabricated metal—*mfg*
2491 Railway crossties, wood: treated—*mfg*
3743 Railway maintenance cars—*mfg*
3743 Railway motor cars—*mfg*
3621 Railway motors and control equipment, electric—*mfg*
4111 Railway operation, local
1629 Railway roadbed construction—general contractors
3531 Railway track equipment: e.g., rail layers, ballast distributors—*mfg*
4011 Railways, interurban
3829 Rain gauges—*mfg*
5699 Raincoat stores—retail
2385 Raincoats, except vulcanized rubber—mfpm—*mfg*
5136 Raincoats, men's and boys'—wholesale
5137 Raincoats: women's and children's—wholesale
2034 Raisins—*mfg*
3423 Rakes, handtools—*mfg*
3523 Rakes, hay (agricultural machinery)—*mfg*
3531 Rakes, land clearing: mechanical—*mfg*
2299 Ramie yarn, thread, roving, and textiles—*mfg*
3297 Ramming mixes, nonclay—*mfg*
3537 Ramps, aircraft—loading—*mfg*
3537 Ramps, loading: portable, adjustable, and hydraulic—*mfg*
3448 Ramps, prefabricated: metal—*mfg*
**** Ranches—see type of ranch
3674 Random access memories (RAMS)—*mfg*
3131 Rands (shoe cut stock)—*mfg*
3433 Range boilers, galvanized iron and nonferrous metal—*mfg*
3861 Range finders, photographic—*mfg*
3589 Ranges, cooking: commercial—*mfg*
3631 Ranges, cooking: household—*mfg*
5064 Ranges, electric—wholesale
5074 Ranges, except electric—wholesale
5722 Ranges, gas and electric—retail
3631 Ranges, household cooking: electric and gas—*mfg*
3743 Rapid transit cars and equipment—*mfg*
5932 Rare book stores—retail
2819 Rare earth metal salts—*mfg*
1099 Rare-earths ore mining
0171 Raspberry farms
3423 Rasps, including recutting and resharpening—*mfg*
2879 Rat poisons—*mfg*
6411 Rate making organizations, insurance
4731 Rate services, transportation
3812 Rate-of-climb instrumentation—*mfg*
2211 Ratine, cotton—*mfg*
3612 Ratio transformers—*mfg*
2499 Rattan ware, except furniture—*mfg*
0279 Rattlesnake farms
2032 Ravioli, canned—*mfg*
2231 Raw stock dyeing and finishing: wool, mohair, and similar animal fibers—*mfg*
2269 Raw stock dyeing and other finishing, except wool—*mfg*
3111 Rawhide—*mfg*
2221 Rayon broadwoven fabrics—*mfg*
5131 Rayon piece goods—wholesale
2823 Rayon primary products: fibers, straw, strips, and yarn—*mfg*
2611 Rayon pulp—*mfg*
2284 Rayon thread—*mfg*
2299 Rayon tops, combing and converting—*mfg*
2282 Rayon yarn, filament: throwing, twisting, winding—*mfg*
2281 Rayon yarn, made from purchased staple: spun—*mfg*
2823 Rayon yarn, made in chemical plants—*mfg*
5199 Rayon yarns—wholesale

2044 Rice, brown—*mfg*
5149 Rice, polished—wholesale
2099 Rice, uncooked: packaged with other ingredients—*mfg*
5153 Rice, unpolished—wholesale
2044 Rice, vitamin and mineral enriched—*mfg*
2241 Rickrack braid—*mfg*
3599 Riddles, sand (hand sifting or screening apparatus)—*mfg*
7999 Riding academies and schools
5699 Riding apparel stores—retail
2329 Riding clothes: men's and boys'—mfpm—*mfg*
7997 Riding clubs, membership
3199 Riding crops—*mfg*
5941 Riding goods and equipment—retail
2339 Riding habits: women's, misses', and juniors'—mfpm—*mfg*
7999 Riding stables
2899 Rifle bore cleaning compounds—*mfg*
3541 Rifle working machines (machine tools)—*mfg*
3484 Rifles and parts, 30 mm. (or 1.18 inch) or less—*mfg*
3841 Rifles for propelling hypodermics into animals—*mfg*
3484 Rifles, high compression pneumatic: 30 mm. (or 1.18 inch) or less—*mfg*
3489 Rifles, recoilless—*mfg*
3944 Rifles, toy—*mfg*
3484 Rifles: BB and pellet—*mfg*
3484 Rifles: pneumatic, spring loaded, and compressed air—except toy—*mfg*
1389 Rig building, repairing, and dismantling: on a contract basis
3469 Rigidizing metal—*mfg*
3714 Rims, wheel: motor vehicle—*mfg*
3961 Rings, finger: gold-plated wire—*mfg*
3255 Rings, glasshouse: clay—*mfg*
3592 Rings, piston—*mfg*
3911 Rings, precious metal—*mfg*
1429 Riprap quarrying, except limestone or granite
4449 River freight transportation, except on the St. Lawrence Seaway
7999 River rafting, operation of
3546 Riveting hammers—*mfg*
3542 Riveting machines—*mfg*
3452 Rivets, metal—*mfg*
3089 Rivets, plastics—*mfg*
2879 Roach poisons—*mfg*
7922 Road companies, theatrical
3531 Road construction and maintenance machinery—*mfg*
5082 Road construction and maintenance machinery—wholesale
1611 Road construction, except elevated—general contractors
2951 Road materials, bituminous: not made in petroleum refineries—*mfg*
2911 Road materials, bituminous: produced in petroleum refineries—*mfg*
3711 Road oilers (motor vehicles)—*mfg*
2911 Road oils, produced in petroleum refineries—*mfg*
7549 Road service, automotive
4785 Roads, toll: operation of
3634 Roasters, electric—*mfg*
0251 Roasting chickens, raising of
3556 Roasting machinery: coffee, peanut, etc.—*mfg*
5137 Robes and gowns: women's and children's—wholesale
2369 Robes, lounging: children's—mfpm—*mfg*
2369 Robes, lounging: girls', children's, and infants'—mfpm—*mfg*
2384 Robes, lounging: men's, boys', and women's—mfpm—*mfg*
2253 Robes, lounging—mitse—*mfg*
5136 Robes, men's and boys'—wholesale
3535 Robotic conveyors for general industrial use—*mfg*
3541 Robots for drilling and cutting—machine type, metalworking—*mfg*
3569 Robots for general industrial use—*mfg*
3541 Robots for grinding, polishing, and deburring—metalworking—*mfg*
3542 Robots for metal forming: e.g., pressing, hammering, extruding—*mfg*
3563 Robots for spraying, painting—industrial—*mfg*
3548 Robots for welding, soldering, or brazing—*mfg*
3559 Robots, plastics: for molding and forming—*mfg*
**** Robots—code according to primary function
5999 Rock and stone specimens—retail
3531 Rock crushing machinery, portable—*mfg*
3532 Rock crushing machinery, stationary—*mfg*
3532 Rock drills, portable—*mfg*
1629 Rock removal, underwater—contractors
1479 Rock salt mining
3275 Rock, gypsum—*mfg*
2512 Rockers, upholstered on wood frames—*mfg*
2511 Rockers, wood: except upholstered—*mfg*
2869 Rocket engine fuel, organic—*mfg*
3489 Rocket launchers, hand-held—*mfg*
3724 Rocket motors, aircraft—*mfg*
3764 Rocket motors, guided missile—*mfg*
3443 Rocket transportation casings—*mfg*

2046 Root starch, edible—*mfg*
3552 Rope and cordage machines—*mfg*
2621 Rope and jute wrapping paper—mitse—*mfg*
3429 Rope fittings—*mfg*
3292 Rope, asbestos—*mfg*
2298 Rope, except asbestos and wire—*mfg*
5085 Rope, except wire rope—wholesale
3496 Rope, uninsulated wire: made from purchased wire—*mfg*
5051 Rope, wire: not insulated—wholesale
3961 Rosaries and other small religious articles, except precious metal—*mfg*
3911 Rosaries and other small religious articles, precious metal—*mfg*
1094 Roscoelite (vanadium hydromica) mining
0181 Rose growers
2821 Rosin modified resins—*mfg*
2899 Rosin sizes—*mfg*
2861 Rosin, produced by distillation of pine gum or pine wood—*mfg*
5169 Rosin—wholesale
3621 Rotary converters (electrical equipment)—*mfg*
3523 Rotary hoes (agricultural machinery)—*mfg*
2754 Rotary photogravure printing—*mfg*
3549 Rotary slitters (metalworking machines)—*mfg*
3545 Rotary tables, indexing—*mfg*
3824 Rotary type meters, consumption registering—*mfg*
3351 Rotating bands, copper and copper alloy—*mfg*
2879 Rotenone bearing preparations—*mfg*
2879 Rotenone concentrates—*mfg*
3728 Roto-blades for helicopters—*mfg*
2621 Rotogravure paper—mitse—*mfg*
2754 Rotogravure printing—*mfg*
2796 Rotogravure printing plates and cylinders—*mfg*
3621 Rotor retainers and housings—*mfg*
3621 Rotors for motors—*mfg*
3524 Rototillers (garden machinery)—*mfg*
2844 Rouge, cosmetic—*mfg*
3291 Rouge, polishing—*mfg*
3523 Roughage mills (agricultural machinery)—*mfg*
2449 Round stave baskets, for fruits and vegetables—*mfg*
2426 Rounds or rungs, ladder and furniture: hardwood—*mfg*
3312 Rounds, tube—*mfg*
5099 Roundwood—wholesale
1389 Roustabout service: on a contract basis
3553 Routing machines, woodworking—*mfg*
2299 Roves, flax and jute—*mfg*
3552 Roving machines (textile machinery)—*mfg*
7999 Rowboat rental
3732 Rowboats, building and repairing—*mfg*
1521 Rowhouse (single-family) construction—general contractors
3949 Rowing machines—*mfg*
6792 Royalty companies, oil
6289 Royalty owners protective associations
2891 Rubber cement—*mfg*
1455 Rubber clay mining
3567 Rubber curing ovens—*mfg*
3061 Rubber goods, mechanical: molded, extruded, and lathe-cut—*mfg*
5085 Rubber goods, mechanical—wholesale
5122 Rubber goods, medical—wholesale
3069 Rubber heels, soles, and soling strips—*mfg*
0831 Rubber plantations
2869 Rubber processing chemicals, organic: accelerators and antioxidants—*mfg*
2899 Rubber processing preparations—*mfg*
3559 Rubber products machinery—*mfg*
5093 Rubber scrap—wholesale
2891 Rubber sealing compounds, synthetic—*mfg*
5999 Rubber stamp stores—retail
2241 Rubber thread and yarns, fabric covered—*mfg*
3559 Rubber working machinery—*mfg*
5199 Rubber, crude—wholesale
3069 Rubber, reclaimed and reworked by manufacturing processes—*mfg*
2822 Rubber, synthetic—*mfg*
3069 Rubber-covered motor mounting rings (rubber bonded)—*mfg*
3069 Rubberbands—*mfg*
3069 Rubberized fabrics—*mfg*
1499 Rubbing stone quarrying
3291 Rubbing stones, artificial—*mfg*
4953 Rubbish collection and disposal
1411 Rubble mining
2819 Rubidium metal—*mfg*
1499 Ruby mining
3728 Rudders, aircraft—*mfg*
2395 Ruffling, for the trade—*mfg*
3069 Rug backing compounds, latex—*mfg*
7389 Rug binding for the trade
3582 Rug cleaning, drying, and napping machines: commercial laundry—*mfg*
7217 Rug cleaning, dyeing, and repairing plants
7699 Rug repair shops, not combined with cleaning
5713 Rug stores—retail
2842 Rug, upholstery, and drycleaning detergents and spotters—*mfg*
2299 Rugbacking, jute or other fiber—*mfg*
2273 Rugs, except rubber or plastics—*mfg*
5023 Rugs—wholesale

7319 Samples, distribution of
7389 Sampling of commodities, not connected with transportation
5211 Sand and gravel dealers—retail
3531 Sand mixers—*mfg*
3599 Sand riddles (hand sifting or screening apparatus)—*mfg*
5032 Sand, construction—wholesale
3149 Sandals, children's: except rubber—*mfg*
3021 Sandals, rubber—*mfg*
1799 Sandblasting of building exteriors—contractors
3471 Sandblasting of metal parts, for the trade—*mfg*
3546 Sanders, hand: electric—*mfg*
3714 Sanders, motor vehicle safety—*mfg*
3553 Sanding machines, except portable floor sanders (woodworking machinery)—*mfg*
3589 Sanding machines, floor—*mfg*
3291 Sandpaper—*mfg*
3554 Sandpaper manufacturing machines—*mfg*
1499 Sandstone, bituminous—quarrying
1411 Sandstone, dimension—quarrying
1429 Sandstone, except bituminous: crushed and broken—quarrying
5812 Sandwich bars or shops
2022 Sandwich spreads, cheese—*mfg*
2013 Sandwich spreads, meat—mfpm—*mfg*
2035 Sandwich spreads, salad dressing base—*mfg*
3634 Sandwich toasters and grills, household: electric—*mfg*
2099 Sandwiches, assembled and packaged: for wholesale market—*mfg*
5149 Sandwiches—wholesale
3842 Sanitary aprons—*mfg*
9631 Sanitary districts—nonoperating
9511 Sanitary engineering agencies—government
5113 Sanitary food containers: paper, paperboard, and disposable plastics—wholesale
2676 Sanitary napkins—mfpm—*mfg*
2656 Sanitary paper food containers, liquid tight—mfpm—*mfg*
3432 Sanitary pipe fittings—*mfg*
5074 Sanitary ware, china or enameled iron—wholesale
3431 Sanitary ware: bathtubs, lavoratories, and sinks—metal—*mfg*
2842 Sanitation preparations—*mfg*
5169 Sanitation preparations—wholesale
1499 Sapphire mining
2221 Saran broadwoven fabrics—*mfg*
2824 Saran fibers—*mfg*
2077 Sardine oil—*mfg*
2091 Sardines, canned—*mfg*
3321 Sash balances, cast iron—*mfg*
3495 Sash balances, spring—*mfg*
3442 Sash, door and window: metal—*mfg*
2431 Sash, door and window: wood and covered wood—*mfg*
5211 Sash, storm: wood or metal—retail
3161 Satchels, regardless of material—*mfg*
2211 Sateens, cotton—*mfg*
4899 Satellite earth stations
3679 Satellite home antennas—*mfg*
4841 Satellite master antenna systems (SMATV) services
4899 Satellite or missile tracking stations, operated on a contract basis
3663 Satellites, communications—*mfg*
2816 Satin white pigments—*mfg*
2221 Satins—*mfg*
3612 Saturable reactors—*mfg*
2621 Saturated felts—mitse—*mfg*
2099 Sauce mixes, dry—*mfg*
3089 Saucers, plastics: except foam—*mfg*
2035 Sauces, meat (seasoning): except tomato and dry—*mfg*
2035 Sauces, seafood: except tomato and dry—*mfg*
2033 Sauces, spaghetti—*mfg*
2033 Sauces, tomato-based—*mfg*
2035 Sauces, vegetable: except tomato and dry—*mfg*
5149 Sauces—wholesale
2035 Sauerkraut, bulk—*mfg*
2033 Sauerkraut, canned—*mfg*
3634 Sauna heaters, electric—*mfg*
5074 Sauna heaters, except electric—wholesale
2452 Sauna rooms, prefabricated: wood—*mfg*
2013 Sausage casings, collagen—*mfg*
3089 Sausage casings, synthetic—*mfg*
5149 Sausage casings—wholesale
3556 Sausage stuffers—*mfg*
2013 Sausages—mfpm—*mfg*
2011 Sausages—mitse—*mfg*
6035 Saving banks, Federal
6035 Savings and loan associations, federally chartered
6036 Savings and loan associations, not federally chartered
6036 Savings banks, State: not federally chartered
3425 Saw blades, for hand or power saws—*mfg*
5072 Saw blades—wholesale
2411 Saw logs—*mfg*
7699 Saw sharpening and repair shops
2421 Sawdust and shavings—*mfg*
2499 Sawdust, reground—*mfg*
5199 Sawdust—wholesale

3541 Sawing and cutoff machines (metalworking machinery)—*mfg*
3553 Sawmill machines—*mfg*
2421 Sawmills, custom—*mfg*
2421 Sawmills, except special product mills—*mfg*
2429 Sawmills, special product: except lumber and veneer mills—*mfg*
3425 Saws, hand: metalworking or woodworking—*mfg*
3546 Saws, portable hand held: power-driven—woodworking or metalworking—*mfg*
3553 Saws, power: bench and table (woodworking machinery)—except portable—*mfg*
3541 Saws, power: metal cutting—*mfg*
3841 Saws, surgical—*mfg*
3931 Saxophones and parts—*mfg*
1799 Scaffolding construction—contractors
5082 Scaffolding—wholesale
3446 Scaffolds, metal (mobile or stationary)—*mfg*
2499 Scaffolds, wood—*mfg*
7699 Scale repair service
3579 Scalers for gummed tape: hand—*mfg*
3829 Scalers, nuclear radiation—*mfg*
7299 Scales, coin-operated: operation of
3596 Scales, except laboratory—*mfg*
5046 Scales, except laboratory—wholesale
3545 Scales, measuring (machinists' precision tools)—*mfg*
7699 Scaling, ship—contractors
2395 Scalloping, for the trade—*mfg*
7299 Scalp treatment service
2819 Scandium—*mfg*
3553 Scarfing machines (woodworking machinery)—*mfg*
2253 Scarfs—mitse—*mfg*
3531 Scarifiers, road—*mfg*
2865 Scarlet 2 R lake—*mfg*
2339 Scarves, hoods, and headbands: women's, misses', and juniors'—mfpm—*mfg*
5136 Scarves, men's and boys'—wholesale
2392 Scarves: e.g., table, dresser—mfpm—*mfg*
2323 Scarves: men's and boys'—mfpm—*mfg*
5137 Scarves: women's, children's and infant's—wholesale
2273 Scatter rugs, except rubber or plastics—*mfg*
5093 Scavengering—wholesale
7922 Scenery design, theatrical
3999 Scenery for theaters, opera houses, halls, and schools—*mfg*
7922 Scenery, rental: theatrical
7999 Scenic railroads for amusement
2759 Schedules, transportation: except lithographed or gravure—*mfg*
2754 Schedules, transportation: gravure printing—*mfg*
2752 Schedules, transportation: lithographed—*mfg*
1061 Scheelite mining
2397 Schiffli machine embroideries—*mfg*
1411 Schist, dimension—quarrying
1542 School building construction—general contractors
4151 School buses
5021 School desks—wholesale
2531 School furniture—*mfg*
2531 School furniture, except stone and concrete—*mfg*
7221 School photographers
5943 School supplies—retail
7999 Schools and camps, sports instructional
8211 Schools for the physically handicapped, elementary and secondary
8211 Schools for the retarded
8249 Schools, correspondence: including branch offices and solicitors
7911 Schools, dance: including children's, and professionals'
8211 Schools, elementary and secondary
7999 Schools, riding
8249 Schools, vocational, except high schools, data processing, or business
3674 Schottky diodes—*mfg*
3944 Science kits: microscopes, chemistry sets, and natural science sets—*mfg*
3231 Scientific apparatus glass, made from purchased glass—*mfg*
3231 Scientific glassware, made from purchased glass—*mfg*
3229 Scientific glassware, pressed or blown: made in glassmaking plants—*mfg*
7699 Scientific instrument repair, except electric
5049 Scientific instruments—wholesale
8621 Scientific membership associations
8733 Scientific research, noncommercial
3829 Scintillation detectors—*mfg*
3634 Scissors, electric—*mfg*
3421 Scissors, hand—*mfg*
3421 Scissors: barbers', manicure, pedicure, tailors' and household—*mfg*
3949 Scoops, crab and fish—*mfg*
3423 Scoops, hand: metal—*mfg*
2499 Scoops, wood—*mfg*
3944 Scooters, children's—*mfg*
3993 Scoreboards, electric—*mfg*
1499 Scoria mining
2841 Scouring compounds—*mfg*
3559 Scouring machines, tannery—*mfg*

2299 Scouring of wool, mohair, and similar fibers—*mfg*
3291 Scouring pads, soap impregnated—*mfg*
3731 Scows, building and repairing—*mfg*
5093 Scrap and waste materials—wholesale
7389 Scrap steel cutting on a contract or fee basis
5093 Scrap, rubber—wholesale
2782 Scrapbooks—*mfg*
5112 Scrapbooks—wholesale
3532 Scraper loaders, underground—*mfg*
3531 Scrapers, construction—*mfg*
3423 Scrapers, woodworking: hand—*mfg*
2013 Scrapple—mfpm—*mfg*
3531 Screeds and screeding machines—*mfg*
3442 Screen doors, metal—*mfg*
2261 Screen printing of cotton broadwoven fabrics—*mfg*
2262 Screen printing of manmade fiber and silk broadwoven fabrics—*mfg*
2759 Screen printing on glass, plastics, paper, and metal, including highway signs—*mfg*
**** Screen printing, textiles—classify on basis of fiber
2893 Screen process ink—*mfg*
3531 Screeners, portable—*mfg*
3532 Screeners, stationary—*mfg*
3569 Screening and sifting machines for general industrial use—*mfg*
5084 Screening machinery and equipment, industrial—wholesale
1499 Screening peat
1231 Screening plants, anthracite
1221 Screening plants, bituminous coal
3089 Screening, window: plastics—*mfg*
3496 Screening, woven wire: made from purchased wire—*mfg*
3442 Screens, door and window: metal frame—*mfg*
2431 Screens, door and window: wood—*mfg*
2511 Screens, privacy: wood—*mfg*
3861 Screens, projection—*mfg*
3953 Screens, textile printing—*mfg*
3541 Screw and nut slotting machines—*mfg*
3423 Screw drivers—*mfg*
3452 Screw eyes, metal—*mfg*
3089 Screw eyes, plastics—*mfg*
3452 Screw hooks—*mfg*
**** Screw machine production of one product—code the product
3451 Screw machine products: produced on a job or order basis—*mfg*
3451 Screw machine products: produced on a job or order basis—*mfg*
3541 Screw machines, automatic—*mfg*
3366 Screw propellers: cast brass, bronze, copper, and copper base—*mfg*
3549 Screwdowns and boxes—*mfg*
3549 Screwdriving machines—*mfg*
3841 Screws, bone—*mfg*
3569 Screws, jack—*mfg*
3452 Screws, metal—*mfg*
2211 Scrim, cotton—*mfg*
3443 Scroll casings—*mfg*
2211 Scrub cloths—mitse—*mfg*
3589 Scrubbing machines—*mfg*
3089 Scrubbing pads, plastics—*mfg*
7999 Scuba and skin diving instruction
3949 Scuba diving equipment, except clothing—*mfg*
8999 Sculptors' studios
3299 Sculptures, architectural: gypsum, clay, or papier-mache—factory production only—*mfg*
3423 Scythes—*mfg*
1499 Scythestone quarrying
3291 Scythestones, artificial—*mfg*
0912 Sea herring, catching of
0919 Sea urchins, catching of
5421 Seafood markets—retail
2091 Seafood products, canned and cured—*mfg*
2092 Seafoods, fresh and frozen—*mfg*
5142 Seafoods, frozen: packaged—wholesale
5146 Seafoods, not canned or frozen packaged—wholesale
3953 Seal presses, notary, hand—*mfg*
5169 Sealants—wholesale
2851 Sealers, wood—*mfg*
2891 Sealing compounds for pipe threads and joints—*mfg*
2891 Sealing compounds, synthetic rubber and plastics—*mfg*
2295 Sealing or insulating tape for pipe, fiberglass coated with tar or asphalt—*mfg*
2891 Sealing wax—*mfg*
3953 Seals, corporation—*mfg*
5085 Seals, gaskets, and packing—wholesale
3953 Seals, hand (dies)—*mfg*
3679 Seals, hermetic: for electronic equipment—*mfg*
2752 Seals, lithographed—*mfg*
2754 Seals: gravure printing—*mfg*
2759 Seals: printing except lithographic or gravure—*mfg*
3548 Seam welding apparatus, gas and electric—*mfg*
3827 Searchlight mirrors and reflectors—*mfg*
3648 Searchlights—*mfg*
7011 Seasonal hotels
2033 Seasonings (prepared sauces), tomato—*mfg*

8322 Senior citizens associations
3861 Sensitometers, photographic—*mfg*
3845 Sentinel, cardiac—*mfg*
3532 Separating machinery, mineral—*mfg*
3569 Separators for steam, gas, vapor, and air (machinery)—*mfg*
2499 Separators, battery: wood—*mfg*
3069 Separators, battery: rubber—*mfg*
3523 Separators, cream: farm—*mfg*
3556 Separators, cream: industrial—*mfg*
3523 Separators, grain and berry: farm—*mfg*
3443 Separators, industrial process: metal plate—*mfg*
7699 Septic tank cleaning service
1711 Septic tank installation—contractors
3272 Septic tanks, concrete—*mfg*
3443 Septic tanks, metal plate—*mfg*
3089 Septic tanks, plastics—*mfg*
5039 Septic tanks—wholesale
3822 Sequencing controls for electric heat—*mfg*
2231 Serges of wool, mohair, and similar animal fibers—*mfg*
2221 Serges, manmade fiber—*mfg*
3629 Series capacitors, except electronic—*mfg*
2836 Serobacterins—*mfg*
1429 Serpentine, crushed and broken—quarrying
1411 Serpentine, dimension—quarrying
2836 Serums, except in vitro and in vivo—*mfg*
8221 Service academies (college)
1799 Service and repair of broadcasting stations—contractors
2339 Service apparel, washable: e.g., nurses', maids', waitresses', laboratory uniforms: women's, misses', and juniors'—mfpm
2326 Service apparel, washable: men's—mfpm—*mfg*
7374 Service bureaus, computer
5063 Service entrance equipment, electrical—wholesale
8322 Service leagues
7299 Service machine operation-coin-operated
7349 Service station cleaning and degreasing service
1542 Service station construction—general contractors
1799 Service station equipment installation, maintenance, and repair—contractors
5013 Service station equipment, automobile—wholesale
5541 Service stations, gasoline—retail
1381 Service well drilling: on a contract basis
3589 Servicing machines, coin-operated: except drycleaning and laundry—*mfg*
1389 Servicing oil and gas wells on a contract basis
1781 Servicing water wells—contractors
2514 Serving carts, household: metal—*mfg*
3621 Servomotors—*mfg*
8322 Settlement houses
2631 Setup boxboard—mitse—*mfg*
5113 Setup paperboard boxes—wholesale
1623 Sewage collection and disposal line construction—general contractors
3589 Sewage treatment equipment—*mfg*
1629 Sewage treatment plant construction—general contractors
7699 Sewer cleaning and rodding
3589 Sewer cleaning equipment, power—*mfg*
1623 Sewer construction—general contractors
1711 Sewer hookups and connections for buildings—contractors
3259 Sewer liner brick, vitrified clay—*mfg*
3259 Sewer pipe and fittings, clay—*mfg*
3321 Sewer pipe, cast iron—*mfg*
5032 Sewer pipe, clay—wholesale
3272 Sewer pipe, concrete—*mfg*
4952 Sewerage systems
5131 Sewing accessories—wholesale
3172 Sewing cases, regardless of material—*mfg*
3999 Sewing kits, novelty: other than sewing cases and cabinets—*mfg*
2517 Sewing machine cabinets and cases, wood—*mfg*
7699 Sewing machine repair shops
5722 Sewing machine stores—retail
3639 Sewing machines and attachments, household—*mfg*
3559 Sewing machines and attachments, industrial—*mfg*
5064 Sewing machines, household: electric—wholesale
5084 Sewing machines, industrial—wholesale
5949 Sewing supplies—retail
5131 Sewing thread, except industrial—wholesale
2284 Sewing thread: cotton, silk, manmade fibers, and wool—*mfg*
3812 Sextants, except surveying—*mfg*
3829 Sextants, surveying—*mfg*
2295 Shade cloth, coated or impregnated—*mfg*
2211 Shade cloth, window: cotton—*mfg*
2591 Shade pulls, window—*mfg*
2394 Shades, canvas—*mfg*
3999 Shades, lamp and candle: except glass and metal—*mfg*
3229 Shades, lamp: glass—*mfg*
3645 Shades, lamp: metal—*mfg*
2591 Shades, porch: made of wood slats—*mfg*
2591 Shades, window: except canvas—*mfg*
1481 Shaft sinking for nonmetallic minerals, except fuels: on a contract basis

1241 Shaft sinking, anthracite mining: on a contract basis
1241 Shaft sinking, bituminous coal and lignite mining: on a contract basis
1081 Shaft sinking, metal mining: on a contract basis
3568 Shafts, flexible—*mfg*
3949 Shafts, golf club—*mfg*
3821 Shakers and stirrers, laboratory—*mfg*
2429 Shakes (hand split shingles)—*mfg*
1459 Shale (common) quarrying-not in conjunction with manufacturing
3295 Shale, expanded—*mfg*
2844 Shampoos, hair—*mfg*
3131 Shanks, shoe—*mfg*
2221 Shantungs, manmade fiber and silk—*mfg*
3541 Shapers and slotters, metal cutting—*mfg*
3553 Shapers, woodworking machinery—*mfg*
3545 Shaping tools (machine tool accessories)—*mfg*
0912 Sharks, catching of
7699 Sharpening and repairing knives, saws, and tools
1499 Sharpening stone quarrying
3991 Shaving brushes—*mfg*
3541 Shaving machines (metalworking)—*mfg*
2844 Shaving preparations: e.g., cakes, creams, lotions, powders, tablets—*mfg*
2253 Shawls—mitse—*mfg*
3545 Shear knives—*mfg*
3542 Shearing machines, power—*mfg*
3111 Shearling (prepared sheepskin)—*mfg*
3421 Shears, hand—*mfg*
3421 Shears, hedge: except power—*mfg*
3421 Shears, metal cutting: hand—*mfg*
3523 Shears, sheep: power—*mfg*
2621 Sheathing paper—mitse—*mfg*
2952 Sheathing, asphalt saturated—mfpm—*mfg*
0751 Sheep dipping and shearing
2879 Sheep dips, chemical—*mfg*
0214 Sheep feeding farms and ranches
0214 Sheep raising farms and ranches
3523 Sheep shears, power—*mfg*
2011 Sheep slaughtering plants—*mfg*
5154 Sheep—wholesale
3211 Sheet glass—*mfg*
3211 Sheet glass blanks for optical or ophthalmic uses—*mfg*
3444 Sheet metal specialties, not stamped—*mfg*
1711 Sheet metal work combined with heating or air-conditioning—contractors
3444 Sheet metal work: cornices, ventilators, skylights, gutters, tanks, etc.—*mfg*
1761 Sheet metal work: except plumbing, heating, or air-conditioning—contractors
3542 Sheet metalworking machines—*mfg*
5736 Sheet music stores—retail
2759 Sheet music, printing (not publishing): except lithographed or gravure—*mfg*
2754 Sheet music: gravure printing (not publishing)—*mfg*
5199 Sheet music—wholesale
3312 Sheet pilings, plain: iron and steel—made in steel works or rolling mills—*mfg*
3316 Sheet steel, cold-rolled: not made in hot-rolling mills—*mfg*
3292 Sheet, asbestos cement: flat or corrugated—*mfg*
3083 Sheet, laminated plastics, except flexible packaging—*mfg*
3081 Sheet, plastics: unsupported—*mfg*
2211 Sheeting, cotton—mitse—*mfg*
3069 Sheeting, rubber or rubberized fabric—*mfg*
2211 Sheets and sheetings, cotton—mitse—*mfg*
3353 Sheets, aluminum—*mfg*
3351 Sheets, copper and copper alloy—*mfg*
2653 Sheets, corrugated and solid fiberboard—mfpm—*mfg*
2392 Sheets, fabric—mfpm—*mfg*
5051 Sheets, galvanized or other coated—wholesale
3069 Sheets, hard rubber—*mfg*
2392 Sheets, hospital: nonwoven textile—*mfg*
5051 Sheets, metal—wholesale
3312 Sheets, steel: made in steel works or hot-rolling mills—*mfg*
5023 Sheets, textile—wholesale
5072 Shelf or light hardware—wholesale
2048 Shell crushing for feed—*mfg*
3351 Shell discs, copper and copper alloy—*mfg*
3483 Shell loading and assembly plants, for ammunition more than 30 mm.—*mfg*
1499 Shell mining
3999 Shell novelties—*mfg*
3312 Shell slugs, steel: made in steel works or rolling mills—*mfg*
2851 Shellac, protective coating—*mfg*
5198 Shellac—wholesale
3523 Shellers, nut (agricultural machinery)—*mfg*
2091 Shellfish, canned and cured—*mfg*
0913 Shellfish, catching of
2092 Shellfish, fresh and frozen—*mfg*
2092 Shellfish, fresh: shucked, picked, or packed—*mfg*
3483 Shells, artillery: more than 30 mm. (or more than 1.18 inch)—*mfg*
3482 Shells, small arms: 30 mm. (or 1.18 inch) or less—*mfg*
8331 Sheltered workshops
2542 Shelving angles and slotted bars, except wood—*mfg*

3496 Shelving without rigid framework, made from purchased wire—*mfg*
2542 Shelving, office and store: except wood—*mfg*
2541 Shelving, office and store: wood—*mfg*
5046 Shelving—wholesale
3479 Sherardizing of metals and metal products, for the trade—*mfg*
3567 Sherardizing ovens—*mfg*
2024 Sherbets and ices—*mfg*
9221 Sheriffs' offices
4492 Shifting of floating equipment within harbors
3499 Shims, metal—*mfg*
2411 Shingle bolts, wood: hewn—*mfg*
2429 Shingle mills, wood—*mfg*
3292 Shingles, asbestos cement—*mfg*
2952 Shingles, asphalt or tar saturated felt: strip and individual—mfpm—*mfg*
5033 Shingles, except wood—wholesale
2429 Shingles, wood: sawed or hand split—*mfg*
5031 Shingles, wood—wholesale
7699 Ship boiler and tank cleaning and repair—contractors
3531 Ship capstans—*mfg*
4499 Ship cleaning, except hold cleaning
3531 Ship cranes and derricks—*mfg*
7361 Ship crew registries
2599 Ship furniture—*mfg*
4491 Ship hold cleaning
1751 Ship joinery—contractors
3999 Ship models, except toy and hobby models—*mfg*
1721 Ship painting—contractors
3366 Ship propellers: cast brass, bronze, copper and copper base—*mfg*
4499 Ship registers: survey and classification of ships and marine equipment
7699 Ship scaling—contractors
3441 Ship sections, prefabricated metal—*mfg*
3531 Ship winches—*mfg*
3357 Shipboard cable, nonferrous—*mfg*
3731 Shipbuilding and repairing—*mfg*
8611 Shipping and steamship company associations
2674 Shipping bags or sacks, including multiwall and heavy duty—mfpm—*mfg*
3412 Shipping barrels, kegs, and pails: metal—light and heavy types—*mfg*
2449 Shipping cases and drums, wood: wirebound—*mfg*
2441 Shipping cases, wood: nailed or lock corner—*mfg*
4731 Shipping documents preparation
2655 Shipping hampers, vulcanized fiber—mfpm—*mfg*
3086 Shipping pads, plastics foam—*mfg*
2621 Shipping sack paper—mitse—*mfg*
2674 Shipping sacks, paper—mfpm—*mfg*
5113 Shipping supplies, paper and disposable plastics (e.g., cartons, gummed tapes)—wholesale
5088 Ships—wholesale
2329 Shirt and slack suits, nontailored: men's and boys'—mfpm—*mfg*
2396 Shirt linings—*mfg*
3965 Shirt studs, except precious metal and precious or semiprecious stones—*mfg*
3911 Shirt studs, precious metal and precious or semiprecious stones—*mfg*
7213 Shirt supply service
2211 Shirting fabrics, cotton—*mfg*
2221 Shirting fabrics, manmade fiber and silk—*mfg*
5699 Shirts, custom made—retail
5136 Shirts, men's and boys'—wholesale
2361 Shirts, outerwear: girls', children's, and infants'—mfpm—*mfg*
2331 Shirts, outerwear: women's, misses', and juniors'—mfpm—*mfg*
2321 Shirts, outerwear; except work shirts: men's and boys'—mfpm—*mfg*
2253 Shirts, outerwear—mitse—*mfg*
2322 Shirts, underwear: men's and boys'—mfpm—*mfg*
2254 Shirts, underwear—mitse—*mfg*
2326 Shirts, work: men's and boys'—mfpm—*mfg*
3714 Shock absorbers, motor vehicle—*mfg*
3542 Shock wave metal forming machines—*mfg*
5139 Shoe accessories—wholesale
2392 Shoe bags—mfpm—*mfg*
2631 Shoe board—mitse—*mfg*
2842 Shoe cleaners and polishes—*mfg*
3131 Shoe cut stock—*mfg*
3131 Shoe cut stock and findings—*mfg*
7389 Shoe designers
2499 Shoe display forms—regardless of material—*mfg*
3149 Shoe dyeing for the trade—*mfg*
7251 Shoe dyeing shops
2211 Shoe fabrics—mitse—*mfg*
3131 Shoe heels, finished wood or leather—*mfg*
3089 Shoe heels, plastics—*mfg*
3069 Shoe heels: rubber, composition, and fiber—*mfg*
5087 Shoe heels—wholesale
3161 Shoe kits, regardless of material—*mfg*
2241 Shoe laces, except leather—*mfg*
3131 Shoe laces, leather—*mfg*
3131 Shoe linings, leather—*mfg*
2259 Shoe linings— mitse—*mfg*

2231 Shrinking cloth of wool, mohair, and similar animal fibers: for the trade—*mfg*
2261 Shrinking cotton broadwoven fabrics for the trade—*mfg*
2262 Shrinking manmade fiber and silk broadwoven fabrics for the trade—*mfg*
7389 Shrinking textiles for tailors and dressmakers
0181 Shrubberies, except forest shrubbery: growing of
3825 Shunts, instrument—*mfg*
3861 Shutters, camera—*mfg*
3442 Shutters, door and window: metal—*mfg*
2431 Shutters, door and window: wood and covered wood—*mfg*
3089 Shutters, plastics—*mfg*
2426 Shuttle blocks: hardwood—*mfg*
3532 Shuttle cars, underground—*mfg*
3552 Shuttles for textile weaving—*mfg*
6321 Sick benefit associations, mutual
3423 Sickles, hand—*mfg*
1011 Siderite mining
1771 Sidewalk construction, except public—contractors
1611 Sidewalk construction, public—contractors
3292 Siding, asbestos cement—*mfg*
2952 Siding, asphalt brick—*mfg*
2421 Siding, dressed lumber—*mfg*
5033 Siding, except wood—wholesale
2621 Siding, insulating: paper, impregnated or not—mitse—*mfg*
2952 Siding, insulating: impregnated—mfpm—*mfg*
3089 Siding, plastics—*mfg*
3272 Siding, precast stone—*mfg*
3444 Siding, sheet metal—*mfg*
1761 Siding—contractors
1479 Sienna mining
2816 Siennas—*mfg*
3496 Sieves, made from purchased wire—*mfg*
3569 Sifting and screening machines for general industrial use—*mfg*
3556 Sifting machines, food—*mfg*
3827 Sighting and fire control equipment, optical—*mfg*
3484 Sights, gun: except optical 30 mm. (or 1.18 inch) or less—*mfg*
3489 Sights, gun: except optical—more than 30 mm. (or more than 1.18 inch)—*mfg*
3827 Sights, telescopic—*mfg*
4522 Sightseeing airplane services
4489 Sightseeing boats
4119 Sightseeing buses
7389 Sign painting and lettering shops
3357 Signal and control cable, nonferrous—*mfg*
2899 Signal flares, marine—*mfg*
3825 Signal generators and averages—*mfg*
3669 Signaling apparatus, electric—*mfg*
5063 Signaling equipment, electrical—wholesale
3612 Signaling transformers, electric—*mfg*
3714 Signals, directional: motor vehicle—*mfg*
3669 Signals: railway, highway, and traffic—electric—*mfg*
2499 Signboards, wood—*mfg*
5046 Signs, electrical—wholesale
5099 Signs, except electric—wholesale
3993 Signs, not made in custom sign painting shops—*mfg*
2211 Silesia, cotton—*mfg*
2819 Silica gel—*mfg*
1446 Silica mining
1446 Silica sand mining
2819 Silica, amorphous—*mfg*
2819 Silicofluorides—*mfg*
3291 Silicon carbide abrasives—*mfg*
3339 Silicon refining, primary (over 99 percent pure)—*mfg*
3674 Silicon wafers, chemically doped—*mfg*
3339 Silicon, epitaxial (silicon alloy)—*mfg*
3339 Silicon, pure—*mfg*
3295 Silicon, ultra high purity: treated purchased materials—*mfg*
2821 Silicone fluid solution (fluid for sonar transducers)—*mfg*
2821 Silicone resins—*mfg*
2822 Silicone rubbers—*mfg*
2869 Silicones—*mfg*
0279 Silk (raw) production and silkworm farms
2262 Silk broadwoven fabric finishing—*mfg*
2221 Silk broadwoven fabrics—*mfg*
2241 Silk narrow fabrics—*mfg*
5131 Silk piece goods—wholesale
7336 Silk screen design
2396 Silk screening on fabric articles—*mfg*
3552 Silk screens for the textile industry—*mfg*
2284 Silk thread—*mfg*
2282 Silk throwing, twisting, winding, or spooling—*mfg*
2281 Silk yarn, spinning—*mfg*
5199 Silk yarns—wholesale
5159 Silk, raw—wholesale
1459 Sillimanite mining
3272 Sills, concrete—*mfg*
1542 Silo construction, agricultural—general contractors
3523 Silo fillers (agricultural machinery)—*mfg*
3272 Silo staves, cast stone—*mfg*
2431 Silo staves, wood—*mfg*
2421 Silo stock, wood: sawed—*mfg*
3251 Silo tile—*mfg*
3523 Silo unloaders—*mfg*
3531 Silos, cement (batch plant)—*mfg*

7319 Sky writing
3211 Skylight glass—*mfg*
1761 Skylight installation—contractors
3444 Skylights, sheet metal—*mfg*
3334 Slabs, aluminum: primary—*mfg*
3331 Slabs, copper: primary—*mfg*
3272 Slabs, crossing: concrete—*mfg*
3339 Slabs, primary: nonferrous metals, except copper and aluminum—*mfg*
3312 Slabs, steel—*mfg*
2325 Slacks (separate): men's and boys'—mfpm—*mfg*
2325 Slacks, jean-cut casual: men's and boys'—mfpm—*mfg*
2369 Slacks: girls' and children's—mfpm—*mfg*
2339 Slacks: women's, misses', and juniors'—mfpm—*mfg*
2253 Slacks—mitse—*mfg*
3531 Slag mixers—*mfg*
3295 Slag, crushed or ground—*mfg*
3552 Slashing machines (textile machinery)—*mfg*
3281 Slate and slate products—*mfg*
1429 Slate, crushed and broken—quarrying
1411 Slate, dimension—quarrying
2441 Slats, trunk: wood—*mfg*
2048 Slaughtering of animals, except for human consumption—*mfg*
2011 Slaughtering plants: except animals not for human consumption—*mfg*
0751 Slaughtering, custom: for individuals
2099 Slaw, cole: in bulk—*mfg*
3423 Sledges (handtools)—*mfg*
3944 Sleds, children's—*mfg*
3429 Sleeper mechanisms, for convertible beds—*mfg*
2399 Sleeping bags—*mfg*
4789 Sleeping car and other passenger car operations, not performed by railroads
3743 Sleeping cars, railroad—*mfg*
3069 Sleeves, pump: rubber—*mfg*
3199 Sleeves, welders': leather—*mfg*
2295 Sleeving, textile: saturated—*mfg*
7991 Slenderizing salons
3556 Slicing machines, fruit and vegetable: commercial types—*mfg*
2241 Slide fastener tapes—*mfg*
3965 Slide fasteners (zippers)—*mfg*
7336 Slide film producers
3999 Slides and exhibits for classroom use, preparation of—*mfg*
3496 Slings, lifting: made from purchased wire—*mfg*
2298 Slings, rope—*mfg*
1455 Slip clay mining
2211 Slipcover fabrics, cotton—*mfg*
2221 Slipcover fabrics, manmade fiber and silk—*mfg*
5714 Slipcover stores—retail
5023 Slipcovers, furniture—wholesale
2392 Slipcovers: made of fabrics, plastics, and other material—except paper—*mfg*
3142 Slipper socks, made from purchased socks—*mfg*
2252 Slipper socks—mitse—*mfg*
3149 Slippers, ballet—*mfg*
3142 Slippers, house—*mfg*
3621 Sliprings for motors and generators—*mfg*
2341 Slips: women's, misses', children's, and infants'—mfpm—*mfg*
2254 Slips—mitse—*mfg*
3579 Slipsheeting machines—*mfg*
3841 Slit lamps (ophthalmic goods)—*mfg*
3549 Slitters, rotary (metalworking machines)—*mfg*
3999 Slot machines—*mfg*
7993 Slot machines, operation of
7999 Slot-car racetracks
3541 Slotting machines (machine tools)—*mfg*
2299 Slubs and nubs (cutting up fibers for use in tweeds)—*mfg*
4953 Sludge disposal sites
3589 Sludge processing equipment—*mfg*
3599 Sludge tables—*mfg*
3355 Slugs, aluminum—*mfg*
3351 Slugs, copper and copper alloy—*mfg*
3555 Slugs, printers'—*mfg*
3251 Slumped brick—*mfg*
4619 Slurry pipeline operation
1389 Slush pits and cellars, excavation of: on a contract basis
2899 Slushing compounds, gun—*mfg*
3482 Small arms ammunition, 30 mm. (or 1.18 inch) or less—*mfg*
2015 Small game dressing—*mfg*
3559 Smelting and refining machinery and equipment, except ovens—*mfg*
3339 Smelting and refining of lead, primary—*mfg*
3341 Smelting and refining of nonferrous metals, secondary—*mfg*
3339 Smelting and refining of zinc, primary—*mfg*
5084 Smelting machinery and equipment—wholesale
3339 Smelting of nonferrous metal, primary: except copper and aluminum—*mfg*
3567 Smelting ovens—*mfg*
3443 Smelting pots and retorts—*mfg*
1031 Smithsonite mining
2339 Smocks: women's, misses', and juniors'—mfpm—*mfg*

2834 Sodium chloride solution for injection, U.S.P.—*mfg*
2899 Sodium chloride, refined—*mfg*
1474 Sodium compounds mining, except common salt
2819 Sodium compounds, inorganic—*mfg*
2819 Sodium cyanide—*mfg*
2869 Sodium glutamate—*mfg*
2819 Sodium hydrosulfite—*mfg*
2812 Sodium hydroxide (caustic soda)—*mfg*
2842 Sodium hypochlorite (household bleach)—*mfg*
2819 Sodium molybdate—*mfg*
2869 Sodium pentachlorophenate—*mfg*
2819 Sodium perborate—*mfg*
2819 Sodium peroxide—*mfg*
2819 Sodium phosphate—*mfg*
2819 Sodium polyphosphate—*mfg*
2834 Sodium salicylate tablets—*mfg*
2843 Sodium salts of sulfonated oils, fats, or greases—*mfg*
2819 Sodium silicate—*mfg*
2819 Sodium silicofluoride—*mfg*
2819 Sodium stannate—*mfg*
2819 Sodium sulfate-bulk or tablets—*mfg*
2869 Sodium sulfoxalate formaldehyde—*mfg*
2819 Sodium tetraborate, not produced at mines—*mfg*
2819 Sodium thiosulfate—*mfg*
2819 Sodium tungstate—*mfg*
2819 Sodium uranate—*mfg*
2819 Sodium, metallic—*mfg*
2515 Sofas, convertible—*mfg*
2512 Sofas, upholstered on wood frames, except convertible beds—*mfg*
3089 Soffit, plastics (siding)—*mfg*
5812 Soft drink stands
2086 Soft drinks, bottled or canned—*mfg*
5149 Soft drinks—wholesale
2298 Soft fiber cordage and twine—*mfg*
2843 Softeners (textile assistants)—*mfg*
7371 Software programming, custom
7371 Software systems analysis and design, custom
7372 Software, computer: prepackaged
5045 Software, computer—wholesale
2861 Softwood distillates—*mfg*
2436 Softwood plywood composites—*mfg*
2436 Softwood veneer or plywood—*mfg*
1629 Soil compacting service—contractors
3531 Soil compactors: vibratory—*mfg*
2879 Soil conditioners—*mfg*
9512 Soil conservation services—government
3321 Soil pipe, cast iron—*mfg*
3523 Soil pulverizers and packers (agricultural machinery)—*mfg*
2899 Soil testing kits—*mfg*
5261 Soil, top—retail
3674 Solar cells—*mfg*
3433 Solar energy collectors, liquid or gas—*mfg*
3433 Solar heaters—*mfg*
1711 Solar heating apparatus—contractors
5074 Solar heating panels and equipment—wholesale
3511 Solar powered turbine-generator sets—*mfg*
1742 Solar reflecting insulation film—contractors
3829 Solarimeters—*mfg*
3341 Solder (base metal), pig and ingot: secondary—*mfg*
3356 Solder wire, bar: acid core and rosin core—*mfg*
3548 Soldering equipment, except soldering irons—*mfg*
2899 Soldering fluxes—*mfg*
3915 Soldering for the jewelry trade—*mfg*
3423 Soldering guns and tools, hand: electric—*mfg*
3423 Soldering iron tips and tiplets—*mfg*
3423 Soldering irons and coppers—*mfg*
3643 Solderless connectors (electric wiring devices)—*mfg*
3111 Sole leather—*mfg*
3625 Solenoid switches, industrial—*mfg*
3492 Solenoid valves, fluid power: metal—*mfg*
3679 Solenoids for electronic applications—*mfg*
3131 Soles, boot and shoe: except rubber, composition, plastics, and fiber—*mfg*
3089 Soles, boot and shoe: plastics—*mfg*
3069 Soles, boot and shoe: rubber, composition, and fiber—*mfg*
5087 Soles, shoe—wholesale
2819 Solid fuel propellants, inorganic—*mfg*
2869 Solid fuel propellants, organic—*mfg*
3674 Solid-state electronic devices—*mfg*
3089 Soling strips, boot and shoe: plastics—*mfg*
3069 Soling strips, boot and shoe: rubber, composition, and fiber—*mfg*
3295 Solite, ground or otherwise treated—*mfg*
2843 Soluble oils and greases—*mfg*
2834 Solutions, pharmaceutical—*mfg*
2865 Solvent naphtha, made in chemical plants—*mfg*
7389 Solvents recovery service on a contract or fee basis
2899 Solvents, carbon—*mfg*
2842 Solvents, degreasing—*mfg*
2842 Solvents, drain pipe—*mfg*
2869 Solvents, organic—*mfg*
2911 Solvents, produced in petroleum refineries—*mfg*
3812 Sonabuoys—*mfg*

8049 Speech pathologists, offices of
3566 Speed changers (power transmission equipment)—*mfg*
3824 Speed indicators and recorders, vehicle—*mfg*
8299 Speed reading courses
3566 Speed reducers (power transmission equipment)—*mfg*
5531 Speed shops—retail
3824 Speedometers—*mfg*
7948 Speedway operation
3339 Spelter (zinc), primary—*mfg*
8099 Sperm banks
0831 Sphagnum moss, gathering of
1031 Sphalerite mining
3443 Spheres, for liquids or gas: metal plate—*mfg*
3841 Sphygmomanometers—*mfg*
5499 Spice and herb stores—retail
2099 Spices, including grinding—*mfg*
5149 Spices—wholesale
3313 Spiegeleisen—*mfg*
3432 Spigots, metal and plastics—*mfg*
2499 Spigots, wood—*mfg*
3312 Spike rods, made in steel works or rolling mills—*mfg*
3399 Spikes, nonferrous metal (including wire)—*mfg*
3315 Spikes, steel: wire or cut—*mfg*
2241 Spindle banding—*mfg*
3552 Spindles, textile—*mfg*
3728 Spinners, aircraft propeller—*mfg*
3542 Spinning lathes—*mfg*
3542 Spinning machines, metal—*mfg*
3552 Spinning machines, textile—*mfg*
3469 Spinning metal, for the trade—*mfg*
2284 Spinning thread: cotton, silk, manmade fibers, and wool—*mfg*
2281 Spinning wool carpet and rug yarn: wool, mohair, or animal fiber—*mfg*
2281 Spinning yarn: cotton, silk, wool, and manmade staple—*mfg*
3496 Spiral cloth, made from purchased wire—*mfg*
2899 Spirit duplicating fluid—*mfg*
2085 Spirits, neutral, except fruit—for beverage purposes—*mfg*
2834 Spirits, pharmaceutical—*mfg*
5182 Spirits—wholesale
3861 Splicers, motion picture film—*mfg*
3542 Spline rolling machines—*mfg*
2449 Splint baskets, for fruits and vegetables—*mfg*
3842 Splints, pneumatic and wood—*mfg*
3111 Splits, leather—*mfg*
1479 Spodumene mining
2499 Spokes, wood—*mfg*
2051 Sponge goods, bakery, except frozen—*mfg*
3312 Sponge iron—*mfg*
3069 Sponge rubber and sponge rubber products—*mfg*
3999 Sponges, bleaching and dyeing of—*mfg*
0919 Sponges, gathering of
3089 Sponges, plastics—*mfg*
3069 Sponges, rubber—*mfg*
3291 Sponges, scouring: metallic—*mfg*
3842 Sponges, surgical—*mfg*
5199 Sponges—wholesale
2231 Sponging and refinishing cloth: wool and similar animal fiber for the trade—*mfg*
7389 Sponging textiles for tailors and dressmakers
2426 Spool blocks and blanks, wood—*mfg*
2282 Spooling yarn: wool, mohair, or similar animal fibers—*mfg*
2282 Spooling yarn: cotton, silk, and manmade fiber continuous filament—*mfg*
2499 Spools, except for textile machinery: wood—*mfg*
2655 Spools, fiber (metal-end or all-fiber)—mfpm—*mfg*
3552 Spools, textile machinery: wood—*mfg*
2656 Spoons, paper: except those made from pressed or molded pulp—mfpm—*mfg*
2679 Spoons, pressed and molded pulp—mfpm—*mfg*
3914 Spoons: silver, nickel silver, pewter, stainless steel, and plated—*mfg*
2321 Sport shirts: men's and boys'—mfpm—*mfg*
7032 Sporting camps
7999 Sporting goods rental
5941 Sporting goods stores—retail
5091 Sporting goods, including firearms, ammunition, and bicycles—wholesale
3949 Sporting goods: except clothing, footwear, small arms, and ammunition—*mfg*
2892 Sporting powder (explosive)—*mfg*
7997 Sports and recreation clubs, membership: except physical fitness
5699 Sports apparel stores—retail
2329 Sports clothing, nontailored: men's and boys'—mfpm—*mfg*
7941 Sports field operation (sports promotion)
7999 Sports instructors, professional: golf, skiing, swimming, etc.
7999 Sports professionals
7941 Sports promotion: baseball, football, boxing, etc.
2253 Sports shirts—mitse—*mfg*
5136 Sportswear, men's and boys'—wholesale
5137 Sportswear: women's and children's—wholesale

3469 Stamping metal, for the trade—*mfg*
3532 Stamping mill mining machinery—*mfg*
2396 Stamping on finished fabric articles—*mfg*
3953 Stamps, hand: time, date, postmark, cancelling, shoe, and textile marking—*mfg*
5961 Stamps, mail-order—retail
5999 Stamps, philatelist—retail: except mail-order
5092 Stamps, philatelist—wholesale
3523 Stanchions and standards, barn—*mfg*
3949 Stand boards—*mfg*
3825 Standard cells—*mfg*
3479 Standardizing of metals and metal products, for the trade—*mfg*
3825 Standards and calibration equipment for electrical measuring, except laboratory—*mfg*
3825 Standing wave ratio measuring equipment—*mfg*
3443 Standpipes—*mfg*
3861 Stands, camera and projector—*mfg*
3537 Stands, ground servicing aircraft—*mfg*
2541 Stands, merchandise display: wood—*mfg*
2542 Stands, merchandise display: except wood—*mfg*
3931 Stands, music—*mfg*
2511 Stands: telephone, bedside, and smoking—wood—*mfg*
2819 Stannic and stannous chloride—*mfg*
3579 Staple removers—*mfg*
3399 Staples, nonferrous metal (including wire)—*mfg*
3315 Staples, steel: wire or cut—*mfg*
3496 Staples, wire: made from purchased wire—*mfg*
5072 Staples—wholesale
3579 Stapling machines, office—*mfg*
4212 Star routes, local
2842 Starch preparations, laundry—*mfg*
2046 Starch, instant—*mfg*
2046 Starch, liquid—*mfg*
2046 Starches, edible and industrial—*mfg*
2842 Starches, plastics—*mfg*
5149 Starches—wholesale
0252 Started pullet farms
7539 Starter and generator repair, automotive
3694 Starter and starter parts, internal combustion engine—*mfg*
3724 Starters, aircraft: nonelectric—*mfg*
3625 Starters, electric motor—*mfg*
3643 Starters, fluorescent—*mfg*
3621 Starting equipment, for streetcars—*mfg*
3643 Starting switches, fluorescent lamp—*mfg*
6022 State banks, commercial
6062 State credit unions, not federally chartered
9411 State education departments
9221 State police
9311 State tax commissions
3679 Static power supply converters for electronic applications—*mfg*
3822 Static pressure regulators—*mfg*
3711 Station wagons (motor vehicles)—*mfg*
3229 Stationers' glassware: inkwells, clip cups, etc.—*mfg*
3069 Stationers' sundries, rubber—*mfg*
5112 Stationery and stationery supplies—wholesale
3269 Stationery articles, pottery—*mfg*
5943 Stationery stores—retail
2759 Stationery: except lithographed or gravure—*mfg*
2754 Stationery: gravure printing—*mfg*
2678 Stationery—mfpm—*mfg*
4013 Stations operated by railway terminal companies
5143 Stations, cream—wholesale
2721 Statistical reports (periodicals), publishing and printing, or publishing only—*mfg*
3621 Stators for motors—*mfg*
3281 Statuary, marble—*mfg*
3299 Statuary: gypsum, clay, papier-mache, scagliola, and metal—factory production only—*mfg*
5199 Statuary—wholesale
2411 Stave bolts, wood: hewn—*mfg*
2429 Staves, barrel: sawed or split—*mfg*
3272 Staves, silo: concrete—*mfg*
3131 Stays, shoe—*mfg*
3053 Steam and other packing—*mfg*
7299 Steam baths
1799 Steam cleaning of building exteriors—contractors
3443 Steam condensers—*mfg*
3589 Steam cookers, restaurant type—*mfg*
3511 Steam engines, except locomotives—*mfg*
1711 Steam fitting—contractors
3494 Steam fittings and specialties, except plumbers' brass goods and fittings, metal—*mfg*
5074 Steam fittings—wholesale
3511 Steam governors—*mfg*
3433 Steam heating apparatus, domestic—*mfg*
4961 Steam heating systems (suppliers of heat)
3443 Steam jet aftercoolers—*mfg*
3443 Steam jet inter condensers—*mfg*
3822 Steam pressure controls, residential and commercial type—*mfg*
3569 Steam separators (machinery)—*mfg*
4961 Steam supply systems, including geothermal
3589 Steam tables—*mfg*

3433 Stokers, mechanical: domestic and industrial—*mfg*
3423 Stone forks (handtools)—*mfg*
3532 Stone pulverizers, stationary—*mfg*
1741 Stone setting—contractors
3559 Stone tumblers—*mfg*
3559 Stone working machinery—*mfg*
5032 Stone, building—wholesale
3272 Stone, cast concrete—*mfg*
5032 Stone, crushed or broken—wholesale
3281 Stone, cut and shaped—*mfg*
3281 Stone, quarrying and processing of own stone products—*mfg*
3423 Stonecutters' handtools—*mfg*
3291 Stones, abrasive—*mfg*
5999 Stones, crystalline: rough—retail
3299 Stones, synthetic: for gem stones and industrial use—*mfg*
3915 Stones: preparation of real and imitation gems for settings—*mfg*
1459 Stoneware clay mining
3269 Stoneware, chemical (pottery products)—*mfg*
1741 Stonework erection—contractors
2599 Stools, factory—*mfg*
2514 Stools, household: metal—*mfg*
2511 Stools, household: wood—*mfg*
2599 Stools, metal: with casters—not household or office—*mfg*
2522 Stools, office: rotating—except wood—*mfg*
2521 Stools, office: wood—*mfg*
3272 Stools, precast terrazzo—*mfg*
3494 Stop cocks, except drain: metal—*mfg*
3432 Stopcocks (plumbers' supplies)—*mfg*
2499 Stoppers, cork—*mfg*
3842 Stoppers, ear—*mfg*
3255 Stoppers, glasshouse: clay—*mfg*
3069 Stoppers, rubber—*mfg*
7219 Storage and repair of fur and other garments for individuals
3691 Storage batteries—*mfg*
5063 Storage batteries, industrial—wholesale
3621 Storage battery chargers, engine generator type—*mfg*
2511 Storage chests, household: wood—*mfg*
3572 Storage devices, computer—*mfg*
2542 Storage fixtures, except wood—*mfg*
2541 Storage fixtures, wood—*mfg*
7219 Storage of furs and other garments for individuals
4226 Storage of goods at foreign trade zones
4214 Storage of household goods: combined with local trucking
4226 Storage of household goods: without local trucking
4922 Storage of natural gas
4221 Storage other than cold storage, farm product
3272 Storage tanks, concrete—*mfg*
3443 Storage tanks, metal plate—*mfg*
1791 Storage tanks, metal: erection—contractors
4222 Storage, frozen or refrigerated goods
4226 Storage, furniture: without local trucking
4225 Storage, general
4226 Storage, special: except farm products and cold storage
1542 Store construction—general contractors
1751 Store fixture installation—contractors
1791 Store front installation, metal—contractors
3469 Store fronts, porcelain enameled—*mfg*
3442 Store fronts, prefabricated: metal, except porcelain enameled—*mfg*
2541 Store fronts, prefabricated: wood—*mfg*
3442 Storm doors and windows, metal—*mfg*
5211 Storm windows and sash, wood or metal—retail
2431 Storm windows, wood—*mfg*
2082 Stout (alcoholic beverage)—*mfg*
3444 Stove boards, sheet metal—*mfg*
3259 Stove lining, clay—*mfg*
3469 Stove parts, porcelain enameled—*mfg*
3444 Stove pipe and flues, sheet metal—*mfg*
2842 Stove polish—*mfg*
7699 Stove repair shops
5722 Stoves and related electric and gas appliances—retail
3589 Stoves, commercial—*mfg*
5064 Stoves, cooking or heating, household: electric—wholesale
5074 Stoves, cooking: except electric—wholesale
3631 Stoves, disk—*mfg*
3631 Stoves, household: cooking—*mfg*
3433 Stoves, household: heating—except electric—*mfg*
3433 Stoves, wood and coal burning—*mfg*
5074 Stoves, wood burning—wholesale
3537 Straddle carriers, mobile—*mfg*
3421 Straight razors—*mfg*
3547 Straightening machinery (rolling mill equipment)—*mfg*
3674 Strain gages, solid-state—*mfg*
3494 Strainers, line: for use in piping systems—metal—*mfg*
3714 Strainers, oil: motor vehicle—*mfg*
3569 Strainers, pipeline—*mfg*
3496 Strand, uninsulated wire: made from purchased wire—*mfg*
2493 Strandboard, oriented—*mfg*
2399 Strap assemblies, tie down: aircraft—except leather—*mfg*

7911 Studios, dance
7221 Studios, portrait photography
3444 Studs, sheet metal—*mfg*
3965 Studs, shirt: except precious metal and precious or semiprecious stones—*mfg*
9121 Study commissions, legislative
3942 Stuffed toys (including animals)—*mfg*
3556 Stuffers, sausage—*mfg*
2411 Stumping for turpentine or powder manufacturing—*mfg*
2411 Stumps—*mfg*
3679 Styli, phonograph record cutting—*mfg*
7389 Styling of fashions, apparel, furniture, and textiles
7389 Styling wigs for the trade
3951 Stylographic pens—*mfg*
2892 Styphnic acid—*mfg*
2865 Styrene—*mfg*
2865 Styrene monomer—*mfg*
2821 Styrene resins—*mfg*
2821 Styrene-acrylonitrile resins—*mfg*
2822 Styrene-butadiene rubbers (50 percent or less styrene content)—*mfg*
2822 Styrene-chloroprene rubbers—*mfg*
2822 Styrene-isoprene rubbers—*mfg*
1221 Subbituminous coal surface mining
1222 Subbituminous coal underground mining
3531 Subgraders, construction equipment—*mfg*
2819 Sublimate, corrosive—*mfg*
3484 Submachine guns and parts—*mfg*
1629 Submarine rock removal—general contractors
5812 Submarine sandwich shops
3731 Submarine tenders, building and repairing—*mfg*
3544 Subpresses, metalworking—*mfg*
4841 Subscription television services
3531 Subsoiler attachments, tractor-mounted—*mfg*
4111 Suburban and urban railway operation
1629 Subway construction—general contractors
4111 Subway operation
3841 Suction therapy apparatus—*mfg*
2261 Sueding cotton broadwoven goods—*mfg*
2262 Sueding manmade fiber and silk broadwoven fabrics—*mfg*
0133 Sugar beet farms
0722 Sugar beets, machine harvesting of
2099 Sugar grinding—*mfg*
2023 Sugar of milk—*mfg*
3556 Sugar plant machinery—*mfg*
2087 Sugar, burnt (food color)—*mfg*
2046 Sugar, corn—*mfg*
2062 Sugar, granulated: made from purchased raw cane sugar or sugar syrup—*mfg*
2063 Sugar, granulated: made from sugar beets—*mfg*
2061 Sugar, granulated: made from sugarcane—*mfg*
2099 Sugar, industrial maple: made in plants producing maple syrup—*mfg*
2062 Sugar, invert: made from purchased raw cane sugar or sugar syrup—*mfg*
2063 Sugar, invert: made from sugar beets—*mfg*
2061 Sugar, invert: made from sugarcane—*mfg*
2063 Sugar, liquid: made from sugar beets—*mfg*
2062 Sugar, powdered: made from purchased raw cane sugar or sugar syrup—*mfg*
2063 Sugar, powdered: made from sugar beets—*mfg*
2061 Sugar, powdered: made from sugarcane—*mfg*
2099 Sugar, powdered—mfpm—*mfg*
2061 Sugar, raw: made from sugarcane—*mfg*
5159 Sugar, raw—wholesale
2062 Sugar, refined: made from purchased raw cane sugar or sugar syrup—*mfg*
5149 Sugar, refined—wholesale
2061 Sugar: clarified, granulated, and raw—made from sugarcane—*mfg*
0133 Sugarcane farms
0722 Sugarcane, machine harvesting of
2396 Suit and coat findings: coat fronts and linings—*mfg*
2396 Suit trimmings, fabric—mfpm—*mfg*
3429 Suitcase hardware, including locks—*mfg*
3089 Suitcase shells, plastics—*mfg*
3161 Suitcases, regardless of material—*mfg*
2211 Suiting fabrics, cotton—*mfg*
2221 Suiting fabrics, manmade fiber and silk—*mfg*
2231 Suitings: wool, mohair, and similar animal fibers—*mfg*
2369 Suits and rompers: children's and infants'—mfpm—*mfg*
2337 Suits, except playsuits and athletic: women's, misses', and juniors'—mfpm—*mfg*
3842 Suits, firefighting: asbestos—*mfg*
2329 Suits, men's and boys': warmup, jogging, snow, and ski—mfpm—*mfg*
5136 Suits, men's and boys'—wholesale
2311 Suits, tailored: men's and boys'—mfpm—*mfg*
2339 Suits, women's, misses', and juniors': ski, swim, snow, play, warmup, and jogging—mfpm—*mfg*
2326 Suits, work: men's—mfpm—*mfg*
2369 Suits: girls' and children's—mfpm—*mfg*

3825 Sweep generators—*mfg*
3825 Sweep oscillators—*mfg*
3589 Sweepers, carpet: except household electric vacuum sweepers—*mfg*
3635 Sweepers, electric: vacuum—household—*mfg*
3589 Sweepers, electric: vacuum—industrial—*mfg*
3711 Sweepers, street (motor vehicles)—*mfg*
2842 Sweeping compounds, oil and water absorbent, clay or sawdust—*mfg*
4959 Sweeping service: road, airport, parking lot, etc.
0161 Sweet corn farms
0161 Sweet pepper farms
0723 Sweet potato curing
0139 Sweet potato farms
2051 Sweet yeast goods, except frozen—*mfg*
2053 Sweet yeast goods, frozen—*mfg*
2869 Sweetners, synthetic—*mfg*
7997 Swimming clubs, membership
7999 Swimming instruction
7389 Swimming pool cleaning and maintenance
1799 Swimming pool construction—contractors
2394 Swimming pool covers and blankets, fabric—mfpm—*mfg*
3089 Swimming pool covers and blankets: plastics—*mfg*
3589 Swimming pool filter systems (home pools)—*mfg*
3648 Swimming pool lighting fixtures—*mfg*
5091 Swimming pools and equipment—wholesale
7999 Swimming pools, except membership
5999 Swimming pools, home: not installed—retail
3949 Swimming pools, plastics—*mfg*
2329 Swimsuits: men's and boys'—mfpm—*mfg*
2339 Swimsuits: women's, misses', and juniors'—mfpm—*mfg*
2253 Swimsuits—mitse—*mfg*
2329 Swimwear, men's and boys'—mfpm—*mfg*
2514 Swings, porch: metal—*mfg*
2511 Swings, porch: wood—*mfg*
2395 Swiss loom embroideries—*mfg*
3644 Switch boxes, electric—*mfg*
3643 Switch cutouts—*mfg*
7389 Switchboard operation of private branch exchanges
3281 Switchboard panels, slate—*mfg*
3613 Switchboards and parts, power—*mfg*
5063 Switchboards, electrical distribution—wholesale
3661 Switchboards, telephone and telegraph—*mfg*
3999 Switches (hair)—*mfg*
3643 Switches for electric wiring: e.g., snap, tumbler, pressure, pushbutton—*mfg*
3613 Switches, electric power: except snap, push button, tumbler, and solenoid—*mfg*
3679 Switches, electronic—*mfg*
5063 Switches, except electronic—wholesale
3625 Switches, flow activated electrical—*mfg*
3822 Switches, pneumatic positioning remote—*mfg*
3462 Switches, railroad: forged—not made in rolling mills—*mfg*
3674 Switches, silicon control—*mfg*
3679 Switches, stepping—*mfg*
3822 Switches, thermostatic—*mfg*
3613 Switchgear and switchgear accessories—*mfg*
5063 Switchgear—wholesale
3613 Switching equipment power—*mfg*
3661 Switching equipment, telephone—*mfg*
3743 Switching locomotives and parts, electric and nonelectric—*mfg*
3949 Swivels (fishing equipment)—*mfg*
3421 Swords—*mfg*
1411 Syenite (except nepheline), dimension—quarrying
1423 Syenite, except nepheline: crushed and broken—quarrying
1459 Syenite, nepheline—quarrying
1041 Sylvanite mining
7929 Symphony orchestras
3829 Synchronizers, aircraft engine—*mfg*
3621 Synchronous condensers and timing motors, electric—*mfg*
3621 Synchros—*mfg*
3825 Synchroscopes—*mfg*
3931 Synthesizers, music—*mfg*
6111 Synthetic Fuels Corporation
3559 Synthetic filament extruding machines—*mfg*
4925 Synthetic natural gas from naphtha, production and distribution
5169 Synthetic rubber—wholesale
3299 Synthetic stones, for gem stones and industrial use—*mfg*
3069 Syringes, fountain: rubber—*mfg*
3841 Syringes, hypodermic—*mfg*
2061 Syrup, cane: made from sugarcane—*mfg*
2046 Syrup, corn: unmixed—*mfg*
2062 Syrup, made from purchased raw cane sugar or sugar syrup—*mfg*
2063 Syrup, made from sugar beets—*mfg*
2087 Syrups, beverage—*mfg*
2066 Syrups, chocolate—*mfg*
5149 Syrups, except for fountain use—wholesale
2087 Syrups, flavoring—*mfg*
5145 Syrups, fountain—wholesale

T

3952 Tailors' chalk—*mfg*
2499 Tailors' pressing blocks, wood—*mfg*
3421 Tailors' scissors—*mfg*
3421 Tailors' shears, hand—*mfg*
5087 Tailors' supplies—wholesale
5699 Tailors, custom—retail
1499 Talc mining
3295 Talc, ground or otherwise treated—*mfg*
2844 Talcum powders—*mfg*
2861 Tall oil, except skimmings—*mfg*
2851 Tallate driers—*mfg*
2077 Tallow rendering, inedible—*mfg*
2076 Tallow, vegetable—*mfg*
3824 Tally counters—*mfg*
3824 Tallying meters: except electrical instruments, watches, and clocks—*mfg*
2032 Tamales, canned—*mfg*
3531 Tampers, powered—*mfg*
3531 Tamping equipment, rail—*mfg*
3489 Tampions for guns more than 30 mm. (or more than 1.18 inch)—*mfg*
2676 Tampons—mfpm—*mfg*
0174 Tangerine groves and farms
7699 Tank and boiler cleaning service
3489 Tank artillery—*mfg*
3255 Tank blocks, glasshouse: clay—*mfg*
7699 Tank cleaning, ship
3795 Tank components, specialized: military—*mfg*
3519 Tank engines and engine parts, internal combustion: military—*mfg*
3743 Tank freight cars and car equipment—*mfg*
3259 Tank liner brick, vitrified clay—*mfg*
3795 Tank recovery vehicles—*mfg*
2331 Tank tops, outerwear: women's, misses', and juniors—mfpm—*mfg*
2361 Tank tops: girls', children's, and infants'—mfpm—*mfg*
2321 Tank tops: men's and boys'—mfpm—*mfg*
2253 Tank tops—mitse—*mfg*
3443 Tank towers, metal plate—*mfg*
7699 Tank truck cleaning service
3824 Tank truck meters—*mfg*
3511 Tank turbines—*mfg*
**** Tanker fleets of oil companies, if separate—code in transportation
3731 Tankers (ships), building and repairing—*mfg*
5088 Tanks and tank components—wholesale
3443 Tanks for tank trucks, metal plate—*mfg*
3272 Tanks, concrete—*mfg*
3261 Tanks, flush: vitreous china—*mfg*
3728 Tanks, fuel: aircraft—*mfg*
3714 Tanks, gas: motor vehicle—*mfg*
3443 Tanks, metal plate: lined—*mfg*
3795 Tanks, military: including factory rebuilding—*mfg*
3585 Tanks, soda water—*mfg*
3443 Tanks, standard and custom fabricated: metal plate—made in boiler shops—*mfg*
2449 Tanks, wood: coopered—*mfg*
3861 Tanks: photographic developing, fixing, and washing—*mfg*
3111 Tanneries, leather—*mfg*
3559 Tannery machines—*mfg*
2869 Tannic acid—*mfg*
2819 Tanning agents, synthetic inorganic—*mfg*
2869 Tanning agents, synthetic organic—*mfg*
3999 Tanning and currying furs—*mfg*
2861 Tanning extracts and materials, natural—*mfg*
7299 Tanning salons
1061 Tantalite mining
1061 Tantalum ore mining
3339 Tantalum refining—*mfg*
5813 Tap rooms (drinking places)
3577 Tape cleaners, magnetic: computer peripheral equipment—*mfg*
7822 Tape distribution for television
3999 Tape measures—*mfg*
5064 Tape players and recorders, household—wholesale
3651 Tape players, household—*mfg*
3577 Tape print units, computer peripheral equipment—*mfg*
7812 Tape production, video or motion picture
7379 Tape recertification service
7622 Tape recorder repair
5731 Tape recorders and players—retail
3572 Tape recorders for data computers—*mfg*
3651 Tape recorders, household—*mfg*
7389 Tape slitting for the trade (cutting plastics, leather, etc. into widths)
3572 Tape storage units, computer—*mfg*
5735 Tape stores, audio and video—retail
3572 Tape transports, magnetic—*mfg*
3842 Tape, adhesive: medicated or nonmedicated—*mfg*
3292 Tape, asbestos—*mfg*
3652 Tape, audio magnetic: prerecorded—*mfg*
2672 Tape, cellophane adhesive—mfpm—*mfg*
3069 Tape, friction: rubber—*mfg*
2672 Tape, gummed: cloth and paper base—mfpm—*mfg*
3965 Tape, hook-and-eye and snap fastener—*mfg*
3695 Tape, magnetic recording: blank—*mfg*
2672 Tape, masking—mfpm—*mfg*
3069 Tape, pressure sensitive (including friction), rubber—*mfg*

3823 Time cycle and program controllers, industrial process type—*mfg*
3821 Time interval measuring equipment, electric (laboratory type)—*mfg*
3429 Time locks—*mfg*
3822 Time program controls, air-conditioning systems—*mfg*
2675 Time recording cards, die-cut from purchased paperboard—*mfg*
7374 Time sharing, computer
3613 Time switches, electrical switchgear apparatus—*mfg*
5063 Time switches—wholesale
7389 Time-share condominium exchanges
6531 Time-sharing real estate: sales, leasing, and rentals
3579 Time-stamps containing clock mechanisms—*mfg*
3579 Time-stamps: containing clock mechanisms—*mfg*
3579 Timeclocks and time recording devices—*mfg*
3873 Timers for industrial use, clockwork mechanism only—*mfg*
3625 Timing devices, mechanical and solid-state, except clockwork—*mfg*
3621 Timing motors, synchronous: electric—*mfg*
0139 Timothy farms
3356 Tin and tin alloy bars, pipe, rods, sheets, strip, and tubing—*mfg*
5051 Tin and tin base metals, shapes, forms, etc.—wholesale
3339 Tin base alloys, primary—*mfg*
3411 Tin cans—*mfg*
2819 Tin chloride—*mfg*
2819 Tin compounds, inorganic—*mfg*
3497 Tin foil, not made in rolling mills—*mfg*
1099 Tin ore mining
2819 Tin oxide—*mfg*
5051 Tin plate bars—wholesale
5051 Tin plate—wholesale
3339 Tin refining, primary—*mfg*
3356 Tin rolling and drawing—*mfg*
2819 Tin salts—*mfg*
3341 Tin smelting and refining, secondary—*mfg*
3312 Tin-free steel—*mfg*
2834 Tinctures, pharmaceutical—*mfg*
3423 Tinners' handtools, except snips—*mfg*
3421 Tinners' snips—*mfg*
3312 Tinplate—*mfg*
3999 Tinsel—*mfg*
7699 Tinsmithing repair, except construction
1761 Tinsmithing, in connection with construction work—contractors
1799 Tinting glass—contractors
2899 Tints and dyes, household—*mfg*
5719 Tinware stores—retail
2396 Tip printing and stamping on fabric articles—*mfg*
1629 Tipple construction—general contractors
3545 Tips, cutting tool—*mfg*
3131 Tips, shoe: regardless of material—*mfg*
5531 Tire (automobile) dealers—retail
5014 Tire and tube repair materials—wholesale
3496 Tire chains, made from purchased wire—*mfg*
2296 Tire cord—*mfg*
2399 Tire covers—mfpm—*mfg*
5531 Tire dealers, automotive—retail
2296 Tire fabric—*mfg*
3559 Tire grooving machines—*mfg*
3563 Tire inflators, hand or compressor operated—*mfg*
7534 Tire recapping
7534 Tire repair shops
3559 Tire retreading machinery and equipment—*mfg*
3559 Tire shredding machinery—*mfg*
7534 Tire studding and restudding
3011 Tire sundries and tire repair materials, rubber—*mfg*
3714 Tire valve cores—*mfg*
5531 Tire, battery, and accessory dealers—retail
5014 Tires and tubes, new—wholesale
3011 Tires, cushion or solid rubber—*mfg*
3089 Tires, plastics—*mfg*
5014 Tires, used—wholesale
3011 Tiring, continuous lengths: rubber, with or without metal core—*mfg*
3089 Tissue dispensers, plastics—*mfg*
2621 Tissue paper—mitse—*mfg*
2676 Tissues, cleansing: mfpm—*mfg*
3264 Titania porcelain insulators—*mfg*
1099 Titaniferous-magnetite mining, valued chiefly for titanium content
3356 Titanium and titanium alloy bars, rods, billets, sheets, strip, and tubing—*mfg*
3369 Titanium castings, except die-castings—*mfg*
3364 Titanium die-castings—*mfg*
3463 Titanium forgings, not made in hot-rolling mills—*mfg*
3356 Titanium from sponge—*mfg*
3339 Titanium metal sponge and granules—*mfg*
1099 Titanium ore mining
2816 Titanium pigments—*mfg*
6541 Title abstract companies
6541 Title and trust companies
6361 Title insurance
6541 Title reconveyance companies
6541 Title search companies
3861 Titlers, motion picture film—*mfg*

3546 Tools, hand: power-driven—woodworking or metalworking—*mfg*
3423 Tools, hand: except power-driven tools and saws—*mfg*
3541 Tools, machine: metal cutting types—*mfg*
5084 Tools, machinists' precision—wholesale
5251 Tools, power and hand—retail
3533 Tools: drilling, etc.—for artesian, gas, and oil wells—*mfg*
3634 Toothbrushes, electric—*mfg*
5064 Toothbrushes, electric—wholesale
3991 Toothbrushes, except electric—*mfg*
5122 Toothbrushes, except electric—wholesale
2844 Toothpastes and powders—*mfg*
2499 Toothpicks, wood—*mfg*
3069 Top lift sheets, rubber—*mfg*
3131 Top lifts, boot and shoe—*mfg*
7532 Top repair, automotive
3069 Top roll covering, for textile mill machinery: rubber—*mfg*
1459 Topaz (nongem) mining
2311 Topcoats: men's and boys'—*mfg*
5145 Toppings, soda fountain—wholesale
3465 Tops, automobile: stamped metal—*mfg*
2675 Tops, bottle; die-cut from purchased paper or paperboard—*mfg*
3259 Tops, chimney: clay—*mfg*
2299 Tops, combing and converting—*mfg*
3466 Tops, jar: stamped metal—*mfg*
2299 Tops, manmade fiber—*mfg*
3714 Tops, motor vehicle: except stamped metal—*mfg*
3089 Tops, plastics (e.g., dispenser, shaker)—*mfg*
3713 Tops, truck—*mfg*
5159 Tops, wool—wholesale
2899 Torches (fireworks)—*mfg*
3489 Torpedo tubes (ordnance)—*mfg*
3483 Torpedoes and parts (ordnance)—*mfg*
2899 Torpedoes, railroad—*mfg*
2892 Torpedoes, well shooting (explosives)—*mfg*
3566 Torque converters, except motor vehicle—*mfg*
3621 Torque motors, electric—*mfg*
3493 Torsion bar springs—*mfg*
3829 Torsion testing equipment—*mfg*
2032 Tortillas, canned—*mfg*
2099 Tortillas, fresh or refrigerated—*mfg*
3824 Totalizing meters, consumption registering, except aircraft—*mfg*
3999 Toupees—*mfg*
4725 Tour operation (travel)
4724 Tourist agencies for the arrangement of transportation, lodging, and car rental
7999 Tourist attractions, natural wonder: commercial
7011 Tourist cabins
7011 Tourist camps
7011 Tourist courts
7999 Tourist guides
7389 Tourist information bureaus
4725 Tours, except sightseeing buses, boats, and airplanes
3728 Tow targets, aircraft—*mfg*
2299 Tow to top mills—*mfg*
7521 Tow-in parking lots
3731 Towboats, building and repairing—*mfg*
3261 Towel bar holders, vitreous china and earthenware—*mfg*
7213 Towel supply service, except wiping
7218 Towel supply service, wiping
2844 Towelettes, premoistened—*mfg*
2621 Toweling paper—mitse—*mfg*
2211 Towels and toweling, cotton: made in weaving mills—*mfg*
2299 Towels and towelings, linen and linen-and-cotton mixtures—mitse—*mfg*
2392 Towels, fabric and nonwoven textiles—mfpm—*mfg*
2676 Towels, paper—mfpm—*mfg*
5113 Towels, paper—wholesale
2259 Towels—mitse—*mfg*
3441 Tower sections, transmission: prefabricated metal—*mfg*
2499 Towers, cooling: wood or wood and sheet metal combination—*mfg*
3443 Towers, tank: metal plate—*mfg*
3443 Towers: bubble, cooling, fractionating—metal plate—*mfg*
3799 Towing bars and systems—*mfg*
7549 Towing service, automotive
4492 Towing services, marine
1521 Townhouse construction—general contractors
2836 Toxins—*mfg*
2836 Toxoids, except in vitro and in vivo—*mfg*
5945 Toy and game stores—retail
3612 Toy transformers—*mfg*
5092 Toys (including electronic)—wholesale
3942 Toys, doll—*mfg*
3069 Toys, rubber: except dolls—*mfg*
3942 Toys, stuffed—*mfg*
3944 Toys: except dolls, bicycles, rubber toys, and stuffed toys—*mfg*
2879 Trace elements (agricultural chemicals)—*mfg*
3483 Tracer igniters for ammunition more than 30 mm. (or more than 1.18 inch)—*mfg*
3952 Tracing cloth (drafting material)—*mfg*
2211 Tracing cloth, cotton—*mfg*
3949 Track and field athletic equipment, except apparel and footwear—*mfg*

3825 Transformers, instrument: portable—*mfg*
3612 Transformers, reactor—*mfg*
3677 Transformers: power supply electronic type—*mfg*
7221 Transient photographers
3674 Transistors—*mfg*
5065 Transistors—wholesale
7319 Transit advertising
9621 Transit systems and authorities—nonoperating
3829 Transits, surveying—*mfg*
7389 Translation service
4923 Transmission and distribution of natural gas
3612 Transmission and distribution voltage regulators—*mfg*
3199 Transmission belting, leather—*mfg*
5063 Transmission equipment, electrical—wholesale
2992 Transmission fluid—mfpm—*mfg*
3714 Transmission housings and parts, motor vehicle—*mfg*
1623 Transmission line construction—general contractors
4911 Transmission of electric power
4922 Transmission of natural gas
7537 Transmission repair, automotive
3441 Transmission towers—*mfg*
3728 Transmissions, aircraft—*mfg*
7537 Transmissions, automotive: installation, repair, or sale and installation
3594 Transmissions, hydrostatic drives—*mfg*
3714 Transmissions, motor vehicle—*mfg*
3663 Transmitter-receivers, radio—*mfg*
3823 Transmitters of process variables, standard signal conversion—*mfg*
5065 Transmitters—wholesale
3663 Transmitting apparatus, radio and television—*mfg*
3671 Transmitting electron tubes—*mfg*
3523 Transplanters—*mfg*
4731 Transport clearinghouse
3731 Transport vessels, passenger and troop: building and repairing—*mfg*
4731 Transportation brokerage
9621 Transportation departments—government
5088 Transportation equipment and supplies, except motor vehicles—wholesale
4449 Transportation of freight on bays and sounds of the oceans
4731 Transportation rate services
9621 Transportation regulatory agencies—government
2754 Transportation schedules, gravure printing—*mfg*
2752 Transportation schedules, lithographed—*mfg*
2759 Transportation schedules, printing: except lithographed or gravure—*mfg*
4011 Transportation, railroad: line-haul
3949 Trap racks (clay targets)—*mfg*
1429 Trap rock, crushed and broken—quarrying
1411 Trap rock, dimension—quarrying
0971 Trapping carried on as a business enterprise
3496 Traps, animal and fish: made from purchased wire—*mfg*
3931 Traps, drummers'—*mfg*
3432 Traps, water—*mfg*
7999 Trapshooting facilities, except membership clubs
2673 Trash bags, plastics film, foil, and coated paper—mfpm—*mfg*
3639 Trash compactors, household—*mfg*
3089 Trash containers, plastics—*mfg*
3443 Trash racks, metal plate—*mfg*
4724 Travel agencies
4724 Travel bureaus
3792 Travel trailer chassis—*mfg*
5561 Travel trailers, automobile: new and used—retail
8322 Traveler's aid centers
6099 Travelers' check issuance
3161 Traveling bags, regardless of material—*mfg*
3671 Traveling wave tubes—*mfg*
1422 Travertine, crushed and broken—quarrying
1411 Travertine, dimension—quarrying
2298 Trawl twine—*mfg*
3731 Trawlers, building and repairing—*mfg*
2599 Tray trucks, restaurant—*mfg*
2441 Trays, carrier: wood—*mfg*
3229 Trays, glass—*mfg*
3272 Trays, laundry: concrete—*mfg*
3496 Trays, made from purchased wire—*mfg*
3861 Trays, photographic printing and processing—*mfg*
3089 Trays, plastics: except foam—*mfg*
3069 Trays, rubber—*mfg*
3634 Trays, warming: electric—*mfg*
3914 Trays: silver, nickel silver, pewter, stainless steel, and plated—*mfg*
2499 Trays: wood, wicker, and bagasse—*mfg*
3011 Tread rubber (camelback)—*mfg*
3949 Treadmills—*mfg*
3069 Treads, stair: rubber—*mfg*
3446 Treads, stair: fabricated metal—*mfg*
9311 Treasurers' offices—government
7218 Treated mats, rugs, mops, dust tool covers, and cloth supply service

7513 Truck rental, except industrial: without drivers
7212 Truck route laundry and drycleaning, not operated by laundries or cleaners
5541 Truck stops—retail
5014 Truck tires and tubes—wholesale
3713 Truck tops—*mfg*
3711 Truck tractors for highway use—*mfg*
5012 Truck tractors—wholesale
3715 Truck trailers—*mfg*
3537 Truck trailers for use in plants, depots, docks, and terminals—*mfg*
5012 Truck trailers—wholesale
4731 Truck transportation brokers
7542 Truck washing
3273 Truck-mixed concrete—*mfg*
4212 Trucking logs
4213 Trucking rental with drivers, except for local use
4231 Trucking terminals, freight: with or without maintenance facilities
4212 Trucking timber
4213 Trucking, except local
4212 Trucking, local: without storage
4214 Trucking, local: combined with storage
3537 Trucks, industrial (except mining): for freight, baggage, etc.—*mfg*
5084 Trucks, industrial—wholesale
3711 Trucks, motor: except off-highway—*mfg*
3531 Trucks, off-highway—*mfg*
5012 Trucks—wholesale
0182 Truffles grown under cover
3931 Trumpets and parts—*mfg*
3429 Trunk hardware, including locks—*mfg*
2441 Trunk slats, wood—*mfg*
5948 Trunks, luggage—retail
3161 Trunks, regardless of material—*mfg*
3443 Truss plates, metal—*mfg*
2439 Trusses, laminated lumber—*mfg*
2439 Trusses, wood—*mfg*
3842 Trusses: orthopedic and surgical—*mfg*
6022 Trust companies (accepting deposits), commercial: State
6021 Trust companies with deposits, commercial: national
6091 Trust companies, nondeposit
6153 Trust deeds, purchase and sale of
6733 Trustees: except for educational, religious, or charitable trusts
6733 Trusts except educational, religious, and charitable: management of
6732 Trusts, charitable: management of
6732 Trusts, educational: management of
6733 Trusts, personal investment: management of
6732 Trusts, religious: management of

3492 Tube and hose fittings and assemblies, fluid power: metal—*mfg*
3354 Tube blooms, aluminum: extruded—*mfg*
3498 Tube fabricating (contract bending and shaping); metal—*mfg*
3469 Tube fins, stamped metal—*mfg*
3492 Tube fittings and assemblies, fluid power: metal—*mfg*
3547 Tube mill machinery—*mfg*
3679 Tube retainers, electronic—*mfg*
3312 Tube rounds—*mfg*
3679 Tube spacers, mica—*mfg*
3825 Tube testers—*mfg*
3679 Tube transformer assemblies used in firing electronic tubes—*mfg*
3354 Tube, aluminum: extruded or drawn—*mfg*
2836 Tuberculins—*mfg*
8069 Tuberculosis and other respiratory illness hospitals
3671 Tubes for operating above the X-ray spectrum (with shorter wavelength)—*mfg*
3844 Tubes, X-ray—*mfg*
3671 Tubes, cathode ray—*mfg*
3499 Tubes, collapsible: for viscous products—tin, lead, and aluminum—*mfg*
3671 Tubes, electron—*mfg*
5065 Tubes, electronic: receiving and transmitting, and industrial—wholesale
2655 Tubes, fiber or paper (with or without metal ends)—mfpm—*mfg*
2655 Tubes, for chemical and electrical uses: impregnated paper or fiber—mfpm—*mfg*
3069 Tubes, hard rubber—*mfg*
3011 Tubes, inner: airplane, automobile, bicycle, motorcycle, and tractor—*mfg*
3312 Tubes, iron and steel: made in steel works or rolling mills—*mfg*
3671 Tubes, klystron—*mfg*
3083 Tubes, laminated plastics—*mfg*
3264 Tubes, porcelain—*mfg*
3317 Tubes, seamless steel—mfpm—*mfg*
3671 Tubes, television receiving type: cathode ray—*mfg*
3082 Tubes, unsupported plastics—*mfg*
3353 Tubes, welded: aluminum—*mfg*
3317 Tubes, wrought: welded, lock joint, and heavy riveted—mfpm—*mfg*
3299 Tubing for electrical purposes, quartz—*mfg*
3292 Tubing, asbestos—*mfg*
3351 Tubing, copper and copper alloy—*mfg*
3599 Tubing, flexible metallic—*mfg*
3229 Tubing, glass—*mfg*
3317 Tubing, mechanical and hypodermic sizes: cold-drawn stainless steel—mfpm—*mfg*

U

V

0742 Veterinary services for pets and other animal specialties
8734 Veterinary testing laboratories
1622 Viaduct construction—general contractors
3221 Vials, glass: made in glassmaking establishments—*mfg*
3231 Vials, made from purchased glass—*mfg*
3089 Vials, plastics—*mfg*
3931 Vibraphones—*mfg*
3829 Vibration meters, analyzers, and calibrators—*mfg*
3531 Vibrators for concrete construction—*mfg*
3999 Vibrators, electric: designed for beauty and barber shops—*mfg*
3612 Vibrators, interrupter—*mfg*
5731 Video camera stores—retail
3651 Video camera-audio recorders, household—*mfg*
3651 Video cassette recorders/players—*mfg*
5064 Video disc players—wholesale
7841 Video disk rental to the general public
7993 Video game arcades
3944 Video game machines, except coin-operated—*mfg*
7221 Video photography, portrait
7539 Video recorder and player rental and leasing
7622 Video recorder or player repair
3695 Video recording tape, blank—*mfg*
7819 Video tape or disk reproduction
7812 Video tape production
5731 Video tape recorder stores—retail
7841 Video tape rental to the general public
5735 Video tape stores—retail
7822 Video tapes, recorded—wholesale
3651 Video triggers (remote control television devices)—*mfg*
3679 Video triggers, except remote control television devices—*mfg*
2013 Vienna sausage—mfpm—*mfg*
2221 Vinal broadwoven fabrics—*mfg*
3523 Vine pullers—*mfg*
2099 Vinegar—*mfg*
2035 Vinegar pickles and relishes—*mfg*
0721 Vineyard cultivation services
0762 Vineyard management and maintenance, with or without crop services
0172 Vineyards
2869 Vinyl acetate—*mfg*
3081 Vinyl and vinyl copolymer film and sheet, unsupported—*mfg*
3292 Vinyl asbestos tile—*mfg*
2295 Vinyl coated fabrics—*mfg*
2851 Vinyl coatings, strippable—*mfg*
2824 Vinyl fibers—*mfg*
1752 Vinyl floor tile and sheet installation—contractors
2851 Vinyl plastisol—*mfg*
2821 Vinyl resins—*mfg*
2824 Vinylidene chloride fibers—*mfg*
2221 Vinyon broadwoven fabrics—*mfg*
3931 Violas and parts—*mfg*
3931 Violins and parts—*mfg*
2835 Viral test diagnostic reagents—*mfg*
2836 Viruses—*mfg*
2823 Viscose fibers, bands, strips, and yarn—*mfg*
3829 Viscosimeters, except industrial process type—*mfg*
3823 Viscosimeters, industrial process type—*mfg*
3423 Vises, carpenters'—*mfg*
3423 Vises, except machine—*mfg*
3545 Vises, machine (machine tool accessories)—*mfg*
2752 Visiting cards, lithographed—*mfg*
2759 Visiting cards, printed: except lithographed or gravure—*mfg*
2754 Visiting cards: gravure printing—*mfg*
8082 Visiting nurse associations
2396 Visors, cap—*mfg*
2044 Vitamin and mineral enriched rice—*mfg*
5499 Vitamin food stores—retail
2834 Vitamin preparations—*mfg*
2833 Vitamins, natural and synthetic: bulk, uncompounded—*mfg*
5122 Vitamins—wholesale
8249 Vocational apprenticeship training
8299 Vocational counseling, except rehabilitation counseling
8211 Vocational high schools
8331 Vocational rehabilitation agencies
8331 Vocational rehabilitation counseling
8249 Vocational schools: except high schools, data processing, or business
8331 Vocational training agencies, except schools
2085 Vodka—*mfg*
3679 Voice controls—*mfg*
4813 Voice telephone communications, except radio telephone
2655 Voids and pans, fiber and cardboard—mfpm—*mfg*
2211 Voiles, cotton—*mfg*
2221 Voiles, manmade fiber and silk—*mfg*
1499 Volcanic ash mining
1429 Volcanic rock, crushed and broken—quarrying
1411 Volcanic rock, dimension—quarrying
3825 Volt-ohm milliammeters—*mfg*

3552 Warp and knot tying machines (textile machinery)—*mfg*
5131 Warp knit fabrics—wholesale
3552 Warping machines (textile machinery)—*mfg*
6399 Warranty insurance, automobile
6351 Warranty insurance, home
3272 Wash foundations, precast terrazzo—*mfg*
2326 Washable service apparel, men's: hospital, professional, barbers', etc.—*mfg*
2499 Washboards, wood and part wood—*mfg*
2211 Washcloths, woven: made in weaving mills—*mfg*
2392 Washcloths—mfpm—*mfg*
2259 Washcloths—mitse—*mfg*
1629 Washeries construction, mining—general contractors
1231 Washeries, anthracite
1221 Washeries, bituminous coal or lignite
3532 Washers, aggregate and sand: stationary type—*mfg*
3565 Washers, bottle: for food products—*mfg*
5072 Washers, hardware—wholesale
3053 Washers, leather—*mfg*
3452 Washers, metal—*mfg*
3861 Washers, photographic print and film—*mfg*
3089 Washers, plastics—*mfg*
2844 Washes, cosmetic—*mfg*
7542 Washing and polishing, automotive
2841 Washing compounds—*mfg*
3469 Washing machine parts, porcelain enameled—*mfg*
7629 Washing machine repair
5064 Washing machines, household: electric—wholesale
3633 Washing machines, household: including coin-operated—*mfg*
3582 Washing machines, laundry: commercial, including coin-operated—*mfg*
2812 Washing soda (sal soda)—*mfg*
7342 Washroom sanitation service
2673 Waste bags, plastics film and laminated—mfpm—*mfg*
5093 Waste bottles and boxes—wholesale
1629 Waste disposal plant construction—general contractors
9511 Waste management program administration—government
4953 Waste materials disposal at sea
5093 Waste rags—wholesale
5093 Waste, rubber—wholesale
2299 Waste, textile mill: processing of—*mfg*
5093 Waste, textile—wholesale
2655 Wastebaskets, fiber (metal-end or all-fiber)—mfpm—*mfg*
3469 Wastebaskets, stamped metal—*mfg*
5093 Wastepaper, including paper recycling—wholesale
3231 Watch crystals, made from purchased glass—*mfg*
3915 Watch jewels—*mfg*
7631 Watch repair shops
3172 Watch straps, except metal—*mfg*
3961 Watchbands, base metal—*mfg*
3911 Watchbands, precious metal—*mfg*
3873 Watchcases—*mfg*
5094 Watchcases—wholesale
3873 Watches and parts: except crystals and jewels—*mfg*
5094 Watches and parts—wholesale
5944 Watches, including custom made—retail
3221 Water bottles, glass—*mfg*
3069 Water bottles, rubber—*mfg*
3088 Water closets, plastics—*mfg*
3431 Water closets: enameled iron, cast iron, and pressed metal—*mfg*
3952 Water colors, artists'—*mfg*
3589 Water conditioners, for swimming pools—*mfg*
5074 Water conditioning equipment—wholesale
9511 Water control and quality agencies—government
3585 Water coolers, electric—*mfg*
2834 Water decontamination or purification tablets—*mfg*
4971 Water distribution or supply systems for irrigation
3589 Water filters and softeners, household type—*mfg*
2819 Water glass—*mfg*
3822 Water heater controls—*mfg*
5064 Water heaters, electric—wholesale
5074 Water heaters, except electric—wholesale
3639 Water heaters, household: including nonelectric—*mfg*
1381 Water intake well drilling: on a contract basis
3599 Water leak detectors—*mfg*
1623 Water main line construction—general contractors
2851 Water paints—*mfg*
3321 Water pipe, cast iron—*mfg*
9511 Water pollution control agencies
1629 Water power project construction—general contractors
3634 Water pulsating devices, electric—*mfg*
1711 Water pump installation and servicing—contractors
5084 Water pumps, industrial—wholesale
3589 Water purification equipment, household type—*mfg*

3442 Windows, louver: all metal or metal frame—*mfg*
2431 Windows, louver: wood—*mfg*
3089 Windows, louver: plastics—*mfg*
3231 Windows, stained glass: made from purchased glass—*mfg*
5211 Windows, storm: wood or metal—retail
3089 Windows, storm: plastics—*mfg*
3523 Windrowers (agricultural machinery)—*mfg*
3714 Windshield frames, motor vehicle—*mfg*
3714 Windshield wiper systems, all types—*mfg*
3231 Windshields, made from purchased glass—*mfg*
3089 Windshields, plastics—*mfg*
3949 Windsurfing boards and equipment—*mfg*
5813 Wine bars
2084 Wine cellars, bonded: engaged in blending wines—*mfg*
2084 Wine coolers (beverages)—*mfg*
5182 Wine coolers, alcoholic—wholesale
5921 Wine, packaged—retail
2084 Wines—*mfg*
5182 Wines—wholesale
3728 Wing assemblies and parts, aircraft—*mfg*
3714 Winterfronts, motor vehicle—*mfg*
2899 Wintergreen oil—*mfg*
3714 Wipers, windshield: motor vehicle—*mfg*
5093 Wiping rags, including washing and reconditioning—wholesale
7218 Wiping towel supply service
5063 Wire and cables, interior—wholesale
3496 Wire and wire products mfpm: except insulated wire, and nails and spikes—*mfg*
3315 Wire carts: household, grocery, and industrial—made in wiredrawing plants—*mfg*
3357 Wire cloth, nonferrous: made in wiredrawing plants—*mfg*
3315 Wire cloth, steel: made in wiredrawing plants—*mfg*
5039 Wire fence, gates, and accessories—wholesale
3315 Wire garment hangers, steel: made in wiredrawing plants—*mfg*
4822 Wire or cable telegraph
3315 Wire products, ferrous: made in wiredrawing plants—*mfg*
3312 Wire products, iron and steel: made in steel works or rolling mills—*mfg*
5051 Wire rods—wholesale
2298 Wire rope centers—*mfg*
5063 Wire rope or cable, insulated—wholesale
5051 Wire rope or cable, not insulated—wholesale
3357 Wire screening, nonferrous: made in wiredrawing plants—*mfg*
5051 Wire screening—wholesale
4813 Wire telephone
3496 Wire winding of purchased wire—*mfg*
3355 Wire, aluminum: made in rolling mills—*mfg*
3496 Wire, concrete reinforcing: made from purchased wire—*mfg*
3351 Wire, copper and copper alloy: made in brass mills—*mfg*
3315 Wire, ferrous: made in wiredrawing plants—*mfg*
3316 Wire, flat: cold-rolled strip—not made in hot-rolling mills—*mfg*
5063 Wire, insulated—wholesale
3356 Wire, nonferrous except copper and aluminum: made in rolling mills—*mfg*
3357 Wire, nonferrous: bare, insulated, or armored—mfpm—*mfg*
5051 Wire, not insulated—wholesale
3315 Wire, steel: insulated or armored—*mfg*
3549 Wiredrawing and fabricating machinery and equipment, except dies—*mfg*
3544 Wiredrawing and straightening dies—*mfg*
3672 Wiring boards—*mfg*
5063 Wiring devices—wholesale
3714 Wiring harness sets motor vehicles: except ignition—*mfg*
5063 Wiring materials, interior—wholesale
5063 Wiring supplies—wholesale
1061 Wolframite mining
9441 Women's bureaus
2861 Wood alcohol, natural—*mfg*
5199 Wood carvings—wholesale
2421 Wood chips produced at mill—*mfg*
2411 Wood chips, produced in the field—*mfg*
5099 Wood chips—wholesale
2861 Wood creosote—*mfg*
5989 Wood dealers, fuel—retail
2861 Wood distillates—*mfg*
3559 Wood drying kilns—*mfg*
2491 Wood fence: pickets, poling, rails—treated—*mfg*
2851 Wood fillers and sealers—*mfg*
1752 Wood flooring—contractors
2499 Wood flour—*mfg*
3131 Wood heel blocks, for sale as such—*mfg*
3131 Wood heels, finished (shoe findings)—*mfg*
2861 Wood oils, product of hardwood distillation—*mfg*
2491 Wood products, creosoted—*mfg*
2611 Wood pulp—*mfg*
3452 Wood screws, metal—*mfg*
5031 Wood siding—wholesale
2851 Wood stains—*mfg*
2429 Wood wool (excelsior)—*mfg*

X

3844 X-ray generators—*mfg*
8734 X-ray inspection service, industrial
8071 X-ray laboratories, including dental (not manufacturing)
5047 X-ray machines and parts, medical—wholesale
3861 X-ray plates, sensitized—*mfg*
2879 Xanthone (formulated)—*mfg*
2865 Xylene, made in chemical plants—*mfg*
3931 Xylophones and parts—*mfg*

Y

3494 Y bends and branches, pipe: metal—*mfg*
4493 Yacht basins, operation of
7389 Yacht brokers
7997 Yacht clubs, membership
0139 Yam farms
5949 Yard goods stores—retail
5131 Yard goods—wholesale
3423 Yardsticks, metal—*mfg*
2499 Yardsticks, wood—*mfg*
2231 Yarn bleaching, dyeing, and finishing: wool, mohair, and similar animal fibers—*mfg*
2269 Yarn bleaching, dyeing, and other finishing: except wool—*mfg*
5949 Yarn shops (knitting)—retail
2281 Yarn spinning: cotton, silk, and manmade staple—*mfg*
3552 Yarn texturizing machines—*mfg*
2282 Yarn, animal fiber: twisting, winding, and spooling—*mfg*
3292 Yarn, asbestos—*mfg*
2281 Yarn, carpet and rug: animal fiber—spinning, twisting and spooling—*mfg*
2823 Yarn, cellulosic: made in chemical plants—*mfg*
2241 Yarn, elastic: fabric covered—*mfg*
3229 Yarn, fiberglass: made in glass plants—*mfg*
2299 Yarn, specialty and novelty—*mfg*
2281 Yarn, spun: cotton, silk, manmade fiber, wool, and animal fiber—*mfg*
2823 Yarn, viscose—*mfg*
2211 Yarn-dyed fabrics, cotton—*mfg*
2281 Yarn: cotton, silk, wool, and manmade staple—*mfg*
2299 Yarn: flax, jute, hemp, and ramie—*mfg*
2299 Yarn: metallic, ceramic, or paper fibers—*mfg*
2241 Yarns, fabric covered rubber—*mfg*
2295 Yarns, plastics coated: made from purchased yarns—*mfg*
5199 Yarns—wholesale
2741 Yearbooks: publishing and printing, or publishing only—*mfg*
2099 Yeast—*mfg*
5149 Yeast—wholesale
7999 Yoga instruction
2023 Yogurt mix—*mfg*
2026 Yogurt, except frozen—*mfg*
2024 Yogurt, frozen—*mfg*
5143 Yogurt—wholesale
8641 Youth associations, except hotel units
8322 Youth centers
8322 Youth self-help organizations

Z

2824 Zein fibers—*mfg*
3674 Zener diodes—*mfg*
3356 Zinc and zinc alloy bars, plates, pipe, rods, sheets, tubing, and wire—*mfg*
3369 Zinc castings, except die-castings—*mfg*
2819 Zinc chloride—*mfg*
3364 Zinc die-castings—*mfg*
3339 Zinc dust, primary—*mfg*
3341 Zinc dust, reclaimed—*mfg*
3497 Zinc foil, not made in rolling mills—*mfg*
2834 Zinc ointment—*mfg*
1031 Zinc ore mining
5052 Zinc ore—wholesale
2851 Zinc oxide in oil, paint—*mfg*
2816 Zinc oxide pigments—*mfg*
2816 Zinc pigments: zinc yellow and zinc sulfide—*mfg*
3356 Zinc rolling, drawing, and extruding—*mfg*
3339 Zinc slabs, ingots, and refinery shapes: primary—*mfg*
3341 Zinc smelting and refining, secondary—*mfg*
1031 Zinc-blende (sphalerite) mining
5051 Zinc—wholesale
1031 Zincite mining
3559 Zipper making machinery—*mfg*
2241 Zipper tape—*mfg*
3965 Zippers (slide fasteners)—*mfg*
5131 Zippers—wholesale
3356 Zirconium and zirconium alloy bars, rods, billets, sheets, strip, and tubing—*mfg*
3339 Zirconium metal sponge and granules—*mfg*
1099 Zirconium ore mining
3931 Zithers and parts—*mfg*
9532 Zoning boards and commissions
8422 Zoological gardens
2052 Zwieback—*mfg*